The IDG Books SECRETS Advantage

Access 97 SECRETS is part of the SECRETS series brought to you by IDG Books Worldwide. We designed the SECRETS series because we know how much you appreciate insightful and comprehensive works from computer experts. Authorities in their respective areas, the authors of the SECRETS books have been selected for their ability to enrich your daily computing tasks.

The formula for a book in the SECRETS series is simple: Give an expert a forum to pass on his or her knowledge to readers. A SECRETS author, rather than the publishing company, directs the organization, pace, and treatment of the subject matter. SECRETS authors maintain close contact with end users through feedback from articles, training sessions, e-mail exchanges, user group participation, and consulting work. Because our authors know the realities of daily computer use and are directly tied to the reader, our SECRETS books have a strategic advantage.

SECRETS authors have the experience to approach a topic in the most efficient manner, and we know that you, the reader, will benefit from a "one-on-one" relationship with the author. Our research shows that readers make computer book purchases because they want expert advice on a product. Readers want to benefit from the author's experience, so the author's voice is always present in a SECRETS series book.

In addition, the author is free to include or recommend useful software in a SECRETS book. The software that accompanies a SECRETS book is not intended to be casual filler but is linked to the content, theme, or procedures of the book. We know that you will benefit from the included software.

You will find what you need in this book whether you read it from cover to cover, section by section, or simply one topic at a time. As a computer user, you deserve a comprehensive resource of answers. We at IDG Books Worldwide are proud to deliver that resource with *Access 97 SECRETS*.

Brenda McLaughlin
Senior Vice President and Group Publisher
Internet: YouTellUs@idgbooks.com

Access 97 SECRETS®

by Cary N. Prague, William C. Amo,
and James D. Foxall

Access 97 SECRETS®

by Cary N. Prague, William C. Amo, and James D. Foxall

IDG Books Worldwide, Inc.
An International Data Group Company

Foster City, CA ♦ Chicago, IL ♦ Indianapolis, IN ♦ Southlake, TX

Access 97 SECRETS®

Published by
IDG Books Worldwide, Inc.
An International Data Group Company
919 E. Hillsdale Blvd.
Suite 400
Foster City, CA 94404
http://www.idgbooks.com (IDG Books Worldwide Web site)

Library of Congress Catalog Card No.: 96-79764

ISBN: 0-7645-3043-7

Printed in the United States of America

10 9 8 7 6 5 4

1B/QV/QS/ZX/IN

Distributed in the United States by IDG Books Worldwide, Inc.

Distributed by Macmillan Canada for Canada; by Transworld Publishers Limited in the United Kingdom and Europe; by WoodsLane Pty. Ltd. for Australia; by WoodsLane Enterprises Ltd. for New Zealand; by Longman Singapore Publishers Ltd. for Singapore, Malaysia, Thailand, and Indonesia; by Simron Pty. Ltd. for South Africa; by Toppan Company Ltd. for Japan; by Distribuidora Cuspide for Argentina; by Livraria Cultura for Brazil; by Ediciencia S.A. for Ecuador; by Addison-Wesley Publishing Company for Korea; by Ediciones ZETA S.C.R. Ltda. for Peru; by WS Computer Publishing Company, Inc., for the Philippines; by Unalis Corporation for Taiwan; by Contemporanea de Ediciones for Venezuela. Authorized Sales Agent: Anthony Rudkin Associates for the Middle East and North Africa.

For general information on IDG Books Worldwide's books in the U.S., please call our Consumer Customer Service department at 800-762-2974. For reseller information, including discounts and premium sales, please call our Reseller Customer Service department at 800-434-3422.

For information on where to purchase IDG Books Worldwide's books outside the U.S., please contact our International Sales department at 415-655-3172 or fax 415-655-3295.

For information on foreign language translations, please contact our Foreign & Subsidiary Rights department at 415-655-3021 or fax 415-655-3281.

For sales inquiries and special prices for bulk quantities, please contact our Sales department at 415-655-3200 or write to the address above.

For information on using IDG Books Worldwide's books in the classroom or for ordering examination copies, please contact our Educational Sales department at 800-434-2086 or fax 817-251-8174.

For press review copies, author interviews, or other publicity information, please contact our Public Relations department at 415-655-3000 or fax 415-655-3299.

About the Authors

Cary N. Prague

Cary Prague is an internationally best-selling author and lecturer in the database industry. He is the owner of Cary Prague Books and Software, the world's largest Microsoft Access add-on vendor. This direct-mail company creates and markets add-on software, books, and video training for personal computer databases. Formerly, he held numerous management positions in Corporate Information Systems, including Director of Managed Care Reporting for MetraHealth (MetLife and Travelers Insurance joint venture); Director of Software Productivity at Travelers Insurance, where he was responsible for software support and training for 35,000 end users, and Director of Corporate Finance, where he was responsible for the selection and installation of Fixed Asset and Payroll Systems; and Manager of Information Centers for Northeast Utilities.

Cary also runs a consulting company, specializing in Microsoft Access applications and training. His clients include many local and national companies, including software companies, manufacturers, public utilities, and broadcast companies. His client list includes Microsoft, Borland International, Otis Elevator, United Healthcare, Pratt and Whitney Aircraft, Rockwell International, and SNET.

He is one of the best-selling authors in the computer database management market, having written over thirty-five books on software that have sold nearly one million copies, including Microsoft Access, Borland dBASE IV, Paradox, R:Base, and Framework. Cary's books include the *PC World Microsoft® Access Bible*, recently on several top 10 national bestseller lists and winner of an award for technical excellence; *dBASE for Windows Handbook*, dBASE IV Programming, winner of the 1989 Computer Press Association's Book of the Year award for Best Software-Specific Book; and *Everyman's Database Primer Featuring dBASE IV.*

Cary has developed and markets several add-on software products for Microsoft Access, including Yes! I Can Run My Business With Access, a business sales and accounting program; The Access Business Forms Library, distributed by Microsoft with Access 2.0 upgrades; The Check Writer (winner of the Microsoft Network Best Access Application award), TabMaster Wizard (which creates tabbed dialogs), User Interface Construction Kit (winner of the 1996 Access Advisor Readers Choice award); and the Command Bar Image Editor and Add-On Image Pack.

Prague, a Microsoft Solutions Provider and Certified Access Professional, is a frequent speaker at seminars and conferences around the country. He has been voted best speaker by the attendees of several national conferences. In the last 24 months, he spoke for Microsoft-sponsored conferences in Kona, Palm Springs, Orlando, Phoenix, Chicago, Toronto, and Boston. He has also spoken at the Borland Database Conference, Digital Consulting's Database

World, Microsoft's Developer Days, Computerland's Technomics Conference, COMDEX, and Compaq Computer's Innovate. He is a contributing editor to *Access Advisor* magazine.

Cary holds a master's degree in computer science from Rensselaer Polytechnic Institute, as well as M.B.A. and Bachelor of Accounting degrees from the University of Connecticut. He is also a Certified Data Processor.

William C. Amo

Bill has over 18 years of experience developing databases and database systems. He is a Microsoft Certified Product Specialist and certified in Microsoft Visual Basic, Microsoft Access, and Windows. He has developed Microsoft Access add-on products sold worldwide, including the Mail Merge Report Wizard and Envelope Report Wizard for Access 2.0 and the TabMaster Wizard for Access 2.0 and Access for Windows 95.

Bill has also written financial applications for mutual fund management and specializes in client/server component development. Bill is currently developing solutions in C++, Visual Basic, and Access for Windows 95 for a leading actuarial consulting firm.

Bill holds a Bachelor of Arts degree in computer science from the State University of New York at Potsdam and a Master of Science degree in computer science from Rensselaer Polytechnic Institute.

James D. Foxall

James Foxall is vice president of Information Management Consultants, Inc., a software development firm in Omaha, Nebraska, that specializes in database applications. James is responsible for managing the development of all Windows applications, including Pursuit, the company's flagship product. Pursuit is a certified Office-Compatible contact and customer information system that has been reviewed in many major software and trade publications. James is an international speaker on Microsoft Access; he holds Microsoft certification in Microsoft Access and Visual Basic. James also develops applications under his own company title (Simtuit Solutions) and licenses their distribution to various resellers. In addition to speaking and writing, James has been featured on numerous television news shows, in trade publications, and in newspaper articles for his technological expertise.

Dedications

This book is dedicated to my friend Joe Chalastra for rescuing me from the depths of work with trips to Sam's, Office Max, and of course Dunkin' Donuts. To Joe, for intellectually stimulating me all the time, for never allowing me to know when you are telling the truth or fabricating the most believable scenarios. You are more fun to be with than any adventure game.

— Cary Prague

To Marianne for your continued support of these projects (Du bist mein Leben).

— Bill Amo

To Laura, my loving wife, for her encouragement and support. Also, to my parents Dave and Linda, my sister Chris, and my grandmother Lucile for always believing in me. In addition, a special dedication to my new niece Amanda; even though she may never get more from this book than using it as a booster chair.

— James Foxall

Credits

Senior Vice President and Group Publisher
Brenda McLaughlin

Managing Editor
Andy Cummings

Acquisitions Manager
Gregory S. Croy

Software Acquisitions Editor
Tracy Lehman Cramer

Marketing Manager
Melisa M. Duffy

Administrative Assistant
Laura J. Moss

Editorial Assistant
Timothy J. Borek

Production Director
Beth Jenkins

Supervisor of Project Coordination
Cindy L. Phipps

Supervisor of Page Layout
Kathie S. Schutte

Supervisor of Graphics and Design
Shelley Lea

Production Systems Specialist
Debbie J. Gates

Development Editor
Pat O'Brien

Copy Edit Coordinator
Barry Childs-Helton

Editor
Chris Katsaropoulos

Project Coordinator
Debbie Stailey

Layout and Graphics
Brett Black
J. Tyler Connor
Dominique DeFelice
Angela F. Hunckler
Drew R. Moore
Brent Savage
Kate Snell

Proofreaders
Henry Lazarek
Christine D. Berman
Melissa D. Buddendeck
Joel K. Draper
Rachel Garvey
Nancy Price
Dwight Ramsey
Robert Springer
Carrie Voorhis
Karen York

Indexer
Rebecca Plunkett

Production Administration
Tony Augsburger
Todd Klemme
Jacalyn L. Pennywell
Leslie Popplewell
Theresa Sánchez-Baker
Melissa Stauffer
Bryan Stephenson

Acknowledgments

First, to Bill Amo and James Foxall, the real secrets behind this book. To Jennifer Reardon and Phuc Phan for once again helping me write and take screen dumps of material I just couldn't look at one more time. To the folks at Cary Prague Books for working so many hours. To Ken Getz, who always answers my questions. To the special people at IDG Books: Our editors, Pat O'Brien (making books and making friends), Barry Childs-Helton (who I like much more as a project manager than as the precise editor he is). To Chris Katsaropoulos, for the most thorough and fair review I have ever seen. To Greg Croy the head pilgrim at the Indy campsite. To our agents, Bill Gladstone and Matt Wagner, for handling the money and keeping only a little. To Bill Ota, John Hawkins, Jeannie Banfield, Pat Edwards, Katie Logan, Geri Bahr, Melissa Holden, Teresa Ogot, and all the folks at *Access Advisor* Magazine and Conferences for giving me a place to write, a place to speak, and a place to exhibit. Finally to my friends and family, who I never see but love so much.

— Cary Prague

To my children Kirsten and Dean for their encouragement, and to my grandson Zachary Carl for bringing me still more happiness. To my co-authors James and Cary for their devotion to the task and for sticking with it through tough times. To the folks at IDG Books for their guidance and a special thanks to Chris Katsaropoulos.

— Bill Amo

To Cary Prague and Bill Amo; I obviously couldn't have done it without you two. To Mike Hartman, for keeping my computer running. To everyone at IDG who made this book possible. To my friends and family for their support and their persistent reminders that there is more to life than just work.

— James Foxall

(The Publisher would like to give special thanks to Patrick J. McGovern, without whom this book would not have been possible.)

Contents at a Glance

Table of Contents

Part VI: Enterprise Computing, Internet, and Client/Server Access 829

Introduction

Welcome to ***Access 97 Secrets*** — the advanced guide to the most powerful features of Microsoft Access 97.

Unlike other *advanced* books that spend the majority of their time rehashing the basics, this book begins and ends with topics on Microsoft Access for the professional developer or power user. This book examines the deepest topics for Microsoft Access 97. We think that Microsoft Access is an excellent database manager and the best Windows database on the market today. We also think it is a uniquely productive environment for developers of serious business applications. Our goal with this book is to share all we know about Access and our best secrets that we have learned since beginning to use Access nearly three years ago.

In the five years since Access 1.0 was released, we have written many mission-critical business systems in Microsoft Access. We learned a great deal and are ready to share all of that knowledge. This book contains many topics for advanced users and developers. You'll find that the book begins with the new features and topics in the language and quickly moves into user interface techniques and data analysis secrets. Then the topics that no one else covers — multiuser systems, the Internet, the Office Developer's Edition, Security, and Help — are covered in detail. Finally, connecting to the outside world, Client/Server back ends, and database replication are demonstrated.

Although each chapter is an integral part of the book as a whole, each chapter can also stand on its own. You can read the book in any order you want, skipping from chapter to chapter and from topic to topic. (Note that this book's index is particularly thorough, so you can refer to the index to find the location of a particular topic in which you're interested.)

The examples in this book have been well thought out and are found on the accompanying CD-ROM, which is packed full of the latest fully working versions of some great Access 97 software as well as demos of many Access add-ons and even Internet-related products. Included in the book are many notes, tips, and techniques (and a whole bunch of secrets) to help you better understand the product.

Although designed to go much further than the limited Microsoft Access developer documentation, this book can easily substitute for the manuals included with Access. This book follows a much more structured approach than the Microsoft Access manuals — going into more depth on almost every topic and showing many different types of examples.

Is This Book for You?

We wrote this book for intermediate and advanced users of Microsoft Access. If you are a novice, you may want to start with our beginners' book, ***Access 97 Bible.*** If, however, you've used Access for a while and want to do more than just create simple tables and forms, then this book is for you. We believe that this book covers Microsoft Access in better detail than any other book currently on the market. We hope that you find this book helpful while working with Access and enjoy the innovative style of an IDG book.

How This Book Is Organized

This book contains 23 chapters, which are divided into six main parts.

Part I: Power Configurations

Part I consists of the first three chapters of the book. In Chapter 1, you learn how Access 97 uses the Windows 95 or Windows NT registry. Chapter 2 covers data — what you need to know to create tables properly and normalize them for real-world applications. In Chapter 3, you learn how to optimize performance in Access 95. You learn the three secret steps that Microsoft won't tell you to increase performance by 200% and reduce your database size by the same amount.

Part II: The Access 97 Language

The next three chapters make up Part II and teach the important new features of the Visual Basic for Applications language. This language replaced Access Basic and is now found in nearly every Microsoft product. In Chapter 4, you learn how to use the new commands and how to avoid the problems that converting an Access 2.0 or Access 95 application can cause. Chapter 5 continues into the underside of the new JET Database Engine and teaches the secrets of Data Access Objects (DAO) as well as how to use all the new commands when dealing with Recordsets and data in Access 97 or Visual Basic. In Chapter 6, you learn about the new ActiveX Controls, formerly called OLE controls, and how to add new features to Access 97. Using OLE, you learn how to make Access 97 work as a server or a client.

Part III: Interface

Part III contains four chapters that offer incredible examples on creating user interface magic. Chapter 7 begins with advanced basics on creating any form. You learn about three-dimensional effects, shortcuts, secrets to quickly aligning controls, and how some of the new form properties really work. In Chapter 8 you see 12 of the best user interface techniques around, including geographic drill-down using maps, how to create tabbed dialogs using only VBA, and intelligent searching and printing dialogs. Chapter 9 covers using the new features in menus and toolbars, including customizing toolbar pictures and adding checkmarks to menu items. Finally, in Chapter 10 you will add new tools to your form toolbelt as you learn to create multipage forms with subforms and really take advantage of combo boxes, list boxes, and option groups.

Part IV: Getting Answers out of Access

Part IV consists of three chapters that really let you understand how to get information out of an Access database. Chapter 11 offers in-depth coverage of advanced queries and filters. You learn how to use parameter queries, update queries, action queries, and even total and crosstabulation queries. Chapter 12 teaches advanced reporting techniques such as how to really control orphaned lines in a report and how to consecutively number multiple reports. Chapter 13 teaches you how to use the business graphics engine, which is part of all Microsoft Office products. You also learn how to create and manipulate pictures and OLE objects (sound, video, and so on) within a Microsoft Access 97 form or report.

Part V: System Functions

This part really gets advanced and goes where no other book has gone before. Chapter 14 contains an advanced look at creating multiuser systems, including how to handle simultaneous updates, transaction processing, and other multiuser secrets. If you distribute runtime applications using the Office 97 Developers Edition, you want to read Chapter 15. Everything you want to know about the Access 97 Setup Wizard (and about using the tools formerly in the Access Developers Toolkit) is contained in this chapter. In Chapter 16 you learn how to create add-ins and libraries, including building wizards. Chapter 17 tells you how to make an application secure and how to make data secure. This chapter offers tips and techniques for creating bulletproof applications. Finally, Chapter 18 covers Help systems, including using the new help engine to create context-sensitive help systems.

Part VI: Enterprise Computing, Internet, and Client/Server Access

This part is the most advanced part of the book and covers topics no one else covers in any depth. Chapter 19 teaches how to integrate an Access 97 application within other Office 97 components. Chapter 20 covers working with external data, including importing, exporting, and attaching to a variety of data sources. Chapter 21 covers Client/Server Databases with a particular attachment (pardon the pun) to Microsoft SQL Server and BackOffice. Chapter 22 includes a complete evaluation and examination of the new database replication features and the Windows 95 Briefcase. The book ends with Chapter 23, which covers all of the Internet features of Access 97.

Part I

Power Configurations

Chapter 1

Using the Windows 95 Registry

In This Chapter

- Understanding predefined keys
- Using the Registry Editor
- Exploring Registry API calls
- Specifying Jet and Access settings
- Using the Setting statements
- Using the SetOption method
- Using user profiles

An Overview of the Registry

In the world of Windows 3.1, applications, as well as Windows itself, store configuration information in .INI files. A hint of a Registry was included in the Windows 3.1 REG.DAT file, mainly for OLE information.

The SYSTEM.INI file stores configuration information pertaining to the system devices and drivers that talk to those devices. The WIN.INI file contains mostly configuration information — the look of Windows — that pertains to the user. Program Manager uses PROGMAN.INI to configure its groups and desktop, and the Control Panel uses an .INI file to store the settings the user chooses.

Applications also use .INI files to store data that users or an administrator can change in order to change the behavior of the application. Some applications use the WIN.INI file in addition to their own .INI file.

Windows 95 still uses SYSTEM.INI and WIN.INI for some configuration data — mostly to be backwards compatible with Windows 3.*x* applications — but stores most of its information in a new file format known as the *Registry*.

You can think of the Registry as a hierarchical structure of nodes. Windows 95 ships with a predefined set of nodes in the Registry. In these nodes, Windows 95 stores information about the computer Windows 95 is running on, the software installed on the computer, the configuration of the computer, and the users defined to the computer. The predefined nodes in the Registry are as follows:

- HKEY_CLASSES_ROOT
- HKEY_LOCAL_MACHINE
- HKEY_CURRENT_CONFIG
- HKEY_CURRENT_USER
- HKEY_USERS
- HKEY_DYN_DATA

You may also see the term *hive* used in documentation about the Registry. For example, you may see the "software hive" or the "system hive" mentioned within HKEY_LOCAL_MACHINE. A hive includes the keys, subkeys, and values from some root within the Registry. The software hive under HKEY_LOCAL_MACHINE means the software key and all subkeys and values under it.

The Registry is physically two separate files: SYSTEM.DAT and USER.DAT. Windows 95 creates backups of these files at startup and places the backups into SYSTEM.DA0 and USER.DA0. You can use these backups to recover the Registry if it becomes damaged.

Windows 95 provides an editor for you to use in order to browse and modify the values in the Registry. This editor is named REGEDIT.EXE and is located in the WINDOWS directory.

Your system may not contain this editor if an administrator has removed it. Changes made with the editor can cause the system to become inoperable; therefore, some administrators remove the editing capabilities to protect the environment. If your system *does* have the editor installed on it, use it with caution. Do not make any changes to values in the Registry until you have a solid understanding of the Registry and the changes you are making.

In this chapter, you use the editor to explore the Registry and its trees of information. Later, you are introduced to values that you can enter with the editor to configure the Jet database engine, the workhorse of database access used by Access and other applications.

You will discover that you also can use the Registry editor to import and export data into and out of the Registry. Files that end with .REG are ASCII format files that the editor creates on export or reads on import. Some application software vendors ship .REG files with their installations and import these files into the Registry programmatically. You can view these .REG files with any ASCII editor such as Notepad; these files have a structure that looks similar to .INI files (see Figure 1-1).

The components of the Registry are known as *keys* and *values*. A tree in the Registry is composed of keys within keys in a hierarchical fashion. The keys below a given key and dependent upon it are known as *subkeys*. Any key can contain one or more values. The structure of a value entry in a key has three parts: a name, a data type, and a value. Each of these components is explored later in this section.

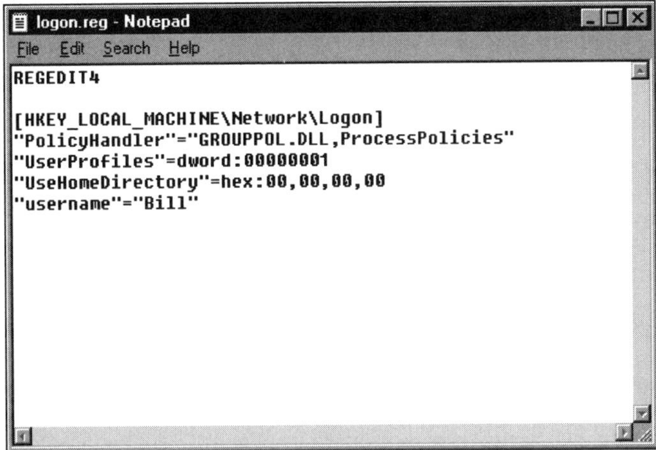

Figure 1-1: Files that you can import into and export from the Registry look similar to .INI files.

Exploring the Predefined Keys

The HKEYs are predefined by Windows 95 and describe the configuration of the computer, including its devices, software, and user preferences.

HKEY is derived from a Windows object known as a *handle*. Handles are familiar to developers working in C or C++ with the 16- or 32-bit API. Windows uses handles to identify system objects such as windows. Access developers also refer to handles with the form property `hWnd`, which returns a handle to the form window.

HKEY_LOCAL_MACHINE stores information about the hardware in the computer, device settings, and some software settings. This key has several subkeys beneath it, which describe various categories of configuration information. Subkeys are sometimes referred to as *branches* to denote the hierarchical structure of the Registry.

Information about the computer's serial ports and any modems installed in the computer are stored in the Hardware subkey.

The Software subkey holds information about the software installed on the computer and some configuration information for this software.

Information about the operating system services and startup information, particularly which device drivers to load, is stored in the System subkey. The startup information is held in a subtree under the System subkey called CurrentControlSet and is further broken down into a Control subkey and a Services subkey.

Remote administration capabilities and network security provider information are held in the Security subkey.

The Network subkey holds current network logon information, and the Config subkey stores a collection of configurations for the local computer.

Hardware device information is held in the Enum subkey. Enum gets its name from the source of the device information in Windows 95, components called *Bus Enumerators*.

The HKEY_USERS key holds the default user configuration information and contains a branch for each user profile defined for the computer. The HKEY_CURRENT_USER key maps to the HKEY_USERS branch for the user currently logged onto the computer.

The Default subkey under HKEY_USERS is used for new users logging onto the computer without a personal user profile.

HKEY_CURRENT_USER contains the configuration data for the user profile currently active on the computer. This information defines the preferences of the user for which the profile was built. If the user hasn't changed any settings, this profile information may be the same as the information found in the default subkey.

The HKEY_CLASSES_ROOT key data is used by the Windows 95 Shell and by OLE applications. It holds the OLE CLSIDs (class identifiers) and the registration information for in-process servers. This key also displays the information carried in the Software\Classes subkey of HKEY_LOCAL_MACHINE, which is divided into two types of subkeys, the Filename extension subkeys and the Class definition subkeys.

Filename extensions associate filename extensions with applications. Class definitions describe properties of each class of document and hold DDE commands for opening and printing files for applications that support DDE.

HKEY_CURRENT_CONFIG points to the Config subkey of HKEY_LOCAL_MACHINE. This key contains the current active configuration among the configurations found in the Config subkey.

Current hardware configuration from loaded device drivers at system startup is stored in a memory resident key called the HKEY_DYN_DATA. This key resides in memory for fast access by the operating system and loaded drivers. The key holds a pointer to a function that returns the values requested by a query to this key. The query is performed by the Registry editor to display the values of the key, and as you will see in the "Exploring Registry API Calls" section, your application can also query these values.

Using the Registry Editor

The Registry Editor that ships with Windows 95 is REGEDIT.EXE. You can find it in the Windows directory or the directory you specified at setup time.

Select Run from the Start menu to start the editor, shown in Figure 1-2, or start it from Windows Explorer.

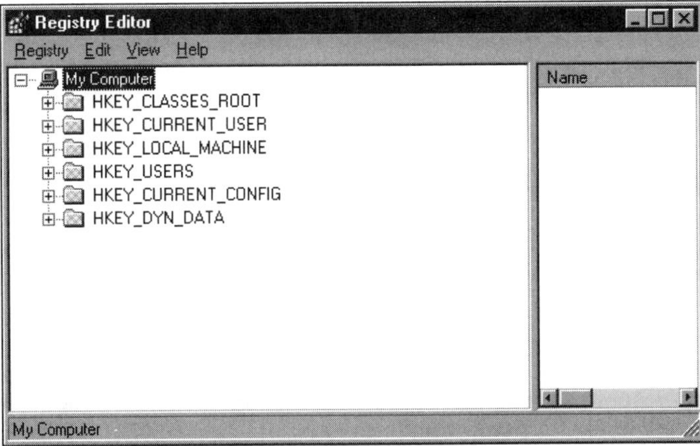

Figure 1-2: The Registry Editor's Tree View displays the predefined keys of the Windows Registry.

Navigating the Tree View

The Editor displays two panes: a Tree View on the left that displays the predefined keys mentioned in the preceding section, and a List View on the right that displays the values of a selected key.

You can navigate the tree by clicking on the plus symbols to the left of the folder icons denoting the keys and subkeys of the tree. As you click on a plus symbol, that key expands to display the subkeys beneath it. Subkeys at the bottom of a tree, or branch, appear without an accompanying plus symbol.

To display the value or values associated with a particular key, click on a folder icon. The values are displayed in the right-hand pane. To size the panes, place the mouse pointer on the center line separating the two panes. The mouse pointer changes to a sizing pointer, and you can adjust the pane width left and right to display more of the pane you are interested in.

You can also navigate the tree with the keyboard. The up- and down-arrow keys navigate through the keys of the tree, displaying the key's values as the key is highlighted. The left- and right-arrow keys collapse and expand the selected key, respectively. If a key is already collapsed or doesn't have subkeys when you press the left arrow, the highlight moves to the parent of the key currently selected. This navigation up the tree continues until the My Computer key is collapsed. Likewise, when you press the right arrow, the highlight navigates through the tree from the selected key down to a bottom subkey.

Pressing Alt+V+l displays the sizing pointer on the panel divider so that you can use the left- and right-arrow keys to size the panels. The Esc key sets the panel width at the size set by the arrow key movement left or right. A subsequent press of the up arrow or down arrow resets the mouse pointer.

Working with keys

Expanding keys within a tree and then collapsing a parent farther up the tree does not collapse the subkeys, but it does hide them from view. Expanding the parent redisplays the previously expanded subtree. This behavior is consistent within a session of the editor, but not between editor sessions. When you close the editor, the current tree view is lost.

If a key contains one or more values, they are displayed in the right pane when you single-click on the key's folder icon. The values contain three parts: a data type, a name, and a value.

The data types are denoted by an icon, as shown in Figure 1-3. The icons containing the letters *ab* are String types, and those containing zeros and ones are Binary types.

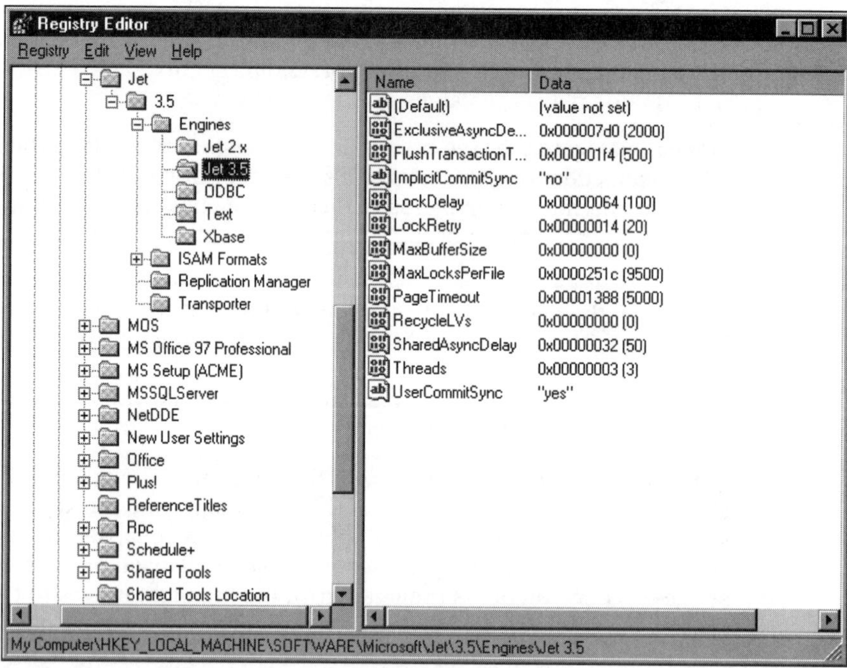

Figure 1-3: The values of a key are displayed in the right-hand pane of the Registry window. The value data types are denoted by icons.

You can modify a value by double-clicking on the entry in the right pane, by selecting Modify from the Edit menu, or by right-clicking on the entry and then selecting Modify from the pop-up menu.

You can add a key to the tree by selecting New Key from the Edit menu or from the pop-up menu that appears when you position the cursor over a key in the tree and right-click. The new key is added below the selected key at the bottom of the branch.

Delete a key by selecting it in the tree and choosing Delete from the pop-up menu you get when you right-click. Alternatively, choose Delete from the Edit menu.

Importing and exporting Registry information

You can import Registry information into the Registry by choosing Import Registry File from the Registry menu. The editor reads the selected .REG file and sets the designated keys and values into the Registry.

Figure 1-4 shows the Registry Editor window with the HKEY_LOCAL_MACHINE key expanded to display the Network\Logon subkey branch. Choosing Export Registry File from the Registry menu brings up the Export Registry File dialog box shown in Figure 1-5.

In the Export Registry File dialog box, choose the folder in which you want to save the exported .REG file and enter a file name in the File name text box. Notice that the Save as type drop-down box defaults to Registration Files, which appends an .REG extension on the end of the file name you enter.

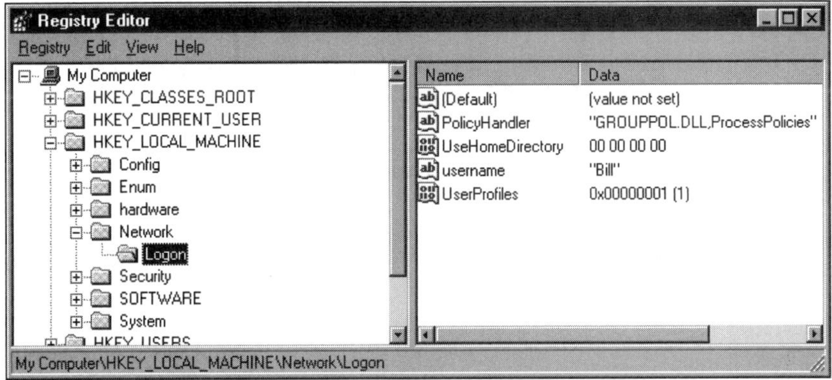

Figure 1-4: The HKEY_LOCAL_MACHINE\Network\Logon branch can be exported to a registration file by selecting Export Registry File from the Registry menu.

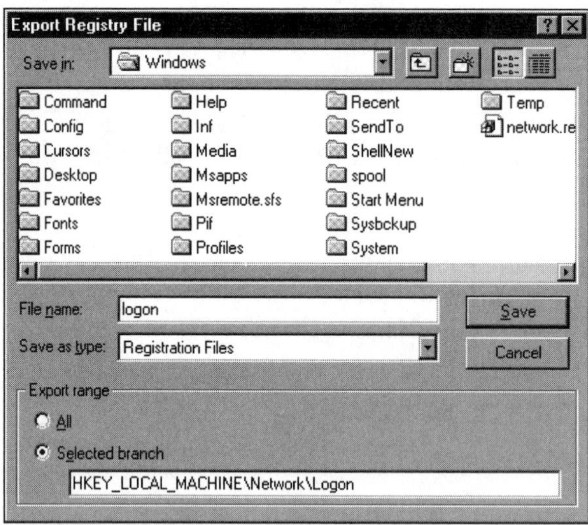

Figure 1-5: The Export Registry File dialog box enables you to specify the file name and range of the Registry that you want to export.

At the bottom of the dialog box is an Export range frame containing two radio buttons. Click on All to export the entire Registry. Click on Selected branch to export the branch displayed in the text box. You can modify the value in the text box to export a branch other than the one you had selected when you brought up the dialog box.

The resulting .REG file, shown in Figure 1-6, has a structure similar to an .INI file and can be edited with any ASCII editor, such as Notepad. You can import this file type into a Registry by using the procedure outlined previously.

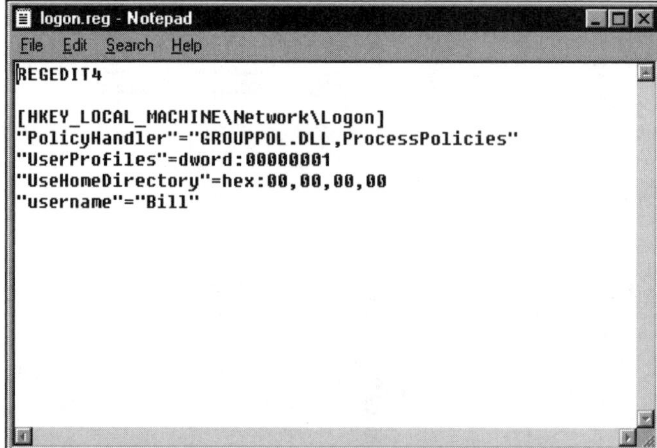

Figure 1-6: The .REG file has an ASCII file format similar to an .INI file and can be imported back into the Registry by using the Registry Editor import capabilities.

Working from the command line

You can import files from the command line by using the following syntax to launch the Registry Editor and cause it to process the specified files:

```
regedit regfile1.reg, regfile2.reg
```

This line entered in a DOS window launches the editor and imports the two files specified. The editor shuts down when the import is completed. To export the entire Registry to a file, use the following command line:

```
regedit /e regfile1.reg
```

You can export a branch by specifying the key to export after the /e file name, as follows:

```
regedit /e regfile1.reg hkey_local_machine\network\logon
```

Exploring Registry API Calls

On CD-ROM

Your Access application can manipulate the Registry by using a few Win32 API calls. You can find declarations for these API calls on the companion CD-ROM in the Defines module in the file CH1.MDB. These declarations are also available from the WINAPI Viewer application that ships with the Office Developers Edition. Table 1-1 summarizes the API calls that you can use to work with the Registry.

Table 1-1 API Calls

API Call	*Description*
RegCreateKeyEx	Creates a key in the Registry
RegDeleteValue	Deletes a named value for the specified key
RegEnumKeyEx	Enumerates the subkeys for the open key specified
RegEnumValue	Enumerates the values for a specified key
RegFlushKey	Writes the attributes of the open key specified to the Registry
RegOpenKeyEx	Opens the specified key for processing
RegQueryInfoKey	Queries a specified key for information
RegQueryValueEx	Queries the value associated with a given open key
RegSetValueEx	Sets the value for a given key
RegDeleteKey	Deletes a given key and all of its values

The following sections outline these functions to describe their purpose. All external .DLL functions used in an Access application must be declared in a code module before being used. All function descriptions in the following sections are prefaced with the declare statement you would use.

RegCreateKeyEx

`RegCreateKeyEx` creates a key in the Registry as a subkey of the key specified by `hKey` in the function call. `hKey` can be a previously created application key or one of the predefined keys. The `hKey` used must be opened with the `KEY_CREATE_SUB_KEY` access flag by using `RegOpenKeyEx`. The syntax is as follows:

```
Declare Function RegCreateKeyEx Lib "advapi32.dll" Alias _
"RegCreateKeyExA" (ByVal hKey As Long, ByVal lpSubKey As String, _
ByVal Reserved As Long, ByVal lpClass As String, ByVal dwOptions As _
Long, ByVal samDesired As Long, lpSecurityAttributes As _
SECURITY_ATTRIBUTES, phkResult As Long, lpdwDisposition As Long) As _
Long
```

The predefined keys can be specified as constants, which are also included in the REGAPI.TXT file or in the API Viewer. These constants are the following:

- `HKEY_CLASSES_ROOT`
- `HKEY_CURRENT_USER`
- `HKEY_LOCAL_MACHINE`
- `HKEY_USERS`

The name of the subkey you want to create is specified in the `lpSubKey` parameter. The `lpClass` parameter specifies the type of key. This can specify any string value you want for the key.

`dwOptions` can be either `REG_OPTION_VOLATILE`, indicating that the key's information is stored in memory and not preserved between restarts of the system, or `REG_OPTION_NON_VOLATILE`, indicating that the information is preserved between system restarts. Non_Volatile is the default.

`samDesired` specifies the desired security access for the key. This value can be a combination of the values found in Table 1-2.

Table 1-2 Reg Security Access Values

API Call	Description
`KEY_ALL_ACCESS`	Combines the query value, notify, create subkey, set value, and enumerate subkey access values

API Call	Description
KEY_QUERY_VALUE	Specifies that Subkey data may be queried
KEY_NOTIFY	Causes a change notification to occur
KEY_CREATE_SUB_KEY	Allows the creation of subkeys
KEY_SET_VALUE	Allows the setting of subkey data
KEY_ENUMERATE_SUB_KEYS	Grants permission to enumerate the subkeys
KEY_EXECUTE	Grants read access
KEY_READ	Combines the enumerate subkey, notify, and query value access permissions
KEY_WRITE	Combines the create subkey and set value access permissions
KEY_CREATE_LINK	Allows the creation of symbolic links

The lpSecurityAttributes parameter points to a SECURITY_ATTRIBUTES structure that specifies the security attributes for the key. This parameter may be NULL.

The phkResult parameter receives the handle of the key that is created. The lpdwDisposition parameter receives either a disposition value of REG_CREATED_NEW_KEY, which indicates that the key was created, or a value of REG_OPENED_EXISTING_KEY, which indicates that the key already exists in the Registry and the parameters passed to the function were not used to modify the key.

RegDeleteValue

The RegDeleteValue function deletes a named value from the key specified in the hKey parameter, which may be an open key or one of the predefined handles. The lpValueName parameter names the value to be deleted from the key. The syntax is as follows:

```
Declare Function RegDeleteValue Lib "advapi32.dll" Alias _
"RegDeleteValueA" (ByVal hKey As Long, ByVal lpValueName As String) _
As Long
```

RegEnumKeyEx

The RegEnumKeyEx function enumerates a subkey of the open key identified by hKey. Each call enumerates a subkey for the given index value specified by dwIndex, which should be zero on the first call. The hKey must have been opened with the KEY_ENUMERATE_SUB_KEYS access. The syntax is as follows:

```
Declare Function RegEnumKeyEx Lib "advapi32.dll" Alias _
"RegEnumKeyExA" (ByVal hKey As Long, ByVal dwIndex As Long, ByVal _
lpName As String, lpcbName As Long, lpReserved As Long, ByVal _
lpClass As String, lpcbClass As Long, lpftLastWriteTime As FILETIME) _
As Long
```

The `lpName` points to the variable that receives the name of the subkey enumerated. The `lpcbName` parameter holds the length of `lpName`.

`lpReserved` must be `NULL`.

The `lpClass` parameter points to a string variable that will receive the class name of the enumerated subkey. If you do not care to receive the class, you may specify `NULL` for this parameter.

`lpftLastWriteTime` is a pointer to a `FILETIME` structure that receives the time the subkey was last written to.

RegEnumValue

This API call enumerates the values of the key specified in `hKey`, which is required to be opened with the `KEY_QUERY_VALUE` access flag. You must call this function for each value of the key. The `dwIndex` specifies the index of the value to be enumerated.

```
Declare Function RegEnumValue Lib "advapi32.dll" Alias _
"RegEnumValueA" (ByVal hKey As Long, ByVal dwIndex As Long, ByVal _
lpValueName As String, lpcbValueName As Long, lpReserved As Long, _
lpType As Long, lpData As Byte, lpcbData As Long) As Long
```

The `lpValueName` parameter receives the value name, and the `lpcbValueName` parameter is the size of the `lpValueName` string. `lpType` receives the type code of the value, `lpData` receives the data of the value, and `lpcbData` specifies the size of `lpData` buffer.

Type codes you may see for values are found in Table 1-3.

Table 1-3 Value Type Codes

API Call	*Value*	*Description*
`REG_BINARY`	3	Binary data
`REG_SZ`	1	A null-terminated string
`REG_EXPAND_SZ`	2	A null-terminated unicode string containing references to environment variables
`REG_MULTI_SZ`	7	An array of null-terminated strings ending with two null characters

API Call	Value	Description
REG_DWORD	4	A 32-bit numeric value
REG_NONE	0	No value type defined
REG_DWORD_LITTLE_ENDIAN	4	A 32-bit numeric value with the high word as the most significant byte (REG_DWORD)
REG_DWORD_BIG_ENDIAN	5	A 32-bit numeric value with the low word as the most significant byte.
REG_LINK	6	A Unicode symbolic link
REG_RESOURCE_LIST	8	A device driver resource list

RegFlushKey

The RegFlushKey function writes the hKey attributes to the Registry. This function returns when all data has been written. The syntax is as follows:

```
Declare Function RegFlushKey Lib "advapi32.dll" Alias _
"RegFlushKey" (ByVal hKey As Long) As Long
```

RegOpenKeyEx

The RegOpenKeyEx function opens a subkey specified by lpSubKey under hKey. samDesired is the same as that specified for RegCreateKeyEx. The syntax follows:

```
Declare Function RegOpenKeyEx Lib "advapi32.dll" Alias _
"RegOpenKeyExA" (ByVal hKey As Long, ByVal lpSubKey As String, ByVal _
ulOptions As Long, ByVal samDesired As Long, phkResult As Long) As
Long
```

The phkResult parameter receives the handle of the opened key.

RegQueryInfoKey

The RegQueryInfoKey function returns information about the key specified by hKey, as follows:

```
Declare Function RegQueryInfoKey Lib "advapi32.dll" Alias _
"RegQueryInfoKeyA" (ByVal hKey As Long, ByVal lpClass As String, _
lpcbClass As Long, lpReserved As Long, lpcSubKeys As Long, _
lpcbMaxSubKeyLen As Long, lpcbMaxClassLen As Long, lpcValues As _
Long, lpcbMaxValueNameLen As Long, lpcbMaxValueLen As Long, _
lpcbSecurityDescriptor As Long, lpftLastWriteTime As FILETIME) As _
Long
```

The lpClass parameter receives the class name of the key, and lpcbClass specifies the size of the lpClass string.

lpcSubKeys receives the number of subkeys contained by hKey. lpcbMaxSubKeyLen receives the length of the longest subkey name, and lpcbMaxClassLen receives the length of the longest subkey class.

lpcValues receives the number of values defined for the key. lpcbMaxValueNameLen receives the longest value name, and lpcbMaxValueLen receives the length of the longest value.

The lpcbSecurityDescriptor parameter receives the length of the security descriptor for the key.

On CD-ROM

lpftLastWriteTime receives a FILETIME structure that denotes the time that key or any of its values was last modified. See the Defines module in CH01.MDB on the CD-ROM for the definition of the FILETIME structure.

RegQueryValueEx

This function returns information about the specified value named in lpValueName. The lpType parameter receives the type of value. These codes are the same as those specified for RegEnumValue. The syntax is as follows:

```
Declare Function RegQueryValueEx Lib "advapi32.dll" Alias _
"RegQueryValueExA" (ByVal hKey As Long, ByVal lpValueName As String, _
ByVal lpReserved As Long, lpType As Long, lpData As Any, lpcbData As _
Long) As Long
```

lpData receives the data of the value, and lpcbData specifies the length of the lpData buffer.

RegSetValueEx

RegSetValueEx sets a value for the key specified by hKey. hKey must have been opened with the KEY_SET_VALUE access flag. The syntax is as follows:

```
Declare Function RegSetValueEx Lib "advapi32.dll" Alias _
"RegSetValueExA" (ByVal hKey As Long, ByVal lpValueName As String, _
ByVal Reserved As Long, ByVal dwType As Long, lpData As Any, ByVal _
cbData As Long) As Long
```

The lpValueName parameter specifies the name of the value to set. If this name does not exist under the hKey, it is added.

dwType specifies the type of data to be stored and is the same as those specified for RegEnumValue.

lpData contains the data to be stored in the value, and cbData specifies the size of lpData.

RegDeleteKey

The subkey under `hKey` designated in `lpSubKey` and all of its values is deleted from the Registry. The `lpSubKey` must have been opened with `DELETE` access. The syntax is as follows:

```
Declare Function RegDeleteKey Lib "advapi32.dll" Alias _
"RegDeleteKeyA" (ByVal hKey As Long, ByVal lpSubKey As String) As _
Long
```

An error occurs if the key specified by `lpSubKey` contains subkeys. Any subkeys must be deleted first. Always delete a tree from the bottom up by using this function.

Listing 1-1 shows how you can use these Registry API functions in an Access application. The code adds a Preferences key to the Registry under the application name and adds a `TimeOut` value to it. CH1.MDB on the CD-ROM that accompanies this book contains this code and the definition of the constants.

Listing 1-1 Using Registry API Functions

```
Dim Result As Long
Dim Disposition As Long
Dim hKey As Long
Dim rc As Long
Dim secattr As SECURITY_ATTRIBUTES

secattr.nLength = 0
secattr.lpSecurityDescriptor = 0
secattr.bInheritHandle = True

' Create the MyApp key under HKEY_CURRENT_USER
rc = RegCreateKeyEx(HKEY_CURRENT_USER, "MyApp", 0, "", _
REG_OPTION_NON_VOLATILE, KEY_ALL_ACCESS, secattr, Result, _
Disposition)
' Open the MyApp key returning handle in hkey
rc = RegOpenKeyEx(HKEY_CURRENT_USER, "MyApp", _
REG_OPTION_NON_VOLATILE, KEY_ALL_ACCESS, hKey)
' Create a Preferences subkey under the MyApp key
rc = RegCreateKeyEx(hKey, "Preferences", 0, "", _
REG_OPTION_NON_VOLATILE, KEY_ALL_ACCESS, secattr, Result, _
Disposition)
' Open the Preferences subkey returning the handle in hkey
rc = RegOpenKeyEx(hKey, "Preferences", _
REG_OPTION_NON_VOLATILE, KEY_ALL_ACCESS, hKey)
' Set a value named Timeout in the Preferences subkey
' and assign a value of 60
rc = RegSetValueEx(hKey, "TimeOut", 0, REG_DWORD, 60, 4)

' Delete a value
```

(continued)

(continued)

```
' Open the MyApp key returning handle in hkey
rc = RegOpenKeyEx(HKEY_CURRENT_USER, "MyApp", _
REG_OPTION_NON_VOLATILE, KEY_ALL_ACCESS, hKey)
' Open the Preferences subkey returning the handle in hkey
rc = RegOpenKeyEx(hKey, "Preferences", _
REG_OPTION_NON_VOLATILE, KEY_ALL_ACCESS, hKey)
' Delete the TimeOut value
rc = RegDeleteValue(hKey, "TimeOut")

' Delete a key

' Open the MyApp key returning handle in hkey
rc = RegOpenKeyEx(HKEY_CURRENT_USER, "MyApp", _
REG_OPTION_NON_VOLATILE, KEY_ALL_ACCESS, hKey)
' Delete the Preferences subkey
rc = RegDeleteKey(hKey, "Preferences")
```

The Registry and Jet

In the absence of any Registry tree for your Access application, Jet gets its settings from the Registry path HKEY_LOCAL_MACHINE\SOFTWARE\Microsoft\Jet\3.5\Engines\Jet 3.5 during startup initialization.

The settings in this path are considered default settings for Jet. You may edit these settings with the Registry editor or through code to set them for all applications that may use Jet on the local machine.

If an application establishes a path in the Registry and sets Jet values there, Jet loads these values in place of those specified in the defaults when your application starts. This is the preferred method for tuning various applications that use Jet.

Access setup establishes the path HKEY_LOCAL_MACHINE\SOFTWARE\Microsoft\Office\8.0\Access\Jet\3.5\Engines\Jet in the Registry. Jet accesses this Registry tree (see Figure 1-7) and loads any settings found there when Access starts up. It loads other settings not specified in this tree from the default path. This ensures that the settings your Access application requires are in effect while your application runs.

Another subkey of interest under the Microsoft\Jet\3.5 key is the ISAM Formats subkey. This subkey contains a key for each data format supported by registered ISAM drivers.

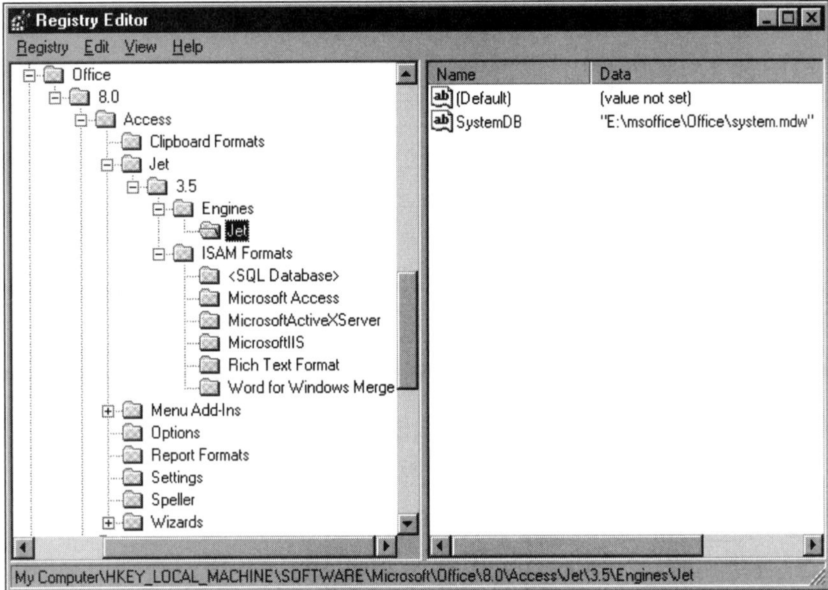

Figure 1-7: The Jet Engine gets its default settings from the HKEY_LOCAL_MACHINE\SOFTWARE\Microsoft\Office\8.0\Access\Jet\3.5\Engines\Jet Registry path during startup.

Xbase settings in the Registry

The settings that affect all applications using Jet to access Xbase ISAM databases are stored in the HKEY_LOCAL_MACHINE\SOFTWARE\Microsoft\Jet\3.5\Engines\Xbase and \Jet\3.5\ISAM Formats keys. Table 1-4 lists values that you may find in the Xbase subkey for FoxPro.

ISAM Basics

ISAM stands for Indexed Sequential Access Method. It is a file access method supported by a two-component file structure containing an index component and a data component. The index contains keys that identify records in the data component. You can search this index for a given record key, and then the corresponding record is fetched by using the record address stored with the key. Indexes can consist of several levels of index. This is what is meant by the Indexed portion of the name. The Sequential portion of the name refers to the capability to scan the file from some point in the data file, record by record in a sequential manner, to some other point deeper in the file.

ISAM is the structure used for most desktop databases in the market today, and Jet can use these databases through their ISAM drivers. The Registry can be used to hold parameters for Jet and for these drivers.

Table 1-4 Xbase Subkey Values for FoxPro

Entry	*Type*	*Description*
`Win32`	`REG_SZ`	The path to the MSXBSE35.DLL used to access FoxPro data.
`NetworkAccess`	`REG_BINARY`	If set to 00, the access to databases and tables is exclusive, regardless of the `OpenDatabase` and `OpenRecordset` methods' exclusive argument.
`PageTimeout`	`REG_DWORD`	The length of time between placing data into an internal cache and invalidating it due to inactivity. The value is specified in 100 millisecond units. The default is 6.
`INFPath`	`REG_SZ`	Specifies the path Jet is to use to look for an .INF file if the file is not located in the same directory as the table.
`CollatingSequence`	`REG_SZ`	The Collating Sequence used by Jet when creating or opening FoxPro tables. This value may be ASCII or International and defaults to ASCII.
`DataCodePage`	`REG_SZ`	Indicates how text pages are stored. May be OEM or ANSI. The default is OEM.
`Deleted`	`REG_BINARY`	Indicates how Jet should handle deleted records. A value of 01 causes Jet not to retrieve or position on records marked for deletion. A value of 00 causes Jet to treat deleted records like any other record. Default is 00.
`Century`	`REG_BINARY`	Indicates how the century components of dates are to be formatted in date-to-string conversions in index expressions.
`Date`	`REG_SZ`	Indicates the date formatting style to use for date-to-string conversions in index expressions. The values are American, ANSI, British, French, DMY, German, Italian, Japan, MDY, USA, and YMD. The default is MDY.

Entry	Type	Description
Mark	REG_DWORD	The decimal value of the character used to separate date parts. The values can be the following: "/" (American, MDY) "." (ANSI) "/" (British, French, DMY) "." (German) "-" (Italian) "/" (Japan, YMD) "-" (USA)
Exact	REG_BINARY	Indicates how string comparisons are handled. The values may be 01 or 00. The 01 value indicates that the strings must match exactly, character for character. 00 indicates that the strings are equivalent if they match character for character until the end of the string on the right side of the expression.

The values you might find for FoxPro 3.0 ISAM Formats are listed in Table 1-5.

Table 1-5 FoxPro 3.0 ISAM Format Values

Entry	Type	Description
Engine	REG_SZ	A value of Xbase
ExportFilter	REG_SZ	A value of Microsoft FoxPro 3.0 (*.DBF)
CanLink	REG_BINARY	A value of 00
OneTablePerFile	REG_BINARY	A value of 01
ISAMType	REG_DWORD	A value of 0
IndexDialog	REG_BINARY	A value of 01
CreateDBOnExport	REG_BINARY	A value of 00
ResultTextImport	REG_SZ	Imports data into the current database from an external file. Changes to data in the database do not change data in the external file.

To affect only the ISAM settings for an Access application, set the preceding values into the HKEY_LOCAL_MACHINE\SOFTWARE\Microsoft\Office\8.0\Access\Jet\3.5\Engines\Xbase and HKEY_LOCAL_MACHINE\SOFTWARE\Microsoft\Office\8.0\Access\Jet\3.5\ISAM Formats keys.

Access settings in the Registry

After installing Access, you can find Jet's defaults in the path HKEY_LOCAL_MACHINE\SOFTWARE\Microsoft\Jet\3.5\Engines\Jet 3.5. If you want to change these defaults, you can edit the values in this path and Jet will use those values instead of its defaults.

Values in this key affect all applications using Jet 3.5 to access an Access database. To apply the values to only Access applications, add the values to the HKEY_LOCAL_MACHINE\SOFTWARE\Microsoft\Office\8.0\Access\Jet\3.5\Engines\Jet key, which Access setup provides. You can find values that you may specify for the Jet key in Table 1-6.

Table 1-6 Jet Key Values

Entry	*Type*	*Description*
PageTimeout	REG_DWORD	The length of time between placing data into an internal cache and invalidating it due to inactivity. The value is expressed in millisecond units. The default is 5000.
LockRetry	REG_DWORD	The number of attempts to access a locked page. Default is 20.
MaxBufferSize	REG_DWORD	The size of the internal cache specified in kilobytes. It must be an integer value greater than or equal to 512. The default is calculated as follows: [(Total Memory in Megabytes - 12 Megabytes) / 4] + 512 Kilobytes.
Threads	REG_DWORD	The number of background threads available to Jet. The default is 3.
UserCommitSync	REG_DWORD	Used for user-specified transactions. The yes default value informs Jet to wait for a commit to finish before returning. A no value enables Jet to perform the commit asynchronously.

Entry	*Type*	*Description*
`ImplicitCommitSync`	`REG_DWORD`	Used for implicit transactions. A yes value informs Jet to wait for the commit to finish before returning. The no default value enables Jet to perform the commit asynchronously.
`ExclusiveAsyncDelay`	`REG_DWORD`	The length of time to defer an asynchronous flush of a database opened exclusively. Specified in milliseconds. The default is 2000. To be effective, `FlushTransactionTimeout` must be set to zero.
`SharedAsyncDelay`	`REG_DWORD`	The length of time to defer an asynchronous flush of a database opened as shared. Specified in milliseconds. The default is 0. To be effective, `FlushTransactionTimeout` must be set to zero.
`SystemDB`	`REG_SZ`	The path and file name of the system database. It is usually the path to SYSTEM.MDW.
`FlushTransaction Timeout`	`REG_DWORD`	Starts asynchronous writes after the specified time has elapsed and no new pages have been added to the Jet cache. Default is 500 milliseconds.
`LockDelay`	`REG_DWORD`	Delays `LockRetry` the specified amount of time between lock requests. Default is 100 milliseconds.
`MaxLocksPerFile`	`REG_DWORD`	A transaction attempting to exceed this value will be split and partially committed.
`RecycleLVs`	`REG_DWORD`	When enabled, Jet recycles long value pages when expanding the database. Default is 0.
`CompactByPKey`	`REG_DWORD`	A 0 value denotes that tables are compacted in base-table order. A non-zero value denotes that tables are compacted in primary-key order.

The Jet\3.5\ISAM Formats key may contain the values found in Table 1-7.

Table 1-7 ISAM Formats/Jet Key Values

Entry	Type	Description
Engine	REG_SZ	Name of the engine
Export or Import Filter	REG_SZ	Microsoft Access (*.MDB;*.MDW;*.MDA)
OneTablePerFile	REG_DWORD	00
IndexDialog	REG_DWORD	00
CreateDBOnExport	REG_DWORD	00

ODBC settings in the Registry

The ODBC driver defaults are found in the key HKEY_LOCAL_MACHINE\SOFTWARE\Microsoft\Jet\3.5\Engines\ODBC in the Registry. Table 1-8 lists the values that you can specify for the ODBC key. Values in this path apply to all applications accessing an ODBC source through Jet.

Table 1-8 ODBC Key Values

Entry	Type	Description
LoginTimeout	REG_DWORD	The number of seconds a login attempt can continue. At the end of this time, the login is considered unsuccessful. 20 seconds is the default.
QueryTimeout	REG_DWORD	The number of seconds a query can continue before being considered unsuccessful.
ConnectionTimeout	REG_DWORD	The number of seconds a connection can be idle before timing out. The default is 600.
AsyncRetryInterval	REG_DWORD	The number of milliseconds between polling the server to determine if an active query has completed. The default is 500.
AttachCaseSensitive	REG_DWORD	Indicates whether to perform a case-sensitive match on table name when attaching tables. A 0 value indicates case-insensitive match, and a value of 1 indicates case-sensitive. The default is 0.

Entry	*Type*	*Description*
AttachableObjects	REG_SZ	A list of server object types for which linking is allowed. The default list is: 'ALIAS', 'SYNONYM', 'SYSTEM TABLE', 'TABLE', 'VIEW'.
SnapshotOnly	REG_DWORD	A value of 1 forces Recordsets to be snapshot types. The default value of 0 allows dynasets and snapshots.
TraceSQLMode	REG_DWORD	A value of 1 causes Jet to trace SQL statements sent to the ODBC source into SQLOUT.TXT. The default value of 0 turns tracing off.
TraceODBCAPI	REG_DWORD	A value of 1 causes Jet to trace ODBC API calls into ODBCAPI.TXT. The default value of 0 turns tracing off.
DisableAsync	REG_DWORD	A value of 0 causes Jet to use asynchronous query execution if it can, and a value of 1 forces synchronous query execution. The default value is 1.
JetTryAuth	REG_DWORD	The default value of 1 causes Jet to try logging into the server using the Access User name and password. If this fails, Jet prompts for login name and password. A value of 0 prompts first.
PreparedInsert	REG_DWORD	A value of 1 causes a prepared insert statement to be used that inserts data into all columns. A value of 0 indicates that a custom insert statement is to be used that inserts only non-null values. The default is 0.
PreparedUpdate	REG_DWORD	A value of 1 causes a prepared update statement to be used that updates data in all columns. A value of 0 uses a statement that updates only columns that change. The default is 0.
FastRequery	REG_DWORD	A value of 1 causes a prepared select statement to be used for parameterized queries. A value of 0 does not use the prepared select. The default value is 0.

The Registry and Access

In addition to the 8.0\Access\Jet subkey, Access sets up other subkeys. The Menu Add-Ins holds the installed add-ins list. The add-ins you see under this subkey are displayed when you choose Add-ins from the Tools menu in Access.

Subkeys you may see under the Menu Add-Ins subkey are Database Splitter, Linked Table Manager, Menu Builder, and Switchboard Manager. The values of these subkeys specify the name of the function that receives control when the add-in is invoked and the name of the library containing the add-in.

Cross-Reference

Other Access subkeys under 8.0\Access\ are Options, Report Formats, Speller, and Wizards. The Wizards subkey contains a key for each type of wizard, and the subkeys under these specify the actual wizards installed. You will find more information on these entries in Chapter 16, "Exploring Add-Ins and Libraries."

Using the Setting Statements

Visual Basic provides statements that you can use to manipulate keys in the Registry. These statements are the `SaveSetting`, `GetSetting`, and `DeleteSetting` statements.

The `SaveSetting` statement modifies or creates a key in the Registry and has the following syntax:

```
SaveSetting AppName:=, Section:=, KEY:=, Setting:=
```

The `AppName` argument specifies the name of the application. The `Section` argument specifies the name of the key where the value will be stored. The `KEY` argument is the name of the value to be stored in the key, and the `Setting` argument is the value to be stored. The labels used in the syntax refer to 16-bit .INI file architecture but operate on the Registry as `AppName:=,Key:=,ValueName:=,Setting:=`.

If you execute the following statement

```
SaveSetting
AppName:="MyApp",Section:="Preferences",KEY:="TimeOut",Setting:="60"
```

the resultant tree in the Registry would be HKEY_CURRENT_USER\Software\VB and VBA Program Settings\MyApp\Preferences, and the value stored in the `Preferences` key would be named `TimeOut` and have a value of `60` with a type of `REG_SZ`.

The `GetSetting` statement returns a value for a specified key in the Registry. It is specified as follows:

```
Dim sVal As String
sVal = GetSetting(AppName:="MyApp", Section:= "Preferences", _
KEY:="TimeOut", Default:="30")
```

The arguments of GetSetting are the same as those for SaveSetting, with the exception of the optional Default argument. The Default argument specifies a value to return if the value specified by KEY is not set in the Registry.

The DeleteSetting statement removes a value or a key from the Registry. Its syntax is the following:

```
DeleteSetting AppName:="MyApp", Section:="Preferences"
```

To delete all values for a key, specify the AppName and Section. Doing so removes all the key's values from the Registry. To delete only a given value for a key, provide the optional value name in the statement, as follows:

```
DeleteSetting AppName:="MyApp", _
Section:="Preferences",KEY:="TimeOut"
```

You should leave at least one value in a key so that errors do not occur when the Registry Editor or an application attempts to open the key. You can insert a default value such as value not set to act as a placeholder.

Using the SetOption Method

You can temporarily override Jet 3.5 Registry settings for your application by using the DBEngine's SetOption method. The values you set with this method remain in effect until your application issues another SetOption or your application closes the DBEngine object.

The SetOption method requires two parameters. The first parameter specifies the name of the Registry value to change, and the second parameter specifies the temporary value to assign to this name. Table 1-9 lists the constants you can use for the first parameter. See Table 1-6 for a description of these keys and the values allowed.

Table 1-9 SetOption Constants

Entry	*Registry Key*
dbExclusiveAsyncDelay	ExclusiveAsyncDelay
dbFlushTransactionTimeout	FlushTransactionTimeout
dbImplicitCommitSync	ImplicitCommitSync
dbLockDelay	LockDelay
dbLockRetry	LockRetry
dbMaxBufferSize	MaxBufferSize
dbMaxLocksPerFile	MaxLocksPerFile
dbPageTimeout	PageTimeout

(continued)

Table 1-9 *(continued)*

Entry	*Registry Key*
dbRecycleLVs	RecycleLVs
dbSharedAsyncDelay	SharedAsyncDelay
dbUserCommitSync	UserCommitSync

Chapter 5, "Working with Data Access Objects (DAO)," discusses the use of DAO objects and the syntax used with objects such as the DBEngine.

Using User Profiles

You can establish a tree within the Registry that contains your own configuration settings to be used for your Access application instead of using the Access settings. This technique enables you to customize the settings for your application without affecting other applications that use Access. The drawback with this technique is the redundancy that it creates in the Registry.

Follow these steps to create your own user profile:

1. Create a Profiles key under HKEY_LOCAL_MACHINE\Software\Microsoft\ Office\8.0\Access.
2. Add a string value named whatever you want to call the profile. `AppProfile` is an example of a profile name.
3. The value of the string should be `\Software\company name\app name\version` number.
4. Create the keys corresponding to the profile string value under the Software key. The mapping here is company name, such as Microsoft; app name, such as Access; and version number, such as 8.0. Substitute your own values when you create the keys.
5. Copy the Access tree — with the exception of the Profiles subkey — to your tree under the version number key. You do this by exporting the \Microsoft\ Office\8.0\Access tree to a .REG file, editing the file with WordPad, and replacing all Microsoft key names with your company name, all Access key names with your app name, and all 8.0 key names with your version number. Do not change any directory paths that contain Access-installed libraries or other objects, unless you have installed these files somewhere else. Remove the Profiles key entry from the file, because you do not want to install this key under your tree.

6. Save the changes in WordPad and go back to the Registry editor and import the file back in.
7. You now have a tree exactly like Access 8.0 with all installed add-ins and wizards, but it's now under your own tree. You can customize this tree for your application without affecting other applications. To use this tree with your application, start Access with a `/profile` command line argument, as follows:

```
Msaccess.exe /profile "AppProfile" app.mdb
```

Cross-Reference

Settings in your profile have precedence over those in the Access tree, which, in turn, have precedence over the settings in the Microsoft\Jet\3.5 tree. To detect that the end user has loaded your application using the correct profile, use the `SysCmd` function in your start-up routine. See Chapter 4, "Understanding Visual Basic for Applications," for information on the `SysCmd` function.

Chapter 2

Relational Databases for Access 97 Developers

In This Chapter

- Understanding an Access 97 database
- Designing a database in seven steps
- Understanding primary keys
- Understanding relations between tables
- Normalization for novices
- Understanding referential integrity
- Using the Lookup Wizard in the table designer

OK, you've tried to understand why you want to use more than one table. When you create an application with two tables, you never can get your system to work. You're tired of all your techno-nerd friends telling you that you have to use more than one table. You've read all the stuff in books that tell you how to use more than one table at a time. You've heard zillions of technical terms, like referential integrity, one-to-many relations, primary and foreign keys, and normalization. (Hey, my database is always normal — I'm OK, my database is OK.) You think to yourself, "I can relate to people; why can't I relate to my database tables?"

The good news is that you're not alone. The *best* news is that Access 97 makes it easy to use multiple tables and accomplish complex database tasks without any programming. The key (pardon the relational humor) is to design your database properly before you start. Access 97 contains a number of tools that help you design your database, including wizards, builders, and the Query Design tool.

The Access 97 form and report wizards automatically create forms and reports that take advantage of multiple related tables. Not only can forms be created instantly that enable you to enter data into multiple lines, but reports can be instantly created for them. In fact, there is even a wizard that can create a complete application. You can select from more than 25 different common business or personal applications.

Generally, you need to first design or select tables that enable relations to be created. Without these tables, you can't begin to take advantage of the power of the Access 97 tools. In this chapter, you learn the very basics of creating and relating multiple tables and the answer to the question, "Why do I need more than one table?" The first task is to define the terms *table* and *database* from an Access 97 relational standpoint.

What Is an Access 97 Database?

A *database* contains one or more tables (as well as other objects, such as queries, forms, and reports). *Tables* are logical groupings of similar data. They consist of Rows (records) and Columns (fields). Most applications have several related tables to present the information in an efficient manner. You've been told countless times that an application that uses multiple tables can manipulate data more efficiently than an application that uses one large table. Well, it's true!

Multiple tables simplify data entry and reporting by decreasing redundant or duplicate data. For example, by defining two tables for an application that uses customer information, you don't need to store customers' name and address information every time they purchase an item. Suppose that you own a toy store. You have many different customers. Each customer may come back many times to buy from you. Each time they may buy many products. Suppose that you had all your information in one database table. Your data might look like the datasheet in Figure 2-1.

Microsoft Access - [Query1 : Select Query]

File Edit View Insert Format Records Tools Window Help

Inv Date	Company	City	Qty	Description	Price
1/8/96	Amo Electronic House	Keenville	5.0	Ren & Stimpy Spell an	$29.99
1/8/96	Amo Electronic House	Keenville	7.0	MEGA Game Wear-Vir	$299.99
1/8/96	Amo Electronic House	Keenville	1.0	The Power Buddy Tape	$32.99
1/12/96	St. Joseph's Children's Hospital	Deerfield Beach	2.0	My First Dollhouse-Wit	$149.99
1/12/96	St. Joseph's Children's Hospital	Deerfield Beach	4.0	The Power Buddy Tape	$32.99
1/12/96	St. Joseph's Children's Hospital	Deerfield Beach	3.0	Adventures of the Lost	$19.99
1/12/96	St. Joseph's Children's Hospital	Deerfield Beach	3.0	Adventures of the Lost	$19.99
1/12/96	St. Joseph's Children's Hospital	Deerfield Beach	10.0	Assorted Stuffed Anima	$19.99
1/12/96	Children's Illustrated	Youngstown	1.0	Wrote Article for Childr	$1,150.00
2/4/96	Children's Illustrated	Youngstown	1.0	Wrote article for Februa	$950.00
2/5/96	Buffy's Electronic Boutique	Atlanta	5.0	MEGA Game Wear-Vir	$299.99
2/5/96	Buffy's Electronic Boutique	Atlanta	3.0	Z-Men Remote Control	$39.99
2/5/96	Buffy's Electronic Boutique	Atlanta	4.0	Ren & Stimpy Spell an	$29.99
2/16/96	Irene's Groovy Scene	North Hampton	2.0	Adventures of the Lost	$19.99
2/23/96	Blue Moon Sporting Goods	Loraine	5.0	Repairing bike-replace	$15.00
2/23/96	Blue Moon Sporting Goods	Loraine	2.5	Replace motor in remot	$25.00
2/24/96	Harrisburg and Associates	Ottawa	6.0	Assorted Stuffed Anima	$19.99
3/1/96	Children's Illustrated	Youngstown	1.0	Wrote Article for Childr	$1,200.00
3/2/96	Sports Palace	Fon-Du-Lac, Syl	1.0	Magic Glow Football	$9.99
3/2/96	Sports Palace	Fon-Du-Lac, Syl	1.0	MEGA Game Wear-Vir	$299.99

Record: 1 of 92

Datasheet View

Figure 2-1: A datasheet showing customers and sales in one table.

Each time you enter a new item for a customer, you have to repeat the information for that customer. You have to reenter the customer's name, address, phone number, credit information, and so on for each item. This is acceptable if each of your customers purchases only one item. If you have to reenter all that information each time a customer purchases multiple items, however, you soon find that you have inconsistent data in your table. First, you would eventually enter something wrong. If you entered the customer's name wrong, you may never find one of his or her orders. You may enter different addresses for the same customer. Which address is correct?

If a customer moves, you have to change many lines in your table. Though you can easily see all your data in one place, it just doesn't make sense in a database management software application like Access 97. You may store data this way in a spreadsheet, but never in a database.

The solution is to divide the data into two or more tables based on logical groupings of data. You have customers, and when they buy merchandise you charge them by issuing an invoice. Each customer may buy from you multiple times. To add even more complexity, each invoice may contain several items, so you need to create several tables: one for customers, one for invoices, and one for invoice items. Whenever you do this, you should also create unique values for each record in a table. This makes locating a specific record easier. You don't want to use the customer's name because you could have two Adam Johnsons in the same town. You don't want to use the name and the address because a whole family may live in the same apartment. One day a customer might walk in and say, "Hi, my name's Larry, this is my brother Darryl, and this is my other brother Darryl." This unique value is called a *primary key*. The primary key can be one or more fields in a table. Before you learn about keys, you have to learn how to create a proper table design.

The Seven-Step Method for Database Design

In order to create tables, you first must complete a series of tasks known as *database design*. The better your design, the better your application. The more you think through your design, the faster you can complete any system. Design is not some necessary evil, nor is its intent to produce voluminous amounts of documentation. The sole intent of design is to enable you to produce a clear-cut path to follow as you implement your design.

In this chapter, you learn only the important parts to designing and creating the tables and relations of any system from a common-sense approach. You learn the relational techniques required to create properly engineered tables. This chapter teaches you the concepts of keys, normalization, relationships, and integrity.

The overall design from concept to reality

All software developers and end users face similar problems. The first set of problems you encounter is with gathering requirements. The end user is typically your client, your coworker, or you. It is important to understand the overall needs of the system before you begin to zero in on the details.

The seven-step design method shown in Figure 2-2 can help you create the system you need at a price (measured in time or dollars) you can afford. The example in this chapter is for a hypothetical toy company named The Toy Box. This company is a medium-sized distributor that services individuals and smaller toy stores across many states. Basically, The Toy Box needs to automate several tasks:

- Entering customer information — name, address, and discount information.
- Entering orders — invoice date, customer information, and the items ordered; the quantity purchased; and the item number. The item description and price are retrieved from a central inventory table.
- Entering inventory items — details of the items sold.
- Asking all types of questions about the information in the database.
- Producing a customer list.
- Producing a monthly invoice report.
- Producing inventory reports.

The design process is an *iterative procedure*. That is, as each new step is finished, you must look again at all the previous steps to make sure that nothing in the basic design has changed. If you decide, when creating a data-entry form, that you need another field not already in the table, then you have to go back and follow each previous step to add the field. Now that you've defined The Toy Box's overall systems in terms of what needs to be accomplished, you can begin the next step of report design.

Report design — Defining the output

You should break down design work to the smallest level of detail of which you are currently aware. You should start each new step by reviewing the overall design objectives. In the case of The Toy Box, the objectives are to track customers, keep a record of orders and inventory, produce invoices, and create a sales summary. The first step is to sketch out on paper what it takes to accomplish each of these objectives. This is usually done in the form of *reports*. You can prototype reports by using unbound controls in the Access 97 report designer or by simply sketching them out on paper.

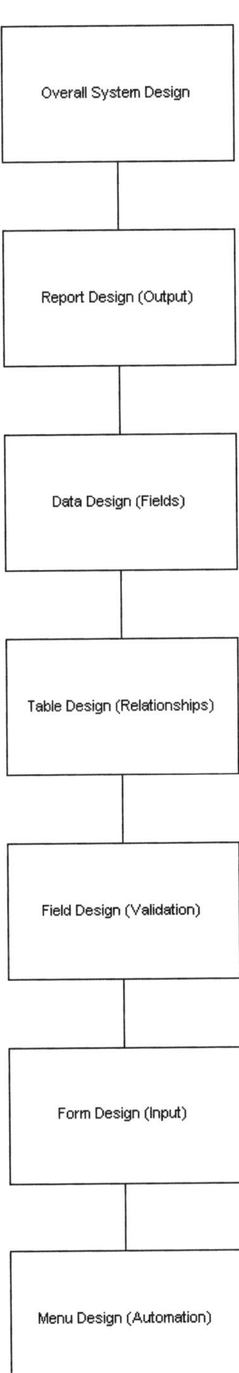

Figure 2-2: The seven-step design flowchart.

When you sketch out reports, you may wonder, "What comes first — the duck or the egg?" Does the report layout come first, or do you first determine the data items and text that make up the report? Actually, these items are conceived together. How you lay out the fields in the conception of a report is not important.

The Toy Box sample design begins with the tasks of tracking sales. The first report that needs to be developed is a standard invoice. This invoice uses information from many sources. Each customer's name and address is shown, along with some tax information. Information particular to each invoice includes the Invoice Date, Customer Order Number, the Payment Terms, and Salesperson. Information about each line item includes the Quantity Shipped, Item Number, Description, Price, and the calculated field Extension (Quantity Shipped × Price). Summary information is also listed, including the Subtotal, Taxes, Freight, and Amount owed. Finally, you can include a checkbox to indicate a paid invoice and to provide a long comment (memo field) for each invoice.

Figure 2-3 shows an example of an invoice report. You can use any tool to sketch it out, even the Access 97 Table and Report Wizards (or a Word document). From this simple report design, you can begin to design the individual tables you need for your application.

The Toy Box

500 Toy Chest Road
Somerset, CA 94567

Invoice Date: [Invoice Date]

[Company]
[Contact Name (First Name/Last Name)]
[Street]
[City, State, Zip/Postal]
Phone: [Phone Number] Fax: [Fax Number]
[Customer Order Number] [Source of Order] [Payment Terms] [Salesperson] [Shipped Via]

[Quantity]	[Description]	[Price]	[Extension]
[Quantity]	[Description]	[Price]	[Extension]
[Quantity]	[Description]	[Price]	[Extension]
[Quantity]	[Description]	[Price]	[Extension]
[Quantity]	[Description]	[Price]	[Extension]
[Quantity]	[Description]	[Price]	[Extension]

[Subtotal]
[Tax Rate 1%] [Tax 1]
[Tax Rate 2%] [Tax 2]
[Freight]
[Amount Owed]

[Paid?] [Comments]

Figure 2-3: A sample report design.

Data design — What fields do you need?

You first want to sketch out each and every report for your application before you start to create your data design. Assume that the invoice report is all you want. From this one report, you can begin to compile all your data and then divide the data into tables. One of the best ways to perform this task is to take each report and list the data items that are found in the report. As you do so, take careful note of the items that are separate and of any fields that are found in more than one report. Make sure that an item with the same name in one report is really the same data item in another report. This is a common-sense approach. Later in the chapter, you see a more scientific process known as *normalization*.

The next step is to determine whether you can begin to separate the data items into some logical arrangement. Later, you have to group these data items into logical table structures and then map them onto data-entry screens that make sense. For example, customer data should be entered as part of a customer table process — not as part of an invoice.

To separate the report fields into table definitions, you must first look at each report. For The Toy Box invoice report, you start by listing the data items that can be classified as belonging to each customer, as shown in Table 2-1.

Table 2-1 Data That Can Be Separated into the Customer Table
Company
First Name
Last Name
Street
City
State
Zip/Postal Code
Phone Number
Fax Number
Tax Rate 1
Tax Rate 2

After extracting the customer data, you can move on to the invoice data. Again, you need to analyze the invoice reports for fields that are part of the sales information. The invoice is a great example of information that occurs once and information that has multiple occurrences. Table 2-2 shows a listing of the fields in the invoice report that occur once and the fields that occur multiple times.

Table 2-2 Data That Can Be Separated into Invoice Tables

Items That Occur Once	*Items That Occur Multiple Times*
Invoice Date	Quantity
Customer Order Number	Description
Source of Order	Price
Payment Terms	Extension
Salesperson	
Shipped Via	
Subtotal	
Tax 1	
Tax 2	
Freight	
Amt Owed	
Paid?	
Comments	

This a good start for the table definitions for The Toy Box. The information for the invoice has been split into two columns. Some of the items are used only once for the invoice, and other items are used for each detail line in the invoice. This is part of the process called normalization.

When you look at Tables 2-1 and 2-2, you may wonder how these three files can be linked together so that Access knows which customer belongs to an invoice and which detail information goes with which invoice. This is done through a process known as *joining,* or *linking.* It is also called *setting relationships.* In order to set these relationships, you must create a unique identifier for each table. Often, this unique identifier is a number or code. You create this identifier by adding one or more fields to each table. It sometimes takes more than one field to create a unique identifier. These fields are called *keys.*

Understanding Primary Keys

Every table should have a *primary key.* The primary key uniquely identifies one record from another. A primary key is made up of one or more fields. For example, a field should be added to the Customer table that uniquely identifies one customer from another. This field may be called the Customer Number field. It can be a Text field and can be set by the user when the record is created, or it can be an AutoNumber field (Counter field in Access

2.0) and can automatically be set when each record is created. The field type of the primary key doesn't matter as long as each record in the table has a different Customer Number (no two records can have the same number) — this is known as *entity integrity* in the world of database management.

By having a different primary key in each record, such as the Customer Number in the Customer table, you can tell two customers apart. This is important, because you can easily have two customers named Fred Smith or Toys R Them in your table.

Theoretically, you could use the customer name plus the customer's address, but two persons named Fred Smith could live in the same town and state. A father and son, Fred David Smith and Fred Daniel Smith, could live at the same address. The goal of setting primary keys is to create individual records in a table that guarantee uniqueness.

Remember that when creating Access 97 tables, if you don't specify a primary key, Access 97 asks if you want one. If you say yes, Access 97 creates a primary key for you. The primary key that Access 97 creates is an AutoNumber data type. It automatically places a new sequential number in the primary key field for each record.

Deciding on a primary key

Most tables have a field or a combination of fields that makes each record unique. The field or fields that make the record unique are known as the primary key for that table. Often, the primary key field is some sort of ID field. The ID field is usually a text type field. The contents of this ID field are usually determined by a simple method that you specify to create the value in the field. Your method can be as simple as a sequential value: 0001, 0002, 0003, 0004, and so on. You also can use the first letter of the real value you are tracking (such as the first letter of the company name) along with a sequence number (such as A001, A002, B001, B002, and so on). Sometimes the method may rely on a specific set of letters and sequential numbers for the field content (as long as each field has a unique value); for example, the first three characters of the company name, a hyphen, and a sequential number. The Customer Number for Toys R Them could be TOY-001. Your method can be a complicated calculation based on information in several fields in the table.

Any rudimentary scheme and a good sequence number always seem to work. Because Access 97 automatically tells you when you try to enter a duplicate key value, you can simply add a duplicate key number to the sequence number. You may think that all these sequence numbers make looking up information in your tables difficult. Just remember that normally you never look up information by an ID field. You generally look up information by the purpose of the table. In Access 97, you can create lookup fields that always display related values while storing the unique key value.

Benefits of a primary key

Have you ever placed an order with a company for the first time, and then the next day decided to increase your order? You call the people at the order desk. Sometimes they ask you for your customer number, and you tell them that you don't know your customer number. This type of thing happens all the time. They then ask you for some other information, usually your zip code or telephone area code. Then, as they narrow down the list of customers, they ask your name and then tell you your customer number (as if you care). Some businesses use phone numbers as a unique starting point. When I call for pizza delivery, I give them my phone number, and they proceed to tell me my wife's name, address, and the last ten types of pizza she ordered. Last week, they didn't even ask for my phone number; they now have Caller ID hooked into their computer screen. Imagine my surprise when they answered the phone, "Good evening, Mrs. Prague" (and I don't even look like my wife!).

Designing the primary key

In order to set relations between the three tables you have designed so far, you need to create a primary key for each proposed table. You start with the Customer fields. As described on the previous pages, you can design a simple primary key that can contain the first three letters of the company name (or the last name if the Company name field was blank) followed by a sequential number. You can create this primary key as a Text field and add it to the top of the table design. (You should try to create your tables with the primary key as the first field.) You can call this field Customer Number.

The main Invoice table is also simple. A single field can be added as the primary key because there will be one record in this table for each invoice number — a simple primary key. In this example, you may want to create a primary key that may be the date and a sequential number. For example, the first record for October 21, 1997, can be 19971021-01, the second invoice on that date can be 19971021-02, and so on. On October 22, the first invoice number can be 19971022-01. These records can be created with an 11-character text field. You also can use a simple sequential number. The first Invoice Number can be 1, the next 2, and so on. But, if a customer calls and doesn't know his or her name (believe it or not, it happens), you can try to find it by the date he or she says the order was placed, or you can find it by the Invoice Number. You can see in Table 2-3 that the Invoice Number has been added to the design.

The primary key in the final table is a little more complicated. A customer can purchase an unlimited number of items on each invoice. Therefore, this Invoice Items table has more than one record for each main invoice record. The Invoice Number field itself is not sufficient to uniquely identify a record in this table. You could add another hyphen and another sequence number. For example, the first item in the first invoice for October 21, 1997, could be 19971021-01-01. The inexperienced database developer would do this and then find that the two invoice tables don't join properly. The reason for this is that when you relate these tables, the two tables do not find a common value. Instead, you have to use two fields: an invoice number field matching the values from the main invoice table and a second field that contains the sequential line number of the number of items for the specific invoice. As you can see in Table 2-3, using two fields for the invoices creates a multiple-field primary key.

Table 2-3 Designing the Primary Keys

Customer Fields	*Invoice Items That Occur Once*	*Invoice Items That Occur Multiple Times*
Customer Number	Invoice Number	Invoice Number
Company	Invoice Date	Line Number
First Name	Customer Order Number	Quantity
Last Name	Source of Order	Description
Street	Payment Terms	Price
City	Salesperson	Extension
State	Shipped Via	
Zip/Postal Code	Subtotal	
Phone Number	Tax 1	
Fax Number	Tax 2	
Tax Rate 1	Freight	
Tax Rate 2	Amt Owed	
		Paid?
		Comments

Why did you have to design two new fields for this multiple-field primary key? Why not just use the Invoice Number and Quantity fields? The answer is that you possibly can have two items with the same quantity ordered. Why not use the Description field? The answer again is that you can have two lines on the invoice ordering the same item. Perhaps you allow a customer to buy ten of a specific item at one price and five more at a reduced price. This situation requires two lines with the same Invoice Number and Description, but it does not create a unique key. You can create a three-field key — Invoice Number, Quantity, and Description — but again, you can have two items purchased with the same quantity and different prices. How about a four-field key created by adding the price field, too? Again, a customer may buy five Lettuce Patch Kids Dolls at $5.50 each and then add five more later in the order at the same price. Though this isn't a normal occurrence, you don't want to limit flexibility, either. Besides, a four-key field is a little tough to follow.

The accepted solution of professional database developers everywhere is a two-key field. The first field in the multiple occurrence table (known as a foreign key) matches the primary key field in the main table. The second key field is simply a sequential number. You can implement this two-field key one of two ways, either by using a text or number field or by using the Access AutoNumber field type for the Line Number field.

Using a text or number field, you can create your data entry form to enter a sequential number starting at 001 or 1 for each item in an invoice. Invoice Number 19971021-01 has as its Line Number field 001 for the first invoice item, 002 for the second line, 003 for the third line, and so on. For the next invoice on October 21, 1997, the Invoice Number is 19971021-02, and its Line Number field is set to 001 for the first invoice item, 002 for the second line, 003 for the third line, and so on. For each new invoice, the numbering begins from 001. However, this requires a fairly complex VBA program to implement.

A simpler solution is to use the Access 97 AutoNumber field type for the Line Number field. It would simply start at 1 and sequentially increase with each new invoice item. For example, if you start using your tables on October 21, 1997, the first Invoice Number might be 19971021-01 and the first line number 1. The next line number is 2, the next 3, and so on. Suppose the first invoice has three items. The next invoice on October 21, 1997, is 19971021-02, and the first item has Line Number 4, the next 5, and so on. Two years later, the first invoice item record for October 21, 1999, has Invoice Number 19991021-01 and perhaps line number 5635 if you had sold 5,634 different items over the past two years.

One more task is to eliminate unnecessary fields. You may ask how a field can be unnecessary. If a field can be calculated at any time and is not dependent on outside factors (such as time), it should not be carried in the table and should be calculated only when it is needed. Unnecessary fields include Extension (Quantity × Price) in the Invoice Items That Occur Multiple Times table and Subtotal and Amount Owed in the Invoice Items That Occur Once table.

Before you begin to create your tables and primary keys, you still have much to design. The next step is to understand relations and learn the concepts of foreign keys.

Understanding Relations Between Tables

Relationships enable data in one table to be matched or joined with data in another table to create a set of data that can be used in a form or report. In Access 97, this joining is commonly done with queries, and the resulting set of data is called a *dynaset*. This dynamic set of data also can be established at the table or relationship level to serve as a basis for those established at the query level. If you can set a relationship at the table level, the relationship is automatically recognized when a multiple-table query is created that uses fields from more than one table. Relationships between tables can be grouped into four types:

- One-to-one
- One-to-many
- Many-to-one
- Many-to-many

When you physically join two tables by connecting fields with like information, you create a relationship that Access 97 recognizes. The relationship that you specify between tables is important. This relationship tells Access 97 how to find and display information from fields in two or more tables. Based on the relationship, your program needs to know whether to look for only one record in a table or for several records. For example, the relationship between the Invoice table and the Invoice Items table is known as a one-to-many relationship. There is always one record in the Invoice table for at least one record in the Invoice Items table. There can be many related records in the Invoice Items table, however, so Access 97 knows to find only one record in the Invoice table and look for any in the Invoice Items table (one or more) that have the same Invoice Number. Figure 2-4 shows this relationship graphically.

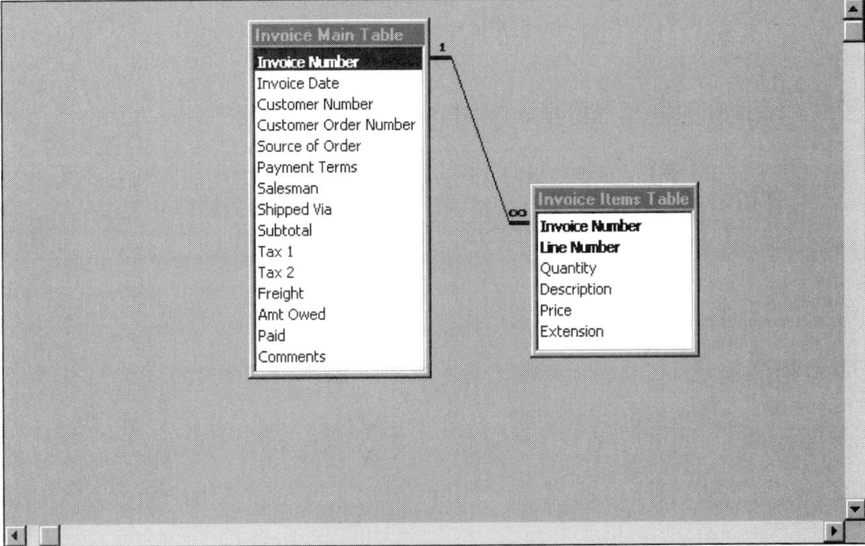

Figure 2-4: A one-to-many relationship.

As you can see in Figure 2-4, a one-to-many relationship exists between the Invoice Main Table and the Invoice Items Table. You should understand the other types of relationships as well.

The one-to-one relationship

The one-to-one relationship is rarely used in database systems, although it can be useful to relate or link two tables together. The one-to-one relationship is rarely used in a single-user system because you can simply move the fields from one table into another. In a multiuser system, files sometimes are split up for local access or security reasons. A good example of a one-to-one relationship that occurs in payroll systems is the payroll and personnel tables. In most companies, nearly everyone can get to the personnel file in order to view and change internal locations, address, or phone information for each employee. The payroll information, which may include salary and raise information, is generally kept separate, and access is granted only to human resources staff. Although both tables are usually keyed by Social Security number, a one-to-one relationship exists between the payroll and personnel files in order to prepare payroll/personnel reports with information from both tables.

The one-to-many relationship

The one-to-many relationship has been thoroughly described in this chapter. This relationship is between two tables in which a single record in one table may have multiple occurrences in another table. This relationship is sometimes called a *parent-child* relationship. The relationship between the Invoice Main Table and the Invoice Items Table shown in Figure 2-4 is a great example of this relationship.

The many-to-one relationship

The one-to-many and many-to-one relationships are actually the same thing. The difference depends on which end of the relation you are looking at. For example, each invoice can have several items. Conversely, there are many items on one order.

An easier way to understand a many-to-one relationship is to look at a table lookup. When displaying a record that has a many-to-one relationship with the primary table, you create a table lookup. For example, when looking at an invoice, you have access to customer information, but this customer information must be looked up. In the table design in Table 2-3, however, there is no way to join Customer and Invoice information.

The Customer table is keyed (the primary key) by the Customer Number field. Each customer is assigned a unique number. Rather than store any of the detailed customer information in the Invoice table, you merely have to repeat this value in the Invoice table. You do this by adding a field named Customer Number to the Invoice table definition. By doing so, whenever a new Invoice is created, the Customer Number is entered into the Invoice record, which enables you to look up information in the Customer Record. Because many invoices may have the same Customer Number, you create a many-to-one relationship.

Understanding foreign keys

The inclusion of a primary key from one table into another table as a lookup key creates a *foreign key*. This key is called foreign because you are storing the primary key from a foreign table. The name of the field is not important. What is important is that the same values are stored, which means that the data types and sizes of the fields in both tables must be identical (or at least compatible). You can join two text fields of differing sizes as long as the values of the field with the larger storage size never exceed the size of the smaller field size.

Primary keys guarantee uniqueness in a table, and you use the primary key field in one table to link to another. The common link field in the other table may not be (and usually isn't) the primary key in the other table. The common link field is a field, or fields, that holds the same type of data that the primary key of the link table holds. The field or fields used to link to a primary key field in another table are known as foreign keys. Unlike a primary key, which must be created in a special way, a foreign key is any field or fields used in a relation. By matching the values (from the primary key to the foreign key) in both tables, two records can be related.

As shown in Figure 2-5, the Customer Number field has been added to the Invoice Main Table as the foreign key. You can also reexamine the keys in the Invoice Items Table. One-to-many relations form interesting situations with respect to primary and foreign keys. The primary key for the Invoice Items Table is a combination of the Invoice Number and Line Number fields, and the Invoice Number is also a foreign key to the relationship with the Invoice Main Table.

This is a good start to creating and relating the tables necessary for this hypothetical system. You may not realize yet that the techniques you have seen so far are really part of a more scientific approach to database management known as normalization. In the next part of this chapter, you learn the basics of data normalization and create the tables and relationships necessary for The Toy Box order entry application.

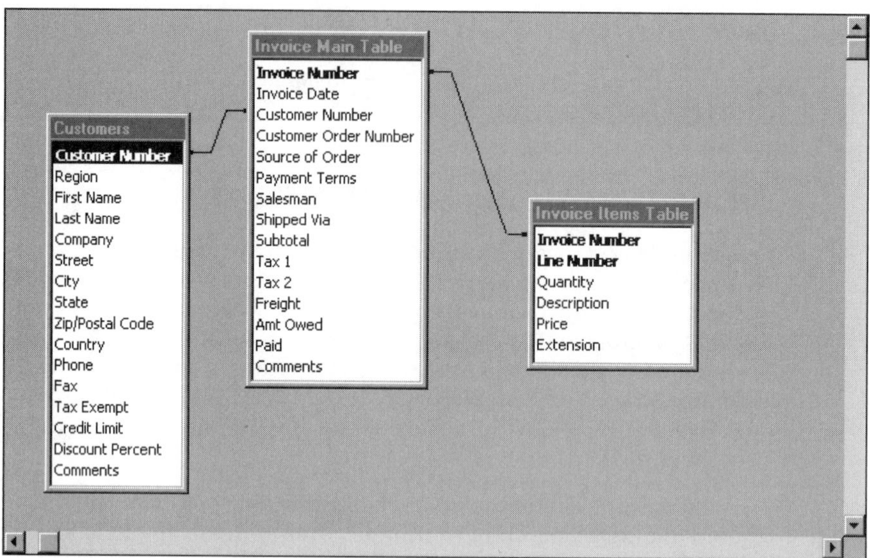

Figure 2-5: Adding a foreign key.

Normalization for Novices

Normalization is the process of breaking apart a single database and then relating the files based on common values. Normalization was developed by E. F. Codd, who is widely considered the father of relational database theory. The goals of normalization are simple:

- Eliminate redundant information
- Increase data integrity
- Make systems more efficient

To illustrate the concepts of normalization, assume that you have retrieved a flat file from an old mainframe system. This file contains thousands of records and about a dozen fields. Like the datasheet shown in Figure 2-1, this file contains the same customer and product information over and over again. The solution is to break up this file into several related tables.

Rule zero: Always key your tables

The key is the key.

Codd's first rule (actually rule zero in his theory of relational databases) is that any table you create must have a unique key. Any item of information must be uniquely identified by three things:

- The database file: In Access, this is the table name.
- The database field: In Access, this is the field name.
- The value of the key for the record: In Access, this is the data value.

In Access, the primary key of a table serves to meet this rule. Codd also states that the primary key should be an index, which is automatic in Access. Any fields you designate as a primary key are always indexed. An *index* is an internal file that maintains the order of a set of values. An index enables data to be searched quickly because the data is always maintained in a known order. Internally, the index file doesn't actually store data but rather a series of pointers to the data. When a value is added, deleted, or changed, rather than rearranging all the values, only a maximum of two pointers have to be changed. To illustrate this simply, assume that an actual data file has three values: A, G, and R. A is the first value in the list. A points to G, and G points to R, which is the last value in the list. A new value K is added. Now, the pointer from G changes to point to K, and a new pointer is added to point from K to R. When finding a value, Access searches through simple lists of pointers rather than searching through potentially millions of bytes of data.

In the example shown in Figure 2-6, there is no key. The Invoice date is merely the date of the invoice. In Figure 2-1, you can see that to uniquely identify a group of records, you must look at the Invoice Date and Customer Name. Looking at both fields prohibits you from processing more than one order each day for a specific customer. To normalize the table, the first task is either to designate one or more fields to be the primary key or to add a new field. In this case, the best decision is to add a new field: Invoice Number. Now that you have added the unique field, you can look at each invoice to see if any of the fields repeat.

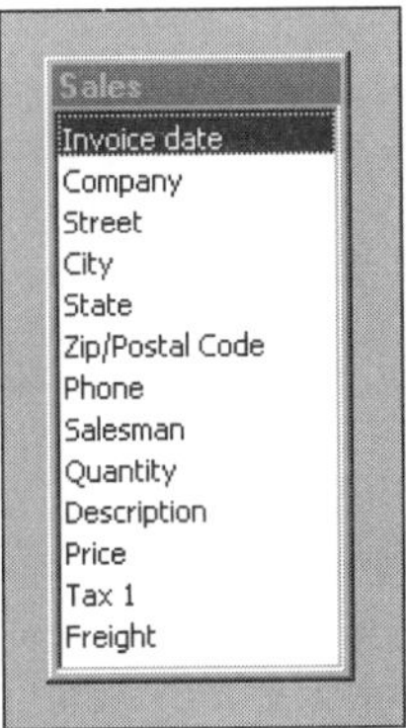

Figure 2-6: A starting point for normalization.

Rule one: Eliminate repeating groups

For each set of related fields, create a separate table and give the table a primary key.

Rule one says to split the data where you have multiple records, known as *repeating groups*. Repeating groups that appear to have a one-to-many relationship are split apart, such as the one-to-many relationship between the invoice data and the line items in each invoice. The Quantity, Description, and Price fields make up the line item data for each invoice. These fields should be separated into a table so that the items that occur once (Invoice Date, Customer Number, Salesman, Tax, and Freight) are separated from the items that occur many times.

This separation creates a relationship between two primary keys. As described earlier in this chapter, however, the Invoice Number in the Sales Detail table is not enough to create uniqueness, so the Line Number field is also added. This is shown in Figure 2-7.

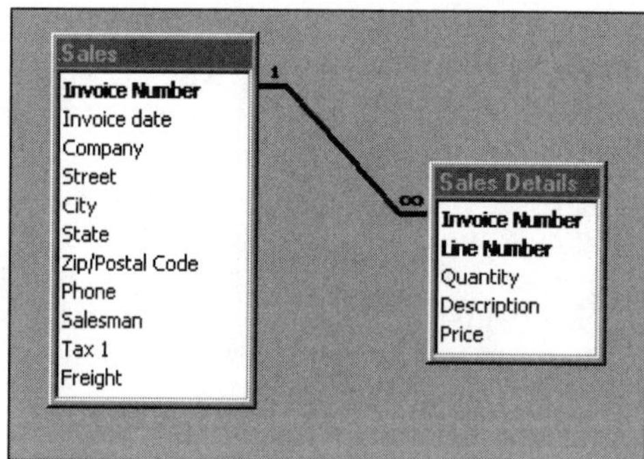

Figure 2-7: Separating Sales and Sales Details information.

Rule two: Examine multifield key relationships

If a field is only related to part of a multifield key, move it to a separate table.

Codd's second rule asks you to examine any table that requires more than a single field key. This requirement is usually a hint that more can be done than just splitting one table into two tables. Rule two specifies that you look to see whether fields in the table are related to only part of a primary key. In this example, only the Quantity field and the fact that a selected product happens to have a price associated with it are related to the invoice number key. The description and price have nothing to do with the Line Number.

Obviously, each invoice had repeating groups. Less apparently, the Description and Price fields repeat for each line item that uses them. You don't see this if you look at only one invoice. If you look across all the records and sort the data differently, the repeating fields become more apparent. If you look through the data, you can see many of the same toys. Seeing these same toys takes a little more experience. You may also notice that the descriptions match wherever the prices match, which lets you know that you can create a table of descriptions and prices. This table is a standard product or inventory table.

The relationship shown in Figure 2-8 is a many-to-one relationship from the Sales Details to the newly created Products table. This relationship is also known as a *lookup table*. Note that the Quantity field remains in the Sales Details table along with the newly added Product Number field, which is also the foreign key. When a customer orders a product, the quantity and product number are entered, and the most up-to-date description and price are used (more about the Price field later).

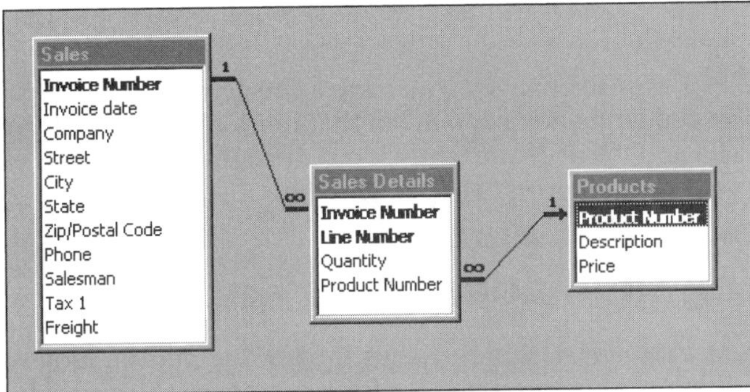

Figure 2-8: Separating the Sales Details and Products information.

Rule three: Examine any remaining groups of information

If fields do not contribute to a description of the key, move them to a separate database file.

Rule three asks you to look for descriptive information that remains in a database table file but is not related to the key. The customer information has nothing to do with the invoice data except to identify who bought the products.

If you look back at Figure 2-1, you can see that the company information is repeated for each item. The customer information should be segregated into a separate table with its own primary key. A linking field (foreign key) must also be added to the Sales table that matches the value in the newly created Customer table. Figure 2-9 shows this change.

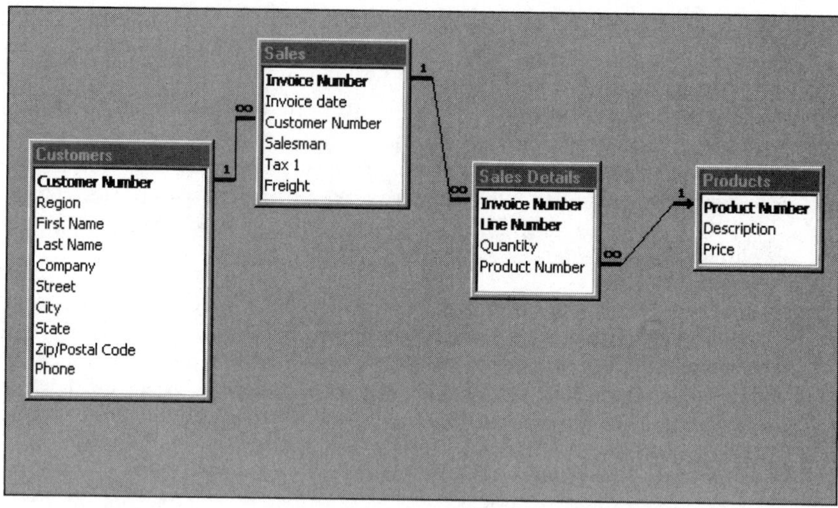

Figure 2-9: Separating the Sales and Customer data.

After you make these changes, you have a third normal form. This form contains no repeating fields, no fields that don't relate directly to the tables' primary key, and, most importantly, no redundant data. Lastly, you must examine your design for time-dependent data.

Handling time-dependent data

The current database design retrieves the product information whenever it needs to. When you print an invoice for a customer, the current description and price are used. What happens if you have a price increase? Suppose you re-invoice the customer a month later, and the five Walk-Out Baseball Games — including Picket Signs — that he or she bought last week at $25.99 each are now $35.00 each. The invoice for $129.95 suddenly becomes $175.00. You may have a fully normalized database, but you don't have happy customers.

This situation is a good example of time-dependent data. You have to return to a second normal form by denormalizing the Price field. You do this by adding the Price field back to the Sales Details table. Rather than just retrieving the price whenever it is needed, when you create the order, the database retrieves the current price and permanently copies it to the Price field in the Sales Details table.

Remembering the normalization rules

The key, the whole key, and nothing but the key, so help me Codd.

The key means that fields cannot repeat but must independently and uniquely describe the database's key; **the whole key** means that in databases with a multifield key, additional fields must describe all of the key; **nothing but the key** means that fields should describe the key only, not other descriptive fields; and **so help me Codd**, of course, refers to the author of the relational database theory.

Understanding Referential Integrity

In addition to specifying relationships between tables in an Access 97 database, you also can set up rules that help maintain a degree of accuracy between the tables. For example, you do not want to delete a customer record in your Customer table if you have related order records in the Orders table. If you did delete a customer record without first deleting the customer's orders, you would have a system that has an order without a customer. This type of problem could be catastrophic.

Imagine being in charge of a bank that tracks loans in a database system. This system has no rules that say, "Before deleting a customer's record, make sure that there is no outstanding loan." It would be disastrous. So, a database system needs to have rules that specify certain conditions between tables — rules to enforce the integrity of information between the tables. These rules are known as *referential integrity.* These rules keep relationships between tables intact in a relational database management system. Referential integrity is a set of rules based on your relationships that prohibits you from changing your data in ways that invalidate the links between tables.

Referential integrity operates strictly on the keys of a table, checking each time a key field, whether primary or foreign, is added, changed, or deleted. If the change to a key creates an invalid relation, it is said to violate referential integrity. You can set up your tables so that referential integrity is enforced automatically.

When tables are linked together, one table is usually called the *parent,* whereas the table it is linked to is usually called the *child.* This is known as a *parent-child relationship.* Referential integrity guarantees that you will never have an orphan, a child record without a parent record. You can have childless parents, but never a parentless child.

Creating relationships

Unless you have a reason for not wanting your relationships to always be active, you should create your table relationships at the table level using the Relationships Builder. If you need to break the table relationships later, you can. For normal data entry and reporting purposes, however, having your relationships defined at the table level makes using a system much easier.

Access 97 has a very powerful Relationships Builder. You can add tables, use drag-and-drop methods to link tables, easily specify the type of link, and set any referential integrity between tables.

You create relationships in the Database window by selecting Edit⇨Relationships, or you can click on the Relationships button on the toolbar. The main Relationships window appears, which enables you to add tables and create links between them.

The main Relationships window is shown in Figure 2-10. When first opened, the Relationships window is a blank surface. You can add tables to the window by using one of several methods:

- Add the tables before entering the Relationships Builder from the Show Table dialog box.
- Click on the Add Tables button on the toolbar.
- Select Relationships⇨Add Table from the Relationships window menu.

You can also click the right mouse button, which calls up the shortcut menu, and select Add Table from the menu. If you select a table by mistake, you can remove it from the window by clicking in it and pressing the Delete key. You can resize each table window to see all the fields in the tables.

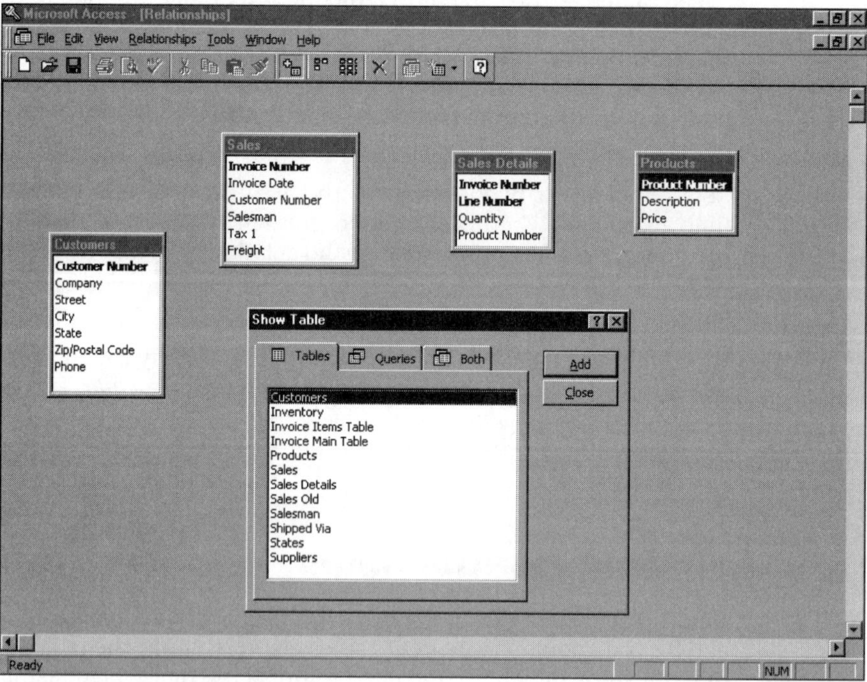

Figure 2-10: The Relationships Builder.

Creating a link between tables

With the tables in the Relationships window, you are ready to create links between the tables. To create a link between two tables, simply select the common field in one table and drag it over to the field in the table you want to link to, then drop it on the common field. This is exactly the same process as joining two tables in a query.

If you select a field for linking in error, simply move the field icon to the window surface. The field icon turns into the international "no" symbol. While it is displayed as this symbol, release the mouse button, and the field linking stops. When you create a link between tables, you see the Relationships dialog box, in which you can further define the relationship.

Specifying relationship options in the Relationships dialog box

The Relationships dialog box has several options that you can specify for a relationship. Figure 2-11 shows the relationship between the Sales and Customers tables. The dialog box tells you which table is the Primary table for the link and whether referential integrity is enforced. The dialog box also tells you the type of relationship (one-to-one or one-to-many) and lets you specify whether you want to allow cascading updates and deletes between linked tables.

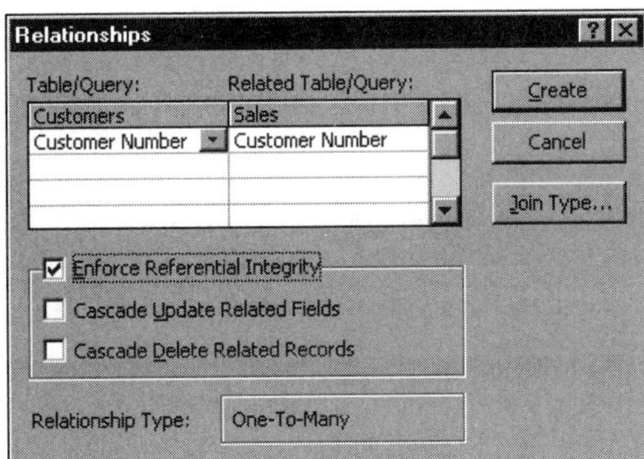

Figure 2-11: The Relationships dialog box.

Specifying the primary table

At the top of the Relationships dialog box (see Figure 2-11) are two table names, Customers and Sales. The Customers table is considered the primary table for this relationship. The link is always made from the one to the many link. Access always figures out which side is the one and which side is the many. The dialog box shows the link fields for each table immediately below the table names. In this example, the link field names are the same in both tables — Customer Number. Remember, it's not the field names that are important; it's the *values* within the fields. If you link two tables by the wrong field, simply select the correct field for each table by using the combo box under each table name.

Note the button labeled Join Type. Clicking on the Join Type button displays a dialog box that enables you to further define the types of joins.

Understanding types of table joins

When you specify a relationship between two tables, you establish rules for the type of relationship, not for viewing the data based on the relationship.

To view data in two tables, you must join them through a link. You establish the link via a common field (or group of fields) between the two tables. The method of linking the tables is known as *joining*. There are three basic types of joins:

- inner joins (equi-joins)
- outer joins
- self-joins

Inner joins (equi-joins)

The default join in Access is known as an *equi-join,* or *inner join.* With this type of join, you tell Access to select all records from both tables that have the same value in the fields that are joined together. This is the most common type of join.

The Access manuals refer to a default join as an equi-join. This join is also commonly referred to as an inner join in relational database theory. The terms are interchangeable and are used as such throughout this chapter.

For an example of an equi-join, recall the Sales and Customers tables. Bear in mind that you are looking for all records from these two tables with matching fields. The Customer Number field is common to both tables, so the equi-join does not show any records for customers who have no orders or for any orders that do not relate to a valid customer number. The rules of referential integrity prevent orders that are not tied to a customer number. Of course, it's possible to delete all orders from a specific customer or to create a new customer record with no orders. As you will learn, referential integrity keeps a customer number from being deleted or changed if an order is related to it.

Regardless of how it happens, you may have a customer in the Customers table who has no orders. Even less likely, but still theoretically possible, is having an order with no customer. If you create a query to show customers and their orders, any record of a customer without orders or of an order without a matching customer record will not be shown in the resulting dynaset.

Finding these "lost" records can be important for you. One of the features of the Relationships Builder is that it can perform several types of joins. Access also can help you find lost records between tables by building a "Find Unmatched Query" using the Query Wizards.

Changing join properties

With the Customers and Sales tables joined, certain join behaviors, or *properties,* exist between the tables. The join property is a rule that says to display all records (for the fields you specify) that correspond to the characters found in the Customer Number field of the Customers table and in the corresponding Customer Number field of the Sales table.

To translate this rule into a practical example, this is what happens in the Customers and Sales tables:

- If a record in the Customers table has a number for a customer not found in the Orders table, that Customer record will not be shown.
- If a record in the Orders table has a number for a customer number not in the Customers table, that Sales record will not be shown.

This makes sense — at least most of the time. You don't want to see records for customers without orders — or do you?

The Join Properties dialog box has three option buttons. Figure 2-12 displays these options for the Sales and Customers tables.

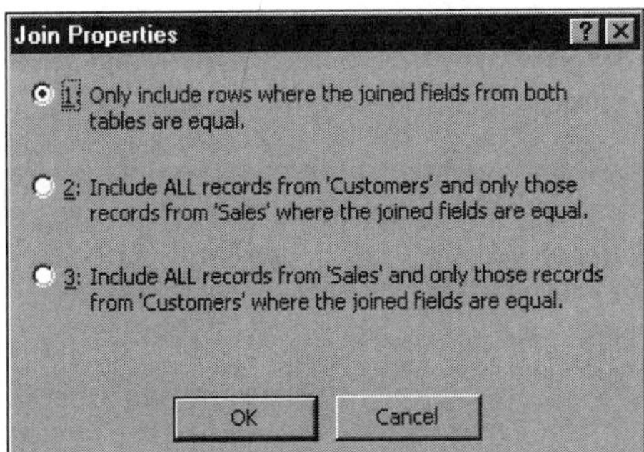

Figure 2-12: The Join Properties dialog box.

The first choice is commonly known as an inner join, and the other two are known as outer joins. These joins control the behavior of Access as it builds the dynaset from the relationship in a query.

Suppose that you want to see all your customers, including those who have no current orders. This would require an outer join. This join tells Access how to interpret any exceptions (possibly errors) between two tables. Should the noncorresponding records be shown or not? With an inner join, the noncorresponding records are not shown. With an outer join, you can show all the records on one side of the relationship or the other.

Outer joins

Unlike equi-joins (inner joins), outer joins show all records in one table while showing only common records in the other. An outer join graphically points to one of the tables. When you look at the join line, it says, "Show all records from the first table while only showing matching records in the other table." There are two types of outer joins — one from each side.

When you create an outer join, the relationship is displayed with an arrow at one end pointing rightward to the other table. Figure 2-13 shows a right outer join. This specifically says, "Show all the data in the Customers table but show only matching records in the Sales table." This shows all Customers, even those without orders.

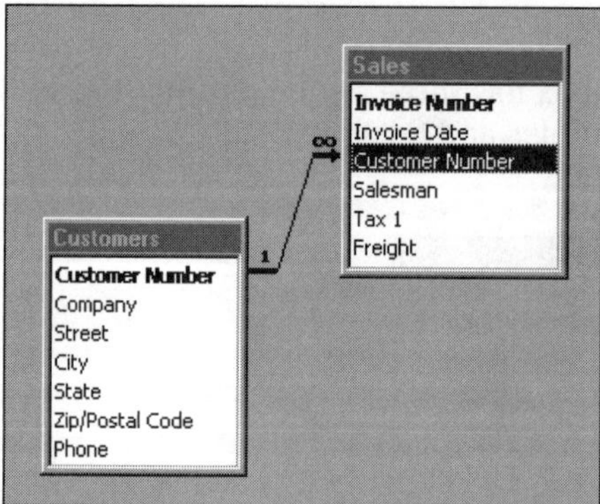

Figure 2-13: A right outer join.

A left outer join, shown in Figure 2-14, says "Show all records from the Sales table while only showing matching records in the Customer table." This identifies an order whose customer number has no matching record in the Customer table. This is also known as a widowed record. While a customer with no orders is acceptable, an order without a matching customer is not.

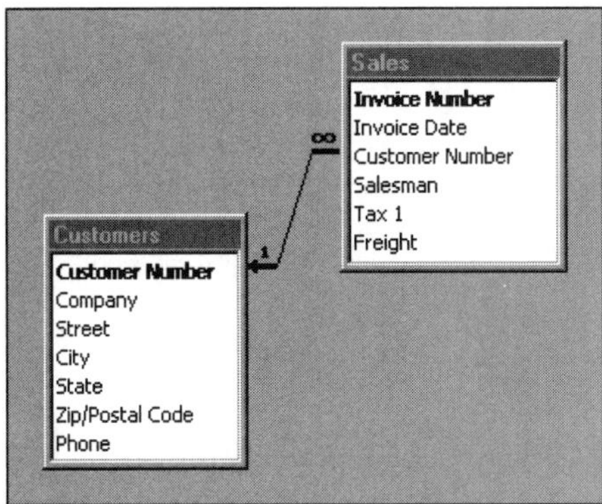

Figure 2-14: A left outer join.

Enforcing referential integrity

After you specify the link and verify the table and link fields, you can set referential integrity between the tables by clicking on the Enforce Referential Integrity checkbox below the table information in the Relationships dialog box (see Figure 2-11). If you choose not to enforce referential integrity, you can add new records, change key fields, or even delete related records without worrying about referential integrity. You can create orphans or parents without children. With normal operations, such as data entry or changing information, referential integrity rules should be in force.

When referential integrity is turned on, a couple global rules apply:

- You cannot change a key field.

  Referential integrity stops you from changing fields, such as the Customer Number, that may be used by other tables, such as the Sales table. This also stops you from changing a field such as Invoice Number, which is used to link the Sales and Sales Details records.

- You cannot delete a record that is used in a relationship.

  Referential integrity stops you from deleting a customer record used by an invoice. It also stops you from deleting an invoice that has detail items. Referential integrity does not stop you, however, from deleting the items.

By turning on referential integrity, you can specify several additional options that enable you to perform the prohibited tasks described in the global rules, but under proper database control.

To specify referential integrity, simply click on the checkbox in front of the Enforce Referential Integrity option shown in Figure 2-11. After you do so, Access 97 activates several of the cascade options in the Relationships dialog box.

Choosing the Cascade Update Related Fields option

If you specify Enforce Referential Integrity in the Relationships dialog box, Access 97 enables you to select the Cascade Update Related Fields checkbox option. This option tells Access 97 that a user can change the contents of a link field (the primary key field in the primary table, such as the Customer Number).

If the user changes the contents of the primary key field in the primary table, Access 97 verifies that the change is a new number (duplicate records cannot exist in the primary table) and then goes through the related records in the other table and changes the link field value from the old value to the new one. This way, if you code your customers by the first two letters of the customer's last name and one of your customers gets married and changes her name, you can change the Customer Number. All changes then ripple through other related records in the system.

Tip

If this option is not checked, you cannot change the primary key field in the primary table that is used in a link with another table. If the primary key field in the primary table is a link field between several tables, this option must be checked for all related tables or it does not work.

Choosing the Cascade Delete Related Records option

If you specify Enforce Referential Integrity in the Relationships dialog box, Access 97 also activates the Cascade Delete Related Records checkbox. By selecting this option, if a user attempts to delete a record in a primary table that has child records, Access 97 first deletes all the related child records and then deletes the primary record. This can be a very useful option for deleting a series of related records. For example, if Cascade Delete is checked and you try to delete a particular customer (who moved from the area) by deleting the Customer record, Access 97 goes to the related tables — Sales and Sales Details — and also deletes all related records for the customer.

If you do not specify this option, Access 97 does not allow you to delete a record that has related records in another table. In these cases, you must first delete all related records in the Sales Details table, then delete the related records in the Sales table, and then, finally, delete the customer record in the Customers table.

To use this option, you must specify Cascade Delete Related Records for all the table relationships in the database. If you do not specify this option for all the tables down the chain of related tables, Access 97 does not allow cascade deleting.

Join lines in the Relationships window

When you create a relationship between two tables, Access 97 automatically creates a thin join line from one table to another. The join line between each table is shown in Figure 2-15.

If you specify that you want to enforce referential integrity, however, Access 97 changes the appearance of the join line. It becomes thicker at each end of the line (alongside the table), and it also has either a 1 or the infinity symbol over the thick bar of the line (on one side of the join line). This bar shows the direction of the one-to-many relationship. The join lines in Figure 2-15 show that referential integrity is enforced.

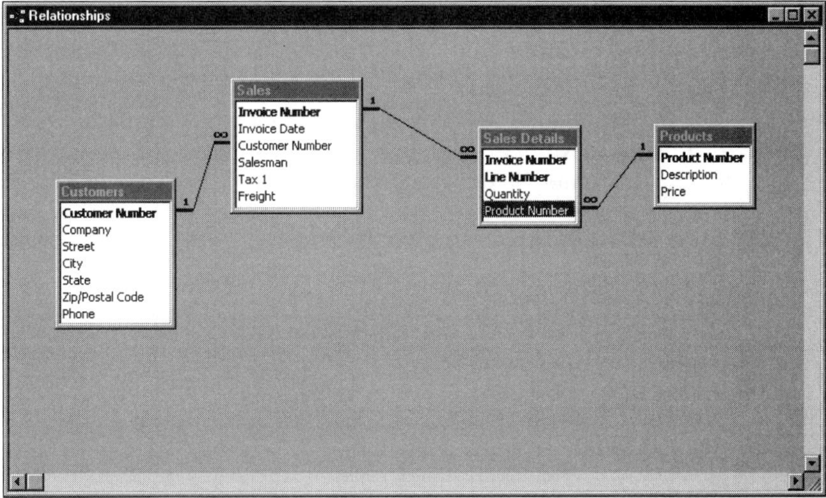

Figure 2-15: The final join lines.

You may specify Enforce Referential Integrity and click on the Create button to create a relationship between two tables and find that Access 97 does not allow you to create a relationship. The reason for this is that you are asking Access 97 to create a relationship supporting referential integrity between two tables that have records that violate referential integrity (the child table has orphans in it).

When this situation occurs, Access 97 warns you by displaying a dialog box. Access 97 returns you to the Relationships window after you click OK, and you need to re-create the relationship. If you are editing an existing join, Access 97 also returns you to the Relationships window by removing the referential integrity option.

To solve any conflicts between existing tables, you can create a Find Unmatched Query by using the Query Wizards to find the records in the many side table that violate referential integrity. Then you can convert the unmatched query to a delete query to delete the offending records. With the offending records gone, you can go back in and set up referential integrity between the two tables.

Using the Lookup Wizard in the Table Designer

When you view a table that is related to another, the table often contains a foreign key. The foreign key, however, is generally the primary key of another table. When looked at through the related table, the foreign key field is often cryptic. Until you relate the two tables and look at the data from a query view, you cannot tell the real value of the field.

For example, Figure 2-16 shows the Invoice table. Note the cryptic value in the Customer Number field. In previous versions of Access, the only way to see the Customer Name was to create a query and look at the resulting dynaset. Access 97 offers a new way to display the Customer Name in a table that contains only a foreign key lookup.

Microsoft Access - [Invoice : Table]

File Edit View Insert Format Records Tools Window Help

Invoice Num	Customer Num	Invoice	Salesperson	Tax 1	Freight	Paid	Comments
940224-01	HA-95020702	2/24/96	Danny	$8.90	$16.95	Yes	
940301-01	CH-95010302	3/1/96	Kevin	$0.00	$15.00	Yes	
940302-01	TR-94030201	3/2/96	Kristen	$24.96	$115.96	Yes	Hold order until all ite
940302-02	AL-95030901	3/2/96	Patricia	$1.32	$0.00	Yes	
940303-01	WE-94030301	3/3/96	Patricia	$15.00	$59.26	Yes	
940303-02	AP-95020701	3/3/96	Kevin	$0.00	$0.00	Yes	
940309-01	LA-95030901	3/9/96	Kevin	$0.00	$60.00	Yes	
940318-01	BL-94031801	2/22/96	Kristen	$71.39	$50.25	No	Have tried to make c
940319-01	MO-94031901	3/19/96	Kevin	$11.81	$25.00	Yes	requested the bikes t
950103-01	AD-95010301	1/3/96	Kristen	$2.10	$0.00	No	Customer had $5.00
950103-02	CH-95010302	1/3/96	Kevin	$0.00	$15.00	Yes	Freight is Overnight S
950108-02	AM-95020601	1/8/96	Patricia	$152.40	$152.22	Yes	sent Fed Ex insured
950112-01	AP-95022802	1/12/96	Danny	$0.00	$185.25	Yes	Hospital overpaid invc
950112-02	CH-95010302	1/12/96	Kevin	$0.00	$15.00	Yes	Freight is cost of shi
950122-01	AD-95010301	1/22/95	Kristen	$6.30	$15.95	Yes	
950201-01	AL-95030901	2/1/96	Danny	$19.86	$0.00	No	
950204-01	CH-95010302	2/4/96	Kevin	$0.00	$13.00	Yes	sent article Standard
950205-01	SW-94020501	2/5/96	Stephen	$94.25	$112.95	Yes	
950207-01	AP-95020701	2/7/96	Patricia	$0.00	$95.00	No	Hold on shipping of S
950207-02	HA-95020702	2/7/96	Kristen	$9.09	$19.75	Yes	

Record: 1 of 34

Datasheet View

Figure 2-16: A confusing foreign key value.

You can change the display of this field by redefining the properties of the Customer Number field in the Invoices table. To start this process, switch to Design view and select the data type of the Customer Number field. When you display the data type list, you will notice that the last item in the list is Lookup Wizard. This is not a data type but rather a way of changing the Lookup properties. Normally, only a single property is listed in the Lookup properties section, but the Lookup Wizard automatically changes this listing to include more than one property.

The Lookup Wizard normally creates a combo box for the field whenever it is used. In a datasheet, you see the related value (Customer Name), not the foreign key (Customer Number). The Lookup Wizard automatically creates the necessary properties for a combo box without requiring you to really understand them.

When you select the Lookup Wizard, the process starts to create a lookup to another table instead of displaying the field value itself. Figure 2-17 shows the first Lookup Wizard screen. There are two choices. The first choice lets you use data from another related table as the displayed value in the field. In this example, you want to display the Customer Name from the Customer table in the Customer Number field in the Invoices table.

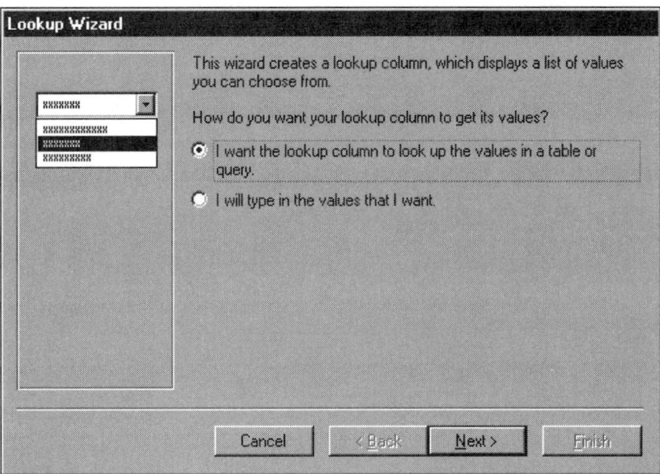

Figure 2-17: Using the Lookup Wizard.

The second choice lets you type in a list of values. You use this choice only when you enter a code such as the Type of Customer field in the Customers table. Perhaps you normally use an option group, and the values are 1, 2, and 3 in this field. Instead, you want to see Retail, Wholesale, and Distributor.

The next screen asks, in effect, "Which table or query contains the fields for the lookup and enables you to choose the table to be used for the lookup?" This screen is the standard table selection wizard screen used in most wizards. To answer the question, you would select the Customers table.

The next wizard screen displays a list of all the fields in the Customers table and enables you to select the fields you want to use in the lookup. This screen is a standard field selection screen. The method involves selecting all the fields in the lookup table that will be used in the display and the field that will hold the actual value. Though you can display more than one field in the table, you generally will display only one field. The second field is stored out of sight and is used for the actual value that belongs to the table.

You need to select both the field in the Customers table that will be displayed and the field that matches the foreign key field (Customer Number) in the Invoice table. In the Customers table, this field is the primary key Customer Number. You would select the Company field first and then the Customer Number field. After selecting and clicking on the Next button, the display and size screen is displayed, as shown in Figure 2-18.

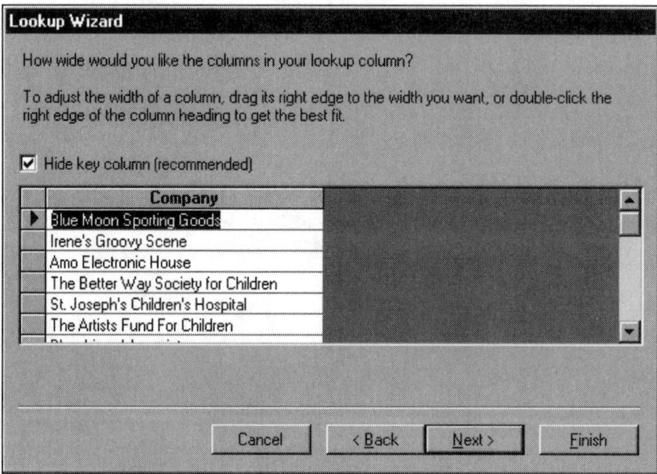

Figure 2-18: Sizing the fields.

A list of the data is displayed from the Customers table. In this example, you want to see only the Customer Name field, and Access has already hidden the Customer Number field by checking the Hide key column checkbox. This sets the column width to 0 in the properties of the combo box.

The next screen asks you which field you want to use to store the actual value in the table. This field is the Customer Number field.

The final screen names the column in your table. The default name is the original name of the column. Accept the default name of Customer Number and click on the Finish button to complete using the wizard. The choices you made are used to fill in the properties sheet of the Customer Number field in the Invoice table.

Figure 2-19 shows the settings in the Invoices table design screen. The Lookup Properties area has significantly changed from a single property to many properties. The first property tells you that the field is now displayed as a combo box whenever it is displayed in a table or as a default when placed on a form. The data type for the Customer Number field, however, is still Text. Even though you chose the Lookup Wizard from the Data Type list, it still creates a text data type. The Lookup Wizard merely changes the lookup properties.

The next two lookup properties define the type of data for the record. In this case, the source of the data in the record is a table or a query. Other choices are Value List (you type each value into the `Row Source` property separated by columns) and Field List (a list of fields in a table).

The `Row Source` displays an SQL statement. SQL (Standard Query Language) is an internal language into which all queries are translated. You can see only a portion of the SQL statement in Figure 2-19. The entire statement is as follows:

```
SELECT [Company], [Customer Number]
```

This statement simply tells Access 97 to use the Company and Customer Number fields from the Customer table. The next property shown in Figure 2-19, `Bound Column`, is set to `2`. This tells Access 97 to use the second column (Customer Number) as the actual value to store in the Customer Number column of the Invoices table. The `Column Count` of `2` tells Access 97 that there are two columns in the SQL statement, and `Column Heads` set to `No` means that when the field list is displayed in the combo box, the name of the column is not displayed. This property is used only when multiple columns are displayed.

The `Column Widths` is set to 2.15";0". This means the first column (Customer Name) is displayed at 2.15", and the second field's length (Customer Number) is set to zero and therefore hidden.

The `List Rows` property tells Access 97 to display (in this example) eight rows when the combo box is opened in the datasheet for the Customer Number field. Finally, the `List Width` property determines the width of the open combo box while the `Limit to List` property means that you cannot type in a value to the Invoices table's Customer Number field that isn't already found in the Customer Number field of the Customers table.

When you display the Invoices table in a datasheet view, as shown in Figure 2-20, you now see the Customer Name instead of the Customer Number in the Customer Number field. Using this method, you can display and limit the selection of any coded field in a table. Using the Lookup Wizard does not change the stored value in the Sales for the Customer Number field. Only the display of the value is changed.

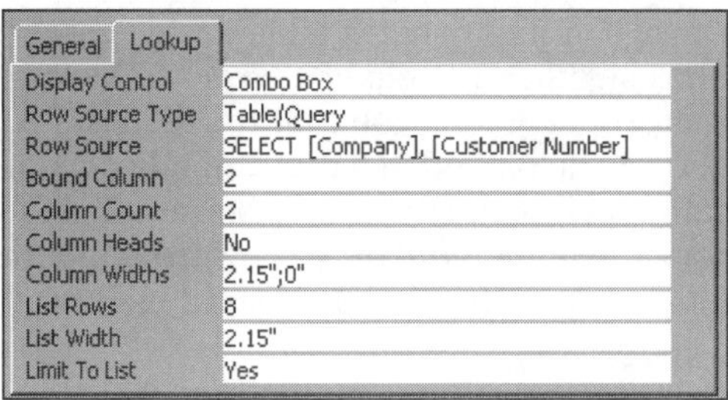

General | Lookup

Display Control	Combo Box
Row Source Type	Table/Query
Row Source	SELECT [Company], [Customer Number]
Bound Column	2
Column Count	2
Column Heads	No
Column Widths	2.15";0"
List Rows	8
List Width	2.15"
Limit To List	Yes

Figure 2-19: Understanding the lookup properties.

Microsoft Access - [Invoice : Table]

File Edit View Insert Format Records Tools Window Help

Invoice Num	Customer Number	Invoice	Salesperson	Tax 1	Freight	Paid
960514-01	August River Toys	5/14/96	Danny	$2.76	$0.00	No
950329-01	The Mother Goose Nursery School	3/29/96	Danny	$19.80	$35.00	Yes
950322-01	Children's Illustrated	3/22/96	Kevin	$0.00	$16.00	No
950321-01	Blue Moon Sporting Goods	3/21/96	Stephen	$4.80	$0.00	Yes
950316-01	The Artists Fund For Children	3/16/96	Patricia	$0.00	$123.75	No
950309-01	Weathervane Recreational Center	3/9/96	Kristen	$0.00	$0.00	Yes
950306-01	Irene's Groovy Scene	3/6/96	Danny	$4.95	$0.00	No
950224-01	Blue Moon Sporting Goods	2/24/96	Kevin	$7.80	$0.00	Yes
950223-01	Blue Moon Sporting Goods	2/23/96	Danny	$8.25	$0.00	Yes
950221-03	Amo Electronic House	2/21/96	Danny	$131.44	$95.95	No
950221-02	August River Toys	2/21/96	Kevin	$1.46	$0.00	Yes
950216-04	Children's Illustrated	2/16/96	Kevin	$0.00	$15.00	No
950216-01	Irene's Groovy Scene	2/16/96	Kevin	$2.33	$0.00	Yes
950208-01		2/8/96	Stephen	$12.52	$0.00	No
950207-02	Harrisburg and Associates	2/7/96	Kristen	$9.09	$19.75	Yes
950207-01	The Better Way Society for Childre	2/7/96	Patricia	$0.00	$95.00	No
950205-01	Buffy's Electronic Boutique	2/5/96	Stephen	$94.25	$112.95	Yes
950204-01	Children's Illustrated	2/4/96	Kevin	$0.00	$13.00	Yes
950201-01	Irene's Groovy Scene	2/1/96	Danny	$19.86	$0.00	No
950122-01	Blue Moon Sporting Goods	1/22/95	Kristen	$6.30	$15.95	Yes
950112-02	Children's Illustrated	1/12/96	Kevin	$0.00	$15.00	Yes

Record: 1 of 34

Datasheet View

Figure 2-20: Displaying a lookup field in a datasheet.

Chapter 3

Optimizing Performance

In This Chapter

- Tuning your computer for maximum performance
- Increasing performance dramatically by keeping your code in a compiled state
- Using light forms
- Using MDE databases for better performance
- Adjusting the Jet registry settings
- Getting the most from your tables
- Tuning your queries for maximum speed
- Getting the most out of your forms and reports
- Using the Table Analyzer Wizard
- Increasing performance by optimizing your VBA code
- Using techniques to increase the *perceived* speed of your application

When Microsoft introduced Access 95, a number of new performance concerns came part and parcel with the new features and functions. Microsoft has made a conscious effort to improve the performance of Access 97 with improvements in compilation techniques and new features such as light forms. The end result is that Microsoft has helped ease your burden, but in no way has it completely taken it from you.

Tip

The published minimum RAM requirement for a computer to run Access for Windows 97 on Windows 95 is 12MB — with an emphasis on *minimum*. On a Windows NT machine, the published minimum is 16MB of RAM. If you are going to do serious development with Access for Windows 97, you should have at least 24MB of RAM or, more preferably, 32MB.

Light Forms — Less Filling, Run Great!

Access 97 gives you the ability to create forms without code modules behind them. When a form doesn't have a code module, it is called a *light form*. Light forms load and display faster than ordinary forms because no code needs to be loaded or compiled when the form is loaded. When you create a new form, it is created as a light form by default. To create a code module for a form, set the form's `HasModule` property to `Yes` (see Figure 3-1).

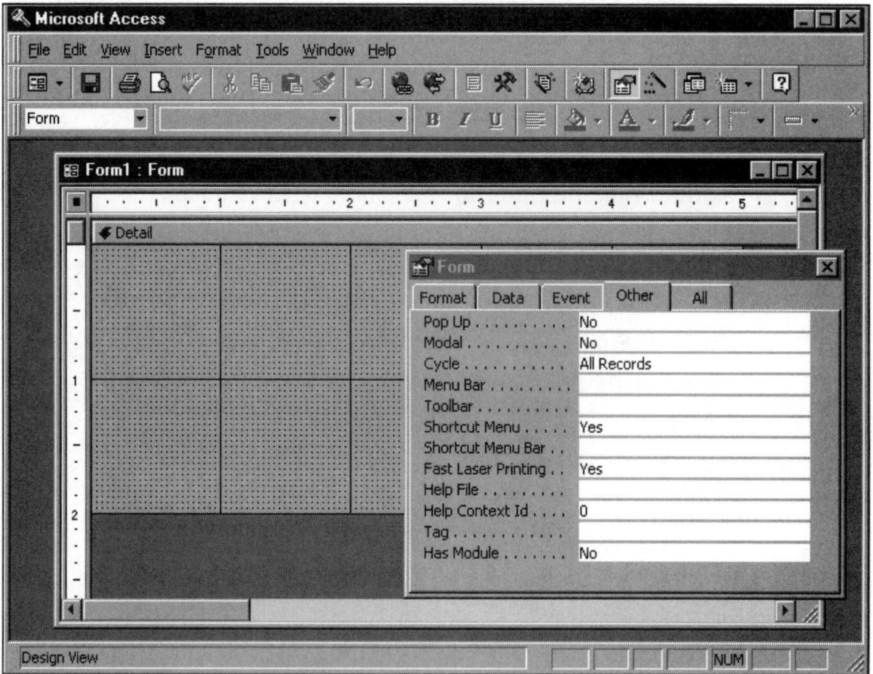

Figure 3-1: You can now create forms that load and display faster because they don't have code modules.

Deleting all of the event procedures in a code module does not turn the form into a light form. Once a form has a module behind it, the only way to remove the code module to make the form a light form is to turn the form's `HasModule` property to `No`.

Just because a light form does not have code behind it doesn't mean the form is a useless, static form; you can attach macros or call functions in standard modules from the events of the form and its controls. For example, if you have a switchboard form, you will need to cause events to happen when the buttons on the form are clicked. As an alternative to creating a form module by setting the form's `HasModule` property to `Yes`, you can call a function in a standard module by creating an expression in the button's click event. Figure 3-2 shows how you would call the function `ShowInventory` when a button is clicked.

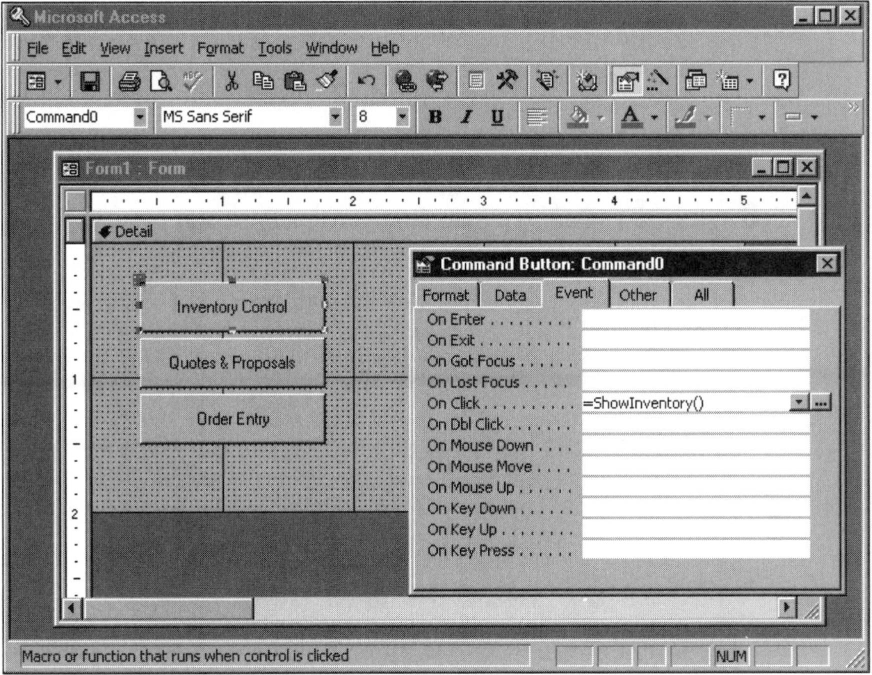

Figure 3-2: You can call functions in standard modules from light forms by creating expressions in the event list.

When a function is designated in an expression of an event procedure, the module containing the function is only loaded and compiled when the procedure is triggered. Thus, in the example above, the module containing the procedure `ShowInventory` is not loaded until the button is clicked. Note: This technique only works for functions; you cannot call a procedure declared with `Sub` because it does not return a value and therefore cannot be used as part of an expression.

Understanding Module Load on Demand

One of the great features of Visual Basic for Applications (the core language that replaced Access Basic in Access 2.0) is the *load on demand* functionality of VBA. Using load on demand, Access only loads code modules as they are needed or referenced. In Access 95, load on demand of modules wasn't fully realized because loading a module loaded the entire module's potential call tree. With Access 97, the load on demand feature truly does help reduce the amount of RAM needed and helps your program run faster.

Because Access does not unload code after it has been loaded into memory, you should periodically close your application while you develop. When developing, there is a tendency to open and work with many different procedures in many different modules. These modules stay in memory until you close Access.

Organizing your modules

First, be aware that when any procedure or variable is referenced in your application, the entire module that contains the procedure or variable is loaded into memory. To minimize the number of modules loaded into memory, you need to organize your procedures and variables into logical modules. For example, it is a good idea to place all `Global` variables in the same module. If even only one `Global` variable is declared in a module, the entire module is loaded into memory. By the same token, you should put only procedures that are always used by your application (such as start-up procedures) into the module containing the `Global` variables.

Access 97 prunes the call tree

The way in which Access 95 performed load on demand imposed serious performance concerns. In Access 95, not only was an entire module loaded when a procedure within it was called, but the potential call tree for that procedure was also called.

A potential call tree consists of all the procedures that *could* be called by the current procedure you are calling. In addition, all the procedures that could be called from *those* procedures are part of the potential call tree as well (see Figure 3-2).

1. If you call Procedure A, the entire module containing Procedure A is loaded.
2. Modules containing variable declarations used by Procedure A are loaded.
3. Procedure A has lines of code that call Procedures B and C — the modules containing Procedure B and Procedure C are loaded. (Even if the call statements are in conditional loops and are never executed, they are still loaded because they could *potentially* be called.)
4. Any procedures that could be called by Procedure B and Procedure C are loaded, as well as the entire modules containing those potential procedures.
5. And so on and so on and…

Fortunately for all Access developers, this complete loading of a potential call tree has been addressed in Access 97. Access 97 includes a new Compile on Demand option (see Figure 3-3) accessed on the Module tab of the

Options form. To access this setting, select Tools➪Options and click the module tab. Access uses this option by default for new databases. Deselecting this option causes Access 97 to behave in a manner similar to that of Access 95, only worse. When the option is deselected, Access 97 will load *and compile* the entire call tree of a module! The distinction here is the compilation of the loaded modules. Whereas Access 95 would load the entire call tree for a module, by default Access 95 would not compile a module until a procedure within the module was actually called. In Access 97, if you deselect Compile on Demand, Access 97 will load and compile all modules in the potential call tree.

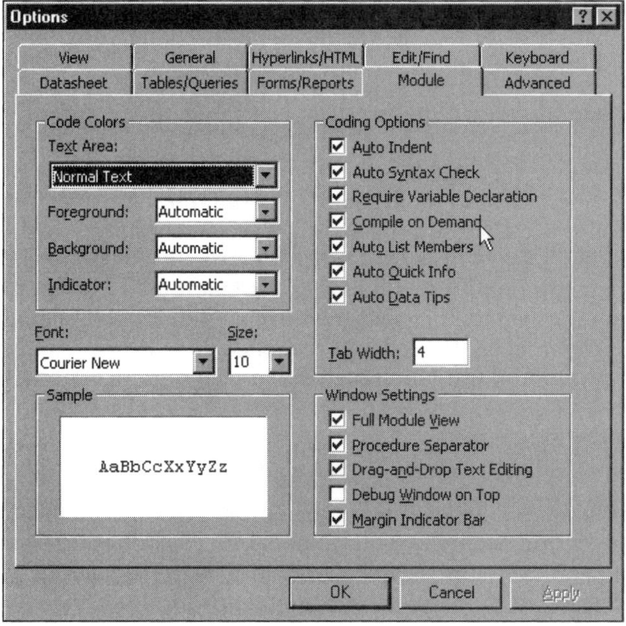

Figure 3-3: For maximum performance, leave the Compile on Demand box checked.

Unless you have a specific reason to do so, you should never deselect the Compile on Demand option. When deselected, you could conceivably cause *all* of the modules in a database to load and compile by simply calling just one procedure.

With the Compile on Demand option selected, Access 97 will not load the entire call tree of a module but will load a portion of the call tree of the executed procedure. For example, if you call procedure A in module A, any modules that contain procedures referenced in procedure A are loaded and compiled. However, Access 97 doesn't take into consideration procedures that may be called from other procedures in module A, and it doesn't look at the potential call tree of the modules loaded because one of their procedures is referenced in procedure A. Because Access 97 only loads modules one-deep from the executed procedure's immediate call tree — not the module's call tree — your applications should load and execute many times faster than they did in Access 95.

Even though there has been a significant improvement in the way modules are loaded and compiled in Access 97, there are still a number of things you can do to reduce the number of modules loaded and compiled. For instance, you should never place infrequently called procedures in a module with procedures that are called often. At times, this may make your modules less logical and harder to conceptualize. For example, you may have a dozen functions that perform various manipulations to Contact information in your application. Ordinarily, you might make one module called `mdlContacts` and place all the contact-related procedures and variables into this one module. Because Access loads the entire module when one procedure or variable in it is called, you may want to separate the contact-related procedures into separate modules (one for procedures that are commonly used and one that contains procedures that are rarely used).

Tip

You need to be aware at all times of the fact that all modules that have procedures referenced in a procedure of a different module are loaded when that procedure is called. In your application, if any of your common procedures reference a procedure that is not commonly used, you will want to place the uncommon procedure in the same module with the common procedures to prevent a different module (containing the uncommon procedures) from being loaded and compiled. You may even decide to use more than two modules if you have very large amounts of code in multiple procedures that are rarely called. Although breaking related procedures into separate modules may make your code a little harder to understand, it can greatly improve the performance of your application.

Tip

When placing related procedures into separate modules, using a standard naming convention can make your application easier to understand. For example, if you have multiple modules containing procedures related to order processing, you could call the module that contains all common procedures `mdlOrder_Common`, and the module that contains less-common procedures `mdlOrders_Rare`. If you want the module name to be more descriptive, you could name the module `mdlOrders_TransactionProcessing`. Whatever method you decide to use, just be sure to use it consistently.

To fully take advantage of Compile on Demand, you have to carefully plan your procedure placement. Third-party tools, such as Total Access Analyzer from FMS, print a complete module reference report. This can be invaluable for visualizing where all the potential calls for various procedures are located.

Distributing MDE files

One way to ensure that your application's code is always compiled is to distribute your database as an .MDE file. When you save your database as an .MDE file, Access compiles all code modules (including form modules), removes all editable source code, and compacts the database. The new

.MDE file contains no source code, but continues to work because it does contain a compiled copy of all of your code. Not only is this a great way to secure your source code, it allows you to distribute databases that are smaller (because they contain no source code) and always keep their modules in a compiled state. Because the code is always in a compiled state, less memory is used by the application and there is no performance penalty for code being compiled at run time.

In addition to not being able to view existing code because it is all compiled, the following restrictions apply:

- You cannot view, modify, or create forms, reports, or modules in Design view.
- You cannot add, delete, or change references to object libraries or databases.
- You cannot change your database's VBA project name using the Options dialog box.
- You cannot import or export forms, reports, or modules. Note, however, that tables, queries, and macros can be imported from or exported to non-MDE databases.

Because of these restrictions, it may not be possible to distribute your application as an .MDE file. For example, if your application creates forms at run time, you would not be able to distribute the database as an .MDE file.

There is no way to convert an .MDE file into a normal database file. Always save and keep a copy of the original database! When you need to make changes to the application, you must open the normal database and then create a new MDE before distribution. If you delete your original database, you will be unable to access any of your objects in design view!

There are some prerequisites to be met before a database can be saved as an .MDE file. First, if security is in user, the user creating the .MDE file must have all applicable rights to the database. In addition, if the database is replicated, you must remove all replication system tables and properties before saving the .MDE file. Finally, you must save all databases or add-ins in the chain of references as .MDE files or your database will be unable to use them.

To create an .MDE file:

1. Close the database if it is currently opened. If you do not close the current database, Access will attempt to close it for you, prompting you to save changes where applicable. When working with a shared database, all users must close the database; Access needs exclusive rights to work with the database.
2. Select Tools⇨Database Utilities and then click on Make MDE File (see Figure 3-4).

3. In the Database To Save As MDE dialog box, specify the database you want to save as an .MDE file, and click on Make MDE (see Figure 3-5).

If you had a database opened when you selected Make MDE File, this step is skipped and Access assumes you want to use the previously opened database. If you wish to use a different database, you will need to cancel creating the .MDE file, close the database, and select Make MDE File again. At that time, you will be asked for the database to save as an .MDE file.

4. In the Database to Save as MDE dialog box, specify a name, drive, and folder for the database. Do not attempt to save the .MDE file as the same file name as the original database.

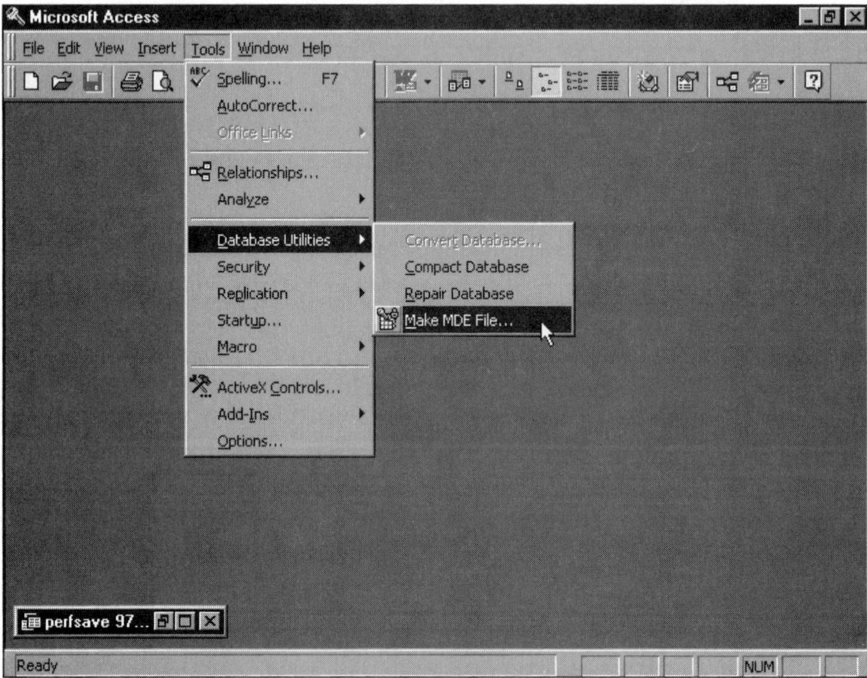

Figure 3-4: Access doesn't convert the existing database into an .MDE file, it creates a new .MDE file for the database.

Do not delete or overwrite your original database! As stated previously, there is no way to convert an .MDE file to a normal database, and you cannot edit any objects in an .MDE file. If you delete or otherwise lose your original database, you will never again be able to access any of the objects in the design environment!

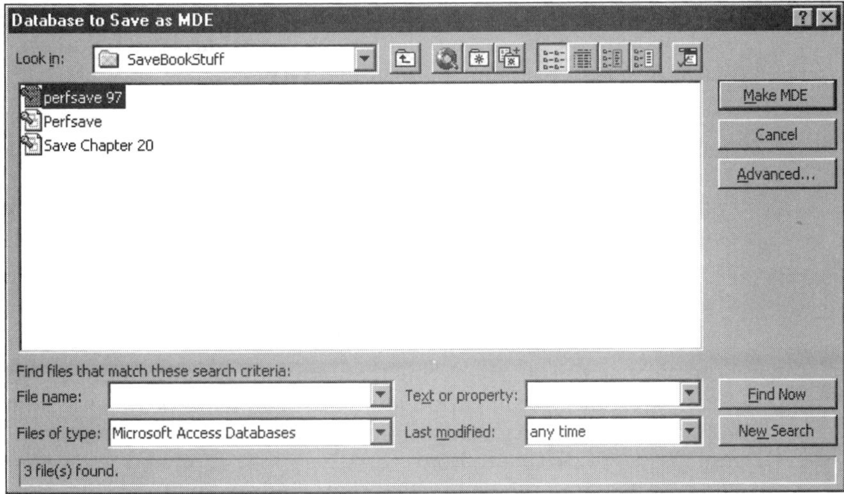

Figure 3-5: If you had a database opened at the time you selected Make MDE File, you will not see this form.

Understanding the Compiled State

Understanding how Access performs Compile on Demand is critical to achieving maximum performance from your Access application. However, it is also paramount that you understand what compilation is and what it means for an application to be in a compiled state. There are actually two types of code in Access, code that you write and code that Access can understand and execute. Before a procedure of VBA code that you have written can be executed, the code must be run through a compiler to generate code in a form that Access can understand — compiled code. Access lacks a true compiler and instead uses precompiled code and an interpreter. The code in the converted form is known as compiled code, or as being in a compiled state. If a procedure is called that is not in a compiled state, the procedure must first be compiled and then the compiled code is passed to the interpreter for execution. In reality, as previously stated, this does not happen at the procedure level, but at the module level; when you call a procedure, the module containing the procedure and all modules that have procedures referenced in the called procedure are loaded and compiled. You can manually compile your code, or you can let Access compile it for you on the fly. It takes time to compile the code, however, so the performance of your application will suffer if you let Access compile it on the fly.

In addition to the time it takes for Access to compile your code at run time, decompiled programs use considerably more memory than code that is compiled. When your application is completely compiled, only the compiled code is loaded into memory when a procedure is called. If you run an application that is in a decompiled state, Access loads the decompiled code and generates the compiled code as needed (explained previously). Access does not unload the decompiled code as it compiles, so you are left with two versions of the same code in memory.

There is one drawback to compiled applications: They use more disk space than their decompiled versions. This is because both the compiled and decompiled versions of the code are stored on disk. This should not often become a problem, but if you have an application with an enormous amount of code, you can save disk space by keeping it in a decompiled state. Remember, there is a trade-off between disk space used and the performance of your database. Most often, when given the choice, a user would rather give up a few megabytes of disk space in exchange for faster applications.

Tip

You may use this space-saving technique to your advantage if you need to distribute a large application and your recipients have a full development version of Access. By distributing the uncompiled versions, you will need much less disk space to distribute the application and the end users can compile it again at their location. If you are going to do this, you should put the entire application into a decompiled state. Fully decompiling an application is discussed later in this chapter.

Putting your application's code into a compiled state

There are only two ways to put your entire application into a compiled state: use the Compile All Modules or the Compile and Save All Modules menu items from the Debug menu on the Modules toolbar (see Figure 3-6). To access the Debug menu, you must have a module open. Generally, you should always use the Compile and Save All Modules command to ensure that all of the code is saved in a compiled state. It can take a long time to compile complex applications, and in general you should only perform a Compile All Modules before you distribute your application or before performing benchmark tests. If you just need to perform syntax checking or compile the modules you currently have open, use the Compile Loaded Modules menu item.

Tip

It is especially important to close your application after performing a Compile All Modules or a Compile and Save All Modules. To compile all your modules, Access needs to load every single one of them into memory. All this code stays in memory until you close down Access.

When you select the Compile Loaded Modules menu item, Access only compiles the modules that are currently open, including the modules of code behind open forms and reports. Compile Loaded Modules does not fully compile your application but works much faster than compiling all of your code. Clicking on the compile button in the toolbar performs a Compile Loaded Modules.

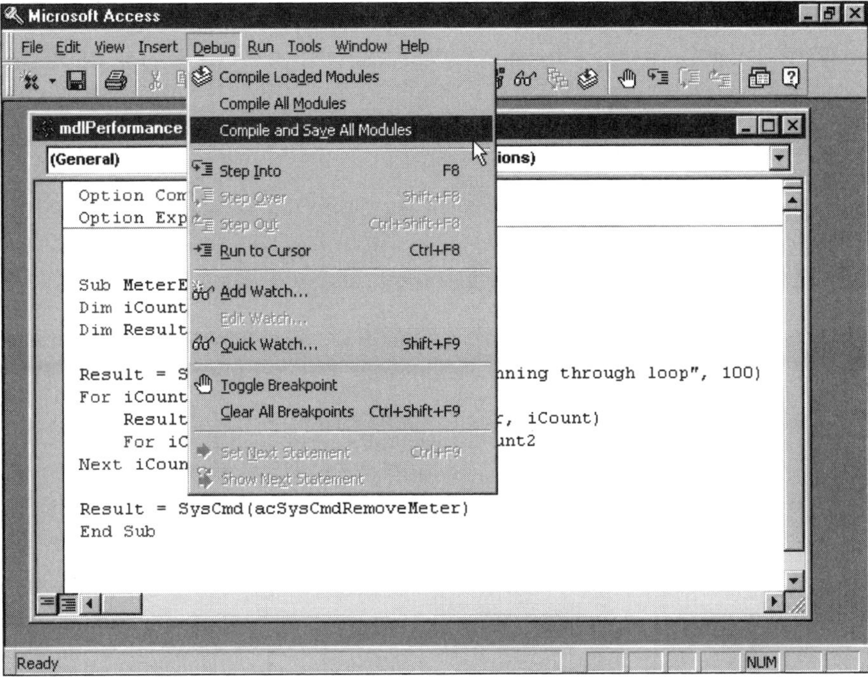

Figure 3-6: Compile All Modules and Compile and Save All Modules are the only ways to fully compile your application.

Although you usually perform Compile Loaded Modules while developing and Compile and Save All Modules only before distribution or performance testing, you will want to use Compile All Modules in one other case: after converting applications from previous versions of Access. When you compile all the modules of your converted application, the compiler alerts you to all the code that needs to be modified before it can be executed in Access 97.

Losing the compiled state

One of the greatest roadblocks to increasing the performance of Access 95 applications was the ease with which an application could be decompiled. When the Access 95 application was in a decompiled state, Access had to constantly compile code as it was called. Losing the compiled state was so easy to do in Access 95, it would often happen without the developer even realizing he had done it.

In Access 97, only portions of code affected by certain changes are put into a decompiled state — not the entire application. This is in itself a tremendous improvement over Access 95.

The following will cause portions of your code to be decompiled:

- Modifying a form, report, control, or module. (If you don't save the modified object, your application is preserved in its previous state.)
- Adding a new form, report, control, or module. (This includes adding new code behind a form.)
- Deleting or renaming a form, report, control, or module.
- Adding or removing a reference to an object library or database by using the References command on the Tools menu.

OK, so you think you have a handle on code that loses its compiled state? Well, here are a couple of "gotchas" that you need to consider:

- If you modify objects such as reports or forms at run time through VBA code, portions of your application are put into an uncompiled state when the objects are modified. (Wizards often do this.)
- If your application creates objects such as reports or forms on the fly, portions of your application are put into an uncompiled state when the objects are created. (Wizards often do this as well.)

Another serious flaw of Access 95 was the fact that an application's entire compiled state was tied to the file name of the database itself. This meant your entire application would lose its compiled state and all code would have to be compiled at the time it was called if you renamed your database, compacted your database into a database of a different name, or copied your database to a database of a different name.

Fortunately, Access 97 has fixed this serious problem. The compiled state of an application is still tied to its name, but now it is tied to its project name rather than its file name. By default, the project name of a database is the same as the file name of the database. You can change the project name of a database by selecting Tools⇨Options and clicking the Advanced tab, as shown in Figure 3-7.

When you change a project name (but not when you change the file name), the entire application loses its compiled state. Because of this, you should change the project name only if absolutely necessary, and you should perform a Compile and Save All Modules immediately after changing the project name.

Distributing applications in a compiled or decompiled state

There are a couple of issues concerning compilation that you should take into consideration when distributing your Access application.

Distributing source code for your application

First and foremost, if you distribute source code and allow your users access to modify or add objects, you must make them completely aware of the compilation issues. If your users do not fully comprehend what is happening with your application's compiled state, you can be sure you will receive phone calls about how your program seems to be getting slower the more the users make changes to objects.

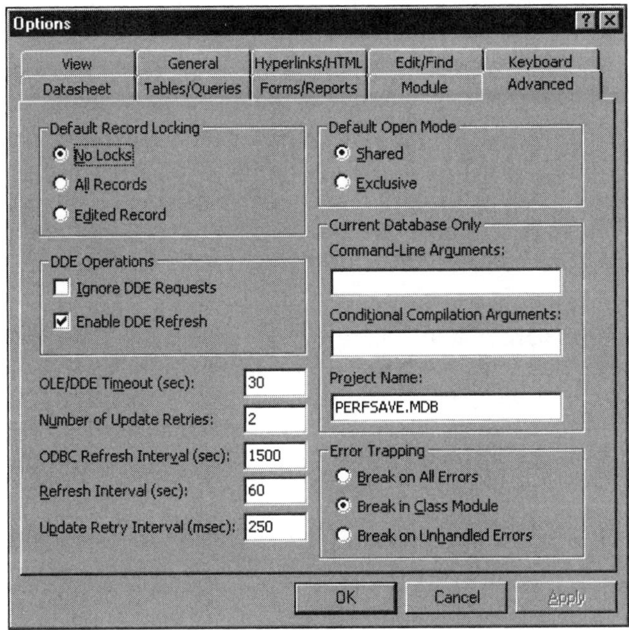

Figure 3-7: Change the project name on the Advanced tab of the Options dialog – but only if absolutely necessary.

Putting an application in a decompiled state

If your application is such that it will be constantly causing itself to lose its compiled state, end users will be making modifications that constantly cause objects to lose their compiled state, or distributed file size is an issue, you may want to consider distributing the database in a fully decompiled state.

To put your entire application into a decompiled state

1. Create a new database.
2. Import all of your application objects into the new database.
3. Compact the new database.

Organizing commonly used code that is never modified into a library

After your application is finished and ready for distribution, you may want to consider putting commonly used code that is never modified by an end user into a library database. A library database is an external database that is referenced from your application database. A little overhead is incurred by having to call code from the library rather than accessing it directly in the parent application, but the benefit is that the library code will never be put into a decompiled state — even if your application creates or modifies objects on the fly or your users add new or modify existing objects. This technique can greatly increase an application's performance and keep the performance consistent over periods of time.

The first step of referencing procedures in an external database is to create the external database with all its modules just as you would an ordinary Access database. Any procedures that you declare as `Private` are not made available to the calling application, so plan carefully what you want and don't want to expose to other databases.

After you have created the database and its modules, you must create a reference to that database in your application database (the database your users will run). To create a reference, first open any module in your application database in Design view. When you have a module in Design view, there will be a new command available from the Tools menu: References (see Figure 3-8). Select Tools⇨References to access the References dialog box (see Figure 3-9).

In the References dialog box, you specify all the references your application needs for using OLE automation or for using other Access databases as library databases. When making a reference to another Access database as opposed to an OLE server created with another development tool such as Visual Basic 4, you will probably need to Browse for the database. Use the Browse dialog box as though you were going to open the external database. After you have selected the external Access database, it shows up in the References dialog box with a check mark to indicate that it is referenced. To remove a reference, access the References dialog box again and deselect the referenced item by clicking on its checked box. After you have made all the references you need to make, click on the OK button.

After a database is referenced, you can call the procedures in the referenced database as though they existed in your application database. No matter what happens in your application database to cause code to decompile, the referenced database always stays in a compiled state unless it is opened and modified directly using Access.

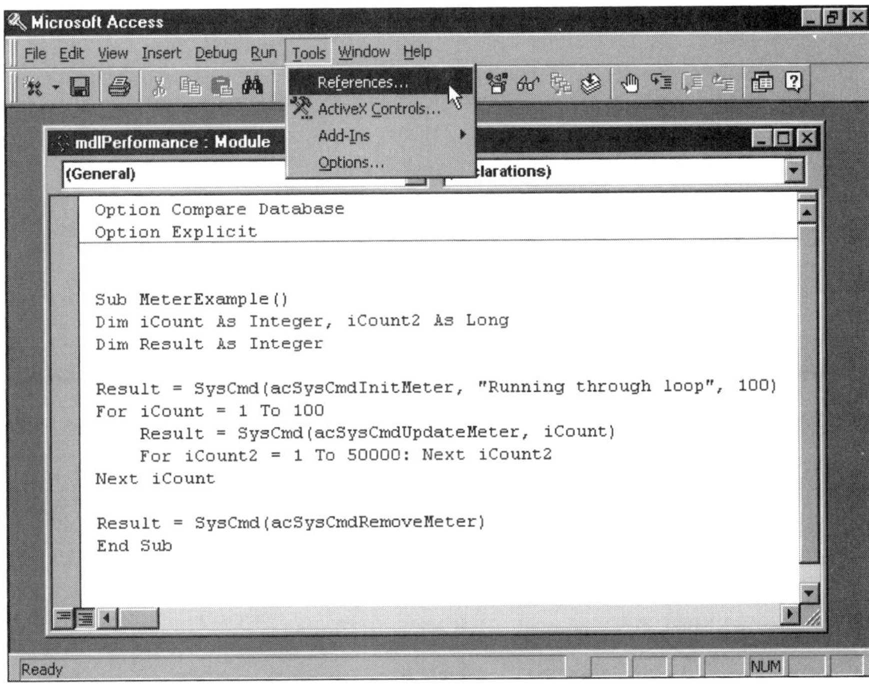

Figure 3-8: The References option only appears on the Tools pull-down menu when you have a module opened and selected in design view.

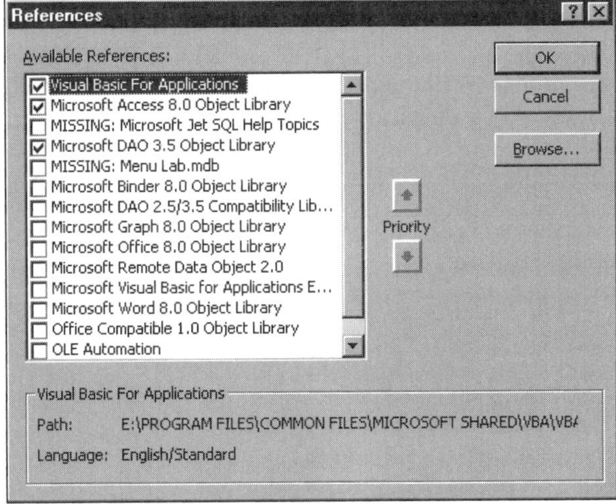

Figure 3-9: The References dialog box is where you resolve references to OLE automation servers and Access library databases.

To reference an external Access database to call its procedures, follow these steps:

1. Create the library database and its modules.
2. Open the database in which you want to use the external procedures.
3. Open any module in design view.
4. Select Tools⇨References.
5. Select the OLE server you wish to register. If it is an Access database, you will probably have to use Browse to locate the database.

Tip

If your application uses add-in databases (a special type of library database), open the add-in database for read-only access. Opening add-ins for read-only access increases performance because Jet does not have to maintain locking information for the add-in database in an .LDB file.

Creating a library reference for distributed applications

If you are distributing your application, references only stay intact if the calling database and the library database are in the same or relative path. For example, if on your machine the main database is in C:\MYAPP and the library database is in C:\MYAPP\LIBRARY, the reference remains intact if the library database is located in the same relative path such as in C:\NEWDIR for the main database and C:\NEWDIR\LIBRARY for the library database. If the relative path will not remain consistent upon distribution, your application's users will have to add the reference manually or you will have to create the reference using VBA code.

In Access 95, it was impossible to create a reference using code. If you distributed your Access 95 application, the end user *had* to create the reference manually. If you distributed your Access 95 application using the Access Developer's Toolkit, it was impossible for the end user to create the reference! Access 95 has a new References collection that you can use to programmatically create references at run time. The following procedure creates a reference to the file whose name is passed to it. For this function to work, the full file name with path must be passed: `bResult = CreateReference("c:\My Documents\MyLib.mdb")`. The procedure is

```
Public Function CreateReference(szFileName As String) As Boolean
    On Error GoTo CreateReferenceError
    Dim ref As Reference

    Set ref = References.AddFromFile(szFileName)
    CreateReference = True

Exit Function

CreateReferenceError:
    MsgBox Err & ": " & Err.Description
```

```
    CreateReference = False
    Exit Function

End Function
```

Tip

You can verify that a reference is set by using the ReferenceFromFile function. To verify a reference, pass the function the full path and file name like this: bResult = ReferenceFromFile("C:\Windows\System\Mscal.ocx"). The function returns True if the reference is valid, False if it is not.

With the advent of the References collection, the primary concern when using libraries — losing references upon distribution — is now gone. There is, however, still one major drawback to library databases: Access does not support circular references. This means that code in your library databases cannot reference variables or call procedures that exist in your parent database.

Whether you distribute your application as one database or as a primary database that uses library databases, if your applications are static (they don't allow modification of objects by end users or wizards and don't perform object modifications on themselves), you should always distribute the databases in a fully compiled state so that your users experience the highest level of performance possible.

Calling procedures in other databases using OLE

An alternative to calling a procedure in a referenced database normally is calling the procedure using the Run method of the Application object. This is essentially using OLE automation within your application. Using the Run method causes Access to load only the module in which the procedure resides because Access doesn't recognize the run statement as it does a call statement or a function call. This technique was very effective in Access 95 because it circumvented the problem of having a procedure's entire call tree loaded. Although this is not the issue it was in Access 95, there are still benefits to using this technique with Access 97.

One benefit of using the Run method is that the database containing the called procedure does not have to be referenced ahead of time as it does when it is a library. This is better for distributed applications where the end user may not have a full version of Access or it is impractical to expect the end user to make the references (such as in a "shrink-wrapped" commercial application).

Access is itself an OLE automation server. However, unlike Visual Basic 4.0, you cannot create OLE objects with methods and properties that can be manipulated from another application that supports OLE automation. The Run method lets you get around this limitation by letting you execute procedures in an Access database from a different program — similar to triggering a method of an object. One consideration when using the `Run` method is that any value returned from the called procedure is ignored; you can trigger a function but cannot receive the result of the function.

For example, suppose you have defined a procedure `OpenForm` in a database named WizCode.mdb. The `OpenForm` procedure accepts a string argument that is the name of the form you want to open. You can call `OpenForm` from your Access application or from any application that supports OLE automation, such as Visual Basic 4.0, using the code shown here:

```
Dim appAccess As New Access.Application
appAccess.OpenCurrentDatabase ("C:\My Documents\WizCode.mdb")
appAccess.Run "WizCode.OpenForm", "Some String"
```

The preceding `Dim` statement works only in an application that has a reference defined for Microsoft Access (just as you define a reference to a library database ahead of time). If no reference is created at design time in the application using the preceding code, the variable would have to be declared as an `Object`, and a reference would have to be created in code like this:

```
Dim appAccess As Object
Set appAccess = CreateObject("Access.Application.7")
```

It is always faster to reference the application at design time and explicitly dimension the object variable rather than resolving the reference using the `CreateObject` command.

Obviously, in distributed applications you need to allow for the external database to be located in different locations. You may choose to install all your databases in the same directory or write a setup program that places the external databases into a directory of the user's choosing and then save the path to the databases in the system registry or a private .INI file. You can then retrieve the path at a later time and use it when creating OLE object references.

Improving Absolute Speed

When discussing an application's performance, the word performance is usually synonymous with speed. In software development, there are actually two different types of speed: absolute and perceived. Absolute speed refers to the actual speed at which your application performs a function, such as how long it takes to run a certain query. Perceived speed is the phenomenon of an end user actually perceiving one application to be faster than another application, even though it may indeed be slower, because of visual feedback provided to the user while the application is performing a task. Absolute speed items can be measured in units of time; perceived speed cannot.

Of course, some of the most important items for increasing actual speed are

- Keeping your application in a compiled state
- Organizing your procedures into "smart" modules
- Opening databases exclusively
- Compacting your databases regularly

You should always open a database exclusively in a single-user environment. If your application is a standalone application (nothing is shared over a network), opening the database in exclusive mode can really boost performance. If your application is run on a network and shared by multiple users, you will not be able to open the database exclusively. (Actually, the first user can open it exclusively, but if so no other user can access the database thereafter.) The preferred method for running an application in a network environment is to run Access and the main code .MDB file locally, and link to a shared database containing the data on the server. If your application is used in this manner, you can open and run the code database exclusively, but you cannot use exclusive links to the shared data.

To open a database exclusively, simply check the Exclusive box on the Open Database dialog box (see Figure 3-10).

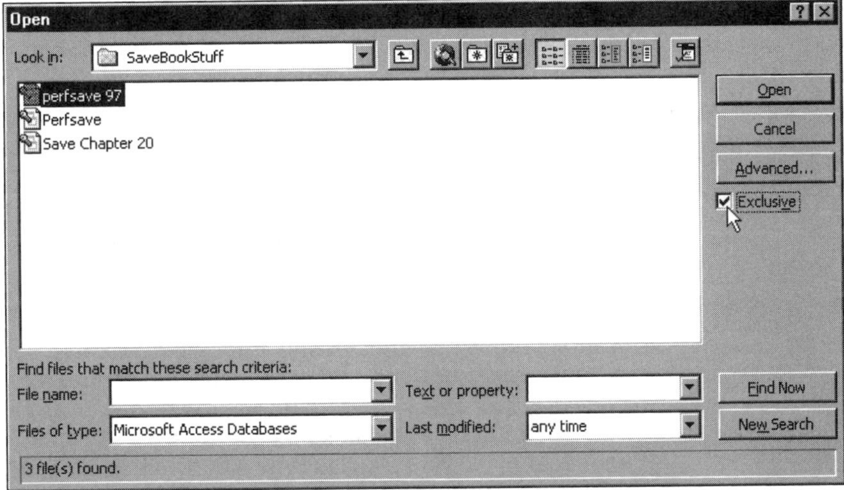

Figure 3-10: Check the Exclusive box when opening a database in a single-user environment to increase the performance of the database.

You can set the default open mode for a database on the Advanced tab of the Options dialog box.

Another often-overlooked way of maximizing your database's performance is to compact your database regularly. When records are deleted from a database, the disk space that held the deleted data is not recovered until a compact is performed. In addition, a database becomes fragmented as data is modified in the database. Compacting a database defragments the database and recovers used disk space.

All of the preceding are excellent (and necessary) methods to help keep your applications running at their optimum performance level, but these are not the only things you can do to increase the absolute speed of your application. Almost every area of development, from forms to modules, can be optimized to give your application maximum absolute speed.

Tuning your system

One very important aspect of performance has nothing to do with the actual application design; that is, the computer on which the application is running. Although it is impossible to account for all the various configurations your clients may have, there are some things you can do for your computer and recommend that end users do for theirs:

- Equip the computer with as much RAM as possible. This often becomes an issue of dollars. However, RAM prices continue to decrease, and adding to a computer's RAM is one of the most effective things you can do to increase the speed of Access.
- Make the `WinCacheSize` parameter for SmartDrive as small as possible, and disable SmartDrive completely on computers with little memory. You need to determine the size to set this at yourself based on your system and its memory configuration. Please consult your Windows manuals for more information on SmartDrive.
- Don't use wallpaper. Removing a standard Windows wallpaper background can free up anywhere from 25K to 250K of RAM, and removing complicated bitmaps or high-color bitmaps can free up even more.
- Eliminate unnecessary TSRs (Terminate and Stay Resident programs). TSRs can be real memory hogs and should not be used unless absolutely needed.
- Close all applications that aren't being used. Windows makes it very handy to keep as many applications as you wish loaded for just the odd chance you may need to use one of them. Although Windows 95 is much better than Windows 3.1 at handling memory for multiple open applications, each running application still uses RAM. On machines with little RAM, unnecessary open applications can degrade performance significantly.
- Ensure that your Windows swap file is on a fast drive with plenty of free space. In addition, if possible you should set the minimum disk space available for virtual memory to at least 25 MB of RAM.
- Defragment your hard drive often. Defragmenting a hard drive allows data to be retrieved from the drive in larger sections, causing fewer direct reads.

Adjusting the Jet registry settings

Access 97 includes a number of registry settings that allow you to tailor Jet functions for maximum performance. The `MaxBufferSize` and the `ReadAheadPages` settings are still there, as well a group of new settings that affects various elements of the Jet engine.

All of the preceding registry entries are found in the \HKEY_LOCAL_MACHINE\SOFTWARE\Microsoft\Jet\3.5\Engines\Jet 3.5 key of the Windows Registry. See Chapter 1 for more information on changing registry settings.

MaxBufferSize

The `MaxBufferSize` setting in the Windows registry controls how Jet uses memory in some operations. The `MaxBufferSize` setting controls the maximum size of the Jet database engine's internal cache (the cache used to store records in memory). The Jet engine reads data in 2K pages and places the data in the cache. After the data has been placed in the cache, it can be used wherever it is needed (in tables, queries, forms, or reports). The default setting for `MaxBufferSize` is 0, which means that Jet calculates the settings based on the formula `((Total RAM in K - 12,288)/4 + 512K)`. On a computer with 16MB of RAM, this equates to a `MaxBufferSize` of 1,536. For computers with minimal memory (8MB), you should set the value to something less than 512K to free up more memory for Access operations. However, for computers with more memory, increase the `MaxBufferSize`.

There is no hard-and-fast rule for what to set the `MaxBufferSize`, but some general guidelines are 2,048K for computers with 16MB, 3,072K for computers with 24MB. Increasing the `MaxBufferSize` enables Jet to read more records into the memory cache, which in turn minimizes disk reads/writes. Note: A higher setting does not always imply a more efficient setting. Setting the value higher than 8MB has not been found to increase performance.

ReadAheadPages

The `ReadAheadPages` setting controls the number of 2K data pages Jet reads ahead when doing sequential page reads. A sequential page read occurs when Jet detects that the data in a current read request is on a data page located on the hard disk adjacent to the data page of the previous request. The default setting for `ReadAheadPages` is 16; you can set the value anywhere between 0 and 31. If you change the setting to 0, Jet does not read ahead pages during sequential scans of data. A lower setting frees more memory for other Access operations; a higher setting uses more memory but enables Jet to access more records quickly in operations performed on sequential records. This setting is most efficient immediately after a database is compacted because compacting defragments the data (makes the data contiguous).

UserCommitSync

The `UserCommitSync` registry setting is used to choose whether Jet processes transactions *synchronously* or *asynchronously*. Setting the `UserCommitSync` setting to `Yes` forces Jet to process transactions synchronously; setting it to `No` forces Jet to process transactions in asynchronous mode. In synchronous mode, Jet processes the entire transaction before returning control to the application. In asynchronous mode, Jet caches the changes to its memory buffer, and immediately returns control to the application while writing the transaction results to disk using background processing. The `FlushTransactionTimeout`, the `SharedAsyncDelay`, and the `ExclusiveAsyncDelay` settings all affect how Jet commits transactions in asynchronous mode.

By default, the `UserCommitSync` registry setting is set to `Yes`; that is, synchronous mode. You should not change this setting to `No`, asynchronous mode, because in such a case control will return to your application before all transactions are committed to disk. Your application won't know whether the transaction was completed properly or not.

For more information on transaction processing see the "Using transactions" section later in this chapter.

ImplicitCommitSync

Jet processes add, delete, and update operations as transactions, even if they are not explicitly wrapped in a transaction. These transactions are known as implicit transactions. The `ImplictCommitSync` setting affects implicit transactions in much the same way that the `UserCommitSync` setting affects explicit transactions. However, the `ImplicitCommitSync` is set to `No`, asynchronous mode, by default. If you change this setting to `Yes` to process implicit transactions synchronously, you will get behavior similar to Access 2.0 in that all add, delete, and update operations are performed immediately and not as a transaction (unless explicitly wrapped in a transaction with `BeginTrans` and `CommitTrans`). Changing this setting to `No` yields much slower performance, so you should leave the setting at its default.

FlushTransactionTimeout

The `FlushTransactionTimeout` setting is the number of milliseconds after which Jet starts committing (writing) a cached transaction to disk. The setting is 50 milliseconds by default, and increasing the setting in a shared database environment can increase performance because more information is cached before writing to disk, causing fewer disk writes. Jet will commit the cached transactions to disk after the `FlushTransactionTimeout` interval is achieved or if the cache exceeds the `MaxBufferSize` setting.

ExclusiveAsyncDelay

The `ExclusiveAsyncDelay` setting is the maximum amount of time in milliseconds that is allowed to pass before asynchronous mode changes start to be committed to disk for a database that is opened exclusively. The default setting is 2,000 (2 seconds), and increasing the value will probably not boost performance unless there is over 32MB of RAM on the computer.

SharedAsyncDelay

The `SharedAsyncDelay` setting is the maximum amount of time in milliseconds that is allowed to pass before asynchronous mode changes start to be committed to disk for a database that is opened in shared mode. The default setting is 50 milliseconds, and increasing this value can yield faster performance. The higher the value used, however, the longer it takes to commit changes so other users can see them and free the locks on the cached records.

PageTimeout

The `PageTimeout` setting is how long Jet waits before checking to see if other users have made changes to the database. After the `PageTimeout` interval has passed, Jet refreshes any changed data into its memory buffer and restarts the interval. The default `PageTimeout` setting is 5,000 milliseconds (5 seconds). Increasing this value can yield faster performance but creates more lag time from when a user changes a record to when you see the change. The Refresh Interval (sec) setting on the Advanced tab of the Options dialog box overrides the `PageTimeout` setting.

Tip

You can cause Jet to immediately update its cache by using the `dbRefreshCache` argument of the `Idle` method in DAO code in a line such as this: `DBEngine.Idle dbRefreshCache`.

LockDelay

The `LockDelay` setting determines how long Jet waits to reattempt a record lock after a record lock attempt has been denied, such as when another user has locked the record. If the time it takes to return a lock denial message is longer than the `LockDelay`, the `LockDelay` setting is ignored and an immediate retry is attempted. The default `LockDelay` setting is 100 milliseconds, and increasing this value on computers accessing a database with frequent locks over a busy network may help reduce network traffic.

MaxLocksPerFile

The `MaxLocksPerFile` setting determines the maximum number of locks that Jet places on a single file. Jet will immediately commit to disk all pending transactions along with associated locks and free their locks if a queued transaction requires more locks than are currently available. By default, the `MaxLocksPerFile` setting is set for 9,500 locks. On a network, if Jet attempts to create more locks than the server can handle, the server returns an error message or may appear to lock up. If this occurs on your network, decrease the `MaxLocksPerFile` setting.

RecycleLVs

Jet uses Long Value pages (LVs) to store data in fields of Memo, OLE Object, and Hyperlink data types. LVs are also used to store data that defines forms, reports, and modules. Databases increase in size when opened in shared mode because Access LVs are constantly being replaced with new LVs as certain database objects are manipulated. The `ReclyceLVs` setting determines when discarded LVs become available for reuse. The default `RecycleLVs` setting is 0, meaning that discarded LVs are only recycled when the last user closes the database. If set to 1, Jet recycles LVs when it determines that there is only one user left using the database — this slows down performance.

Tip

The only way to free the disk space used by discarded LVs is to compact the database — another reason why you should compact your databases frequently.

Getting the most from your tables

In addition to all of the technical issues discussed in the preceding sections, it is advantageous to get back to the basics when designing your applications. Tools such as Access enable novices to create relational databases quickly and easily, but they do not teach good database design techniques in the process. An exception to this statement is the Table Analyzer Wizard, which is discussed later in this chapter. Even though the Table Analyzer Wizard offers suggestions that are often helpful in learning good design technique, its recommendations should *never* be taken as gospel. The Table Analyzer has proven to be wrong on many occasions.

Entire volumes of text have been devoted to the subject of database theory. Teaching database theory is certainly beyond the scope of this chapter (or even this book). There are, however, many basics of good database design with which you should be familiar.

Creating efficient indexes

Indexes help Access find and sort records more efficiently (in other words, faster). Think of these indexes as you would think of an index in a book. To find data, Access looks up the location of the data in the index and then retrieves the data from its location. You can create indexes based on a single field or based on multiple fields. Multiple-field indexes enable you to distinguish between records in which the first field may have the same value. If they are defined properly, multiple-field indexes can be used by Rushmore query optimization, the technology Jet uses to optimize the speed at which queries execute based on the search and sort fields of the queries and indexes of the tables included in the queries, to greatly speed queries (see the "Getting the most from your queries" section).

Deciding which fields to index

Two typical mistakes made by people new to database development are not using indexes and using too many indexes (usually putting them on every field in a table); both of these are serious mistakes — sometimes a table with indexes on every field may give *slower* performance than a table with no indexes. Why? When a record is saved, Access also must save an index entry for each defined index. This can take time and use a considerable amount of disk space. The time used is usually unnoticed when there are just a few indexes, but many indexes can require a huge amount of time for record saves and updates. In addition, indexes can slow some action queries (such as append queries) when the indexes for many fields need to be updated while performing the query's operations.

Figure 3-11 shows the index property sheet for a sample Customer table.

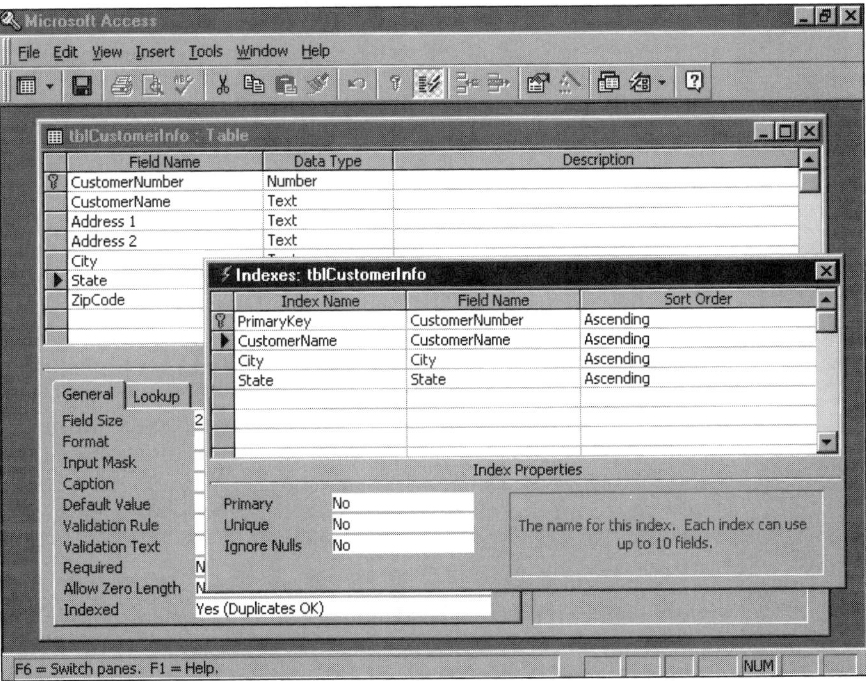

Figure 3-11: Note that common search fields such as City and State are indexed.

When you create a primary key for a table, the field (or fields) used to define the key is automatically indexed, and you can index any field unless the field's data type is Memo or OLE Object. You should consider indexing a field if all the following apply:

- The field's data type is Text, Number, Currency, or Date/Time.
- You anticipate searching for values stored in the field.

- You anticipate sorting records based on the values in the field.
- You will join the field to fields in other tables in queries.
- You anticipate storing many different values in the field. (If many of the values in the field are the same, the index may not significantly speed up searches or sorting.)

When defining an index, you have the option of creating an ascending (the default) or a descending index. Jet can use a descending index when optimizing queries only when the equal sign (=) operator is used. If you use an operator other than the equal sign, such as <, >, <=, or >=, Jet cannot use the descending index. If you plan on using operators other than an equal sign on an index, you should define the index as an ascending index.

Using multiple-field indexes

If you often search or sort by two or more fields at the same time, you can create an index for that combination of fields. For example, if you often set criteria for LastName and FirstName fields in the same query, it makes sense to create a multiple-field index on both fields.

When you sort a table by a multiple-field index, Access first sorts by the first field defined for the index. If there are records with duplicate values in the first field, Access then sorts by the second field defined for the index, and so on. This creates a drill-down effect. For a multiple-field index to work, there *has* to be search criteria defined for the first field in the index, but not for additional fields in the index. In the preceding example, if you were to search for someone with the first name *Robert* but don't specify a last name to use in the search, the second field in the index would not be used. If you need to perform searches on the second field in a multiple-field index, but are not always specifying criteria for the first field in the index, you should create an index for the second field in addition to the multiple-field index. Continuing with the LastName, FirstName index, if you wanted to search for the first name *John*, the multiple-field index would not be used because you would be attempting to search only on the second field in the index.

Normalizing your tables

Another issue that is not often understood by novice database designers is *normalization*. Normalization is the process of splitting (or joining) data into optimized tables. For example, if you needed to keep the following information to track multiple invoices for customers, you could put all the information in one table, such as the one shown in Figure 3-12.

```
CustomerName
Address1
Address2
City
State
ZipCode
InvoiceNumber
ItemSold
```

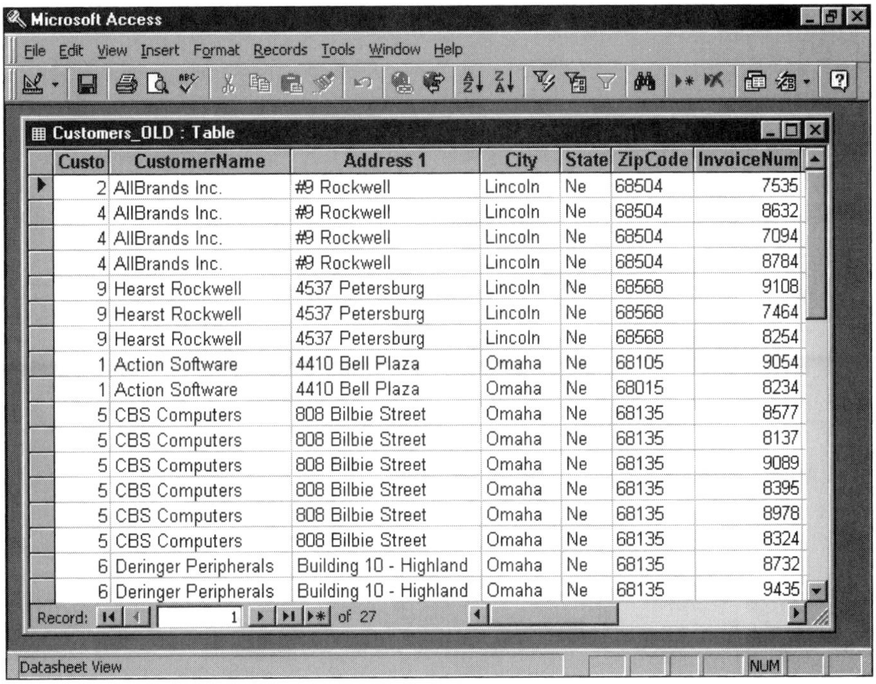

Microsoft Access

Customers_OLD : Table

Custo	CustomerName	Address 1	City	State	ZipCode	InvoiceNum
2	AllBrands Inc.	#9 Rockwell	Lincoln	Ne	68504	7535
4	AllBrands Inc.	#9 Rockwell	Lincoln	Ne	68504	8632
4	AllBrands Inc.	#9 Rockwell	Lincoln	Ne	68504	7094
4	AllBrands Inc.	#9 Rockwell	Lincoln	Ne	68504	8784
9	Hearst Rockwell	4537 Petersburg	Lincoln	Ne	68568	9108
9	Hearst Rockwell	4537 Petersburg	Lincoln	Ne	68568	7464
9	Hearst Rockwell	4537 Petersburg	Lincoln	Ne	68568	8254
1	Action Software	4410 Bell Plaza	Omaha	Ne	68105	9054
1	Action Software	4410 Bell Plaza	Omaha	Ne	68015	8234
5	CBS Computers	808 Bilbie Street	Omaha	Ne	68135	8577
5	CBS Computers	808 Bilbie Street	Omaha	Ne	68135	8137
5	CBS Computers	808 Bilbie Street	Omaha	Ne	68135	9089
5	CBS Computers	808 Bilbie Street	Omaha	Ne	68135	8395
5	CBS Computers	808 Bilbie Street	Omaha	Ne	68135	8978
5	CBS Computers	808 Bilbie Street	Omaha	Ne	68135	8324
6	Deringer Peripherals	Building 10 - Highland	Omaha	Ne	68135	8732
6	Deringer Peripherals	Building 10 - Highland	Omaha	Ne	68135	9435

Record: 1 of 27

Datasheet View

Figure 3-12: Notice the amount of duplicated data in this non-normalized table.

Placing all the information in one table creates a large database with duplicated data; this table is not normalized. The basic ideas behind normalization are *reduce the amount of redundant data* and *break data into logical tables*. When you have redundant data, you are not only increasing disk space used to store the data, you are also slowing down searches and increasing the chance that data will be entered inaccurately. For example, if you wanted a list of all Invoices for Microsoft Corporation, and a data entry person entered an order for Microsoft Corp., it would not show up in your search. A better alternative to the preceding table is to break the data elements into two tables: a customer table and an invoice table (see Figure 3-13).

The next step is to create a join for these two tables (see Figure 3-14). Now, customer data has to be entered once and only once. Also, if customer data needs to be changed (such as changing the address information when a customer moves), the change can be made in only one place. Searches also become much faster because there is less data to deal with in any one table. These tables are normalized tables.

Give careful thought to the normalization of your tables. In very rare cases on extremely large databases it may become more efficient to denormalize certain aspects of the database, but, in general, you should always normalize your databases to make them as efficient as possible.

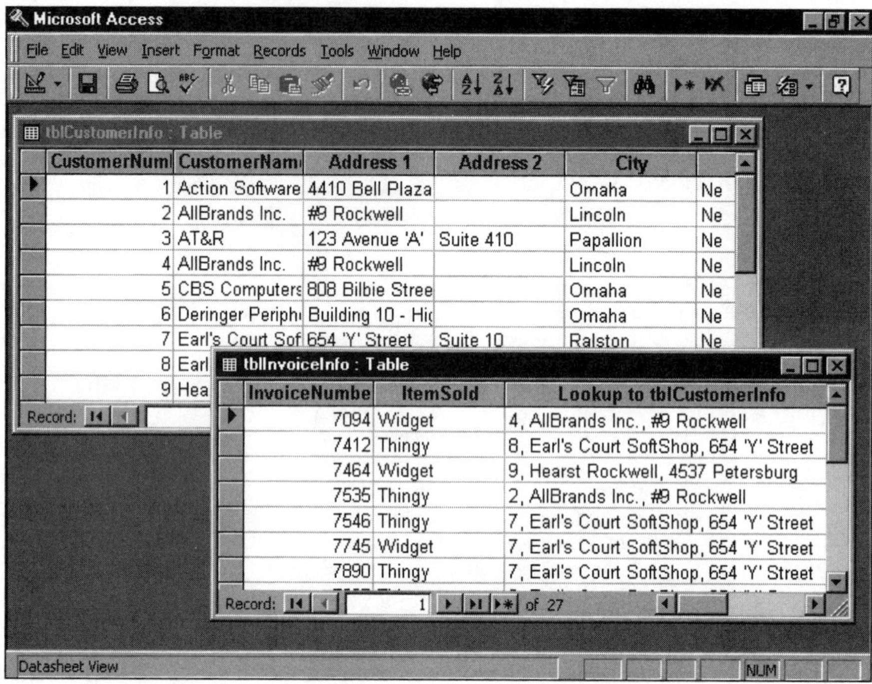

Figure 3-13: The data has now been split into two tables to reduce redundancy.

Using the Table Analyzer Wizard

Absolutely nothing can substitute for experience and education when it comes to proper table normalizing. However, Access has attempted to improve the learning curve with a tool called the Table Analyzer Wizard. The Table Analyzer Wizard looks at an existing table and attempts to determine if the table is normalized. If the wizard believes the table is not normalized, it makes suggestions to you on how to normalize the table. It then allows you to modify or accept its suggestions, and it creates new, normalized related tables containing the data from the original table.

This tool can be extremely helpful if you have just imported a flat file database (see Chapter 17) and are not very familiar with what the imported database contains. In a situation such as this, the Table Analyzer Wizard can greatly speed up the process of understanding and normalizing the data.

You should use the Table Analyzer Wizard's suggestions only as general guidelines when normalizing your database. The Table Analyzer Wizard has shown to be inaccurate under some circumstances; at times it is not even close. This section teaches you how to use the Table Analyzer Wizard, but it is to your benefit to learn how to normalize your own databases as quickly as possible so that you will not need to rely on the suggestions of the Table Analyzer Wizard.

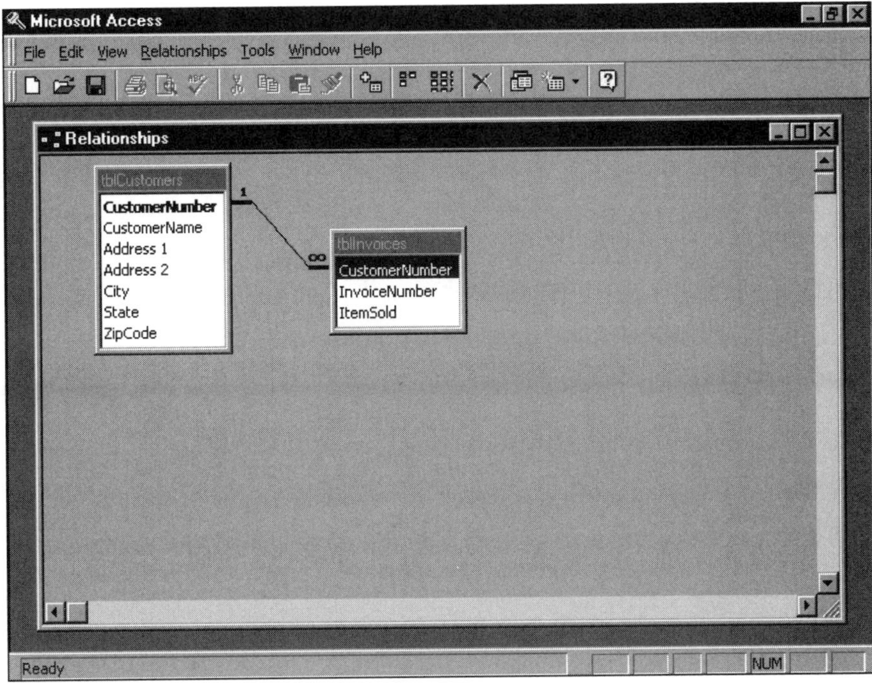

Figure 3-14: By creating a join with referential integrity, you ensure that the customer data is always related to the proper invoices regardless of what customer data may change.

When you have a table and need some help normalizing the data, use the Table Analyzer Wizard. To start the Table Analyzer, select Analyze⇨Table from the Tools menu (see Figure 3-15).

The first two pages of the Table Analyzer are simply help screens (see Figure 3-16 and Figure 3-17). They introduce you to some basic concepts of normalization and what the Table Analyzer is going to attempt to do. On each of these pages, you can click on the Show me an example buttons to view examples of non-normalization. After viewing each page, click on the Next button.

If you don't want to see the first two help pages of the Table Analyzer Wizard, uncheck the button on the third page that says Show introductory pages?

The following fields belong to a sample table called Customers. Figure 3-18 shows the table in datasheet view. In the figure, observe the duplication of account information for each invoice entered. This data would be better organized if the customer information were put into one table and the invoices were put into a different table. They could then be linked by the unique customer number. Then, each customer would only need to have the information stored once. The Table Analyzer can look at this table and make these recommendations.

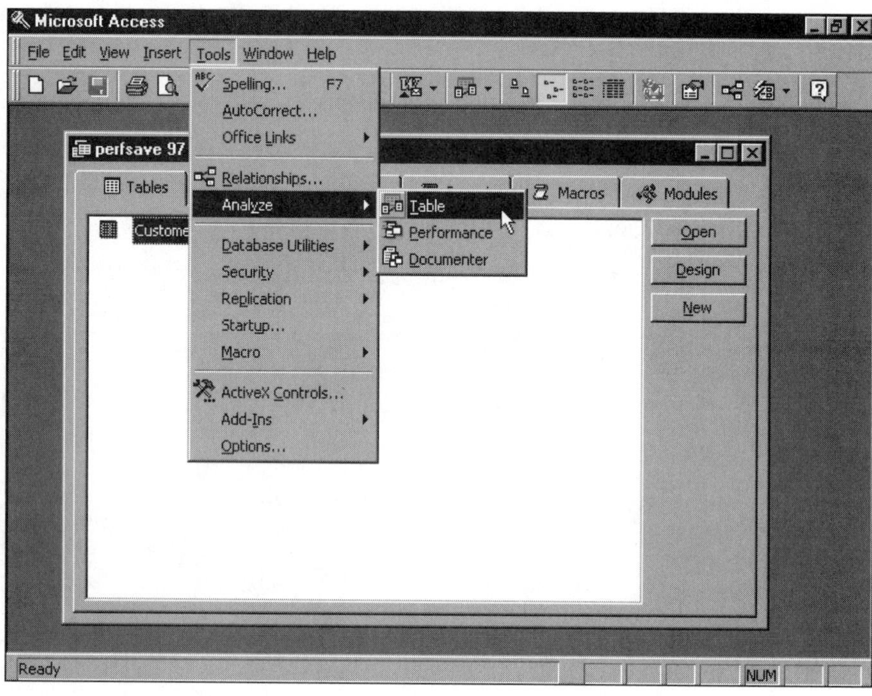

Figure 3-15: Starting the Table Analyzer Wizard.

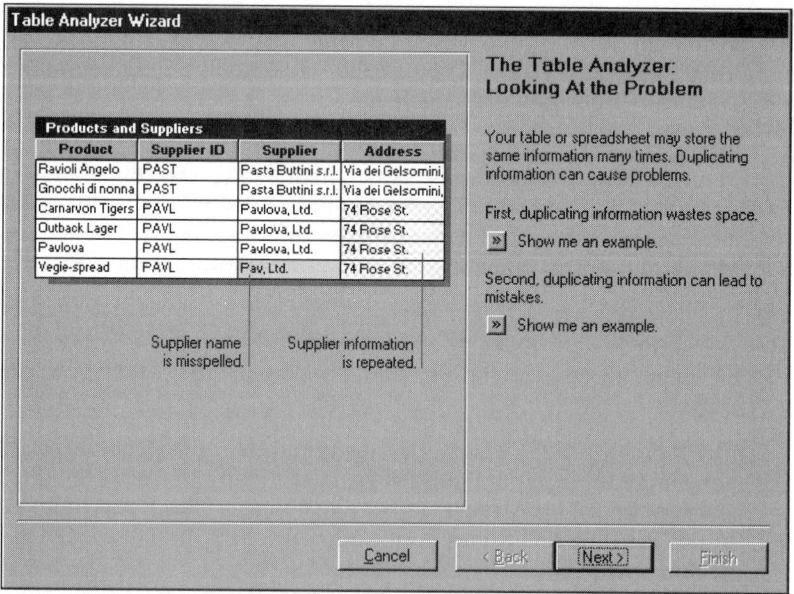

Figure 3-16: Page 1 of the Table Analyzer Wizard introduces you to the problems of a non-normalized database.

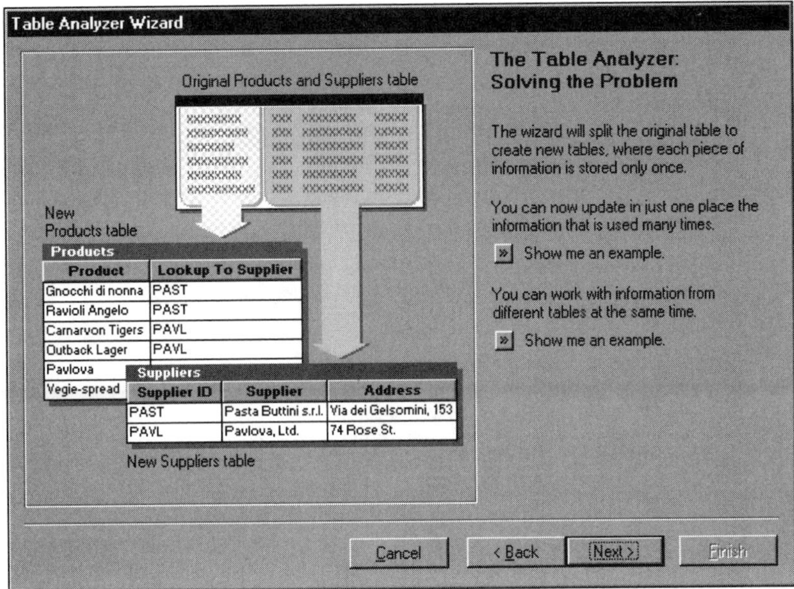

Figure 3-17: Page 2 of the Table Analyzer Wizard talks about what it can do to help normalize your table.

```
CustomerNumber
CustomerName
Address 1
Address 2
City
State
ZipCode
InvoiceNumber
ItemSold
```

The Table Analyzer looks for certain key words such as Customer and Number or Invoice and Number to help it understand a table. If you use standard names for your fields, you may have better luck using the Table Analyzer Wizard.

Because the first two pages are introductory pages and can be disabled, from this point we refer to the page shown in Figure 3-19 (Page 3) as Page 1 instead of Page 3, and all page references are adjusted accordingly.

Page 1 of the Table Analyzer is used to select the table you want to analyze; you can analyze only one table at a time. Note also that your original table is not modified but new tables are created. When you have selected the table to analyze, click on the Next button.

Microsoft Access

File Edit View Insert Format Records Tools Window Help

Customers : Table

Custo	CustomerName	Address 1	City	State	ZipCode	InvoiceNum	
2	AllBrands Inc.	#9 Rockwell	Lincoln	Ne	68504	7535	Thi
4	AllBrands Inc.	#9 Rockwell	Lincoln	Ne	68504	8632	Wi
4	AllBrands Inc.	#9 Rockwell	Lincoln	Ne	68504	7094	Wi
4	AllBrands Inc.	#9 Rockwell	Lincoln	Ne	68504	8784	Thi
9	Hearst Rockwell	4537 Petersburg	Lincoln	Ne	68568	9108	Thi
9	Hearst Rockwell	4537 Petersburg	Lincoln	Ne	68568	7464	Wi
9	Hearst Rockwell	4537 Petersburg	Lincoln	Ne	68568	8254	Thi
1	Action Software	4410 Bell Plaza	Omaha	Ne	68105	9054	Wi
1	Action Software	4410 Bell Plaza	Omaha	Ne	68015	8234	Wi
5	CBS Computers	808 Bilbie Street	Omaha	Ne	68135	8577	Wi
5	CBS Computers	808 Bilbie Street	Omaha	Ne	68135	8137	Wi
5	CBS Computers	808 Bilbie Street	Omaha	Ne	68135	9089	Thi
5	CBS Computers	808 Bilbie Street	Omaha	Ne	68135	8395	Thi
5	CBS Computers	808 Bilbie Street	Omaha	Ne	68135	8978	Wi
5	CBS Computers	808 Bilbie Street	Omaha	Ne	68135	8324	Wi
6	Deringer Peripherals	Building 10 - Highland	Omaha	Ne	68135	8732	Wi
6	Deringer Peripherals	Building 10 - Highland	Omaha	Ne	68135	9435	Thi

Record: 1 of 27

Datasheet View NUM

Figure 3-18: Much-duplicated data is usually a sure sign that a table is not normalized.

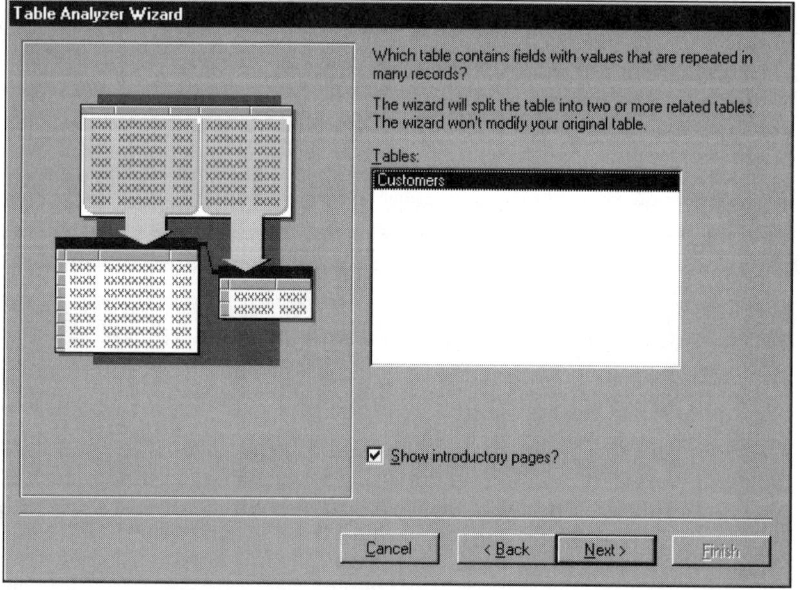

Figure 3-19: Use page 1 of the Table Analyzer to select the table you want to analyze.

Page 2 is where you need to make an important decision: You need to specify if you want the Table Analyzer to decide what fields go in what tables or if you want to decide how to split the table (see Figure 3-20). If you elect to make the decisions, you are in effect just using the Table Analyzer as a fancy tool to manually split your table. By telling the Table Analyzer you want it to decide on how to split the table, you are giving it free reign to work its magic and normalize your table. Note that you can override any and all recommendations before any new tables are created.

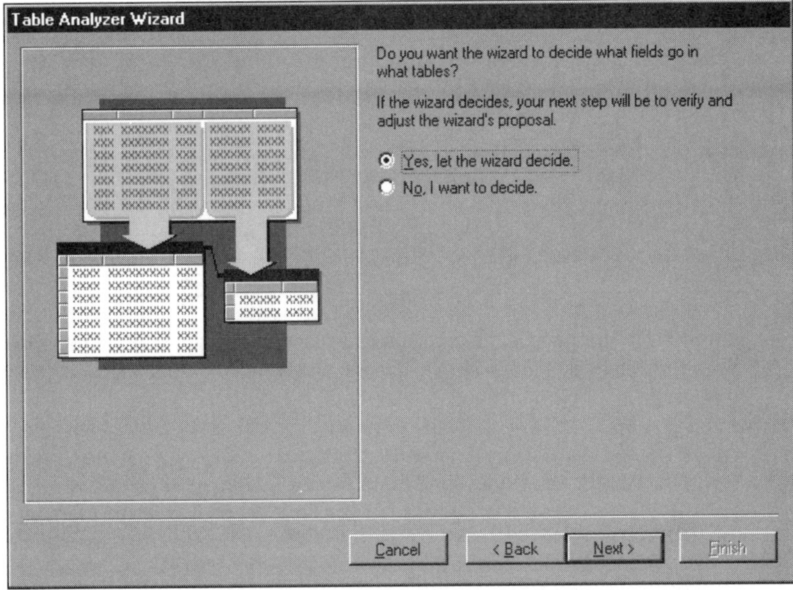

Figure 3-20: If you want to have the Table Analyzer do its stuff, you need to tell it to decide how to split the table.

After you tell the Table Analyzer to make recommendations on how to split your table, click on the Next button. When you do so, a page like that in Figure 3-21 is shown. This page looks similar to the relationship definition window in Access. It shows you the new tables it believes need to be created to normalize your original table. Notice in Figure 3-21 that the Table Analyzer correctly assessed that the customer information needs to be separated from the invoice data. It also correctly assessed that the CustomerNumber is the unique identifier of the customer data and assigns it as the primary key for the customer table and then created a join to a lookup field in the invoice table. In this example, the Table Analyzer hits the nail right on the head, so you don't need to alter its recommendation. If the Table Analyzer had been wrong with its suggestion, you could drag fields between the tables in any way you saw fit. Because the Table Analyzer is right in this instance, you only need to name your new tables.

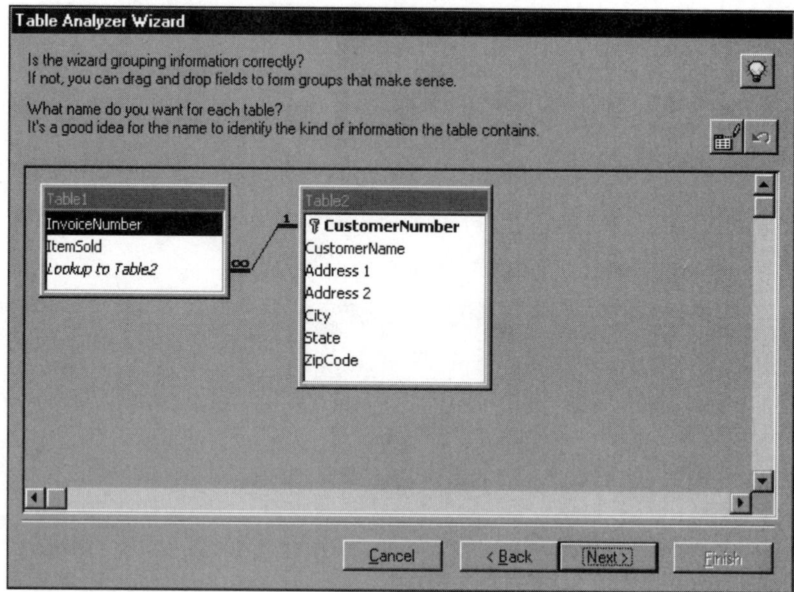

Figure 3-21: This page is the critical step in using the Table Analyzer to normalize your table. Look carefully at its recommendations and make any changes you believe are necessary.

Tip

At the top-right of the latter pages of the Table Analyzer Wizard is a little button with a picture of a light bulb. Click on this button for tips on using the Table Analyzer Wizard.

To name the new tables, click on the table to give it the focus and then click on the button in the upper-right of the page that has the picture of a table and a pencil on it. When you click on the edit table name button, you are shown the form in Figure 3-22. To name a different table, select any field of the table to give it the focus and click on the edit table button again. When you are through naming the new tables, click on the Next button.

The next step to normalizing your tables using the Table Analyzer is to tell the wizard what the unique keys are for each table. The Table Analyzer attempts to determine the keys, but you will probably have to help. You don't need to specify a primary key, but you should do so. In Figure 3-23, the multiple-field key for tblInvoiceInfo was created by selecting both the InvoiceNumber and the ItemSold while holding the Shift key and clicking on the Set Unique Key button (the button with the key). If no fields make good primary keys, you can click on the Add Generated Unique Key button (the button with the key and the plus sign) to have Access add a field of type autonumber to the table and set it as the primary key. When you have added keys to the new tables, click on the Next button to continue.

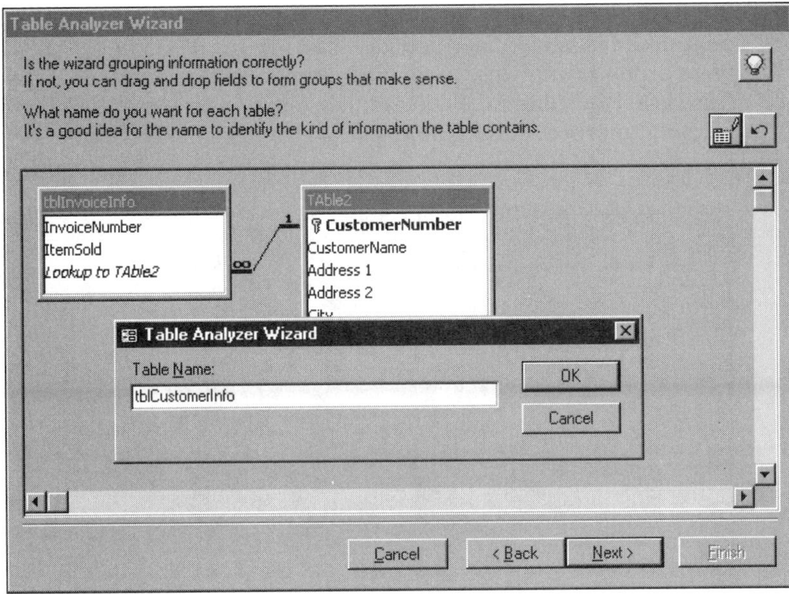

Figure 3-22: Although you can rename your tables in the database window after the Table Analyzer creates them, it is more convenient to name them here before they are saved.

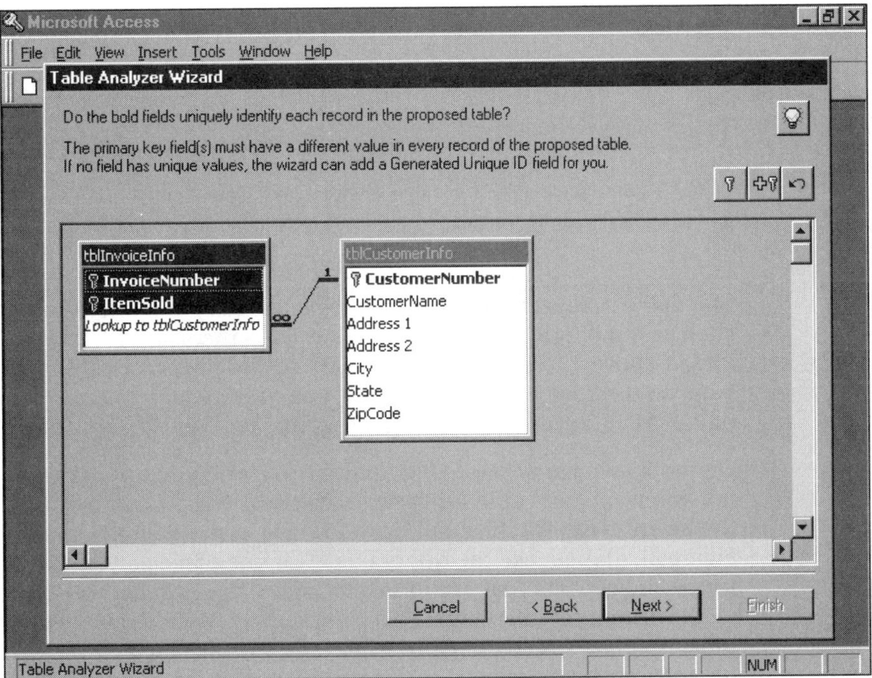

Figure 3-23: All of your tables should have primary keys. Add them here to any new tables where the Table Analyzer did not assign a field as a primary key.

In this example, the Table Analyzer Wizard has noticed that some fields designated as related actually don't appear to be related. The Table Analyzer prompts you when situations such as this occur (see Figure 3-24). In this case, the Table Analyzer is mistaken, so you would select Yes. After electing to proceed, the Table Analyzer shows the fields that are in question.

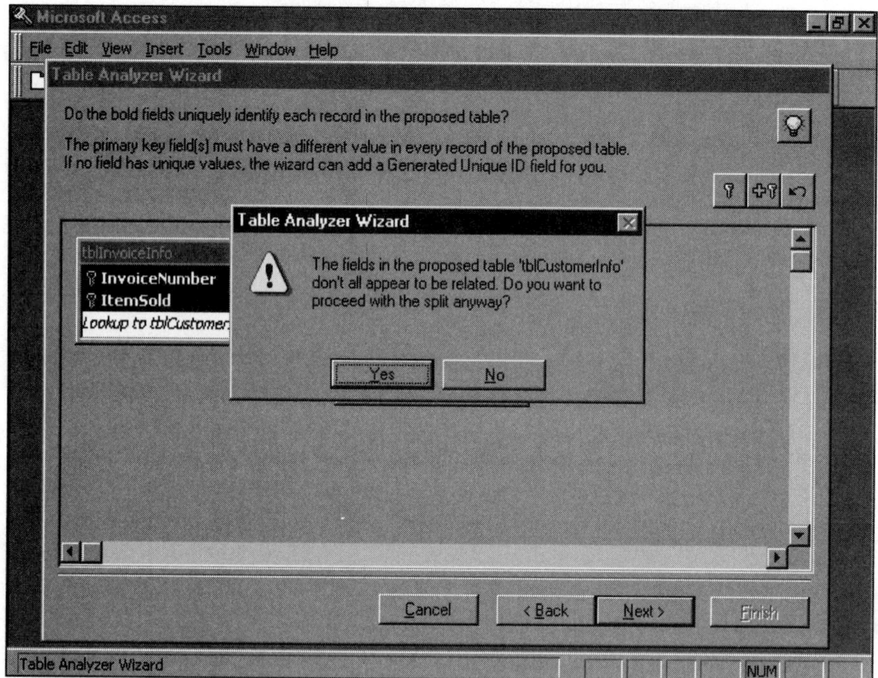

Figure 3-24: Occasionally, the Table Analyzer finds something that it does not think is proper and asks for your input.

The Table Analyzer searches the fields of each record for discrepancies such as minor spelling deviations. If it finds records with minor discrepancies, it shows them to you and lets you decide which is the appropriate value to use (see Figure 3-25). After you have resolved discrepancies, click on the Next button to proceed to the final page of the wizard.

On the final page of the Table Analyzer Wizard, you are asked whether or not you want the Table Analyzer to create a query that uses the data from the newly created tables but has the same name as your original table (see Figure 3-26). Because the query has the same name as your original table, all forms and reports that are based on your original table will continue to work without modification. This is extremely useful if you are normalizing a table that has already been used to create forms and reports. Note that your original table is renamed, not overwritten. You can also tell Access to display help on working with your new tables by checking the box at the bottom of the final page. When you are satisfied with your selections, click on the Finish button to split your tables.

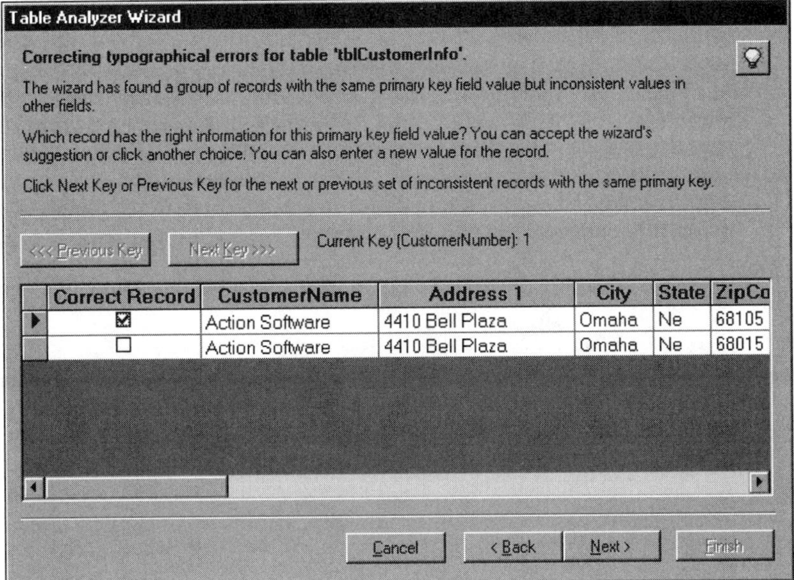

Figure 3-25: In this case, the Table Analyzer found two different ZIP codes for what appears to be the same record. It shows the conflict to you and asks you to resolve it.

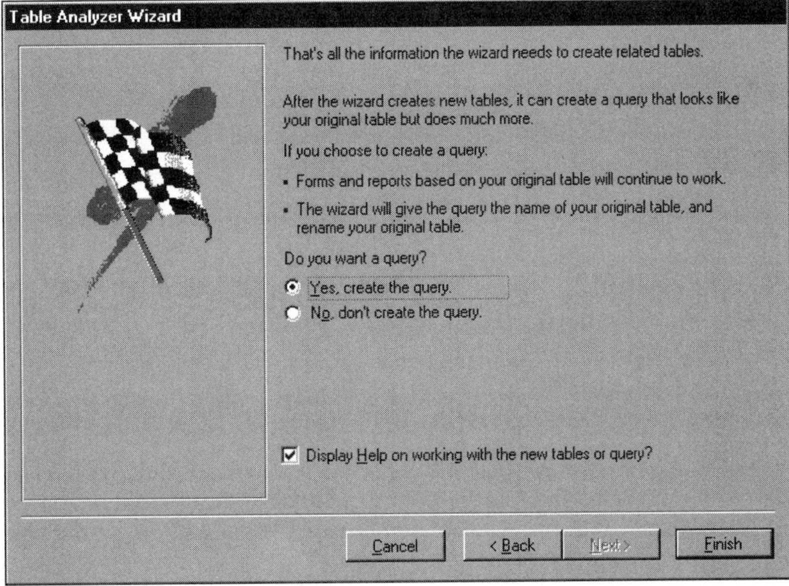

Figure 3-26: The Table Analyzer Wizard asks if you want to create a query and name it the same as your original table.

Figure 3-27 shows the results of the Table Analyzer's analysis of the Customers table. It has created two new related tables called tblCustomerInfo and tblInvoiceInfo and renamed the original table to Customers_OLD because it has created a new query called tblCustomers. Now the data is normalized, and existing forms and reports continue to function. At this point, you can delete the original table.

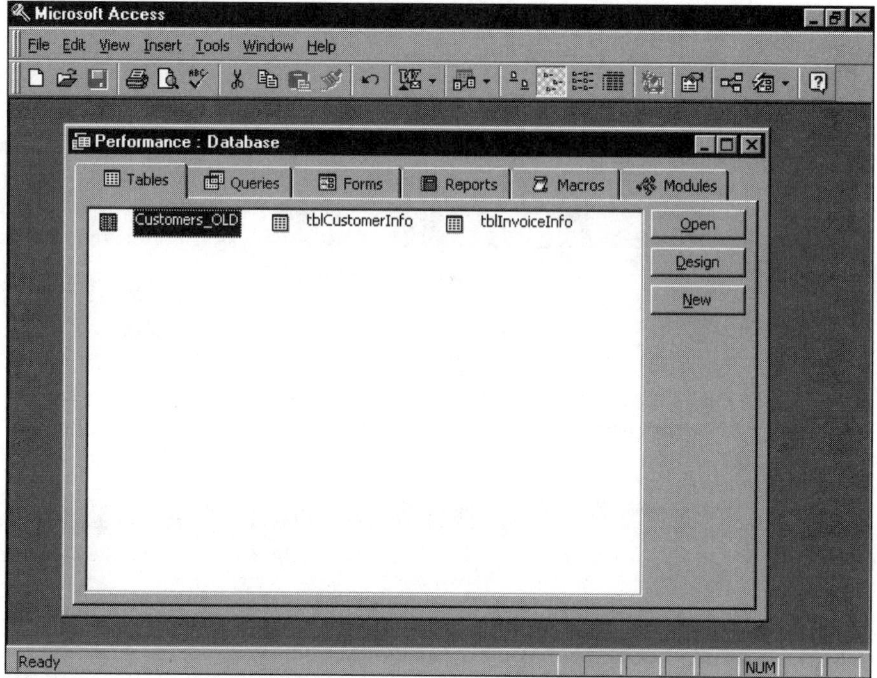

Figure 3-27: The results of the Table Analyzer's analysis of the Customers table.

It is always advisable to back up your database before deleting any tables — just in case you make a mistake.

Getting the most from your queries

The performance problems of many Access applications lie in the design of their queries. Database applications are all about looking at and working with data, and queries are the heart of determining what data to look at or work with. Queries are used to bind forms and reports, fill list boxes and combo boxes, make new tables, and for many other functions within an Access application. Because they are so widely used, it is extremely important to optimize your queries. A query that is properly designed can provide results in minutes to hours faster than a poorly designed query that returns the same result set.

- When designing queries and tables, you should create indexes for all fields used in sorts, joins, and criteria fields. Indexes enable Jet to quickly sort and search through your database. In addition, sorting and searching is much faster if the indexes are unique rather than non-unique.
- When possible, use a primary key in place of a regular index when creating joins. Primary keys don't allow nulls and give the Rushmore query optimizer more ways to use the joins.
- Limit the columns of data returned in a select query to only those columns you need; if you don't need the information from a field, don't return it in the query. Queries run much faster when they must return less information.
- When you need to return a count of the records returned by an SQL statement, use `Count(*)` instead of `Count([FieldName])`; `Count(*)` is considerably faster. `Count(*)` counts records that contain null fields; `Count([FieldName])` checks for nulls and disqualifies them from being counted. If you specify a field name instead of using the asterisk, `Count` does not count records that have a null in the specified field. You may also replace `FieldName` with an expression, but this slows down the function even further.
- Avoid using calculated fields in nested queries. A calculated field in a subordinate query considerably slows down the top-level query. You should use only calculated fields in top-level queries, and then only when necessary.
- When you need to group records by the values of a field used in a join, specify the Group By for the field that is in the same table as you are totaling. You can drag the joined field from either table, but using Group By on the field from the table you are totaling yields faster results.
- Domain Aggregate functions, such as `DLookup` or `DCount`, used as expressions in queries, slow down the queries considerably. Instead, you should add the table to the query or use a subquery to return the information you need.
- Just as with VBA code modules, queries are compiled. To compile a query, Jet's Rushmore query optimizer evaluates the query to determine the fastest way to execute the query. If a query is saved in a compiled state, it runs at its fastest the first time you execute it. If it is not compiled, it takes longer the first time it executes because it must be compiled, and then runs faster in succeeding executions. To compile a query, run the query by opening it in datasheet view and then close the query without saving it. If you make changes to the query definition, run the query again after saving your changes and then close it without saving it.
- If you really want to squeeze the most out of your queries, you should experiment by creating your queries in different ways (such as specifying different types of joins). You will be surprised at the varying results you achieve.

Getting the most from your forms and reports

Forms and reports can slow an application by taking a long time to load or process information. You can do a number of things to increase the performance of forms and reports.

Minimizing form and report complexity and size

One of the key elements to achieving better performance from your forms and reports is reducing their complexity and size. To reduce a form's or report's complexity and size

- Minimize the number of objects on a form or report. The fewer objects used, the less resources needed to display and process the form or report.
- Reduce the use of subforms. When a subform is loaded, two forms are in memory — the parent form and the subform. Use a list box or a combo box in place of a subform whenever possible.
- Use labels instead of text boxes for hidden fields; text boxes use more resources than labels do. Hidden fields are often used as an alternative to creating variables to store information. You cannot write a value directly to a label like you can to a text box, but you can write to the label's caption property like this: `Label1.Caption = "MyValue"`.
- Move some code from a form's module into a standard module. This enables the form to load faster because the code doesn't need to be loaded into memory. If the procedures you move to a normal module are referenced by any procedures executed upon loading a form (such as in the form load event), moving the procedures will not help because they are loaded anyway as part of the potential call tree of the executed procedure.
- Don't overlap controls on a form or report.
- Place related groups of controls on form pages. If only one page is shown at a time, Access does not need to generate all the controls at the same time.
- Use light forms whenever possible. Light forms have no code module attached to them, so they load and display considerably faster than forms with code modules.
- Use a query that returns a limited result set for a form's or report's RecordSource rather than use a table. The less data returned for the RecordSource, the faster the form or report loads. In addition, return only those fields actually used by the form or report.

Using bitmaps on forms and reports

Bitmaps on forms and reports make an application look attractive and also help convey the purpose of the form or report (like in a wizard). Graphics are always resource intensive, so you should use the fewest number of graphic objects on your forms and reports as possible. This helps minimize form and report load time, increase print speed, and reduce the resources used by your application.

Often you will display pictures that a user never changes and that are not bound to a database. Examples of such pictures would be your company logo on a switchboard or static images in a wizard. When you want to display an image such as this, you have two choices:

- Use an Unbound Object Frame
- Use an Image control

If the image will never change and you don't need to activate it in form design view, use an Image control. Image controls use fewer resources and display faster. If you need the image to be a linked or embedded OLE object that you can edit, use an Unbound Object Frame. You can convert OLE images in Unbound Object Frames.

If you have an image in an Unbound Object Frame that you no longer need to edit, you can convert the Unbound Object Frame to an Image control by selecting Change To⇨Image from the Format menu.

When you have forms that contain unbound OLE objects, you should close the forms when they are not in use to free resources. Also avoid using bitmaps with many colors — they take considerably more resources and are slower to paint than a bitmap of the same size with fewer colors.

If you want to display an Unbound OLE object but don't want the user to be able to activate it, set its `Enabled` property to `False`.

Speeding list boxes and combo boxes

It is important to pay attention to the optimization of list boxes and combo boxes when optimizing your application. There are a number of steps you can take to make your combo boxes and list boxes run faster.

- When using multipage forms that have list boxes or combo boxes on more than one page, consider not setting the `RowSource` of the list boxes or combo boxes until the actual page containing the control is displayed.
- Index the first field displayed in a list box or combo box. This enables Access to find entries that match text entered by the user much faster.
- Although not always practical to do so, try to refrain from hiding a combo box's bound column. Hiding the bound column causes the control's searching features to slow down considerably.

- If you don't need the search capabilities of AutoExpand, set the `AutoExpand` property of a combo box to `No`. Access is then relieved of constantly searching the list for entries matching text entered in the text portion of the combo box.
- When possible, make the first non-hidden column in a combo or list box a text data type, not a numeric one. To find a match in the list of a combo box or list box, Access must convert a numeric value to text in order to do the character-by-character match. If the data type is text, Access can skip the conversion step.
- Often overlooked is the performance gain achieved by using saved queries for `RecordSource` and `RowSource` properties of list boxes and combo boxes. A saved query gives much better performance than an SQL `SELECT` statement because an SQL query is optimized by Rushmore on the fly.

There is one problem with combo boxes that has been introduced in Access 97 that poses a performance concern. Because Access 97 now supports hyperlinks, Access has to perform a little additional work when first painting a combo box; it needs to determine the data type of the combo box. The result is that the combo box takes a little longer to paint — up to a couple of seconds on some computers. If your combo box is a bound combo box, this is not a problem because Access gets the data type from the ControlSource's data type. In addition, if you save a RowSource for the combo box when you save the form, Access determines the data type from the RowSource and doesn't need to determine the data type at run time. The only time this paint delay is an issue is when you have an unbound combo box that has its RowSource set programmatically. When this is the case, the combo box will take slightly longer to paint the first time it is displayed.

Getting the most from your modules

Perhaps the area where you'll be able to use smart optimization techniques most frequently is in your modules. For example, in code behind forms, you should use the Me keyword when referencing controls. This approach takes advantage of Access 97 capabilities; using Me is faster than creating a form variable and referencing the form in the variable. Other optimization techniques are simply smart coding practices that have been around for many years. You should try to use the optimum coding technique at all times. When in doubt, try many different methods to accomplish a task and see which one is fastest.

Tip

Consider reducing the number of modules and procedures in your application by consolidating them whenever possible. There is a small memory overhead incurred for each module and procedure you use, so consolidating them may free up some memory.

Using appropriate data types

You should always explicitly declare variables using the `Dim` function rather than arbitrarily assign values to variables that have not been Dimmed. To assure that all variables in your application are explicitly declared before they are used in a procedure, select Tools⇨Options and then set the Require Variable Declarations option on the Modules tab.

Use integers and long integers rather than singles and doubles when possible. Integers and long integers use less memory, and they take less time to process than singles and doubles. Table 3-1 shows the relative speed of the different data types available in Access.

Table 3-1 Data Types and Their Mathematical Processing Speed

Data Type	*Relative Processing Speed*
Integer/Long	Fastest
Single/Double	Next to Fastest
Currency	Next to Slowest
Variant	Slowest

In addition to using integers and long integers whenever possible, you should also use integer math rather than precision math when applicable. For example, to divide one long integer by another long integer, you could use the following statement:

```
x = Long1 / Long2
```

This statement is a standard math function that uses floating-point math. The same function could be performed using integer math with the following statement:

```
x = Long1 \ Long2
```

Of course, integer math isn't always applicable. It is, however, commonly applied when returning a percentage. For example, you could return a percentage with the following precision math formula:

```
x = Total / Value
```

However, you could perform the same function using integer math by first multiplying the `Total` by `100` and then using integer math like this:

```
x = (Total * 100) \ Value
```

You should also use string functions ($) where applicable. When you are manipulating variables that are of type String, use the string functions (for example, `Str$()`) as opposed to their variant counterparts (`Str()`). If you are working with variants, use the non-$ functions. Using string functions when working with strings is faster because Access doesn't need to perform type conversions on the variables.

When you need to return a substring by using `Mid$()`, you can omit the third parameter to have the entire length of the string returned. For example, to return a substring that starts at the second character of a string and returns all remaining characters, you would use a statement like this:

```
szReturn = Mid$(szMyString, 2)
```

When using arrays, use dynamic arrays with the `Erase` and `ReDim` statements to reclaim memory. By dynamically adjusting the size of the arrays, you can ensure that only the amount of memory needed for the array is allocated.

Tip

In addition to using optimized variables, consider using constants when applicable. Constants can make your code much easier to read and will not slow your application if you compile your code before executing it.

Writing faster routines

There are a number of ways you can make your procedures faster by optimizing the routines they contain. If you keep performance issues in mind as you develop, you will be able to find and take advantage of situations like those discussed here.

Some Access functions perform similar processes but vary greatly in the time they take to execute. You probably use one or more of these regularly, and knowing the most efficient way to perform these routines can greatly affect your application's speed:

- `For/Next` statements are faster than `Select Case` statements.
- The `IIF()` function is much slower than a standard set of `If/Then/Else` statements.
- The `With` and `For Each` functions accelerate manipulating multiple objects and/or their properties.
- Change a variable with `Not` instead of using an `If . . . Then` statement. (For example, use `x = Not(y)` instead of `If y = true then x= false.)`
- Instead of comparing a variable to the value `True`, use the value of the variable. (For example, instead of saying `If X = True then . . .`, say `If X then . . .`.)
- Use the `Requery` method instead of the `Requery` action. The method is significantly faster than the action.
- When using OLE automation, resolve references when your application is compiled rather than resolve them at run time using the `GetObject` or `CreateObject` functions.

Using control variables

When referencing a control on a form many times in a loop, it is much faster to first dimension a control variable to reference the control like this:

```
Dim ctrl as Control
set ctrl = Me![CustomerNumber]
```

You can then reference the variable rather than reference the actual control. Of course, if you don't need to set values in the control but rather use values from a control, you should simply create a variable to contain the value rather than the reference to the control.

Tip

If you need to set the value of a property of a control but the property may already contain the value, check the value first and only write to the property if its current value is not correct.

Using field variables

The preceding technique also applies to manipulating field data when working with a Recordset in VBA code. For example, you may ordinarily have a loop that does something like this:

```
...
Do Until tbl.EOF
MyTotal = MyTotal + tbl![OrderTotal]
Loop
```

If this routine loops through many records, you should use the following code snippet instead:

```
Dim MyField as Field
...
Set MyField = tbl![OrderTotal]
Do Until tbl.EOF
MyTotal = MyTotal +MyField
Loop
```

The preceding code executes much faster than code that explicitly references the field in every iteration of the loop.

Increasing the speed of finding data in code

Use the `FindRecord` and `FindNext` methods on indexed fields. These methods are much more efficient when used on a field that is indexed. Also, take advantage of bookmarks when you can. Returning to a bookmark is much faster than performing a `Find` method to locate the data.

The procedure shown in Listing 3-1 is an example of using a bookmark. Bookmark variables must always be Dimmed as variants, and you can create multiple bookmarks by Dimming multiple variant variables. The following code opens the tblCustomers table, moves to the first record in the database, sets the bookmark for the current (first) record, moves to the last record, and finally repositions back to the bookmarked record. For each step, the `debug.print` command is used to show the relative position in the database as evidence that the current record changes from record to record.

Listing 3-1 Using a Bookmark to Mark a Record

```
Public Sub BookmarkExample()
Dim rs As Recordset, bk As Variant
Set rs = Workspaces(0).Databases(0).OpenRecordset("tblCustomers", _
dbOpenTable)

' Move to the first record in the database
    rs.MoveFirst
    ' Print the position in the database
    Debug.Print rs.PercentPosition

' Set the bookmark to the current record
    bk = rs.Bookmark

' Move to the last record in the database
    rs.MoveLast
    ' Print the position in the database
    Debug.Print rs.PercentPosition

' Move to the bookmarked record
    rs.Bookmark = bk
    ' Print the position in the database
    Debug.Print rs.PercentPosition

rs.Close
Set rs = Nothing

End Sub
```

Using transactions

Transaction processing is the act of queuing multiple database transactions such as record updates and then committing them as a whole. If any one of the queued transactions fails, all successful transactions are undone and any remaining transactions are canceled.

Transactions are typically used in applications dealing with financial data to maintain data integrity. For example, if you transfer money from one account to another, you would subtract an amount from one table and add the amount to another table. If either update fails, the accounts no longer balance. By wrapping these record updates in a transaction, you assure that the data remains intact because if either update fails, neither update is performed. In Access 2.0, you could greatly increase the speed of your application by wrapping Recordset operations in transactions. In Access 97, Access uses transactions internally, and wrapping your code in transactions tends to decrease the transaction's performance.

Eliminating dead code and unused variables

Before distributing your application, remove any *dead code* — code that is not used at all — from your application. Oftentimes you will find entire procedures, or even modules, that once served a purpose but are no longer called. In addition, it is not uncommon to leave variable declarations in code after all code that actually uses the variables has been removed. By eliminating dead code and unused variables, you reduce the amount of memory your application uses and the amount of time it takes to compile code at run time.

Tip

Although not easy and often impractical, removing large numbers of comments from your code can decrease the amount of memory used by your application.

Other things you can do to increase the speed of your modules include opening any add-ins your application uses for read-only access and replacing procedure calls within loops with in-line code. Also, don't forget one of the most important items: Deliver your applications with the modules compiled.

Increasing network performance

Cross-Reference

The single most important action you can take to make sure your networkable applications run at their peak performance is to run Access and the application database on the workstation and link to the shared network database. Running Access over the network is much slower than running it locally. For more information on sharing data, see Chapter 14, "Creating Multiuser Systems."

Using the Performance Analyzer

Access includes a wonderful tool to help you better optimize your applications: the Performance Analyzer Wizard. The Performance Analyzer looks at the objects in your application and makes suggestions to you about things you can do to optimize your objects. Often, the Performance Analyzer alerts you to a potential problem discussed in this chapter. For example, the Performance Analyzer tells you which modules in your database don't have `Option Explicit` set. It then recommends that you set `Option Explicit` and tells you why.

To run the Performance Analyzer Wizard, select Analyze➪Performance from the Tools menu, as shown in Figure 3-28.

When you first run the Performance Analyzer, you need to select the type of objects to analyze by using the tabs at the top of the dialog box. To view all of the objects in the database, click the All tab. After selecting the type of object (such as Form, Report, Table, or All), you must select the specific objects to analyze. You can use the Select All and Deselect All buttons to save time. Figure 3-29 shows a large Access database with all its forms selected for analysis.

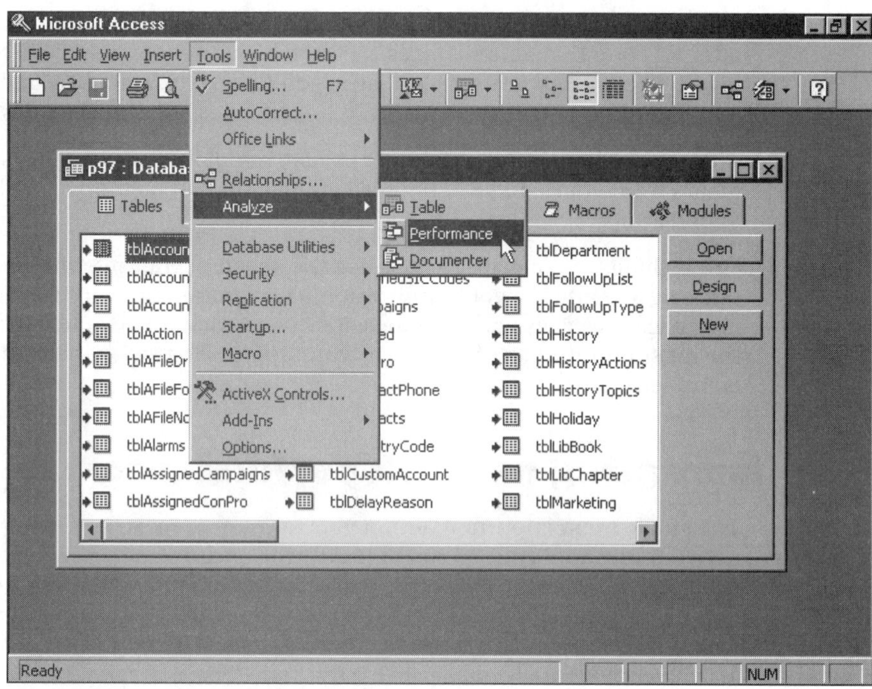

Figure 3-28: Select the Performance Analyzer Wizard using the Tools menu.

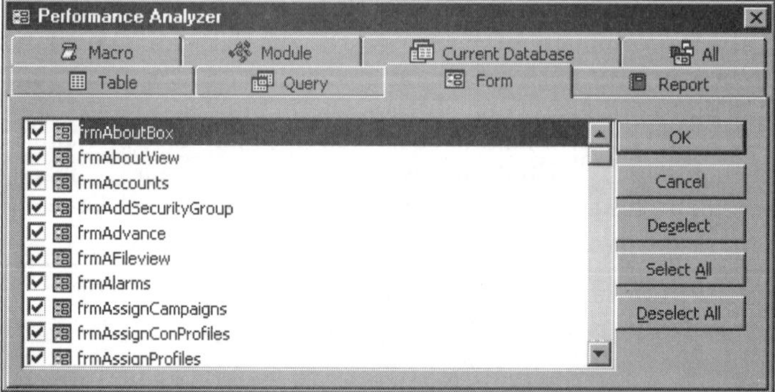

Figure 3-29: You can analyze all objects in a database or just few specific objects.

Figure 3-30 shows the results of analyzing all the forms in the database. Notice that the suggestions in the figure are all covered in depth in this chapter. The Performance Analyzer can make suggestions and recommendations, offer hints, and fix things automatically. If you have a question about its recommendation for a certain item, click on that item. The Performance Analyzer gives you more information about what it thinks needs to be done with the object.

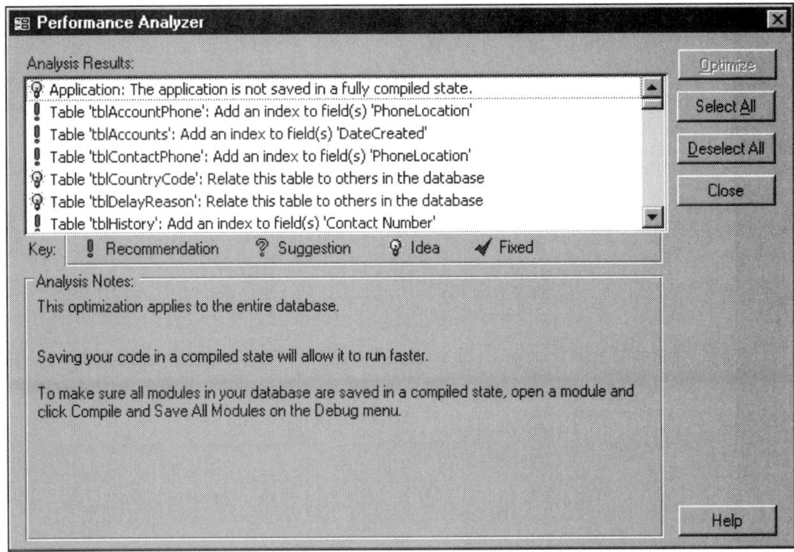

Figure 3-30: You should periodically analyze your objects to make sure you take advantage of all possible optimization strategies.

The more you are exposed to the issues expressed by the Performance Analyzer Wizard, the more it becomes second nature to use the optimization strategies as you work.

Improving Perceived Speed

Perceived speed is how fast your application appears to run to the end user. Many techniques can increase the perceived speed of your applications. Perceived speed usually involves supplying visual feedback to the user while the computer is busy performing some operation, such as constantly updating a percent meter when Access is busy processing data.

Using a splash screen

Most professional Windows programs employ a splash screen. Most people think the splash screen is simply to show the product's name and copyright information as well as the registered user's information; this is not entirely correct. The splash screen greatly contributes to the perceived speed of an application. It shows the user that something is *happening*, and it gives users something to look at (and hence occupy their time) for a few seconds while the rest of the application loads.

To create a splash screen, create a basic form with appropriate information such as your application information, logo, and registration information. Then set this form as the Display Form in the Start Up dialog box. Setting the form as the Display Form ensures that the splash screen is the first form that is loaded. You then want to call any initialization procedures from the `On Open` event of the splash form. You may find that a light form that calls code or a macro displays faster than putting the startup code in the form's module. After all the initialization code has been run, close down the splash form. There are a few issues to remember when using splash forms:

- Never use custom controls in a startup form. Custom controls take time to load and consume resources.
- Minimize code in startup forms. Use only code that is absolutely necessary to display your startup form and use a light form if possible.
- The startup form should call only initialization procedures. Be careful about call trees; you don't want your startup form triggering the loading of many modules in your application.

Loading and keeping forms hidden

If there are forms that are displayed often, consider hiding them rather than closing them. To hide a form, set its `Visible` property to `False`. When you need to display the form again, set its `Visible` property back to `True`. Forms that remain loaded consume memory, but they display more quickly than forms that must be loaded each time they are viewed. In addition, if you are morphing a form or report (changing the way the form or report looks by changing form and control properties), keep the form hidden until all changes are made so that the user doesn't have to watch the changes take place.

Using the hourglass

When your application needs to perform a task that may take a while, use the hourglass. The hourglass cursor shows the user that the computer is not locked up but is merely busy. To turn on the hourglass cursor, use the `Hourglass` method like this:

```
DoCmd.Hourglass True
```

To turn the hourglass back to the default cursor, use the method like this:

```
DoCmd.Hourglass False
```

Using the percent meter

In addition to using the hourglass, you should consider using the percent meter when performing looping routines in a procedure. The percent meter gives constant visual feedback that your application is busy, and it shows the user in no uncertain terms where it is in the current process. The following code demonstrates using the percent meter in a loop to show the meter starting at 0 percent and expanding to 100 percent, 1 percent at a time:

```
Dim iCount As Integer, iCount2 As Long
Dim Result As Integer

Result = SysCmd(acSysCmdInitMeter, "Running through loop", 100)
For iCount = 1 To 100
    Result = SysCmd(acSysCmdUpdateMeter, iCount)
    For iCount2 = 1 To 50000: Next iCount2      ' This creates a _
pause so the meter is readable
Next iCount

Result = SysCmd(acSysCmdRemoveMeter)
```

The first step for using the percent meter is initializing the meter. You initialize the meter by calling the `SysCmd` function like this:

```
Result = SysCmd(acSysCmdInitMeter, "Running through loop", 100)
```

The `acSysCmdInitMeter` in this line is an Access constant that tells the function that you are initializing the meter. The second parameter is the text you want to appear to the left of the meter. Finally, the last value is the maximum value of the meter (in this case, 100 percent). You can set this value to anything you want. For example, if you were iterating through a loop of 504 records, you could set this value to 504. Then you could pass the record count at any given time to the `SysCmd` function; Access decides what percentage the meter should show filled.

After the meter has been initialized, you can pass a value to it to update the meter. To update the meter, you call the `SysCmd` function again and pass it the `acSysCmdUpdateMeter` constant and the new update meter value. Remember, the value that you pass the function is not necessarily the percent displayed by the meter.

Through judicious use of the techniques discussed in this chapter, you will be able to increase the performance of your Access application to the highest level possible.

Part II

The Access 97 Language

Chapter 4

Understanding Visual Basic for Applications

In This Chapter

- Editing code with the VBA editor
- Compiling and debugging your code
- Viewing objects available to the VBA environment
- Exploring SysCmd and other useful functions
- Discovering new keywords, functions, and language constructs

Visual Basic for Applications (VBA) is a full-featured development language nested within an application host, such as Access 97. OLE automation, which you'll explore in Chapter 6, makes VBA available to its host as an embedded application.

Setting Options for the VBA Editor

To enter your code into modules, whether they are standard or class modules, you use the VBA editor window.

This editor is more user-friendly than the editor found in previous versions of Access. One of the most helpful features is color-coded text to indicate keywords, comments, non-keyword text, and breakpoints.

You can customize the editor window by selecting Options from the Tools menu and then selecting the Module tab (see Figure 4-1).

You use the Code Colors section in the Module tab to set the colors of various parts of the editor window. You can set the color of the text to show when a syntax error has been detected, the text of keywords, the comment text, and identifiers such as your variable and procedure names. You use the Indicator color to set the color of indicators such as the Breakpoint indicator and the Execution Point indicator. If you have the Margin Indicator Bar checked in the Window Settings frame, these indicators appear in the left margin of the module window. The Breakpoint indicator appears as a small circle when you set a breakpoint. The Execution Point indicator appears as a small arrow when execution is paused at a statement. You also can set fonts and sizes of the module window text on the Module tab.

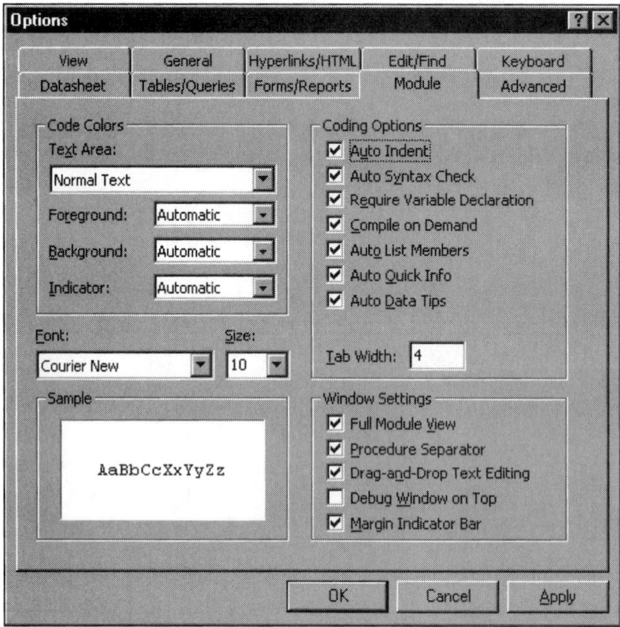

Figure 4-1: The Module tab in the Options dialog box enables you to customize the editor window.

Checking the Auto Indent checkbox in the Coding Options section causes the insertion point to be placed directly below the first character of the current typing line when you press the Enter key.

Placing a check mark in the Auto Syntax Check checkbox causes a check of your statements for proper syntax upon entering them and the display of a Syntax Error message box if the statement is not coded correctly. Clearing this checkbox color marks the statement with the Syntax Error color if the statement is in error, but the VBA editor does not issue an error message.

When you check the Require Variable Declaration checkbox, the VBA editor automatically inserts an Option Explicit statement into the General declarations section of new modules. Clearing this checkbox does not remove the Option Explicit statement if one is present. With Option Explicit, VBA requires that all variables used in the code be declared prior to use.

The next section, "Compiling and Debugging Your Code," covers the Compile On Demand checkbox and the Conditional Compilation Arguments text box located on the Advanced tab.

The next two checkboxes in the Coding Options section are concerned with features that aid in coding statements in the module window. Checking Auto List Members causes a list of relevant methods or properties to appear after you type an object name and period. You can choose from the list or continue to type the rest of the statement yourself. Auto Quick Info provides a tip box that shows the syntax of the method you are entering. The tip box appears whenever you enter a space or an open parenthesis after the name of a procedure or method. Auto Data Tips provides the value of a variable in a tip box whenever the program execution is paused and you place the mouse pointer over a variable in the scope of execution. This is a quick method of inspecting variables during your debugging sessions.

Check the Full Module View checkbox in the Window Settings section to display the procedures of a module sequentially within the editor window. With this view, choosing a procedure name from the Proc drop-down list in the module editor scrolls the edit window to bring the procedure into view and places the insertion point below the procedure definition statement. Using the toggle buttons in the lower-left corner of the module window, you can switch between Procedure View and Full Module View. Procedure View shows only the procedure selected in the Procedure list at the top of the window. Selecting these toggle buttons does not affect the setting of the Full Module View checkbox. Leaving the Full Module View checkbox unchecked yields the Procedure view.

Checking the Procedure Separator places a line between procedures that is visible in Full Module View to delineate the boundaries of the procedures in the module.

Drag-and-Drop Text Editing enables you to move selected text from one point in your module to another. Select one or more lines of code, or even text within a line, and then click and hold the left mouse button while dragging the text to another point in the module. When the caret appears at the point you want to insert the text, release the mouse button; the text is dropped at the caret location.

In versions prior to Access 97, the Debug window behaved as a pop-up form, always on top of other windows. Using the Debug Window on Top checkbox, you now have the option of having the Debug window always on top or behind the window with focus.

Command line arguments can be entered at run time with the `/Cmd` command line switch when starting Access. Using the Command function returns values entered as command line arguments. When debugging your application, you may want to enter a command line argument from inside the Access environment to emulate the entry of the arguments from the command line. You do this by entering a value in the Command Line Arguments text box on the Advanced tab of the Options dialog box (see Figure 4-2). Enter the value you expect to be returned from the Command function.

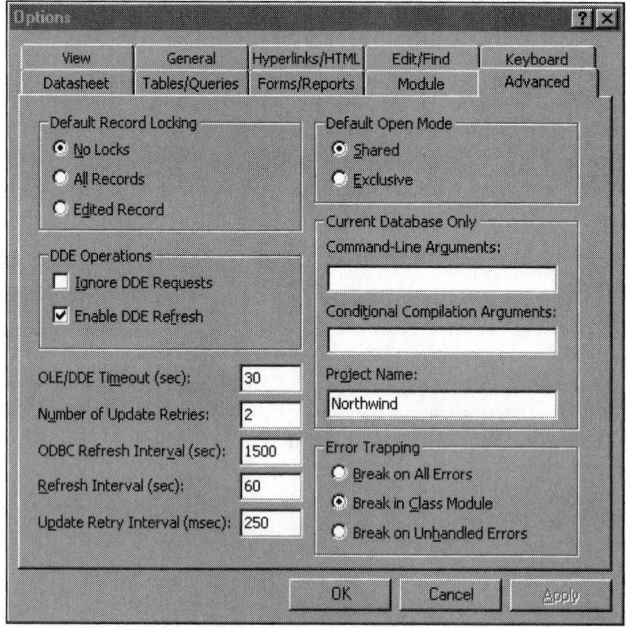

Figure 4-2: The Advanced tab in the Options dialog box enables you to customize the error trapping options, set conditional compilation arguments, specify command line arguments, and set a number of other environment options.

The Error Trapping section gives you three options for handling errors. Checking Break on All Errors causes Visual Basic to ignore any error-handling routine you have established for a module and displays the error as if you hadn't provided an error routine. Clearing this checkbox enables your own error routines.

Break in Class Module causes execution to break when an error occurs in a class or standard module and no On Error statement has been specified. Break on Unhandled Errors breaks execution when an error occurs in a procedure that is not in a class module and no error handling is specified by an On Error statement.

Compiling and Debugging Your Code

Visual Basic must compile your code before executing it. By default, Visual Basic compiles a module when a procedure in it is called, providing the called module is not already compiled; this is known as *on-demand compilation.*

On-demand compilation

With on-demand compilation, only called modules are compiled. On-demand compilation improves performance by compiling only *what* is needed *when* it is needed.

You can change this compilation behavior in a number of ways. You can clear the Compile On Demand checkbox in the Module tab of the Options dialog box, for example, which forces VBA to compile all modules that may be called by a procedure in the running module. With on-demand compilation turned off, VBA compiles the loaded module containing the called procedure and all modules that the loaded module references, whether or not those modules will be called.

Tip

Compiling your modules before run time achieves the best performance. Choose Compile and Save All Modules from the Debug menu. This forces VBA to compile every module in the database and save them. Doing this compile before releasing your application to end users eliminates the need for VBA to compile the code at run time.

The Debug menu also contains Compile Loaded Modules and Compile All Modules selections. You can choose these options to force VBA to compile the modules currently loaded in memory or all modules in the project whether they are loaded or not.

Debugging your code

If the compilation of your code doesn't produce any error messages, your next step is to debug it. This step is where the VBA debugger comes into action. By setting breakpoints — points where you want the execution to pause or break — in your code and stepping through a routine statement by statement, you can do the following:

- Follow the execution path to determine whether the code is taking the expected branches
- Stop where you want to inspect variables for proper values

Your application usually will contain several forms, modules, and reports. You can embed Visual Basic code in all these components, and you will want to test all of it for proper operation before releasing your application to end users.

Three popular methods for monitoring the behavior of your application exist:

- Stepping through your code with the debugger Step methods
- Embedding `Debug.Print` statements at various points in your code
- Embedding `MsgBox` statements at various points in your code

Embedding Debug.Print and MsgBox statements

The last two techniques are handy for a quick view of a particular execution path in your application without stepping through the code with the debugger. For example, you may want to evaluate the code that adds a new customer to the database or the code that makes adjustments to an inventory-tracking database and then view variables at certain key points in the execution path.

With these techniques, you insert the Print or MsgBox statements at points in the execution path of the routines you are interested in and then review the results. The Print or MsgBox statements should contain the variables that you want to monitor, such as the result of a calculation, the return value of a function, or a variable that controls an If statement or a Select Case statement.

Tip

Using the MsgBox approach, you see the results as they occur. Be sure to include a label indicating where the MsgBox is in the execution path. With the Debug.Print statements, you review the results in the Debug Window after the execution path completes. This technique also requires good labels for the printed results so that you know where the variable is being evaluated in the execution path.

You may want to use something like the following two options:

```
MsgBox "In Calculate_Balance Proc: variable_name is: _
" & variable_name
```

or

```
Debug.Print "In Calculate_Balance Proc: variable_name is: _
" & CStr(variable_name)
```

The variable name being displayed may be a non-string data type and require conversion to a string to be concatenated to the label. In the preceding Debug.Print statement, the CStr function converts the variable to a string data type. There are many other data conversion functions available. Search the Access Help file for *Conversion Functions* for a list of available functions.

The MsgBox and Debug.Print techniques are also useful for evaluating KeyDown, KeyUp, and KeyPress event procedures, where use of the debug Step technique may interfere with the Key events.

Tip

If you insert debugging statements into your code, label them with a standard comment that can be found with the Find command. Use a label that stands out when scrolling through the code, such as *** DEBUG *** or *** TEST ***. This labeling is helpful in finding your inserted debugging code when you want to pull those statements out. Another method is to insert debug statements within conditional compile statements and use a constant to activate this code (see "Conditional compilation," later in this chapter). With this technique, you remove or change the constant to deactivate the debug statements when you have finished debugging. This technique is elegant but can be problematic if the constants are missed or forgotten and your application is released into production with your debugging statements active.

Stepping through code with breakpoints

The technique of stepping through your code is usually used to evaluate a small set of one or more procedures. This technique is slower than using `MsgBox` or `Print` statements, but you have more control over the code and can even change the execution path at will.

At the point you want to begin monitoring in the execution path, set a breakpoint to pause execution. You set this breakpoint by placing the insertion point on the line of code you want to break on and then pressing F9. You also can choose Toggle Breakpoint from the Debug menu or from the pop-up menu activated by clicking the right mouse button, or click on the breakpoint button (the button with the hand icon) on the toolbar. Setting a breakpoint color codes the statement in the breakpoint color set on the Module tab of the Options dialog box. If you have the Margin Indicator Bar turned on in the Module Options tab, setting a breakpoint also places a breakpoint indicator in the margin next to the statement on which the breakpoint is placed.

Using the Add Watch dialog box is another method of setting a breakpoint. Place the insertion point on an expression and choose Add Watch from the Debug menu. Select Break When Value Is True or Break When Value Changes in the Watch Type frame. This choice pauses execution at the statement, causing the selected condition, and brings up the Debug window displaying the expression.

When you run your application and the execution gets to your breakpoint, execution stops before executing the breakpoint statement. At this time, you may examine variables that are *in scope,* which means variables that are currently allocated either locally within the current procedure or globally within the current module or project.

Using the Debug window

You can display a variable's current value on demand by using the Quick Watch feature. Place the caret at the beginning, end, or on a variable name — it doesn't have to be the breakpoint statement — and then choose Quick Watch (Shift+F9) from the Debug menu or toolbar. This action displays a dialog box containing the variable's current value. With Auto Data Tips checked in the Module Options tab, you can see the variable's value by placing the mouse cursor over the variable name to display a tips window. You can use this method to inspect a variable of a basic data type or a user-defined structure member but not entire structures.

From the Quick Watch dialog box, you can click on the Add button to add the variable to the Debug Window watch expressions, which provides you with a continuous display of the variable's current value. If the Debug Window is not displayed, adding the watch expression displays it. A Debug

Window containing a watch variable is shown in Figure 4-3. You can watch the variable value as you step through your code. This feature saves you from bringing up the Quick Watch window every time you want to see the value of a variable.

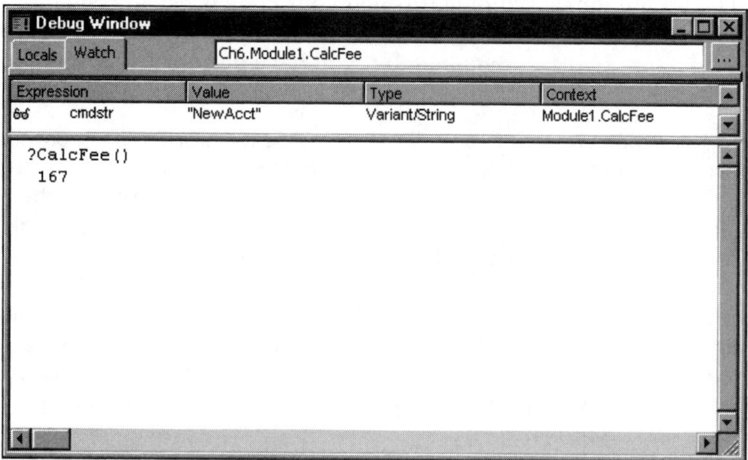

Figure 4-3: You can use the Debug Window to execute code as well as display watch expressions and any variable within scope.

The Debug Window does much more than display watch expressions. You can display any variable in this window by preceding the variable name with a question mark, and you can execute any Visual Basic statement, including calls to sub or function procedures. These statements are executed in the Immediate pane of the window. Figure 4-3 shows a statement that displays the return value of a call to a function named `CalcFee()` in CH6.MDB (on the CD-ROM that accompanies this book). Type your expression in the Immediate pane (the lower pane) and then press the Enter key. The value of the expression appears on the next line. To execute Sub procedures, do not precede the statement with a question mark.

You can set a variable's value in the Immediate pane by typing an assignment statement, such as `variable = value`. In this case, you do not precede the expression with a question mark. Press Enter to execute the expression. This technique is very useful if your code has produced the wrong value for a variable and you want to set the variable to the proper value or you want to test a routine with a value that causes a particular execution path to be taken. This feature saves you from restarting the code for every value you want to test or every time you find a problem. Temporarily fix the problem in the Immediate pane and continue testing.

After you have inspected the variables you want to see, you can continue the execution of your code. You have several options available for doing so.

Press F8 or choose Step Into from the Debug menu to execute the current statement. If this statement is a call to a sub or function procedure, Step Into displays the procedure and halts execution at the first executable statement in the called procedure. F8 executes your code line by line. If you accidentally step into a procedure you don't want to step through line by line, you can choose Step Out (Ctrl+Shift+F8) from the Debug menu to continue executing the procedure and return to the calling procedure line immediately following the call. This is the same behavior you would have achieved had you chosen Step Over at the call to the procedure.

Shift+F8 invokes Step Over sub and function calls. You can use this approach when you aren't interested in following the execution path into a procedure. Unlike Step Into, Step Over does not stop execution in the called procedure but stops on the next executable statement after the call returns.

Run To Cursor on the Debug menu (Ctrl+F8) executes code from the current statement up to but not including the statement where the caret is positioned. If you use this option, be sure that you position the caret on a statement that will definitely be in the execution path. Don't position it on a branch of an `If` statement unless you are sure that branch will be taken.

You can control the next statement to be executed by choosing Set Next Statement from the Debug menu. When execution of your code has paused, position the insertion point on the statement you want to execute next and choose Set Next Statement. This statement can be one that has already been executed or one that will be executed later in the execution path. When you continue execution, the statement marked with Set Next Statement is executed instead of the statement following the point where execution paused. You can also set the next statement by dragging the execution point indicator in the margin to the statement you want to execute next.

To resume normal execution to the end of the current execution path or to the next breakpoint in the execution path, choose Continue (F5) from the Run menu or click on the Continue button on the toolbar.

Choose the Reset (Alt+F5) option from the Run menu or from the toolbar to reset the program. After resetting, you may restart the same execution path or choose another action to test.

To toggle off a breakpoint, position the insertion point on the statement containing the breakpoint and use any of the toggle breakpoint options. To clear all breakpoints, choose Clear All Breakpoints (Ctrl+Shift+F9) from the Debug menu. This action toggles off all breakpoints set in all modules. Toggling off breakpoints removes them from the module, forcing you to reset them when needed.

Conditional compilation

Visual Basic normally compiles all code presented to it line by line. You can alter this behavior with compiler directives, which are statements intended as instructions for the compiler at compile time but that are not part of your application code.

You use the #If compiler directive to provide conditional compilation, as shown in the following example:

```
#If expression Then
   statements
[#ElseIf expression-n Then
   [statements]]
[#Else
   [statements]]
#End If
```

The expression is a compiler constant set with #Const or a constant set in the Conditional Compilation Arguments text box in the Advanced tab of the Options dialog box.

When using a #Const, set it in the module that contains the #If statement (preferably in the General declarations section) so that you can find and change it quickly. The form of the #Const statement is as follows:

```
#Const constant_name = value
```

Use the constant_name in the #If expression, as in the following example:

```
#Const DEBUGGING = -1
#If DEBUGGING Then
   nLoop = 10
#Else
   nLoop = rsAcctRecords.RecordCount
#End If
For k = 0 To nLoop - 1
    ...
Next k
```

If you use the Conditional Compilation Arguments text box to set the Const, do not include the #Const directive; just set the constant name, an equal sign, and a value. You can specify multiple values by separating them with a colon.

In the preceding example, the compiler compiles the code in the Then branch or the Else branch, depending on the value of DEBUGGING. Keep in mind that this statement is evaluated at compile time, not run time. In other words, the compiled code ends up containing either nLoop = 10 or nLoop = rsAcctRecords.RecordCount, but not both.

This technique is the one mentioned earlier in this chapter for inserting debug statements into your code. Turn on debugging code by setting the DEBUGGING constant to True and turn it off by setting it to False.

Your application may have a target group of users that will never execute a particular portion of code. Using conditional compilation directives, you can trim this code out of the application to reduce the size of the distributed code.

Using the New Keyword

The New keyword allocates an instance of an object defined by Visual Basic or an object defined by some other OLE Automation server. The object being allocated must be externally creatable; that is, outside the object's server application. The object cannot be a dependent object type, which can be referenced only with the aid of another related object.

To determine whether an object can be created externally, consult the OLE server application's documentation. Dependent objects depend on the existence of another object and need to be created through the use of a method of the preexisting object; you cannot use New to create these types of objects.

The syntax for using New in a Dim statement to instantiate a new object variable is

```
Dim variable_name[([subscripts])] As New object_type
```

As indicated in the syntax, you may create an array of New object__type. If, for example, you want to create two new tables in your application, you can use code such as the following example:

```
Dim dbDatabase As Database
Dim tdArray(1) As New TableDef
Dim fField As Field, ndxIndex As Index
Set dbDatabase = CurrentDb()
tdArray(0).Name = "Item"
Set fField = tdArray(0).CreateField("ItemID", DB_TEXT, 50)
tdArray(0).Fields.Append fField
Set ndxIndex = tdArray(0).CreateIndex("PrimaryKey")
With ndxIndex
   .Primary = True
   .Unique = True
   .Fields = "ItemID"
End With
tdArray(0).Indexes.Append ndxIndex
dbDatabase.TableDefs.Append tdArray(0)
```

Cross-Reference

The second Dim statement declares an array of two elements of type TableDef object (see Chapter 5, "Working with Data Access Objects," for details on creating and using TableDefs).

After declaring the array, any array element can be used as a TableDef object to define a new table in the current database. The With statement sets several properties of the index object. With statements are covered later in this chapter.

You also can use the New keyword with the Set statement. This syntax creates the object and sets a reference to it in variable_name. The following is an example:

```
Dim variable_name As object_type
Set variable_name = New object_type
```

Use the `Private` and `Public` keywords with `New`, as in the following example, to create object variables that are either hidden or accessible from certain parts of the application. See the next section, "Understanding the Public and Private Keywords," for details.

```
Private variable_name [([subscripts])] As New object_type
Public variable_name [([subscripts])] As New object_type
```

Object variables created with `Private` are accessible only within the module or procedure in which they are defined. Using `Public` extends the accessibility to all modules.

Understanding the Public and Private Keywords

The `Public` and `Private` keywords define the accessibility of the variables and procedures they declare.

Using `Dim` to declare a variable at the module level (in the General Declarations of a module) implies that the variable is accessible to all procedures within that module, but not accessible to procedures outside the module.

Replacing `Dim` with the `Private` keyword makes no change in the accessibility of the variable; the variable remains known only within the module. Replacing `Dim` with the `Public` keyword, however, extends the accessibility of the variable to all modules within the project.

Sub and Function procedures that you add to a module are `Public` by default; they are known to all modules in the project. Event procedures within a Form or Report module are `Private` by default, so they are known only within the containing module.

You can change the accessibility of your procedures by adding the `Private` keyword to the procedure definition. This addition makes the procedure available to the other procedures in the same module but not to procedures in other modules.

Cross-Reference

Procedures in other databases can also use the Public procedures in your database through referencing, which is explained in Chapter 6, "Working with OLE and ActiveX Controls." You can hide your Public procedures from referencing databases by including an `Option` statement in the module, as follows:

```
Option Private Module
```

This statement in the General Declarations enables procedures in your project (the containing database) to use the public procedures in the module but prevents a referencing database from seeing those procedures.

Using the Collection Object

Visual Basic for Applications supports a `Collection` object that you can use to hold items of any data type.

You can use a collection in the same way you use an array to store integers, strings, or items of other data types. The `Collection` object provides methods for adding items to the collection, removing items from the collection, and inspecting items in the collection.

Cross-Reference

In Chapter 6, "Working with OLE and ActiveX Controls," you learn about creating your own application objects. Some of these objects use a collection to provide a collection property.

You can dimension a collection to hold your application objects — objects you define — by using the `New` keyword, as shown here:

```
Dim AppObjects As New Collection
```

Tip

The name `AppObjects` denotes that this object is a collection of objects of type `AppObject`, an object type you are defining for your application. You should always use a plural name for collection-type objects and indicate the type of object in the collection as shown in the preceding code sample.

To add an `AppObject` to the collection, use the `Add` method of the `Collection` object, as follows:

```
AppObjects.Add AppObject, AppObjectKey
```

The `AppObjectKey` specifies a key by which you can retrieve the `AppObject` from the collection by using the `Item` method.

If you need to insert the new object at a specific position in the collection, you can specify an index as in the following example:

```
AppObject.Add AppObject,AppObjectKey,2
```

The preceding statement adds the new `AppObject` to the collection before the second object already in the collection.

You can achieve the same results by using the after argument instead of the before argument as shown here:

```
AppObject.Add AppObject,AppObjectKey, , 1
```

This statement doesn't specify the before argument, and the after argument instructs the `Add` method to insert the new `AppObject` into the collection after the first object already in the collection.

In place of the numerical designations for position, you can use the keynames of the objects in the collection. If object one has a keyname of `AppObjectOne` in a collection, for example, you can insert a new object after object one with the following method:

```
AppObject.Add AppObject,AppObjectKey, , "AppObjectOne"
```

Both the numerical and keyname specifications of position must refer to an existing object. If the position specifies an object not in the collection, you get a `subscript out of range` error.

Attempting to add an object with a key that is already present in the collection yields a 457 error, `This key is already associated with an element of this collection.`

After adding objects to the collection, you may refer to the individual object properties by specifying the collection name, as in this example:

```
Dim niObjNdx As Integer
For niObjNdx = 1 To AppObjects.Count
   MsgBox "Object " & Str$(niObjNdx) & " name is _
" & AppObjects(niObjNdx).Name
Next niObjNdx
```

The preceding example loops through each item in the `AppObjects` collection and displays the object's `Name` property. Note that the items of `AppObjects` are indexed from 1, not 0, and the loop stops after visiting the number of items indicated by the collection's `Count` property.

The `MsgBox` statement refers to the collection by item index, using the loop control variable, `niObjNdx`. For each item indexed, the item's `Name` property is accessed for display in the message box.

Remember that this syntax refers to object properties in the collection just as you would refer to those properties as a single object variable, as shown here:

```
Dim AppObject As Object
...
Set AppObject = AppObjects(niObjNdx)
MsgBox "Object " & Str$(niObjNdx) & " name is " & AppObject.Name
```

`Name`, as used here, is a property of the object type stored in the collection. You can refer to `Name` by using the collection, as in `AppObjects(index).Name`, or by setting a variable of the `AppObject` type or a generic `Object` type equal to an item in the collection and then referring to `Name` by using the object variable as shown in the preceding code.

The collection object provides an `Item` method that you can use to address an item in the collection, much like the indexing syntax just discussed. The following is an example:

```
Set AppObject = AppObjects.Item(niObjNdx)
```

The `Item` method takes one argument to indicate the position of the item in the collection. As with the `Add` method position arguments, you can specify the `Item` method position as a numerical position or as a keyname.

To remove an item from the collection, use the collection's `Remove` method. This method also takes one argument, and that argument can be numerical or string to specify the item in the collection to remove, as in the following statement:

```
AppObjects.Remove(1)
```

If other objects are in the collection, their positions are adjusted upward. In other words, if you remove item one, the item that was item two becomes item one, and the item that was item three becomes item two, and so on. Using this method, you can develop a loop to remove all objects in a collection, as in this example:

```
Dim niObjCount As Integer
niObjCount = AppObjects.Count
While AppObjects.Count > 0
     AppObjects.Remove(1)
Wend
```

When you start working with objects in Chapter 6, you'll find that the Visual Basic `Collection` object is a very useful object to have around.

Using the For Each ... Next Looping Construct

You use the `For Each` statement to loop through the elements of a collection or array. The statement has the following syntax:

```
For Each element In collection
   [statements]
   [Exit For]
   [statements]
Next [element]
```

The collection component of the statement can refer to an array or a collection of objects. An *element* is a Variant data type if the collection refers to an array, or it can be an object within the collection to which you are referring.

You can include any other Visual Basic statements within the loop delimited by the `Next` keyword. You can exit the loop either by exhausting the elements in the collection or by executing the `Exit For` statement.

An example of the `For Each` statement to loop through the elements of an array follows:

```
Dim sArray(5) As String
Dim vElement
. . .
For Each vElement In sArray
   If sArray(vElement) = "Delinquent Account" Then
      Exit For
```

```
   Else

   ...

   End If
Next vElement
```

In this example, sArray is a string array that is being examined for a delinquent account. If the array contains an occurrence of this string, the code exits the loop; otherwise, the loop continues until all elements of the array have been inspected.

To iterate through a collection of objects — the Forms collection, for example, which is a collection of open forms — you can use the following method:

```
Dim oGeneric As Object
For Each oGeneric In Forms
   If oGeneric.Name = "Account Form" Then
   ...

      Exit For
   End If
Next oGeneric
```

oGeneric refers to an element of the collection of open Forms. The loop continues until all open forms have been inspected or until the process finds a form with the name Account Form.

Using the With ... End With Construct

Often, while working with objects in a Visual Basic program, you set properties and invoke methods of a given object.

In referring to object properties and methods, you must qualify the object you are addressing. In other words, each reference to a property or method must have the object variable as a prefix in a statement, such as the following:

```
ObjectVariable.ObjectProperty = some value
```

or

```
ObjectVariable.ObjectMethod()
```

If you are referring to only a few properties, the full syntax isn't so bad; if you must set several properties of an object and invoke several methods, using a shorthand notation may be helpful.

Using the With . . . End With statement helps reduce the typing you have to do and also helps to group object operations together.

The syntax of the `With` statement is the following:

```
With object
   [statements]
End With
```

An object variable is named in the `With` statement and implies that all statements within the construct containing a dot notation refer to the named object.

The following example sets properties and invokes methods of an open form:

```
Dim oGeneric As Object
DoCmd.OpenForm "Account Form"
Set oGeneric = Forms("Account Form")
With oGeneric
   .Caption = "Accounts"
   .Detail.BackColor = 16711680
   .SetFocus
   DoCmd.MoveSize 0, 0
End With
```

The `OpenForm` method of the `DoCmd` object opens the `Account Form`. The subsequent `Set` statement sets the generic object variable `oGeneric` to point to the open form.

With this form object, the code sets the form's `Caption` and the `BackColor` properties of the form's detail section. Notice that each statement within the `With` construct starts with a dot, implying that the object pointed to by `oGeneric` is the target of the statement.

The `MoveSize` method of the `DoCmd` object acts on the currently active form to move or size the form, or both. The code invokes the form's `SetFocus` method to set the focus on the form before using the `MoveSize` method to move it.

As you can see from the use of the `DoCmd.MoveSize` statement in the example, all statements inside the construct need not be a direct reference to the object specified in the `With` statement.

Wrapping with the Line-Continuation Character

In Access 2.0 Basic, the user was required to put a statement on one line. You could not break a line and wrap it around to the next line. Access Basic either complained or gave you unexpected results when you ran the code.

With Visual Basic for Applications, you now have a line-continuation character you can use to inform the compiler that you are continuing your statement on the following line.

This capability is especially helpful when you put together a long SQL string. It's nice to be able to see the entire statement within the visible page without scrolling. The compiler, of course, doesn't care whether your string is on one line or on many lines, but it's much easier for humans not to scroll around the screen while deciphering an SQL string.

You specify the line-continuation character with a space followed by an underscore, as shown in the following example. You cannot continue a string with the line-continuation character, and you cannot have a comment on the same line.

```
Dim sSomeString As String
sSomeString = "Select [Account Number], [Account Name] From " _
& "[Accounts] Where [State] = 'CT'"
```

To continue the string, you must end the string prior to using the line-continuation character and then concatenate the continuation of the string on the next line, as shown in the preceding statement.

Using Named Arguments

With Visual Basic for Applications, you can call a sub or function procedure with named arguments or positional arguments.

Using *positional arguments* means passing them in order, as defined in the sub or function definition. Here's an example:

```
Sub CalcFee(AcctTotal As Currency, ContractMonths As Integer)
```

Calling this subroutine with positional arguments looks like this:

```
CalcFee ncTot_Acct, 24
```

The order of the arguments in the call to `CalcFee` must follow the order defined by the `CalcFee Sub` definition statement.

You can also call `CalcFee` by using the names of the arguments, `AcctTotal` and `ContractMonths`. With this approach, the positions of the arguments in the call are not important, as follows:

```
CalcFee ContractMonths:= 24, AcctTotal:= ncTot_Acct
```

You can use the `Optional` keyword in a sub or function definition to indicate that an argument is optional. In the following example, the type of `ContractMonths` changes from `Integer` to `Variant` because `Optional` arguments must be Variants.

```
Sub CalcFee(AcctTotal As Currency, Optional ContractMonths As _
Variant)
```

The call to `CalcFee` defined this way can take either the preceding form or the following form:

```
CalcFee AcctTotal:=ncTot_Acct
```

This call to `CalcFee` passes the `AcctTotal` argument but not the `ContractMonths` argument. How should the `CalcFee` subroutine determine whether the optional argument is present? It can use the `IsMissing` function, as in the following example:

```
Sub CalcFee(AcctTotal As Currency, Optional ContractMonths As _
Variant)
If IsMissing(ContractMonths) Then
   AcctFee = (AcctTotal/12) * .10
Else
   AcctFee = (AcctTotal/ContractMonths) * .10
End If
```

`IsMissing` returns `True` if the optional argument is not passed to the routine; otherwise, `IsMissing` returns `False`.

Using Parameter Arrays

If you need to create a procedure to process an array of arguments, you can specify an argument as a `ParamArray` in the procedure definition statement without specifying the size of the array. Note that in the following example, the size of the `ItemCosts` array of variants is not specified:

```
Public Function Calc_OrderCost(ParamArray ItemCosts() As Variant) As _
Currency
```

This function takes a `ParamArray` argument, which can contain any number of variants. If you use the `ParamArray` argument, it must be of type `Variant` and it must be the last argument specified in the definition statement.

A function passing a `ParamArray` can pass any number of arguments, as in the following example:

```
Dim ItemCost(10) As Currency
Dim ncReturn As Currency
. . .
ncReturn = Calc_OrderCost(ItemCost(0), ItemCost(1), ItemCost(2))
...
ncReturn = Calc_OrderCost(ItemCost(0), ItemCost(1), ItemCost(2), _
ItemCost(3))
```

The first call to `Calc_OrderCost` passes three arguments, whereas the second call passes four arguments. The `Calc_OrderCost` function needs to determine the number of arguments passed to it by using the `Ubound` function, which returns the upper bound of the argument array, as shown here:

```
Public Function Calc_OrderCost(ParamArray ItemCosts() As Variant) As _
Currency
   Dim niNdx As Integer
```

```
   Dim ncTotCost As Currency
   For niNdx = 0 To UBound(ItemCosts)
      ncTotCost = ncTotCost + ItemCosts(niNdx)
   Next niNdx
   Calc_OrderCost = ncTotCost
   Exit Function
```

Consider the difference between passing the individual elements of the ItemCost array versus passing the array itself. If the array itself was passed to Calc_OrderCost, the UBound function would return 0, indicating one argument passed in. If the function is coded to sum the arguments passed in as separate cost values, as shown in this example, it would cause a Type Mismatch runtime error if it attempted to treat the array as a currency value.

Using the Is Functions

This section explores the use of functions you can use to discover a variable's type, the validity of a variable's value, a variable's state, or the state of the application. The functions covered in this topic are grouped together by the prefix Is.

You use IsArray to discover whether or not a variable is an array. The function takes one argument (the variable to be checked) and returns True if the variable is an array — otherwise, False — as illustrated here:

```
Sub Calc_Total(CostArray As Variant)
If IsArray(CostArray) Then
   ...
Else
   ' Error routine
End If
```

To discover whether an expression will produce a number, you can use the IsNumeric function. This function takes a numeric or string expression and returns True if the expression can evaluate to a number, False otherwise, as in the following:

```
Dim sPriceInput As String
sPriceInput = InputBox("Enter the current price.", "Price Input")
If IsNumeric(sPriceInput) Then
 ...
Else
   MsgBox "Price entered is not numeric."
End If
```

You can check for valid dates with the IsDate function. IsDate takes a date or string expression and returns True if the expression can be converted to a date or False otherwise, as follows:

```
Dim sDateInput As String
```

```
sDateInput = InputBox("Enter the price date.", "Price Date Input")
If IsDate(sDateInput) Then
 ...
Else
   MsgBox "Date entered is not valid."
End If
```

Be careful when you use this function. It returns `True` if the expression passed to it is a valid date or if the expression can be converted to a date. If the function returns `True`, do not assume that the expression is a date in the format you have established in the control panel Regional Settings. If you check an expression with `IsDate` and, receiving `True`, expect the first two characters of the expression to be the month, you may be surprised, as shown in the next example:

```
Dim sDate As String
sDate = "15/10/95"
If IsDate(sDate) Then
   MsgBox "The month is " & Left$(sDate,2)
Else
   MsgBox "Date is not valid."
End If
```

When you run this code, `IsDate` returns `True` and you see the message `The month is 15`. If you were to use this result in a calculation instead of merely displaying it, no doubt your result would be wrong.

To correct for this situation, either use the `Format` function to format the date as you expect it or use one of the date functions. In this example, using the `Month` function instead of using `Left$` would return the proper month.

After declaring a variant variable and before assigning it a value, the variant is considered empty. You can also set a variant variable to empty by using the `Empty` keyword, as follows:

```
Dim vVariable As Variant
...
vVariable = Empty
```

The `IsEmpty` function returns `True` if the variant variable is in the `Empty` state either initially or after being set with the `Empty` keyword, as in the following code:

```
If IsEmpty(vVariable) Then
  ...
End If
```

After initializing a variant variable, it is no longer considered empty, and the `IsEmpty` function returns `False`. If the variable's data is not valid, it is `Null` data; another function, the `IsNull` function, can detect this state.

`IsNull` returns `True` if the variable contains `Null` data and `False` otherwise, as shown here:

```
If IsNull(vVariable) Then
...
End If
```

A variable becomes Null when the keyword `Null` is assigned to the variable or if an expression being assigned to the variable results in a Null value.

You can determine whether a variable is an OLE Automation object, including Access objects such as a `Form` object, by using the `IsObject` function. `IsObject` returns `True` if the expression passed to it is an `Object` type; otherwise, it returns `False`. Following is an example:

```
Dim oObject As Form
Set oObject = Forms![Customer]
...
If IsObject(oObject ) Then
 ...
End If
```

The "Using Named Arguments" section introduced the `IsMissing` function. You use this function to determine whether an optional argument has been passed to a procedure. If the argument has not been passed, `IsMissing` returns `True`; otherwise, it returns `False`, meaning that you can access the argument. The following is an example of using this function:

```
Sub CalcFee(AcctTotal As Currency, Optional ContractMonths As _
Variant)
If IsMissing(ContractMonths) Then
    AcctFee = (AcctTotal/12) * .10
Else
    AcctFee = (AcctTotal/ContractMonths) * .10
End If
```

Variants can hold a data type known as a `vbError`. The variant variable becomes an error value through the return value of the `CVErr` function, as follows:

```
vVariantVariable = CVErr(45000)
```

To test for the `vbError` value, use the `IsError` function. `IsError` takes a variant as an argument and returns `True` if it holds the `vbError` type, `False` otherwise.

Tip

Together, you can use the `vbError` data type, the `CVErr` function, and the `IsError` function as the basis of your error-handling infrastructure. Consider using these throughout the design of your application; they improve the readability of the code and deal consistently with errors within the application.

Using the Array Function

You can use the Array function to create an array in a variant variable, as in the following:

```
Dim vVariable As Variant
vVariable = Array(10, 20, 30)
...
ReDim Preserve vVariable(3)
vVariable(3) = 40
```

In this example, a variant variable is assigned the result of the Array function, which is a three-element array.

The arguments of the function are the elements you want to assign to the array, and the number of the arguments determines the upper bound of the array. In this example, the upper bound is two.

As the example shows, you can use the resulting array like any other array created with the Dim statement, but note that the variant can be treated as a dynamic array even though the array being assigned to it was not declared as dynamic. The next example shows this use.

The result of using the Array function is the same as creating an array with the Dim statement and assigning it to a variant variable, as shown here:

```
Dim vVariable As Variant
Dim niArray(2)
niArray(0) = 10
niArray(1) = 20
niArray(2) = 30
vVariable = niArray
ReDim Preserve vVariable(3)
vVariable(3) = 40
```

The Array function cannot create multidimensional arrays, whereas the Dim statement can. The Array function produces only a single-dimension array; however, assigning the array to a variant variable enables the array to be resized.

Using the Nz Function

If any part of an expression contains a Null value, the entire expression is Null. For that reason, you cannot use the following statement to determine whether a variant variable is Null:

```
If vVariantVariable = Null Then   'does not work
...
End If
```

The preceding If statement always returns False, because the expression being evaluated contains a Null value. Using the IsNull function described previously properly evaluates the variable for Null.

The same results occur if a variant variable in an expression contains a Null value. Sometimes this situation is acceptable; at other times, you must add code to handle the null condition.

The Nz function saves additional work when a Null expression is unacceptable. Its syntax is as follows:

```
Nz(variant_variable[, value_returned_if_null])
```

If you pass only a variant variable, the function returns zero or a zero-length string if the variable is null. The context of the function in the expression determines whether a number or a string is returned. If the variable is not null, the function returns the variable's value.

If zero or a zero-length string is not appropriate for your application, you can specify an alternative value as the value_returned_if_null optional argument. The Nz function in the following example specifies that the string "Not Available" be returned in place of a zero-length string.

```
Dim vVariable As Variant
Dim vTotal As Variant
vTotal = Null
vVariable = Nz(vTotal, 1) * (0.1)
MsgBox "The commission is " & Nz(vVariable, "Not Available")
```

Using the BuildCriteria Method

When you design a query in the query design grid, you have the option of specifying a criteria expression to qualify the selection of records. You can enter your criteria expression by following a few simple rules, but when you leave the cell in which you enter the expression, Access takes care of parsing it and ensuring that it is in the correct form.

This parser is available to you in code as well. You can accept strings from users in the same way the strings would be entered in the query design grid, and you can force the parsing of the entered string into a complete and correct criteria expression. You accomplish this task through the BuildCriteria method of the Application object. Its syntax is as follows:

```
BuildCriteria(field, fieldtype, expression)
```

You can specify the Application object qualifier, but it is not required because it is implied. The field argument is the field for which the criteria apply, equivalent to the column into which you specify the criteria in the query design grid.

The `fieldtype` argument specifies the data type of the field, and the `expression` is the criteria expression to be parsed. The following is an example of using this method:

```
Dim sInput As String
Dim sCriteria As String
sInput = InputBox("Enter the Criteria for Customer Name: ", _
"Criteria")
sCriteria = BuildCriteria("CustomerName", dbText, sInput)
...
```

The returned string can be used wherever a criteria expression is required, as in the `Filter` property of a form or report, or in the `OpenReport` action.

Note that if the user enters double quotation marks in the string, `BuildCriteria` accepts them and wraps them inside its own set of double quotation marks. This approach is not accepted in the query design grid. Single quotation marks are accepted as they are entered, and the method adds no quotation marks.

If the user misspells a keyword, such as *lke* for *like,* `BuildCriteria` does not complain; it merely takes *lke* as part of the string value to compare against and prefixes the expression with the keyword *Like*. For example, if the user enters **lke "De*"**, the preceding `BuildCriteria` statement parses the entry into `CustomerName Like "lke "De*""`, which fails if used as a filter expression.

Exploring the SysCmd Function

Many Access applications need to retrieve information about the environment they are running in or get the status of a particular database object in order to function properly. `SysCmd` is a function you can use in these instances.

`SysCmd` takes an action argument that determines the behavior of the function. These action arguments can be placed into three categories:

- Access runtime information
- Progress meter management
- Database object state information

Maybe you've developed an application that is dependent on a particular Registry profile being used. When the user starts your application, he or she should be using a `/profile` command line argument to specify the profile name. To ensure proper operation of your application, your start-up code can check to see what profile the user specified and take appropriate action. The `SysCmd` function does this is as follows:

```
Dim RetVal
```

```
RetVal = SysCmd(acSysCmdProfile)
If RetVal = "MyProfile" Then
    ' OK to continue
Else
   MsgBox "Please start application with profile 'MyProfile'"
   ' Close down the app here
End If
```

You can retrieve the path to msaccess.exe by specifying the action constant `acSysCmdAccessDir` and the path to the system workgroup file by using `acSysCmdGetObjectState`. Both return the path into the return value variable.

During long-running operations in your application, it's good practice to keep the end user informed as to the progress of the operation. A simple progress meter in the status bar or a text message in the status bar keeps the end user informed as to what is happening. Using the progress meter management actions with `SysCmd` is a quick method of displaying a task's progress.

To use the progress meter, you must first initialize it with a value that represents 100 percent completion. The following initialization uses a value of 100 to indicate completion:

```
RetVal = SysCmd(acSysCmdInitMeter, "Processing", 100)
```

The text message is placed before the progress meter in the status bar to indicate the activity taking place. This text is optional.

Updating of the progress meter is done by sending an `acSysCmdUpdateMeter` argument and a value equal to or less than the initial value specified with the `acSysCmdInitMeter` action. `SysCmd` calculates a percentage of the `Init` value using the `Update` value and fills the progress meter according to this percentage. Passing the value 25 fills the meter by 25 percent, a value of 50 by 50 percent, and so on, until completely filling it by passing a value of 100.

The progress meter can be removed by sending `SysCmd` an action argument of `acSysCmdRemoveMeter` or by changing the text with an action of `acSysCmdSetStatus`. To reset status bar text, use an action of `acSysCmdClearStatus`.

By sending `SysCmd` an action of `acSysCmdGetObjectState`, you can get the state of a database object. You may want to know whether the end user has opened a particular form. By using the following call, you can find out whether the form is open or not:

```
RetVal = SysCmd(acSysCmdGetObjectState, acForm, "Account Entry")
If RetVal = acObjStateOpen Then
   ' the form is open
Else
   ' the form is not open
End If
```

If the form is not open, `RetVal` has a value of zero. Other values that `acSysCmdGetObjectState` can return are `acObjStateNew` to indicate a new object and `acObjStateDirty` to indicate a design change that has not yet been saved.

Using the New Data Types

Visual Basic for Applications adds three new variable data types to those available in Access 2.0 Basic: `Boolean`, `Byte`, and `Date`.

The `Boolean` data type, also referred to as `Bool`, has two possible values: `True` and `False`. This data type is appropriate for variables that act as flags to indicate the state of an object or as function return values to indicate success or failure.

Some application designers develop a standard that has all application functions returning a `Boolean` type that will indicate the success or failure of the function. If a function failure is detected, the error is either determined through another application-defined function call, such as `GetLastError`, or the error code variable is passed as one of the arguments to all functions and the function returns the error on failure and zero otherwise.

A numeric variable evaluates to a `Boolean True` if it is non-zero or to `False` if zero. Converting a `Boolean` to a numeric value yields `-1` if the Boolean variable is `True` and zero if `False`. You can use the `CBool` function to convert a numeric or string expression to a `Boolean` data type.

A popular function for Access developers is the `RGB` function. This function returns `RGB` color values for the red, green, and blue color intensities passed to it. These color intensity arguments are values in the range 0 to 255, each an unsigned eight-bit value, or byte.

The `Byte` data type is used for arguments such as the `RGB` color intensities or any other variables that need to represent a value from 0 to 255, the highest positive value possible in eight bits.

Tip

Because the `Boolean` data type takes two bytes (16 bits) and the `Byte` data type takes only one byte (8 bits), you can save memory by using the `Byte` data type for variables that denote only `True` and `False` values. A value of zero in the `Byte` variable is `False`, and any other value is `True`. You may also assign `True` and `False` to the `Byte` variable, as in the following:

```
Dim byByte As Byte
...
byByte = True
```

If you need to convert an expression to a `Byte` value, pass the expression as an argument to the `CByte` function. `CByte` converts the expression to a `Byte` value if the expression evaluates to a value in the range of 0 to 255; otherwise, an error occurs.

Working with dates

Most business applications use dates on forms and reports; these applications usually need to calculate date values. The Date data type is useful for this purpose.

Date variables store their values as IEEE 64-bit floating-point numbers. The date/time values that you can store in Date variables range from 1 January 100 to 31 December 9999, and times range from 0:00:00 to 23:59:59.

You may assign any numeric or string expression that is recognizable as a valid date.

When assigning numeric values, digits to the left of the decimal point are converted to the date portion, and the digits to the right of the decimal are converted to the time portion. Midnight is 0 and noon is .5.

You must bracket a Date literal by # symbols, such as #10/20/95#.

The CDate function can be used to convert an expression to a date. The date formats recognized by CDate are dependent on the locale setting of your system, which you set in the control panel Regional Settings. Use the Date tab of the Regional Settings Properties dialog box to set the short date and long date display styles. Use the Time tab to set the time display style.

With a short date style of M/d/yy set in the Date properties tab, CDate returns 10/20/95 for each of the following statements:

```
Dim dtDate As Date
dtDate = CDate(#20/10/95#)
dtDate = CDate("20/10/95")
dtDate = CDate("20 October 1995")
```

Visual Basic also changes the date literal in the first statement to a literal in the short date format at compile time. Entered as #20/10/95#, the compiler changes it to #10/20/95# under the m/d/yy date style setting.

The last statement is passing a long date to the CDate function. CDate does not accept the name of the day of the week in the expression. Passing "Friday, 20 October 1995" results in an error.

To determine whether the expression is convertible through the CDate function, use the IsDate function, as described in the section "Using the Is Functions."

Visual Basic provides several other functions for working with dates. Some of these are used to extract the day, month, and year parts. The Day function returns the day value, 1 – 31, of the date expression passed to it. Month extracts the month value, 1 – 12, out of the date passed to it. Year returns the year of the date passed.

These date extraction functions all return Null if the date passed to them evaluates to Null. This behavior is a good application of the Nz function described previously. Using Nz, you can return a default date part instead of Null.

You can use a set of Time functions to extract the time components from a date expression. The Hour function returns the hour, 0 – 23, of the date passed to it. Minute returns the minute, 0 – 59, and Second returns the seconds, 0 – 59, of the date passed.

The Weekday function returns the day of the week as a number, as shown in Table 4-1.

Table 4-1 Visual Basic Constants Returned by the Weekday Function

Constant	*Value*	*Meaning*
vbSunday	1	Sunday
vbMonday	2	Monday
vbTuesday	3	Tuesday
vbWednesday	4	Wednesday
vbThursday	5	Thursday
vbFriday	6	Friday
vbSaturday	7	Saturday

By default, Sunday is the first day of the week. You can specify the first day of the week by using the following syntax:

```
Weekday(date, [firstdayofweek])
```

Now returns the current date and time as set either in the control panel Date/Time Properties or by the execution of the Date and Time statements.

You can change the Date and Time settings by using the Date and Time statements. The functions with the same name return the Date and Time separately. The following code example illustrates the values returned from Now, Date( ), Time( ), and the use of the Date statement:

```
Dim dtDate As Date
dtDate = Now
MsgBox "Now = " & dtDate
dtDate = Date
MsgBox "Date = " & dtDate
dtDate = Time()
MsgBox "Time = " & dtDate
Date = #10/1/95#
```

After executing the last statement, which sets the system date, rerunning the code displays the Oct 1 date. The date and time set by the Date and Time statements are also displayed in the Date/Time properties in the control panel.

Three useful functions for calculating with dates are the DateAdd, DateDiff, and DatePart functions.

DateAdd adds an interval of time to a given date, returning the sum as a variant of type vbDate, as shown here:

```
DateAdd(interval, number, date)
```

The interval is specified as a string value, as shown in Table 4-2.

Table 4-2 The Interval Argument Takes a String Setting

String	Meaning
yyyy	Year
q	Quarter
m	Month
y	Day of year
d	Day
w	Weekday
ww	Week
h	Hour
n	Minute
s	Second

Using DateAdd, you can add or subtract an interval from the date you pass to the function. For example, you can determine the next quarter date by using the following:

```
Dim dtCurQtr As Date
...
DateAdd("q",1, dtCurQtr)
```

Using the quarter interval causes DateAdd to add or subtract, depending on the sign of the number argument, three months to the date argument. This method yields a quarterly date relative to the date argument, but it isn't necessarily the last day of the month. If you ask DateAdd to subtract one quarter from 6/30/95, for example, you get 3/30/95. You achieve the same result by subtracting three months, as in the following:

```
DateAdd("m", -3, dtCurQtr)
```

To determine the last day of a month, you can devise your own date function. Here's one possibility:

```
Public Function LastDay(dtDate As Date) As Date
Dim dtNextMonth
dtNextMonth = DateAdd("m", 1, dtDate)
dtNextMonth = DateValue(DatePart("m", dtNextMonth) & "/" & _
DatePart("yyyy", _
   dtNextMonth))
LastDay = DateAdd("d", -1, dtNextMonth)
End Function
```

This `LastDay` function determines the last day of the date passed into it by calculating the first day of the next month and then subtracting one day from that date. First, the function uses `DateAdd` to add one month to the input date. Next, it calculates the first day of the next month by extracting the month and the year (using the `DatePart` function) and then strings them together to form an mm/yyyy date. When this date is passed to the `DateValue` function, the function returns the date as mm/1/yy. (Instead of using `DateValue`, the program could have just concatenated `"/1/"` between the `DateParts`.) Lastly, the function subtracts one day from the first of the next month to yield the last day of the month for the date passed into the function.

This sample function introduces the `DatePart` function, which you use to extract parts of a date.

`DatePart` extracts the interval specified by the first argument from the date specified by the second argument. The interval designation is shown in Table 4-2 and is the same as that used for `DateAdd`.

A simpler method of determining the last day of the month, and many other useful date calculations, uses the following `DateSerial` function:

```
DateSerial(year, month, day)
```

Looking at `DateSerial`, it seems at first that it merely returns a date, given the month, day, and year components. The power of the function, however, lies in the capability of the function to compute dates by using relative arguments.

You specify the last day of the month calculation by using `DateSerial` as follows:

```
Public Function LastDay(dtDate As Date) As Date
LastDay = DateSerial(Year(dtDate), Month(dtDate) + 1, 0)

End Function
```

The first argument of `DateSerial` uses the `Year` function to extract the year from the input date. The second argument extracts the month from the input date and then adds one to it to get the next month. Finally, the last argument, expressed as 0, indicates that the function should subtract one from the first day of the next month, which yields the last day of the previous month, the month passed into the `LastDay` function. This third argument is perhaps better understood if written as a relative expression, 1 –1, one day before the first.

You can determine the number of intervals between two dates by using the `DateDiff` function, whose syntax is as follows:

```
DateDiff(interval, date1, date2)
```

The interval specification is one of those found in Table 4-2. The date arguments can be any date type variable or expression that evaluates to a valid date. If `date1` is later than `date2`, the return interval is negative.

What type is it?

When you dimension variables in your application, you give them a type according to their intended purpose, using the following syntax:

```
Dim variable As type
```

The type specifier can be any of the following:

- `Byte`
- `Boolean`
- `Integer`
- `Long`
- `Currency`
- `Single`
- `Double`
- `Date`
- `String`
- `String* length`
- `Object`
- `Variant`
- A user-defined type
- OLE Automation object type

If you omit the `As type` part of the `Dim` statement, the variable defaults to `Variant`.

Visual Basic for Applications provides a number of functions to determine the type of a variable.

The `TypeName` function returns the name of the type of the variable passed to it, using the following syntax:

```
TypeName(varname)
```

The returned name may be any of the following:

- `Objecttype`
- `Byte`
- `Integer`
- `Long`
- `Single`
- `Double`
- `Currency`
- `Date`
- `String`
- `Boolean`
- `Error`
- `Empty`
- `Null`
- `Object`
- `Unknown`
- `Nothing`

If a variant is passed to `TypeName`, the function returns the current subtype of the variant, `Empty` if the variant has not been assigned a value, or `Nothing` if the variant has no value or has been set to `Nothing`.

The `objecttype` may be any OLE Automation object type, but `Object` is returned for a generic object variable that supports OLE Automation.

If the variable passed is an array, `TypeName` returns the type of the array with parentheses appended to the type name. If the variable is an array of variants, the name returned is `Variant()`.

Whereas `TypeName` returns the name of the variable type, `VarType` returns a code for the type of the variable, which you use as follows:

```
VarType(varname)
```

Return values from `VarType` are listed in Table 4-3.

Table 4-3 The Returned Type Code from the VarType Function

Constant	*Value*	*Variable Type*
`vbEmpty`	0	Uninitialized
`vbNull`	1	Null (no valid data)
`vbInteger`	2	Integer
`vbLong`	3	Long integer
`vbSingle`	4	Single-precision floating-point number
`vbDouble`	5	Double-precision floating-point number
`vbCurrency`	6	Currency
`vbDate`	7	Date
`vbString`	8	String
`vbObject`	9	OLE Automation object
`vbError`	10	Error
`vbBoolean`	11	Boolean
`vbVariant`	12	Variant (used only with arrays of Variants)
`vbDataObject`	13	Non-OLE Automation object
`vbByte`	17	Byte
`vbArray`	8192	Array

If the variable passed to `VarType` is an array, the return value is the sum of `vbArray` plus the type of array.

You can use `TypeOf` in an `If` statement to determine the type of an object variable, as shown here:

```
If TypeOf object_name Is objecttype Then
   ...
End If
```

If the `TypeOf` statement specifies a variable of type `Control`, for example, one of the following values may be specified as `objecttype`:

- `Label`
- `Rectangle`
- `Line`
- `Image`
- `CommandButton`
- `OptionButton`
- `Checkbox`
- `OptionGroup`

- BoundObjectFrame
- TextBox
- ListBox
- ComboBox
- Subform
- ObjectFrame
- PageBreak
- CustomControl
- ToggleButton
- TabControl

You can obtain valid `objecttype` specifiers from the Object Browser. See Chapter 6, "Working with OLE and ActiveX Controls," for details on using the Object Browser.

Handling Errors

Error handling is a significant part of any well-designed application. In fact, some design guidelines recommend that you design the error-handling architecture before you design the normal flows of the application. Although this practice is rarely found in projects — everyone is too anxious to get to the good stuff — it does have some merit. Concentrating on error conditions involved in a particular problem domain can lead you to some interesting insights into the problem and force you to dig a little deeper into how the system works.

Whether you design your error handling first, last, or during the rest of the application, Visual Basic for Applications provides you with plenty of facilities for handling errors.

To set an error trap within a procedure, include an `On Error` statement at the point you want your error trapping to be active, as in the following:

```
Public Function SomeFunction()
On Error GoTo ProcErrHandler
...
Exit Function
ProcErrHandler:
' Error Handling Code
Exit Function
```

In this function, an `On Error GoTo` statement at the beginning of the function activates error trapping for the entire procedure, until the procedure exits. Another `On Error GoTo` statement following the first resets error trapping.

The `On Error GoTo` statement directs execution to the error-handling routine at the label `ProcErrHandler`. The `Exit Function` previous to the label forces normal execution of the function to exit, preventing entry into the error-handling routine.

You may place any code you want within the error-handling routine. At this point, you determine what the error was and process it accordingly. More on this later.

Another form of the On Error statement directs execution to the statement following the statement raising the error, as it would had the error not occurred. That statement is as follows:

```
On Error Resume Next
```

With this error trapping active, either you ignore errors as they occur and continue executing your code or you check for errors after executing a statement. Following is an example:

```
Public Function SomeFunction()
On Error Resume Next
...
ncTot = ncOrder + ncPrevBal
If Err Then
   ...
End If
Exit Function
```

You can place as many On Error statements as you want in a procedure. As execution proceeds, the last On Error statement executed is the one that controls the handling of an error, should it occur.

To turn off error trapping, use an On Error GoTo 0 statement. This statement removes any error trapping that may be active within the procedure. Error trapping still occurs, however, if a calling procedure higher in the call tree has error trapping active.

When an error occurs in a procedure, the procedure's error handler, if trapping is active, receives control. If trapping is not active in the procedure, the first calling procedure in the call tree containing active error trapping receives control. If no procedure in the call tree has error trapping active, a critical error is raised by Access and the application halts.

The same search up the call tree occurs if calls are being made out of error handlers. For example, consider a call tree where procedure A calls procedure B and B raises an error. In B's error handler, a call is made to procedure C, and C raises an error but doesn't have error trapping enabled. In this situation, control passes back to procedure B, but because B's error handler is active already, control must pass on to B's caller. Procedure A handles the error if it has error trapping; otherwise, the application halts.

The Err object

After your error handler is active, you most likely want to determine which error occurred. If a system-level error occurred, information about the error is found in the Err object.

The Err object's Number property contains the error code, and the Description property contains descriptive text about the error code. The

`Number` property is the default property. In the preceding code example, which uses `On Error Resume Next`, the code checks `Err` for a non-zero value. This procedure is actually a reference to the `Err` object's `Number` property. You could have specified `Err.Number` in place of `Err`.

The `Error` function used in Access 2.0 Basic yields the same information as the `Err Description` property.

The source of the error is present in the `Source` property. This property identifies the original source of the error even if the error has been passed back to your application through several levels of application objects.

Tip

These three properties are helpful in determining the error and possibly in handling it. You can code your error handler to be aware of certain error codes or ranges of error codes and to take steps either to correct an error or to work around it. If messages are presented to the user either real-time in a message box or off-line in a log file, you should include all three properties — `Number`, `Description`, and `Source` — in the message. The more information you can give the user concerning an error, the better.

You can use the `Err` object to generate user-defined errors. If you detect an error situation in your application — a sales commission rate out of range, for example — you can set the `Err` object `Number` and `Description` properties that describe the error and raise the error condition by using the `Err` object's `Raise` method. This technique has the same effect as a system-level error in that the procedure's error handler receives control, as in the following:

```
If nSalesCommRate > nRateLimit Then
   Err.Raise Number:=2074, Description:= _
"Commission Rate Out Of Range"
End If
```

The information in the `Err` object is cleared whenever an `On Error` statement is executed, a `Resume` statement is executed, or the current procedure is exited. You can explicitly clear the `Err` information by using the `Clear` method, as follows.

```
Err.Clear
```

If your application calls DLL functions, you should check the `Err` object's `LastDLLError` property after the function returns. This property contains the DLL error code if the function failed. Because an error condition is not raised for these errors, you should check the property to determine the success of the call.

The Error value

As mentioned earlier, you can assign an `Error` value to a variant variable through the use of the following `CVErr` function:

```
vVariable = CVErr(2074)
```

This capability is useful for procedures that need to report an error back to a calling procedure. If you use the Err object's Raise method within the procedure to raise the error condition, the procedure's error handler can report the error condition, or an interpretation of the error, back to the calling procedure by returning a variant with an Error value, as in the following:

```
Public Function CalcCommission(nSalesCommRate, nCommission)
On Error GoTo CCErrHandler
Dim vSuccessFail As Variant
vSuccessFail = 0
...
If nSalesCommRate > nRateLimit Then
   Err.Raise Number:=2074, Description:= _
"Commission Rate Out Of Range"
End If
CalcCommission = vSuccessFail
Exit Function
CCErrHandler:
   vSuccessFail = CVErr(Err.Number)
   CalcCommission = vSuccessFail
   Exit Function
```

The calling procedure uses the IsError function in this case to determine the success of the call, as in the following example:

```
If IsError(CalcCommission(nSalesCommRate, nCommission)) Then
   ...
End If
```

Using Resume and Resume Next

If your error-handling routine can correct the condition causing the error or wants to bypass the statement causing the error, it can use two variations of the Resume statement.

Resume by itself passes execution back to the statement that caused the error and attempts to execute it again. If it raises the error again, your error-handling procedure is again entered. If you're using the Resume statement, you should increment a counter in the error handler each time the error handler is entered. If some limit to this counter is reached, abort the Resume behavior and exit the procedure.

Resume Next causes execution to resume at the statement following the one that caused the error. You can use this technique only if you are certain that the statement in error is noncritical and can be bypassed or if your error handler has made a correction on behalf of the failed statement.

Cross-Reference

In Chapter 5, "Working with Data Access Objects," you learn about Data Access Object (DAO) errors, the Error object, and the Errors Collection. Using the error-handling facilities of DAO and Visual Basic for Applications, you can develop a sound architecture for handling run-time errors.

Chapter 5

Working with Data Access Objects

In This Chapter

- Understanding the Data Access Object hierarchy
- Looking at the Data Access Object type library
- Using Data Access Objects through their properties and methods
- Working with DAO Lab on the companion CD-ROM
- Using the Error object and Jet error handling
- Exploring DAO collections
- Using TableDef and QueryDef objects
- Using Recordsets, including dynasets and snapshots
- Looking at record locking in a multiuser environment
- Using attached tables
- Considering performance when using Jet and DAO

Open an Access database, and you see components such as Tables, Queries, Forms, Reports, Macros, and Modules. Dig a little deeper, and you find things such as `Indexes` and Relationships. These components are what you use to define a database application, the basic goals being to store and retrieve data and then present it to your end user in a meaningful way.

Hidden under all these layers is a system of programs that interprets and executes your requests for data. Some code must be responsible for understanding what you want when you make a request to read or write data to one or more tables on disk. When you base a form on a query that reads `Select [Customer last name], [Customer Phone], [Customer Zip] From Customers Where City = "New York"` , some code must interpret this request, figure out how to get what you want to see, retrieve the data, and manage it until you are finished with it.

Understanding the Data Access Object Hierarchy

The system of programs that does the work of database management in Access is collectively called the *Microsoft Jet database engine,* or just *Jet.* Jet stands between your application and the data on disk; it manages security, query interpretation, and data access management, including reading, writing, data type conversion, indexing, locking, validation, and transaction management (see Figure 5-1).

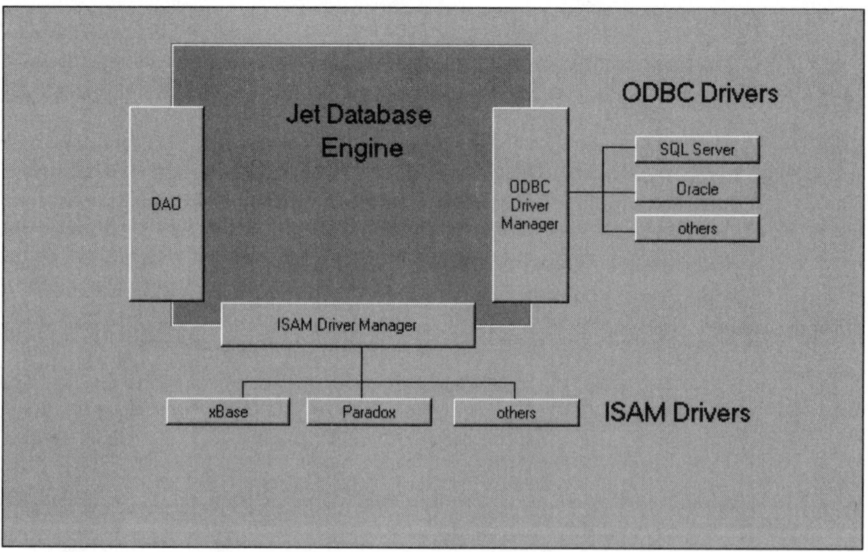

Figure 5-1: The Jet database engine also provides interfaces with other ISAM-type databases through ISAM drivers and server-based databases through ODBC drivers.

When Jet is working with native Access tables, it does its own data access. When requests for data in other table formats (*external data*) are processed, Jet depends on a series of drivers to handle the reading and writing. These drivers might be ISAM drivers (such as Paradox and Btrieve) or Xbase (such as FoxPro or dBASE). When the requirement is for access to server-based databases, such as SQL Server, Jet depends on ODBC to handle the request.

As you can see, Jet is the heart of the Access database. Access 97 uses version 3.5 of Jet, and in this chapter, you explore how your applications can use Jet to access and manipulate your database objects directly from code.

Talking to Jet through Data Access Objects

Data Access Objects (DAO) provide a comprehensible, object-based interface that enables you to work with the Jet database engine. DAO exposes a set of objects that have meaning in the world of databases, no matter what the source of the data. DAO depends on Jet to do the physical data management.

Access itself defines some of the components you use to build your database application, and Data Access Objects define others. This chapter addresses these objects after a review of the hierarchy of objects DAO provides (see Figure 5-2).

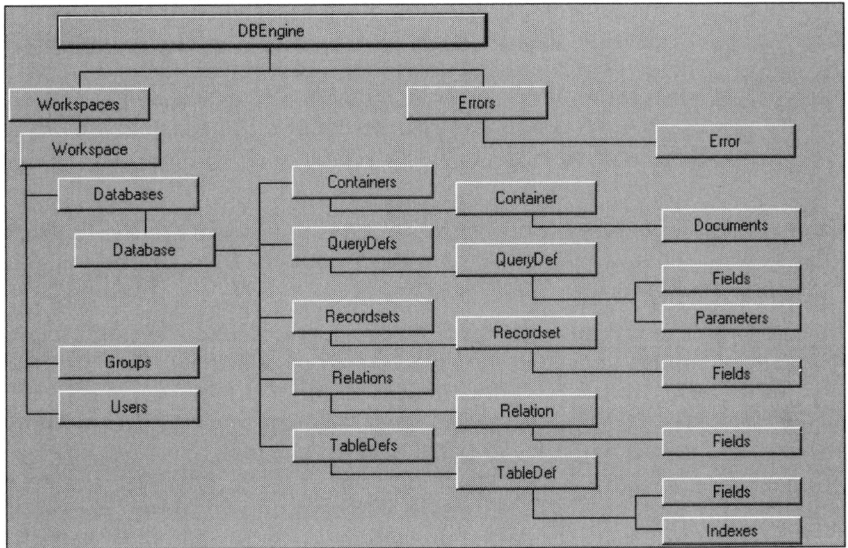

Figure 5-2: The Data Access Objects hierarchy offers a rich set of objects with which to build database applications.

Looking at the DAO type library

DAO enables its functionality via Automation, just as ActiveX Controls and applications such as Excel do. The objects, properties, and methods the OLE Automation applications make available are specified in a *type library.* See Chapter 6 for more information on Automation and ActiveX Controls.

Access 97 ships with two DAO type libraries. The DAO2535.TLB describes a DAO 2.5/3.5 compatibility layer, which is used when you convert your Jet 2.5 databases to Access 97. The DAO2535.TLB is used for full compatibility with your existing code. The DAO 3.5 object library is found in DAO350.DLL and is used for full compatibility with the latest version of DAO.

The Object Browser enables you to explore the objects provided by various Automation applications, including those shipped with Access 97 and those you obtain from other vendors.

Become familiar with the References dialog box and the Object Browser. Other Microsoft development products (such as Visual Basic 4.0) also use these tools; these tools will become more prevalent as software's use of OLE components increases.

To discover the objects DAO exposes, browse through the DAO type library by using the following procedure:

1. From a form module or module window, choose Object Browser from the View menu or from the shortcut menu, or press F2.
2. In the Project/Library drop-down list, choose the DAO – Microsoft DAO 3.5 Object Library. (If you didn't choose the DAO 3.5 library in the References dialog box, you can follow the procedure presented in Chapter 6, "Working with OLE and ActiveX Controls," to select the DAO 3.5 library, or you can choose the library here that you did set up with the References dialog box.)
3. The Classes list box lists all the collections and objects provided by the DAO library. Choose the `<globals>` entry in this list to display the constants you can use in DAO methods. Click on another entry, such as `DBEngine`.
4. The Members list box lists the properties and methods available for the object chosen in the Classes list box. For the `DBEngine` object, you see entries such as `CompactDatabase`, `CreateWorkspace`, `DefaultPassword`, and so on. Click on an entry in this list to see its syntax in the lower panel of the dialog box.

If you are coding a procedure and want to refer to the syntax of a particular method, you can use the preceding procedure and then click on the Paste Text button to paste the syntax statement into your code at the current cursor position.

Table 5-1 summarizes the objects included in the Data Access Object Version 3.5 hierarchy.

Table 5-1 Objects Contained in the Data Access Object Hierarchy, Version 3.5

Object	*Description*
`DBEngine`	Represents the Jet database engine. This top-level object contains all other DAO objects. There is only one instance of `DBEngine` in any given application, and there is no collection of `DBEngine` objects. This object is the one you reference to compact and repair your database through VBA code.

Object	*Description*
`Error`	An `Error` object consists of information pertaining to an error that occurred from a Jet/DAO operation. The object is a member of the `Errors` collection, and you can think of it as a list of errors from the lowest level of the operation to the highest level, such as errors returned from a database driver to those returned from Jet/DAO.
`Workspace`	A `Workspace` object contains the open databases within a user session and also offers methods and properties for maintaining transactions across the open databases and for maintaining security. The `Workspace` object is a member of the `Workspaces` collection.
`Database`	The `Database` object refers to a database open in the associated `Workspace` object.
`User`	The `User` object represents the user in session with the associated `Workspace` object. More than one user may be in session at a time, and they are contained in the `Users` collection.
`Group`	The `Group` object contains multiple users, or members, and grants to those users common permissions. The group referred to is the group in session with the associated workspace. The `Groups` collection lists all groups in session.
`TableDef`	The `TableDef` object represents a saved definition of a local or attached table in the associated `Database` object.
`QueryDef`	The `QueryDef` represents a saved query in the associated database. Its `SQL` property defines the SQL statement used to define the returned Recordset. When you build a query with the Query Builder in Access, its resulting SQL statement text is recorded in this property.
`RecordSet`	This object represents the records resulting from the execution of a query or the records in a table. As a developer, you'll deal with this object frequently in your applications.
`Field`	The columns of a table that appear in table design or in a datasheet are known as *fields.* The `Field` object defines the properties and method applicable to a column, and the `Fields` collection contains all `Field` objects in an associated table, query, Recordset, relation, or index.
`Index`	The `Index` object describes an index on the associated table. Indexes provide an order to the records accessed in the table and provide for faster access to specific records when values for one or more fields in the index's `Fields` collection are either completely or partially specified.
`Parameter`	`QueryDefs` may contain parameters, which are placeholders for criteria values to be determined at run time.

(continued)

Table 5-1 *(continued)*

Object	Description
`Relation`	Relations can be established for a database that enable Jet to enforce referential integrity. Relations define the relationship between two tables, and the subordinate `Fields` collection defines the fields involved in the relationship.
`Container`	`Container` objects are built in and represent data access objects such as tables, relations, and databases, and Access objects such as reports, forms, and modules. Each container object holds security information about the object it represents.
`Document`	`Document` objects represent instances of objects of the type of its associated container. For example, the Access `Forms` container contains a `Document` object for each form in the database. Additionally, the document holds security information for the object instance it represents.

Understanding DAO Methods and Properties

The best way to learn what the DAO objects are about is to explore them firsthand. Experience with the objects, properties, and methods in a "laboratory" type of environment gives you the skills you need to write Access 97 procedures to manipulate your database objects.

Introduction to the DAO Lab

The DAO Lab located in the file CH5.MDB on the CD-ROM that accompanies this book provides a view of the MDB's Data Access Objects and enables you to explore the properties of the DAO objects and collections (see Figure 5-3).

The components of the Lab include the following:

- The DAO Lab form used to display the objects, instances of objects, and properties
- A form to display any selected property in the properties list box
- The DAO Objects table used to hold the list of objects
- The DAO Props table used to list the properties of a selected object

The information displayed in the DAO Lab form is stored in the DAO Objects table and the DAO Props table. The DAO Objects table is populated with a function, `Refresh_Tree`, that enumerates the collections of DAO objects and stores their names, types, and parent information. The DAO Props table is populated by the code behind the Properties command button on the DAO Lab form. This table is a work table that is deleted and refreshed each time an object's properties are displayed in the properties list box. This table holds the name and value of each property object belonging to the object selected in the Instances list box.

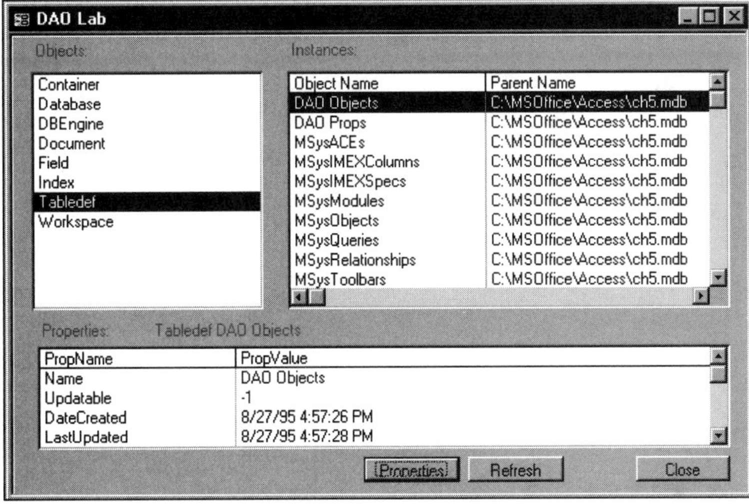

Figure 5-3: The DAO Lab Form displays the instances of DAO objects and their properties.

When the DAO Lab form loads, the Objects list box selects the distinct object types from the DAO Objects table. The Instances list box selects all objects of the type selected in the Objects list box. The Properties list box selects the records from the DAO Props table. These records are the properties of the object last displayed.

To rebuild the hierarchy, click on the Refresh button at the bottom of the form. This action causes the `Refresh_Tree` function (see Listing 5-1), located in the DAO Lab module, to run and enumerate all objects through their collections in DAO.

Listing 5-1 The Refresh_Tree Function

```
Function Refresh_Tree()
' Refresh the DAO Objects Table
On Error Resume Next
DoCmd.Hourglass True
Dim dbDatabase As Database
```

(continued)

(continued)

```
Dim wsWorkspace As Workspace
Dim tdTabledef As TableDef
Dim qdQuerydef As QueryDef
Dim pmParameter As Parameter
Dim cnContainer As Container
Dim doDocument As Document
Dim fdField As Field
Dim nxIndex As Index
Dim rsDAOObj As Recordset, rsRecSet As Recordset
Dim relRelation As Relation
Dim sSQLStmt As String
Dim ObjID As Long, DBEngineID As Long, WorkspaceID As Long, _
DatabaseID As Long
Dim TabledefID As Long, QuerydefID As Long, IndexID As Long, _
RelationID As Long
Dim ContainerID As Long
Dim iWS As Integer, iDB As Integer, iTD As Integer, iFD As Integer
Dim iNX As Integer, iQD As Integer, iPM As Integer, iRL As Integer
Dim iCN As Integer, iDO As Integer

Set dbDatabase = DBEngine.Workspaces(0).Databases(0)

' Remove the records from the DAO Objects table

sSQLStmt = "Delete from [DAO Objects]"
dbDatabase.Execute sSQLStmt

' List the DAO Objects into the DAO Objects table

Set rsDAOObj = dbDatabase.OpenRecordset("DAO Objects", dbOpenTable)
' Insert the DAO Hierarchy root
rsDAOObj.AddNew
rsDAOObj![Object Name] = "DBEngine"
rsDAOObj![Object Type] = "DBEngine"
EngineID = 0
ObjID = 0
rsDAOObj![Object ID] = ObjID
rsDAOObj![Parent ID] = EngineID
rsDAOObj.Update
' List the workspaces
For iWS = 0 To Workspaces.Count - 1
   Set wsWorkspace = Workspaces(iWS)
   rsDAOObj.AddNew
   rsDAOObj![Object Name] = wsWorkspace.Name
   rsDAOObj![Object Type] = "Workspace"
   rsDAOObj![Parent Name] = "DBEngine"
   ObjID = ObjID + 1
   rsDAOObj![Object ID] = ObjID
   rsDAOObj![Parent ID] = EngineID
   rsDAOObj.Update
   WorkspaceID = ObjID
   ' List the Databases
   For iDB = 0 To wsWorkspace.Databases.Count - 1
```

```
Set dbDatabase = wsWorkspace.Databases(iDB)
rsDAOObj.AddNew
rsDAOObj![Object Name] = dbDatabase.Name
rsDAOObj![Object Type] = "Database"
rsDAOObj![Parent Name] = wsWorkspace.Name
ObjID = ObjID + 1
rsDAOObj![Object ID] = ObjID
rsDAOObj![Parent ID] = WorkspaceID
rsDAOObj.Update
DatabaseID = ObjID
' List the TableDefs
For iTD = 0 To dbDatabase.TableDefs.Count - 1
   Set tdTabledef = dbDatabase.TableDefs(iTD)
   rsDAOObj.AddNew
   rsDAOObj![Object Name] = tdTabledef.Name
   rsDAOObj![Object Type] = "Tabledef"
   rsDAOObj![Parent Name] = dbDatabase.Name
   ObjID = ObjID + 1
   rsDAOObj![Object ID] = ObjID
   rsDAOObj![Parent ID] = DatabaseID
   rsDAOObj.Update
   TabledefID = ObjID
   ' List the Fields
   For iFD = 0 To tdTabledef.Fields.Count - 1
      Set fdField = tdTabledef.Fields(iFD)
      rsDAOObj.AddNew
      rsDAOObj![Object Name] = fdField.Name
      rsDAOObj![Object Type] = "Field"
      rsDAOObj![Parent Name] = tdTabledef.Name
      ObjID = ObjID + 1
      rsDAOObj![Object ID] = ObjID
      rsDAOObj![Parent ID] = TabledefID
      rsDAOObj.Update
   Next iFD    'Next Field
   ' List the Indexes
   For iNX = 0 To tdTabledef.Indexes.Count - 1
      Set nxIndex = tdTabledef.Indexes(iNX)
      rsDAOObj.AddNew
      rsDAOObj![Object Name] = nxIndex.Name
      rsDAOObj![Object Type] = "Index"
      rsDAOObj![Parent Name] = tdTabledef.Name
      ObjID = ObjID + 1
      rsDAOObj![Object ID] = ObjID
      rsDAOObj![Parent ID] = TabledefID
      rsDAOObj.Update
      IndexID = ObjID
           ' List the Index Fields
           For iFD = 0 To nxIndex.Fields.Count - 1
           Set fdField = nxIndex.Fields(iFD)
           rsDAOObj.AddNew
           rsDAOObj![Object Name] = fdField.Name
           rsDAOObj![Object Type] = "Field"
           rsDAOObj![Parent Name] = nxIndex.Name
           ObjID = ObjID + 1
```

(continued)

(continued)

```
                rsDAOObj![Object ID] = ObjID
                rsDAOObj![Parent ID] = IndexID
                rsDAOObj.Update
             Next iFD    'Next Field
         Next iNX    'Next Index
      Next iTD   ' Next TableDef
      ' List the QueryDefs
      For iQD = 0 To dbDatabase.QueryDefs.Count - 1
         Set qdQuerydef = dbDatabase.QueryDefs(iQD)
         rsDAOObj.AddNew
         rsDAOObj![Object Name] = qdQuerydef.Name
         rsDAOObj![Object Type] = "Querydef"
         rsDAOObj![Parent Name] = dbDatabase.Name
         ObjID = ObjID + 1
         rsDAOObj![Object ID] = ObjID
         rsDAOObj![Parent ID] = DatabaseID
         rsDAOObj.Update
         QuerydefID = ObjID
          ' List the Fields
         For iFD = 0 To qdQuerydef.Fields.Count - 1
              Set fdField = qdQuerydef.Fields(iFD)
              rsDAOObj.AddNew
              rsDAOObj![Object Name] = fdField.Name
              rsDAOObj![Object Type] = "Field"
              rsDAOObj![Parent Name] = qdQuerydef.Name
              ObjID = ObjID + 1
              rsDAOObj![Object ID] = ObjID
              rsDAOObj![Parent ID] = QuerydefID
              rsDAOObj.Update
         Next iFD    'Next Field
          ' List the Parameters
         For iPM = 0 To qdQuerydef.Parameters.Count - 1
              Set pmParameter = qdQuerydef.Parameters(iPM)
              rsDAOObj.AddNew
              rsDAOObj![Object Name] = pmParameter.Name
              rsDAOObj![Object Type] = "Parameter"
              rsDAOObj![Parent Name] = qdQuerydef.Name
              ObjID = ObjID + 1
              rsDAOObj![Object ID] = ObjID
              rsDAOObj![Parent ID] = QuerydefID
              rsDAOObj.Update
         Next iPM    ' Next Parameter
      Next iQD   ' Next QueryDef
   '   List the Relations
      For iRL = 0 To dbDatabase.Relations.Count - 1
         Set relRelation = dbDatabase.Relations(iRL)
         rsDAOObj.AddNew
         rsDAOObj![Object Name] = relRelation.Name
         rsDAOObj![Object Type] = "Relation"
         rsDAOObj![Parent Name] = dbDatabase.Name
         ObjID = ObjID + 1
         rsDAOObj![Object ID] = ObjID
```

```
        rsDAOObj![Parent ID] = DatabaseID
        rsDAOObj.Update
        RelationID = ObjID
        ' List the Fields
        For iFD = 0 To relRelation.Fields.Count - 1
             Set fdField = relRelation.Fields(iFD)
             rsDAOObj.AddNew
             rsDAOObj![Object Name] = fdField.Name
             rsDAOObj![Object Type] = "Field"
             rsDAOObj![Parent Name] = relRelation.Name
             ObjID = ObjID + 1
             rsDAOObj![Object ID] = ObjID
             rsDAOObj![Parent ID] = RelationID
             rsDAOObj.Update
        Next iFD    'Next Field
     Next iRL   'Next Relation
     '   List the Containers
     For iCN = 0 To dbDatabase.Containers.Count - 1
        Set cnContainer = dbDatabase.Containers(iCN)
        rsDAOObj.AddNew
        rsDAOObj![Object Name] = cnContainer.Name
        rsDAOObj![Object Type] = "Container"
        rsDAOObj![Parent Name] = dbDatabase.Name
        ObjID = ObjID + 1
        rsDAOObj![Object ID] = ObjID
        rsDAOObj![Parent ID] = DatabaseID
        rsDAOObj.Update
        ContainerID = ObjID
        ' List the Documents
        For iDO = 0 To cnContainer.Documents.Count - 1
             Set doDocument = cnContainer.Documents(iDO)
             rsDAOObj.AddNew
             rsDAOObj![Object Name] = doDocument.Name
             rsDAOObj![Object Type] = "Document"
             rsDAOObj![Parent Name] = cnContainer.Name
             ObjID = ObjID + 1
             rsDAOObj![Object ID] = ObjID
             rsDAOObj![Parent ID] = ContainerID
             rsDAOObj.Update
        Next iDO    'Next Document
     Next iCN   'Next Container
  Next iDB   ' Next Database
Next iWS  ' Next Workspace
rsDAOObj.Close
DoCmd.Hourglass False
Exit Function
End Function
```

Prior to the enumeration, the routine clears the table by executing an SQL delete statement, as follows:

```
sSQLStmt = "Delete from [DAO Objects]"
dbDatabase.Execute sSQLStmt
```

After clearing the table, the function proceeds through each DAO collection and stores the object name, type, and parent name for each object found. Every object receives a unique ID. The object's ID and the ID of the parent object are stored with the object record. These IDs are used to create a chain of an object's parents up to the Engine level whenever the user requests the display of an object's properties.

After the `Refresh_Tree` function finishes adding all objects to the table, the list boxes are requeried to rebuild their contents. The user may then select an object type from the Object list box. After the user makes the selection, the Instances list box is requeried to reflect the instances of the object type in the DAO Objects table.

To display an object's properties, select an object instance and click on the Properties command button. The code behind the Properties command button calls the `GetParentHier` function (see Listing 5-2), which walks the object hierarchy in the DAO Objects table from the current selected object up to and including the parent `Workspace`. The code accomplishes this task by using each object's parent ID to select the next upper level parent. As it locates each level, the code stores the name, type, and object ID in the `ParentHier` array, as follows:

```
Type Hier
   ParentName As String * 100
   ParentType As String * 50
   ParentID As Long
End Type

Dim ParentHier(6) As Hier
Dim nMaxNdx As Integer
```

When the `GetParentHier` function finishes, the `ParentHier` array contains a complete chain from `Workspace` down to object instance. This chain is used to set object variables that qualify the parents of the selected object and to display the object's properties. There is no assumption as to which parent object a given object is located under, and the properties displayed are current values.

Listing 5-2 The GetParentHier Function

```
Private Function GetParentHier(ObjectID) As Integer

On Error GoTo GetParentErrHandler

Dim dbDatabase As Database
Dim rsParent As Recordset
Dim nCurObj As Long
Dim nParentHierNdx As Integer

Set dbDatabase = DBEngine.Workspaces(0).Databases(0)
nCurObj = ObjectID
nParentHierNdx = -1
```

```
Do
   SQLStmt = "SELECT [Object Name],[Object Type],[Object ID],[Parent _
ID] FROM [DAO Objects] WHERE [Object ID] = " & nCurObj
   Set rsParent = dbDatabase.OpenRecordset(SQLStmt, dbOpenSnapshot)
   If rsParent.EOF Then
      Exit Do
   End If
   nParentHierNdx = nParentHierNdx + 1
   ParentHier(nParentHierNdx).ParentName = rsParent![Object Name]
   ParentHier(nParentHierNdx).ParentType = rsParent![Object Type]
   ParentHier(nParentHierNdx).ParentID = rsParent![Object ID]
   If Trim(UCase(ParentHier(nParentHierNdx).ParentType)) = _
"WORKSPACE" Then
      Exit Do
   End If
   nCurObj = rsParent![Parent ID]
   rsParent.Close
Loop
nMaxNdx = nParentHierNdx
rsParent.Close
GetParentHier = False
Exit Function
GetParentErrHandler:
MsgBox "Error: " & Str$(Err) & ": " & Error$(Err)
GetParentHier = Err
Exit Function
End Function
```

This technique enables the program to display current properties on demand and supports objects no matter which parent chain they have. If the code finds a `Field` object named `[Customer Name]` in a table open in a database under workspace zero, and a `Field` object with the same name is located in a table of a database open in workspace one, the properties display needs to position on the correct `Field` object in order to display its properties to the user. Building the parent chain (the hierarchy) at the time the display is requested simplifies table design, but it complicates code. Of course, you can build the chain with SQL statements using self joins, but the technique presented here is a little more straightforward, and you can see what's going on.

Double-clicking on a property in the properties list box displays the `Zoom` form and the entire string of the selected property value. This technique is helpful for displaying a long `Connect` string or `Relation` name.

Using the Error object

The `DBEngine Errors` collection and the `Error` objects it contains are new to DAO with Version 3.5. The `Errors` collection contains an `Error` object for each error that occurred during a data access operation.

The Error objects detail the errors from the last data access operation; the objects are contained in the Errors collection from the lowest-level error to the highest-level error. These levels refer to the various components a data access operation passes through from your request to the physical data access and back to your application.

Most data access operations involving an Access database entail only one Error object, the one from DAO, and this Error is equal to the Err code made available by Visual Basic.

Secret

In application procedures containing DAO code, it's a good idea to check the Err code against the Errors(0).Number in your error-handling routine to determine the type of error to be handled, a Visual Basic error or a DAO error.

The Errors collection is cleared when the next data access operation generates an error. If an operation results in an error that prohibits entry into the collection, the collection may not be valid for the current operation. To determine the validity of the collection for the current operation, check the first Error object Number DBEngine.Errors(0).Number against the Err code returned by Visual Basic. If the two are equal, you can use the collection to list the Error objects for the operation.

Listing 5-3 shows an error routine you can use to scan through the Errors collection and to display all errors that occurred from the data access operation that raised the error.

Listing 5-3 An Errors Collection Routine

```
Public Sub Show_Errors(ErrCd As Integer)
   Dim errErr As Error, txtErr As Control
   Dim i As Integer

' List the DAO errors collection
   Set txtErr = txtErrors

   If (Errors.Count = 0) Or (Errors(0).Number <> ErrCd) Then
      txtErr.Value = "No Information Available"
   Else
      For i = 0 To Errors.Count - 1
         Set errErr = Errors(i)
         txtErr.Value = txtErr.Value & Str$(errErr.Number) & ": _
" & _ errErr.Description & Chr$(13) _                        & Chr$(10)
      Next i
   End If

   txtErr.Locked = True
   Exit Sub
End Sub
```

Exploring collections

`Errors` is just one of the collections found in DAO. Also present are `TableDefs`, `QueryDefs`, `Recordsets`, `Workspaces`, and `Databases`, to name a few. You can find each of the collections in the DAO Lab `Refresh_Tree` function.

The `Refresh_Tree` function in the DAO Lab form walks through each DAO collection to determine the names of each object in the collection. The `For loop` that lists the objects in a collection is controlled by the `collection_name.Count` property, which holds the number of objects in the collection. The `Count` property of the `TableDefs` collection is shown in the following example controlling the enumeration of the `TableDef` objects in the Database referenced by the `Database` object variable named `dbDatabase`:

```
For iTD = 0 to dbDatabase.TableDefs.Count - 1
    ...
Next iTD
```

You can use a collection name to reference an object in the collection. For example, to reference the first `TableDef` in the `TableDefs` collection, you can use the ordinal position of the object within the collection, as shown here:

```
sTableName = dbDatabase.TableDefs(0).Name
```

The `Name` property does not refer to a property of the `TableDefs` collection but instead refers to a property of the zero `TableDef` (the first `TableDef`) in the collection. Likewise, you can refer to all other `TableDef` properties in this manner.

If you know the name of an object in a collection, such as `DAO Objects` in the `TableDefs` collection of the CH5.MDB database, you can use the name instead of the ordinal position, as in the following:

```
MsgBox "DAO Objects DateCreated Is: " & dbDatabase.TableDefs _
("DAO Objects").DateCreated
```

The preceding `MsgBox` displays the `DateCreated` property value of the `DAO Objects TableDef`.

You can add objects to some collections by using the collection's `Append` method. You may want to track a user's session activity, report on it at the end of the session, and then remove the statistics before closing the application. You can build a session table at start-up and add the table to the database. Listing 5-4 is an example of how you can accomplish this goal.

Listing 5-4 Adding a TableDef to a Database

```
Dim dbDatabase As Database
Dim tblTableDef As TableDef
Dim fldField As Field
```

(continued)

(continued)

```
Set dbDatabase = CurrentDb()

' Create a new TableDef in the Database
Set tblTableDef = dbDatabase.CreateTableDef("User Session")

' Create the User Name Field
Set fldField = tblTableDef.CreateField("User Name", dbText, 40)
tblTableDef.Fields.Append fldField

' Create the Login Date/Time Field
Set fldField = tblTableDef.CreateField("Login Date_Time", dbDate)
tblTableDef.Fields.Append fldField

' Create the Activity Field
Set fldField = tblTableDef.CreateField("Activity", dbText, 50)
tblTableDef.Fields.Append fldField

' Create the Activity Date/Time Field
Set fldField = tblTableDef.CreateField("Activity Date_Time", dbDate)
tblTableDef.Fields.Append fldField

' Append the new table to the TableDefs Collection
dbDatabase.TableDefs.Append tblTableDef
```

If you want the fields in your table to have an order different from the order that you append the fields to the `TableDef`, set the zero-based `OrdinalPosition` property of the `Field` object before appending, as follows:

```
Set fldField = tblTableDef.CreateField("Activity Date_Time", dbDate)
fldField.OrdinalPosition = 2
tblTableDef.Fields.Append fldField
```

The preceding code sets the `Activity Date_Time` field as the third field in the `User Session` table. To order the fields alphabetically by field name, set the `OrdinalPosition` value of all fields to the same value.

You can think of collections as lists in memory. The list is created when you first reference the collection. To ensure that the collection you are working with in memory is in sync with the physical store in the database, use the `Refresh` method of the collection. This approach is especially important in a multiuser environment where other users can also maintain collections in the database.

To remove the `User Session` table from the database, you use the `TableDefs` collection `Delete` method, as shown here:

```
Set dbDatabase = CurrentDb()
Set tblTableDef = dbDatabase.TableDefs("User Session")
dbDatabase.TableDefs.Delete tblTableDef.Name
```

Collection methods, such as Append and Delete, are only applicable to objects that are physically stored in the database. Collections that are built in to memory by the DBEngine do not recognize Append and Delete. Table 5-2 shows where you can use the Append and Delete methods.

Table 5-2 Append and Delete Usage

Collection	*Use Append*	*Use Delete*
DBEngine.Workspaces	No. Use CreateWorkspace.	No. Use Close.
Workspace.Databases	No. Use OpenDatabase or CreateDatabase.	No. Use Close.
Database.TableDefs	Yes	Yes
TableDef.Fields	Yes, if the TableDef Updatable property is True.	Yes, if the TableDef Updatable property is True.
TableDef.Indexes	Yes, if the TableDef Updatable property is True.	Yes, if the TableDef Updatable property is True.
Index.Fields	Yes, if the Index object has not yet been appended into the TableDef.Indexes collection.	Yes, if the Index object has not yet been appended into the TableDef.Indexes collection.
Database.QueryDefs	Yes	Yes
QueryDef.Fields	No	No
QueryDef.Parameters	No	No
Database.Recordsets	No. Use OpenRecordset.	No. Use Close.
Recordset.Fields	No	No
Database.Relations	Yes	Yes
Relation.Fields	No	No
Database.Containers	No	No
Container.Documents	No	No
Container.Properties	Yes	Yes
Document.Properties	Yes	Yes
Workspace.Users	Yes	Yes
User.Groups	Yes	Yes

(continued)

Table 5-2 *(continued)*

Collection	*Use Append*	*Use Delete*
`Workspace.Groups`	Yes	Yes
`Group.Users`	Yes	Yes
`DBEngine.Errors`	No	No

The `Containers` and `Documents` collections hold information about saved DBEngine and Access objects. As you can see in Table 5-2, your application code cannot append to or delete from these collections. You can, however, add your own properties to the objects in these collections.

For Access 97, Containers hold information on saved forms, reports, macros, and modules. The DBEngine uses Containers to hold information on tables, table relationships, queries, and the database in which all of these objects are stored.

Each `Container` object has a dependent `Documents` collection. The `Document` objects in the `Documents` collection hold the properties of a specific object of the type implied by the parent container. The `Forms Container` object, for example, contains a collection of `Form Document` objects that hold information about the `Forms` saved in the database.

Do not confuse the `Forms Document` collection with the `Forms` collection that Access maintains. The collection that Access maintains is a list of Forms Access has *open*. The `Forms Document` collection holds information on all Forms *saved* in the database.

To see the kind of information stored in `Container` and `Document` objects for your application, see the DAO Lab display of these objects.

Each object in the DAO hierarchy has one or more properties that describe the object's behavior and attributes. Each of these properties is itself an object in the `Properties` collection of the parent object. For example, the `TableDef` object created previously has properties such as `Name`, `Updatable`, and `DateCreated`. You can access the `Name` property by using the following:

```
tblTableDef.Name
```

Alternatively, you can refer to the `Name` property by using the `Properties` collection of the `TableDef` object, as follows:

```
tblTableDef.Properties("Name")
```

The syntax `tblTableDef.Properties("Name").Name` refers to the `Name Property` of the `Property` object in the `tblTableDef` object `Properties` collection with a `Name` of `Name`. This syntax returns `Name` as the value, meaning that the property referred to is the `Name` property. The syntax `tblTableDef.Properties("Name")` returns the name of the `TableDef` and is the same value as that returned by `tblTableDef.Properties("Name"). Value`.

Both the preceding statements refer to the same property. The latter statement refers to the Property object of the TableDef's Properties collection that has the value of Name. This latter syntax is rarely used in favor of the first form, but the Properties collection is useful in informational applications such as DAO Lab. The Refresh_Tree function in DAO Lab uses the Properties collection to list the properties of Containers and Documents.

Exploring TableDef and QueryDef objects

The preceding section illustrates how you can create a TableDef and append it to the TableDefs collection of a database. Now, let's explore the TableDef object in more detail and take a look at QueryDef objects and creating and maintaining them in code.

Defining the TableDef and QueryDef objects

A TableDef object describes every physical table stored in the database or linked from an external source. Likewise, for every query stored in the database, an associated QueryDef object describes it. The TableDef object defines the fields in the physical table, identifies the indexes on the table, and holds properties pertaining to the characteristics of the table. The QueryDef object defines the characteristics of the stored compiled query, including the show fields of the query and the SQL string defining the query.

Using the TableDef properties

The RecordCount property of a local TableDef object indicates the number of records in the table. If no records are in the table, this property value is 0. For attached tables, this property value is -1.

Attributes of a TableDef indicate various characteristics of the table. You may set the Attributes property when you build your TableDef, but after appending the TableDef to the TableDefs collection, the property may only be read.

The value of an Attribute may contain more than one constant. For example, an Attribute may be an attached table and have the user and password information for the attached table stored with the connection information. In this case, the sum of the constants dbAttachedTable and dbAttachSavePWD is the value of the Attributes property. To test the property for a given value, use the bitwise And operator with the constant for which you are testing. To test for an attached table in a non-ODBC database, use the following statement:

```
Set tblTabledef = dbDatabase.TableDefs("DAO Objects")
If (tblTabledef.Attributes And dbAttachedTable) <> 0 Then
   MsgBox "Table is an attached table.", 64, "Attributes Test"
Else
   MsgBox "Table is not an attached table.", 64, "Attributes Test"
End If
```

The preceding code would yield the message `Table is not an attached table`, because the DAO Objects table is local to the CH5.MDB database.

The `Connect` property holds information about the source of an attached table. The first value in the `Connect` string is the database type. Subsequent values denote parameters specific to the database type. An attached Jet database does not specify a database type, so this member is not present in the connect string. The parameter for the Jet database type is the path to the source table. If you develop a database called MyDB.MDB and attach the CH5.MDB DAO Objects table, the resulting TableDef in your database will have a connect string that looks something like the following:

```
yourtabledef.Connect = ";C:\MSOFFICE\OFFICE\SAMPLES\CH5.MDB"
```

Note the lack of a database type specifier that indicates that the source is a database type that uses the Jet engine for access. The path portion of the string is the path into which you installed the CH5.MDB.

If you attach an ODBC table — one that resides in Microsoft SQLServer, for example — your connect string looks something like the following:

```
yourtabledef.Connect = _
"ODBC;DSN=Pubs;APP=Microsoft Access -97
Secrets;WSID=yourID;DATABASE=pubs"
```

The database type in this string indicates an ODBC source, and the DSN parameter is the Data Source Name of the data source specified in the ODBC setup. Chapter 21, "Working with Client/Server Databases," covers this setup. The Database that contains the source of the attached table is the Pubs database, which ships with Microsoft SQLServer as a sample database.

Other parameters than what you see here may be specified in an ODBC connect string. For a table local to the database in which you are working, the connect string is empty.

You can attach a table through code by modifying this connect string property. To do so, you need to specify the source of the database that contains the table to which you want to attach. The connect string does not refer to the table name you are attaching. To specify the name of the table you want to attach, use the `SourceTableName` `TableDef` property.

The `SourceTableName` property holds the name of the attached table as it appears in the source database. In the preceding case, where you attached to the CH5.MDB DAO Objects table from MyDB.MDB, the `SourceTableName` property of the resulting `TableDef` is as follows:

```
yourtabledef.SourceTableName = "DAO Objects"
```

See the "Working with Attached Tables" section in this chapter for an example of how you can attach to a table in code.

The `Updatable` property of a `TableDef` object indicates whether you can change the table definition. The values of this property are `True` (which means you can change the TableDef) and `False` (which means you cannot change the TableDef). For newly created local tables, the default setting is `True`. For attached tables, the setting is `False`.

If the value of this property is `False`, you cannot change the properties of the `TableDef` object itself and you cannot change the setting of most `Field` objects in the `TableDef Fields` collection. You can, however, modify settings that apply to the display of the field in your application.

TableDef properties

Some properties of a `TableDef` object are not available for a newly created TableDef. The Table Properties dialog box Access displays while in table design mode offers the properties `Description`, `Validation Rule`, `Validation Text`, `Display Expression`, `Filter`, and `OrderBy`. `Validation Rule` and `Validation Text` are present as `TableDef` properties even if they don't have values. The other properties in this dialog box, however, are not present in the list of the `Properties` collection of a TableDef after you create it.

You can explore the behavior of these properties in the DAO Lab by using the following procedure:

1. Pick a TableDef from the DAO Lab Instances and click on the Properties button to display the `TableDef` properties. You discover that the properties list displays 12 properties. None of the properties listed includes `Filter`, `Description`, or `OrderBy`, as shown in the Properties dialog box in table design.
2. From the database container window, open the table whose properties you just viewed in datasheet mode. Choose one of the columns and click on the right mouse button to display the menu.
3. Choose Sort Ascending.
4. Next, close the table, answer Yes to the prompt to save changes, and open it in Design mode. Click on the right mouse button to display the menu and then choose Properties. The Table Properties dialog box shows the properties mentioned previously. Notice that the `OrderBy` property shows the field name you set the sort order on. The question now is, "Where is this stored in the data access hierarchy?"
5. To find out, go back to DAO Lab and select the TableDef you've been working with and look at the properties list once again. This time, you notice an `OrderBy` property listed.

This example is a case of adding a property to the TableDef on an as-needed basis. Explore a little further and find out what happens when you remove the sort order from the Properties dialog box.

Using the TableDef methods

You use the CreateField method illustrated here to create a new field in the DAO Objects TableDef; the new field holds the number by which the object is listed in the collection. The procedure sets up the database and TableDef object variables and then issues a TableDef object CreateField statement. The new field will have a name of Object Number and a type of Integer. After the field has been created, the Fields collection's Append method adds the field to the TableDef, as follows:

```
set fldField = tblTableDef.CreateField("Object Number",dbInteger)
tblTableDef.Fields.Append fldField
```

Tip

To see the constants that DAO recognizes, follow these steps:

1. Bring up the Object Browser and select DAO – Microsoft DAO 3.5 Object Library in the Libraries/Databases drop-down list.
2. Select Constants in the Modules/Classes list box.
3. All the DAO constants are listed in the Members list box. Choose a constant from the list to see the value of the constant in the display pane.

The RefreshDate property used in the DAO Lab form is a user-defined property added to the DAO Objects TableDef for the purpose of saving the last date and time the table was refreshed. User-defined properties are available for many of the DAO objects, and you can establish them by using the TableDef CreateProperty method, as shown here:

```
Dim dbDatabase As Database
Dim tblTableDef As TableDef
Dim proProperty As Property

Set dbDatabase = CurrentDb()

' Create a new TableDef in the Database
Set tblTableDef = dbDatabase.TableDefs("DAO Objects")
Set proProperty = tblTableDef.CreateProperty("RefreshDate", dbText, _
Now)
tblTableDef.Properties.Append proProperty
```

The RefreshDate property is intended for display only, so it is created with the dbText property type instead of the dbDate type. The Now function, which returns the system date and time as a variant of type VarType 7 (date), sets the value of the property.

A user-defined property is relevant for the object for which it is defined but not for all objects of a given type. The RefreshDate property, for example, is valid for the DAO Objects TableDef but not for other TableDefs.

User-defined properties are persistent after you append them to the object. To delete a user-defined property, such as `RefreshDate`, use the `Delete` method of the `Properties` collection, as in the following:

```
tblTableDef.Properties.Delete "RefreshDate"
```

To create an index on the DAO Objects table, use the `TableDef` method `CreateIndex`. Use `CreateIndex` to create and name an index object. After you do so, you may define the field or fields from the TableDef on which the index is based. You may also set other index properties, as shown in Listing 5-5.

Listing 5-5 Creating an Index for a Table

```
Dim dbDatabase As Database
Dim tblTableDef As TableDef
Dim ndxIndex As Index, fldField As Field

' Create new Index object.
Set dbDatabase = CurrentDb()
Set tblTableDef = dbDatabase.TableDefs("DAO Objects")
Set ndxIndex = tblTableDef.CreateIndex("ObjName")
Set fldField = ndxIndex.CreateField("Object Name")
ndxIndex.Primary = True
ndxIndex.Required = True
ndxIndex.Fields.Append fldField
' Append it to Indexes collection.
tblTableDef.Indexes.Append ndxIndex
```

The code creates an index on the `Object Name` field of the DAO Objects table and designates it as the Primary index. The `Required` property of the index is set to `True` to disallow Null values in the indexed field or fields. You could also set this property for the `Object Name` field object of the `TableDef Fields` collection.

After setting the index properties, you can append the index field to the `Fields` collection of the index and append the index itself to the `Indexes` collection of the TableDef.

Working with QueryDef objects

A `QueryDef` object describes a query stored in a database. Queries against Jet databases are stored in compiled form. *Compiled* means that the Jet SQL parser and optimizer have examined the SQL statement making up the query and devised the best method for executing the query and carrying out the SQL commands. The optimizing method used by Jet is known as a *least-cost* method and depends on current statistics about the database objects referenced by the query. These statistics are updated whenever you compact the database. The stored query can be considered a plan that Jet uses for accessing the database when executing the query.

By storing the queries in their compiled form, Jet can execute them much more quickly than queries presented as SQL strings for execution. Presented as an SQL string, Jet must check the query for proper syntax, as well as figure out what the query wants to do and the best way to do it, before the actual execution and getting the results.

You can define many different types of queries in a `QueryDef` object. When you define a query in the Query Design dialog box, known as the *QBE (Query By Example) grid*, you can select the type of query by selecting the QueryType drop-down list in the toolbar or by selecting the query type from the Query menu. This type selection is stored in the QueryDef's type property as a numeric code.

Not all queries need to be defined in terms of Access SQL. You can specify some queries in terms of an external database engine such as Microsoft SQL Server. These types of queries are known as *SQL PassThrough* queries because Jet passes them through to the external engine without examining them, leaving this task for the external engine.

Another type of query offers the option of specifying criteria values for the query's `WHERE` clause at execution time. This type of query is known as a *Parameter* query, and the `QueryDef` object of such queries contains a parameters collection for specifying the criteria values.

Using the QueryDef methods and properties

You create a QueryDef in a Database object by using the `CreateQueryDef` method of the `Database` object, as in the following:

```
Dim dbDatabase As Database
Dim qryQueryDef As QueryDef

Set dbDatabase = CurrentDb()
Set qryQueryDef = dbDatabase.CreateQueryDef("qryObjects")
```

This code creates a QueryDef called `qryObjects` in the current database. Although it is a `QueryDef` object, it does not represent an executable query because the QueryDef has no specified SQL statement.

You can specify the SQL statement for the QueryDef when the QueryDef is created by giving the `CreateQueryDef` method an SQL statement as the second argument, as in the following example:

```
SQLStmt = "SELECT [Object Name], [Object Type] FROM [DAO Objects]"
Set qryQueryDef = dbDatabase.CreateQueryDef("qryObjects",SQLStmt)
```

In defining what the query is to do, an SQL statement is created and stored in the QueryDef's `SQL` property. If the `CreateQueryDef` statement doesn't specify an SQL statement, then you must set it after the `CreateQueryDef` statement and before using the QueryDef, as follows:

```
Set qryQueryDef = dbDatabase.CreateQueryDef("qryObjects")
qryQueryDef.SQL = _
"SELECT [Object Name], [Object Type] FROM [DAO Objects]"
```

As you define a query in the QBE grid, you can inspect the SQL statement that will be stored in the `SQL` property by selecting SQL from the View menu or by selecting the QueryView drop-down list in the toolbar.

You can inspect the `Type` property of a QueryDef to determine the type of query the QueryDef defines. The `Type` property is read-only for `QueryDef` objects, and you can inspect it after using the `QueryDef` collection's `Refresh` method. The values and their meanings are listed in Table 5-3.

Table 5-3 QueryDef Type Property Values

Type Value	*Query Type*	*DAO Constant*
0	Select	`dbQSelect`
16	Crosstab	`dbQCrosstab`
32	Delete	`dbQDelete`
48	Update	`dbQUpdate`
64	Append	`dbQAppend`
80	Make-table	`dbQMakeTable`
96	Data-definition	`dbQDDL`
112	PassThrough	`dbQSQLPassThrough`
128	Union	`dbQSetOperation`
144	PassThrough not returning records	`dbQSPTBulk`
240	Action	`dbQAction`

SQL PassThrough queries are sent to the external database engine specified in the `Connect` property. Because Jet does not inspect the SQL being passed, it doesn't know whether to expect records back from the query or not. To inform Jet of the expected results of the query, you can set the `ReturnsRecords` property, as shown in the example here. The values for this property are `True` (the query returns records) and `False` (the query does not return records).

```
qryQueryDef.Connect = "ODBC;DSN=Pubs;APP=Microsoft Access -97 _
Secrets;WSID=yourID;DATABASE=pubs"
qryQueryDef.SQL = "SELECT au_lname, au_fname, phone FROM authors"
qryQueryDef.ReturnsRecords = True
```

Setting the `Connect` property tells Jet that this query is an SQL PassThrough query. The `ReturnsRecords` property defaults to `True`, so it is not necessary to set this property unless the query does not return records. If the query does return records and the `ReturnsRecords` property is set to `False`, the result is a trappable error.

Although not as efficient as a PassThrough query, you can define the same query to be non-PassThrough as long as the `SQL` property contains SQL that Jet can understand and the table or tables specified in the `From` clause are attached tables. To change the preceding QueryDef to non-PassThrough, change the `Connect` property to a zero-length string and ensure that the table name matches the name of the attached table.

In the non-PassThrough case, Jet evaluates the query by using the information contained in the attached TableDef and then formulates calls to the external database engine to satisfy the SQL statement.

To see the difference between a query against an attached ODBC table and one designated as SQL PassThrough, follow the procedures outlined in the following steps to trace the activity between Jet and ODBC:

1. Run REGEDIT.EXE and open the HKEY_LOCAL_MACHINE window.
2. Open the tree path: SOFTWARE\Microsoft\Jet\3.5\Engines\ODBC
3. If no ODBC key exists, create one by choosing Edit⇨New Key while positioned on the Engines Key.
4. Use Edit⇨New⇨String Value to add the following settings:

   TraceSQLMode as type REG_SZ String value 1

   TraceODBCAPI as type REG_SZ String value 1
5. Close the Registry Editor.

After setting these Registry values and reopening Access, run the query as a non-PassThrough query and then close the datasheet view. Minimize Access and open the ODBCAPI.TXT file located in the Access directory. This file lists the ODBC API calls that Jet passed to ODBC to run the query and display the results. The SQLOUT.TXT file in the same directory displays the SQL sent to ODBC. Print the files and delete or rename them.

Now go back to Access and run the query as an SQL PassThrough query. View the resulting text files and compare them to the non-PassThrough query. You'll notice a big difference in the two queries, with the non-PassThrough query causing considerably more ODBC activity to display the same results.

SQL PassThrough QueryDefs can contain any valid external database engine SQL and, in the case of Microsoft SQL Server, the names of stored procedures.

If your QueryDef defines an action query, one that doesn't return records, you can use the `QueryDef Execute` method to run the query. Dimension a `QueryDef` object and use the database `QueryDefs` collection to set the object variable to reference your QueryDef, as in the following:

```
Dim qryQueryDef As QueryDef
Dim dbDatabase As Database
Set dbDatabase = CurrentDb()
Set qryQueryDef = dbDatabase.QueryDefs("your querydef")
```

To execute the query, use the Execute method, as follows:

```
qryQueryDef.Execute
```

The Execute method gives a trappable error if the query returns records, because no buffer has been established to handle returned records and no means of referencing the returned records has been declared.

To determine the number of records affected by the Execute method on an SQL non-PassThrough query, check the QueryDef's RecordsAffected property, as in this example:

```
Dim nlNumRecsAff As Long
nlNumRecsAff = qryQueryDef.RecordsAffected
If nlNumRecsAff > 0 Then
   MsgBox Str$(nlNumRecsAff) & " records were updated"
Else
   MsgBox "No records updated"
EndIf
```

As with the TableDef object, Access also adds properties to the QueryDef object. To see the properties of a QueryDef object, choose a QueryDef from the DAO Lab instances list and click on the properties button. Remember that some properties may not be present until Access sets them. The sort order of a queries datasheet view, for example, yields an OrderBy property in the QueryDef object, just as it did in the TableDef object.

If your query does return records, you can use the QueryDef's OpenRecordset method to deal with the results. Recordsets are explored in the "Using Recordsets" section of this chapter. For QueryDef objects, you can open a Recordset as a *dynaset* or *snapshot* type. The dynaset type means that you can update the records contained in the Recordset. The snapshot type means that the records in the Recordset are read-only. SQL Pass-Through queries return only snapshot-type Recordsets.

Using parameters

QueryDef objects may contain a Parameters collection. These QueryDefs are known as *parameter queries* and are useful when a particular Where clause of a query cannot be stated before run time.

Parameters are placeholders for values that specify the criteria of a Where clause. This type of query is very useful for implementing Find or Filter features in your application, because you can specify the parameters from values collected from the user.

The QueryDef object does not have a CreateParameter method, you cannot append to the Parameters collection, and you cannot delete parameters from the Parameters collection. The only available method for creating parameters is to specify the PARAMETERS keyword in the SQL statement of the QueryDef.

Place the parameters first in the SQL statement, using the following syntax:

```
PARAMETERS [parameter 1] type; [parameter 2] type; ...
```

To create a parameter query for the DAO Objects table where you want to enter the type of object to select from the table, you can use the following:

```
Dim SQLStmt As String
Dim dbDatabase As Database
Dim qryQueryDef As QueryDef
SQLStmt = "PARAMETERS [Enter Object Type] TEXT; "
SQLStmt = SQLStmt & "SELECT [Object Name] FROM [DAO Objects] "
SQLStmt = SQLStmt & "WHERE [Object Type] = [Enter Object Type]"
Set DBDatabase = CurrentDb()
Set qryQueryDef = dbDatabase.CreateQueryDef("qryParamQuery")
qryQueryDef.SQL = SQLStmt
qryQueryDef.Close
```

If you open this query from the Access Database window, you get a dialog box prompting you to `Enter Object Type`. After entering the type of object you want to see — `QueryDef`, for example — the query runs and Access displays a datasheet of objects having object types of `QueryDef`.

To run this query from code and to specify the parameter before running the query, you can use the following code:

```
Dim dbDatabase As Database
Dim qryQueryDef As QueryDef
Dim rsRecordSet As Recordset
Set dbDatabase = CurrentDb()
Set qryQueryDef = dbDatabase.QueryDefs("qryParamQuery")
qryQueryDef("Enter Object Type") = "querydef"
Set rsRecordset = qryQueryDef.OpenRecordset()
```

The resulting Recordset contains all objects of type `QueryDef` if any exist in the DAO Objects table.

Using Recordsets

Recordsets are objects that you use to manipulate records. The `Recordset` object is built in memory when you open the Recordset. The `Recordsets` collection of a database object contains all open Recordsets. When you close a Recordset, the `Recordset` object is removed from memory and from the `Recordsets` collection.

The `OpenRecordset` method is available for the `Database`, `TableDef`, and `QueryDef` objects. In addition, you can apply it to another `Recordset` object. The `Recordset` object is a memory object composed of one or more *buffers* that hold the records contained in the Recordset. The relationships between the records in the Recordset and their source in the database tables are maintained in various ways and are explained later in this chapter.

You can create four types of Recordsets. A *table-type* Recordset is considered an open buffer on the table itself. When creating this type of Recordset, you can specify only a table name as the source in the `OpenRecordset` method. The table name cannot be an attached table.

A *dynaset*-type Recordset is an updatable set of records composed of two buffers. One holds the unique keys of the records in the Recordset, and the other holds the data fields specified in the source of the `OpenRecordset`.

The third type of Recordset is the *snapshot-type* Recordset. This type consists of a buffer holding the data fields specified in the source of the `OpenRecordset`.

A fourth type of Recordset is a special type of snapshot called the *forward-only-type* Recordset. This Recordset is used in cases where you only need to scroll forward through a data source and only need to read the data, so no updating is involved. This Recordset can take advantage of Jet's *read-ahead buffering* to gain performance in reading data.

The population of these buffers is explained later in this section.

Table Recordsets

Using a table-type Recordset is usually the fastest of the three types, because you are opening the table directly and so don't require the overhead of selecting records. The table-type Recordset manages a buffer that holds the current record's data and reflects any changes that may have been made by other users in a multiuser environment.

Using the OpenRecordset method

You can open the Recordset by specifying the name of a table in the `OpenRecordset` method of a `Database` object, or you can open the Recordset by using the `OpenRecordset` method of a `TableDef` object, as in the following two examples:

```
Set rsRecordset = dbDatabase.OpenRecordset _
("DAO Objects",dbOpenTable)
```

or

```
Set rsRecordset = dbTableDef.OpenRecordset(,dbOpenTable)
```

Note that the table you specify as a source or the `TableDef` object you use cannot be an attached table.

You can edit this Recordset, and in a multiuser environment, the Recordset reflects the changes made by others. The options you can use with the table-type Recordset are `dbDenyWrite` and `dbDenyRead`.

The `dbDenyWrite` option specifies that other users are blocked from making changes to the table while you have the Recordset open. Other users can read the table, however.

The dbDenyRead option tells Jet to open the Recordset and prevent other users from reading the table.

The dbReadOnly option indicates that you want to open the table for reading but not for updates. You use this option if your application requires only browsing of the table.

BOF and EOF properties

After opening the Recordset, you should determine whether records are available. If no records are in the Recordset, the Recordset's BOF (Beginning of File) and EOF (End of File) properties are set to True. If EOF is False, then at least one record is in the Recordset.

At the time the Recordset opens, you are positioned at the first record, if any exist. Moving to a position prior to this record sets the BOF property to True but doesn't affect the setting of the EOF property.

Moving through the Recordset beyond the last record sets the EOF property to True and leaves the BOF property unmodified.

Navigating with the Move methods

Using the Move methods and the BOF and EOF properties, you can set up a loop to visit every record in the Recordset, as shown in Listing 5-6.

Listing 5-6 Setting Up a Loop to Visit Every Record in the Recordset

```
Dim dbDatabase As Database
Dim rsRecordset As Recordset
Dim niTableCount As Integer

Set dbDatabase = CurrentDb()
Set rsRecordset = dbDatabase.OpenRecordset("DAO Objects",dbOpenTable)
Do While Not rsRecordset.EOF
   If rsRecordset![Object Type] = "tabledef" Then
      niTableCount = niTableCount + 1
   End If
   rsRecordset.MoveNext
Loop
rsRecordset.Close
dbDatabase.Close
MsgBox "There are " & Str$(niTableCount) & " tables in DAO Objects"
```

The preceding code starts at the first record, if any, and visits each record in the Recordset until the EOF property is True. To work through the table from the last record to the first, use the code in Listing 5-7.

Listing 5-7 Working from the Last Record to the First

```
Dim dbDatabase As Database
Dim rsRecordset As Recordset
Dim niTableCount As Integer

Set dbDatabase = CurrentDb()
Set rsRecordset = dbDatabase.OpenRecordset("DAO Objects",dbOpenTable)
rsRecordset.MoveLast
Do While Not rsRecordset.BOF
   If rsRecordset![Object Type] = "tabledef" Then
      niTableCount = niTableCount + 1
   End If
   rsRecordset.MovePrevious
Loop
rsRecordset.Close
dbDatabase.Close
MsgBox "There are " & Str$(niTableCount) & " tables in DAO Objects"
```

This code does a `MoveLast` on the Recordset to position the record pointer at the last record in the Recordset. You use the `MovePrevious` method to move toward the beginning of the Recordset until the `BOF` property becomes `True`.

When the Recordset is opened, the code does not need to issue a `MoveFirst` method, because the `OpenRecordset` implies `MoveFirst`. At any time in the use of the Recordset, however, you can issue a `MoveFirst` to reset the record pointer to the first record in the Recordset.

Locating records with Seek and Find methods

If you need to locate a particular value in the table, you can use this technique of visiting every record and checking it for the value for which you are looking. In tables with very few records — say, fewer than 100 — this means is acceptable to the user waiting for the results. On tables with thousands of records, however, this approach may not be acceptable.

Tip

You can find what you need with a faster technique. The table-type Recordset has a `Seek` method, which uses an index to locate values in the Recordset.

`Seek` uses an index specified by the Recordset's `Index` property to locate the first record in the Recordset that matches the values supplied in the arguments of the `Seek` method, as in the following example:

```
Dim dbDatabase As Database
Dim rsRecordset As Recordset

Set dbDatabase = CurrentDb()
Set rsRecordset = dbDatabase.OpenRecordset("DAO Objects",dbOpenTable)
rsRecordset.Index = "PrimaryKey"
```

```
rsRecordset.Seek "=","DBEngine"
If rsRecordset.NoMatch Then
MsgBox "DBEngine is not in the DAO Objects table"
Else
   MsgBox "DBEngine found"
End If
```

The preceding code uses the index of the DAO Objects table named `PrimaryKey`. This index name is set into the Recordset's `Index` property. This index is the one that `Seek` uses to locate the record.

The `Seek` method searches the index, looking for an entry equal to `DBEngine`. If it finds one, the record pointer is set on this record in the Recordset and the `NoMatch` property is set to `False`. If the `Seek` method doesn't find an entry, the `NoMatch` property is set to `True`.

You can use any existing index on the table referenced in the `OpenRecordset` to locate records. `PrimaryKey` happens to be the default index name when you build a primary key index, a unique index, on a table. You can name this index something other than `PrimaryKey`, and you can create additional indexes on the table. (See "Exploring TableDef and QueryDef objects," earlier in this chapter, for details on creating indexes.)

Some indexes have only one field in them, and some have more than one field. To use an index with more than one field in a `Seek`, specify the `Seek` statement, as in the following:

```
Dim fieldxvalue As String, fieldyvalue As String
fieldxvalue = "some value"
fieldyvalue = "some other value"
rsRecordset.Index = "multifield index"
rsRecordset.Seek "=", fieldxvalue,fieldyvalue
```

The index used here is an index named `multifield index`, and the values in the index being sought are contained in the variables `fieldxvalue` and `fieldyvalue`.

`Seek` can locate the first record matching the specified criteria. If an index contains non-unique values and you want to locate all such values in the Recordset, you need to use `Seek` to get to the first record and then use a `MoveNext - Test record` approach to visit all other records with that value, as in Listing 5-8. DAO doesn't offer a `SeekNext` method.

Record pointer and current record

The term *record pointer* in Access is analogous to using your finger to go through a list, such as a phone book. As you open to the page of interest in the phone book, you position your finger at the first entry on the page. You inspect that entry, the *current record*, and then move your finger to the next entry in the list. You've just done a `MoveNext`, and your finger, the record pointer, is positioned on a new record. Continuing down the list, you eventually end up beyond the last entry in the column. If you consider the column to be a Recordset, you have an `EOF` condition.

Listing 5-8 Visiting All Records with Non-Unique Values Using MoveNext

```
Dim dbDatabase As Database
Dim rsRecordset As Recordset
Dim niTableCount As Integer

Set dbDatabase = CurrentDb()
Set rsRecordset = dbDatabase.OpenRecordset("DAO Objects",dbOpenTable)
rsRecordset.Index = "Object Types"
rsRecordset.Seek "=","tabledef"
If rsRecordset.NoMatch Then
   MsgBox "Tabledef objects are not in the DAO Objects table"
Else
   Do
      niTableCount = niTableCount + 1
      rsRecordset.MoveNext
      If rsRecordset.EOF Or rsRecordset![Object Type] <> "tabledef" _
Then
         Exit Do
      End If
   Loop
   MsgBox "There are " & Str$(niTableCount) & _
" tables in DAO Objects"
End If
```

Why does the preceding approach work? When you set the `Index` property of the Recordset, you are essentially ordering the records in the Recordset by that index. In this case, all records are ordered by the `Object Type` field so that all records having an `Object Type` of `TableDef` are together. Using the `MoveNext` method and inspecting the field value until either an `EOF` condition occurs or the field value changes is equivalent to what you would expect from a `SeekNext` method, if one existed.

Using bookmarks

To refresh a record's fields to see other users' changes, you can set the Recordset's `Bookmark` property equal to itself, as follows:

```
rsRecordset.Bookmark = rsRecordset.Bookmark
```

This line releases any editing done on the record and refreshes the field values that were there prior to editing. You can use this technique at any time after invoking the `Edit` method and prior to invoking the `Update` method.

This technique works in a Recordset based on Jet engine type tables or any tables that support bookmarks. To determine whether the Recordset supports bookmarks, you can check the Recordset `Bookmarkable` property. If this property is `True`, then you can use bookmarks; otherwise, you cannot use them.

You can use bookmarks to mark a particular record to which you want to return after moving away from it, as follows:

```
Dim varBookmark
...
varBookmark = rsRecordset.Bookmark
rsRecordset.MoveLast
...
rsRecordset.Bookmark = varBookmark
```

The preceding code saves the current record bookmark into a variable and then moves to the last record in the Recordset. Later in the code, you achieve a return to the record by setting the Recordset `Bookmark` property equal to the saved bookmark.

Updating and locking

In order to update the Recordset, you must ensure that the Recordset's `Updatable` property is `True`. If it is true, then you can update at least one of the fields in a record. Some fields may not be updatable, but to discover this status, you must check the `Updatable` property of the field itself.

To edit the Recordset, you need to consider what type of locking you will use. *Pessimistic* locking locks a page (2KB of data) in the Recordset at the time you start editing a record. This locking prevents other users from making changes to the record you are editing and all other records in the page being locked.

Optimistic locking locks a page at the time of update. While the record is being edited, no lock is taken, enabling other users to make changes to the records in the page.

The choice of pessimistic or optimistic locking depends on a number of factors that only you can evaluate for your application. Consider the following factors:

- The size of records in the Recordset. If your records are small, causing many records to fit in a 2KB page, the result is that many records will be locked each time you cause a lock to be taken. If your editing procedure holds the lock for a long duration, then a very good chance exists that other users will be waiting much of the time.
- The number of users doing updates. The larger the population of users doing updates, the greater the chance for clashes. Likewise, a small population of users does not generally clash as much. If all users, however, are concentrating on the same small subset of the Recordset, clashes are likely to occur no matter what the population size.
- The type of activity being applied. Updating records is one type of activity that you need to understand, but you need to consider adding records too. If many users are entering data on the Recordset, clashes are likely to occur because all users are attempting to append to the bottom pages of the Recordset. If the Recordset is indexed, clashes also occur in the index pages as new index values are added.

The Windows multitasking environment

In the Windows 3.*x* environment, the locking issue was a concern generally in a multiuser installation where multiple machines were sharing a database on a file server. Multiple applications sharing a database from the same machine was not a frequent concern. With Windows 95 and Windows NT, however, multiple tasks running on the same machine accessing the same database is more of a possibility. The capability to multitask the machine and run several Access applications at once will likely become a more common occurrence. This scenario is still a multiuser situation, but on the same machine. Locking is a consideration here, too, because multiple applications are accessing the same shared database. In fact, this method is open to you for testing your application targeted for a multiuser environment. Run two instances of Access and your application on the same machine to test your error handling and your handling of record locking situations.

To set your choice of locking, you use the `LockEdits` property. Setting `LockEdits` to `True`, which is the default locking strategy for Jet `Workspaces`, establishes pessimistic locking. With this setting, a lock is taken when you issue the `Edit` method and then is released when you issue the `Update`, `Close`, or `CancelUpdate` methods, or one of the `Move` methods.

Setting the `LockEdits` property to `False` establishes optimistic locking. A lock is taken at the time you issue the `Update` method and then is released after the change is made. This setting holds the lock the least amount of time but requires that you deal with clashes with other users' changes that may occur.

If you use the `LockEdits` option of the `OpenRecordset` method, using `dbPessimistic` equates to setting the `LockEdits` property to `True` and any other options results in `LockEdits` being set to False.

Listing 5-9 is an example of an error-handling routine you can use to deal with locking errors you may encounter in a multiuser environment. This routine uses the `Errors` collection to display error descriptions to the end user and to check for locking error codes. Note that if the Visual Basic `Err` variable does not equal the `Number` property of the first `Error` object in the `DBEngine Errors` collection, the error is not a DAO error. The routine checks for this at the top of the error-handling procedure.

Listing 5-9 An Error-Handling Procedure for Dealing with Multiuser Clashes

```
On Error GoTo DBErrHandler
Const TRYLIMIT = 3
Const WAITTIME = 5
Dim TryCount As Integer, UserAction As Integer
Dim CurTimerVal As Long
Dim dbDatabase As Database
Dim rsRecordset As Recordset
```

(continued)

(continued)

```
Set dbDatabase = CurrentDb()
Set rsRecordset = dbDatabase.OpenRecordset _
("SELECT * FROM [Customers]", dbOpenDynaset)
If rsRecordset.EOF Then
   rsRecordset.Close
   Set dbDatabase = Nothing
   Exit Sub
End If
rsRecordset.LockEdits = False
rsRecordset.Edit
rsRecordset![Cust St] = "MA"
rsRecordset.Update
rsRecordset.Close
Set dbDatabase = Nothing
Exit Sub

DBErrHandler:
If Err <> Errors(0).Number Then
   MsgBox "Not a dao error", vbCritical
   Exit Sub
End If

Select Case Errors(0).Number
   Case 3186, 3188, 3189, 3260
      TryCount = TryCount + 1
      If TryCount > TRYLIMIT Then
         UserAction = MsgBox(Errors(0).Description, vbExclamation + _
vbRetryCancel)
         If UserAction = vbRetry Then
            TryCount = 0
         Else
            Exit Sub
         End If
      End If
      Idle dbFreeLocks
      CurTimerVal = Timer
      Do While Timer < CurTimerVal + WAITTIME  'Wait WAITTIME _
seconds
         DoEvents
      Loop
      Resume
   Case 3197
      UserAction = MsgBox(Errors(0).Description & "Apply changes?", _
vbQuestion + vbYesNo)
      If UserAction = vbYes Then
         Resume
      Else
         rsRecordset.CancelUpdate
      End If
   Case Else
      MsgBox Errors(0).Description, vbCritical
      Exit Sub
End Select
```

The `Edit` method informs Jet that you are making changes to the current record. When you issue the `Update` method, the changes you made are committed to the table, assuming that transactions are not being used. If you move off the record, close the Recordset, use the `CancelUpdate` method, or use the bookmark to refresh the fields — before issuing the `Update` — you lose your changes.

Make special note that a record is pulled into the edit buffer at the time you issue the `Edit` method. With optimistic locking, you get a trappable error if you issue an `Update` method and the record you are attempting to update in the table was changed by another user since you issued the `Edit` method, not since you opened the table Recordset. If you issue the `Edit` after another user or task has completed its update, your edit buffer contains the updated fields and your `Update` succeeds, unless another update precedes you.

Adding records

To add records to the Recordset, use the `AddNew` method. You use this method in place of the `Edit` method when adding a new record. Any default values specified in the TableDef are applied to the record if you do not set those fields. As with the `Edit` method, the record is committed to the table when you issue the `Update` method. Remember that clashes can occur here as well as in editing, even though your record may be unique.

To position the current record on the last record modified or added in the Recordset, you can use the `LastModified` property. This property returns a bookmark, and you can use it to set the `Bookmark` property of the Recordset to make the last modified record the current record. Use the following syntax:

```
rsRecordset.Bookmark = rsRecordset.LastModified
```

Use the `Delete` method to delete the current record. After deleting, the current record is still positioned at the deleted record; however, you cannot refer to the record or recover it unless you are using transactions (see "Using transactions," later in this chapter).

In a table-type Recordset, the `RecordCount` property is a true number of the number of records in the table. This number reflects additions and deletions by other users immediately. The `PercentPosition` property indicates the position of the current record relative to the value of the `RecordCount` property.

You can use the `PercentPosition` property to move the current record. A value of 0 yields the first record in the Recordset, and a value of 100 yields the last record in the Recordset. A value of 70 yields a record position that is roughly 70 percent into the Recordset from the beginning. Using this property to position to a record is not recommended, however, because the result is not always exact. Setting the `PercentPosition` to 70, for example, in a Recordset of four records yields the second record as the current record, whereas you may have expected the third record.

The Close method

When you have finished processing the Recordset, close it by using the `Close` method. This method removes the Recordset from the `Recordset` collection of the database in which it was opened and invalidates the `Recordset` object.

The DAO Lab

To see your `Recordset` objects in the DAO Lab, you must add code to the `RefreshTree` routine to list Recordsets and add them to the DAO Objects table. You must also refresh the DAO Lab form after a Recordset has been opened and before it has been closed because the Recordset is not a persistent object that is stored in the database. After refreshing the DAO Objects table supporting the DAO Lab with open Recordsets, you may close the Recordsets; they remain visible in the DAO Lab object hierarchy due to their presence in the DAO Objects table. In this case, however, clicking on properties to view the `Recordset` properties results in an `Object Not Found` message because no Recordset is open for inspection.

Dynaset Recordsets

A dynaset Recordset is the set of records resulting from the execution of a select query statement or a stored select query defined by a `QueryDef` object. You can create this type of Recordset to select records from a local or attached table.

Understanding the dynaset

Dynasets actually consist of two sets of records internal to Jet. One of these sets is known as the *keyset.* The keyset is a set of keys or bookmarks that uniquely identify the rows of the selected records. The actual data values retrieved are known as the *rowset.* As a developer, you need only refer to the dynaset as a whole, using its methods and properties to manipulate it. Jet maintains the keyset and rowset for you.

When you create a dynaset, Jet populates the internal keyset with keys from the record source. As you refer to the fields of a particular record in the dynaset, Jet fetches the current values of the record from the associated tables. This process enables Jet to provide the most-current values of the records making up the dynaset, even those recently changed by other users if the tables you are referencing are shared in a multiuser environment.

Insertions of new records by other users in a multiuser environment are not reflected in the dynaset because the key of the new record is not resident in the keyset and Jet only fetches data values from this keyset. To see the new records added to the underlying tables, you need to force Jet to rebuild the keyset. To force this rebuilding, you use the Recordset's `Requery` method. More on this procedure later.

If another user deletes a record contained in your dynaset, you see a "hole" when you visit the deleted record. This hole is made evident to your code by issuing a trappable error. This behavior occurs because the keyset still contains the key of the deleted record even after the record it refers to has been deleted by the other user. When Jet uses the key to fetch the data values for the record, it discovers that the record is not found (the hole) and issues a trappable error to your program. Records your program deletes are removed from the dynaset immediately, however, and do not create holes.

Creating dynasets

Dynasets are created with the `OpenRecordset` method of a database, QueryDef, TableDef, or another Recordset object.

To create a dynaset from an SQL string, you use the following code:

```
Dim dbDatabase As Database
Dim rsRecordset As RecordSet

Set dbDatabase = CurrentDb()
Set rsRecordset = dbDatabase.OpenRecordset("SELECT [Object _
Name],[Object Type] FROM [DAO Objects] WHERE [Parent Name] = _
'CH5.MDB'",dbOpenDynaset)
```

The preceding code creates a dynaset in the current database, using an SQL string constant. Because the source of the Recordset is a query, the `dbOpenDynaset` option need not be specified because a dynaset would be created anyway.

Remember that Jet must parse this statement prior to executing it and returning records into the Recordset. This approach is somewhat slower than using a query already parsed but can be useful in some situations. If a data source is small and the result of the query can be returned in an acceptable amount of time, the overhead of the parsing may not be a factor. Your own situation should dictate whether you choose to code an SQL string or build a QueryDef. Generally, the guideline is to use QueryDefs wherever possible.

To yield the same result using a QueryDef, you can create the QueryDef ahead of time and then specify its name in the `OpenRecordset`, as follows:

```
Dim dbDatabase As Database
Dim rsRecordset As RecordSet

Set dbDatabase = CurrentDb()
Set rsRecordset =
dbDatabase.OpenRecordset("qryDBChildren",dbOpenDynaset)
```

This method saves the overhead of parsing the query SQL at run time because Jet has already done that job at the time the query was created. Jet need only run the query and return the results.

You can collect the components of a query from the end user and define a QueryDef at run time by using the following code:

```
Dim dbDatabase As Database
Dim rsRecordset As Recordset
Dim qryQueryDef As QueryDef
Dim sSQLStmt As String

Set dbDatabase = CurrentDb()
' Collect the sSQLStmt from the user here
Set qryQueryDef = dbDatabase.CreateQueryDef("qryUserQuery",sSQLStmt)
Set rsRecordset = qryQueryDef.OpenRecordset(,dbOpenDynaset)
qryQueryDef.Close
```

When this code is executed, you realize the overhead of creating the QueryDef due to the parsing required on the entered SQL string. When the query is used again in the application as the source of the dynaset, the dynaset is created more quickly because the SQL string has already been compiled, as shown in the following code:

```
Set rsRecordset = _
dbDatabase.OpenRecordset("qryUserQuery",dbOpenDynaset)
```

You can create a dynaset by specifying a table name. Unlike a table-type Recordset, a dynaset can specify an attached table as the data source. If the table named in the `OpenRecordset` statement is an attached table, then a dynaset Recordset is created by default. Specifying the `dbOpenDynaset` option isn't necessary in this situation. If the table name is a local table, however, the `dbOpenDynaset` option needs to be present or a table-type Recordset is created instead of a dynaset.

It is good programming practice to always specify the type of Recordset being created. Because it is sometimes difficult to determine the type of Recordset from the `OpenRecordset` statement, this specification helps to improve the readability of your code by stating the type.

To specify a table name as the data source, use a statement such as the following:

```
Set rsRecordset = dbDatabase.OpenRecordset("Pubs",dbOpenDynaset)
```

Another means of creating a dynaset is to specify another dynaset or table Recordset as the source, as follows:

```
Dim dbDatabase As Database
Dim rsRecordset1 As Recordset
Dim rsRecordset2 As Recordset

Set dbDatabase = CurrentDb()
Set rsRecordset1 =
dbDatabase.OpenRecordset("qryObjects",dbOpenDynaset)
Set rsRecordset2 = rsRecordset1.OpenRecordset(,dbOpenDynaset)
```

Running a query creates Recordset1 in the preceding code. The first Recordset is used to create rsRecordset2. Both are dynasets and both contain the same set of records at this point.

Dynasets are updatable if the Updatable property is True. As in the case of the table-type Recordset, the Updatable property is True if at least one of the fields in the Recordset is updatable.

A dynaset is not updatable if any one of the following applies:

- The database object was opened as read-only.
- The underlying tables or fields are read-only.
- The underlying table permissions do not allow the current user to update.
- The underlying ODBC or Paradox tables do not have a unique index.

Be aware that your code creating these Recordsets is being executed on behalf of the user logged into a Jet session. All of the user's permissions to objects referenced in the session apply and may prohibit updating and even reading. Always be sure to code error routines to handle these types of situations.

OpenRecordset options that apply to dynasets are dbAppendOnly, dbDenyWrite, dbSeeChanges, dbInconsistent, and dbConsistent.

dbAppendOnly opens the Recordset for appending new records. Other actions, such as updating and deleting, are not allowed with this option and result in a trappable error if someone attempts them.

If you require that other users be denied access to the records in your dynaset, you can specify the dbDenyWrite option. Although other users can read the records contained within your dynaset, they cannot modify them and they cannot add records. You have exclusive control over the dynaset records until you close the dynaset. This option reduces the need for an elaborate error-handling procedure, but it also reduces concurrency in the database.

The dbSeeChanges option tells Jet to notify you with a trappable error if another user is editing the record you are attempting to edit. Suppose that User A is editing a shared table named Customers in datasheet view and has the No Locks option selected in Tools⇨Options⇨Advanced. Another user, User B, executes the following code at the same time. If User A changes the first record after User B has created the Recordset and set the LockEdits to False, No Locks, User B raises a trappable error when the Update method is issued against the Recordset. Jet raises an error, notifying User B that the data has changed, as shown in the following code:

```
Set dbDatabase = CurrentDb()
Set rsRecordset = dbDatabase.OpenRecordset("Customers", _
dbOpenDynaset, dbSeeChanges)
rsRecordset.LockEdits = False
```

```
rsRecordset.Edit
rsRecordset![Cust Name] = "newname"
rsRecordset.Update
rsRecordset.Close
```

With `No Locks`, Jet doesn't check conflicts until the `Update` method is issued, which is an example of optimistic locking. In this situation, the elimination of `dbSeeChanges` from the `OpenRecordset` statement does not raise an error. Jet applies the update without notification.

The `dbInconsistent` and `dbConsistent` options refer to the edit behavior of multitable dynasets where a one-to-many relationship has been defined. If you have a customers table, for example, with a Customer Number defined as the primary key, and you have an orders table where Customer Number is a non-key field defined with the same data type as the Customer Number of the Customers table, you can establish a one-to-many relationship between the two tables in a join such as the following:

```
sSQLStmt = "SELECT Customers.*,Orders.* FROM Customers INNER JOIN _
Orders ON Customers.[Customer Number] = Orders.[Customer Number]"
Set rsRecordset = _
dbDatabase.OpenRecordset(sSQLStmt,dbOpenDynaset,dbConsistent)
```

When you use `dbConsistent`, you must ensure that records added or updated on the many side of a one-to-many relationship refer to keys that are present on the one side. If you add a record to the many side that does not specify a valid related value from the one side via the join, then a trappable error results. Likewise, when updating records on the one side, you must ensure that the key field does not take on a value that would leave records orphaned on the many side.

Using the `dbInconsistent` option enables the update of records on the one side that cause orphans on the many side. This action does not cause an error unless you have set on Force Referential Integrity in a `Relation` object. With referential integrity on, a trappable error is raised whenever orphans will result from an update.

Tip

You can reduce the need for resources if you open the Recordset by using a `LockEdits` option of `dbReadOnly`. This action essentially results in the same behavior as a snapshot Recordset in that you cannot update records in or add records to the dynaset. The difference is in the way dynaset records are fetched, enabling you to see changes by other users as they occur. The snapshot, as you'll see shortly, takes a picture of the data at a point in time, the point at which the Recordset is opened, but the dynaset fetches records as needed. Being ReadOnly, Jet doesn't need to be concerned with maintaining locks for your dynaset.

Using the Move methods

The Move methods that applied to the table Recordset apply to the dynaset Recordset, too. In a multiuser environment, however, movement through the dynaset does not show any new records added by other users, whereas the table Recordset does.

To visit every record in a dynaset, you can use the code shown in Listing 5-10.

Listing 5-10 Visiting Every Record in a Dynaset

```
Dim dbDatabase As Database
Dim rsRecordset As Recordset
Dim niTableCount As Integer

Set dbDatabase = CurrentDb()
Set rsRecordset = dbDatabase.OpenRecordset _
("DAO Objects",dbOpenDynaset)
Do While Not rsRecordset.EOF
   If rsRecordset![Object Type] = "tabledef" Then
      niTableCount = niTableCount + 1
   End If
   rsRecordset.MoveNext
Loop
rsRecordset.Close
dbDatabase.Close
MsgBox "There are " & Str$(niTableCount) & " tables in DAO Objects"
```

Note that the only difference between this code and that used in the table Recordset is the specification of the Recordset type in the `OpenRecordset` statement.

As you use `MoveNext` to move through a dynaset, Jet fetches one or more records and increments the `RecordCount` property. The `RecordCount` property reflects the total number of records in the dynaset when Jet has fully populated the Recordset.

You can force Jet to fully populate the dynaset by using the `MoveLast` method. This action causes Jet to fetch all the records (keyset) of the dynaset and reflect the number fetched in the `RecordCount` property. Note that as your application deletes or adds records in the dynaset, the `RecordCount` property is adjusted. As other users add records or delete records, the dynaset `RecordCount` property is not affected. To reflect the activity of other users, you have to rebuild the dynaset by using the `Requery` method.

Using the Find methods

To locate a specific record in a dynaset, you need to use the `Find` methods, as shown in Listing 5-11. You cannot use the `Seek` method you used against a table Recordset against a dynaset-type Recordset.

Listing 5-11 Using the Find Methods

```
Dim dbDatabase As Database
Dim rsRecordset As Recordset
Dim niTableCount As Integer, sCriteria As String

Set dbDatabase = CurrentDb()
Set rsRecordset = dbDatabase.OpenRecordset _
("DAO Objects",dbOpenDynaset)
sCriteria = "[Object Type] = 'tabledef'"
rsRecordset.FindFirst sCriteria
Do While Not rsRecordset.NoMatch
   niTableCount = niTableCount + 1
   rsRecordset.FindNext sCriteria
Loop
rsRecordset.Close
dbDatabase.Close
MsgBox "There are " & Str$(niTableCount) & " tables in DAO Objects"
```

The code in Listing 5-11 counts all the `TableDef` objects in the DAO Objects table. Instead of visiting every record using `MoveNext` and inspecting the `Object Type` field for a value of `TableDef`, this code uses the `Find` methods to locate all records with `ObjectType` equal to `"TableDef"`.

The `FindFirst` method finds the first occurrence of the specified criteria. You specify the criteria argument used with the `Find` methods just as you do in an SQL `Where` clause, except that you do not use the keyword `Where` in the criteria string.

If a `Find` method does not locate a record matching the specified criteria, the `NoMatch` property is set to `True`. If `Find` locates a match, however, the `NoMatch` is `False`. The code uses this property to control the `Do` loop, which counts the records matching the criteria. Inside the loop, the `FindNext` method locates the next record with the criteria. Whereas `FindFirst` starts its search from the beginning of the dynaset, `FindNext` starts searching from the current position.

You may also use `FindLast` to locate the last record with the specified criteria and `FindPrevious` to locate the record previous to the current position.

Using AbsolutePosition and PercentPosition

Two new Recordset properties first made available in Access for Windows 95 are `AbsolutePosition` and `PercentPosition`. Both of these properties are related to the `RecordCount` property.

`AbsolutePosition` indicates the position of the current record with respect to the current value of `RecordCount`. The minimum value of `AbsolutePosition` is `0`, indicating the first record in the Recordset, and the maximum value is `RecordCount -1`. If no records are in the Recordset, the value of `AbsolutePosition` is `-1`.

You can set the value of AbsolutePosition to set the current record. Remember that its value is zero-based, so use 0 to set the current record at the first record. If you set the value equal to or greater than the value of RecordCount, the result is a 3001 Invalid argument trappable error.

PercentPosition indicates the relative position of the current record as a percentage of the total RecordCount. Its value range is from 0 to 100. You should ensure that the Recordset is fully populated before using this property; otherwise, its value isn't very meaningful to your end user.

You can set PercentPosition to a value between 0 and 100 percent to set the current record. Depending on the number of records in the Recordset, the value used to set PercentPosition may not be equal to the value read from this property after setting it.

PercentPosition is handy as an indicator of relative position as your end user scrolls through the Recordset. This method is not recommended for setting the current record.

The code in Listing 5-12 illustrates the effects of using AbsolutePosition and Bookmark to position the current record pointer. To see the results, insert this code behind a command button on a form.

Listing 5-12 Positioning the Current Record Pointer Using AbsolutePosition and Bookmark

```
Dim dbDatabase As Database
Dim rsRecordset As Recordset
Dim sSaveBookmark As String

Set dbDatabase = CurrentDb()
Set rsRecordset = dbDatabase.OpenRecordset("DAO Props", _
dbOpenDynaset)

MsgBox "RecordCount before MoveNext is: " & _
Str$(rsRecordset.RecordCount)
rsRecordset.MoveNext
MsgBox "RecordCount after MoveNext is: " & _
Str$(rsRecordset.RecordCount)

rsRecordset.AbsolutePosition = 4
MsgBox "Field 0 at record 4 is: " & rsRecordset.Fields(0)
sSaveBookmark = rsRecordset.Bookmark

rsRecordset.AbsolutePosition = 2
rsRecordset.Delete
MsgBox "AbsolutePosition after delete is: " & _
Str$(rsRecordset.AbsolutePosition)

rsRecordset.AbsolutePosition = 4
MsgBox "Field 0 at record 4 after deleting record 2 is: " & _
rsRecordset.Fields(0)
```

(continued)

(continued)

```
rsRecordset.Bookmark = sSaveBookmark
MsgBox "Field 0 at saved bookmark after deleting record 2 is: " & _
rsRecordset.Fields(0)
```

This code uses the DAO Props table in CH5.MDB. The DAO Lab uses this table to hold the properties of the object you select in the Lab form. You can use any table for this example, but be sure to specify `dbOpenDynaset` as the Recordset type. The `AbsolutePosition` property isn't valid with the table-type Recordset or snapshot-type Recordsets that only allow forward movement through the Recordset (a Forward-Scrolling-Only Recordset).

The code establishes the Recordset and then displays the value of the `RecordCount` property. Next comes a `MoveNext` method, and the `RecordCount` value again is displayed. Notice that Jet fetches more than one record with a `MoveNext` method.

The `AbsolutePosition` property is then set to `4` to set the current record pointer at the fifth record. You need to use a value you are sure is within the bounds of the `RecordCount` value. The first field's value is displayed to identify the current record. After identifying the record, its bookmark is saved in order to return to this record later in the code.

Next, the code sets the `AbsolutePosition` value to `2` and deletes the record. This action deletes the third record in the Recordset. To see what this delete method does to the `AbsolutePosition` property, the value of the property is displayed. Note that it is `-1` after the deletion, indicating that its value is invalid.

The current record is then set to `4` again by using `AbsolutePosition`, as was done previously, and the display shows the first field's value. Assuming distinct values in the first field of the Recordset, you see a different value from what you saw when you first displayed the fourth record. This difference is due to the `Delete` method decrementing the `RecordCount`. The fifth record in the Recordset after the deletion was the sixth record before the deletion took place. `AbsolutePosition` of `4` is referencing a different record.

The program then sets the Recordset's `Bookmark` property to the value of the bookmark in the string variable. This bookmark is the one saved earlier in the code, when you first visited the fifth record. After setting the current record pointer by using the bookmark, the first field is displayed and this time it is the same value you saw before the deletion took place.

The lesson here is that you should not depend on `AbsolutePosition` to get you to a particular record in an updatable Recordset. For this purpose, always use the `Bookmark` property.

CopyQueryDef method

You can use a Recordset's `CopyQueryDef` method to create another `QueryDef` object, as shown in the following code. This method is only available for Recordsets that have a QueryDef as a source.

```
Dim dbDatabase As Database
Dim rsRecordset As Recordset
Dim qryCopy As QueryDef
Dim qryOrig As QueryDef

Set dbDatabase = CurrentDb()
Set qryOrig = dbDatabase.QueryDefs("qryCustomers")
Set rsRecordset = qryOrig.OpenRecordset(, dbOpenDynaset)
Set qryCopy = rsRecordset.CopyQueryDef
```

The `CopyQueryDef` method can be useful for accessing the Recordset's SQL statement and creating a duplicate query in a procedure receiving a Recordset as an argument.

Rebuilding the Recordset with the Requery method

When referring to tables shared in a multiuser environment, your dynaset can quickly become outdated. As other users add records that qualify as members in your dynaset, you do not see these records because Jet's keyset underlying the dynaset does not contain the new record keys.

Likewise, as other users delete records that are members of your dynaset, your code experiences trappable errors as you attempt to access those deleted records. Jet still retains the key of these records in its keyset and doesn't realize that they have been deleted until accessing the data.

To bring your dynaset up to date, you need to rebuild it by using the `Requery` method. `Requery` executes the dynaset's record source, which causes Jet to repopulate the keyset. This action removes records that were deleted by other users and adds records that were added by other users.

Recordsets built from tables do not support the `Requery` method. In this case, the Recordset's `Restartable` property is set to `False`, and using the `Requery` method causes a trappable error. See the following example:

```
Dim dbDatabase As Database
Dim rsRecordset As Recordset

Set dbDatabase = CurrentDb()
Set rsRecordset = dbDatabase.OpenRecordset _
("DAO Objects",dbOpenDynaset)

...

If rsRecordset.Restartable Then
   rsRecordset.Requery
End If
```

You can also specify another query to be executed instead of the original query. Using this option is essentially the same as using `OpenRecordset`, as follows:

```
rsRecordset.Requery qryNewQuery
```

Snapshot Recordset

A third type of Recordset supported by DAO is the snapshot. This Recordset is a read-only Recordset and is useful for activities where you only need access to the data but do not require updating. Unlike the dynaset, the snapshot consists of the actual data records specified in the record source, not just the keys.

You can create the snapshot three ways: using the `OpenRecordset` method specifying another snapshot as the source object; using the `dbOpenSnapshot` flag with the `OpenRecordset` method of a database object, and using the `dbOpenForwardOnly` as the Recordset type to create a forward-only snapshot.

Snapshots reflect the state of the records contained in them at the time the snapshot was created. After that, Jet does nothing to keep the snapshot up to date with changes to the underlying records.

If another user in a multiuser environment changes a record contained in your snapshot, you do not see those changes. If another user deletes a record, you do not notice the deleted record. To see the effects of other users' changes, you must rebuild the snapshot by using `Requery` or recreate it by using `OpenRecordset`.

ForwardOnly Recordset

Using `dbOpenForwardOnly` as a type in the `OpenRecordset` method restricts movement in the resulting snapshot to forward scrolling. This technique requires less overhead because data fetched isn't required to be cached for subsequent visits. Use this option whenever possible to improve the performance of your application.

Using Clones and RecordsetClones

Access itself uses Recordsets to navigate and modify tables underlying the forms you create and bind to a table or query. Your code can access these Recordsets by referencing the `RecordsetClone` property of a form.

Tip

Setting a `Recordset` object variable to the `RecordsetClone` property of a form creates a copy of the Recordset underlying the form. You can use this Recordset as you do any other `Recordset` variable. This capability enables you to access the same records available to the form view, independently of the form itself.

The code shown in Listing 5-13 in the SumUnits form of CH5.MDB sums the UnitsOnOrder fields for the supplier of the current record in the form. This process yields a total of all units on order from a given supplier across all products from that supplier.

Listing 5-13 Using the RecordsetClone Property of the SumUnits Form

```
Dim rsRecordset As Recordset
Dim sSupplier As String, totUnits, criteria As String
Dim fdUnitsOnOrder As Field

Set rsRecordset = Forms!SumUnits.RecordsetClone
rsRecordset.Bookmark = Forms!SumUnits.Bookmark
sSupplier = rsRecordset!SupplierID
criteria = "[SupplierID] = " & sSupplier
Set fdUnitsOnOrder = rsRecordset!UnitsOnOrder
rsRecordset.FindFirst criteria
While Not rsRecordset.NoMatch
   totUnits = totUnits + fdUnitsOnOrder
   rsRecordset.FindNext criteria
Wend
txtTotUnits = totUnits
```

The `Recordset` variable `rsRecordset` is assigned the value of the SumUnits form's `RecordsetClone` property. This assignment creates a copy of the form's Recordset and points the `Recordset` variable to it.

The form's `Bookmark` property is assigned to the Recordset's bookmark to synchronize the current record of the Recordset with that of the form's Recordset. This synchronization takes place to pick up the current record's `SupplierID` value through the RecordsetClone. The code could have referenced this field's value through the form as well.

The code next sets a criteria string to enable searching of the `RecordsetClone` for all records containing the current `SupplierID`.

Because the code loops through all records of the Recordset and references the UnitsOnOrder field inside the `While` loop, it is usually more efficient to assign the referenced field to a field object variable and reference this variable's default property, the `Value` property. The next statement in the code carries out this task.

The `FindFirst` method of the Recordset locates the first occurrence of the `SupplierID` in the RecordsetClone. The code then goes into a `While` loop until the `Find` raises a `NoMatch` condition. The loop adds the value of the UnitsOnOrder field through the `Field` variable `Value` property until all records for the `SupplierID` have been added.

The total of `UnitsOnOrder` is then assigned to the text box in the form's footer for display to the user.

You can use the `Bookmark` property in reverse of the way it is used here. If you locate a particular record in the RecordsetClone, you can synchronize the form to it by setting the form's Bookmark equal to the `Bookmark` property of the RecordsetClone, as follows:

```
Forms!SumUnits.Bookmark = rsRecordset.Bookmark
```

This technique is very useful for implementing a find routine on your form. Use a Find button to associate a text box to collect the value to search for from the user. Behind the Find button, search the RecordsetClone for the value specified in the text box. If found, set the form's bookmark equal to the RecordsetClone's bookmark to move the form's current record to the record found in the search. The FindCustomer form of CH5.MDB demonstrates this process.

At times, you may want to create another Recordset based on the same records as a current Recordset. You can use this second Recordset to move independently of the original.

To create a copy of an existing Recordset, use the RecordsetClone method, as shown here:

```
Dim rsRecordset As Recordset
Dim rsRecordsetClone As Recordset

...

Set rsRecordset = dbDatabase.OpenRecordset("qryQuery",dbOpenDynaset)
Set rsRecordsetClone = rsRecordset.Clone
rsRecordsetClone.MoveFirst
```

You can use the code used with the form RecordsetClone with a Recordset created in code. Using the rsRecordsetClone, you can move through the records independently of the rsRecordset. You can implement finds or accumulations in the copy while holding your current record position in the original Recordset. This capability eliminates the need to manage bookmarks within a single Recordset.

The clone reflects any record modifications made in one Recordset because the clone and the original are the same Recordset but with different record pointers.

Working with Attached Tables

When you open a table contained within the current database, CurrentDb(), you are opening a *local* table, sometimes referred to as a *base* table. Jet is aware of the table location in the currently open database.

Jet can access tables in external databases, including FoxPro, dBASE, Paradox, ODBC sources (such as SQL Server), and even Excel spreadsheets and text files. You can also attach Access 2.0 and Access 95 tables. A variety of methods are available to access these external databases. One method, and usually the best performing, is *attached* tables.

Attaching, or *linking,* to external database tables involves telling Jet where the database containing the table is located and which table in the database to reference. The Connect property provides location information. The SourceTableName property provides the table information. Both properties are properties of the TableDef object.

The following code segment adds an attached Access table from the NWIND.MDB sample that ships with Access 97 to the current database:

```
Dim dbDatabase As Database
Dim tdTabledef As TableDef

' Create an attached table
Set dbDatabase = CurrentDb()

Set tdTabledef = dbDatabase.CreateTableDef("Suppliers")
tdTabledef.Connect = _
";DATABASE=c:\msoffice\office\samples\northwind.mdb"
tdTabledef.SourceTableName = "Suppliers"
dbDatabase.TableDefs.Append tdTabledef

Set tdTabledef = dbDatabase.CreateTableDef("Categories")
tdTabledef.Connect = _
";DATABASE=c:\msoffice\office\samples\northwind.mdb"
tdTabledef.SourceTableName = "Categories"
dbDatabase.TableDefs.Append tdTabledef
```

The code first creates a `TableDef` object by using the `CreateTableDef` method of the `Database` object. The developer chooses the name supplied for the TableDef, which can be any legal name. The name need not be the same as the table name in the external database, but it helps to document your application if you do use the external name.

After creating the TableDef, the `Connect` property is set to inform Jet of the database's location. The `Connect` property consists of several parts, depending on the type of external database being referenced. The first argument of the connect string is a database type specifier, but for Jet databases, you do not enter this argument. Subsequent parameters specify the path to the database, as indicated in Table 5-4.

Table 5-4 Connect Property Arguments

Type of Database Being Referenced	*Type Specifier DATABASE=*	*Database Path:*
Jet database	`"[database];"`	`"drive:\path\filename.MDB"`
dBASE III	`"dBASE III;"`	`"drive:\path"`
dBASE IV	`"dBASE IV;"`	`"drive:\path"`
dBASE 5	`"dBASE 5;"`	`"drive:\path"`
Paradox 3.*x*	`"Paradox 3.x;"`	`"drive:\path"`
Paradox 4.*x*	`"Paradox 4.x;"`	`"drive:\path"`
Paradox 5.*x*	`"Paradox 5.x;"`	`"drive\path"`

(continued)

Table 5-4 *(continued)*

Type of Database Being Referenced	*Type Specifier DATABASE=*	*Database Path:*
Btrieve	`"Btrieve;"`	`"drive:\path\filename.DDF"`
FoxPro 2.0	`"FoxPro 2.0;"`	`"drive:\path"`
FoxPro 2.5	`"FoxPro 2.5;"`	`"drive:\path"`
FoxPro 2.6	`"FoxPro 2.6;"`	`"drive:\path"`
Excel 3.0	`"Excel 3.0;"`	`"drive:\path\filename.XLS"`
Excel 4.0	`"Excel 4.0;"`	`"drive:\path\filename.XLS"`
Excel 5.0	`"Excel 5.0;"`	`"drive:\path\filename.XLS"`
Excel 7.0	`"Excel 7.0;"`	`"drive:\path\filename.XLS"`
HTML Export	`"HTML Export;"`	`"drive:\path"`
HTML Import	`"HTML Import;"`	`"drive:\path\filename"`
Text	`"Text;"`	`"drive:\path"`
ODBC	`"ODBC; DATABASE=defaultdatabase; UID=user; PWD=password; DSN=datasourcename; LOGINTIMEOUT=seconds"`	None

You specify the path to the sample NWIND.MDB as the path parameter completing the `Connect` property. With this specification, Jet has enough information to locate the database.

The next statement sets the `SourceTableName` property to specify the name of the table in the connect string database to reference. This example is attaching the Suppliers table.

These two properties are sufficient to enable Jet to complete the attachment. The next statement appends the TableDef to the database `TableDefs` collection, which causes Jet to attempt the attachment. If the attempt is successful, the attached table appears in the Access database container window with an attached table icon.

The benefit of the attachment is that Jet locally stores information about the attached table. This information consists of the location information just discussed and information about the table's fields, which Jet uses whenever you access the attached table.

Because the attached table is an external table and the information about it is stored locally, if the table is changed in some way, renamed, or relocated, you must inform Jet of the change. To give Jet this information, you use the `RefreshLink` method of the database object, as follows:

```
Dim dbDatabase As Database
Dim tdTabledef As TableDef

' ReLink the attached tables
Set dbDatabase = CurrentDb()
Set tdTabledef = dbDatabase.TableDefs("Suppliers")
tdTabledef.RefreshLink
Set tdTabledef = dbDatabase.TableDefs("Categories")
tdTabledef.RefreshLink
```

You need an error-handler routine, as you should have in every procedure, to handle the connection error should the link to the database or table fail. In your error routine, you can prompt the user for the current location information or read it from an application .INI file or Registry entry if the error was a connection error. You then can reestablish the connection string and attempt the link again. You may want to add a counter to the error routine to count the connection attempts and fail the application if the attempts exceed a certain limit.

To determine whether a table is an attached table or a local table, you can check the `Connect` property. Local tables have an empty string.

Although attached tables provide a performance benefit, they do have some limitations. If you run the DAO Lab and inspect the properties of an attached table, you see that the `Updatable` property is set to `False`. This setting means that you cannot change the table definition from within the current database.

You are prevented from opening a table Recordset on an attached table source. You can open a snapshot or dynaset Recordset, but attempting to open a table Recordset yields an invalid operation error. You can circumvent this limitation by using the `OpenDatabase` method of the `Workspace` object. `OpenDatabase` is discussed in the "Using the OpenDatabase method" section of this chapter.

To remove an attached table from a database, use the `Delete` method of the `TableDefs` collection, as follows:

```
dbDatabase.TableDefs.Delete "Suppliers"
```

This method removes only the link information from the database; it does not delete the physical table, as it would if the table were local.

Chapter 21, "Working with Client/Server Databases," presents more details on using attached ODBC tables and views.

Considering Performance

This section presents some performance improvement techniques you should consider when building your application. Ideally, you achieve the best performance if you have the database exclusively dedicated to your application. This dedication certainly improves your application speed, but it severely impacts other users trying to accomplish their work.

Exclusive use of the database is an alternative, however, especially for heavy maintenance work, when multiuser access is not critical. When multiuser access is necessary, you need to find methods of balancing performance and concurrency.

ODBC performance considerations are presented in Chapter 21, "Working with Client/Server Databases."

Using GetRows

If your application needs to loop through a number of records for one reason or another, you can improve performance by pulling the records into an array and looping through the array instead of the Recordset.

Accessing a table on disk every time you need to refer to a record can add considerable overhead to your application. Using a snapshot can improve performance, but this technique also adds a small overhead to your code in that referencing the fields of the Recordset requires code to map the DAO field reference to the actual field in the Recordset row.

Bringing the records into an array in memory can speed up the processing because disk read operations are reduced or eliminated, especially if your application requires several passes over a given set of records. `GetRows` is a method of building an array of records in memory and can be a valuable addition to your application. You use `GetRows` as shown in Listing 5-14.

Listing 5-14 Using GetRows to Build an Array of Records in Memory

```
Dim dbDatabase As Database
Dim rsRecordset As Recordset
Dim niMaxRows As Integer, niRow As Integer
Dim SQLStmt As String
Dim varOrders
Const NUMROWS = 10

Set dbDatabase = CurrentDb()
```

```
SQLStmt = "SELECT [Order Number],[Product ID],[Quantity] FROM _
Orders"
Set rsRecordset = dbDatabase.OpenRecordset(SQLStmt, dbOpenSnapshot)

While Not rsRecordset.EOF
   varOrders = rsRecordset.GetRows(NUMROWS)
   niMaxRows = UBound(varOrders, 2) + 1
   For niRow = 0 To niMaxRows
      ' do something with varOrders(0,niRow)    Order Number
      ' or with varOrders(1,niRow)                   Product ID
      ' or with varOrders(2,niRow)                   Quantity
   Next niRow
Wend
rsRecordset.Close
Exit Sub
```

The code in Listing 5-14 creates a snapshot of records from the Orders table in CH5.MDB consisting of three columns: Order Number, Product ID, and Quantity.

After creating the snapshot, the program enters a loop until the Recordset `EOF` is `True`. Inside the loop, the `GetRows` method fetches `NUMROWS`, in this case `10`, into an array named `varOrders`, which you have defined as a variant. After each `GetRows` method, the program uses a `For` loop to cycle through the returned records from the first record to the upper bound of the array, because there is no guarantee that all 10 records were returned. Inside the `For` loop, the code references the fields it needs in the array.

`GetRows` returns an array of two dimensions. The first dimension is the field, and the second dimension is the row. The first field of the first row, the Order Number, is `varOrders(0,0)`, and the second field of the first row, the Product ID, is `varOrders(1,0)`.

After every `GetRows`, the current record is the record after the last one fetched into the array. If the number of records requested, in this case `10`, is not available, `GetRows` returns the number remaining. By using the `Ubound` function, you can determine how many records `GetRows` returns, as in the following:

```
niMaxRows = UBound(varOrders, 2) + 1
```

`Ubound` returns the highest subscript value of the array for the dimension specified. Because you want to know how many rows are present, the `Ubound` function looks at the second subscript. The array is zero-based, so it adds `1` to the result to get the number of rows.

This method does its processing on the array rather than on the snapshot Recordset to save the expense of referencing the Recordset fields in a loop. The savings, of course, depends on what the program needs to do with the records, how many fields it needs to reference, and how many times it needs to visit each record.

Additionally, if the Recordset contains any memo fields, the code fetches those fields into the array as well.

Using Field objects

In referencing the fields of a Recordset inside a loop that visits a large number of records, use `Field` objects instead of field references.

Whenever a field reference such as `rsRecordset!field` is found in your code, it must be mapped to a specific field location within the record. This mapping adds a slight overhead to the code, and inside a loop through a large number of records, the overhead can be very time consuming.

To remove the overhead, replace the field references with `Field` objects that already point to the field locations, as illustrated here:

```
Dim fldQuantity As Field, fldCustNumber As Field

Set fldQuantity = rsRecordset!Quantity
Set fldCustNumber = rsRecordset![Cust Number]

While Not rsRecordset.EOF
   If fldCustNumber = 7 Then
     rsRecordset.Edit
     fldQuantity = fldQuantity + 5
     rsRecordset.Update
     End If
   rsRecordset.MoveNext
Wend
```

In this code, the references to the field objects use the default properties of the `Field` objects, the `Value` properties, to access the field's contents.

Using indexes

Indexes on tables enable Jet to optimize your queries. An index can speed up the selection of data when the index is based on a `Where` clause in the query, and an index can speed up the access of data across multiple tables related through a join. To use the phone book analogy, you can locate phone numbers much more quickly by using the keys at the top of the pages to narrow your search rather than paging through each page of the phone book looking for a name.

Tip

Although techniques for speeding up the sequential search of a Recordset are available, indexes give the best performance improvement. You should carefully consider the choice of indexes, however, because they also play a role in updates. Each index selected must be maintained whenever the column (or columns) on which the index is based changes value. Such changes can impact the use of the index by other users because the index must be locked for a brief time while Jet updates it. Locking on the table records and the index records can impact not only other users of the database but your application throughput as well.

The choice of indexes for the database is a result of a design step known as *data access modeling*. Data access modeling is a phase of the design process in which you consider the database accesses required by your code and by users through forms. This step occurs later in the design, after developing the data model or structure of the database — which is also a concern for performance — and before implementation. The access model also needs to be revisited from time to time during the life of the application because requirements and database use are always changing.

In addition to speeding up queries, indexes also provide better performance for ordering your data in a table Recordset. If you can use a table Recordset and the data needs to be ordered, especially in large tables, use an index rather than the `Sort` property of the Recordset.

Using transactions

When you use the update method of a Recordset, Jet takes a lock on the page containing the record to be updated, preventing other users from changing the data until the record is updated with your update. After applying the update, Jet releases the lock, enabling other users to gain access to it.

This action involves multiple disk I/O to carry out the update request. In a large update operation, many of these disk writes occur, each of which takes a considerable chunk of time in which the CPU is doing nothing for your application.

In addition to slowing down your application, updates on a table-by-table basis can corrupt the integrity of your database if one table is updated but another table's update fails. Your application can become complicated very quickly if you attempt to handle these partial updates through code.

To speed up the application throughput and to preserve the integrity of your data, you can use *transactions* to do the updating. By determining a complete unit of work for your application, a set of updates that need to be completed together, and encasing that unit of work in a transaction, you can preserve the integrity of the database and simplify your code.

The transaction is a method of the `Workspace` object and applies to all databases open in the workspace. Before using transactions, always check the `Transactions` property of the database or Recordset being updated to ensure that transactions are supported. See Listing 5-15 for an example.

Listing 5-15 Setting a Workspace Object to Enable Transaction Processing

```
On Error GoTo ErrHandler

Dim dbDatabase As Database
Dim rsRecordset As Recordset
Dim qryQueryDef As QueryDef
Dim wsWorkspace As Workspace
Dim transactive As Integer

Set wsWorkspace = Workspaces(0)
Set dbDatabase = CurrentDb()

Set qryQueryDef = dbDatabase.QueryDefs("qryCustOrders")
qryQueryDef("CustNbr") = 7
Set rsRecordset = qryQueryDef.OpenRecordset(dbOpenDynaset)
rsRecordset.LockEdits = False

transactive = rsRecordset.Transactions
If Not transactive Then
   MsgBox "Transactions not supported"
Else
   wsWorkspace.BeginTrans
End If

While Not rsRecordset.EOF
   rsRecordset.Edit
   rsRecordset![Quantity] = 15
   rsRecordset.Update
   rsRecordset.MoveNext
Wend

If Not transactive Then
Else
   wsWorkspace.CommitTrans
End If
rsRecordset.Close
Exit Sub

ErrHandler:
  MsgBox "Error: " & Str$(Err) & ":" & Error$(Err)
  If Not transactive Then
  Else
     wsWorkspace.Rollback
  End If
  Exit Sub
```

The code sample in Listing 5-15 sets a workspace object to enable the transaction processing. The transaction starts with the `wsWorkspace.BeginTrans` statement. At this point, all update activity is buffered until the procedure encounters either a `CommitTrans` or a `Rollback`. In this sample, the code issues a `Rollback` if an error is raised during the updates. If all updates succeed, the code issues a `CommitTrans` statement to save all updates to disk.

The locking considerations presented earlier in this chapter are also valid with transactions. The BeginTrans does not lock tables, but, depending on the edit strategy in place as specified by the LockEdits property, the Edit or Update method takes locks. The difference between transactions and updates without transactions is that the locks taken inside transactions are held until the transaction is committed or rolled back.

Remember that if multiple databases are open in the workspace and have been changed since the transaction occurred, committing or rolling back the transaction affects all the databases. You can specify a Database object to issue the transaction statements. When looking at this situation in code, it implies that the transaction applies only to the database specified, but actually it applies to the workspace in which the Database object is open. This capability is convenient but confusing, so it is not recommended. Use a Workspace object to maintain transactions.

Using the OpenDatabase method

Attached tables have the limitation of your not being able to open them as table Recordsets. Because table Recordsets are usually faster to work with than other types of Recordsets and you can use Seek to locate records through the use of an index instead of using the slower Find methods, using a table Recordset has significant advantages for performance.

Instead of using attached tables, you can open the table's containing database directly by using OpenDatabase and then set a Recordset to the desired table, as in the following:

```
Set database = [workspace.]OpenDatabase(dbname[, exclusive[, read- _
only[, source]]])
To open the NWIND.MDB database directly in code, use the following:
Dim dbDatabase As Database
Dim rsRecordset As Recordset

Set dbDatabase = _
OpenDatabase("C:\MSOFFICE\OFFICE\SAMPLES\NORTHWIND.MDB", False, _
False, _ "")
```

After opening the database, you can set your Recordset, as follows:

```
Set rsRecordset = dbDatabase.OpenRecordset("Suppliers", dbOpenTable)
```

With the Recordset opened as a table Recordset, you may now perform a Seek by using any index available. Had you attempted to open the Suppliers table as an attached table, Jet would have issued an Invalid Operation error.

The difference between the direct reference and the attached is that in the direct open method, Jet needs to determine the connection and characteristics of the objects being referenced every time the reference is made; Jet knows nothing about the database you are opening or the table you are referencing. Jet needs this information to satisfy your access requests.

With attached tables, Jet already has the information it needs cached in the local database. When you look at an attached table in DAO Lab, you can see the table's `Fields` collection, its connect string, and other properties. Jet uses all this information to access the table and to build queries. If you open the table's database directly, Jet needs to collect the missing information dynamically in order to access the data.

Although you can open ODBC data sources in the same way, it is better not to do so because the amount of overhead required to retrieve the necessary information is far greater than for a local database. In fact, if a network is between Jet and the database you are opening, carefully consider the choice of using attachments or directly opening the database.

Chapter 6

Working with OLE and ActiveX Controls

In This Chapter

- Understanding Automation
- Using type libraries and references
- Using the Object Browser
- Using OLE objects in your application
- Using Microsoft Access objects
- Exploring ActiveX controls

OLE 2.0 offers many features to the application developer to enable application integration. *Linking and embedding* are two features supported by Access that allow your application forms and reports to exhibit documents from other applications. Through linking and embedding, an OLE server application can provide its objects, particularly the objects visible to the end user, to a client application. The client can then present these objects through its own interface and, if desired, can use the server to edit the objects.

Automation is another integration feature of OLE. Automation enables a client application to manipulate a server's objects through the management of the object's properties and methods. Automation often provides a rich set of functionality that is available through VBA code. Using Automation, for example, your application can create a Word document or an Excel worksheet, edit those objects, possibly based on input from your application's end user, and save those objects. The Word or Excel documents resulting from your editing through Automation are no different from those resulting from direct end-user interaction with Word or Excel. Automation is remote control, whether on the same machine or across the network.

A third feature of OLE supported by Access is *ActiveX controls*. ActiveX controls are embeddable objects that provide properties, methods, and events just like built-in Access controls. Your applications can be greatly enhanced — and you can save hours of development time — through the use of the many controls available from Microsoft and other vendors.

This chapter focuses on how you can use Automation and ActiveX controls to build robust and feature-rich Access applications.

Understanding Automation

Applications that offer their object models to other applications are called *automation servers*. Applications that use another application's object model are called *automation controllers*. Access 97 is both an automation server and an automation controller. This means that applications such as Excel, Word, and others can work with Access objects such as forms and reports without the end user of those applications ever seeing Access on the desktop. Likewise, as a controller, Access can use the objects of Excel and Word, plus others that are written to perform server functions.

Objects are managed through their properties and methods. The *properties* of an object describe the object's behavior and identify the object. The object's *methods* enable a client to create an *instance* of an object and to manipulate the state of the object, possibly changing some of its properties.

Chapter 5, "Working with Data Access Objects," presented the Data Access Object hierarchy as a set of objects that enable an application to create and manipulate databases, tables, queries, Recordsets, fields, and others. The DAO server application exposes these objects to other applications. None of the objects supported by DAO is visible to the end user. The client application, such as Access, must present the user interface. DAO is an example of OLE Automation used to integrate the functionality of the Jet engine with client applications that want to provide database features.

Type libraries and references

Automation servers provide a library describing the objects they expose. The library is known as a *type library* and contains descriptions, properties, and methods of all the objects the server provides. The usual type library file suffixes are .TLB and .OLB, but the file may also be contained inside the server .EXE or .DLL, eliminating the need for a separate .TLB or .OLB file.

If a client application wants to use an object, such as a DAO Database object, a reference to DAO's type library enables VBA to check the usage of object properties and methods. Without the type library reference, VBA does not recognize a statement such as `Dim dbDatabase As Database`; VBA issues an error message that states `User-defined type is not defined`. Visual Basic assumes that `Database` should have a `Type ... End Type` definition and doesn't realize that `Database` is a DAO object.

Visual Basic can check the validity of a reference to an object's properties and methods if VBA knows about the type library describing the object. For example, consider the following code:

```
Dim niCount As Integer
Dim dbDatabase As Object

Set dbDatabase = DBEngine.OpenDatabase("C:\MSOffice\Access\CH6.MDB")
niCount = dbDatabase.TableDef.Count
```

Without a reference to the DAO type library, this code compiles without error, but running it results in the error message `Run-time error 438, object doesn't support this property or method`. Visual Basic invoked the `DBEngine` to create the database object and set a reference to it in the generic `Object` variable. When the statement to retrieve the database object's `TableDef` collection `Count` property is executed, DAO returned the error, because `TableDef` is specified instead of `TableDefs`.

With a reference to the DAO 3.5 type library, you can change the generic object type from `Object` to `Database`. At compile time, rather than at run time, Visual Basic can determine that `TableDef` doesn't support a `Count` property or method. You receive the error message `Property or method not found` at compile time instead of waiting until run time to discover the error. Using a reference to provide Visual Basic with information about external objects at compile time is known as *early binding*. Using generic object types instead of specific object types, even if you have a reference to the appropriate type library, doesn't enable Visual Basic to verify external objects until run time. This is known as *late binding*.

You can see from this small example that type library references are not necessary for Automation. Had the preceding error been corrected by adding an `s` to `TableDef` and leaving the `dbDatabase` variable as a generic `Object` type, the code would have executed properly. The disadvantage is that errors in object references are not discovered until run time and the code would run more slowly due to Visual Basic's need to verify object references.

A reference to a type library can also aid coding. After establishing the type library reference, you can use the Object Browser to view a list of the objects offered by the server and their properties and methods. Selecting a method provides a syntactically correct statement that you can paste into your code. This feature can help reduce errors and accelerate development.

To add a reference into your project, follow these steps:

1. While in design mode of any module, open the Tools menu and choose References.
2. If the object server library is already registered in the system Registry, you can check it from the Available References list box (see Figure 6-1).
3. If the server library is not yet registered, you can click on the Browse button to locate it and then select it in the Add Reference dialog box.
4. As you select libraries in the Available References list box, the Path in the Result frame displays the path to the type library.

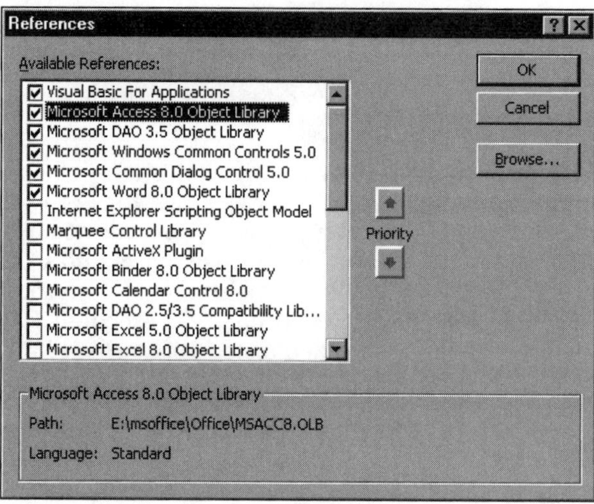

Figure 6-1: Use the References dialog box to add references to OLE server type libraries into your project.

If a .TLB or .OLB is not available but you suspect that a server provides objects, you can attempt to choose the application .EXE or .DLL in the Add Reference dialog box. If a type library is not provided by the .EXE or .DLL, you get the following message:

```
Can't add a reference to the specified file
```

Adding a type library reference through the Add Reference dialog box also registers the library in the system Registry. The next time the References dialog box is opened in any project, the Available References list box displays the added library.

Using the References collection

VBA enables you to use the `References` collection to add and remove references to other projects and type libraries in code. In addition to the methods made available for adding and removing references, there are associated events — the `ItemAdded` event and the `ItemRemoved` event — that you can code to perform some processing when a reference is added or removed.

References added in code to the `References` collection are *persistent,* that is, they remain associated with the database after closing the database. After it's added, the reference will be available in the Object Browser until it is removed either through the `Remove` method or manually through the References dialog box.

CH6.MDB, which is on the CD-ROM that accompanies this book, shows an example of adding a reference in code. The frmExamples form contains a References command button with the following code:

```
Private Sub cmdReferences_Click()
 On Error GoTo RefErrHandler
  Dim oRef As Reference

  ' Initialize the references variable
  Set RefEvent = References

  ' Add a reference to Word 97
  Set oRef = RefEvent.AddFromFile("E:\MSoffice\Office\msword8.olb")

  Exit Sub
RefErrHandler:
  MsgBox Err.Description, 16, "References Error"
  Exit Sub
End Sub
```

In order to detect when a reference is added to or removed from the project, a `References` variable is declared with the `WithEvents` option. This option enables you to detect the `References` collection `ItemAdded` and `ItemRemoved` events. In the code example, a variable called `RefEvent` is declared in the class module declarations, as shown here:

```
Public WithEvents RefEvent As References
```

`RefEvent` is an object variable, a `References` object variable. Before it can be used, it must be set to the `References` collection of the `Application` object.

After the event variable is set, it can be used to add a reference. In this case, a reference to Word 97 is being added to the project with the `AddFromFile` method. `AddFromFile` specifies the path and file name of the desired type library, as follows:

```
  Set oRef = RefEvent.AddFromFile("E:\MSoffice\Office\msword8.olb")
```

Because the event object variable `RefEvent` is used as the `References` collection, it's `ItemAdded` event fires after the reference to Word 97 is added to the project. By selecting the `RefEvent` from the frmExamples module object list, you have access to the two events supported by the `References` collection. In the example code, a message box was added to the `ItemAdded` event procedure to display the name, path, and version of the library being added. That code is as follows:

```
Private Sub RefEvent_ItemAdded(ByVal Reference As Access.Reference)
  MsgBox "Reference " & Reference.Name & " added. Path is: _
 " & Reference.FullPath & vbCrLf & _
    "Version is: " & Reference.Major & "." & Reference.Minor
End Sub
```

Note that the `ItemAdded` event procedure receives a `Reference` object representing the library being added. The procedure then uses several properties of the `Reference` object to display the desired information.

A more realistic application of `References` would use this code in a class module. If your class requires a particular object — a Word document, for example — you could establish a reference to the Word type library when your class is instantiated and remove the reference when the class was no longer needed. The questions now are "How does your class know when it is being created?" and "How does it know when it is no longer needed?" The answer to these questions lies in two class module events that are covered in the "Examining class modules" section later in this chapter.

Using the Object Browser

After an OLE Server's type library is added to a project, opening the Object Browser displays the objects described in the library.

While in module design mode, you have three ways of choosing Object Browser: the View menu, the F2 function key, or the Object Browser toolbar button (see Figure 6-2).

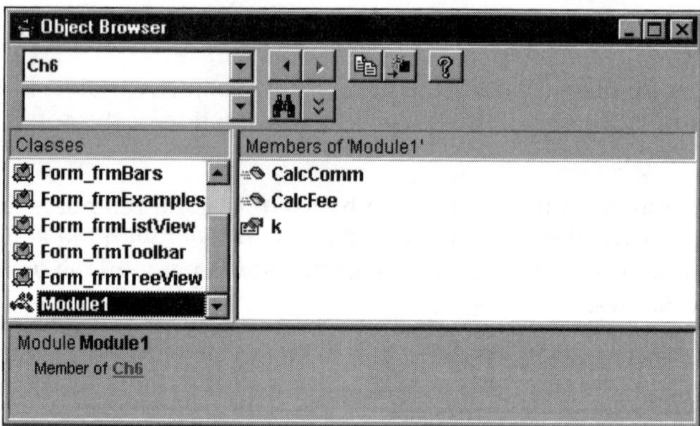

Figure 6-2: The Object Browser displays the objects exposed by an OLE server and the properties and methods available for each object.

The OLE type libraries that have been added to the project through the References dialog box or through code are listed in the Project/Library drop-down list box. Selecting one of these libraries displays the available classes in the Classes list box. Selecting one of the classes displays the methods and properties in the Members list box.

After choosing a method or property in the Members list box, you can copy the member syntax to the Clipboard and paste it into your code module where desired.

Using Objects in Your Application

Through OLE, you can enhance your Access application in powerful ways. You can open and manipulate Excel worksheets, you can create Word documents, and you can use a growing collection of other applications from within your own application. You can use many of these objects without your end user ever seeing another application on the screen.

This section presents an overview of using objects in your application code. In addition to learning how to create and manipulate OLE objects exposed by other applications, you'll see how to develop your own objects by using Class modules. Property procedures, a new feature of Access, implement the properties of your objects, and standard sub and function procedures provide the methods. You also learn how you can use Access as an OLE server to expose your application objects to any OLE Controller application.

Creating objects

You manipulate an object's methods and properties through object variables defined in your application. These variables are declared to be either a generic or a specific object type. The variables are set with a reference to an instance of an object corresponding to that type.

You can declare a variable to be a generic type `Object` and assign any Automation object type to it, as follows:

```
Dim  objGeneric As Object
```

You can declare other object types that are more specific than `Object` but still generic. Examples of these object types are `Form`, `Control`, and `Report`. DAO offers generic types, such as `Field`, `Table`, `Query`, and `Relation`. Variables of these types can refer to any object of the type declared for the variable. For example, a variable declared as type `Form` can refer to any form in your application, whereas a variable declared as `frmCustomer` can refer only to an instance of the specific form named frmCustomer. Attempting to assign any other form reference to the `frmCustomer` variable causes a `Type Mismatch` error at run time. Use the following syntax:

```
Dim F As [Form_frmCustomer]

DoCmd.OpenForm "frmCustomer "
Set F = Forms![frmCustomer]
```

The `Dim` statement declares `F` as a variable of type `Form` class and specifically references the `Form` class `frmCustomer`. `Form` and `Report` modules are always `Class` modules, as opposed to `Standard` modules. More on this subject follows later in this chapter.

After declaring the object variable, you can instantiate an object and assign it to the variable. You can create the object instance in several ways, depending on the implementation of the object within the server application.

Using the New keyword

Chapter 4, "Understanding Visual Basic for Applications," introduced the New keyword for creating new instances of objects. When using this keyword in an automation controller application, the object being instantiated must be externally creatable. *Externally creatable objects* are those that the server application can create without a dependency on a higher-level object. You need to check your object server's documentation to learn which objects are externally creatable, if any. Usually, you'll find that the server provides at least one externally creatable object. In servers that provide an object hierarchy, such as Access, the top root object is externally creatable. Within Office 97, most applications have an externally creatable object known as Application, and it sits at the root of the application's object hierarchy.

In Access, the top-level externally creatable object is the Application object. You can declare your object variable that points to this object by using the New keyword, as in the following:

```
Dim objAccess As New Access.Application

objAccess.OpenCurrentDatabase _
filepath:="C:\MSOffice\Office\Samples\Orders.Mdb"
```

The Dim statement declares the object variable objAccess to be a New instance of an Access application. The statement itself, however, does not instantiate an instance of Access when the statement is executed.

The new Access Application object is instantiated when the first reference to it is made. In this code example, the execution of the OpenCurrentDatabase method of the Application object starts an instance of Access. Running this code from within Access then results in two instances of Access running on your machine. Obviously, this technique is not one you want to use very often. The server capabilities of Access are meant to be used by other applications, such as Excel, Word, Visual Basic, and so on, much like your use of Excel from within your Access application.

You can force the instantiation of the Application object before the first reference to it. Use the New keyword in a Set statement, as follows:

```
Dim objAccess As Object

Set objAccess = New Access.Application
objAccess.OpenCurrentDatabase ("C:\MSOffice\Access\Samples\Orders.Mdb")
```

In this example, Access launches when the Set statement is executed rather than when the OpenCurrentDatabase method is executed.

You cannot instantiate an instance of an Access Form object in a controller application using New, as shown in the following statements, because the form depends on an Application object and its methods to bring it to life.

```
Dim objForm As New Form_Account

objForm.Rank = 10     ' Fails
```

This code is fine within the Access database in which the Form_Account lives, because the Application object on which the form depends is implied to be the running Access instance.

In an external OLE Controller application, the compiler flags the reference to the New Form_Account because Form_Account is unknown. Access does not provide a reference for Form_Account and does not enable a form to be externally creatable. A technique you can use to instantiate a new form in a controller application is presented in the following code:

```
Dim objBaseForm As Access.Form
Dim objForm As Access.Form
Dim objAccess As Object

Set objAccess = New Access.Application
objAccess.OpenCurrentDatabase ("C:\MSOffice\Office\Samples\CH6.Mdb")
Set objBaseForm = objAccess.DoCmd.OpenForm "frmExamples"
Set objForm = objBaseForm.NewAcct()
objForm.Rank = 10
```

A form within the application can contain a method — the NewAcct method in this example — that instantiates a New Form_Account form and returns a reference to that form. With this technique, a controller application can create new instances of the Account to gain admission to its property procedures and methods. The form object instantiated with the New keyword is not a member of the Forms collection. More on this technique is presented later in this chapter (see the section "Exploring property procedures" for details).

The Application object, whether implied or explicitly created, is required to gain access to the dependent objects of the Access object hierarchy.

Using the CreateObject method

CreateObject is a method of Visual Basic for Applications that creates an Automation object. You can use it instead of the New keyword. To create an instance of Word, for example, and set a reference to its Application object, use the following code:

```
Dim objWord As Object

Set objWord = CreateObject("Word.Application")
```

This code instantiates a Word Application object that starts the Word server application and returns a reference to the objWord variable. You can then use this object variable to manipulate Word objects through the Word Object hierarchy.

Unlike the New keyword used in a Dim statement, the CreateObject method causes the immediate instantiation of an object instance. The object creation doesn't wait for a reference to one of the object's methods or properties.

The Word `Application` object instantiation does not run another instance of Word if Word is already running when the `CreateObject` method is executed. Servers differ in how they respond to the request to create one of their objects. You'll also find that some servers will launch but will not display a window to service your object create request. Access launches as a visible process.

Using the GetObject method

When you want a reference to an object that already exists in a file, you can use the `GetObject` method to set your object variable, using the following syntax:

```
GetObject([pathname][, class])
```

If you specify a zero-length string for the path name argument and then a class name for the class argument, `GetObject` behaves like `CreateObject` and returns a reference to a newly created object of type class.

The following `GetObject` method instantiates an Access Application and opens the specified Orders database. The reference to the `Application` object is returned in the `objAccess` variable.

```
Dim objAccess As Object

Set objAccess = GetObject("C:\MSOffice\Office\Samples\Orders.Mdb")
```

Specify the optional class argument to specifically point to a version of the application server or to a specific object within the file if the server supports direct reference. In the preceding `GetObject` statement, assuming you have Access 95 and Access 97 installed on your machine, you could specify that you want an instance of Access 97 instead of Access 95 by using the following:

```
Set objAccess = _
GetObject("C:\MSOffice\Office\Samples\Orders.Mdb","Access.Application.8")
```

Specifying `Access.Application.8` rather than `Access.Application.7` will cause Access 97 to be used as an object server instead of Access 95.

Using Object properties and methods

You obtain an object's properties and methods through an object variable reference and the *dot syntax*. You can use the Object Browser to determine what properties and methods are available, but you need the object server documentation or help file to find how to use them.

In Access, you see the *dot* (`.`) *operator* and the *exclamation* (`!`) *operator* used in expressions. The exclamation operator denotes that the word following refers to a user-defined type, such as a form, report, or control. The dot operator denotes a type defined by Access or Visual Basic for Applications as a property or method. The following syntax is an example:

```
Forms![Account]![Account Name].Text = "CPBS Inc."
```

The preceding statement uses the ! operator to refer to the form [Account] in the open forms collection and to the control [Account Name] on the [Account] form. The dot operator used here refers to the Text property of the [Account Name] control (a Text box control).

Be aware that controls usually have a default property associated with them. For the Text box control, the Text property is the default property, so that if an expression refers to the control and the property is not specified, the default property is used. You can then write the preceding statement as follows:

```
Forms![Account]![Account Name] = "CPBS Inc."
```

This particular statement works if the text box has the focus. If it doesn't have the focus, you can use the Value property instead of the Text property to assign the string to the text box.

Examining class modules

Class modules are a means of supporting custom objects within your application. You can define a class module to contain several properties and methods through the use of Property procedures and function procedures. After your class is defined, your application can instantiate an object of your class and use its properties and methods in the same way you use other Access or Office objects.

Create a class module by choosing Class Module from the Insert menu. You'll notice that class modules have two event procedures associated with them, the Initialize event and the Terminate event.

The Initialize event fires whenever an instance of your class is created, and the Terminate event fires when all references to the class have been removed. You can insert code into the Initialize event procedure to set up references needed by the class and to initialize data used by the class. Likewise, the Terminate event procedure can contain code to remove references and to perform any clean-up operations before the class is removed from memory.

CH6.MDB (on this book's CD-ROM) contains a class module called WelcomeLetter. The intent of this class is to use Word 97 to create a welcome letter for a new account. A procedure in the application could establish a WelcomeLetter object when a new account is added to the database and use the WelcomeLetter's Account property to set the Account number of the new account to receive a welcome letter. To issue the letter, the application would use the WelcomeLetter's Create method.

To instantiate a WelcomeLetter object, your application would use the following:

```
Dim clientletter As New WelcomeLetter
```

or

```
Dim clientletter As Object
Set clientletter = New WelcomeLetter
```

When the `clientletter` object is created, the `WelcomeLetter Initialize` event is fired and the class can set a reference to Word 97's type library in order to use Word objects in creating the welcome letter for the new account. The Word reference is established by using the `References` collection, as discussed in the section "Using the References collection" earlier in this chapter. Note the special handling in the `Initialize` and `Terminate` event procedures of an existing reference to Word 97. This processing is necessary to avoid duplicate reference errors and to avoid removing a reference used by another part of the application.

To create the welcome letter through Word 97, your application needs to set the Account number and name properties of the `WelcomeLetter` class as follows:

```
clientletter.Account = newacctnumber
clientletter.AccountName = newacctname
```

After setting the required properties, the welcome letter can be created by using the `Create` method:

```
clientletter.Create()
```

When the application no longer needs the `WelcomeLetter` object, the `clientletter` object variable is set to `Nothing`. If this variable is the only or last reference to the `WelcomeLetter` class, the class' `Terminate` event will fire and the event procedure will execute.

Although useful as a step toward object design in your own application, the Access class module cannot be referenced directly from outside the application. References to your database from other Access databases cannot see your class modules. To use your classes, you need to establish public functions in standard modules in your database that the referencing database can call. These functions can use the classes in your database and act as a bridge between your class and the external database.

This same problem occurs in Automation. Because non-Access applications cannot establish a reference to an Access database, they must resort to the use of Automation by using Access as an automation server. Doing so, however, still does not expose your classes to the external application. You need to establish bridging functions in standard modules or forms to gain access to your classes. This technique is illustrated in the section "Using Access objects," later in this chapter.

The next section introduces the development of properties in your class. You'll discover how to create properties that accept values, retrieve values, and yield object references.

Exploring property procedures

Property procedures enable you to define procedures that act like object properties. The dot operator in front of your property procedure name in an expression executes the procedure code.

You can create three types of property procedures. `Property Let` assigns a value to a property, and `Property Get` returns a property value. The `Property Set` procedure sets a reference to an object.

Property procedures are implemented as form, report, or class module procedures and thus become custom properties of the parent form, report, or class module. Using property procedures enables you to implement data hiding in custom objects. *Data hiding* prevents procedures outside of the class from directly accessing private variables. Using property procedures presents a controlled access path to the private data of the custom object in a familiar dot syntax manner.

The procedure definition statements specify the scope of the procedures, which may be `Private` or `Public`. `Private` procedures are visible only to the module in which they are defined. `Public` procedures are visible to all procedures in all modules.

Building Property Let procedures

The `Property Let` procedure statement defines the procedure that assigns a value to the property, as follows:

```
Private niRank As Integer

Public Property Let Rank(ByVal vNewValue As Variant)

   If IsNumeric(vNewValue) Then
      niRank = vNewValue
   Else
      Err.Number = 600
      Err.Description = "Rank must be numeric."
   End If

End Property
```

The preceding `Rank` property procedure can be defined in an Account form, for example, to give an account a rank for later processing in the application.

The procedure stores the value assigned to the property in a private variable defined in the General Declarations section of the form. Because this variable, `niRank`, is private, only procedures within the form can refer to it. The variable is not visible to procedures outside the containing form.

A procedure in the application instantiates an Account form and sets the rank as follows:

```
On Error Resume Next
Dim F As New Form_Account
```

```
F.Rank = 10
If Err Then
   MsgBox Err.Description, 16, "Application Error"
   Exit Sub
End If
Exit Sub
```

Building Property Get procedures

`Property Get` procedures return the value of the property assigned with the `Property Let` procedure, as shown here:

```
Public Property Get Rank() As Integer

   Rank = niRank
   Exit Property

End Property
```

The `Property Get` procedure being defined in the same form as the `Private` variable `niRank` means that the variable is visible to the procedure and is directly accessible. The property is referenced as follows:

```
Dim niWorkRank As Integer
Dim F As New Form_Account
F. Rank = 10...            'using property Let procedure
niWorkRank = F.Rank'using property Get procedure
```

Building Property Set procedures

On CD-ROM

If your application object has a property that is itself an object, you can establish a `Property Set` procedure to give the object property a value. In CH6.MDB on the CD-ROM, the `Account` object contains a `SubAccount` property that references another `Account` object.

The `objSubAcct` variable is declared as a `Private` variable in the Account form, just as `niRank` was. The `Property Set` procedure in the form gives this variable a value by setting it to the object reference passed into the procedure, as in the following:

```
Private objSubAcct As Object
Public Property Set SubAccount(Acct As Object)
   Set objSubAcct = Acct
End Property
```

To retrieve the `SubAccount` property, an application uses a `Property Get` procedure, which returns the `SubAccount` reference as an `Object`. Here's an example:

```
Public Property Get SubAccount() As Object

   Set SubAccount = objSubAcct

End Property
```

Using Property procedures

On CD-ROM

CH6.MDB on this book's CD-ROM contains a form that illustrates the use of the property procedures just introduced. The command button labeled Property Procs in frmExamples contains code that instantiates two `Account` objects (`F1` and `F2`), assigns a `Rank` and a `SubAccount` to `F1`, and then assigns a `Rank` to the `F2 SubAccount`. The `SubAccount Rank` is then accessed through the `SubAccount` property of `F1`, as shown in Listing 6-1.

Listing 6-1 Accessing a Custom Property through an Object Property

```
Dim F1 As New Form_Account
Dim F2 As Form_Account

F1.Rank = 10
If Err Then
   MsgBox Err.Description, 16, "Application Error"
   Exit Sub
End If

Set F2 = NewAcct()
Set F1.SubAccount = F2
F2.Rank = 5
MsgBox "SubAccount Rank is " & Str$(F1.SubAccount.Rank) ' Access _
Rank of SubAccount

Exit Sub

Public Function NewAcct() As Form

   Set NewAcct = New Form_Account

   Exit Function

End Function
```

The `NewAcct` procedure is a method that external Automation controllers can call to create new instances of the Account form. This procedure returns a reference to a `Form_Account` form object, which you then can use to refer to the Account's `Rank` and `SubAccount` properties. "Using Access objects," later in this chapter, gives an example of this use.

Exploring Microsoft Access Objects

Access 97 is an automation server that can provide access to your application databases from any application that can act as an automation controller.

Applications written in Visual Basic 4.0 or Excel, for example, can use VBA to instantiate an Access application object to gain access to your database and its objects. Microsoft Access can present the features of your application or the functionality of Access itself to OLE controller applications.

As an automation server, Access can carry out its tasks in the background in response to the controlling application, such as Microsoft Excel. The server capability enables the Access interface to be used either from within Access or from outside Access, which enhances the value of your application on the desktop.

The Access Object hierarchy

The objects that Access exposes are arranged in a hierarchy, as depicted in Figure 6-3.

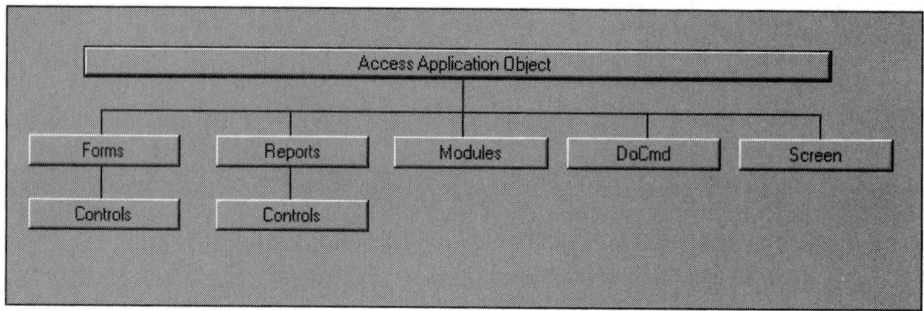

Figure 6-3: The Access Objects are arranged in a hierarchy in which all objects are dependent on the Application object.

Using the Access object in an Automation controller application, such as Microsoft Excel 97, requires the creation of an Access `Application` object before referencing any other object. Creating the `Application` object instantiates an instance of Access and provides a base object through which you can reference all other objects in your database.

The `Forms` and `Reports` objects represent the open Forms and Reports in the database. Use the `DoCmd` object to open your forms and reports in addition to executing any other command the `DoCmd` object supports.

`Controls` collections are properties of open forms and reports. You can access the properties of every control on a form or report through a reference to these collections.

The `DBEngine` object refers to the Jet engine instance associated with the instance of Access created for the `Application` object. Through the `DBEngine` object, you can access the complete set of DAO objects in your database.

Use of the `Screen` object enables you to reference the active object on the screen, which could be a form, report, or control with current focus.

The `References` collection is a set of `Reference` objects currently selected for the database. Using this collection, you can programmatically set and remove references in the database, as discussed in the section "Using the References collection."

On CD-ROM

The next section uses a Microsoft Excel 97 workbook, Secrets.XLS, which you can find on the book's CD-ROM, to illustrate the use of Access as an automation server. A reference to Access 97 is added to the project by using the References dialog box on the Tools menu while in the Visual Basic editor.

Using Access objects

The example presented earlier in "Using Property procedures" illustrates the creation of new instances of `Form` objects and the use of their property procedures. This example creates `Account` objects within the same database. This section explains the same example but uses Automation from Microsoft Excel 97.

A workbook was created in Excel, the Secrets97.XLS workbook, with a command button placed on Sheet1. The code behind this button's `Click` event procedure is shown in Listing 6-2.

Listing 6-2 Visual Basic Code Controlling the Creation and Use of Account Objects in CH6.MDB

```
Private Sub cmdAccess_Click()

   On Error Resume Next

   Dim aplAccess As Object
   Dim FBase As Access.Form
   Dim F1 As Access.Form
   Dim F2 As Access.Form
   Dim sMsg As String

   MousePointer = vbHourglass
   Set aplAccess = CreateObject("Access.Application.8")
   aplAccess.OpenCurrentDatabase "C:\Book\CH6\CH6.MDB"
   aplAccess.DoCmd.OpenForm "frmExamples"

   Set FBase = aplAccess.Forms("frmExamples")
   Set F1 = FBase.NewAcct()
   F1.Rank = 10

   Set F2 = FBase.NewAcct()
   Set F1.SubAccount = F2
   F2.Rank = 5
   sMsg = "Account F1 Rank is " & Str$(F1.Rank) & vbCrLf
   sMsg = sMsg & "F1 SubAccount Rank is " & Str$(F1.SubAccount.Rank) _
    & vbCrLf
   MsgBox sMsg, vbInformation, "OLE Lab"

   aplAccess.DoCmd.Close acForm, "frmExamples"
   aplAccess.CloseCurrentDatabase
   Set aplAccess = Nothing
   MousePointer = vbDefault
   Exit Sub
End Sub
```

The first task of the procedure is to establish an instance of an Access Application object through which other objects are referenced, as follows:

```
Dim aplAccess As Object
Dim FBase As Access.Form
Dim F1 As Access.Form
Dim F2 As Access.Form
Dim sMsg As String

Set aplAccess = CreateObject("Access.Application.8")
aplAccess.OpenCurrentDatabase "C:\Book\CH6\CH6.MDB"
aplAccess.DoCmd.OpenForm "frmExamples"
```

The CreateObject function creates the new instance of the Access Application and assigns its reference to an Object variable, aplAccess.

To open CH6.MDB, you use the OpenCurrentDatabase method of the Application object, and you use the DoCmd object's OpenForm method to open the frmExamples form. This form contains the NewAcct procedure this application uses as a method to create a new instance of an Account form.

You reference the form's NewAcct method through the form variable Fbase, which has been declared as an Access.Form. Because NewAcct returns a reference to a Form_Account object, the Set statement sets form variable F1, which now can be used to access the Form_Account properties, as shown here:

```
Set FBase = aplAccess.Forms("frmExamples")
Set F1 = FBase.NewAcct()
F1.Rank = 10
```

After the Form_Account form variable is set, you can use the form's Property Let procedure to set the Form_Account's Rank property.

To further illustrate the property procedures, the code sets another Form_Account object reference into form variable F2 and sets its Rank property. This Account is used as a SubAccount to F1, and therefore you use the F1 SubAccount Property Set procedure to assign the F2 reference to F1 SubAccount property, as follows:

```
Set F2 = FBase.NewAcct()
Set F1.SubAccount = F2
F2.Rank = 5
```

Tip

Using a form procedure within the application database to instantiate new application objects (such as Form_Accounts that use the New keyword within the Access procedure) provides an automation controller with the capability to create new application objects. Controller applications cannot refer to these objects directly because Access does not provide a type library for application-defined objects to applications other than Access itself.

The last tasks of the code are closing out the forms, closing the database, and then freeing the Application object, like this:

```
aplAccess.DoCmd.Close acForm, "frmExamples"
aplAccess.CloseCurrentDatabase
Set aplAccess = Nothing
```

To free the Access `Application` object from memory, the object variable used to refer to the application is set to `Nothing`.

Although the preceding example uses Excel to illustrate Automation to an Access server, you can use any other application or language that provides automation controller support.

Using ActiveX Controls

In addition to the standard toolbox controls available to you in form or report design mode, you can add custom controls from third-party vendors, from the Office Developers Edition (ODE), or that you have developed yourself.

ActiveX controls are built on the OLE 2.0 foundation and are generally distributed as .OCX files. These controls are usually installed in the Windows system directory and may have one or more extension DLLs associated with them.

If you are versed in C++, you can develop your own ActiveX controls. Microsoft Visual C++ 4.2 has ActiveX control development integrated into it and comes with several example projects that illustrate the construction and use of ActiveX controls.

The Office Developers Edition, an enhanced version of Microsoft Office, contains several custom controls you can add to your applications. You can find help on these controls in MSODTCTL.HLP.

The ODE ships the `ImageList`, `ListView`, `ProgressBar`, `Slider`, `StatusBar`, `TreeView`, and `Toolbar` controls that are contained in COMCTL32.OCX. The ODE setup installs this file into your Windows system directory.

The `ImageList` control is a collection of `ListImage` objects that are referenced by other controls that use images, such as the `TreeView` and `Toolbar` controls. `ImageList` is not visible at run time and acts as an image repository for other controls.

The `ListView` control displays items in views similar to those found in Windows 95 folders. You can display items in columns with or without icons. The ListView's Report view is extremely useful for displaying multiple column information and enabling the user to sort on those columns.

You can display the progress of a task with the `ProgressBar` control. This control fills in a rectangle to show how much of a task has been completed. You can use this control in place of the `SysCmd` progress meter discussed in Chapter 4, "Understanding Visual Basic for Applications."

You can display application status information with the `StatusBar` control. This control contains a collection of `Panel` objects in which you display any information you want your end user to see.

A `Slider` control displays a slider with or without tick marks. Movement of the slider can be accomplished via the mouse or keyboard. You can orient the Slider either horizontally or vertically, and it can be used to enable the selection of a value or range of values.

With the `Toolbar` control, you create a collection of `Button` objects for an application toolbar. Buttons can display pictures or text and can have ToolTips associated with them. The Toolbar can be set up to allow the user to customize the toolbar at run time.

A `TreeView` control contains a list of `Node` objects that are displayed in a hierarchy. Each node in the hierarchy can display + and – signs to indicate expansion and compression of sub nodes under a parent; an image from the `ImageList` control can be associated with a node.

Two other controls that ship with the ODE are the `RichTextBox` and `Common Dialog` controls contained in RICHTX32.OCX and COMDLG32.OCX, respectively. These controls are also installed in the Windows system directory.

The `RichTextBox` control provides a standard text box control for editing text and adds formatting features — such as bold, italic, and color text; superscripts and subscripts; and paragraph formatting. The control also can read and write its contents in .RTF format.

`Common Dialog` presents a standard dialog box, such as Open or Save File. Other dialog boxes that this control can present are Color, Font, and Printer.

Installing the controls should register them in the system Registry. In the case of the ODE setup, all the custom controls are registered at the time of installation and are available to you through the Insert menu in Form and Report design mode.

If a control is not registered, it doesn't appear in the ActiveX Control dialog box when you choose Insert ActiveX Control from the menu (see Figure 6-4).

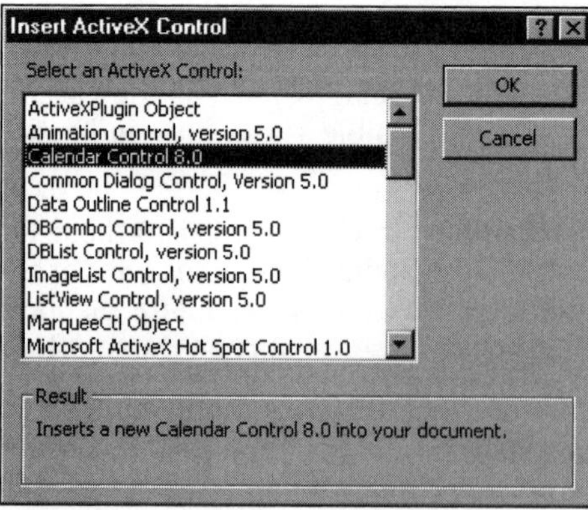

Figure 6-4: Use the Insert ActiveX Control dialog box to insert registered custom controls into a form or report.

To register a control or remove it, use the following procedure:

1. While in form or report design mode, choose ActiveX Controls from the Tools menu.
2. In the resulting ActiveX Controls dialog box, click on the Register button (see Figure 6-5).

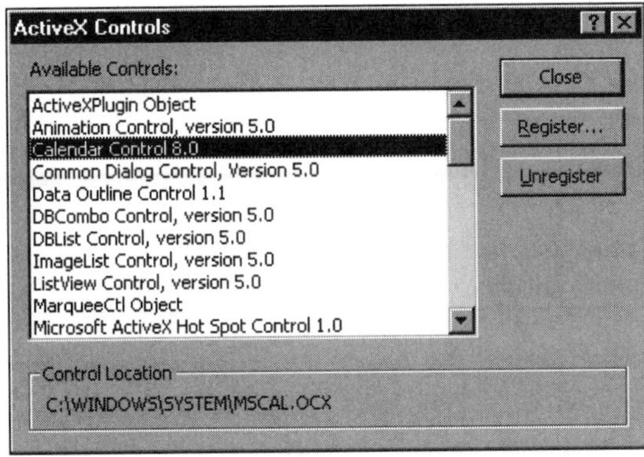

Figure 6-5: The ActiveX Controls dialog box registers or unregisters custom controls in the system Registry.

3. To register the control in the system Registry, locate the .OCX custom control file in the Add ActiveX Control dialog box and click on OK. This step also adds the control to the Insert ActiveX Control dialog box. After registering the control, use the References dialog box to add a reference to the control .OCX file. Doing so enables you to use the constants defined by the control and enables Visual Basic to check your code for errors when using the methods and properties of the control in your code modules.
4. To unregister a control and remove it from the Insert ActiveX Control dialog box, select the control in the Available Controls list box and click the Unregister button.

Registering or unregistering an .OCX file causes all controls in the file to be registered or unregistered. In the case of the ODE, unregistering the `ImageList` control also removes the `ListView`, `ProgressBar`, `Slider`, `StatusBar`, `TreeView`, and `Toolbar` controls.

Place a custom control on your form or report by selecting it from the Insert ActiveX Control dialog box displayed after choosing ActiveX Control from the Insert menu.

After you select the control on the form and then click the right mouse button to display the pop-up menu, you have two choices of properties dialog boxes. Select the custom control name to display the tabbed properties dialog box specific to the control. Select the Properties option to display the properties common to all custom controls. The tab labeled Other in the Properties dialog box contains the specific properties found in the ActiveX Control Properties dialog box.

The Data properties associated with the custom control are shown in Table 6-1.

Table 6-1 The Data Properties of Custom Controls

Property	*Description*
`OLE Class`	A description of the kind of object contained in the frame (read only)
`Class`	Specifies the type of OLE object
`Enabled`	Specifies whether the control can receive the focus

Using the Common Dialogs control

The `Common Dialogs` control presents a standard dialog box for opening, saving, setting color and fonts, and printing files.

Using the `Common Dialogs` control enables you to control certain options that appear in the dialog boxes according to the requirements of your application and retrieve information from the user of your application. You can present the same dialog boxes to your user that other Windows 95 applications present without the need to declare and call a Windows 95 Application Programming Interface (API) function such as `GetOpenFileName`. Because the `Common Dialogs` control handles the necessary management of required API structures, such as the `OPENFILENAME` structure required by the `GetOpenFileName` function and the access to the user-entered data, you save yourself a great deal of work by using this control.

The Files dialog box

Use the Files dialog box when you need to prompt the end user for a file name to open or save.

The Open dialog box appears when the control's `ShowOpen` method is executed or the `Action` property is set to `1` (see Figure 6-6). Using the `ShowSave` method or setting the `Action` property to `2` causes the Save As dialog box to appear (see Figure 6-7).

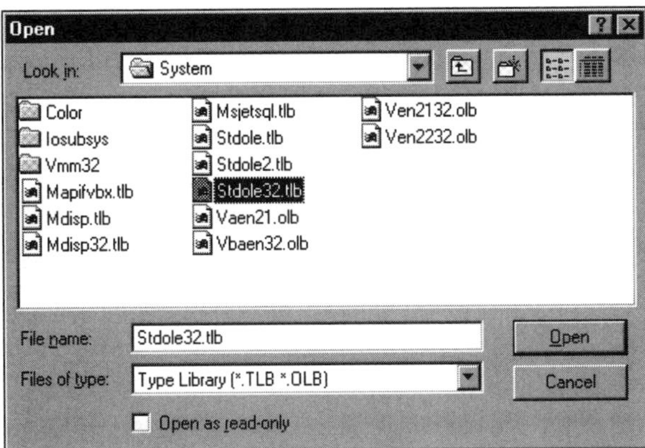

Figure 6-6: The Common Dialogs control used as an Open dialog box.

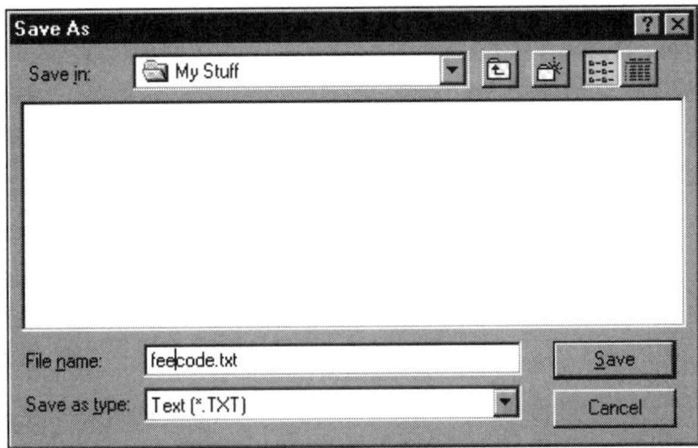

Figure 6-7: The Common Dialogs control used as a Save As dialog box.

Before displaying the dialog box, you can set the `Filter` property to limit the types of files listed in the dialog box's File list box. Use the `Filter` property setting to fill the Type list box with one or more file type specifications, as follows:

```
ActiveXCtl20.Filter = _
"OLE Control (*.OCX)|*.OCX|Type Library (*.TLB *.OLB)|*.TLB;*.OLB"
ActiveXCtl20.FilterIndex = 2
ActiveXCtl20.ShowOpen
```

The preceding filter setting specifies that only files of type .OCX or files of type .TLB and .OLB are to be displayed in the files list box, depending on the selection in the Type list box. The default type is set with the `FilterIndex`, which is based on `1`. This code fragment displays .TLB and .OLB files when the Open dialog box is first displayed.

The `Flags` property values for the Open and Save dialog boxes are listed in Table 6-2.

Table 6-2 Flags Property Settings for the File Open and Save As Dialog Boxes

Flag Constant	Flag Value	Flag Description
cdlOFNAllowMultiselect	&H200&	Enables multiple selections in the File name list box. The `FileName` property returns a string containing the names of the selected files delimited by spaces.
cdlOFNCreatePrompt	&H2000&	Causes the dialog box to prompt the user to create a file. Specifying this flag sets the `PathMustExist` and `FileMustExist` flags.
cdlOFNExtensionDifferent	&H400&	After closing the dialog box, this flag indicates that the extension of the returned file name is different from the extension specified by the `DefaultExt` property. If the `DefaultExt` property is `Null`, the file extension matches the `DefaultExt`, or the file has no extension, this flag is not set.
cdlOFNFileMustExist	&H1000&	Limits the user to entering only names of existing files in the File name text box. This flag sets the `PathMustExist` flag.
cdlOFNHideReadOnly	&H4&	Hides the read only check box.
cdlOFNNoChangeDir	&H8&	The dialog box sets the current directory to what it was when the dialog box was opened.
cdlOFNNoReadOnlyReturn	&H8000&	Specifies that the Read Only attribute of the returned file will not be set and the file will not be in a write-protected directory.

Flag Constant	*Flag Value*	*Flag Description*
`cdlOFNNoValidate`	`&H100&`	The common dialog box will allow invalid characters in the returned file name.
`cdlOFNOverwritePrompt`	`&H2&`	If the file to be saved in the Save As dialog box already exists, a message box appears asking the user to confirm overwriting the file.
`cdlOFNPathMustExist`	`&H800&`	Limits the user to entering only valid paths.
`cdlOFNReadOnly`	`&H1&`	Causes the read only checkbox to be initially checked when the dialog box is opened. When the dialog box is closed, this flag indicates the state of the read only checkbox.
`cdlOFNShareAware`	`&H4000&`	Specifies that sharing violation errors will be ignored.
`cdlOFNShowHelp`	`&H10&`	Selects the Help button to appear in the dialog box.

The `DialogTitle` property sets the title of the dialog box. If `DialogTitle` is not specified, the default title indicating the type of dialog box is used.

The `InitDir` property specifies the initial file directory in the directory list box.

After the user has selected a file and clicks on the Open or Save button, the `FileTitle` property contains the name of the file to open or save. `FileTitle` does not contain path information.

The `FileName` property contains the name of the file, with the path prepended. If the `AllowMultiselect` flag is specified, the `FileName` property contains the path followed by the names of the files selected, each separated with a space.

The `DefaultExt` property specifies a default file name extension, which is appended to the file name when the file is saved and no extension is provided.

The Print dialog box

The Print dialog box enables the user to select a destination printer and to specify certain parameters for the print job. The `ShowPrinter` method displays the dialog box shown in Figure 6-8.

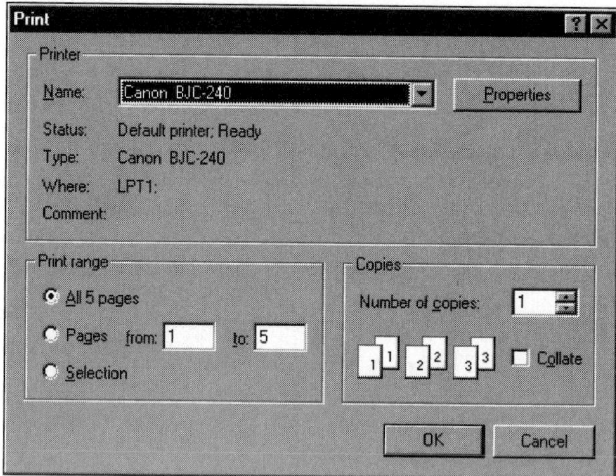

Figure 6-8: The Common Dialogs control used as a Print dialog box.

As in other common dialog boxes, you can specify the Print dialog box options before displaying the dialog box by using the `Flags` property. The valid `Flags` property settings are shown in Table 6-3.

Table 6-3 Print Dialog Box Flag Property Constants

Flag Constant	*Flag Value*	*Flag Description*
`cdlPDAllPages`	`&H0 (0)`	Sets or returns the state of the All option button in the Print range frame.
`cdlPDCollate`	`&H10 (16)`	Sets or returns the state of the Collate checkbox.
`cdlPDDisablePrintToFile`	`&H80000 (524288)`	Disables the Print to File checkbox.
`cdlPDHelpButton`	`&H800 (2048)`	Displays the Help button.
`cdlPDHidePrintToFile`	`&H100000 (1048576)`	Hides the Print to File checkbox.
`cdlPDNoPageNums`	`&H8 (8)`	Disables the Pages option button and the from: and to: text boxes in the Print range frame.
`cdlPDNoSelection`	`&H4 (4)`	Disables the Selection option button in the Print range frame.

Flag Constant	*Flag Value*	*Flag Description*
`cdlPDNoWarning`	`&H80 (128)`	Prevents a warning message from being displayed when there is no default printer.
`cdlPDPageNums`	`&H2 (2)`	Sets or returns the Pages option in the Print Range frame.
`cdlPDPrintSetup`	`&H40 (64)`	Causes the system to display the Print Setup dialog box instead of the Print dialog box.
`cdlPDPrintToFile`	`&H20 (32)`	Sets or returns the state of the Print to File checkbox. Setting this flag places a check in the checkbox (and vice versa).
`cdlPDReturnDC`	`&H100 (256)`	Returns a device context in the `hDC` property for the printer selection made in the dialog box.
`cdlPDReturnIC`	`&H200 (512)`	Returns an information context in the `hDC` property for the printer selection made in the dialog box.
`cdlPDReturnDefault`	`&H400 (1024)`	Returns the default printer name.
`cdlPDSelection`	`&H1 (1)`	Returns or sets the state of the Selection option button in the Print range frame.
`cdlPDUseDevModeCopies`	`&H40000 (262144)`	Disables the Copies edit control when the printer driver doesn't support multiple copies. If multiple copies is supported, setting this flag indicates that the default printer setting for the number of copies will be used.

To specify a Print range of All in the dialog box, set the `Flags` property to `cdlPDAllPages`. To specify that only the Selection be printed, set the `Flags` property to `cdlPDSelection`. If you want to specify a page range in the from: and to: text boxes, set the `Flags` property to `cdlPDPageNums`. Using `cdlPDPageNums` by itself, however, is not sufficient for enabling the from: and to: text boxes, as you'll see shortly.

You can disable the Pages and Selection options by setting the Flags to cdlPDNoPageNums and cdlPDNoSelection, respectively. Specify both flags to disable both options, as follows:

```
CommDlg.Flags = cdlPDNoPageNums Or cdlPDNoSelection
```

If you want a Pages range shown to the user when the dialog box is displayed, you need to set the Min, Max, FromPage, and ToPage properties. Setting these properties also sets the Flags to cdlPDPageNums.

Set the Min property to the minimum page number that the user can specify in the from: text box. The Max property holds the maximum page number allowed. If the user tries specifying a page number outside of this range, the dialog box displays an error message and asks for a valid range between the Min and Max property settings.

In addition to the Min and Max properties, you must set the FromPage and ToPage properties before the Pages option is enabled. The FromPage and ToPage values must be within the Min and Max range.

When the user closes the dialog box, you can check the FromPage and ToPage properties for the values set by the user. To determine whether the from: and to: values should be used, check the Flags property to determine whether cdlPDPageNums is present.

Note that the Common Dialogs control is a Windows 95 Common Control and that it is slightly different from the dialog box displayed by Access. In a word processor, the Selection option is appropriate, but within a database application such as Access, Selected Records replaces Selection as an option. For example, when you print a report from a Print Preview window, Access doesn't enable the Selected Records option. From a displayed form, however, in both form and datasheet view, Selected Records is available.

The Common Dialogs control Selection option is useful in your applications when you want to print a selection of application objects, such as Accounts or Customers.

If the printer supports multiple copies, the Copies property can be set in code or by the user to specify the number of copies desired. Setting the cdlPDUseDevModeCopies flag forces either one copy or the default setting for the printer, depending on the printer driver's capabilities.

Setting the CancelError property to True raises an error condition if the user cancels out of the dialog box. Your procedure displaying the dialog box needs to have an On Error statement directing the execution of the program to an error routine containing code to deal with the cancellation.

If you want the user's selections in the Print dialog box to become the new Default Printer settings everywhere in the system, set the PrinterDefault property to True before displaying the dialog box. Any printer selection and settings the user makes are also saved in the Registry as the default printer. Setting this property to False doesn't impact the default printer and applies only to your application.

The hDC property is either a device context handle or an information context handle, depending on the Flag setting. Setting the Flag to cdlPDReturnDC returns the device context handle, but cdlPDReturnIC returns an information context handle. The device context that returns corresponds to the printer selected in the dialog box and can be used anywhere a device context handle is required (including Windows 95 API calls). The information context cannot be used for printing, but it is useful in certain Windows 95 API calls for retrieving information about the selected printer and printer driver capabilities.

The Font dialog box

The ShowFont method displays a dialog box that enables users to select a screen or printer font (see Figure 6-9).

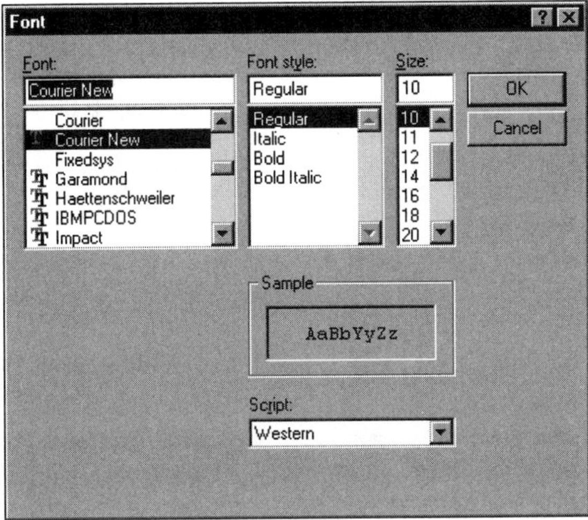

Figure 6-9: The Common Dialogs control used as a Font dialog box.

The Min and Max properties set or determine the smallest and largest font sizes displayed in the Size list box.

The hDC property identifies the device context for the default printer or the printer selected in the Printer dialog box. The Fonts dialog box uses this property whenever you specify a reference to a printer font.

The Flags property setting for the Fonts dialog box can take the values shown in Table 6-4.

Table 6-4 Available Flags Property Settings for the Font Dialog Box

Flag Constant	*Flag Value*	*Flag Description*
cdlCFApply	&H200&	Enables the Apply button in the dialog box.
cdlCFANSIOnly	&H400&	Limits the user to selecting the fonts that use the Windows character set.
cdlCFBoth	&H3&	Lists available printer and screen fonts in the dialog box.
cdlCFEffects	&H100&	Enables strikethrough, underline, and color effects.
cdlCFFixedPitchOnly	&H4000&	Lists only fixed-pitch fonts.
cdlCFForceFontExist	&H10000&	Limits the user to selecting only fonts that exist. An error message is displayed if the user attempts to select a nonexistent font.
cdlCFLimitSize	&H2000&	Limits font sizes appearing in the Sizes list box to the range specified by the Min and Max properties.
cdlCFNoSimulations	&H1000&	Prohibits graphic device interface (GDI) font simulations.
cdlCFNoVectorFonts	&H800&	Prohibits vector-font selections.
cdlCFPrinterFonts	&H2&	Limits the list of fonts to those supported by the printer, specified by the hDC property.
cdlCFScalableOnly	&H20000&	Limits the selection of fonts to those that can be scaled.
cdlCFScreenFonts	&H1&	Limits the list of fonts to the screen fonts supported by the system.
cdlCFShowHelp	&H4&	A Help button is displayed in the dialog box.
cdlCFTTOnly	&H40000&	Limits the selection to TrueType fonts.
cdlCFWYSIWYG	&H8000&	Limits the selection of fonts that are available both on the printer and on screen. Also requires setting the Both and ScalableOnly flags.

After the user closes the Fonts dialog box, you can determine the user's selections and apply them to any object that accepts font properties, such as a text box control. For example, the dialog properties `FontName`, `FontBold`, `FontSize`, `FontItalic`, and `FontUnderline` can be applied to the corresponding properties of a text box control on a form or report.

The Color dialog box

The `ShowColor` method of the `Common Dialogs` control displays the Color dialog box (see Figure 6-10). This dialog box enables users to create a custom color or to choose a color from a palette.

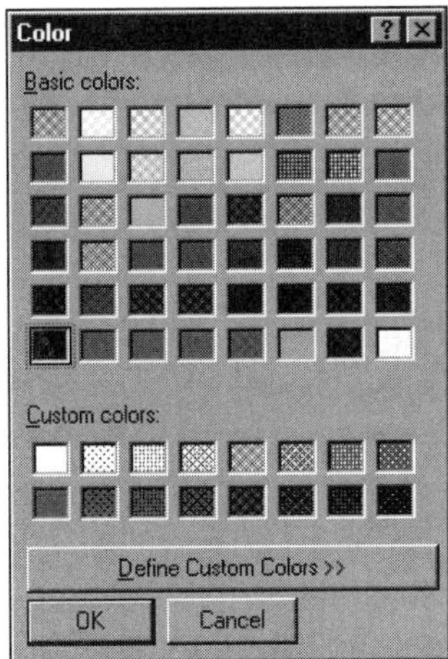

Figure 6-10: The Common Dialogs control used as a Color dialog box.

The `Flags` property settings available for the Color dialog box are shown in Table 6-5.

Table 6-5 Available Flags Property Settings for the Color Dialog Box

Flag Constant	*Flag Value*	*Flag Description*
`cdlCCFullOpen`	`&H2&`	Displays the Create Custom Colors portion of the dialog box when the dialog box is created. If this flag is not specified, the user must choose the Define Custom Colors command button to display this portion of the dialog box.

(continued)

Table 6-5 *(continued)*

Flag Constant	*Flag Value*	*Flag Description*
`cdlCCPreventFullOpen`	`&H4&`	Disables the Define Custom Colors command button.
`cdlCCRGBInit`	`&H1&`	Sets the initial color value.
`cdlCCShowHelp`	`&H8&`	Displays a Help button in the dialog box.

Use the `Color` property of the dialog box to get the selected color value. This value can be assigned to any property that accepts an `RGB` value, such as the `BackColor` property of a form's Detail section.

Creating an ImageList

Many of the custom controls use images in their user interface. Instead of storing these images within their own address space, they refer to another control, the `ImageList` control, to reference the images they need. This method is a shareable resource with lower memory requirements.

The `ImageList` control is a collection of `ListImage` objects. The `ListImage` object contains a `Picture` property with a bitmap or icon image and an identity for the image in the form of a key or index.

`ListImage` objects are added to the `ListImages` collection through the `Add` method or through the design-time property sheet.

Using the ImageList property sheet, you select the dimensions of the images stored in the control on the General tab (see Figure 6-11). Select one of the fixed dimensions, or specify a custom dimension in the Height and Width text boxes. These settings are specified in pixels and affect the `ImageHeight` and `ImageWidth` properties of the control. These settings apply to all `ListImage` objects in the collection. You cannot set these properties while images are loaded into the control.

Tip

The Images tab controls the images stored in the control (see Figure 6-12). The Insert Picture button provides a Select Picture dialog box where you can select the images. As you select each image, the Index property of the `ListImage` object is incremented in the dialog box and you can provide a Key for the image. It is recommended that you give each image a unique Key name, because the Index may change at run time if your application adds or removes images.

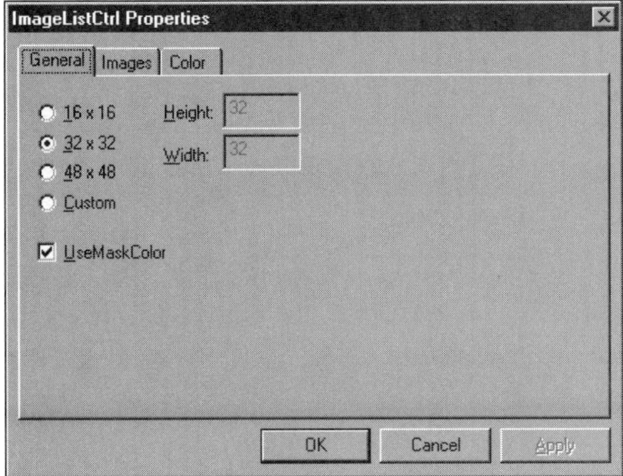

Figure 6-11: Use the General tab of the ImageList control property sheet to specify the ImageHeight and ImageWidth of all ListImage objects in the ImageList control.

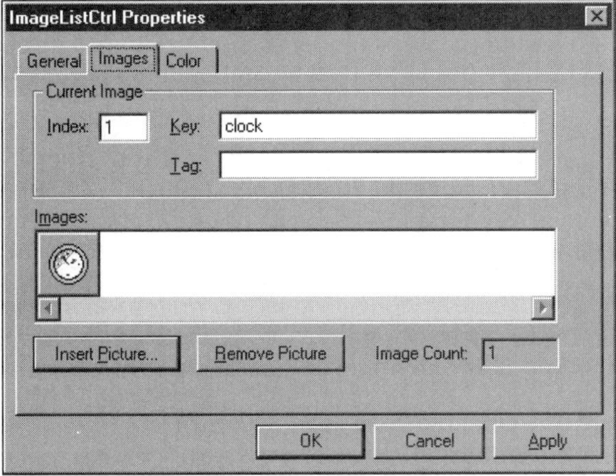

Figure 6-12: The Images tab of the ImageList property sheet provides a dialog box for adding and removing images in the control.

You can set the `ImageList` control's `BackColor` and `MaskColor` properties in the Color tab of the property sheet (see Figure 6-13). The `BackColor` property refers to the background color of all `ListImage` objects. The `MaskColor` property is used in the `Draw` and `Overlay` graphical methods, which are discussed shortly.

You may also add `ListImage` objects in code by using the `ListImages Add` method, as follows:

```
Dim imgLisImage As ListImage
Set imgLisImage = _
ImageList1.ListImages.Add(,"Account1",LoadPicture("c:\images\acct.ico"))
```

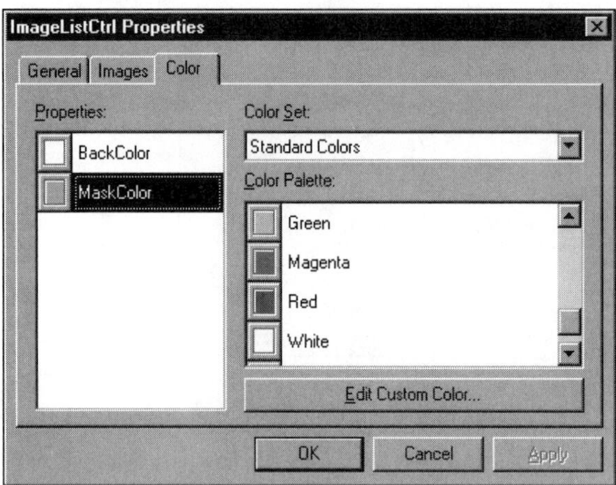

Figure 6-13: The Color tab enables you to set the BackColor and MaskColor properties for all ListImage objects.

The first argument in the method represents the `Index` of the image and may be omitted to assign the next sequential index value. The second argument represents the Key on the image and must be unique within the collection.

Specify the Index of a `ListImage` in the `Remove` method to remove an image from the collection. After doing so, the Index properties of the remaining `ListImage` objects are changed to keep the objects sequentially numbered within the collection.

To remove all images from the collection in one operation, use the `Clear` method. This method is faster than the `Remove` method in a loop. You can use the `Clear` method before loading an `ImageList` with a new set of images at run time.

The `ImageList` and `ListImage` objects implement some graphical methods that you may find useful.

The `ExtractIcon` method of a `ListImage` object returns a reference to an icon extracted from the picture stored in the `ListImage` object. You can use this reference anywhere you need an icon in your application. If the `Picture` property of the `ListImage` contains an icon image type, you need not use the `ExtractIcon` method because you can refer to the `Picture` property directly. The frmToolbar form in CH6.MDB, located on this book's CD-ROM, uses this technique to assign an icon to the mouse pointer so that the appearance of the pointer will change whenever the mouse pointer passes over the toolbar.

You can use the `ListImage Draw` method to draw the image on a device context, such as the one returned in the Print Dialog's `hDC` property, as illustrated here:

```
Dim imgLisImage As ListImage

imgLisImage.Draw(Prnt Dlg.hdc, x,y, imlTransparent)
```

The `Draw` method may optionally specify the position of the image within the device context and a style to be applied to the image. Styles you can use with the `Draw` method are listed in Table 6-6.

Table 6-6 Style Options for the ListImage Draw Method

Style Constant	Style Value	Description
imlNormal	0	(Default) Draws the image with no change.
imlTransparent	1	Draws the image using the MaskColor property to determine which color of the image will be transparent.
imlSelected	2	Draws the image dithered with the system highlight color.
imlFocus	3	Draws the image dithered and striped with the highlight color, creating a hatched effect to indicate that the image has the focus.

Note that the `imlTransparent` style uses the property color setting of the `MaskColor` property to mask out the matching color in the image drawn on the device. That portion of the image becomes transparent.

You can use the `ImageList Overlay` method to combine two `ListImage` objects. This method refers to two `ListImage` objects by `Index` or `Key` value and returns an image combined by overlaying the second image onto the first and using the `MaskColor` property setting to make transparent the matching `MaskColor` color in the overlaying image.

Creating toolbars with the Toolbar control

The `Toolbar` control is a collection of `Button` objects that you can customize to make your application easier to use.

To create a simple toolbar for a form, select the `Toolbar` control from the list of custom controls in the Insert ActiveX Control dialog box and draw it on your form.

If the `Toolbar` control is not listed in the available controls list box, follow the procedure outlined in the "Using ActiveX Controls" section of this chapter to add the `Toolbar` control to the list.

To align the toolbar at the top of your form, set the `Top` and `Left` properties of the control to zero.

Using the procedures outlined in the "Creating an ImageList" section of this chapter, add an `ImageList` to your form and load a few icons or bitmaps into it for display on your toolbar.

The Toolbar control properties sheet

Ensure that the `Toolbar` control is selected and then click the right mouse button to display the pop-up menu. Select the Toolbar Control Object Properties option to display the Toolbar Control Properties sheet.

The General tab

Use the General tab in the Toolbar Properties dialog box to set the properties that apply to the entire toolbar (see Figure 6-14). Check the AllowCustomize check box if you want to enable the end user of your application to customize the toolbar at run time by double-clicking on the toolbar. This action displays the Customize Toolbar dialog box, shown in Figure 6-15, and enables the user to add, move, and remove buttons on the toolbar.

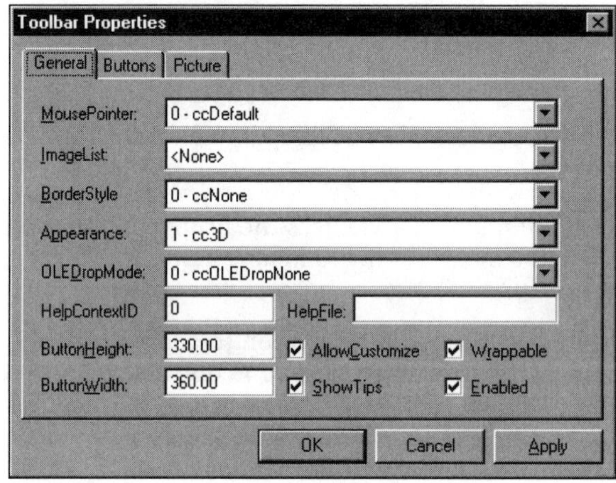

Figure 6-14: The Toolbar Properties dialog box General tab enables you to customize the toolbar properties that apply to the entire toolbar.

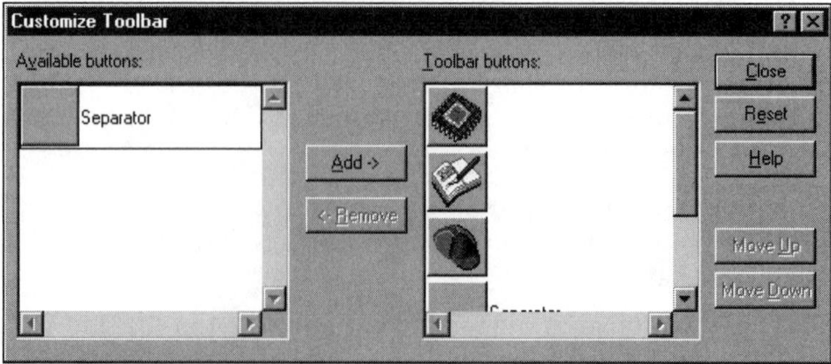

Figure 6-15: The end user of your application can customize your toolbar with the Customize Toolbar dialog box.

Checking the ShowTips checkbox in the Toolbar Properties dialog box enables the display of ToolTips associated with each button. You set ToolTips text on the Buttons tab.

The Enabled checkbox is checked by default, indicating a value of `True` and enabling the toolbar to respond to any user event, such as clicking on a toolbar button. Clearing the checkbox — a `False` value — disables the toolbar. When disabled, none of the event procedures of the toolbar are executed as a result of a user action.

Checking the Wrappable checkbox in the Toolbar Properties dialog box wraps the buttons of the toolbar if the form containing the toolbar is resized; otherwise, the buttons are clipped.

You can select a mouse pointer style by selecting from the MousePointer drop-down list. Selecting MousePointer `99 - Custom Mouse Pointer` enables you to specify the mouse pointer picture by using the Picture tab of the dialog box.

To associate pictures with the toolbar buttons, you need to assign an `ImageList` control to the `ImageList` property in code. This procedure is illustrated later in this section.

`ButtonHeight` and `ButtonWidth` set the height and width of the buttons on the toolbar you specify under the Buttons tab.

The Buttons tab

As mentioned in the beginning of this section, a toolbar consists of a collection of button objects. Each button has a set of properties and methods that can be used from code in your application.

Using the Buttons tab, you can add and remove button objects on your toolbar and set some of their properties (see Figure 6-16). Each button added with the Insert Button button receives an Index value, which you can use to refer to the button in the `Buttons` collection.

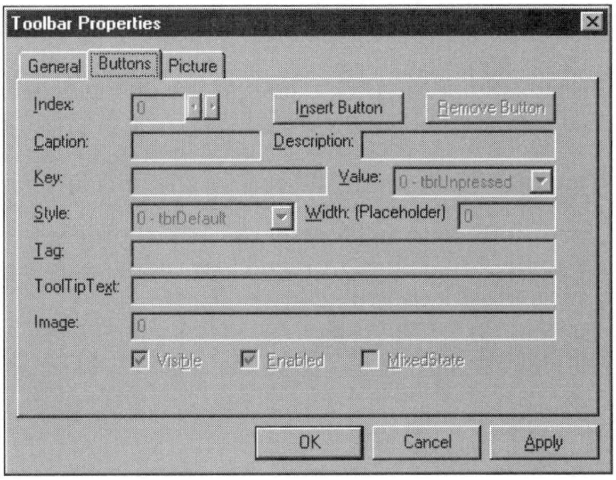

Figure 6-16: The Buttons tab enables you to insert or remove button objects and set their properties.

In addition to using a button's `Index` value, you can set a Key, which is a text string that can uniquely identify the button. By setting a Key for button one in a toolbar to "ButtonOne", your code could refer to this button as follows:

```
Toolbar1.Buttons(1)                'Use Button Index
```

or

```
Toolbar1.Buttons("ButtonOne")      'Use Button Key
```

If you want a button to contain text, set the `Caption` property to the text that will appear on the button face.

The Style drop-down list offers five settings. The `0 - Default (Button)` style results in a button that appears pressed when you click the mouse button down over the button and as raised when the mouse button is released. This action is independent of other buttons in the toolbar.

A Style of `1 - Check` toggles the button between pressed and raised states with each mouse button click. While pressed, the button's `Value` property is `1 - Pressed`, and while raised, its value is `0 - Unpressed`.

Selecting a Style of `2 - Button Group` causes the button to behave like a checked button style, but the button's value state affects the state of other buttons in the same group. A Button Group is defined as all buttons with Style 2 between button separators. When a button in a group is pressed, the other buttons of the same group are raised.

Using a Style of `3 - Separator` doesn't yield a button on the toolbar but a spacing that can be used to separate visible buttons and delimit button groups.

The Style `4 - Placeholder` is currently not available in Access. This style will be used in later versions to hold other controls, such as drop-down list boxes.

You can use the `Tag` property in the dialog box to store any data you want to associate with the button. You may want to assign a special value to each button's `Tag` property that is displayed in a status box on your form or is assigned to a variable whenever the button is pressed.

If you check ShowTips under the General tab of the dialog box, you can set the ToolTip that appears when the mouse passes over the button by setting the `ToolTipText` property in the Buttons tab of the dialog box. Set this property to a string that displays the purpose of the button when pressed.

To display a picture on the button face, set the `Image` property in the Buttons tab to a number other than zero and less than the number of images in the associated `ImageList` control specified in the `ImageList` property. The number entered in the `Image` property corresponds to the index of the image you inserted into the `ImageList` control. This property is set in code after setting the associated ImageList to the ToolBar's `ImageList` property.

The Visible and Enabled checkboxes set the state of the button as it appears to the user. Unchecking the Enabled checkbox disables the button on the toolbar so that the button recognizes no mouse or keyboard events.

Checking the MixedState checkbox grays the button. This graying is described as having an *indeterminate state*. Use this property if the button refers to a common property among a group of objects in your application and the property value is not consistent throughout the group.

You can use MixedState on a toolbar button as follows. You may, for example, have a list box of customers in your application and a toolbar button with the Check style to change the status of a customer between Paid Up (a button Value of `Unpressed`) and Delinquent (a button Value of `Pressed`). As you select a customer in the list box and check the value of the customer's Paid status, you set the button `Value` property accordingly. If a selection of two or more customers was made, however, and some were Paid Up and some were Delinquent, you could not set the `Value` property of the button to either `Pressed` or `Unpressed`. In this case, you can set the `MixedState` property to `True`; the button grays to alert the end user of the different statuses for the selected customers.

The Picture tab

If you set the `MousePointer` property under the General tab to `99 - Custom Mouse Pointer Icon`, you can specify the icon to be used as a mouse pointer with the Picture tab.

The MousePointer picture specified here appears when the mouse passes over the toolbar. Click on the Browse button and select the icon you want to assign to the mouse pointer. In this release of the toolbar control, the Property Name applied to the selected icon remains constant as `MouseIcon`. Click on the Clear button to remove the icon from the property.

The Object property

Controls may contain certain properties that may be named the same as properties defined by Access. The behavior of the Access property may be different from that of the custom control.

To reference the custom control property instead of the Access property, use the control's `Object` property. This use is illustrated in the assignment of an `ImageList` to the Toolbar, as shown here:

```
ActiveXCtl12.ImageList = ActiveXCtl13.Object
```

Determining the parent of the toolbar

The toolbar's `Parent` property returns the form that has the toolbar. You can use this property to access the parent form's properties and other controls. The `Parent` property is read-only. Its syntax is as follows:

```
MsgBox "The toolbar is on form " & ActiveXCtl12.Parent.Name
```

Invoking the Customize dialog box from code

When you have set the `AllowCustomize` property to `True`, the end user can invoke the Customize dialog box by double-clicking on the toolbar at run time. You can also invoke this dialog box in code through the `Customize` method, as in the following:

```
ActiveXCtl12.Customize
```

To ensure that the `Customize` property is set to `True` so that the dialog box is enabled, preface the customize method statement with the following:

```
ActiveXCtl12.AllowCustomize = True
```

Using the SaveToolbar and RestoreToolbar methods

If end users can customize the application toolbar, it's likely that you will want the customized toolbar displayed in the next application session. As shown in Figure 6-17, the `SaveToolbar` method saves the toolbar in the system Registry under the HKEY_CURRENT_USER key in the subkey you specify, as follows:

```
Dim niKey As Integer
Dim sSubKey As String
Dim sValue As String

niKey = 1
sSubKey = "Chapter 6"
sValue = "Toolbar"
ActiveXCtl12.SaveToolbar niKey, sSubkey, sValue
```

To restore the customized toolbar, use the `RestoreToolbar` method, as follows:

```
Dim niKey As Integer
Dim sSubKey As String
Dim sValue As String

niKey = 1
sSubKey = "Chapter 6"
sValue = "Toolbar"
ActiveXCtl12.RestoreToolbar niKey, sSubkey, sValue
```

Keep in mind that the saved toolbar is stored in the Registry of the current machine. If you move the application to another machine, you should export the user's toolbars and other specific Registry data for your application. See the section "Using the Registry Editor," in Chapter 1, "Using the Windows 95 Registry," for the steps to import and export Registry information.

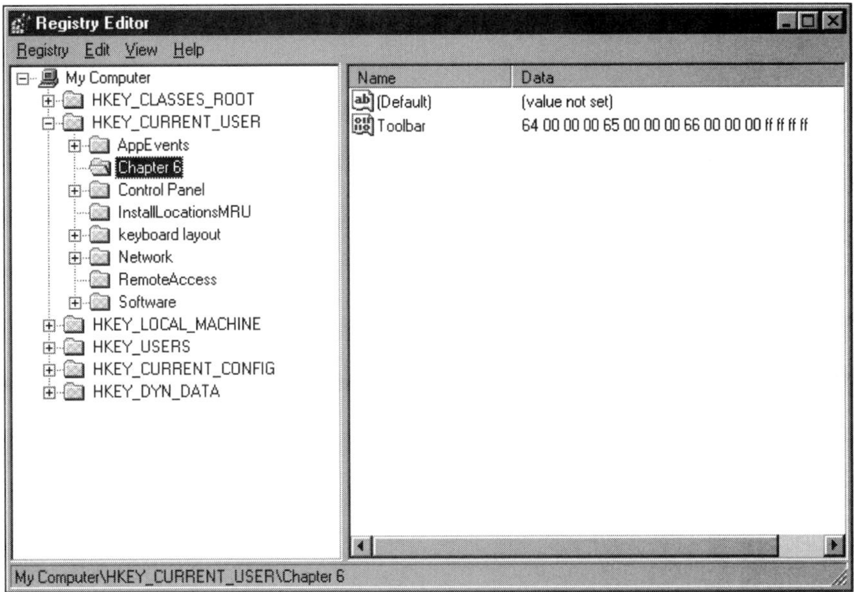

Figure 6-17: The Toolbar information is stored in the Registry of the local machine under the HKEY_CURRENT_USER key.

The ButtonClick and Click events

Insert code into the `ButtonClick` event of the toolbar control to initiate processing of the Button passed into the procedure as an argument. This button argument is a `Button` object and can be used to obtain the properties and methods of the `Button`.

It is recommended that you specify a Key for each button you establish on the toolbar. The `Key` property can then determine which button was clicked and react accordingly. The Index of the button is unreliable (especially if users are allowed to customize the toolbar).

The `Click` event of the toolbar fires whenever the user clicks on the toolbar where no buttons are placed; it occurs before the `ButtonClick` event. The `Click` event usually is not coded.

Using the Change event

The `Change` event fires whenever the user dismisses the Customize toolbar dialog box or when you use the `RestoreToolbar` method.

You can use this event to save the toolbar with the `SaveToolbar` method or to perform an action in response to restoring the toolbar.

If you set the Tag property of the toolbar in a session of your application, it remains as long as the toolbar is loaded, even if you use the RestoreToolbar method.

Adding a button in code

The Buttons collection has an Add method, which you use to add Button objects to the collection, as follows:

```
ActiveXCtl12.Buttons.Add 1, "Calculate", , 0, 4
ActiveXCtl12.Buttons("Calculate").ToolTipText = "Calculate Commission"
```

The preceding code uses the Add method to add a new button to ActiveXCtl12 at the first position on the toolbar. A Key of Calculate is assigned to the new button; it's given a default button Style and an Image index of 4 in the associated ImageList control. No caption is assigned to the button.

After the new button is added to the toolbar, its ToolTipText property is set to display Calculate Commission whenever the mouse passes over the button.

Another method of setting the same button, addressing each property separately, is with the following code fragment:

```
Dim btnButton As Button

Set btnButton = ActiveXCtl12.Buttons.Add
btnButton.Key = "Calculate"
btnButton.Style = 0
btnButton.Image = 4
btnButton.ToolTipText = "Calculate Commission"
```

This code yields the same results as in the first example, except the button is added to the *end* of the Buttons collection by default instead of the first position. Because the Index property is Read Only, you cannot set it specifically as you can the other properties.

To remove a button from the toolbar's Buttons collection, use the Remove method, as follows:

```
ActiveXCtl12.Buttons.Remove ActiveXCtl12.Buttons.Count
```

The preceding code fragment removes the last button of the Buttons collection, using the Buttons collection Count property to determine the last index value.

You can specify any valid index number to remove. Remember, removing or adding a button other than the last button changes the index values of the remaining buttons. It is not recommended that you use index values in your code unless you are enumerating the button of the collection for some reason. Addressing a button by its index value may not always address the same button; the `Add` and `Remove` methods can change the order of buttons, and the user can also change the order with the Customize dialog box. The best approach is assigning a Key to each button and using these keys to address the buttons in the collection.

On CD-ROM

CH6.MDB, located on the CD-ROM that accompanies this book, contains an example of using the `ToolBar` control in form frmToolbar. The `Form_Load` event assigns the `ImageList` control, `ActiveXCtl13`, and also adds the buttons to the toolbar, `ActiveXCtl12`, as shown in Listing 6-3.

Listing 6-3 Initializing a Toolbar Control in the Form_Load Event Procedure

```
Private Sub Form_Load()
   Dim btnWrk As Button

   ' Set up the toolbar buttons collection

   ActiveXCtl12.ImageList = ActiveXCtl13.Object
   Set btnWrk = ActiveXCtl12.Buttons.Add(1, "Button1", , _
tbrButtonGroup, 1)
   btnWrk.ToolTipText = "Inside My Computer"
   Set btnWrk = ActiveXCtl12.Buttons.Add(2, "Button2", , _
tbrButtonGroup, 2)
   btnWrk.ToolTipText = "Antique My Computer"
   Set btnWrk = ActiveXCtl12.Buttons.Add( , , , tbrSeparator)
   Set btnWrk = ActiveXCtl12.Buttons.Add(3, "Button3", , tbrDefault, _
3)
   btnWrk.ToolTipText = "Mystery My Computer"

   ' Set the toolbar properties

   With ActiveXCtl12
      .BorderStyle = ccFixedSingle
      .Height = ActiveXCtl12.ButtonHeight + 50
      .Width = Me.Width
      .MouseIcon = ActiveXCtl13.ListImages(4).Picture
      .MousePointer = ccCustom
  End With

End Sub
```

Using the TreeView control

When you need to display a hierarchical view in your application, the `TreeView` custom control is a good choice.

The TreeView provides for the display of information in a hierarchical (tree) fashion. Each node in the view is a parent or child node (or both) in the hierarchy, and its function in the hierarchy can be denoted by a distinct picture and text. The nodes can be expanded and compressed while the user navigates through the hierarchy, and each node can have one picture when it is expanded and another picture when it is compressed.

The nodes in the TreeView are `Node` objects and are members of the `Nodes` collection property of the control. You can add nodes to the collection by using the `Add` method.

The frmTreeView sample form in CH6.MDB on the CD-ROM that accompanies this book uses the `TreeView` control to display the organization of Accounts within a business (see Figure 6-18). The accounts in this business are arranged into primary parent or home accounts; each has zero or more subaccounts. In turn, each subaccount does business through a number of sites; each site has one or more departments. The form contains a `Refresh_TreeView` procedure that selects the data for building the hierarchy from the Account, Site, and Department tables and adds nodes at the appropriate levels in the `TreeView`.

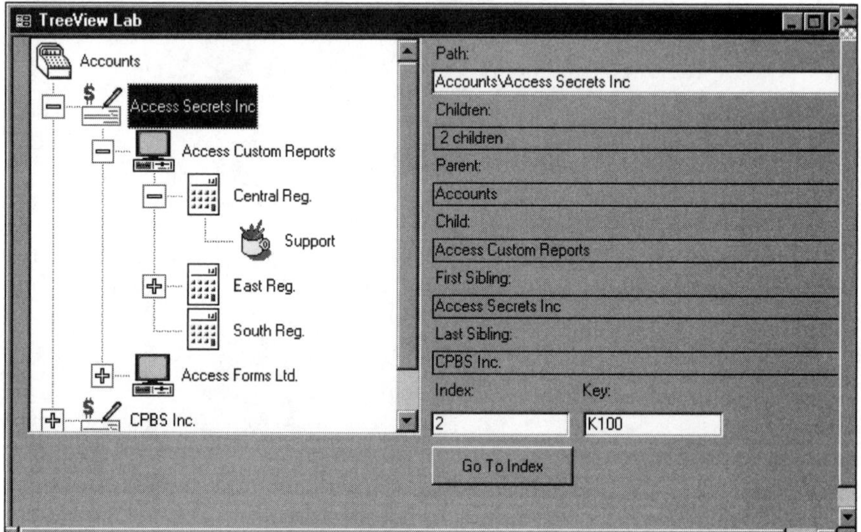

Figure 6-18: The frmTreeView form in CH6.MDB is an example of the use of the TreeView control to display a hierarchy within an application.

You can set TreeView-specific properties in code or by using the TreeView Control Properties sheet, as shown in Figure 6-19.

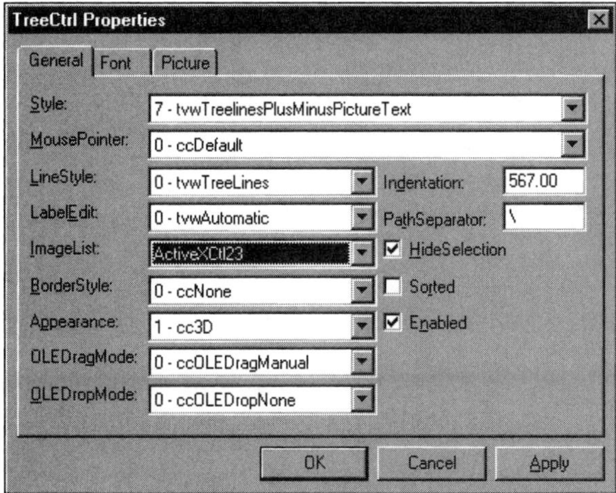

Figure 6-19: You can use the TreeView Control Properties sheet to establish some of the TreeView properties, or you can set them in your code.

The TreeView properties sheet

The General tab enables you to set the Style of the TreeView. The styles denote various combinations of image, text, level connecting lines, and symbols that indicate expanded and compressed nodes. The `Style` property lets you choose from eight styles.

You can select a MousePointer, which is displayed whenever the mouse passes over the `TreeView` control. Select `99 - Custom MousePointer`, and the MousePointer uses the icon specified in the `MouseIcon` property, which you can set in the Picture tab.

LabelEdit specifies the type of editing allowed on the `Node` objects displayed. If you select `0 - Automatic`, users can edit the text of the nodes. When this editing occurs, the `BeforeLabelEdit` and `AfterLabelEdit` events fire, enabling you to react to the change. If you select `1 - Manual`, your code must enable the edit capability by using the `StartLabelEdit` method.

Use the PathSeparator text box to specify the character that the node object's `FullPath` property uses to delimit nodes in the path. The `FullPath` property specifies the `Text` properties of all `Node` objects that are ancestors of the selected node. The PathSeparator character goes between the text of each node in the path from the root to the selected node.

Use the Font tab to select a font for the text displayed in the TreeView.

The `Refresh_TreeView` procedure in frmTreeView adds a root node to the TreeView, under which all other nodes are added as children, as illustrated in Listing 6-4.

Listing 6-4 The Refresh_TreeView Procedure

```
Public Function Refresh_TreeView(ctlTreeView As CustomControl) As _
Integer

    On Error GoTo RTErrHandler

    Dim dbDatabase As DATABASE
    Dim rsAccounts As Recordset
    Dim rsSubAccounts As Recordset
    Dim rsSites As Recordset
    Dim rsDepts As Recordset
    Dim SQLStmt As String
    Dim objNode As Node

    If ctlTreeView.OLEClass = "TreeCtrl" Then
    Else
       Refresh_TreeView = False
       Exit Function
    End If

     ctlTreeView.ImageList = Me!ActiveXCtl23.Object
    Set objNode = ctlTreeView.Nodes.Add(, , "acct", "Accounts", 1)
    objNode.ExpandedImage = 2      ' Image 2 for expanded node.

    Set dbDatabase = CurrentDb()
    SQLStmt = "SELECT [Account_ID],[Account_Name] FROM [Account] _
WHERE [Account_Parent] = 0 ORDER BY [Account_Name]"
    Set rsAccounts = dbDatabase.OpenRecordset(SQLStmt, _
DB_OPEN_SNAPSHOT)

    Do While Not rsAccounts.EOF
        ' add an account node
        Set objNode = ctlTreeView.Nodes.Add(1, tvwChild, "K" & _
CStr(rsAccounts![Account_ID]), _
(rsAccounts![Account_Name]), 3)
        ' get the sub accounts
        SQLStmt = "SELECT [Account_ID],[Account_Name] FROM [Account] _
WHERE [Account_Parent] = _
           " & Str$(rsAccounts![Account_ID]) & _
" ORDER BY [Account_Name]"
        Set rsSubAccounts = dbDatabase.OpenRecordset(SQLStmt, _
DB_OPEN_SNAPSHOT)
        Do While Not rsSubAccounts.EOF
           ' add the subaccount node
           Set objNode = ctlTreeView.Nodes.Add("K" & _
CStr(rsAccounts![Account_ID]), tvwChild, "K" & _
CStr(rsSubAccounts![Account_ID]), (rsSubAccounts![Account_Name]), 4)
           ' get the sites for subaccount
           SQLStmt = _
"SELECT [Site_ID],[Site_Name] FROM [Site] WHERE [Account_ID] = " _
```

```
           & Str$(rsSubAccounts![Account_ID]) & _
" ORDER BY [Site_Name]"
           Set rsSites = dbDatabase.OpenRecordset(SQLStmt, _
DB_OPEN_SNAPSHOT)
           Do While Not rsSites.EOF
                ' add the site node
                Set objNode = ctlTreeView.Nodes.Add("K" & _
CStr(rsSubAccounts![Account_ID]), tvwChild, "K" & _
 CStr(rsSites![Site_ID]), (rsSites![Site_Name]), 6)
                ' get the departments for the site
                SQLStmt = "SELECT [Dept_ID],[Dept_Name] FROM _
[Department] WHERE [Site_ID] = " _
                    & Str$(rsSites![Site_ID]) & " ORDER BY _
[Dept_Name]"
                Set rsDepts = dbDatabase.OpenRecordset(SQLStmt, _
DB_OPEN_SNAPSHOT)
                Do While Not rsDepts.EOF
                   ' add the department node
                   Set objNode = ctlTreeView.Nodes.Add("K" & _
CStr(rsSites![Site_ID]), tvwChild, "K" &  _
CStr(rsDepts![Dept_ID]), (rsDepts![Dept_Name]), 7)
                   rsDepts.MoveNext
                Loop
                rsDepts.Close
                rsSites.MoveNext
           Loop
           rsSites.Close
           rsSubAccounts.MoveNext

        Loop
        rsSubAccounts.Close
        rsAccounts.MoveNext

    Loop
    rsAccounts.Close
    Refresh_TreeView = True
    Exit Function

RTErrHandler:
    Refresh_TreeView = False
    Exit Function
End Function
```

A control reference is passed into the procedure, and the procedure checks to ensure that the control is a `TreeView` custom control. If it isn't, the procedure returns `False`.

Next, the images for the TreeView are attached to the TreeView through the `ImageList` property. This property is set to point to the `ImageList` control on the form. Note that you must refer to the `ImageList` control's `Object` property when setting the `ImageList` property.

Adding nodes to the Tree

You use the Add method of the Nodes collection to add the root node to the TreeView, as follows:

```
Add(relative, relationship, key, text, image, selectedimage)
```

The relative argument can specify an index or key of an existing node. If specified, the new node is added to the collection relative to the specified node and according to the relationship argument. Constants that you can specify for the relationship are in Table 6-7.

Table 6-7 Relative Argument Constants of the Nodes Add Method

Relative Argument Constant	*Constant Value*	*Description*
tvwLast	1	The new Node object is placed after all other nodes at the same level of the node named in the relative argument.
tvwNext	2	The new Node object is placed after and at the same level as the node named in the relative argument.
tvwPrevious	3	The new Node object is placed before and at the same level as the node named in the relative argument.
tvwChild	4	(Default) The new Node object becomes a child node of the node named in the relative argument.

Specify a Key for the node in the key argument. This key must be unique within the collection. The text argument is the text displayed with the node, and the image is the index of the image in the associated ImageList control that you want to have displayed for the node. If you want the node to display a different image when the node is selected, specify the image's index in the selectedimage argument.

The Add method returns a reference to a Node object, which you set into a Node object variable. With this reference, you can set other Node properties, such as the ExpandedImage property, which is the index of the image to be displayed for the node when the node is in an expanded state.

The rest of the Refresh_TreeView procedure steps through the Accounts, Sites, and Departments tables as it builds a hierarchy through the table relationships. Children are added by using an add method that specifies appropriate relative and relationship arguments to properly insert the child nodes into the hierarchy, as shown here:

```
Set objNode = ctlTreeView.Nodes.Add(1, tvwChild, "K" & _
CStr(rsAccounts![Account_ID]), _
(rsAccounts![Account_Name]), 3)
```

The key argument must be an alphanumeric key starting with an alpha character. Because the `Account_Ids` in the Account table are numeric values, the `Refresh_TreeView` procedure adds a constant `K` to the front of each node key as it inserts them.

The NodeClick event

The `TreeView` control's `NodeClick` event procedure uses several `Node` object properties to display information about the node the user selected, which is passed into the `NodeClick` event procedure. The entire procedure is shown in Listing 6-5.

Listing 6-5 The NodeClick Event Procedure

```
Private Sub ActiveXCtl0_NodeClick(ByVal Node As Object)

   Dim sNodeText(6) As String
   Dim objNode As Node
   Dim ndx As Integer

           txtPath.Value = Node.FullPath
   lblChildren.Caption = Str$(Node.Children) & " children"
   txtIndex.Value = Node.Index
   txtKey.Value = Node.Key
   ' Get the Root lable
   Set objNode = Node.Root
   If objNode Is Nothing Then
   Else
      sNodeText(ndx) = objNode.Text
      ndx = ndx + 1
   End If
   ' Get the Parent label
   Set objNode = Node.Parent
   If objNode Is Nothing Then
      lblParent.Caption = ""
   Else
      lblParent.Caption = objNode.Text
      ndx = ndx + 1
   End If
   ' Get the Child label
   Set objNode = Node.Child
   If objNode Is Nothing Then
      lblChild.Caption = ""
   Else
      lblChild.Caption = objNode.Text
      ndx = ndx + 1
   End If
   ' Get the FirstSibling label
   Set objNode = Node.FirstSibling
```

(continued)

(continued)

```
    If objNode Is Nothing Then
       lblFirstSibling.Caption = ""
    Else
       lblFirstSibling.Caption = objNode.Text
       ndx = ndx + 1
    End If
    ' Get the LastSibling label
    Set objNode = Node.LastSibling
    If objNode Is Nothing Then
       lblLastSibling.Caption = ""
    Else
       lblLastSibling.Caption = objNode.Text
       ndx = ndx + 1
    End If
    ' Get the Previous label
    Set objNode = Node.Previous
    If objNode Is Nothing Then
    Else
       sNodeText(ndx) = objNode.Text
       ndx = ndx + 1
    End If
    ' Get the Next label
    Set objNode = Node.Next
    If objNode Is Nothing Then
    Else
       sNodeText(ndx) = objNode.Text
    End If
End Sub
```

The family of nodes

As noted earlier, the `FullPath` property of a `Node` object yields the text of all nodes in the ancestry tree of the selected node. Each node's text is separated by the PathSeparator character.

The `Children` property can be read to determine whether the node has any child nodes beneath it. This property returns the number of children nodes that exist below the selected node.

You obtain information about the selected node's relatives in the tree by using the properties that return node references to set a `Node` object variable and then accessing the resulting node's `Text` property.

The `Root` property returns a reference to the root of the tree. The `Parent` property returns a reference to the parent of the selected node. In the Accounts example, a `Site` node's `Parent` property returns a reference to a `SubAccount` node.

You obtain the immediate child node reference from the `Child` property. As with all other properties returning object references, if the referenced object is not present, the resulting property value is `Nothing`.

FirstSibling and LastSibling properties refer to the first and last nodes at the same level in the hierarchy as the selected node. If the selected node is the first or last node at that level, a self-reference is returned.

The Previous and Next properties refer to the previous and next nodes at the same level as the selected node.

Expanding and collapsing nodes

Use the Node object's Expanded property either to expand a node in code or to determine whether a node is in an expanded state. Setting this property to True expands the node; False collapses it.

When a node is expanded or collapsed, either through code or by the user, the TreeView Expand and Collapse events occur.

Setting a node's Selected property to True selects that node. This property is used in the frmTreeView behind the GoTo button to set the selection on the selected Index, as follows:

```
Private Sub cmdGoto_Click()

   Dim ndx As Integer
   If IsNumeric(txtIndex.Value) Then
      ndx = Val(txtIndex.Value)
      If ndx > 0 And ndx < ActiveXCtl0.Nodes.Count Then
         ActiveXCtl0.Nodes(ndx).Selected = True
         ActiveXCtl0.Nodes(ndx).EnsureVisible
         ActiveXCtl0_NodeClick (ActiveXCtl0.Nodes(ndx))
         ActiveXCtl0.SetFocus
      End If
   End If
End Sub
```

The selected node is returned from the TreeView's SelectedItem property and can be used to reference the properties and methods of the selected node.

Using the ListView control

Another Windows 95 Common Control you'll find useful in your applications is the ListView control. This control is the one you see on the right side of the Windows 95 Explorer window and in the Folders on the desktop.

Views and icons

The ListView control contains a ListItems property, which is a collection of ListItem objects. These ListItems appear in the ListView control in one of four views, which you select in the View property by using an appropriate constant (see Table 6-8).

Table 6-8 Constants for Selecting the Desired View

View Constant	*Value*	*Description*
`lvwIcon`	0	Each `ListItem` object is displayed as a full-sized (standard) icon with a text label. The Default view.
`lvwSmallIcon`	1	Each `ListItem` object is displayed as a small icon with a text label. The items are listed horizontally.
`lvwList`	2	Each `ListItem` object is displayed as a small icon with a text label. The items are listed vertically, each on its own line.
`lvwReport`	3	Each `ListItem` object is displayed as a small icon with a text label. Additional information about each `ListItem` object can be assigned to subitems. The icons, text, and subitem entries appear in columns, with the leftmost column containing the small icon, followed by the text. Additional columns display the text for each of the subitems in the ListItem.

Before you can display icons with `ListItem` objects in a view, you must associate the `ListView` control with an `ImageList` control. This takes two `ListView` properties. Use the `Icons` property to specify the source of images for the Icon view, and use the `SmallIcons` property to specify the image source for the SmallIcon view.

Each `ListItem` object also has properties, `Icon` and `SmallIcon`, for specifying the `ListImage` index or key of the ListItem's `Icon` and `SmallIcon`, as shown here:

```
Dim liItem As ListItem

Me!ActiveXCtl9.Icons = ActiveXCtl10.Object
Me!ActiveXCtl9.SmallIcons = ActiveXCtl11.Object
...
liItem.Icon = 1           ' ListImage 1 in ActiveXCtl10 ImageList
liItem.SmallIcon = 1   ' ListImage 1 in ActiveXCtl11 ImageList
```

Adding items to the list

You can specify both `Icons` and `SmallIcons` in the `Add` method when adding a `ListItem` object, as follows:

```
OLEControl0.ListItems.Add(index, key, text, icon, smallicon)
```

As with the `TreeView` control's `Nodes Add` method, the `index`, `key`, and `text` give the new `ListItem` an identity within the collection and a label within the `ListView`. The `Icon` and `SmallIcon` arguments specify the `ListImage` indexes of the associated `ListImage` control.

Removing ListItems requires the use of the Remove method, as shown here:

```
ActivXCtl9.ListItems.Remove index
```

The index argument represents the index of the ListItem to remove. If you specify a string for the index, the string is interpreted as the key of the ListItem to remove. If you specify a number, it is interpreted as the index number of the ListItem to remove. Using the Clear method removes all ListItem objects.

You can reference a specific item in the ListItems collection with the Item method, as shown in the following code; however, it is not necessary to use this method explicitly because it is the default method of the ListItems collection:

```
ActiveXCtl9.ListItems.Item(index)
```

Here, too, you may specify a key instead of the index of the desired ListItem to reference.

ColumnHeaders and SubItems

You can store additional data with a ListItem object, which makes this control a valuable addition to your project. Each ListItem can have SubItems associated with it. The SubItems property is an array of strings that you can use to store additional information about the object represented by the ListItem.

To assign SubItems, you must first build a ColumnHeaders collection. ColumnHeaders is a property of the ListView control and defines a collection of ColumnHeader objects. Each ColumnHeader describes a column within the ListView when the View property is set to lvwReport.

Although adding ColumnHeaders to the control enables the Report view to display columns of data, it also enables the use of SubItems, which can be used with any selected view. The SubItem strings are displayed within the Report's columns, starting in column two. If you don't want the ColumnHeaders displayed in the view, set the ListView HideColumnHeaders property to True.

The ColumnHeaders Add method adds ColumnHeader objects to the control. After establishing ColumnHeaders, you may specify (ColumnHeaders - 1) SubItems for each of the ListItem objects, because the first ColumnHeader is reserved for the ListItem itself, as shown here:

```
Dim colHeader As ColumnHeader
Dim liItem As ListItem
Dim rsSites As RecordSet

Set colHeader = Me!ActiveXCtl9.ColumnHeaders.Add(, "Site", "Site", _
2500)
Set colHeader = Me!ActiveXCtl9.ColumnHeaders.Add(, "City", "City", _
2500)
Set colHeader = Me!ActiveXCtl9.ColumnHeaders.Add(, "State", "State", _
1500)
```

```
Set liItem = ActiveXCtl9.ListItems.Add(, "K" & _
CStr(rsSites![Site_ID]), _
      rsSites![Site_Name], niSiteIcon, niSiteIcon)
liItem.SubItems(1) = rsSites![Site_City]
liItem.SubItems(2) = rsSites![Site_State]
```

Aligning text

You may specify a fifth argument in the ColumnHeaders Add method for the Alignment of the ColumnHeader text. Valid specifications are listed in Table 6-9.

Table 6-9 ColumnHeader Text Alignment Constants

ColumnHeader	*Constant*	*Value Description*
lvwColumnLeft	0	Text is left-aligned.
lvwColumnRight	1	Text is right-aligned.
lvwColumnCenter	2	Text is centered.

Lists containing ghosts

If your ListView displays items that may need to denote a state different from the other items in the list, you can set an item's Ghosted property to True. This action grays the item's icon but not the text. Although the item is grayed, it is not disabled. If you have code in the ItemClick event procedure and you want to take a different action for Ghosted items, check the Ghosted property at the beginning of the procedure and act accordingly.

Arranging items in the list

You can set the arrangement of items in a list in the ListView Arrange property. The values you may specify are shown in Table 6-10.

Table 6-10 ListView Arrange Property Constants

Arrange Constant	*Value*	*Description*
lvwNoArrange	0	None.
lvwAutoLeft	1	Items are aligned along the left side of the control.
lvwAutoTop	2	Items are aligned along the top of the control.

Sorting the list

Three ListView properties are used to sort the items displayed in a view: `Sorted`, `SortOrder`, and `SortKey`. To sort a list, do the following:

1. Set the `SortOrder` property to either `lvwAscending (0)` for Ascending order or `lvwDescending (1)` for Descending order.
2. Specify which SubItem to sort on by setting the `SortKey` property either to a number for one of the SubItems or to `0` to sort by the item's text.

Setting the `Sorted` property to `True` displays the list sorted according to these settings. Report view is not required to use a SubItem SortKey.

In Report view with ColumnHeaders visible, you can let the user change the order of the list with code in the `ColumnClick` event to change the SortKey according to the column clicked, as in the following:

```
Private Sub ActiveXCtl9_ColumnClick(ByVal ColumnHeader As Object)

   Me!ActiveXCtl9.SortOrder = lvwAscending
   Me!ActiveXCtl9.SortKey = ColumnHeader.Index - 1
   Me!ActiveXCtl9.Sorted = True

End Sub
```

In this procedure, if the user has clicked the first column, the SortKey is set to zero, which causes a sort by the item's text. If the user clicks on column two, the first subitem controls the order of the list, and so on. This feature is one your users will welcome.

Selecting multiple items

Another feature that comes in handy is the MultiSelect capability. Setting the `MultiSelect` property to `True` enables the user to select multiple items in the list. The Shift key selects all items from the previous selection up to and including the current selection. The Ctrl key enables selection of items anywhere in the list.

`MultiSelection` is used in the `frmListView` to print a report of selected sites.

Finding items in the list

You can implement a Find feature for your list with the `FindItem` method. This method searches for text in an item's text property, its tag property, or one of its subitems. You specify which property to search in the method's second argument by using one of the constants in Table 6-11.

Table 6-11 The Second Argument of the FindItem Method Specifies the Property to Search

Property Constant	*Value*	*Description*
lvwText	0	Text. Searches the Text property.
lvwSubItem	1	SubItem. Searches the SubItems property.
lvwTag	2	Tag. Searches the Tag property.

The match argument in the FindItem method, the last argument, specifies the match method to use if searching the Text property. Use lvwWholeWord (0) to match the first whole word within the Text string or lvwPartial (1) to match a partial string starting at the beginning of the text.

Secret

To find matches subsequent to the first, set the third argument to the index of the first match, as shown in Listing 6-6. This setting causes the FindItem method to start its search at the item that has the specified index. The cmdFind button uses the FindItem method to search the Text property of the ListView for a partial match to the text entered by the user into the txtFind text box.

Listing 6-6 The FindItem Method Used to Search the Text Property of the ListView

```
Private Sub cmdFind_Click()

   Dim liListItem As ListItem

   If IsNull(txtFind.Value) Then
      Exit Sub
   End If

   Set liListItem = ActiveXCtl9.FindItem(txtFind.Value, lvwText, , _
lvwPartial)

   If liListItem Is Nothing Then
      MsgBox "Item not found"
      Exit Sub
   End If

   liListItem.Selected = True
   ActiveXCtl9.Refresh

End Sub
```

After the FindItem returns a ListItem reference, you can set the item's Selected property to True and refresh the ListView to show the selection.

Using the ProgressBar and StatusBar controls

It's a good idea to tell users about the state of your application and indicate the progress of a lengthy process. The `StatusBar` control is appropriate for displaying certain state information, such as a mode, keystate, and page numbers. This information is displayed in one of the `Panel` objects in the StatusBar's `Panels` collection. Use the `ProgressBar` control to indicate the progress of a process by filling a rectangle with blocks to show how much of the process has been completed.

On CD-ROM

The CH6.MDB database on this book's CD-ROM contains an example of the `ProgressBar` and `StatusBar` controls in the frmBars: Form (see Figure 6-20). The progress of the summation is displayed in the first panel and the running sum in the second panel of the StatusBar at the bottom of the form.

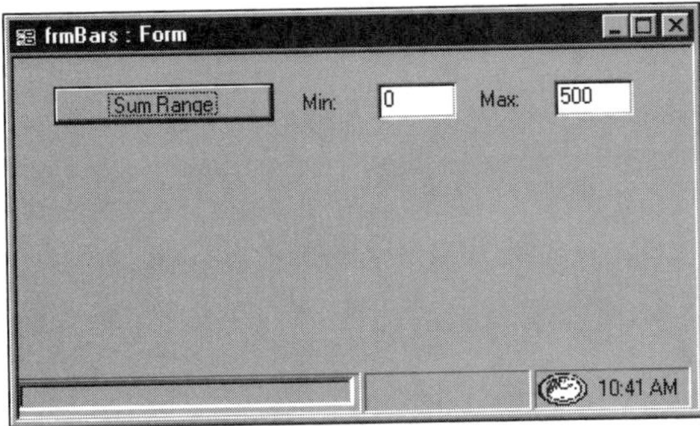

Figure 6-20: The frmBars: Form sums the range of numbers entered in the Min and Max text boxes.

The Sum Range button's `Click Event` procedure is in Listing 6-7. The Min and Max text boxes are checked for valid numbers; a default is used if either is invalid. These numbers from Min to Max are added together and the running sum is displayed in the StatusBar.

Listing 6-7 The Sum Range Button's Click Event Procedure

```
Private Sub cmdProgress1_Click()

   On Error GoTo ProgErrHandler

   Dim pbProgressBar As CustomControl
   Dim sbStatusBar As CustomControl
   Dim nsIncr As Single, nsAccum As Single

   Set pbProgressBar = ActiveXCtl11
   Set sbStatusBar = ActiveXCtl12
```

(continued)

(continued)

```
    If IsNumeric(txtMin.Value) Then
       pbProgressBar.Min = txtMin.Value
    Else
       txtMin.Value = 0
       pbProgressBar.Min = txtMin.Value
    End If
    If IsNumeric(txtMax.Value) Then
       pbProgressBar.Max = txtMax.Value
    Else
       txtMax.Value = 500
       pbProgressBar.Max = txtMax.Value
    End If

    pbProgressBar.Value = txtMin.Value
    For nsIncr = txtMin.Value To txtMax.Value
       nsAccum = nsAccum + nsIncr
       pbProgressBar.Value = nsIncr
       ' Show the running sum in the status bar
       sbStatusBar.Panels(2).Text = Format(nsAccum, "#,##0.00")
       If nsIncr Mod 10 = 0 Then
          sbStatusBar.Refresh
       End If
    Next nsIncr
    sbStatusBar.Refresh
    pbProgressBar.Value = 0
    Exit Sub

ProgErrHandler:
    sbStatusBar.Panels(2).Text = "Error"
    pbProgressBar.Value = 0
    Exit Sub
End Sub
```

In form design, the ProgressBar was positioned over the `StatusBar` control's first panel and brought to the front by selecting the control and choosing Bring To Front on the Format menu. This action gives the ProgressBar the effect of being included in the StatusBar panel. The Border Style of the ProgressBar is Transparent, because the panel border encloses it.

The frmBars: Form `Load` procedure sets the width of the first panel to the width of the ProgressBar, as follows:

```
Private Sub Form_Load()
   Dim pbProgressBar As CustomControl
   Dim sbStatusBar As CustomControl
   Dim pnlPanel As Panel

   Set pbProgressBar = ActiveXCtl11
   Set sbStatusBar = ActiveXCtl12
   sbStatusBar.Panels(1).Width = pbProgressBar.Width + 50
   Set pnlPanel = sbStatusBar.Panels.Add(, , , sbrTime)
   Set pnlPanel.Picture = _
Me!OLEControl2.ListImages("clock").ExtractIcon
End Sub
```

The Min and Max text box values are assigned to the `ProgressBar Min` and `Max` properties. This assignment sets the range the ProgressBar uses to determine the amount of space in the control to fill with blocks, based on the value in the `Value` property.

The `Value` property is initialized with the `Min` value and then assigned the value of the loop counter as the `For` loop proceeds to add the numbers in the range. This technique causes the ProgressBar to update its display.

To display the running sum in the `StatusBar` control, the code sets the second panel's `Text` property with the value of the accumulator. The `Style` property of these panels was set to `0 - Text` in the StatusBar Properties Sheet. Other Styles you can use are shown in Table 6-12.

Table 6-12 StatusBar Panel Style Properties

Style Constant	*Value*	*Description*
`sbrText`	0	Displays text and a bitmap. This value is the default.
`sbrCaps`	1	CAPS LOCK key status. Displays `CAPS` in bold when the Caps Lock mode is on, and dimmed when it is off.
`sbrNum`	2	NUM LOCK key status. Displays `NUM` in bold when the Number Lock mode is on, and dimmed when it is off.
`sbrIns`	3	INS key status. Displays `INS` in bold when the Insert mode is on, and dimmed when it is off.
`sbrScrl`	4	SCROLL LOCK key status. Displays `SCRL` in bold when the Scroll Lock mode is on, and dimmed when it is off.
`sbrTime`	5	Time. Displays the current time in the system format.
`sbrDate`	6	Date. Displays the current date in the system format.

The StatusBar is only refreshed on every tenth iteration of the loop in order to reduce the time it takes to complete the process, as indicated in the following code:

```
If nsIncr Mod 10 = 0 Then
   sbStatusBar.Refresh
End If
```

When the summation process is complete, the StatusBar is refreshed one last time and the ProgressBar is set to zero to indicate that the process has finished, as in this code:

```
sbStatusBar.Refresh
pbProgressBar.Value = 0
```

The `Form Load` procedure adds a panel to the `Panels` collection to display the current time. The `Panels` collection `Add` method accomplishes this task, as follows:

```
sbStatusBar.Panels.Add(index, key, text, style, picture)
```

You can assign the picture argument an icon either through the `LoadPicture` function or by using the `ListImage ExtractIcon` method, as the `Form Load` procedure does.

To remove a panel, use the `Panels Remove` method, specifying the index or key of the panel to remove from the collection.

The `Style` property of the StatusBar can be set to `sbrNormal (0)`, which shows all `Panel` objects, or `sbrSimple (1)`, which displays only one large panel. Notice that Access uses the `sbrSimple` style in its bottom left panel and the `sbrNormal` style in its bottom right panel.

When you use `sbrSimple`, set the text in this panel with the `StatusBar SimpleText` property.

Use of ActiveX controls and the Automation features available in Access 97 can greatly enhance the look and feel of your application and make your job as a developer much easier. There are many sources of third-party custom controls on the market. You may find some of them a worthwhile investment to add features to your applications and to reduce your overall development time.

Part III

Interface

Chapter 7

Form Layout

In This Chapter

- Defining controls and properties
- Using the Tab control
- Creating, selecting, and manipulating controls
- Creating a standard data-entry form
- Learning about label and text box control techniques
- Creating a multiple-page form
- Using form and page headers and footers
- Enhancing text controls by controlling font size and style
- Applying special display effects to forms
- Adding a background picture to a form
- Using AutoFormat and the Format Painter
- Printing a form
- Converting a form to a report

Controls and properties form the basis of forms and reports. Therefore, you must understand the fundamental concepts of controls and properties before you begin to apply them to forms and reports. Even if you have been using Access for several years, you may not know some of the following fundamentals and secrets of using even the simplest of controls:

- A text label is more powerful than a command button for creating visual effects when you need a push button.
- You can move and resize a single control or move a group of controls one pixel at a time without using a mouse.
- You can create cartoonlike animation by using an Access form's On Timer event.

If some of these are secrets to you, you will want to read the next several chapters carefully. You should learn the basics first before you learn some of the best-kept form secrets. Feel free to skip ahead if you think the beginning of this chapter is too basic for your knowledge level.

What Is a Control?

A control has many definitions in Access. Generally, a control is any object on a form or report, such as a label or text box. Values are entered into controls and displayed by the use of a control. A control can be bound to a table field, but it can also be an object, such as a line or rectangle. Calculated fields are also controls, as are pictures, graphs, option buttons, checkboxes, and objects. Some controls aren't part of Access but are developed separately; they are called *OLE custom controls* (also known as OCX and ActiveX controls). These controls extend the base feature set of Microsoft Access.

Whether you're working with forms or reports, creating and using controls is done with essentially the same process. In this chapter, you see controls explained from the perspective of a form.

The different control types

You find many different control types on a form or report. These types include the controls that you can create by using the toolbox shown in Figure 7-1. In this book, you learn how to create and use the most frequently used controls listed in Table 7-1. In this chapter, you learn when to use each control and how these controls work.

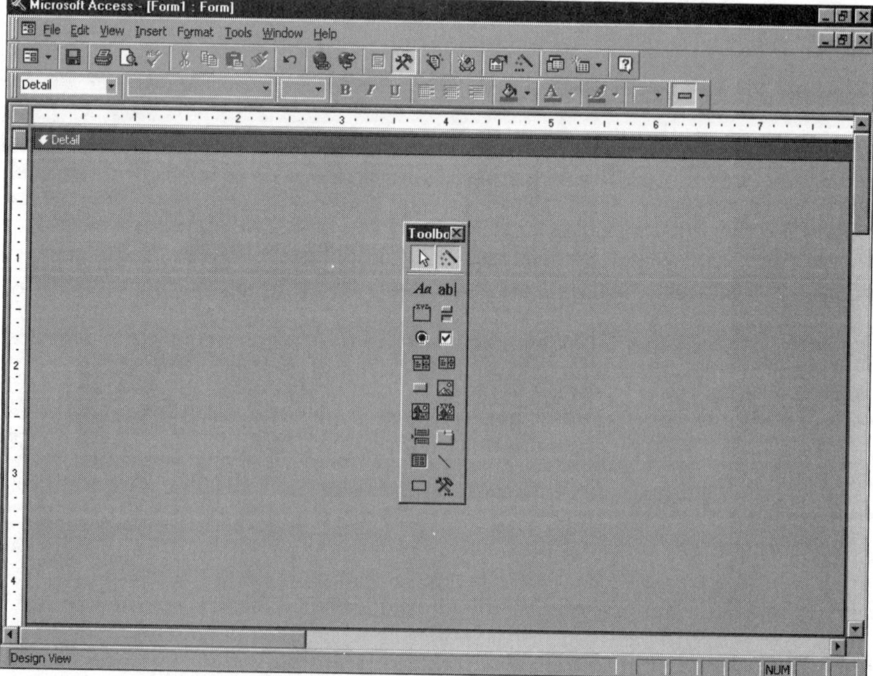

Figure 7-1: A new blank form and the toolbox.

Table 7-1 Controls You Can Create in Access Forms and Reports

Basic Controls	
Label	Literal text is displayed in a label control.
Text box	Data is typed into a text box.
Enhanced Data-Entry and Data-Validation Controls	
Option group	Holds multiple option buttons, checkboxes, or toggle buttons.
Toggle button	A two-state button, up or down, which usually uses pictures or icons.
Option button	Also called a *radio button,* this button is displayed as a circle with a dot when the option is on.
Checkbox	Another two-state control, shown as a square that contains an X if it's on, an empty square if it's off.
Combo box	A pop-up list of values that allows entries not on the list.
List box	A list of values that is always displayed on the form or report.
Command button	Also called a *push button,* this button is used to call a macro or run a Basic program to initiate an action.
Tab Control	Use to create a tabbed form with several pages or a tabbed dialog box.
Subform/Subreport	Displays another form or report within the original form or report.
Graphic and Picture Controls	
Image	Displays a bitmap picture with very little overhead.
Unbound object frame	This frame holds an OLE object or embedded picture that is not tied to a table field. It includes graphs, pictures, sound files, and video.
Bound object frame	Holds an OLE object or embedded picture that is tied to a table field.
Line	A single line of variable thickness and color that is used for separation.
Rectangle	A rectangle can be any color or size. It can also be filled in or blank. The rectangle is used for emphasis.
Page break	Usually used for reports, it denotes a physical page break.

If the toolbox is not displayed, select View⇨Toolbox or click on the toolbox icon to display the toolbox.

The toolbox can be moved, resized, and anchored on the window. You can anchor it to any border, grab it, and resize it in the middle of the window.

The Control Wizard icon does not create a control but rather determines whether a wizard is automatically activated when creating some of the controls. The option group, combo box, list box, subform/subreport, object frame, and command button controls all have wizards that are started when a new control is created.

Understanding bound, unbound, and calculated controls

The three basic types of controls are

- Bound controls
- Unbound controls
- Calculated controls

Bound controls are those that are bound to a table field. When you enter a value into a bound control, Access automatically updates the table field in the current record. Most of the controls that let you enter information can be bound, including OLE fields. Bound controls can be most data types, including text, dates, numbers, Yes/No, pictures, and memo fields.

Unbound controls are controls that retain the value entered but do not update any table fields. You can use these controls for text display; for values to be passed to macros, lines, and rectangles; or for holding OLE objects (such as a bitmap picture) that are not stored in a table but on the form itself. Unbound controls are sometimes called *variables,* or *memory variables.*

Calculated controls are based on expressions, such as functions or calculations. Calculated controls are also Runbound, because they do not update table fields. An example of a calculated control is `=[Hours] * [Salary Rate]`. This control calculates the total of two table fields for display on a form.

Examples of these three control types are shown in Figure 7-2. The picture of the sunset, which is the company's logo, and the text "Sunset Adventure Tours" are unbound controls. The controls below the text and logo that contain field names, including the picture, are bound controls. You also see one calculated control, which is the person's age. You can see that the function `DateDiff` is used to calculate the number of years from the Date of Birth bound control to the function `Now( )`, which returns the current date.

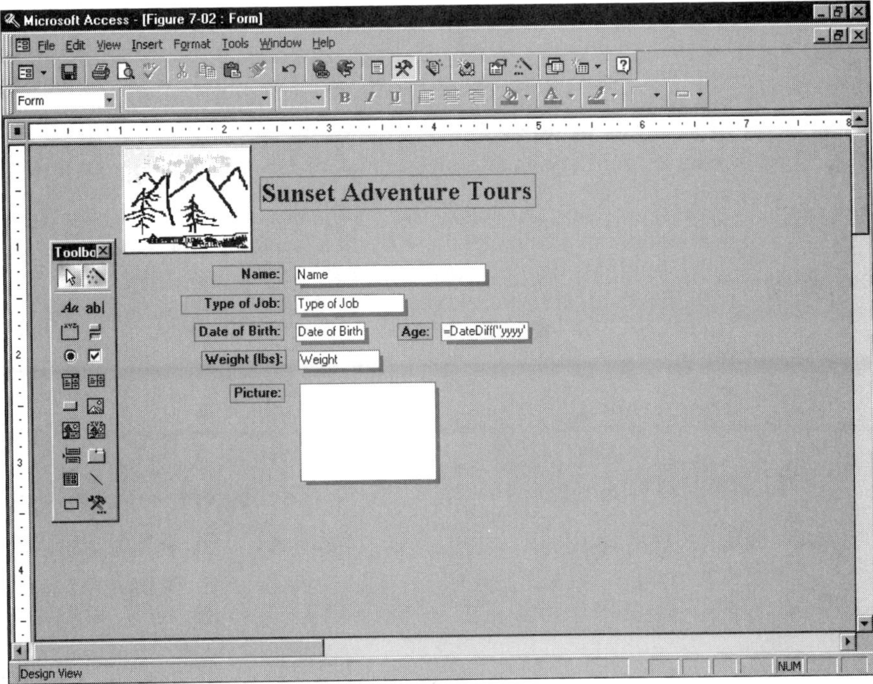

Figure 7-2: The three control types.

Standards for Using Controls

Most of you reading this book have used Microsoft Windows, and you've probably used other applications in Windows, such as word processing applications (Word for Windows, WordPerfect for Windows, or WordPad) and spreadsheet applications (Excel, 1-2-3 for Windows, or Quattro Pro). Using a Windows application and designing one, however, are very different propositions.

The controls in Microsoft Access have specific purposes. Their use is not decided by whim or intuition. Rather, a logical method exists that determines which control should be used for each specific situation. Experience will show you that correct screen and report designs lead to more-usable applications.

Label controls

A *label control* displays descriptive text, such as a title, a caption, or instructions on a form or report. Labels can be separate controls, which is common when they are used for titles or data-entry instructions. When labels are used for field captions, they are often attached to the control that they describe.

Labels can be displayed on a single line, or they can occupy multiple lines. Labels are unbound controls that accept no input. You use them strictly for one-way communication; they are read and that's all. You can use labels on many types of controls. Figure 7-3 shows many uses of labels, including titles, captions, button text, and button and box captions. You can use different font styles and sizes for your labels, and you can boldface, italicize, and underline them.

You should capitalize each word in a label, except for articles and conjunctions, such as *the, an, and, or,* and so on. You can follow several guidelines for label controls when you use them in other controls, as you can see in Figure 7-3. The following list explains some of these guidelines for placement:

Command buttons: Inside the button

Checkboxes: To the right of the checkbox

Option buttons: To the right of the option button

Text box: Above or to the left of the text box

List or combo box: Above or to the left of the box

Group box: On top of and replacing part of the top frame line

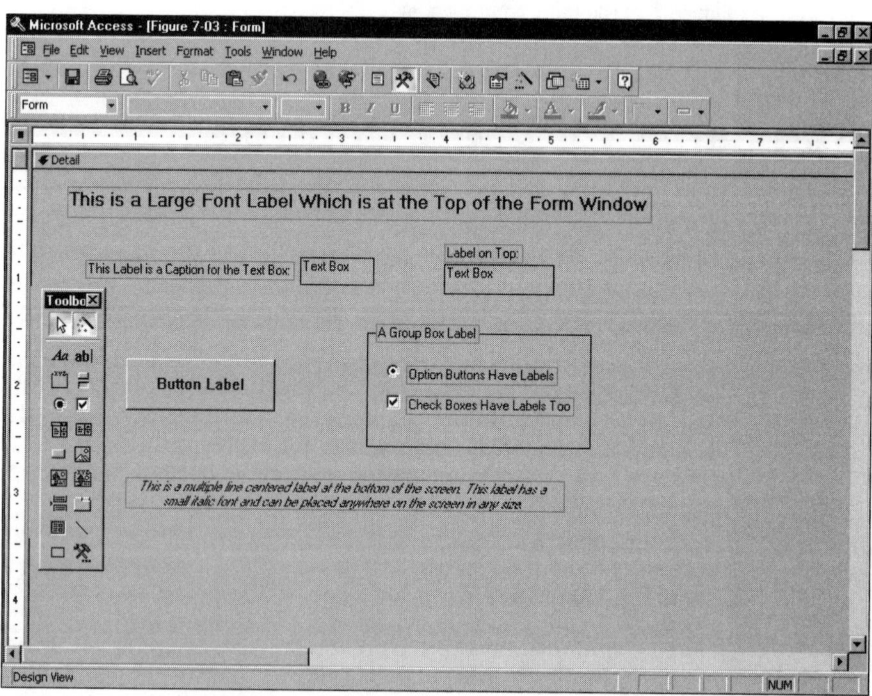

Figure 7-3: Sample label controls.

Text box controls

Text boxes are controls in which the user types information or data. In a text box, you can accept the current text, edit it, delete it, or replace it. Text boxes can accept any type of data, including Text, Number, Date/Time, Yes/No, and Memo data types. Text boxes can be bound or unbound. You can use text box fields from tables or queries, and the text box can also contain calculated expressions. A text box is the most used control, because editing and displaying data are the main purposes of any database system.

Text boxes should have an associated label to identify the purpose of the text box. Text boxes can contain multiple lines of data. When you use a text box to display Memo field data, you normally use a multiple-line text box. Data that is too long for the text field width automatically wraps within the field boundaries. Figure 7-4 shows several different text boxes in the Form view. Notice how the different data types vary in their alignment within the text boxes. The Comments text box displays multiple lines in the resized text box, which also has a scroll bar added.

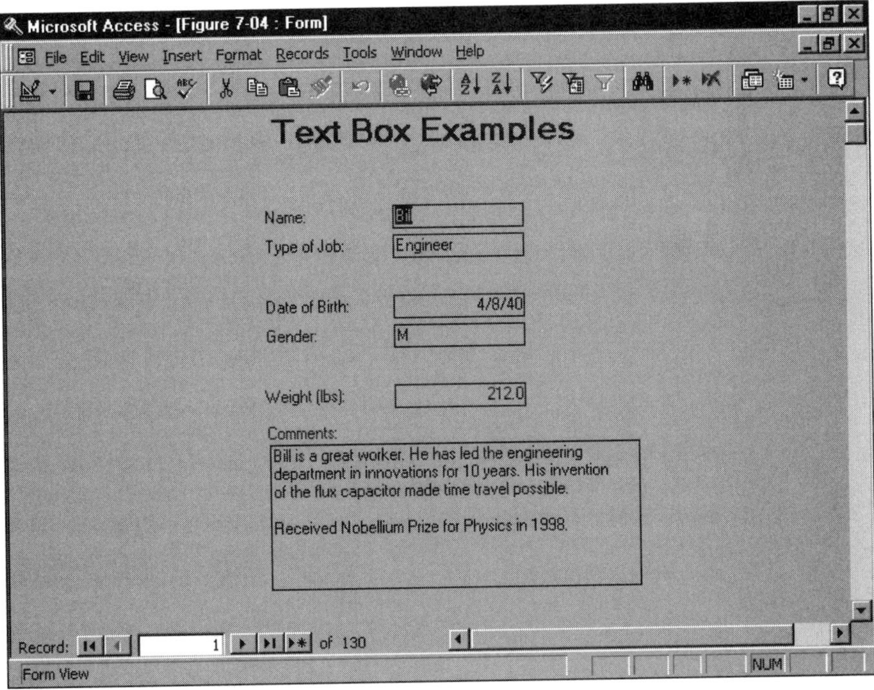

Figure 7-4: Sample text box controls.

Toggle buttons, option buttons, and checkboxes

The following three types of buttons act in the same way, but their visual display is very different:

- Toggle buttons
- Option buttons (also known as radio buttons)
- Checkboxes

These controls are used with Yes/No data types. Each of these buttons can be used individually to represent one of two states, whether Yes or No, On or Off, or True or False. Table 7-2 describes the visual representation of these controls.

Table 7-2 Button Control Visual Displays

Button Type	*State*	*Visual Description*
Toggle button	True	Button is sunken
Toggle button	False	Button is raised
Option button	True	Circle with a large solid dot inside
Option button	False	Hollow circle
Checkbox	True	Square with a check in the middle
Checkbox	False	Empty square

Toggle buttons, option buttons, and checkboxes return a value of – 1 to the bound table field if the button value is Yes, On, or True, and a value of 0 if the button is No, Off, or False. You can enter a default value to display a specific state. The control is initially displayed in a Null state if no default is entered and no state is selected. The Null state's visual appearance is the same as in the No state.

Although you can place Yes/No data types in a text box, using one of these controls is better. The values that are returned to a text box are very confusing, especially because Yes is represented by – 1 and No is represented by 0.

The checkbox is the commonly accepted control for two-state selection. Toggle and option buttons are nice but not always appropriate. Each of these controls can also use pictures instead of a text caption to represent the two states. Figure 7-5 shows these buttons, including text box values and toggle buttons.

As you can see in Figure 7-5, you can change the look of the option button or checkbox by using the special effects options from the formatting toolbar.

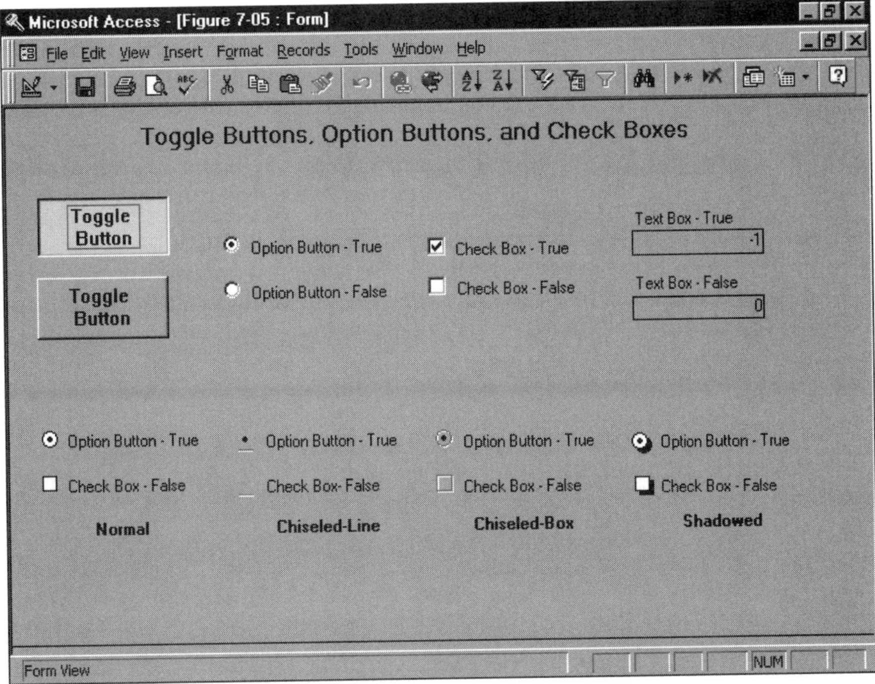

Figure 7-5: Sample toggle buttons, option buttons, and checkboxes.

Tip

You can format the display of the Yes/No values in the Datasheet or Form view by setting the Format property of the text box control to Yes/No, On/Off, or True/False. If you don't use the Format property, the datasheet will display – 1 or 0. Using a default value also speeds up data entry by setting as the default the value that is selected most often.

Option groups

An *option group* can contain multiple toggle buttons, option buttons, or checkboxes. When these controls are placed inside an option group box, they work together instead of individually. Rather than represent a two-state Yes/No data type, controls within an option group return a number based on the position in the group. Only one control within an option group can be selected at one time. The maximum number of buttons in an option group should be four. If you need to exceed that number, you should switch to a drop-down list box (unless you have plenty of room on your screen).

An option group is generally bound to a single field or expression. Each button inside passes a different value back to the option group, which in turn passes the single choice to the bound field or expression. The buttons themselves are not bound to any field but to the option group box.

Figure 7-6 shows three types of buttons in an option group box. The toggle button option group and the option button option group have the second choice selected. The checkboxes are not part of an option group but are independent, and the first and third choices are selected. When you make a new selection in an option group, the current selection is deselected. For example, in the middle option group box in Figure 7-6, if you click on Option Button 3, the solid dot appears to move to the third circle, and the second circle becomes hollow.

The option button is the generally accepted control for use within an option group. You should use checkboxes only in two-state or multiple-state selections when more than one selection is allowed in a group, as shown in Figure 7-6.

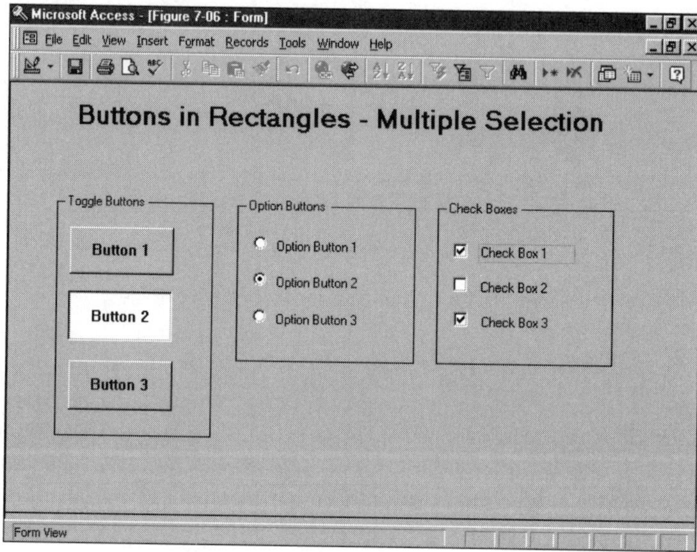

Figure 7-6: Three types of option groups.

List boxes

A *list box* control displays a list of data on screen just as a pull-down menu does, but the list box is always open. You can highlight an item in the list by moving the cursor to the desired choice and then pressing Enter or clicking the mouse to complete the selection. You can also type the first letter of the selection to highlight the desired entry. After you select an item, the item's value is passed back to the bound field.

List boxes can display any number of fields and any number of records. By sizing the list box, you can make it display more or fewer records.

Access 97 list boxes feature a Multi-Select property that enables you to select more than one item at a time. The results are stored in an array and must be used with VBA.

List boxes are generally used when there is plenty of room on screen and you want the operator to see the choices without having to click on a drop-down arrow. A vertical — and even horizontal — scroll bar is used for displaying records and fields that are not visible when the list box is in its default size. The highlighted entry will be the one currently selected. If no entries are highlighted, either a selection has not been made or the selected item is not currently in view. Only items in the list can be selected.

You also have a choice of whether to display the column headings on list boxes. Figure 7-7 displays list boxes with three layout schemes.

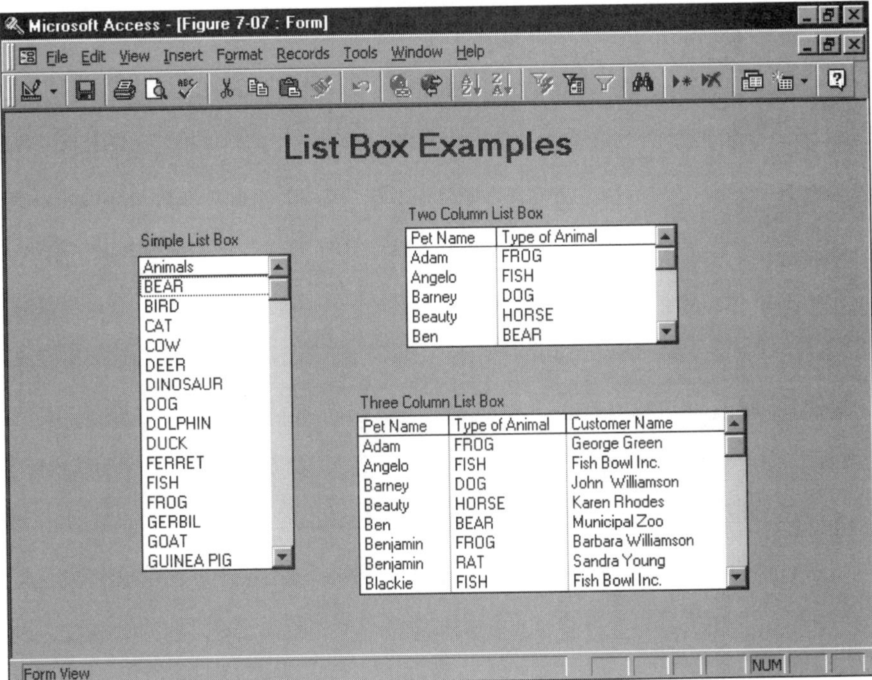

Figure 7-7: Sample list boxes.

Combo boxes

In Access, combo boxes differ from list boxes in two ways:

- The combo box is initially displayed as a single row with an arrow that enables you to open the box to the normal size.
- As an option, the combo box enables you to enter a value that is not on the list.

In Figure 7-8, you see a list box and two combo boxes (one open and one closed).

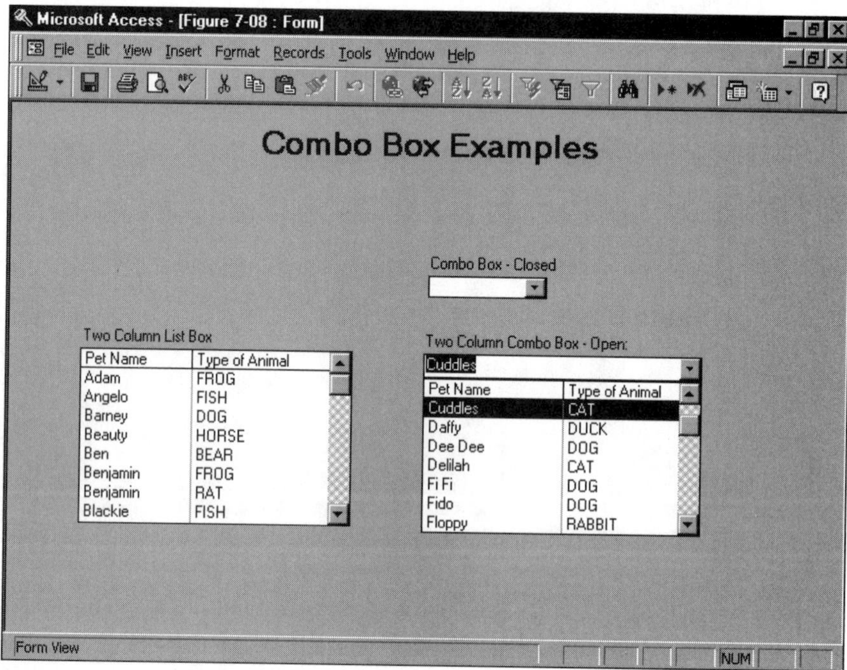

Figure 7-8: A list box and two combo boxes, one open and one closed.

Using the Access 97 Tab Control

Today, most serious windows applications contain tabbed dialog boxes. Tabbed dialog boxes look very professional, and they enable you to have many screens of data in a small area by grouping similar types of data and using tabs to navigate between the areas.

Microsoft Access 97 introduces a *native* (built-in) tab control similar to one that has been in Visual Basic for many years.

Microsoft Access 2.0 and Access for Windows 95 did not contain a tab control, but Microsoft provided a free .OCX tab control, which has been available on CompuServe for the last several years. Several other methods for creating tabbed dialog boxes also have been known, such as using lines, rectangles, and either command buttons or even label controls.

Creating a new form with the Access 97 tab control

The Access 97 tab control has been added to the standard form design toolbar. This control is called a tab control because it looks like the tabs on a file folder. Figure 7-9 shows the Access 97 forms design screen with the toolbar. The tab control icon is labeled, and the design screen shows a tab control already under construction.

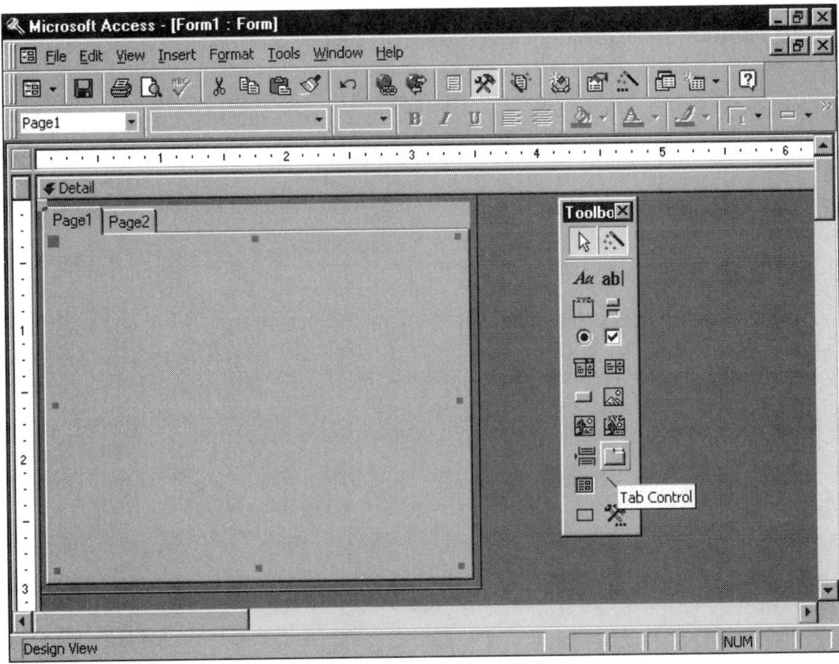

Figure 7-9: Creating an Access 97 tab control.

You create a new tab control the way you create any Access control. You select the tab control, as shown in the figure, and then draw a rectangle to indicate the size of the control. When the tab control is initially shown, it is displayed with two tab pages.

Each tab you define creates a separate page. As you choose each tab in design view, you see a different page. You can place other controls on each page of the tab control. In fact, you can have multiple rows of tabs each having their own page. You can place new controls onto a page or copy and paste them from other forms or other pages. You cannot drag and drop between pages of a tab control. To change the active page for the tab control, just click on the page you want and it will become active (even in design mode).

You insert new pages by selecting the Insert⇨Tab Control Page option or by right clicking on a tab and choosing the Insert command. The new page is inserted before the selected page. You delete pages by selecting a tab and pressing the Delete key, by choosing the Edit⇨Delete menu option, or by right-clicking on a tab and choosing the Delete page command.

Warning

Deleting pages with the Delete page command deletes the active page and all the controls on it.

You must move controls away from the border of a tab control before resizing the control to be smaller.

Access 97 tab control properties

Like any control, the tab control has a variety of properties. The tab control has a separate set of properties for the tab control itself as well as for each page of the tab control. Figure 7-10 shows the property window for the tab control itself. Notice that there is no `Control Source` property. The tab control is only a container for other controls. The form itself can be bound to a table or query, and each control you place on a tab page can be bound to a table field. The tab control and its pages, however, cannot be bound by themselves to a data source.

The tab control itself has many properties found in most controls, such as a name, `Status Bar Text`, `Visible`, `Enabled`, `Tab Stop`, and the position and size properties. The tab control also has several unique properties. Note the properties `Multi-Row`, `Style`, `Tab Fixed Height`, and `Tab Fixed Width`. These properties are only found in a tab control and are explained later in this chapter

Access 97 tab control page properties

Each page also has a unique set of properties, as shown in Figure 7-11. These properties include the page name or caption (which can be different, though the caption is what you see on the tab). You can also have a picture beside the caption. The `Page Index` is like the tab order on a form. It indicates which page comes first and starts at 0. The rest of the properties are generic control properties.

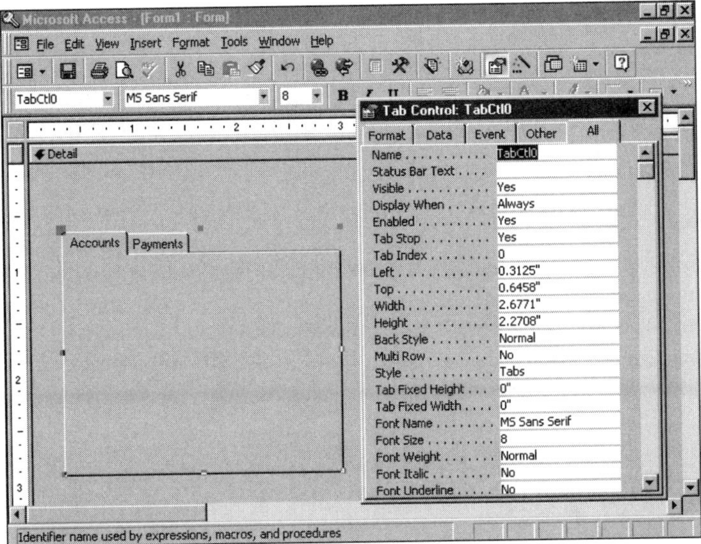

Figure 7-10: Tab control properties.

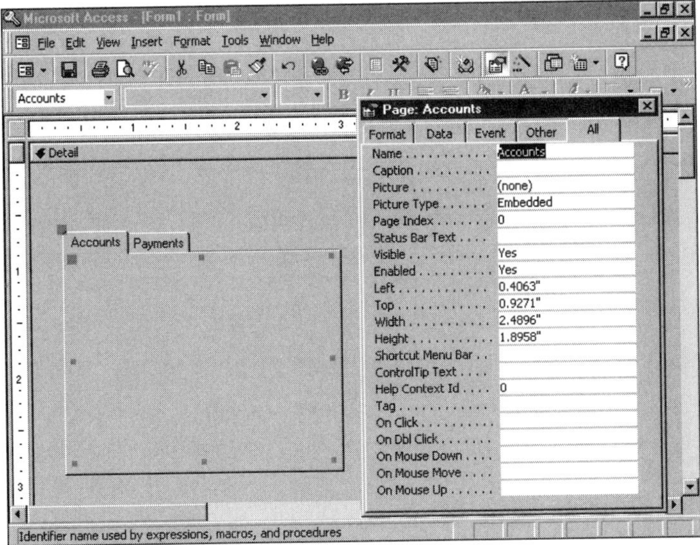

Figure 7-11: Tab control page properties.

Working with a number of rows

The first unique property for a tab control is Multi Row. This is either Yes or No; the default is No. When you change the value to Yes and you have more tabs than will fit in the width of the tab control, the tabs jump to a new row. If you make the tab control wider, the tab may return to a single row. You can create as many rows as you have vertical space to hold them. The tab control itself can be as wide as the form width allows. Figure 7-12 shows one-, two-, and three-row tab controls. Note that the middle tab control has an uneven number of tabs on each row. This is perfectly acceptable, and the tabs will grow to fill the available space. The tab control at the bottom of the screen was sized too small to fit the number of tabs, and the Multi Row property was set to No. For that reason, navigation buttons appear to fill the space. You use these navigation buttons to reach the remainder of the tabs.

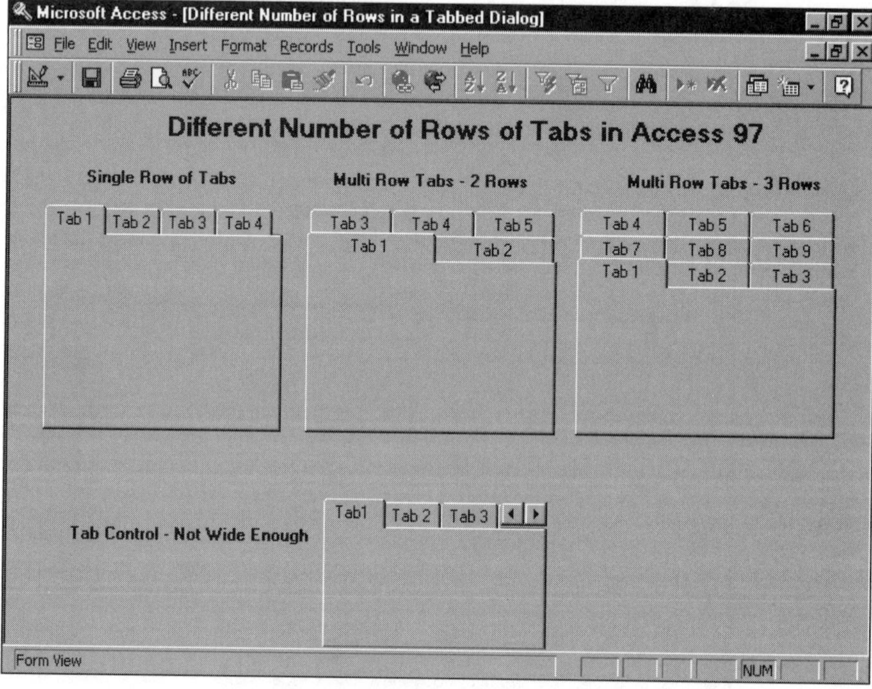

Figure 7-12: Using the Multi Row property.

Setting the height and width of the tabs

Two properties affect the size of the tabs in the tab control. These are the `Tab Fixed Height` and `Tab Fixed Width` properties. Generally, these properties allow you to set the width of the tab in inches, centimeters, or whatever is your local unit of measurement. The default for both of these controls is `0`. When the properties are set to `0`, each tab is wide enough and tall enough to accommodate its contents. If needed, the width of each tab is increased to span the entire width of the tab control. If the properties are greater than 0, the tab is the exact size specified.

The Style of a tab control

The next unique property is the `Style` property, which has three settings: `Tabs`, `Buttons`, and `None`, as you can see in Figure 7-13. The Tabs setting is the default and creates the standard square tabs. The Buttons setting makes the tabs into buttons, surrounded by a button. The effect shown in Figure 7-13 looks more like the Access 95 `Tab Strip` control than an actual tab control, and leaves only the buttons and the tab control set to the first page. You cannot see the rectangle, as you can with the `Tabs` setting. The third setting, `None`, removes the tabs from the tab control and leaves an empty gray area. When using this setting, the tab control can act like a multipage form, which is easier to control than a standard multipage form, because you don't have to worry about navigation from one page to the next.

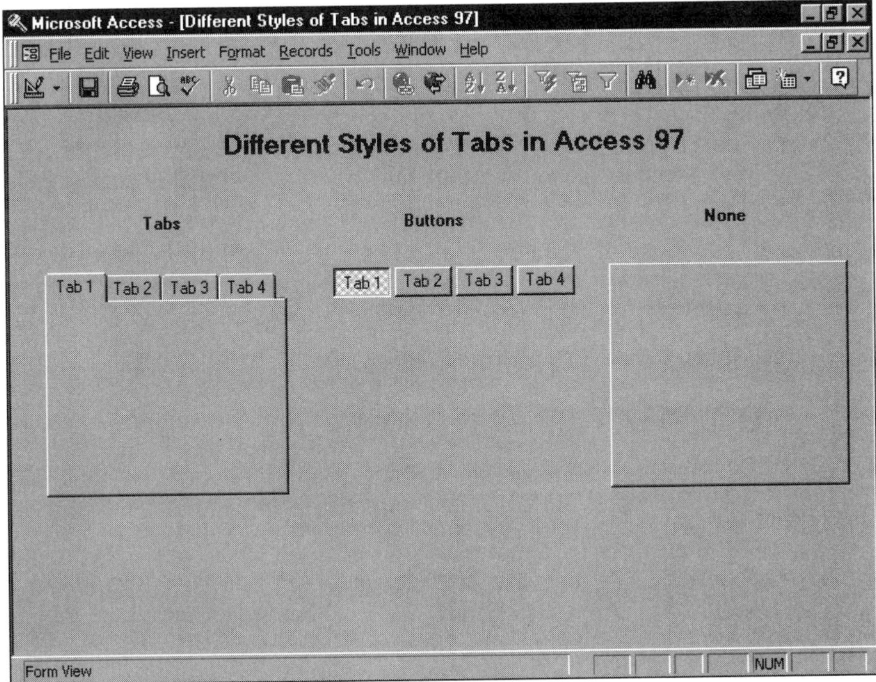

Figure 7-13: Using the Style property.

Changing the page order

Another feature of the tab control is the capability to change the order of the pages (tabs) in the same way that the tab order of the controls on the form can be changed. Figure 7-14 shows the Page Order dialog box. The Page Order lists the text on each tab and enables you to use the Move Up and Move Down buttons to rearrange the pages on the tab control.

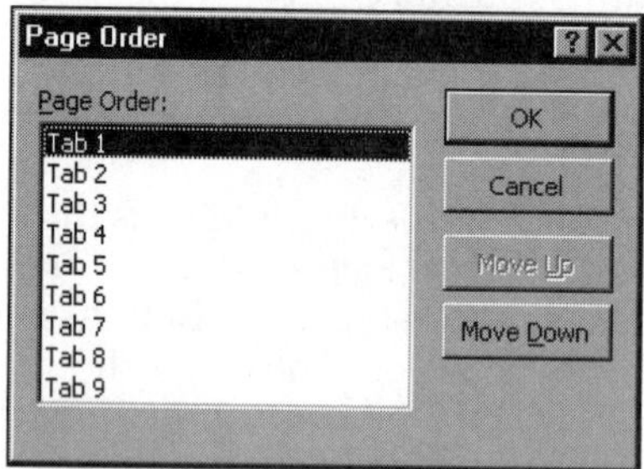

Figure 7-14: Changing the page order.

Using the tab order on a form and the tab control itself

If you have a tab control on a form and you choose View⇨Tab Order, the tab control shows up as a single control in the Tab Order dialog box. The controls inside the tab control do not show in this dialog box.

To set the tab order for controls within a particular page of a tab control, choose the Tab order command from the tab control's right-click menu, or go to the property sheet for the tab control and click on the builder for the tab index property. You must set the tab order for each page individually.

Tabbing out of the last control inside a tab control page brings you to the next control in the tab order for the form itself. You cannot jump between pages.

Adding pictures to the tab control

The page properties of the tab control have no unique properties, but one of the common properties enables you to add a picture to the tab just before the tab text. You use the `Picture` property just as you would on a command button, toggle button, image control, or unbound OLE object.

You can type in the full path and name of the bitmap or icon file or use the Access 97 Picture Builder to select a picture. Figure 7-15 shows the tab control on the Print Reports Tabbed dialog box with one picture already completed and another being selected. Note that in Figure 7-15, the picture of a printer is already beside Page 1. When you select this picture in the Picture Builder, the document picture will appear next to Page 2.

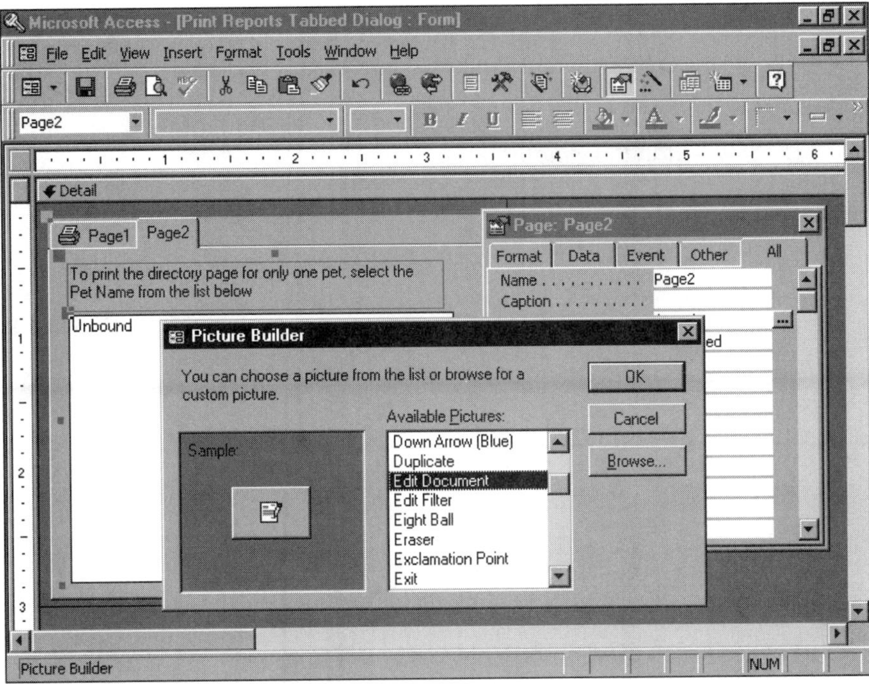

Figure 7-15: Adding a picture to a tab.

Creating New Controls

Now that you have learned about the controls that you can use on a form or report, you should learn how to add controls to a form and how to manipulate them in the Form Design window. Although the Form Wizards can quickly place your fields in the Design window, you still may need to add more fields to a form. There are also many times when you simply want to create a report from a completely blank form.

The two ways to create a control

You can create a control in either of two ways:

- Dragging a field from the Field List window to add a bound control
- Clicking on a button in the toolbox and then adding a new unbound control to the screen

Using the Field List window

The Field List window shown in Figure 7-16 displays all the fields in the open table/query that was used to create a form. This window is movable and resizable and also displays a vertical scroll bar if there are more fields than will fit in the window.

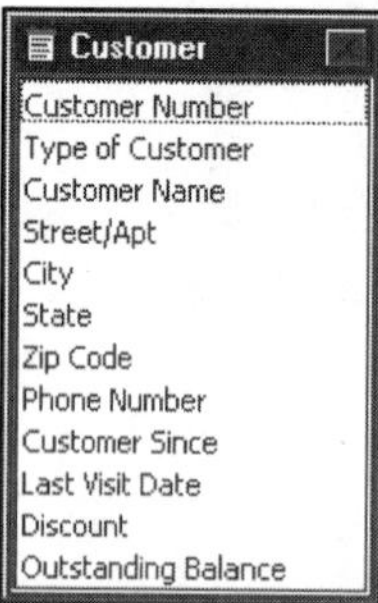

Figure 7-16: The Field List window.

You can display the Field List window in two ways:

- Click on the Field List button in the toolbar. (This button looks like a table.)
- Select View⇨Field List from the Form menu bar.

After you resize or move the Field List window, it remains that size for all forms, even if it is toggled off or if the form is closed. The window is set to its default size only if you exit Access.

When a field is dragged from the Field List window, it generally creates a bound text box on the Form Design screen. If you drag an OLE field from the Field List window, you create a bound object frame. You can select the type of control by first selecting a control from the toolbox and then dragging the field to the Form Design window. This creates the selected control and binds it to the control source (field) selected in the Field List.

When you drag fields from the Field List window, the first control is placed where you release the mouse button. Make sure that there is enough space to the left of the control for the labels. If there is insufficient space, the labels will slide under the controls. The following list describes several distinct advantages of dragging a field from the Field List window:

- The control is automatically bound to the field that you dragged.
- Field properties inherit table-level formats, status-bar text, and data-validation rules and messages.
- The label text is created with the field name as the caption.

Using the toolbox

By using the toolbox buttons to create a control, you can decide what type of control will be used for each field. If you don't create the control by dragging it from the Field List window, the field will be unbound with a default label name, such as Field3 or Option11. After you create the control, you can decide what field to bind the control to, enter any text you want for the label, and set any properties you want.

The basic deciding factor in choosing between the Field List and the toolbox is whether the field exists in the table/query or whether you want to create an unbound or calculated expression. By using the Field List window and the toolbox together, you can create bound controls of nearly any type. You will find, however, that some data types do not allow all the control types found in the toolbox. For example, if you attempt to create a graph from a single field, you simply get a text box.

Secret

In Access 97, you can change the type of control after you create it and set all the properties for the control. For example, suppose that you create a field as a text box control and you want to change it to a list box. You can use Format⇨Change To to change the control type. Obviously, you can only change from some types of controls to others. Anything can be changed to a text box control. Option buttons, toggle buttons, and checkboxes are interchangeable, as are list and combo boxes.

Dragging a field name from the Field List window

The easiest way to create a text box control is to drag a field from the Field List window. When the Field List window is open, you can click on an individual field and drag it to the Form Design window. This window works exactly as a Table/Query window in QBE. You also can select multiple fields and then drag them to the screen together. The techniques you can use include the following:

- Selecting multiple contiguous fields by holding down the Shift key and clicking on the first and last field you want
- Selecting multiple noncontiguous fields by holding down the Ctrl key and clicking on each field you want
- Double-clicking on the table/query name in the window's top border to select all the fields

After you select one or more fields, you can drag the selection to the screen. Each of the controls is made up of a label control and a text box control. Access automatically attaches the label control to the text box. You can work with these controls as a group or independently, and you can select, move, or delete them. Each control label has a caption matching the field name, and the text box control displays the bound field name used in the text box control.

Creating unbound controls with the toolbox

You can create one control at a time by using the toolbox. You can create any of the controls listed in the toolbox. Each control becomes an unbound control that has a default label and a name.

Tip

If you simply click on the Form Design window, Access creates a default-sized control.

In Figure 7-17, note the difference between the controls that were dragged from the Field List window and the controls that were created from the toolbox. The Field List window controls are bound to fields in a table and are appropriately labeled and named. The controls created from the toolbox are unbound and have default names. Notice that control names are automatically assigned based on the type of control and a number.

Later, you learn how to change the control names, captions, and properties. By using properties, you will quickly be able to name the controls and bind the controls to specific fields.

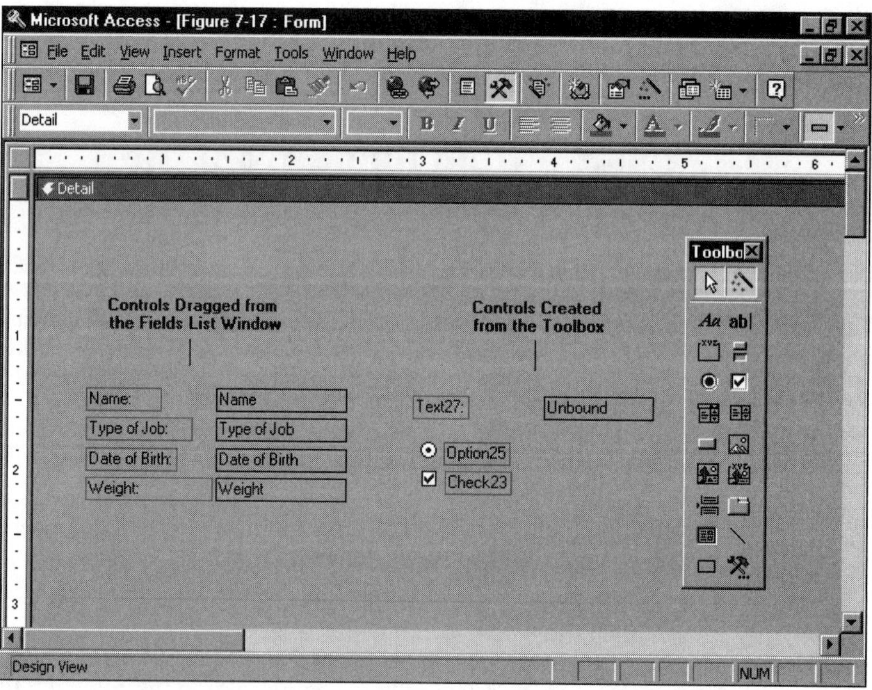

Figure 7-17: Bound and unbound controls.

Selecting Controls

After you have a control on the Form Design window, you can begin to work with it. The first step in working with controls is to select one or more controls. A selected control appears with *handles* around the control box area. A selected control generally has from four to eight handles. A handle appears as a small square and is generally located on the corners of a control box and also at the midpoint of the sides, depending on the size of the control. The handle in the upper-left corner is larger than the other handles and is used to move the control. The other handles are used to size the control. Figure 7-18 shows these controls.

The pointer tool in the toolbox must be on for you to select a control. The pointer always appears as an arrow pointing diagonally to the upper-left corner. If you selected another button in the toolbox and then selected the Lock button in the toolbox, you must click on the pointer again to change the cursor to a selection pointer. If you use the toolbox to create a single control, Access automatically reselects the pointer as the default cursor.

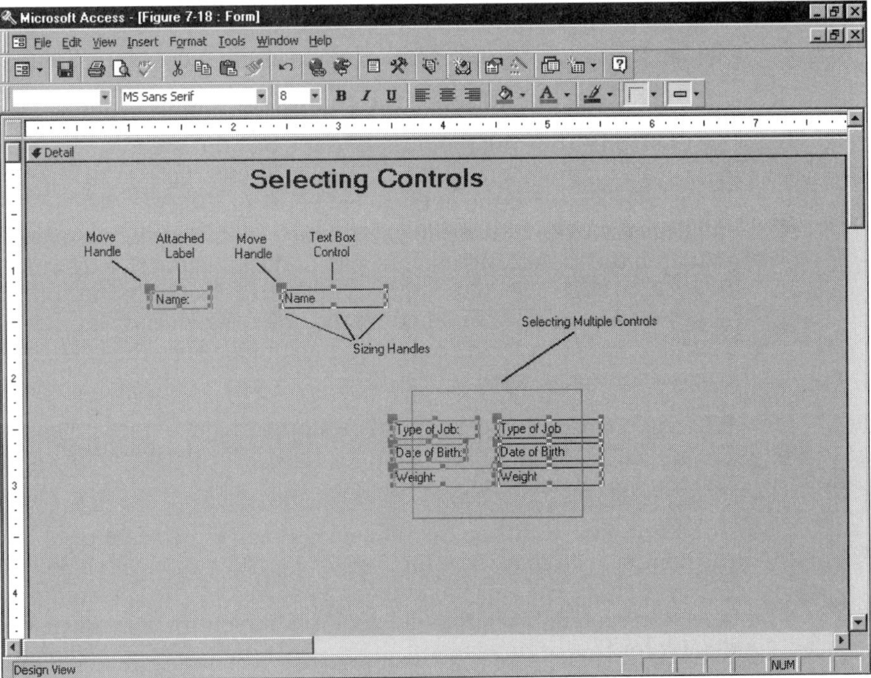

Figure 7-18: A conceptual view of selecting controls.

Deselecting selected controls

You should practice deselecting any selected controls before you select another control. You can deselect a control by simply clicking on an unselected area of the screen that does not contain a control. When you do so, the handles disappear from any selected control.

Selecting a single control

You can select any single control simply by clicking anywhere on the control. When you click on a control, all the handles appear. If the control has an attached label, the handle for moving the label appears as well. If you select a single label control that is part of an attached control, all the handles in the label control are displayed and only the move handle is displayed in the attached control.

Selecting multiple controls

You can select multiple controls in the following ways:

- Click on each desired control while holding down the Shift key.
- Drag the pointer through the controls you want to select.
- Click on either ruler and drag to the desired area.

Figure 7-18 shows some of these concepts graphically. When you select multiple controls by dragging the mouse, a light gray rectangle appears as you drag the mouse. When you select multiple controls by dragging the pointer through the controls, be careful to select only the controls you want to select. Any control touched by the line or enclosed within it is selected. If you want to select labels only, you must make sure the selection rectangle encloses only the labels.

When you click on a ruler, an arrow appears and a line is displayed across the screen. You can drag the cursor to widen the line. Each control that the line touches is selected.

If you find that controls are not selected when the rectangle passes through the control, you may have the `Selection Behavior` global property set to `Fully Enclosed`. This means that a control will be selected only if the selection rectangle completely encloses the entire control. The normal default for this option is `Partially Enclosed`. You can change this option by first selecting Tools➪Options and then selecting Forms/Reports Category in the Options tabbed dialog box. The option `Selection Behavior` should be set to `Partially Enclosed`.

By holding down the Shift key, you can select several noncontiguous controls. This enables you to select controls on totally different parts of the screen, cut them, and then paste them together somewhere else on screen.

Manipulating Controls

Creating a form is generally a multistep process. The next step is to make sure that controls are properly sized and moved into the correct position.

Resizing a control

You can resize controls by using any of the smaller handles on the control. The handles in the control corners enable you to make the field larger or smaller in width and height — all at the same time. You use the handles in the middle of the control sides to size the control larger or smaller in one direction only. The top and bottom handles control the height of the control, whereas the handles in the middle of the sides change the control width.

When a corner handle is touched by the cursor in a selected control, the cursor becomes a diagonal double arrow. You can then hold down the mouse button and drag the control size handles to the desired size. If the cursor touches a side handle in a selected control, the cursor changes to a horizontal or vertical double-headed arrow.

You can resize a control in very small increments by using the Shift+arrow keys. This also works with multiple controls selected. The size of the controls changes by only one pixel at a time.

Moving a control

After you select a control, you can move it. Use either of these methods to move an unselected control:

- Click on the control and drag it to a new location.
- Select the control and then place your cursor *between* any two move handles on the control's border.

As soon as you enter an area of a selected control that can be clicked on and moved, your cursor changes to a hand button.

If the control has an attached label, you can move both the label and the control by this method. It doesn't matter whether you click on the control or the label; they are moved together.

You can move a control separately from an attached label by simply grabbing the move handle of the control and moving it. You also can move the label control separately from the associated control by selecting the move handle of the label control and moving it separately.

Figure 7-19 shows a label control that has been separately moved to the top of the text box control. When you pass the cursor over an edge of the selected control, a hand cursor indicates that the controls are ready to be moved together.

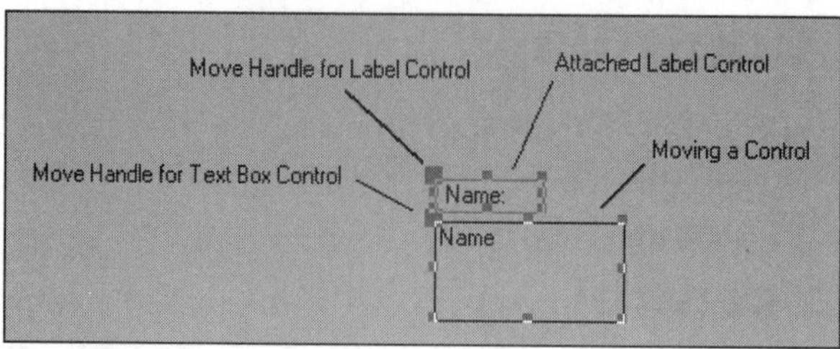

Figure 7-19: Moving a control.

Secret

You can move a control in small increments with the keyboard by using the Ctrl+arrow keys after a control or group of controls has been selected.

Secret

You can restrict the direction in which a control is moved so that it maintains alignment within a specific row or column. To do this, hold down the Shift key as you press the mouse button to select and move the control. The control moves only in the direction you first move it, whether horizontally or vertically.

Tip

You can cancel a move or a resizing operation by pressing Esc before you release the mouse button. After you complete a move or resizing operation, you can click on the Undo button or select Edit⇨Undo Move or Edit⇨Undo Sizing to undo the changes.

Aligning controls

You may want to move several controls so that they are all aligned (lined up). The Format⇨Align menu has several options, as shown in Figure 7-20. The following list describes the options:

- Left — Aligns the left edge of the selected controls with that of the leftmost selected control
- Right — Aligns the right edge of the selected controls with that of the rightmost selected control
- Top — Aligns the top edge of the selected controls with that of the topmost selected control
- Bottom — Aligns the bottom edge of the selected controls with that of the bottom-most selected control
- To Grid — Aligns the top-left corners of the selected controls to the nearest grid point

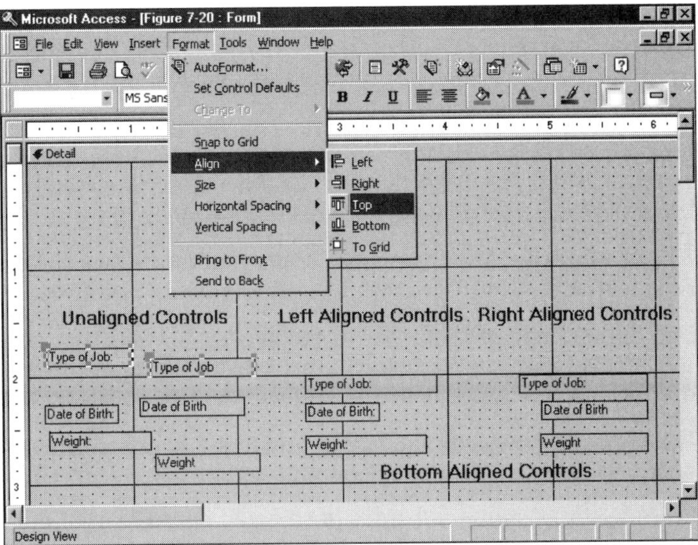

Figure 7-20: Aligning controls and the grid.

By selecting from this menu, you can align any number of controls. When you choose one of the options, the control that is closest to the desired selection is used as the model for the alignment. For example, suppose you have three controls and you want to left align them. They will be aligned based on the control farthest to the left in the group of the three controls.

Figure 7-20 shows several groups of controls. The first group is not aligned. The label controls in the second group of controls have been left aligned. The text box controls in the third group have been right aligned. Each label and its attached text box have been bottom aligned.

Each type of alignment must be done separately. In this example, you can left align all the labels or right align all the text boxes at once. However, you would have to align each of the label and text control bottoms separately, which would take three separate alignments.

You may notice a series of dots in the background of Figure 7-20. This series of dots is called the grid, which assists you in aligning controls. The grid is displayed by selecting View⇨Grid.

You can use the Format⇨Snap to Grid option to align new controls to the grid as you draw or place them on a form. This option also aligns existing controls when you move or resize them.

When Snap to Grid is on and you draw a new control by clicking on and dragging the form, Access aligns all four corners of the control to points on the grid. When you place a new control just by clicking on the form or report, only the upper-left corner is aligned.

As you move or resize existing controls, Access lets you move only from grid point to grid point. When Snap to Grid is off, Access ignores the grid and lets you place a control anywhere on the form or report.

You can temporarily turn off Snap to Grid by holding down the Ctrl key before you create a control (or while you're creating or moving it).

The Size option on the Format menu has several options that assist you in sizing controls based on the value of the data, the grid, or other controls. The options of the size menu are as follows:

- **To Fit** — Adjusts the height and width of controls to fit the font of the text they contain
- **To Grid** — Moves all sides of selected controls in or out to meet the nearest points on the grid
- **To Tallest height** — Sizes selected controls so that they have the same as the tallest selected control
- **To Shortest height** — Sizes selected controls so that they have the same as the shortest selected control
- **To Widest** — Sizes selected controls so that they have the same width as the widest selected control
- **To Narrowest** — Sizes selected controls so that they have the same width as the narrowest selected control

You can change the grid's *fineness* (number of dots) from form to form by using the `GridX` and `GridY` Form properties. The grid is invisible if its fineness is greater than 16 units per inch horizontally or vertically. (Higher numbers indicate greater fineness.)

Another pair of alignment options exists that can make a big difference when aligning the space between multiple controls. The options Horizontal Spacing and Vertical Spacing change the space between controls based on the space between the first two selected controls. If the controls are across a screen, use the horizontal spacing. If they are down a screen, use the vertical spacing.

Deleting a control

If you find that you no longer want a specific control on the Form Design window, you can delete it by selecting the control and pressing Delete. You can also select Edit⇨Delete to delete a selected control or Edit⇨Cut to cut the control to the Clipboard.

You can delete more than one control at a time by selecting multiple controls and pressing one of the Delete key sequences. If you have a control with an attached label, you can delete the label only by clicking on the label itself and then selecting a delete method. If you select the control, both the control and the label are deleted.

Attaching a label to a control

If you accidentally delete a label from a control, you can reattach it by first re-creating the label control on the form, then cutting it to the Clipboard, reselecting the text box control it was originally attached to, and then pasting the label to the control. This reattaches a label to a control so that they work together.

Copying a control

You can create copies of any control by duplicating them or by copying them to the Clipboard and then pasting them where you want them. If you have a control for which you entered many properties, or if you formatted the control a certain way, you can copy it and revise only the properties, such as the control name and bound field name, to make it a different control. This method is also useful when you have a multiple-page form and you want to display the same values on different pages and in different locations.

What Are Properties?

Properties are named attributes of controls, fields, or database objects that you can use to modify the characteristics of the control, field, or object. These attributes can be the size, color, appearance, or name. A property also can modify the behavior of a control, such as by determining whether the control is editable or visible.

Properties are used extensively in forms and reports for changing the characteristics of controls. Each control has properties. In a form, the form itself also has properties, as does each section of a form. The same is true for reports. The report itself has properties, as does each report section and each individual control. The label control also has its own properties, even if it is attached to another control.

Properties are displayed in a *property sheet.* The property sheet is also commonly called a *property window,* because it is an actual window. The first column contains the property names, whereas you enter properties in the second column. Figure 7-21 shows a property sheet for a Birth Date text box.

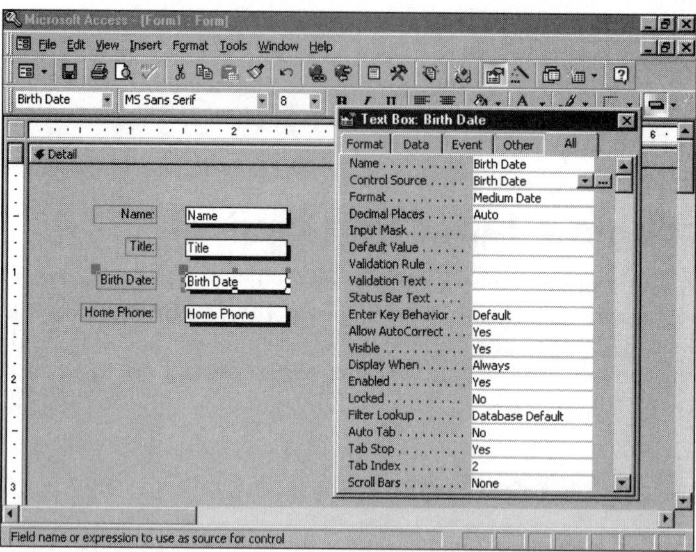

Figure 7-21: The property sheet for a text box.

Viewing a control's properties

The following lists several ways to view a control's properties:

- Select View➪Properties from the menu bar.
- Click on the control and then click on the Properties button in the toolbar.
- Double-click on any control.
- Right-click and choose Properties from the shortcut menu.

Figure 7-21 shows a partial property sheet. The sheet has been resized to make it larger. By widening the property sheet, you can see more of the property values, and by increasing the vertical size, you can see more controls at one time. The vertical scroll bar lets you move between various properties. Only the text box control has more properties than can fit on screen at one time. Because the property sheet is a true window, it can be moved anywhere on screen and resized to any size. It does not, however, have Maximize or Minimize buttons.

The property window is a tabbed dialog box that enables you to see all the properties for a control. You can limit the view, however, to specific properties. The specific groups of properties include the following:

- Format These properties determine how a label or value looks: font, size, color, special effects, borders, scroll bars.
- Data These properties affect how a value is displayed and the control it is bound to: control source, formats, input masks, validation, default value, and other table-level properties.
- Event Event properties are the named events, such as a mouse click, adding a record, pressing a key for which you can define a response (in the form of a call to a macro or an Access Basic procedure), and so on.
- Other Other properties shows additional characteristics of the control, such as the name of the control or the description that appears on the status bar.

The properties displayed in Figure 7-21 are the specific properties for Birth Date. The first two properties, `Name` and `Control Source`, reflect the field name Birth Date.

The `Name` is simply the name of the control itself. You can give the control any name you want. Unbound controls have names such as Field11 or Button13. When a control is bound to a field, it automatically is named to match the bound field name.

The `Control Source` is the name of the table field to which the control is bound. In this example, the Home Phone field is the name of the field in the table. An unbound control has no control source, whereas a calculated control's control source is the calculated expression, as in the example `=[Weight] * .65`.

The following properties are always inherited from the table definition of a field for a text box or other type of control. Figure 7-21 shows some of these properties inherited from any table:

- `Format`
- `Decimal Places`
- `Status Bar Text` (from the field Description)
- `Input Mask`
- `Caption`
- `Default Value`
- `Validation Rule`
- `Validation Text`

Changes made to a control's properties don't affect the field properties in the source table.

Each type of control has a different set of properties, as do objects such as forms, reports, and sections within forms or reports. In the next few chapters, you learn about many of these properties as you use each of the control types to create complex forms and reports.

Changing a control property

You can display properties in a property sheet, and you can change the properties using many different methods. The following is a list of methods you can use to change properties:

- Entering the desired property in a property sheet
- Directly changing a property by changing the control itself
- Using inherited properties from the bound field
- Using inherited properties from the control's default selections
- Entering control color selections using the palette
- Changing text style, size, color, and alignment by using the toolbar buttons

You can change a control's properties by simply clicking on a property and typing the desired value.

In Figure 7-21, an arrow and a button with three dots are displayed to the right of the `Control Source` property entry area. Some properties display the arrow in the property entry area when you click in the area. This tells you that a pop-up list of values is provided from which you can choose. If you click on the down arrow in the `Control Source` property, you find that the choices are a list of all fields in the open table.

The button with the three dots is the Builder button, which is used to open one of the many builders in Access 97, including the Macro Builder, the Expression Builder, and the Module Builder.

Some properties have a list of standard values such as `Yes` or `No`, whereas others display varying lists of fields, forms, reports, or macros. The properties of each object are determined by the object itself and what the object is used for.

Access 97 provides the capability to cycle through property choices by repeatedly double-clicking on the choice. For example, double-clicking on the `Display When` property alternately selects `Always`, `Print Only`, and `Screen Only`.

Creating a Standard Data Entry Form

When you have decided to create a data entry form, you must start by assembling the data necessary for the data entry form. You can bind a form either to a single table or to a query. If you use a query to assemble your data, the query presents the form with a set of data indistinguishable from a single table. However, make sure that you have not created a query that cannot be updated. If you have, your data entry form will be read-only and you will not be able to enter or change data on the form. Data entry forms should almost always be based on a table, and you should use relational links with subforms to display data and update data from related tables. When you have assembled your data, you can begin creating a form.

Creating a new form and binding it to data

You can create a form by clicking on the New button in the Database window when the Forms tab is selected. You can also select Insert⇨Form from the main Access menu.

Figure 7-22 shows the standard New Form dialog box with the Inventory table selected as the data source for the new form.

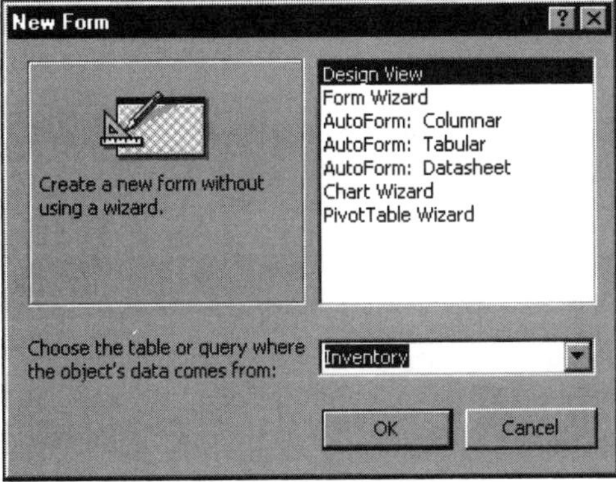

Figure 7-22: The New Form window.

When you select the Design View choice, an empty form is created on the screen. If you want to automatically place some or all of your fields into the form, you can use one of the Form Design wizards.

You can see the property window displayed on screen in the empty form shown in Figure 7-23. Notice that Inventory is the Record Source for the form. This means that the data from the Inventory table will be used when the form is viewed or printed. The fields from the query are available for use in the form design and appear in the Field List window.

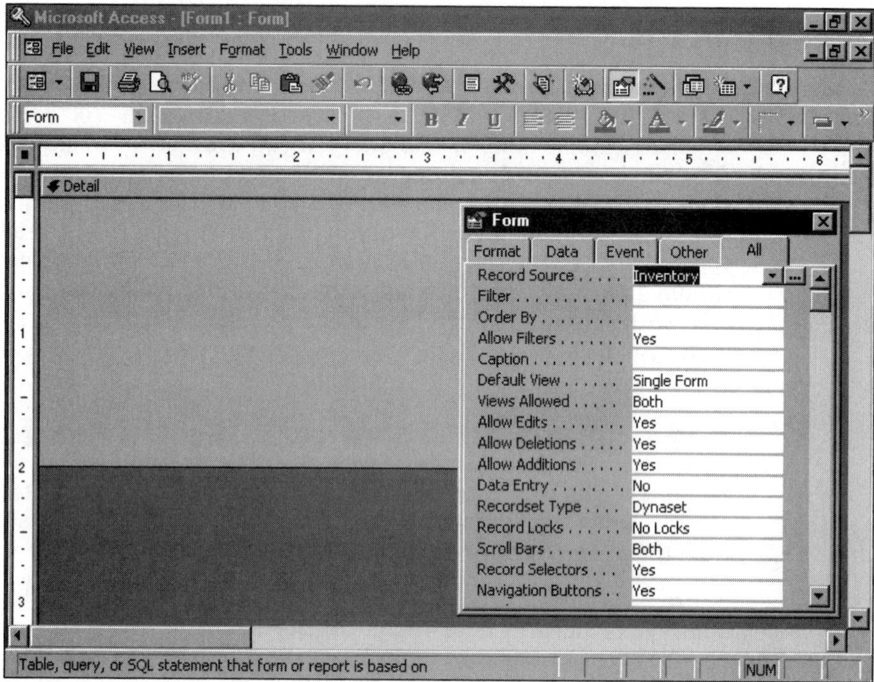

Figure 7-23: The blank Form Design window.

Tip

If you need to create a form that contains no field controls, you may want to create a blank form that is not bound to a query. You can do this simply by not selecting a table/query when you select Design View in the New Form dialog box.

Defining the form display size

When you are creating your form, you must resize the workspace of the form. The light gray area in the form shown in Figure 7-23 is your workspace. If you place controls in the dark gray area outside the workspace, however, the workspace expands automatically until it is larger than the area in which you placed the control. The size of the workspace depends on the size of your form. If you want the form to fill the screen, you should size it to the size of your screen. This depends on your screen resolution. You can fit more on screen if you are using a Super VGA screen size of 800 x 600 or 1024 x 1024 than you can if you are using the standard VGA size of 640 x 480. However, because you never know who may use a form you create, you should stay with the smallest size that any anticipated user may have.

A maximized standard VGA screen set to 640 x 480 in Windows 95 can display a full-screen size of approximately 6 1/4 inches × 3 7/8 inches. This includes the space for the title bar, menu bar, and toolbar at the top, the record-pointer column down the left side, the vertical scroll bar areas down the right side, and the navigation buttons/scroll bar and status line at the bottom. Of course, you can control most of these elements by setting the form properties.

The easiest way to set the form size is simply to use your mouse to grab the borders of the light gray area and resize it as you want. If you can grab either the top or bottom borders, your cursor turns into a double arrow. If you grab the corner, the cursor becomes a four-headed arrow, and you can size both sides at the same time. If you set the form size to 6 1/4 inches × 3 7/8 inches, no form scroll bars should appear.

If you add controls beyond the right border, you have to scroll the form to see these controls. Generally, this is not acceptable in a form. If you add controls beyond the bottom border, you have to scroll the form to see these controls as well. This is acceptable, because the form becomes a multiple-page form. Later in this chapter, you learn how to control multiple-page forms.

Changing form properties

You can set many form properties to change the way the entire form is displayed. Some of the most important properties shown in Figure 7-24 are described in Table 7-3.

Some of these properties work together to create certain behaviors in the form that are worth noting in more detail here. Other property characteristics are noted later in this chapter.

Embedding a filter or sort in a form

The first two properties in a form enable you to save an active filter definition and sorted order with a form. When you use Filter by Selection or Filter by Form as you sort your data or select criteria filters, their definitions are copied to the `Filter` and `Order By` properties of the form. For example, if you decide to filter the Inventory data by only records for the Inventory category of Books and also sort the data by Subcategory, you would find `((Category)="BOOKS")` in the `Filter` property and `Subcategory` in the `Order By` property. If the filter is active when you close or save the form, the properties are saved with the form and the filter is reactivated the next time the form is opened.

The next form property, `Allow Filters`, determines whether the user can create a new filter while using the form. By changing the `Allow Filters` property to `No`, you deactivate the filter buttons in the form.

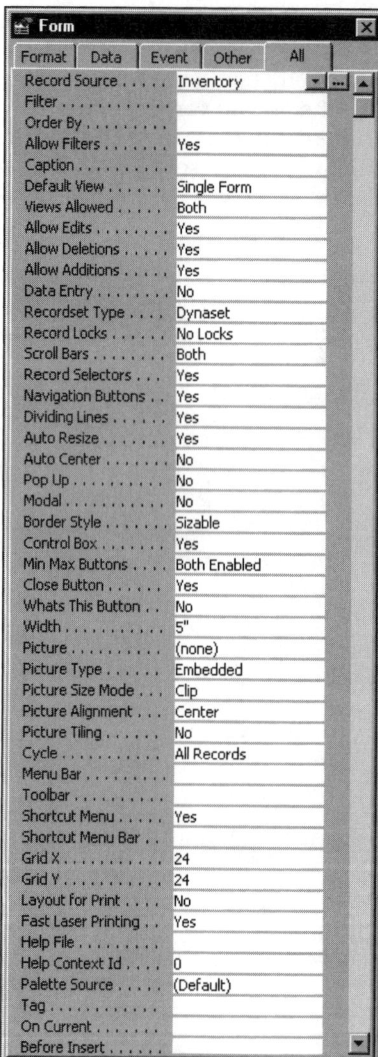

Figure 7-24: Form properties.

Changing the title bar text with the Caption property

Normally, the title bar displays the name of the form after it is saved. By changing the `Caption` property, you can display a different title in the title bar when the form is run. The caption you enter overrides the actual name of the saved form.

Using the Startup Properties dialog box `Application Title` property, you can also remove or change the Microsoft Access label that is displayed first in every title bar.

Setting the various views

Two properties determine how your form displays records: `Default View` and `Views Allowed`. The `Views Allowed` property has three settings: `Form`, `Datasheet`, and `Both`. The default setting is `Both`, which enables the user to switch between Form and Datasheet view. If the `Views Allowed` property is set to `Datasheet`, you cannot select the Form button and the View⇨Form menu, and you can only view the data as a datasheet. If the `Views Allowed` property is set to `Form`, you cannot select the Datasheet button and the View⇨Datasheet menu, and you can only view the data as a form.

The `Default View` property is very different. This property determines how the data is displayed when the form is first run. Three settings are possible: `Single Form`, `Continuous Forms`, and `Datasheet`. The first setting, `Single Form`, displays one record per form page, regardless of the size of the form. The next setting, `Continuous Forms`, is the default. This setting tells Access to display as many detailed records as will fit on screen. Normally, you use this setting when you define a very small form in height and many records can be displayed at one time. The final `Default View` setting, `Datasheet`, simply displays the form as a standard datasheet when run. You generally want only one record per display, so you would change this property to `Single Form`.

Eliminating the Record Selector Bar

The `Record Selector` property determines whether you see the vertical bar on the left side of the form that lets you select the entire record. This vertical bar is the one with the editing icon seen in datasheets. Primarily used in continuous (multiple-record) forms or datasheets, a right-pointing triangle indicates the current record; a pencil icon indicates that the record is being changed. Though the Record Selector Bar is important for datasheets, you probably don't want it for a single record form. You can eliminate it by simply changing the `Record Selector` property of the form to `No`. Nothing is more amateurish than a form displaying a single record that shows a Record Selector bar down the left side.

Table 7-3 Form Properties

Property	*Description*
Caption	Displayed in the title bar of the displayed form.
Default View	Determines the type of view when the form is run.
Single Form	One record per page.
Continuous Forms	As many records per page as will fit (Default).
Datasheet	Standard row and column datasheet view.

(continued)

Table 7-3 *(continued)*

Property	***Description***
Views Allowed	Determines whether the user can switch between the two views.
Form	Form view only is allowed.
Datasheet	Datasheet view only is allowed.
Both	Form view or Datasheet view is allowed.
Allow Filters	Specifies whether records in a form can be filtered.
Allow Edits	Prevents or allows editing of data, making the form read-only for saved records.
Yes/No	You can or cannot edit saved records.
Allow Deletions	Used to prevent records from being deleted.
Yes/No	You can or cannot delete saved records.
Allow Additions	Used to determine whether new records can be added.
Yes/No	You can or cannot add new records.
Data Entry	Used to determine whether form displays saved records.
Yes/No	Only new records are displayed/All records are displayed.
Recordset Type	Used to determine updateability of multitable forms; replaces Access 2.0 Allow Updating property.
Dynaset	Only default table fields can be edited.
Dynaset (Inconsistent Update)	All tables and fields are editable.
Snapshot	No fields are editable (Read-Only form).
Record Locks	Used to determine multiuser record locking.
No Locks	Record is only locked as it is saved.
All Records	Locks all form records while using the form.
Edited Records	Locks only the current record being edited.
Scroll Bars	Determines whether any scroll bars are displayed.
Neither	No scroll bars are displayed.
Horizontal Only	Displays only the horizontal scroll bar.
Vertical Only	Displays only the vertical scroll bar.
Both	Displays both the horizontal and vertical scroll bars.
Record Selectors	Determines whether vertical record selector bar is displayed (Yes/No).
Navigation Buttons	Determines whether navigation buttons are visible (Yes/No).

Property	*Description*
Dividing Lines	Determines whether lines between form sections are visible (Yes/No).
Auto Resize	Opens form to display a complete record (Yes/No).
Auto Center	Centers form on the screen when opened (Yes/No).
Pop Up	Form is a pop-up form that floats above all other objects (Yes/No).
Modal	A modal form is used when you must close the form before anything else can be done. Disables other windows. When Pop Up is set to Yes, it also disables menus and the toolbar, creating a dialog box (Yes/No).
Border Style	Determines form's border style.
None	No border or border elements (scroll bars, navigation buttons).
Thin	Thin border, not resizeable.
Sizeable	Normal form settings.
Dialog	Thick border, title bar only; not sizeable; use for dialog boxes.
Control Box	Determines whether control menu (Restore, Move Size...) is available (Yes/No).
Min Max Buttons	
None	No buttons displayed in upper-right corner of form.
Min Enabled	Minimize Button only is displayed.
Max Enabled	Maximize Button only is displayed.
Both Enabled	Minimize and Maximize buttons are displayed.
Close Button	Determines whether the close button in the upper-right corner is there and whether the Close menu item in the control menu is displayed (Yes/No).
Whats This Button	Determines whether Screen Tips are displayed when the Shift-F1 help is used.
Width	Displays the value of the width of the form. Can be entered or is filled in as you adjust the width of the work area.
Picture	Enters the name of a bitmap file for the background of the entire form.
Picture Size Mode	
Clip	Displays the picture at its actual size.
Stretch	Fits picture to the form size (Non-Proportionally).
Zoom	Fits picture to the form size (Proportionally). This may result in the picture not fitting in one dimension (Height or Width).

(continued)

Table 7-3 *(continued)*

Property	Description
Picture Alignment	
Top Left	The picture is displayed at the top left corner of the form or report window or image control.
Top Right	The picture is displayed at the top right corner of the form or report window or image control.
Center	(Default) The picture is centered in the form or report window or image control.
Bottom Left	The picture is displayed at the bottom left corner of the form or report window or image control.
Bottom Right	The picture is displayed at the bottom right corner of the form or report window or image control.
Form Center	The form's picture is centered horizontally in relation to the width of the form and vertically in relation to the topmost and bottom-most controls on the form.
Picture Tiling	Used when a small bitmap is used and you want to overlay multiple copies of the bitmap. For example, a single brick can become a wall.
Cycle	
All Records	Tabbing from the last field of a record moves to the next record.
Current Record	Tabbing from the last field of a record moves to the first field of that record.
Current Page	Tabbing from the last field of a record moves to the first field of the current page.
Menu Bar	Used to specify an alternate menu bar. Builder button lets you create a new menu bar if you want.
Shortcut Menu	Determines whether shortcut menus are active.
Shortcut Menu Bar	Used to specify an alternate shortcut menu bar.
Grid X	Determines the number of points per inch when the X grid is displayed.
Grid Y	Determines the number of points per inch when the Y grid is displayed.
Layout for Print	Determines whether the form uses screen fonts or printer fonts.
Yes	Printer fonts
No	Screen fonts
Fast Laser Printing	Prints rules instead of lines and rectangles (Yes/No).

Property	Description
Help File	Name of the compiled help file to assign custom help to the form.
Help Context ID	ID of the context-sensitive entry point in the help file to display.
Has Module	Determines whether a form or report has a class module.

Placing fields on the form

The next step is to place the necessary fields onto the form. When you place a field on a form, it is no longer called a field; it is called a *control*. A control has a control source (a field to which the control is bound). Therefore, you see the terms control and field used interchangeably in this chapter.

As you've learned, the process of placing controls on your form consists of three basic tasks:

- Displaying the Field List window by clicking on the Field List button in the toolbar
- Clicking on the desired toolbox control to determine the type of control that is created
- Selecting each of the fields that you want on your form and dragging the fields to the Form Design window

Selecting the fields for your form

Selecting a field in the Field List window is the same as selecting that field from a query field list. The easiest way to select a field is simply to click on it. As you click on a field, it is highlighted. When a field is highlighted, you can drag it to the Form window.

You can highlight contiguous (adjacent) fields in the list. To do this, click on the first field you want in the field list and then move the cursor to the last field you want; hold down the Shift key as you click on the last field. The block of fields between the first and last field is displayed in reverse video as you select them. You can then drag the block of fields to the Form window.

You can highlight noncontiguous fields in the list by clicking on each field while holding down the Ctrl key. Each field is then displayed in reverse video and can be dragged as part of the group to the Form Design window.

Unlike the query field list, you cannot also double-click on a field to add it to the Form window.

Dragging fields onto your form

After you select the proper fields from the table, all you need to do is drag the fields onto the form. Depending on whether you choose one or several fields, the cursor changes to reflect your selection. If you select one field, you see a Field icon, a box containing text. If you select multiple fields, you see a Multiple Field icon instead. These icons are the same cursor icons you've seen in the Query Design screens. Figure 7-25 shows the process of dragging fields to the form.

Note that there are two controls for each field you dragged onto the form. When you use the drag-and-drop method for placing fields, Access automatically creates a label control that uses the name of the field and is attached to the text control to which the field is bound. Note that in Figure 7-25, the Category field is displayed as a combo box automatically, because this is one of the properties of the Inventory table. The Category field is created as a Lookup field and would display the actual categories in the Inventory table.

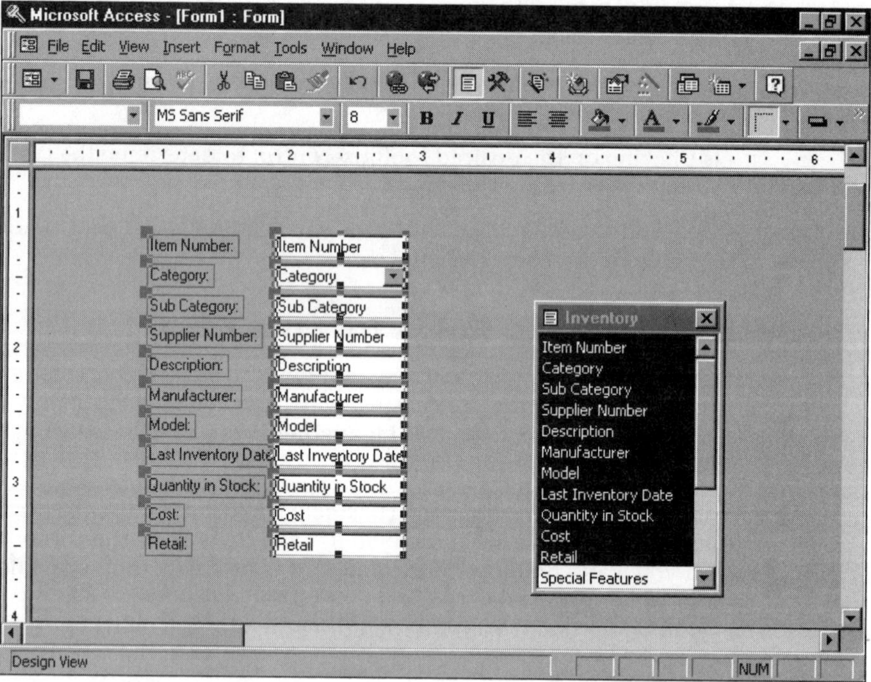

Figure 7-25: Dragging fields to the form.

Label and Text Box Control Techniques

You've already seen how attached label controls are automatically created. You drag a field from the Field List window to a form with the Text Box button selected in the toolbox; this creates a text box control and also a label control attached to the text box control. But sometimes you want to add text label controls by themselves to create headings or titles for the form.

Creating unattached labels

To create a new, unattached label control, you must use the toolbox — unless you copy an existing label.

Tip

To create a multiple-line label entry, press Ctrl+Enter to force a line break where you want it in the control.

Modifying the text in a label or text control

To modify the text in a control, click on the inside of the label. The cursor changes to the standard Windows text cursor, an I-beam. Also notice that the formatting toolbar icons become grayed out and are not selectable. This is because within a label control — or any control — you cannot apply specific formatting to individual characters.

You can now make any edits you want to the text. If you drag across the entire selection so that it is highlighted, whatever is in this area is replaced by anything new that you type. Another way to modify the text is to edit it from the control's property window. The second item in the property window is `Caption`. In the `Caption` property, you can also edit the contents of a text or label control (for a text control, the property is called `Control Source`) by clicking on the edit box and typing.

Tip

If you want to edit or enter a caption that is longer than the space in the property window, the contents will scroll as you type. Alternatively, you can press Shift+F2 to open up a zoom box that gives you more space to type.

Changing the control type

You may notice in Figure 7-25 that the Category field is a combo box, the default control type that can be defined in the table using the Lookup Wizard. If you decide that you want to change the control type, you first select the desired field and then select Format⇨Change To⇨Text Box to change the control type to a text box. Text boxes can be interchanged with list and combo boxes. Checkboxes can be interchanged with option and toggle buttons.

Setting the tab order

When you've finished moving all your controls into position, you should test the form. If you run the form and use the Tab key to move from field to field, you may notice that the cursor does not move from field to field in the order you expect. The cursor begins in the first field but may not tab from field to field in the order you want. The order may seem strange, but it will be the original order in which the fields were added to the form.

This is called the *tab order* of the form. The form's default tab order is always the order in which the fields were added to the form. You don't have to move the fields around, but if you do, you may want to change the order. Although you may make heavy use of the mouse when designing your forms, the average data entry person still uses the keyboard to move from field to field.

When you need to change the tab order of a form, select the View⇨Tab Order menu option in the Design window to change the order to match your layout, as shown in Figure 7-26.

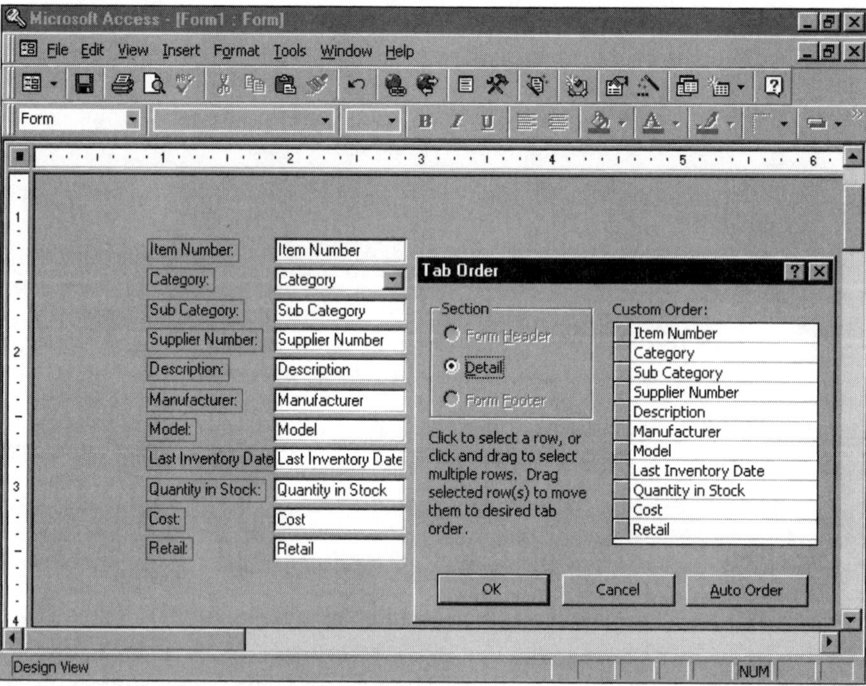

Figure 7-26: The Tab Order dialog box.

The Formatting toolbar

Access 97 features a second toolbar known as the Formatting toolbar. This toolbar is more fully described later in this chapter. Toolbars are really windows. You can move any toolbar by dragging it from its normal location and placing it in the middle of a form, and you can change its size and shape. Some toolbars can be docked to any edge of the screen, such as the left, right, or bottom. The Formatting toolbar, however, can be docked only at the top of the screen.

The Formatting toolbar integrates objects from the Access 2.0 Form Design toolbar and the palette. The first area of the Formatting toolbar on the left side is used to select a control. When you have multiple pages of controls and you want to select a control on page 3 or a control that is behind another, this combo box makes it easy. The next few objects on the Formatting toolbar are used to change text properties. The next two combo boxes enable you to change the font style and size. Remember, you may have fonts that others do not have. Do not use an exotic font if the user of your form does not have the font. After the font style and size combo boxes are icons for Bold, Italic, and Underlining a text control. Beyond those are alignment icons for left, center, and right text alignment. The last five pull-down icons are used to change color properties, line types and styles, and special effects.

The Tab Order dialog box enables you to select either one row or multiple rows at a time. You can select multiple contiguous rows by clicking on the first row and then dragging down to select multiple rows. After the rows are highlighted, you can drag the selected rows to their new position.

The Tab Order dialog box has several buttons at the bottom of the box. The Auto Order button places the fields in order from left to right and top to bottom, based on their position in the form. This button is a good place to start when you have significantly rearranged the fields.

Each control has two properties that interact with this screen. The `Tab Stop` property determines whether pressing the Tab key will land on the field. The default is `Yes`; changing the `Tab Stop` property to `No` removes the field from the tab order. When you set the tab order, the control's `Tab Index` property is set. In this example, the Item Number field is set to 1, the Category is set to 2, and so on. Whenever you move around fields in the Tab Order dialog box, the `Tab Index` properties of those (and other) controls are changed.

Adding multiple-line text box controls for Memo fields

Multiple-line text box controls are used for Memo data types. The Features field in the Inventory table is a Memo field. When you add a Memo field to a form, make sure that there is plenty of room in the text box control to enter large amounts of text. You can use several ways to make certain that you allow enough space.

The first way is to resize the text box control and make it large enough to accommodate any text you may enter into the Memo field. This kind of resizing, however, is rarely possible. Usually, the reason you create a Memo field is to hold very large amounts of text. The text can easily be larger than the entire form can display.

One of the options in a text box control is a vertical scroll bar. By adding scroll bars to your Memo field text box control, you can allow for any size of data entry. You can add a vertical scroll bar to the text box control by changing the control's Scroll Bars property to Vertical, as shown in Figure 7-27.

When you run the form, the scroll bar appears only after you move into the Comments Memo field.

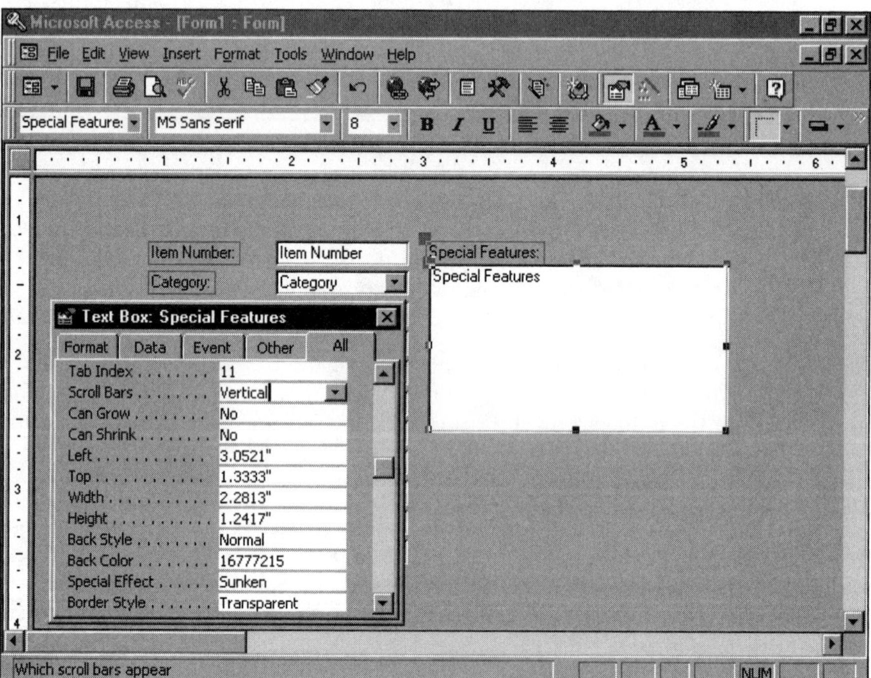

Figure 7-27: Adding a multiple-line text box control.

Creating a Multiple-Page Form

Suppose that you want to add more information to a form that has little room left on the form to add more fields or labels. You can create a larger form or you can just make the screen bigger by changing to a higher screen resolution — but this means getting the necessary hardware. Another solution is to create a *multiple-page form.*

Why use multiple-page forms?

You use multiple-page forms when all your information won't fit on one page or when you want to segregate specific information on separate pages. By using multiple-page forms, you can display less information on a page, making a complicated form look less cluttered. You can also place data items that are not always necessary on the second or even the third page, which makes data entry easier for the user on the first page.

You can have as many pages as you need on a form, but the general rule is no more than five pages. In addition, the form has a 22-inch size limitation. By using a macro or VBA, you can attach other forms to buttons on the form; then you can call up the other pages as you need them by selecting a button.

Changing defaults for attached label positioning

Attached label controls are called compound controls because the two controls are *attached.* At times, you may want to disable this feature, which you can do by changing a default property named `Auto Label`. When you set `Auto Label` to `Yes`, you automatically create a label control that bears the name of the field to which the text control is bound. And with `Auto Label` in effect, a label is automatically created every time you drag a field onto a form. Follow these steps to change the Auto Label default:

1. Display the toolbox if it is not already displayed.
2. Display the property window if it is not already displayed.
3. Click on the Text Box button in the toolbar. The title of the property window should be Default Text Box.
4. Scroll down until you see the `Auto Label` property.
5. Click on the Auto Label text box.
6. Change the contents in the text box to No.

The next property, `AutoColon`, automatically places a colon following any text in a new label if the value of the property is set to `Yes`.

Two properties control where the label appears relative to the control itself. These are the `Label X` and `Label Y` properties. `Label X` controls the horizontal position of the label control relative to the text box control. The default is `-1` (to the left of the text box control). As you make the value a smaller negative number, as with `-.5`, you decrease the space from the attached label to the control. If you want the label after the control (as

(continued)

(continued)

you may for an option button), you use a positive number, such as `1.5`, to move the label to the right of the control.

`Label Y` controls the vertical position of the label control relative to the text box control. The default is `0`, which places the label on the same line as the text box control. If you want to place the label above the control, change `Label Y` to `-1` or a larger negative number. The last option, `Label Align`, lets you control the alignment of the text within the label.

If you change the `Auto Label` default to `No` and drag fields from the Field List window to the form, you see no label controls attached. The `Auto Label` property is in effect only for this form. Because you don't need to add further labeled fields to this form, you can leave the setting of `Auto Label` as `No`.

When you add pages to a form, you can move between the pages by using the PgUp and PgDn keys, or you can program navigation keys by using macros or VBA.

You can create a multiple-page form only when the `Default View` property of the form is set to `Single Form`.

Adding a page break

You can add page breaks to a form by adding a page break control. This control is found in the bottom-left part of the toolbox and is an icon that looks like two pieces of paper. When you click on the control in the toolbar, you simply place it on the left edge of the form where you want the page break to be. Figure 7-28 shows a second page added to the Inventory form.

Using Form and Page Headers and Footers

The most common use of a page or form header is to repeat identification information. When you have a second page, you don't see the text header. In Access forms, you can add both form and page sections. Sections include headers, which come before the detail controls, and footers, which come after the detail controls.

The different types of headers and footers

Several types of headers and footers can appear in a form:

- Form header — Displayed at the top of each page when viewed and at the top when the form is printed

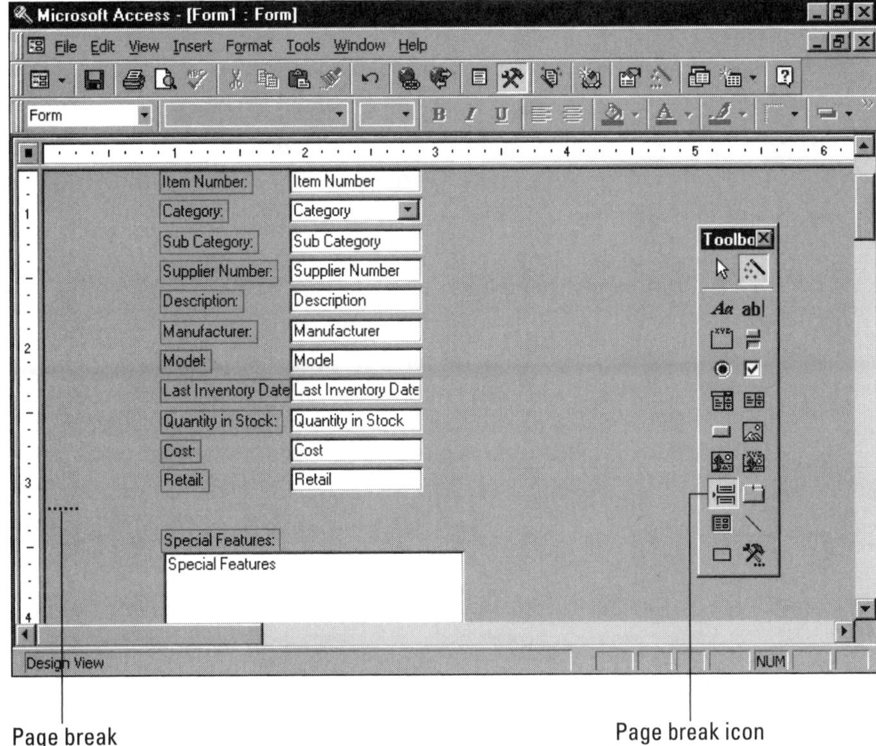

Figure 7-28: Adding a new page and a page break.

- **Page header** — Displayed only when the form is printed; prints after the form header
- **Page footer** — Appears only when the form is printed; prints before the form footer
- **Form footer** — Displayed at the bottom of each page when viewed and at the bottom of the form when the form is printed

Form headers and footers are used in the displayed form and optionally can be used in a printed form. Page headers and footers are displayed only when a form is printed. Generally, unless you print the form as a report, you won't use the page headers or footers. Because you can easily create reports in Access and even save a form as a report, you won't find much use for page headers and footers.

Creating a form header and footer

You create form headers and footers by selecting View➪Form Header/Footer (see Figure 7-29). When you select this menu option, both the form header and form footer sections are added to the form.

You can add page headers and footers by selecting View➪Page Header/Footer.

Sometimes, when you display a form with an added header or footer, you lose that much space from the Detail section. You must adjust the size of your Detail section to compensate for this space.

In the example shown here, you may need to make the height of the Detail section smaller because you moved the text label control to the Form Header section and moved the other controls up in the Detail section. You also have to close the Form Footer section because you are not using it.

You change the size of a section by placing the cursor on the bottom border of the section, where it turns into a two-headed arrow. You can then drag the section border up or down.

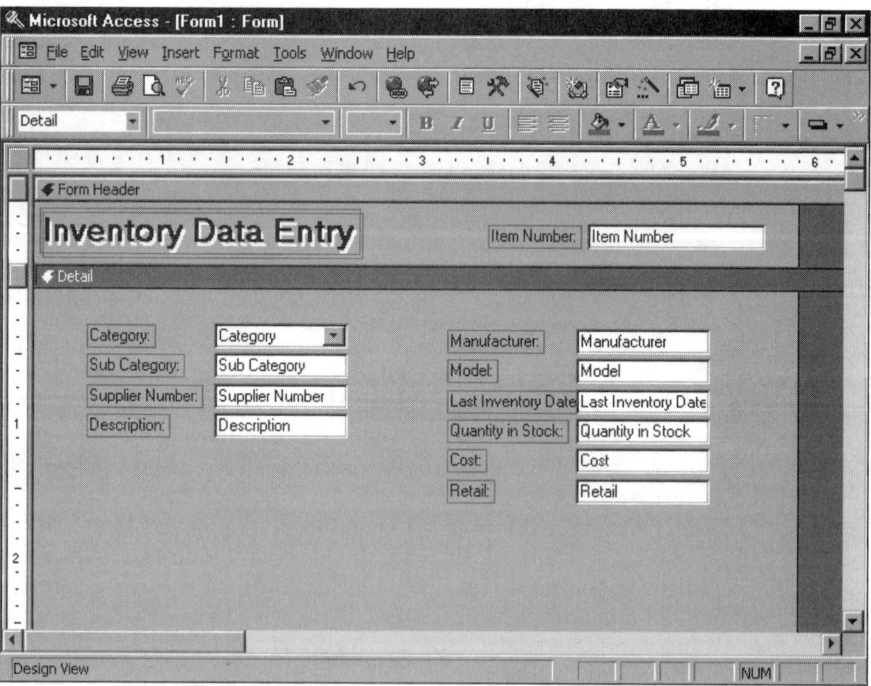

Figure 7-29: Adding a form header.

When you display a form with a header or footer section, you see the sections separated from the Detail section by a line. The form headers and footers are literally anchored in place. If you create a scrollable or a multiple-page form, the headers and footers remain where they are while the data in the Detail section moves.

Changing the header dividing line

Form headers and footers are automatically separated from the Detail section by a solid black line. In Access 97, you can remove this line by changing the Form property `Dividing Line` to `No`, which also makes the form appear seamless. This procedure is especially important if you have a background bitmap on the entire form and you are using form headers or footers and want a single look.

Making a Good Form Look Great

The Access Form Designer has the capability to do with a form what any good desktop publishing package can do with words. Just as a desktop publishing package can enhance a word-processed document to make it more readable, the Form Designer can enhance a database form to make it more usable.

With the Access Form Designer, you can draw attention to areas of the form that you want the reader to notice. Just as a headline in a newspaper calls your attention to a particular news story, an enhanced section of a form calls attention to the information it contains.

The Access Form Designer gives you a number of tools to make the form controls and sections visually stand out:

- Lines and rectangles
- Color and background shading
- 3-D effects (raised, sunken, etched, chiseled, shadowed)
- Background pictures
- Form headers and footers

In this section, you learn how to enhance your forms by adding special text features to create shading, shadows, lines, rectangles, and 3-D effects. Figure 7-30 shows you a form after some special effects have been added.

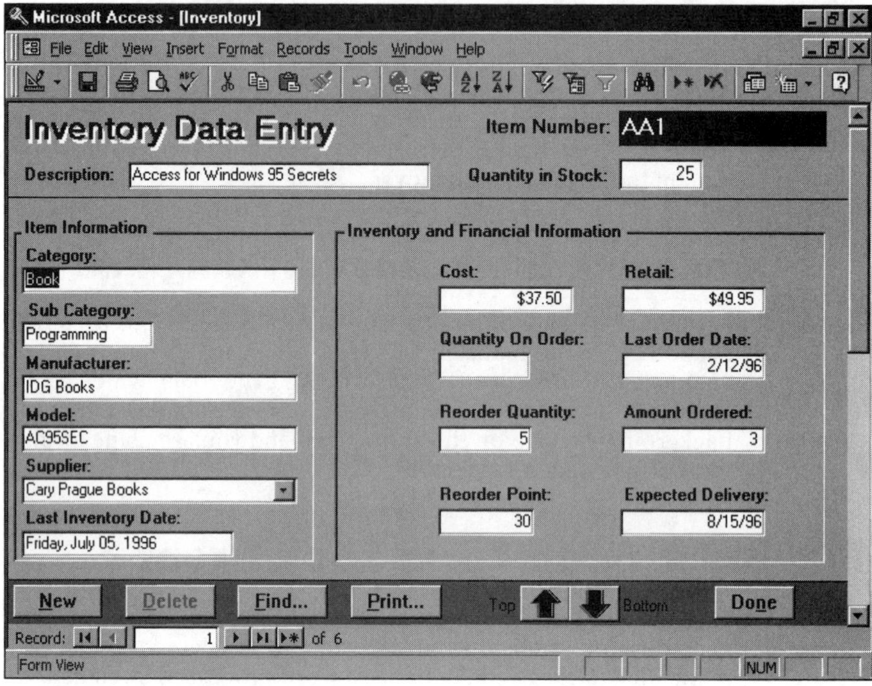

Figure 7-30: An enhanced form.

Understanding WYSIWYG

Access has a WYSIWYG ("what you see is what you get") Form Designer. As you create your controls on-screen, you instantly see what they look like in your form. If you want to see what the data will look like during your form design, the on-screen preview mode enables you to see the actual data in your form design without using a hard-copy device.

The Access Form Designer enables you to add color and shading to your form text and controls. You can also display them in reverse video, which shows white letters on a black background. You can even color or shade the background of form sections. As you specify these effects, you see the change instantly on the Design screen.

Using the formatting windows and toolbar

The most important controls for enhancing a form are the formatting windows and the Formatting toolbar. The following is a list of the five available formatting windows:

- Background color for shading
- Foreground color for text

- Border color for lines, rectangles, and control borders
- Line thickness for lines, rectangles, and control borders
- Special effects, such as raised, sunken, etched, chiseled, or shadowed

The Formatting toolbar can be displayed and removed from the screen by selecting View⇨Toolbars and then selecting Formatting, or by right-clicking on the toolbar area and selecting Formatting.

You can tell the currently selected color in the three color icons (background, foreground, and border) by looking in the small square in each picture icon.

You modify the appearance of a control by using a formatting window. To modify the appearance of a control, select the control by clicking on it. Then click on the formatting windows you need in order to change the control's options. Figure 7-31 shows all five of the formatting windows.

A *formatting window* is a window, just like the toolbox or the field list. You can move a formatting window around the screen. However, you cannot change its size or anchor it as you can a toolbar to a window border. A formatting window can remain on screen all the time, and you can use it to change the options for one or more controls. You close a formatting window by clicking on the Close button or reselecting the icon in the formatting toolbar.

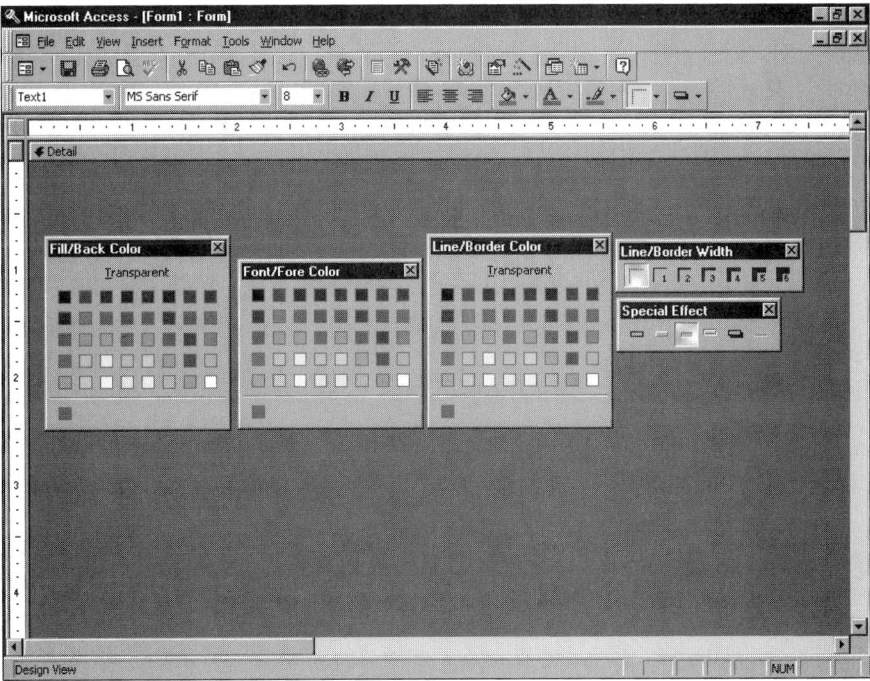

Figure 7-31: The various formatting windows.

Use the foreground text and background color windows to change the color of the text or the backgrounds of a control. You can make a control's background transparent by selecting the Transparent Back Color window button. The border color window changes the color of control borders, lines, and rectangles. When you press the Transparent button of the Border Control window, the border on any selected control becomes invisible.

The Border Thickness window controls the thickness of control borders, lines, and rectangles. A line can be the border of a control or a standalone line control. You define the thickness of the line by using the thickness buttons. You can select from the following line sizes: hairline, 1 point, 2 points, 3 points, 4 points, 5 points, and 6 points.

You also have a window to determine the line type, including solid line, dashed line, and dotted line.

A point is approximately 1/72 of an inch and is a unit of measurement that denotes character height.

When you are finished with a formatting window, you can close it by clicking on the X in the upper-right corner of the window.

Creating special effects

Figure 7-32 shows some of the special effects that can be easily created for controls by using the special effects formatting window. In the figure, you see that controls with a gray background color show off special effects much better than those with white. In fact, a form background in gray or a dark color is almost mandatory for seeing most special effects. Each of these special effects is described in the next section.

Special effects can be applied to rectangles, label controls, text box controls, checkboxes, option buttons, and option group boxes. Anything that has a box or circle around it can be raised, sunken, etched, chiseled, or shadowed.

By simply selecting the control and adding the special effect, you can make your forms look much better and draw attention to the important areas of the form.

Flat

In Figure 7-32, you see a pair of boxes that have both been created without any special effects. As you can see in Figure 7-32, the flat box stands out better when set against the gray background.

You can also increase the width of the border lines to make the box more prominent by using the Border Width window. The Border Color window lets you change the color of the box. A thick white box also stands out well.

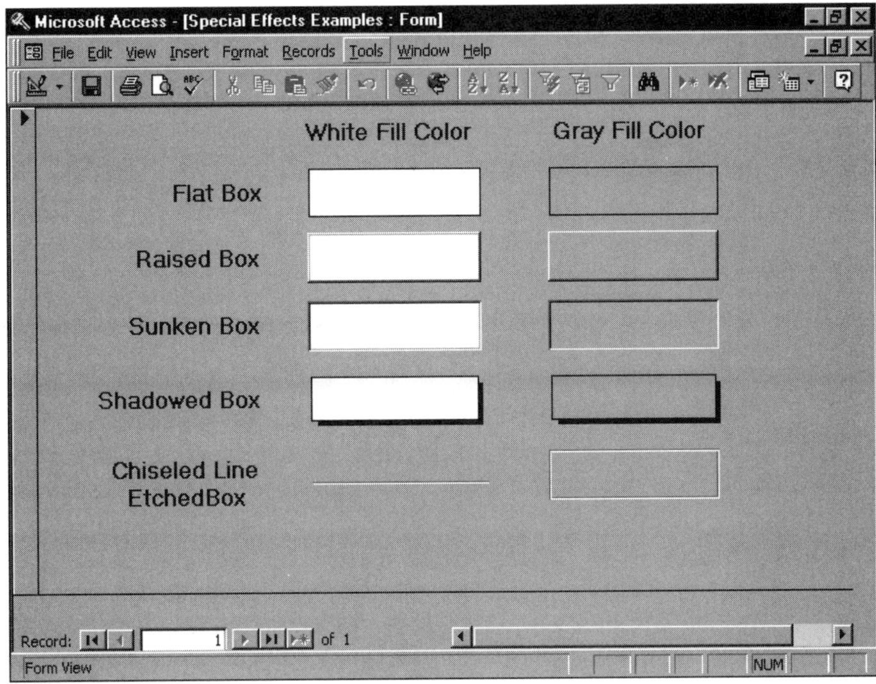

Figure 7-32: Special effects.

Raised

The raised box is best when used for a rectangle that surrounds other controls or for label controls. The raised box provides the best effect in a dark color against a dark background. As you can see in Figure 7-32, the raised box is difficult to see with a white fill color. By increasing the width of the box, you can make the control appear to be higher than it really is. You achieve the raised 3-D effect by contrasting the white left and top borders with the black right and bottom borders.

Sunken

The sunken special effect is the most dramatic and most often used. This look is the standard Windows 95 format in the Form Wizard and the default control format in Access 97. As you can see in Figure 7-32, either the white or the gray fill color looks very good on a gray form background. You can also increase the width of the border to give the effect of a deeper impression. The sunken 3-D effect is achieved with black left and top borders and white right and bottom borders. The sunken effect also works well with checkboxes and option buttons.

Shadowed

The shadowed special effect places a solid, dark-colored rectangle behind the original control. The second rectangle is slightly offset to give the shadowed effect. As you can see in Figure 7-32, the black shadow works well behind the white or gray filled box. You can change the border color to change the shadow color.

Etched

The etched effect is perhaps the most interesting of all the special effects. This look is, in effect, a sunken rectangle with no sunken inside area. Windows 95 makes heavy use of etched rectangles.

Chiseled

The chiseled effect adds a chiseled line underneath a selected control.

Changing the form's background color

If you are typically going to view your form on screen instead of printing it, you may want to color the background. A light gray background (the Windows 95 default) seems to be the best neutral color for all types of lighting and viewing conditions. If you want to change the background for the Form Header and Detail sections, you select the desired section and then select the appropriate background color.

Tip

When you change the background color of form sections, you also want to change the background of individual label controls for a more natural look. Generally, the background of a label control does not look good if it doesn't match the background of the form itself.

Enhancing Text-Based Controls

Generally, before you start enhancing display items with shading or special effects, you first must get the label text and data right. When your enhancements include label and text box control changes, you should begin with them.

Enhancing label and text box controls

You can enhance label and text box controls in several ways:

- Changing the text font typeface (Arial, Times New Roman, Wingding)
- Changing the text font size (4 – 200)
- Changing the text font style (bold, italic, underline)
- Changing the text color (using a formatting window)
- Adding a shadow

Creating a text shadow

Text shadows give text a 3-D look by making the text appear to float above the page while its shadow stays on the page. This effect uses the same basic principle as a shadowed box. Text shadows, however, are created using these steps:

1. Duplicate the text.
2. Offset the duplicate text from the original text.
3. Change the duplicate text to a different color (usually a lighter shade).
4. Place the duplicate text behind the original text.
5. Change the original text background color to Clear.

When you duplicate the original text, the duplicate copy is automatically offset below the original text. When you place the duplicate text behind the original, it is hidden. You display it by placing the original text in front. If the offset or distance from the other copy is too great, the effect will not look like a shadow. By adjusting one of the label controls slightly, you can perfect the shadowed appearance.

Although the shadow text looks great and appears to be correct on screen, it won't print correctly on most monochrome printers. What most printers produce is two lines of black text, which looks horrible. If you plan to print your forms and do not have a printer that prints text in color or prints many shades of gray using graphics rather than text fonts, you should avoid using shadowed text on a form.

Changing text to reverse video display

Text really stands out when you create white text on a black background. This setup is called *reverse video* because the text is white against a black background rather than the usual black letters on white. You can convert text in a label control or text box to reverse video by changing the Back Color to black and the Fore Color to white. To change a text control to reverse video, follow these steps:

1. Select the text box control (not the label control).
2. Select Black from the Back Color formatting window.
3. Select White from the Fore Color formatting window.

If you use less-expensive laser printers, the printers may not produce reverse video in the printed form because of a limitation of the printer drivers.

Displaying label or text box control properties

As you change values in a label control or text box control by using a formatting window, you are actually changing their properties. Figure 7-33 displays the property window for the label control in the form header you just modified. As you see in Figure 7-33, many properties can be affected by a formatting window. Table 7-4 shows the various properties and their possible values for both label and text box controls.

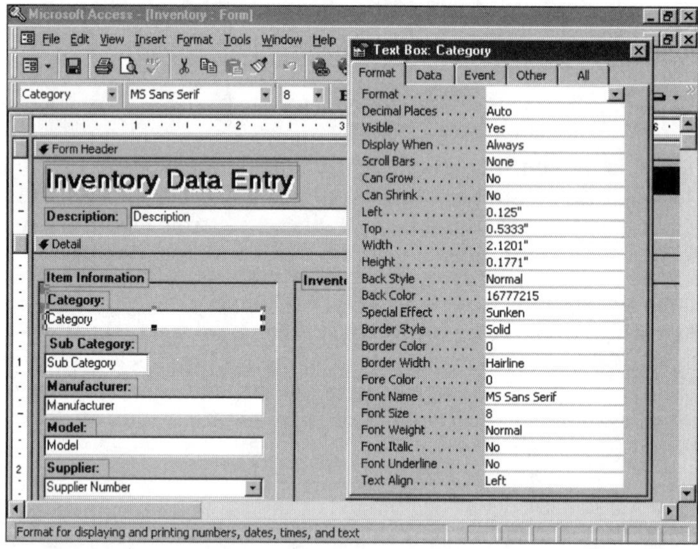

Figure 7-33: Text box control properties.

Table 7-4 Label or Text Box Format Properties

Property	*Options*	*Description*
Format	Various numeric and date formats	Determines how the data is displayed.
Decimal Places		Number of decimal places for a numeric field.
Visible	Yes/No	Yes — Control is displayed normally, No — Control is invisible when displayed.
Display When	Always, Print Only, Screen Only	Determines when the control is displayed.

Property	Options	Description
Scroll Bars	None, Vertical, Horizontal, Both	Specifies when scroll bars are displayed.
Can Grow	Yes/No	If multiple lines of text are in the control, the size of the text box gets larger.
Can Shrink	Yes/No	If fewer lines of text are in the control than the initial size, the height of the text box gets smaller.
Left	Position of the left corner of the control in the current measure (include a measurement indicator, such as cm or in, if you use a different unit of measurement).	Specifies the position of an object on the horizontal axis.
Top	Position of the top corner of the control	Specifies the position of an object in the current measure on the vertical axis.
Width	The width of the control	Specifies the width of an object in the current unit of measure.
Height	The height of the control	Specifies the height of an object in the current unit of measure.
Back Style	Transparent or Normal	Determines whether a control's background is opaque or transparent.
Back Color	Any available background color	Specifies the color for the interior of the control or section.
Special Effect	Flat, Raised, Sunken, Shadowed, Etched, or Chiseled	Determines whether a section or control appears flat, raised, sunken, shadowed, etched, or chiseled.
Border Style	Transparent or Normal Dashes, Dots (Lines/Boxes Only)	Determines whether a control's border is opaque or transparent.
Border Color	Any available border color	Specifies the color of a control's border.
Border Width	Hairline, 1pt, 2pt, 3pt, 4pt, 5pt, or 6pt	Specifies the width of a control's border.
Fore Color	Any selection from a formatting window	Specifies the color for text in a control or the printing and drawing color.

(continued)

Table 7-4 *(continued)*

Property	*Options*	*Description*
Font Name	Any system font name that appears on the toolbar; depends on the fonts installed	Specifies the name of the font used for text or a control.
Font Size	Any size that is available for a given font	Specifies the size of the font used for text or a control.
Font Weight	Extra Light, Light, Normal, Medium, Semi-bold, Bold, Extra Bold, and Heavy	Specifies the width of the line that Windows uses to display and print characters.
Font Italic	Yes/No	Italicizes text in a control.
Font Underline	Yes/No	Underlines text in a control.
Text Align	General (default), Left, Center, and Right	Sets the alignment for text in a control.

Although you can set many of these controls from the property sheet, you'll find that it's much easier to initially drag the control to set the `Top`, `Left`, `Width`, and `Height` properties, or to use a formatting window to set the other properties of the control.

Tip

Access lets you press the Ctrl+arrow keys to move the selected control a very small amount in the direction of the arrow key you choose.

Displaying Images in Forms

You can display a picture in a form by using image frames. This feature is different than a bound OLE control, which is used to store an OLE object (sound, video, Word, or Excel documents) with a data record, or an unbound OLE object, which is used to store OLE objects (sound, video, Word, or Excel documents) on a form itself.

Note

Image controls are used only for non-OLE objects such as Paintbrush (.BMP) pictures. Unlike OLE objects (which can be edited but use huge amounts of resources), the image control adds only the size of the bitmap picture to overhead. Using many OLE objects in Access causes resource and performance problems. New and existing applications should only use image controls when displaying pictures that don't change or need to be edited.

Tip

In Access 2.0, many people learned to select an unbound OLE object picture and then select Edit⇨Save As Picture. Although this selection process broke the OLE connection, it did not fix the resource problem.

You can add an image control to your form by either pasting a bitmap from the Clipboard or embedding a bitmap file that contains a picture.

Suppose that you have a logo for your company scanned as a bitmap file. An image object can be displayed in one of three ways:

- **Clip** Displays picture in its original size
- **Stretch** Fits picture into the control regardless of size; often displayed out of proportion
- **Zoom** Fits picture into the control either vertically or horizontally and maintains proportions; often results in white space on top or right side

To add a logo to the form, select the Image button in the toolbox. Click on the left corner below the title and drag the box so that it creates a rectangle. The Insert Picture dialog box appears, as shown in Figure 7-34.

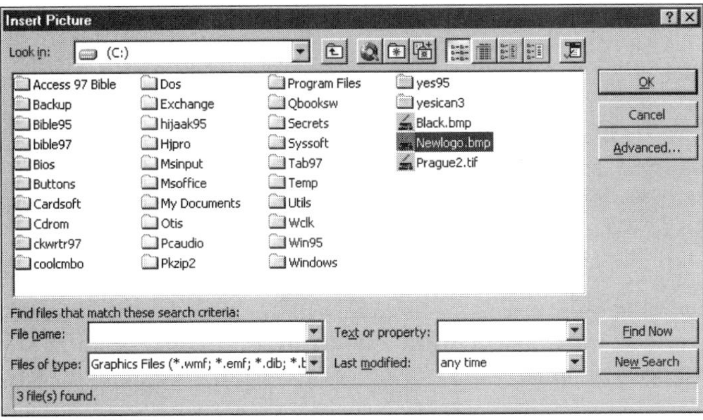

Figure 7-34: Creating an image dialog box.

From this dialog box, you can select the type of picture object you want to insert into your form. The dialog box supports many picture formats, including .WMF, .EMF, .DIB, .EPS, .CDR, .DRW, .BMP, .TIF, .PCX, .ICO, .WPG, .JPG, .PCT, or any picture format your copy of Windows 95 supports. Next, you can select your logo and click on the OK button. If the file does not already exist and you want to create a new object, such as a Paintbrush Picture, you must create an unbound OLE frame instead of an image.

Adding a Background Bitmap

If you want to emphasize a form even further or add a really fun effect, you can add a background bitmap to any form, just as you added one control behind another (see Figure 7-35). In Access 97, you do this by using the form's Picture properties. The following is a list of three properties with which you can work:

- `Picture` — The name of the bitmap picture. This can be any image-type file.
- `Picture Size Mode` — `Clip`, `Stretch`, or `Zoom`. `Clip` only displays the picture at its actual size starting at the `Picture Alignment` property. `Stretch` and `Zoom` fill the entire form from the upper-left corner of any header to the lower-right corner of any footer.
- `Picture Alignment` — `Top-Left`, `Top-Right`, `Center`, `Bottom-Left`, `Bottom-Right`, and so on. Only used when the Clip Picture Size Mode is used.
- `Picture Tiling` — `Yes/No`. When a small bitmap is used with Clip mode, the bitmap across the entire form repeats. For example, a brick becomes a brick wall.

Tip

The use of background bitmaps can give your form some interesting capabilities. You can go even further by incorporating the bitmap into your application. A bitmap can have buttons tied to macros or VBA code placed in the right locations. For example, to help the office staff look up a patient, you can create a form that has a map with three states behind it. By adding invisible buttons over each state, the operator can then click on the state to select the state to look in for the patient records. (See the next chapter for a good look at this technique.)

You can also scan in a paper form and use that as the form background, placing fields on top of the scanned form itself without having to spend too much time re-creating the form, which gives the phrase filling out a form a whole new meaning.

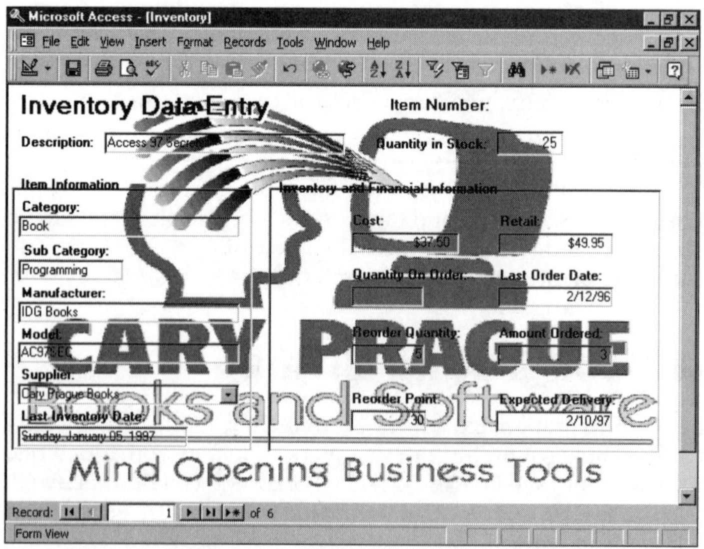

Figure 7-35: A bitmap picture behind a form.

Using AutoFormat

You can change the format of an entire form by using a new feature in Access 97 known as *AutoFormat*. This feature is the first menu option in the Format menu. AutoFormat enables you globally to change all fonts, colors, borders, background bitmaps, and virtually every property on a control-by-control basis. This feature works instantly and completely and is totally customizable.

When you select Format⇨AutoFormat, a window appears, as shown in Figure 7-36. This window lets you select from the standard AutoFormats or any you have created. The figure is shown after clicking on the Options button, which further lets you apply fonts, colors, or border style properties separately.

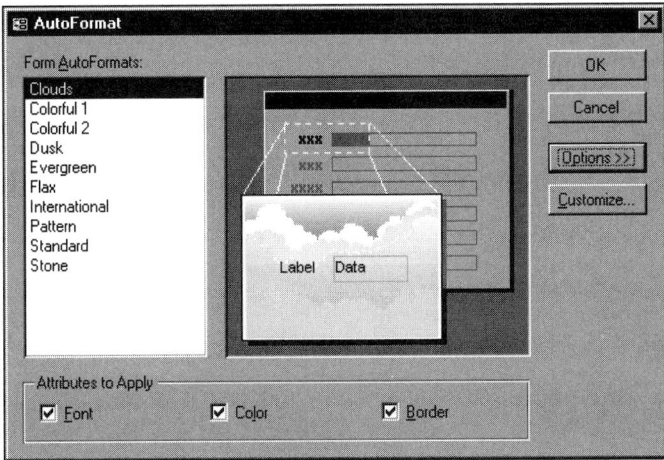

Figure 7-36: Selecting AutoFormat.

As shown in the figure, you can choose the Clouds AutoFormat type to change the style of the control fonts and colors and also change the background bitmap. As you move between the different AutoFormats, you can see an example of the look in the preview area to the right of the selections.

If you choose the Clouds AutoFormat, you see a series of messages indicating that there is no style set for various objects (such as lines and rectangles) because the Clouds AutoFormat only contains formatting instructions for label and text controls. You can add the current formatting to the Clouds AutoFormat (actually updating the AutoFormat), or you can leave the current formatting for each control type as you go through the process.

Customizing and adding new AutoFormats

You can modify existing AutoFormats or define new ones by simply creating a form, setting various form properties, and then starting AutoFormat. Though AutoFormat will totally change the look of your form, it does its job on a control-type-by-control-type basis, which means that it can format a label differently than a text box and differently than a line or rectangle. This feature also lets you define your own formats for each and every control type, including the background bitmap.

When you have created a form that you want to use as the basis for an AutoFormat, you can select AutoFormat and then click on the Customize button. Another window lets you update the currently selected format, add a new format, or delete the currently selected format.

Copying individual formats between controls

A subset of the AutoFormat technology is the Format Painter. This tool enables you to copy formatting properties from one individual control to another. To use the Format Painter, you first select the control whose properties you want to use. Then select the format painter icon in the toolbar (a picture of a paintbrush next to the Paste icon). Your cursor changes to a paintbrush. Click on the control you want to update, and the properties are copied from the originally selected control to the newly selected control.

Printing a Form

You can print a form by simply selecting the File➪Print option and entering the desired information in the Print dialog box. Printing a form is like printing anything else. You are in a WYSIWYG environment, so what you see on the form is essentially what you get in the printed hard copy. If you added page headers or page footers, you see them at the top or bottom of the printout.

Converting a Form to a Report

By right-clicking on the form name in the database container and selecting Save As Report, you can save the form design as a report. The entire form is placed in the report form. If the form has form headers or footers, these are placed in the Report Header and Report Footer sections. If the form has page headers or footers, these are placed in the Page Header and Footer sections in the report. When the design is in the Report Design window, you can enhance it by using the report design features. This feature enables you to add group sections and additional totaling in a report without having to re-create a great layout.

Chapter 8

User Interface Secrets and Techniques

In This Chapter

- Building a Switchboard
- Creating animated switches and gauges
- Combining multiple form pages into a tabbed dialog box
- Using progress meters for time-consuming events
- Assigning a key field automatically
- Morphing controls at run time
- Creating a geographic drill-down interface

Great user interfaces are an art and a science. No matter how good a developer you are, you must follow the scientific rules of human interface design to create a great user interface. Though you must design and implement an application that can be used by its operators, you must entice users with your application and conform to their needs and idiosyncrasies.

There are many standards for developing systems under Microsoft Windows. These include the *Windows Interface Standard Design Guide* (Microsoft Press 1994, 1995) and, for Microsoft Office Compatible applications, the *Microsoft Office Compatibility Guidelines* (Microsoft 1995). If you are interested in the *Microsoft Office Compatibility Guidelines,* call Microsoft at (206) 882-8080.

Note the word *Guidelines* in the *Office Compatibility Guidelines.* A *guideline* is a *suggestion.* Great user interfaces apply these suggestions while remaining sufficiently flexible to be familiar to the users. This flexibility is the art behind the science.

When you first demonstrate an application to a new client or a group in your company, if they don't say "Wow!" or "Great!" in the first 30 seconds, chances are that you have failed. If you implement the techniques presented in this chapter, your users will say "Wow!" many times during your first demonstration.

An application's most important goal is to function correctly. The *interface,* however, is what computer users see and what they invariably use to accomplish their tasks. Without a productive and user-lovable interface, your system may not be accepted — regardless of how well the system accomplishes its tasks.

The secrets behind great user interfaces are the following:

- Adherence to commonly accepted standards
- Simple navigation between functions and tasks
- Resemblance to the age-old manual processes
- Liberal use of pictures and other visual cues that make a user feel comfortable

Some call it sexy or jazzy, but the reality is that today, with increasing accessibility of multimedia and computers that talk or make sounds, you must do everything you can to focus users on accomplishing each task successfully. When the creative side of the brain is occupied with visual cues, the technical side of the brain also works better.

On CD-ROM

This chapter presents the secrets and techniques you need to create great user interfaces. The techniques include tools from simple switchboards to tabbed dialog boxes that display pages of data in a single screen or drill-down through layers of data with maps. The examples in this chapter are included in the Access database file CH8.MDB, which you can find on the CD-ROM that accompanies this book.

Building a Better Switchboard

A simple *switchboard,* or menu, is the most common Access user interface that you may see. However, you can create a plethora of interfaces with simple bitmaps, command buttons, and a little imagination.

The books switchboard

Figure 8-1 shows an interface created with a form and a bitmap of a book repeated several times. Each book is a separate bitmap. This interface started with a single book bitmap that was pasted to a form. You can duplicate any of the bitmaps; if they are OLE-type objects, you can double-click on them, launch an image editor, and change their color. You can also change the size, as shown in Figure 8-1.

This switchboard consists of a form, several bitmap-graphic objects, text objects, and command buttons. The secret of this technique is overlaying transparent command buttons on a graphic image for invisible selection. Each book has a command button on top of the button; the `Transparent` property of the command button is set to `Yes`. This creates an invisible button. The command button is placed over as much of the bitmap as possible, and then the command button is brought to the front of the objects (bitmap, text, or button) by using the Form Design command Format⇨Bring to Front.

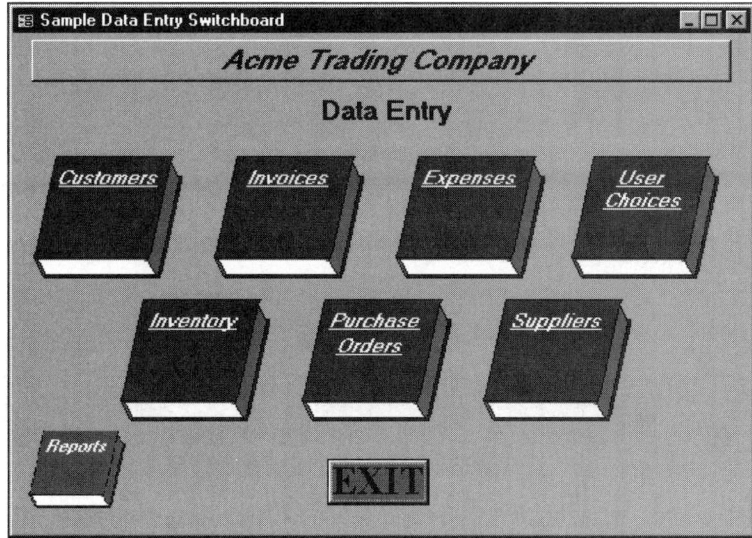

Figure 8-1: The switchboard user interface uses bitmaps and command buttons to combine many user steps into one single button push.

The design of the Book switchboard is shown in Figure 8-2. As you can see, the bitmap is placed on the form. The bitmap `Size Mode` property must be set to `Stretch`. This ensures that when the form is displayed at different screen resolutions, the bitmaps are always displayed correctly. With the `Size Mode` set to `Stretch`, you can make the bitmap any size you want.

As you can see in Figure 8-2, the `Command Button` is placed over the bitmap, and its `Transparent` property is set to `Yes`. Because the button is invisible, the button's caption is also invisible. This is why you must also place a text element on the bitmap in this example to give the book a title.

It is important that the command button cover as much of the bitmap as possible so that the user can click anywhere on the bitmap. You can reissue the command button to any size. Unfortunately, command buttons are always rectangular. You may need to use more than one command button to cover a nonrectangular area. When the user clicks on any part of the book covered by the large button or multiple buttons, your application can use a macro or VBA program.

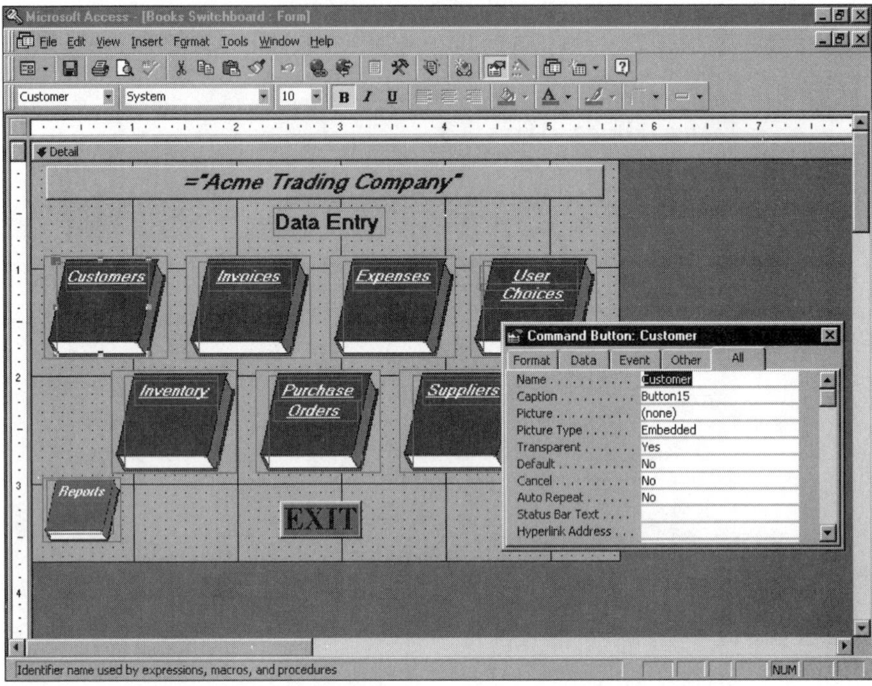

Figure 8-2: The invisible command buttons on the switchboard are placed over the bitmaps.

One last secret of bitmaps: Use Paintbrush-type bitmaps (.BMP). They take the least amount of space and use fewer resources. Most important, if the bitmap type is OLE, change it to a Picture. You do this by selecting the bitmap and then choosing Edit➪Paintbrush Picture Object➪Change to Picture on the form design menu. If you have a different application associated with your graphic, such as CorelDraw or Microsoft Imager, you will see that application instead of Windows Paintbrush. Though you can double-click on most bitmap objects and change them, after you change them to a Picture, they are uneditable. Make sure that you make all of your changes before changing an OLE-class bitmap to a Picture.

A command button picture switchboard

Although the books switchboard has pizzazz, it requires large, scalable bitmaps and a single theme for the bitmap buttons. Instead of using the Transparent button technique of placing an invisible button on top of a bitmap, place the picture on top of the button itself. This type of interface is found traditionally in executive information systems. You can use any icon-size bitmap.

Good user interface design means icons should be remembered, not recognized. You must train the user on the function of the icon. In most applications, the easiest way is to provide a redundant cue. Generally, this is a textual explanation, as shown in Figure 8-3, or ToolTip-type help.

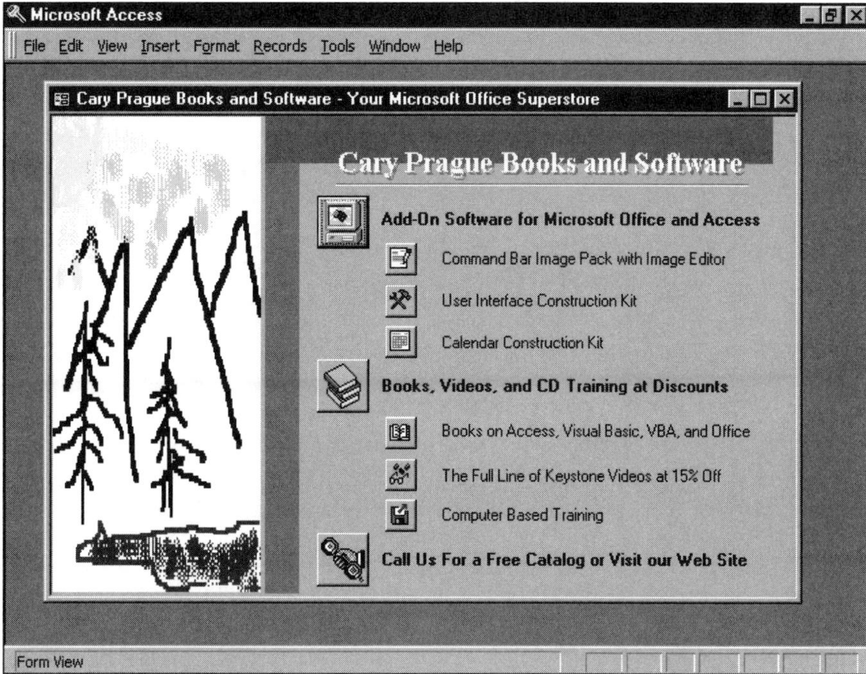

Figure 8-3: Placing a picture on a command button provides a visual label in addition to a text label.

Although you can resize OLE-type bitmaps, you cannot resize a picture placed on top of a button. Alternatively, you can use simple icon-size (32 x 32 pixels) buttons with an additional text label. Most graphics libraries you can purchase include icon files used in Program Manager icons. A Picture switchboard (shown in Figure 8-3), however, uses command buttons.

Figure 8-4 shows the Design view of the Alternative Switchboard. To give this switchboard a sharp look, two large, colored rectangles are first drawn on the form. The form background is set to dark gray, which enhances the 3-D effect. The form itself has the usual switchboard properties set (`Auto Resize – Yes`, `Auto Center – Yes`; `No Control Box`, `Record Selector`, or `Scroll Bars`). After the form is ready, you add the command buttons and text.

Each command button is aligned in a vertical row. The `Picture` property is used to embed the already-created bitmap picture, as shown in the preceding figure, where the `Picture` property is being used to enter the name and location of the bitmap file. Two label objects make the icon understandable: One is just a row of dashes; the other is the actual reason to "push" the button.

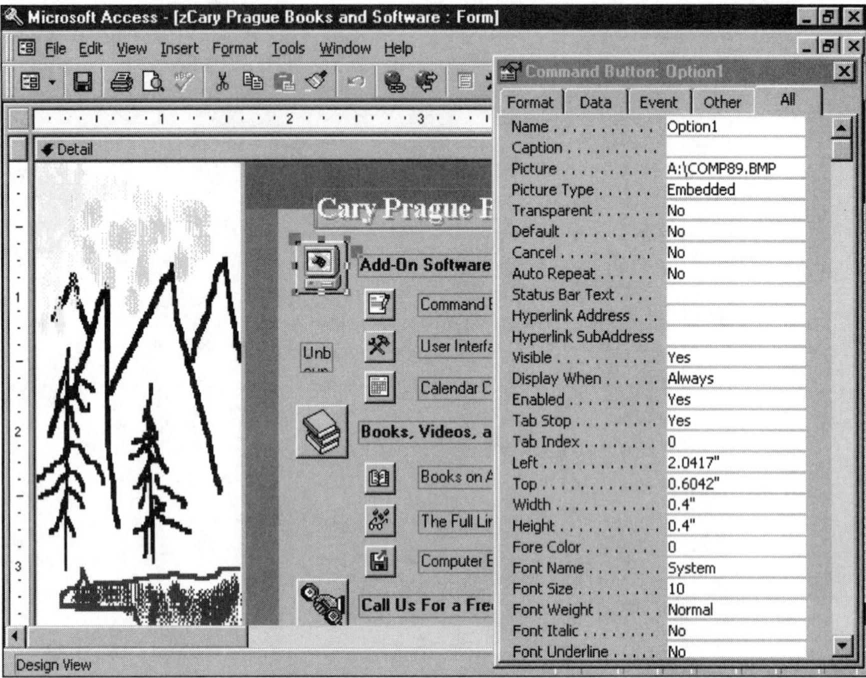

Figure 8-4: 3-D effects and bitmap icons give the switchboard a sharp look.

Animated Switches and Gauges

After you have completed the switchboard as the navigational component of your user interface, you should turn your attention to data-entry screens. Anyone can create a simple form with labels and text boxes. What distinguishes professional applications from average ones is their use of *graphical objects* and *visual cues*. Great systems don't run just one way. You should give the user choices that control how the system runs.

For example, in an inventory system you can switch on various options or switch them off. Switches can be created with simple checkboxes or they can look like switches. Sometimes, you may have more than one choice. For example, a form may be used for several types of data entry. Each type of data entry may require a different form. You may want to let users pick the default form from a list of forms for their specific needs. You can use an option group with simple option or toggle buttons, or you can use a list or combo box. It is much better, however, to do it graphically. Figure 8-5 shows animated switches and a graphical option group.

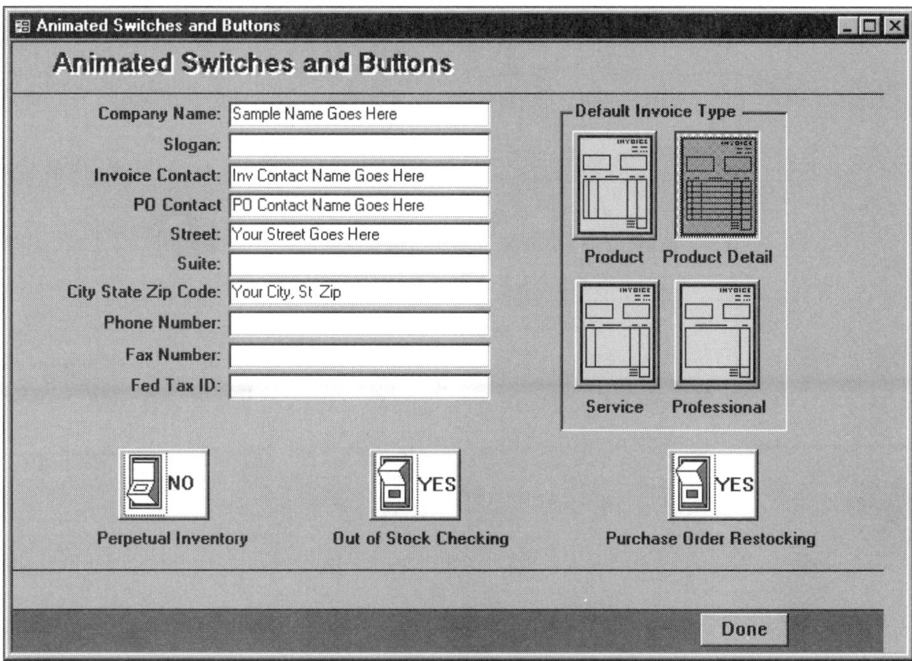

Figure 8-5: Combining graphical objects and visual cues gives the user more than one way to use the system.

Finally, you may want to display a value or a ratio of values graphically. While the data changes, you manipulate the look of the graph to indicate changes. The following section provides you with these tools to enhance your systems.

Animated Yes/No switches

Checkboxes are boring objects. They appear either as empty rectangles or as rectangles with a checkmark inside. Because these are actually two-state switches, they should *look like* switches. The following techniques provide the necessary bitmaps and code to make any checkbox into a real switch.

Figure 8-6 shows the Design view of the Animated Switches and Buttons form. All you need to make a switch are two bitmap pictures embedded on command buttons (one an On switch, one an Off switch) sized the same and placed on top of each other, and a simple checkbox (plus a little code or a simple macro). The switch changes the value of the checkbox, which generally is bound to a field in a table.

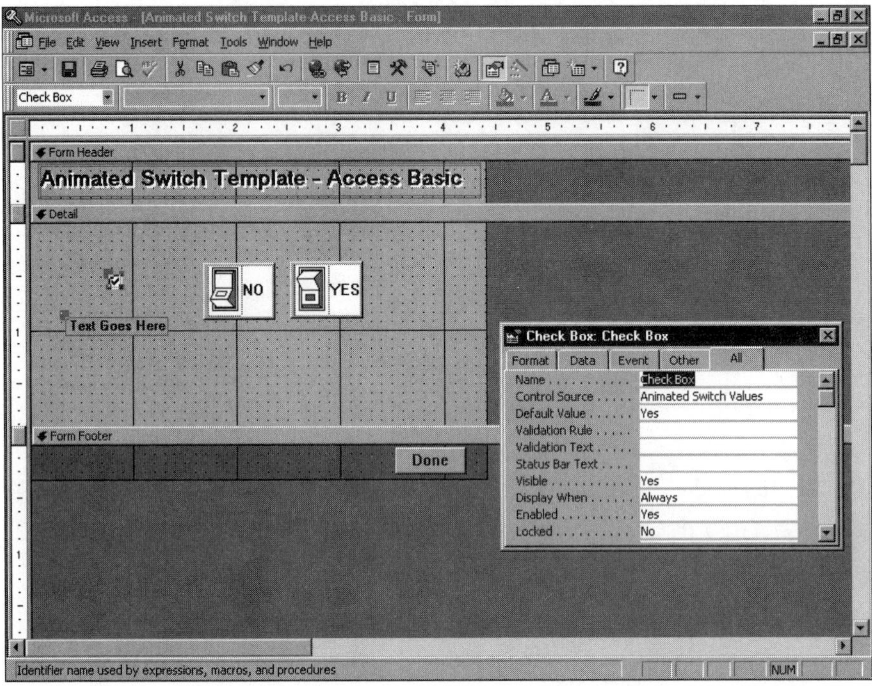

Figure 8-6: The secret of the switch technique is placing two bitmap pictures on command buttons combined with a simple checkbox.

The Perpetual Inventory checkbox is a standard Microsoft Access checkbox. The first secret of this interface component is manipulating the checkbox value each time you click on a switch button. The second secret is knowing which switch button is being clicked on and reacting appropriately. The key is manipulating the `Visible` property of the selected and nonselected switch buttons.

While the button that is pressed is visible, the other button remains invisible. This is controlled by either a macro or an Access Basic program. Based on the switch button that was pressed, the controlling program runs a code sequence that changes the currently visible switch's `Visible` property to `No`, changes the currently invisible switch's `Visible` property to `Yes`, and changes the checkbox value to the opposite of the previous value.

Creating animated switches with VBA code

You should start by creating a standard Access checkbox. This step is important; ultimately, the checkbox is the object whose value the switches manipulate. After you create a checkbox and place the two command buttons with embedded pictures on your form, you can create the VBA code that is called by the form and button events. Figure 8-7 shows the code window for opening the form.

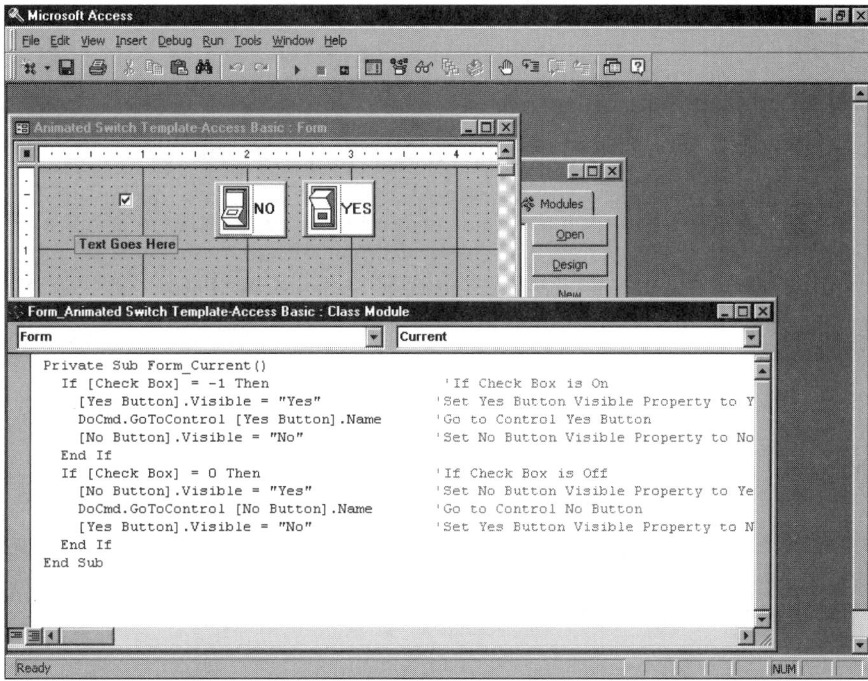

Figure 8-7: The On Open event sets the switch to the proper state when the form opens.

The VBA code is attached to the form's `On Open` property as an `[Event Procedure]`. This sets the switch to the proper state, based on the current value of the checkbox in the first record that is used. You also must add this code to the form's `On Current` property, which changes the switch when you move from record to record. The `On Current` property is triggered each time a different record becomes the current record when you move between records. The `On Current` property also handles new records, whether the default value is `Yes` or `No`. The initial null state is treated as a `No`, the way the macro is coded. You can follow the process through the comments in Figure 8-7.

You also need to set the `On Click` property for both the Yes Button and the No Button to run the proper VBA code. Figure 8-8 shows the code for the Yes Button's `On Click` event. The Yes Button code is triggered when the Yes Button is clicked on. You can click on this button when the checkbox state is `Yes`; it means that you want to change the checkbox's state to `No`. As you can see in the following Yes Button program, the No Button is first made visible and then the focus is shifted to the No Button. Then the Yes Button is made not visible. This is possible only if the focus is on a different object. This is why the focus is shifted to the button that will eventually be the visible button. Finally, the checkbox state itself is changed.

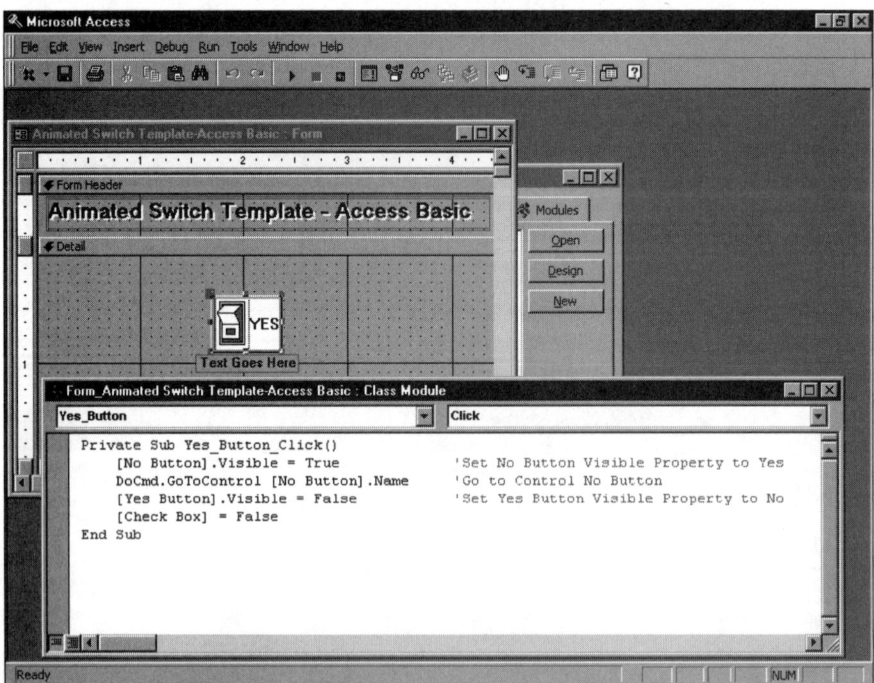

Figure 8-8: The Yes Button On Click event makes the Yes Button invisible and the No Button visible.

As you can see in the No Button program (shown in Figure 8-9), the Yes Button is first made visible and then the focus is shifted to the Yes Button. Next, the No Button is made not visible. Finally, the checkbox state itself is changed.

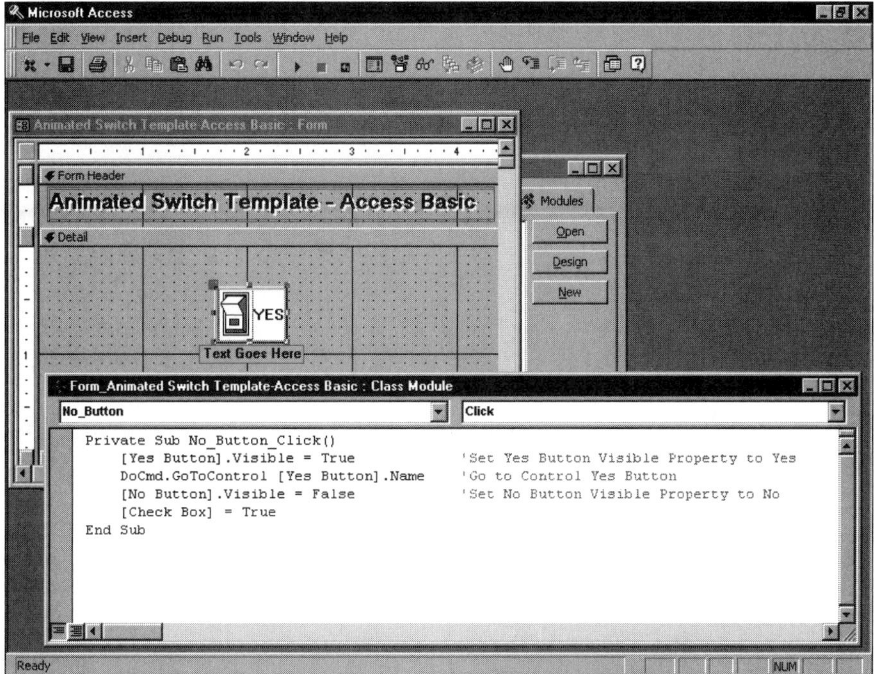

Figure 8-9: The No Button On Click event makes the No Button invisible and the Yes Button visible.

Animated toggle buttons

The toggle button is an interface component used in place of option buttons (*radio* buttons) when you want to represent a selection graphically. Figure 8-10 shows a group of toggle buttons for selecting the Default Invoice Type. When you click on a Default Invoice Type, it becomes sunken and out of focus while the others become sharp.

Unlike some of the other interfaces in Access, there is no plug-and-play approach to animated toggle buttons. This interface is shown simply to demonstrate a better way of representing a group of choices than standard option buttons.

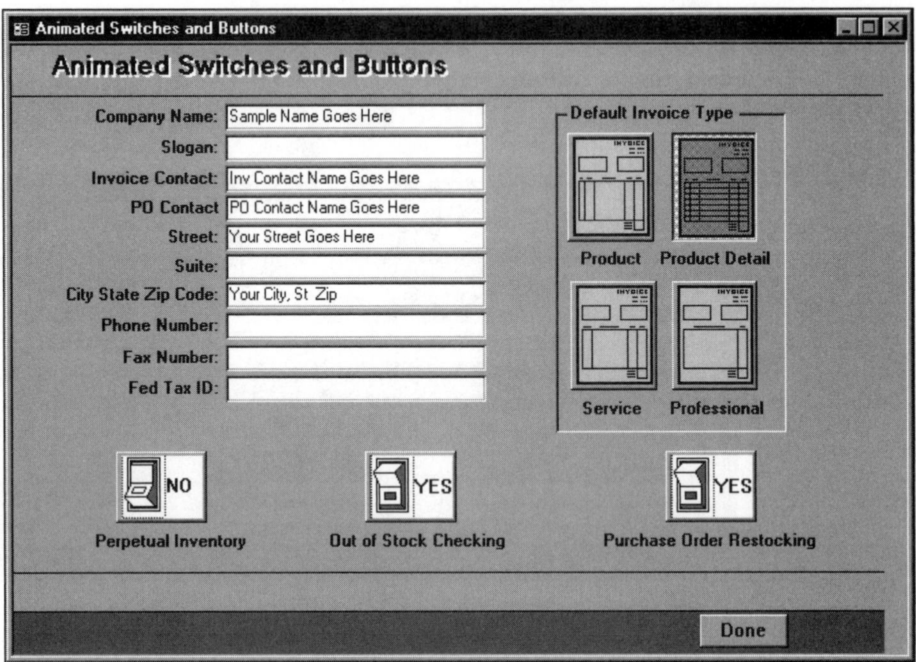

Figure 8-10: Using toggle buttons to graphically represent a selection from a group of objects.

To create a group of toggle buttons for your application, you first must create the bitmaps that will represent each choice. They should all be the same size (unless your selections reflect size). Remember: Like command buttons, pictures you embed on a toggle button cannot be resized. After you complete the pictures and save them as bitmaps or icon files, you can create your toggle buttons.

For toggle buttons to function as a group that allows only one to be selected at a time, you first must create an option group. After creating the option group, you can add your toggle buttons (by embedding the pictures on the buttons), resize the buttons to fit the pictures, and resize the option group to fit the toggle buttons.

When you click on each toggle button, the button that is selected appears sunken and its picture is dimmed. The other button pictures are displayed normally. This technique gives your users a better interface than selecting standard option buttons.

Simple gauges

Graphical displays of the ratio of two or more values can be crucial in some systems. In Figure 8-11, the Stock Level (defined as the Quantity in Stock/ Reorder Point) instantly tells the inventory manager that it is time to order more product.

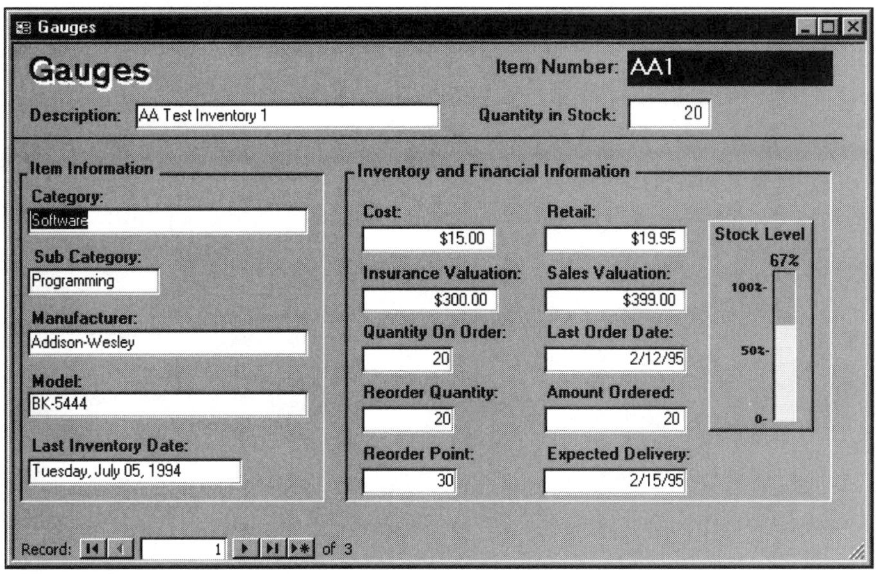

Figure 8-11: Using a gauge enables users to analyze data quickly.

You have two ways to display graphics in Microsoft Access. The first is a graph control. But if you have ever created a graph in Microsoft Access, you know that it is time consuming, difficult to maintain, and slower than molasses running uphill. Microsoft Graph was never meant to be used as a quick analytical tool. Another way to display a set of values graphically is a simple graph created from simple objects, such as colored rectangles.

In the Gauges example, you can see in the Stock Level that the graph is on 67 percent. This is done with a set of colored rectangles embedded within a set of three-dimensional rectangles. You can create the colored bar by manipulating and coloring a rectangle, or you can create it by displaying an appropriate colored rectangle from a series. In this product, we use a series of rectangles. Later (in the section on animated progress meters), you see an example that manipulates a single rectangle.

To calculate a bar graph value, you need only three items: a numerator (the top number in a division), a denominator (the bottom number in a division), and the percentage calculation. To create the bar graph, you need only some simple rectangles, a few label or text-box objects, and a small VBA program.

Understanding the gauge control

Figure 8-12 shows the Gauges Template form with all its components separated. Though you can't see the exact colors in the gray scale figure, there are several different color sets in the bars. When the bars get bigger, their color changes, which is a secondary visual cue.

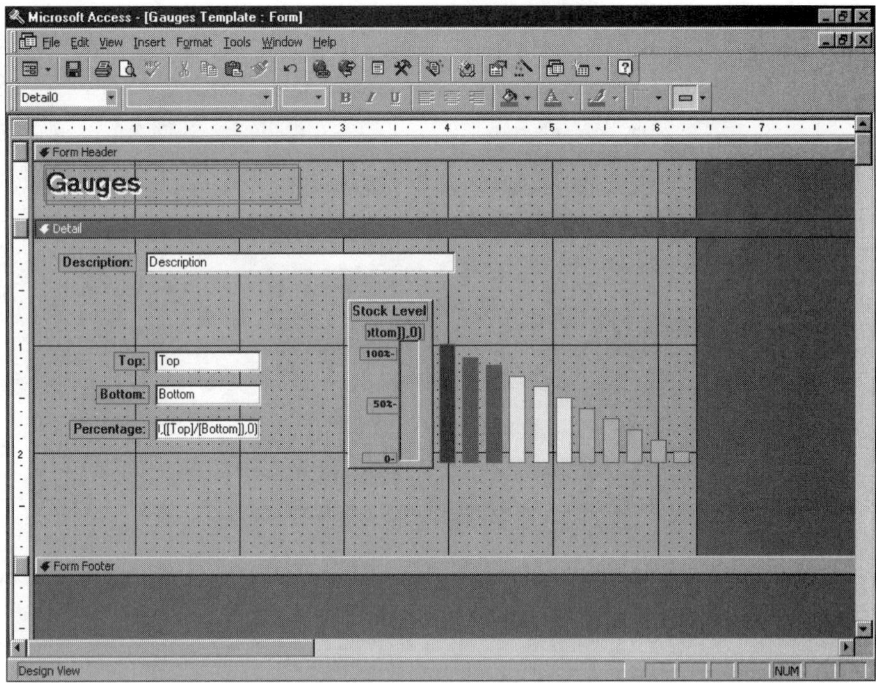

Figure 8-12: Using rectangles to create a gauge.

All the rectangle bars are stacked on top of each other and fit in the sunken area of the gauge rectangle itself.

By using the `Visible` property of the bars to make one bar visible at a time, you can make the graph change from record to record in accordance with the changing value of the calculation. This example is only shown as a VBA program. Even if you don't understand VBA, you can easily change the call to the gauge module without ever seeing the gauge module.

The gauge itself is built from several controls. The first control is a gray, raised rectangle. Then a sunken gray rectangle is embedded in the raised rectangle; the sunken rectangle is where the colored bars are placed.

The scale is made with three text labels; in this example, they use the Small Fonts font, set to 6 points. You can also use 6-point Arial.

You can change the size of the gauge to any size you want and change the rectangles appropriately. The program itself does not need to be changed, which you will see in the following pages.

A text box above the gauge displays the current ratio as a percentage. Figure 8-13 shows the calculation for the ratio percentage. Notice that the calculation takes into account a possible zero-divide condition. The calculation `[ =IIf([Bottom]<>0,([Top]/[Bottom]),0)]` says that if the value of `Bottom` isn't zero, then divide top by bottom and display it as a percent, or else display 0.

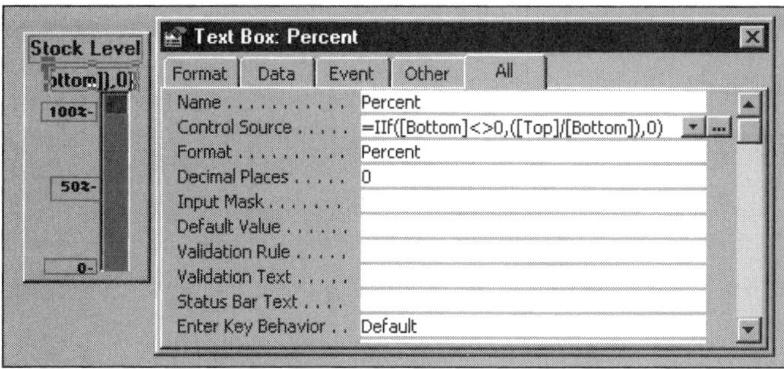

Figure 8-13: Displaying the current ratio as a percent.

Also notice that the graph is made to show values over 100 percent. Generally, after a ratio is over 100 percent, it isn't important how much over it is. Using the techniques for the simple gauge, you should be able to make the graph represent any number you want, including negative numbers.

The gauge works by showing only one bar at a time, based on the result of the `Percent` calculation. As Figure 8-12 illustrates, there are 11 separate rectangles, named Gauge1 through Gauge11. Only one rectangle is displayed at a time.

A single VBA program is called by the events that trigger a change in the graph. This program is stored as a separate VBA module named `Gauge` because it is called from at least three places:

- Forms' `On Current` event
- The control that has the `Top` (numerator) value's `After Update` property
- The control that has the `Bottom` (denominator) value's `After Update` property

Displaying the gauge value with a program

Listing 8-1 shows the VBA program that is called each time a record is made current or either the numerator or denominator is changed. First X is calculated, and then (based on the result) the appropriate gauge rectangle is made visible. There are also checks for a zero denominator to avoid divide-by-0 errors or null values for the numerator or denominator. In the following example, the Gauge module contains one function named ShowGauge().

Listing 8-1 Using a VBA Program to Update the Gauge

```
Function ShowGauge (AnyForm As Form, _
Numer As Control, Denom As Control)  'Declare Parameters
  Dim X As Single                    'Declare the percent
  AnyForm![Gauge1].Visible = 0  'Make sure all colored
  AnyForm![Gauge2].Visible = 0  'fills start invisible
  AnyForm![Gauge3].Visible = 0
  AnyForm![Gauge4].Visible = 0
  AnyForm![Gauge5].Visible = 0
  AnyForm![Gauge6].Visible = 0
  AnyForm![Gauge7].Visible = 0
  AnyForm![Gauge8].Visible = 0
  AnyForm![Gauge9].Visible = 0
  AnyForm![Gauge10].Visible = 0
  AnyForm![Gauge11].Visible = 0
 If Denom <> 0 Then    'Trap for division by zero error
   If IsNull(Numer) Or IsNull(Denom) Then 'If either
     End                                  'field is null
   End If                                 'no comparison
                                          'possible
   X = Numer / Denom   'Do percent calculation and fill
                       'variable

  If X > 0 And X <= .15 Then      'Conditional statements
    AnyForm![Gauge1].Visible = -1  'to set visible
  ElseIf X > .15 And X <= .25 Then 'properties of color
    AnyForm![Gauge2].Visible = -1  'fill rectangles.
  ElseIf X > .25 And X <= .35 Then
    AnyForm![Gauge3].Visible = -1
  ElseIf X > .35 And X <= .45 Then
    AnyForm![Gauge4].Visible = -1
  ElseIf X > .45 And X <= .55 Then
    AnyForm![Gauge5].Visible = -1
  ElseIf X > .55 And X <= .65 Then
    AnyForm![Gauge6].Visible = -1
  ElseIf X > .65 And X <= .75 Then
    AnyForm![Gauge7].Visible = -1
  ElseIf X > .75 And X <= .85 Then
    AnyForm![Gauge8].Visible = -1
  ElseIf X > .85 And X <= .95 Then
    AnyForm![Gauge9].Visible = -1
  ElseIf X > .95 And X <= 1 Then
```

```
    AnyForm![Gauge10].Visible = -1
  ElseIf X > 1 Then
    AnyForm![Gauge11].Visible = -1
  End If
 End If
End Function
```

You can modify the number of gauge rectangles and change this program to accommodate them. For example, you can create 21 gauges and change the value for every 5 percent, or you can have just four rectangles that each represent 25 percent. As long as the number of rectangles on the form corresponds to the result of the program, everything works fine.

Calling the ShowGauge program

The call to the `ShowGauge` function passes three parameters: the name of the form, the control storing the value of the numerator, and the control storing the value of the denominator. The `ShowGauge` program is called the same way from the form's `OnCurrent` property and also from the `AfterUpdate` properties of any value that changes the graph percentage value. These are usually the numerator or denominator values. In Figure 8-14, you can see that these are the `Top` and `Bottom` values.

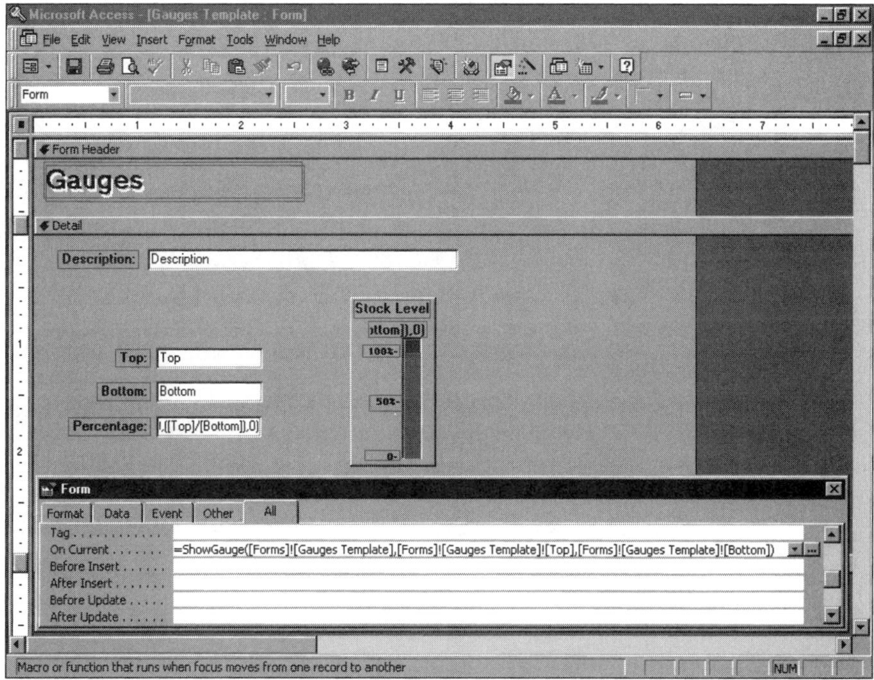

Figure 8-14: Calling the ShowGauge function.

Selecting a range of dates with a calendar

One of the biggest deficiencies in most applications is that they attempt to force the user into traditional date ranges. Systems that enable the user to choose from a year, month, or week do not let the nonfiscal or nontraditional company measure its data. A year defined as January 1 through December 31, or a month defined as the 1st through the 30th (or 28th, 29th, or 31st) may not work for many companies. A company's internal reporting period may start with the 20th of a month and end with the 19th of the next month. One of the world's largest soft drink companies uses a 13-period year. A fiscal year may consist of any 12-month period, but the periods do not need to be equal periods, nor are 12 periods required. Never predefine periods for your system; instead, let users choose the period to display or report from their data.

Figure 8-15 illustrates an interface that enables users to select the data they want. For simplicity, the examples and standard VBA code cover a single year; they assume that each month starts on the first day and ends on the last day of the month. As you will see in the VBA module, you easily can adjust the concept of a month to start or end on different dates.

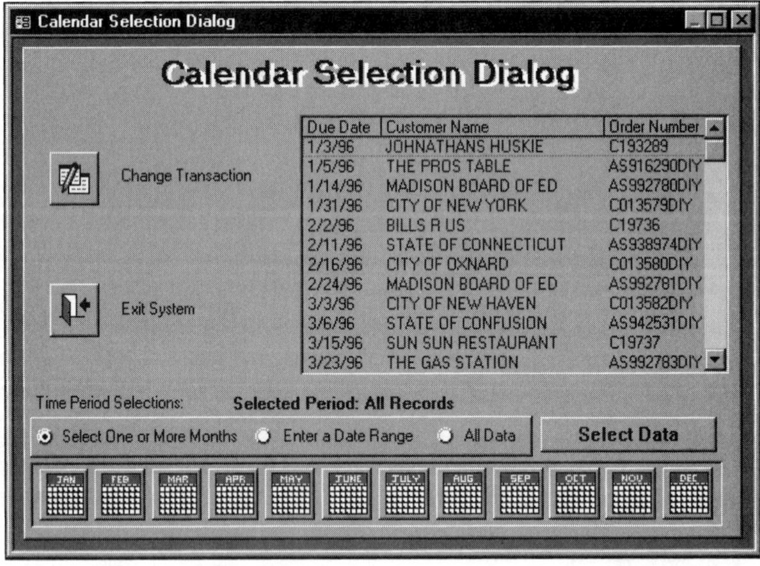

Figure 8-15: A calendar interface is a flexible way for your users to choose date ranges.

Understanding the calendar interface

The calendar interface consists of two main sections:

- The Calendar Selection area
- The Data Display area

The Calendar Selection area at the bottom of the form determines how to search for the data and then actually allows the selection of a range of dates. A set of option buttons controls what the user sees. The first option button, Select One or More Months, displays the 12 monthly calendars and resets all of them so that none is selected. You can then click on one calendar to see one month of data in the current year, or you can click on two or more months to select from a range of days from the first day of the first selected month to the last day of the last selected month. The second option button, Enter a Date Range, displays two text boxes that let you enter any dates. For example, you can enter a range of dates from March 3, 1997, through June 11, 1998. The last choice is preset to select all records from the table. Each time a selection is made, the selection is also shown above the option group as a secondary visual cue.

The area where the small calendars appear is actually two sets of controls layered on top of each other. As you can see in Figure 8-16, these layers are shown separated. The Data Display area is simply an unbound list box, which displays the data within the selected dates. Here you can select a record and click on the Change Transaction button (shown separately in Figure 8-16) to display a form with the selected record, or you can double-click on the record in the data display area.

Creating the calendar interface

Though the CH8.MDB file contains this entire interface for you to use, it is important to understand how the interface is created. The calendar interface consists of three parts:

- The Option Group for selecting the proper calendar view
- The Graphical Calendar view
- The Text Box Calendar selectors

The first part that is created is the Graphical Calendar view. This is a series of toggle buttons and a rectangle. The first rectangle is created and sunken for a 3-D effect. Next, 12 equally sized toggle buttons are created without an option group. The toggle buttons of this interface component do not act in tandem; without an option group, more than one toggle button can be selected at a time. After the 12 standard toggle buttons are created, you can embed a graphic on each one and resize the toggle button slightly larger than the toggle button. Figure 8-17 shows the toggle buttons for the 12 months of the year.

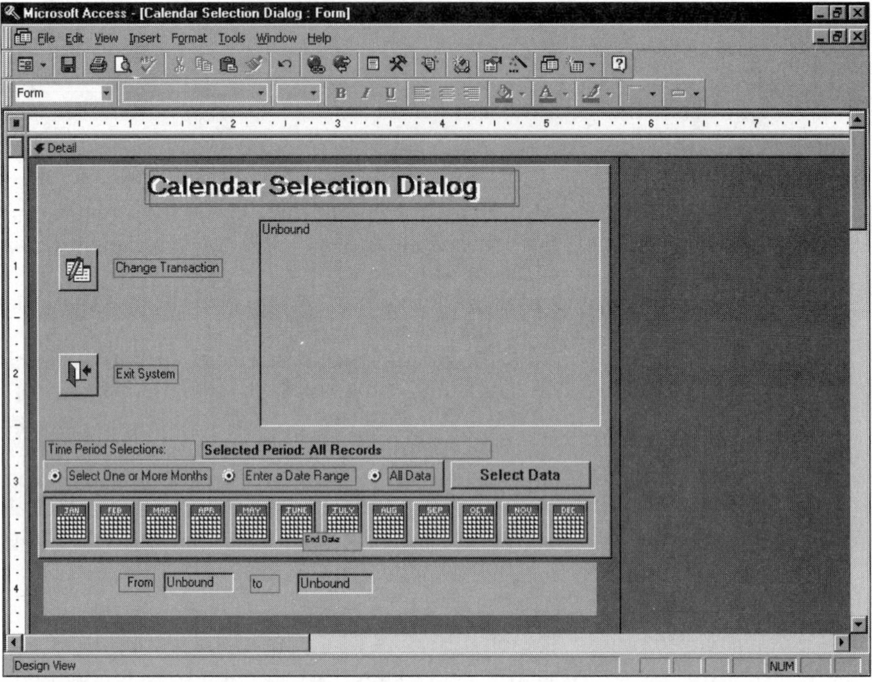

Figure 8-16: Combining various interfaces for entering date ranges. The Change Transaction button displays a form with the selected record.

Figure 8-17: Using toggle buttons for selecting the twelve months of the year.

Later in this section, you see how VBA code can manipulate the visible properties of the rectangle and the toggle buttons and how the up and down states of the toggle buttons are manipulated.

The second part of the interface is the Text Box Calendar selectors. As shown in Figure 8-18, these are simply two unbound text boxes that capture the user's input, plus some text box labels. In fact, when the user clicks on the calendars and clicks on the Select Data button, the calculated dates are stored in these text boxes.

Figure 8-18: Using unbound text boxes to capture and store the actual date ranges.

Figure 8-19 shows the last part of the interface, which consists of a single option group with three option buttons. Each option button triggers one of the views. When the toggle buttons are clicked on or dates are entered in the text boxes and the Select Data button is clicked on, the data displayed in the Data Display area is updated based on the selections in the toggle buttons or the text boxes.

Figure 8-19: An option group that lets the user specify how to input the date range.

Working with your data

The Calendar Selection dialog box example uses a simple three-field table that contains an Order Key, a date field named Due Date, and a customer field. Obviously, the table must contain a date field for date selection to be relevant. The other fields, the size of the list box, and the number of fields depends upon your specific application.

In Figure 8-20, the Order Search list box is filled by an SQL statement (which also has a corresponding query design) that displays three fields. The secret is the `WHERE` clause. The `WHERE` clause selects only data that has a date value between the `From Date` and the `To Date`.

```
WHERE (([Sample Calendar Data].[Due Date] Between _
[Forms]![Calendar Selection Dialog]![From Date] And _
[Forms]![Calendar Selection Dialog]![To Date])
```

When you create your SQL statement, you can use any fields you want if a date field is somewhere in the list box.

Understanding the calendar events and programs

Only four events and VBA programs control this entire interface. The first is the `On Open` event of the form. This event sets the text box to the widest range of dates that you want and requeries the Data Display area list box, which displays the data. The VBA program for the `On Open` form event is shown in Figure 8-21. In this example, the dates from 1/1/96 through 12/31/99 are set, and then the Data Display area is requeried to display all the data for the default dates.

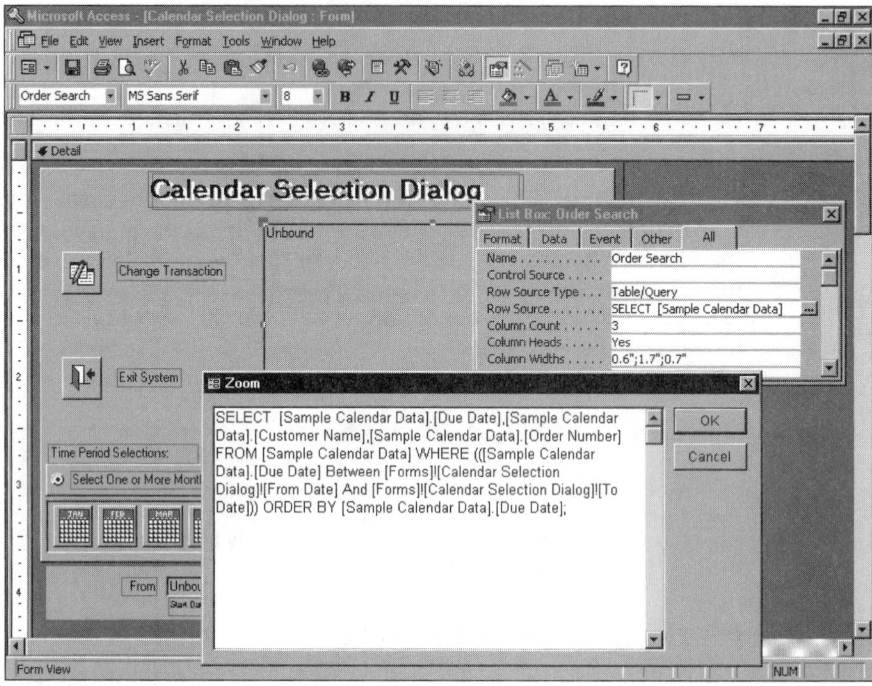

Figure 8-20: Updating the data based on the date range selection.

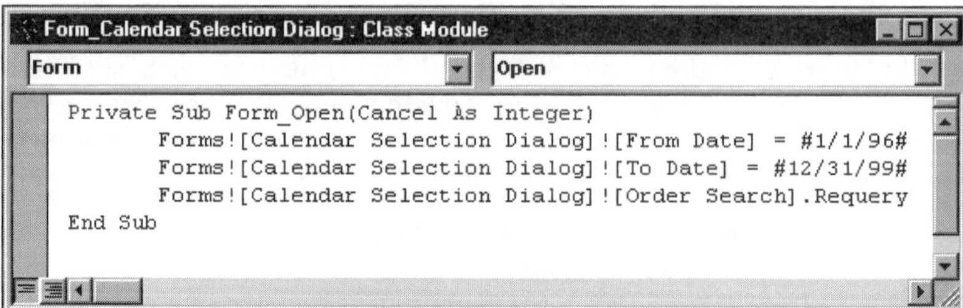

Figure 8-21: Initializing the date range when the form opens.

The next event is the `AfterUpdate` event for the Calendar View option group. This event runs a VBA program, shown in Listing 8-2, each time the option group item is changed. The first group of statements makes the Text Box Calendar selectors visible, which hides the Calendar Toggle Buttons. The `Else` statement does the opposite, which makes the Calendar Toggle Buttons visible. The last two blocks of code (only partially shown) manipulate the buttons first, making them all raised; if All Records is selected, the buttons are sunken.

Listing 8-2 Updating the Interface When the Date Range Changes

```
Private Sub Date_Selection_AfterUpdate()
    If [Date Selection] = 2 Then   'Enter a Date Range
                                   'Chosen'
        [Time Period Divider].Visible = True
        [From Text].Visible = True
        [To Text].Visible = True
        [From Date].Visible = True
        [To Date].Visible = True
        [Start Date Text].Visible = True
        [End Date Text].Visible = True
   Else: [Time Period Divider].Visible = True
        [Time Period Divider].Visible = False
          'Either Calendar View or Select All Data Chosen
        [From Text].Visible = False
        [To Text].Visible = False
        [From Date].Visible = False
        [To Date].Visible = False
        [Start Date Text].Visible = False
        [End Date Text].Visible = False
   End If
    For T = 1 To 12                    'Sets all Toggle
      MonthNo = "Month" + Trim(Str(T)) 'Buttons To the Up
                                       '(Unselected)
                                       'Position
      Me(MonthNo) = 0
    Next T
If [Date Selection] = 3 Then   'If All Records is
                               'Selected
  For T = 1 To 12                    'Sets all of the
                                     'Toggle Buttons
     MonthNo = "Month" + Trim(Str(T))'To the Down
                                     '(Selected) Position
     Me(MonthNo) = -1
  Next T
 End If
End Sub
```

The next event is the VBA code associated with clicking on the Select Data button. When this button is pressed, the currently visible interface is scanned and the specified dates are entered or copied to the text boxes, and then the Order Search List box is requeried to display the new data.

The first part of the Select Data button's `On Click` event is partially displayed in the Listing 8-3. This block of code determines which of the buttons, if any, were pressed.

Listing 8-3 Determining Which Toggle Button Was Pressed

```
Private Sub Select_Data_Click()
  If [Date Selection] = 1 Then  'Selection is Being Made
                                'from the Calendar Toggle
                                'Buttons
   Fst = 0                      'Set Variables to
                                'determine the First and
                                'Last Months
   Lst = 0
   For T = 1 To 12
        MonthNo = "Month" + Trim(Str(T))
        If Not (IsNull(Me(MonthNo))) Then
           If Me(MonthNo) Then  'If Feb is down
               If Fst > 0 Then  'and a month was
                                'already set to first
                    Lst = T     'then set last to Feb
                Else            'Else if no month was set
                                'set to first and Feb is
                                'down
                    Fst = T     'Set Feb to first
                End If
            End If
        End If
    Next T
   If Fst = 0 Then      'If no month is set to first
                        'then no month was selected
     Response = MsgBox("No Months Selected", _
48, "Date Selection Failed")
     Else
      If Lst = 0 Then     'If a month was set to first
                          'but no month was set to last
       Lst = Fst          'Only one month was set and it
                          'is now set to last too
      End If
~~~~~~~~~~~~~~~
~~~~~~~~~~~~~~~
```

The preceding code only determines which buttons (if any) were pressed and sets the first-month and last-month values. Listing 8-4 shows the next part of the code, which is used to set the actual values in the text boxes.

Listing 8-4 Determining the Month, Day, and Year

```
CurYr = Year(Date)           'Grab the current year
      Select Case Lst
       Case 4, 6, 9, 11             '30 Day Last Month
         NumDays = 30
       Case 1, 3, 5, 7, 8, 10, 12  '31 Day Last Month
         NumDays = 31
       Case 2
         Leap = CurYr Mod 4         'Check for 28 or 29 Day February
         If Leap = 0 And CurYr <> 2000 Then
           NumDays = 29
          Else: NumDays = 28
```

```
          End If
        End Select
        FstCap = Fst & "/1" & "/" & CurYr
                      'Set the From and To Date Text Boxes
        LstCap = Lst & "/" & NumDays & "/" & CurYr
        Forms![Calendar Selection Dialog]![From Date] = _
        DateValue(Fst & "/1" & "/" & CurYr)
        Forms![Calendar Selection Dialog]![To Date] = _
        DateValue(Lst & "/" & NumDays & "/" & CurYr)
        DoCmd.ApplyFilter , "[Due Date] Between _
        Forms![Calendar Selection Dialog]![From Date] _
        and Forms![Calendar Selection Dialog]![To Date]"
        [Period].Caption = "Selected Period: " & FstCap _
        & " To " & LstCap  'Reset the caption
    End If
  End If
  If [Date Selection] = 2 Then 'If a From and To Date was _
'Entered
    If Forms![Calendar Selection Dialog]![From Date] _
    > Forms![Calendar Selection Dialog]![To Date] Then
      Response = MsgBox("Start Date After End _
Date -     No Data Selected", 48, "Date Selection Failed")
      Exit Sub
     Else
      DoCmd.ApplyFilter , "[Due Date] Between _
      Forms![Calendar Selection Dialog]![From Date] _
      and Forms![Calendar Selection Dialog]![To Date]"
      [Period].Caption = "Selected Period: " & _
      Forms![Calendar Selection Dialog]![From Date] & _
      " To " & Forms![Calendar Selection Dialog]![To Date]
     End If
  End If
  If [Date Selection] = 3 Then 'Reselect All Records and
     DoCmd.ShowAllRecords       'reset the From and To _
'dates
     [Period].Caption = "Selected Period: All Records"
     Forms![Calendar Selection Dialog]![From Date] = _
     #1/1/95#
     Forms![Calendar Selection Dialog]![To Date]= _
     #12/31/99#
  End If
  Forms![Calendar Selection Dialog]! _
  [Order Search].Requery            'Redisplay the data
'in the List Box

End Sub
'Only one month was set and it is now set to last too
```

The Current Year is set first because the interface works only with the current year. If you want to span two years or more, you must modify the code to select a year as well as a month. For example, if you want to select six months from the previous year and the first six months of the present year, you might select the current year for January through June; for July through December, you might select the number of the current year minus 1.

Next, a standard algorithm determines the number of days for the last month. This program selects the first day of the first month to the last day of the last month. Even leap years are taken into account. The To and From date boxes are built by concatenating the parts of the date. Finally, the calculated values are placed into the actual text boxes. After the dates are set, the filter is applied to the records and the list box requeried. If the dates were actually typed into the From and To date boxes, they are verified for accuracy before the filter is applied. If All Records is selected, then the filter is removed from the table.

Displaying a form with selected data in the list box

Figure 8-22 illustrates a command button that displays the selected record in the list box on a form. When the Change Transaction button is clicked on, a form enables the user to view or edit the transaction. Listing 8-5 shows the code for this procedure; just modify the code to make it work with your form.

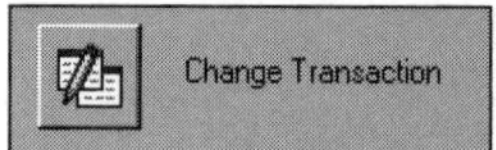

Figure 8-22: Using a command button to edit the selected data.

Listing 8-5 **Using VBA Code to Display a Form for Editing the Transaction**

```
Private Sub Change_Transaction_Click()
'  On Error GoTo Err_Chg_Click
  If IsNull(Forms![Calendar Selection Dialog]! _
  [Order Search]) Then
   Response = MsgBox("You Did Not Select a Record _
   to Search For", 16, "No Record Selected")
   Exit Sub
  End If
'  DoCmd OpenForm "Form Name Goes Here"
'  DoCmd SelectObject A_Form, "Form Name Goes Here"
'  DoCmd GoToControl Forms![Form Name Goes Here]! _
   [Key Field Here].Name
'  DoCmd FindRecord Forms! _
   [Calendar Selection Dialog]![Order Search]

Exit_Chg_Click:
    Exit Sub
Err_Chg_Click:
    MsgBox Error$
    Resume Exit_Chg_Click
```

```
End Sub
Err_Chg_Click:
    MsgBox Error$
    Resume Exit_Chg_Click

End Sub
```

The same code is also added to the `On Dbl Click` event of the list box. This way, you can also double-click on the needed list box item to select it and open a form for that record.

Using the Calendar control

New types of controls are being sold today: ActiveX controls. These are plug-in controls that extend the functionality of OLE-enabled applications. For Visual Basic, these types of controls (called .OCX or .VBX controls) have been around for years.

The `Calendar` control displays a monthly calendar that you can insert into a form. Figure 8-23 shows a typical use of the calendar control. As each day of the month is clicked on, the day number is highlighted and the box around the day number is sunken. The entire design can be modified through the control's properties dialog box.

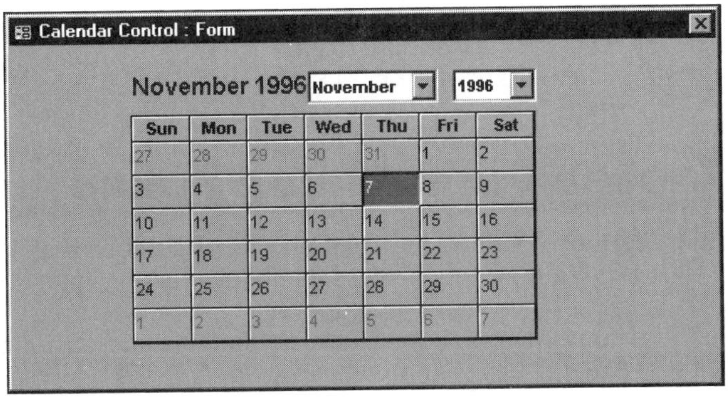

Figure 8-23: The Calendar control is an easy way to enter a date.

The `Calendar` control supports properties that you can use to set and retrieve the date and to control the appearance of the calendar. Figure 8-24 shows the calendar object's General properties page. The `Calendar` control also supports methods that you can use to set the day, month, and year; to show an About box; and to refresh the calendar. It also supports events that notify your application when the user has moved to a new date on the calendar, when the user has clicked or double-clicked on a date, and when the user has pressed a key.

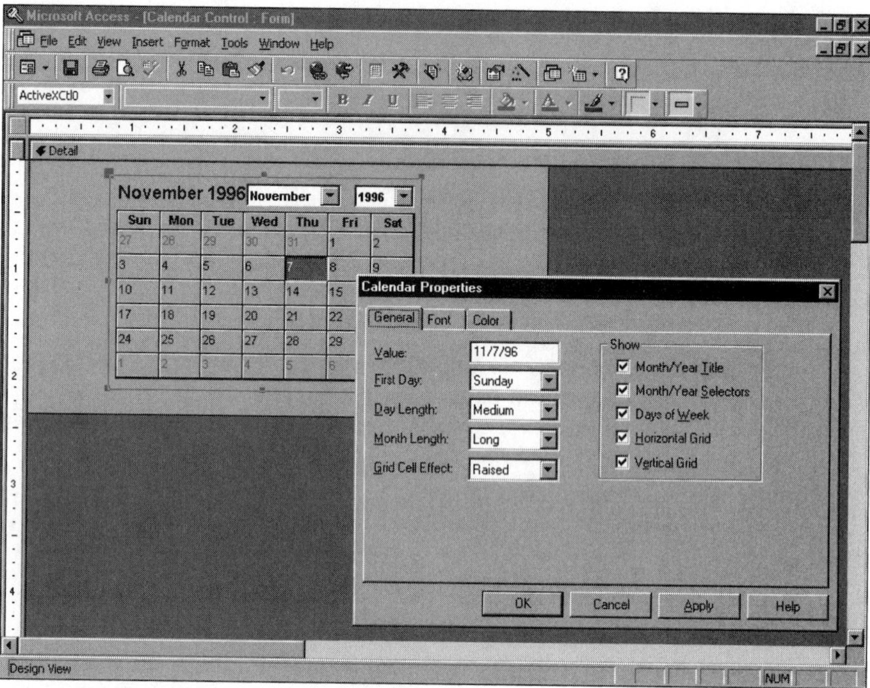

Figure 8-24: The design view of a Calendar control.

Creating Tabbed Form Dialog Boxes

Today, most serious Windows applications contain tabbed dialog boxes. Tabbed dialog boxes look very professional. They display many screens of data in a small area by grouping similar types of data with tabs to navigate between the groups. Microsoft Access itself contains an ActiveX control for creating tabbed dialog boxes automatically.

Figure 8-25 shows a typical use of a tabbed dialog box. When each tab is clicked on, the tab is highlighted, the tab text is put in bold, and the area of tab changes.

Understanding tabbed forms

You can use the tab control to create a tabbed form with several pages or a tabbed dialog box. You can copy or add other controls onto a tab control. Right-click on the `Tab` control in the design grid to modify the number of pages, the page order, the selected page's properties, and the selected tab control properties. Figure 8-26 shows a tab control in design view.

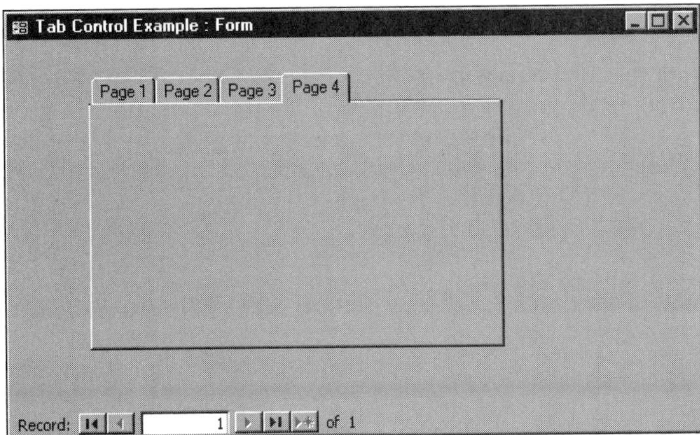

Figure 8-25: Tabbed dialog boxes enable you to display many screens of data in a small area.

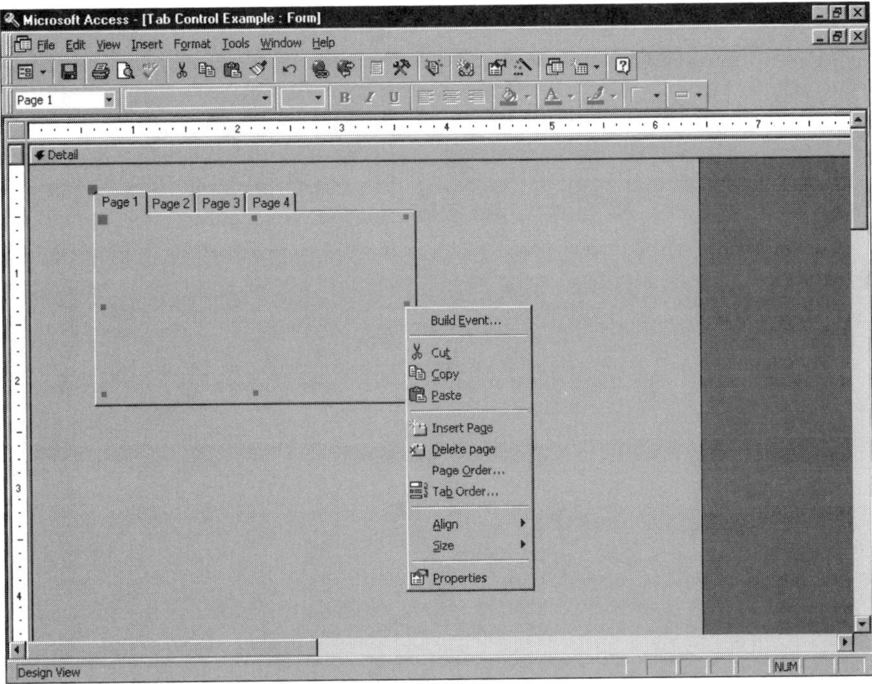

Figure 8-26: Displaying the shortcut menu for a tab control.

Creating your own tabbed form

Although the built-in tab control is a quick and easy way to design a tabbed dialog box, its capabilities are limited. The tabs can appear only at the top of the form, for example, and you cannot change the font or color of a tab's label. The good news is that by using either multipage forms or multiple subforms and a simple bitmap with a little imagination and a little work, you can create your own tabbed control.

Figure 8-27 shows how a simple set of controls produces the tabbed effect. The controls have been separated to show the four distinct layers. The layers include the following:

- `Label` or `Text Box` controls containing the text for each tab.
- Raised Tab bitmaps; only one is visible at a time to give the selected effect.
- One bitmap containing all the unselected tabs.
- The body of the form, which contains a single subform.

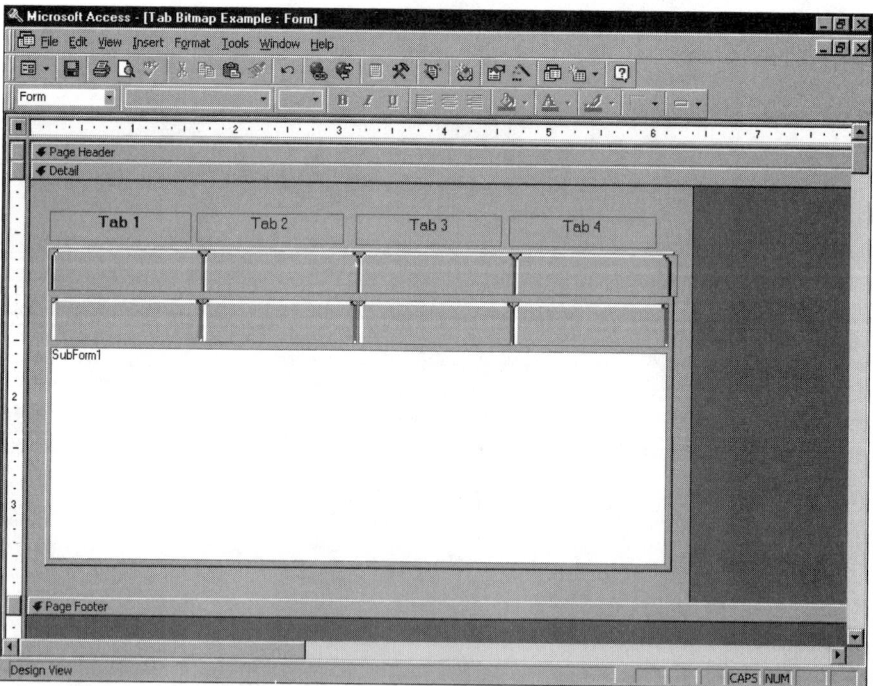

Figure 8-27: The tabbed dialog box uses just four types of interface objects.

Using just these controls, you can create any type of tabbed dialog box. A standard example of this technique is demonstrated in the following section.

Creating the tabbed form

The first step to creating the tabbed form is to place one of the tab bitmaps on the form. This book's CD-ROM includes a set of bitmaps of various numbers of tabs. (There's a complete list of bitmap names and their functions later in this section.) The bitmaps are placed on the form as unbound OLE objects. You can do this by first placing an Unbound OLE Object frame on a form and then selecting Create From File from the Insert Object dialog box, shown in Figure 8-28, that appears when a new unbound OLE object is placed on the desktop.

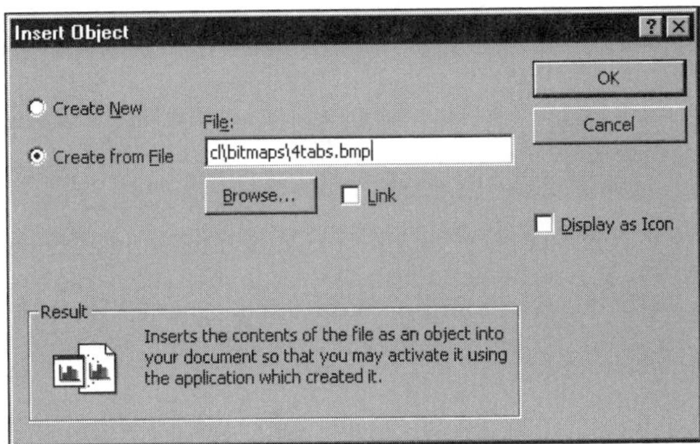

Figure 8-28: Adding a bitmap to the form.

After you select the correct bitmap, the bitmap image is displayed on the form. In this example, the bitmap 4TABS.BMP, as shown in Figure 8-29, is the unselected row of four tabs. After the bitmap is on the form, you can change it to the needed size. You also need to add a second bitmap: the raised bitmap that will be used for the second layer. The second bitmap is placed on top of the multiple-tab bitmap to show the selected tab; this second bitmap is on the CD-ROM as TABRAISD.BMP. Figure 8-29 shows these unsized bitmaps.

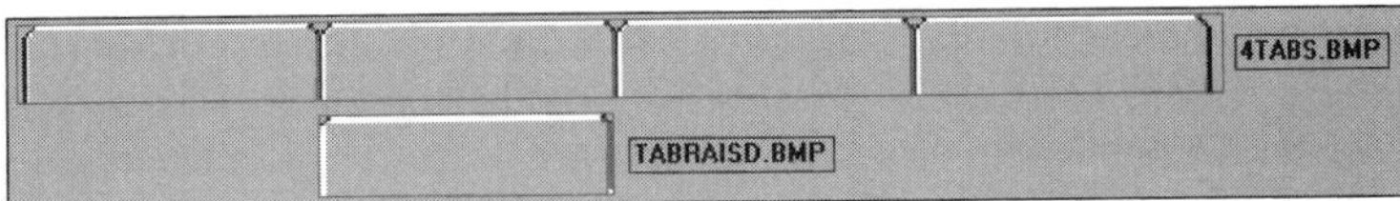

Figure 8-29: Using bitmaps to display the selected tab and the unselected tabs.

You should first size the multiple-tab bitmap to the needed size. While you size the multiple-tab bitmap, you should use the `Stretch` setting of the bitmap's `Size` property. After this is done, you must properly size the raised bitmap so that it gives the appearance of being a selected tab. Though you may not be able to see this in a two-dimensional screen figure, you can see it on your computer screen. As shown in Figure 8-30, the visual trickery is accomplished by creating the raised bitmap slightly larger than the tab it goes over and then placing it directly on top of the first tab in the multiple-tab bitmap.

Figure 8-30: The selected tab is represented by a raised bitmap that is slightly larger than the unselected tab directly underneath.

So far, the figure doesn't show that it looks much like a tab control. Adding a rectangle below it and either raising or lowering the rectangle, however, gives the tab control more definition. Adding the text fields and boldfacing the one on the raised tab adds even more visual acuity. Figure 8-31 shows the same form with a raised rectangle added.

After the raised bitmap is properly sized and positioned, you should set the `Visible` property of the raised bitmap to `Yes` for the first tab. Then duplicate the raised tab for the number of tabs in the tab control and position each raised tab over the tabs in the multiple-tab bitmap. Next, change the `Visible` property to `No` for all the raised tabs except the first. Make sure that each of the raised tabs are on top of the multitab bitmap. The set of raised tabs is the middle layer of the control.

The next step is to add the label controls and their captions. In this example, the tabs are simply labeled Tab 1, Tab 2, Tab 3, and Tab 4. The label controls should be added and centered across the entire width of each raised tab. As you will see, the label control will be used as a button to change the selected tab and therefore must cover the entire raised tab bitmap. The labels should be centered, and the first tab's label control should be boldfaced as well. Make sure that the text controls are on top. You can use the Format⇨Bring to Front menu option to bring the label to the front. Make sure that the label control's Border and Back Color options are set to Clear.

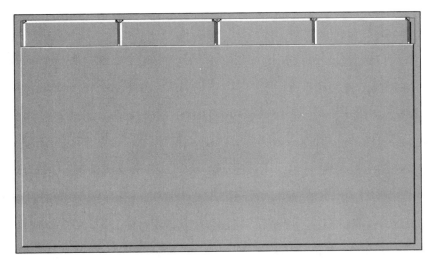

Figure 8-31: Adding a raised rectangle to the tabbed dialog box gives the tab control more definition.

After you have completed the controls, you can add a simple VBA program to the `On Click` event of each label control to change the visible raised bitmap and to boldface the selected tab's text caption. After this is working, you will see how to make the tabs show different subforms.

Creating a program to change tabs

The program to change the appearance of the selected tab is very simple. You simply make the selected raised tab visible while making all other tabs not visible. Then boldface the selected tab's caption while making sure that all other nonselected tabs' text label captions are not bold. This program is added to the `On Click` event of each label control. Any control can have an `On Click` event, and because the label control is on top, it is easiest to use it. Figure 8-32 shows the program and the text labels on the forms design screen.

Note in the Tab Bitmap example that the label controls were named `TabText1`, `TabText2`, `TabText3`, and `TabText4`, and the raised bitmaps were named `RaisedTab1`, `RaisedTab2`, `RaisedTab3`, and `RaisedTab4`. In this module example, because this is the `On Click` event for the first tab, only the first tab's caption and tab are boldface and made visible. All others are "unboldfaced" and the raised tab is made invisible.

Each tab's label control (`TabText1-4`) has a similar code block added to the `On Click` event of the label control. Though you can make the raised bitmaps into command buttons and use the `Picture` property to embed the raised-button bitmap, you would have no way to add text to the button; you can have either a picture or text on a command button, not both.

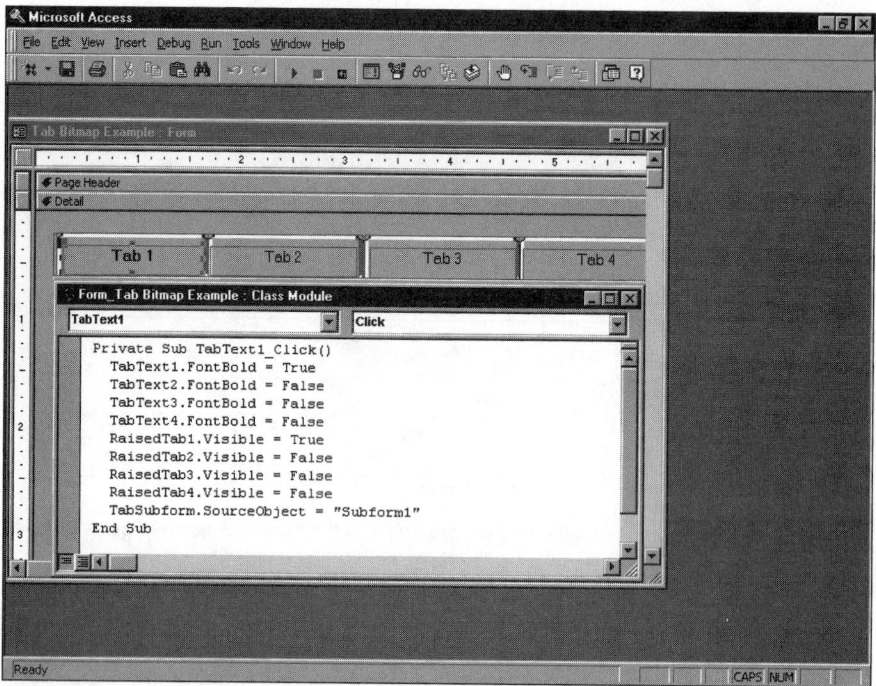

Figure 8-32: The On Click event of the label controls makes the proper raised tab visible.

After you have applied this program for each label control (making the appropriate changes for each tab), test the program. As you click on each tab, the raised tab should move when a different one is made visible, and the new text should be boldfaced. You can also program tabbed dialog boxes with only one raised bitmap by physically moving the bitmap's location, but the visible/invisible technique is easier to apply and maintain.

Changing areas of the form as tabs are pressed

The final step is connecting the change in a tab to what happens below the tabs. Though there are many ways to do the next part of the tab control technique, this task is generally done with *subforms*. You can use one multipage subform, or you can use one subform for each page. You can place anything you want on the pages (even more tabbed controls). Though you have seen the secret of moving the tab and changing the text, you now must learn to work with several simple subforms or one multipage subform.

The Tab Bitmap Example form uses four separate subforms. As shown in Figure 8-33, one subform control, named `TabSubform`, is embedded in the raised rectangle.

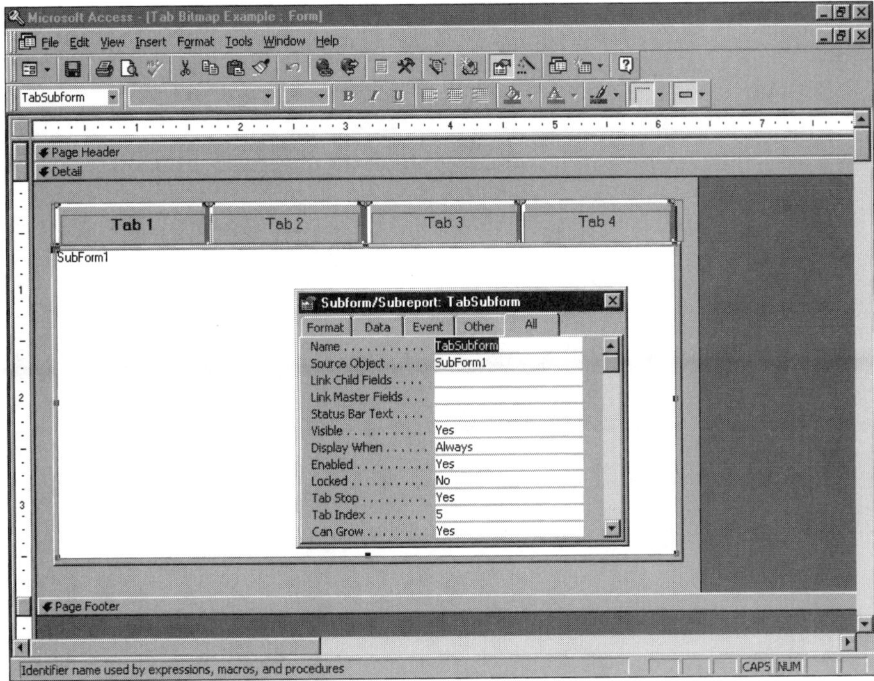

Figure 8-33: Use subforms to change the data area of the form to correspond to the selected tab.

This subform control shows that the `SourceObject` (the name of the subform form) is `Subform1`. This is the name of a subform in the CH8.MDB database container. When the form is displayed initially with the first tab highlighted, this subform's content is displayed in the area below the tabs. In this example, one line of code is added to the `On Click` events to change the subform used. The line of code that is added to the first tab's `On Click` event is as follows:

```
TabSubform.SourceObject = "Subform1"
```

The other three `On Click` events also would have a line added that changes the `SourceObject` property to the required subform when the tab is pressed.

The `On Click` event code makes `Subform1` the form displayed in the subform control. For each of the other tabs, you add the line of code to display the subform for that tab. You use a different form for each tab; however, each form should be the same size. As you move from tab to tab, you want to make sure that controls positioned in each subform are placed consistently. This avoids jumping while users move from tab to tab (or form to form).

Figure 8-34 shows the Tab Bitmap Example in Form mode. As you can see in the figure, when you click from tab to tab, the name of the subform changes in the body of the form. There are four subforms — each has only one large text object with the name of the form. You can put anything in each of the subforms. Because each of the subforms has its own record source, you can display data from a different table or query for each tab. You can also link the subforms to the main form's data and even change the main form data as a tab is changed. What you are doing is the equivalent of clicking on four different buttons.

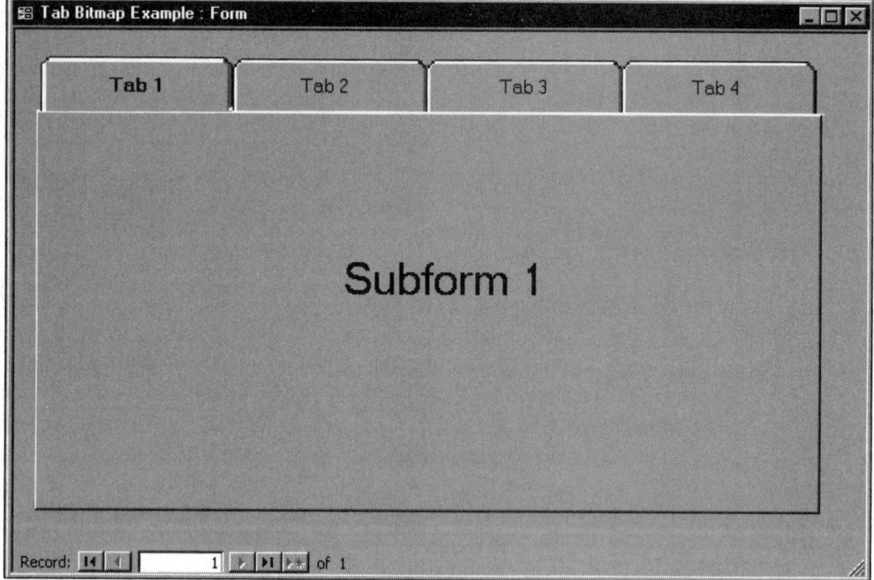

Figure 8-34: Clicking on each tab updates the subform name in the body of the form.

Creating a tabbed form dialog box

You do not always need to use a form as a full-screen form. You can also use a tabbed dialog box as part of a larger form. Figure 8-35 is another example of the use of a three-tabbed form dialog box.

This example is exactly the same as the preceding example, except that the tabs and the subform area are smaller and enclosed within a chiseled rectangle. You can make the subform work in tandem with the OK and Cancel buttons if you want. If you look at the `On Click` event code for the three tabs, you can see that no subforms are in this example. The text Subform 1 Goes Here is just a line of text that is changed. Obviously, you can make this example work with multiple subforms, as you saw in the preceding technique. The purpose of this example is simply to show a different number of tabs, a smaller area, and what a tabbed area looks like when used as a dialog box. You can add controls in other parts of the main form and then use the tabbed area to display groups of controls, thereby saving valuable real estate. Another common use for the tabbed dialog box is as a display for data sorted multiple ways. You use the tabs to display and change the sort and then use the OK button to select a record for display.

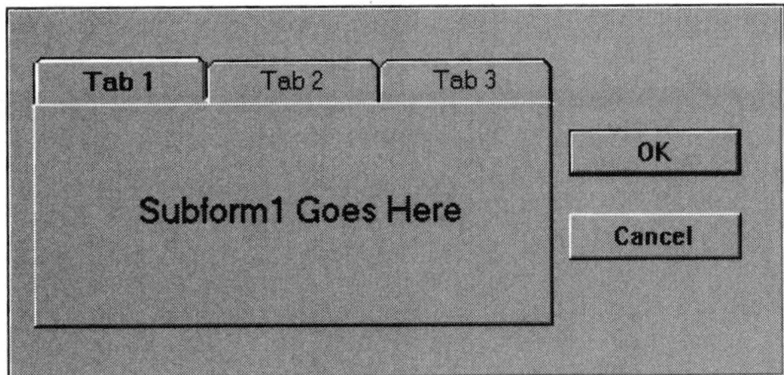

Figure 8-35: Tabbed dialog boxes can be used as part of a larger form.

There is one more way to create a tabbed dialog box. You can place all the controls you need on different pages of a single multipage subform. Multipage subforms are a little more difficult to use than the multiple subform method; you must precisely line up your controls on each page and you must manipulate the pages rather than the subforms. When the pages contain many combo-box controls, it may take some time to display the first page while all controls are filled on all pages.

The following example not only describes how to use multiple pages but also shows multiple lines of tabs.

Using multipage, multiline tabbed dialog boxes

Figure 8-36 shows another type of tabbed dialog box. This type has two rows of tabs. As with other tabbed dialog boxes, the tabs change appearance when you click on them. When you click on any of the tabs in the back row, the back row becomes the front row. This enables you to bring the back row into focus and even group the two rows of tabs.

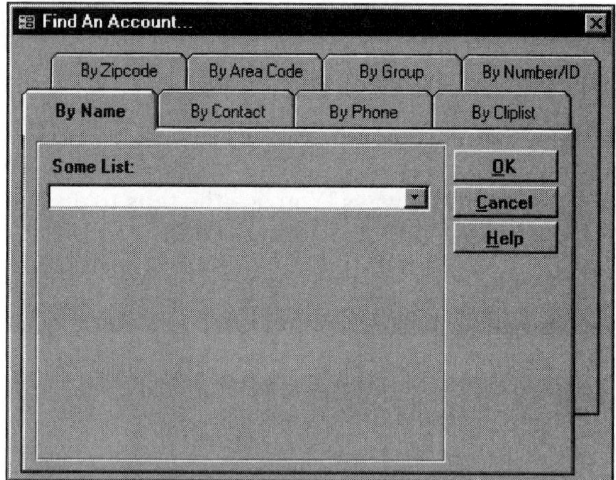

Figure 8-36: Multiline tabbed dialog boxes enable you to stack infinite rows of tabs.

Also important: This tabbed dialog box uses only one subform. The subform has eight pages, all created in the same form. As each tab is selected, the VBA code moves the subform to the right page and displays the subform below the tabs. There are two ways to handle multipage subforms. One method is to place the tabs on a main form and change the page of the following subform. Another way is to use only one multipage form. The tabs exist only once at the top of page 1 of the form. As you select a tab, the entire tabbed bitmap and its controls are moved to the top of the page for the selected tab. Then a new page appears in the body of the form. Although this method has some small performance advantages, it is very cumbersome to use and so we won't describe it here.

Creating a multipage subform for a tabbed dialog box

Figure 8-37 shows the Design mode of a multipage subform. You can see the first three pages and the top of the fourth. Each page is exactly the same length, and the page break control is used to mark the beginning of a new page (or the end of the preceding one).

The correct page of the subform is displayed below the tabs in the main form. This figure has been modified to show a one-inch gap between pages. In reality, there is a two-inch gap in this subform. The size of the gap corresponds to the size of the display area in the main form (in this example, approximately two inches high).

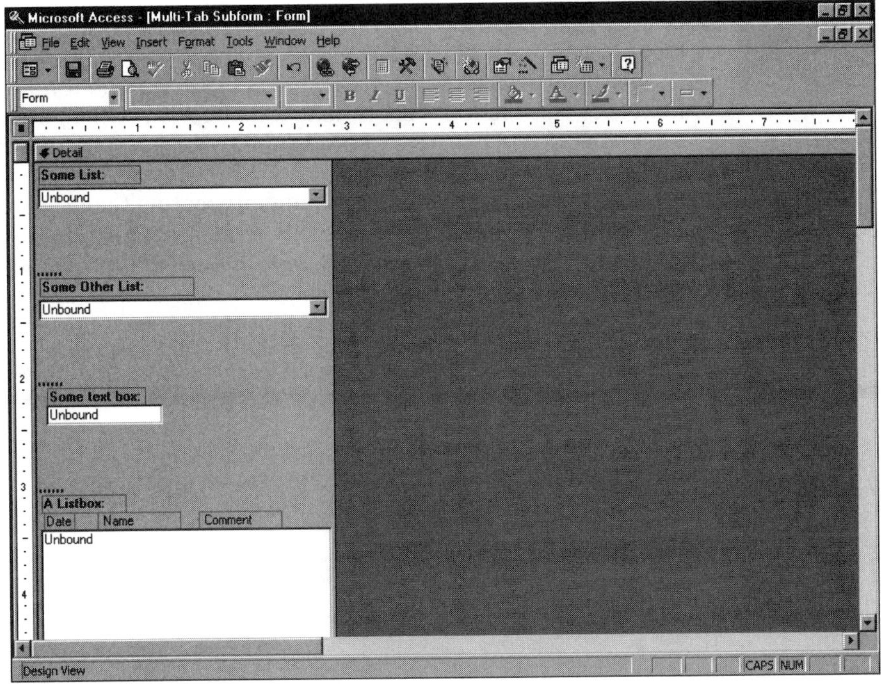

Figure 8-37: Creating a multipage subform.

You may also notice that the width of the form is a little more than two inches. Again in this case, the width of the main form display area for the subform is a little more than two inches.

After you create the multipage subform (or the multiple one-page subforms of the previous examples), you can program your tabs to display the correct page or subform. You have already seen how to use multiple subforms.

The code behind the form is complex, but you can understand it if you are familiar with VBA code. You need to understand two secrets. First, this technique uses one transparent button across each set of four tabs and uses the location of the mouse to determine which tab is pressed. The other secret is that the buttons are numbered 0 – 7, and this is used to position the correct page when pressed.

Progress Meters

Progress meters are valuable for giving users feedback about how close an operation is to completion. This is almost mandatory when performing operations that take a long time. For example, OLE automation with VBA can take up to several minutes to output data. A progress meter is very helpful in this situation and may be the only thing preventing the user from rebooting the machine during a long operation. Common operations that need progress meters include sorting, searching, deleting, and any other operations that take more than a few seconds.

Creating a progress meter with a pop-up form

Figure 8-38 shows a progress meter form reaching 100 percent.

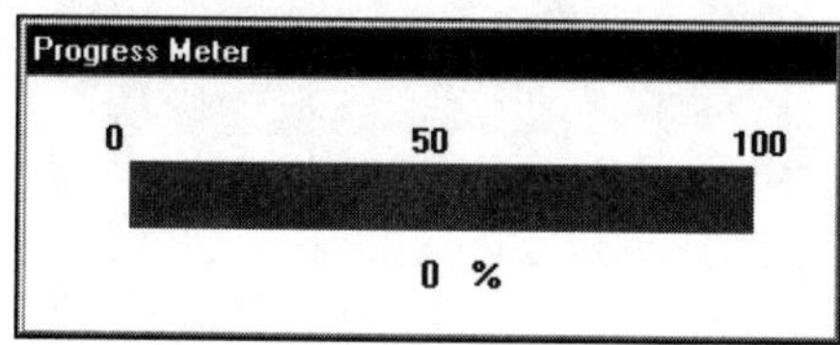

Figure 8-38: Using a progress meter to keep the user advised of the estimated time to completion of the task.

This progress meter has some advantages over the standard Microsoft Access progress meter. The progress meter supplied with Access uses the status bar to display the meter and isn't always as visible as you may like. The progress meter shown in Figure 8-38 pops up in the middle of the screen and is very visible. However, the meter supplied with Access usually appears faster because it requires less overhead to run (although the difference may not be noticeable with longer tasks). The speed of the pop-up meter can be controlled by updating the meter every X percent. Therefore, when the form meter is set for fast execution, it appears as fast as the built-in meter.

The progress meter form (named Progress Meter in the CH8.MDB file) is created from a few simple controls. As you can see in Figure 8-39, the form includes one rectangle and several label controls. The label controls on top represent 0, 50, and 100. If you want, you can create a more detailed scale. The label control at the bottom can be updated while the meter progresses.

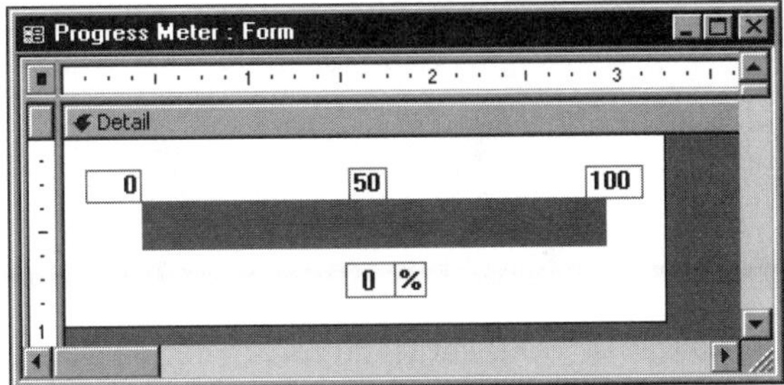

Figure 8-39: Creating a progress meter.

In Design mode, the rectangle is shown fully completed. In reality, the width of the rectangle is manipulated by the program that displays the progress. The width is reset to 0 when the progress meter starts and is slowly built back to its original length.

Using the Progmeter procedure

The `Progmeter` procedure, shown in Figure 8-40, displays and controls the progress of the meter. You just pass a percentage from 0 to 100 to the procedure that displays the meter. Any invalid percentage will be corrected by the procedure. You must pass a 0 to initialize the meter. The meter closes when the percentage reaches 100. Using the preceding form to create the meter, you can change the meter's appearance to your liking (as long as the meter is a rectangle). For example, you can create a vertical meter instead of a horizontal one.

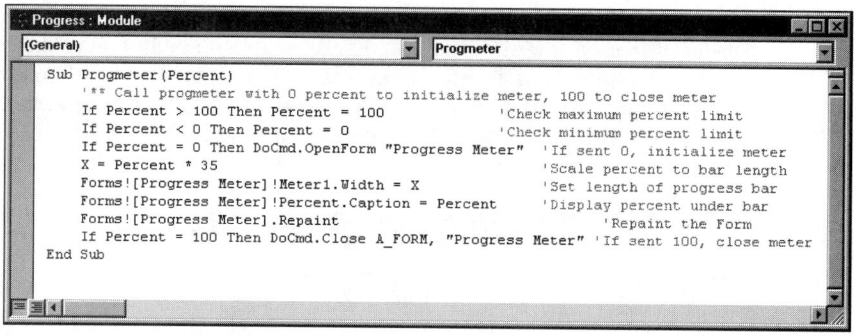

```
Progress : Module
(General)                    Progmeter

Sub Progmeter(Percent)
    '** Call progmeter with 0 percent to initialize meter, 100 to close meter
    If Percent > 100 Then Percent = 100                'Check maximum percent limit
    If Percent < 0 Then Percent = 0                    'Check minimum percent limit
    If Percent = 0 Then DoCmd.OpenForm "Progress Meter"  'If sent 0, initialize meter
    X = Percent * 35                                     'Scale percent to bar length
    Forms![Progress Meter]!Meter1.Width = X              'Set length of progress bar
    Forms![Progress Meter]!Percent.Caption = Percent     'Display percent under bar
    Forms![Progress Meter].Repaint                            'Repaint the Form
    If Percent = 100 Then DoCmd.Close A_FORM, "Progress Meter" 'If sent 100, close meter
End Sub
```

Figure 8-40: Updating the progress meter.

Notice the line `X = Percent * 35` in the sample code. This line makes the bar proportional to the form and should be changed for custom meters. The length of the bar is measured in *twips*, and there are 1,440 twips to an inch. Therefore, because the meter is 2 1/2 inches long, it is also about 3,500 twips in length. The rest of the procedure changes the width of the filled rectangle and then updates the percent text on the meter. The form is then repainted, which updates the meter on the screen.

This routine is called whenever you want to update the progress meter. It is up to you to decide how often this is done. Normally, you call the progress meter only when it is likely to be updated. If you know there are 1,000 records, you may call the meter every 10 records; if there are 10,000 records, you may call the meter every 100 records.

Figure 8-41 shows the code for the sample application named Progress Meter Form. Note the calls to the `Progmeter` procedure.

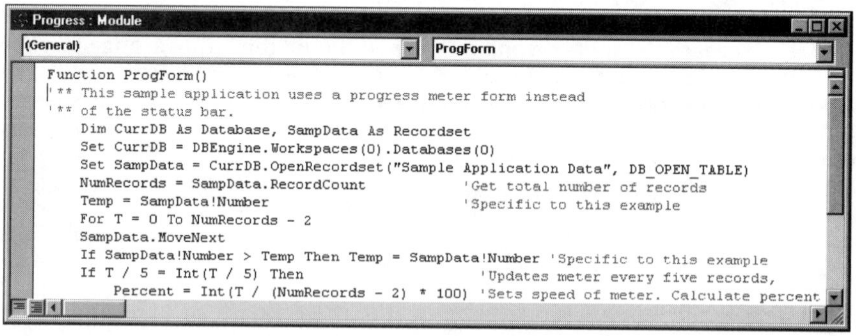

```
Progress : Module
(General)                    ProgForm

Function ProgForm()
'** This sample application uses a progress meter form instead
'** of the status bar.
    Dim CurrDB As Database, SampData As Recordset
    Set CurrDB = DBEngine.Workspaces(0).Databases(0)
    Set SampData = CurrDB.OpenRecordset("Sample Application Data", DB_OPEN_TABLE)
    NumRecords = SampData.RecordCount              'Get total number of records
    Temp = SampData!Number                         'Specific to this example
    For T = 0 To NumRecords - 2
    SampData.MoveNext
    If SampData!Number > Temp Then Temp = SampData!Number 'Specific to this example
    If T / 5 = Int(T / 5) Then                      'Updates meter every five records,
        Percent = Int(T / (NumRecords - 2) * 100) 'Sets speed of meter. Calculate percent
```

Figure 8-41: Calling the procedure to update the progress meter.

The first few statements open the Recordset. In this example, the Recordset is a table named Sample Application Data. (You would substitute your table or query here.) The next statements count the total number of records in the Recordset. This is necessary in order to calculate the percent of the file that you have processed. The following lines are specific to your application. When you are deleting or processing the data, those lines go next. In this example, the procedure is searching for the highest value.

In the Progress Meter Form example, the progress meter update routine is called every five records. You can speed up the meter execution by changing the line `If T/5 = Int( T / 5)`, which displays each pass that is evenly divisible by. This means that the meter isn't refreshed as often as possible, so its execution is faster. There are many ways of controlling this cycle, and the choice of technique is really application dependent. The next line calculates the percentage value that is passed to the `Progmeter` procedure. This must be calculated from information in your application; the `Progmeter` procedure does not calculate percentages. The percentage can be calculated in the `Progmeter` form, if you want. This requires you to pass the number of records to the sub procedure when initializing it.

Automatic Key Field Numbering

One of the requests most frequently received by accounting software companies is the capability of automatically numbering a key field. With a key field that numbers automatically, the customer, invoice, or purchase order number is always unique and is easy to track. For example, when a new invoice is created, the next available unique invoice number is automatically used. This saves users the time of looking up the next available number and typing it.

This section introduces two numbering schemes. The first method is straight sequential numbering. In straight sequential numbering, each new record is numbered one higher than the current highest value. Figure 8-42 shows a number formatted to 5 digits, `00001`, which is incremented according to the highest entry in a table. The second method combines the current date and a sequential number to assign a unique ID number. For example, if today is May 11, 1996, and you have already created eleven invoices today, the next invoice can be numbered 960511-12 (96 for 1996, 05 for May, 11 for the 11th of May, and 12 as the smallest unused integer for this date). This way, no new invoices can have the same number before the year 2096!

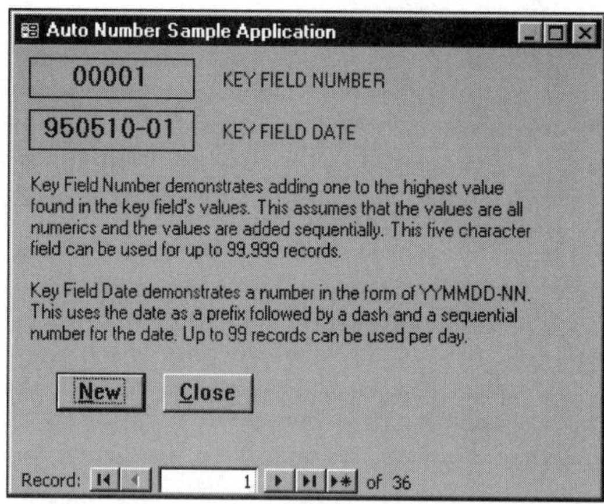

Figure 8-42: Auto-numbering the key field saves time and errors.

Creating sequential automatic key field numbering

The New button in the Auto Number Sample Application example contains the program code for both numbering schemes. Figure 8-43 shows the code for determining the next sequential number. The program is very simple.

Form_Auto Number Sample : Class Module

New_Button | Click

```
Private Sub New_Button_Click()
  DoCmd.GoToRecord A_FORM, "Auto Number Sample", A_NEWREC 'Change Table Name
  Dim YICDB As Database, YICTB As Recordset
  Dim Temp, Temp2

 'Sequential Numbering
    Set YICDB = DBEngine.Workspaces(0).Databases(0)
    Set YICTB = YICDB.OpenRecordset("Sample Table", DB_OPEN_TABLE)
    Temp = 0
    Do Until YICTB.EOF                              'Loop through all records
       If Val(YICTB![Key Field Number]) > Temp Then
          Temp = Val(YICTB![Key Field Number])      'Temp assigned highest #
       End If
       YICTB.MoveNext
    Loop                                            'Format highest+1 as text
    Me![Key Field Number] = Format$(Str$(Temp + 1), "00000")
      YICTB.Close
```

Figure 8-43: Determining the next sequential number.

First, a Recordset is opened and a temporary variable (TEMP) is set to 0. All the records are scanned for the value of the key field. When the value is higher than the value of TEMP, then TEMP is assigned that value. The VAL ()

function converts the characters of the Key Field Number to a numeric value. When the loop ends, the value of TEMP contains the highest sequential number. Finally, the key field value for the new record in the form (and in the table) is set to the value of TEMP + 1. Remember, the key value is stored as a text field; the value must be formatted as a string and the leading 0 must be shown if you want numbers less than 10000 to show with leading zeros.

When there are no records, the value of TEMP is 0 and the first number is 00001. You don't need to number the records sequentially. If you want to number the records by 5s, you can add 5 to the value of TEMP. This creates numbers that are five digits apart: 00005, 00010, 00015, and so on. Using this code, you can do anything with numeric values to create unique sequences.

There are other ways to calculate the highest value. You can also use a MAX function and execute an SQL statement to check all the records. Generally, this is the fastest way to find the highest value.

Creating date-based automatic key field numbering

The other method of automatic key field numbering demonstrated here uses a date as a prefix and adds a sequential number that is reset to 1 for each new date. Figure 8-44 shows the code found in the New button's On Click event property below the sequential numbering code. Only one code block is used for a form.

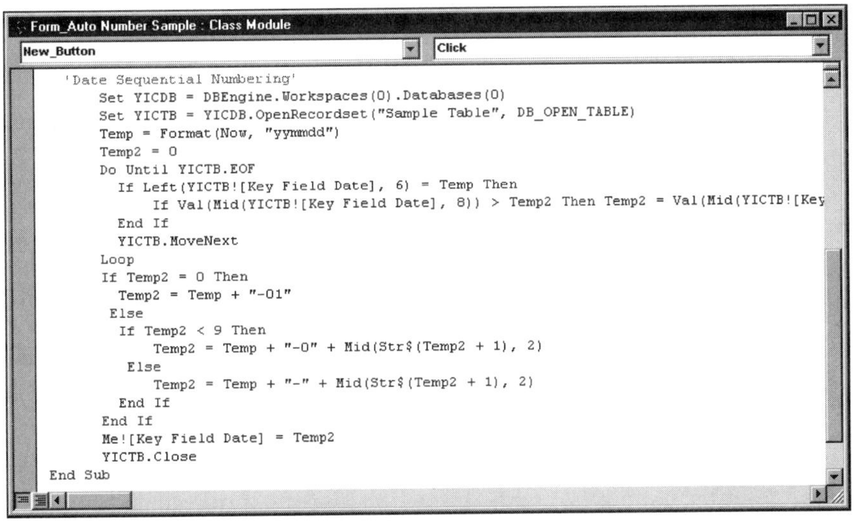

Form_Auto Number Sample : Class Module

New_Button | Click

```
    'Date Sequential Numbering'
        Set YICDB = DBEngine.Workspaces(0).Databases(0)
        Set YICTB = YICDB.OpenRecordset("Sample Table", DB_OPEN_TABLE)
        Temp = Format(Now, "yymmdd")
        Temp2 = 0
        Do Until YICTB.EOF
          If Left(YICTB![Key Field Date], 6) = Temp Then
              If Val(Mid(YICTB![Key Field Date], 8)) > Temp2 Then Temp2 = Val(Mid(YICTB![Key
          End If
          YICTB.MoveNext
        Loop
        If Temp2 = 0 Then
          Temp2 = Temp + "-01"
         Else
          If Temp2 < 9 Then
              Temp2 = Temp + "-0" + Mid(Str$(Temp2 + 1), 2)
           Else
              Temp2 = Temp + "-" + Mid(Str$(Temp2 + 1), 2)
          End If
        End If
        Me![Key Field Date] = Temp2
        YICTB.Close
  End Sub
```

Figure 8-44: Generating a number with a date prefix.

First, a Recordset is created and two temporary variables are created. The first (`TEMP`) is set to today's date. The second (`TEMP2`) is set to `0`. All the records are scanned to find any records that have the current date. The date-number scheme has two parts: a date code, which is always six digits, and a second part consisting of digits that represent an item number for that day. The program uses parsing to check both parts of the date-number code. It checks the first six digits of the current record to see if they are equal to those of today's date. If they are equal, it then finds the greatest number in the second half of the code. You'll notice that the last half is displayed as two digits on the sample application form. The program actually looks at the rest of the digits after position 8, which is the dash. This way, the counter can roll above 100 (if the total field length is greater than 9).

`TEMP2` is set to the highest sequential number found for the current date. If there are no records for the current date, then `TEMP2` is `0` after the search. The new key value is today's date plus `-01`. If `TEMP2` is greater than `0`, then `1` is added to that value and the new key value is set to today's date plus `-##`, where `##` is the value of `TEMP2+1`. Finally, the form control is set to the new key value.

This method can be used for any type of prefix, not just a date. You can use the first three letters of the last name, or the company name, or anything else. You may also want to add other features to your application's auto-numbering scheme. One popular feature is the capability of handling deleted records. When numbers aren't sequential because of deleted records, should vacant numbers be used or skipped? The preceding examples ignore that issue, because the sample application looks only for the highest value. You may want to handle vacant numbers for slow-turnover numbers (for example, employee numbers). It may be more efficient to ignore the blank numbers on fast turnovers, such as invoice numbers.

Finding the next available number is easy. It just requires checking whether the next number is greater than the current number + 1. If the next number is greater, use the current number + 1 as the next number and stop checking. This is true in both numbering schemes because the date-number scheme uses a sequential number for the second half of the code. There are many other features you can add with the date-number scheme, such as showing numbers entered on a certain day. You may also want to consider using the first few letters of a customer or company name as the prefix instead of the date. Either way, the code is only modified slightly.

Control Morphing

The word *morph* means change. Control morphing can have several meanings. In this context, *control morphing* is the capability of a control (most often list boxes, combo boxes, or subforms) to change its appearance while a program is running. This is possible because you can change properties of a control at run time. In this section, you learn techniques for morphing various controls. Unlike other sections of this chapter, this section demonstrates techniques instead of giving you a plug-and-play solution.

Changing a list box's contents with an option group

One of the simplest things you can do to morph a control is change the display and sort order of a combo box or list box by using a simple option group with option buttons. Figure 8-45 shows this method. When one of the option buttons is clicked on, the fields and sort order of the combo box change.

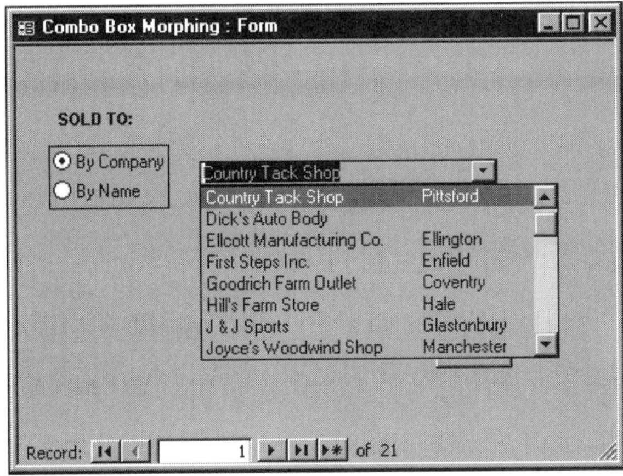

Figure 8-45: Changing the look of controls at run time.

To create this type of interface, which enables users to search for data many ways using a single list or combo box, you first must create the list or combo box control. Set all the properties to the control's default settings. These properties include the `Row Source Type`, `Row Source`, `Column Count`, `Column Widths`, and `Bound Column`. You can also change the `List Rows` and the `List Width`. Figure 8-46 shows the design view for the Combo Box Morphing example.

Combo Box: SOLD TO CUSTOMER

Format | Data | Event | Other | All

Name	SOLD TO CUSTOMER
Control Source	
Format	
Decimal Places	Auto
Input Mask	
Row Source Type	Table/Query
Row Source	SELECT Customers.[Last Name], Customers.[First Name], Customers.[Customer Number] FROM Customers ORDER BY Cust
Column Count	3
Column Heads	No
Column Widths	0.6";1.4";0"
Bound Column	3
List Rows	8

Figure 8-46: Creating the control to be morphed.

After you create the default list box or combo box, you can create the option group that changes some of the list box or combo box properties. The option group can be created by using the Option Group Wizard. Typically, you enter the option button text values right into the wizard screens. When you complete the option group, the last step is to add the code to morph the list or combo box when an option button is selected.

You do this by using the option group's `After Update` event property. Each time an option button is selected, a different set of property settings is copied into the combo box control. When the combo box is opened, a new set of fields in a different sorted order can be displayed. If you use a list box, you see the contents change immediately. In fact, the selected data in a combo box morphs to show the new first column value. In this example, the last name is replaced by the company name in the closed combo box.

Programming the combo box to morph

The program that is attached to the option group's `After Update` property is fairly straightforward, as shown in Listing 8-6.

Listing 8-6 Updating the Combo Box List

```
Private Sub Customer_Display_AfterUpdate()
  If [Customer Display] = 1 Then
     [Sold to Customer].RowSource = ""
     [Sold to Customer].ColumnWidths ="1.5 in;1.0in;0 in"
     [Sold to Customer].RowSource = _
     "Select [Company],[City],[Customer Number] _
     From [Customers] Order By [Company];"
    Else
     [Sold to Customer].RowSource = ""
     [Sold to Customer].ColumnWidths ="1.5 in;1.0in;0 in"
     [Sold to Customer].RowSource = _
     "Select [Last Name],[First Name],[Customer Number] _
     From [Customers] Order By [Last Name];"
  End If
End Sub
```

Because there are only two selections, a simple `If-THEN-ELSE` construct is used. (If there are three or more option buttons, use a `CASE` construct.)

The first line in the program, `[Sold to Customer].RowSource = ""`, sets the `Row Source` to null. This is a critical step for managing large files. The control morphing will still work without this first step, but the combo or list box's `Row Source` is queried each time you change any of the properties at run time. For example, if you have 10,000 records, it may take 12 seconds to open the combo box because the box first must be filled by running the query. Twelve seconds will be required every time you change any property — even when you just change the column widths! By first setting the row source to null, the query runs with no data each time you change a property, thereby improving performance dramatically.

`RowSource` should always be the last property you change in this technique, setting it back to the fields and order you want to display in the combo or list box.

Changing a subform display

When displaying data in a one-to-many relationship, you often use a subform. Sometimes, however, you may want different views of your data. Suppose that you have a great deal of information about your customers and their sales in several tables. You design a form that shows each customer on a page with his or her sales in a subform. You probably have many fields in your tables. You want to see only some of the fields for retail customers and other fields for wholesale customers. Rather than design two completely different forms to look at your customers in two different ways, you can design one form that does both.

Figure 8-47 shows an example of a single record in a subform. Normally, you would have some type of one-to-many data relationship for this situation. The important part is that the look of the subform changes when you move to different records. This is done by a program attached to the form's `OnCurrent` property. This event is triggered when you move from one record to another. Actually, two separate forms are used by a single subform container. One form is used for retail customers (`Type of Customer = "Retail"`); another form is used for wholesale customers.

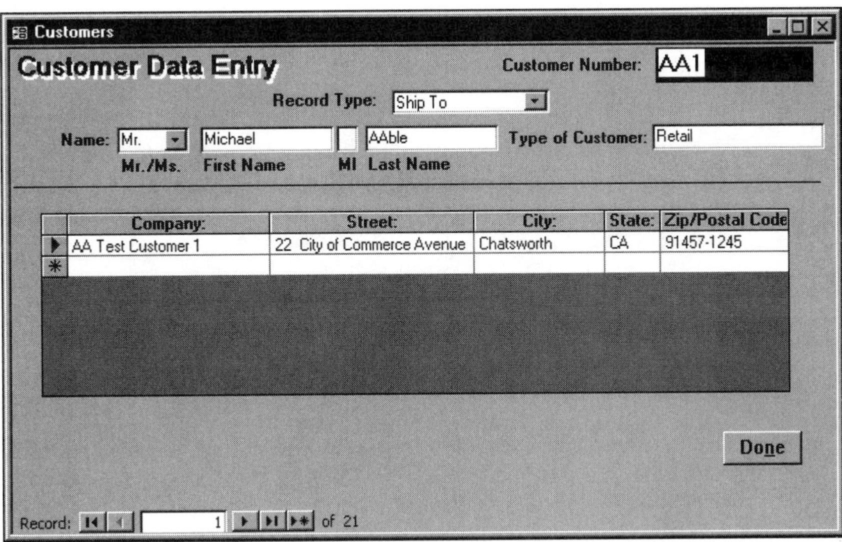

Figure 8-47: Updating the contents of the subform as you move from record to record.

In the Subform Morphing example form, note that the second subform does not use all the subform container space. You shouldn't create two subforms of different sizes. If the two subforms are the same, the fields from each subform would fit precisely within the subform container. You can change the size and location of the subform container to match each set of fields, but it isn't the most efficient way to morph this type of control. When you change the size of a control, there is a noticeable change in the form, which can be distracting to the user — like a visual slap in the face. By keeping dimensions constant, the control changes smoothly.

By understanding how to change a subform display while moving from record to record, you can easily create subforms that morph based on the data. The secret to morphing a subform is to first create as many forms as you need to fill the single subform container. Then, as shown in Figure 8-48, you change the subform container's `SourceObject` property by using the form's `OnCurrent` property.

Form_Subform Morphing : Class Module

Form | Current

```
Private Sub Form_Current()
  If [Type of Customer] = "Retail" Then
    [Customer Subform].SourceObject = "Subform Morphing Retail"
   Else
     [Customer Subform].SourceObject = "Subform Morphing Wholesale"
  End If
End Sub
```

Figure 8-48: Morphing the subform control.

The subform's `SourceObject` property is always a form name. Each form you create can be used as a subform if its `DefaultView` property is a datasheet or a continuous form. When the `SourceObject` property is changed, the contents of the subform are changed.

By morphing the subform, you can eliminate the need for many forms based on a data value. This way, when a certain type of record needs additional information, you can use a different subform to display it.

As you can see in the simple procedure for the Subform Morphing form's `OnCurrent` event, when the value of the control `Type of Customer` is `"Retail"`, the `SourceObject` of the subform is changed to the form named `Subform Morphing Retail`. When the value of the control `Type of Customer` is `"Wholesale"`, the `SourceObject` of the subform is changed to the form named `Subform Morphing Wholesale`.

In the next section, you see very advanced applications of the subform morphing techniques to perform geographic drill down by manipulating multiple sets of graphical bitmaps using morphing combo boxes, transparent buttons, and option groups.

Geographic Drill Down

The Geographic Drill Down interfaces come with maps from several countries, including the United States, Canada, Australia, and several European countries. Maps also are included for U.S. regions, states, and counties. In this section, you learn how to use these maps to drill down from summarized information and display detail information about an area of the country and a selected time period.

These are not geodesic maps (by zip code, latitude, or longitude). These are simple bitmap graphics that are manipulated using techniques you learn in this section. You can copy the example files into your application and specify your data instead of the sample files. If you want geodesic maps to use with your Microsoft Access data, you can use a product called MapLinx for Windows. This product includes many types of maps and reads many types of data, including Microsoft Access. You can even purchase MapLinx for Windows city and street-level maps, primarily using zip-coded data.

In this section, you learn how to use and modify three basic interfaces for geographic drill down. Figure 8-49 shows a simple United States map that displays data for the selected state and time period. Also shown is a drill down by state and by county. When you click on a state, a summary for all state data is displayed. When you click on the picture of the state itself, a county map opens and lets you select data by county. Using this technique, you can substitute regions, cities, sales territories, or even street-level maps. The examples on your CD-ROM also include the capability of showing multiple maps (U.S., Canada, Europe, Australia) on one page.

Creating a simple United States map drill down with macros

The Geographic Drill Down form, shown in Figure 8-50, displays a map of the United States. As you click on a state, the rectangle to the right of the map displays the name of the selected state, a picture of the state, and selected detail data for the state.

The Geographic Drill Down form contains several areas. The area to the left contains the map of the United States, and on each state, a button that allows each state area to be selected. The maps are nothing more than embedded picture files in a standard Access object frame. By embedding the files into the object frames, you do not need to ship the original picture files with the application.

The right side of the form contains areas to display the results each time a state is selected. To understand the techniques in these forms, you first must understand the data files and data model used by any form for a graphical drill down technique.

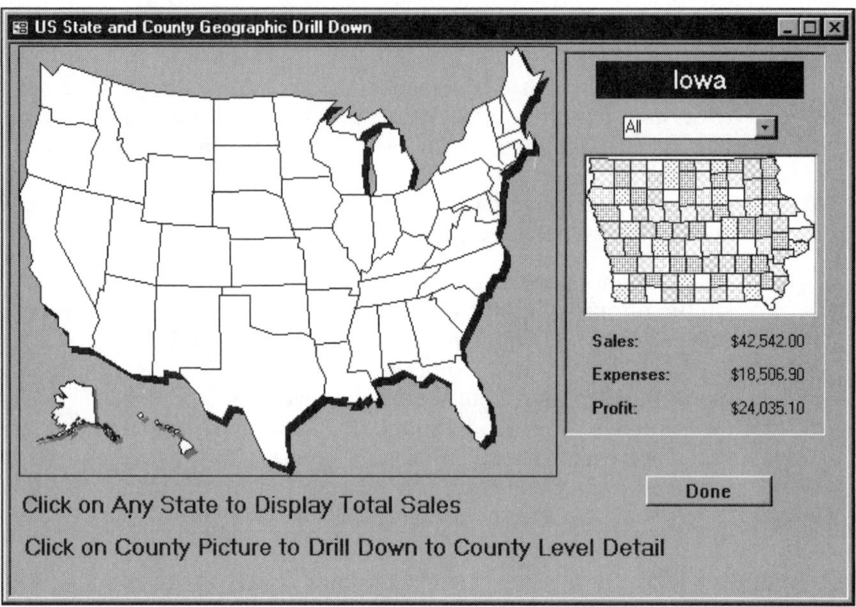

Figure 8-49: The geographic drill down interface provides a graphical way of representing data by geographic area.

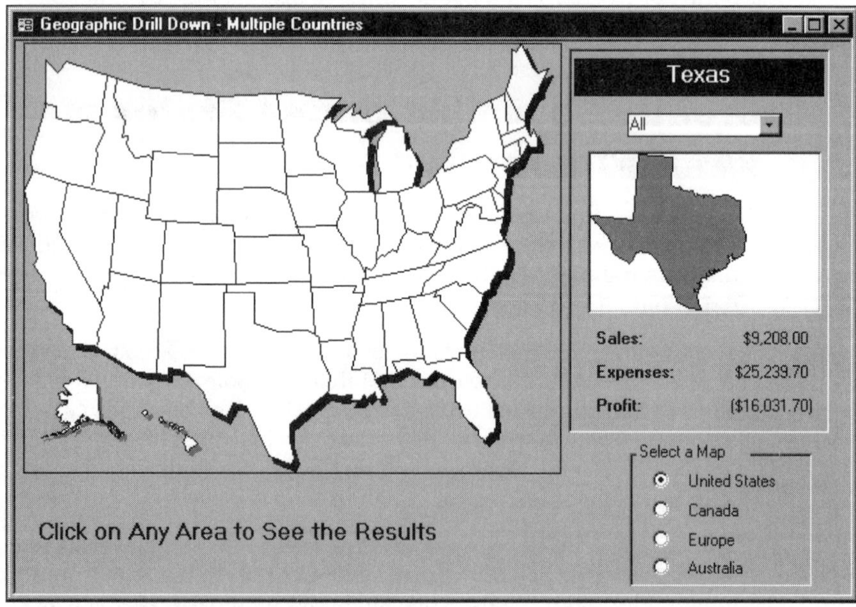

Figure 8-50: Displaying detail data for a state.

Understanding a graphical drill down data model

Each interface of this type requires two types of data. One type is the graphical data (pictures) used to display selected areas of the map as well as the map itself. The other type is the data that is displayed when a user selects an area of the map.

On CD-ROM

The first part of the data you should understand is the table that contains the names of the states and the pictures of the states. In the CH8.MDB file on this book's CD-ROM, this table is named US States. As you can see in Figure 8-51, this table contains several fields. Each field's purpose is described in the Description area of the table design.

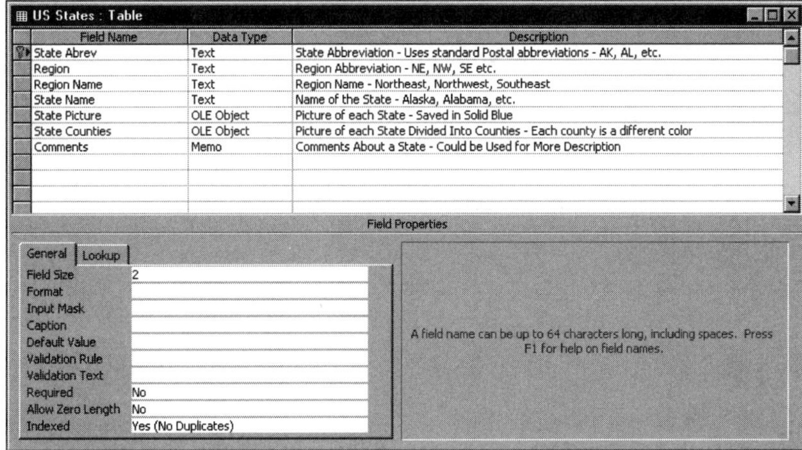

Figure 8-51: The US States table contains the names of the states and their pictures.

This table already contains the state abbreviations, names for each state, pictures of each state, and pictures of each state divided by county. (Note that there are no counties in Alaska and Hawaii.) Because everyone defines regions differently, the region information has not been filled in. You can group states to make your own regions or sales territories and then report on the groups.

If you simply display the data in the table using a standard Access datasheet, you see only the textual data and the word Picture where the OLE Objects are. To embed the pictures (and to see the embedded pictures), you must use a form. A form has been created on your database; the form contains the textual data and a bound OLE object frame for each picture. Figure 8-52 shows the US State Data form.

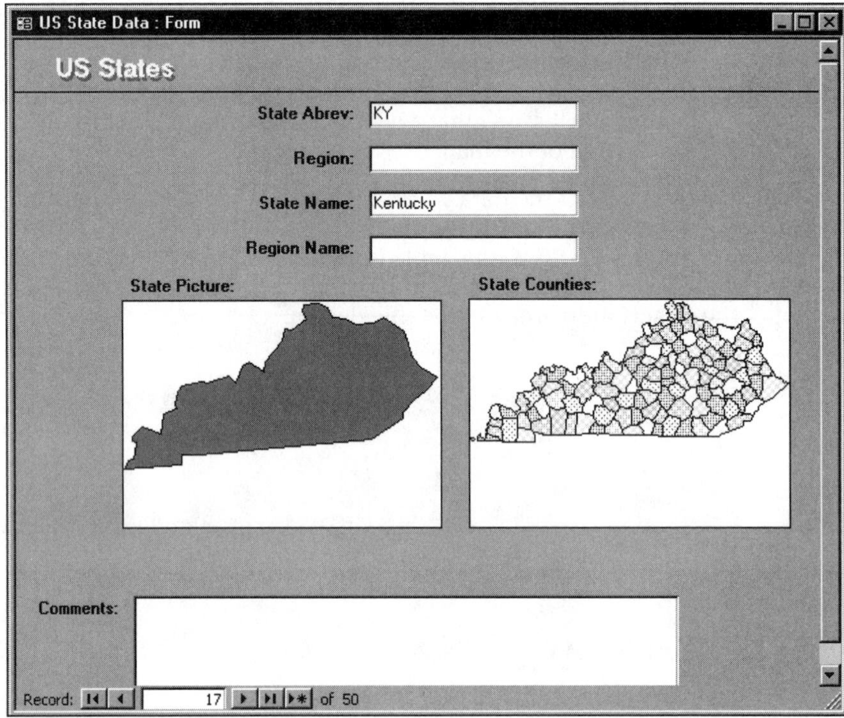

Figure 8-52: You must use a form to view the state pictures stored in the table.

All the clip art included in CH8.MDB comes from royalty-free clip art collections. To embed these maps in a form, select your favorite piece of clip art from your favorite package and then copy it to the Windows Clipboard. After the clip art is on the Clipboard, you can select the correct record in the form, select the bound object frame, and Paste the picture into the frame.

If you paste the picture from an OLE-enabled application (such as CorelDraw, Designer, Draw, or Arts and Letters), you can double-click on the picture, launch the source application, and edit the picture. However, OLE-enabled pictures use a great deal of storage space. After the picture has been embedded in the form, you can select the picture and then choose Edit⇨Object⇨Save as Picture to break the OLE connection and save the picture as a standard bitmap.

By using the state abbreviation as the key field for the table, you can pull any of the pictures out of the table by using standard data access techniques, which you will learn in this section.

Besides the graphical data, any other data that you want to use to display, count, summarize, or otherwise use on the form for the selected state must be keyed into the table. In this example, the data consists of a Sales number and an Expenses number. As you can see in Figure 8-53, the data is keyed only by state, date, and county (for Connecticut). To keep the example files small, only a limited set of data was included. The Region column isn't used for the examples in this section.

Microsoft Access - [US Sales Data : Table]

File Edit View Insert Format Records Tools Window Help

State Abrev	Date	County	Region	Sales	Expenses	Comments
ID	9/1/95			$9,898.00	$34,434.00	
AL	2/1/95			$4,433.00	$4,343.00	
AR	2/1/95			$643.00	$122.00	
ME	2/1/95			$2,343.00	$7,565.00	
VT	2/1/95			$2,345.00	$2,323.00	
NH	2/1/95			$4,665.00	$1,233.00	
MA	2/1/95			$3,455.00	$3,445.00	
CT	2/1/95	Hartford		$1,234.00	$673.00	
RI	2/1/95			$356.00	$776.00	
NY	2/1/95			$7,644.00	$555.00	
NJ	2/1/95			$2,234.00	$1,121.00	
PA	2/1/95			$34,554.00	$12,554.00	
VA	2/1/95			$676.00	$5,456.00	
WV	2/1/95			$54.00	$455.00	
DE	2/1/95			$4.00	$2,323.00	
MD	2/1/95			$4,444.00	$43,344.00	
NC	2/1/95			$3,333.00	$656.00	
SC	2/1/95			$7,655.00	$7,676.00	
GA	2/1/95			$7,787.00	$6,755.00	
FL	2/1/95			$55,666.00	$98,978.00	
MS	2/1/95			$444.00	$545.00	
TN	2/1/95			$3,334.00	$4,454.00	
KY	2/1/95			$33,445.00	$33,223.00	
OH	2/1/95			$966.00	$33.00	
IN	2/1/95			$456.00	$334.00	
MI	2/1/95			$4,567.00	$545.00	

Record: 1 of 283

Datasheet View CAPS NUM

Figure 8-53: By assigning the State Abrev as the key field in the table, you can retrieve data quickly for each state.

The trick to creating a usable data model is breaking the data into the smallest usable component. This way, the data can be summarized in natural hierarchies when needed. In the US State Data example, the data would be separated as follows:

```
TOTAL SALES
   BY YEAR            A HIERARCHY OF DATES
      BY MONTH
         BY DAY
   BY REGION          A HIERARCHY OF LOCATIONS
      BY STATE
         BY COUNTY
```

Dates have a natural hierarchy. A date can be broken into years (groups of quarters), quarters (groups of months), months (groups of weeks), weeks (groups of days), and days (the smallest unit of measure). This enables you to filter only the records that meet your needs or to summarize to any level. In this example, you can display data for all dates or for a single selected month. You can change the form to select any period of time using the techniques you learn here.

Locations have a hierarchy that is user defined according to the area you are mapping. In a map of the world, the hierarchy can be continents, countries, regions, and cities. In the United States, there are regions (groups of states), states (groups of counties), counties (groups of cities), cities (groups of streets), streets (groups of addresses), and addresses (the smallest unit of measure).

Creating a form with a background map or picture

To create a form with an embedded picture, you can either paste a picture from the Windows Clipboard, which automatically creates an unbound object frame, or you can create an unbound object frame and then select a file to use as the picture. Using this technique, you can use any type of graphic that makes sense to you, including pictures of your salespeople, pictures of your products, or even other maps. Use your imagination. Graphical interfaces can be fun! Figure 8-54 illustrates embedding a picture on a form.

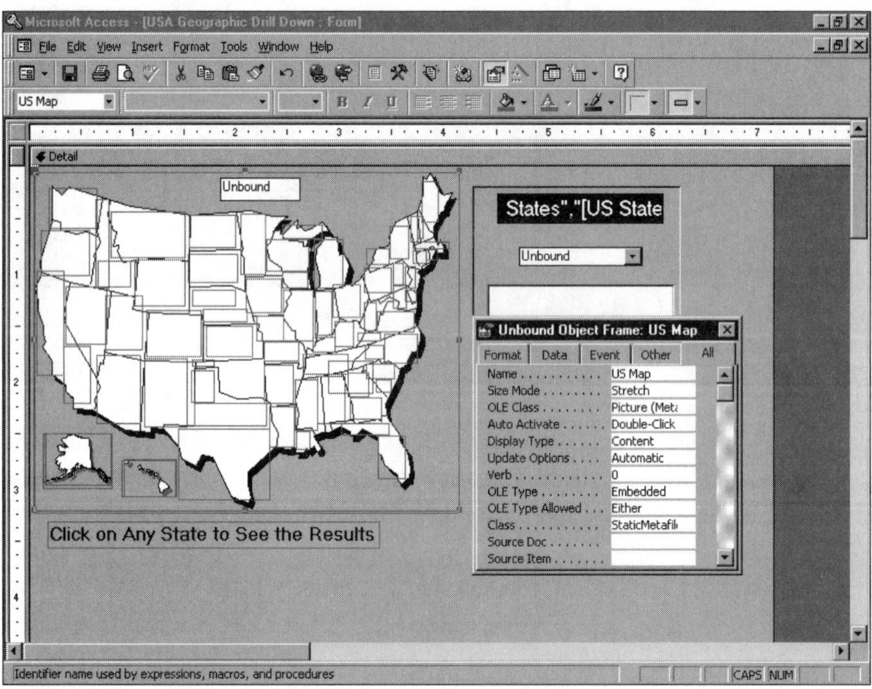

Figure 8-54: Embedding a picture on a form.

After you have the picture on your form, you add command buttons on top of each and every part that you want to designate as a different object of the picture. In the USA Geographic Drill Down example, the states are specified as the objects. Each state area in the object frame has one or more command buttons on top of the area of the picture that is bounded by the state.

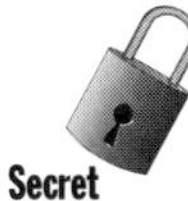

Some irregularly shaped states may require more than one command button so that you can click anywhere within a state's borders to select data.

Creating invisible command buttons

Figure 8-55 illustrates the Design view of the US States Map form; the figure shows the command buttons for the United States picture object frame. Notice that the buttons do not appear as buttons; they are small rectangles. These buttons are clear — no text or pictures. This is accomplished by setting the `Transparent` property for each of the command buttons to `Yes`. They become invisible when the form opens, and they appear as clear rectangles when the form is in design view.

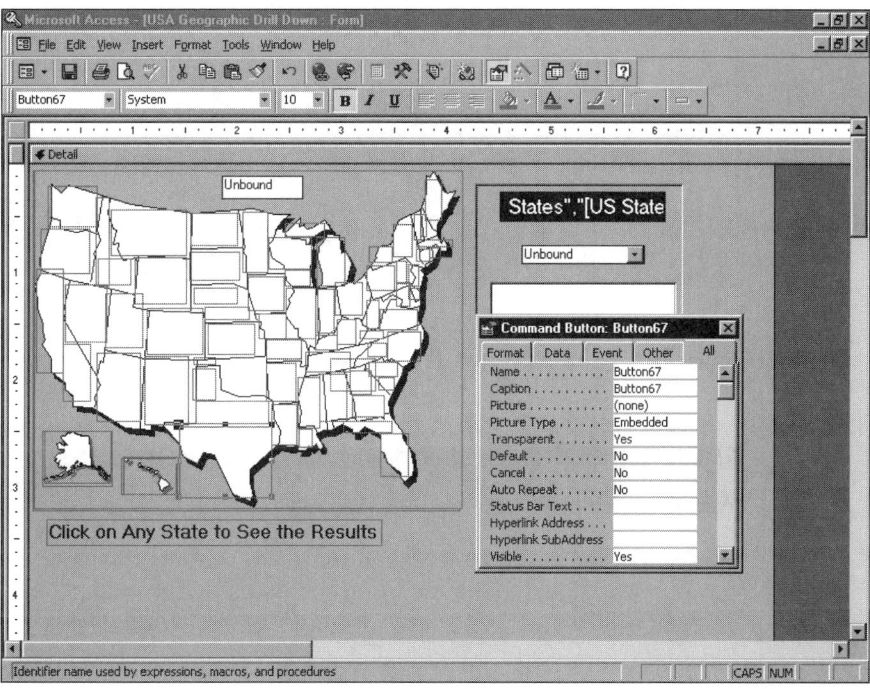

Figure 8-55: Creating the command buttons for each state.

Storing a variable in a hidden control

Figure 8-56 shows the Pick State text box at the top of the form design. The Pick State's `Visible` property is set to `No` so that the control isn't visible when the form is run. The field is needed only as an intermediate value holder. The Pick State text box is used as a storage area for the value passed to the calculated fields in the detail information rectangle. The calculated fields use the abbreviated state name to look up the detail information in the database. By using a hidden control, you can pass data from one control on the form to another.

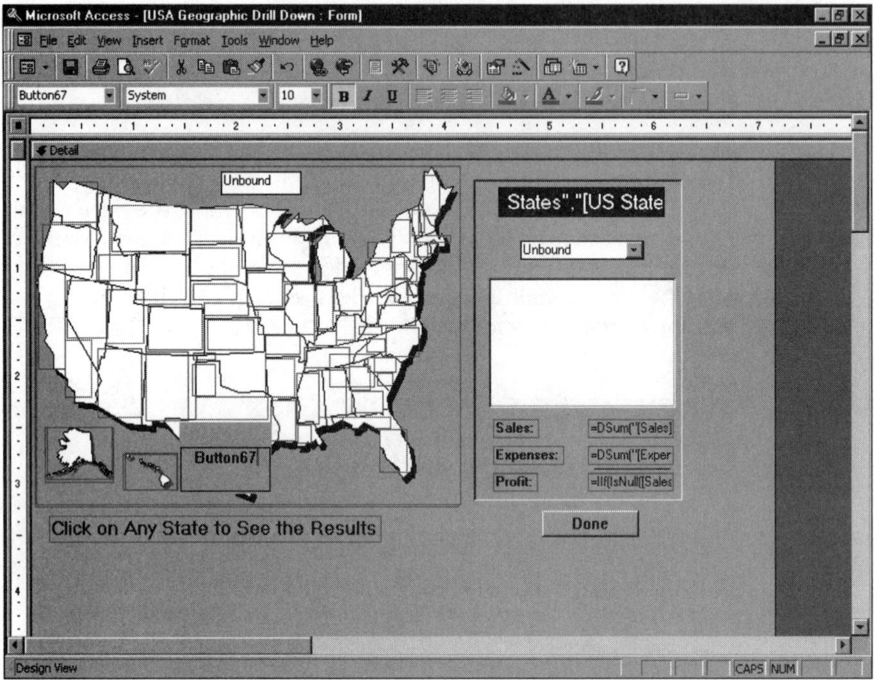

Figure 8-56: By using a hidden control, you can pass data from one control on the form to another.

Updating the results of the calculations

When you click on a state, the detail information does not update automatically. The `Requery` action (in the state's `On Click` event) updates the contents of the State Name Display text box to show the name of the currently selected state. The `Requery` action forces the record pointer to retrieve a different row from the table according to the result of the calculation in the State Name Display text box.

The rectangle on the right side of the form displays the state's detail information. The name of the state appears at the top of the rectangle. A picture of the state appears in the center of the rectangle. The Monthly Result information (Sales, Expenses, and Profit) for the state is displayed below the state's picture. The combo box above the picture is used to filter information for one month or for the entire year.

Displaying the state name and picture

The State Name Display text box is a calculated field. Figure 8-57 shows the expression for the calculation. The `DLookUp` function looks up the `State Name` in the `US States` table where the table's `State Abrev` is the same as the value in the `Pick State` text box.

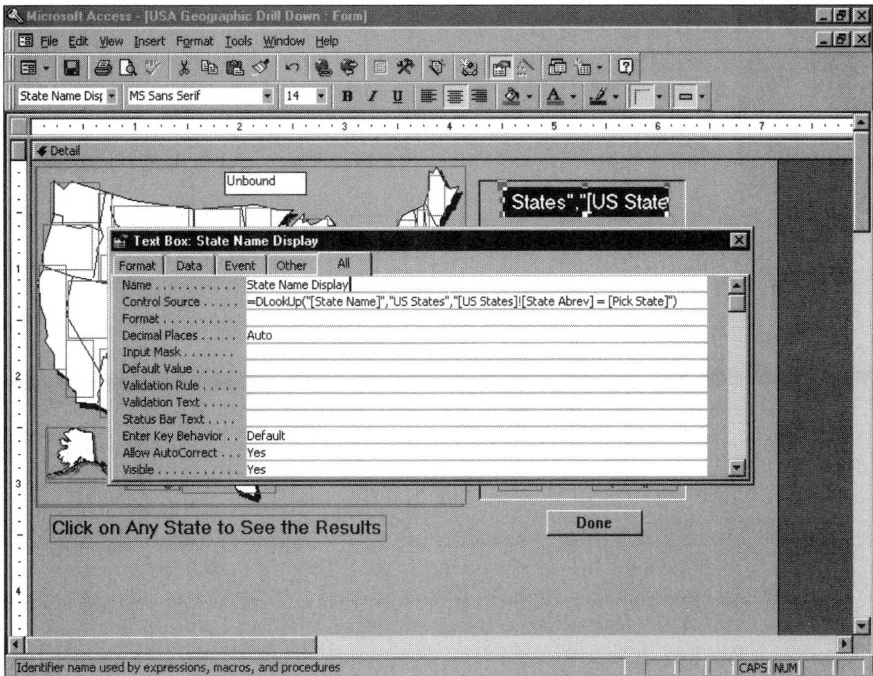

Figure 8-57: Using the DLookUp function to retrieve the state's name from the table.

The state's picture is displayed in a bound object frame. It isn't bound to a table but bound to a calculation. As you learned, the US States table includes a picture of each state in the State Picture column. The bound object frame uses the `DLookUp` function to retrieve the picture to display in the frame.

In case you are not familiar with the `DLookUp` function, it contains three parts. The first part is the name of the field to be retrieved from the specified table. In this example, this is the `State Name` or `State Picture`. The second part is the table name. This is `US States`, which contains the state name and picture. Finally, the last part tells the table the record to retrieve. The `DLookUp` function always returns a single record. The line `"[US States]![State Abrev] = [Pick State]"` tells the calculation to retrieve the record in the `US States` table where the `State Abrev` in the table `US States` is equal to the value of the `Pick State` control found in the USA Geographic Drill Down form.

Table 8-1 summarizes the calculations for the controls that display the state name and picture. The table shows that the calculations for retrieving the state name are essentially the same for both the text box and the bound picture.

Table 8-1 The Calculations for Retrieving the State Name

Control	*Control Source*
State Name Display	=DLookUp("[State Name]","US _ States","[US States]![State Abrev] _ = [Pick State]")
State Picture	=DLookUp("[State Picture]","US _ States","[US States]![State Abrev] _ = [Pick State]")

Displaying the numeric data for each state

The last part of the calculations displays the data from the US Sales Data table containing data by state, county, and date. Instead of using a DLookUp function, which retrieves one record, you need to use a DSum function to summarize all the data that meets the criteria. The criteria are all data for a specified state. All data, regardless of date, region, or county, are summarized when the record's state is equal to the selected state in the map. Without date criteria, the calculations would be simple, as shown in Table 8-2.

Table 8-2 Using the DSum to Summarize the Data for a State

Control	*Control Source*
Sales	=DSum("[Sales]","US Sales Data","[US Sales _ Data]![State Abrev] = [Pick State]"
Expenses	=DSum("[Expenses]","US Sales Data","[US Sales _ Data]![State Abrev] = [Pick State]"
Profit	=IIf(IsNull([Sales]),0,[Sales])-[Expenses]

The USA Geographic Drill Down example, however, is a little more complicated. Note the date combo box in Figure 8-58. This combo box uses a simple Value List combo box Row Source Type, the text All, and the months January 1996 through December 1996. When the value is selected from the combo box, the calculations are updated. The calculations in Table 8-2 do not account for a filtering for a single month. A second condition must be added to the DSum command to accomplish that.

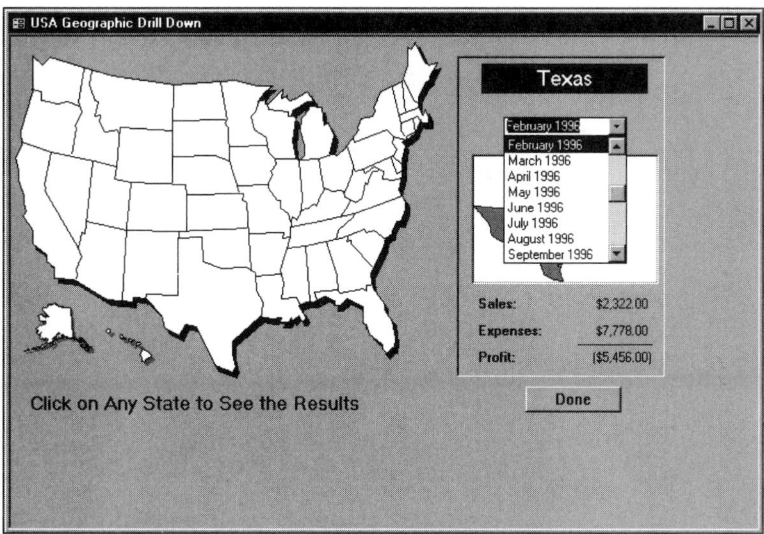

Figure 8-58: Filtering the state's data for a single month.

Filtering records used in a calculation

The Sales and Expenses information initially appears for all the rows that match a selected state in the US Sales Data table. You can use the combo box in the detail information area to limit the Sales and Expenses information to one month.

Table 8-3 illustrates the calculation for limiting the Sales figures to the item selected in the combo box. Notice that the `IIF (Immediate IF)` function is used to check the selected value in the `SelectMonth` combo box. If `All` is selected, then `DSum` retrieves all the Sales figures in the US Sales Data table for the matching state value. When a specific month is selected, `DSum` retrieves only the Sales figures from the US Sales Data table where the month and year of the Date column match the `SelectMonth` month and year. (Notice that the `Format` function in Table 8-3 converts the value in the Date column to match the format of the value in the combo box.)

Table 8-3 Adding Dsum Criteria to Filter Data for a Single Month

Control	*Control Source*
`Sales`	`=DSum("[Sales]","US Sales _ Data","IIf([SelectMonth].Value = 'All', [US _ Sales Data]![State Abrev] = [Pick State], _ [US Sales Data]![State Abrev] = [Pick State] _ and (Format([US Sales Data]![Date], 'mmmm _ yyyy') = [SelectMonth].Value)) ")`
`Expenses`	`=DSum("[Expenses]","US Sales _ Data","IIf([SelectMonth].Value = 'All', [US _ Sales Data]![State Abrev] = [Pick State], _ [US Sales Data]![State Abrev] = [Pick State] _ and (Format([US Sales Data]![Date], 'mmmm _ yyyy') = [SelectMonth].Value)) ")`
`Profit`	`=IIf(IsNull([Sales]),0,[Sales])-[Expenses]`

If you want to give the user the capability to enter a range of dates, you can change the calculations to select records between two dates. This gives you complete flexibility for the date filtering in the example.

Creating a multilevel drill down with VBA

This example takes the preceding example and goes a few steps further. Figure 8-59 demonstrates drilling down to a second level. In this example, the Connecticut counties are used for a second level of drill down. The map is displayed in a subform instead of a simple bound object frame. This enables you to reuse the subform for multiple types of analysis.

Using a subform to display the map

Subforms are simply forms displayed with another form. Look at the subform in Figure 8-60 named Country Subform. The `SourceObject` is the form named zUS State Map, which contains essentially the same map as in the previous examples.

The subform named Country Subform isn't linked because it really doesn't display data. Rather, it is used simply to display the subform containing the US Map.

Though this form looks very similar to the previous examples, it is very different in the way that the map interacts with other forms in the database.

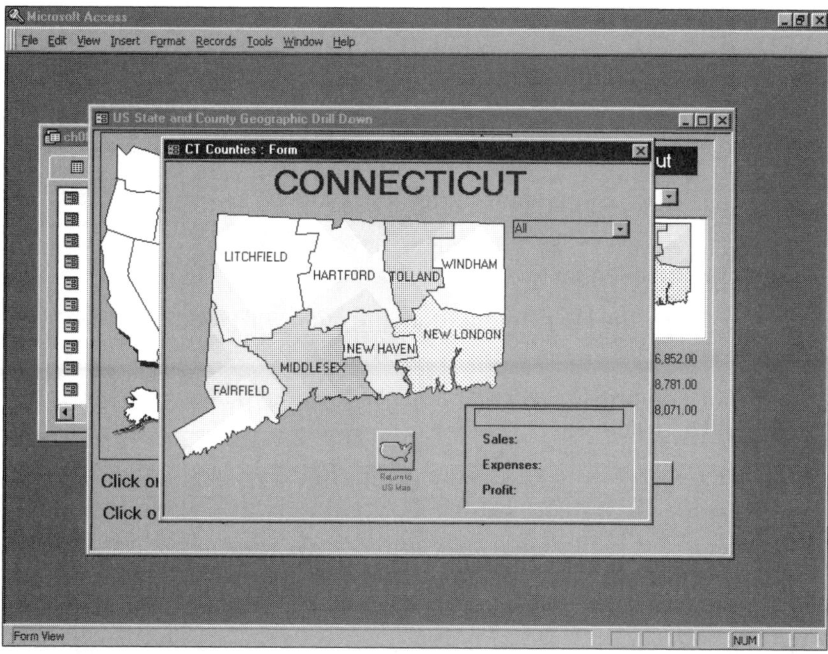

Figure 8-59: Drilling down to a second level.

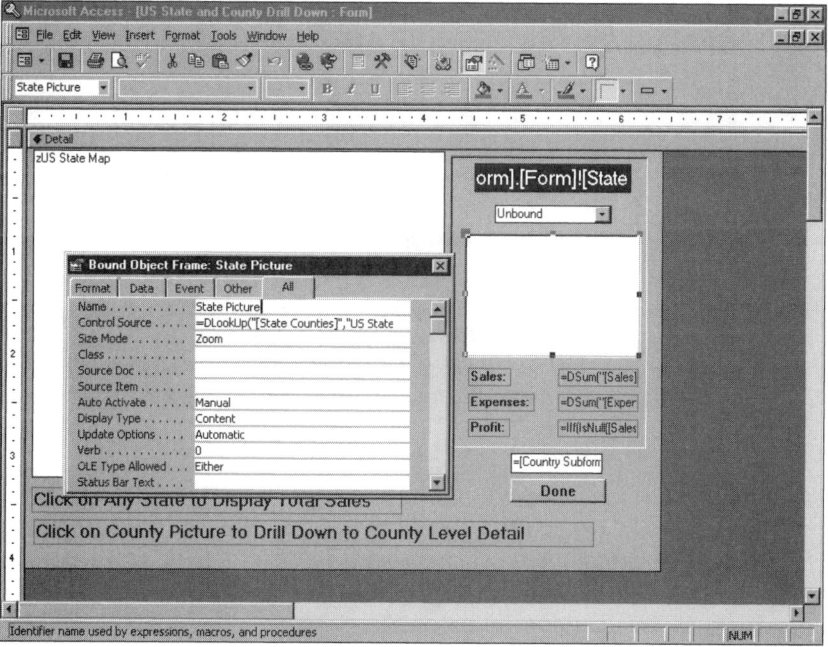

Figure 8-60: Using a subform to display the picture.

One of the differences is how controls are referenced. Because all the state selections actually occur at the subform level, controls on the subform must be referenced from the main form for the calculations to work. For example, the display of the state name uses the following reference:

```
=[Country Subform].[Form]![State Name Display]
```

This is actually a shortcut for this syntax:

```
=Forms![US State and County Drill Down]! _
[Country Subform].[Form]![State Name Display]
```

By using the shortcut method, the code will work if you rename the main form.

The subform in Figure 8-61 shows the map displayed in an unbound object frame.

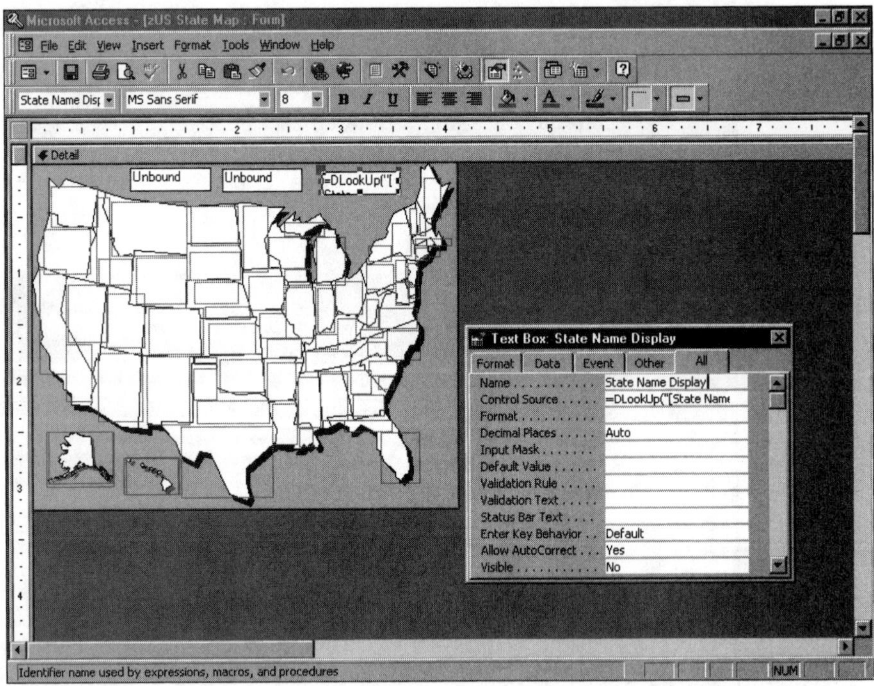

Figure 8-61: The map displayed in a subform.

One of the major differences you may see are the three text boxes on the subform. Where the original example used only the text box named Pick Box to store the abbreviation, this subform uses two additional text boxes for interform communication.

The second text box on the subform is named State Name Display. Where the main form simply referenced this control, the control on the subform uses the `DLookUp` function to retrieve the state name. This field is necessary because of some quirks in Microsoft Access's subform control referencing model; it is explained more fully later in this section.

```
=DLookUp("[State Name]","US States","[US States]! _
[State Abrev] = [Pick State]")
```

The third text box is named TypeCode. This is used to communicate with a common module of functions. By using the `TypeCode` control, many forms can call the same routine.

Calling the common module

Rather than use a macro library that requires a different macro for each state, this example uses a single function called `DisplayState`. The `DisplayState` function receives the abbreviation of the state and then sets the value of Pick State. After this value is set and the State Name Display is requeried, all the calculations can be executed. The state name is retrieved and passed back to the main form for display, the picture is retrieved, and the sales and expense calculations are executed. Figure 8-62 illustrates calling the function from the form.

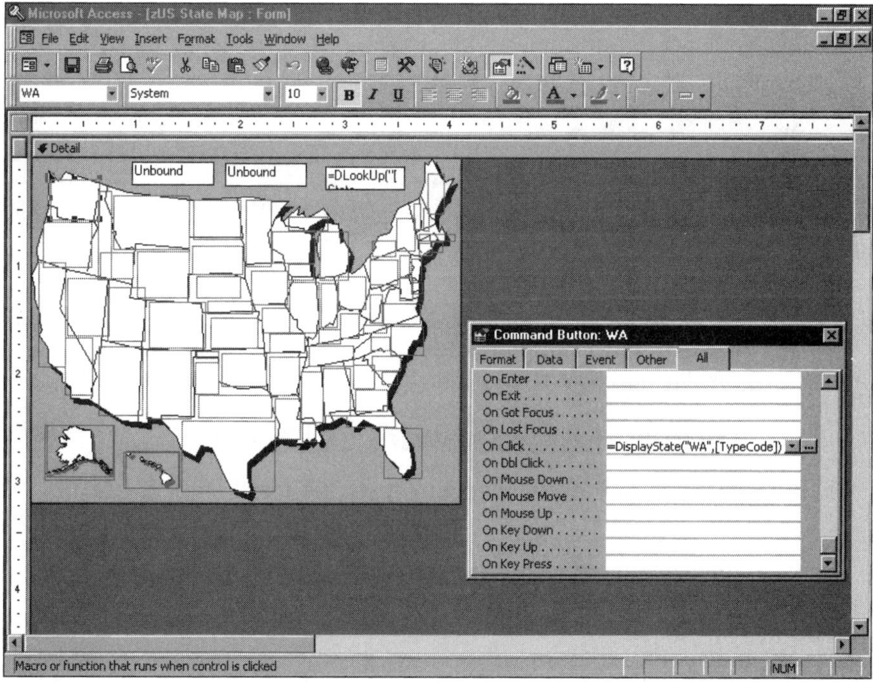

Figure 8-62: Calling the DisplayState function to update the form with the state's information.

The DisplayState function is located in the module named Geographic Functions. As you can see in Figure 8-63, the function DisplayState is called and passed two values. The first value is the state abbreviation. Each button passes the abbreviation for its state. The second value is named TypeCode. In this example, TypeCode is set to "Counties" in the main form's OnOpen event. The code to set the value of TypeCode for the US State and County Drill Down form is the following:

```
Me![Country Subform].Form!Typecode = "Counties"
```

When a state is selected, the DisplayState function is called and the value of Pick State is set, as shown in Figure 8-63. The StateName Display control is then requeried. Finally, the whole form is refreshed. Without the refresh statement, certain parts of the form (such as the state name) do not work. Again, this should not be necessary, but strange quirks in the Microsoft Access control referencing model mean you must refresh the form.

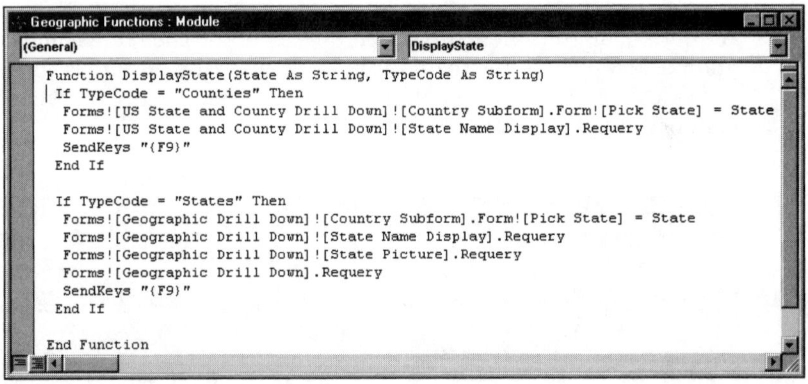

```
Geographic Functions : Module
(General)                                   DisplayState

Function DisplayState(State As String, TypeCode As String)
 If TypeCode = "Counties" Then
  Forms![US State and County Drill Down]![Country Subform].Form![Pick State] = State
  Forms![US State and County Drill Down]![State Name Display].Requery
  SendKeys "{F9}"
 End If

 If TypeCode = "States" Then
  Forms![Geographic Drill Down]![Country Subform].Form![Pick State] = State
  Forms![Geographic Drill Down]![State Name Display].Requery
  Forms![Geographic Drill Down]![State Picture].Requery
  Forms![Geographic Drill Down].Requery
  SendKeys "{F9}"
 End If

End Function
```

Figure 8-63: The DisplayState function performs the updates and refreshes the form for the selected state.

When you understand the differences in control referencing and see some of the detail-level complexities, you can begin to see how to change the form to display and how to use the county forms.

Displaying the county subform

The methods for displaying the County picture are exactly the same as for displaying the US Map picture. However, the DLookUp functions need to be modified to retrieve the County picture from the table, instead of the State picture. The DLookUp statement for retrieving the County picture from the US States table is as follows:

```
=DLookUp("[State Counties]","US States" _
"[US States]![State Abrev] =[Pick State]")
```

The control that displays the county picture is named State_Picture. Users can click on this control to display a pop-up form. In the US State and County Geographic Drill Down example, four county forms have been created and connected to the interface. The rest are left for you to create if you want. Figure 8-64 shows the code to display the appropriate pop-up form for each of the four states.

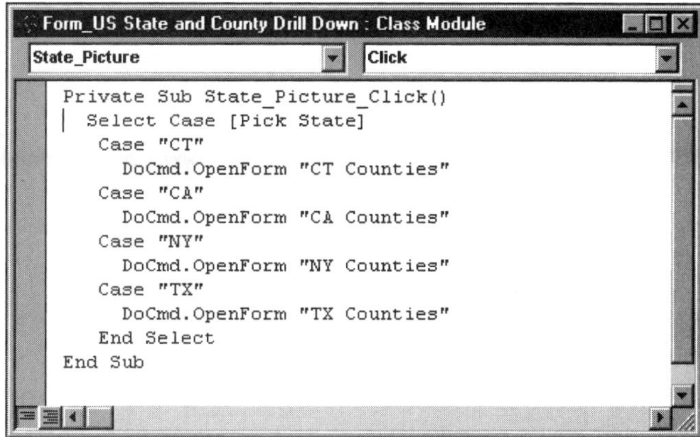
Form_US State and County Drill Down : Class Module
State_Picture
Click
Private Sub State_Picture_Click()
Select Case [Pick State]
Case "CT"
DoCmd.OpenForm "CT Counties"
Case "CA"
DoCmd.OpenForm "CA Counties"
Case "NY"
DoCmd.OpenForm "NY Counties"
Case "TX"
DoCmd.OpenForm "TX Counties"
End Select
End Sub

Figure 8-64: Programming the On Click event to display a pop-up form when clicking on a state.

Creating a county display form

The county display form is similar to all the other main form examples discussed in earlier sections. The only differences are that the calculations of sales and expense data must take into account the selection of date, state, and county. Figure 8-65 shows the Design View for the CT Counties form.

Creating this form required the following tasks:

- A new form was created and named CT Counties.
- The Connecticut Counties picture was selected in the US State Data form and copied to the Clipboard.
- The Connecticut Counties picture was pasted as an unbound bitmap to the new form.
- The names of the counties were added as labels to the map picture.
- Transparent buttons were added to each county, and the SetCounty function was added to each button.
- The Date Selector and Financial Information controls were copied from the main form.

- The `Financial Information` controls were modified for the county selection technique.
- A new control named `PickState` was created and preset to `"CT"` (for Connecticut).

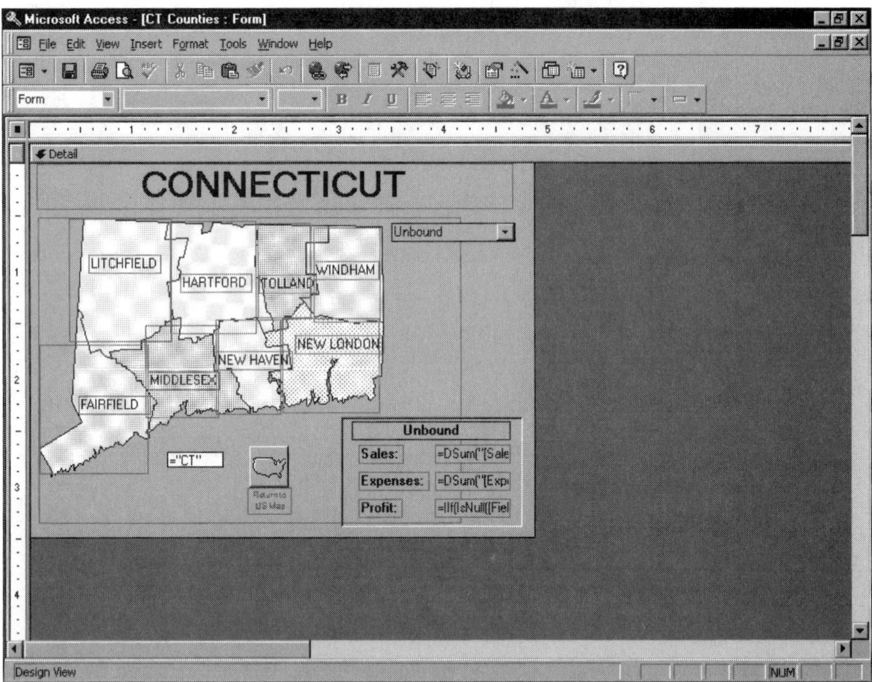

Figure 8-65: The design for the county display form is like the design of the main form.

The primary difference between this form and the main form is that the command button for each county calls the `SetCounty` function. The `Geographic Functions` module is the best place to store the `SetCounty` function. An example of the call for the `OnClick` event for a county is

```
=SetCounty("Hartford")
```

Figure 8-66 shows the code for the `SetCounty` function. This code simply sets the value of `PickCounty` to the value of the passed county name and then refreshes the form.

The calculations for displaying the county detail information, shown in Table 8-4, are a degree more complicated than summarizing the data for a state and date. An `AND` connector connects the three distinct filters for date, state, and county.

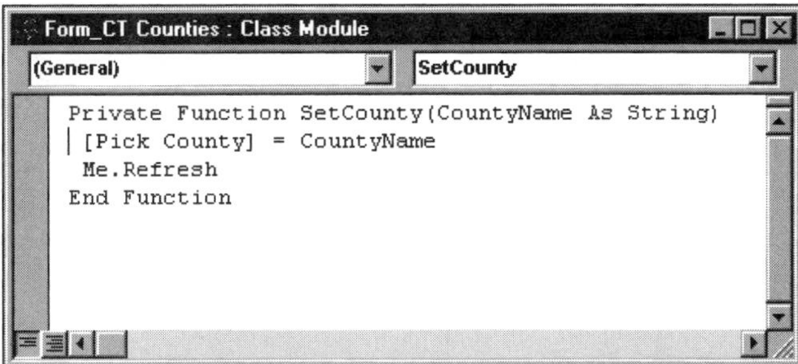

```
Private Function SetCounty(CountyName As String)
 [Pick County] = CountyName
 Me.Refresh
End Function
```

Figure 8-66: Using a function to display the detail information for a county.

Table 8-4 Adding County Criteria to the DSum Function

Control	*Control Source*
Sales	=DSum("[Sales]","US Sales _ Data","IIf([SelectMonth].Value = 'All',([US _ Sales Data]![State Abrev] = [Pick State] and _ [US Sales Data]![County] = [Pick County]), _ [US Sales Data]![State Abrev] =[Pick State] _ and [US Sales Data]![County] = [Pick County] _ and (Format([US Sales Data]![Date], 'mmmm _ yyyy') = [SelectMonth].Value)) ")
Expenses	=DSum("[Expenses]","US Sales _ Data","IIf([SelectMonth].Value = 'All', [US _ Sales Data]![State Abrev] = [Pick State] and _ [US Sales Data]![County] = [Pick County], _ [US Sales Data]![State Abrev] = [Pick State] _ and [US Sales Data]![County] = [Pick County] _ and (Format([US Sales Data]![Date], 'mmmm _ yyyy') = [SelectMonth].Value)) ")
Profit	=IIf(IsNull([Sales]),0,[Sales])-[Expenses]

Creating a form for multiple countries

The last (and most complicated) example of a geographic drill down interface is one that can display multiple maps in one form. This involves changing the `SourceObject` of the subform while the form is running. Figure 8-67 shows the form Geographic Drill Down displaying the Canadian Provinces map.

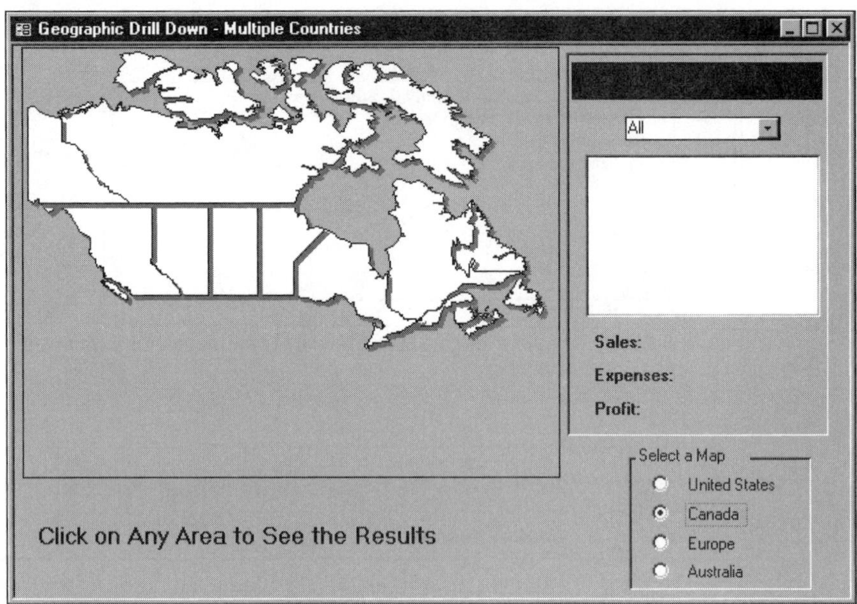

Figure 8-67: A single form can display multiple countries.

For the United States map, the form uses the subform zUS State Map. Additionally, the form uses three other subforms: zCanada Province Map, zEurope Country Map, and zAustralia Territory Map. The Canadian subform has been completed; the European and Australian maps simply have been placed on the forms.

Creating controls to change country

The Geographic Drill Down form uses a subform to display each country's map; each map is a separate form. Each form contains the object frame for the map's picture file and all of the necessary command buttons.

As shown in Figure 8-68, an option group, named Country, is used to change the `SourceObject` of the subform container. When you click on an option in the option group, the `AfterUpdate` event runs to display the selected country. Because you are actually loading a different form into the subform container, you have complete control over any changes.

In the Geographic Drill Down example, you can see that there are three text boxes in the bottom left corner. These text boxes maintain a link between the main form and the specified subform. The first text box is PickState, which is used to maintain a link to the United States subform. The second is PickProvince, which is used to maintain a link to the Canadian subform. If you connect the other two maps, you need similar text boxes. These are again due to quirks in Microsoft Access's reference model. You must also redundantly have a link to the `TypeCode` (passed by the selected State, Province, Country, or Territory) from the global routine in the `Geographic Function` module.

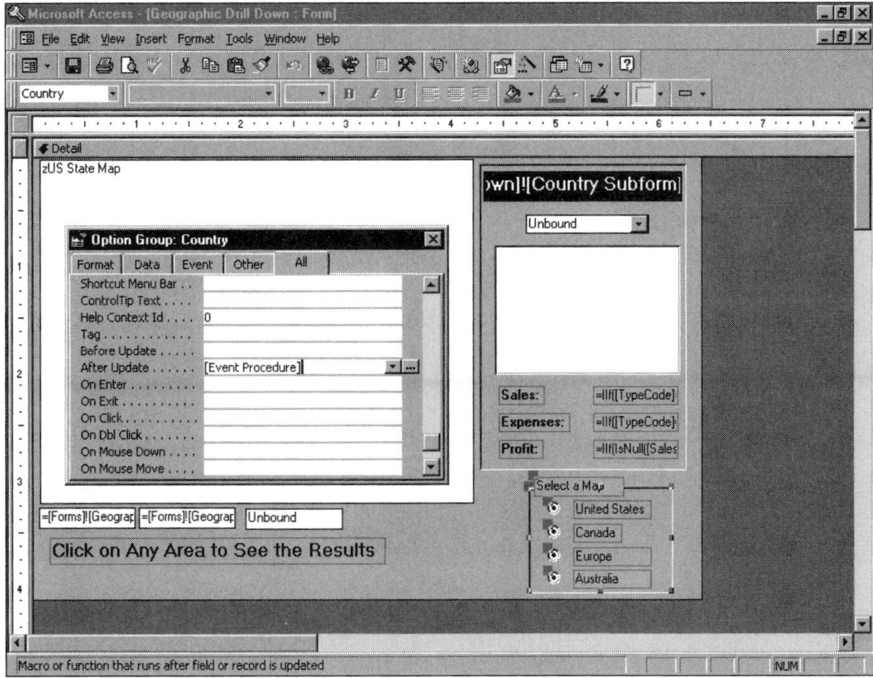

Figure 8-68: The Country option group is used to control the dislayed country.

When an option button is selected, the subform container's (Country Subform's) `SourceObject` property changes. The `TypeCode` variable is also changed and is used by the global routine. Notice that the value of `TypeCode` is set both on the main form and the subform. Again, this is necessary because of Access's subform referencing problems. Basically, Access tends to lose track of control references while using morphing subforms. The final line of VBA code in each case (US and Canada) resets the `ControlSource` of the `State Name Display` (USA) or the `Province Name Display` (Canada). Listing 8-7 shows the `AfterUpdate` code for the Country option group.

Listing 8-7 Updating the Displayed Country Using the AfterUpdate Event of an Option Group

```
Sub Country_AfterUpdate ()
  Select Case Country
    Case 1
      Me![Country Subform].SourceObject = "zUS State Map"
      Me![Country Subform].Form!TypeCode = "States" _
      TypeCode = "States"
      [State Name Display].ControlSource = _
"=[Forms]![Geographic Drill Down]! _
      [Country Subform].[Form]![State Name      Display]"
```

(continued)

(continued)

```
      Case 2
        Me![Country Subform].SourceObject = _
        "zCanada Province Map"
        Me![Country Subform].Form!TypeCode = "Provinces"
        [State Name Display].ControlSource = _
        "=[Forms]![Geographic Drill Down]! _
        [Country Subform].[Form]![Province Name    Display]"
        TypeCode = "Provinces"
      Case 3
        Me![Country Subform].SourceObject = _
        "zEurope Country Map"
        Me![Country Subform].Form!TypeCode = "Countries"
        TypeCode = "Countries"
      Case 4
        Me![Country Subform].SourceObject = _
        "zAustralia Territory Map"
        Me![Country Subform].Form!TypeCode = "Territories"
        TypeCode = "Territories"
    End Select
End Sub
```

Using the Canadian subform to display provinces

To understand how much the interfaces are similar, you can examine the Canadian Province subform, shown in Figure 8-69. Like the United States subform, three fields maintain the link to the main form. These are `TypeCode` (set to `Provinces`); `Pick Province`, which stores the selected `Province`; and the `Province Name Display` control.

When a province is selected, the same techniques you learned earlier in this section are used to display a province in the picture box and to update the financial calculations. For the Canadian example, two tables store the data: Canadian Provinces stores the Province abbreviation, Province Name, and Province Picture, and Canadian Sales Data stores the Sales and Expense information by Province and (optionally) by city.

When a province is selected, a global routine is run to set the value of `Pick Province` and to recalculate all the controls. Each province passes the abbreviation of the province and the `Type Code` (`Provinces`) to the routine, as follows:

```
=DisplayProvince("NW",[TypeCode])
```

The `DisplayProvince` program (shown in Listing 8-8) is virtually identical to the `DisplayState` program (shown in Listing 8-9) for the United States display.

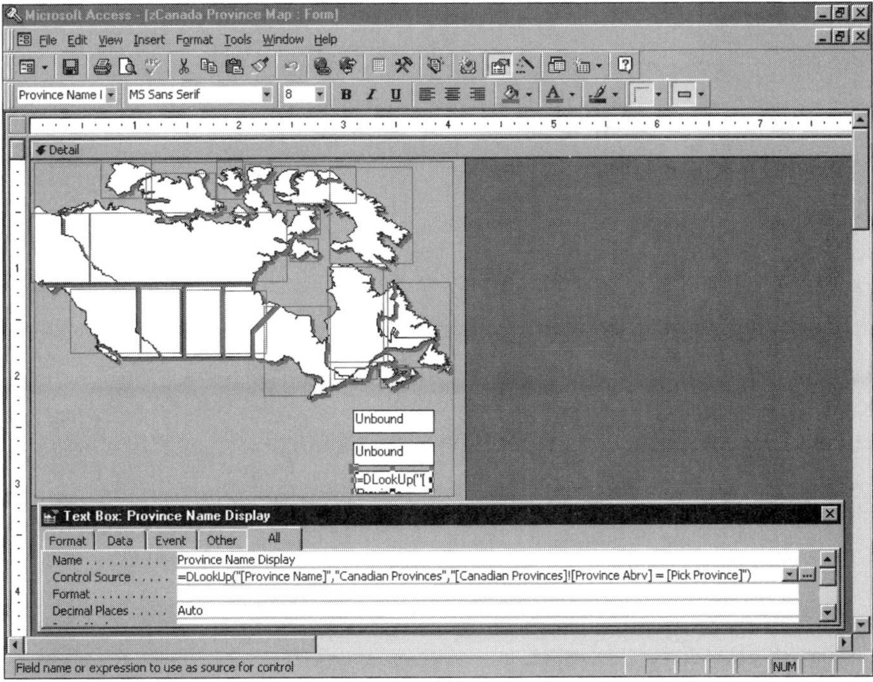

Figure 8-69: Similar to the US Map interface, the Canada Province Map uses a DLookUp function to display detail information for a province.

Listing 8-8 Canadian Program Called from zCanada Province Map Selections

```
Function DisplayProvince _
(Province As String, TypeCode As String)
  If TypeCode = "Provinces" Then
   Forms![Geographic Drill Down]! _
   [Country Subform].Form![Pick Province] = Province
   Forms![Geographic Drill Down]! _
   [State Name Display].Requery
   Forms![Geographic Drill Down]![State Picture].Requery
   Forms![Geographic Drill Down].Requery
   SendKeys "{F9}"
  End If
End Function
```

Listing 8-9 United States Program Called from zUS State Map Selections

```
Function DisplayState (State As String, _
TypeCode As String)
 If TypeCode = "States" Then
  Forms![Geographic Drill Down]![Country Subform].Form! _
  [Pick State]= State
  Forms![Geographic Drill Down]! _
  [State Name Display].Requery
  Forms![Geographic Drill Down]![State Picture].Requery
  Forms![Geographic Drill Down].Requery
  SendKeys "{F9}"
 End If
End Function
```

The calculations for handling multiple countries use an `IIF` branch for each country that is hooked up to the interface and the appropriate `DLookUp` function to retrieve the right text or picture. Figure 8-70 shows the `Control Source` code for the US and Canada for the selected picture.

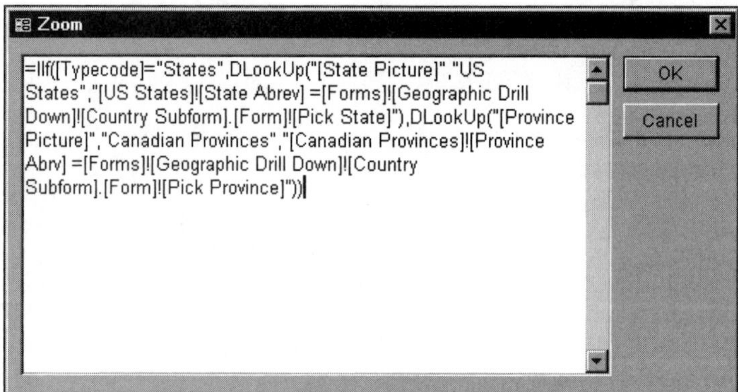

Figure 8-70: Using an IIF branch to display the appropriate picture based on the TypeCode value.

Displaying the multicountry calculations

The field State Name Display, which is used to display the name of the selected state or province, is morphed when a user clicks on the option group button. Table 8-5 lists the calculations. The morphing is necessary because Access simply will not maintain the link between the subforms. This technique may also be more efficient with a large volume of data.

Table 8-5 Control Source Calculations for the Geographic Drill Down Controls

Control	*Calculation*
`State Name Display` (United States Only)	`= [Forms]![Geographic Drill Down]! _ [Country Subform].[Form]![State Name _ Display]`
`State Name Display` (Canada Only)	`= [Forms]![Geographic Drill Down]! _ [Country Subform].[Form]![Province _ Name Display]"`
`State Picture`	`=IIF([Typecode]="States",DLookUp("[State _ Picture]","US States","[US _ States]![State Abrev] _ =[Forms]![Geographic Drill _ Down]![Country Subform].[Form]![Pick _ State]"),DLookUp("[Province _ Picture]","Canadian _ Provinces","[Canadian _ Provinces]![Province Abrv] _ =[Forms]![Geographic Drill _ Down]![Country Subform].[Form]![Pick _ Province]"))`
`Sales`	`=IIF([TypeCode]="States",DSum("[Sales]","US _ Sales Data","IIF([SelectMonth].Value _ = 'All', [US Sales Data]![State _ Abrev] =[Pick State],[US Sales _ Data]![State Abrev] =[Pick State] and _ (Format([US Sales Data]![Date], 'mmmm _ yyyy') = [SelectMonth].Value)) _ "),DSum("[Sales]","Canadian Sales _ Data","IIF([SelectMonth].Value = _ 'All', [Canadian Sales _ Data]![Province Abrev] =[Pick _ Province], _ [Canadian Sales Data]![Province _ Abrev] =[Pick Province] and _ (Format([Canadian Sales Data]![Date], _ 'mmmm yyyy') = _ [SelectMonth].Value)) "))`

(continued)

Table 8-5 *(continued)*

Control	*Calculation*
Expenses	`=IIF([TypeCode]="States",DSum("[Expenses]","US _ Sales Data","IIF([SelectMonth].Value _ = 'All', [US Sales Data]![State _ Abrev] = [Pick State], _ [US Sales Data]![State Abrev] = [Pick _ State] and (Format([US Sales _ Data]![Date], 'mmmm yyyy') = _ [SelectMonth].Value)) _ "),DSum("[Expenses]","Canadian Sales _ Data","IIF([SelectMonth].Value = _ 'All', [Canadian Sales _ Data]![Province Abrev] =[Pick _ Province], _ [Canadian Sales Data]![Province _ Abrev] =[Pick Province] and _ (Format([Canadian Sales Data]![Date], _ 'mmmm yyyy') = _ [SelectMonth].Value)) "))`
Profit	`=IIF(IsNull([Sales]),0,[Sales])- _ [Expenses]`

The display of the picture and all the financial calculations, for some unknown reason, works fine by using an `IIF` function that uses the value of `TypeCode` and runs the correct `DLookUp` reference to the correct picture or `DSum` function to the correct values in either `US Sales Data` or `Canadian Sales Data`.

As you add more countries, these calculations continue to grow. That's when you should convert the calculations into a common module routine to handle any country to display on the form.

On CD-ROM

As you have learned in this section, you can perform a rather complex geographic drill down while armed with nothing but a clip-art library and some data. The CH8.MDB database file on this book's CD-ROM also includes maps of continents and other countries. You can use any clip art with this technique.

Chapter 9

Working with Menus and Toolbars

In This Chapter

- Creating great menus and toolbars using command bars
- Creating menu accelerator keys with key assignment macros
- Customizing Access's built-in command bars
- Manipulating menu and toolbar command items
- Using the Application object to hide and show command bars

Access 97 offers you powerful and easy-to-use tools to create menus and toolbars for your application. With the introduction of the new *command bar object,* creating menus and toolbars in Access has never been easier. There are still some limitations on what you can do with them while they're in use, however. In this chapter, you learn how to maximize the capabilities of Access's menus and toolbars. In addition, you find many tips for effectively designing and organizing your menus and toolbars.

What's So Special About Menus?

One of the greatest features of Windows applications is their consistent use of the *graphical user interface (GUI)* for interacting with and navigating through the programs. GUI applications use graphics elements such as drop-down list boxes, spin buttons (small buttons with up and down arrows used to increment and decrement numeric fields), scroll bars, and buttons with pictures in place of plain text characters (which are typical of DOS applications). Although you may rely heavily on your mouse for performing design tasks while in Windows, many Windows users are keyboard users; they prefer to use a mouse only when absolutely necessary. Data-entry people, in particular, never take their hands off the keyboard. Many software companies receive support calls from angry customers because a common function is only accessible with a mouse. Menus, and their associated hot keys and accelerator keys, are the easiest way for a user who relies on the keyboard to navigate through your application. Figure 9-1 shows an example of Microsoft Office application menu bars.

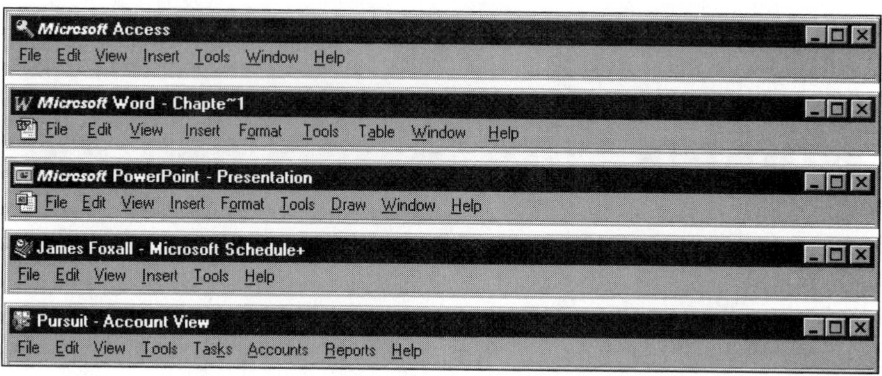

Figure 9-1: Menu bars are similar and consistent throughout the Office suite.

Tip

New users of an application often scan the menus before ever opening a manual. By providing comprehensive menus, you make your application more intuitive, so it is easier to learn and use.

Toolbars Are Shortcuts

Just as menu bars are staples for keyboard users, mouse-oriented users use toolbars to quickly execute functions of your applications. Think of toolbars as mouse shortcuts. In general, you should have one toolbar for every menu in your program. When you display a menu, you should also display a corresponding toolbar. Figure 9-2 shows an example of a toolbar.

Tip

A toolbar generally contains shortcuts for functions often used within your application. Each toolbar button should have a corresponding menu item, but not all menu items need an associated toolbar button. Toolbar real estate is usually limited, so reserve your toolbar buttons for the most frequently used functions of a form.

Cross-Reference

Two types of toolbars are available to you with Access: Microsoft Access's built-in toolbars and custom toolbars that you create. Access includes a number of built-in toolbars that you can modify. If you will always run your application with the full development version of Access, this may be the easiest way for you to use toolbars. If you plan to distribute your application with the runtime version of Access (using the ODE Tools), however, you will not be able to display Access's built-in toolbars; you must create *custom* toolbars. The ODE Tools are covered in detail in Chapter 15, "Distributing Applications with the Office Developer Edition."

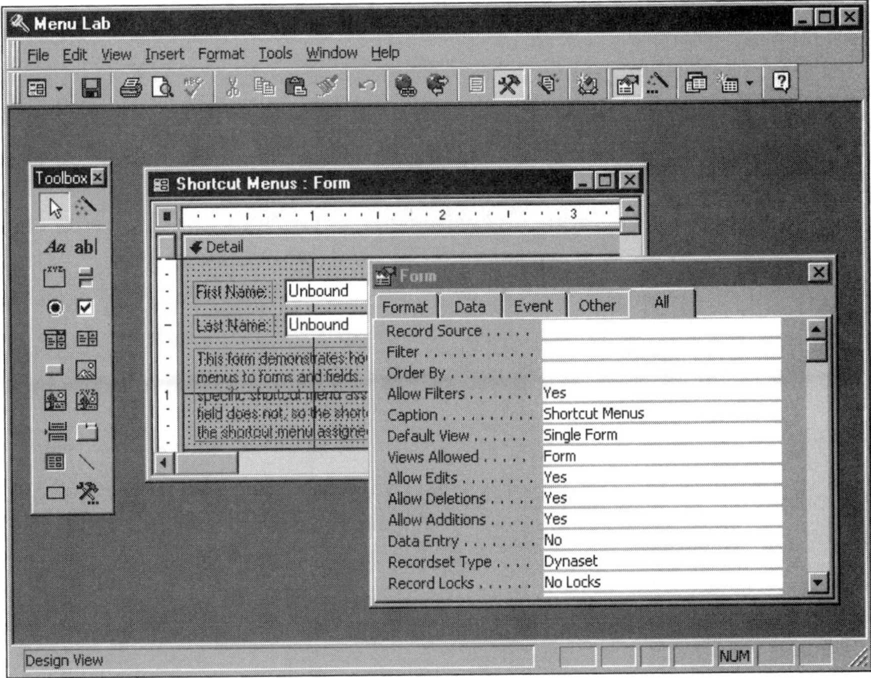

Figure 9-2: Access uses many different toolbars to make it easier for you to perform various functions.

Creating Great Menus and Toolbars Using Command Bars

In Access 95, a menu was a collection of macros. New to Access 97 is the *command bar* object. All menus, toolbars, and shortcut menus are types of command bars. You determine the type of command bar by setting the command bar's `Type` property.

Command bars can be one of the following types:

- Menus
- Toolbars
- Shortcut menus

Command bars are fully customizable and much more intuitive to use than menu macros.

Converting menu macros to command bars

To convert menu macros created in Access 2.0 or Access 95 to command bars, select the macro to convert in the Database window, and then select Tools⇨Macro⇨Create Menu from Macro (see Figure 9-3). When the menu has been successfully converted, it appears at the top of the Access window (see Figure 9-4). After the menu command bar has been created from the menu macro, you can customize it using the techniques described in this chapter.

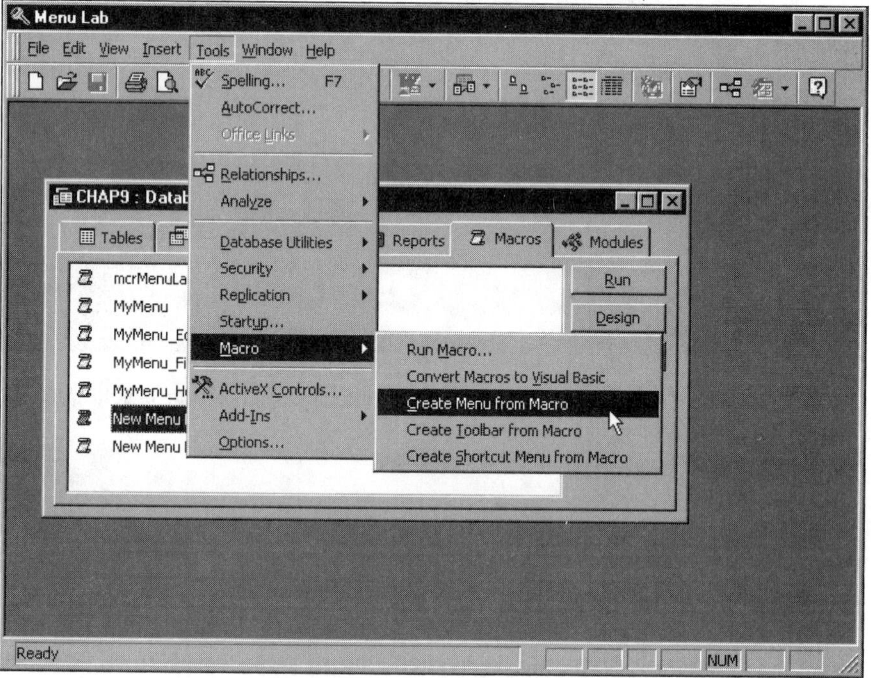

Figure 9-3: You can convert menu macros from previous versions of Access by selecting the macro to convert and then selecting Tools⇨Macro⇨Create Menu from Macro.

You do not need to explicitly convert every submenu macro. When you convert a top-level menu macro, all submenu macros are converted as well.

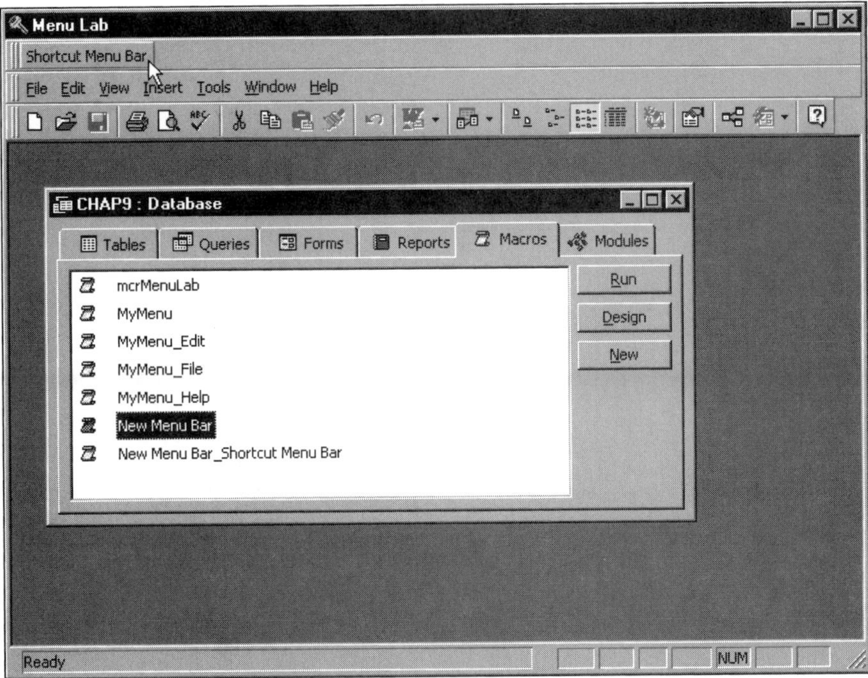

Figure 9-4: Custom menus appear at the top of the Access window after they are converted from macros.

Creating custom command bars

You create new command bars by using the Customize dialog box. To create a new command bar using the dialog box, select View➪Toolbars➪Customize from the Database Window toolbar (see Figure 9-5.) After selecting Customize, the Microsoft Office Assistant appears, ready to help you — if it has been installed. The Office Assistant is a new form of help that is shown as an animated figure. Programming the Office Assistant is discussed in Chapter 19, "Integrating Office Applications." You can turn off the Assistant if you want.

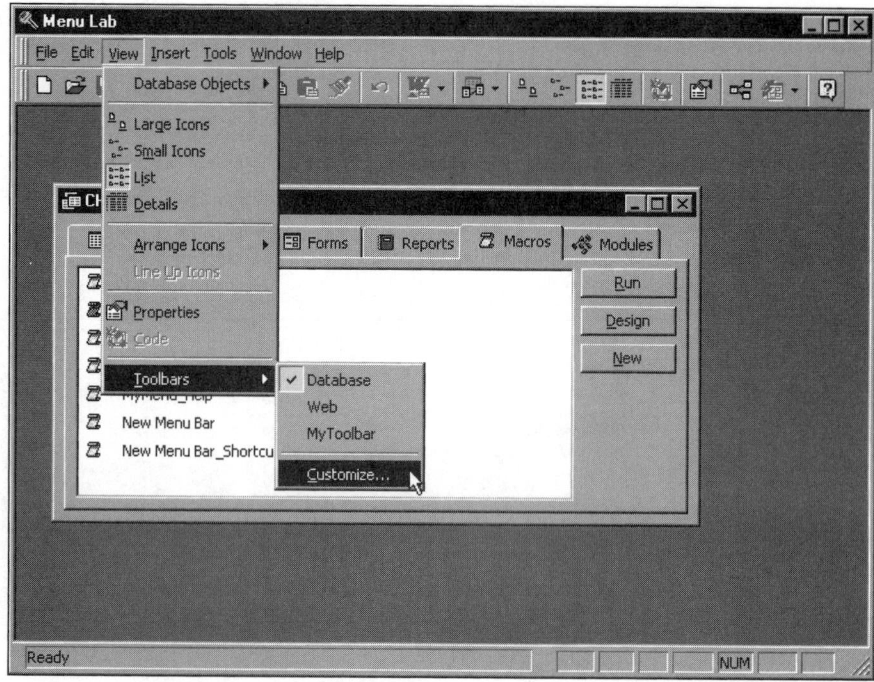

Figure 9-5: Accessing the Customize dialog box.

Tip

You can still create menus by using macros, but as a general rule, you should always create new menus as command bars, using the Customize dialog box. If you do create menu macros, you will need to convert them as just described to take advantage of the new features of command bars.

From the Toolbars tab of the Customize dialog box shown in Figure 9-6, click on New and then enter a name for your new command bar (see Figure 9-7).

After naming your custom command bar, it appears, floating on your desktop (see Figure 9-8). Note that no items are on the command bar; it is completely blank. You need to add command items to the command bar (discussed later in this chapter).

Tip

You can drag your new command bar to the top of the window so that it appears like a normal menu or toolbar. Then you can tear it off at any time to make it float again.

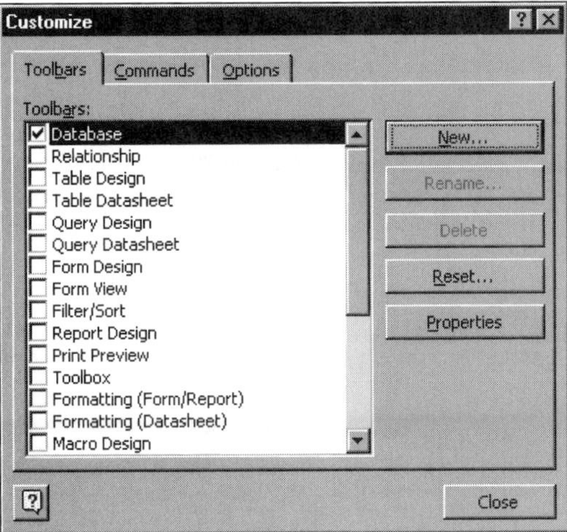

Figure 9-6: Menus and toolbars are all created in the same way, by clicking on New in the Toolbars tab of the Customize dialog box.

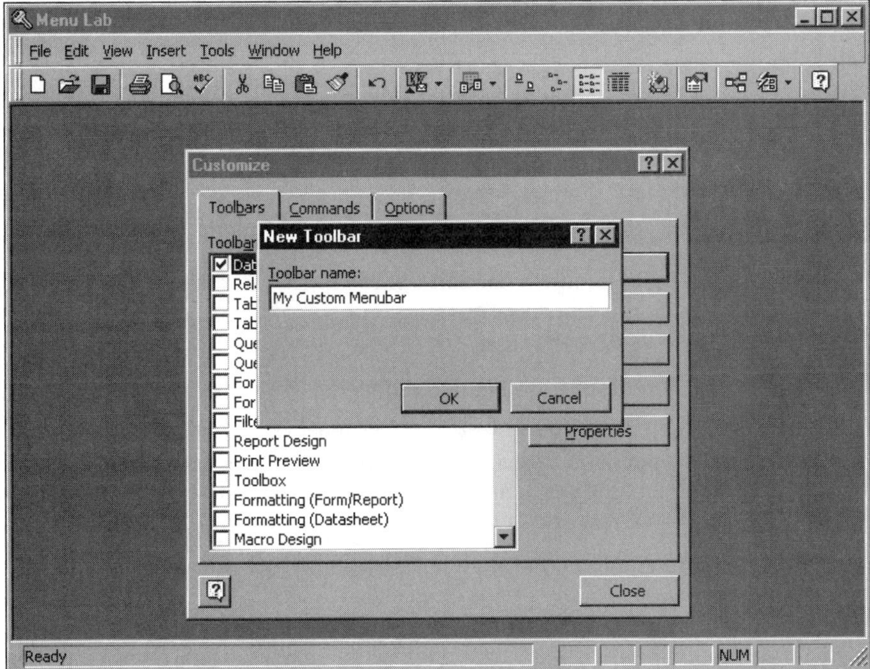

Figure 9-7: The first step to creating a custom command bar is to give it a name.

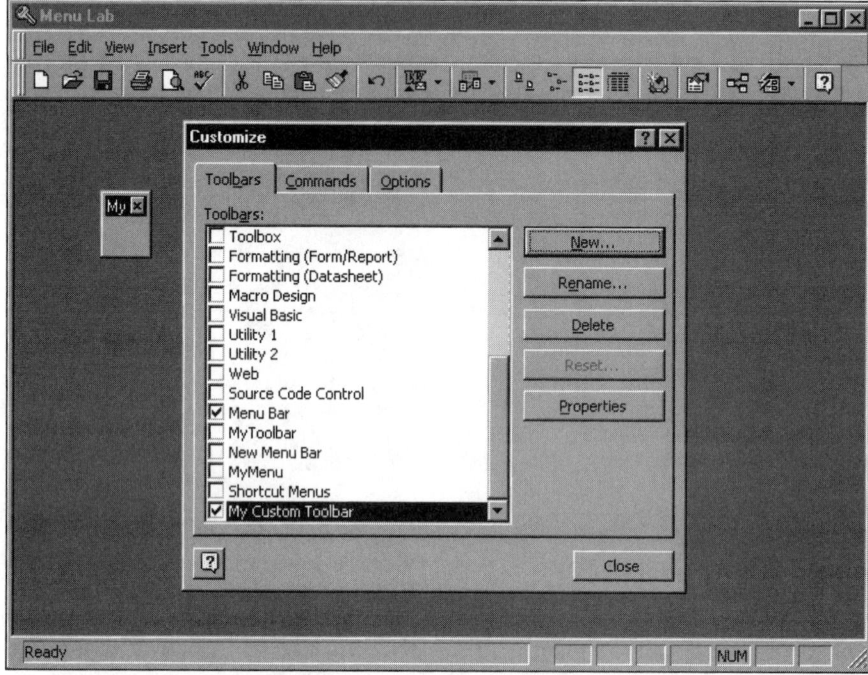

Figure 9-8: A new command bar appears, floating and empty.

Setting a command bar's Type: Toolbar, Menu, or Popup

By default, all new command bars are toolbars. To turn a command bar into a menu, you edit its properties; specifically, you set its `Type` property. To change a command bar to a menu, follow these steps:

1. Select the new command bar from the list on the Toolbars tab.
2. Click on the Properties button in the Customize dialog box to display the properties for the command bar (see Figure 9-9). If the desired custom command bar is not selected in the drop-down list of the Toolbar Properties dialog box, you must select it.
3. Change the command bar's `Type` property from `Toolbox` to `Menu`.

Figure 9-9: You can change the default toolbar to a menu by changing its Type property.

In addition to `Type`, a number of other properties affect your menu bar. The following properties of a menu bar appear in the Toolbar Properties dialog box:

- **Docking.** Determines if and how your menu may be docked.
- **Show on Toolbars Menu.** Determines whether your menu appears on the View⇨Toolbars submenu.
- **Allow Customizing.** You can prevent users from changing the menu by deselecting this checkbox.
- **Allow Resizing.** Determines whether users can resize the menu.
- **Allow Moving.** Determines whether users can move the menu.
- **Allow Showing/Hiding.** Determines whether users can show and hide the menu.

When you are satisfied with the property settings, click on Close to save the changes and close the Toolbar Properties dialog box.

Creating submenus

New command bars are always blank. The only items you should add to menu bars are *submenus.* Submenus are the drop-down menus that appear when a user selects an item on the main menu bar. To create a submenu for your new menu bar, click on the Commands tab of the Customize dialog box and then select New Menu from the Categories list (see Figure 9-10). From the Commands tab, drag the text `New Menu` in the Commands box and drop it on your custom menu. A submenu is then created with the name New Menu (see Figure 9-11).

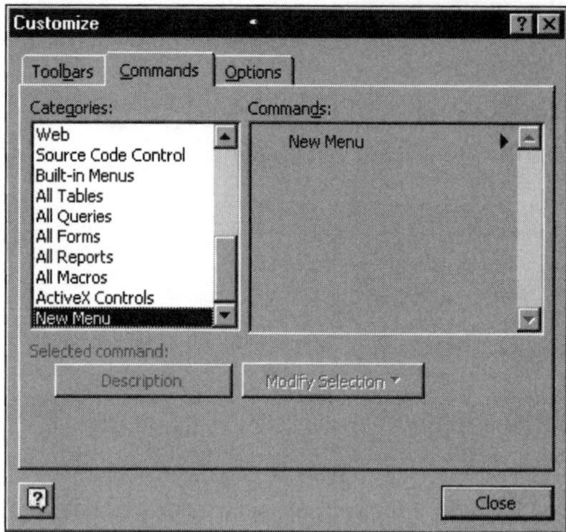

Figure 9-10: Creating submenus is tricky if you don't know the proper way to do it.

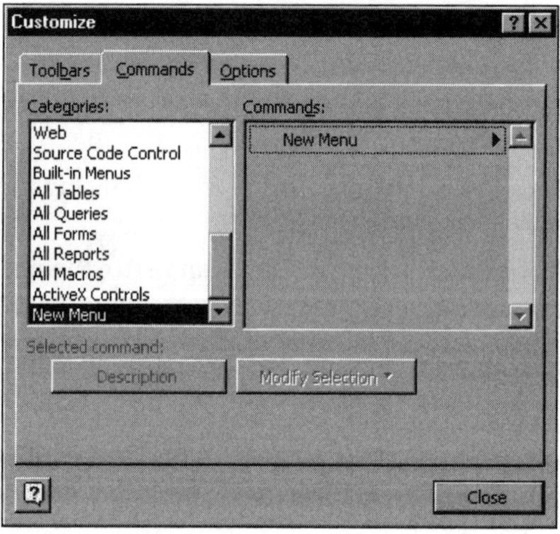

Figure 9-11: You can create as many submenus as you like by dragging the text New Menu and dropping it on your menu.

After you add a submenu to a menu bar, you cannot change it to a toolbar or popup menu.

Submenus have a set of properties, just as menu bars do. To change the properties of a submenu, right-click on the submenu and select Properties to display the Properties dialog box (see Figure 9-12). You can modify the following properties of a submenu:

- **Caption.** The `Caption` property is the text that is displayed for the submenu. In this example, it has been changed to `File`.
- **ToolTip.** The ToolTip is the text displayed in a yellow popup balloon when the user positions the pointer over the menu caption and leaves it there for a few seconds.
- **On Action.** You can call a macro or a function when the submenu is selected. Leave this field blank for submenus, and fill it in for items appearing on the submenus.
- **Help File.** The `Help File` property is where you designate the name of a custom Help file (if any) that is to be called if the user presses F1 with the submenu selected.
- **Help ContextID.** If you specify a Help file, the `Help ContextID` property is used to specify which help topic in the custom Help file is displayed when the user presses F1 while the submenu is selected.
- **Parameter.** This parameter is passed to the function specified in the `On Action` property, if any.
- **Tag.** The `Tag` is an optional text property that is not used by Access itself but that you can reference in event procedures. Tags are essentially string variables, and your application may store information in the Tag property to be recalled at any time.

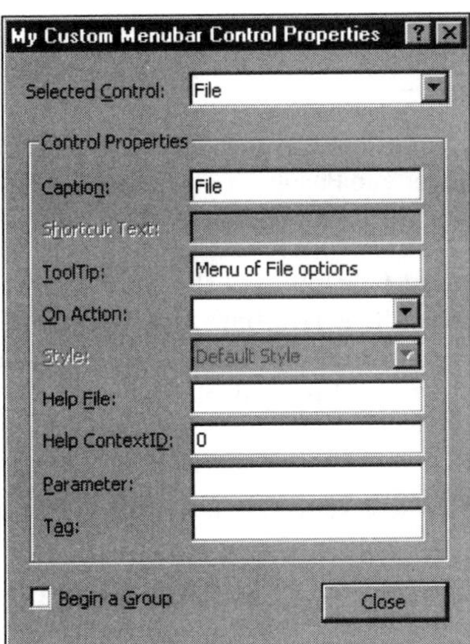

Figure 9-12: Submenu properties differ from the properties of menu bars.

When you are satisfied with the properties for the selected submenu, click on Close to save the properties and close the Properties dialog box.

Creating shortcut menus

Shortcut menus are menus that appear when you right-click on an object. You probably already take advantage of shortcut menus in many applications, including the design environment of Access. You can now give your application's users this valuable time-saver.

You can assign shortcut menus to forms. In addition, if you want, you can assign a different shortcut menu to every control on a form.

You create shortcut menus the same way you create standard menus: by first creating a new command bar and then changing its `Type` property. After you have created a new command bar, setting its `Type` property to `Popup` makes it a shortcut menu. When you change the `Type` property to `Popup`, the message in Figure 9-13 appears.

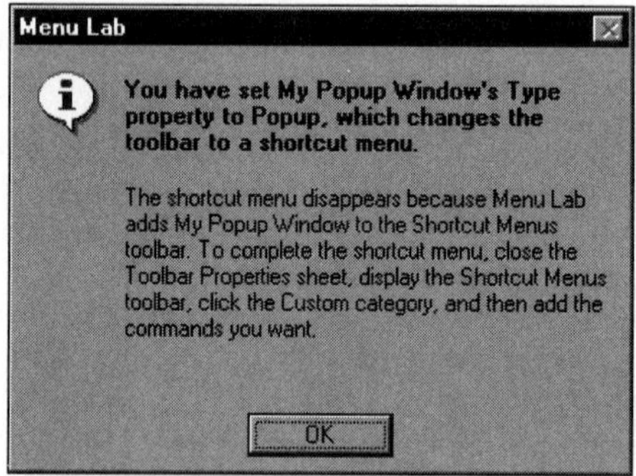

Figure 9-13: Shortcut menus do not appear as ordinary menus, and you are warned of this when you set a command bar's Type property to Popup.

To view or edit a submenu, you must first display the Shortcut Menus toolbar by selecting its checkmark on the Toolbars tab or by double-clicking on it in the list (see Figure 9-14). Custom shortcut menus that you create appear under the Custom menu item on the right of the Shortcut Menus toolbar.

Adding command items to menus and toolbars

The final step to creating a new menu or toolbar is to add command items. You add items to the submenu by using the Commands tab of the Customize dialog box.

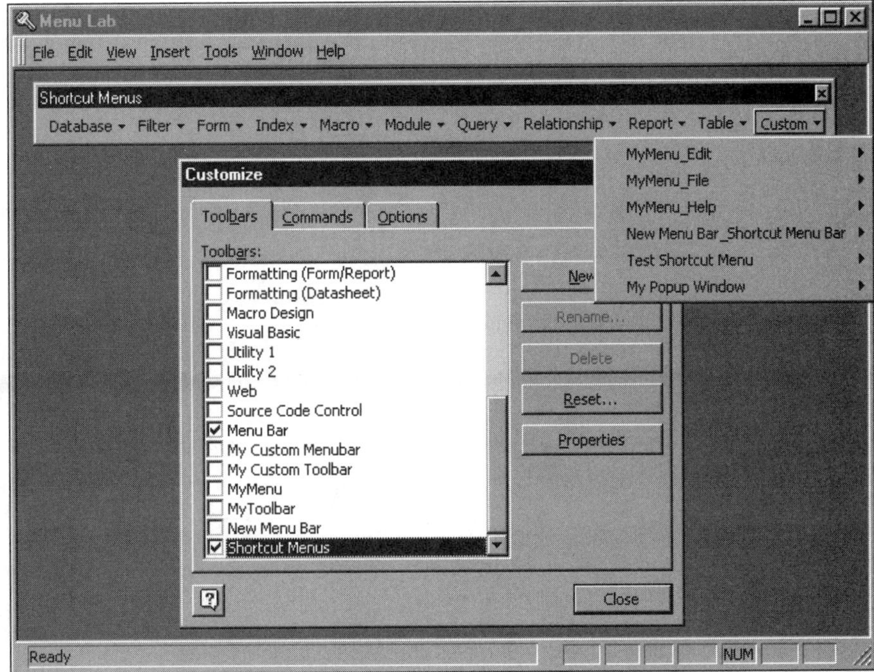

Figure 9-14: You edit all shortcut menus on the Shortcut Menus toolbar.

The Commands tab (refer to Figure 9-11) consists primarily of two elements:

- A category list
- A view of commands for the selected category

The Categories list shows all available command categories, such as Form and Query Design. When you select a category, Access displays all the available commands for that category. In addition to the standard categories, you also receive the opportunity to display all tables, queries, forms, reports, and macros. This makes it easy to execute a macro or open a form, for example, directly from a menu or toolbar.

To add a command to a menu or toolbar, first select the category that contains the command you want to add to the toolbar. When the desired command is displayed in the Commands box, drag the command to the menu or toolbar. When you are dragging an item over a menu or toolbar, an I-beam cursor is displayed where the command would be placed if you dropped it. When you are satisfied with the location of the I-beam cursor, release the mouse button to drop the command in place.

To place a command on a submenu, first drag the command over the caption of the submenu to force the submenu to open. Then position the cursor over the drop-down portion of the submenu and drop the item by releasing the mouse button. If you drop the item appropriately, it appears as an item on the submenu, as shown in Figure 9-15.

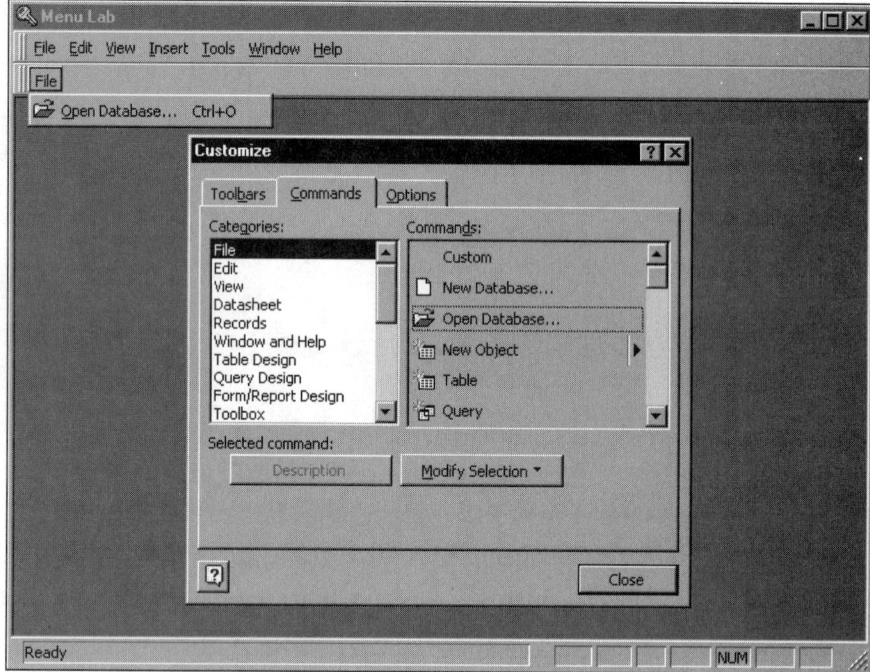

Figure 9-15: Dropping commands on submenus creates instant menu items.

Another way to add a command to a menu or toolbar is simply to drag an object from the Database window. For example, to open a form by clicking on a toolbar button, simply drag that form from the Database window to the desired toolbar.

After a command is added to a menu or toolbar, you alter its properties and appearance by using its shortcut menu displayed by right-clicking on the command item (see Figure 9-16). To display the shortcut menu for a command item, right-click on the item in question. If the command item appears on a submenu, click once on the submenu caption to display the submenu, and then right-click on the command item in question. Figure 9-17 shows the properties for the Open Database command that was dragged to a submenu.

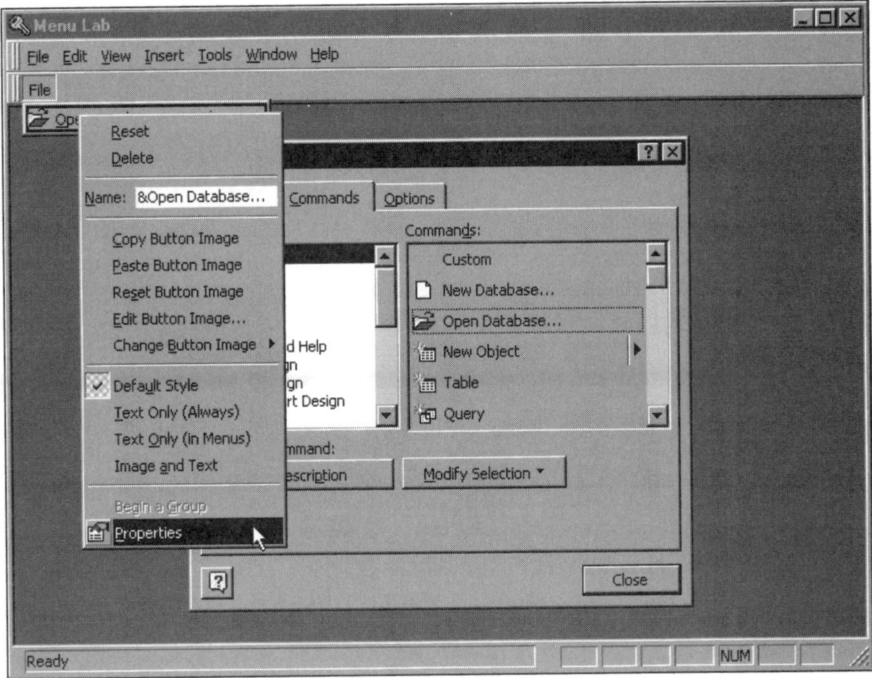

Figure 9-16: Command items have additional features that are not available for submenus and menu bars.

Custom Popup 1 Control Properties

Selected Control: &Open Database...

Control Properties

Caption:	&Open Database...
Shortcut Text:	Ctrl+O
ToolTip:	&Open Database...
On Action:	
Style:	Default Style
Help File:	ACTIP80.HLP
Help ContextID:	8195
Parameter:	
Tag:	

☐ Begin a Group   Close

Figure 9-17: When you drag and drop an Access command on a menu, toolbar, or submenu, many of the command's properties are filled in for you.

Removing command items from a menu or toolbar

To remove a command item, simply drag the desired command item from one toolbar to the Access desktop or the Customize dialog box. If you drag a command item and drop it on another toolbar, the toolbar button is removed from the original toolbar and placed on the toolbar you dropped it on. This also works for menu bars, and items can be dragged from menu bars to toolbars and from toolbars to menu bars as well.

Obviously, you can drag command items only when you are in Customize mode. If you attempt to drag an item during normal operation, you simply trigger the command to execute.

Moving command items on a menu or toolbar

You should always attempt to place command items into logical groups. You can move command items on a menu or toolbar or move items from one command bar to another. Microsoft Word, for example, separates paragraph alignment buttons from text formatting buttons. To move a command item on a menu or toolbar, with the Customize dialog box displayed, drag the command item to the desired location. To move a command item from one command bar to another, drag the item to the location on the new command bar where you want to move the item.

As just stated, command items are often placed into logical groups; all items belonging to the same group are displayed flush with each other; a separator is used between items of different groups. To create a separator space between two items, display the properties for the item that is to start a new group and then select the Begin a Group checkbox.

Calling a function from a command item

In Access 95, you could only call macros from menu and toolbar items. Now, you can call functions from command items by entering an equal sign (=) and the name of the function in the `On Action` property of the command item. If the procedure you are calling is expecting a parameter to be passed with it, enter the parameter in the `Parameter` field. Also, return values are ignored.

You cannot call procedures declared as `Sub` from the `On Action` property; you can only call procedures declared with `Function`. To call a function, enter the following text in the `On Action` field:

```
=functionname()
```

Adding ToolTips to command items

Every command item can display a ToolTip. ToolTips are floating "balloon help" that appear when a user places the pointer over an object and leaves it there for a few seconds. To change the ToolTip of a command item, follow these steps:

1. Open the shortcut menu of the command item for which you want to set the ToolTip.
2. Select Properties.
3. Type the toolbar button's ToolTip help in the ToolTip field.
4. Click on Close to accept your changes.

Tip

A shortcut to accessing the Customize dialog box is to right-click on any toolbar and select Customize.

Changing button faces on menus and toolbars

You can give your application a distinct look and feel by changing the images displayed for menu and toolbar items. Although it can be a great deal of fun to create very customized toolbars, you should refrain from reinventing the wheel. If a command item performs a function that is standard among many applications, such as a Save function, you should use its standard image. Although you may have a better image for a Save button than the standard image of a diskette, you should constantly be thinking about *what your users expect.* Remember: You are not entering an art show. The primary purpose of menus and toolbars is to make your application easier and more intuitive to use. The standard Save toolbar button image is used in every product in the Microsoft Office suite and throughout most other commercial applications. When you must create custom toolbar buttons that are not standard, by all means be creative; put on your artist's cap and have fun. However, always remember that your toolbar images should be intuitive to the user. Design images that make their functions obvious.

There are three methods for customizing the image of a command item (toolbar button):

- Copy and paste an image by using the Clipboard.
- Select a bitmap from Access's supplied images.
- Design an image using the built-in Button Editor.

You access all these methods by the shortcut menu for each command item. To display the shortcut menu of a command item you want to edit, right-click on the command item (see Figure 9-18).

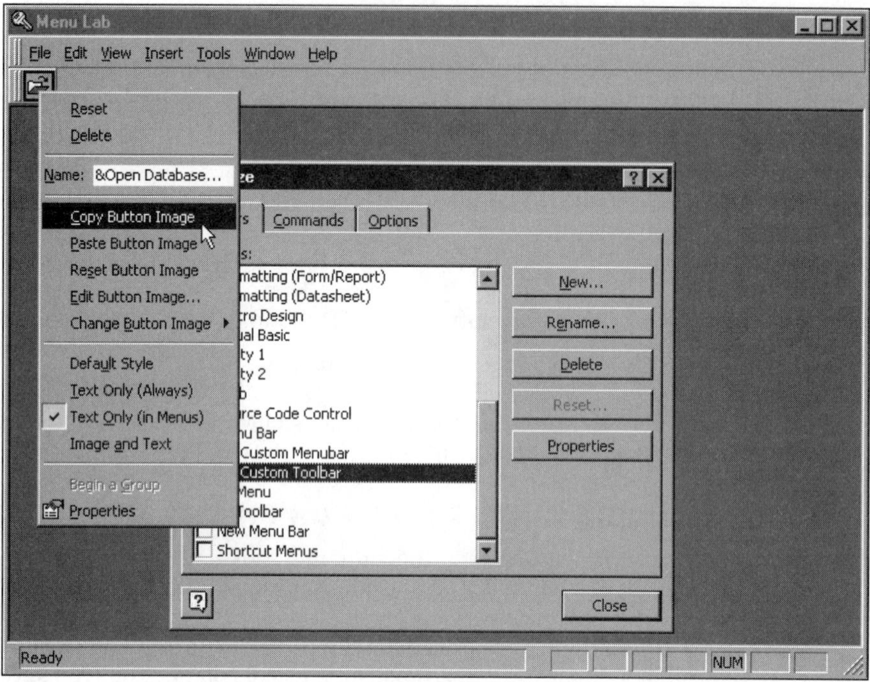

Figure 9-18: You can change a toolbar button's image by using its shortcut menu.

Copy and paste an image by using the Clipboard

You can use the Windows 95 Clipboard to transfer a bitmap from an image editing application to a toolbar button in your Access application. To use the Clipboard to transfer an image, do the following:

1. Display the image in the graphics editor of your choice.
2. Use the editor's function to copy the image to the Clipboard.
3. Open the shortcut menu of the command item you want to change.
4. Select Paste Button Image.

You also can copy the image from one command item to another. To do this, follow these steps:

1. Open the shortcut menu of the command item from which you want to copy the image.
2. Select Copy Button Image.
3. Open the shortcut menu of the command item you want to change.
4. Select Paste Button Image.

If you paste an image to a button and decide that is really not what you wanted to do, you can undo the paste, as follows:

1. Open the shortcut menu of the toolbar button where you want to undo the paste.
2. Select Reset Button Image.

The button is reset to its original image.

If you paste an image that is larger than the command item, Access automatically scales the image to the button. This can create undesired effects such as distorting the picture.

Select from supplied bitmaps

Access contains a library of 42 toolbar button images that you can assign to your command items. To select an image from this library of button images, follow these steps:

1. Open the shortcut menu of the command item whose image you want to change.
2. Select Change Button Image. The Change Button Image submenu appears, as illustrated in Figure 9-19.
3. Select the desired image by clicking on it.

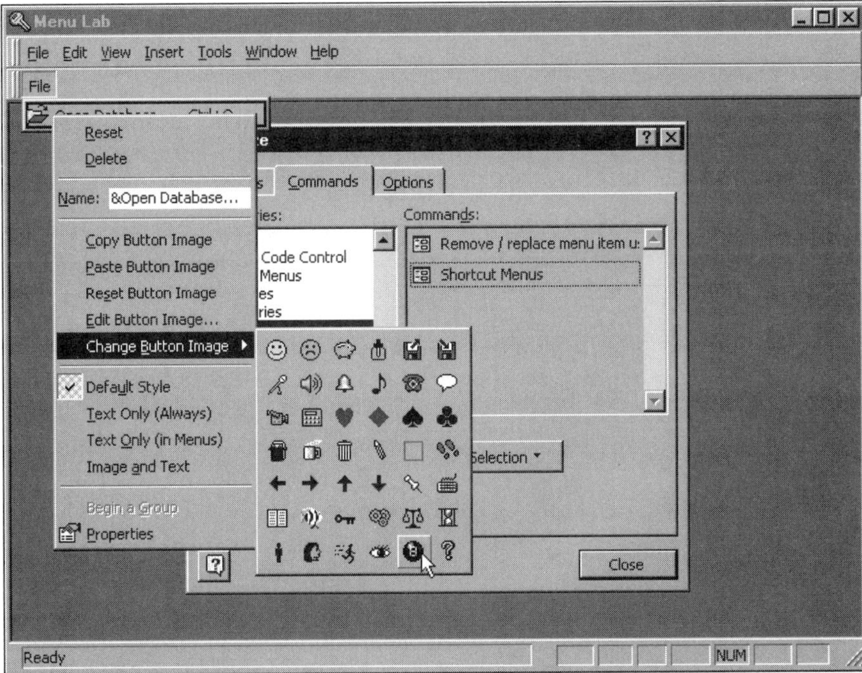

Figure 9-19: The Change Button Image menu enables you to select an image from Access's small image library.

One sorely missed function that has yet to be addressed by Access is the capability to load an image from a file just as you do for a command button. To load an image from a file, open the image in an image editor (such as Windows 95 Paintbrush), copy the image to the Clipboard, and then paste the image to the command item.

To reset a command item to its original image after you have selected an image from the Change Button Image library, do the following:

1. Open the shortcut menu of the command item where you want to undo the paste.
2. Select Reset Button Image.

Using the built-in Button Editor

The third way to change a button image is to use the built-in Button Editor that is included with Access. To use the Button Editor, you do the following:

1. Open the shortcut menu of the command item that you want to change.
2. Select Edit Button Image. The Button Editor is shown in Figure 9-20.

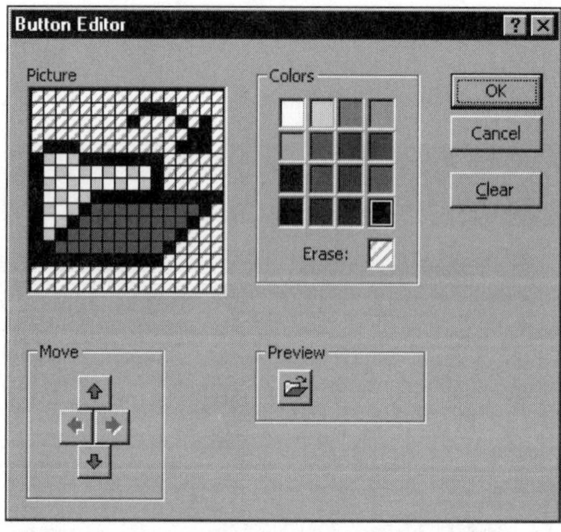

Figure 9-20: The Access Button Editor enables you to design your own buttons.

The Button Editor is a very basic image editor. It consists of four sections:

- An enlarged picture of the button
- A color palette
- A full-size button preview
- Move buttons that shift the image

To edit a button image, click on the color that you want to paint with in the color palette, and then draw on the exploded view of the button by dragging with the left mouse button. The preview section continuously shows you how your changes make the button look at normal size. You can use the Move buttons to shift the entire button image up, down, left, or right. To clear the button image and start from scratch, click on the Clear button. When you have finished making changes to the image, click on OK to use the edited image on your toolbar button, or click on Cancel to leave the toolbar button the way it was before you started editing the image.

Use images of text *only* when absolutely necessary. An example of when text on a button is appropriate is the text formatting buttons in Word, where a letter B is shown in bold to boldface selected text, a letter I is shown in italics to italicize selected text, and so forth.

If you want to start your new image design with an existing image from a standard toolbar button, do the following:

1. Add the command item to a toolbar.
2. Use the Button Editor to change the command item's image.
3. Copy the changed image to the desired command item. After you have copied the image to the desired command item, you can delete the original command item.

Giving a command item a hot key

Every command item on each submenu should have a *hot key*. A hot key is a character in the name of an item that appears underlined, and executes the menu item immediately when a user presses the character while the submenu is displayed. The hot key must be unique for the submenu it is on, but the hot key may be used on other submenus. For example, you can assign the hot key P to both Print on the File menu, and Paste on the Edit menu, but you cannot define P as the hot key for both Print and Page Setup on the File menu. The hot key need not be the first character of the menu item, so you could use the A of Page Setup as a hot key to prevent duplicate hot keys under one menu. In addition, you should assign only one hot key to a menu item. To make a character of the caption a hot key, prefix the character with an ampersand & (Shift+7). Refer to Figure 9-21 for an example of hot keys.

The three types of keyboard shortcuts

Windows menus have three different types of shortcuts: access keys, hot keys, and shortcut keys. *Access keys* open a pull-down menu when used in conjunction with the Alt key. *Hot keys* enable you to select a menu item from an open pull-down menu with the touch of a single key. Both access keys and hot keys are denoted by an underlined character on the menu item. *Shortcut keys* are keyboard shortcuts for often-used menu items and are active at all times. A shortcut key may be a single keystroke, such as the Delete key, or it may be a combination of Shift, Ctrl, or Alt with a single key; Ctrl+X is a common shortcut key for selecting Edit⇨Cut. Shortcut keys are displayed at the right of their corresponding menu item. All these keyboard shortcuts are discussed in detail in this chapter.

Top-level menu item hot keys are called *access keys*. You can open a pull-down top-level menu item by pressing the Alt key and the menu item's access key at the same time. For example, you can press Alt+F to open the Access File pull-down menu. After the File menu is displayed, you can press the hot key of any menu items that are displayed.

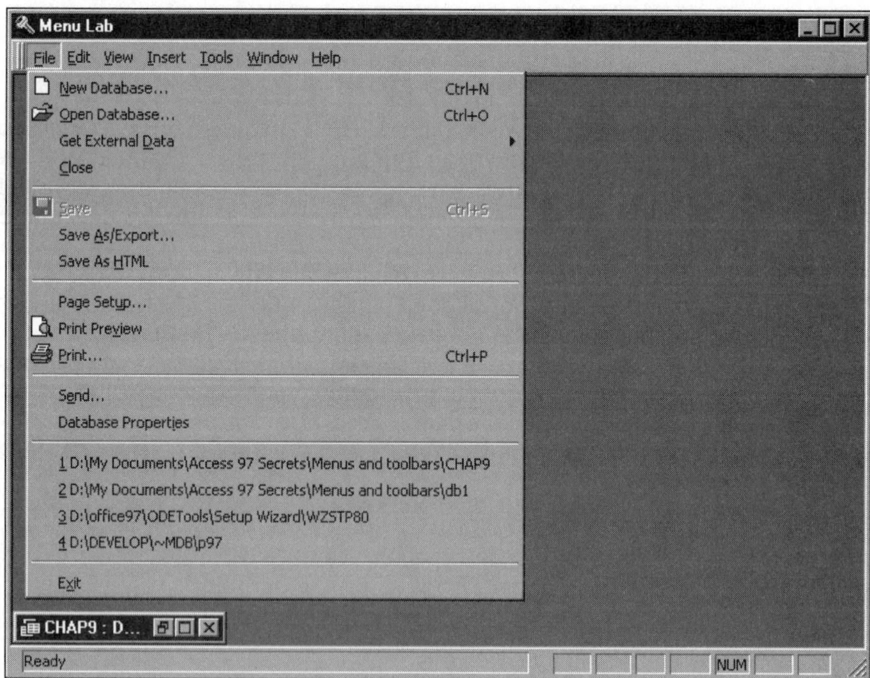

Figure 9-21: The Access File menu. Each menu item has a hot key.

Attaching command bars to forms and reports

After you have created your custom menus and toolbars, you must attach them to their corresponding forms and reports. Attaching menus and toolbars to forms and reports is a simple matter of setting the `Menu Bar`, `Toolbar`, or `Shortcut Menu Bar` property for each form and report. Figure 9-22 shows the property sheet of a form that uses MyMenu as its menu bar. When you set a form's `Toolbar`, `Menu Bar`, or `Shortcut Menu Bar` property, the designated command bar replaces the default that Access would ordinarily display.

Secret

Most people don't realize this, but you can add a custom menu to a report. The menu is shown when the form is displayed in Print Preview (see Figure 9-23). To add a custom menu to a report, open the report in design view and set its `Menu Bar` property just as explained above for forms.

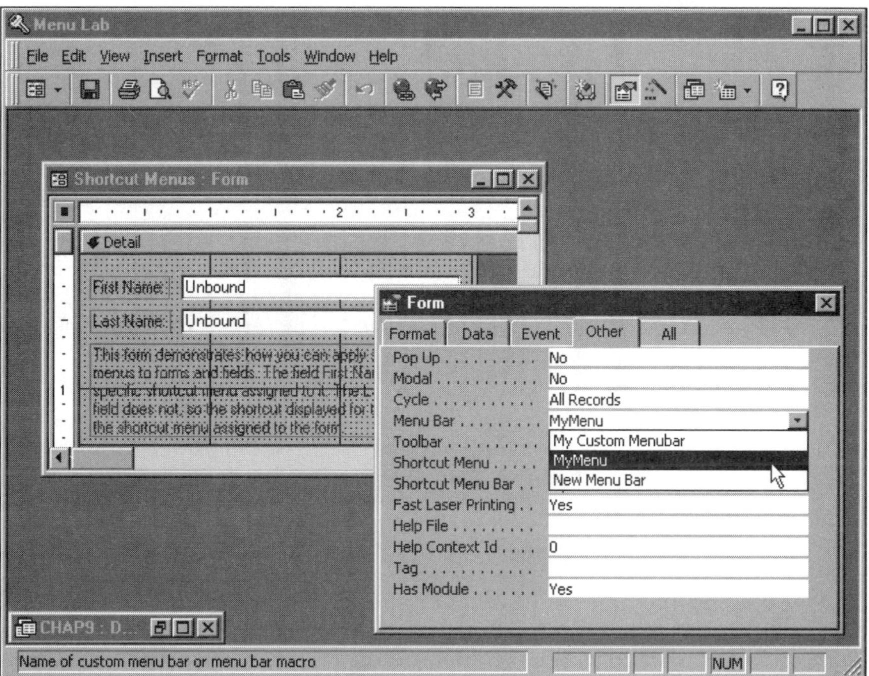

Figure 9-22: Setting the menu bar for the form Shortcut Menus to MyMenu.

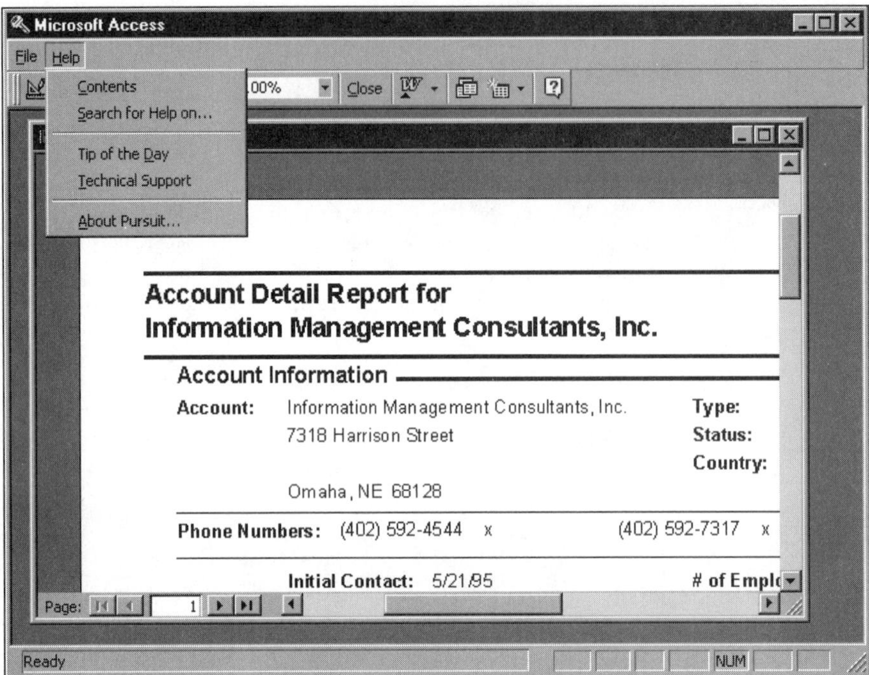

Figure 9-23: A report shown in Print Preview with a custom menu.

Not only can you set toolbars and menus at design time, you can also change the menu or toolbar of a form at run time by using VBA code. For example, if you wanted to change the menu bar of form frmCustomer to My Other Menu, you enter a line of code like this:

```
frmCustomer.Menubar = "My Other Menu"
```

If you want to set a form's menu bar to Access's default menu bar or to the default menu bar you designated in the Setup dialog box, set the `Menu Bar` property to " " as follows:

```
frmCustomer.Menubar = ""
```

You may want to have different menu bars for a form if the menu needs dramatic changes at run time. For minor changes to the menu bar, however, you should use the techniques described later in this chapter.

Note

In order for shortcut menus to be displayed for a form or objects on a form (see Figure 9-24), you must set the form's `Shortcut Menu` property to `Yes`. If this property is set to `No`, shortcut menus will not be displayed, regardless of the shortcut menu assignments you have made to the form and its reports.

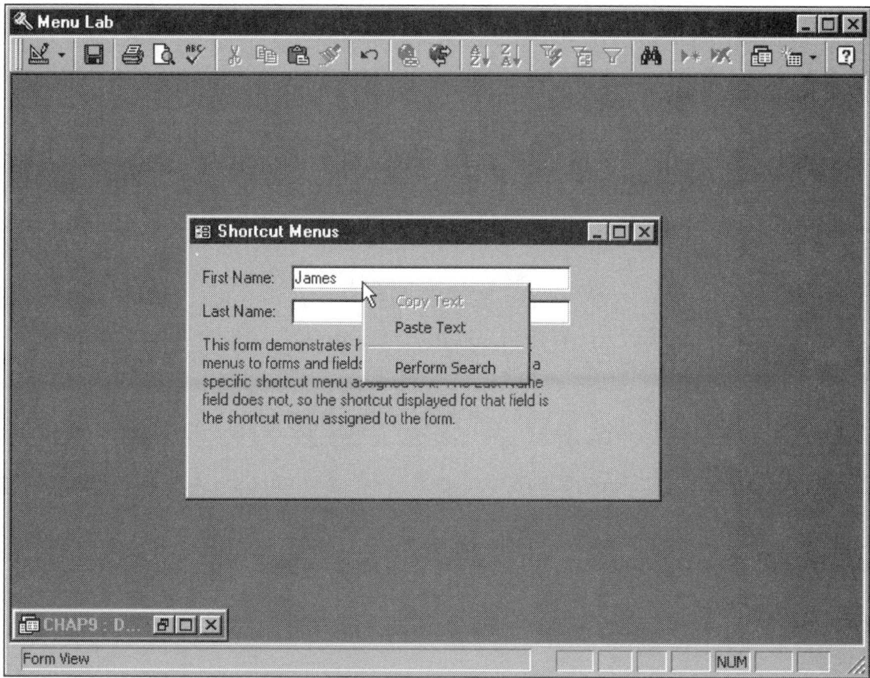

Figure 9-24: Shortcut menus help application users get their jobs done faster.

Tip

If you do not specify a shortcut menu to use for a form that has shortcut menus enabled, Access displays its own default shortcut menus. If you are planning to add shortcut menus to your application, create a default shortcut menu for the form and then create specific shortcut menus for each control. If you do this, you can ensure that users will never see a default shortcut menu when they right-click on a control that does not have its own shortcut menu assigned.

Creating Menu Accelerator Keys with Key Assignment Macros

Although menu access keys (the keys that open pull-down menus when combined with the Alt key) and menu item hot keys (the shortcut keys for selecting a menu item from an open pull-down menu) make it easy to select a menu item, power users are always looking for faster shortcuts. To make your application as efficient as possible, you need to give your users the ability to select commonly used items with one key or key combination: a shortcut key.

Unlike menu item hot keys, which are only active while a pull-down menu is open, shortcut keys, or *accelerator keys,* are active at all times that the menu or toolbar is visible. A shortcut key may be one key, such as the Delete key, or it may be a key combined with Shift, Ctrl, or Alt. Unlike hot keys that should be assigned to every menu item, shortcut keys need to be assigned only to the most frequently selected menu items. Shortcut keys are shown on pull-down menus to the right of their corresponding menu items. You can specify the text for a shortcut key by setting the `Shortcut Text` property for the command item. Note, however, that this text is display only. To implement shortcut keys, you need to use the Autokeys techniques described in this chapter. See Figure 9-25 for an example of how Access assigns shortcut keys used for commonly selected menu items.

Creating intuitive shortcut keys

Microsoft offers a program where applications can be certified as Microsoft Office Compatible. All Microsoft Office Compatible applications share three characteristics:

- Common menu structures
- Common toolbar structures
- Common shortcut key definitions

For an application to be certified Microsoft Office Compatible, it not only needs to have shortcut keys, but the shortcut keys must also be consistent with the other Microsoft Office products. For example, if you have a Print menu item, you must use the Ctrl+P shortcut key. Even if you don't plan on submitting your application for Office Compatibility certification, you should still attempt to use the same shortcut keys as Office, where applicable. This consistency lowers the learning curve for your application and helps your users become more productive in less time.

Adding shortcut keys to your application should be simple; unfortunately, it's not. Although it is a common request, Microsoft has yet to properly address the issue of shortcut keys. Currently, it is a tedious chore in Access because it involves using numerous AutoKeys macros. Autokeys macros let you assign macros to key combinations; when the user presses a defined key combination while in your database, the assigned macro is executed. You probably will want to add shortcut keys only to small applications or commercial applications that you plan to release on a large scale. Figure 9-25 shows an example of a simple AutoKeys macro.

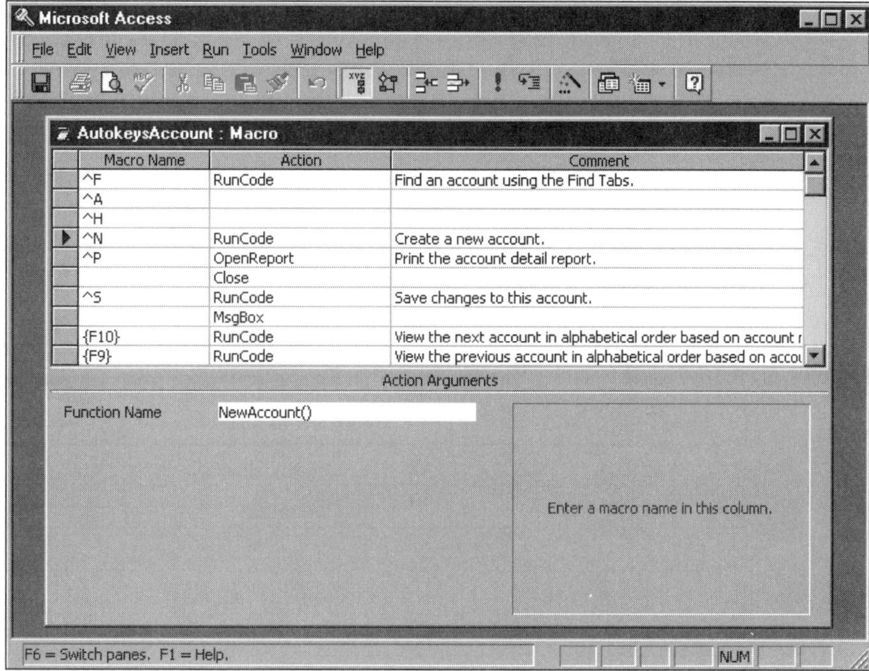

Figure 9-25: A simple AutoKeys macro.

Adding shortcut keys to your application

Adding shortcut keys requires these three steps:

1. Create an AutoKeys macro for every menu used in your application. If two forms use identical menus, you need to create only one AutoKeys macro.
2. Add the shortcut keys to the text of their corresponding menu items by setting the items' `Shortcut Text` properties.
3. Add code to your forms' `On Activate` events that tells Access which AutoKeys macro to use for each form.

Each AutoKeys macro needs to contain a definition of every shortcut key that can be selected on a form. To create an AutoKeys macro, make sure that the `Names` property is visible in Design mode of the Macro window, and then enter a key combination for each accelerator key in the `Names` property; use one macro for each accelerator key.

Tip

Here's another good reason to have your custom menu items execute functions rather than call macros. While using AutoKeys macros to create accelerator keys, changes of a menu item's action must also be made to the

AutoKeys macro. If you use macro actions, you need to change them in the `On Action` property of the command item and in the corresponding AutoKeys macro. If your menu items and AutoKeys macro items call the same function, however, changes made to that function are applied to both the menu items and the accelerator keys.

Table 9-1 shows the key combinations you can use to make key assignments in an AutoKeys macro group. These key combinations are a subset of the syntax used in the `SendKeys` statement in Visual Basic. In the following table, ^= Ctrl, + = Shift, and % = Alt.

Table 9-1 Valid AutoKeys Combinations

SendKeys Syntax	*Key Combination*
^ A or ^ 4	Ctrl + any letter or number key
^ {F1}	Any function key
{F1}	Ctrl + any function key
+{F1}	Shift + any function key
{INSERT}	Ins
^ {INSERT}	Ctrl+Ins
+{INSERT}	Shift+Ins
{DELETE} or {DEL}	Del
^ {DELETE} or ^ {DEL}	Ctrl+Del
+{DELETE} or +{DEL}	Shift+Del

If you assign a set of actions to a key combination that is already being used by Access (for example, Ctrl+C for Copy), the actions you assign this key combination replace the Access key assignment. Some keys, such as PgUp and PgDn, still are not trappable in Access for Windows 95.

Tip

If you precede your AutoKeys macro group names with AK, they are easier to track and manage. For example, you may give an AutoKeys macro group for form MyCustomers the name AK_MyCustomers. This keeps all AutoKeys macros together in the Database Window so that you can easily identify them in the list.

Synchronizing the AutoKeys macros with your forms

After creating your AutoKeys macros and setting the `Shortcut Text` property for all corresponding menu items, you must synchronize each AutoKeys macro group with each form as it is displayed. Unfortunately,

Access does not let you set an AutoKeys macro property for a form the way you can assign a menu, so you must do this with Visual Basic code.

Access allows only one AutoKeys macro to be in effect at any given time. If you name a macro AutoKeys, it is used as the default AutoKeys macro when your application first starts. In Access 2.0, you can specify any macro as the default AutoKeys macro in the Options dialog box under Keyboard settings. As of Access 95, you no longer can do this. Hopefully, Microsoft will add this property to the Startup options in a future release.

You can change the macro that is used as the AutoKeys macro by using the `SetOption` method of the `Application` object. To synchronize your AutoKeys macros with your forms, you need to change the AutoKeys macro each time a form is activated. Figure 9-26 shows the code that changes the AutoKeys macro to the AutoKeys Account macro when the from Accounts form is activated. Whenever you designate a macro as the AutoKeys macro, it remains as the AutoKeys macro, even after the form that executed the code is closed. Therefore, you must apply one or both of the following techniques:

- Set the proper AutoKeys macro in the `On Activate` event of each form.
- Reset the AutoKeys macro to a default macro when a form is closed.

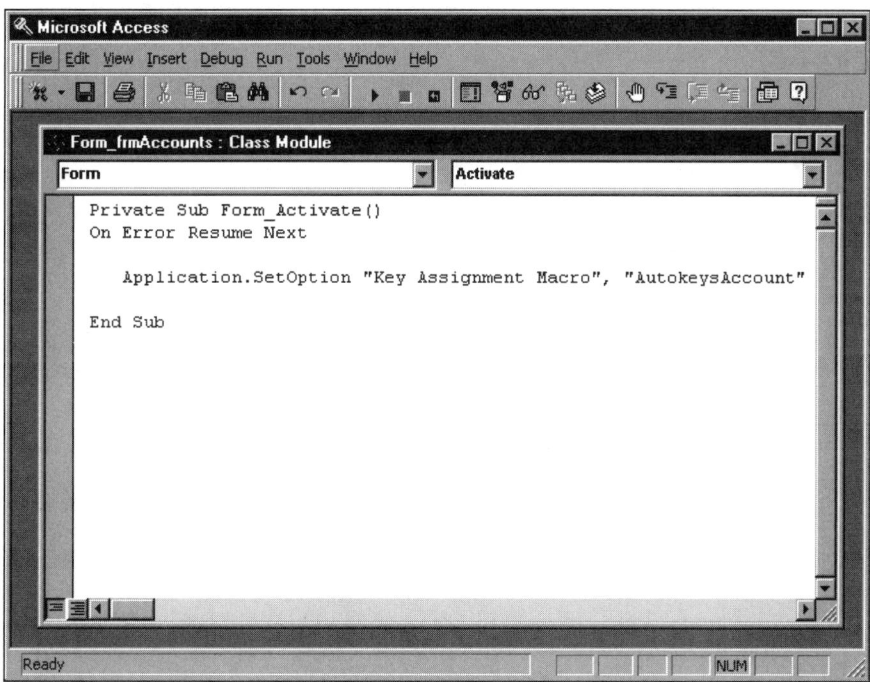

Figure 9-26: Code used in a form's On Activate event to designate AutoKeys Account as the AutoKeys macro.

Customizing Access's Built-In Command Bars

You can customize Access's built-in command bars in the same manner as you customize custom command bars. To customize an existing command bar, follow these steps:

1. Select View➪Toolbars➪Customize.
2. Display the command bar you want to customize, if it is not already displayed, by selecting the checkbox next to the command bar in the list on the Toolbars tab of the Customize dialog box.
3. Make your desired changes, as described in "Creating custom command bars."

Manipulating Menu and Toolbar Command Items

Just as it is important to create well-planned menus and toolbars, it is also important for your menus and toolbars to adjust dynamically to such events as user input and changes of your application's state. In Access 2.0, it was possible only to change menus by using program calls to the Windows API. Access 95 added some new menu-controlling macros but still required API calls to perform some functions. Now, you have complete control over items on menus and toolbars.

Enabling and disabling menu and toolbar items

The change you probably will make most often to your menu and toolbar items is enabling and disabling them. You disable an item while the function accessed from that item is currently unavailable. For example, if your menu or toolbar item is New Record, you disable the item while the form with this menu bar is positioned at a new record.

You no longer need to use macros to set certain characteristics of command items on menus and toolbars. Using the `CommandBarControls` collection, you can access and manipulate each command item of a menu or toolbar.

The first step in manipulating a command item is to get a reference to the command bar containing the item. To create an object reference to a command bar, dimension a variable as `Object`, and set the variable to the command bar using the `CommandBars` function, as shown in the following example. This code references the command bar object whose name is passed as the szBarName parameter, and sets the control whose index is iIndex to the Enabled state equal to the bState parameter:

```
Public Function SetEnabledState(szBarName As String, iIndex As _
Integer, bState As Boolean)
On Error Resume Next          ' Every procedure should have
                              ' error handling code!
Dim cbar As Object

Set cbar = CommandBars(szBarName)

cbar.Controls(iIndex).Enabled = bState

End Function
```

The Commandbars() function accepts one argument, the command bar name. After you have referenced the command bar, you can use the Controls collection to iterate through each command item (control) on the command bar.

Unlike almost all collections in Visual Basic for Applications, the Controls collection is not zero based. To reference the first control of a command bar, you reference Commandbar.Control(1), not Commandbar.Control(0) as you would expect. You can determine the number of command items on a command bar by referencing the Control collection's Count property, as follows:

```
iCount = cbar.Controls.count
```

Hiding and showing menu and toolbar items

Hiding and showing items on menus used to take calls to the Windows API. Now, using the Controls collection of the command bar object, you can easily hide and show items by setting their Visible property. The following code accepts the same parameters as the code in the preceding example. This code, however, sets the control's Visible state rather than the enabled state:

```
Public Function SetVisibleState(szBarName As String, iIndex As _
Integer, bState As Boolean)
On Error Resume Next          ' Every procedure should have
                              ' error handling code!
Dim cbar As Object

Set cbar = CommandBars(szBarName)

cbar.Controls(iIndex).Visible = bState

End Function
```

Adding controls to a menu or toolbar at run time

In addition to referencing command items using the Controls collection of a command bar object, you can add new command items to a command bar as well. To add a new command item to a command bar, use the Add method of the CommandBarControls collection. For example, to add a new button to the command bar named "MyCustomToolbar" that calls the procedure MyFunction when selected, you use the following code:

```
Dim myBlankBtn as Object
Set myBlankBtn = CommandBars("MyCustomToolbar").Controls.Add

With myBlankBtn
     .Caption = "My New Button"
     .OnAction = "=MyFunction()"
End With
```

After you have created a new command item, you can change any or all of its properties as shown in the preceding two examples.

Using the Application Object to Hide and Show Command Bars

The Application object is an Access object that references your application. The Application object contains all Microsoft Access objects and collections, including the Forms collection, the Reports collection, the Screen object, and the DoCmd object. You can use the Application object to apply methods or property settings to your entire Access application. One of these properties is the Menubar property.

To see how Access uses different menus to help you perform different tasks, try this:

1. Open a form in Design view and look at the menu bar that is displayed.
2. Select the Database Explorer.

Did you notice how the menu bar changes when the Database Explorer gets the focus? Try selecting the form in design view again and watch the menu bar change. Although you cannot change these menus, it is possible to create new menus for the Application object. You may create these menus from scratch, or you can use existing menus as templates.

Controlling what menu the Application object displays

You can display custom menus for the `Application` object in two ways:

- Change the `Menu Bar` property of the Startup options for your database. You can access the `Startup` properties of a database by selecting Startup from the Tools menu of the Database window, or by right-clicking on the Database window itself (see Figure 9-27).

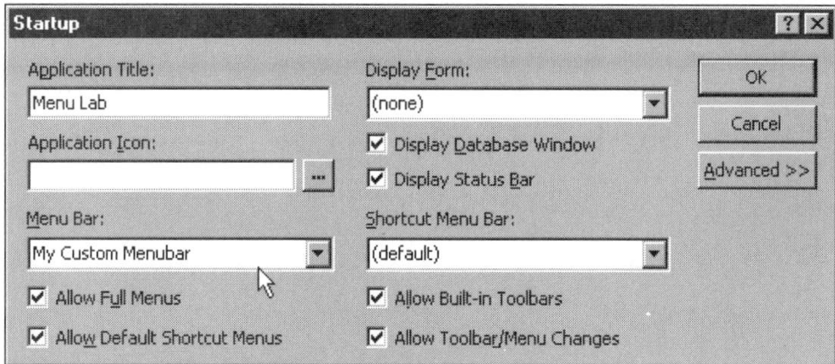

Figure 9-27: The Startup dialog box with a custom menu selected.

- Set the `Application.Menubar` property directly by using VBA code. Figure 9-28 shows code that displays the menu defined by the macro My Menu Bar Macro for the `Application` object. To set the `Application` object menu bar back to the default menu bar, set the property to a zero-length string.

Although you can change the `Application` object's menu to any custom menu you choose, you cannot cause the menu bar to change automatically like Access does. You must change the menu by using code every time you want a different menu to appear. You should set the `Application` object's menu to a generic custom menu when your application first starts, and then assign other custom menus to your forms and reports. To do this, it is best to set the Startup Menu Bar option to a generic custom menu, and then use VBA code if you need to change the Application's menu bar later. This makes your application's menus appear consistent at all times, whether or not the current form or report has its own custom menu defined.

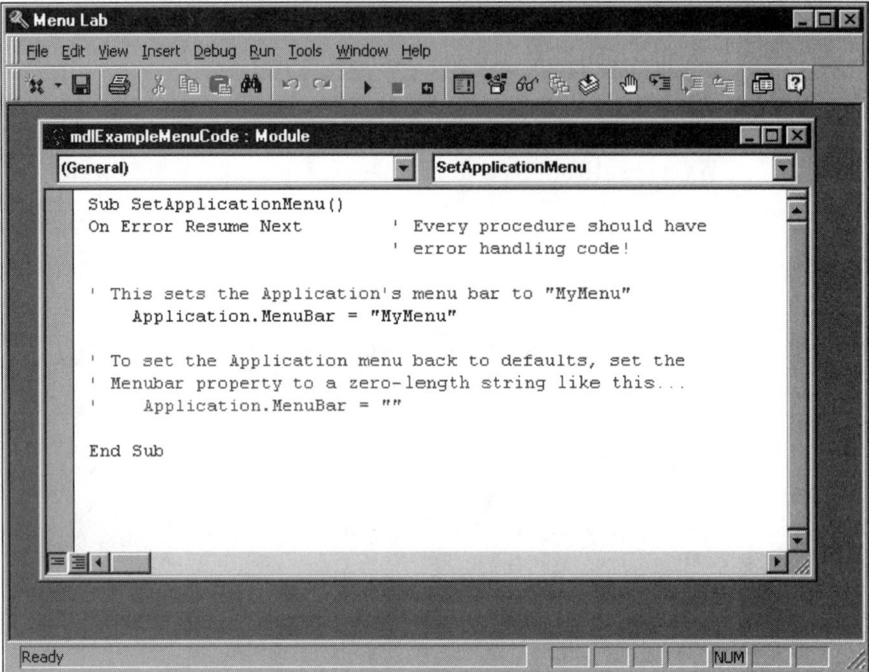

Figure 9-28: Code to change the Application object's menu bar.

Tip

By setting your `Application` object's menu to a standard custom menu, you prevent your users from ever getting a standard Access toolbar *if you hide the Database window.* This is important for most of your custom applications, because Access's standard menu bars contain more functionality than you probably want to give your users. When creating a default menu, use a simple menu structure, such as the following:

```
FILE
   Exit Application
HELP
   About Application
```

When a form or report gets the focus, its menu bar always overrides the `Application` object's menu bar.

Hiding and displaying toolbars

After you have defined all the toolbars for your application, you need to control when and which toolbars are displayed. Menus and toolbars attached to forms and reports automatically appear when the form or report is opened and then disappear when the form or report is closed. Toolbars can also be hidden or shown at any time by using the ShowToolbar macro action or the `ShowToolbar` method in Visual Basic code.

Hiding Access's built-in toolbars

When you are using a set of custom toolbars, the first thing you want to do is hide all of Access's built-in toolbars. To disable Access's built-in toolbars throughout your entire application, display the Startup dialog box by right-clicking on the Database window and then selecting Startup. On the Startup dialog box, uncheck the box that says Allow Built-in Toolbars.

The Allow Built-in Toolbars option is a property of the database. As such, you can turn built-in toolbars on or off at run time. The property name is `AllowBuiltinToolbars`. This property is not available until after it has been set once. Therefore, if you are writing code to modify this property, you need to include an error trap that detects whether the property does not yet exist and then create the property using VBA code. Figure 9-29 shows VBA code to manipulate this property.

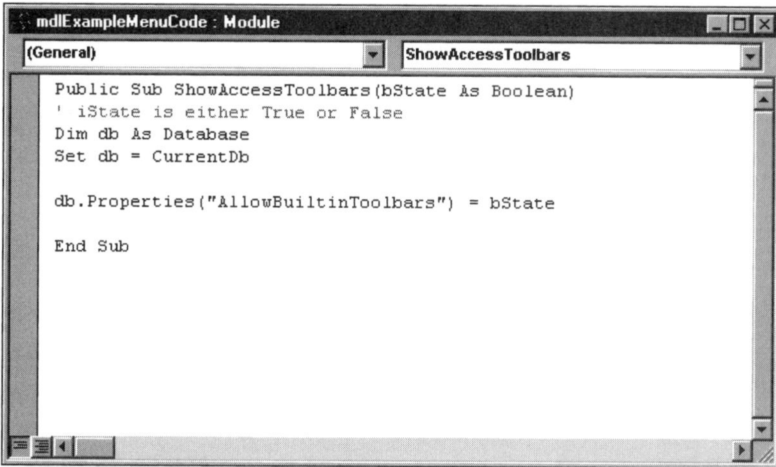
mdlExampleMenuCode : Module
(General)
ShowAccessToolbars
Public Sub ShowAccessToolbars(bState As Boolean)
' iState is either True or False
Dim db As Database
Set db = CurrentDb
db.Properties("AllowBuiltinToolbars") = bState
End Sub

Figure 9-29: Use this function to hide or show Access's built-in toolbars.

Secret

You can cause the `AllowBuiltinToolbars` property to become available by changing the setting in the Startup dialog box and then saving your change. After the value has been set, you can reference it in code.

Note

Changes to the `AllowBuiltinToolbars` setting do not take effect until Access is restarted.

You cannot turn off all built-in toolbars easily by using macros. To disable a toolbar using a macro, you use the `ShowToolbar` macro action. The `ShowToolbar` action enables you to manipulate only one toolbar at a time. When you use the `ShowToolbar` action, you must specify the toolbar you want to hide or show, and specify a `Show` value (see Figure 9-30).

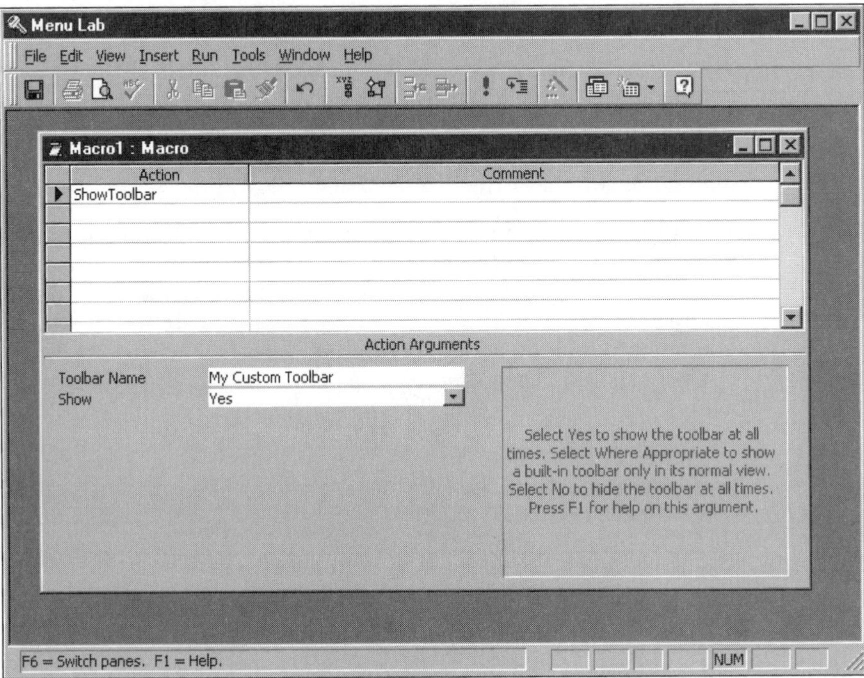

Figure 9-30: Use the ShowToolbar macro action to show or hide a toolbar.

The Show value must be one of the following:

- Yes
- Where Appropriate
- No

If you set the value to `Yes`, the toolbar is displayed and remains visible at all times. If you set the value to `No`, Access permanently hides the toolbar; the toolbar will not be displayed until the `Show` property is changed. The `Where Appropriate` value tells Access to show the built-in toolbar when appropriate and hide it the rest of the time. For example, the Form Design toolbar should be shown only while a form is in Design view. If this toolbar's `Show` value is `Yes`, the toolbar is always displayed; if it is set to `Where Appropriate`, the toolbar is shown only while a form in Design view is given the focus.

Displaying toolbars using Visual Basic

To display a specific toolbar at run time, you can use the `ShowToolbar` macro action previously discussed, or you can use the `ShowToolbar` method in VBA code. The `ShowToolbar` method belongs to the `DoCmd` object.

The syntax for the `ShowToolbar` method is as follows:

```
DoCmd.ShowToolbar sztoolbarname [, show]
```

You provide two parameters to the `ShowToolbar` method: `sztoolbarname` and `show`. The first parameter, `sztoolbarname`, is the name of the toolbar you want to show or hide. The `show` parameter must be one of the following intrinsic constants:

- `acToolbarYes`
- `acToolbarWhereApprop`
- `acToolbarNo`

These intrinsic constants correspond to the same `Show` values available with the `ShowToolbar` macro action previously discussed. To show a toolbar called MyToolbar, for example, you use the following line of code:

```
DoCmd.ShowToolbar "MyToolbar", acToolbarYes
```

Allowing users to modify your custom toolbars

You can allow users to modify your toolbars, just as you can modify Access's built-in toolbars. If you do not want users to be able to customize your toolbars, you must disable this option, because custom toolbars are customizable by default.

To prevent users from customizing your toolbars, do one of the following:

- Uncheck the Allow Toolbar Changes box on the application's Startup dialog box.
- Set the `AllowToolbarChanges` property of the `Application` object to `False`.

The `AllowToolbarChanges` property is a database property. Figure 9-31 shows how to prevent users from changing your toolbars.

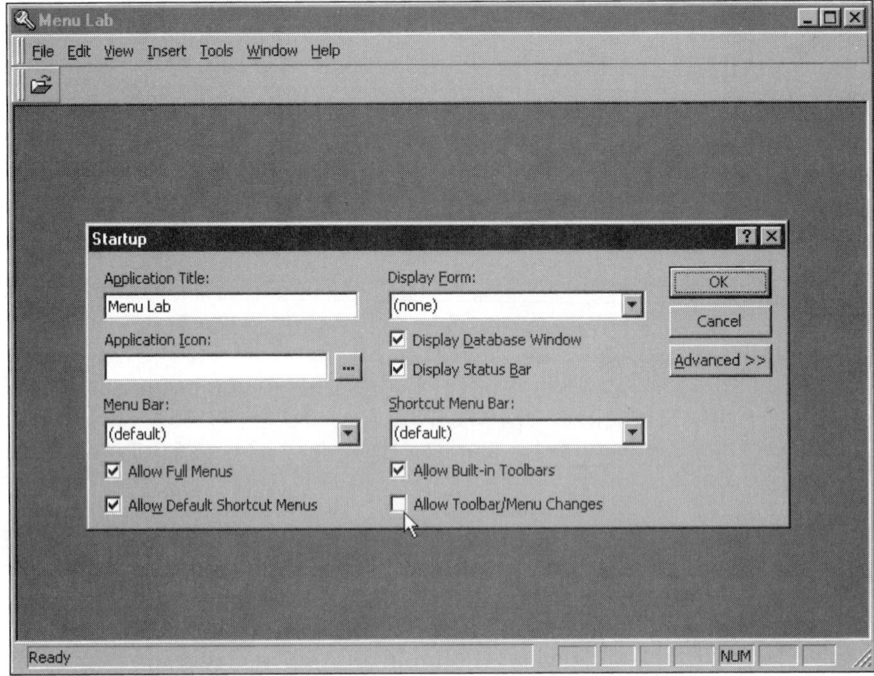

Figure 9-31: Disabling the Allow Toolbar Changes option for the current database.

If you allow users to customize your toolbars, you should make sure that the users are running their *own* copy of your application. Changes to custom menu bars are saved in the database, and they are applied to all users of that database. If all your users run the same copy of your application on a network and one user changes a toolbar, all subsequent users that log into your application will see the changed toolbar.

Chapter 10

Form Branching Techniques

In This Chapter

- Taking four related tables and creating one relational form
- Creating combo boxes, based on a query, that retrieve and display information
- Building a subform and embedding it into the main form
- Building buttons that call macros to display other forms for new data entry
- Setting form and control event properties to control navigation and form behavior
- Embedding pictures on buttons for a more appealing look
- Creating a module to post data from one table to another
- Creating complex calculations using data from both a form and a subform

In this chapter, you learn how to build relational forms, which use data from multiple tables. You learn a variety of topics, including creating subforms, creating list and combo boxes, using combo boxes within a subform, using form headers and footers, and creating totals from a subform. You also learn how to create simple menus to help you navigate from one form or report to another.

Microsoft Access 97 has one of the best form design tools available on a personal computer today. This feature, coupled with its underlying database architecture and the functionality of controls and properties, makes creating complex forms very straightforward. Each form is made up of controls — these include bound controls that allow data entry and display, unbound controls such as lines and boxes, controls that allow the display and manipulation of relational data using subforms, and calculated controls that you use to display complex expressions that can involve multiple tables and query dynasets. Data validation controls such as option buttons, checkboxes, list boxes, and combo boxes complete the toolbox of the form designer.

Creating a complex form that uses multiple dynasets and the event properties of form controls can really enhance data entry and display. A well-made form can make a clerical data-entry person more productive while eliminating repetitive errors and speeding up navigation. For the professional analyst or manager, complex forms can improve the ability to react to changing business requirements and make correct decisions.

In this chapter, you learn how to create the form pictured in Figure 10-1. This Invoice form requires knowledge of some of the more complex design techniques you can learn in Microsoft Access. You see how to build this form by using a simple methodology that you can apply to any complex form. It is assumed that you have created forms already, mastered table and query creation, and have used property sheets to set control properties. You should also be familiar with the Palette, Field List, and Toolbox.

Understanding the Invoice Table Relationships

The Invoice form, shown in Figure 10-1, uses four tables, one query, four forms, a macro library, and a small module function written in Access Basic.

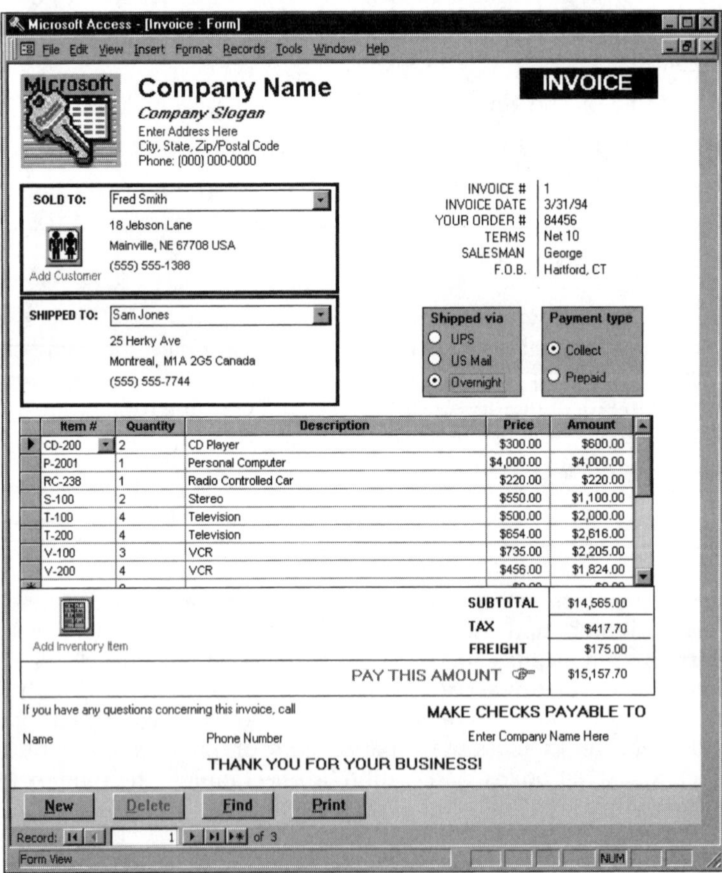

Microsoft Access - [Invoice : Form]

File Edit View Insert Format Records Tools Window Help

Company Name

Company Slogan

Enter Address Here
City, State, Zip/Postal Code
Phone: (000) 000-0000

INVOICE

SOLD TO: Fred Smith
18 Jebson Lane
Mainville, NE 67708 USA
(555) 555-1388
Add Customer

INVOICE # 1
INVOICE DATE 3/31/94
YOUR ORDER # 84456
TERMS Net 10
SALESMAN George
F.O.B. Hartford, CT

SHIPPED TO: Sam Jones
25 Herky Ave
Montreal, M1A 2G5 Canada
(555) 555-7744

Shipped via: UPS / US Mail / Overnight

Payment type: Collect / Prepaid

Item #	Quantity	Description	Price	Amount
CD-200	2	CD Player	$300.00	$600.00
P-2001	1	Personal Computer	$4,000.00	$4,000.00
RC-238	1	Radio Controlled Car	$220.00	$220.00
S-100	2	Stereo	$550.00	$1,100.00
T-100	4	Television	$500.00	$2,000.00
T-200	4	Television	$654.00	$2,616.00
V-100	3	VCR	$735.00	$2,205.00
V-200	4	VCR	$456.00	$1,824.00

Add Inventory Item

SUBTOTAL	$14,565.00
TAX	$417.70
FREIGHT	$175.00
PAY THIS AMOUNT	$15,157.70

If you have any questions concerning this invoice, call

Name Phone Number

MAKE CHECKS PAYABLE TO
Enter Company Name Here

THANK YOU FOR YOUR BUSINESS!

New Delete Find Print

Record: 1 of 3

Form View NUM

Figure 10-1: The completed Invoice form.

As shown in Figure 10-2, the relationship between the Invoice table and the Invoice Lineitems table is *one-to-many*. For each record in the Invoice table, there can be many corresponding records in the Invoice Lineitems table. The Invoice Customers and Inventory tables are used as lookup tables. A *many-to-one* relationship exists from the Invoice table to the Invoice Customers table. You may have many invoices that contain a record for a customer in the Invoice Customers table. Note that in the Invoice table there are two fields used as relational lookups to the Invoice Customers table.

The Invoice table records all the general information contained in the invoice with one record for each invoice. Its primary key field is Invoice #. The Invoice Lineitems table provides information about the items in an invoice — item numbers, descriptions, and prices. Each invoice can have many different lineitems. The Invoice Lineitems table is linked to the Invoice table by the Invoice # field. It has a two-field primary key, Invoice # and Item #, which makes each record unique. This limits you, however, because you cannot have the same item number on a specific invoice twice.

The Invoice Customers table has the names and addresses of your customers. The table is linked by its key field, Customer Number, to the Sold to Customer and Ship to Customer fields in the Invoice table. The Inventory table contains information about the items that you sell. The table is linked by its key field, Item Number, to the Item # field in the Invoice Lineitems table.

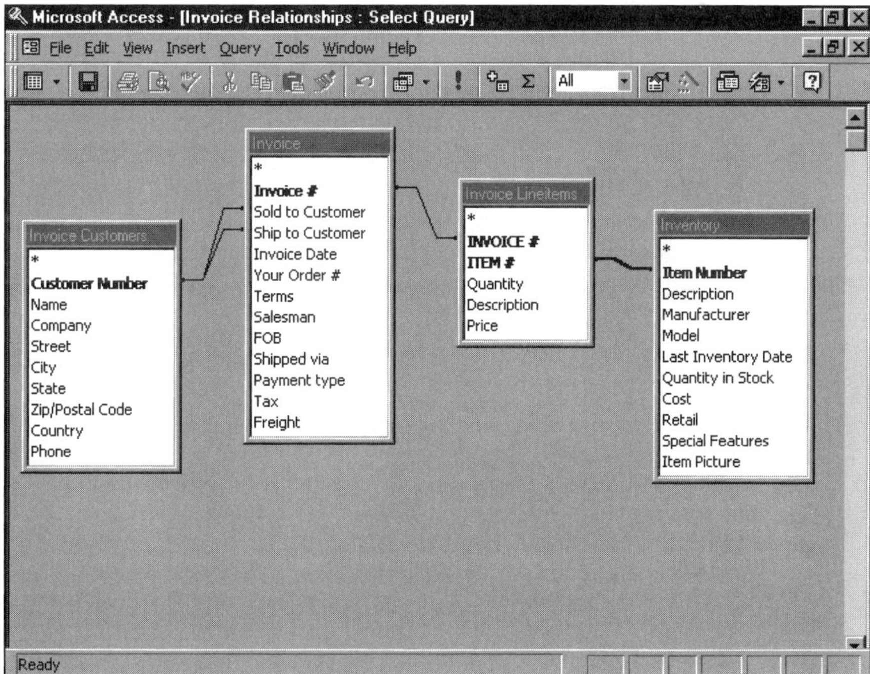

Figure 10-2: The Invoice form table relationships.

In reality, the relationships shown in the query diagram are not created with a query. The relationships are established with subform links, combo box lookups, macros, and modules. This relationship could be built if a standard report was desired and all the related information needed to be brought together using various report sections.

Creating the Main Invoice Form

The table diagram in Figure 10-2 shows you the tables necessary for this form and how the tables are related. Table 10-1 describes the components of the Invoice database that are necessary to create the Invoice form.

Table 10-1 Components of the Invoice Database

Table	*Form*	*Report*
Main Form	Invoice	Invoice
Subform	Invoice Customers	zlnvoiceCustomers
Subform	Invoice Lineitems	zlnvoiceLineitems
New Customer Form	Invoice Customers	zlnvoiceNewCustomer
New Inventory Form	Inventory	zlnvoiceNewInventory

You can create the basic Invoice form either from a New form or from a Form Wizard. In this example, because a majority of fields are used from both the Invoice and Invoice Lineitems, it is more efficient to use the Main/Subform Form Wizard.

When you create the New form, you select the Invoice table as the starting point. After clicking on the FormWizards button, you select the Form Wizard, as shown in Figure 10-3. This step will let you create both the main Invoice form and the subform zlnvoiceLineitems. Remember, the wizard lets you select not only the fields, but also the name of the table to use for the form and the subform.

The wizard first asks you to select the table/query for the main form. Assuming that you have already built the Invoice table, you can select that table for the form. Next, the wizard lets you select the fields for the Invoice form. You should select all the fields. You then select the Invoice Lineitems table and choose the fields for the subform. Again, you should use all the fields. Then, Access 97 will automatically understand the one-to-many relationship and allow you to choose between creating a form/subform or a form with a button to open a linked form. You want to choose the default, which is a main form and a subform. Then, you can choose the layout for the subform. The datasheet is the layout you will want here. You will want to choose the tabular layout if you need to customize the column headers. In this example, the datasheet is sufficient. You choose the style of the form.

Because you will manually manipulate the form design aesthetics after the form is created, you should select the Standard look for the form. Finally, the form is named Invoice and the subform is named Invoice Lineitems Subform.

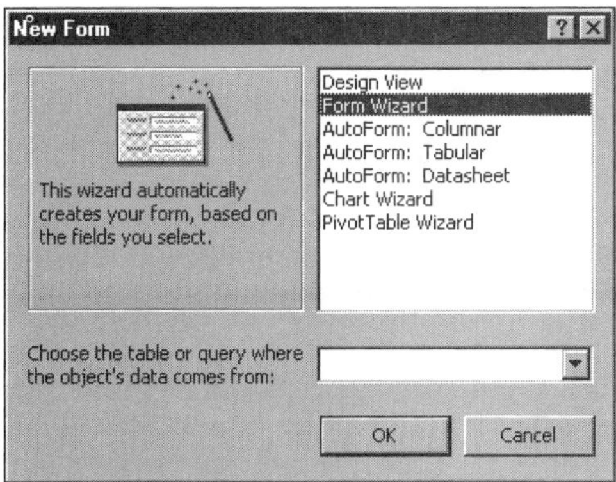

Figure 10-3: Selecting the Form Wizard.

When you are finished, the Invoice form design is displayed, as shown in Figure 10-4. You can then begin to move the fields into position for the top portion of the invoice. You can also test the design by switching to form view and entering a record into the table datasheet.

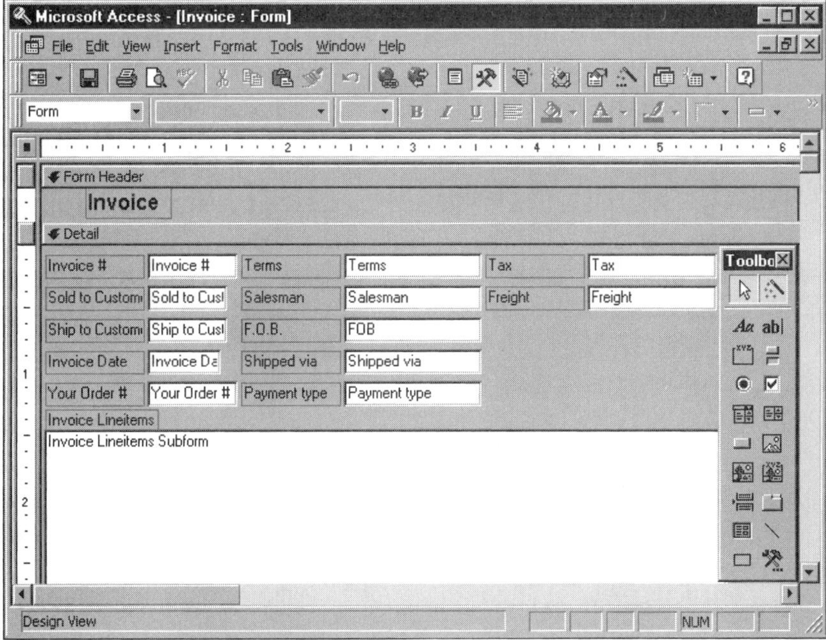

Figure 10-4: The main/subform default design.

Rearranging and reformatting invoice form fields

Each field is created as a text box control. You need to delete some fields to change their control type. You must complete many tasks to get the form to look like the one shown in Figure 10-1.

First, remove the Invoice title in the Form Header. The Form Header section will not be used in this form, so you should close the header by dragging the separator line between the Form Header section and the Detail section.

Next, move all the fields from their original positions to their approximate final positions. The Sold To Customer and Shipped To Customer fields stay on the left side of the form.

You must also do some work with the Palette. You need to change the background color of the entire form from gray to white. Finally, add the labels that appear in the top part of the form. The Access logo in Figure 10-1 was captured with a screen capture program and expanded by using an unbound OLE object control. The rest of the text objects are simply unbound label controls.

When you complete these steps, the form should look similar to Figure 10-5.

As you can see in Figure 10-5, the form is already starting to look like an invoice. The next step is to continue working on the top of the Invoice form by changing the text box controls Shipped Via and Payment type into option button controls. Notice in Figure 10-5 that these controls display numbers. An option button control normally returns a number to the underlying table. In this example, the field data type is Number Integer.

Creating the option button groups

Many forms use option buttons. Generally, these controls have two states (on or off) when used by themselves. When used as part of an option group, you can select one value from a list of values, as follows:

Button Type	*State*	*Symbol*
Option Button	True	◉
Option Button	False	○

An *option group* can contain multiple option buttons. When these controls are placed inside an option group box, they work together. Controls within an option group return a number based on the position in the group. Only one control within an option group can be selected at one time. The maximum number of buttons in an option group should be four. When you exceed that number, unless you have a lot of room on your screen, you should switch to a pop-up list box.

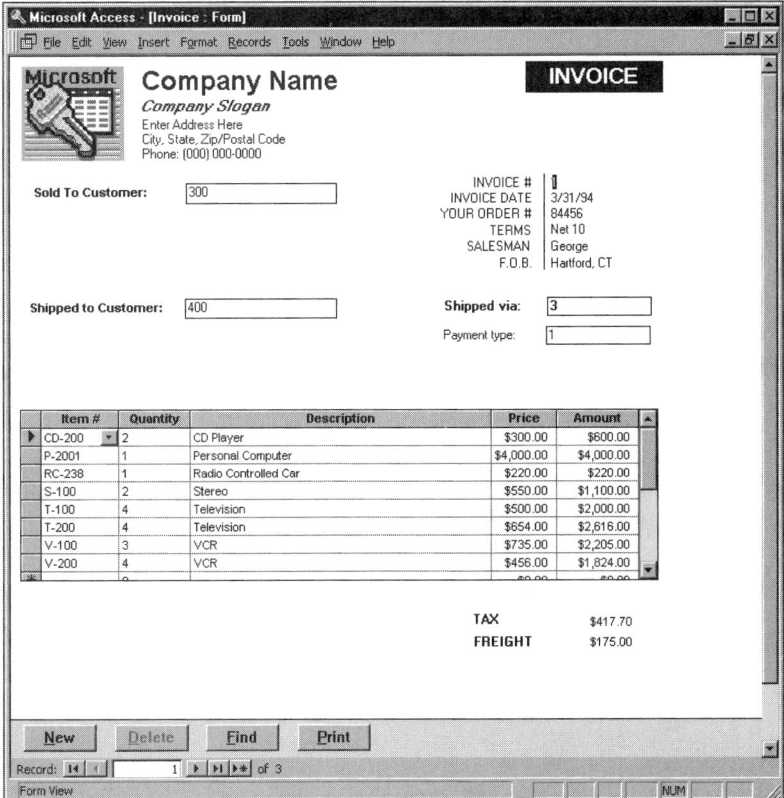

Figure 10-5: The invoice after initial field rearrangement and formatting.

An option group is generally bound to a single field or expression. Each button inside passes a different value back to the option group, which in turn passes the single choice to the bound field or expression. The buttons themselves are not bound to any field but to the option group box.

To change the Shipped Via control into an option group, you must first delete the existing text box control. The easiest way to create any new control is to use the toolbox and the field list window. By making this change, you automatically bind the control to the field.

To create an option group, use the Option Group icon in the toolbox. When this icon is pressed (or sunken), open the Field List window and drag the Shipped Via field name to the approximate desired position on the form. This step creates an empty option group rectangle with the text Shipped Via in the top border. You can grab the text label move handle and move the text inside the top border for its final positioning. By using the Palette, you can also change the Back Color of the option group itself to gray to match the final Invoice form, as shown in Figure 10-1. You may also want to change the label's font style to bold. If the Control Wizard's icon is on, the first Option Group Wizard screen is displayed. In this chapter, you learn how to work without wizards.

After you create the option group control, you must add the individual buttons. One word of caution — you cannot simply copy and paste buttons into an option group control. You must create them inside the option group control or they will not be properly bound to it. Remember, the option group control itself is bound to the table field (in this example, Shipped Via). The individual option buttons will be bound to the option group control.

To create an option button, click on the option button icon in the toolbox. When the icon is selected, the cursor changes to look like the option group icon. You can then anchor the cursor inside the option group and drag the cursor until a small rectangle appears. When you release the mouse button, the option button and a text label appear. The Access default places the text label control on the left and the option button on the right. You can drag the option button label to the other side of the option button control after it is displayed. You can save this step by first modifying the default label position of the option button label control by changing the Default Option Button `LabelX` property to .8 in. from –.12 in. This correctly puts the button on the left of the label control.

When the three option button controls are positioned one above the other, you have to modify the text labels. The first should be UPS; the second, US Mail; and the last, Overnight. If you look at the property window for each option button control, you see that the first control's `Option Value` property is 1; the second, 2; and the third, 3. The option group controls `Control Source` property is, of course, Shipped Via.

When you finish the first option group so that it looks like the final version in Figure 10-1, you can test it by displaying the form in Form view. You should be able to select the buttons, and if you then check the value of the Shipped Via field in the Invoice table, it should correspond to the last selected option button. Perform the same steps to complete the Payment Type option group controls, and you are finished with this part of the form.

Creating subform lookups with combo boxes

In the final Invoice form, combo boxes have been used in the areas marked Sold To and Shipped To in order to simplify data entry. When you click on the down arrow to the right of each of these fields, a list of customers drops down below the field, and you can select from among the choices. These are created in several steps. First, make the combo box and test it to make sure that a list of your customers is displayed. Next, the subform is created separately and then embedded into the Invoice form. You are creating two different combo boxes and embedding two subforms. The form used for both subforms is the same. The `Link Master Fields` property of the subform, however, is different to point to each combo box. The `Link Child Fields` property of both subforms points to the same form you create.

First, take a look at Figure 10-1. Note that the entire area of each address box is enclosed in a rectangle. Both rectangles are a little thicker than the default thickness. Create the rectangles for each area and change the thickness to the third width setting. This gives you some space with which to work. You can always adjust it later if you need more room.

You will probably want to delete the existing text box controls for each address box. Next, add an unbound label control in each box. The top one's text will be SOLD TO:, and the bottom one's text will be SHIPPED TO:.

The combo boxes are added next. Click on the combo box icon in the toolbar. Then drag the Sold to Customer field from the property window to the inside of the top rectangle you previously created. The combo box appears. Next, delete the unnecessary label, keeping the combo box control. You should also resize the combo box control to fill the rectangle horizontally.

The next step is to enter the combo boxes' properties. In this example, you want to see only the name of the customer, though you want the customer number to be stored in the Invoice table's Sold to Customer field. You do this by creating a multifield combo box with the bound column different from the column being displayed. You will be using the Invoice Customers table for the source of the combo boxes display.

You need to display the Name field while storing the Customer Number field. Figure 10-6 shows the completed combo box control and the top portion of the property window for the completed control.

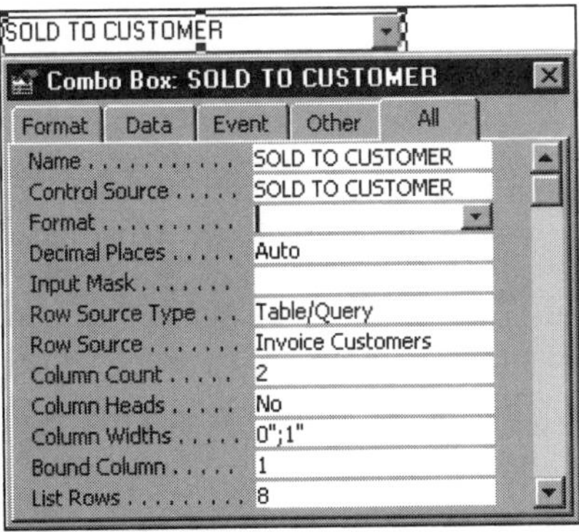

Figure 10-6: The completed combo box.

The `Name` and `Control Source` properties were automatically filled in when you dragged the Sold to Customer field from the field list. You still have to specify the rest of the properties. In this example, the combo box uses the first two fields in the Invoice Customers table so that you don't have to create a separate query for the combo box. If you wanted to rearrange fields or sort the combo box list, you would have to first create a query for the combo box display.

The `Row Source Type` property is set to `Table/Query`. Other choices include `Value List` and `Field List`. The `Row Source` property is set to `Invoice Customers`.

This is the name of the table that the combo box looks at to create the list of values. You want to use the first three columns so that the `Column Count` property is set to `3`. In reality, you will only display two columns. The `Column Heads` property is set to `No` — you don't need to see the column header when displaying two obvious columns.

The `Column Widths` property is set to `0";1";1.5"`. This setting hides the first column (Customer Number), while displaying only the Name and Company fields. The Bound Column, which returns a value to the Control Source, is the first column (the hidden Customer Number). The value of Customer Number from the Invoice Customers table is copied to the Control Source/Sold to Customers field in the Invoice table when its name is chosen in the combo box.

If you did all this correctly, you can run the form, select the combo box, and display a list of your customers. In reality, you probably want to create a query for the Row Source to display your customers in a sorted order. When the first combo box is created and tested, you can create the second combo box by using the Ship to Customer field and changing the properties for the combo box to the identical properties of the other combo box (except, of course, for the `Name` and `Control Source`).

The next step is to create, embed, and link the subform that both combo boxes will change when used. The subform is created like any Access form. This subform needs to be very compact because it must display several fields in a small area. Figure 10-7 shows the completed form with the special form properties you need.

The form zInvoiceCustomers is created with just three lines. The first line simply contains the Street. The second line is a calculated expression that combines the City, State, and Zip/Postal Code fields. Any text fields can be combined, or (in computer terms) *concatenated,* by using the & character.

The last line is the Phone. You could eliminate this line, which would make Company the first line. As designed, this area holds only three lines.

Notice the Form properties in the Properties Window in Figure 10-7. The `Default View` is set to `Single Form` so that only one record is displayed at a time. The `Default Editing` property is set to `Read Only` because this subform is to be used strictly as a lookup into the Customer table. Finally, the `Allow Editing` property is set to `Unavailable` so that a menu choice cannot be used to override the `Read Only` condition. The `Scroll Bars` property is set to `Neither` so that the form appears as a small rectangular block with only the fields shown.

The `Record Selectors` property is set to `No`, so the Record Selection Bar is not displayed.

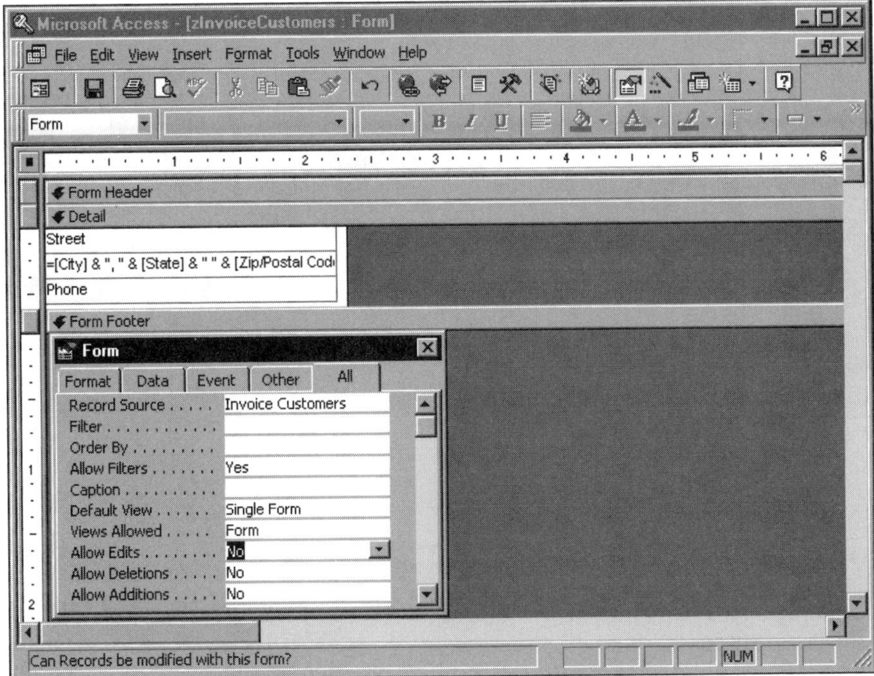

Figure 10-7: Creating the subform.

When all this is completed, you can embed the zInvoiceCustomers form as a subform on the main Invoice form. You can do this two ways:

- Select the Subform icon from the toolbox and then drag an unbound subform rectangle into the proper position.
- Drag the form to be used as the subform directly from the database container onto the main form.

When you drag a form from the database container and place it on another form, a bound subform is automatically created, sized to the borders of the form used as the subform. If the primary keys match (usually in a one-to-many relationship), it automatically creates the links between the Parent and Child forms. In this example, you will be manually relating the foreign key, Sold to Customer in the Invoice table, to the primary key — Customer Number in the Invoice Customers table. The completed property window for the zInvoiceCustomers subform is shown in Figure 10-8.

When you drag the form, the subform appears. A text label appears above the subform rectangle. You can delete the label — it is not necessary — and adjust the location and size of the subform rectangle.

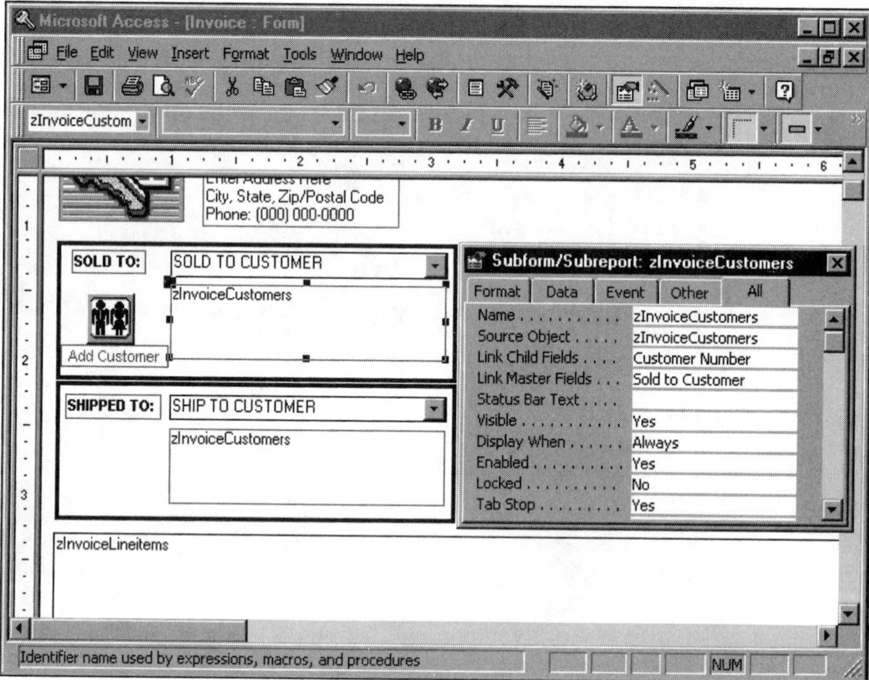

Figure 10-8: The subform properties.

In Figure 10-8, you can see the property window for the zInvoiceCustomers subform. The `Link Master Fields` property is set to `Sold to Customer`, and the `Link Child Fields` is set to `Customer Number`. This sets the link from the Invoice table to the Invoice Customers table.

When you finish this process, you should be able to perform all the steps necessary to complete the Shipped To box, which includes adding the combo box and creating the subform. Remember, the only difference is that the next combo box's `Control Source` property is `Ship to Customer`. You can copy the subform from the first rectangle to the second. You have to change the subform's `Link Master Fields` property to `Ship to`

`Customer`, but leave the `Link Child Fields` as `Customer Number`. If you copy the subform, the `Name` property will probably be named something like `zInvoiceCustomers2`, because two controls cannot have the same name even if all the properties are the same.

Understanding Event Properties, Macros, and Code

Before you begin to create macros or VBA programs and add macro calls to various event properties of your form and form controls, you should have a conceptual understanding of what a macro is and how to use event properties to trigger macros.

What is a macro?

A *macro* is an object just like other Access objects (tables, queries, forms, and reports). You create a macro to automate a particular task or series of tasks. Each task can be considered the result of one or more steps — each step being an action found in the VBA language. Access macros can also be used to simulate menu choices or mouse movements.

Unlike macros in spreadsheets, Access macros are not usually used to duplicate individual keystrokes or mouse movements. Rather, Access macros perform specific user-specified tasks, such as opening a form or running a report. Every task you want Access to perform is known as an *action*. Access provides 48 actions that you can select and perform in your macros. For example, you can create a macro that opens a form, copies a value to another form control, closes the form, and displays a message.

Macro actions are created in a macro design window. The macros are run by entering the macro name in the event properties of a form or report.

Understanding events

You can run the actions stored in macros in one of two ways — by menu choice or by using event properties. Macros are run based on a user action triggering an event. For example, the user clicks on a command button to activate a macro that opens a form. To accomplish this, Access uses a concept called an *event*. An Access event is the result or consequence of some action performed by the user. An Access event can be when a user moves from one record to another (in a form), closes a report, or clicks on a command button on a form. Access can recognize many different events in forms and reports. Some of these events are listed in Table 10-2.

Table 10-2 Common Access Events

Event	*Description*
On Current	Making a record the current record
Before Update	Changing any data in a form or report before updating
After Update	Changing any data in a form or report after updating
On Insert	Inserting a new record
On Delete	Deleting an existing record
On Open	Opening a form
On Close	Closing a form
On Menu	Selecting a choice from a user-created menu
Before Update	Changing data in a control before updating
After Update	Changing data in a control after updating
On Enter	Selecting a control
On Exit	Leaving a control
On DblClick	Double-clicking on a control
On Click	Pressing a command button
On Open	Opening a report
On Close	Closing a report
On Format	Laying out the data in a report section (band)
On Print	Printing the data in a report section (band)

When a user performs any one of the events that Access recognizes, you can have Access trigger a macro. Access can recognize an event through the use of the special event properties for forms, controls (fields), and reports.

Opening a popup form with a command button

Command buttons are used to perform an action. A command button can be added by using the toolbox to create the command button. You can then add the desired action by using the `On Click` event property of the command button. The action is generally a call to a macro or VBA program.

Figure 10-9 shows a command button and the text Add Customer below the button added to the left of the Sold to Customer combo box. Initially, the button will display text on the button face corresponding to the name of the command button. For example, Button30. If you have a library of clip art, you could fill in the name of a .BMP picture in the `Picture` property of the button. You can also click on the Builder button which displays the Picture Builder that Access supplies, which includes more than 100 pictures. This display embeds the picture on the button, as you can see in Figure 10-9. Once you have added the button, you will want to go to its event properties and add some code behind the `On Click` event. In this example, you simply want to open the zInvoiceNewCustomer form as found in the CHAP10.MDB database file on your CD-ROM.

You create a procedure by going to the event, in this example `On Click`, and selecting `Event Procedure` from the combo box list. You can then click the builder button and a blank procedure window opens. To open the zInvoiceNewCustomer form you enter the program shown in Figure 10-10. The program uses the `DoCmd.OpenForm` action to open the form named ZInvoiceNewCustomer. This allows you to display the new customer form while still having the Invoice form open in the background.

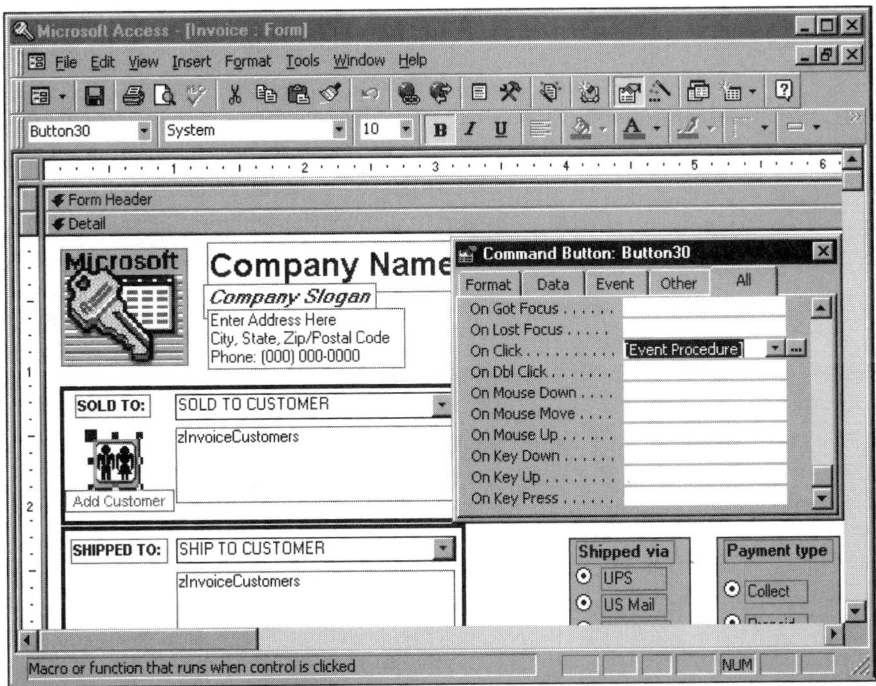

Figure 10-9: Creating the command button to open the new Customer form.

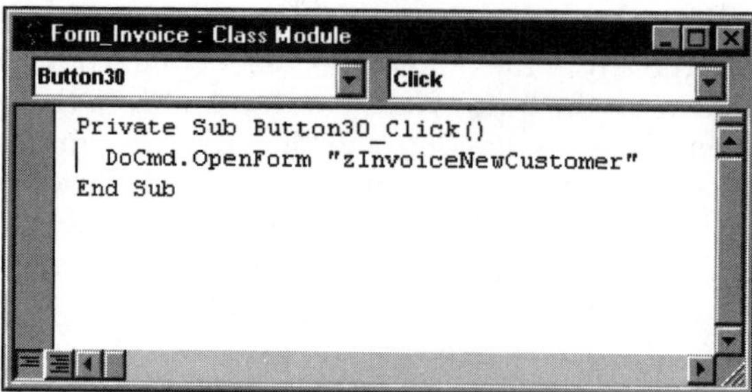

Figure 10-10: A simple VBA program to open a form.

You can now test your button by running the Invoice form and clicking on the new customer button. However, you will find several problems. First, if you created the zInvoiceNewCustomer form from a wizard, the form would open up as a full-screen form. What you want is to have the form open as a popup form. To do this, you have to resize the form in the design screen and then change some of the form properties. In fact, you also have to create a VBA program so that the form opens automatically on a new blank record.

You can easily change the size by trial and error. First, display the zInvoiceNewCustomer form in Design mode. Resize it and switch into form view until the form is displayed with no extra space inside the borders and approximately in the center of the screen. When you save a changed form in design view, it retains its new size and position when displayed.

You also need to change some of the form properties in the zInvoiceNewCustomer form. You can set form properties in Design mode by displaying the property window and then clicking on the small white rectangle in the upper-left corner of the form. The properties `PopUp` and `Modal` are set to `Yes`, as shown in Figure 10-11. `PopUp` enables the form to appear as a window on top of another window when displayed. In this example, you want it to appear on top of the Invoice form window. `Modal` requires you to finish your work in the Popup form before leaving it. You cannot switch to another window as long as the Modal window is open.

You still must create several Event Procedures and use them in this form. The first is a procedure to automatically open the form and position the record pointer to a new record, as shown in Figure 10-12. This procedure is attached to the zInvoiceNewCustomer form. To do so, you enter the single line of VBA code in the `On Open` Event Property procedure of the zInvoiceNewCustomer form.

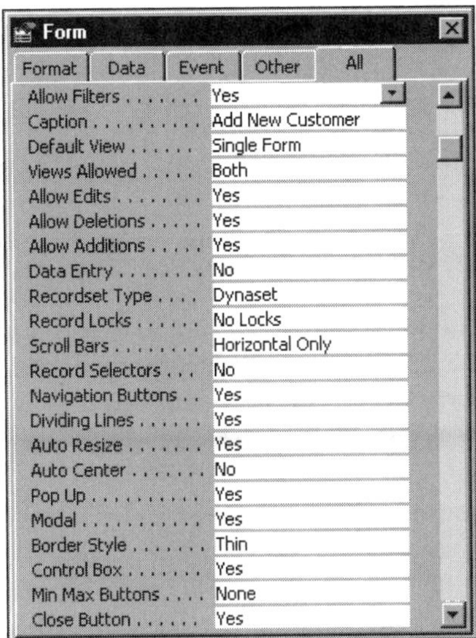

Figure 10-11: Changing the zInvoiceNewCustomer form to a modal pop-up.

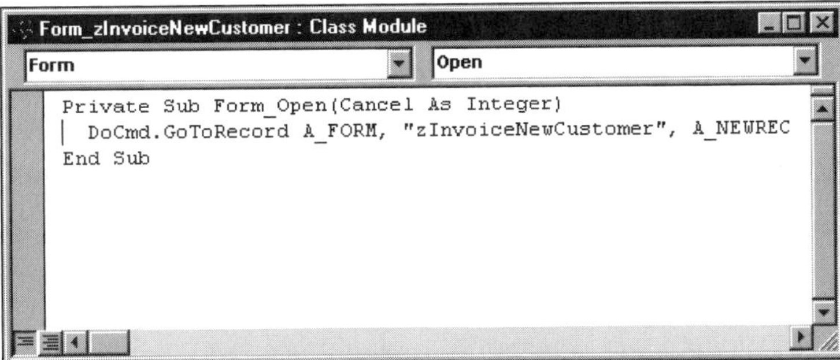

Figure 10-12: A procedure to display a new record.

The final procedure should be created to close the zInvoiceNewCustomer form and then requery the record source that is used for the combo boxes for the Ship to Customer and Sold to Customer combo box controls. You should add a button to the zInvoiceNewCustomer form to do these items. This step adds the newly added customer to the combo box list, which is necessary because the combo box only queries the Customer table for the customers when the Invoice is first opened.

This code includes the following three VBA statements:

```
DoCmd.Close acForm, "zInvoiceNewCustomer"
   DoCmd.Requery "SOLD TO CUSTOMER"
   DoCmd.Requery "SHIP TO CUSTOMER"
```

Tip

You can still use the old constant A_FORM instead of acForm for most DoCmd methods that require an object type. The acForm is called an intrinsic constant because it is already defined as a variable in Access itself. In Figure 10-12, you could have used the new intrinsic constant acDataForm for A_FORM and acNewRec for A_NEWREC.

Working with the invoice lineitems subform

When you have completed all the tasks for the main Invoice form and its popup subform for new customers, you can begin to modify the zInvoiceLineitems form to make it more functional and more aesthetically pleasing. When the Main/Subform Wizard was used to create the subform, it created the subform as a datasheet. You can do this procedure by changing the Default View property. This property enables you to determine how the form is initially displayed when opened, which is critical when a form is used as a subform.

Understanding a form's default view property

Forms can be displayed in one of three default views:

- **Single form:** Displays a single record
- **Continuous form:** Displays multiple records in a customized view
- **Datasheet:** Displays multiple records with little control

Most forms are displayed as a single form. A datasheet enables you only to control the width of the rows and columns and the overall font used in the display. A continuous form gives you far more flexibility and lets you control the following:

- Text labels in the form header, including multiple-line column headers
- Color and font of the column headers
- Color and font in the line items
- Multiple line items (two or more lines of information per row)

Datasheets are easier to use but limit your ability to customize the display. Figure 10-13 shows an example of a continuous form.

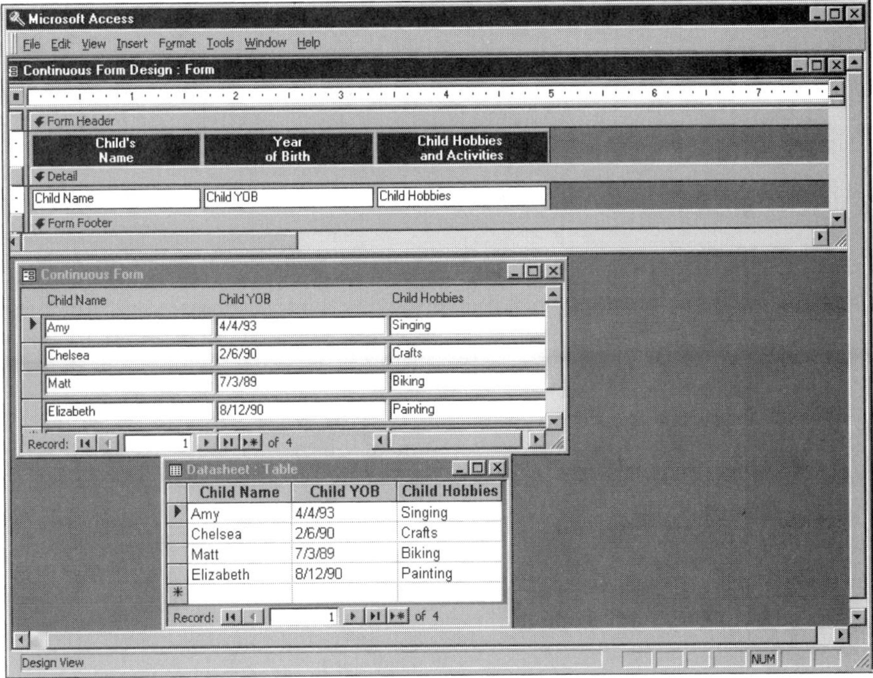

Figure 10-13: Continuous forms and datasheets.

To customize a continuous form subform, you need to change the column heading information found in the Form Header and also change the data found in the Detail section of the form. It is much easier to line up items and create a more personalized look using a continuous form.

You should use a datasheet only when the information being displayed is simple, with few totals or other calculations. Because you have little control over labels and colors, the `Continuous Forms` property setting is the best choice.

In the example in this chapter, you use a datasheet because it contains fairly simple information.

Modifying the zInvoiceLineitems datasheet

When you currently display the form, your subform datasheet should look like Figure 10-14. You still have many tasks to do. These tasks include the following:

- Creating the calculation for the extension of Quantity*Price
- Resizing the Datasheet columns so that they all fit within the subform space

- Hiding the INVOICE # column
- Changing the ITEM # column to a combo box lookup

The ITEM # combo box displays a list of inventory items and automatically fills in the Description and Price.

Invoice Lineitems : Table

INVOICE #	ITEM #	Quantity	Description	Price
1	CD-200	2	CD Player	$300.00
1	P-2001	1	Personal Compı	$4,000.00
1	RC-238	1	Radio Controllec	$220.00
1	S-100	2	Stereo	$550.00
1	T-100	4	Television	$500.00
1	T-200	4	Television	$654.00
1	V-100	3	VCR	$735.00
1	V-200	4	VCR	$456.00
15	C-100	2	Camera	$680.00
15	T-200	1	Television	$654.00
2	P-2001	3	Personal Compı	$4,000.00
2	T-200	5	Television	$654.00

Record: 1 of 12

Figure 10-14: The zlnvoiceLineitems subform in its original state.

The zInvoiceLineitems datasheet is modified by displaying it in design view. Before you adjust the columns, however, you need to create the calculated column, which is done in the Form Design view.

Multiplying two numbers in a datasheet or continuous form row

In Figure 10-15, you can see a calculation being created in the Amount field. The zInvoiceLineitems subform uses a datasheet in its calculation, so the result is shown in the Form view. If a continuous form were used, the text boxes would be shown horizontally across the Detail section of the form.

First, you must create a new text box control. You do this by using the toolbox. Because it will be an unbound text box control (the data will not be saved to any table, just displayed on the form), the value `=[Quantity]*[Price]` is entered into the `Control Source` property of the Amount text box. This step displays the calculation in the Amount field when the form is displayed.

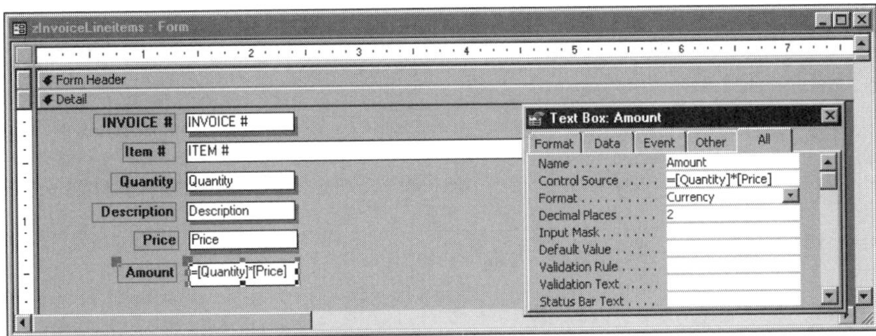

Figure 10-15: Creating the Amount column for the datasheet.

Resizing the datasheet

When the calculation is added to the form, you can display the form in datasheet view to see the approximate sizes of the columns. You now see an additional column, Amount. This field should correctly display the calculation of `Quantity*Price`.

Correctly sizing the datasheet involves a lot of trial and error. The first task, however, is to hide the INVOICE # column. You have three ways to do this:

- Change the INVOICE # control's `Visible` property to `No` in the form's Design view.
- Resize the column width to 0 by dragging the right column border all the way to the left in the datasheet view.
- Select the INVOICE # column and choose Hide Columns from the datasheet's Layout menu bar.

Any of these methods can accomplish the task. When you hide the INVOICE # column, you begin the trial-and-error approach. You then save the datasheet. (Make sure that you save the form in datasheet view or else column width changes won't be saved.) Then display the Invoice form and see how the datasheet is displayed. Perhaps you have extra space. You can reduce the width of the subform control in the Invoice form or increase the width of some of the columns.

Perhaps you don't have enough space. You then have to shrink some of the columns or increase the width of the subform control. In this example, you will probably find that you have extra space. You may want to increase the width of the Description column and decrease the width of the Quantity and ITEM # columns.

You may also notice that the original column headers created by the wizard contain a colon after the name. You may want to modify each label control's `Caption` property to remove the ending colon. When you are finished, your zInvoiceLineitems datasheet should look something like Figure 10-16.

zInvoiceLineitems : Form

Item #	Quantity	Description	Price	Amount
CD-200	2	CD Player	$300.00	$600.00
P-2001	1	Personal Computer	$4,000.00	$4,000.00
RC-238	1	Radio Controlled Car	$220.00	$220.00
S-100	2	Stereo	$550.00	$1,100.00
T-100	4	Television	$500.00	$2,000.00
T-200	4	Television	$654.00	$2,616.00
V-100	3	VCR	$735.00	$2,205.00
V-200	4	VCR	$456.00	$1,824.00
C-100	2	Camera	$680.00	$1,360.00
T-200	1	Television	$654.00	$654.00
P-2001	3	Personal Computer	$4,000.00	$12,000.00
T-200	5	Television	$654.00	$3,270.00
*	0		$0.00	$0.00

Figure 10-16: The final datasheet.

One more task you may need to do in the Invoice form is to increase or decrease the height of the subform control. This change enables you to control the number of items that can be displayed at one time. Make sure that your test data contains more records than can fit in the displayed subform. If you don't, when the vertical scroll bar appears the first time you have a lot of records, the subform may no longer look correct when the form is displayed.

Before you move on to the totals for the form, you still have to change the ITEM # control to a control that displays data from the Inventory table and lets the user choose from a combo box list. This change is far more complicated than the combo box controls you saw earlier, because you have to create multiple columns in the list, and sort the list by Manufacturer (a field not in the datasheet but in the Inventory table) and Description.

This combo box also has to trigger a VBA routine from the `After Update` property of the combo box that copies the Description and Price field values from the Inventory table to the zInvoiceLineitems table when a record is selected.

Creating a combo box control for multiple fields

You may want the combo box for the ITEM # lookup of the Inventory table to display four fields (shown in Figure 10-17). These fields cannot be displayed as they are by using the Inventory table as the Row Source of the combo box. When you want to display fields in a different order than they appear in the table design, or if you want to display the records within the combo box in a sorted order, you must first create a query before creating the combo box.

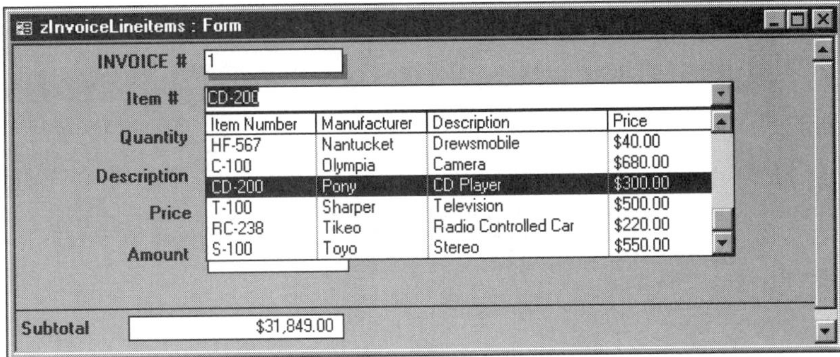

Figure 10-17: The combo box displayed.

The query that you need to create for the combo box is shown in Figure 10-18. The fields are placed in the necessary order in the Query Design pane. Notice that the Inventory values are to be sorted by Manufacturer and Description. When you create the query, you can enter the properties for the combo box control. Also notice in the last column that the Retail field is labeled Price by using the notation `Price:Retail` in the query.

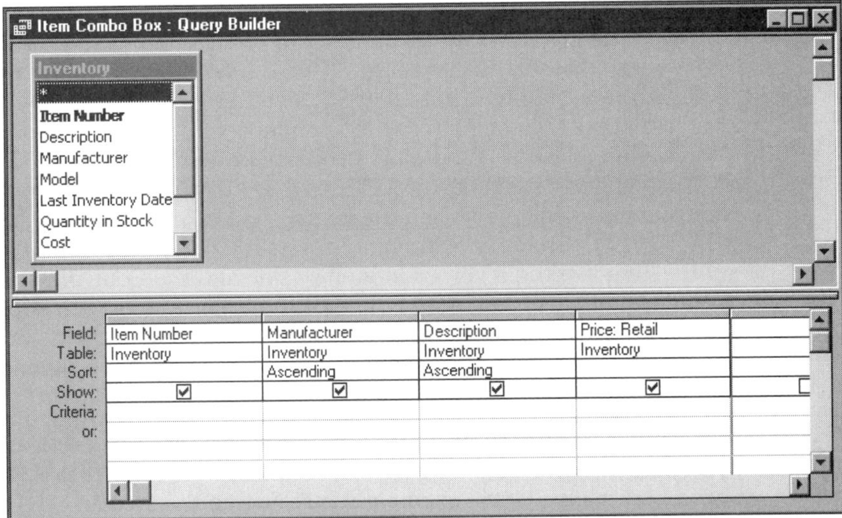

Figure 10-18: The query for the combo box.

After you create the query, you can create the combo box. You must first delete the existing Item # text box control and then create the new combo box by using the Item # field as the Control Source. Figure 10-19 shows the properties that are necessary for the Item # combo box.

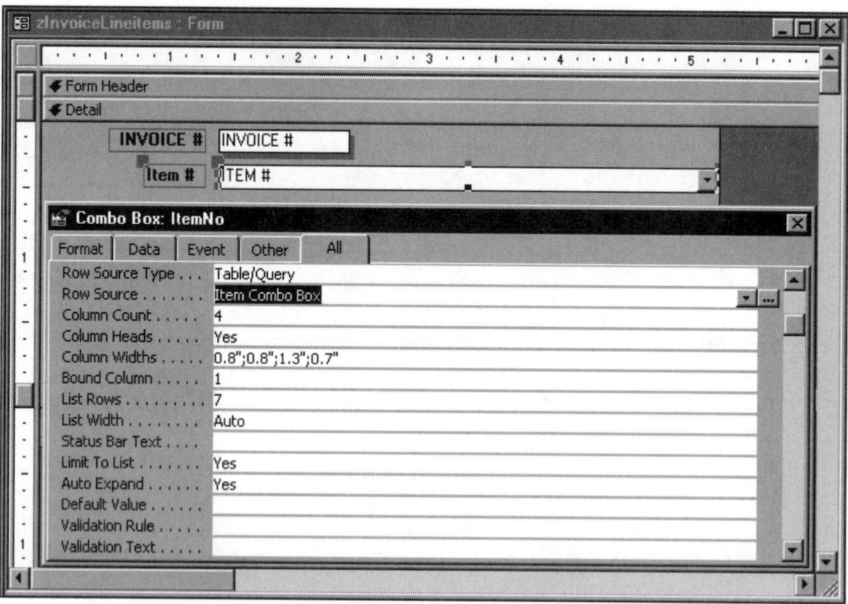

Figure 10-19: The property sheet for the combo box.

Note that the `Row Source Type` is set to `Table/Query` and the `Row Source` is the query that was just created, `Item Combo Box`. Because you want to display four columns, the `Column Count` property is set to `4`. You should display column heads when you have more than two columns. In this example, the `Column Heads` property is set to `Yes`. The `Column Widths` property is set to `0.8";0.8";1.3";0.7"` in order to properly size the columns for display when the combo box is open. The `Bound Column` is set to `1` so that the first column, Item #, is filled in to the bound control source Item # in the Invoice Lineitems table and the Control Source of the zInvoiceLineitems form. Also note that the `Limit to List` property is set to `Yes`. This setting means that you cannot add an item that is not on the list. It also means that you must provide a way to add new inventory when in the Invoice form. You see this later in this chapter.

The last task for the subform is to copy the Description and Price fields from the Inventory table to the zInvoiceLineitems form. This is the classic second normalized form example. You must do this because if a customer buys an item today and next week the price of the item changes, the customer must still receive today's price. If you just performed a relational lookup to the Inventory table, the new price would appear. So, you have to copy the Price field to the Line Item table.

The best way to do this — or any posting routine — is with a simple VBA program. You do this by using the `After Update` property. This event is triggered after the record is chosen in the combo box.

Creating a posting routine in VBA

The VBA function shown in Figure 10-20 is fairly simple and performs the tasks necessary to copy the Price and Description fields from the selected record in the Inventory table to the same fields in the zInvoiceLineitems form.

Module1 : Module

(General) LookUpDescriptionAndPrice

```
Function LookUpDescriptionAndPrice(tForm As Form, tItemNo As String)
Dim tDB As Database, tTB As TABLE
   Set tDB = CurrentDb()
   Set tTB = tDB.OpenTable("Inventory")
   tTB.INDEX = "Item Number"
   tTB.Seek "=", tItemNo
   tForm.price = tTB.retail
   tForm.Description = tTB.Description
   tTB.Close
End Function
```

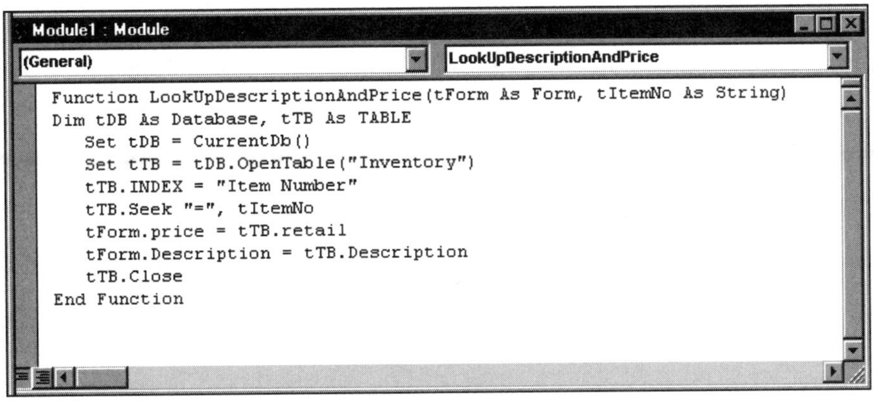

Figure 10-20: A VBA posting routine.

The call from the `After Update` property from the combo box is shown here. The name of the VBA function is called `LookUpDescriptionAndPrice`. Two parameters are used to pass information to the VBA function. The first parameter is the name of the form, which contains the fields that will be posted to. These fields are the Description and Price fields in the zInvoiceLineitems subform displayed in the main Invoice form. The notation may seem complex, but it is quite normal, and you should understand the standard expression notation in Access. The second parameter is the field in the form that is to be used as the lookup into the Inventory table. Following is the code:

```
=LookUpDescriptionAndPrice(Forms![Invoice]![zInvoiceLineitems]
.Form,Forms![Invoice]![zInvoiceLineitems].Form![ItemNo])
```

The VBA routine itself is stored in a module library shown in Figure 10-20 (called Module1 in this example). This is a function, as VBA routines usually are. Two parameters are passed to the function. The first is the name of the form; the second is the field used for the lookup into the Inventory table. Variables are set up for the database and the table in the second line of the module.

The third line of the function sets the variable `tDB` to the current open database. This setting is needed to correctly reference the Inventory table. The next line uses the variable `tTB` to open the Inventory table in the current database. The fifth line sets the index used in the search to `"Item Number"`, and the actual search (`Seek`) of the selected Item Number (using the value passed from the `After Update` call) is the `tItemNo` variable.

The line `tTB.Seek "=", tItemNo` performs the actual search for the matching record in the Inventory table. No error-checking logic exists here, because a value has to be found as the combo box list also uses the Inventory table. Because the `Seek` has to be successful, the next two lines set the value of the Price field in the subform to the value of the Retail field from the Inventory table and the Description field as well. This does the actual posting. The final two lines in the function close the open database from memory for VBA and end the function.

You can create the module and add the calling line to the `After Update` property in the combo box. You won't be able to try it, however, unless you test it from the Invoice form, because the call uses the notation from the Invoice form in its calling expression. Remember, when referencing a subform control from a main form, you have to fully qualify the expression. That is why the call uses the following notation:

```
Forms![Invoice]![zInvoiceLineitems].Form![ItemNo].
```

You must still add a button to add a new inventory record on demand. This addition uses the exact same logic as the Add New Customer button that was shown earlier in this chapter, except that it would use and reference the zInvoiceNew Inventory form. You would also have to add macros for the open, close, and new functions for the Inventory form as already shown in the new customer form explanations. If you have completed all of the tasks outlined in the chapter to this point, your form should look like Figure 10-21 when you look at it in form view.

Completing the totals on the form

The mathematical formulas on the invoice form are very simple and either sum a column of values or multiply two values in a datasheet. One of the more complex tasks you can do is create a summary calculation in a subform and then use it in the main form. The Invoice form provides one of the best examples of calculations in both forms and subforms.

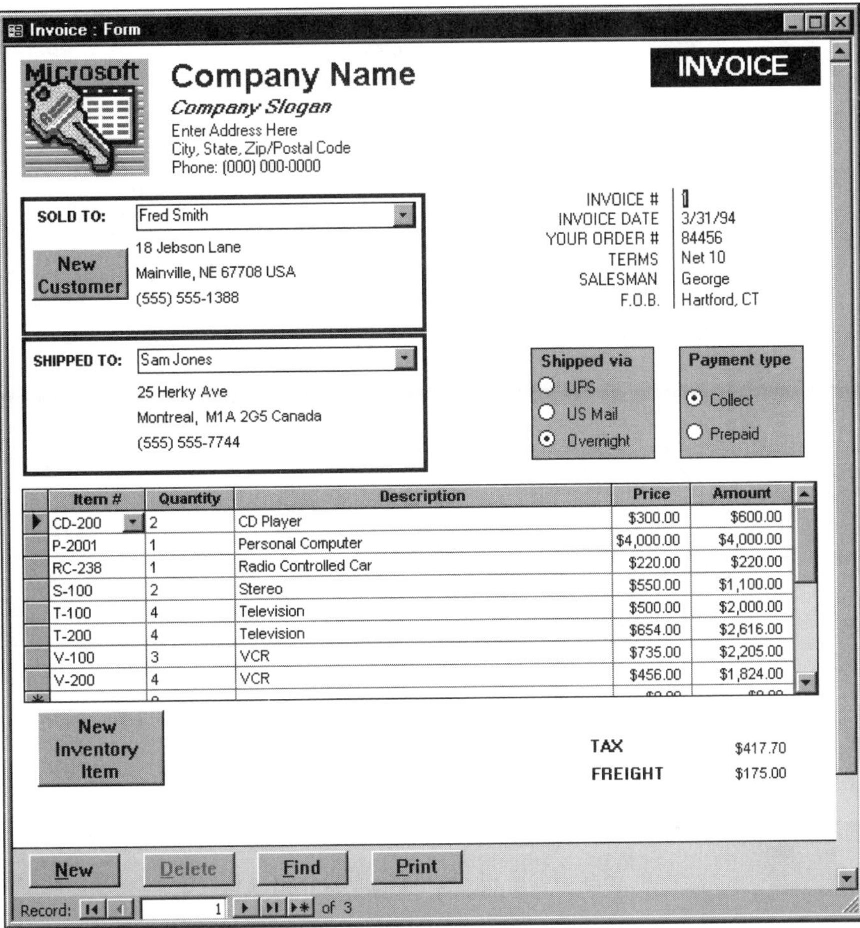

Figure 10-21: The partially completed invoice form.

Calculating the sum of a column

If you look back to Figure 10-1, you can see the SUBTOTAL field on the Invoice form. The subtotal control, however, is only a reference to the sum of the lineitems, which must be calculated on the zInvoiceLineitems form. The Form Footer Section of the zInvoiceLineitems form calculates the sum of a group of records. As shown in Figure 10-22, the calculation uses the Sum function and the fields Quantity and Price.

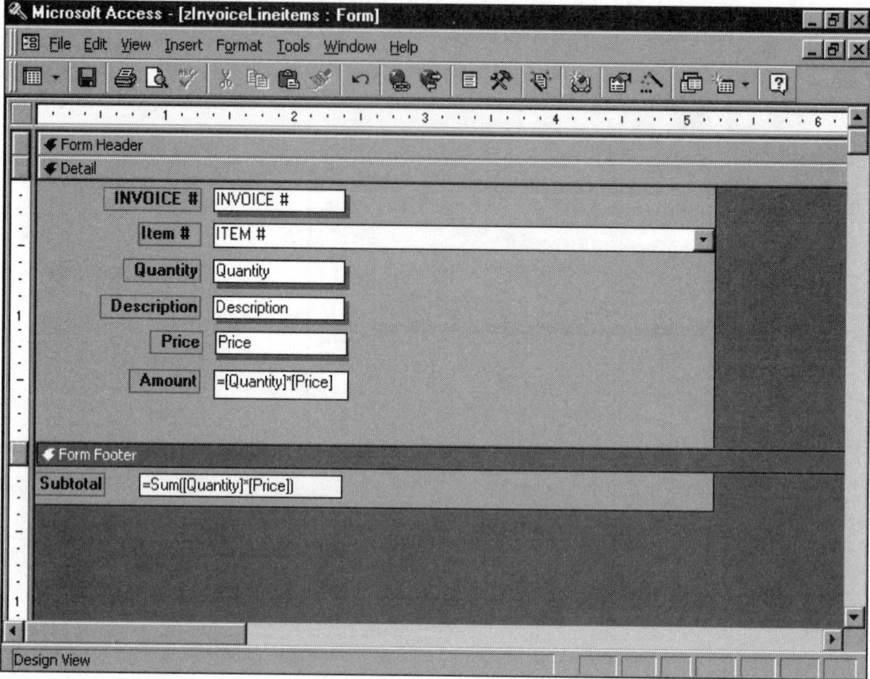

Figure 10-22: Calculating a sum of the lineitems.

In Figure 10-22, you can see the calculation `=Sum([Quantity]*[Price])`. This calculation should seem surprising. Why isn't the field name `Amount used`? This choice is simply a limitation of Access. You must repeat the calculation in a summary field. If you forget this step, you get an error message and the calculation does not occur. When the calculation is created, you can use the form field in the main form.

If you were to display the form, you would see that the Subtotal field displays the total of all records in the Invoice Lineitems table. When this field is used through the subform, however, only the referenced records for the specific Invoice Number are used.

Displaying a total from a subform in a master form

After you have created the calculations necessary in the subform, you can use them in the master form. The Subtotal field is displayed in the main form by referencing the field created in the subform. Figure 10-23 displays this reference.

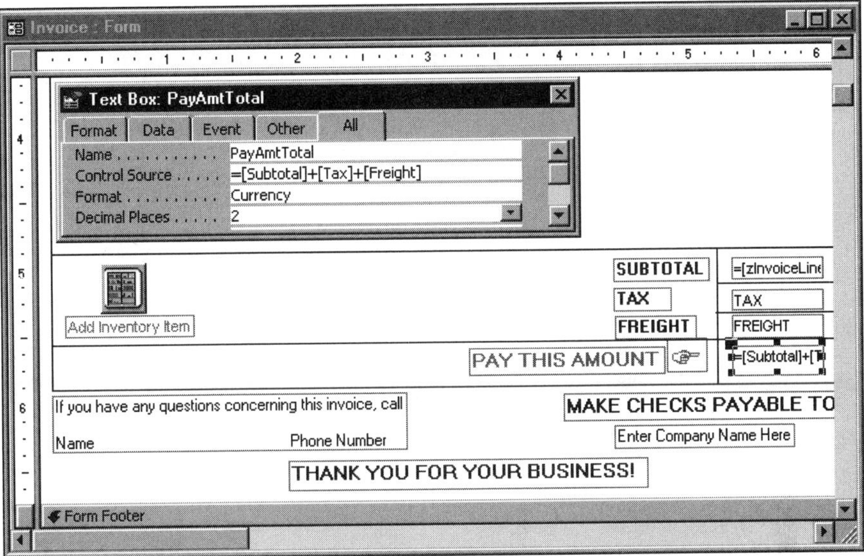

Figure 10-23: The bottom of the invoice form with subtotal calculations.

The calculation `=[zInvoiceLineitems].Form![Subtotal]` references the Subtotal field in the zInvoiceLineitems form. When you have created the field in the master form by referencing a subform field, you can use it for the master form calculation. Notice that in Figure 10-23 a series of lines and rectangles were added to make the form look more polished.

As you can partially see in Figure 10-23, the Pay This Amount field uses the expression `=[Subtotal]+[Tax]+[Freight]`. Because the Subtotal field is in the master form, no reference is necessary. The hand in the Pay This Amount is created with the Wingding True Type font standard in Windows 95.

The very bottom of the screen shows a series of unbound text boxes. You can make these whatever you want for your company on your form.

Creating complex forms with branching, subforms, and buttons is easy if you follow a logical approach to creating and using them.

Part IV

Getting Answers out of Access

Chapter 11

Manipulating Data with Queries and Filters

In This Chapter

- Using multiple-table queries
- Understanding table joins
- Using total queries
- Exploring crosstab queries
- Using parameter queries
- Creating action queries
- Using lookup tables and joins
- Using SQL statements in queries
- Using Filter by Selection
- Using Filter by Form
- Applying a filter in code

In this chapter, you work with advanced queries and filters. We assume that you have a sound understanding of simple select queries and how to build them by using the Query By Example (QBE) grid.

Using the queries in this chapter, you can calculate totals for records, summarize data in row-and-column format, run a query that obtains criteria by prompting the operator of the query, update records, append records to a table, create a new table with fields chosen from other tables, and filter records from a query for display in a form or report.

The Customers, Orders, Order Details, and Products tables from the Northwind sample database that ships with Access have been used to build the queries discussed in this chapter.

Adding More Than One Table to the Query Window

After you create the tables for your database and decide how the tables are related to one another, you are ready to begin creating multiple-table queries to obtain information from several tables at the same time.

By adding more than one table to a query and selecting fields from the tables in the query, you can view information from your database just as though the information from the many tables were in one table.

Suppose that you want to send a letter to all customers who last placed an order more than 90 days ago. To collect this data, you have to get the information from two separate tables: Customers and Orders. You can use the Customers and Orders tables and create for all customers a query in which the CustomerID field in the Customers table equals the CustomerID field in the Orders table and in which the difference between today's date and the OrderDate is more than 90 days. Because of the relationship between Orders and Customers on CustomerID, you have access to the order information for each customer. You can then use the related information from the query to create a report.

The first step in creating a multiple-table query is to open each table in the Query window. The following steps show how to open the Customers and Orders tables in a single query:

1. Click on the Query tab in the Database window.
2. Click on the New button to create a new query.
3. Choose New Query and click on OK in the New Query dialog box.
4. Select the Orders table (double-click on the table name).
5. Select the Customers table (double-click on the table name).
6. Click on the Close button in the Show Table dialog box.

You can also add each table by highlighting the table separately in the list and clicking on Add.

The top pane of the Query Design window is shown in Figure 11-1 with two tables: Orders and Customers.

Figure 11-1: The Query Design window with two files added.

You can add more tables by choosing Query⇨Show Table from the Query Design menu or by clicking on the Show Table button.

Working with the Table/Query Pane

As shown in Figure 11-1, each table is connected by a single line from the primary key field to the foreign key field. You learn in this chapter how to move the table designs so that the lines are displayed correctly.

When Access displays each set of related tables, it places a line between the two tables. This *join line* is a line that graphically represents the link between two tables. In Figure 11-1, the join line goes from the Orders table to the Customers table to connect the two CustomerID fields.

This link is created automatically because a relationship has been set in the Database window. If Access already knows what the relationship is, it automatically creates the link for you when the tables are added to a query. The relationship is displayed as a join line between two tables.

If referential integrity is checked in the relationship between two tables, Access displays a thick portion of the line directly at the table window, similar to the line shown in Figure 11-1. Notice that the line is initially heavy and then becomes thinner between the Orders and Customers boxes (it's heavy on both sides). This line variation tells you that referential integrity has been set up between the two tables in the Relationships Builder. If a one-to-many relationship exists, the many relationship is denoted by an infinity sign (∞).

If you have not specified a relationship between two tables and the following conditions are true, Access 97 automatically joins the tables:

1. Both tables have a field with the same name.
2. The field with the same name in both tables is of the same type (text or numeric, for example).
3. The field is a primary key field in one of the tables.

Access 97 automatically joins the tables if a relationship exists. You can turn off this feature, however, by removing the (default) check from the Enable AutoJoin box in the Global Options tabbed dialog box. To display this dialog box, choose Tools⇨Options⇨Table/Queries and then remove the check.

Understanding the Limitations of Multiple-Table Queries

When you create a query with multiple files, limitations exist on which fields you can edit. You can generally change data in a query dynaset, and your changes are saved to the underlying tables. Normally, you cannot edit a primary key field if referential integrity is in effect and if the field is part of a relationship unless the Cascade Update Related Fields box has a check in it.

To be able to update a table from a query, a value in a specific record in the query must represent a single record in the underlying table. You cannot, therefore, update fields in a crosstab query or total query because both group records to display grouped information. Rather than display the underlying table data, these types of queries display records of data that are calculated and stored in a non-updatable table called a *snapshot.*

Updating limitations

In Access 1.*x*, only the records on the many side of a one-to-many relationship were updatable. That capability has changed in Access 2.0 and Access 97. Table 11-1 lists the updatability for fields in a table. As shown in the table, queries based on one-to-many relationships are updatable in both tables (based on how the query was designed). Any query that creates a snapshot, however, is not updatable.

Table 11-1 Updatability Rules for Queries

Type of Query or Field	*Updatable*	*Comments*
One table	Yes	
One-to-one relationship	Yes	
One-to-many relationship	Mostly	Restrictions based on design methodology (see text).
Crosstab	No	Creates a snapshot of the data.
Total query (Sum, Avg, and so on)	No	Works with grouped data to create a snapshot.
Unique Value property is Yes	No	Shows unique records only in a snapshot.
SQL-specific queries	No	Union and passthrough work with ODBC data.
Calculated field	No	Recalculates automatically.
Read-only fields	No	If opened, read-only or on read-only drive (CD-ROM).
Permissions denied	No	Insert, Replace, or Delete is not granted.
ODBC tables with no primary key	No	A primary key (unique index) must exist.
Paradox table with no primary key	No	A primary key file must exist.
Locked by another user	No	Cannot be updated while a field is locked by another.

Overcoming query limitations

You can see in Table 11-1 that queries and fields in tables sometimes are not updatable. Any query that performs aggregate calculations or that is an ODBC-based SQL query is generally not updatable. All others can be updatable. When your query has more than one table and some of the tables have a one-to-many relationship, some fields may not be updatable, based on the design of the query.

A unique index (primary key) and updatability

If a query uses two tables that have a one-to-many relationship, the "one" side of the join must have a unique (primary key) index on the field that is used for the join. If not, the fields from the one side of the query cannot be updated.

How to replace existing data in a query with a one-to-many relationship

All the fields in the many-side table normally are updatable in a one-to-many query; the one-side table can update all the fields except the primary key (join) field. This situation is usually sufficient for most database application purposes. You normally never change the primary key field in the one-side table because it is the link to the records in the joined tables.

You may, however, sometimes want to change the link field contents in both tables (make a new primary key in the one-side table and have the database program change the link field in all the related records from the many-side table). With Access 97, you can — by defining a relationship between the two tables and using referential integrity. If you define a relationship and enforce referential integrity in the Relationships Builder, two checkboxes are activated. If you want to allow changes (updates) to the primary key field, put a check in the Cascade Update Related Fields box, as shown in Figure 11-2. You then can change the primary key field in a relationship, and Access automatically updates to the new value the link field in the related records in other tables.

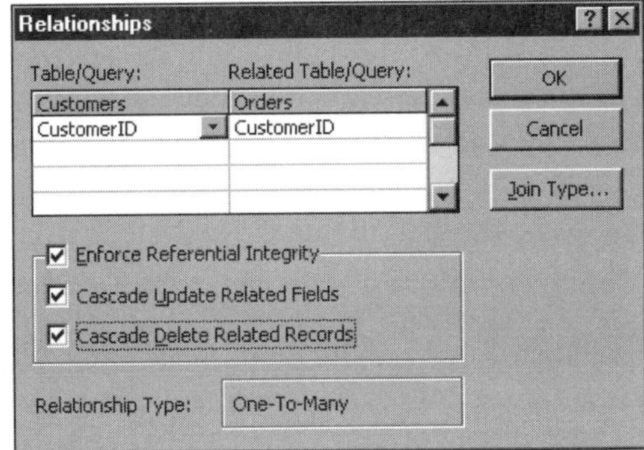

Figure 11-2: The Relationships Builder dialog box with referential integrity turned on.

Design tips for updating fields in queries

There are several tips you should remember when designing multitable queries that you want to use to update fields. Many queries are read-only if you are not careful (when you build them) to make sure they allow editing and updating of data.

- If you want to use AutoLookup between forms, be sure to include in your form the join field from the many-side table (rather than the one-side table). Also, use a combo box or list box to display this field.
- If you want to add records to both tables in a one-to-many relationship, be sure to include the join field from the many-side table and show the field in the datasheet. You then can add records beginning with either table. The one-side join field is copied automatically to the many-side join field.
- If you do not want any updatable fields, set the `Allow Edits` property of the form to `No`.
- If you do not want to update some fields on a form, set the `Tab Stop` property for the control (field) to `No` for these fields.
- If you want to add records to multiple tables in a form, remember to include all (or most) of the fields from both tables. Otherwise, you will not have a complete record of the data in your form.

Temporary non-updatability in a one-to-many relationship

When you update records on the one side of a one-to-many query, you cannot change the many-side join field until you save changes to the one side. You can quickly save changes to the one side by pressing Shift+Enter or choosing File➪Save Record from the menu. After you save the one-side changes, you can change the join field in the many-side record.

Creating Query Joins

You can create joins between tables in the following three ways:

- Create relationships between the tables when you design the database (by choosing Tools➪Relationships from the Database window menu or by clicking on the Relationship button on the toolbar).
- Choose for the query two tables that have a field with the same type and name and that is a primary key field in one of the tables.
- Create joins in the Query window at the time you create a query.

The first two methods are automatic. If you create relationships when you design the tables in your database, Access automatically displays join lines based on those relationships when you add the related tables to a query. It also automatically joins two tables that have a common field, and that field is a primary key in one of the tables.

You may sometimes add to a query some tables that are not already related to a specific file, as in these examples:

- The two tables have a common field, but it does not have the same name.
- A table is not related — and cannot be related to the other table (for example, the Customers table cannot be directly joined to the Order Details table).

If you have two tables that are not automatically joined and you want to relate them, you join them in the Query Design window. When you join tables in the Query Design window, a permanent join is not created between the tables. Rather, the join (relationship) applies only to the table for the query on which you are working.

This relationship is unlike those that are set at the database level, which are joined automatically whenever you work with the two tables in a query.

All tables in a query must be joined to at least one other table. If you place two tables in a query and do not join them, for example, Access creates a query based on a *Cartesian product* (also known as a *cross product*) of the two tables. A Cartesian product means that if five records are in table 1 and six records are in table 2, the resulting query will have 30 records (5 × 6) that probably will be useless to you.

Joining tables

To join the Customers and Orders tables in the query grid, follow these steps:

1. Select the CustomerID field in the Customers table in the Table/Query Pane.
2. Drag the highlighted field to the Orders table (as you drag the field, the Field icon is displayed).
3. Drop the Field icon on the CustomerID field in the Orders table.

The Field icon first appears in the CustomerID field of the Customers table; it then moves to the Orders table. As the Field icon moves between tables, it changes to the symbol indicating that the icon cannot be dropped in the area between the tables. When the icon moves over the CustomerID field, it changes back to the Field icon, indicating that it can be dropped in that location. When you release the mouse button, the join line is displayed.

You also can create joins that make no sense. When you view the data, however, you get less-than-desirable results. If two joined fields have no values in common, no records are selected in your datasheet.

You can select either table first when you create a join.

Never create a meaningless join. For example, do not join the City field from the Customers table to the ShipName field in the Orders table. Although Access lets you create this join, the resulting dynaset has no records in it.

Deleting joins

To delete a join line between two tables, you select the join line and click on the Delete key. You can select the join line by placing the cursor on any part of the line and clicking one time. For example, create a new query by adding the Customers and Orders tables to a query, and then follow these steps to delete the join line between the two tables:

1. Select the join line between the CustomerID fields in the Orders table and the Customers table by placing the cursor on the line and clicking the mouse button.
2. After the join line is highlighted, press the Delete key.

After Step 2, the line should disappear. If you delete a join line between two tables that have a relationship set at the database level, the broken join is effective only for the query in which you broke the join. When you exit the query, the relationship between the two tables remains in effect for other operations, including subsequent queries.

You can also delete a join by selecting it and choosing Edit⇨Delete.

If you delete a join between two tables and the tables remain in the Query window unjoined to other tables, you get unexpected results in the datasheet because of the Cartesian product Access creates from the two tables. The Cartesian product is effective for only this query. The underlying relationship remains intact.

Access enables you to create multiple-field joins between tables (you can draw more than one line). Remember that the join normally must be between two fields that have the same data and data type, or else the query does not find any records from the datasheet to display. This is usually done for tables that have multifield keys.

Understanding Table Joins

Access understands all types of table and query relations, which include the following:

- One-to-one
- One-to-many
- Many-to-one
- Many-to-many

When you specify a relationship between two tables, you establish rules for the type of relationship, not for viewing the data based on the relationship.

To view data in two tables, you must join them through a link. You establish the link by way of a common field (or group of fields) between the two tables. The method of linking the tables is called *joining*. In a query, tables with established relationships are shown as already joined. Within a query, however, you can create new joins or change an existing join line.

Just as different types of relationships exist, different types of joins also exist. This section describes these types of joins:

- Equi-joins (inner joins)
- Outer joins
- Self-joins
- Cross-product joins (Cartesian joins)

Using inner joins (equi-joins)

The Access default join is known as an *inner join,* or *equi-join*. In this type of join, you tell Access to select all records from both tables that have the same value in the fields that are joined.

The Access manuals refer to a default join as an equi-join. In relational database theory, this join is also commonly referred to as an inner join. These terms are interchangeable and are used that way throughout this chapter.

For an example of an equi-join, recall the Customers and Orders tables. Keep in mind that you are looking in these two tables for all records with matching fields. Because the CustomerID field is common to both tables, the equi-join does not show any records for customers who have made no orders or with any orders that do not relate to a valid customer ID. The rules of referential integrity prevent order records not tied to a customer ID. It's possible, of course, to delete all orders from a customer record or to create a new customer record with no orders, but an order should always be related to a valid customer. Referential integrity should prevent a customer ID from being deleted or changed if an order is related to it.

Regardless of how it happens, the Customers table can have in it a record of a customer who has no orders. It is less likely, but still theoretically possible, to have an order with no customer. If you create a query to show customers and their orders, any record of a customer without orders or an order record without a matching customer record is not shown in the resulting dynaset.

It can be important for you to find these "lost" records. One of the features of a query is that it performs several types of joins.

Tip

Access can help you find lost records between tables by using the Query Wizard to build a Find Unmatched Query.

Changing join properties

With the Customers and Orders tables joined, certain join behaviors, or *properties,* exist between the tables. The join property is a rule that says to display (for the fields you specify) all records that correspond to the characters found in the CustomerID field in the Customers table and in a corresponding CustomerID field in the Orders table.

To translate this rule into a practical example, look at what happens in the Customers and Orders tables:

- If a record in the Customers table has a number for a customer not found in the Orders table, that Customer record is not shown.
- If a record in the Orders table has a number for a customer ID not in the Customers table, that Order's record is not shown.

This system makes sense, at least most of the time. You don't want to see records for customers without orders (or do you?).

A join property is a rule operated by Access. This rule tells Access how to interpret any exceptions — possibly errors — between two tables. The rule asks, "Should the noncorresponding records be shown?"

Access has several types of joins, each with its own characteristics or behaviors. Access lets you quickly change the type of join by changing its properties. You can change join properties by selecting the join line between tables and double-clicking on the line. Figure 11-3 shows the Join Properties dialog box that is displayed when you select the join line between the Customers and Orders tables.

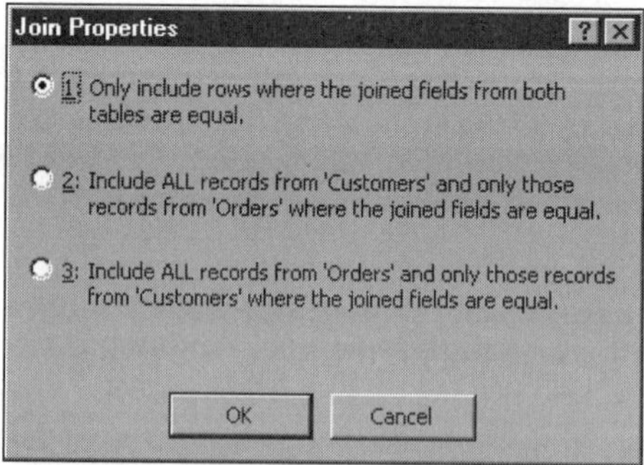

Figure 11-3: The Join Properties dialog box.

The first option in the dialog box is known as an inner join, and the other two are known as *outer joins*. These joins control the behavior of Access as it builds the dynaset from the query.

Your Query Design window should display two tables in the top pane of the Query window: Orders and Customers. In the following sections, these tables are used as examples of how inner and outer joins operate.

Displaying an inner join

To display an inner join, follow this procedure:

1. In the QBE pane, select the fields CustomerID and ContactName from the Customers table and the fields OrderID and OrderDate from the Orders table.
2. Next, display the dynaset by clicking on the Datasheet button on the toolbar. The datasheet should look like Figure 11-4, displaying each customer, all the customers' orders, and the order date for each order. Scroll through the records until you reach the bottom of the datasheet.

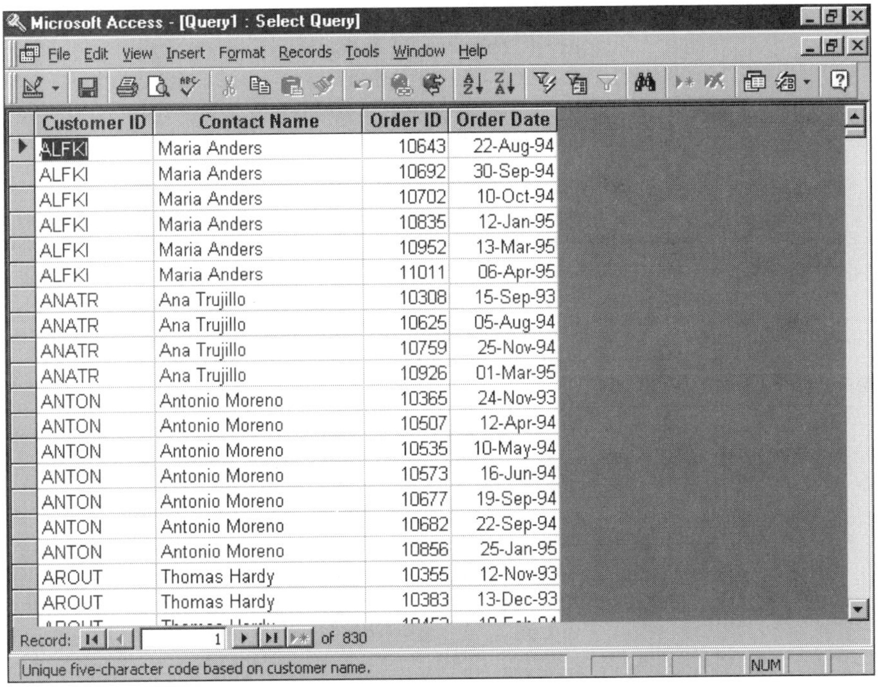

Microsoft Access - [Query1 : Select Query]

File Edit View Insert Format Records Tools Window Help

Customer ID	Contact Name	Order ID	Order Date
ALFKI	Maria Anders	10643	22-Aug-94
ALFKI	Maria Anders	10692	30-Sep-94
ALFKI	Maria Anders	10702	10-Oct-94
ALFKI	Maria Anders	10835	12-Jan-95
ALFKI	Maria Anders	10952	13-Mar-95
ALFKI	Maria Anders	11011	06-Apr-95
ANATR	Ana Trujillo	10308	15-Sep-93
ANATR	Ana Trujillo	10625	05-Aug-94
ANATR	Ana Trujillo	10759	25-Nov-94
ANATR	Ana Trujillo	10926	01-Mar-95
ANTON	Antonio Moreno	10365	24-Nov-93
ANTON	Antonio Moreno	10507	12-Apr-94
ANTON	Antonio Moreno	10535	10-May-94
ANTON	Antonio Moreno	10573	16-Jun-94
ANTON	Antonio Moreno	10677	19-Sep-94
ANTON	Antonio Moreno	10682	22-Sep-94
ANTON	Antonio Moreno	10856	25-Jan-95
AROUT	Thomas Hardy	10355	12-Nov-93
AROUT	Thomas Hardy	10383	13-Dec-93

Record: 1 of 830

Unique five-character code based on customer name. NUM

Figure 11-4: The datasheet for an inner join.

Note that each of the 830 records has entries in all four fields: Every record displayed from the Customers table has a corresponding record or records in the Orders table.

When you double-click on the join line between the Customers and Orders tables in the query design window, you see that the join property for these two tables becomes the first selection shown in the Join Properties dialog box (refer to Figure 11-3). This type of join is an inner join, or equi-join. Equi-joins are the most common type of joins between tables. These joins show only the records that have a correspondence between tables.

Creating an outer join

Unlike equi-joins (inner joins), you use *outer joins* to show all records in one table while showing common records in the other. An outer join graphically points to one of the tables. When you look at the join line, it says — in effect — "Show all records from the main table (the one missing the arrow) and show only matching records in the table being pointed to."

Return to the Query Design window and again double-click on the join line between Customers and Orders.

Click on the second option in the Join Properties dialog box, which includes all records from the Customers table and only those records from the Orders table in which the joined fields are equal. Then click on OK. Note that the join line now has at one end an arrow pointing to the right to the Orders table. In database terminology, this arrow is known as a *left outer join.*

Click on the Datasheet button to display this dynaset. Everything looks the same as before. Page down until you see record number 189. You should see a record for CustomerID FISSA, which is Diego Roel, who has no corresponding entry in either the OrderID or OrderDate field (see Figure 11-5). This record results from selecting the second join property ("include all records from Customers") in the Join Properties dialog box.

Unlike equi-joins, outer joins show all corresponding records between two tables and records that do not have a corresponding record in the other table. In Figure 11-5, you see a record for Diego Roel but no corresponding record for any orders.

If you have changed the display order of the tables since adding them to the Query window, Access does not follow the table order you set up; rather, it uses the original order in which you selected the tables. Because the information is usually the same in either table, it doesn't make a difference which field is selected first.

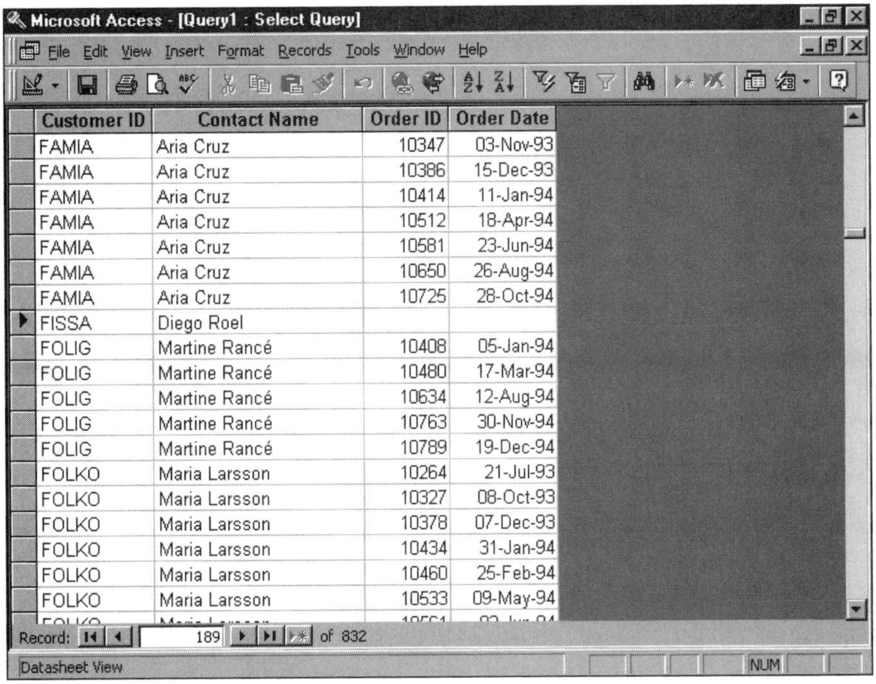

Microsoft Access - [Query1 : Select Query]

File Edit View Insert Format Records Tools Window Help

Customer ID	Contact Name	Order ID	Order Date
FAMIA	Aria Cruz	10347	03-Nov-93
FAMIA	Aria Cruz	10386	15-Dec-93
FAMIA	Aria Cruz	10414	11-Jan-94
FAMIA	Aria Cruz	10512	18-Apr-94
FAMIA	Aria Cruz	10581	23-Jun-94
FAMIA	Aria Cruz	10650	26-Aug-94
FAMIA	Aria Cruz	10725	28-Oct-94
FISSA	Diego Roel		
FOLIG	Martine Rancé	10408	05-Jan-94
FOLIG	Martine Rancé	10480	17-Mar-94
FOLIG	Martine Rancé	10634	12-Aug-94
FOLIG	Martine Rancé	10763	30-Nov-94
FOLIG	Martine Rancé	10789	19-Dec-94
FOLKO	Maria Larsson	10264	21-Jul-93
FOLKO	Maria Larsson	10327	08-Oct-93
FOLKO	Maria Larsson	10378	07-Dec-93
FOLKO	Maria Larsson	10434	31-Jan-94
FOLKO	Maria Larsson	10460	25-Feb-94
FOLKO	Maria Larsson	10533	09-May-94

Record: 189 of 832

Datasheet View NUM

Figure 11-5: A datasheet with a left outer join.

Click on the Design button on the toolbar to return to the Query Design window. When you created the outer join for the Customers table with the Orders table, Access changed the appearance of the graphical join line to show an arrow at one end. As shown in Figure 11-6, the arrow points toward the Orders table. This arrow tells you that Access has created an outer join and therefore shows you all records in the Customers table and only those that match in the Orders table.

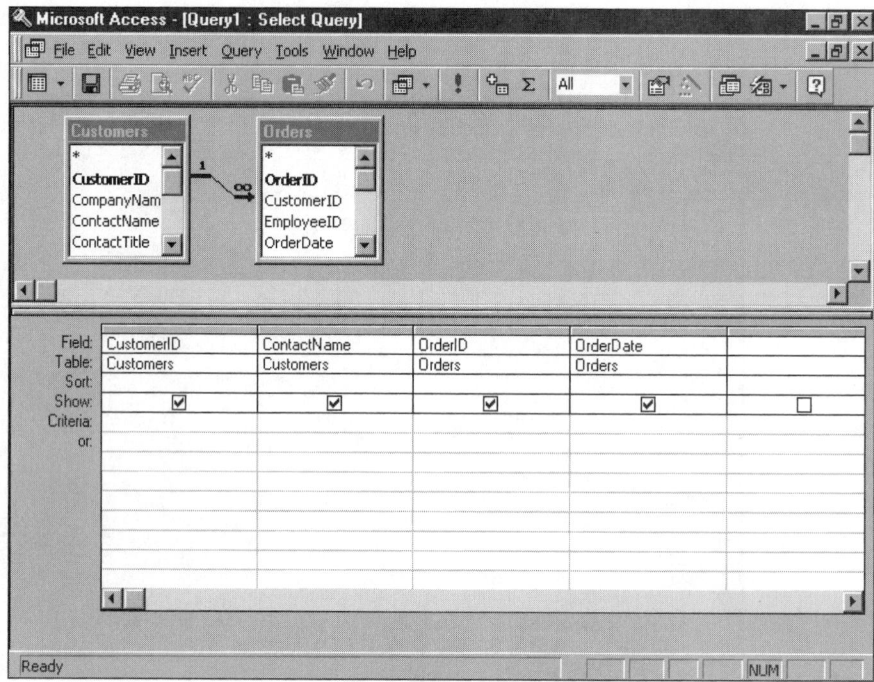

Figure 11-6: The Table/Query Pane shows a left outer join.

Creating another outer join

Return to the Query Design window, and again double-click on the join line between the Customers and Orders tables.

Choose the third option ("include all records from Orders") in the Join Properties dialog box, and then click on OK. Note that the arrow on the join line now points to the Customers table, as shown in Figure 11-7. In database terminology, this arrow is a *right outer join.* You can see the join type by inspecting the SQL window in Query Design mode. You see either the statement `LEFT JOIN` or the statement `RIGHT JOIN`, depending on the join type you chose in the Join Properties dialog box. You can find out more about these statements later in this chapter.

Click on the Datasheet button to display this dynaset. Because the referential integrity rules set up for the Customers and Orders tables prevent you from entering an order without a related customer, you do not see any records in the datasheet in which CustomerID and ContactName are blank. All 830 records are displayed.

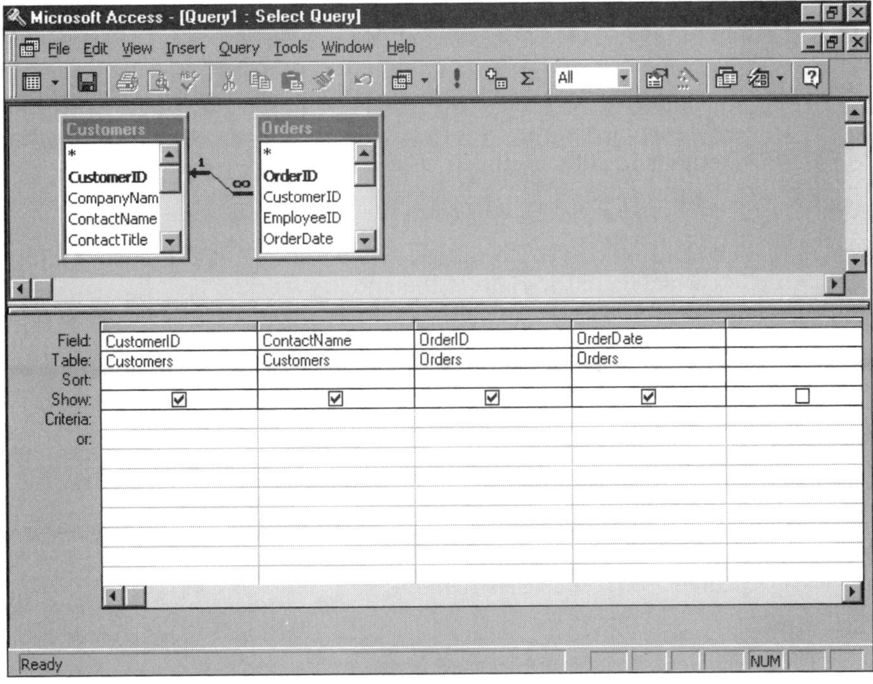

Figure 11-7: The Table/Query Pane shows a right outer join.

Creating Queries That Calculate Totals

Many times, you want to find information in your tables based on total-type data. You may want to find, for example, the total number of orders you have processed or the total amount of freight spent on orders last year. Access supplies the tools to fulfill these queries without the need for programming.

Access totals calculations by using nine aggregate functions that enable you to determine a specific value based on the contents of a field. For example, you can determine the average freight of all orders, the maximum and minimum freight amounts of all orders you have processed, or the total count of all records in which the order date is between two dates. Performing each of these examples as a query results in a dynaset of answer fields based on the mathematical calculations you requested.

To create a total query, you use a new row in the QBE pane: the Total row.

Displaying the Total row in the QBE pane

To create a query that performs a total calculation, you create a select query and then activate the Total row in the QBE pane. After you open a new query using the Orders table, you can use either of these two selection methods to activate the Total row.

- Choose View⇨Totals from the Query Design menu.
- Click on the Totals button on the toolbar. It's the Greek letter sigma (Σ), which is to the right of the midway mark.

Figure 11-8 shows the Total row after it has been added to the QBE pane. Note that the Totals button has been chosen on the toolbar and that the Total row is placed in the QBE pane between the Table and Sort rows.

If the toolbar is not visible, choose View⇨Toolbars from the Query Design menu. Then choose Query Design and close the dialog box.

If you do not see the Table row on-screen, the Total row is between the Field and Show rows. You can activate the Table row by choosing View⇨Table Names from the Design menu.

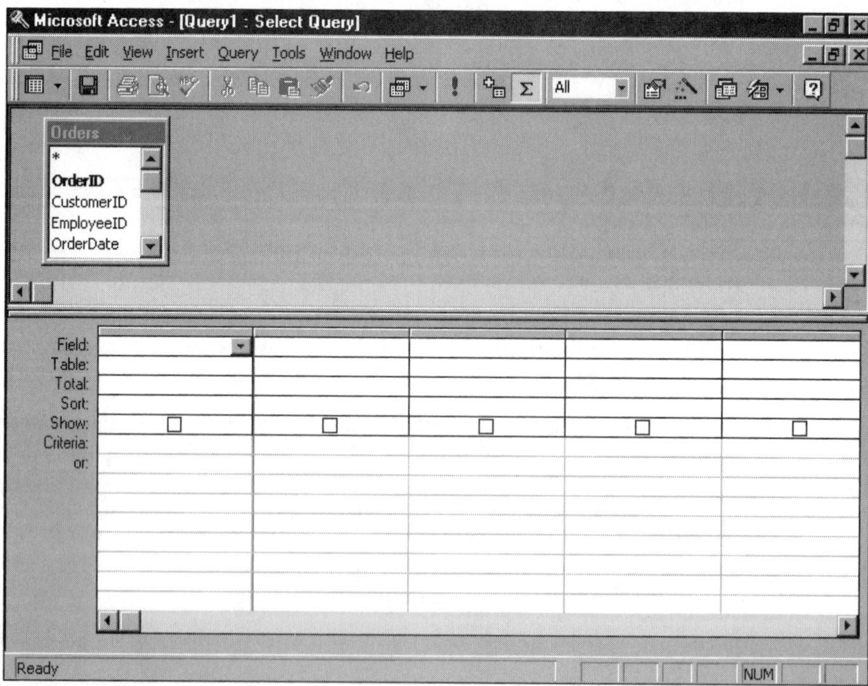

Figure 11-8: Activating the Total row in the QBE pane.

What is an aggregate function?

The word *aggregate* implies gathering a mass (a group or series) of items and working on this mass as a whole — a total. An *aggregate function,* therefore, is a function that performs some mathematical function on an entire group of records. The function can be a simple *count* or a *complex expression* you specify, based on a series of mathematical functions.

Removing the Total row from the QBE pane

To deactivate the Total row in the QBE pane, simply click on the Totals button or choose from the Totals/View menu. The Totals button is a toggle that turns the display of the Total row on or off.

Understanding the Total row options

You can perform total calculations against all records or groups of records in one or more tables. To perform a calculation, you must choose one of the options from the drop-down list box in the Total row for every field you include in the query, including any hidden fields (Show option turned off). Figure 11-9 shows the drop-down list box in the Total row in the OrderID field.

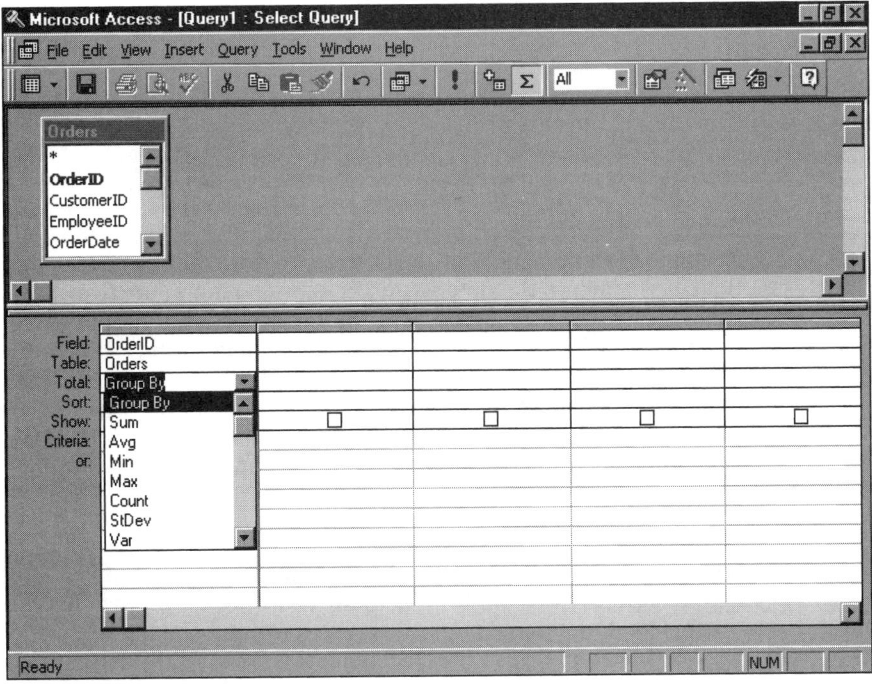

Figure 11-9: The drop-down list box in the Total row.

The 12 options in the Totals list box can be divided into four distinct categories:

- Group By
- Aggregate
- Expression
- Total field record limit

Table 11-2 lists each category, its number of Total options, and its purpose.

Table 11-2 Total Option Categories

Category	*Number of Options*	*Purpose of Operator*
Group By	1	Groups common records to perform aggregate calculations against
Aggregate	9	Specifies a mathematical or selection operation to perform against a field
Expression	1	Groups several total operators and performs the group totals
Total field	1	Limits records before totaling, performing a total calculation against a certain group of fields

Note that the aggregate category has nine options. Its options are used by the other three categories.

Group By category

The Group By category has one option, the Group By option, which you use to specify a certain field in the QBE pane that will be used as a grouping field. If you select the field OrderDate, for example, the Group By option tells Access to group all records with the same order date. This option is the default for all Total cells; when you drag a field to the QBE pane, Access automatically selects this option. Figure 11-9 shows that it is also the first choice in the drop-down list box. These groups of records are used for performing an aggregate calculation against another field in the query. This subject is discussed in detail later in this chapter.

Expression category

Like the Group By category, the Expression category has only one option: Expression (the second-from-last option in the drop-down list box). You use this option to tell Access that you will use one or more aggregate calculations in the Field cell in the QBE pane to create a calculated field. You may want to create a query that shows each customer and how much freight the customer paid, based on the customer's orders. This process requires that you create a calculated field that uses a sum aggregate against the Freight field in the Orders table. This type of calculation is discussed in detail later in this chapter.

Total Field Record Limit category

The Total Field Record Limit category is the third category that has a single option: the Where option (the last choice in the drop-down list box). When you choose this option, you tell Access that you want to specify limiting criteria against an aggregate type field, as opposed to a Group By or an Expression field. The limiting criteria are performed before the aggregate options are executed.

Suppose that you want to create a query, for example, that counts all orders by the ShipVia method that have order dates of less than 30 days. Because the OrderDate field is not to be used for a grouping and isn't used to perform an aggregate calculation, you specify the Where option. By doing so, you tell Access to use this field only as a limiting criteria field — before it performs the aggregate calculation (counting types of ShipVia methods). This type of operation is also discussed in detail later in this chapter.

Aggregate category

Unlike the other categories, the Aggregate category has nine options: Sum, Avg, Min, Max, Count, StDev, Var, First, and Last. These options are displayed as the second through tenth options in the drop-down list box. Each option performs an operation. Seven of the options perform mathematical operations, and two perform simple selection operations. When you choose one of these options, Access finds (calculates or determines) some answer or value and supplies it to a cell in the resulting dynaset. You may want to determine, for example, the maximum (Max) and minimum (Min) freight of each order in the Freight field in the Orders table. On the other hand, you may want to determine the total number (Count) of orders in the Orders table. You use these aggregate options to solve these types of queries.

These types of options are what most people think of when they hear the words "total query." Each of the options performs a calculation against a field in the QBE pane of the query and returns a single answer in the dynaset. As an example, there can be only one maximum freight for all orders. Several orders may have the same maximum freight amount, but only one freight amount is the largest.

The other three categories of options can be used against any type of Access field (Text, Memo, or Yes/No, for example). Some of the aggregate options, however, can be performed only against specific field types. You cannot, for example, perform a Sum option against Text type data, and you cannot use a Max option against an OLE object.

Table 11-3 lists each aggregate option, describes what it does, and indicates which field types you can use with it.

Table 11-3 Total Row Aggregate Options

Option	*Finds*	*Field Type Support*
Count	Number of non-Null values in a field object	Counter, Number, Currency, Date/Time, Yes/No, Text, Memo, OLE object
Sum	Total of the values in a field	Counter, Number, Currency, Date/Time, Yes/No
Avg	Average of values in a field	Counter, Number, Currency, Date/Time, Yes/No
Max	Highest value in a field	Counter, Number, Currency, Date/Time, Yes/No, Text
Min	Lowest value in a field	Counter, Number, Currency, Date/Time, Yes/No, Text
StDev	Standard deviation of values in a field	Counter, Number, Currency Date/Time, Yes/No
Var	Population variance of values in a field	Counter, Number, Currency, Date/Time, Yes/No
First	Field value from the first record in a table or query	Counter, Number, Currency, Date/Time, Yes/No, Text, Memo, OLE object
Last	Field value from the last record in a table or query	Counter, Number, Currency, Date/Time, Yes/No, Text, Memo, OLE object

Performing totals on all records

You can use total queries to perform calculations against all records in a table or query. For example, you can find the total number of orders in the Orders table, their average freight amount, and the maximum freight amount of the orders. To create this query, follow these steps (your query should look similar to Figure 11-10):

1. Select the Orders table.
2. Click on the Totals button on the toolbar to turn it on.
3. Double-click on the OrderID field in the Orders table.
4. Double-click on the Freight field in the Orders table.

5. Double-click on the Freight field in the Orders table again.
6. In the Total cell of OrderID, select Count.
7. In the Total cell of Freight, select Avg.
8. In the second Total cell of Freight, select Max.

The query in Figure 11-10 calculates the total number of order records in the Orders table as well as the average freight amount of all orders and the largest freight amount of all the orders.

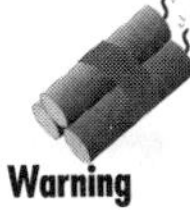

The Count option in the Total cell can be performed against any field in the table (or query). Count eliminates any records, however, that have a Null value in the field you select. You may want to select the primary key field on which to perform the Count total, therefore, because this field cannot have any Null values, which ensures an accurate record count.

If you click on the Datasheet button on the toolbar, you should see a query similar to Figure 11-11. Notice that the dynaset has only one record. When you perform calculations against all records in a table or query, the resulting dynaset has only one record.

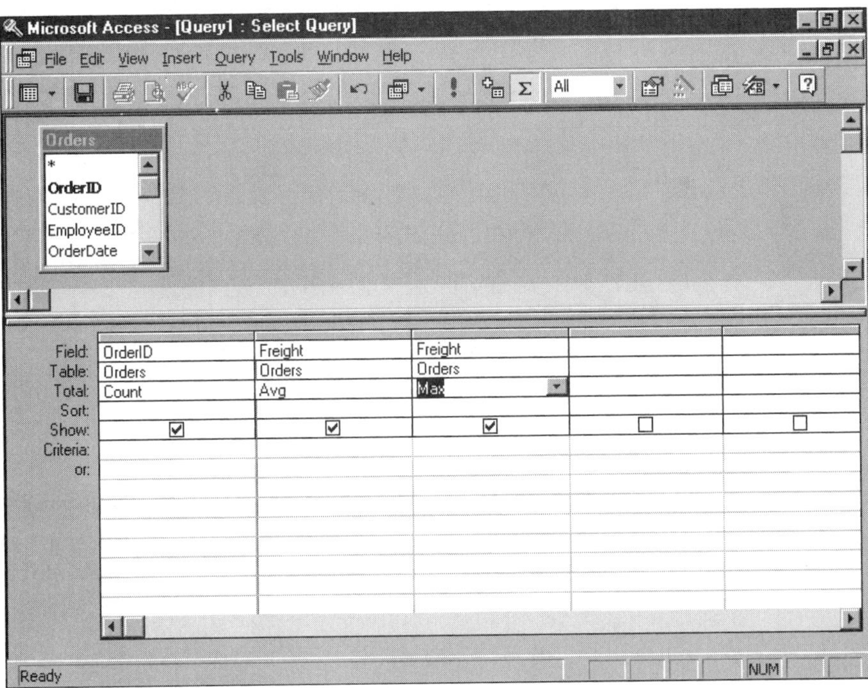

Figure 11-10: A query against all records in the Orders table.

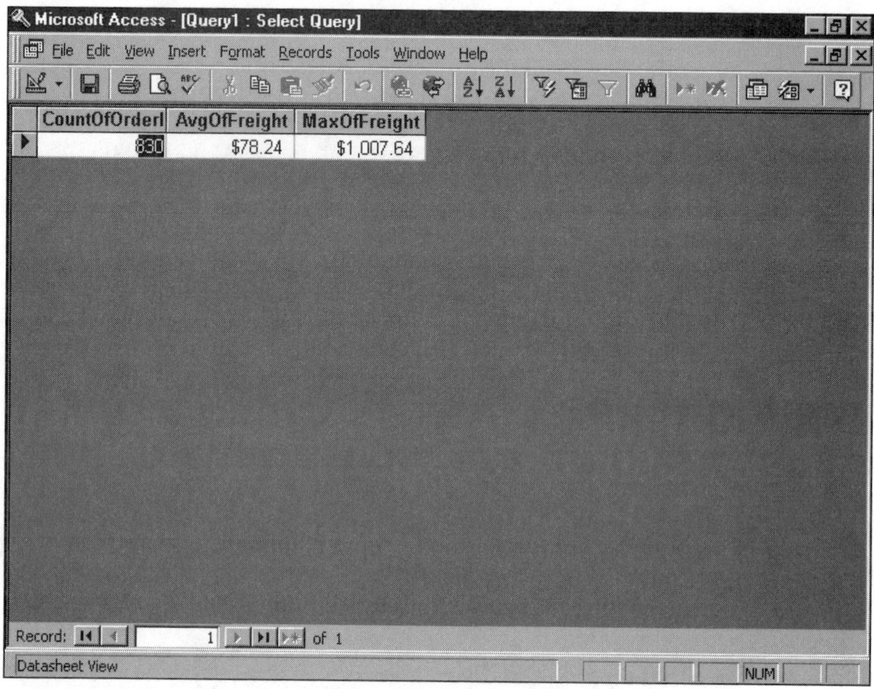

Figure 11-11: This datasheet of a dynaset was created from a total query against all records in a table.

Access creates a default column heading for all Total fields in a totals datasheet, like the one shown in Figure 11-11. The heading name is a product of the name of the total option and the field name. The heading names in the figure, therefore, are CountOfOrderID, AvgOfFreight, and MaxOfFreight. You can change the column heading name to something more appropriate by renaming the field in the QBE pane in the Design window. As with any other field you want to rename, you simply place the cursor at the beginning of the field cell you want to rename (to the left of the field name). Then type the name you want to display, followed by a colon.

Performing totals on groups of records

You will most often want to perform totals on a group of records rather than on all records. For example, you may want to calculate the total number of orders you have processed for each day in the past month. In other words, you want to create a group for each order date and then perform the total calculation against each of these groups. In database parlance, this process is known as *control break totaling*.

Calculating totals for a single group

When you create your query, you specify which field or fields to use for grouping the totals and which fields to perform the totals against. In the preceding example, to group the OrderDate field, you select the Group By option in the Total cell. Follow these steps to create the query:

1. Open a new query and select the Orders table.
2. Click on the Totals button (Σ) on the toolbar to turn it on.
3. Double-click on the OrderDate field in the Orders table.
4. Double-click on the OrderID field in the Orders table.
5. In the Total cell in the OrderDate field, select Group By.
6. In the Total cell in the OrderID field, select Count.

The query in Figure 11-12 groups all like order dates and then performs the count total for each order date. Unlike what happens when you perform totals against all records, this query produces a dynaset of many records — one record for each order date. Figure 11-13 shows what the datasheet looks like if you click on the Datasheet button on the toolbar.

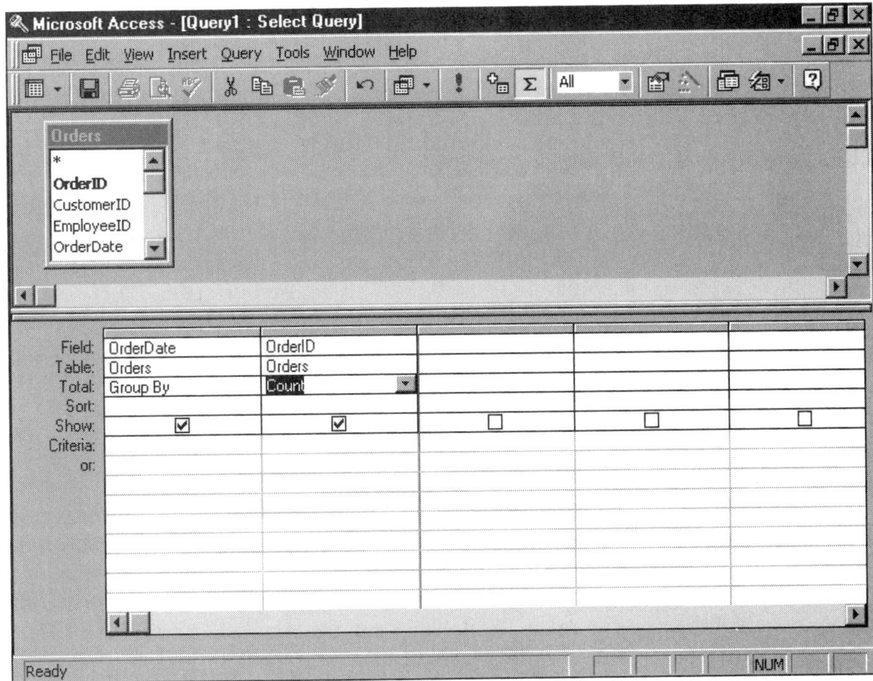

Figure 11-12: Totals against a group of records.

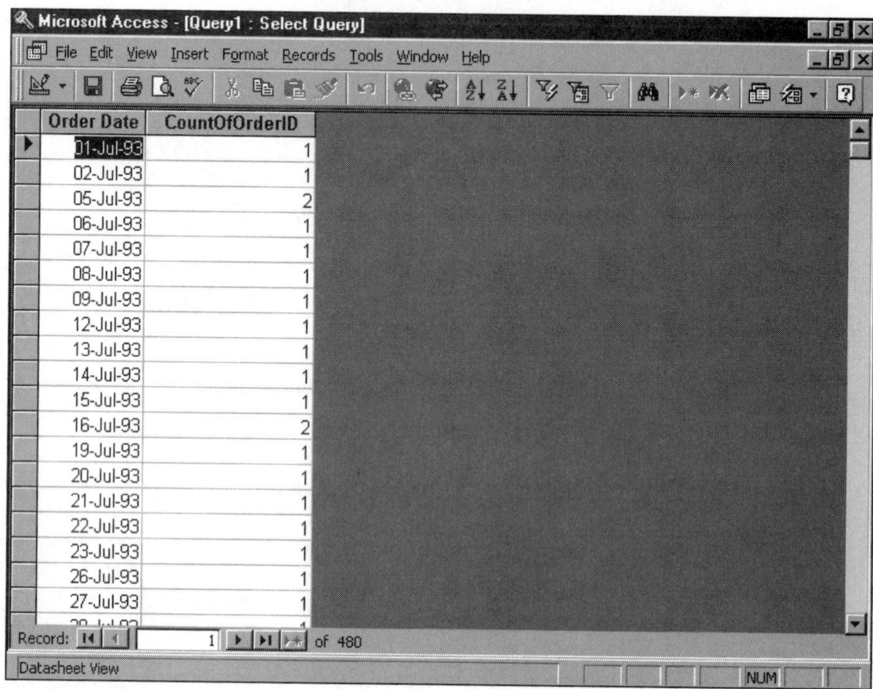

Figure 11-13: A datasheet of totals against the group OrderDate field.

The dynaset in Figure 11-13 has a single record for each order date. Note that the count was performed against each order date: one on 1-Jul-93, two on 5-Jul-93, and so on. Also notice that the Group By field displays one record for each unique value in that field. The OrderDate field is specified as the Group By field and displays a single record for each order date, showing 01-Jul-93, 02-Jul-93, 05-Jul-93, and so on. Each of these records is shown as a row heading for the datasheet, indicating a unique record for each specified order date that begins with the Group By field content. In this case, each unique record is easy to identify by the single-field row heading under OrderDate.

Calculating totals for several groups

You can perform group totals against multiple fields and multiple tables as easily as you can with a single field in a single table. You may want to group by both customer and order date to determine the number of orders a customer placed on each date. To create a total query for this example, add the Customers table to the query in Figure 11-12 and then add the CustomerID field. Specify Group By in both Total fields (CustomerID and OrderDate).

This query, shown in Figure 11-14, uses two tables and also groups by two fields to perform the count total. The query first groups by OrderDate and then by CustomerID. When you click on the Datasheet button on the toolbar, you see a datasheet similar to the one in Figure 11-15.

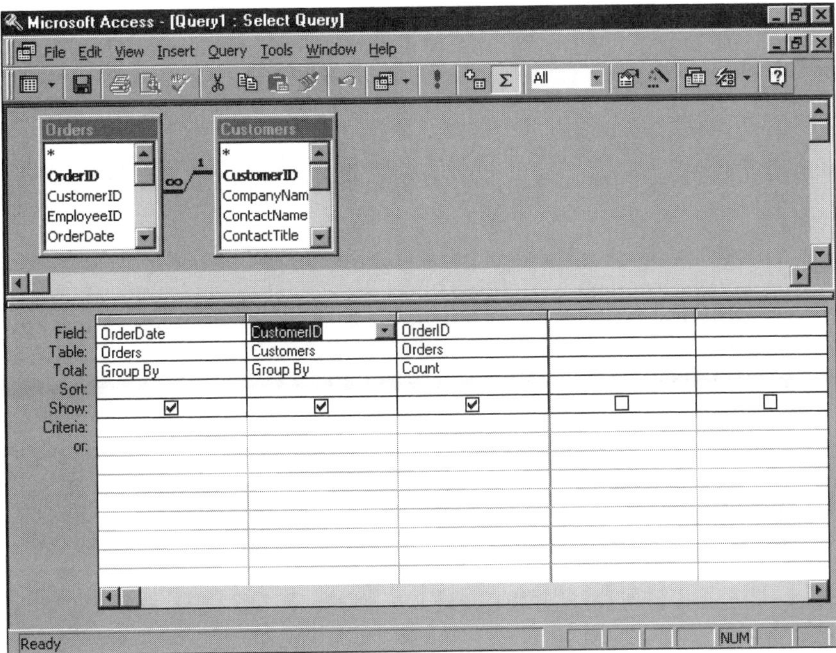

Figure 11-14: A multiple-table, multiple-field Group By total query.

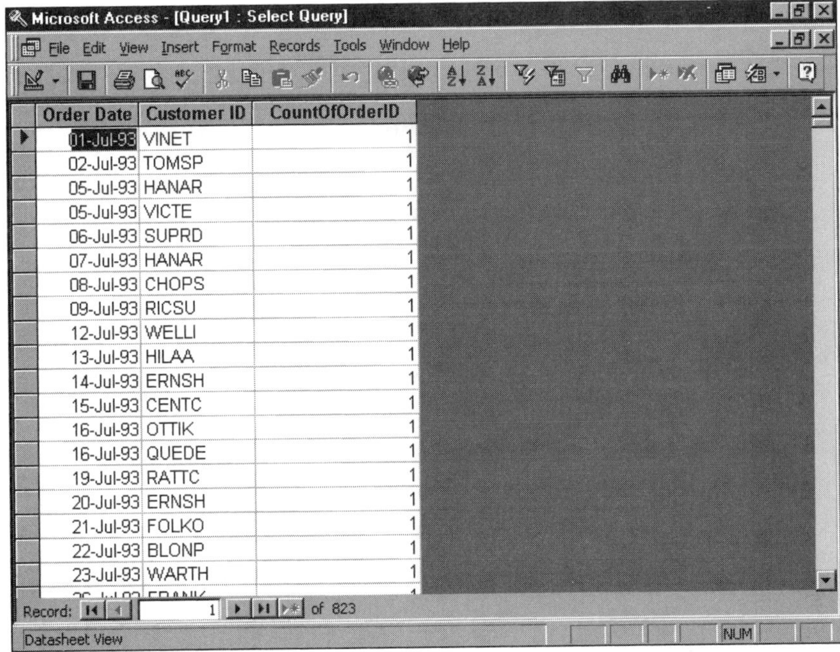

Figure 11-15: A datasheet from a multiple-field Group By query.

The datasheet in Figure 11-15 shows two records for the order date 05-Jul-93, which has two orders. The datasheet has a unique record based on two Group By fields: CustomerID and OrderDate. The unique row headings for this datasheet are created, therefore, by combining both fields — first the OrderDate and then the CustomerID.

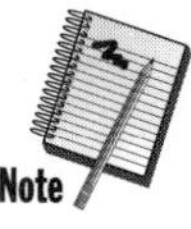

You can think of the Group By fields in a total query as fields that specify the row headings for the datasheet.

Access groups records based on the order of the Group By fields in the QBE pane (from left to right). Therefore, you should pay attention to the order of the Group By fields. Although the order does not change the aggregate totals of the fields, the order of the Group By fields determines how you see the results in the datasheet. If you place the Order Date field before the CustomerID field, the resulting datasheet shows the records in order first by date and then by customer.

By changing the order of the Group By fields in a total query, you can look at your data in new and creative ways.

Specifying criteria for a total query

In addition to being able to group records for total queries, you can specify criteria to limit the records that are processed or displayed in a total calculation. When you specify record criteria in total queries, you have several options available. You can create criteria against these three fields:

- A Group By field
- An Aggregate Total field
- A Non-Aggregate Total field

Using any one or all three of these criteria types, you can easily limit the scope of your total query to a finite number of criteria.

A Group By field

To limit the scope of records used in a grouping, you specify criteria in the Group By fields. For example, you may want to calculate the average freight amount of only two ShipVia types. To do so, you must specify criteria on the Group By field ShipVia. This query looks like the one shown in Figure 11-16.

By specifying criteria in the Group By field, the aggregate calculations are performed on only those records that meet the Group By criteria. In Figure 11-16, the count and average freight amount are performed only for orders that have the specified ShipVia types. This calculation results in a two-record dynaset, with one for each ShipVia type.

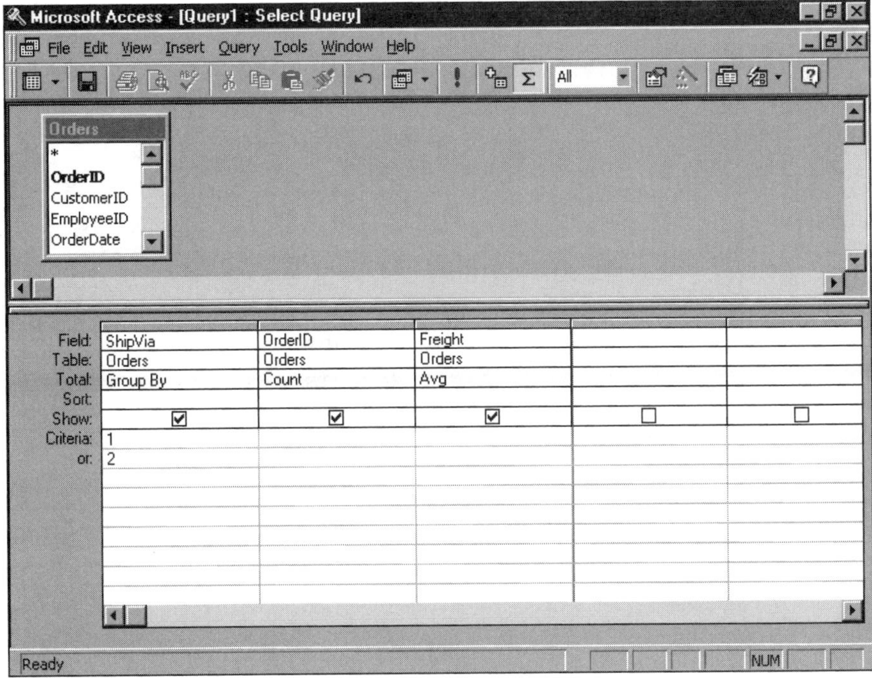

Figure 11-16: Specifying criteria in a Group By field.

An Aggregate Total field

At times, you may want a query to calculate aggregate totals first and then display only those totals from the aggregate calculations that meet specified criteria. In other words, you want Access to determine all totals for each Group By field and then use the criteria to limit the data in the Total field before creating the resulting dynaset.

A query to find the average freight amount of all orders, grouped by ShipVia type, in which the average freight amount of any order is greater than $20 should look like Figure 11-17. Note that the criterion >20 is placed in the Aggregate Total field Freight. This query calculates the average freight amount of all orders grouped by ShipVia type. Then the query determines whether the calculated totals for each record are greater than 20. Records greater than 20 are added to the resulting Recordset, and records less than or equal to 20 are discarded. Note that the criteria are used after the aggregate calculations are performed.

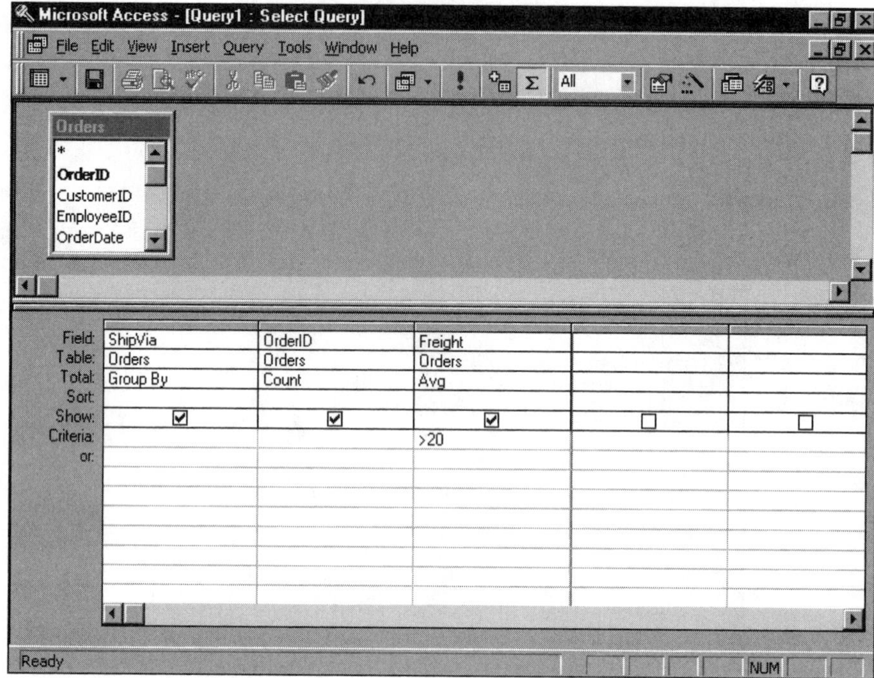

Figure 11-17: A query with a criterion set against an Aggregate Total field.

Non-Aggregate Total field

The example in Figure 11-17 limits the records after performing the calculations against Total fields. You also can specify that you want Access to limit the records based on a Total field before performing total calculations. In other words, you limit the range of records against which the calculation is performed. Doing so creates a criterion similar to the first type of criterion; the field against which you want to set a criterion is not a Group By field.

You may want to display, for example, the total amount of freight charged for orders having a freight amount of less than $15. You should use the Freight field to specify a criterion, but you should not perform any calculations against this field or use it to group by. In fact, you shouldn't even show the field in the resulting datasheet.

Figure 11-18 shows what the query should look like. Note the use of the Where Total option in the last Freight column.

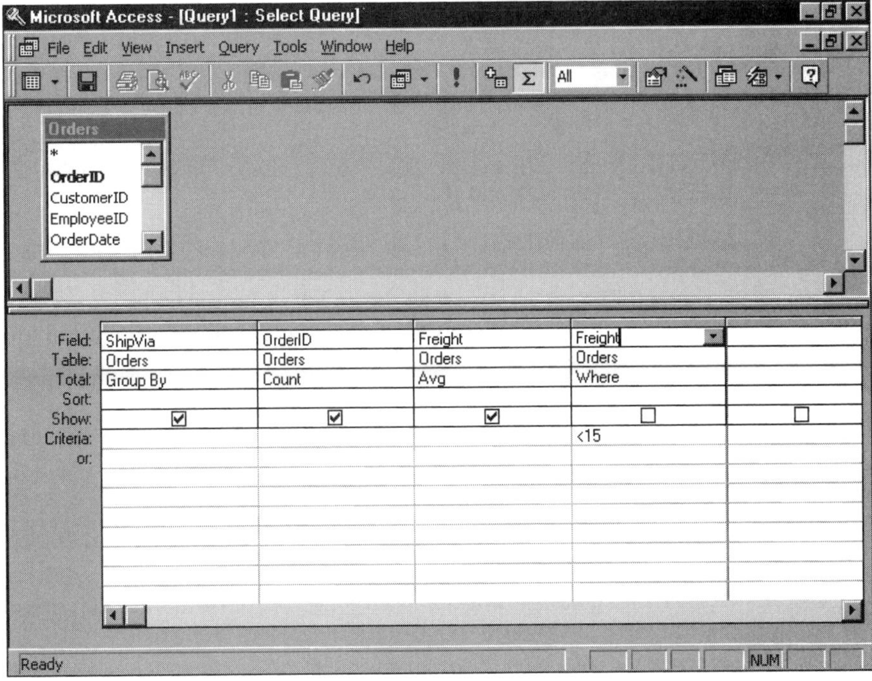

Figure 11-18: Specifying a criterion for a non-aggregate field.

Access automatically turns off the Show cell whenever it encounters a Where option in a field's Total cell. Access understands that you are using the field only to specify criteria because you don't want to see it.

In the query you just completed, Access displays only those records for orders that have freight amounts of less than $15. All other records are discarded.

When you specify a Where option in a Total cell, you cannot show the field. The reason is that Access uses the field to evaluate the Where criteria before performing the calculation. The contents are usable, therefore, only for the limiting criteria. If you try to turn on the Show cell, Access displays an error message.

Creating Crosstab Queries

With Access, you can use a specialized type of total query, the *crosstab,* to display summarized data in a compact and readable format. A crosstab query summarizes the data in the fields from your tables and presents the resulting dynaset in row-and-column format.

Understanding the crosstab query

A *crosstab query* is simply a two-dimensional summary matrix created from your tables. This query presents summary data in a spreadsheet-like format you create from fields you specify. In this specialized type of total query, the Total row in the QBE pane is always active. You cannot toggle off the Total row in a crosstab query.

In addition, the Total row in the QBE pane is used for specifying a Group By total option for both the row and column headings. Like other total queries, the Group By option specifies the row headings for the query datasheet and comes from the actual contents of the field. Unlike other total queries, however, the crosstab query also obtains its column headings from the value in a field (table or calculated) rather than from the field names.

The fields used as rows and columns must always have a Group By in the Total row. Otherwise, Access reports an error when you attempt to display or run the query.

For example, you may want to create a query that displays the OrderDate field as the row heading and the customer's country as the column heading, with each cell containing a total for each order date in each country. Table 11-4 shows what the query should look like.

In this table, the row headings are specified by OrderDate. The column headings are specified by Country. The cell content in the intersection of any row and column is a summary of records that meet both conditions. The 17-Apr-96 row that intersects the Belgium column, for example, shows that there is one order from the country of Belgium. The 21-Apr-96 row that intersects with the Brazil column shows that there is one order from the country of Brazil.

Table 11-4 shows a simple crosstab query created from the fields OrderDate and Country, with the intersecting cell contents determined by a Count total on any field in the Orders table.

Table 11-4 A Typical Crosstab Query Format

OrderDate	*Belgium*	*Brazil*	*Canada*
17-Apr-96	1		
18-Apr-96	1		
19-Apr-96	1		
20-Apr-96			1
21-Apr-96		1	1

Creating the crosstab query

Now that you have a conceptual understanding of a crosstab query, it's time to create one. To create a crosstab query like the one described in Table 11-4, follow these steps:

1. Begin a new query and select the Customers and Orders tables.
2. Double-click on the OrderDate field in the Orders table.
3. Double-click on the Country field in the Customers table.
4. Double-click on the OrderID field in the Orders table.
5. Choose Query⇨Crosstab in the Query Design menu, or click on the Query Type button on the toolbar. (This step drops down a box that lists the types of queries.)
6. In the Crosstab cell in the OrderDate field, select Row Heading.
7. In the Crosstab cell in the Country field, select Column Heading.
8. In the Crosstab cell in the OrderID field, select Value.
9. In the Total cell in the OrderID field, select Count.

Your query should look similar to Figure 11-19. Notice that Access inserted a new row labeled Crosstab between the Total and Sort rows in the QBE pane.

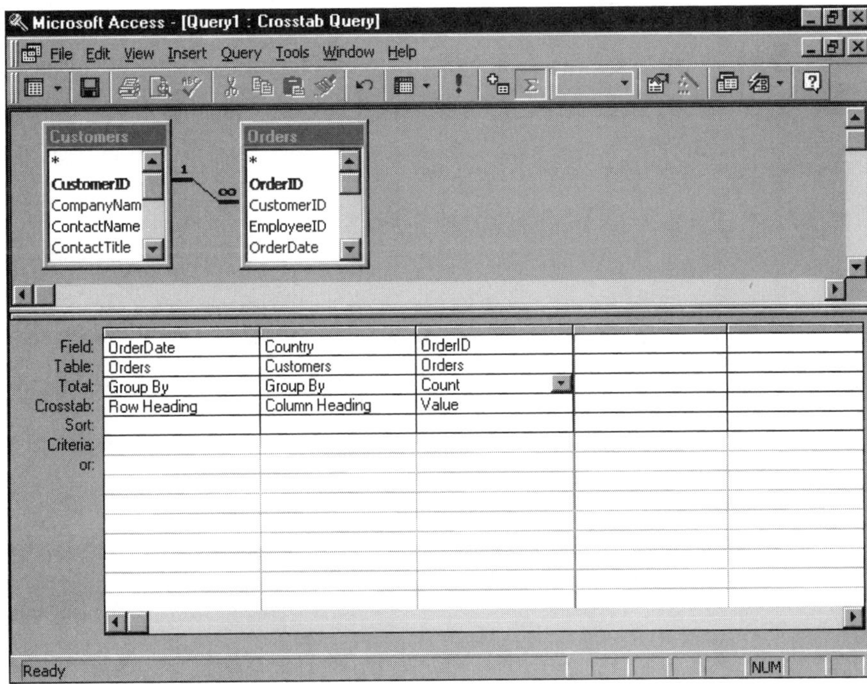

Figure 11-19: Creating a crosstab query.

As Figure 11-19 demonstrates, you must specify a minimum of three fields for crosstab queries:

- Row heading
- Column heading
- Value (of summary)

These three fields are specified in the appropriate Crosstab cells of the fields. After you specify the contents for the three Crosstab cells, you specify Group By in the Total cell in both the Row Heading and the Column Heading fields and an aggregate Total cell operator (such as Count) for the Value field.

If you have done this procedure correctly, clicking on the Datasheet button on the toolbar reveals a datasheet similar to the one shown in Figure 11-20.

Notice that the dynaset is composed of distinct (nonrepeating) rows of orders, 21 columns (one for each country in the customer's table), and summary cell contents for each order against each country; that is, Brazil has no orders on 18-Apr-95, Belgium has one order, and Brazil has one on 21-Apr-95.

Order Date	Argentina	Austria	Belgium	Brazil	Canada
07-Apr-95					
10-Apr-95	1	1			
11-Apr-95				1	
12-Apr-95					
13-Apr-95					
14-Apr-95					
17-Apr-95			1		
18-Apr-95			1		
19-Apr-95				1	
20-Apr-95					
21-Apr-95				1	
24-Apr-95		1		1	
25-Apr-95	1				
26-Apr-95				1	
27-Apr-95					
28-Apr-95					
01-May-95				1	
02-May-95		1			
03-May-95					

Figure 11-20: The datasheet for a crosstab query.

Entering multiple-field row headings

When you're working with crosstab queries, you can specify only one Value field and one Column Heading field. You can, however, add more than one Row Heading field. By adding multiple Row Heading fields, you can refine the type of data you want displayed in the crosstab query.

Suppose that you're interested in seeing the order dates from the last crosstab query refined to the level of CustomerID. In other words, you want to see how many orders you have on each order date from each customer within each country. This type of query is shown in Figure 11-21. Notice that two Crosstab cells show Row Heading for the fields OrderDate and CustomerID. Access groups the crosstab rows first by OrderDate and then by CustomerID. Access specifies the group order from left to right.

If you click on the Datasheet button on the toolbar, Access presents a datasheet similar to the one shown in Figure 11-22. Note that the row heading depends on both the OrderDate and CustomerID fields. The dynaset is displayed in order first by OrderDate (01-Jul-93, 02-Jul-93, and so on) and then by CustomerID within the order date (VINET, TOMSP, and so on).

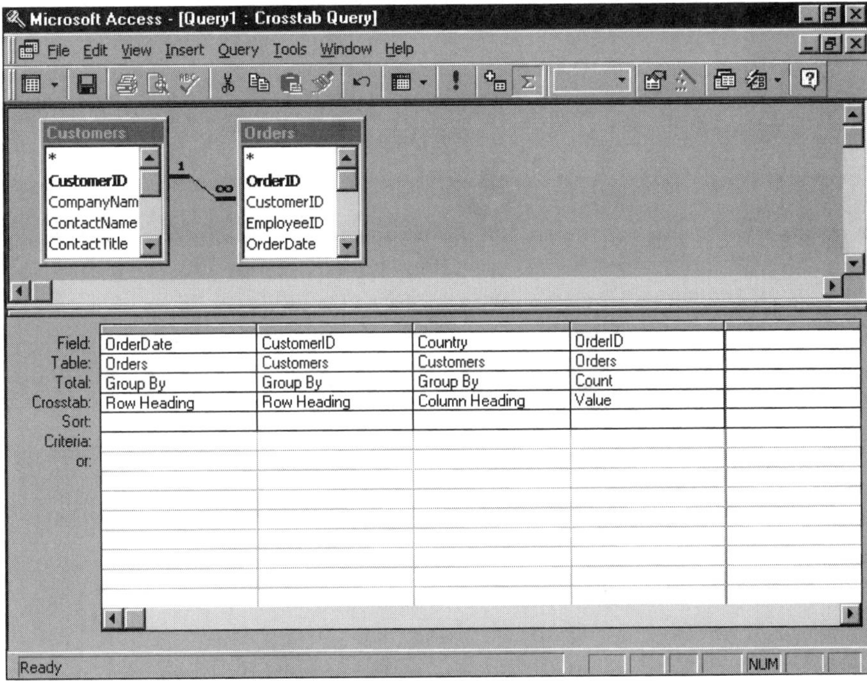

Figure 11-21: A crosstab query using two fields for the row heading.

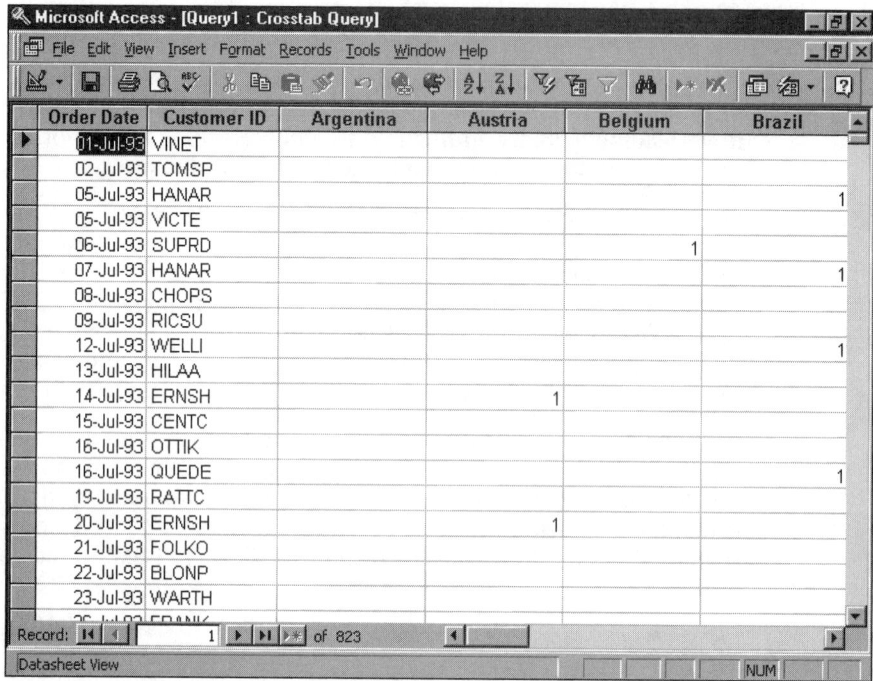

Figure 11-22: A datasheet with multiple-field row headings in a crosstab query.

Tip

A crosstab query can have several row headings but only one column heading. If you want to display a several-field column heading and a single-field row heading, simply switch your heading types. Then change all the multiple-field column headings to multiple-field row headings and change the single-row heading to a single-column heading.

Specifying criteria for a crosstab query

When you work with crosstab queries, you may want to specify a record criteria for the crosstab. Criteria can be specified in a crosstab query against any of these types of fields:

- A new field
- A Row Heading field
- A Column Heading field

A new field

You can add criteria based on a new field not displayed in the crosstab query. For example, you may want to create the crosstab query you see in Figure 11-23, in which the two fields OrderDate and CustomerID are used as the row heading. However, you want to see only records in which the contact title is Owner. To specify a criterion, simply follow these additional steps:

1. Begin with the crosstab query shown in Figure 11-21.
2. Double-click on the ContactTitle field in the Customers table.
3. Select the Criteria cell in the ContactTitle field.
4. Type **Owner** in the cell.

The Crosstab cell in the ContactTitle field should be blank. If it is not, select the (not shown) that you will see if you pull down the Crosstab combo box to blank the cell.

Your query should now resemble the one shown in Figure 11-23. Notice that you added a criterion in a field not displayed in the crosstab query.

Now that the new criterion is specified, you can click the Datasheet button on the toolbar to see a datasheet similar to the one shown in Figure 11-24.

Note that the datasheet in Figure 11-24 shows only columns in which at least one of the intersecting row cells has a value.

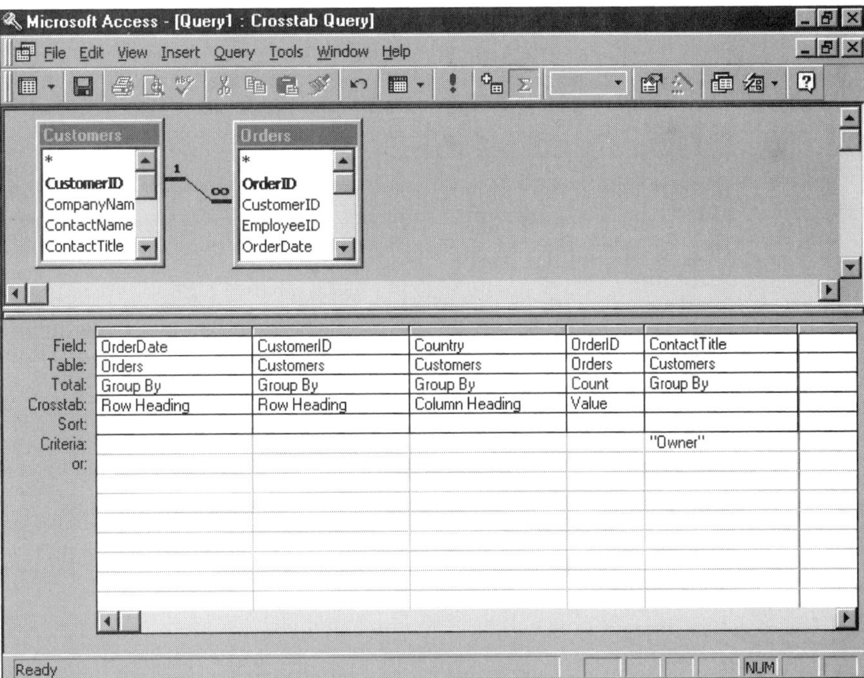

Figure 11-23: Specifying a criterion in a crosstab query in a new field.

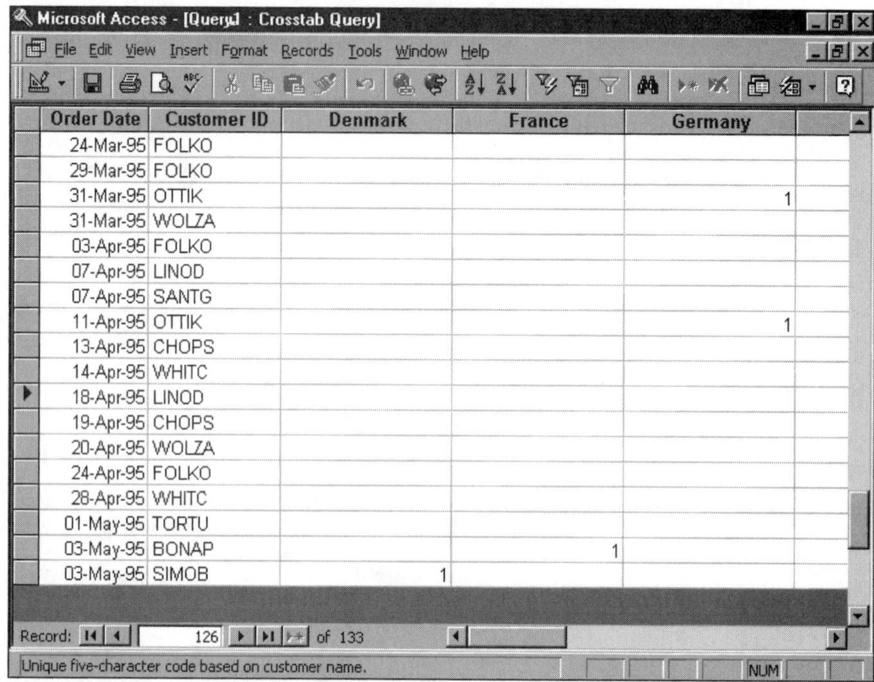

Order Date	Customer ID	Denmark	France	Germany
24-Mar-95	FOLKO			
29-Mar-95	FOLKO			
31-Mar-95	OTTIK			1
31-Mar-95	WOLZA			
03-Apr-95	FOLKO			
07-Apr-95	LINOD			
07-Apr-95	SANTG			
11-Apr-95	OTTIK			1
13-Apr-95	CHOPS			
14-Apr-95	WHITC			
18-Apr-95	LINOD			
19-Apr-95	CHOPS			
20-Apr-95	WOLZA			
24-Apr-95	FOLKO			
28-Apr-95	WHITC			
01-May-95	TORTU			
03-May-95	BONAP		1	
03-May-95	SIMOB	1		

Figure 11-24: The datasheet after specifying a criterion in a new field.

A Row Heading field

In addition to being able to specify criteria for a new field, you can specify criteria for a field being used as a row heading. When you specify a criterion for a row heading, Access excludes any rows that do not meet the specified criterion.

You may want to view a crosstab query for all orders for which the customer ID is EASTC. To create this query, begin with the crosstab query shown in Figure 11-21. If you created the preceding sample query, simply remove the ContactTitle column from the QBE pane. Make the QBE pane look like the one shown in Figure 11-25. When you view this query, you see only records from the customer ID EASTC.

You can specify criteria against any field used as a Row Heading field. You can even specify criteria for multiple Row Heading fields to create a finely focused crosstab query.

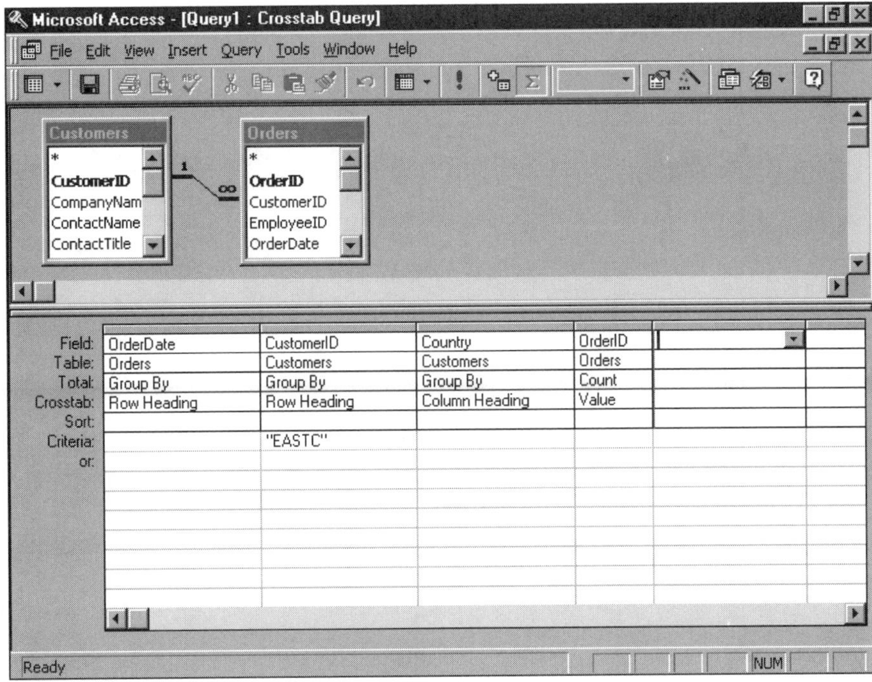

Figure 11-25: Criterion set against a Row Heading field.

A Column Heading field

You also can specify criteria for the field being used as the column heading. When you specify the criteria for a column heading, Access excludes any columns that don't meet your specified criteria.

Suppose that you want a crosstab query for any order placed from customers in the USA and Canada. To create this query, again begin with the crosstab query shown in Figure 11-21. If you created the query in the preceding example, simply remove the criterion for the CustomerID field from the QBE pane. The QBE pane should look similar to the one shown in Figure 11-26.

Note that the specified criterion is placed in the Criteria cell in the Column Heading field Country. When you click the Datasheet button on the toolbar, you should see a datasheet that has only two column headings: Canada and USA. The other headings have been eliminated.

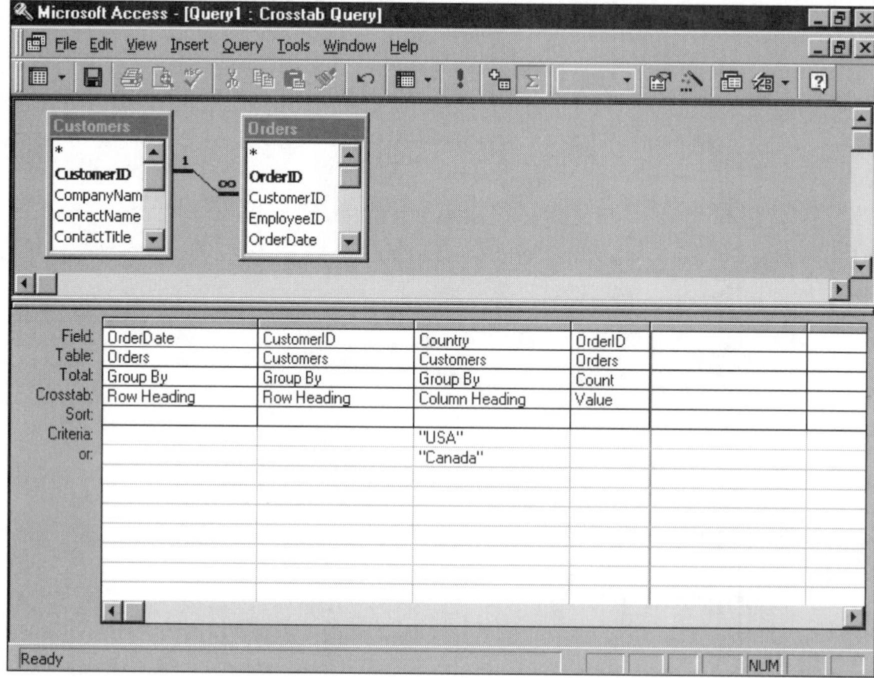

Figure 11-26: A criterion specified against the Column Heading field.

Tip

You cannot specify a criterion in a field used as the Value field for the crosstab query. To specify a criterion based on this field, however, simply drag the field again to the QBE pane and set a criterion against this second copy of the field while keeping the Crosstab cell empty.

Specifying fixed-column headings

At times, you may want more control over the appearance of your column headings. By default, Access sorts column headings in alphabetical or numerical order. This sort order can be a problem if you are working with date columns. Your columns are more readable if you put the columns in chronological (rather than alphabetical) order. To solve this problem, you can use the Fixed Column Headings option in the Query Properties dialog box. This option lets you make these choices:

- Specify an exact order for the appearance of the column headings.
- Specify fixed column headings for reports and forms that use crosstab queries.

To specify fixed column headings, follow these steps:

1. Begin with the crosstab query shown in Figure 11-26. Move the mouse pointer to the top half of the query screen and click one time.
2. Click on the Properties button (a hand holding a piece of paper) on the toolbar or choose View⇨Properties from the Query Design menu.
3. Select the Column Headings text box.
4. Type **USA,Canada** in the box.

The Query Properties dialog box should look like the one shown in Figure 11-27. When you move the mouse pointer to another entry area, Access converts your text into `"USA", "Canada"` in the Query Properties dialog box.

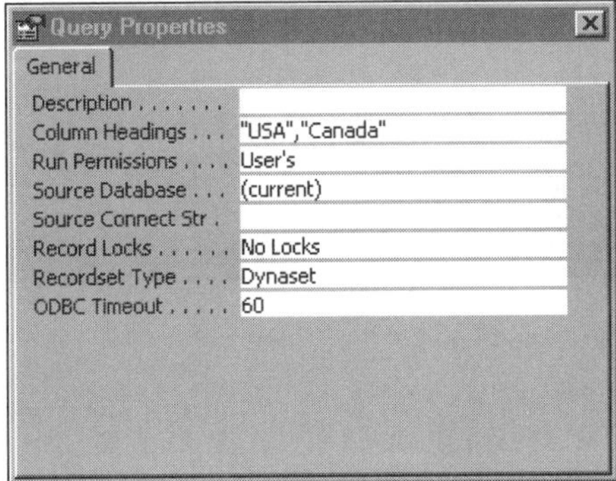

Figure 11-27: The Query Properties dialog box.

The datasheet should now look like the one shown in Figure 11-28. The order of the column headings is reversed from the alphabetical ordering Access chose.

The column names you enter must exactly match the query headings. If you enter `US` rather than `USA`, Access accepts the heading without reporting an error. When you display the query, however, no records for that column are displayed.

You can enter column names without separating them with semicolons. To do so, enter each name on a new line (press Ctrl+Enter to move to a new line).

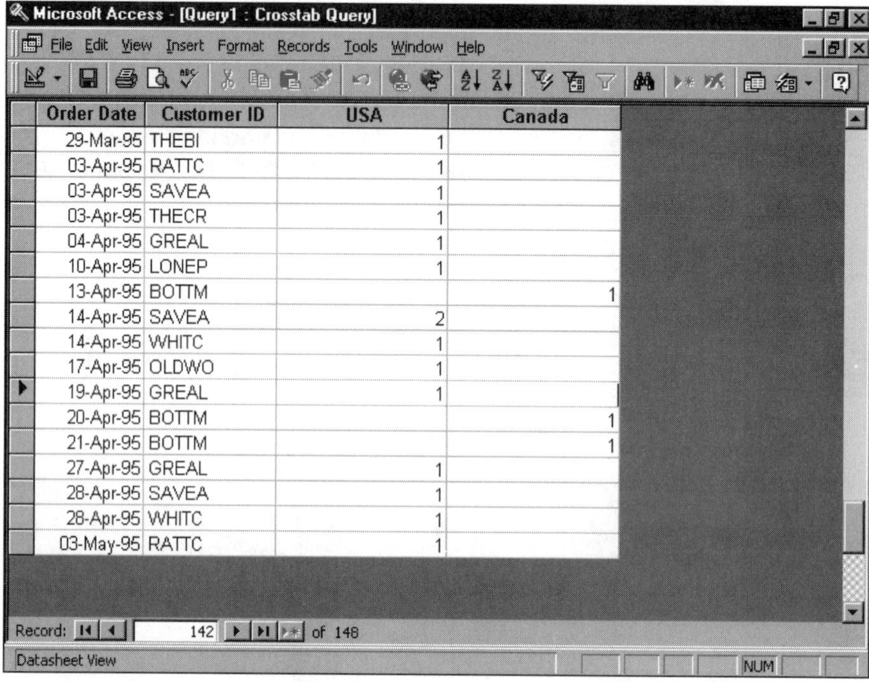

Order Date	Customer ID	USA	Canada
29-Mar-95	THEBI	1	
03-Apr-95	RATTC	1	
03-Apr-95	SAVEA	1	
03-Apr-95	THECR	1	
04-Apr-95	GREAL	1	
10-Apr-95	LONEP	1	
13-Apr-95	BOTTM		1
14-Apr-95	SAVEA	2	
14-Apr-95	WHITC	1	
17-Apr-95	OLDWO	1	
19-Apr-95	GREAL	1	
20-Apr-95	BOTTM		1
21-Apr-95	BOTTM		1
27-Apr-95	GREAL	1	
28-Apr-95	SAVEA	1	
28-Apr-95	WHITC	1	
03-May-95	RATTC	1	

Figure 11-28: The datasheet with a specified column order.

Using the Crosstab Query Wizard

Access 97 employs several Query Wizards, which are helpful additions to the query-design process. One especially helpful wizard, the Crosstab Query Wizard (see Figure 11-29), is an excellent tool to help you quickly create a crosstab query.

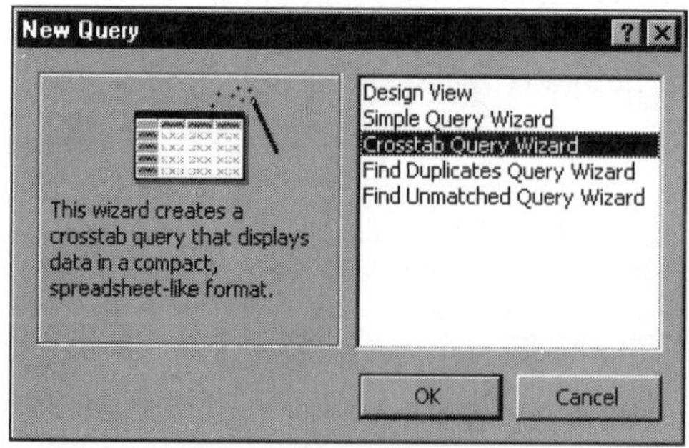

Figure 11-29: Choosing the Crosstab Query Wizard.

Some limitations exist, however. Those limitations are the following:

- To use more than one table for the crosstab query, you must create a separate query that has the tables you want for the crosstab query. For example, you may have a Group By row heading from the Orders Table (OrderDate) and a Group By column heading from the Customers table (Country). The Crosstab Query Wizard enables you to select only one table or query for the row and column headings.

  The workaround: Create a query of the Customers and Orders tables. Select the all fields reference for each one, and then save this intermediate query. Use this intermediate query as the record source for the wizard.

- You cannot specify a limiting criterion for the wizard's query.

  The workaround: Make the wizard perform the query, and then go in and set the limiting criterion.

- You cannot specify column headings or column orders.

  The workaround: Again, have the wizard create the query, and then modify it.

To use the crosstab query, simply click on the New button and then select the Crosstab Wizard (third one from the top) in the dialog box. Click on OK and follow the Access on-screen prompts to provide the following information:

- Table or query name for the source
- Fields for the row headings
- Fields for the column headings
- Field for the body
- Title

After you specify these items, Access creates your crosstab query and runs it for you.

Creating a Parameter Query

You can automate the process of changing criteria for queries you run regularly by creating *parameter queries.*

Understanding the parameter query

A parameter query, as its name suggests, is a query you create that prompts users for a quantity or constant value every time the query is executed. Specifically, a parameter query prompts users for criteria every time it is run, thereby eliminating the need to open the query in Query Design mode to change the criteria manually.

Parameter queries are also useful with forms or reports, because you can have Access prompt users for criteria when the form or report is opened.

Creating a single-parameter query

You may have queries that require minor modifications to the criteria of a field every time they are run. Suppose that you have a query that displays all orders for a specific customer. If you run the query often, you can design a parameter query to prompt users for a customer ID whenever the query runs. To create the query, follow these steps:

1. Beginning with a select query, select the Customers and Orders tables.
2. Double-click on the CustomerID field in the Customers table.
3. Double-click on the ContactName in the Customers table.
4. Double-click on the OrderID field in the Orders table.
5. Click on the Criteria cell for CustomerID.
6. Type **[Enter a Customer ID]** in the cell.
7. Deselect the Show cell in the CustomerID field if you don't want this field to be displayed in the datasheet.

That's all there is to creating a single-parameter query. Your query should resemble the one shown in Figure 11-30.

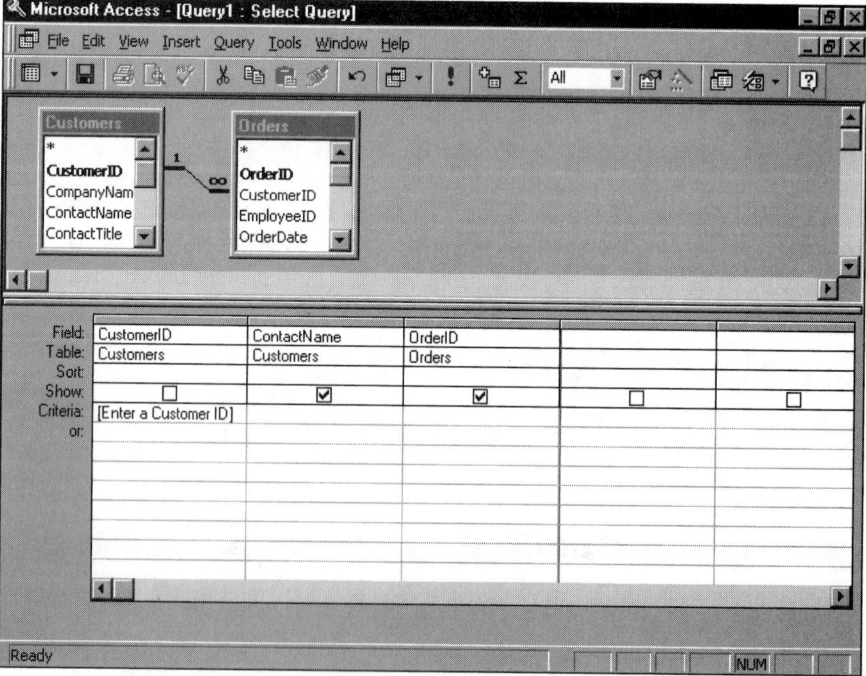

Figure 11-30: A single-parameter query.

In the preceding example, you created a parameter query that prompts users for a customer ID by displaying the message `Enter a Customer ID` every time the query is run. Access converts a user's entry to an "equals" criterion for the CustomerID field. If a user enters a valid number, Access finds the correct records.

When you specify a prompt message for the parameter, you should make the message meaningful yet brief. When the parameter query is run, Access displays as many as (approximately) 50 characters of any prompt message. Messages longer than that are truncated to approximately the first 50 characters.

Running a parameter query

To run a parameter query, click on either the Run button or the Datasheet button on the toolbar. An Enter Parameter Value dialog box is displayed and prompts users for a value, as shown in Figure 11-31.

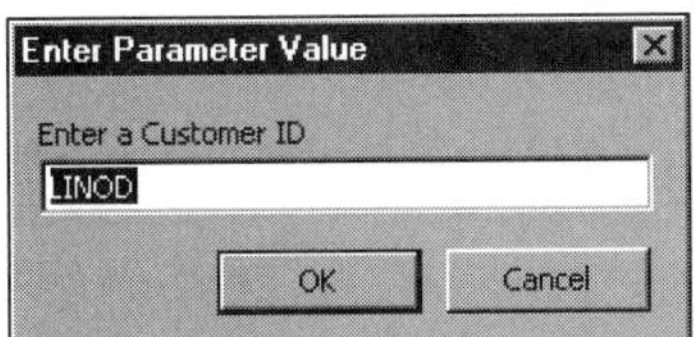

Figure 11-31: The Enter Parameter Value dialog box.

After a user enters a value or presses Enter, Access runs the query, based on the criterion that was entered. If the criterion is valid, the datasheet shows records that match the criterion; otherwise, the datasheet displays no records.

You are not limited to creating a query with a single parameter. You can create a query that asks for multiple criteria by entering parameters in the criteria cells, as in the preceding example.

Access defaults to the prompt order of left to right, based on the position of the fields and their parameters. You can override the prompt order, however, by choosing Query➪Parameters and specifying an order.

Understanding Action Queries

The term *action query,* as you can guess, is a query that does something more than simply select a specific group of records and present them to you in a dynaset. The word action suggests the performance of some operation. By definition, action means that you do something to influence or affect something. *Action* is synonymous with *operation, performance,* and *work,* which is exactly what an action query does: It performs some specific operation or work.

An action query can be considered a select query that is given the duty of performing some operation or work against a specified group of records in a dynaset.

When you create a query, Access automatically creates a select query. You can specify a different type, such as an action query, from the Query Design menu. From this menu, you can choose from several types of action queries (Make Table, Update, Append, and Delete).

Like select queries, action queries create a dynaset you can view in a datasheet. To see the dynaset, you simply click on the Datasheet button on the toolbar. Unlike select queries, however, action queries perform some action when you click on the Run button (the one with the exclamation point) on the toolbar. The action performed is the action specified in the QBE pane in the Query Design window.

You can quickly identify an action query in the Database window by the special exclamation point icon next to the action query name. Each of the four different types of action queries has a different icon, as shown in Figure 11-32.

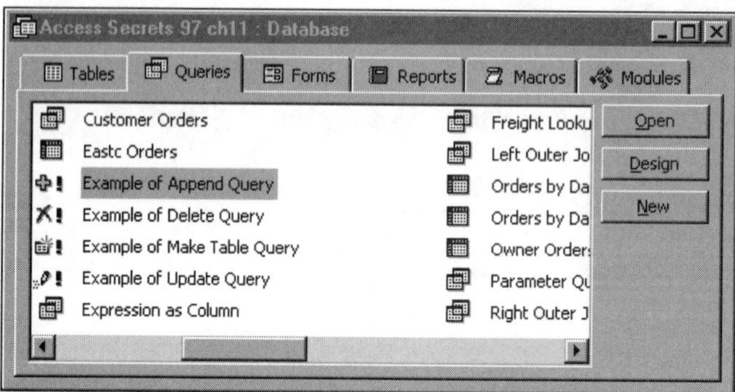

Figure 11-32: The Queries tab in the Database window shows select queries and action queries.

Using action queries

You can use action queries to accomplish the following tasks:

- Delete specified records from a table or group of tables
- Append records from one table to another
- Update information in a group of records
- Create a new table from specified records in a query

This list describes a couple of practical uses for action queries:

- You want to create history tables and then copy all inactive records to these tables. (A record is considered inactive if a customer has not placed an order in more than three years.) You decide to remove the inactive records from your active database tables.

  What to do? Use a make-table query to create the history tables and a delete query to remove the unwanted records.

- One of your old customers places an order and you want to bring the customer information back into your active file from your backup files.

  What to do? Use an append query to add records from your backup tables to your active tables.

Action queries change, add, or delete data. As a result, you should always observe these rules:

- Back up your table before performing the query.
- Create and view the action query (click on the Datasheet button on the toolbar) before performing an action query.

Understanding the process of action queries

Because action queries are irreversible, you should follow this four-step process when you work with them:

1. Create the action query by specifying the fields and the criteria.
2. View the records selected in the action query by clicking on the Datasheet button on the toolbar.
3. Run the action query by clicking on the Run button on the toolbar.
4. Check the changes in the tables by clicking on the Datasheet button on the toolbar.

If you follow these steps, you should be able to use action queries relatively safely.

Viewing the results of an action query

Action queries perform a specific task — which is often a destructive task. Be careful, therefore, when you use them. Before you run the action query, it is important to view the changes to be made and to verify afterward that the anticipated changes were made. Before you learn how to create and run an action query, you should review the process for seeing what your changes will look like before you change a table permanently.

Viewing the query before using update and delete queries

You can click on the Datasheet View button to see on which set of data the action query will work. Meanwhile, when you're updating or deleting records with an action query, the actions take place on the underlying tables of the query that's in use. To view the results of an update or a delete query, therefore, you can click on the Datasheet button to see whether the records were updated or deleted.

If your update query made changes to the fields you used to select the records, you may have to look at the underlying table or change the selection query to see the changes. If you deleted a set of records with an action button, for example, the resulting select dynaset of the same record criterion shows that no records exist. By removing the delete criterion, you can view the table and verify that all the specified records have been deleted.

Switching to the result table of a make-table or append query

Unlike the update or delete queries, make-table and append queries copy resultant records to another table. After specifying the fields and the criteria in the QBE pane in the Query Design window, the make-table and append queries copy the specified fields and records to another table. When you run the queries, the results take place in another table, not in the current table.

Clicking on the Datasheet button shows you only a dynaset of the criteria and fields that were specified, not the actual table that contains the new or added records. To view the results of a make-table or append query, you have to open the new table and view the contents to verify that the make-table or append query worked correctly. If you don't plan to use the action query again, do not save it — delete it.

Reversing action queries

Action queries copy or change data in underlying tables. After Access executes an action query, you cannot reverse it. When you're working with action queries, therefore, you should consider creating a select query first to make sure of the record criteria and selection for the action query.

Because of the destructive nature of action queries, you should always make a backup of the underlying tables before you perform an action query.

Creating an action query

The process of creating an action query is similar to creating a select query. You specify the fields for the query and any scoping criteria (see the "Scoping criteria" sidebar).

In addition to specifying the fields and criteria, you specify an action-specific property: Append to, Make new table, Update to, or Delete where.

Scoping criteria

Action queries can use any expression composed of fields, functions, and operators to specify any limiting condition you want to place on the query. *Scoping criteria* are a form of record criteria. Record criteria are normally thought of as a filter to tell Access which records to find or leave out of the dynaset. Because action queries do not create a dynaset, you use scoping criteria to specify a set of records to be operated on by Access.

Creating an update action query to change values

This section describes how to handle an event that requires you to change many records.

Suppose that you want to discount by 15 percent the unit price on all orders for Jack's New England Clam Chowder that were placed after 19-Apr-96.

It's possible to update each record in the table individually by using a form or a datasheet. The use of a select query dynaset to make these changes, however, takes a long time. This method is not only time-consuming but also inefficient — especially if you have numerous records to change. In addition, this method lends itself to typing errors as you enter new text in fields.

The best way to handle this type of event is to use an update action query, because the query makes many changes in just one operation. By using action queries, you save time and eliminate many of the typos that crop up in manually edited records.

To create an update query that performs these tasks, follow this two-phase process:

1. Create a select query. View the data you want to update by clicking on the Datasheet button.
2. Convert the select query to an update query. Then run the update query after you are satisfied that it will affect only the records you want.

Creating a select query before an update action

The first step in making an update query is to create a select query. In this example, the query is for all customers who live in Mountain View and who own horses. To create this query, follow these steps:

1. Create a new query using the Orders and Order Details tables.
2. Select the OrderDate field from the Orders table and the ProductID and Discount fields from the Order Details table.

3. Specify a criterion of **>#4/19/ 96#** in the OrderDate field and **41** (the product ID for Jack's New England Clam Chowder) in the ProductID field.
4. The Select Query Design window should now resemble the one shown in Figure 11-33. Note that the QBE pane shows all three fields but shows criteria in only the OrderDate and ProductID fields.
5. Examine the datasheet to make sure that it has only the records you want to change. Return to the design surface when you are finished.

You are now ready to convert the select query to an update query.

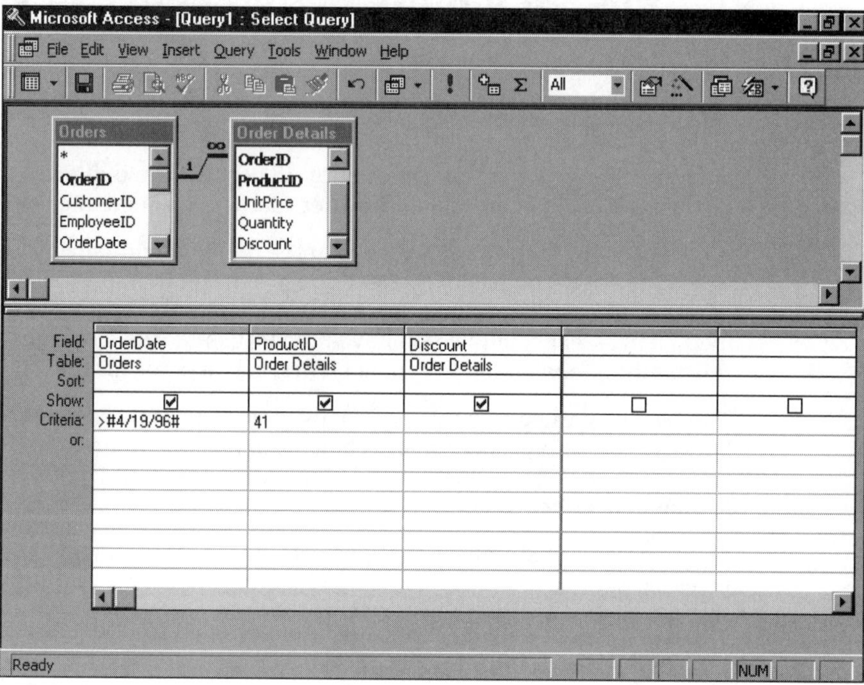

Figure 11-33: Entering a select query.

Converting a select query to an update query

After you create a select query and verify the selection of records, it's time to create the update query. To convert the select query to an update query, follow these steps:

1. Select Query➪Update from the Query Design menu.
2. Access changes the title of the Query window from Query1: Select Query to Query1: Update Query. Access also adds the Update To property row to the QBE pane, as shown in Figure 11-34.
3. In the Update To cell in the Discount field, enter **15**.
4. Click on the Run button on the toolbar (or choose Query➪Run from the Query Design menu).
5. Access displays the dialog box shown in Figure 11-35.
6. Click on the Yes button to complete the query and update the records. Otherwise click on No to stop the procedure (no records are updated).

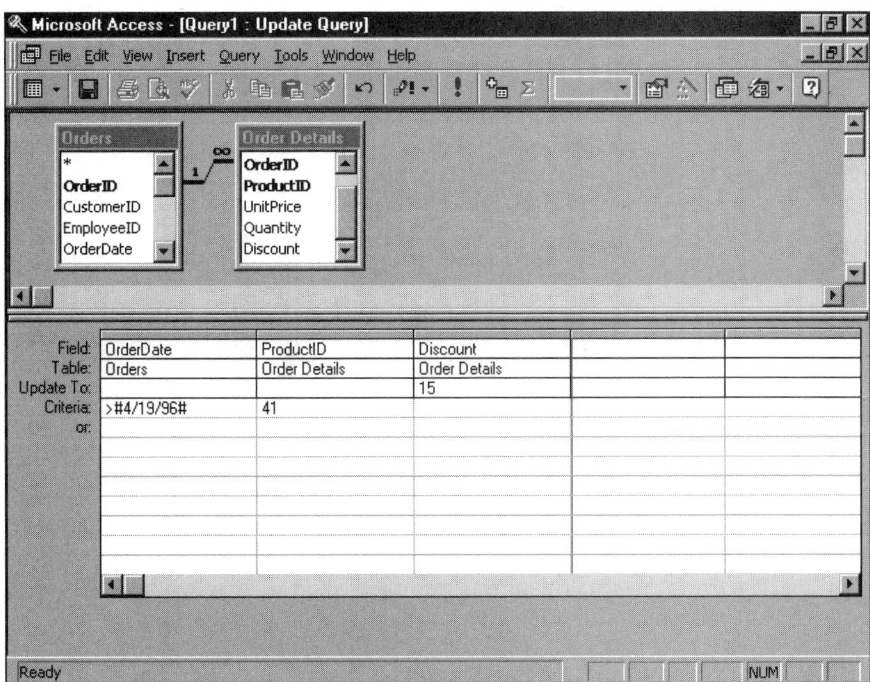

Figure 11-34: The Update Query Design pane.

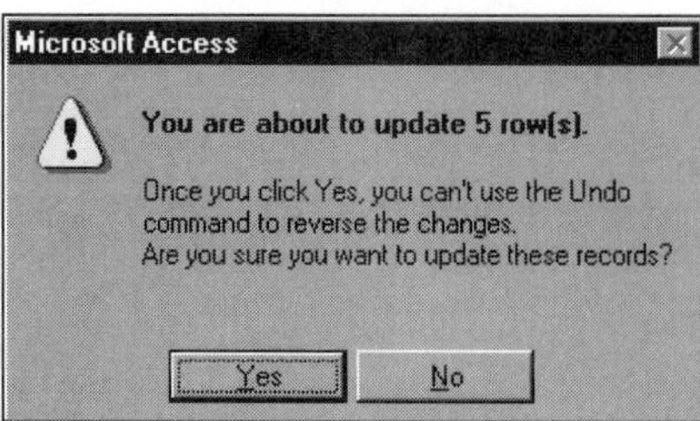

Figure 11-35: Access asks whether you're sure that you want to update your records.

If you are changing tables attached to another database, you cannot cancel the query.

You can change more than one field at a time by filling in the Update To section of any field you want to change. You can even change the field contents of fields you used for limiting the records (criteria).

After completing the update query, you should check your results. You can do so by changing the update query back to a select query (click on the Select Query button on the toolbar). After you have changed the query back to a select query, you can review your changes in the datasheet.

If you update a field that was used for a limiting criterion, you must change the criterion in the select query to the new value to verify the changes.

Creating a new table by using a make-table query

You can use an action query to create new tables based on scoping criteria. To make a new table, you create a make-table query. Consider the following example of a particular task for which you would want to create a make-table query.

Jack, the owner of Jack's New England Clam Chowder, has approached you for help with a mailing list of customers who have ordered his chowder. His company wants to send these customers a coupon for a new product he plans to introduce soon. Jack plans to create the mailing labels and send the form letters if you supply a table of customer information, including customer names and addresses. Jack also stipulates that because this mailing is a trial process, only customers who have placed orders in the past six months should receive letters.

You've decided to send the company the requested table of information. So now you have to create a new table from the Customers, Orders, and Order Details tables. To accomplish this task, you create a make-table query that performs these actions.

You decide to create a make-table query for all customers who have placed an order for Jack's New England Clam Chowder in the past six months. In this example, assume that the date six months ago was February 1, 1996. Follow these steps to create this query:

1. Create a new query using the Customers, Orders, and Order Details tables.
2. Select Make Table from the Query Type button on the toolbar.
3. Access displays the Make Table dialog box, as shown in Figure 11-36.

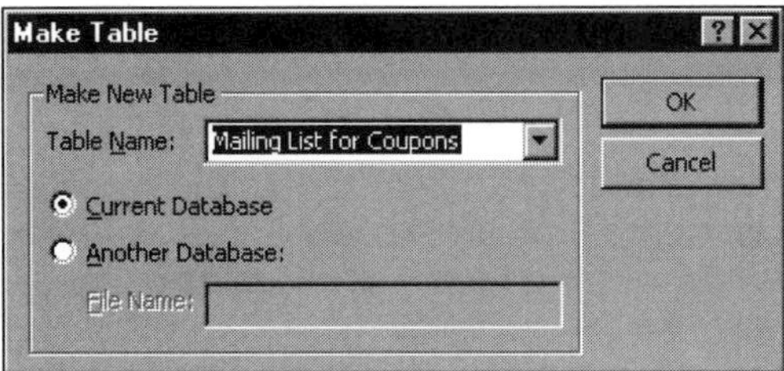

Figure 11-36: Give your table a name in the Make Table dialog box.

4. Type **Mailing List for Coupons** in the Table Name field and either press Enter or click on OK. After you click on OK, note that the name of the window changes from Query1: Select Query to Query1: Make Table Query.
5. Select the mailing information fields (from ContactName through PostalCode) from the Customers table and the fields OrderDate from the Orders table and ProductID from the Order Details table.
6. Specify the criterion **41** in the ProductID field and >**#2/1/96#** in the OrderDate field.
7. The Query Design window should resemble the one shown in Figure 11-37. Note that the fields are resized so that all are displayed in the QBE pane. Two fields, ProductID and OrderDate, contain criteria.
8. To view the dynaset, click on the Datasheet View button on the toolbar.
9. Make sure that the dynaset has only the records you specified.
10. Click on the Design button to switch back to Query Design view.
11. Deselect the `Show` property of the OrderDate field.
12. Do not copy this field to the new table Mailing List for Coupons. Only those fields with a checkmark in the checkbox of the Show row are copied to the new table. By deselecting a field with a criterion set, you can base the scoping criteria on fields that are not copied to the new table.

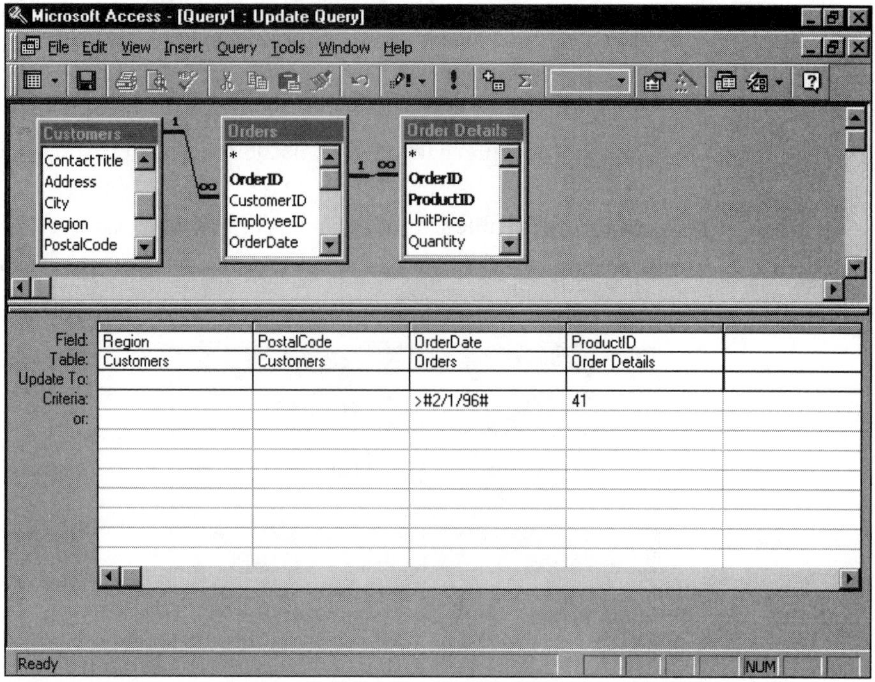

Figure 11-37: The Customers, Orders, and Order Details tables are in the top pane; the fields ContactName, Address, City, Region, PostalCode, ProductID, and OrderDate are in the bottom pane.

13. Click on the Run button on the toolbar or choose Query➪Run from the Query Design menu.
14. Access indicates the number of records it will copy to the new table (see Figure 11-38).

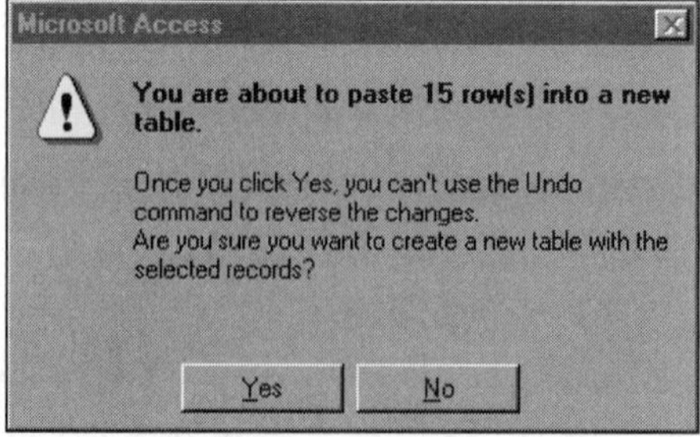

Figure 11-38: The dialog box for copying records.

15. Click on the Yes button to complete the query and make the new table. Otherwise, click on No to stop the procedure (no records are copied).

When you're creating numerous make-table queries, you have to select Make Table from the Query Type button on the toolbar or choose Query⇨Make Table from the menu to rename the make-table query each time. Access assumes that you want to overwrite the existing table if you don't reselect the make-table option. Before performing the new make-table query, the program warns you of what it's about to do.

After you complete the make-table query, you should check your results: Open the new table Mailing List for Coupons, which has been added to the database container.

When you create a table from a make-table query, the fields in the new table inherit the data type and field size from the fields in the query's underlying tables; no other field or table properties are transferred, however. If you want to define a primary key or other properties, you have to edit the design of the new table.

You also can use a make-table action query to create a backup of your tables before you create action queries that change the contents of the tables. Backing up with this method does not copy the table's properties or primary key to the new table.

To copy any database object (table, query, form, or other object) while the Database window is displayed, follow these steps:

1. Highlight the object you want to copy.
2. Press Ctrl+C (or choose Edit⇨Copy) to copy the object to the Clipboard.
3. Press Ctrl+V (or choose Edit⇨Paste) to paste the object from the Clipboard.
4. Enter the new object name (table or form, for example) and click on OK in the dialog box. If the object is a table, you also can specify Structure with or without the data and append it to an existing table.

Creating a query to append records

As the word append suggests, an append query attaches or adds records to a specified table. An append query adds to another table the records from the table you are using. The table to which you want to add records must already exist. You can append records to a table in the same database or in another Access database.

Append queries are useful for adding information to another table based on some scoping criteria. Append queries are not always the fastest way, however, to add records to another database. If you want to append all fields and all records from one table to a new table, for example, the append query is not the best way to do it. Instead, use the Copy and Paste options on the Edit menu when you're working with the table in a datasheet or form.

You can add records to an open table. You don't have to close the table before adding records. Access does not, however, automatically refresh the view of the table that has records added to it. To refresh the table, press Shift+F9. This action requeries the table so that you can see the appended records.

When you're working with append queries, you have to be aware of these rules:

- If the table to which you are appending records has a primary key field, the records you add cannot have Null values or duplicate primary key values. If so, Access does not append the records.
- If you add records to another database table, you must know the location and name of the database.
- If you use the asterisk (*) field in a QBE row, you cannot also use individual fields from the same table. Access does not append the records because it "thinks" that you're trying to add field contents twice to the same record.
- If you append records with an AutoNumber field (an Access-specified primary key), do not include the AutoNumber field if the table to which you are appending records also has the field and record contents. (Doing so causes the problem specified in the first rule in this list.) Do not use the AutoNumber field if you are adding to an empty table and you want the new table to have a new AutoNumber number (order number) based on the criteria.

If you follow these simple rules, your append queries will perform as expected and become a useful tool.

The following example helps illustrate the use of append queries. Suppose that every February you archive all records of orders that were processed during the preceding year. To archive the records, you perform two steps: Append the records to existing backup files, and then delete the records from the active database.

In this case, you want to add records to the backup tables for past orders in your active tables. In other words, you copy records from two tables — Orders and Order Details. To perform this exercise, you need two backup files. To create the backup files, follow these steps:

1. Press F11 or Alt+F1 to display the Database window.
2. Click on the Tables tab to display the list of tables.
3. Click on the Orders table to highlight it.

4. Press Ctrl+C (or choose Edit⇨Copy) to copy the object Orders table to the Clipboard.
5. Press Ctrl+V (or choose Edit⇨Paste) to display the Paste Table As dialog box.
6. Click on Structure Only in the Paste Options section of the dialog box (or press Tab to move to the Paste Options section and then press S).
7. Click on the Table Name box and type **Orders Backup**.
8. Click on OK (or press Enter after typing the file name).
9. Open the Orders Backup table (it should be empty), and then close the table.

Repeat this process for the Order Details tables and name it Order Details Backup.

To create an append query that copies the past order records, follow this two-step process:

1. Create a select query to verify that only the records you want to append are copied.
2. Convert the select query to an append query and run it.

When you're using the append query, only fields with names that match in the two tables are copied. Suppose that you have a small table with six fields and another with nine. The table with nine fields has only five of the six field names that match fields in the smaller table. If you append records from the smaller table to the larger table, only the five matching fields are appended. The other four fields remain blank.

Creating the select query for an append query

To create a select query for all orders processed (placed) last year along with their order details, follow these steps:

1. Create a new query using the Orders and Order Details tables.
2. Select the OrderDate field from the Orders table.
3. Specify a criterion of **<#1/1/96#** in the OrderDate field.
4. Go to the datasheet and make sure that all the OrderDate field contents indicate orders placed in 1996.
5. Return to Query Design mode. With the select query created correctly, you are ready to convert the select query to an append query.

Converting to an append query

After you create the select query and verify that it is correct, you have to create the append query. In fact, you have to create *two* different append queries — one for each of the tables Orders and Order Details — because append queries work with only one table at a time. For this example, first copy all fields from the Order Details table, and then copy all the fields from the Orders table.

To convert the select query to an append query and run it, follow these steps:

1. Deselect the `Show` property of the OrderDate field.
2. Select Query⇨Append from the Query Design menu.
3. Access displays the Append dialog box, as shown in Figure 11-39.

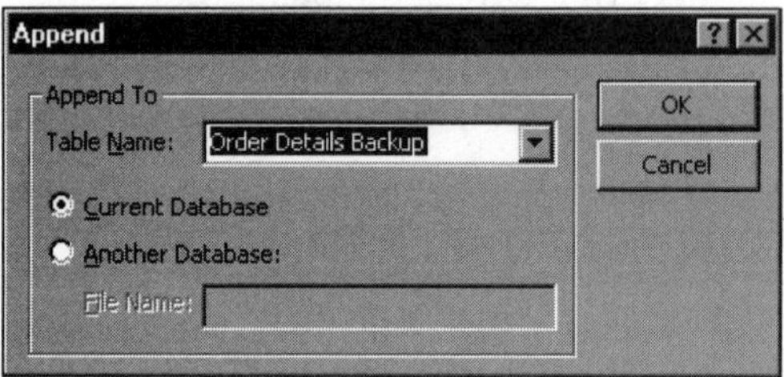

Figure 11-39: The Append dialog box.

4. Type **Order Details Backup** in the Table Name field, and either press Enter in the field or click on OK in the dialog box.
5. To select all fields, drag the asterisk (*) field from the Order Details table to the QBE pane.
6. The QBE pane should look like Figure 11-40. Access automatically fills in the Append To field under the All fields selector column.
7. Click on the Run button on the toolbar (or choose Query⇨Run from the Query Design menu).
8. Access displays a dialog box with a warning message that you cannot undo your changes.

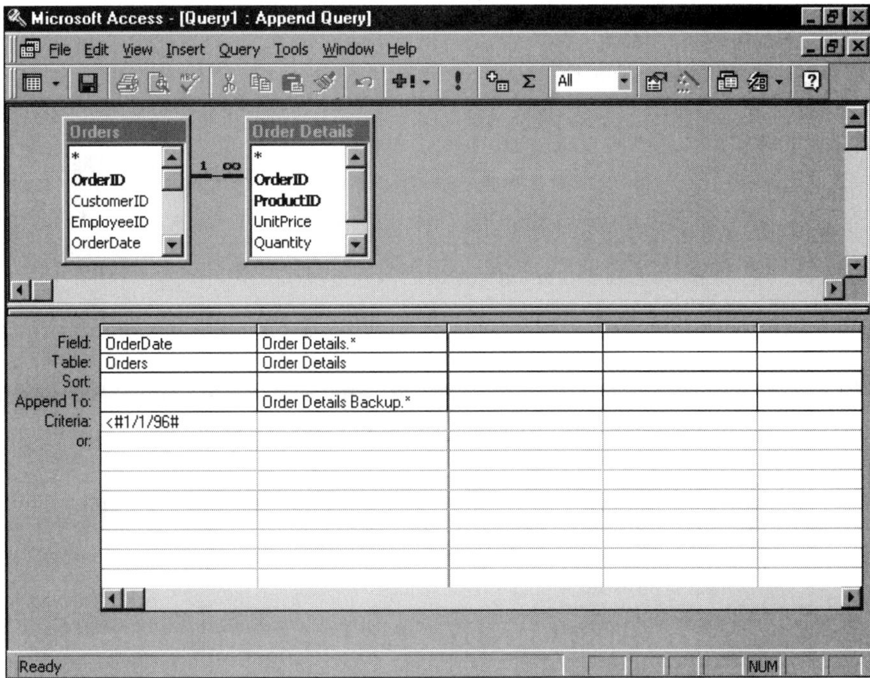

Figure 11-40: The QBE pane for an appended query.

9. Click on the Yes button to complete the query and copy (append) the records to the backup table. Click on No to stop the procedure (no records are copied).

After you back up the past Order Detail records, repeat Steps 2 through 5 for the Orders table. Before you append fields from this table, however, you must remove the preceding all selector field (Order Details.*) from the QBE pane.

If you create an append query by using the asterisk (*) field and you also use a field from the same table as the asterisk to specify a criterion, you must remove the criterion field from the Append To row. If you don't, Access reports an error. Remember that the field for the criterion is already included in the asterisk field. If you leave the Show on, it tries to append the field twice and repeats the error. Access halts the append query and appends no records to the table.

After you complete the two append table queries, check your results: Go to the Database window, select each of the two backup tables (Orders backup and Order Details backup), and view the new records.

Creating a query to delete records

Of all the action queries, the delete query is the most dangerous. Unlike the other types of queries you've worked with, delete queries delete records from tables permanently and irreversibly.

Like other action queries, delete queries act on a group of records based on scoping criteria.

A delete action query can work with multiple tables to delete records. To delete related records from multiple tables, however, you must do the following:

- Define relationships between the tables in the Relationships Builder.
- Check the Enforce Referential Integrity option for the join between tables.
- Check the Cascade Delete option for the join between tables.

When you work with one-to-many relations without defining relationships and turning on the Cascade Delete option, Access deletes records from only one table at a time. Specifically, Access deletes the many side of the relation first. Then you must remove the many-side table from the query and delete the records from the one side of the query.

This method is time-consuming and awkward. When you delete related records from one-to-many relationship tables, make sure that you define relations between the tables and put a checkmark in the Cascade Delete box in the Relationships Builder.

Because of the permanently destructive action of a delete query, you should always make backup copies of your tables before working with them.

The following example helps illustrate the use of Access action queries. In this case, you have a large number of records to delete.

Suppose that you want to delete all records of past orders and that you have already copied all past order records to backup tables in the append query section. The tables you are working with have these relations:

One order has many details.

The relation is a one-to-many relationship. As a result, if you don't define permanent relations between the tables and turn on the Cascade Delete option, you have to create two separate delete queries. (You have to delete queries from the Order Details and Orders tables — in that order.)

With relations set and the Cascade Delete option turned on, however, you simply have to delete the records from the Orders table; Access automatically deletes all related records. In this example, assume that you have already appended the records to another table — or that you have made a new table of the records you are about to delete, set up permanent relations between the two tables, and turned on the Cascade Delete option.

To create a cascading delete query for all orders that were processed last year along with their order details, follow these steps:

1. Create a new query using the Orders and Order Details tables.
2. Choose Query⇨Delete Query from the Query Design menu.
3. Notice that the name of the window changes from Select Query:Query1 to Delete Query:Query1.
4. Select the OrderDate field from the Orders table.
5. Specify the criterion **<#1/1/96#** in the OrderDate field.
6. The Delete Query Design window is shown in Figure 11-41. The only field (and its criterion) that must appear in this delete query is the first field, OrderDate.

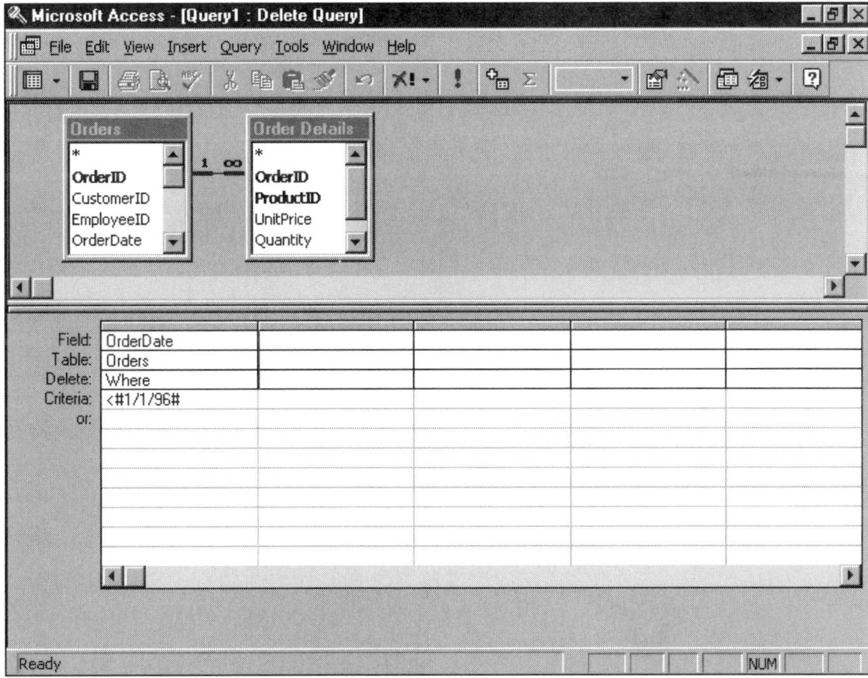

Figure 11-41: The delete query QBE pane.

7. Verify that only records for 1996 are on the datasheet.
8. Return to the Design window.
9. Click on the Run button on the toolbar (or choose Query➪Run).
10. Access displays a dialog box with a warning message that you will not be able to undo your changes. The program does not specify how many rows will be deleted from the other tables that may be linked to the table you selected.
11. Click on the Yes button to complete the query. The records are removed from the two tables. When you click on the Yes button, Access deletes the records in the related Order Details table and then deletes the records in the Orders table. Click on No to stop the procedure (no records are copied).

Remember that a delete query permanently and irreversibly removes the records from the table or tables. It is important, therefore, to back up the records you want to delete before you delete them.

After completing the delete query, you can check your results by simply clicking on the Datasheet button on the toolbar. If the delete query worked correctly, you see no records in the datasheet.

You have now deleted all records of past orders from the database tables Orders and Order Details.

Delete queries remove entire records, not just the data in specific fields. If you want to delete values in only specific fields, use an update query to change the values to empty values.

Creating other queries with the Query Wizard

This chapter described earlier how to use a Query Wizard to create a crosstab query. Access has three other wizards that can help you maintain your databases:

- Find Duplicate Records Wizard: Shows any duplicate records in a single table based on a field in the table
- Find Unmatched Records Wizard: Shows all records that do not have a corresponding record in another table (a customer with no orders, for example, or an order with no customer)
- Archive Wizard: Lets you back up records in a single table and then delete records you just backed up

Both the Duplicate Records Query and the Archive Query work on a single table. The Unmatched Records Query compares records from one table with records from another.

These wizards are listed when you first start a new query along with all the other wizards (the Crosstab Wizard, for example).

The Find Duplicate Records Wizard

The Find Duplicate Records Wizard helps you quickly create a query that reports which records in a table are duplicated, based on some field or fields in the table. Access asks which fields you want to use for checking duplication and then prompts you to enter another field or fields you may want to see in the query. Finally, Access asks for a title and then creates and displays the query.

This type of query can help you find duplicate key violations, which is a valuable trick when you want to make a unique key field with the data from an existing table. If you try to create a unique key field and Access reports an error, you know that you have either nulls in the field or duplicate records. This query helps you find duplicate records.

The Find Unmatched Records Wizard

The Find Unmatched Records Wizard helps you quickly create a query that reports any orphan or widow records between two tables.

An *orphan* is a record in a many-side table that has no corresponding record in the one-side table. If an order in the Orders table does not have a corresponding customer in the Customers table, for example, the order is an orphan.

A *widow* is a record in the one side in a one-to-many or one-to-one table that does not have a corresponding record in the other table (for example, a customer who has no orders in the Orders table).

Access asks for the names of the two tables you want to compare and the link field name between the tables. Then the program prompts you for the fields you want to see in the first table and a title. Access then creates the query.

This type of query can help you find records that have no corresponding records in other tables. If you create a relationship between tables and try to set referential integrity but Access reports that it cannot activate it, this query enables you quickly to find the records that are violating integrity.

The Archive Records Wizard

The Archive Records Wizard helps you quickly create a query that backs up records for a specific criterion and then deletes the records from the current table (at a user's request). The query is composed of two queries: a make-table query and a delete query. This query works with only one table at a time, however, and is based on a single field criterion (based on a field in the table).

Access prompts you for the table you want to archive and then for a single field criterion for which you want to archive. The program then reports the number of records to be archived and shows them to you for verification. It also asks whether you want to delete the records after archiving. Finally, Access prompts you for a title and runs the query. When the query runs, the program again prompts you to verify that you want to archive the records. If you answer Yes, the records are copied to a table by the same name, with Arc added to the back of the name.

This type of query can help you back up any table not related to other tables (lookup tables, for example).

Saving an action query

The process of saving an action query is the same as the process of saving any other query. From Design mode, you can save the query and continue working by clicking on the Save button on the toolbar or by choosing File⇨Save from the Query Design menu. If you're saving the query for the first time, Access prompts you for a name in the Save As dialog box.

You can also save the query and exit, either by choosing File⇨Close or by double-clicking on the window menu button (in the top left corner of the Query window) and answering Yes to the question in the dialog box about saving changes to the design.

Another method of saving the query is to press F12.

Running an action query

After you save an action query, you can run it by simply double-clicking on its name. Access warns you that an action query is about to be executed and asks you to confirm before it continues with the query.

Troubleshooting action queries

When you're working with action queries, you have to be aware of several potential problems. While you're running the query, any of several messages may appear, including messages that several records were lost because of key violations or that records were locked during the execution of the query. This section discusses some of these problems and how to avoid them.

Data-type errors in appending and updating

If you attempt to enter a value not appropriate for the specified field, Access doesn't enter the value: It simply ignores the incorrect values and converts the fields to Null values. When you're working with append queries, therefore, Access appends the records, but the fields may be blank.

Key violations in action queries

When you attempt to append records to another database that has a primary key, Access does not append records that contain the same primary key value.

Access does not let you update a record and change a primary key value to an existing value. You can change a primary key value to another value under these conditions:

- The new primary key value does not already exist.
- The field value you are attempting to change is not related to fields in other tables.

Access does not let you delete a field on the one side of a one-to-many relationship without first deleting the records from the many side.

The program does not let you append or update a field value that will duplicate a value in a unique index field, a field in which the index property is set to Yes (No Duplicates).

Record-locked fields in multiuser environments

Access does not perform an action query on records locked by another user. When you're performing an update or append query, you can choose to continue and change all other values. Remember, however, that by allowing Access to continue with an action query, you won't be able to determine which records were left unchanged.

Text fields

When Access appends or updates to a Text field that is smaller than the current field, the program truncates any text data that doesn't fit in the new field. Access does not warn you that it truncated the information.

Using Lookup Tables and Joins

A *lookup table* is a database table you can use to validate the entry of information. Also, you can use the table to find additional information based on a key value. It is by definition a many-to-one relationship, which means that many records in the primary table can reference information from one record in the lookup table. By definition, a lookup table can be permanent or transient:

- Permanent: A table created solely for lookup purposes
- Transient: A table used as a lookup table or a primary table

An example of a transient lookup table is the Shippers table. When you're working with a form to add order information, the Shippers table becomes a lookup table based on the ShipVia field. Although the Shippers table is a primary table of the database, in this form it may become a lookup table for the Orders table.

Working with lookup tables in queries requires an understanding of joins and how they work. For example, you may be interested in displaying an order form and want to look up the Shipper Company Name based on the ShipVia number of the order record that's displayed. The Company Name information comes from a lookup table: Shippers.

To create this query, follow these steps:

1. Select the Order and Shippers tables, and join them if they are not already joined.
2. Double-click on the ShipVia field in the Orders table.
3. Double-click on the CompanyName field in the Shippers table.

Your query should look like the one in Figure 11-42.

After you create the query, you can select the Datasheet option from the Query View button on the toolbar to display a dynaset of the lookup values.

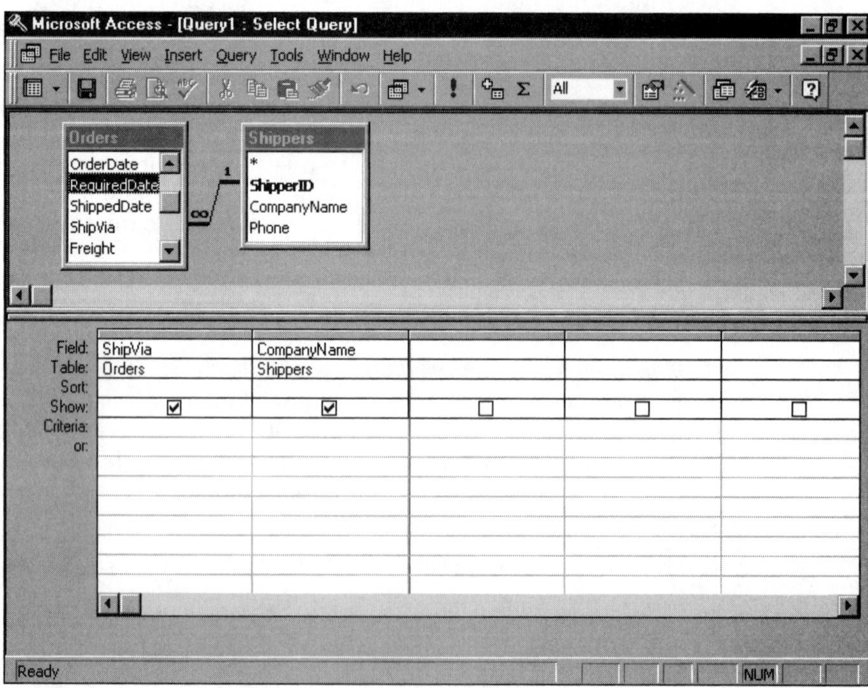

Figure 11-42: Creating a lookup table query.

Using the DLookUp()Function for Lookup Tables

Another way to find specific lookup information based on a field is to use the DLookUp() function to create a calculated field. You use DLookUp() to find information in a table that is not open. The general syntax for DLookUp() is

```
DLookUp("[Field to display]",
"[Lookup Table]", _
"<Criteria for Search>")
```

"[Field to display]" is the field in the lookup table you want to find.

"[Lookup Table]" is the table in which the field you want to display is located.

"<Criteria for Search>" is the criteria the lookup function uses.

Although Access suggests that Criteria for Search is not necessary, if you want to use a different criterion for each record, Criteria for Search is essential. When you use DLookUp(), the criteria format is critical. The format of the Criteria for Search is as follows:

```
"[Field in Lookup Table] = _
'<Example Data>' "
```

You can substitute any valid Access operator for the equal (=) operator.

'<Example Data>' (note the single quotation marks) is usually a literal. If the data is a field in the current table, you must use the following syntax:

```
" & [Field in This Table] & "
```

Note that the field is surrounded by double quotation marks (") and ampersands (&).

Although this seems complex, building a calculated field using the DLookUp() function can be a simple way to create a query for use in a form or report. For example, create a query that finds the freight in the Orders table:

1. Select the Order Details table.
2. Double-click on the OrderID field in the Order Details table.
3. Type **Freight:DLookUp ("[Freight]","[Orders]","[OrderID]= "&[OrderID])** in an empty field in the QBE pane.

When you enter the field name of the current table in the criteria for the DLookUp() function, you *cannot* use spaces. After the equal sign, you type the entry in this format:

```
double quote — ampersand _
— [field name]
```

If OrderID were a Text field, you would have to enclose the OrderID field specification in single quotation marks. Because the field is numeric it needs no surrounding single quotation marks.

The following figure shows what the query looks like after you enter the calculated field Freight (note that you do not see the entire formula you entered):

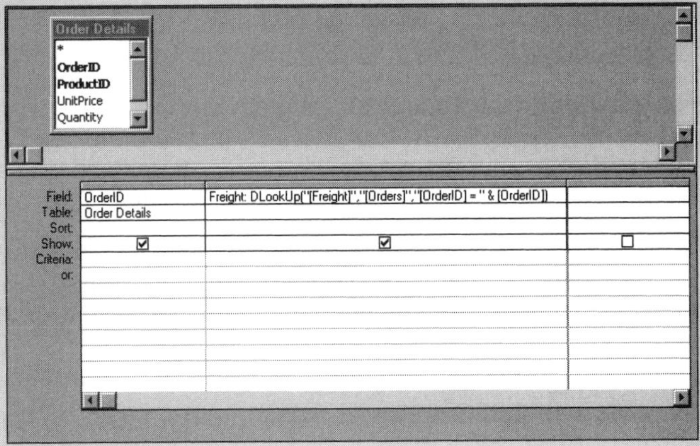

If you are having problems typing Step 3, press Shift+F2 to activate the Zoom window. When the window is displayed, the entire contents are highlighted; press F2 again to deselect it and move to the end of the contents.

If you choose the Datasheet option in the Query View button on the toolbar, you see a datasheet that displays the freight values resulting from the `DLookUp()` function.

Using calculated fields

Queries are not limited to actual fields in tables. You can also use a *calculated* field, a field created by performing some calculation. You can create a calculated field in many different ways. For example, you can create a calculated field by using these methods:

- Use the ampersand (&) to concatenate two Text type fields.
- Perform a mathematical calculation on two Number type fields.
- Use an Access function to create a field based on the function.

In the following steps, you create a simple calculated field, Total Due, from the UnitPrice and Quantity fields in the Order Details table. To create the calculated field, follow these steps:

1. Create a new query using the Order Details table.
2. Select the UnitPrice and Quantity fields from the Order Details table.
3. Click on an empty Field cell in the QBE pane.
4. Press Shift+F2 to activate the Zoom box.
5. Type **Total Due: [UnitPrice]×[Quantity]**.
6. Click on OK in the Zoom box or press Enter.

After completing these steps, your query should look like Figure 11-43. Total Due is the calculated field name for the expression `[UnitPrice]×[Quantity]`.

The field name and expression are separated by a colon. This total is for all order details, because no limiting criteria or related tables are specified in the query. To show this total for each customer, you have to add to the query the Customers and Orders tables with their defined relationships, the CompanyName and OrderID fields. This query then displays the total due (minus the cost of freight) for each customer's order.

Access 97 has an Expression Builder you can use to help create any expression — a complex calculated field for a query, for example. In the following steps, you create a calculated field named Next Order Date that displays a

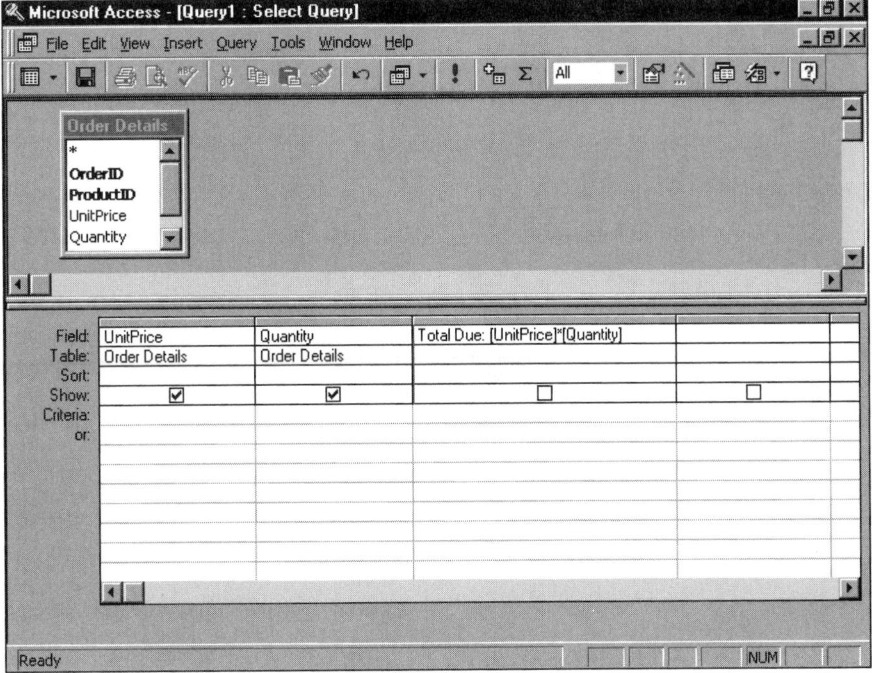

Figure 11-43: Creating a simple calculated field.

date six months later. You can use this date for a letter report you plan to send to all customers. The date is based on the last Order Date field in the Orders table. To create this calculated field, follow these steps:

1. Create a new query using the Customers and Orders tables.
2. Select ContactName from the Customers table and OrderDate from the Orders table.
3. Click on an empty Field cell in the QBE pane.
4. Activate the Expression Builder by clicking on the Builder button on the toolbar (the wand) or click the right mouse button on Menu on Demand and select Build.
5. Access displays the Expression Builder dialog box, as shown in Figure 11-44.
6. Now build the expression **DateAdd("m",6,[Orders]![OrderDate])** for the calculated field.
7. In the bottom left window of the Expression Builder dialog box, click on the folder in the Functions tree to expand it.
8. Select Built-in Functions (double-click on it).
9. Access displays information in the two windows to the right.

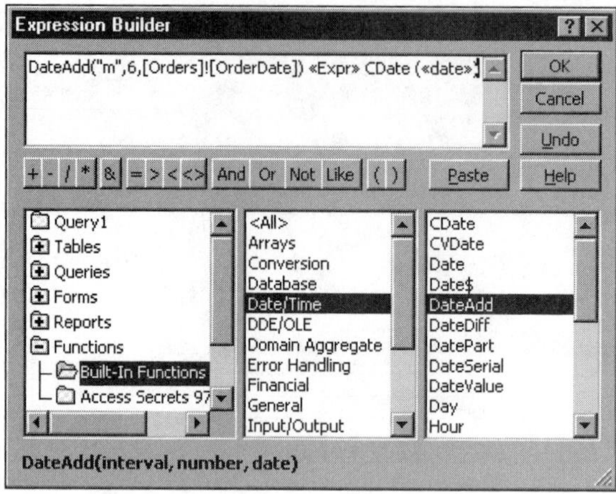

Figure 11-44: The Expression Builder dialog box.

10. Move to the third window, which lists all the functions.
11. Select the `DateAdd` function (double-click on it).
12. Access displays the function in the top left window with information about the necessary parameters.
13. Move to the top left window and click on the parameter `<interval>`.
14. Type **"m"**.
15. Click on `<number>` and replace it with **6**.
16. Click on `<date>` and highlight it.
17. Move back to the bottom left window and click on the Tables folder.
18. Select the Orders table by clicking on it.
19. Select `[OrderDate]` from the middle window on the bottom row (double-click on it).
20. Access places the table and field name in the last part of the `DateAdd` function.
21. Click on OK in the Expression Builder.
22. Access returns to the QBE pane and places the expression in the cell for you.
23. Access automatically assigns a name for the expression, by labeling it `ExprX`. Should your field now show, change the name of the expression from Expr1 to Next Order Date by simply overwriting it.

The `DateAdd()` function lets you add six months to `Orders.OrderDate`. The `m` signifies that you are working with months rather than days or years.

You can type the calculated field directly, of course, but the Expression Builder is a valuable tool when you create complex expressions that are difficult to remember.

Finding the number of records in a table or query

To determine quickly the total number of records in an existing table or query, use the `Count(*)` function. This is a special use of the `Count()` function. To determine the total number of records in the Orders table, for example, follow these steps:

1. Start a new query using the Orders table.
2. Click on the first empty Field cell in the QBE pane.
3. Type **Count(*)** in the cell.

Access adds the calculated field name Expr1 to the cell in front of the `Count()` function.

When you look at the datasheet, you see a single cell that shows the number of records for the Orders table.

If you use this function with the asterisk wildcard (*), this field is the only one that can be shown in the datasheet. That is the reason you entered the expression `Count(*)` in an empty QBE pane.

You can also use the `Count(*)` function to determine the total number of records that match a specific criterion. You may want to know, for example, how many orders in the Orders table have a ShipCountry of Germany. Follow these steps to determine the number of orders in the table:

1. Start a new query and select the Orders table.
2. Click on the first empty Field cell in the QBE pane.
3. Type **Count(*)** in the cell.
4. Double-click on the ShipCountry field in the Orders table.
5. Deselect the Show cell in the ShipCountry field.
6. Type **Germany** in the Criteria cell in the ShipCountry field.

If you choose the Datasheet option from the Query View button on the toolbar, Access again displays only one cell in the datasheet, which contains the number of orders in the Orders table that have a ShipCountry of Germany.

Remember that only the field that contains the `Count(*)` function can be shown in the datasheet. If you try to display any additional fields, Access reports an error.

Finding the top (n) records in a query

Access 97 not only enables you to find the number of records in an existing table or query but also helps you find the first (n) records in a query. The first (n) records can be a set number or a percentage of the records in the query.

Suppose that you want to identify the top ten orders you have processed — in other words, you want to find the orders for the customers who have paid the most amount of money to your business. To determine the top ten orders and their customers, follow these steps:

1. Create a new query using the Customer, Orders, and Order Details tables.
2. Select CompanyName from the Customers Table and OrderID from the Orders table.
3. Build a Total Due field from the Order Details table, as you did earlier in this chapter (refer to Figure 11-43). Click on the Totals button (the sigma — Σ) on the toolbar.
4. Change Group By under the Total Due field to Sum.
5. Sort the Total Due field in descending order.
6. The resulting query should look like the one shown in Figure 11-45.

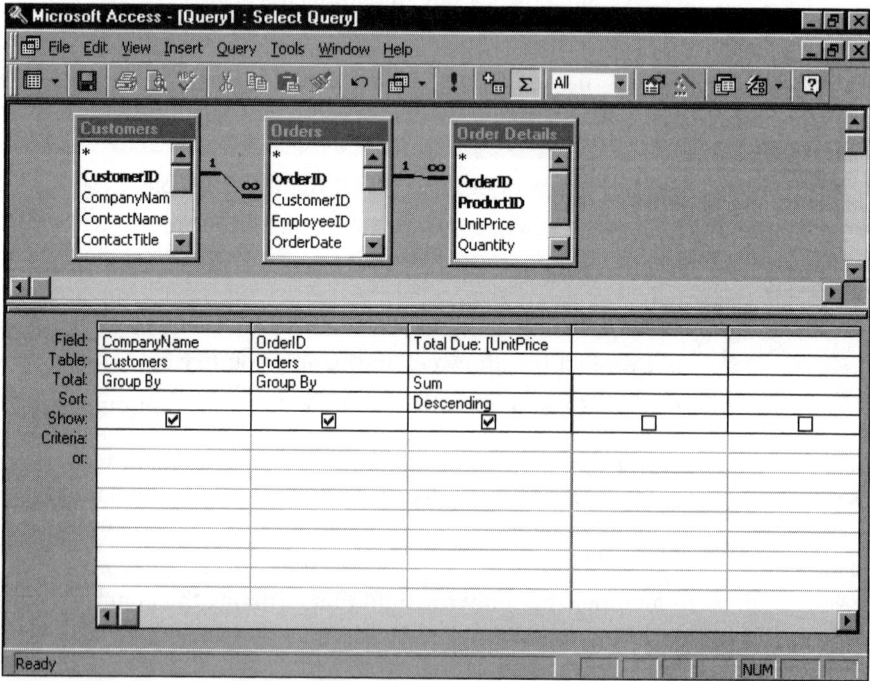

Figure 11-45: A total query with two Group By fields and a sum.

7. Click on the combo box next to the Totals button on the toolbar. The choices are 5, 25, 100, 5%, 25%, or All. You can also enter your own number of records or percentage of records in the table you want to see.
8. Enter **10** in the Top Values property cell to select the top 10 records.

You are ready to run your query. When you click on the Query View button on the toolbar, you should see the top ten money-producing records in the dynaset.

Creating SQL-specific queries

Access 97 has added three query types you create only by entering SQL statements. You cannot create these queries by using the QBE pane; instead, you type the appropriate SQL statement directly in the SQL view window. This list describes what you can do with the new SQL-specific queries in Access:

- Union query: Combine common fields from more than one table or query into one Recordset
- Pass-through query: Send SQL commands directly to any SQL database server in the SQL database server's SQL syntax.
- Data-definition query: Create or alter database objects directly in Access databases.

To create any of these queries, pick the type you want to create by choosing Query⇨SQL Specific.

Union queries

A *union* query lets you quickly combine several tables that have common fields. The resulting snapshot Recordset is not updatable.

A union query has two or more SQL `SELECT` statements. Each `SELECT` statement requires the same number of fields in the same order.

When you run a union query, it creates a snapshot rather than a dynaset. A snapshot-type Recordset is not updatable.

Pass-through queries

A *pass-through* query sends SQL commands directly to an SQL database server (Microsoft SQL Server or Oracle, for example). You send the command by using the syntax the specific server requires. Be sure to consult the documentation for the appropriate SQL database server.

Never attempt to convert a pass-through query to another type of query. If you do, Access erases the entire SQL statement you typed.

When you work with pass-through queries, you should not perform operations that change the state of the connection. If you halt a transaction in the middle of processing it, for example, you may get unexpected results.

Data-definition queries

Of the three new SQL-specific queries, the data-definition query is least useful. Everything you can do with it, you can also do by using the Access design tools. A data-definition query is an efficient way, however, to create or change database objects. You can use any of these SQL statements with a data-definition query:

- `CREATE TABLE`
- `ALTER TABLE`
- `DROP TABLE`
- `CREATE INDEX`
- `DROP INDEX`

Understanding how queries save field selections

When you open a query design, you may notice that the design has changed since you last saved the query. When you save a query, Access rearranges fields and even eliminates fields based on several rules:

- Fields in which the Show box is not checked but criteria are specified are moved to the rightmost columns in the QBE pane.
- Fields in which the Show box is not checked are eliminated from the QBE pane column unless they have sorting directives or criteria.

Because of these rules, your query may look much different after you save and reopen it.

Renaming fields in queries

When you work with queries, you can rename a field to describe the field's contents more clearly or accurately. You may want to rename the CompanyName field to Customer Name, for example. The ability to rename fields is useful when you work with calculated fields or calculate totals; Access automatically assigns names such as Expr1 or AvgOfFreight. The process of renaming fields in Access queries is extremely simple. To change the display name of the CompanyName, for example, follow these steps:

1. Select the Customers table.
2. Double-click on the CompanyName field in the Customers table.

3. Place the cursor in front of the first letter of CompanyName in the Field cell.
4. Type **Customer Name:** (be sure to include a colon).

When you name a query field, you should delete any names that Access has assigned (on the left of the colon). You should remove the calculated field name Expr1, for example, when you name the field.

If you rename a field, Access uses only the new name for the heading of the query datasheet or a control source in a form or report that uses the query. Any new forms or reports you create based on the query, therefore, use the new field name. Access does not change the actual field name in the underlying table.

If you want to change the name that appears only on the datasheet, change the `Captions` property of the field cell to display the new name. This then appears only when you view the datasheet; it does not show up in Query Design view.

When you're working with renamed fields, you can use an expression name (the new name you specified) in another expression within the same query. You may have a calculated field called First Name, for example, that uses several Access functions to separate an individual's first name and last name. For this calculated field, you can use the field name you created rather than the Access default name.

Using query-design options

You can specify three default options when you work with a query design. You can view and set these options by choosing Tools⇨Options from the main Query Design menu and then clicking on the Tables/Queries tab.

You can set the following four items for queries:

- Output All Fields
- Run Permissions
- Show Table Names
- Enable AutoJoin

Access uses these default options when you open a new query. The default for Show Table Names and Output All fields is generally No. The Run Permissions option offers you a choice of either owners or users (the default). The Enable AutoJoin option controls whether tables with no relationships set are automatically joined by common field names. Table 11-5 briefly describes each query-design option and its purpose.

Table 11-5 Query-Design Options

Option	*Purpose*
Output All Fields	Shows all fields in the underlying tables or only the fields displayed in the QBE pane.
Run Permissions	Restricts use in a multiuser environment. Users restricted from viewing the underlying tables can still view the data from the query.
Enable AutoJoin	Tables with no relationships set are automatically joined by common field names.
Show Table Names	Set to Yes, shows the Table row in the QBE pane; set to No, hides the Table row.

Note

When you set query design options, they do not take effect for the current query. You use these options to specify actions for only new queries. To show table names in the current query, choose View⇨Table Names from the main Query Design menu. To specify the other two options for the current query, choose View⇨Properties.

Setting query properties

To set query properties, either click on the Properties button on the toolbar, click the right mouse button to choose Properties from the shortcut menu, or choose View⇨Properties from the main Query Design menu. Access displays a Query Properties dialog box. Your options depend on the query type and the table or field with which you are working. Tables 11-6 and 11-7 show the query properties you can set.

Table 11-6 Field-Level Properties

Property	*Purpose*
`Alias`	A custom name for the table
`Source`	The connecting string and database

Table 11-7 Query-Level Properties

Property	*Description*	*Query*	*Select*	*Cross-tab*	*Update*	*Delete*	*Make-Table*	*Add-Table*
`Description`	Text that describes table or query	X	X	X	X	X	X	
`Output All Fields`	Shows all fields from underlying tables in query	X				X	X	
`Top Values`	The number of highest or lowest values to be returned	X				X	X	
`Unique Values`	Returns only unique field values in the dynaset	X				X	X	
`Unique Records`	Returns only unique record for the dynaset	X		X	X	X	X	
`Run Permissions`	Establishes permissions for specified user	X	X	X	X	X	X	
`Source Database`	External database name for all tables or queries in query	X	X	X	X	X	X	
`Source`	Name of application	X	X	X	X	X	X	
`Connect Str`	Used to connect to external database							
`Record Locks`	Records locked while query runs (usually action queries)	X	X	X	X	X	X	
`ODBC Timeout`	Number of seconds before reporting error for opening DB	X	X	X	X	X	X	

(continued)

Table 11-7 *(continued)*

Property	*Description*	*Query*	*Select*	*Cross-tab*	*Update*	*Delete*	*Make-Table*	*Add-Table*
`Filter`	Filter name loaded automatically with query	X	X	X	X	X	X	
`Order By`	Sort automatically loaded with query	X	X	X	X	X	X	

You can use the query-level and field-level properties in the same manner as you use the properties in forms, reports, and tables. Field-level properties are displayed when you select a table and the Properties window is displayed. The query-level properties that are displayed when you click depend on the type of query being created.

Viewing SQL Statements in Queries

When you use graphical Query By Example, Access converts what you create into an SQL statement. When you run your query, Access executes this SQL statement.

SQL is a standardized language that many relational databases use to query and update tables. Although SQL is relatively simple to learn and use, Access does not require that you know how to use it or even that you use it. Access uses SQL, but you don't ever have to know that SQL is there.

If you are familiar with SQL, you can view and edit an SQL statement. If you make changes to an SQL statement, Access automatically reflects the changes in the QBE pane for you.

To view an SQL statement that Access creates, choose View➪SQL from the Query menu. Figure 11-46 shows a typical SQL statement that displays the fields `CompanyName`, `OrderDate`, and `RequiredDate`.

To modify an existing SQL statement or to create your own, you enter your changes directly in the SQL dialog box. To add new lines in the dialog box, you press Ctrl+Enter. This is also true for adding data to a Memo field.

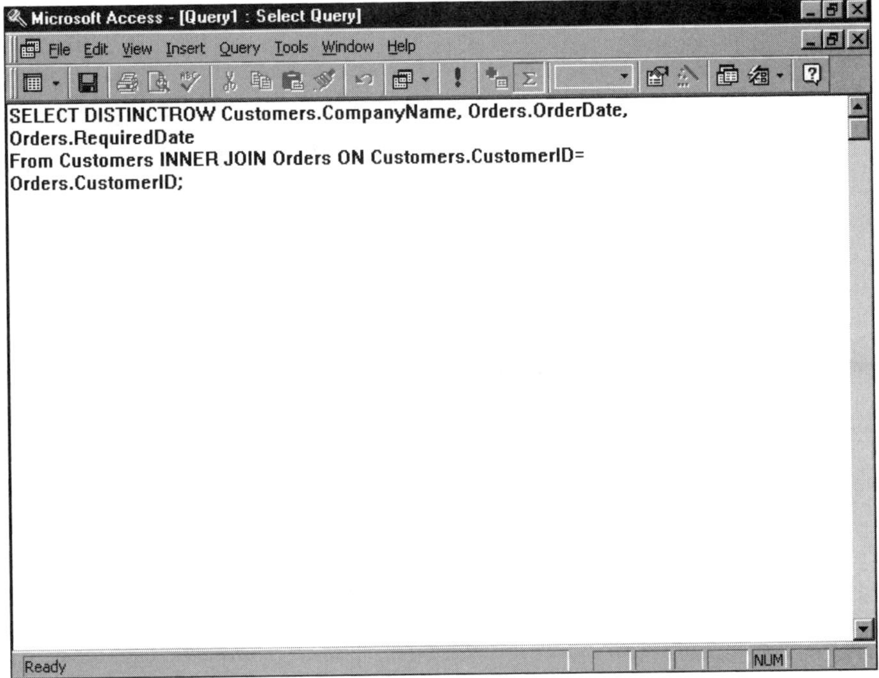

Figure 11-46: An SQL statement in Access.

You can use SQL statements directly in expressions, macros, forms, and reports. You can use an SQL statement, for example, in the `RowSource` or `RecordSource` properties of a form or report. To do so, you don't even have to know how to use SQL. Rather, you can simply create the SQL statement (by selecting specific records, for example) in the Query window. Activate the SQL dialog box and press Ctrl+C to copy the entire SQL statement you created. Switch to the location in which you want to use the statement and press Ctrl+V to paste the statement (in the `RowSource` property of the property sheet, for example).

You can create SQL statements in the SQL dialog box. If you write your own SQL statement or edit one, Access updates the Query window when you exit the dialog box: It adds tables to the top portion and adds fields and criteria to the QBE pane.

Until now, you have created queries using the Access Query Designer. You have even learned that you can choose View⇨SQL View to examine the SQL statement that Access builds.

As you already know, one way to learn SQL statements is to build a query graphically and then view the corresponding SQL statement, as shown in Figure 11-46.

Table 11-8 shows the most-common SQL commands and explains their purposes.

Table 11-8 Common SQL Commands

Command	*Purpose of SQL Statement*
SELECT	(A required keyword.) A command/keyword that starts an SQL statement and that is followed by the names of the fields you select from the table or tables (if more than one is specified in the FROM clause/command).
FROM	(A required keyword.) A clause/keyword that specifies the name of the table or tables that hold the fields you specify in the SELECT command.
WHERE	A command that specifies any condition used to filter, or limit, the records to be viewed; used only when you want to limit the records to a specific group based on the condition.
ORDER BY	A command that specifies in which order you want the resulting data set (the selected records Access found and returned) to be displayed.

Using these four basic SQL commands, you can build powerful SQL statements you can use in your Access forms and reports.

The DISTINCTROW keyword

The DISTINCTROW keyword in the SQL statement in Figure 11-46 is an optional predicate keyword Access uses as a restricter keyword to specify which records should be returned. This predicate keyword is not used by other SQL database languages. Access uses it to limit the display of duplicate records based on the values of the entire record. It works in the same way as the DISTINCT predicate in other SQL languages, except that DISTINCT works against duplicate fields within the SELECT statement. DISTINCTROW works against their records (even fields that are not in the SELECT statement). This subject is covered in more detail later in this chapter.

The SELECT command

The SELECT command, or clause, is the first word in a select query or make-table query. You use the SELECT command to specify the field or fields you want displayed in the results table.

After specifying the keyword SELECT, you have to specify the fields you want to display. When you specify more than one field, use a comma between the fields, with this general syntax:

```
SELECT Field_one, Field_two, Field_three, ...
```

where Field_one and Field_two are replaced with the name of the table field.

Note that each field in the list is separated by the use of a comma. To specify the company name and country from the Customers table, for example, you specify the following:

```
SELECT CompanyName, Country
```

Brackets around field names

Whenever you specify a field name that has spaces within the name, Access requires you to place the field name in brackets.

To view fields from more than one table, you should specify the name of the table in which the field will be found. When you want to select fields from both the Customers and Orders tables, for example, the SELECT clause looks like this:

```
SELECT Customers.[CompanyName], Customers.[Country], _
Orders.[OrderDate], Orders.[RequiredDate]
```

When you build a query in Access, it automatically places the table name before the field name. In reality, you have to specify the table name only if more than one table in the SQL statement has fields with the same name. Both the Customers table and Orders table, for example, have a field named [CustomerID]. If you want to select [CustomerID] in your SQL statement, you must specify which [CustomerID] to use — the one in Customers or the one in Orders, as shown in this SQL SELECT clause:

```
SELECT Customers.[CustomerID], [CompanyName], Country, [OrderDate], _
[RequiredDate]
```

Table names

Although table names are not required for nonduplicate fields in an SQL statement, you should use them for clarity.

You can use the asterisk (*) wildcard to specify that all fields should be selected. To select all fields from more than one table, specify the table, a period (.), and then the name of the field (in this case, the asterisk).

SELECT predicates

When you create a SELECT SQL statement, several predictors can be associated with the SELECT clause:

- ALL
- DISTINCT
- DISTINCTROW
- TOP

You use these predictors to restrict the number of records that are returned. They can work in conjunction with the WHERE clause in an SQL statement.

The ALL predicate is the default. It selects all records that meet the WHERE condition specified in the SQL statement. ALL is optional because it is the default value.

The DISTINCT predicate is used when you want to omit records that contain duplicate data in the fields specified in the SELECT clause. For example, if you create a query and want to look at the Customer ID and the dates on which a customer has placed orders, you use this SELECT statement:

```
SELECT DISTINCT [CustomerID], [OrderDate]
```

If a customer in the Orders table has placed two orders on the same date, you see only one record in the resulting datasheet. The DISTINCT predicate tells Access to show only one record if the fields you selected have duplicate values (the same customer ID and order date). Even though two different records are in the Orders table, only one is shown. DISTINCT eliminates duplicates based on the fields you select for viewing.

The DISTINCTROW predicate is unique to Access. It works in a manner similar to DISTINCT, with one big difference: DISTINCTROW looks for duplicates based on *all* fields — not just selected fields — in the table or tables. If a customer has two different order records in the Orders table, for example, and you use the predicate DISTINCTROW (replacing DISTINCT) in the preceding SQL statement, both records are displayed. DISTINCTROW looks for duplicates in all the fields in the Customers and Orders tables. If any field is different (in this case, the order ID and others), both records are displayed in the datasheet.

The TOP predicate, which is also unique to Access, lets you restrict the number of displayed records based on the WHERE condition of the TOP <number> of values. For example, TOP 10 displays only the first ten records that match the WHERE condition. TOP can be used, for example, to display the top number of customers who have spent money with your company.

The TOP predicate has an optional keyword, PERCENT, that you can use to display the top number of records based on a percentage rather than on a number.

The FROM clause in an SQL statement

As its name suggests, the `FROM` clause (command) specifies the tables (or queries) that hold the fields named in the `SELECT` clause. This required clause tells SQL where to find the records.

When you work with one table, as in the original example, the `FROM` clause simply specifies the table name:

```
SELECT [CompanyName], Country,
FROM Customers
```

When you work with more than one table, you can supply a `TableExpression` to the `FROM` clause to specify which data is retrieved. In a `FROM` clause, you set the relationship between the two or more tables being linked in the resulting datasheet.

A `TableExpression` can be one of three types:

- `INNER JOIN...ON`
- `RIGHT JOIN...ON`
- `LEFT JOIN...ON`

`INNER JOIN...ON` is used to specify the traditional Access equi-join. To join Customers to Orders via the CustomerID field in the `FROM` clause, for example, you use this command:

```
SELECT Customers.[CompanyName], Orders.[OrderDate]
FROM Customers INNER JOIN Orders ON Customers.[CustomerID] = _
Orders.[CustomerID]
```

Note that the `FROM` clause specifies the main table to use — Customers. The `INNER JOIN` portion of the `FROM` clause then specifies the second table to be used — Orders. The `ON` portion of the `FROM` clause then specifies which fields are used to join the table.

The `LEFT JOIN` and `RIGHT JOIN` work in exactly the same way except that they specify an outer join rather than an inner (equi-) join.

The WHERE clause in an SQL statement

You use the `WHERE` clause (command) in an SQL statement to specify any condition you want to set. Unlike the `SELECT/DELETE...` and `FROM` clauses, the `WHERE` clause is optional. Use it only when you want to specify a particular condition.

The original SQL statement began, for example, by specifying this `WHERE` clause:

```
WHERE (Customers.[CustomerID]="EASTC")
```

The WHERE condition can be any valid expression. It can be a simple one-condition expression, as in the preceding line, or a complex expression based on several criteria.

If the WHERE clause is used, it must follow the FROM clause of the SQL statement.

The ORDER BY clause

You use the ORDER BY clause to specify a sort order. This clause sorts the displayed data by the field or fields specified after the clause. ORDER BY can sort in either ascending or descending order. For example, you can specify a sort order by CustomerID, as follows:

```
ORDER BY Customers.[CustomerID];
```

The end of an SQL statement

Because an SQL statement can be as long as 64,000 characters, you need a way to tell the database language that you have finished creating a statement. SQL statements end with a semicolon (;).

Access is forgiving about your use of the ending semicolon. If you forget to place one at the end of an SQL statement, Access assumes that it should be there and runs the SQL statement as though you had typed one there.

If you accidentally place a semicolon inside an SQL statement, Access reports an error and attempts to tell you where it occurred.

By using SELECT, FROM, WHERE, and ORDER BY, you can create some powerful SQL statements to display and view data from your tables. For example, you can build an SQL statement that does the following:

1. Selects the Customer's CompanyName, Country, OrderID, and OrderDate fields
2. Joins from the Customers and Orders tables where the Customers and Orders tables are linked by the CustomerID
3. Displays only records in which the CustomerID is EASTC
4. Sorts the data in order by OrderDate

The SQL statement you use may look like this:

```
SELECT [CompanyName], Country, [OrderID], [OrderDate]
FROM Customers INNER JOIN Orders ON Customers.[CustomerID] = _
Orders.[CustomerID]
WHERE [CustomerID] = "EASTC"
ORDER BY Orders.[OrderDate];
```

This short discussion of SQL statements serves as an overview and describes how to create statements in Access 97. You can use several other clauses (commands) with SQL statements. SQL is relatively easy to understand and work with and offers several benefits over creating graphical queries and using queries.

Working with Filters

By using a filter applied against a table or query Recordset, you can display just the set of records you want to work with. Filters are especially useful when you use them in conjunction with forms in which you want to enable users to specify a subset of records from the Recordset on which the form is built. You may want to include a control on the form on which users specify the limiting criteria to display the records they want to see.

On a form that displays orders, for example, you can put a text box in which users enter a date to represent the order date for orders to be displayed. The date value in the text box is then used to specify a filter for selecting orders from the form's record source. More on this technique later.

Access 97 includes two types of filters that are useful in your applications: Filter by Selection and Filter by Form.

Using Filter by Selection

Filter by Selection is an Access 97 technology that enables you to instantly select records on the basis of the current value you have selected. Suppose that you move your cursor to the ShipCountry column in a datasheet that displays order records. When you click on the Sort Ascending button, Access sorts the data by ShipCountry. When you highlight any of the records that contain Germany and click on the Filter by Selection button, Access selects only the records in which ShipCountry is Germany. After you select Germany and click on the Filter by Selection button in the Orders table (which has 830 records), you see only 122 records, and all have the value of Germany in the ShipCountry field.

You may also notice that the navigation button area tells you that the table is currently filtered. In addition, the Apply Filter/Remove Filter icon (the third filter icon, which looks like a large funnel) is pressed, indicating that a filter is in use. When you toggle this button, it removes all filters. The filter specification does not go away; it is simply turned off.

Filter by Selection is additive. You can continue to choose values and then click on the Filter by Selection button each time. If you place your cursor in the Ship City column in a record in which the value of Ship City is Frankfurt A.M. and click on the Filter by Selection button, you see only 15 records — the orders being shipped to Frankfurt, Germany.

If you want to specify a selection and then see everything that *doesn't* match the selection, right-click the datasheet and click on the Filter Excluding Selection option. You choose this option to select everything except the records with the selected value.

Filter by Selection provides incredible opportunities for drill-down into successive layers of data. As you add to Filter by Selection, it continues to add to its own internal query manager. Even when you click on the Remove Filter button to redisplay all the records, Access still stores the query specification in memory.

If you click on the button again (now called Apply Filter), only the filtered records are displayed.

Filter by Selection has some limitations. Most important, all the choices are `AND`ed together, which means that the only operation you can perform is a search for records that meet *all* the conditions you specify.

Using Filter by Form

Another option, Filter by Form, enables you to create a more complex analysis of data. Clicking on the Second Filter button changes the datasheet to a single record. Every field in the displayed record becomes a combo box in which you can choose from a list of all values for that field. On the bottom of the form, you can specify the `OR` conditions for each group of values you specify. If you click on an Or tab, you can enter a second set of conditions.

Suppose that you want to see orders being shipped to France in addition to those for Germany. To specify this second condition, you click on an Or tab and either enter or select France in the ShipCountry column. The filter then displays orders for Germany and France.

You can have as many conditions as you want. If you want even more advanced manipulation of your selections, you can choose Records⇨Filter⇨Advanced Filter/Sort to display a QBE screen used to enter more-complex filters.

Using filtering in code

You don't have to use Datasheet view in order to use Filter by Selection or Filter by Form. You can use these filter methods with your application forms, too, by using the same steps you use for datasheets.

In addition to using these techniques, you can use the `ApplyFilter` method in code placed behind a command button. The `ApplyFilter` method takes two arguments: a filter name and a `WHERE` condition. Both are optional. You usually use either one or the other but not both unless you want to filter the filter. If neither argument is used, the filter stored in memory is applied and produces the same effect as clicking on the Apply Filter button on the toolbar.

If you have a form that displays orders and you want to provide a feature that enables users to filter the orders by order date, follow these steps:

1. On your Orders form, place an unbound text box named Filter OrderDate.
2. Place a command button on the form with the caption &Filter Orders.
3. In the `On Click` event of the command button, place the following code:

```
DoCmd.ApplyFilter , "[OrderDate] = #" & [Filter OrderDate] & "#"
```

In these steps, the `ApplyFilter` method of the `DoCmd` object is being used with the `WHERE` argument. Because the `Filter` argument is not specified, you must use a leading comma before the `WHERE` argument.

The field used in the `WHERE` argument, `[OrderDate]`, must be a field in the `RecordSource` of the form. The pound sign (#) symbols are used to enclose the date string entered in the text box named Filter OrderDate to indicate to Access that this string is a Date string literal. Note that we haven't checked for a valid date here, but you should always perform validity checks on values entered by users and notify them if an invalid value has been entered.

Open this form in Form View, enter a date in the Filter OrderDate text box, and click on the Filter Orders button. You should see orders with the order date you entered only if orders with that OrderDate value are in the Orders table.

Now that you know how to filter the displayed orders, you need a method for turning off the filter so that you can see all the orders: `ShowAllRecords`.

Place another command button on your form with the caption Show All Orders. In the `On Click` event of this button, place a `DoCmd.ShowAllRecords` statement. When you click on this button in Form View, the filter is turned off and all orders are again displayed.

Chapter 12

Getting the Most out of Access 97 Reports

In This Chapter

- Desktop publishing a report
- Previewing the report layout
- Printing a report
- Adding calculations and summaries to reports
- Modifying a report at run time
- Creating a Mail Merge report without Word
- Using the Mail Merge Wizard with Word

Creating reports can be a challenging assignment, especially if you don't have all of your data in a row (or is that ducks in a row?). After your data is in order, though, any report is easy. In Chapter 11, "Manipulating Data with Queries and Filters," you learned some of the advanced methods for creating a query. Many times, it takes several queries to get your data lined up.

The report writer is simply a piece of software that processes a stream of data and rearranges the data into a more readable form. Common formatting includes grouping the data into like groups of one or more fields; sorting the data differently from the original format; or creating subtotals, totals or calculations using the raw data.

Creating reports that do these tasks is fairly simple and you can even use the Access 97 report wizard to accomplish them. In this chapter, you will see some of the lesser known capabilities of reports in Access 97.

Desktop Publishing a Report

The Access Report Writer lets you design reports exactly the way you want to see them. In other words, Access has a WYSIWYG (what-you-see-is-what-you-get) report writer. As you place controls in the design window, you instantly see how they will look in your report. If you want to see how the data will look, you can take advantage of several types of on-screen preview modes. These modes enable you to see the actual data without outputting to a hard-copy device.

Figure 12-1 shows the hard copy of a final report. Notice how the special effects significantly enhance the report's readability. Important information, such as the customer, invoice number, and shipping information, is easily understood at a glance. Readers need only look at an option button or checkbox, rather than a numeric code or text.

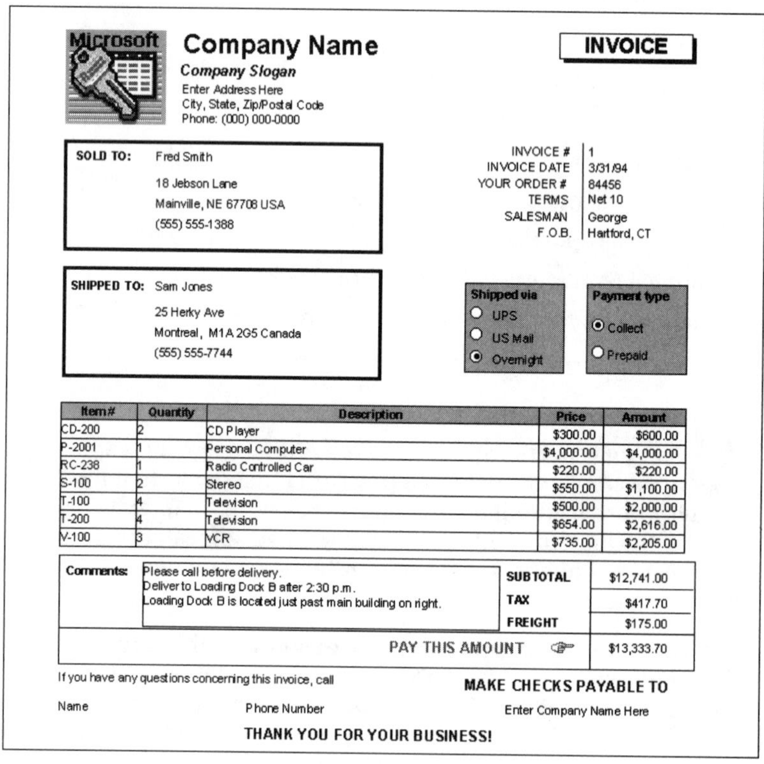

Microsoft

Company Name

Company Slogan

Enter Address Here
City, State, Zip/Postal Code
Phone: (000) 000-0000

INVOICE

SOLD TO: Fred Smith
18 Jebson Lane
Mainville, NE 67708 USA
(555) 555-1388

INVOICE # 1
INVOICE DATE 3/31/94
YOUR ORDER # 84456
TERMS Net 10
SALESMAN George
F.O.B. Hartford, CT

SHIPPED TO: Sam Jones
25 Herky Ave
Montreal, M1A 2G5 Canada
(555) 555-7744

Shipped via
UPS
US Mail
(•) Overnight

Payment type
(•) Collect
Prepaid

Item#	Quantity	Description	Price	Amount
CD-200	2	CD Player	$300.00	$600.00
P-2001	1	Personal Computer	$4,000.00	$4,000.00
RC-238	1	Radio Controlled Car	$220.00	$220.00
S-100	2	Stereo	$550.00	$1,100.00
T-100	4	Television	$500.00	$2,000.00
T-200	4	Television	$654.00	$2,616.00
V-100	3	VCR	$735.00	$2,205.00

Comments: Please call before delivery.
Deliver to Loading Dock B after 2:30 p.m.
Loading Dock B is located just past main building on right.

SUBTOTAL	$12,741.00
TAX	$417.70
FREIGHT	$175.00
PAY THIS AMOUNT	$13,333.70

If you have any questions concerning this invoice, call

Name Phone Number

MAKE CHECKS PAYABLE TO

Enter Company Name Here

THANK YOU FOR YOUR BUSINESS!

Figure 12-1: A report with special effects.

Understanding WYSIWYG Printing

You can add color, shading, or reverse video (white letters on a black background) to add emphasis to your report text and controls. You can even color or shade the background of report sections; you see the effect immediately. Although what you see on the Report Design screen appears to be exactly what you'll get when you print, you should be aware of some factors that affect just how close what you see is to what you really get.

The first problem is with fonts. If you use Windows 95 and TrueType fonts, typically about 95 percent of your fonts appear perfectly, both in the Report Design window on screen and in the hard-copy report. A common problem is that letters don't all fit on the report even though they appear to fit in the Report Design window. Another problem is that controls shift very slightly from perfect alignment. For example, although the Report Design window shows that the word Invoice fits perfectly in the report, when you view the report in print preview mode or send it to a printer, only the letters *Invoic* may print out. The final *e* simply vanishes.

Other problems occur when you place controls very tightly within a rectangle or group box. In fact, most of the time, the print preview modes are perfect for determining what the hard copy will look like, whereas the Report Design window view may differ slightly. The print preview (or hard copy) should be your only method of determining when your report is complete. Make sure you're using the right Windows screen driver when previewing a report; you can get vastly different results depending on the driver. For example, a dot-matrix driver is probably only 100–150 dpi (dots per inch), whereas an HP LaserJet 4 can be 600 dpi; higher values mean higher resolution (a clearer image).

Using the formatting windows and toolbar

The formatting windows and Formatting toolbar provide important tools for enhancing controls in a report. You can use the five formatting windows to change a control's background and foreground colors, the border color and thickness, and to apply special effects such as raised, sunken, etched, chiseled, or shadowed.

The Formatting toolbar can be displayed and removed from the screen by selecting View➪Toolbars and then selecting Formatting or by right-clicking on the toolbar area and selecting Formatting.

You can tell the currently selected color in the three color icons (background, foreground, and border) by looking in the small square in each picture icon.

To modify the appearance of a control, you use a formatting window. First select the control, then click on one of the formatting windows.

A formatting window can remain on the screen at all times so that you can use it to change the options for one or more controls. To keep the formatting window on-screen, first click on the down arrow of the option on the Formatting toolbar to display the window, and then drag the window to the design area. To close a formatting window, click on the window's Close button.

Changing the report's background color

If you typically print a report without previewing it, you may want to use a white background. A white background is the best choice for printed output. To make use of color for printed output, you can design your report with a white background, then use colored paper when you print. You can emphasize the report header and footer areas by using a light gray background. To color a header or footer section, select the desired section and then select the appropriate background color.

Tip

When you change the background color of report sections, you also want to change the background color of the section's controls to match the background color of the section.

Enhancing text-based controls

You can make label controls stand out by applying some simple formatting techniques. You can change the type style of the text font. Some good standard fonts to use for printed output include Arial, Times New Roman, or even Wingdings for special effects. You can use different font sizes (4 points to 200 points) and styles (bold, italic, underline) to emphasize different sections. For example, use a larger font size for labels in the report header section and a smaller font for the data in the detail section. You can print column headings in bold and underline them as well.

Using the AutoFormat button

Access has an AutoFormat button that can assign predefined styles to a report and its controls. To use the AutoFormat functions, click on the AutoFormat button in the toolbar when you're in a report design. Access shows the AutoFormat dialog box for reports (Figure 12-2). Select the desired AutoFormat and click on OK to complete the formatting. All of your controls (and the overall look of the form) will be changed as shown in the AutoFormat preview.

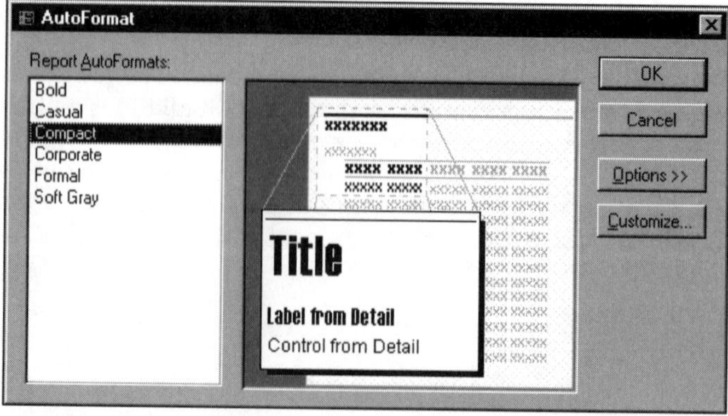

Figure 12-2: The AutoFormat dialog box.

Tip

Although you can set many of these controls from the property sheet, it's much easier to use the Formatting toolbar to set the other properties of the control. Access (like other Microsoft Office products) has a Format Painter in the standard toolbar. This excellent and convenient tool allows you to copy styles from one selection to the next. Simply click on the item whose style you want to copy, then click on the Format Painter icon, and then click on the item that needs the style change.

Adding special effects

Figure 12-3 shows some of the special effects that can be easily created for controls using the special effects formatting window.

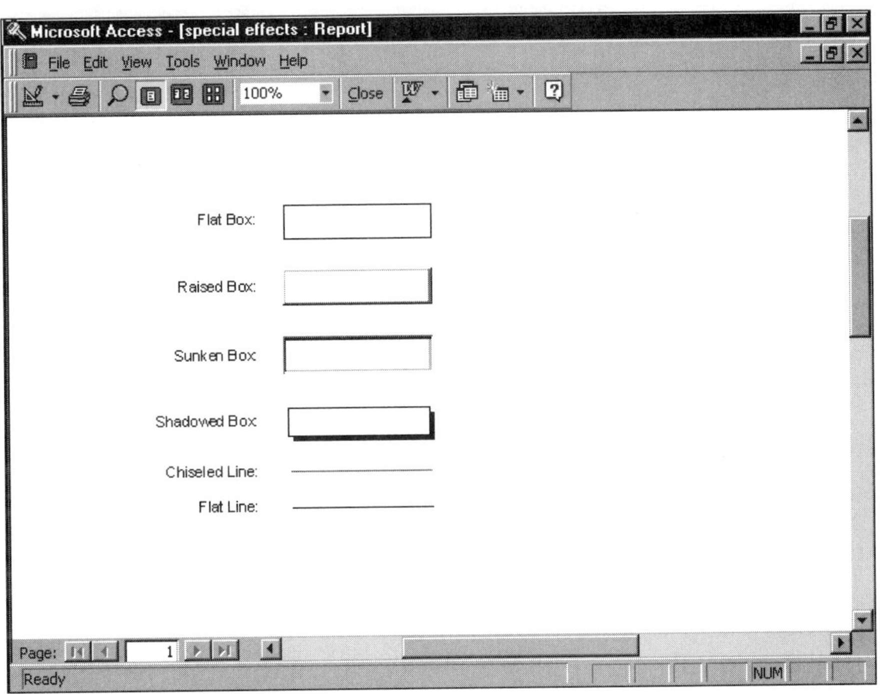

Figure 12-3: Special effects.

Special effects can be applied to rectangles, label controls, text box controls, checkboxes, option buttons, and option group boxes. Anything that has a box or circle around it can be raised, sunken, etched, chiseled, or shadowed.

By simply selecting the control and adding the special effect, you can make your reports look much better and draw attention to the important areas of the report.

Creating a text shadow

Text shadows create a three-dimensional look. They make the text appear to float above the page while shadows stay on the page. You can create text shadows using these techniques:

- Duplicate the text
- Offset the duplicate text from the original text
- Change the duplicate text to a different color (usually a lighter shade)
- Place the duplicate text behind the original text
- Change the original text with the Back Color Transparent button

Access has a shadow effect in the Special Effects button on the Formatting toolbar. This effect creates a shadow only on boxes or on text boxes, not on the text itself.

Although the on-screen shadow looks great, it does not print correctly on most monochrome printers. Normally you just get two lines of black text that look horrible. Unless you have a printer that prints text in shades of gray (using graphics rather than text fonts) or a color printer that prints gray, avoid using shadowed text on a report.

A better idea than to shadow the text is to shadow the label box. You can easily do this by deleting the duplicate text label, selecting the original label, and changing the special effect to Shadowed. This displays a cleaner look, as shown in the Invoice text box in Figure 12-1.

Using reverse video

Text really stands out when you present it as white text on a black background. This technique is called reverse video because the foreground and background colors of the text control are the opposite colors of the report itself. To change a text control to reverse video you would

1. Select the text box control (not the label control).
2. Select Black from the Back Color formatting window.
3. Select White from the Fore Color formatting window.

Some of the less-expensive laser printers do not support reverse video.

Sinking controls

Generally, sunken controls do not work on a white background. If you want to use a sunken control in a report, use a gray background for the control. In Figure 12-1, for example, the Shipped via and Payment type controls can be sunken because they have a gray background.

Raising controls

Just as you can sink a control, you can raise one. Raised controls, like sunken controls, look much better on a gray or dark background. To emphasize the Shipped To and Sold To rectangles of the Invoice report, you could make the rectangles raised and the background gray.

Working with lines and rectangles

You can use lines and rectangles (commonly called boxes) to make certain areas of the report stand out or to bring attention to desired areas of the report. In Figure 12-1 you saw several groups of lines and rectangles that were used to emphasize data in the report.

The two lines in Figure 12-3 are actually rectangles. The chiseled line is a chiseled rectangle that is shrunken vertically to display only a single line. The flat line is a flat rectangle that is shrunken vertically to display only a single line.

Secret

When you want to draw lines in your report, you should use the rectangle method instead of the line control. In Access, print previewing a report that displays line controls uses up system resources. The resources are not recovered when the report window is closed. Using the rectangle method avoids this system resource problem.

Tip

You may notice that when you create a rectangle, it blocks out the controls beneath it. You can make the controls reappear by sending the rectangle to the background or by making the background transparent.

If you want to emphasize an area of the report, you can add a shadow to any control. Most commonly, rectangles and text boxes are the types of controls given this effect. You can create a shadow using either of these two methods:

- Add a solid-color rectangle that is slightly offset and behind the original control.
- Use the built-in Shadowed special effect in the Formatting window.

If the background is light or white, you need a dark-colored rectangle. If the background is dark or black, you need a light-colored or white rectangle.

Working with multiple-line text box controls

Some fields, like very large text fields or Memo-type fields, contain more data than can fit in a normal text box control. In order to display all of the data, you need to display it on multiple lines.

In the sample report, the Comments text box control in the page footer area sometimes contains data that takes up more than one line. The way the text box control is sized, you can only see up to four lines of data. There are two methods to display multiple lines of text in a text box control.

- Resize the control vertically to allow more lines to display.
- Set the control's `Can Grow` or `Can Shrink` properties.

When you resize a control by making it larger vertically, it uses as much space as you allow for it — less space than required if the value exceeds the allowable space. For example, if you resize the Comments text box control to display two lines, the control displays only one or two lines for every invoice. If the data for the Comments field is longer than two lines, only the first two lines will display. The remaining Comments data will be missing.

Rather than resizing the control vertically, a better solution to this problem is to use the `Can Grow` or `Can Shrink` properties of the text box control. If you change the value of the `Can Grow` property to `Yes`, the control grows vertically if there are more lines than can be displayed in the default control. Another solution is to resize the control so that it's larger and then use the `Can Shrink` property to remove any blank lines if the value of the data does not use the full size of the control.

When you set the `Can Grow` property in a text box control to `Yes`, you automatically set this property for the detail, group header and group footer, or report header and report footer sections.

To see the effect of the `Can Grow` and `Can Shrink` properties, display the report in the Print Preview window. Notice the Description lines and Comment text box in Figure 12-4, which shows the Print Preview window. If you look at the print preview in Zoom mode, you'll see that the spaces between the records are the same because the Description text uses only one line. If any description were two lines, more space would be allotted for the text. The comments box will grow as the text expands. If more than four comment lines of text are present, the Pay This Amount field begins immediately below the end of the comment text box.

Displaying images in reports

You can display a picture, such as a Paintbrush (.BMP) file, in a report by using image frames. This feature is different than a bound OLE control, which is used to store an OLE object (sound, video, Word or Excel documents) with a data record, or an unbound OLE object, which is used to store OLE objects on a report itself.

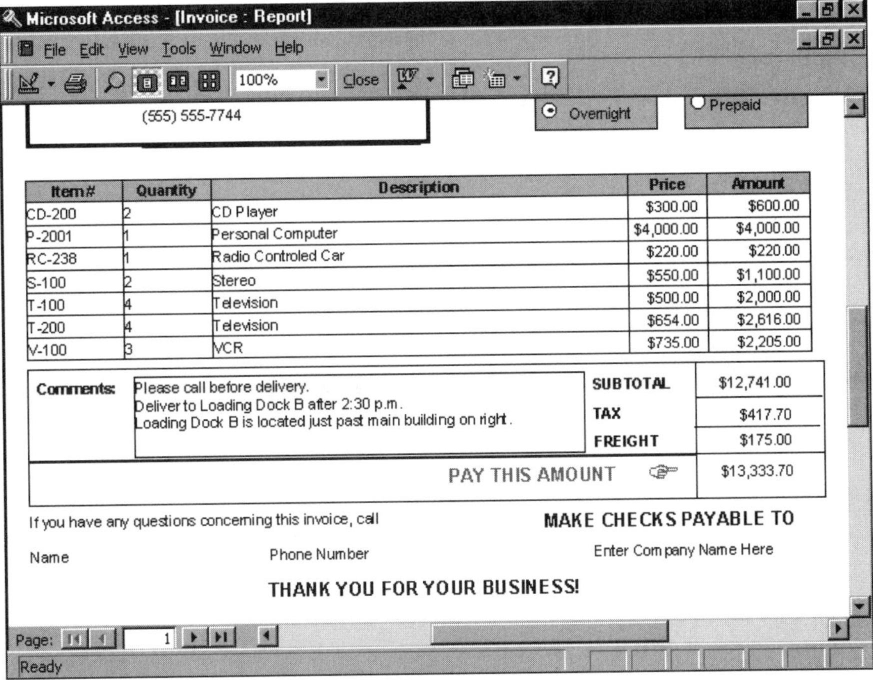

Figure 12-4: Displaying the Print Preview window.

Image controls are used for objects that will only be displayed or printed. OLE controls, on the other hand, are used when you need to be able to edit the picture file. OLE controls consume huge amounts of resources. Using many OLE objects in Access causes resource and performance problems. An Image control adds only the size of the bitmap picture to overhead. You should use image controls whenever you are displaying a picture that does not change or does not need to be updated.

You can add an image object to your report by pasting a bitmap from the Clipboard, or by either embedding or linking a bitmap file that contains a picture.

To add a logo to the report, select the Image control in the toolbox. Click on the left corner below the title and drag the box so that it creates a rectangle. The Insert Picture dialog box appears, as shown in Figure 12-5.

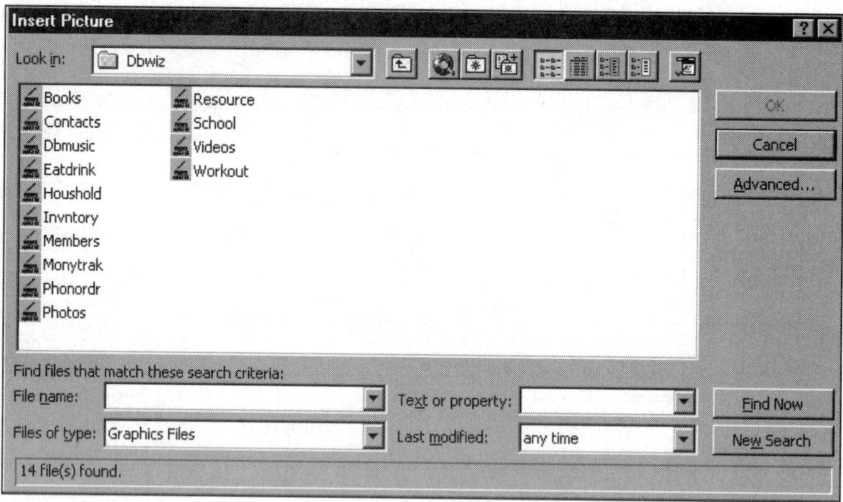

Figure 12-5: Creating an image with the Insert Picture dialog box.

From this dialog box, you can select the type of picture object you want to insert into your form. The dialog box supports many picture formats, including .BMP, .TIF, .WMF, .PCX, .ICO, .WPG, .JPG, .PCT, or any other picture format your copy of Windows 95 supports. Next, you can select your logo and click on the OK button. If the file does not already exist and you want to create a new object, such as a Paintbrush Picture, you must create an unbound OLE frame instead of an image.

Previewing the Report Layout

As you design your report, you will want to get an idea of what the report really looks like so far. You may need to preview the report's layout many times before it is complete. If you print the report to the printer each time, you can end up killing a lot of trees. Access 97 provides a couple of methods for viewing reports on-screen.

Using the Print Preview window

In Figure 12-4 you saw how the Print Preview window enables you to view your report. Figure 12-6 shows a report displayed in a page preview. Print Preview lets you see your report with the actual fonts, shading, lines, boxes, and data that will be on the printed report. When the print preview mode is in a zoomed view, you can press the mouse button, which changes the mouse pointer to a magnifying glass, to change the view to a page preview (where you can see the entire page). You can use the horizontal and vertical scroll bars to move around the page, or move from page to page by using the page controls at the bottom left corner of the window.

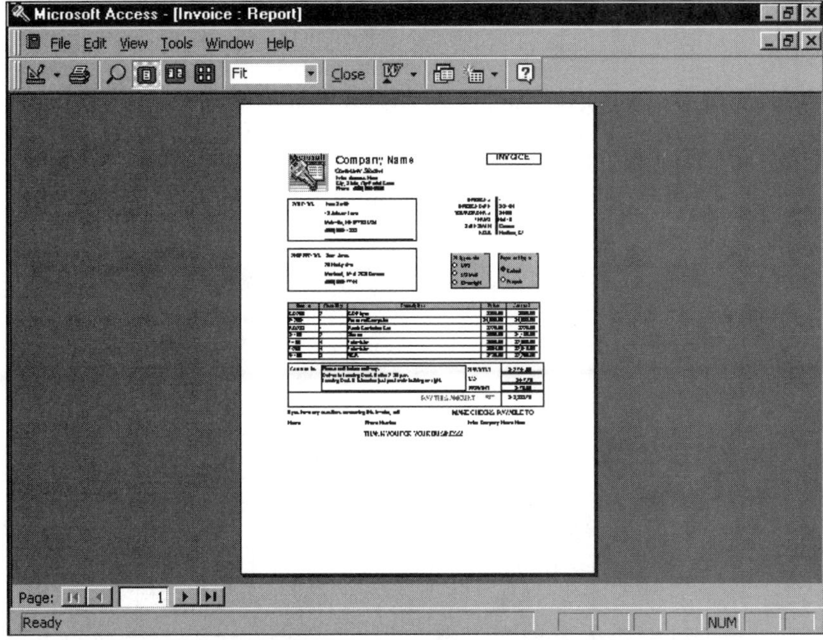

Figure 12-6: Displaying a report in page preview mode.

The *one page* mode of the Print Preview window displays an entire page of the report. The cursor is shaped like a magnifying glass in Print Preview windows; using this cursor during page preview lets you select a portion of the page and then zoom in to that portion for a detailed view.

You can use the navigation buttons (located in the lower left section of the Print Preview window) to move between pages, just as you would use them to move between records in a datasheet.

The first six buttons displayed on the toolbar provide quick access to printing tasks:

■ Design	Displays the Report Design screen
■ Print	Displays the Print dialog box
■ Zoom	Toggles in and out of Page Preview and Zoomed view
■ One Page	Displays a single page in Print Preview
■ Two Pages	Displays up to two pages at a time in the Print Preview window
■ Four Pages	Displays up to four pages at a time in the Print Preview window
■ Zoom Control	Select Percent of Size to Zoom (200%, 150%, 100%, 75%, 50%, 25%, 10%, Fit)
■ Close	Returns to Design view

In Access 97 you can view up to 12 pages on a single screen. As you can see in Figure 12-7, the View➪Pages menu command lets you select 1, 2, 4, 8, or 12 pages to preview. In Figure 12-7, four pages have been selected. You can also right-click on the Print Preview page and select pages or the Zoom percentage. When you use the shortcut menus, you can select up to 20 pages to preview at a time; you can also determine their arrangement in rows and columns (2 × 4, 5 × 4, 3 × 4, and so on).

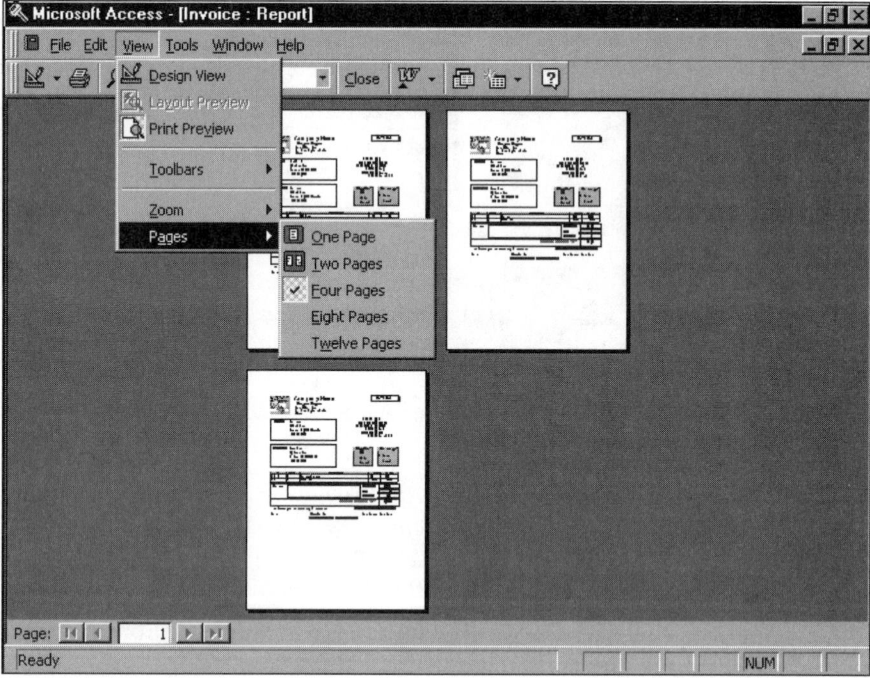

Figure 12-7: Multipage Print Preview mode.

If you are satisfied with the report after examining the preview, simply click on the Print button on the toolbar and print it. If you are not satisfied with your report, click on the Close button to return to the Report Design window and make further changes.

Using layout previews

Layout preview is different from a print preview. A print preview uses a query's dynaset; layout preview displays sample data (ignoring criteria) or joins in an underlying query.

The purpose of a layout preview is strictly to show you the field placement and formatting. Thus, you can create a report design without having to assemble your data properly; in a large query, this can save a considerable amount of time. You can see a sample preview by one of two methods: Select View⇨Layout Preview, or click on the Report View button and then select the Layout Preview icon (the bottom one) in the Report Design toolbar. If you entered Print Preview from the Report Design window, you can switch back to the Report Design window by clicking on the Close Window button. If you entered from the Database window, clicking on the Close Window button returns you there.

You can also zoom in to a layout page preview on the sample data or print the sample report from the Layout Preview window.

Printing a Report

You can print one or more records in your form (exactly as they look on screen) from several places:

- Select File⇨Print in the Report Design window.
- Click on the Print button in the Preview window.
- Select File⇨Print in the Database window with a report highlighted.

If you are in the Print Preview window, your actual data prints. If you are in the Layout Preview window, only sample data prints.

The Print dialog box

Once you decide to print your report, the Print dialog box is displayed, as shown in Figure 12-8. The Print dialog box lets you control several items by giving you the following choices:

- Name — Lets you select the printer
- Print Range — Prints the entire report or selected pages
- Copies — Lets you select the number of copies
- Collate — Lets you select whether or not to collate copies
- Print to File — Prints to a file rather than the printer

The Print dialog box that is displayed is specific to your printer and based on your setup in Microsoft Windows. Although each printer is different, the dialog box is essentially the same from printer to printer. Generally, the dialog box for dot-matrix and impact printers includes a few more options for controlling quality than does the dialog box for laser printers.

Assuming you set up a printer in Microsoft Windows 95, you can click on OK to print your form. Your form is printed using the font you selected for display (or the nearest printer equivalent). The printout contains any formatting in the form, including lines, boxes, and shading. Colors are converted to shades of gray on a monochrome printer.

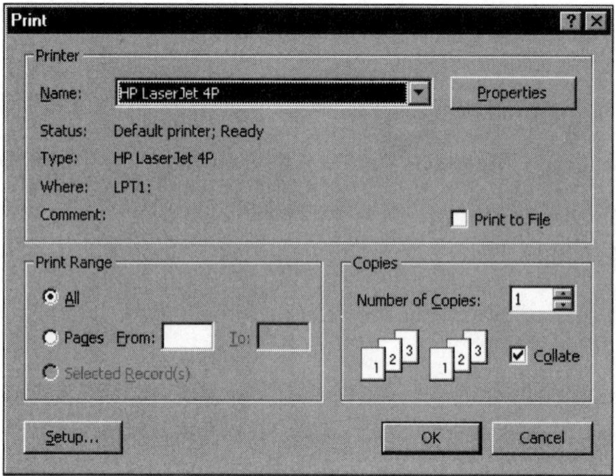

Figure 12-8: The Print dialog box.

If you need to make further changes to your Windows printer options, you can click on the Properties button in the Print dialog box. The Properties dialog box sets up your printer, not your report. If you want to fine-tune the setup of your report, use the Setup button (which provides more options).

You can display print setup options in other ways as well, including the following:

- Selecting File⇨Page Setup from the Report Design window
- Selecting File⇨Page Setup from the Database window

The Page Setup dialog box

The Page Setup dialog box, shown in Figure 12-9, is divided into three tabs: Margins, Page, and Layout.

- Margins   Lets you set the page margins. Also includes the option to Print Data Only.
- Page   Lets you select page orientation, paper size and source, and printer device.
- Layout   Lets you select grid settings, item size, and layout items.

In the Page tab, you can control the Orientation of the report. There are two choices: Portrait and Landscape. Clicking on the Portrait button changes the report so that the page is taller than it is wide. Clicking on the Landscape button changes the report orientation so that the page is wider than it is tall.

Tip

A good way to remember the difference between landscape and portrait is to think of paintings. Portraits of people are usually taller than wide; landscapes are usually wider than tall. When you click on either button, the page icon (letter A) changes to show your choice graphically.

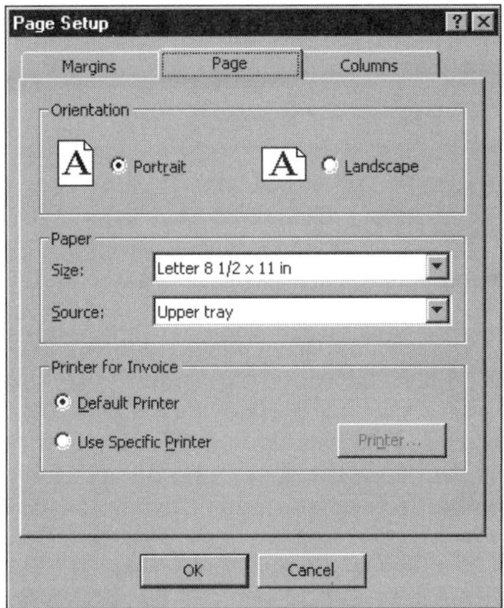

Figure12-9: The Page tab in the Page Setup dialog box.

The Paper section indicates the size of the paper you want to use, as well as the paper source (for printers that have more than one source available). Clicking on Source displays a drop-down list of paper sources available for the printer you selected. Depending on the printer selected, you may have one or more paper trays or manual feed available. Click on the source you want to use.

Clicking on Size displays a drop-down box showing all the paper sizes available for the printer (and paper source) you selected. Click on the size you want to use.

If you click on the Data Only check box in the Margins tab, Access prints only the data from your report and does not print any graphics. (This feature is handy if you use preprinted forms.) Also, printing complex graphics slows down all but the most capable printers; not printing them saves time.

The Margins section, shown in Figure 12-10, displays (and allows you to change) the left, right, top, and bottom margins. To change one or more of these settings, click on the appropriate text box and type in a new number.

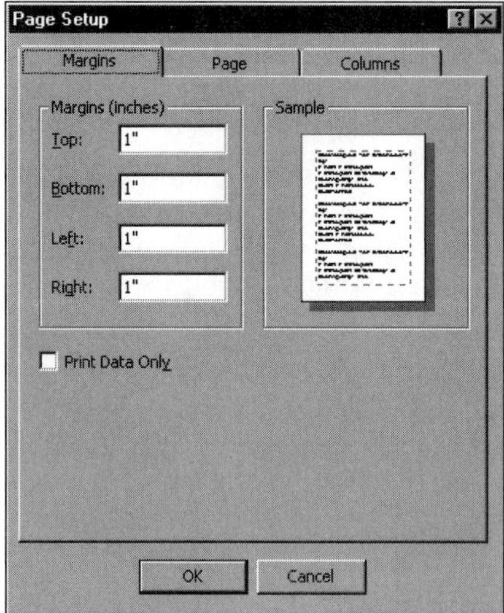

Figure 12-10: The Margins tab in the Page Setup dialog box.

Page Setup settings are stored with each report. It's therefore possible to use several different printers for various reports, as long as you don't use the default Windows printer. This can also be a problem, though, because if you exchange files with another user who doesn't have the same printer installed, the other user must modify the Page Setup settings in order to print.

Someone may send you a report you can't view or print because a Windows printer driver you don't have was used. If the report was created with a driver not installed on your system, Access will display a dialog box and let you print with your default printer.

Adding Calculations and Summaries to Reports

In this section of the chapter, you will see how to use advanced calculations and report summaries. It is assumed that you have a sound understanding of simple calculations and how to create calculated fields in a report. Using the calculations in this chapter, you can calculate totals for records and summarize data in row-and-column format.

The Customer Sales History report displays information about items purchased by a customer over a period of time. This report displays data that lists the Invoice Number, Invoice Date, and the total of each invoice. The data is summarized for each customer and then a grand total is created for the entire report. The report can display multiple invoices for the same customer. Finally, totals are shown for each customer, including the total invoice amount, any tax, and freight. A sample hard-copy printout of the report is shown in Figure 12-11.

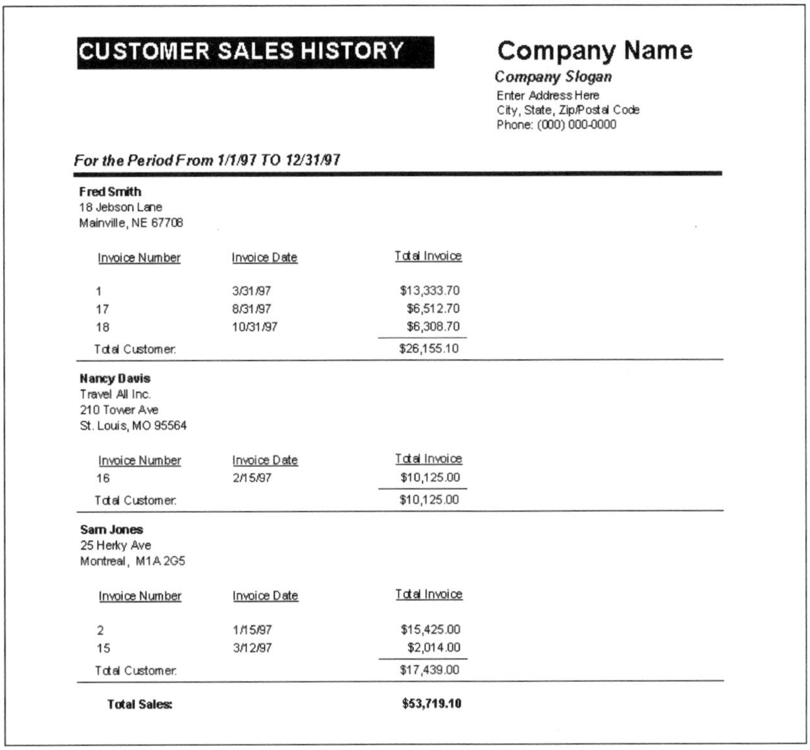

CUSTOMER SALES HISTORY

Company Name
Company Slogan
Enter Address Here
City, State, Zip/Postal Code
Phone: (000) 000-0000

For the Period From 1/1/97 TO 12/31/97

Fred Smith
18 Jebson Lane
Mainville, NE 67708

Invoice Number	Invoice Date	Total Invoice
1	3/31/97	$13,333.70
17	8/31/97	$6,512.70
18	10/31/97	$6,308.70
Total Customer:		$26,155.10

Nancy Davis
Travel All Inc.
210 Tower Ave
St. Louis, MO 95564

Invoice Number	Invoice Date	Total Invoice
16	2/15/97	$10,125.00
Total Customer:		$10,125.00

Sam Jones
25 Herky Ave
Montreal, M1A 2G5

Invoice Number	Invoice Date	Total Invoice
2	1/15/97	$15,425.00
15	3/12/97	$2,014.00
Total Customer:		$17,439.00

Total Sales: **$53,719.10**

Figure 12-11: The sample Customer Sales History page.

The Customer Sales History report is an excellent example of the advanced report-writing features in Access — sorting and grouping, group summaries, and text expressions. Following is a summary of what the Customer Sales History design includes:

- Your company name, slogan, address, and phone number on the top of every page
- Customer information (customer name, street/apartment number, city, state, and ZIP code)
- Invoice Number
- Invoice Date
- A subtotal that summarizes each invoice's details (total amount for the invoice)
- A subtotal that summarizes the total invoice amounts for each customer
- A report grand total that summarizes all of the invoice amounts for all customers listed in the report.

The report design also addresses the following considerations:

- The report must be sorted by the fields Customer, Invoice Date, and Invoice Number.
- One or more invoices belonging to the same customer can appear on each printed page.
- One or more customers can appear on each printed page.
- If there is more than one invoice for a customer, the invoices should be listed in date then invoice number order.

The design for this report is shown in Figure 12-12. As you can see, each section displays either a field control or a calculated control. With the exception of several lines and rectangles, the report consists primarily of text box controls.

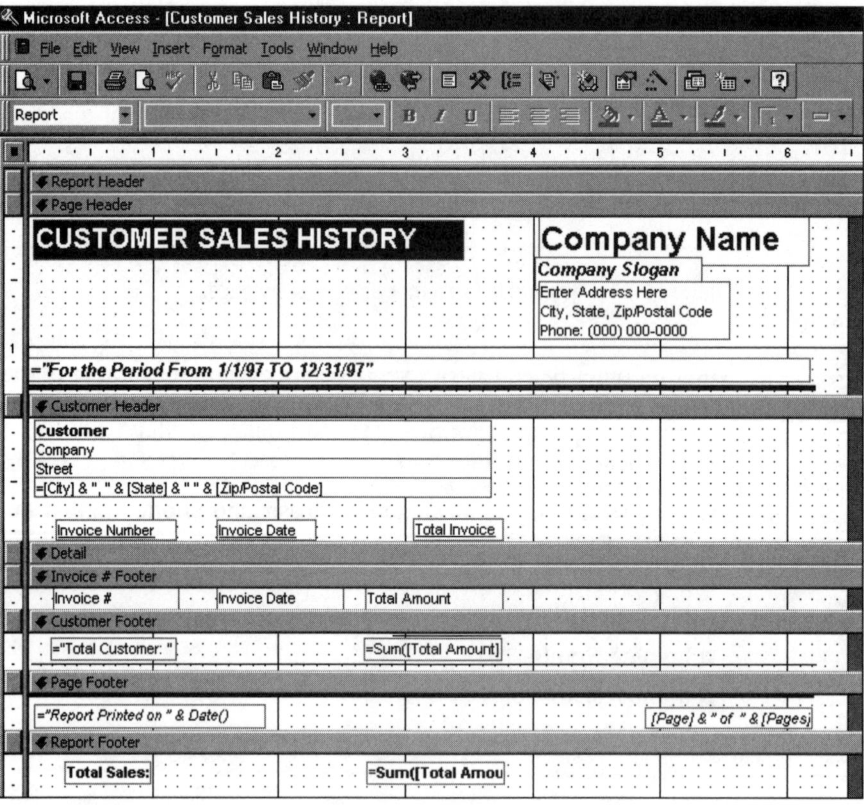

Figure 12-12: The design for the Customer Sales History report.

Designing and creating the query for the report

The Customer Sales History report uses fields from several tables. Although the design in Figure 12-12 shows the position and contents of each control, it is equally important to perform a data design that lists each table field or calculated control. This data design should include the purpose of the field or control and the table in which the field originates. Using such a design plan, you can be sure to build a query that contains all the fields you may need. Table 12-1 lists these controls, the section in the report where they are used, and the originating table. Important: Do this type of data design before creating the query from which you build your report.

Table 12-1 Data Design for the Customer Sales History Report

Report Section	*Control Purpose*	*Type of Control*	*Table Field/ Calculation*	*Table*
Page header	Name and address	Label controls (3)		
Page header	Report date range	Calculated text box		
Customer header	Customer name	Bound text box	Customer Name	Invoice Customers
Customer header	Street	Bound text box	Street	Invoice Customers
Customer header	City St Zip	Calculated text box	City	Invoice Customers
Customer header	City St Zip	Calculated text box	State	Invoice Customers
Customer header	City St Zip	Calculated text box	Zip Code	Invoice Customers
Customer header	Column headers	Label Controls(3)		
Invoice footer	Invoice Number	Bound text box	Invoice #	Invoice
Invoice footer	Invoice date	Bound text box	Invoice Date	Invoice
Invoice footer	Sum of Total Amount	Bound text box	[Total Amount]	Calculate Total Extensions
Customer footer	Text label	Label control		
Customer footer	Cust Sum of Total Amount	Calculated text box	Sum([Total Amount])	Calculate Total Extensions

(continued)

Table 12-1 *(continued)*

Report Section	*Control Purpose*	*Type of Control*	*Table Field/ Calculation*	*Table*
Page footer	Date printed	Calculated text box	Text + Date	
Page footer	Page number	Calculated text box	Text + Page Number	
Report footer	Text label	Label control		
Page footer	Report Total Amount	Calculated text box	Sum([Total Amount])	Calculate Total Extensions

After you complete the data design for a report, you can scan the Table column to determine the tables necessary for the report. When you create the query, you may not want to select each field individually; if not, use the asterisk (*) field to select all the fields in each table. This way, if a field changes in the table, the query can still work with your report.

Warning

Remember that if a table field name changes in your query, you'll need to change your report design. If you see a dialog box asking for the value of a specific field when you run your report — or the text `#Error` in place of one of your values after you run it — chances are a table field has changed.

After examining Table 12-1, you will see that the query for the report uses data from two tables. The table Calculate Total Extensions by Invoice is actually the result of another query. These tables are all joined together in the Customer Sales History query, as illustrated in Figure 12-13.

The query Calculate Total Extensions By Invoice uses data from two tables to calculate the extended amount (Price × Quantity) for each invoice. The Calculate Total Extensions By Invoice query is illustrated in Figure 12-14.

Designing test data

The final step, and one that should never be overlooked, is to check the results your report displays. Before you create your complete report, you should have a good understanding of your data. One way is to create a query using the same sorting order the report will use, and create any detail line calculations. You can then check the query's datasheet results and use them to check the report's results. When you are sure the report is using the correct data, you can be sure it will always produce great results. Normally you can make a copy of the report query, adding the sorting orders and using only the detail fields you need to check totals. You can then add the numbers manually, or convert the query to a Total query to check group totals. Figure 12-15 shows the datasheet produced by this query; you can compare the results of each task in the report design to this datasheet.

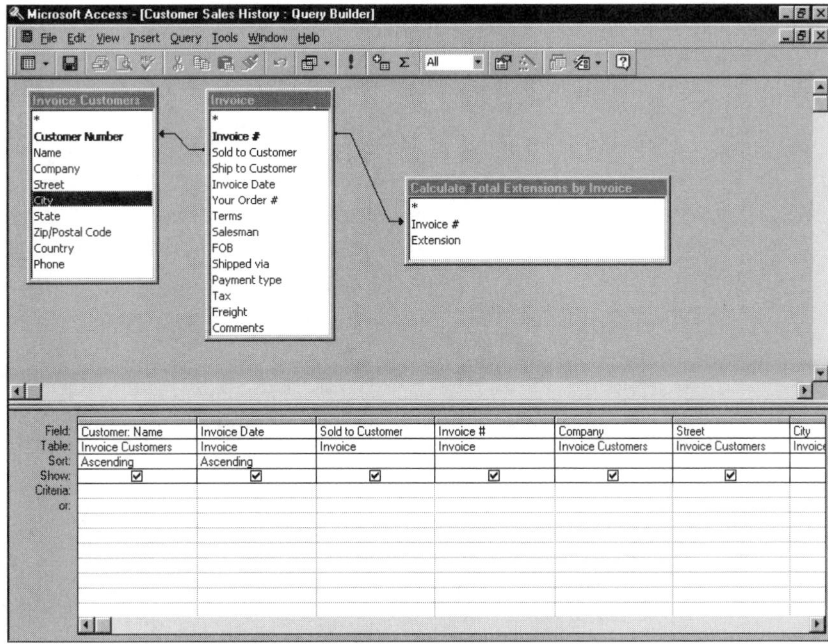

Figure 12-13: The Query Design window for the Customer Sales History query.

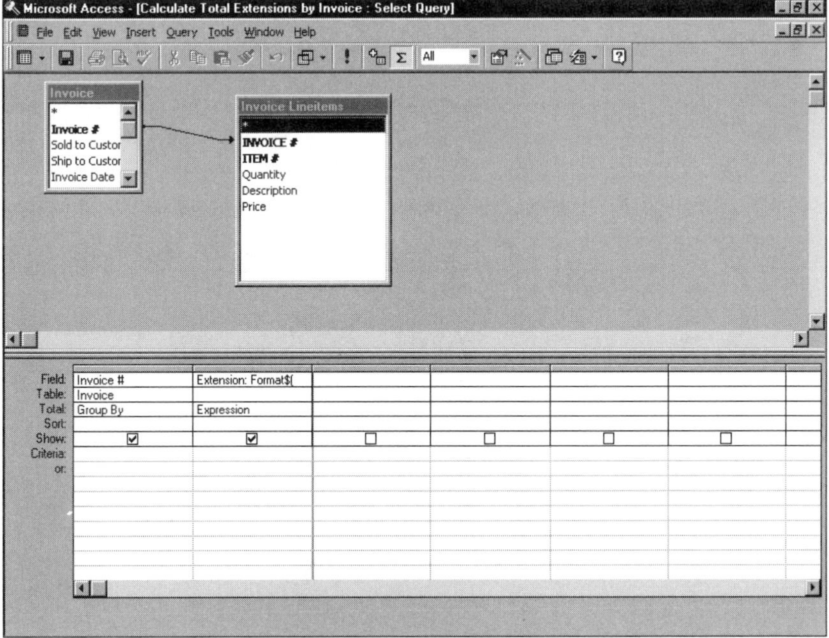

Figure 12-14: The Query Design window for the Calculate Total Extensions by Invoice query.

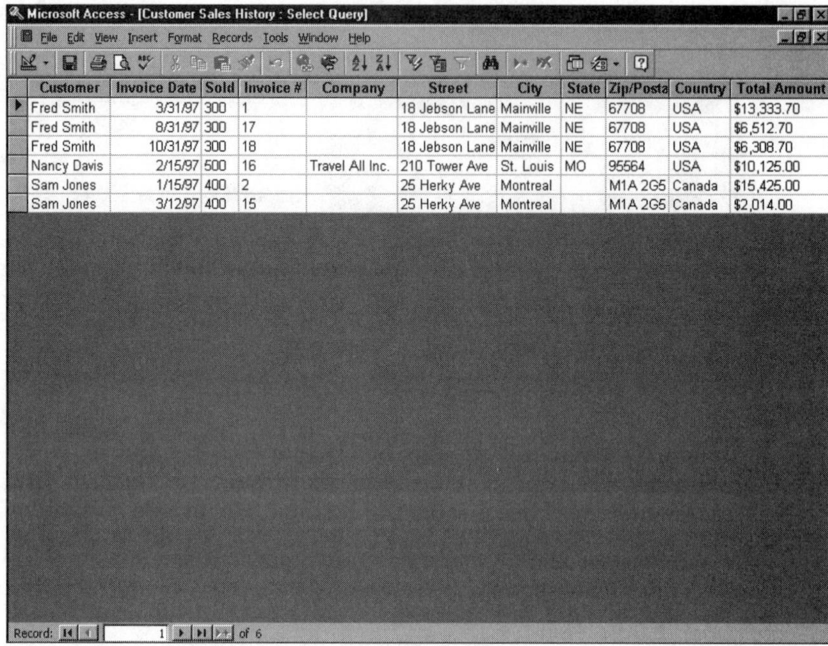

Microsoft Access - [Customer Sales History : Select Query]

Customer	Invoice Date	Sold	Invoice #	Company	Street	City	State	Zip/Posta	Country	Total Amount
Fred Smith	3/31/97	300	1		18 Jebson Lane	Mainville	NE	67708	USA	$13,333.70
Fred Smith	8/31/97	300	17		18 Jebson Lane	Mainville	NE	67708	USA	$6,512.70
Fred Smith	10/31/97	300	18		18 Jebson Lane	Mainville	NE	67708	USA	$6,308.70
Nancy Davis	2/15/97	500	16	Travel All Inc.	210 Tower Ave	St. Louis	MO	95564	USA	$10,125.00
Sam Jones	1/15/97	400	2		25 Herky Ave	Montreal		M1A 2G5	Canada	$15,425.00
Sam Jones	3/12/97	400	15		25 Herky Ave	Montreal		M1A 2G5	Canada	$2,014.00

Record: 1 of 6

Figure 12-15: The datasheet for checking data results.

Creating the sorting orders

Even though you can specify the sorting order in your report's query, you must also specify the sorting order when you create the report. Access ignores the underlying query sorting. In the Customer Sales History report, there are three sorting levels: Customer, Invoice Date, and Invoice Number. The report definition includes a group header and footer for the Customer field, and a group footer only for the Invoice Number. Before you can add a grouping, you must first define the sort order for the report. Figure 12-16 shows the completed Sorting and Grouping box.

Sorting and Grouping

Field/Expression	Sort Order
Customer	Ascending
Invoice Date	Ascending
Invoice #	Ascending

Group Properties

Group Header	Yes
Group Footer	Yes
Group On	Each Value
Group Interval	1
Keep Together	Whole Group

Select a field or type an expression to sort or group on

Figure 12-16: Creating the sorting orders.

Tip

To see more of the Field/Expression column, you can drag the border between the Field/Expression and Sort Order columns to the right.

Note

After a group header or footer is defined, the first column of the Sorting and Grouping box for the field you created in the header or footer displays a grouping icon (which is the same icon you see when you select the Sorting and Grouping button on the toolbar).

Controlling widows and orphans

When you print or display a report, Access automatically inserts page breaks according to the parameters defined in the report's Page Setup dialog box. When you group information in a report, you need to control where Access places a page break. For example, you might want a group header to always print on the same page with the first item in the detail section.

You can use the `Keep Together` property for a group in a report to keep parts of a group — including the group header, detail section, and group footer — together on the same page. Figure 12-16 shows that the `Keep Together` property for the Customer group is set to `Whole Group`. The report will print all of the data for each customer on the same page, including all of the data in the Customer header, the Invoice Number footer, and the Customer footer. At the start of each new customer's data, if all of the information will not fit in the space remaining on the current page, Access will break the page and start the new customer's data on the next page.

The `Keep Together` property for a group uses the following settings.

Setting	***Description***
`No`	Prints the group without keeping the group header, detail section, and group footer on the same page
`Whole Group`	Prints the group header, detail section, and group footer on the same page
`With First Detail`	Prints the group header on a page only if it can also print the first detail record

Note

A group includes the group header, detail section, and group footer. If you set the `Keep Together` property for a group to `Whole Group` and the group is too large to fit on one page, Access will ignore the setting for that group. Similarly, if you set this property to `With First Detail` and either the group header or detail record is too large to fit on one page, the setting will be ignored.

The `Keep Together` property setting in the Sorting and Grouping dialog works in conjunction with the `Keep Together` property of the section. In the Customer Sales History report, the Customer group header `Keep`

`Together` property in the Sorting and Grouping dialog box is set to `Whole Group`. Then, the `Keep Together` property for the Customer group header section is set to `Yes`. Figure 12-17 illustrates setting the `Keep Together` property for the Customer header section.

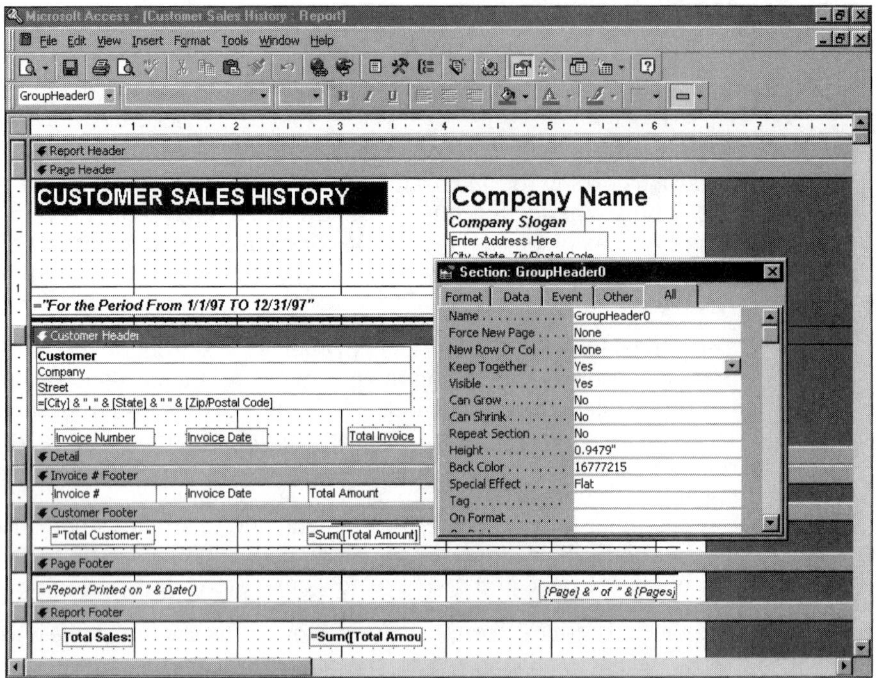

Figure 12-17: Setting the Keep Together property.

If the `Keep Together` property for a section is set to `No` and the `Keep Together` property for a group is set to `Whole Group` or `With First Detail`, then the `Keep Together` property setting for the section is ignored.

Adding page breaks

Although the `Keep Together` properties allow you to control how Access automatically inserts page breaks, for some reports you want to insert a page break for a certain section of the report every time it prints. For the Invoice report, for example, you want each invoice to print on a new page.

You can use the `Force New Page` property to specify whether report sections (header, detail, footer) print on a separate page, rather than on the current page. In the Invoice report, the `Force New Page` property setting for the Invoice Number footer is set to `After Section`. When the report prints, Access will start a new page after every invoice footer section, regardless of how much space remains on the page. Figure 12-18 shows the `Force New Page` property setting for the Invoice report's Invoice Number footer.

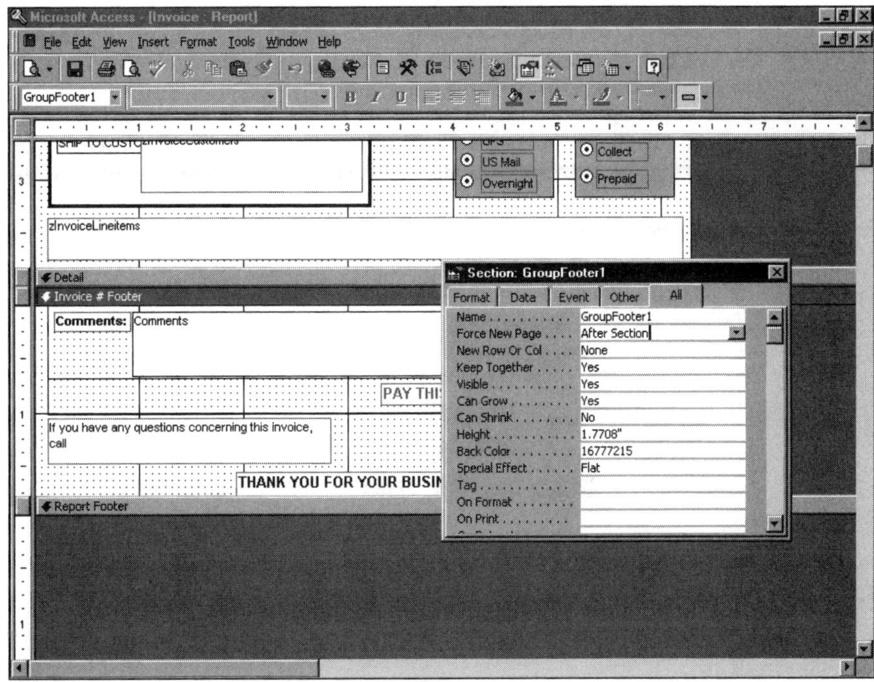

Figure 12-18: Setting the Force New Page property.

The `Force New Page` property uses the following settings:

Setting	*Description*
`None`	The current section (the section for which you're setting the property) is printed on the current page.
`Before Section`	The current section is printed at the top of a new page.
`After Section`	The section immediately following the current section is printed at the top of a new page.
`Before & After`	The current section is printed at the top of a new page, and the next section is printed at the top of a new page.

Note

The `Force New Page` property does not apply to page headers or page footers.

Tip

If you want to break a page within a section, just insert a page break control from the Toolbox.

Completing the Customer header and footer sections

When you specify a group header or footer for a field in the Sorting and Grouping dialog box, Access automatically creates the header or footer section in your report design. Figure 12-19 illustrates the Customer header and footer sections for the Customer Sales History report. The first four controls are text controls that display data from the Invoice Customers table. The City, State, and Zip/Postal Code fields are concatenated together to display as one calculated field. Concatenating these fields saves space by compressing any trailing spaces in the city name, adding a comma after city, and also by compressing the space between State and Zip/Postal Code. The remaining fields are label controls used to describe the values in the columns in the Invoice Number footer section.

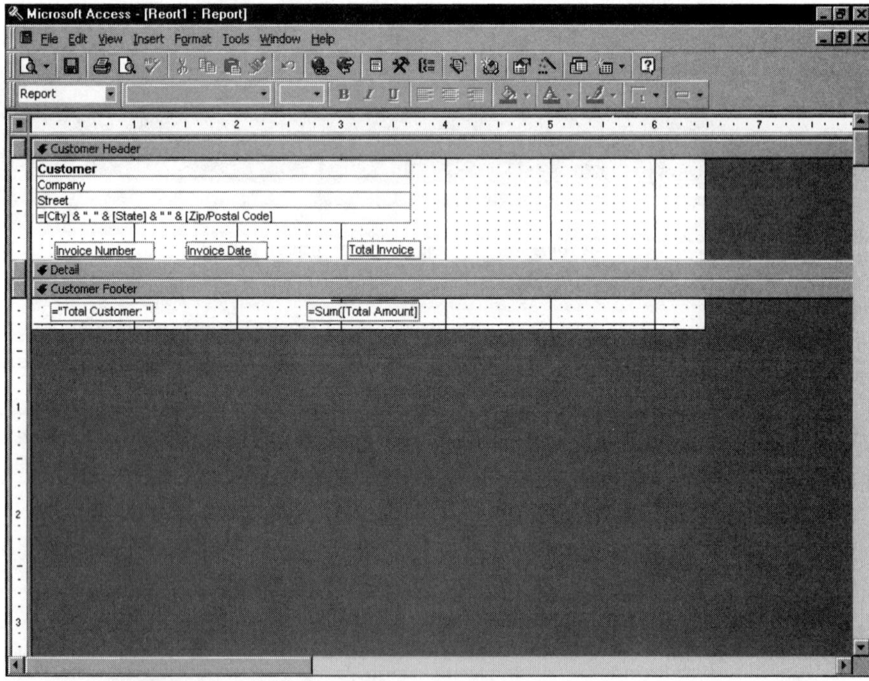

Figure 12-19: Creating the Customer header and footer.

The Customer footer section contains two controls: a label control and a text box control. The text box control expression sums the total of all the Total Amount values displayed for a customer's invoices. The value automatically resets to zero at the start of each new customer that prints in the report.

Creating a sum of numeric data within a group is very simple. Following is the general procedure for summing group totals for bound text controls:

1. Create a new text control in the group footer (or header).
2. Enter the expression **=Sum([Control Name])** where `Control Name` is a valid field name in the underlying query or the name of a control in the report.

Warning

If, however, the control name is for a calculated control, you will have to repeat the control expression. Suppose, for example, that in the Invoice footer you entered the following expression into the text box control named `[Total Invoice]` to display the total of all the Invoice lines:

```
=Sum([Price] * [Quantity])
```

Then, in the Customer footer you create a text box control containing the expression:

```
=Sum([Total Invoice])
```

If you try this, it won't work; this is simply a limitation of Access. To create a sum for the totals in the Invoice section, you have to enter

```
=Sum([Price] * [Quantity])
```

Note that the line displayed in the Customer footer is actually a flat rectangle. The rectangle delineates the section from the other sections. It serves as a *bottom cap* for the customer sections and helps to separate one customer's data from the next.

In addition, note that there is no space between the top of the controls and the top of the section. Notice also how the controls in the footer section line up with the column headings in the header section. Aligning the controls properly is critical to making the report display in an orderly row-and-column layout.

Creating the Invoice Number footer section

The Invoice Number group footer, shown in Figure 12-20, creates a group break on Invoice Number, which causes each customer's individual invoices to be grouped together. This is the section where the invoice totals are displayed.

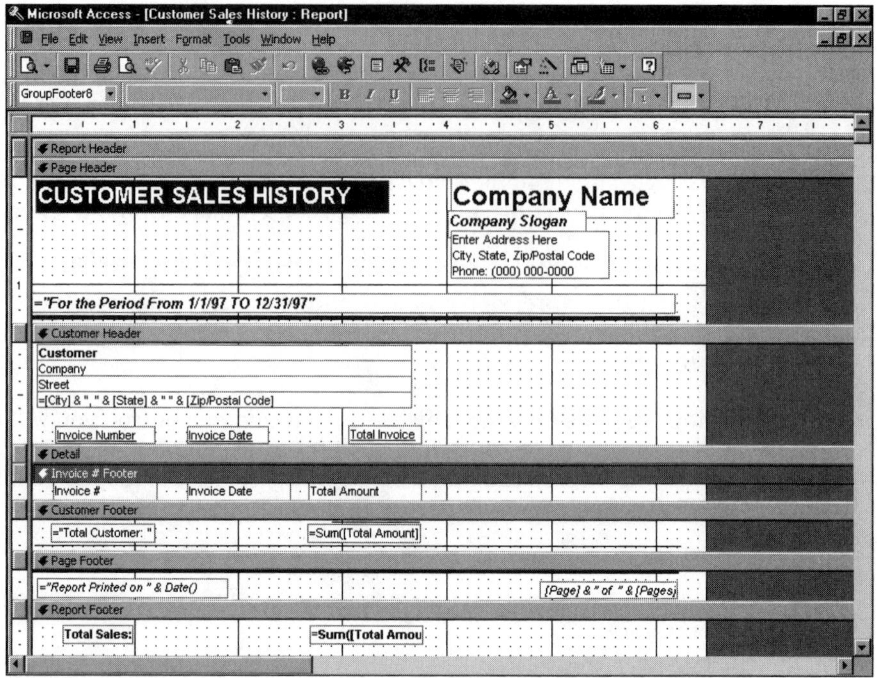

Figure 12-20: The Report Design window for the Invoice Number group footer.

The Invoice Number group footer is where you subtotal each invoice for a customer. This section lists the total of the invoice line items for each invoice in this section. In fact, even if there is only one invoice record for a customer, a summary is displayed.

The Invoice Number footer section contains three bound controls. The bound controls display the Invoice Number, Invoice Date, and Invoice Total Amount fields.

Creating the page header and footer controls

Most applications include a reports menu that contains multiple preformatted or "canned" reports. Generally, these canned reports are formatted in a row-and-column layout. Depending on the number of fields included in the report, the report may be in either portrait or landscape orientation. When you create reports for an application, you should give all of the reports with similar layouts a consistent visual appearance. Every report should have a page header and page footer. All of the portrait style row-and-column reports should have the same page header and footer, with only the report title changing from report to report. Likewise, all of the landscape style row-and-column reports should have consistent page headers and footers.

The page header appears at the top of every page in the Customer Sales History report. The page header and footer controls are not controlled by the Sorting and Grouping box; you have to select View⇨Page Header/Footer. In this report, the page header has been open all the time, as shown in Figure 12-21.

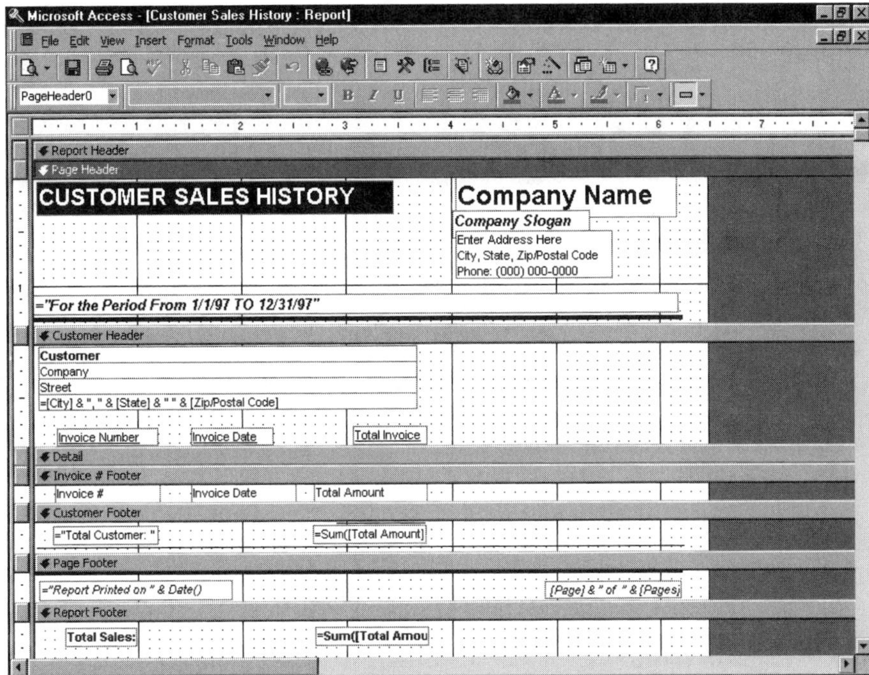

Figure 12-21: The page header.

The page header in the Customer Sales History report provides a way to display the company's name, address, and phone number. The section also contains the report date range and a horizontal line at the bottom to visually separate it from the rest of the page. By default, the page header and footer are created and displayed automatically when a new report is created. All you have to do is change the height and add the proper controls.

The page footer appears at the bottom of every page in the report. This section, as shown in Figure 12-22, displays the date the report was printed along with the page number. The horizontal line at the top of the section helps delineate the page footer from the rest of the report.

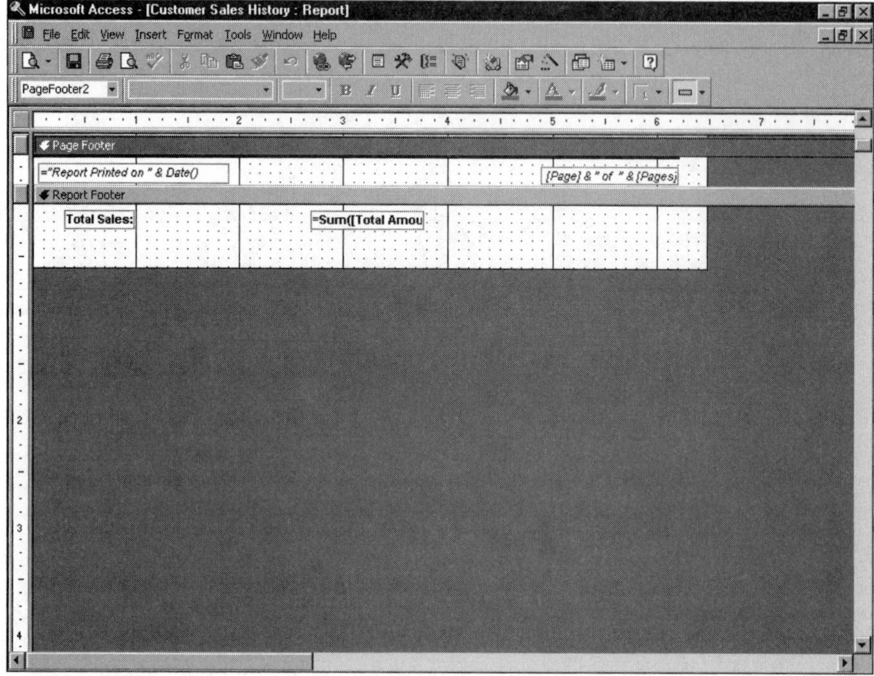

Figure 12-22: The page footer.

Access offers several built-in functions that let you display and manipulate date and time information. The easiest to start with is the `Date()` function, which returns the current system date when the report is printed or previewed.

Another date function Access offers is `DatePart( )`, which returns a numeric value for the specified portion of a date. The syntax for the function is

```
DatePart(interval,date,firstweekday,firstweek)
```

where `interval` is a string expression for the interval of time you want returned, and `date` is the date to which you want to apply the function.

A new feature in Access 97 provides a way of automatically adding the date and time to a report. Choosing Insert⇨Date and Time automatically inserts a calculated text box control into the report's page header or footer. Figure 12-23 shows the Date and Time dialog box. Using this dialog box, you can specify to include the date and time, just the date, or even just the time. You can also specify the format for printing the date and time.

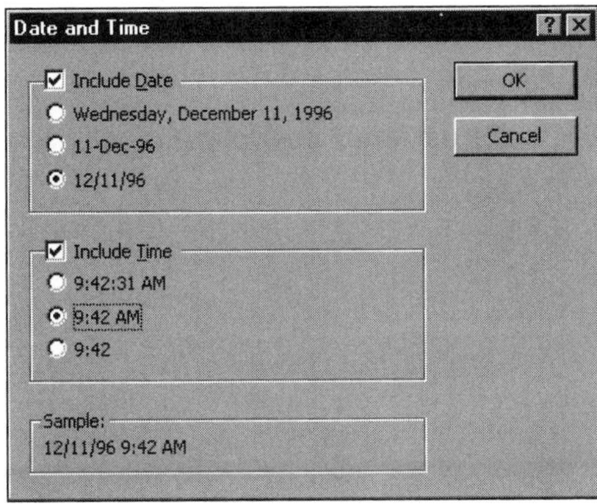

Figure 12-23: The Date and Time dialog box.

To number the pages in your report, Access provides the `Page` function. You access it by using it in an expression in a text control that returns the current page of the report. As with all expressions, one that has the `Page` property in it must be preceded by an equal sign (=).

A new feature in Access 97 provides a way to automatically add a page number to a report. Choose Insert⇨Page Numbers to insert a calculated text box control that automatically includes the page number in the report's page header or footer. Figure 12-24 shows the Page Numbers dialog box. Using this dialog box, you can specify format, alignment, position, and whether to print the page number on the first page of the report.

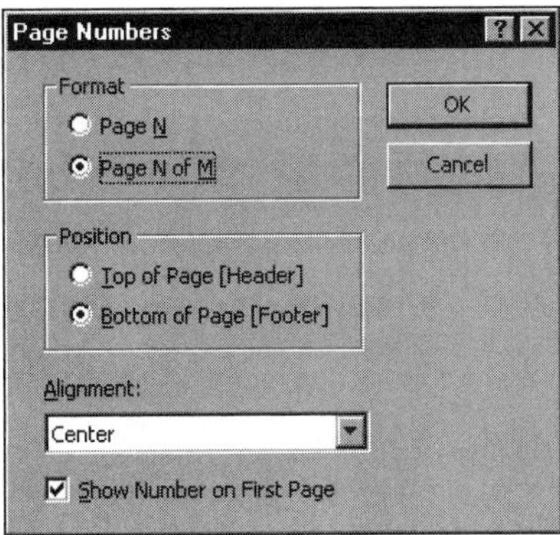

Figure 12-24: The Page Numbers dialog box.

Modifying a Report's Design at Run Time

By using calculated fields and event procedures, you can make changes to a report that affect the fields it prints or even its page layout. For example, you can change the title of the report or print just the summary sections of the report.

In Figure 12-25, the Print Invoice dialog box displays an option group called Print Report that displays four reports. You can select one or more of the reports to print at the same time. The Print Messages option allows you to include special message text in the footer sections of the reports. The Messages tab, shown in Figure 12-26, provides up to five different messages that you can print. The Messages tab also provides two Report Title fields that you can use to print titles at the top of each report. The Summary Only option on the Print tab allows you to eliminate the detail section of the reports.

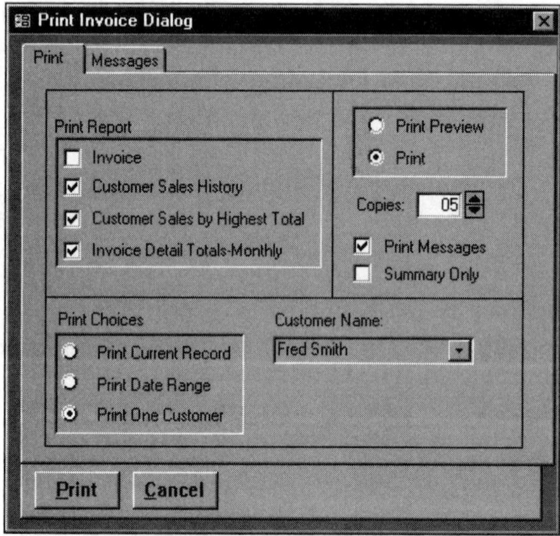

Figure 12-25: The Print tab of the Print Invoice dialog box.

Changing the report's title

You can change the title of the report every time it prints. The Messages tab of the Print Invoice dialog box, shown in Figure 12-26, provides two text box controls called First Title and Second Title. You can use these text box controls to enter one or two title lines for your reports.

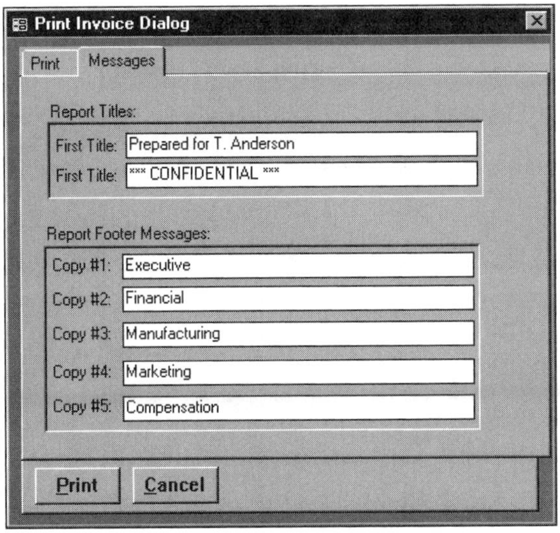

Figure 12-26: The Messages tab of the Print Invoice dialog box.

Each of the reports contains two calculated text box controls that get their values from the First Title and Second Title fields in the Print Invoice dialog. Figure 12-27 shows the design view of the page header section illustrating the calculated text box controls.

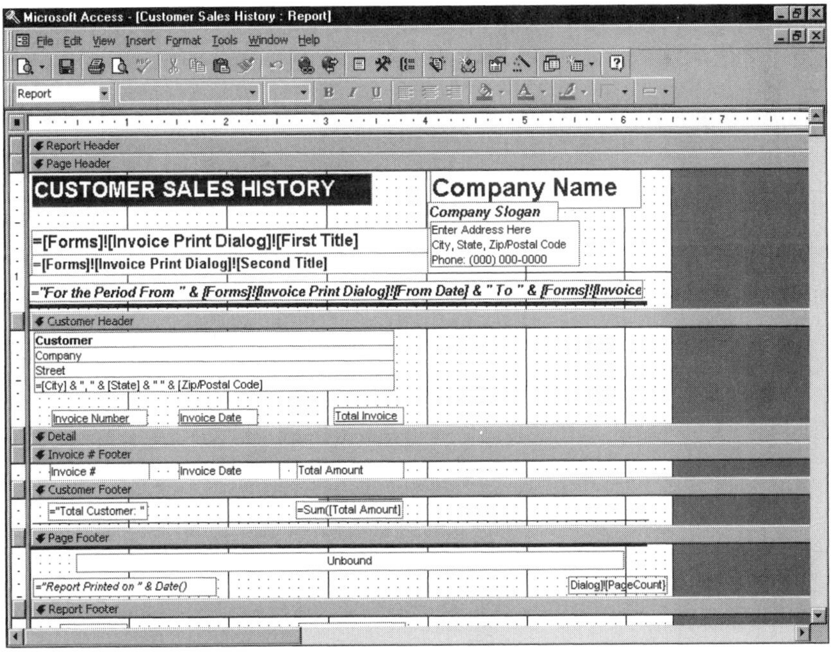

Figure 12-27: Modifying a report's titles.

The third line of the report title area prints the date range used in the report's query. The Print Choices option group in the Print Invoice Dialog contains a Print Date Range option which you can use to specify the From Date and To Date to use for the reports. The default values for the date range fields are January 1, 1997 and December 31, 1997. You can enter any other time period. Figure 12-28 shows the Print Date Range option.

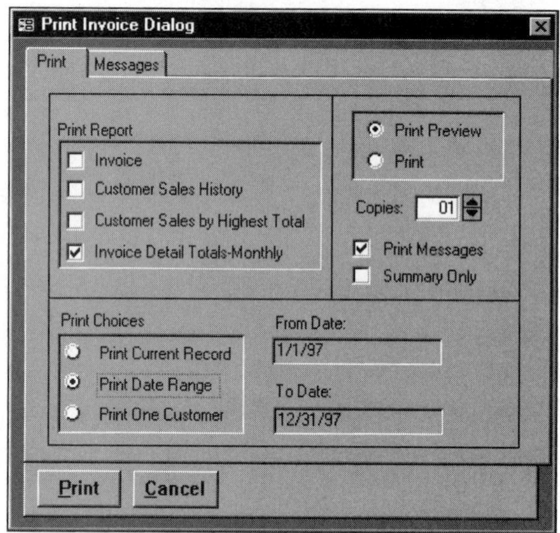

Figure 12-28: Specifying a date range for a report.

When the query for the report runs, it looks at the date range in the Print Invoice Dialog. Figure 12-29 shows the design view of one of the report queries. The query checks the Invoice Date field to see if it is between the dates entered in the Print Invoice Dialog.

Changing the report's page footers

You can print special text in the page footer section of each report whenever it prints. As shown in Figure 12-30, the page footer of the Customer Sales History report includes an unbound text box control named Message. Using the Print Invoice Dialog Messages tab, you can print a different message on each copy of the report for up to five copies.

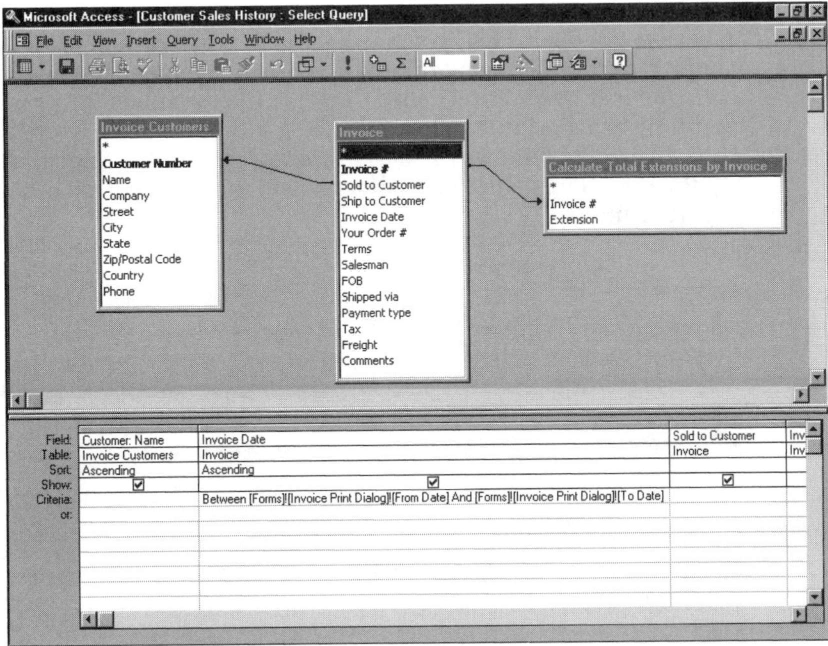

Figure 12-29: Passing date range parameters to a query.

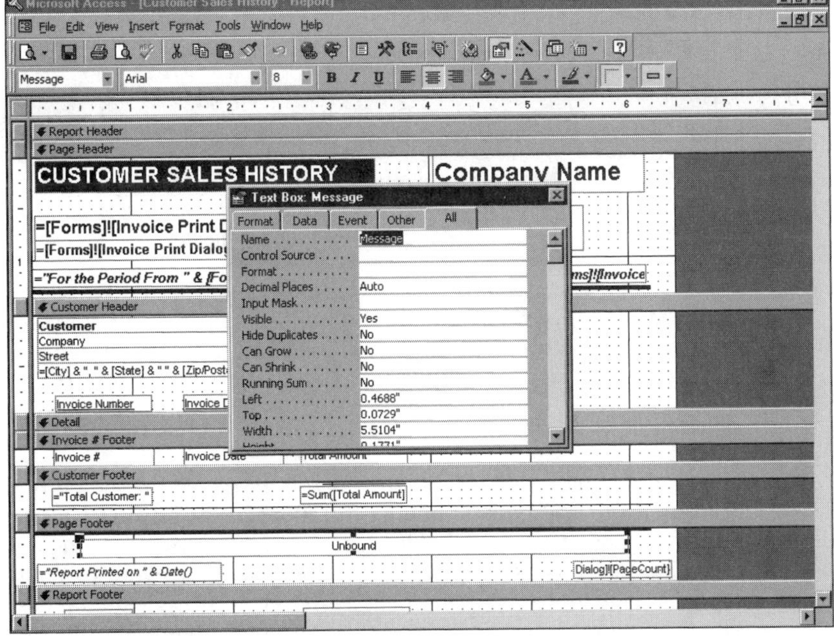

Figure 12-30: Printing special text in a page footer.

Printing the appropriate messages in a report's page footer requires a few special techniques. First, you need a way to keep track of which copy number is currently being printed. The Print Invoice Dialog uses an invisible unbound text box control called `CopyNum` to store the number of the copy currently being printed. When the dialog box first opens, its default value is zero. Figure 12-31 shows the design view of the Print Invoice Dialog illustrating the CopyNum field. The CopyNum field updates as each copy of the report prints.

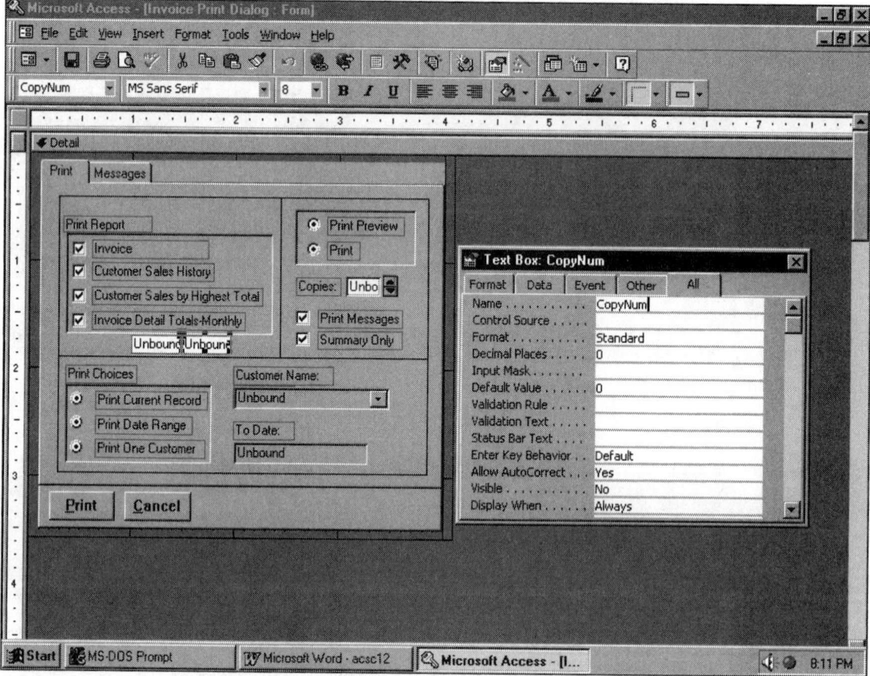

Figure 12-31: Storing the value of the current copy number.

The next technique is to update the field that stores the copy number being printed. Click on the Print button in the Print Invoice Dialog to begin printing; the CopyNum field is updated as each copy of the report prints. The `Print_Button_Click` event procedure for the Print button, shown in Figure 12-32, updates the CopyNum field.

The final technique is to print the correct message for the copy being printed. If the first copy is being printed, then the `Copy #1` value in the Print Invoice Dialog should print. Likewise, if the fifth copy is being printed, then the value for `Copy #5` should print. The `OnFormat` event procedure for the report's page footer, shown in Figure 12-33, controls which message prints. The procedure uses a `Select Case` statement to update the Message field with the appropriate value from the Print Invoice Dialog.

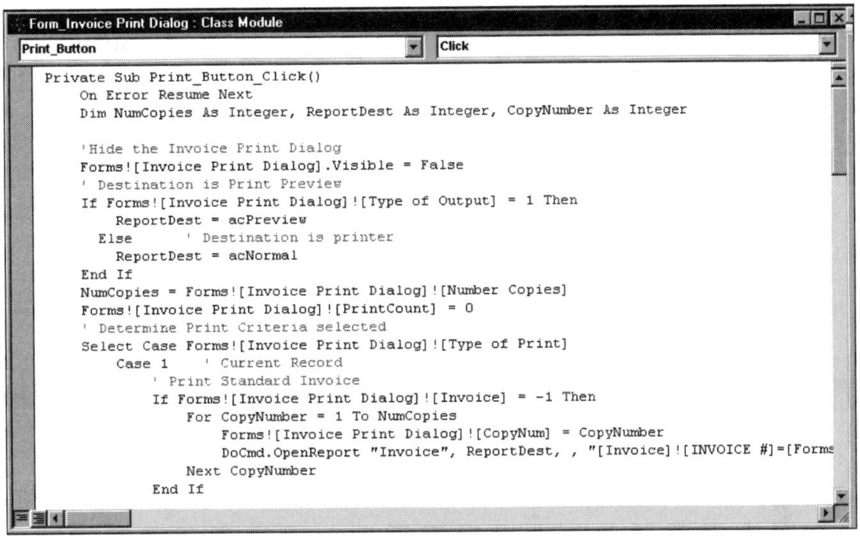

```
Form_Invoice Print Dialog : Class Module
Print_Button                                Click

Private Sub Print_Button_Click()
    On Error Resume Next
    Dim NumCopies As Integer, ReportDest As Integer, CopyNumber As Integer

    'Hide the Invoice Print Dialog
    Forms![Invoice Print Dialog].Visible = False
    ' Destination is Print Preview
    If Forms![Invoice Print Dialog]![Type of Output] = 1 Then
        ReportDest = acPreview
      Else      ' Destination is printer
        ReportDest = acNormal
    End If
    NumCopies = Forms![Invoice Print Dialog]![Number Copies]
    Forms![Invoice Print Dialog]![PrintCount] = 0
    ' Determine Print Criteria selected
    Select Case Forms![Invoice Print Dialog]![Type of Print]
        Case 1    ' Current Record
            ' Print Standard Invoice
            If Forms![Invoice Print Dialog]![Invoice] = -1 Then
                For CopyNumber = 1 To NumCopies
                    Forms![Invoice Print Dialog]![CopyNum] = CopyNumber
                    DoCmd.OpenReport "Invoice", ReportDest, , "[Invoice]![INVOICE #]=[Forms
                Next CopyNumber
            End If
```

Figure 12-32: Updating the value of the current copy number.

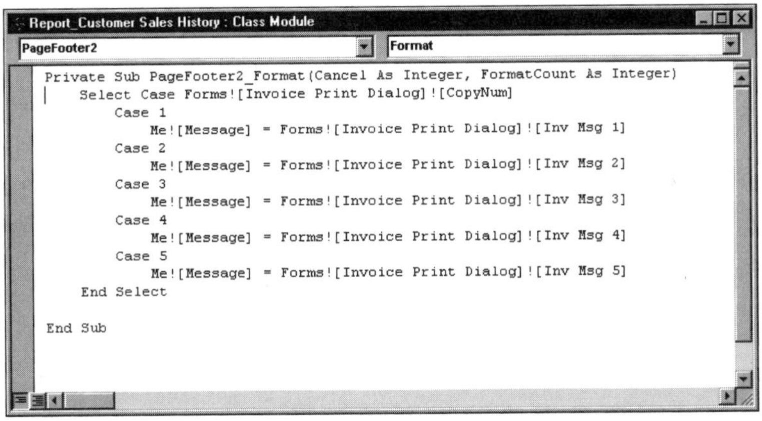

```
Report_Customer Sales History : Class Module
PageFooter2                                 Format

Private Sub PageFooter2_Format(Cancel As Integer, FormatCount As Integer)
    Select Case Forms![Invoice Print Dialog]![CopyNum]
        Case 1
            Me![Message] = Forms![Invoice Print Dialog]![Inv Msg 1]
        Case 2
            Me![Message] = Forms![Invoice Print Dialog]![Inv Msg 2]
        Case 3
            Me![Message] = Forms![Invoice Print Dialog]![Inv Msg 3]
        Case 4
            Me![Message] = Forms![Invoice Print Dialog]![Inv Msg 4]
        Case 5
            Me![Message] = Forms![Invoice Print Dialog]![Inv Msg 5]
    End Select

End Sub
```

Figure 12-33: Printing the correct message in the page footer.

Hiding a report's detail information

Most reports include a section of detail information grouped by some category. The categories, or groups, as they are called in report design, usually show the sum total of the detail information.

In many organizations, there are typically two types of workers who use reports: those who need to see both the detail information and the group summary information and those who only want to see the summarized information. The workers who only care about the summarized information do not want to wade through often large amounts of detail information just to get to the information they need. They want to see the same report with the detail data eliminated.

The Print Invoice Dialog, shown in Figure 12-25, provides a checkbox for printing only the summary information in the reports. When the report prints, it checks the value of the Summary Only checkbox to determine whether or not to print the detail information. The `OnFormat` event procedure of the detail section for the Customer Sales by Highest Total report controls whether or not the detail section prints. The `OnFormat` event procedure is shown in Figure 12-34. If the Summary Only field is checked, then the `Format` event is canceled for the detail section so that it will not print.

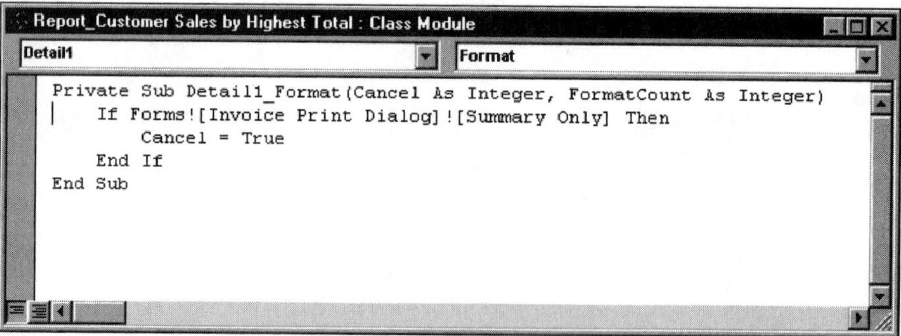
Report_Customer Sales by Highest Total : Class Module
Detail1
Format
Private Sub Detail1_Format(Cancel As Integer, FormatCount As Integer)
If Forms![Invoice Print Dialog]![Summary Only] Then
Cancel = True
End If
End Sub

Figure 12-34: Suppressing the detail section.

Adding consecutive page numbers to multiple reports

When printing several reports at the same time, you may want to number the pages with consecutive numbers instead of starting each new report with page one. Instead of using the page number function that is built into Access, you will need to create your own numbering scheme.

Building your own page numbering scheme requires a few special techniques. First, you need a way to keep track of the page number that is currently being printed. The Print Invoice Dialog uses an invisible unbound text box control called `PageCount` to store the number of the page currently being printed. When the dialog box first opens, its default value is zero. Figure 12-35 shows the design view of the Print Invoice Dialog illustrating the PageCount field. The PageCount field is updated as each of the reports prints.

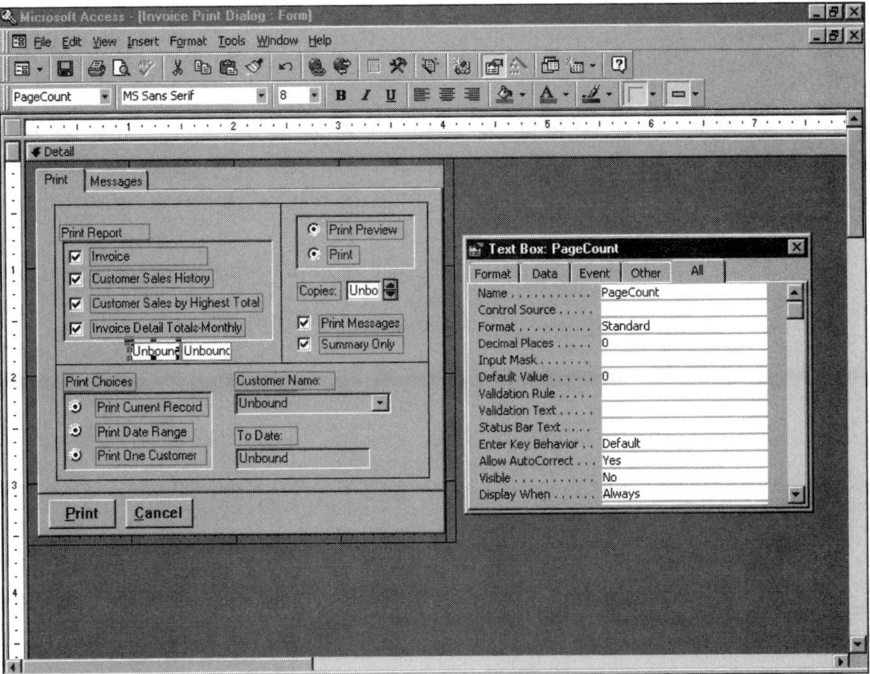

Figure 12-35: Storing the value of the current page number.

The next technique is to update the field that stores the page number being printed. As each page of the report prints, the PageCount field is updated. The `OnPrint` event procedure for the report's page footer, shown in Figure 12-36, updates the PageCount field in the Print Invoice Dialog. The procedure simply adds one to the current value in the field.

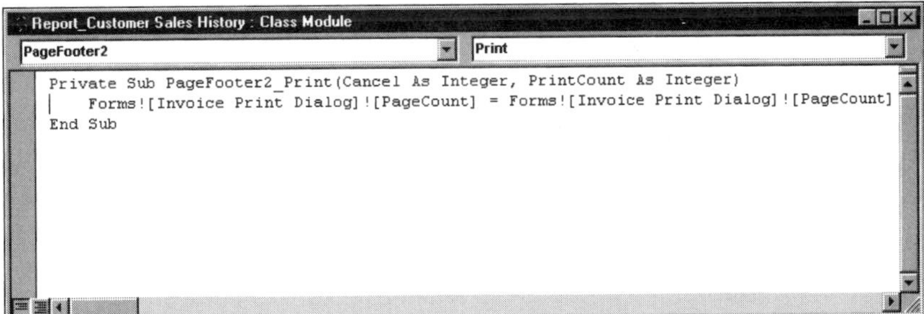

Figure 12-36: Updating the value of the current page number.

The final technique is to print the correct page number for the page being printed. Since the Print Invoice Dialog keeps track of the current value of the page number, you can just copy the value to a field in the report's page footer. As shown in Figure 12-37, the page footer of the Customer Sales History report includes a calculated text box control named `PageNum`. The `PageNum` text box control gets its value from the PageCount field in the Print Invoice Dialog.

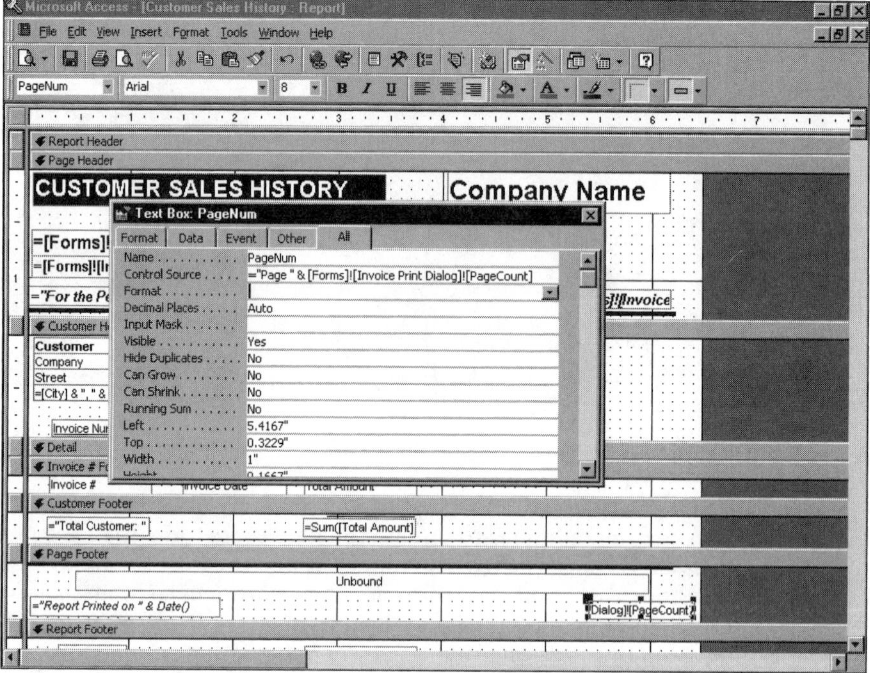

Figure 12-37: Printing the correct page number in the page footer.

Creating Mail Merge Reports

Most organizations need to create form letters, commonly known as mail merges. The Access report writer helps you create this type of report. A mail merge report is simply a report containing large amounts of text that have embedded database fields. For example, a letter may contain the amount owed by a customer and the name of a product within the body of the text.

The problem is to control the word wrap. This means that the text may take more than one line, depending on the length of the text and the embedded field values. Different records may have different length values in their embedded fields. One record may use two lines in the report, another may use three, yet another may require only one.

Access itself does not have the specific capability to perform mail merging. Access 97 contains a Report Wizard that exports your data to Word and launches Word's Print Merge feature. But what happens if you don't use Microsoft Word? As you see in this section, Access can indeed perform a mail merge with nearly the same precision as any Windows word processor!

A typical form letter is shown in Figure 12-38. Many of the data fields embedded in this letter come from an Access query. The letter itself was created entirely with the Access Report Writer, as were its embedded fields.

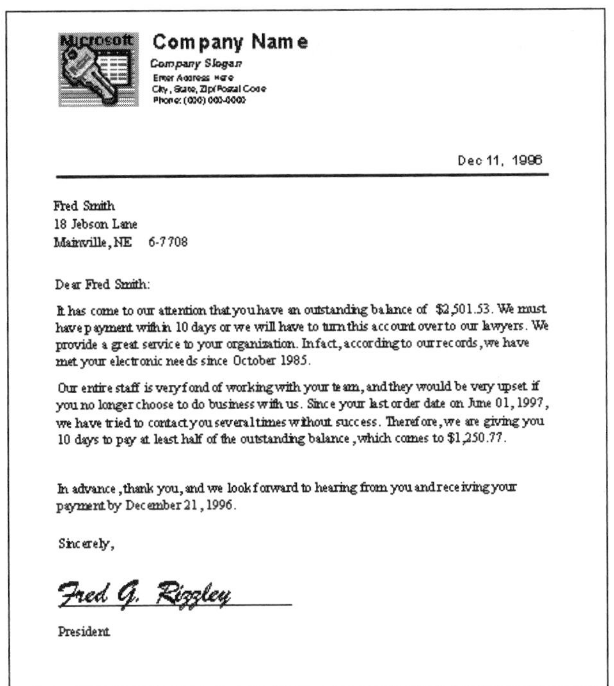

Company Name
Company Slogan
Enter Address Here
City, State, Zip/Postal Code
Phone: (000) 000-0000

Dec 11, 1996

Fred Smith
18 Jebson Lane
Mainville, NE 6-7708

Dear Fred Smith:

It has come to our attention that you have an outstanding balance of $2,501.53. We must have payment within 10 days or we will have to turn this account over to our lawyers. We provide a great service to your organization. In fact, according to our records, we have met your electronic needs since October 1985.

Our entire staff is very fond of working with your team, and they would be very upset if you no longer choose to do business with us. Since your last order date on June 01, 1997, we have tried to contact you several times without success. Therefore, we are giving you 10 days to pay at least half of the outstanding balance, which comes to $1,250.77.

In advance, thank you, and we look forward to hearing from you and receiving your payment by December 21, 1996.

Sincerely,

Fred G. Rizzley

President

Figure 12-38: A letter created with the Access Report Writer.

Assembling data for a mail merge report

A mail merge report is just like any other report. As with any report, its Control Source must be based on a table or query. Figure 12-39 displays the query used for the letter.

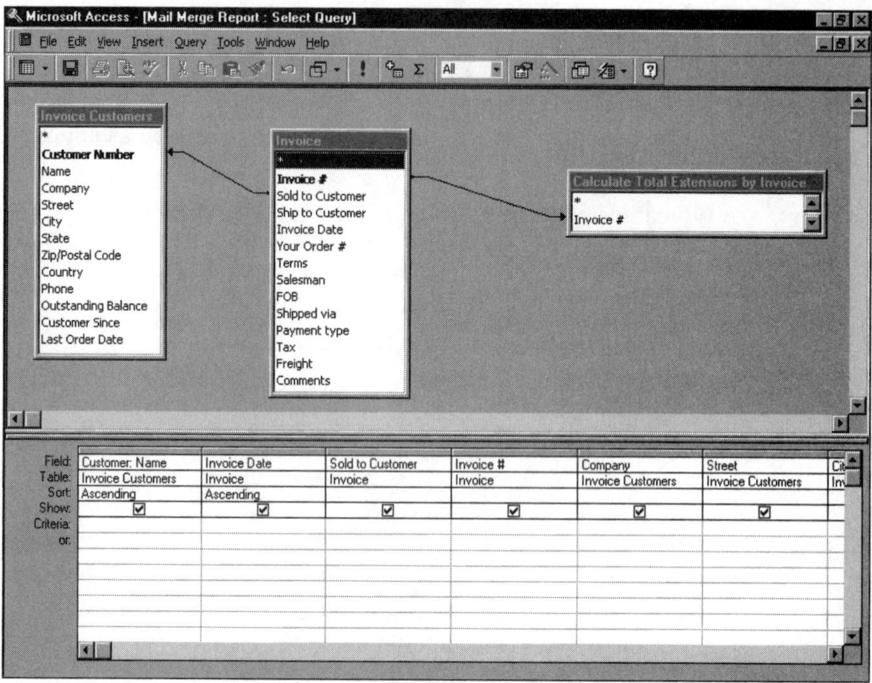

Figure 12-39: A query for a mail-merge report.

Table 12-2 shows the fields or functions embedded in the text box controls used to create the letter. Compare the values found in each line of the letter (shown in Figure 12-38) to the fields shown in the table. Later in this chapter, you'll see how each field or function is embedded in the text.

Table 12-2 Fields Used in the Mail Merge Report

Field Name	*Table*	*Usage in Report*
Date()	Function	Page header; displays current date; formatted as mmmm dd, yyyy
Customer	Invoice Customers	Page header; displays customer name
Street	Invoice Customers	Page header; displays street in the address block
City	Invoice Customers	Page header; part of city, state, ZIP code block

Field Name	*Table*	*Usage in Report*
State	Invoice Customers	Page header; part of city, state, ZIP code block
ZIP Code	Invoice Customers	Page header; part of city, state, ZIP code block; formatted as @@@@@-@@@@
Customer	Invoice Customers	Detail; part of salutation
Outstanding Balance	Invoice Customers	Detail; first line of first paragraph; formatted as $#,##0.00
Customer Since	Invoice Customers	Detail; fourth line of first paragraph; formatted as mmmm yyyy
Last Order Date	Invoice Customers	Detail; second/third line of second paragraph; formatted as mmm dd, yyyy
Outstanding Balance ×.5 Calculation	Invoice Customers	Detail; fourth line of second paragraph; formatted as $#,##0.00
Date Add(); Now()	Function;	Detail; second line of third paragraph; Date Add adds ten days to system date; formatted as mmmm dd, yyyy

Creating a mail merge report

After you assemble the data, you can create your report. Creating a mail merge report is much like creating other reports. Frequently a mail merge has only a page header and a detail section. You can, however, use sorting and grouping sections to enhance the mail merge report (although normally form letters are fairly consistent in their content).

Usually the best way to begin is with a blank report. The Report Wizards don't really help you create a mail merge report. After you create the blank report, you can begin to add your controls to it.

Creating the page header area

Generally a form letter has a top part that includes your company's name, address, and possibly a logo. You can print on preprinted forms that contain this information, or you can scan in the header and embed it in an unbound object frame. Usually the top part of a form letter also contains the current date along with the name and address of the person or company to whom you're sending the letter.

Figure 12-40 shows the page header section of the mail merge report. In this example, an unbound bitmap picture that contains a company logo is inserted. The text for the company information is created with individual label controls. As you can see in the top half of the page header section, the current date is also displayed along with a line to separate the top of the header from the body of the letter. You can see the calculated text box control's properties at the bottom of Figure 12-40.

The `Format( )` and `Date( )` functions are used to display the date with the full text for month, followed by the day, a comma, a space, and the four-digit year. The date expression is entered as

```
=Format(Date( ),"mmmm dd, yyyy")
```

and then automatically changed to

```
=Format(Date(),"mmmm dd"","" yyyy")
```

This expression takes the system date of 12/11/96 and formats it as December 11, 1996.

The customer name and address fields are also displayed in the page header. The standard concatenated expression is used to display the city, state, and ZIP code fields:

```
=[City] & ", " & [State] & " " & Format([Zip Code],"@@@@@-@@@@")
```

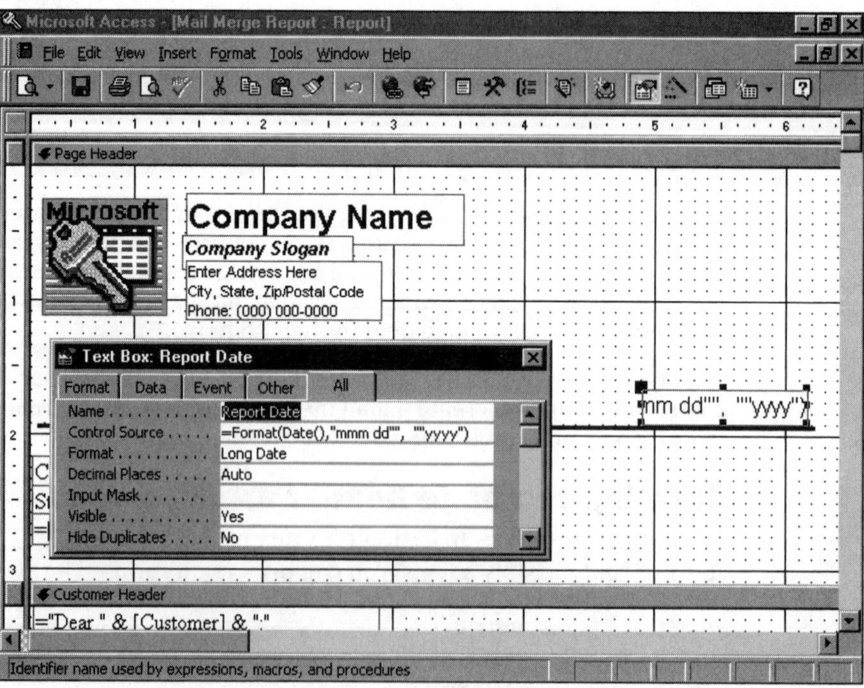

Figure 12-40: The page header section of a mail merge report.

Working with embedded fields in text

The body of the letter is shown in Figure 12-41. Each paragraph is one large block of text. A standard text box control is used to display each paragraph. The text box control's `Can Grow` and `Can Shrink` properties are set to `Yes`. This allows the text to take up only as much space as needed.

Embedded in each text block are fields from the query or expressions that use the fields from the query. In the page header section, for example, the `&` method is used to concatenate the city, state, and ZIP code. Although this method works for single concatenated lines, it does not allow word wrapping, which is critical to creating a mail merge report. If you use this method in large blocks of text, you get only a single truncated line of text.

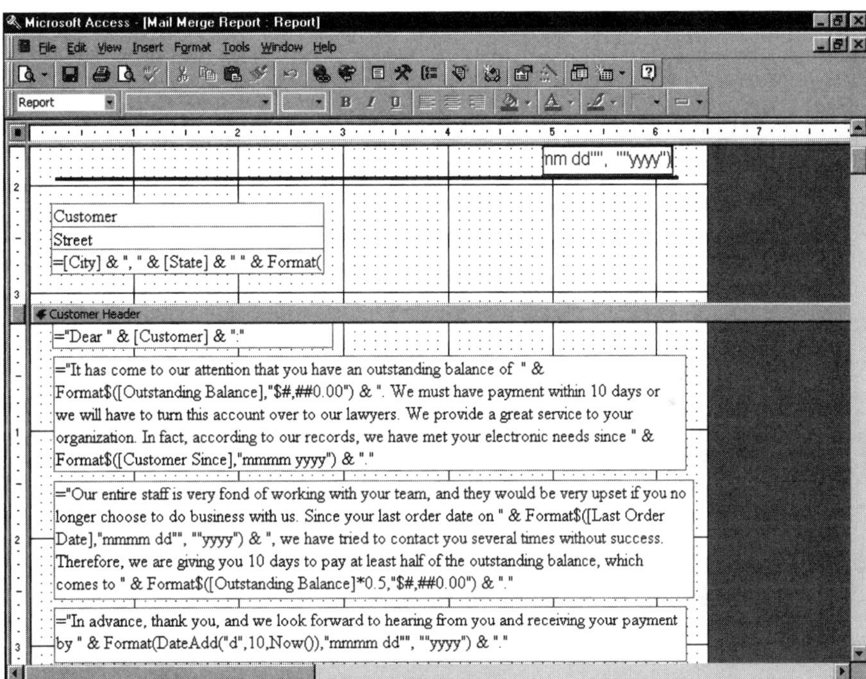

Figure 12-41: The body of the letter in the Report Design window.

The first text block is a single-line text box control that concatenates the text "Dear" with the field Customer. Notice that there are some special symbols within the first text box control. Remember that each text box is made up of smaller groups of text and expressions. By using the `&` character, you can concatenate them.

The expression ="Dear" & [Customer] & ":" begins with an equal sign and a double quote. Because the first item is text, it's surrounded by " characters. [Customer] needs to be enclosed in brackets because it's a field name; it should also be surrounded by & characters for concatenation. The colon at the end of the expression appears in the letter; it too is text, and must be surrounded by double quotes.

The next control produces the first paragraph of the letter. Notice that there are five lines in the text box control, but only four lines in the first paragraph of the letter (as shown in Figure 12-38). If you compare the two figures carefully, you'll see that the text box for the date is on the fifth line of the paragraph in the text control, whereas it's in the fourth line of the paragraph in the printed letter. This is a good example of word wrap. The number of lines shrank to fit the data.

The first line of the text control simply displays a text string. Notice that the text string is both enclosed in double quotes and concatenated to the next expression by the & character. The second line begins with an expression:

```
Format$([Outstanding Balance],"$#,##0.00") & "."
```

The expression converts the numeric expression to text, and formats the field Outstanding Balance so that it shows a dollar sign, a comma (if the value is 1,000 or more), and two displayed decimal places. Without this format, the field would have simply displayed 381 for the first record rather than $381.00.

The rest of the second line of the paragraph through the end of the fourth is one long text string. It's simply enclosed in double quotes and concatenated by the & character. The last line of the first paragraph contains an expression that formats and converts a date field. The expression Format$([Customer Since],"mmmm yyyy") formats the date value to display only the full month name and the year. (The date format in the page header demonstrated how to display the full month name, day, and year.)

Warning

The maximum length of a single concatenated expression in Access is 254 characters between a single set of quotes. To get around this limitation, just end one expression, add an & character, and start another. The limit on the length of an expression in a single text box is 2,048 characters (almost 40 lines)!

The last line of the second paragraph formats a numeric expression, but it also calculates a value within the format function. This is a good example of an expression within a function. The calculation [Outstanding Balance] x .5 is then formatted to display dollar signs and a comma if the number is 1,000 or more.

The last paragraph contains one text string and one expression. The expression advances the current date Now() by 10 days by using the expression DateAdd("d",10,Now()).

The bottom of the letter is produced using the label controls as shown in Figure 12-41. These label controls display the closing, the signature, and the owner's title. The signature of Fred G. Rizzley is created here by using the Script font. Normally you would scan in the signature and then use an unbound frame object control to display the bitmap picture that contains the signature.

Remember to set the `Force New Page` property of the Customer header section to `After Section` so there is always a page break after each letter.

Printing the mail merge report

You print a mail merge report in exactly the same way you would any other report. From the Print Preview window, you can simply click on the Print button. From the Report Design window, you can select File⇨Print. The report is printed out like any other report.

Chapter 13

Working with OLE Objects and Business Graphics

In This Chapter

- Exploring the types of objects you can create
- Discovering the differences between bound and unbound objects
- Discovering the differences between linking and embedding
- Storing bound and unbound objects
- Modifying an existing OLE object from your form design
- Creating and linking a graph to a form
- Creating a new graph using a Form Wizard
- Customizing a graph

Access provides many powerful tools for enhancing your forms and reports. These tools enable you to add pictures, graphs, sound, and even video to your database applications. Chart Wizards make it easy to build business graphs and add them to your forms and reports. New features, borrowed from Microsoft Office 97, make your use of Access forms more productive than ever. In this chapter, you learn about the different types of graphical and OLE (Object Linking and Embedding) objects you can add to your system and how to manipulate them to create professional and productive screen displays and reports.

Understanding Objects

Access 97 gives you the capability to embed pictures, video clips, sound files, business graphs, Web pages, Excel spreadsheets, and Word documents into your forms and reports, as well as link to any OLE object. In addition to using Access objects in your forms, you can directly edit the objects from within your form, including HTML documents.

Types of objects

Access 97 generally can add any type of picture or graphical object to a form or report. The program also can interact with any application through DDE (Dynamic Data Exchange) or OLE. You can interact with OLE objects with great flexibility. For example, you can link to entire spreadsheets, ranges of cells, or even individual cells.

Access can embed and store any binary file within an object frame control, including sound and full-motion video. As long as you have the software driver for the embedded object, you can play or view the contents of the frame.

You can bind these objects to a field in each record (*bound*) or to the form or report itself (*unbound*). Depending on how you want to process the OLE object, you can either place the copy directly in the Access database (*embed* it) or tell Access where to find the object (*link* it) and place it in the bound or unbound object frame in your form or report. The following sections describe the different ways you can use embedding and linking to process and store both bound and unbound objects.

Using bound and unbound objects

A *bound* object is an object that is displayed and potentially stored within a field of a record in a table. Access can display the object in a form or print it on a report. A bound object is bound to an OLE object data type field in the table. If you use a bound object in a form, you can add and edit pictures or documents record by record in the same way as you can add and edit values. To display a bound OLE object, you use a bound object frame.

In Figure 13-1, the Organization's logo is a bound object. Each record stores a scanned image of the logo of each Organization in the Customers table field named Logo. You can insert a different picture for each record.

An *unbound* object is an object that is not stored in a table but is placed on the form or report. An unbound object control is the graphical equivalent of a label control. Rather than belonging to a field of a record, these controls are generally used for OLE objects in a form or report. Unbound objects don't change from record to record.

An image control that displays a picture is another example of an unbound object. An unbound OLE object frame enables you to edit an object by double-clicking on it and launching the source application (PC Paintbrush, Word, Excel, or a sound or video editor or recorder, for example). An image control, however, displays only a bitmap picture (usually .BMP, .PCX, or .WMF) that cannot be edited.

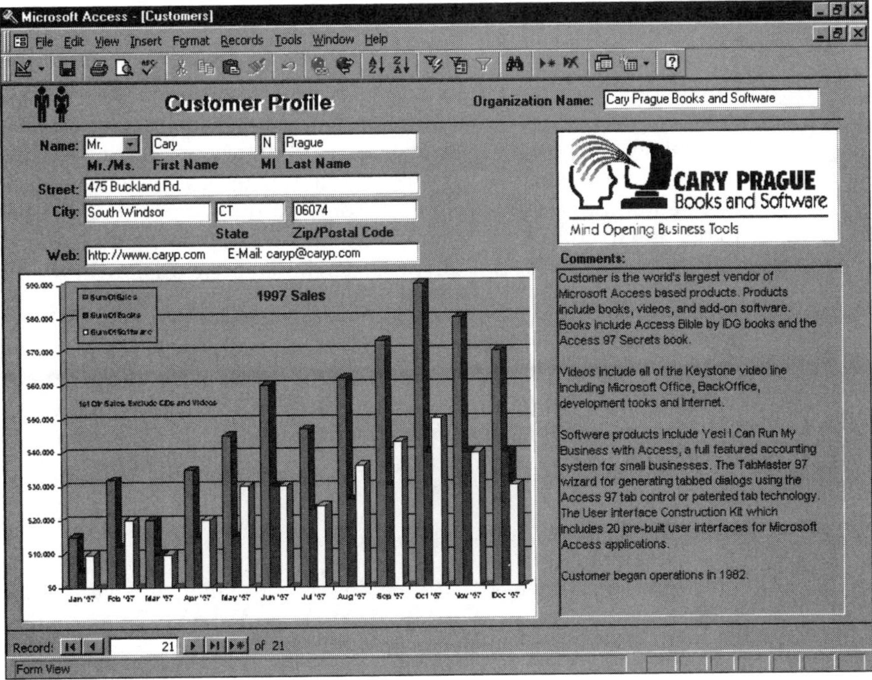

Figure 13-1: Bound and unbound objects.

You should always use the image control for unbound pictures, because it uses fewer resources than an OLE control and significantly increases performance.

In Figure 13-1, the picture of the man and woman in the form header is an image control. The logo is a bound OLE object, and the graph is an unbound object. Although the graph is unbound, a data link exists from the graph template to the data on the form. The graph is updated, therefore, every time data in the record changes.

Linking and embedding

The basic difference between linking and embedding objects within a form or report is that embedding the object causes a copy of the object to be stored within your database. Linking an object from another application does not cause the object to be stored in your database; rather, the external location of the object is stored.

Linking an object gives you two benefits:

- You can make changes by using the external application, even without opening Access.
- The external file does not use any space in the Access .MDB database file.

If you move the external file to another directory or rename the file, the link to Access is broken and opening the Access form may cause an error.

One of the benefits of embedding is that you don't have to worry about someone changing the location or the name of the linked file. Because it is embedded, it is part of the Access .MDB database file. Embedding does have its costs, however. The first cost is that it takes up space in your database — and sometimes a great deal of it. Some pictures can occupy several megabytes of hard disk space. In fact, if you embed a 30-second .MPEG video clip in your database for one record, the clip can use up 5 or more megabytes of space. Imagine the space used by 100 records with video.

After an object is embedded or linked, you can use the source application (Excel or Paintbrush, for example) to make changes to the object directly from the form. To make changes to these objects, all you have to do is display the object in Access and double-click on it. This step automatically launches the source application and enables you to make changes to the object.

When you save the object, it is saved within Access.

Suppose that you have written a document-management system in Access and have embedded a Word file in an Access form. When you double-click on the image of the word document, Word is automatically launched and you can edit the document.

When you open the external application and make changes to the object, the changes are made to the external file rather than within your database.

To edit an OLE object, you must have the associated OLE application installed in Windows. If you have embedded an Excel .XLS file but don't own Excel, you can view the spreadsheet or use its values, but you cannot edit or make changes to the spreadsheet.

Embedding Objects

You can embed objects in both unbound and bound object frames as well as in image frames. Embedding places the object directly in the Access database, and it is stored in either the form or report design or in a record of a table.

Embedding an unbound object

You can embed an unbound object in a form or report in one of two ways:

- Simply paste an object on the form or report — an image or unbound object frame that contains the object is created.
- Create an unbound object frame or image frame and then insert the object or picture into the frame.

Pasting an unbound object

If the object you want to insert is not an OLE object, you must paste the object on the form. First, the object must be created by using the external application. Then you can select the object in the external application and choose Edit⇨Cut or Edit⇨Copy. After you have cut or copied the object to the Windows 95 Clipboard, you can display the Access 97 form or report and choose Edit⇨Paste from the menu.

This procedure automatically creates an unbound object frame for an OLE object or an image frame for a picture and embeds the pasted object in it.

If the object you paste into a form is an OLE object and you have loaded the OLE application, you can still double-click on the object to edit it. You can highlight a range of cells in an Excel worksheet, for example, and then cut and paste the highlighted selection into an Access form or report. You can highlight a paragraph of text in Word and cut and paste it on the Access form or report. You can use this method to cut and paste both OLE and non-OLE objects on a form or report, but other methods are available for adding an OLE object.

Inserting an image type object

You also can use another method to embed OLE objects or pictures into an unbound object frame or image frame. Suppose that you want to embed a file containing a Paintbrush picture. In Figure 13-1, the picture of the two people is displayed on the form in the form header in an image frame. You can embed the picture by either pasting it into the image frame or inserting the object into the image frame. You can create an empty image frame by first clicking on the Image Frame button on the toolbar. Then you can create the image frame by clicking on the form and drawing a rectangle.

After you create an Image frame, the Insert Picture dialog box appears, as shown in Figure 13-2. It displays the image objects you have on your system. In this example, the picture is chosen from a library of small buttons. After you highlight the picture you want to use, click on OK, and the picture appears in the image frame (see Figure 13-1).

Changing the display of an image

After you add an image to a form or report, you may want to change the size of the object or object frame. If you embed a small picture, you may want to adjust the size of the object frame to fit the picture. Similarly, you may want to reduce the size of a picture to fit a specific area on your form or report.

You can change the appearance and proportions of the object you embed by changing the size of the image frame and setting the `Size Mode` property. Figure 13-3 shows three choices for the `Size Mode` property:

- **Clip:** Shows the picture by using the actual size and truncating both right and bottom. Use `Clip` only when the frame is the exact size of the picture or when you want to crop the picture.

- **Stretch:** Fits the picture within the frame but distorts the proportions of the picture. `Stretch` is useful when you have pictures in which you can accept a slight amount of distortion.
- **Zoom:** Fits the picture proportionally within the frame but may result in extra white space. Although the use of this option fits the picture to the frame and maintains its original proportions, empty space may appear within the frame.

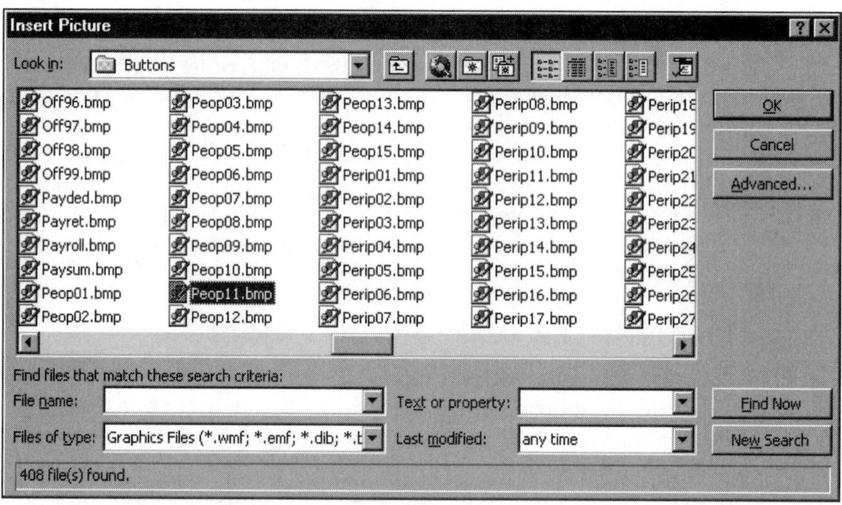

Figure 13-2: The Insert Picture dialog box.

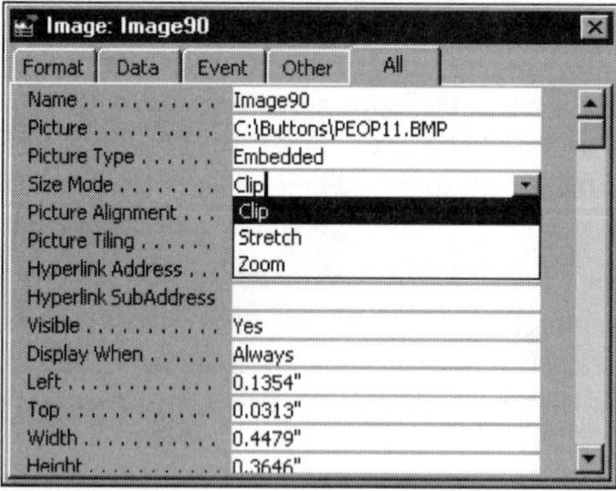

Figure 13-3: Various scaling options.

To return the chosen object to its original size, select the object and choose Format➪Size➪To Fit from the Format menu.

Embedding bound objects

You can store pictures, spreadsheets, word-processing documents, or other objects as data in a table. For example, you can store a Paintbrush picture, an Excel worksheet, or an object created in any other OLE application.

You store objects in a table by creating a field with a data type of OLE object. After you create a bound object frame, its control source can be bound to the OLE object field in the table. You can then embed an object into each record of the table by using the bound object frame.

Secret

You also can insert objects into a table from the Datasheet view of a form, table, or query, although the objects cannot be displayed other than in Form view. When you switch to Datasheet view, you see text describing the OLE class of the embedded object. If you insert a .BMP picture into an OLE object field in a table, for example, the text "Picture" or "Paintbrush Picture" appears in Datasheet view.

Creating a bound OLE object

After you have created an OLE object in your table, creating a bound OLE frame in the form is essentially the same as creating an image control or an unbound object frame. The only difference is that the bound object frame has a control source property to bind the frame to a table field.

You enter the control source property in the same way you enter a control source for any other type of control.

Adding a picture to a bound object frame

After you define the bound object frame control and place it on a form, you can add pictures to it in several ways. You can paste a picture into a record or insert a file object into the frame. You insert the file object for a bound frame in almost the same way as for an unbound object or image frame. The only difference is that, whereas an image frame has a picture inserted on the design screen, a bound object frame has a picture inserted in Form view.

To insert a picture or other object into a bound object frame, you display the form in Form view, move to the correct record (each record can have a different picture or object), select the bound object frame, and then choose Insert Object from the form menu. The dialog box is a little different. Because you can insert any OLE object (a picture, in this example), you first have to choose Create from File and then choose the first option, Bitmap Image. You can then choose the picture. When you finish, the picture or object is displayed in the space used for the bound object frame in the form.

If you create the object rather than embed an existing file, some applications display a dialog box asking whether you want to close the connection and update the open object. Choose Yes, and Access embeds the object in the bound object frame (or in the datasheet field along with text that describes the object, such as “Paintbrush Picture”).

After you embed an object, you can open its source application and edit the object from your form or report by selecting the object in Form view and double-clicking on it.

Editing an embedded object

After you have placed an embedded object on a form, you may want to modify the object. You can edit an OLE object in several ways. Typically, you can simply double-click on the object. This launches the source application and lets you edit the object. When you double-click on an object that is a picture, the screen changes to an image-editing environment in which Windows Paint menus and functions are available.

Windows 95 supports full in-place editing of OLE objects. Rather than launch a different program, the menus and look of the screen change as Windows Paint's functionality is temporarily added to Access.

If you make any changes, you are prompted to update the embedded object before continuing.

In most cases, you can modify an OLE object by double-clicking on it. When you attempt to modify either a sound or video object, however, you cannot modify it — double-clicking on the object causes it to “play” or display the player. To edit or play this type of object, you must choose from the Edit menu the last option in the menu, which will be different depending on the type of OLE Object with which you are working.

You also can convert some embedded OLE objects to static images by selecting the OLE Object and then selecting the Change to Picture option from the Edit menu option of the forms design menu. This process breaks all OLE links and simply displays a picture of the object.

Linking Objects

In addition to being able to embed objects, you can link them. You can link to external application files in much the same way as you embed them. The difference is that the object itself is not stored in the form or report or database table; rather, information about the link is stored in the form, report, or table. This storage system saves valuable space in the .MDB file and enables you to edit the object in the source application without having to make it go through Access.

When you create a link from information in another application (a Microsoft Excel file, for example) to a field in a table, the information is still stored in its original file.

Suppose that you decide to use the OLE object field to store an Excel file containing additional information about sales. If the Excel file contains sales broken down by category, you may want to link the information from the month record to this file.

Before linking information in a file to a field, you must first create and save the file in the source application. In Figure 13-1, you can see a graph of the customer's sales for 1997. Suppose that you want instead to display an Excel worksheet maintained by a different department in your organization. To view this Excel worksheet, you first have to launch Excel and select the information you want to link, as shown in Figure 13-4.

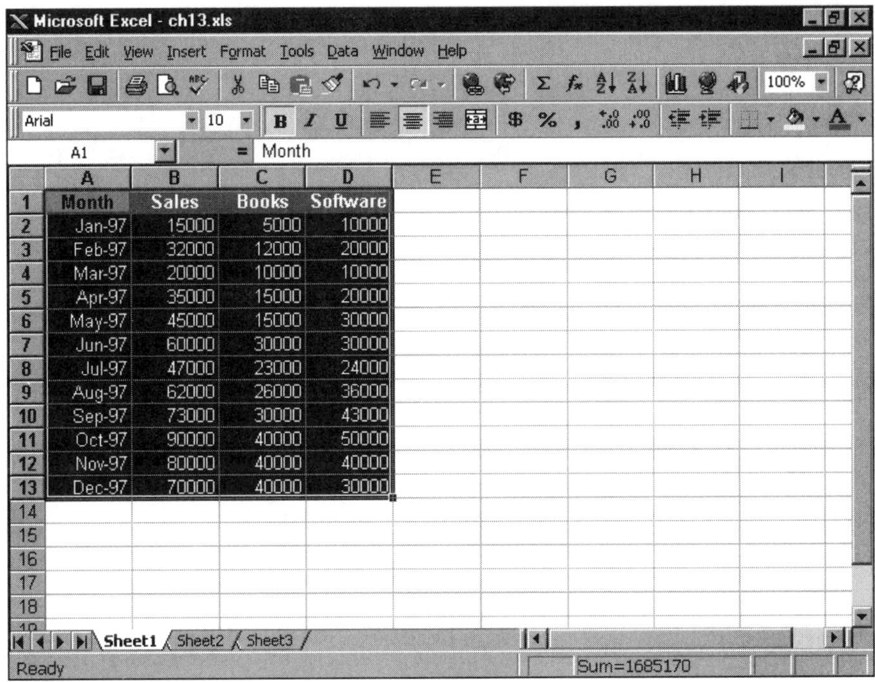

Month	Sales	Books	Software
Jan-97	15000	5000	10000
Feb-97	32000	12000	20000
Mar-97	20000	10000	10000
Apr-97	35000	15000	20000
May-97	45000	15000	30000
Jun-97	60000	30000	30000
Jul-97	47000	23000	24000
Aug-97	62000	26000	36000
Sep-97	73000	30000	43000
Oct-97	90000	40000	50000
Nov-97	80000	40000	40000
Dec-97	70000	40000	30000

Figure 13-4: Copying a range from Microsoft Excel.

Next, you choose Edit⇨Copy. After you copy the range to the Clipboard, you can paste it into a bound object frame in the Access form by choosing the Paste Special option from the Edit menu, as shown in Figure 13-5.

The linked Excel worksheet appears in the bound object frame. Access creates the link and either displays the object in the bound object frame or links it to the datasheet field and displays text that describes the object, such as "Microsoft Excel." When you double-click on the picture of the worksheet, Excel is launched and you can edit the data.

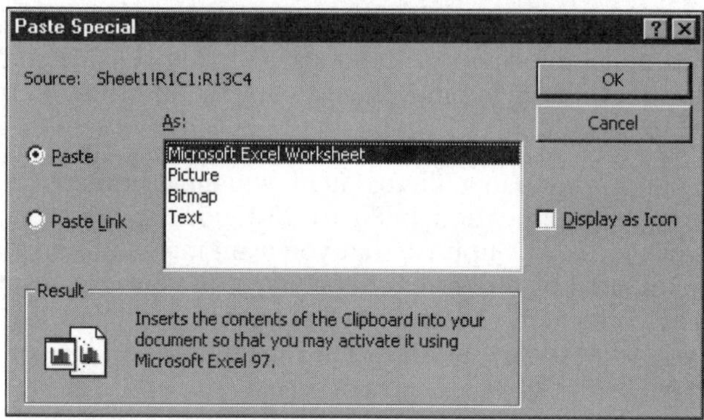

Figure 13-5: Pasting a linked worksheet.

Understanding the Different Ways to Create a Graph

Access has the capability to incorporate *graphs* (also known as *charts*) within a form or report. You can create graphs with the Microsoft Graph application included in your Access package, or you can create a graph by using any of the other OLE applications. A graph is typically just a specialized type of bound or unbound object frame.

You can graph data from any of your database tables or data that is stored within other applications, such as Excel. With Microsoft Graph, you can create a variety of styles of graphs, such as bar graphs, pie charts, and line charts. Because Microsoft Graph is an embedded OLE application, it does not work as a stand-alone application. You must run it from within your Access program.

After you embed a graph, you can treat it as any other OLE object. You can modify the graph from Design view in your form or report by double-clicking on the graph. You can also edit the graph from Form or Datasheet view in a form. The following sections describe how to build and process graphs that use data from within an Access table, as well as from tables of other OLE applications.

Access provides two ways to create a graph and place it on a form or report:

- You can use the Microsoft Graph form or Report Wizard to create a graph as a new form or report or to add it to an existing form or report.
- You can click on the Unbound Object frame button in the toolbox from Form Design mode and choose Microsoft Graph 97 Chart to add a graph to an existing form and link it to a table data source.

Unless you are already an experienced Microsoft Graph user from using earlier versions of Access or Excel, it is much easier to create a new graph from the toolbox. If you examine the toolbox, however, you do not see a Chart icon. You must first customize the toolbox to add a graph to an existing form by using the Chart Wizard.

Customizing the Toolbox

If you are an experienced Access user, you may notice for the first time that the Graph icon (now called the Chart Icon) button is missing from the Access 97 toolbox. This optional item has been left for you to add to the toolbox. Like toolbars, you can (fortunately) customize the toolbox.

The easiest way to customize the toolbox is to right-click on it, display the shortcut menu, choose Customize, and then select the Commands tab on the tabbed dialog box. Select the Toolbox choice from the list of toolbars. You can then choose the various Toolbox icons (tasks) from the list of icons, as shown in Figure 13-6. Click on the Chart icon, which is the picture of a graph and has the word Chart to the right of it, and drag it to the toolbox. This step permanently adds the missing icon.

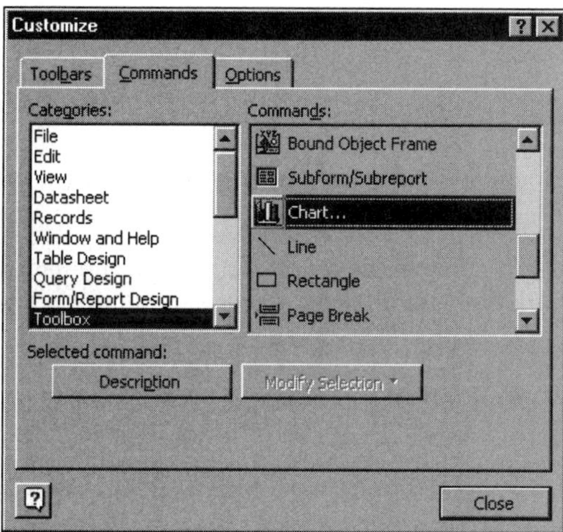

Figure 13-6: Customizing the Toolbox toolbar.

Before you enter a graph into a form or report based on data from one or more of your tables, you typically must first specify — for both types of graph creation — which table or query will supply the data for the graph. When you set up your query, you should keep several rules in mind:

- Make sure that the fields containing the data to be graphed are selected.

- Be sure to include the fields containing the labels that identify the data.
- Include any linking fields if you want the data to change from record to record.

Embedding a Graph in a Form

As you read earlier in this chapter, you can both link and embed objects in your Access tables, and you can create and display objects on your Access forms and reports.

Suppose that you want to create a graph based on the data shown in the Excel worksheet in Figure 13-4. This graph represents monthly sales by showing the sale dates and the dollars received from the sale of books, software, and total sales. When you move through the Customers table, the form links to a Sales table by customer, recalculates each customer's sales, and displays the data in a graphical format. Look back at Figure 13-1 to see the completed form in the Form view you create.

Assembling the data

As a first step in embedding a graph, you must make sure that the information you need for the graph is provided for in the query or table associated with the form. In this example, the sales date and several numeric values are used as the basis of the graph, and the customer's Organization name field from the Sales table is used as a link to the data on the form. This link enables the data in the graph to change from record to record.

Sometimes you have to create a query when you want data items from more than one table. In this example, you can select all the data you want directly from the wizard, and the query (an SQL statement) is built for you automatically.

Adding a graph to a form

You can begin creating a graph with the wizard by clicking on the Graph button in the toolbox. Next, position the chart icon in the upper-left position for the new graph and drag the rectangle to the size you want on the form. After you size the blank area for the graph and release the mouse button, Access activates the Chart Wizard used to embed a graph in the form.

As shown in Figure 13-7, this wizard dialog box enables you choose the table or query from which you want to select the values. By using the row of option buttons under the list of tables, you can view just the tables, just the queries, or all the tables and queries.

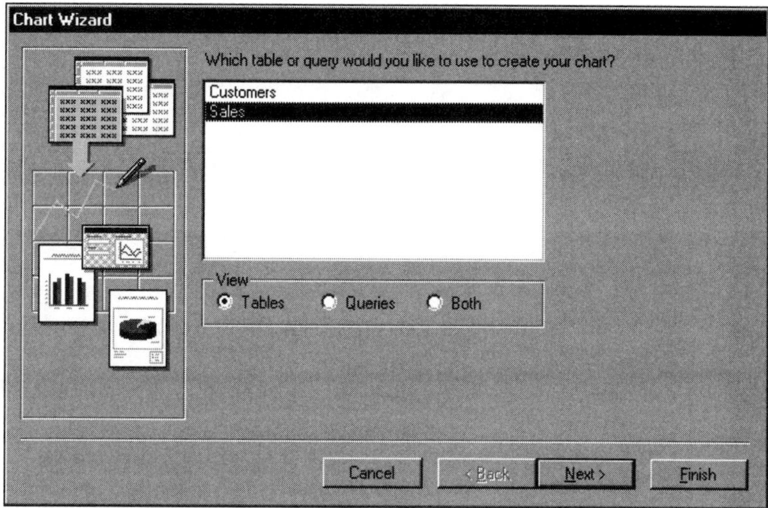

Figure 13-7: Choosing the table for the source of data for the graph.

In this example, you choose the Sales table as the source for the graph. When you click on Next to display the next wizard dialog box, the Chart Wizard enables you to choose the fields you want to include in your graph.

In this example, you choose all the fields except the Organization field. This field is used later to link the graph with the customer. You can use the standard wizard selection buttons or double-click on each field you want to include. After you choose the fields, click on Next to display the next wizard dialog box.

In the next dialog box that is displayed, you can choose the type of graph you want to create and whether the data series will appear in rows or columns. In this example, you choose a 3-D column chart (see Figure 13-8) and later customize it by using many of the graph options. As you click on each of the graph types, an explanation is displayed in the box on the right side of the dialog box.

Because a column chart is the easiest chart style to work with, it's a good place for you to begin.

When you click on Next, the dialog box shown in Figure 13-9 appears. It automatically makes certain choices for you and lets you change its assumptions. In the figure, the Month field has been chosen for the x-axis, and the Sales field is used in the y-axis to determine the height of the bars.

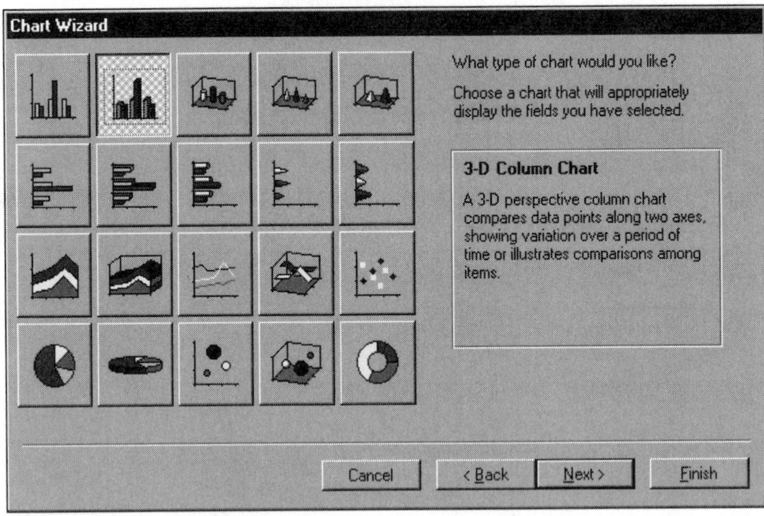

Figure 13-8: Choosing a chart type.

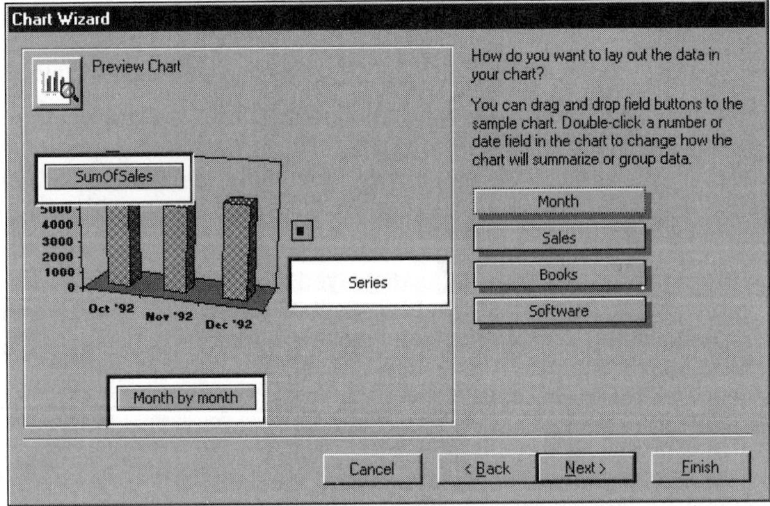

Figure 13-9: Laying out a chart's data elements.

This dialog box is different from the Access 2.0 Graph Wizard: It replaces three or four Access 2.0 Wizard dialog boxes with a single dialog box. In this one, you can graphically choose the fields you want to use in your graph and drag them to the simulated graph window.

In Figure 13-9, the Chart Wizard dialog box is divided into two areas. The right side simply displays the fields with which you have chosen to work. The left side displays a simulated graph and enables you to drag fields from the list of fields on the right to the axis area. To change the Month field chosen for you for the x-axis, for example, you can drag the field from the left side to the right side of the dialog box. Likewise, to make a selection, you can drag a field name from the right side of the dialog box to the proper axis on the left side.

If you have chosen several numeric fields (as in this example), you can drag multiple fields to the left side for multiple series. Each of these fields appears in a legend. As long as you are grouping differently, you can also drag the same field to both the x-axis and the Series indicator. You can group the Month by month, for example, and use it again in a series grouped by year. Without using the Month field a second time as the series variable, you see one bar for each month in sequential order (for example, Jan95, Feb95, Mar95, and continuing with Dec95, Jan96, and Feb96). By adding Month as a series variable and grouping it by year, you get pairs of bars. Multiple bars (each one in a different color and representing a different year and a legend for each year) are displayed for each month.

Figure 13-10 shows the Chart Wizard dialog box. In this example, the Access 97 assumptions are acceptable. Note in the figure that each field on the left side of the dialog box is a button. When you double-click on one of these buttons, you can additionally define how the data is used in the graph.

The x-axis variable is typically either a date field or a text field. The y-axis field is almost always a number, although it can be a count of values. Only numeric and date fields can be further defined. The y-axis variables can be further defined. If you double-click on any of the Sales fields on the left side of the dialog box, the dialog box shown in Figure 13-11 is displayed, in which you can define summarization options for the field.

Remember that many records may be available for a specific summarization. The example in this figure shows only one value for each month, but it could just as easily show the numerous daily sales records that need to be "rolled up" into their respective month and years.

In Figure 13-11, Sum has been chosen as the summarization type. You could change it to Average if there were multiple entries in the data to graph the average sales in a month rather than sum all the sales amounts.

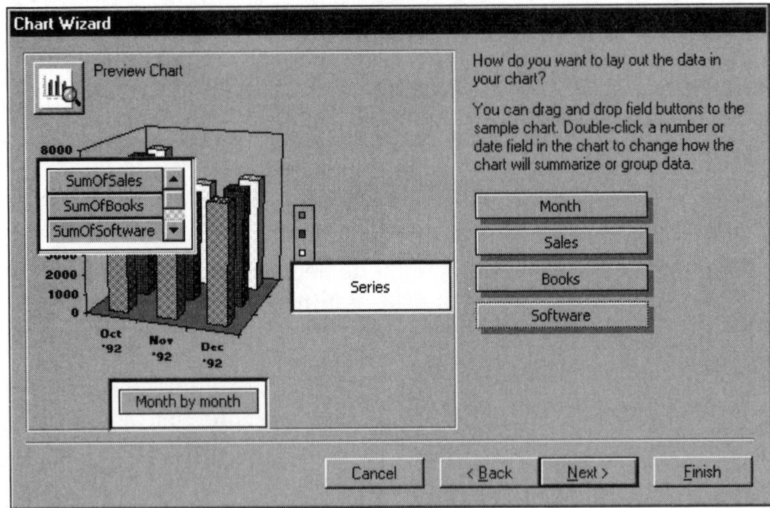

Figure 13-10: Adding several y-axis elements.

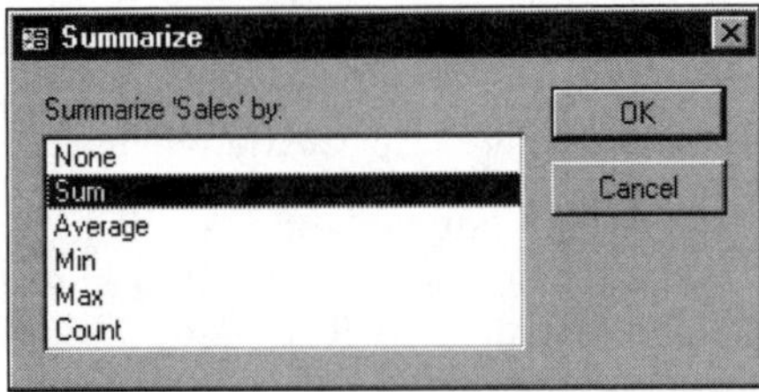

Figure 13-11: Selecting summarization options.

You must supply a numeric variable for all the selections except Count, which can be any data type.

You can click on the Chart Wizard's Preview Chart button at any time to see the results of your choices.

The dialog box shown in Figure 13-12 enables you to choose the date hierarchy, from larger to smaller rollups. The choices range from Year to Minute. In this example, to see all the detail data for many dates within a month, you choose Month to view all the records, because the data is already in Months.

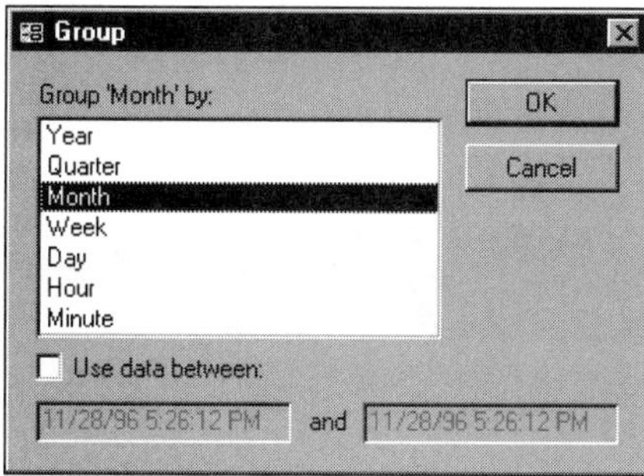

Figure 13-12: Choosing group options for a date field.

After you choose a date hierarchy in the wizard dialog box, click on Next to display the field-linking dialog box, as shown in Figure 13-13. If you run the Chart Wizard from inside an existing form, you have the option to link a field in the form to a field in the chart. Even if you don't specify the field when you choose the chart fields, as long as the field exists in the selected table, you can make the link. In Figure 13-13, Access has correctly chosen the Organization field from both the Customer form and the Sales table. This way, as you move from record to record (which is keyed by Organization) on the Customer form, the graph changes to display data for only that Organization.

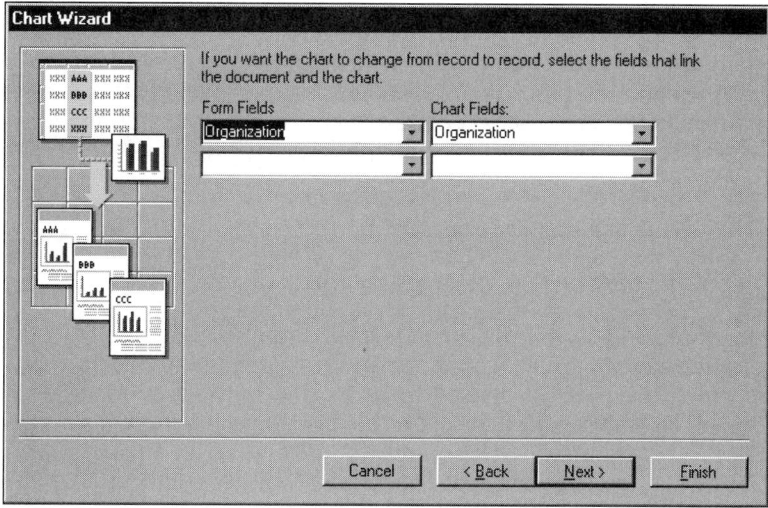

Figure 13-13: Linking fields between the form and the graph.

In the final Chart Wizard dialog box, as shown in Figure 13-14, you enter a title and determine whether a legend is necessary. In the figure, `1997 Sales` is entered as the chart title, and a legend will be displayed.

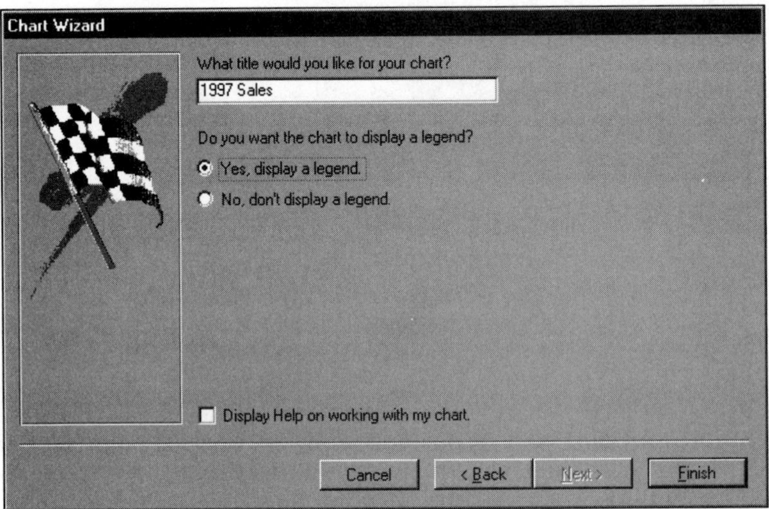

Figure 13-14: Specifying a chart title and legend.

After you complete all the entries and click on the Finish button, the sample chart appears in the graph object frame in the Form Design window, as shown in Figure 13-15. The link to the individual Organization is not established and the graph is not recalculated to show only the sales for the specific Organization's record unless you view the graph in form view. The graph that's shown is just a sample preview that doesn't use any of your data.

You can click on the Form View button on the toolbar to display the Customer form and recalculate the graph. Figure 13-16 shows the final graph in Form view. You may notice that it still needs some work to look good.

Figure 13-15 shows the graph and its property sheet. You display a graph by using a *graph frame,* which displays its data in either Form view or Design view. Take note of some of the properties in the property sheet. The `Size Mode` property is initially set to `Clip`. You can change this property to `Zoom` or `Stretch`, although the graph should always be displayed proportionally. You also can size and move the graph to fit on your form. When you work with the graph in the graph window, the size of the graph you create is the same as it is in the Form Design window.

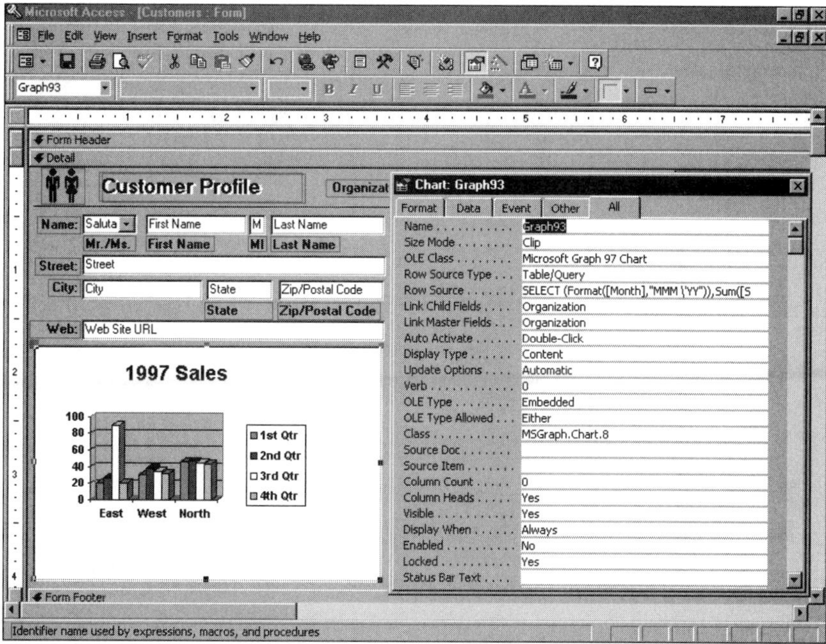

Figure 13-15: The graph in the Form Design window.

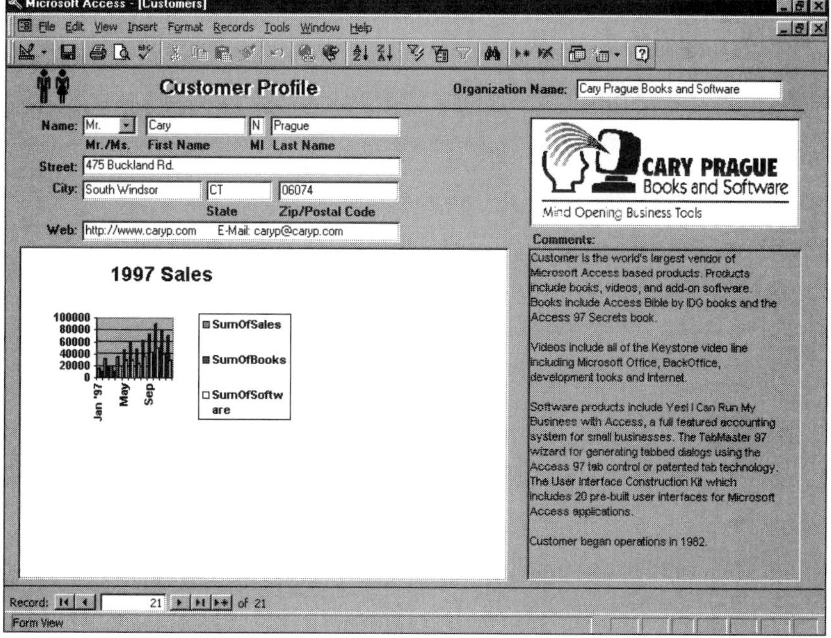

Figure 13-16: Recalculating the graph in form view.

The OLE Class property is Microsoft Graph 97 Chart. This is automatically linked by the Chart Wizard. The Row Source comes from the table or query you used with the graph but is displayed as an SQL statement, which is passed to the graph. The SQL statement (you can read more about SQL later) that was created for this graph is shown here:

```
SELECT (Format([Month],"MMM \'YY")),Sum([Sales]) AS _
[SumOfSales],Sum([Books]) AS [SumOfBooks],Sum([Software]) AS _
[SumOfSoftware] FROM [Sales]   GROUP BY (Year([Month])*12 + _
Month([Month])-1
```

Tip

You might want to change the SQL statement to the following:

```
SELECT [Month],Sum([Sales]) AS [Total Sales],Sum([Books]) AS [Book _
Sales],Sum([Software]) AS [Software Sales] FROM [Sales] GROUP BY _
[Month];
```

This revised code changes the legend so that it doesn't say SumOfSoftware but rather just Software on the graph.

The next two properties, Link Child Fields and Link Master Fields, control the linking of data to the form data. Using link properties, you can link a graph's data to each record in a form. In Figure 13-16, the Organization from the current Customer record is linked to sales records with the same Organization.

To change the appearance of a graph, you can double-click on the graph in Design view to open Microsoft Graph. After you make the changes you want, you can choose File⇨Exit to return to Access and go back to Design view.

Customizing a Graph

After you create a graph within Access, you can make enhancements to it by using the tools in Microsoft Graph. As demonstrated in the preceding section, it takes only a few mouse clicks to create a basic graph. This section describes a number of ways to enhance your graph and make it a powerful presentation and reporting tool.

In many cases, the basic chart you create represents the idea you want to present. In other cases, however, you may want to create a more illustrative presentation. You can use any of the following enhancements to produce a better presentation:

- Enter freeform text to highlight specific areas.
- Change attached text for a better display of the data being presented.
- Annotate the graph with lines and arrows.
- Change certain graphics objects with colors and patterns.
- Move and modify the legend.

- Add gridlines to better display the data.
- Manipulate the 3-D view to show your presentation more accurately.
- Add a bitmap for a more professional presentation.
- Change the graph type to show the data in a different graphics format (bar, line, or pie, for example).
- Add or modify the data in the graph.

After the graph is displayed in the Microsoft Graph application, you can begin to make changes to it.

Understanding the graph window

In the graph window, shown in Figure 13-17, you can work with and customize a graph. As you can see, the graph window has two windows:

- **Datasheet:** A spreadsheet of the data used in the graph
- **Chart:** The chart displayed for the selected data

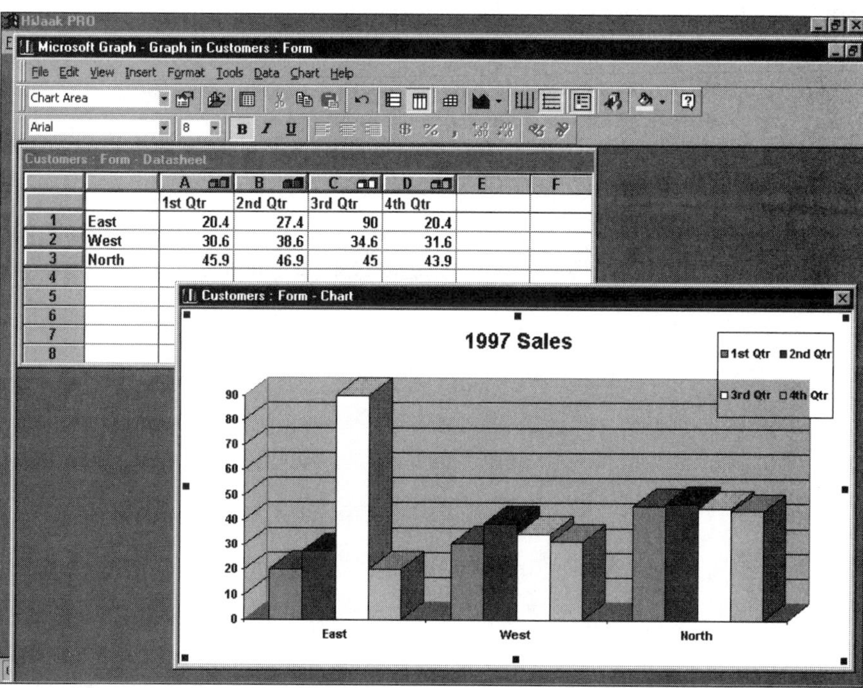

Figure 13-17: The graph window.

The data in the datasheet contains sample data. Unless you create your own sample data for this graph by either typing in real data or by copying data from an actual data source (in this example, the Excel spreadsheet would work), you will only work with the sample data. The authors of this book believe this to be a major bug in the software. In both Access 2.0 and Access 95, after you displayed the graph once in Form view, your real data was available. You should put in some sample data to help you better understand how to customize the look of the chart.

You can change the look of the graph by resizing the chart window. Note in Figure 13-17 that you see a wider graph window, which enables you to see labels better.

The bigger the graph window, the better looking the chart.

Any data you add, change, or delete in the datasheet is reflected immediately in the graph. After you change the datasheet in the graph window, you can even tell Access whether to include each row or column when the graph is drawn.

Data in a linked record is changed, however, only as long as the mouse pointer is on that record. After you move the pointer off the record, the changes are discarded.

Most important, in the chart portion of the graph window, you can change the way the graph is displayed. By clicking on objects (attached text, for example) or areas of the graph (columns, for example), you can make changes to them. You can double-click on an object to display a customization dialog box or make selections from the menus at the top of the window.

Working with attached text

Text generated by the program is called *attached text,* which includes the graph items in this list:

- Graph title
- Y-axis value
- X-axis category
- Data series and points
- Y-axis overlay value
- X-axis overlay value

After the initial graph is displayed, you can change any text attached to the graph. You can click on a text object to change the text, for example, or double-click on any of the text items in the preceding list and then modify their properties.

You can choose from the following six categories of settings to modify an attached text object:

- **Font:** Text font, size, style, and color
- **Alignment:** Alignment and orientation
- **Colors and Lines:** Fill Colors, Borders, and Arrows
- **Size:** Size and Scale (usually used for axis labels)
- **Properties:** Whether to change the size as the graph gets bigger or smaller
- **Margins:** Left, Right, Top, and Bottom

The Font options enable you to change the font assignment for text within a text object, as shown in Figure 13-18. The Format Chart Title dialog box is a standard Windows dialog box for choosing fonts and their characteristics. In this one, you can choose font, size, style, color, and background effects.

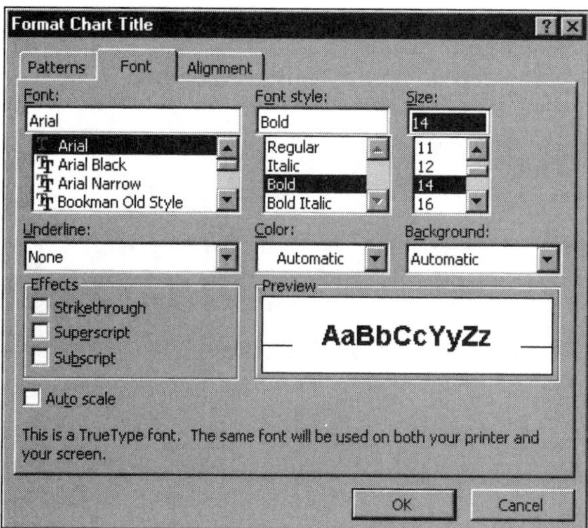

Figure 13-18: The Font tab of the Format Chart Title dialog box.

As you make font changes, a sample of the change is displayed in the Preview box.

Using the Alignment tab in the dialog box, you can set the horizontal alignment (left, center, or right), the vertical alignment (top, center, or bottom), and the orientation, with four options available for displaying text in either horizontal or vertical format.

The most important part of the Alignment tab is the Orientation setting. Although it is not important to change any of these settings for some titles, it is necessary to change the settings for titles that normally run vertically, such as axis titles.

Sometimes, you may want to add text to your graph to present your data more clearly. You can place this *freeform,* or *unattached,* text anywhere on your graph and combine it with other objects to illustrate your data. Figure 13-19 shows freeform text being entered on a graph.

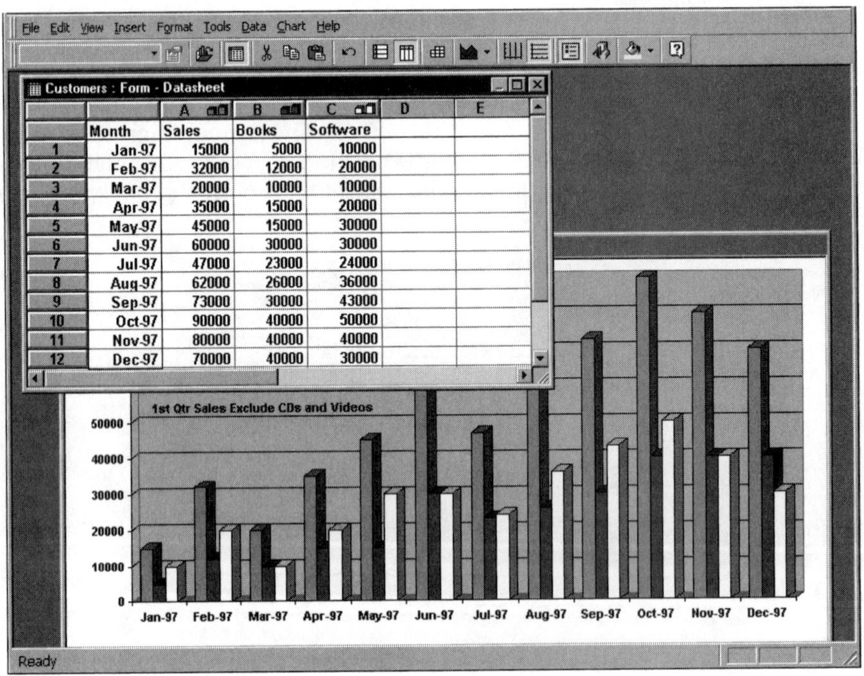

Figure 13-19: Freeform text on a graph.

To enter freeform text, simply type it in the graph and then drag it into position at the location where you want the text to be displayed. You also can format the text by right-clicking on it, choosing Format⇨Object, and then changing the font or any other text properties.

Note in Figure 13-19 that the sample data has been replaced with the data from the Excel worksheet.

Changing the axis label formats

You may have noticed that the y-axis is not formatted to represent dollars. The x-axis has been preformatted, in fact, to display the months in numerical rather than (the default) alphabetical order.

If you enter month data in your graph in the format of Jan, Feb, Mar, and Apr, for example, it is sorted in alphabetical order on the graph: Apr, Aug, Dec, Feb, and so on. To prevent Access from using this sort order, always enter your month data as numbers (1–12) or as true date data and then format the values by using the standard date format. In this example, the data was simply entered as Jan-97, Feb-97, Mar-97, and so on, and then it was formatted by using the mmm date format to display only the month. To format the x-axis, you select the axis and then choose Format⇨Selected Axis. Figure 13-20 shows the axis being formatted for the month. Note that a custom format is being used, not one of the date formats.

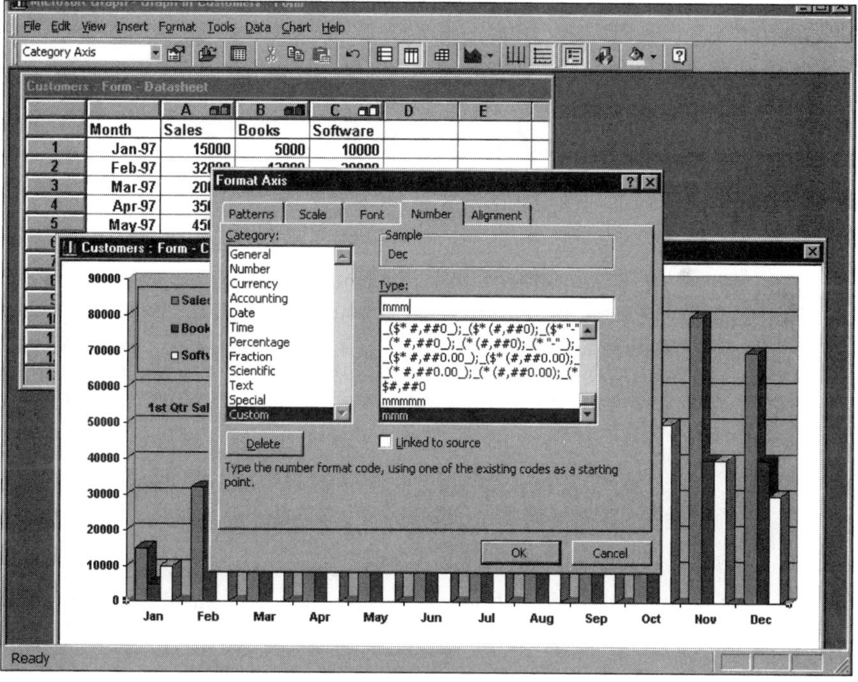

Figure 13-20: Formatting the Category axis.

To make the y-axis (the Series axis) represent dollar amounts, you have to format it as currency. To do so, select the y-axis and then choose Format⇨Selected Axis. In Figure 13-21, the Number tab is displayed, and Currency is highlighted.

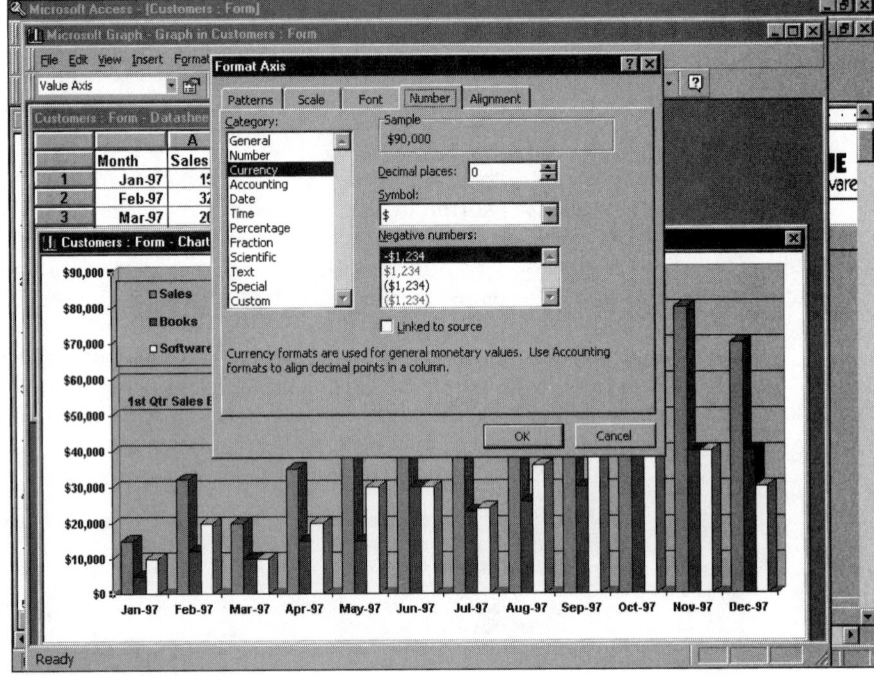

Figure 13-21: Formatting the Series axis.

Note in the figure that the graph area has been made larger and that it now occupies the entire window. The legend and graph title have been moved inside the graph area by simply selecting them and dragging them to another location. As you click your mouse with the pointer on different areas of the graph, you can see that almost everything can be selected and visually manipulated.

Changing the graph type

After you create your initial graph, you can experiment with graph types to make sure that you choose the type that most appropriately represents your data. Microsoft Graph provides a wide range of graphs from which to choose — just a few clicks of your mouse can change the type of graph presentation.

To choose a different graph type, choose Chart⇨Chart Type from the menu in the chart window to display the chart types. When you choose any of the graph options, a window opens to display all the graphing options available for the chosen graph type, as shown in Figure 13-22. You can click on the option you want in order to redisplay your graph with a new type.

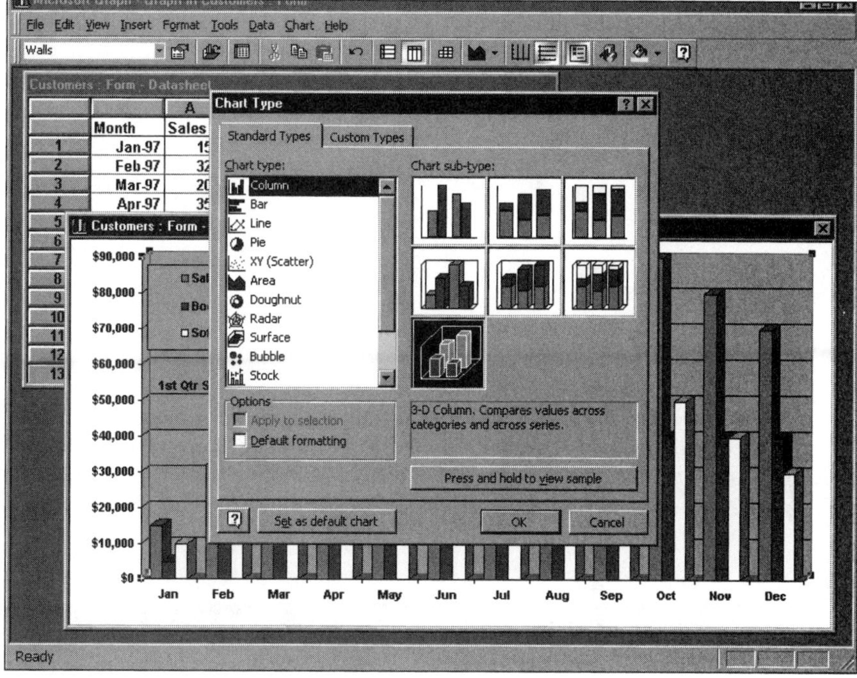

Figure 13-22: Choosing the chart type.

Changing the bar color and pattern

If you plan to print your graph in monochrome colors, you should always adjust the patterns so that they are not all solid colors. You can change the color or pattern of each bar by double-clicking on any bar in the category you want to select.

Modifying gridlines

Gridlines are lines that extend from an axis across the plotting area of a graph to help you read the graph properly. You can add two types of gridlines to a graph: an x-axis gridline and a y-axis gridline. If your graph is three-dimensional, an additional gridline is available for the z-axis.

You can add gridlines for any axis on a graph.

You can work with gridlines on your graph by choosing Chart⇨Chart Options and then choosing Gridlines from the tabbed dialog. On the left wall are the Series (y-axis) gridlines, and on the back wall are the Value (z-axis) gridlines. On the floor are the Category (x-axis) gridlines. You can set whether or not each of these walls have major or minor gridlines. When you double-click on one of these areas in the graph itself, you can change the line type used in it.

Manipulating three-dimensional graphs

For any of the three-dimensional chart options, you can modify these graph display characteristics:

- Elevation
- Perspective
- Rotation
- Scaling
- Angle and height of the axes

You can change the 3-D view by selecting the graph, right clicking, and selecting 3-D View. When the dialog box shown in Figure 13-23 appears, you can either enter the values for the various settings or use the six large buttons with arrows on them to rotate in real time the icon representing the graph. When you see a view you want to use for the graph, click on OK. Your chart then changes to that perspective.

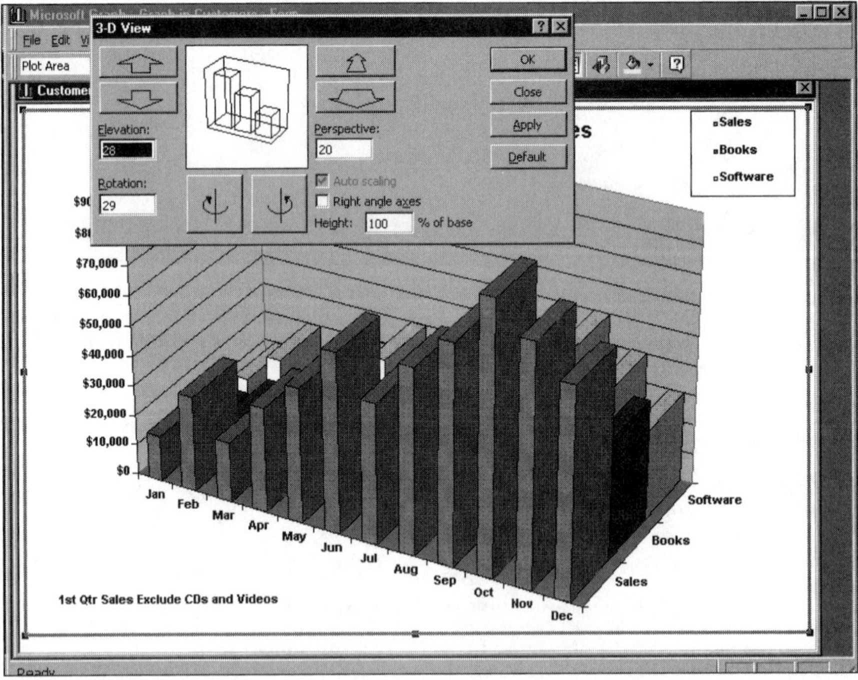

Figure 13-23: Using the Format 3-D View dialog box to change a graph's perspective.

The Elevation button controls the height at which you view the data in the graph. Elevation, measured in degrees, can range from –90 to 90 degrees.

An elevation of 0 degrees displays the graph as though your line of vision were level with the center of the graph. An elevation of 90 degrees shows the graph as it would look if you were viewing it from above the center of the graph; a –90-degree elevation shows the view you would see from below the center of the graph.

The Perspective button controls the amount of perspective in your graph. Adding more perspective makes data markers at the back of the graph look smaller than those at the front of the graph. This option provides a sense of distance to the data markers that are farther away. If your graph contains a large amount of data, you may want to use a greater perspective so that data markers in the back appear smaller relative to those near the front.

The perspective value is the ratio of the front of the graph to the back of the graph. The value can range from 0 to 100. A perspective of 0 makes the back edge of the graph as wide as the front edge. You can experiment with these settings to get the effect you want.

The Rotation buttons control the rotation of the entire plotting area. Rotation, measured in degrees, can range from 0 to 360. A rotation of 0 displays your graph as you view it from directly in front of it. A rotation of 180 degrees displays the graph as though you were viewing it from the back. (This setting visually reverses the plotting order of your data series.) A rotation of 90 degrees displays your graph as though you were viewing it from the center of the side wall.

If you have selected Right angle axes, you can use the Auto scaling checkbox to scale a three-dimensional graph so that it is closer in size to the two-dimensional graph using the same data. To activate this option, click on the Right angle axes and then select the Auto scaling checkbox so that a checkmark appears in the box. When you activate this option, whenever you switch from a two-dimensional graph to a three-dimensional graph, the scaling is adjusted automatically.

Two options in the Format 3-D View dialog box pertain specifically to the display of the axes. To control the orientation of the axes, you can click on the Right angle axes checkbox. All axes are then displayed at right angles to each other.

If the Right angle axes checkbox has a checkmark in it, you cannot specify the perspective for the three-dimensional view.

The Height text box contains the height of the z-axis and the walls relative to the width of the base of the graph. The height is measured as a percentage of the length of the x-axis. A height of 100 percent makes the height equal to the x-axis. Similarly, a height of 50 percent makes the height half the length of the x-axis. You can set this height percentage to a number greater than the 100 percent setting to make the height of the z-axis greater than the length of the x-axis.

If you change the Height setting, your change is not displayed in the sample graph shown in the 3-D View dialog box.

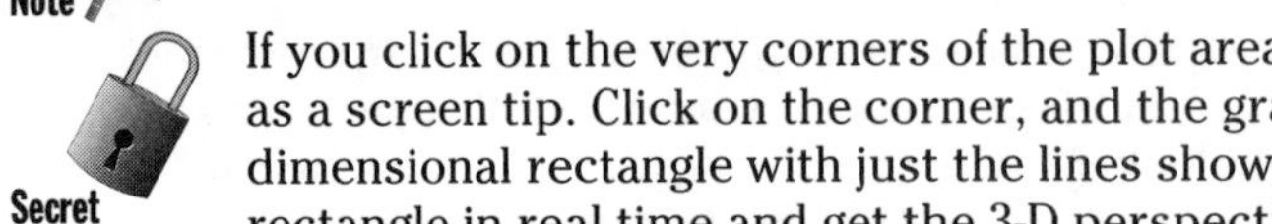

If you click on the very corners of the plot area, the word `corner` appears as a screen tip. Click on the corner, and the graph becomes a three-dimensional rectangle with just the lines showing. You can rotate this 3-D rectangle in real time and get the 3-D perspective you want.

After you have made the changes you want, you can choose File⇨Exit& Return the form name To in order to return to the Form Design dialog box. You may want to make one more change, however: Because a graph frame is really an unbound object frame, you can change its border type and background. Figure 13-24 shows the original graph after the border has been changed to an etched special effect and the background has been colored light gray to match the background of the form. This makes the graph stand out more than by using just a white, sunken background.

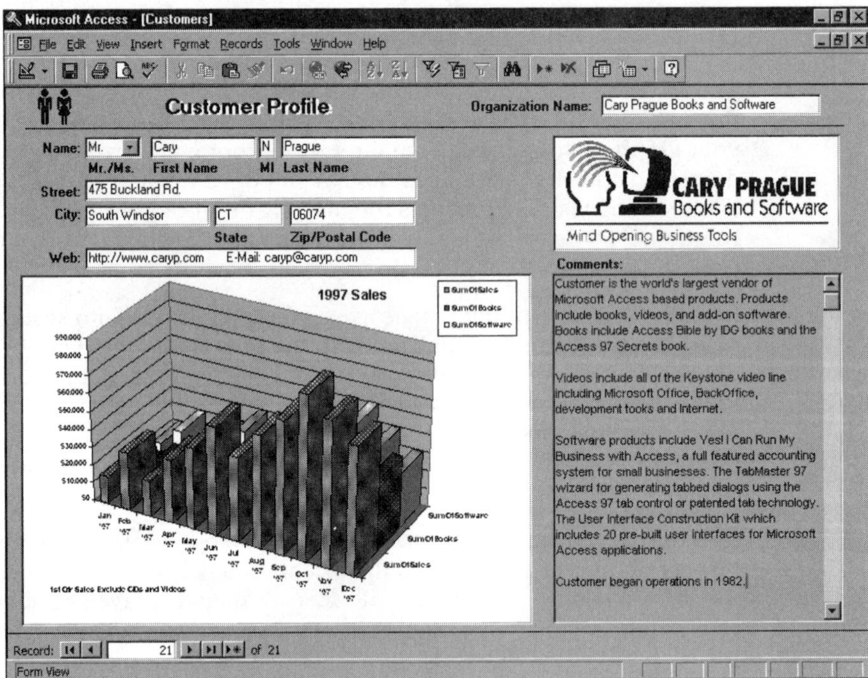

Figure 13-24: The final graph.

Now you understand the differences between linking graphs and other OLE objects to your forms and embedding the objects in your forms. You create a graph by using the Chart Wizard, and you use Microsoft Graph to customize the graph to fit your needs. You embed or link a full range of graphs to your forms with just a few keystrokes. Access, because of its Windows compatibility, has the power to share data, pictures, and other objects with any other OLE-compatible products.

Part V

System Functions

Chapter 14

Creating Multiuser Systems

In This Chapter

- Deciding on an installation configuration
- Splitting code objects from tables
- Identifying the current user of a database
- Controlling record locking

Multiuser applications exploit the power of real-time relational database systems. By placing a shared database file on a network, many different users can access up-to-the-minute data on an as-needed basis. Access includes quite a bit of built-in functionality and features that you can use to make your databases stable and secure in a multiuser situation. Making a database a true multiuser database is a little more involved than just placing the database on a network drive, however. When setting up an Access application for use on a network, you need to be concerned with a number of things, including the following:

- The placement of the application and database files
- The security permissions granted to database users and groups of users
- The protection of data integrity using Access's locking schemes

Cross-Reference

Security permissions are discussed in great detail in Chapter 17, "Securing an Access Application." This chapter focuses on the other elements of creating a multiuser database application in Access, such as increasing network Performance and record locking techniques.

Deciding on an Installation Configuration

The first decision you are faced with when creating a multiuser Access application is where to place the application files. You may elect to install Access in one of two ways:

- Install all Access files on the network, which allows all users to run the same copy of Access from the shared network drive.
- Install Access on each workstation, and have only the database file shared among the users on the network.

Running Access over the network

Many developers who are new to networking Access applications choose to install Access on the network drive, as described in the first option. Running Access over the network does have the following advantages:

- Little or no disk space is used on the workstations.
- Software updates are easy because only one set of files needs to be updated.

Although this is the easiest solution, it is in no way the *best* solution. While running Access, a large amount of disk access occurs. When all of the files are located on the network, this constant disk access must occur over the network lines. This disk time degrades network performance and significantly slows down the Access application.

Running Access on local workstations

To overcome the performance problem of running access over the network, you can run Access locally at each workstation, accessing only the shared data from the network drive. Because the network connection is used only for data transmission, not to load or execute Access, Access starts and runs faster.

The only real disadvantage in this situation is the increased maintenance overhead. When any installation of Access or your application database files needs to be updated, it needs to be updated at *every* workstation, not just once on the shared server.

Fortunately, Access's Setup Wizard has a feature to minimize the work of installing Access on a number of workstations: the *administrator switch*. When you run the Setup program with the administrator switch, both an administrator version of Access and a custom Setup program are placed on the network drive in the folder of your choosing. After this administrator version is in place on the network server, each workstation installs the program to its local drive by running this custom Setup program from the network server. The networked Setup eliminates the need to carry the CD-ROM (or worse — many diskettes) to each workstation.

To set up Access in this way, you must do the following:

1. Install Access to the network with the **/a** administrator switch (see Figure 14-1).
2. Place the shared database on the network drive.
3. Install Access on each workstation by running the Setup program from the network.

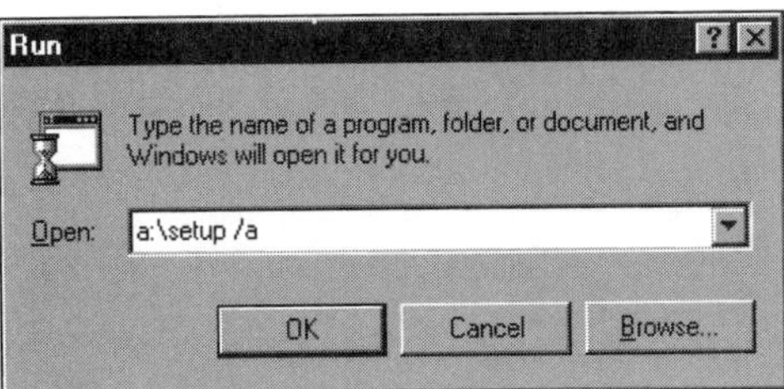

Figure 14-1: The /a switch installs the Administrative version of Access to the network drive.

If you create a custom setup program for your Access application using the ODE Tools' Setup Wizard, users of your database can perform an administrative install of your runtime Access application in the same way the install is performed for Access itself.

To have Access perform a typical installation automatically with no user prompts or interventions, use the **/q** parameter (for Quiet) when running the Setup program on the network drive from the workstation.

Sharing a workgroup file

If you are using user-level security for your database, you need to determine where to keep the shared workgroup files. Workgroup files (discussed in Chapter 15) contain all the user, group, and permissions information for the objects in your database. You can choose to install the workgroup file on each workstation, or you can place the workgroup file on the server for all users to share. Generally, it is much better to have just one workgroup file on the shared network drive and have all workstations use that shared workgroup file. By sharing a single workgroup file, maintenance is much easier and safer. For example, if a user has left your company, you can remove the user or related permissions from one shared workgroup file and that user will no longer have rights to the database. If, however, workgroup files are located on different workstations, you must distribute the changed workgroup file to all of the workstations. If you miss one individual workstation, the deleted user can use Access at the unchanged workstation and open the database with all the original rights he or she possessed.

Splitting Your Code Objects from Your Tables

The biggest disadvantage of running any application in a network environment is performance. To maximize your multiuser application performance, you should start by installing Access at the workstation level, using the technique discussed in the section "Running Access on local workstations."

This is only a start, however. In addition, you should split your tables from all the other objects in your database into a separate database (see Figure 14-2).

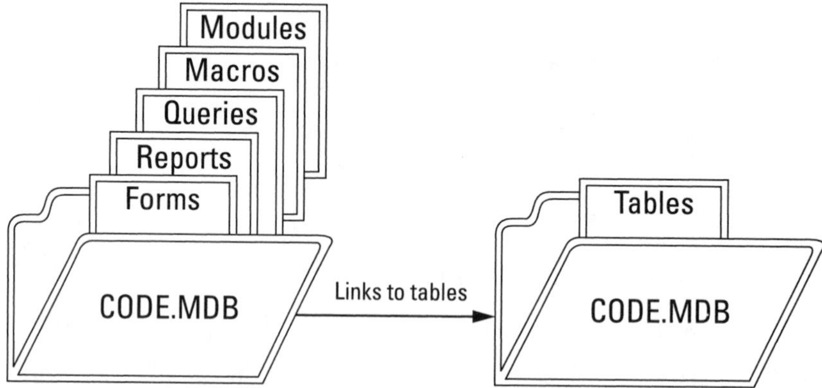

Figure 14-2: Splitting your objects into two databases greatly increases the performance of your Access application.

Splitting and using external tables is discussed in great detail in Chapter 17, "Securing an Access Application."

After successfully splitting your application's objects into two separate databases — a database that contains tables and a database that contains code objects (forms, macros, modules, queries, and reports) — you should distribute the code database to each workstation. Your application will run more quickly and forms will load much more quickly when the database containing your code objects is opened on the local workstation. The table database should reside on the shared network drive, with the workstations linking to that database. Splitting your database in this manner adds some maintenance overhead — all application database changes must be distributed to each workstation — but this also gives you two key advantages:

- All users are running the application at the best possible performance level.
- All users are sharing the same set of data.

Identifying the Current User of a Database

It is possible to retrieve the login name of the user currently using the database by using the `UserName` property of the `Workspace` object. If you do not employ user-level security, or if you let a number of users log into a database as the same user, this information may not be of use to you. The following procedure displays the user name of the currently logged in user:

```
Public Sub ShowUser()
      MsgBox "The current user is " & Workspaces(0).UserName
End Sub
```

Controlling Record Locking

The foundation of creating an efficient and dependable multiuser database is to understand and correctly apply *record locking*. Record locking determines which user can add, edit, or delete any record in the database at any given time. This is extremely important when multiple users access the data simultaneously; if two users attempt to update a record at the exact same time, Access needs to know whose changes to accept.

Note

When a lock is put on a record, any number of users can view the record in a read-only mode. Only the user who initiated the lock, however, has the capability to modify the locked record.

Jet stores all locking information in a file that has the same name as the opened database, but with the extension .ldb. If there is no .ldb file when the database is opened (such as when the database is opened for the first time), Access creates a new .ldb file for the database.

Secret

At times, you may get an error indicating that a database or object is exclusively locked by a user, even when no user is accessing the database. If this occurs, you should immediately repair and compact the database. If the error persists, the .ldb file may be corrupt; delete the .ldb file and try again to open the database.

Understanding page locking

Unlike many databases, Access employs *page locking* rather than record locking. A page is a block of data 2,048 bytes (2K) long. Access stores all data on the disk in pages. Pages can contain one record or a number of records, depending on the size of the record. Longer records may span multiple pages, whereas many small records may fit together on one page. When a record is locked, the entire page that contains the record is locked; consequently, all records on that page are locked. If the database contains a number of small records, it is possible that a user editing one record can prevent (lock out) other users from editing numerous other records.

Tip

Memo fields and OLE fields contain pointers to the actual data. This helps minimize the number of pages that are locked while editing one of these long fields.

You have control over when pages are locked and for how long they remain locked. It is important to understand the different types of locking and to apply the proper strategy for your situation. The two locking strategies you can use are as follows:

- Optimistic record locking
- Pessimistic record locking

Using optimistic record locking

In situations where it is uncommon for multiple users to access the same records at the same time, you can employ a method of locking that only locks the record (and the record's page) at the precise time that an update is written to the disk. In DAO code, the lock is placed only when the Update method is performed, and it is released after the update is completed. This prevents users from locking pages for long periods of time and greatly reduces the number of locking conflicts encountered. The disadvantage of optimistic record locking occurs when two users make changes to the same record and then attempt to commit (update) their changes to the database. Only the changes from the user who first triggers the update are saved; changes from the other user are lost. If users of your database will not often be modifying the same records at the same time, using optimistic locking will eliminate locking conflicts within your database almost entirely. Pursuit, a commercial Access application that is designed to be inherently multiuser, uses optimistic locking, allowing multiple users to work with the same records. Out of the hundreds upon hundreds of people using Pursuit in a network environment, almost none has ever encountered a locking conflict.

Using pessimistic record locking

When using pessimistic record locking, Access locks only the record currently being edited. In DAO code, a page is locked as soon as the `Edit` method is initiated on the Recordset. The lock is then released when a `CommitTrans`, `Rollback`, or `Update` is performed. After a record is locked, other users have only the capability to view the locked data, not modify or delete it. The drawback of pessimistic locking is that other users cannot edit any records that exist on the same page as the locked record (as with optimistic locking); records and their pages stay locked for a much longer time. You should only employ pessimistic record locking if you have a very specific reason to do so, such as when developing accounting applications where data integrity needs to be assured by wrapping all debits and credits in transactions.

Setting a database's multiuser defaults

Default record locking settings can be set for an entire database. These settings are located on the Advanced tab of the Options dialog box (see Figure 14-3) accessed from the Tools⇨Options menu item. In addition, you can set multiuser options in VBA code by using the `SetOption` method of the `Application` object.

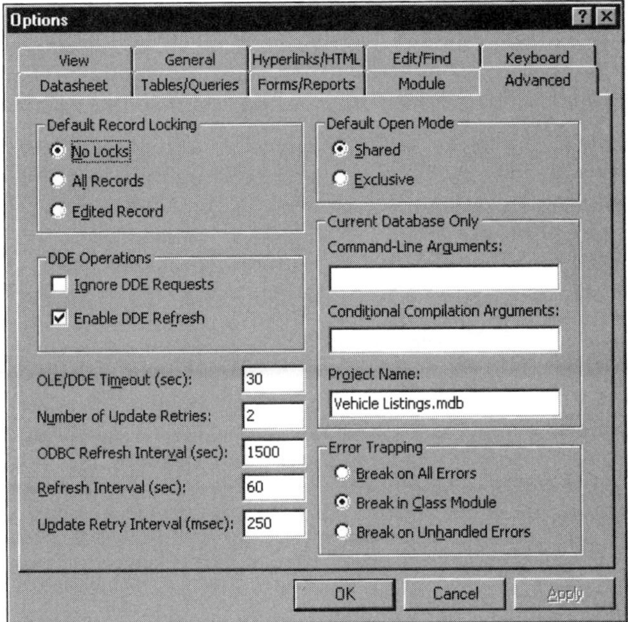

Figure 14-3: Default multiuser options are set for a database by using the Options dialog box.

There are basically four locking parameters defined on this tab:

- The default locking scheme to use
- The default open mode for the database
- The interval to pass before Access attempts to retry saving a changed record that is locked
- The number of retries Access will attempt in order to update a locked record

Setting the default open mode for a database

The default open mode dictates whether the database is opened exclusively or for shared access. A database can be opened exclusively only if no other users currently have the database open. After a database is opened exclusively, no other users can open the database. If a user attempts to open a database that has already been opened exclusively by another user, he will receive the error `Database <name> is exclusively locked`. To use Access in a multiuser environment, all users must open the database in Shared mode.

You can prevent users from opening a database exclusively by removing the Open Exclusive permission for the user to the Database object. (For information on adding and removing permissions, see Chapter 15.)

Setting locking defaults

The Default Record Locking setting dictates what locking scheme to employ, unless otherwise specified in the application. Table 14-1 shows you the available locking options.

Table 14-1 Default Record Locking Options

Option	*Description*
No Locks	Does not lock the record you're editing; only locks the record during the update. This is also referred to as optimistic locking.
All Records	Locks all records in the form or datasheet (and underlying tables) you're editing for as long as you have it open.
Edit Records	Locks the record you're editing. The is also referred to as pessimistic locking.

When using transaction processing in VBA code, pessimistic locking is used regardless of the settings for the Recordset being edited.

If you set the default to All Records, all records in a Recordset or underlying table are locked when a user initiates an edit of a record. If a user starts to change a record and then goes to lunch, he or she leaves the entire underlying Recordset in a locked state. For this reason, you should set the default to All Records only when absolutely necessary.

Setting the retry interval for updating locked records

The final group of locking settings dictates how many times Access attempts to update a record that is locked by another user and how long to wait between attempts. Unless you are accessing a database using ODBC, the settings you need to be concerned with are as follows:

- Number of Update Retries
- Refresh Interval
- Update Retry Interval

If a user attempts to update a record that has a lock placed on it, Access waits the specified Update Retry Interval (in milliseconds) and attempts to update the record again. If the record is still locked, Access continues attempting to update the record until it is successful or reaches the Number of Update Retries. If you use the default locking scheme of No Locks, the default number and interval should be sufficient. If you use the All Records or Edit Records locking scheme, you may need to experiment with the settings to provide satisfactory results. If you encounter a number of locking conflicts, try increasing first the Refresh Interval then the Number of Update Retries to reduce the conflicts.

Setting the record locking scheme for forms

It is possible to override the default record locking scheme for a form. To specifically set the record locking scheme for a form's underlying recordset or table, you set the `Record Locks` property of the form (see Figure 14-4).

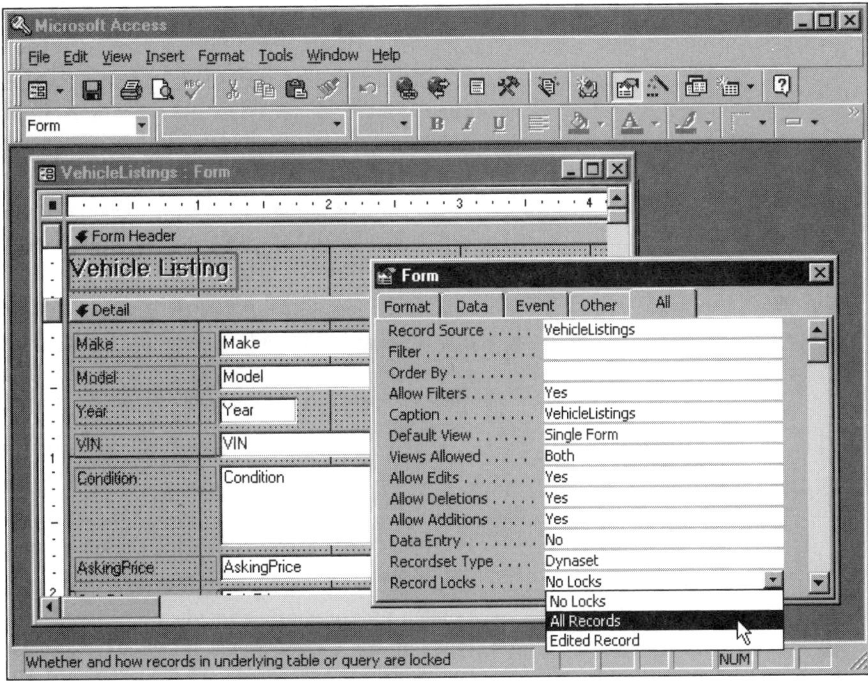

Figure 14-4: You can control the type of record locking employed at the form level.

In general, the default record locking setting should be sufficient for most of the forms in your database. Being able to change the setting at the form level, however, allows greater control over the locking of Recordsets.

Setting the record locking scheme for Recordsets

You can override the default record locking when creating a Recordset in VBA code. The `OpenRecordset` method of the database object enables you to specify a constant that dictates the locking scheme to use on the Recordset. Following is the format for opening a Recordset in VBA code:

```
Set recordset = object.OpenRecordset (source, type, options, _
lockedits)
```

By specifying constants for the `options` and `LockEdits` parameters, you control the locking method employed on the `Recordset` object.

Table 14-2 lists the available constants for the `options` parameter.

Table 14-2 Available Constants for the Options Parameter

Constant	*Description*
`dbAppendOnly`	Enables users to append new records to the Recordset, but prevents them from editing or deleting existing records (Microsoft Jet dynaset-type Recordset only).
`dbSQLPassThrough`	Passes an SQL statement to a Microsoft Jet-connected ODBC data source for processing (Microsoft Jet snapshot-type Recordset only).
`dbSeeChanges`	Generates a runtime error if one user changes data that another user is editing (Microsoft Jet dynaset-type Recordset only). This is useful in applications where multiple users have simultaneous read/write access to the same data.
`dbDenyWrite`	Prevents other users from modifying or adding records (Microsoft Jet Recordset objects only).
`dbDenyRead`	Prevents other users from reading data in a table (Microsoft Jet table-type Recordset only).
`dbForwardOnly`	Creates a forward-only Recordset (Microsoft Jet snapshot-type Recordset only). This is provided only for backward compatibility—you should use the `dbOpenForwardOnly` constant in the type argument instead of using this option.
`dbReadOnly`	Prevents users from making changes to the Recordset (Microsoft Jet only). The `dbReadOnly` constant in the `lockedits` argument replaces this option, which is provided only for backward compatibility.
`dbRunAsync`	Runs an asynchronous query (ODBCDirect workspaces only).

Constant	Description
dbExecDirect	Runs a query by skipping SQLPrepare and directly calling SQLExecDirect (ODBCDirect workspaces only). Use this option only when you're not opening a Recordset based on a parameter query. For more information, see the *Microsoft ODBC 3.0 Programmer's Reference.*
dbInconsistent	Allows inconsistent updates (Microsoft Jet dynaset-type and snapshot-type Recordset objects only).
dbConsistent	Allows only consistent updates (Microsoft Jet dynaset-type and snapshot-type Recordset objects only).

The constants dbConsistent and dbInconsistent are mutually exclusive, and using both causes an error. Supplying a LockEdits argument when options uses the dbReadOnly constant also causes an error.

To specify more than one parameter, such as dbDenyRead and dbDenyWrite, separate them in the parameter section with a plus (+) sign, as follows:

```
Set rsObject = dbObject.OpenRecordset ("tblTableName", dbDenyRead + _
dbDenyWrite, dbAppendOnly)
```

Table 14-3 lists all of the constants for the LockEdits argument.

Table 14-3 Constants for the LockEdits Argument

Constant	Description
dbReadOnly	Prevents users from making changes to the Recordset (default for ODBCDirect workspaces). You can use dbReadOnly in either the options argument or the LockEdits argument, but not both. If you use it for both arguments, a run-time error occurs.
dbPessimistic	Uses pessimistic locking to determine how changes are made to the Recordset in a multiuser environment. The page containing the record you're editing is locked as soon as you use the Edit method (default for Microsoft Jet workspaces).
dbOptimistic	Uses optimistic locking to determine how changes are made to the Recordset in a multiuser environment. The page containing the record is not locked until the Update method is executed.
dbOptimisticValue	Uses optimistic concurrency based on row values (ODBCDirect workspaces only).
dbOptimisticBatch	Enables batch optimistic updating (ODBCDirect workspaces only).

For example, to open a table as a Recordset object so that other users can only add new records and where pessimistic locking is enforced, you use a line of code like the following:

```
Set rsObject = dbObject.OpenRecordset ("tblTableName", dbOpenTable, _
dbAppendOnly, dbPessimistic)
```

In addition to specifying a LockEdits parameter when opening the Recordset, you can set the locking scheme in code by setting the LockEdits property of the Recordset object. If you set LockEdits to True, pessimistic locking is used; setting LockEdits to False enforces optimistic locking on the Recordset.

Refreshing DAO collections in a multiuser environment

DAO collections in VBA code are treated like snapshots: If one user makes modifications to a collection a different user is referencing in code (by adding, modifying, or deleting objects in the collection), the collection object referenced by the other user does not reflect the changes until the collection object is refreshed using the Refresh method. The following code refreshes the table object named tblDefObject:

```
tblDefObject.Refresh
```

The Refresh method may take some time on very large collections. Use it only when necessary.

Although it takes some extra consideration and a little time to properly implement, Access's relational database power and flexibility really shine when used correctly in a multiuser environment.

Chapter 15

Distributing Applications with the Office Developer Edition

In This Chapter

- Defining the startup parameters of the application
- Testing the application
- Polishing the application
- Creating comprehensive and intuitive menus and toolbars
- Bulletproofing the application
- Separating the code objects from the tables in the application
- Documenting the application
- Creating a help system for the application
- Implementing a security structure for the application
- Creating distribution disks using the Access Developer's Toolkit

You are indeed lucky if you have the luxury of developing only single user, in-house applications and never have to worry about distributing an application within a company or across the country. Most developers have to worry about application distribution sooner or later. You don't have to develop commercial software to be concerned with distribution — when you develop an application to be run on a dozen workstations in one organization, you need to distribute your application.

This chapter covers all the above points to some degree. However, because some of the listed items, such as splitting tables and creating help systems, are covered in detail in other chapters, this chapter focuses primarily on using the Setup Wizard in the Office Developer Edition Tools.

Preparing Your Application for Distribution

There are many issues to be concerned with when preparing an Access application for distribution. Distributing your application properly not only makes installing and using the application easier for the end user but also makes updating and maintaining the application easier for yourself. In addition, you can lower the amount of support required for your application by including comprehensive online help.

Defining the startup parameters of the application

An Access database has a number of startup parameters that can greatly simplify the process of preparing your database for distribution (see Figure 15-1). You can access the startup parameters for a database by selecting Tools⇨Startup menu or by right-clicking on the database window and selecting Startup. You can still use an Autoexec macro to execute initialization code, but the Startup parameters form enables you to set up certain aspects of your application to reduce the amount of startup code you have to write. It is extremely important to set up the startup parameters correctly before distributing your Access application.

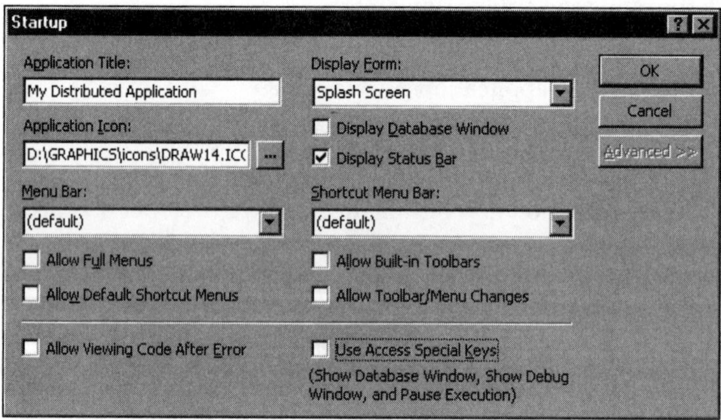

Figure 15-1: The Startup parameters form enables you to take control of your application from the moment a user starts it.

Setting the Application Title

The text you provide in the Application Title field displays on the main Access title bar. You should always specify an Application Title for your distributed applications. If you do not, Microsoft Access appears on the title bar of your application.

Application Icon

The icon you specify on the Startup form is displayed on the title bar of your application and in the task switcher (Alt-Tab) of Windows 95. If you do not specify your own icon, Access displays the default Access icon, so you should always provide an application-specific icon for your application.

Menu Bar

The menu bar field is used to specify a custom menu to use as the default menu bar. If you do not supply a custom menu bar, Access uses its own default menu bar, which may be inappropriate for your application.

Allow Full Menus

This setting determines whether Access displays its menus with all options available to the user or if it disables items used to create or modify objects. If you supply custom menus for all your forms and reports and set the Menu Bar property to a custom menu bar, this setting has no effect.

If you supply your own menu bars or use Access's menu bars but do not allow full menus, you must deselect Allow Built-in Toolbars or supply your own custom toolbars for each form. If you do not, the built-in toolbars may make available features to which you do not want users to have access.

Allow Default Shortcut Menus

The Allow Default Shortcut Menus setting determines whether or not Access displays its own default shortcut menus when a user left-clicks on an object.

Display Form

The form you select in this field is immediately displayed when your application is run. When the form is loaded, the `Form Load` event fires if there is any code in it, eliminating the need to use an Autoexec macro. You should consider using a splash screen (discussed later in this chapter) as your startup Display Form.

Display Database Window

With most distributed applications, you may never want your users to have direct access to any of your forms or other database objects. Deselecting this option hides the Database Window from the user at startup. Unless you also deselect the option Use Access Special Keys (discussed later), users can press F11 to unhide the database window.

Display Status Bar

You can deselect the Display Status Bar option to completely remove the status bar from the screen. However, the status bar is an incredibly informative and easy-to-use tool; it displays the various key-states automatically, as well as displaying Status Bar Text for the active control. Instead of hiding the status bar, you should make full use of it and only disable it if you have a very good reason to do so.

Shortcut Menu Bar

This setting is similar to the Menu Bar option discussed previously, only it allows you to specify a menu bar to use as the default shortcut menu bar when a user right-clicks on an object. Using custom shortcut menus that have functionality specific to your application is always preferable.

Allow Built-in Toolbars

Deselecting this option prevents Access from displaying any of its built-in toolbars. In general, you should always deselect this option and provide your own custom toolbars that you can display using the `ShowToolbar` method in the `Activate` event of your forms.

Allow Toolbar/Menu Changes

Deselecting this option prevents users from modifying either Access's built-in toolbars or your own toolbars, whichever you choose to use. Once again, you almost always want to deselect this item to prevent your users from gaining access to features that you do not want them to have.

Allow Viewing Code After Error

The Allow Viewing Code After Error setting is not applicable if you distribute your application with the Office Developer Edition Tool's Setup Wizard. However, if your users run your application with a full version of Access and you select this option, they can access your code if an error occurs by clicking on the Debug button in the error dialog box. You should always deselect this option when distributing your application.

Use Access Special Keys

If you select this option, users of your application can use keys specific to the Access environment to circumvent some security measures, such as hiding the database window. If you deselect this option, the following keys are disabled:

- F11 and Alt+F1. These keys show the database window if it is hidden and bring it to the front.
- Ctrl+Break. This key causes a break in your code and then displays a code module with the currently executing procedure displayed.
- Ctrl+F11. This key is used to toggle between using a custom menu bar for a form and using a built-in menu bar.

You should always deselect this option when distributing the application.

Using the Startup options form saves you many lines of code that you would ordinarily need to perform the same functions and allows you to control your application's interface from the moment the user starts it. Always verify the Startup options before distributing your application.

Testing the application before distribution

After you finish adding features and have everything in place within your application, you need to take some time to thoroughly test the application. Testing may sound obvious, but this step apparently is overlooked by many developers and is evident by the amount of buggy software appearing on the shelves of your local software stores. If you don't believe this to be true, check out the software support forums on CompuServe; almost every major commercial software application has some patch available or known bugs that need to be addressed.

Distributing an application that is 100 percent bug free is almost impossible. The nature of the beast in software development is that if you write a program, someone can and will find a way to break it. Specific individuals even seem to have a black cloud above their heads and can usually break an application (hit a critical bug) within minutes of using it. If you know of such people, hire them! They can be a great asset when testing your application.

While working through the debugging process of an application, categorize your bugs into one of three categories:

- **Category 1: Major ship-killing bug.** These bugs are absolutely unacceptable, such as numbers in an accounting application that don't add up the way they should or a routine that consistently causes the application to terminate unexpectedly. If you ship an application with known Category 1 bugs, prepare yourself for a lynch party from your customers!
- **Category 2: Major bug that has a workaround.** Category 2 bugs are fairly major bugs, but they do not stop users from performing their tasks. For instance, a toolbar button that does not call a procedure correctly is a bug. If the toolbar button is the only way to run the procedure, this bug is a Category 1 bug. If, however, a corresponding menu item calls the procedure correctly, the bug is a Category 2 bug. Shipping an application with a Category 2 bug is sometimes necessary. Although shipping a bug is officially a no-no, deadlines sometimes dictate that exceptions need to be made. Category 2 bugs will annoy your users but should not send them into fits.

  If you ship an application with known Category 2 bugs, document them! Some developers have a "Don't say anything and act surprised" attitude when users find a Category 2 bug. This attitude can frustrate users and waste considerable amounts of their time by forcing them to discover not only the problem but also the solution. For example, if you were to ship an application with the Category 2 bug just described, you could include a statement in your application's README file that reads something like this:

  ```
  The foobar button on the XYZ form does not correctly call
  procedure suchandsuch. Please use the corresponding menu
  item suchandsuch found on the tools pull-down menu. A
  patch will be made available as soon as possible.
  ```

- **Category 3: Small bugs and minor nits.** Category 3 bugs are small issues that in no way affect the workings of your application. They may be misspellings of captions or incorrect colors of text boxes. Category 3 bugs should be fixed whenever possible but should never take precedence over Category 1 bugs, and they should take precedence over Category 2 bugs only when they are so extreme that the application looks completely unacceptable.

By categorizing your bugs and approaching them systematically, you can create a program that looks and behaves as its users think it should. Sometimes you may feel like you will never finish your Category 1 list, but you will. You will surely be smiling the day you check your bug sheet and realize that you're down to a few Category 2s and a dozen or so Category 3s! Although you may be tempted to skip this beta testing phase of development, don't. You will only pay for it in the long run.

Not all Access features are available when an application is run with the Access runtime (discussed with the Setup Wizard later in this chapter). You can operate in the runtime environment and use the full version of Access to test for problems with your code and with the runtime environment by using the `/Runtime` command line option when starting your Access application. Click on Run on the Windows Start menu or create a shortcut. The following example command line starts Access and opens the Invoices database in the runtime environment:

```
C:\OFFICE95\ACCESS\MSACCESS.EXE /RUNTIME
C:\MYAPPS\INVOICES.MDB
```

You should always test and debug your application in the runtime environment if you plan to distribute the application with the Office Developer Tool's Setup Wizard.

Polishing your application

When your application has been thoroughly tested and appears ready for distribution, spend some time polishing your application. Polishing your application consists of

- Giving your application a consistent look and feel
- Adding common, professional components
- Adding clear and concise pictures to buttons
- Using common, understandable field labels and button captions

Giving your application a consistent look and feel

First and foremost you should decide on some design standards and apply them to your application. This is incredibly important if you want your application to look professionally produced. Figure 15-2 shows a form with samples of different styles of controls.

You must make design decisions such as

- Will text boxes be sunken, flat with a border, flat without a border, chiseled, or raised?
- What backcolor will the text boxes be?
- What color will the forms be?
- Will you use chiseled borders to separate related items or opt for a sunken or raised border?
- What size will buttons on forms be?
- For forms that have similar buttons, such as Close and Help, in what order will the buttons appear?
- Which accelerator keys will you use on commonly used buttons such as Close and Help?

Making your application look and work in a consistent manner is the single most important thing you can do to make it appear professional. For ideas on design standards to implement in your applications, spend some time working with some of your favorite programs and see what standards they utilize. In the area of look and feel, copying from another developer is generally not considered plagiarism but rather often looked upon as a compliment. Copying does not extend, however, to utilizing another application's icons or directly copying the look and feel of a competitor's product; this is very bad practice. An example of a good look and feel is the Microsoft Office Compatible program. An application may be certified Office Compatible by meeting certain user-interface requirements laid out by Microsoft Corporation. One such program is Pursuit (see Figure 15-3). Pursuit is a certified Office Compatible application developed in Visual Basic using the Jet engine. Pursuit uses the same menu structures as all the Office applications such as Word, Access, Excel, and so on. In addition, toolbars are also similar because Pursuit uses the same positioning guidelines and, where applicable, the same button image as Microsoft uses. The benefits of making an application look like an Office application are saving the developer time by giving clear and concise guidelines for interface features and helping end users by lowering the learning curve of the application.

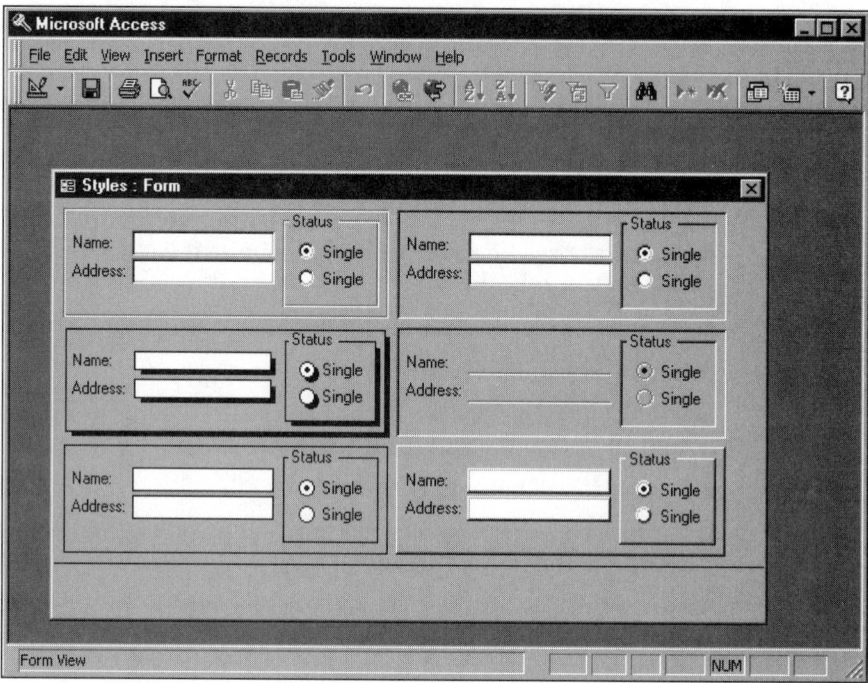

Figure 15-2: You can decide on any interface style you like for your application. However, once you decide on a style, use it consistently.

Although you may not want to have your application independently tested and certified Office Compatible, you may want to check out the specifications and use some of the ideas presented to help you get started designing your own consistent application interfaces.

Adding common professional components

Cross-Reference

Most commercial/professional applications have some similar components. The two most common components are the splash screen and the about box. The splash screen is discussed in greater detail in Chapter 3, "Optimizing Performance." Be aware that the splash screen not only aids in increasing perceived speed of an application but also gives the application a polished, professional appearance from the moment a user runs the program. Figure 15-4 shows the implementation of Pursuit's splash screen.

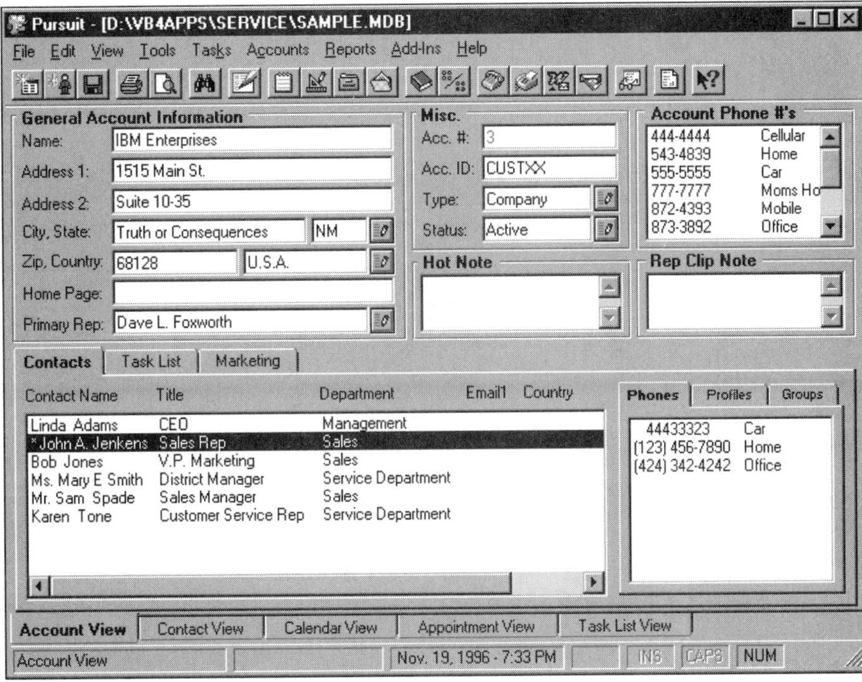

Figure 15-3: Pursuit utilizes the Office interface to make it much more intuitive and to lower the learning curve.

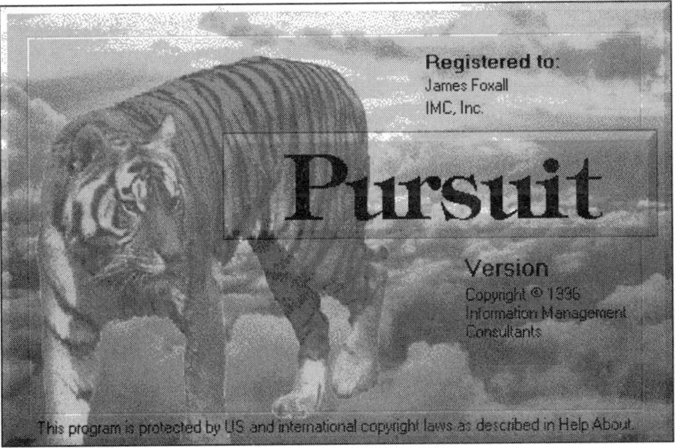

Figure 15-4: A splash screen not only increases perceived speed of your application but also gives your application a professional appearance.

Figure 15-5 shows the very same form used for the Access version of Pursuit's splash screen. This form is included on the CD-ROM that comes with this book. Import this form into your application and use it as a template for creating your own splash screen.

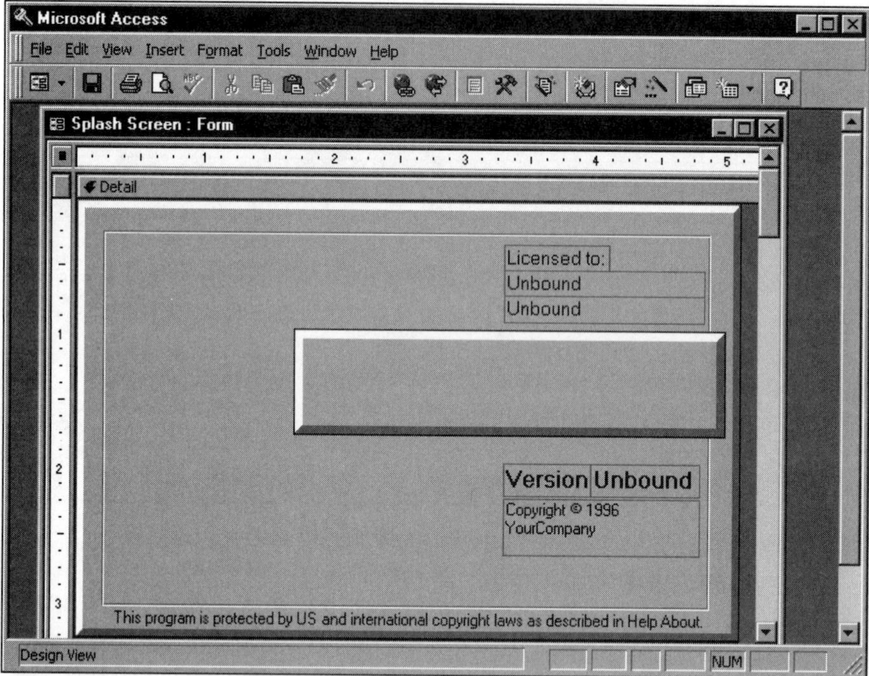

Figure 15-5: Use this form as a template to create your own splash screens for your applications.

Your splash screen should contain the following items:

- The application's title
- The application's version number
- Your company information
- A copyright notice

In addition, you may want to include the licensee information and/or a picture on the splash screen. If you use a picture on your splash screen, make it relevant to your application's function. For example, Word 6.0's splash screen shows a pen and a piece of paper. If you like, you can use clip art for your splash screen; just be sure that the picture is clear and concise and doesn't interfere with the text information presented on your splash screen.

To implement the splash screen, have your application load the splash form before it does anything else (consider making your splash screen the Start form). When your application finishes all of its initialization procedures, close the form. Make the splash form a light form and be sure to convert any bitmaps you place on your splash screen to pictures to decrease the splash form's load time.

The second component that you should implement is an about box (see Figure 15-6). The about box should contain your company and copyright information, as well as the application name and current version. Including your application's licensee information (if you keep such information) in the about box is a good idea as well. The about box serves as legal notice of your ownership and makes your application easier to support by giving your users easy access to the version information. Some advanced about boxes call other forms that display system information (Figure 15-6 has one additional button – System Info). You can make the about boxes as fancy as you want, but usually a simple one works just fine.

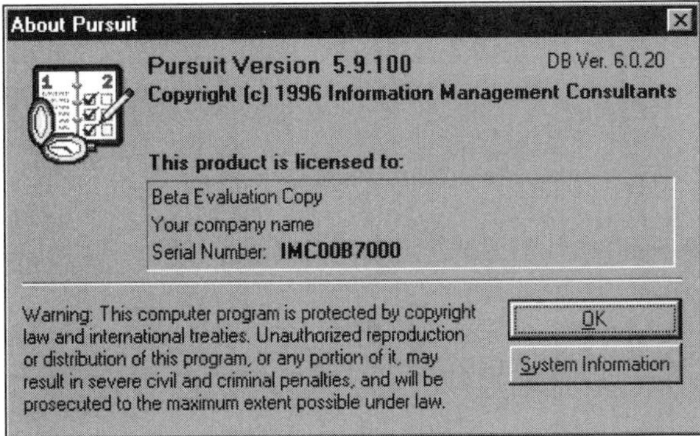

Figure 15-6: The implementation of an about box is a polishing technique that also provides useful information to the user and protects your legal interests.

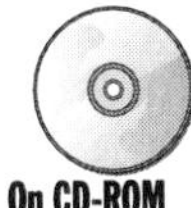

The form shown in Figure 15-7 is a template about box that can be found on the CD-ROM that accompanies this book. Import this form into your application and customize it to fit your needs. The about box should be a modal form (it should keep the focus until the form is closed) and should not have minimize or maximize buttons available to the user.

The about box should be accessible from a Help pull-down menu on all menu bars. The submenu title should be About MyApplication. Of course, substitute MyApplication with your application's actual name.

The splash screen and the about box may seem trivial, but they can greatly enhance your application's appeal. They take little time to implement and should be included in all your distributed applications.

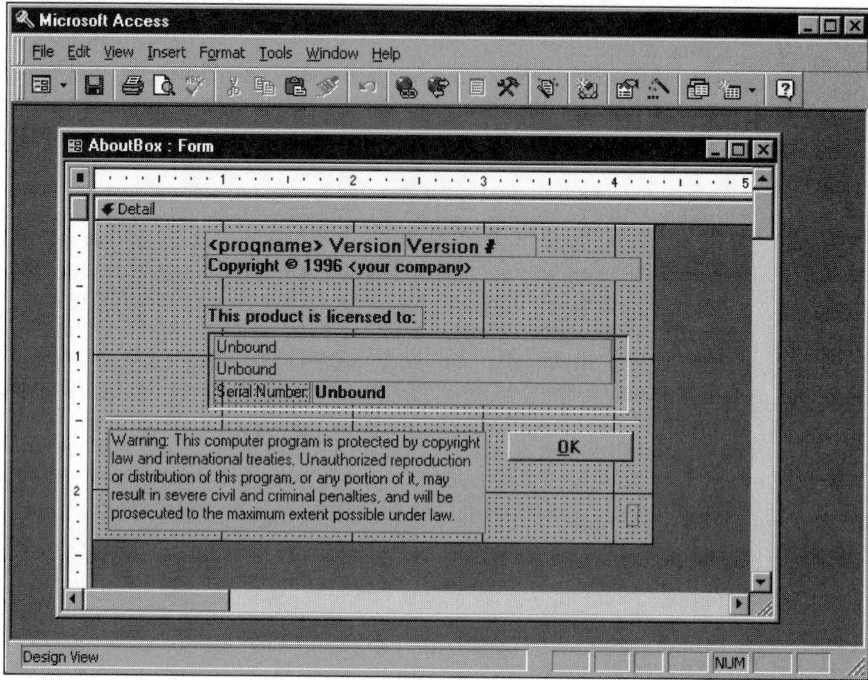

Figure 15-7: You can import and customize this about box template form to meet your needs.

Adding clear and concise pictures to buttons

Most users love pictures, and most developers love to use pictures on buttons. Studies have shown that clear and concise pictures are more intuitive to understand and are more easily recognizable than textual captions. Most developers, however, are not graphic artists and usually slap together buttons made from any clipart images that are handy. These ugly buttons make an application look clumsy and unprofessional. In addition, pictures that do not clearly show the function of the button make the application harder to use.

If your budget permits, consider hiring a professional design firm to create your button pictures. A number of professional image galleries and a number of tools to create and edit buttons are available.

Select or create pictures that end users easily recognize. Avoid abstract pictures or pictures that require specific knowledge to understand them, such as wiring symbology. Figure 15-8 shows a sample of good picture buttons.

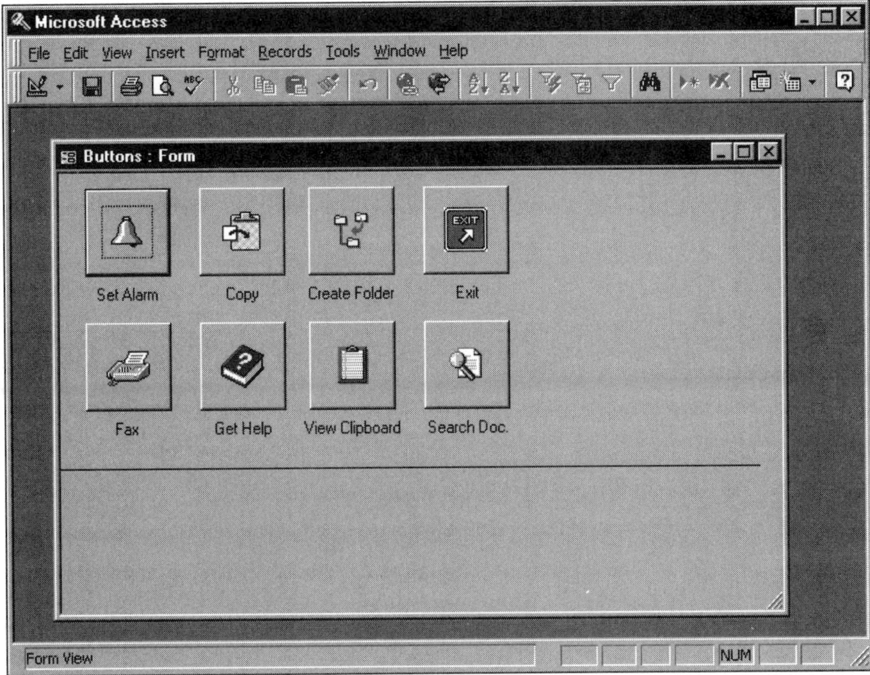

Figure 15-8: Use buttons with common or easy-to-recognize images that convey the function of the button.

Well-thought-out picture buttons can really make your application look outstanding, as well as easier to use.

Using understandable field labels and button captions

You should attempt to standardize the field labels and captions in your application. For example, if you call a database field Item Comment on one form, you should call it Item Comment on all other forms that contain the field. If you call it Item Remark on one form and Item Comment on another form, you will confuse the users.

Tip

If you use the Form Wizards to create forms based on the same tables, you can ensure consistent field labels by assigning captions to the table's fields in Table Design view. To do this, open the table in Design view, select the field to create a caption for, and enter the caption text in the `Caption` property of the field as shown in Figure 15-9. Whenever you drag the field onto a form or create a form from the table with a wizard, the proper caption is used.

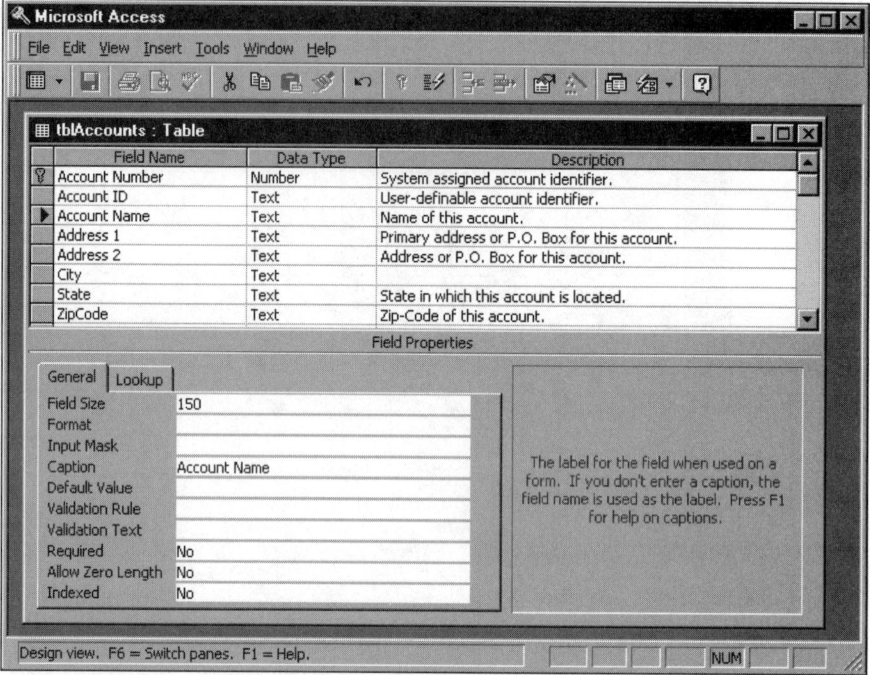

Figure 15-9: You can save yourself time and eliminate consistency errors by giving fields captions in table design view.

Just as important (and probably more so) is standardizing button captions. For example, if you have buttons on many different forms that call context-sensitive help for your application, you should not have one button with the label Help while another form has a button labeled Get Help. In addition to standardizing button captions, you should always standardize button placement where applicable. For example, if you have many different forms that always have OK, Cancel, and Help buttons, these buttons should always appear in the same order (see Figure 15-10). You may have additional buttons, but these three should always appear in a consistent place and should also adhere to a specific order.

For application-specific functions, give your button captions intuitive and descriptive text, but avoid being too wordy. Also, most professional applications never have buttons with multiple line captions, so you should always try to avoid them. Use the same labels and captions throughout your application whenever possible. Never change standard captions such as Close or OK unless absolutely necessary; you will only confuse the end users.

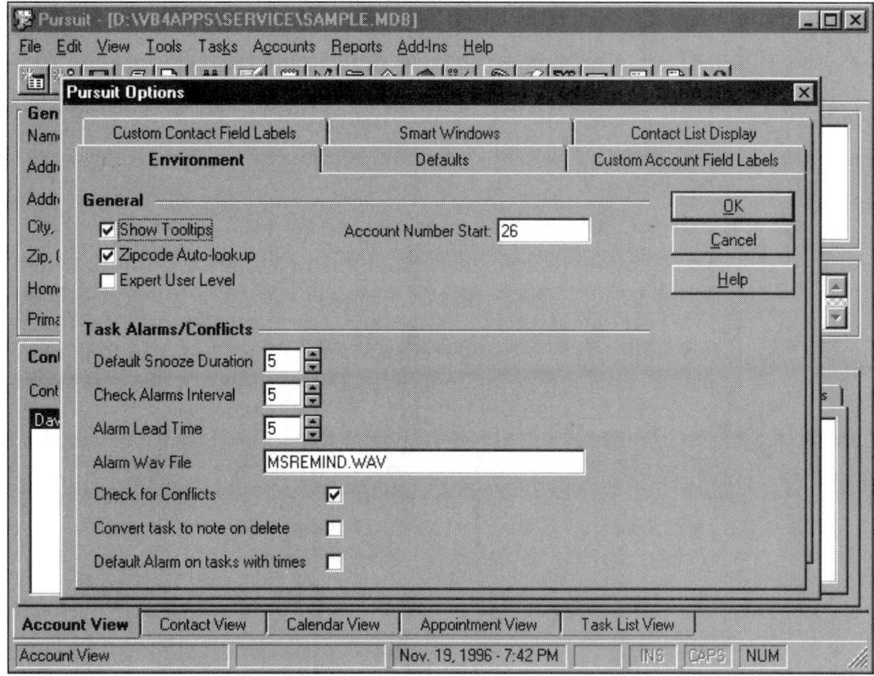

Figure 15-10: Tabbed dialog forms often have similar sets of buttons. Like buttons should stay consistent across tabs as well as forms.

Creating comprehensive and intuitive menus and toolbars

Before you even consider distributing an application, you need to make the application as intuitive as possible. Menus and toolbars are absolutely vital for usability with any Windows application. Chapter 9, “Working with Menus, Toolbars, and the Database Explorer,” is devoted to teaching you how to create great menus and toolbars.

Bulletproofing an application

Bulletproofing your application is an additional stage that should be completed parallel with debugging and performed again after the application is working and debugged. Bulletproofing an application is the process of making the application idiot-proof. It involves trapping errors that can be caused by users, such as invalid data entry, attempting to run a function when the application is not ready to run the function, and allowing users to click on a Calculate button before all needed data has been entered. To bulletproof your applications, you can

- Use modal forms for critical data entry.
- Test conditions before executing a function.
- Disable buttons and fields when they are not applicable.
- Use error trapping on all VBA procedures.

Using modal forms for critical data entry

When it is vital that certain data be entered as a complete step before a function can be executed, use a modal form to capture the data. Figure 15-11 shows a modal form used to enter modem settings before the application can dial the phone. Using modal forms causes users to deal with the requested information immediately before they can move forward. If the form was nonmodal, users could possibly either click on a button or select a menu item that calls a function that may conflict with the auto-dialer (such as launching fax software that needs to use the same communications port) or change data that may be critical for the dialing function (such as changing a phone number after the auto-dialer was initiated). Whenever possible, you should allow users to Cancel the function.

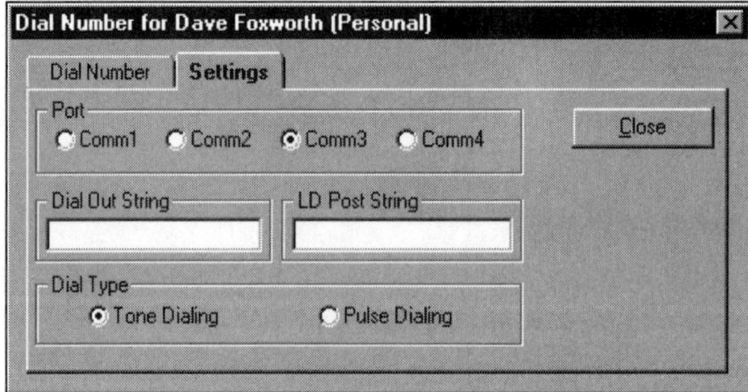

Figure 15-11: Modal forms force the user to deal with specific pieces of information at one time.

Testing conditions before executing functions

Rather than check for certain conditions at various stages (which could cause the function to perform a task for a long time before signaling the user that more information is needed) or risk the function generating an error, check ahead of time for the conditions on which a function relies. For example, most Access applications work with lists of items. Providing the user with buttons to perform list functions such as adding or deleting a list item is quite common. Figure 15-12 shows a form containing a list with buttons that enable the user to work with the list's contents.

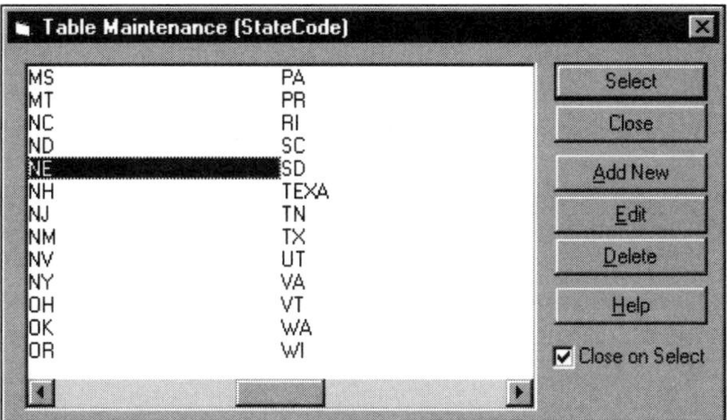

Figure 15-12: If the user clicks on a button, you must make sure that the system is in a state to perform that function, such as making sure a list item is selected here.

With list maintenance forms such as these, you always need to verify that a valid list item is selected before you run a delete or edit procedure. The following code shows how to verify that an entry is selected in a sample list box:

```
Function IsValidSelection (ctrl as Control) as Boolean
    If IsNull(ctrl) or ctrl = "" then
           IsValidSelection = False
    Else
           IsValidSelection = True
    End If
End Function
```

You can call this function when any of the list maintenance buttons are clicked, and pass to it the list box in question. If an item is selected in the list, the function returns true; if nothing is selected, the function returns false. You call this function before ever executing code for the selected button, such as Delete Item. Calling this function ensures that the application does not attempt to perform a function on a zero-length string or a null if no item is selected and helps ensure that your application runs smoothly, even in the event users request your application to do something when the application is not in a state to execute the request.

Disabling buttons and fields when they are not applicable

You can take the previous topic of validating conditions one step further. You can evaluate conditions on the fly and use the `Enabled` property of controls to prevent users from initiating functions when they shouldn't. When a control's `Enabled` property is set to `False`, the control is visible but the user cannot change the contents of the control (such as in a text box) or fire any events of the control (such as clicking on a button). Using the previous example, you could check the field value on the `After Update` event. If a valid item is selected, enable the appropriate buttons, such as Edit and

Delete in this example. When you requery a list, set its value to "" and disable the appropriate buttons. This is better than checking the conditions when a button is clicked on because it gives the user immediate visual feedback as to what can and cannot be done at any point in time.

Using error trapping on all VBA procedures

One of the most important elements of bulletproofing an application is making sure that the application never crashes; that is, never ceases operation completely and unexpectedly. Although preventing crashes also falls under debugging your application, it is important to note that you should put error trapping on each and every procedure in your application, even if you use just `On Error Resume Next`. When running an application distributed with the Office Developer Tools' Setup Wizard, any untrapped error encountered in your code causes the program to terminate completely. Your users cannot recover from such a crash, and serious data-loss may occur. Your users have to restart the application after such an application error.

Separating the code objects from the tables in the application

As discussed in Chapter 20, "Working with External Data," you should separate your code objects (forms, reports, queries, modules, and macros) from your table objects. Many benefits are gained from distributing these objects in separate .MDB files:

- Network users benefit from speed increases by running the code .MDB (the database containing the queries, forms, macros, reports, and modules) locally and accessing only the shared data on the network.
- Updates can easily be distributed to users.
- Data can be backed up more efficiently because only one file is needed to back up, and disk space and time are not used to continuously back up the code objects.

All professionally distributed applications, especially those intended for network use, should have separate code and data database (.MDB) files.

Documenting the application

Most developers dislike writing documentation; it's simply no fun and can be quite frustrating and time-consuming. However, you can save the users of your applications many hours of time by providing them with pertinent information. Even if you do not plan to distribute a full user's manual, take time to document how to perform the most common functions in your application. If you have created shortcuts, make sure to share them with the users.

Creating a help system

Although documentation is extremely important for getting users started with your application, well-written and thorough context-sensitive help is just as important. Help puts pertinent and informative information at users' disposal with just a click of the mouse or a push of a button. See Chapter 18, "Creating Help Systems in Access 97," for information on creating help files for your Access applications.

Implementing a security structure

The final item to consider before distributing your application is the level at which you wish to secure your application. You can secure specific individual objects or secure your entire application. If it is important to you to secure design permissions for all your objects to protect your source code, you need to be aware that you cannot rely solely on Microsoft's word that the security in Access works. The security model of Access 2.0 was touted by Microsoft as being the most secure available. It has been discovered that an average Access developer can unsecure an Access 2.0 database with ease in about five minutes, with only minimum coding! Although no method for unsecuring a secured Access 97 application has yet been discovered, a method may be uncovered in the future. You must understand and accept this risk when you distribute a secured Access application. Chapter 17, "Securing an Access Application," discusses the Access security model in detail.

Creating Distribution Disks Using the Office Developer Edition Tools

When you finish your application and you are ready to distribute it to your customers, you need a way to distribute the application. Distribution includes delivering all files necessary to run your application on some form of media, such as floppy disk, CD-ROM, or electronic distribution like the Internet. The media should include some sort of setup program that automates copying the files to the user's computer, sets up any shortcut items, registers necessary controls, and sets values in the system registry. Microsoft offers you a solution to the distribution problem: the Office Developer Edition Tools.

What are the Office Developer Edition Tools?

You purchase the Office Developer Edition tools, or ODE Tools, separately from Microsoft Access. The ODE Tools replace the Access Developer's Toolkit of previous versions of Access. The ODE Tools include a Setup Wizard that automates the creation of distribution media, as well as creates a setup file that your end users run to automate the installation procedure to their hard drive. All of this functionality is available to you in various third-party installation tools. With these third-party tools, some tasks are easy to accomplish and some are not. However, the ODE Tools offer something unavailable with other installation applications: They enable your application to run on a computer that does not have Access installed on it. Unlike Visual Basic, Access does not create executables that you can distribute to others. Instead, your application must be run within Access, which presents a problem when you want to distribute your applications commercially or to clients who will run your application on a number of networked computers; obviously, you cannot distribute Microsoft Access. As a solution to this problem, Microsoft has created a runtime mode of the Access executable. The ODE Tools include this runtime executable file. When you distribute your application with the ODE Tools' Setup Wizard, end users can run your application within the Access runtime environment without needing to purchase a full version of Access. This is all (mostly) transparent to users; they do not realize that Access is running in the background. Certain design interfaces are hidden from users so that they cannot create Access applications with the runtime executable. Purchasing the ODE Tools gives you the licensing rights to distribute your application with the runtime environment to an unlimited number of users, with no royalty fees! So, even if you plan to create your setup program with a third-party tool, you need to purchase one copy of the ODE Tools for the legal rights to distribute your application with the runtime files.

In addition to a Setup Wizard and the runtime environment, the ODE Tools include a number of royalty-free custom controls (.OCXs) that you can use to enhance the functionality of your applications, an Access Language Reference Guide, and a sample Developer's CD that allows you to experience firsthand some top-notch developer support facilities. The ODE Tools are worth the purchase price for these features alone.

When you distribute your application with the Setup Wizard, you can configure your custom Setup program to

- Copy your application's files to specified locations on a user's hard disk.
- Create Windows shortcuts that start your application or program files.
- Add Windows Registry keys and entries for your application.
- Group files, shortcuts, and Registry keys and entries into components that users can select to install or uninstall.
- Install other Access files, such as drivers for accessing various data sources and any .OCX custom controls used by your application.
- Run an application or open a file after the Setup program is finished installing your application.

Restrictions of the Office Developer Edition Tools

The Access runtime environment is an excellent (and currently the only) way to distribute your applications to users who do not own a licensed copy of Microsoft Access. As stated earlier, the Access runtime is almost transparent to the user. Unfortunately, some limitations do exist with the release version of the ODE Tools. Some of these issues affect the behavior of your application; some are problems inherent in the Setup Wizard itself. You need to be aware of the limitations, and you probably want to make your end users aware of some of them as well.

Known limitations of the Access 97 ODE Tools include

- Runtime applications that do not include custom help files generate errors when referring to the Access help file. As stated earlier, you should always attempt to distribute applications with help systems. Even a rudimentary help system is better than no online help at all.

  Tip

  If you elect not to ship a help file with your application, you can avoid Access generating an error by not providing a Help menu item on any of your custom menus and by creating an Autokeys Macro that traps the F1 key. The F1 key does not have to do anything in the macro. Simply including it in the Autokeys macro causes the macro to trap the F1 key when it is pressed. This prevents it from being passed to the Access runtime, calling up the help file.

- Attempting to close a runtime application with the `CloseCurrentDatabase` method generates an error. The runtime version of Access does not run without an application loaded and therefore generates the error if you attempt to close the current database. To terminate your application, use the `Quit` method of the `DoCmd` object.

- Uninstalling Microsoft Access 97 breaks applications installed with a custom Setup program. Unfortunately, Access's uninstall program does not know when a runtime Access application is installed on the computer, and it changes registry settings that are crucial to running your runtime Access application.

  Tip

  You should include the file MSARNREG.EXE in your list of files to distribute. This file is located in C:\PROGRAM FILES\COMMON FILES\MICROSOFT SHARED\MICROSOFT ACCESS RUNTIME folder under Windows 95 and in the C:\WINDOWS\MSAPPS\MICROSOFT ACCESS RUNTIME folder on Windows NT machines. The file installs when you install the ODE Tools on your computer. This program fixes the registration database so that your ODE Tools application works again. You will want to document the program for your users, and you may want to consider creating a shortcut or adding a menu item to your start menu to run the program.

- Uninstalling Visual Basic 4.0 breaks applications installed with the ODE Tools. Unfortunately, there is no fix for this. The uninstall program for Visual Basic 4 removes files that are essential to Access runtime applications. The only remedy is to reinstall the Access runtime application. You definitely want to document this for your users.
- The Setup Wizard does not support Administrative (setup /a) and Run From Network Server installations. Performing a network install places all the Setup files onto a server drive so that all workstations on the network can run the Setup program from the server rather than from floppy disk. If you distribute your application to run in a network environment, instruct your users to copy all files from each diskette in the distribution set to the same directory on the network and then run the Setup program in this directory from each workstation.
- Reinstalling your application with the custom Setup program fails if the user has performed a Maintenance Removal of Workgroup Administrator. A user can do this by re-running the Setup program and deselecting the Workgroup Administrator component (discussed later). If a user removes the Workgroup Administrator component and attempts to reinstall your Access runtime application, the install fails. Attempting to run the Setup program again after the failure results in a successful install.

Tip

You can prevent end users from removing the Workgroup Administrator component by setting the component to Hidden on the Components page of the Setup Wizard. This setting is discussed later in this chapter.

- Very large components (100+ MB) show negative numbers in your custom setup program. This bug does not affect the installation or workings of your ADT application, but it may confuse end users. Most developers almost never have components this large. However, if you experience this problem, consider breaking the offending component into smaller components.
- Removing the component in single-component setup does not remove the entire application. There is no workaround for this. If users want to remove the application completely, they must use the Remove All button.
- The Setup Wizard is unable to use exclusively locked files. If you try to add a file in the Setup Wizard that is exclusively locked by another user or another application, the Setup Wizard responds with an `Application-defined or object-defined` error. When users trigger this error, Access cancels the creation of your custom Setup program disk images. When creating disk images with the Setup Wizard, you should close all possible applications in order to avoid potential lock conflicts.

Using the Setup Wizard to create distribution disks

Now that you are familiar with what the Setup Wizard is supposed to do and aware of some of the pitfalls, you are ready to use the Setup Wizard to create setup disks for your application. Start the Setup Wizard by selecting Microsoft ODE Tools⇨Setup Wizard from the Start Menu. When you first run the wizard, you will see the form shown in Figure 15-13. If you previously saved a set of options with the Setup Wizard and wish to continue working with them, check the appropriate radio button. To create a new setup definition, leave the default radio button checked and click on the Next button.

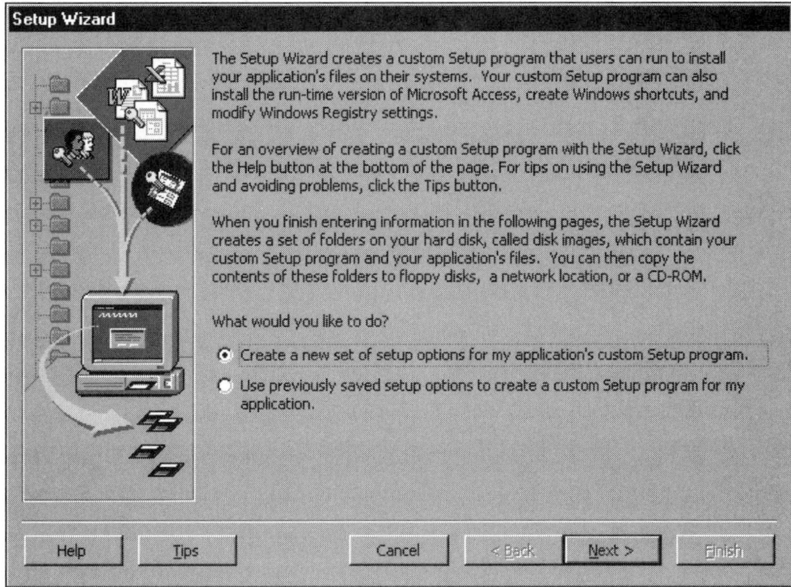

Figure 15-13: The first page of the Setup Wizard allows you to select between creating a new set of setup options or working with a set you have already saved.

Specifying files to distribute

You define the files to include in your distribution set on the second page of the Setup Wizard (see Figure 15-14). You do not need to explicitly select the Access files to include, you will be given the option later to install the Access runtime files. You do, however, need to specify at least one Access database file to be distributed. In addition to your main database file, you may wish to also distribute auxiliary databases, icons, text files, help files, .OCX controls, custom .DLLs, or any other support files your application requires, as shown in Figure 15-14.

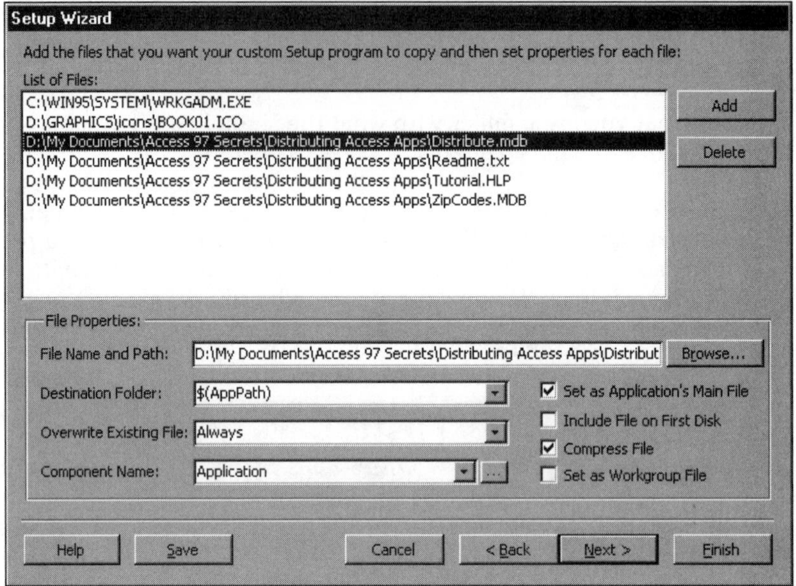

Figure 15-14: The Setup Wizard offers you many ways to tailor what and how files are installed on users' computers.

Warning

If you include files that do not have three-character extensions, your custom Setup program will fail. This occurs because of the way the Setup Wizard compresses files. If you need to use files with one- or two-character extensions, rename them in the final image folders so that they contain three characters. For example, a file named READ.ME is named READ.M_ in the disk images. To correct your custom Setup program, rename this file READ.ME_.

You can set a number of properties for each file you include. These properties affect how and where each file is installed on the users' machines, what component the file belongs to, and how the file is stored on the distribution disks.

Each file has the following properties:

- File Name and Path
- Destination Folder
- Overwrite Existing File
- Compress File
- Include File on First Disk

- Set as Application's Main File
- Set as Workgroup File
- Component Name

Specifying the file name and path

The file name and path is the file name and location of the file on your computer that you wish installed on the user's computer. The Setup Wizard uses a copy of this file when placing it onto the distribution disks. This property is set automatically when you add a file using the Add button. If you wish to select a different file or a file in a different location, click on the Browse button next to the name and path. If you select a file using the Browse button, the newly selected file replaces the originally selected file and is not added as a new file to the distribution set.

Destination Folder

The destination folder is the folder on the end users' computers into which you want the file placed. There are three default folders available for you to choose from:

- `$(AppPath)`: This folder is designated by the user running your custom Setup program. Think of AppPath as being a variable used to hold the user-selected folder. Your main application database should always be placed in the AppPath folder. In addition, you should always place your help files with the application files, so the help files should also have AppPath specified as their destination folder.
- `$(WinPath)`: This is the Windows folder on the user's machine. Once again, think of WinPath as a variable. At run time, the Setup Wizard determines what folder Windows resides in and places all files that have WinPath as their destination folder in that Windows folder. You should generally avoid placing a file in the Windows folder unless that file is an update to a file that already resides in the Windows folder.
- `$(WinSysPath)`: This folder is the System folder found below the Windows folder. WinSysPath is similar to WinPath in that at run time the Setup Wizard resolves where the Windows System folder resides and places the appropriate files there. You should place .DLL and .OCX files in the system folder because these files are common components. Avoid placing application-specific files in the System folder.

Although not immediately apparent, you are not limited to placing your files in only these three folders. You may also specify a subfolder below your AppPath folder. To do this, use the following syntax:

```
$(AppPath)\subfolder
```

Replace the word `subfolder` with the actual folder name. For example, if you want to create a folder called DATA under your main application folder, specify the following folder as the destination folder:

```
$(AppPath)\DATA
```

The Setup Wizard determines the AppPath folder name at run time by letting the user specify the folder. It then creates the folder if it does not currently exist and creates any subfolders specified in the `Destination Folder` property of included files.

Tip

If you include a large number of files and offer many components for installation, consider grouping the files or components into subfolders. Grouping makes future updates much easier and makes your application component architecture easier to understand when troubleshooting — if you need to replace a file for component A, you know what subfolder in which to look. Keeping only the main application files in the application folder is best whenever possible.

Overwrite Existing File

A file to be installed in your custom Setup program may already exist on the user's computer. Most .DLLs and many .OCXs are used by numerous other applications and will probably reside on the computer prior to installing your application. The Setup Wizard also encounters existing files when the user reinstalls the application without removing the first installed copy.

By default, the Setup Wizard uses internal version numbers of the files in question to determine what gets written to (or stays on) the user's system. Many files, such as .DLLs and .EXEs, contain internal version numbers, but files such as database files and text files do not. If one or both of the files in question do not contain a version number, the Setup Wizard resolves the conflict based on one of the following file replacement options that you specify:

- `Older`: When you specify `Older`, the Setup Wizard overwrites the existing file only if it is older than the file being installed.
- `Always`: The Setup Wizard always replaces the existing file with the file on your distribution disks.
- `Never`: The Setup Wizard never overwrites the existing file.

Secret

There is a caveat you need to be aware of when using the `Older` parameter. As recommended many times in this book, you should separate your code objects from your tables into two different database files. Logic then tells you to specify the `Overwrite Existing File: Older` option when installing your code database to ensure that your new code updates overwrite your previous code databases. The problem with this is that every time you open an Access database, the file's date and time are updated.

When distributing Access database files that contain only code objects, you should specify `Always` overwrite existing files. When distributing empty databases with all table objects, you should specify `Never` overwrite existing file to avoid overwriting the users' existing data with a new, empty dataset. If you do indeed wish your users to install from scratch, instruct them to remove their data database first before reinstalling your application.

In general, here are excellent guidelines for what to overwrite using the `Overwrite Existing File` property:

- `Always`: Database files containing only code objects, icons, README text files, or files that you are always certain are outdated or corrupted on all users' machines
- `Never`: Empty database files containing only table objects
- `Older`: .DLLs, .OCXs, Help files, and most other files

If you distribute a custom workgroup file, you need to determine what to use for its `Overwrite Existing File` property. If the databases you are distributing are updates that have new or modified objects in them, you may have to choose `Always` to overwrite the workgroup database file to ensure that all the objects in your application are usable due to possible security conflicts. If your end users are allowed to modify the Workgroup database file, they may possibly have added new users prior to running your current custom Setup program. If this happens, your end users have to re-create these new users if you overwrite the existing workgroup database file with the workgroup file on your distribution disks.

Compress File

The Setup Wizard uses this property to determine whether or not to compress the file on the distribution disks; compressing the files significantly reduces the number of disks created for a distribution set. The only time you should not compress a file is when a user may need to access the file directly from the distribution disks before or without installing your application — such as a README file.

Include File on First Disk

You can force the Setup Wizard to place a file on the first distribution disk by selecting this property. In general, you should do this only for files that you elect not to compress because compressed files are useless unless users are familiar with Microsoft's decompression utility. README files should always reside on the first disk in an uncompressed state. Obviously, a limited amount of space is available on each disk, and if you specify files whose cumulative size exceeds the size of the first disk (which also must contain the files needed for your custom Setup program), the Setup Wizard places some of the files on disk two as it sees fit.

Set as Application's Main File

This property is used to tell the Setup Wizard which file is the main application database file. Only one file can be designated as the Application's Main File.

Tip

If you have split your code objects from your table objects as recommended, you should set the application's main file to be the database file containing the code objects (forms, modules, and so on).

Set as Workgroup File

If you have created a custom workgroup file, you must not only include it in the distribution file set but also select this property for the workgroup file. Only one file may be specified as the workgroup file. If you do not include a custom workgroup file in your distribution set, the Setup Wizard includes and installs the default workgroup file automatically.

Note

If you attempt to add the workgroup file that the Setup Wizard is currently using to your distribution file set, you get an error indicating that permission to the file has been denied. If you wish to include this file in your distribution set, close the Setup Wizard and Access, make a copy of the workgroup database file, and include the copy in your list of files.

Component Name

You have the ability to specify components (or file sets) to be installed on the end user's computer. Components are useful for giving the user the ability to install optional functions or features of your application, such as a tutorial, online help files, or additional databases. By default, all files are members of the Application component. The Application component is always installed, regardless of what other components are or are not selected at the time of install.

To create additional components, click on the Build button next to the Component Name field. Access then shows you the Components Builder form shown in Figure 15-15.

A component definition consists of five items:

- The name of the component
- The types of installations in which the component may be installed
- A textual description of the component and its contents
- Whether the component is displayed in the components list
- Whether the component is required for all installations or whether it is optional

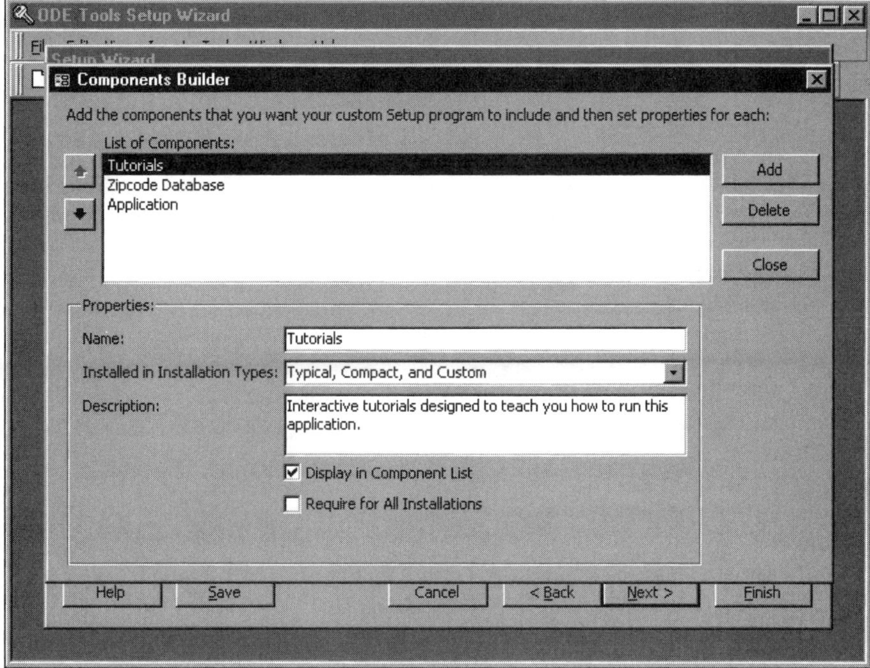

Figure 15-15: The Components Builder enables you to give users incredible flexibility in what they can select to be installed on their computer.

When end users run your custom Setup program, they are given the option to perform a Typical, Compact, or Custom installation. A Typical installation is a complete installation; that is, all components and files are installed on the user's computer. A Compact installation is used primarily for laptop computer installations where hard drive space may be limited; you should designate only those files that are absolutely vital to the operation of your application to be part of a Compact installation. A Compact installation usually does not contain items such as tutorials or extended help. When users elect to perform a Custom installation, they are given a list of all available components and are allowed to pick and choose the components they want to have installed on their computer. If a component must be installed in order for your application to work, you need to include it in all three types of installations and set its `Require for All Installations` property to `True`. If you do not set this property to `True`, users have the option of deselecting the component when performing a Custom installation.

After you have designated all the files to include in your distribution set and have set all their properties, click on Close to close the Components Builder, then click on the Next button to continue the wizard.

Defining shortcuts for your custom Setup program

The next page of the Setup Wizard is used to define the shortcuts that your custom setup program creates (see Figure 15-16 and Figure 15-17). Shortcuts are used to launch applications and open documents — anything you can do with a command line — and you can create as many of these shortcuts as you like. You should create a shortcut to run your main application, and you may also consider creating shortcuts to repair and compact your data or launch your help program.

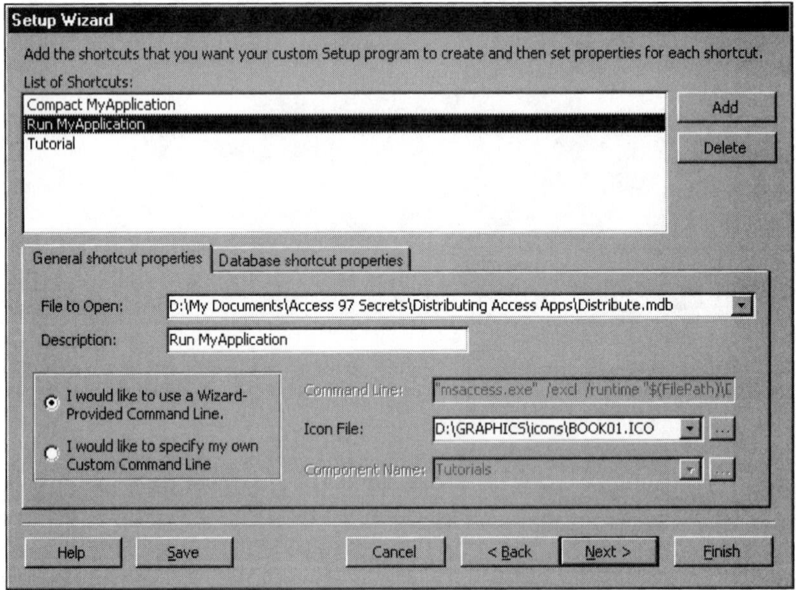

Figure 15-16: You can create shortcuts using the Access Setup Wizard.

To create a shortcut, first click on the Add button. The Setup Wizard then creates a shortcut with a placeholder named New Shortcut. By default, this shortcut is designed to start the Access runtime with your main application database file. When a user clicks on a shortcut that uses these default parameters, the user starts your application.

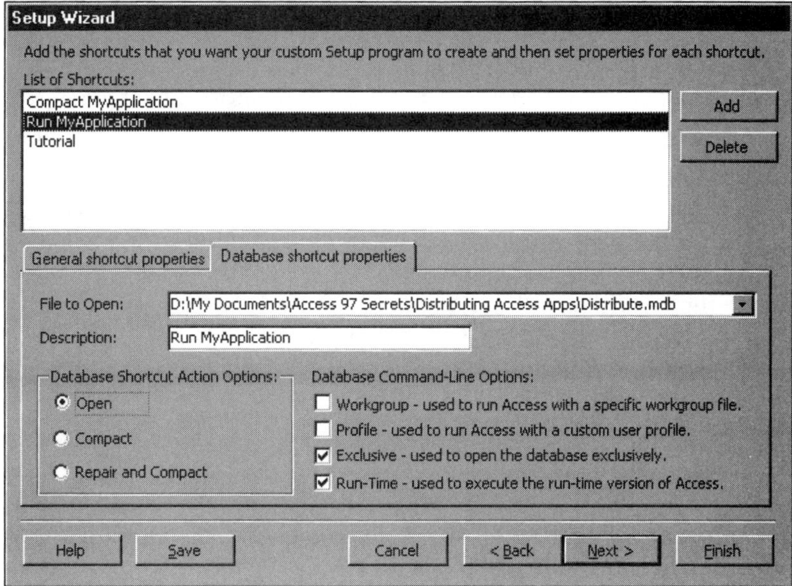

Figure 15-17: The Setup wizard has built-in Access database parameters for you to choose from.

Many different properties are associated with a shortcut, and you need to understand these properties to get your shortcuts to perform the duties you want them to perform. The properties for each shortcut are

- Description
- File to open
- Command line style
- Database command line options
- Database shortcut action options
- Component name

Description

The description is the text displayed under the icon when the shortcut appears on the desktop. When changing properties for a shortcut, Access references the shortcut by its description. If you change a shortcut's description, that change is reflected in the list of shortcuts. When you select a different shortcut from the list of shortcuts, any property changes you have made are saved immediately. You cannot undo property changes from the shortcuts page.

Although the Setup Wizard does not enforce the rule, shortcut descriptions cannot be longer than 40 characters. In addition, no shortcut description may contain the following characters: comma (,), forward slash (/), square brackets ([ ]), angled brackets (<>), or parentheses(). If you use any of these characters in a shortcut's description, your custom setup program will fail.

File to Open

This property is the name of the file you want the shortcut to open or run on the user's computer. The file specified must be a file you have designated to be installed by the Setup Wizard, or it must be one of the Access files the Setup Wizard installs automatically unless you explicitly create a command line (discussed below). Although the Setup Wizard lists the file's path on the computer creating the setup disks, the Setup Wizard resolves the location of the file on the user's computer when it installs the file, and that path is reflected in the final shortcut.

When creating shortcuts in Windows 95, the shortcuts must be resolved by Windows at the time they are created. To resolve shortcuts, you must specify a full path to the file, or you must specify a program that exists in the Windows search path. For example, WORDPAD.EXE does not require a path because Windows knows it is in the Windows folder. However, MYCUSTOM.EXE would be an invalid shortcut unless you precede the file name with a full path or a keyword such as `$(FilePath)` or `$(AppPath)`.

It is possible to create a shortcut to open or run a file not included in your distribution set but that you know resides on the end user's computer (such as WordPad). To create such a shortcut, leave the File to Open field blank, set the Command line Style to "I would like to specify my own Custom Command Line" (see next section), and enter the command line used to open or run the desired file.

If you create shortcuts for Access components, the command line must be in lowercase letters. For example, when creating a shortcut to the Microsoft Access Setup program, use setup.exe, not Setup.exe or SETUP.EXE. Other Access files that follow this restriction are msaccess.exe, wrkgadm.exe, and replman.exe. If you do not enter the entire program name in lowercase letters, the Setup Wizard will not recognize your shortcuts.

Command Line style

You have two options to create a command line for the item executed by the shortcut: "I would like to use a Wizard-Provided Command Line" and "I would like to specify my own Custom Command Line." If you use the wizard-provided command line, you cannot modify the command line. Instead, the wizard creates the command line that it thinks is most appropriate for the file. If the file to be opened is an Access database file, you can select the command line parameters to use on the Database Shortcut Properties page discussed later.

If you elect to create your own command line, all default command line options are grayed out, but you are allowed direct access to the command line field. In your custom command line, you can use the same placeholders you use to specify the location to install files. These placeholders are described in Table 15-1.

Table 15-1 Command-Line Placeholders

Placeholder	*Description*
`$(AppPath)`	The folder where your application is installed
`$(WinPath)`	The folder where Windows is installed
`$(WinSysPath)`	The System subfolder of the Windows program folder
`$(FilePath)`	The folder where the file you specified is installed
`$(WorkgroupFile)`	The folder where the Workgroup file is installed if your custom Setup program installs a custom Workgroup file

If you would like to refer to specific user profiles located in the System Registry of the end user's system in the command line, you can use the placeholder `$(Profile)`. In a command line that runs Access (or your database file that uses the Access runtime), you can put this placeholder after the `/Profile` command line option instead of entering the profile name itself. You can create custom registry entries with the Setup Wizard, which is discussed later in this chapter.

Tip

Creating your own command line gives you a vast amount of control over what the shortcut does. If you specify a file name in the command line that includes spaces, you must enclose the file name and path in quotation marks or the shortcut will not work.

Database command line options

When a shortcut opens an Access database file and you elect to use the wizard-provided command line, the Database Shortcut Properties are enabled. Clicking the Database shortcut properties tab displays the following options:

- **Workgroup.** When you include a custom Workgroup file in your distribution set, the command line must contain a reference to it or the default Workgroup file will be used and your application may not run. To add the Workgroup switch to the command line, check this box.
- **Profile.** The Access runtime uses a Windows Registry profile to provide options for running your application. If you include this option, the Setup Wizard includes the `/Profile` command line option on the Access command line to run your database and sets the profile to that of your application. Note that you can also do this manually as previously discussed.

- **Exclusive.** The Access runtime can open your application databases for exclusive use so that no other user can open them. The performance of your application will be improved if you run your application with this switch; however, the database will not be available for simultaneous use by multiple users.
- **Runtime.** You will almost always use this switch when distributing your applications. It forces the application database to be open in runtime mode so that users cannot access the design features of Access. Unless you want your users to specifically have access to Access's design features, always check this box! If a version of Microsoft Access won't be installed on the user's computer, make sure to include the Microsoft Access Run-Time component with your custom Setup program using the Select Microsoft Office Components page of the Setup Wizard (discussed later).

Database Shortcut Action Options

Whenever you open an Access database, you must select a Database Shortcut Action Option. The options available are Open (run) the database, Compact the Database, or Repair and Compact the database.

If you create a shortcut based on an Access database file that uses a Database Shortcut Action option other than Open, do not change the `File to Open` property to anything other than an Access database file. If you do change it, you generate an invalid command line, which in turn causes a General Protection Fault in your custom Setup program. You can prevent this from happening by setting the Shortcut Action option to Open before modifying the `File to Open` property or by deleting the shortcut and then re-creating it. If you do create an invalid command line, you can fix it by removing the `/compact` parameter from the resultant command line.

Icon File

The icon specified here appears on the user's desktop for the shortcut. When the user double-clicks on the icon, Windows executes the shortcut. You may type in the name and path of an icon or use the Build button to locate an icon.

When using custom icons for shortcuts, the icon must be installed with the file the shortcut will open, or it must already reside on the end user's machine. You should always include a shortcut's icon within the same component that the shortcut resides in to ensure that the icon is available on the end user's computer. If the icon you specify cannot be found, a generic Windows icon is used in its place.

Component name

You must specify a component in which to include the shortcut. By default, the file the shortcut opens is selected. You can change the component setting, but you should never need to.

To create a shortcut that uninstalls your application, create a shortcut with a custom command line of `setup.exe /U`. If you want the Setup program to remove components that are shared with other applications, use `setup.exe /UA`. Shared components are not removed if another application requires them; however, using the `/U` parameter and leaving the shared components on the user's system are safer.

When you finish creating all the shortcuts for your custom Setup program, click on the Next button to continue.

You can save the current custom setup definition at any time by clicking on the Save button and then specifying a file name for the shortcut definition template. You can then reload this definition by selecting "Use previously saved setup options to create a custom Setup program for my application" on the first page of the Setup Wizard.

Creating Registry Values with your custom Setup program

The Setup Wizard enables you to specify custom registry keys to be created on the end user's system (see Figure 15-18). Creating Registry entries replaces creating .INI entries in Windows 3.1. The System Registry is so important that an entire chapter of this book (Chapter 1, "Using the Windows Registry") is devoted to it. A certain number of Registry entries are created automatically by the Setup Wizard in order to run the Access runtime and use certain services such as Jet. If you want to create additional Registry entries, you can do so using the Setup Wizard, but you do not have to create custom Registry entries for your application.

To create a Registry key, click on the Add button. Each Registry key has a number of properties that you can set. These properties are

- Top-Level for Key
- Path to Key
- Value Name
- Base Value Data on File
- Value Data
- Value Data Type
- Component Name

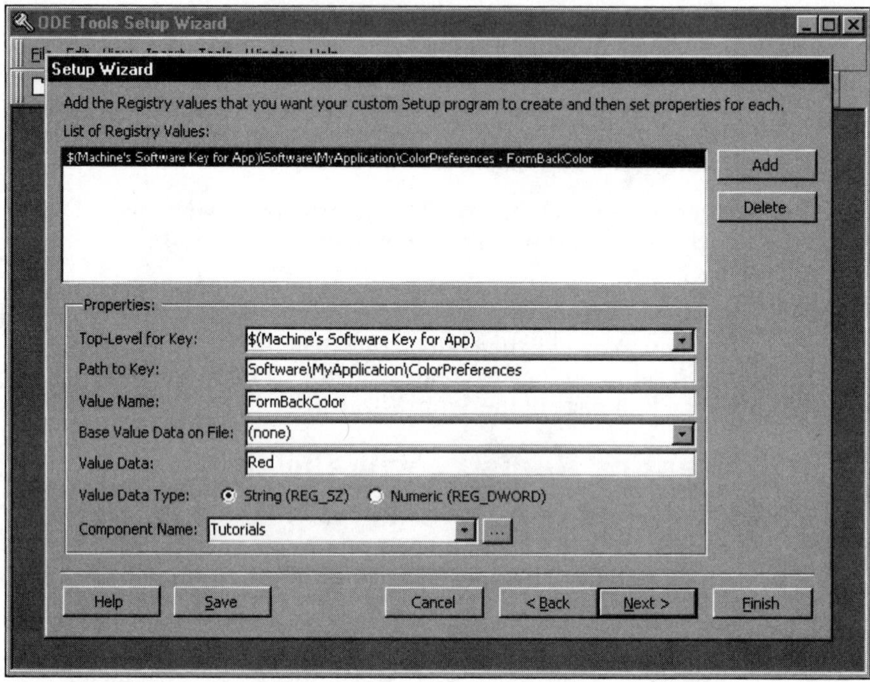

Figure 15-18: The Setup Wizard enables you to define custom Registry settings for your application.

Top-Level for Key

The top-level key is the root location in the Windows Registry from which you want to create this key. This is like selecting a root directory under which a subdirectory is to be created. You must choose from the following Registry root locations:

- `$(Machine's Software Key for App)`. This is the profile key for your application on the user's machine. Use this location to store settings that apply to all users on the computer or to create custom options (such as file paths to auxiliary items) for your application. You can force the Access runtime to use your custom Registry settings by using the Profile option when creating a shortcut. This key is placed in the HKEY_LOCAL_MACHINE and has the path SOFTWARE\Company\ApplicationName\ApplicationVersion. You specify these parameters on the Applications Details page of the Setup Wizard discussed later in this chapter.
- `$(User's Software Key for App)`. This is the user key for your application. You use this key location to create options such as application preferences for specific users. This key is placed in the HKEY_CURRENT_USER and has the path

SOFTWARE\COMPANY\APPLICATIONNAME\APPLICATIONVERSION. Note that this path is the same as the previous path, only the root key is different.

- `HKEY_CLASSES_ROOT`. Windows stores associated files and extensions, as well as other shell information, in this location. If you create executable files with another development tool, such as Visual Basic 4 or Visual C++, and want to associate a file extension with the executable, you create that association here.
- `HKEY_LOCAL_MACHINE`. Windows stores information specific to the computer in this key. You probably will never need to write information to this key, but at times you may wish to retrieve information from this key.
- `HKEY_CURRENT_USER`. Windows stores information specific to the user in this key. These user settings are global, as opposed to user settings specific to your application. You may retrieve values from this key, but you will rarely have to write values to it.
- `HKEY_USERS`. Windows stores the default user configuration in this key. You probably will not use this key when installing normal applications.

Path to Key

You specify additional path information to the Registry key in this property. The Setup Wizard then uses the root location and the Path to Key together to work with your Registry entry. When specifying Paths to Keys, separate values in the path with a backslash, just as you would folders in a file path name — for example, SOFTWARE\MYAPPLICATION\COLORPREFERENCES.

If you need to use a percent sign (%) in a Registry Entry, you need to use two percent signs instead like this %%. If you use just one percent sign, your custom Setup program will fail.

Value Name

In this property, you specify the actual Registry entry that you wish to create or change. For example, following through with the path SOFTWARE\MYAPPLICATION\COLORPREFERENCES from the preceding paragraph, you may want to change the setting for `Value Name` to `FormBackColor`.

Leave this box blank to create or change the value of a Registry key instead of an entry.

Base Value Data on File

If the Registry entry that you are creating or editing must be set to a file name, you can select a file that your custom Setup program installs using the dropdown list for this property. When you select a file from the list, the Setup Wizard adds the final installed path and file name to the Registry.

Value Data

Value Data is the actual data to store in the Registry entry. If you elected to base the value data on a file, that file's information is shown here. If the value you're setting is a string, you can use the standard placeholders `$(AppPath)`, `$(WinPath)`, `$(WinSysPath)`, `$(FilePath)`, and `$(WorkgroupFile)` to symbolize file paths. Once again, the Setup Wizard resolves these file paths at run time and places the correct value in the Registry keys.

Value Data Type

You must specify the data type of the data you are storing in the Registry. You can specify that the data is string data or numeric data. Numeric entries can be from 0 to 4294967295.

Component Name

You must specify a component that the Registry entry belongs to. Just as with shortcuts, a Registry key by default is created in the same component as the file it is based on, but you can override this property. You may click on the Build button next to Component Name to create a new component.

When you have created all the Registry entries for your application, click on the Next button.

Specifying additional components

Access applications often make use of additional components such as replication or ISAM drivers that allow them to work directly with other databases such as Paradox or dBase. Rather than force you to manually include all the necessary support files and .DLLs for such components, the Setup Wizard gives you the ability to select the specific components used by your application (see Figure 15-19). When you select a component, the Setup Wizard automatically includes all the necessary files for the component on the distribution disks. Then, when a user runs your custom Setup program, the Setup program installs all the additional component files in their proper location and makes all necessary changes to the System Registry.

The Setup Wizard allows you to select from the following components:

- Microsoft Access Runtime Version
- Microsoft Excel ISAM Drivers
- Paradox ISAM Drivers
- Text and HTML ISAM Drivers
- Lotus ISAM Drivers
- Xbase ISAM Drivers
- Microsoft Graph 97 Runtime Version
- Workgroup Administrator

- Microsoft Replication Manager
- ODBC Support with SQL Server
- Microsoft Exchange and Outlook ISAM
- ODBC Direct

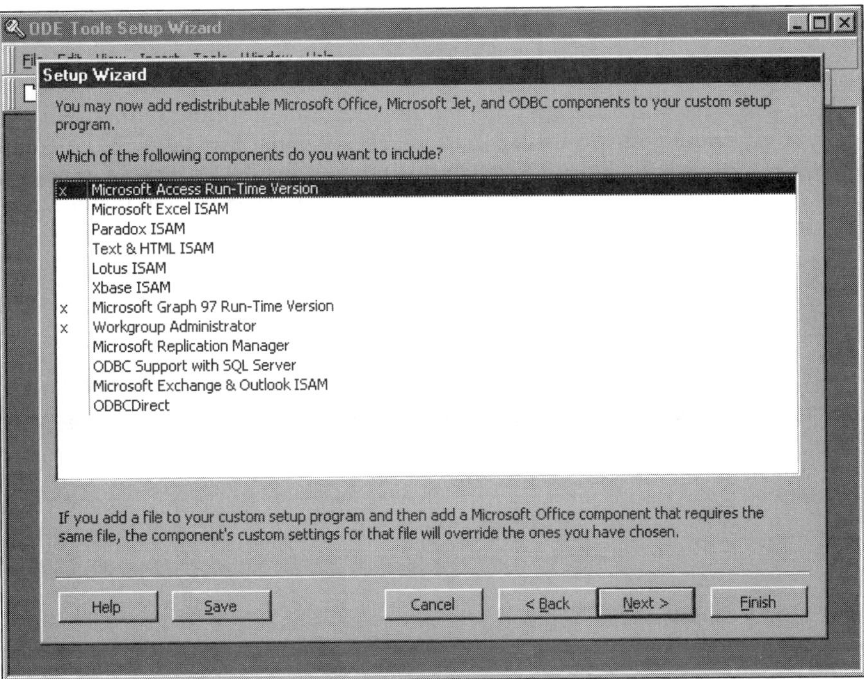

Figure 15-19: The Setup Wizard saves you time and eliminates errors by allowing you to choose prebuilt components to distribute.

Each component you select on this page is added to the component list of your application. You have the option (discussed later in this chapter) of hiding these components from the end user running your application. In addition, the Setup Wizard automatically includes other components required by the components you select. For example, if your application includes a Workgroup information file, the Setup Wizard automatically includes the Workgroup Administrator program.

Unless you are creating a custom Setup program simply to distribute your database to users that already have Access, you need to select the Microsoft Access Runtime Component. Note that the Runtime component is not selected by default, so you need to select it if you need it. Including this component increases your distribution set by several disks.

If you have included charts or graphs in any of your forms or reports, you must include the Microsoft Graph 97 Runtime Version component. And, of course, if your application uses the new Replication features of Access, you must include the Microsoft Replication Manager.

When you have selected all the components you wish to include in your distribution set, click on the Next button to continue.

Reordering your custom Setup program's component list

After you have specified all the files and prebuilt components that you want included in your distribution set, you must fine-tune all the components, as shown in Figure 15-20. On this page of the Setup Wizard, you define the order in which the components appear, what type of installation each component is included in, and the description of each component as displayed displayed in your custom Setup program when a user highlights the component.

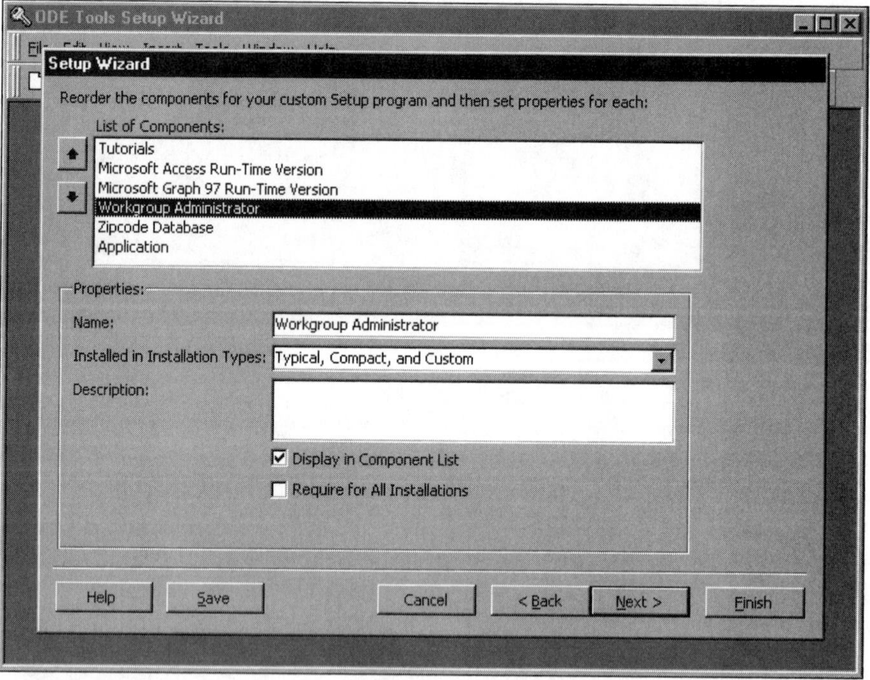

Figure 15-20: Making sure your that components are understandable and installed appropriately is important to ensuring that users successfully install your application.

Each component name should uniquely identify the component. In addition, the component description should tell the users enough about the component so that they understand what is included within the component and can decide whether or not they need to install it.

As stated earlier, when end users run your custom Setup program, they can select the type of installation they want to perform. The following three installation types are available:

- Typical
- Compact
- Custom

This page of the Setup Wizard allows you to specify the type of installation in which each component is available. Any components that you feel the average user will want installed should be included in a Typical installation. Compact installations are generally performed on laptops or computers where hard drive space is minimal; therefore, you should include only those components that are absolutely necessary for your application to run in the Compact installation type.

When users select Custom as the installation type, they are given a list of all the available components from which to choose. This list is displayed in the order defined in the list of components on this page of the Setup Wizard. To move a component in the list, select the component and then click on one of the two arrow buttons to the right of the list: the up arrow to move the list item up one position in the list, and the down arrow to move the list item down one position in the list.

Many of the additional components, such as the ISAM components, don't need to be shown in the component list. Showing the end user such components serves no purpose and usually confuses him or her. To hide a component from the end user, uncheck the Display in Component List checkbox. The Microsoft Access Runtime Version is an excellent component to hide. If you want to keep Access behind the scenes, there is no reason the user even needs to know the runtime is being installed. You need to show this component only if the end users may already have Access installed and you want to allow them to use their existing copy of Access to run your application database.

If a component must always be installed, check the Require for All Installations checkbox. If you select this checkbox, the end user will still be able to deselect it, but your custom Setup program will display a warning message saying that the application will not function without the component. Deselecting the Require for All Installations checkbox enables users to reinstall specific components or install components that were not installed the last time the Setup program was run.

You should force your custom Setup program to always install your main application file on the end user's machine. To do this, mark the component containing the main application file as hidden and select to have it installed with Minimal, Typical, and Custom installations. Without this file, users cannot use your custom Setup program to uninstall your application successfully.

Spend some time on this page and carefully think through all the scenarios a user may come up with. You want to make sure that the proper components are always installed at the appropriate times. When you are finished defining the components' order and their properties, click on the Next button to continue.

Defining the application information for your custom Setup program

At this point in the Setup Wizard, all files you wish to distribute and the components they belong to should have been defined. The next step is to provide the Setup Wizard with your application's information to be used in your custom Setup program (see Figure 15-21). The Setup Wizard uses this information to tailor the appearance of your custom Setup program.

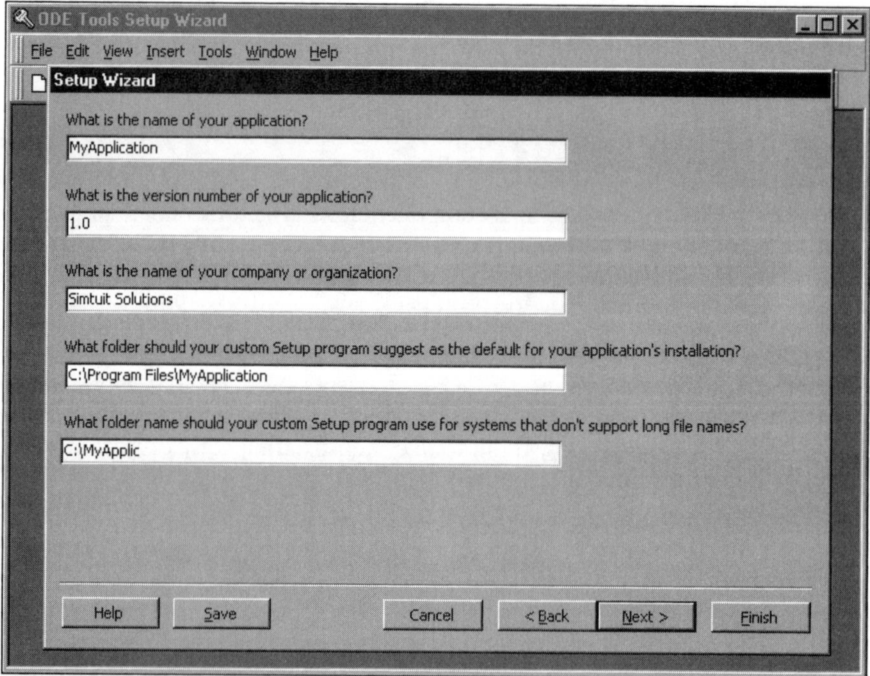

Figure 15-21: This page of the Setup Wizard is used to tailor the appearance of your custom Setup program.

The information that you must provide for your custom Setup program includes

- The name of your application
- The version number of your application
- The name of your company or organization
- The default folder in which to install your application
- A default directory in which to install your application on systems that do not support long file names

Setup displays the name of your application on the various screens and title bars of your custom Setup program.

You cannot use quotation marks in the application name. As a general rule, in fact, you should avoid using quotation marks in any text required by the Setup Wizard.

End users running your custom Setup program can elect to install your application in any folder they specify. However, standard practice is to supply a default folder. The default folder is merely a recommendation; end users have the ability to override this default at run time and install the application into any directory they choose. Most users elect to use the default folder, which makes technical support of your application a little easier because you know the location of your application on most users' machines. In addition to specifying a folder name, you can specify a default directory for computers that do not support long file names.

When you have finished specifying the application information for your custom Setup program, click on the next button to continue.

Running an executable file when your Setup program is finished

You can have your custom Setup program run an executable file when your Setup program is finished (see Figure 15-22). If you want your custom Setup program to run a file that is included in your distribution set, you may select it from the list. The Setup Wizard will then create a default command line for the file.

If you have your custom Setup program run a file that you include in your distribution set, be sure to include that file in a component that is always installed. Otherwise, your installation will finish, but the file cannot be run and the custom Setup program displays a message saying that the installation failed.

You can have your custom Setup program run files that are not included in your distribution set or modify the command line used to run a file that is included in your distribution set. As with other pages of the Setup Wizard, the path placeholders `$(AppPath)`, `$(WinPath)`, `$(WinSysPath)`, `$(FilePath)`, `$(WorkgroupFile)`, and `$(Profile)` can all be used.

One of the most common uses of running an executable when your Setup program finishes is to display a README file. The following example takes advantage of the path placeholders and the fact that Notepad is installed (by default) on all Windows 95 machines in the Windows directory. To have your installation display using Notepad a README.TXT file that was installed into your application directory, use this command line:

```
"$(WinPath)\Notepad.exe" "$(AppPath)\Readme.txt"
```

Your custom Setup program resolves the path placeholders at run time, runs Notepad from the Windows directory, and opens the README.TXT file found in the application directory.

The custom Setup program does not make use of file associations like File Manager does in Windows 3.1. You cannot elect to run a .TXT file and expect the Setup program to resolve the association and launch the appropriate program (Notepad). You must have the command line in the Setup Wizard run an executable and pass it the associated file to open. This is done by specifying the name and path of the executable and then name and path of the file to open with the executable, as shown in the preceding example. If you do not specify an executable, your Setup program will not complete successfully.

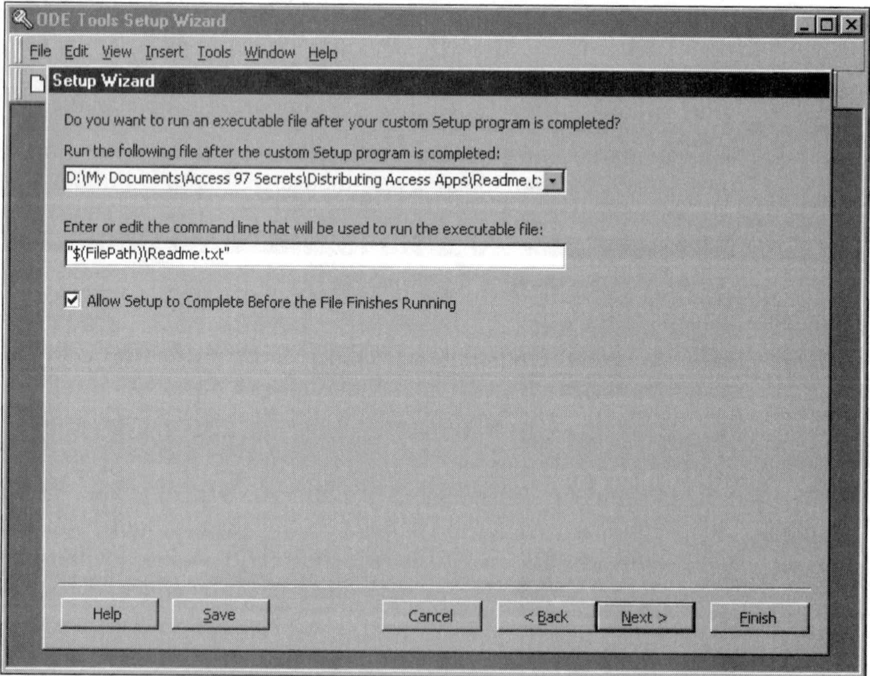

Figure 15-22: When your custom Setup program is finished, you can have it run an executable.

Tip

If a specific command line is not working for you, remove the quotation marks that enclose the file argument and try to run the command line again.

The Setup Wizard offers you one additional parameter when you elect to run an executable program: Allow Setup to Complete Before the File Finishes Executing. The help text for the ODE Tools explains this checkbox as follows:

If you select this check box, the Setup program displays the 'Setup was completed successfully' message box before the file or application you've specified has finished executing. If you don't select this check box, it will appear to the user that the Setup program is still running while the file that you specified is executing, and the message won't be displayed until after execution complete.

Generating a distribution file set

The final step to creating a custom Setup program using the Setup Wizard is specifying where to place the disk images, what type of installation to create, whether or not to store the compressed files that are created, and what folder they should be stored in if you do decide to store the compressed files (see Figure 15-23).

First specify where you want to place the images of the distribution disks. The Setup Wizard creates folders under the folder you specify, one folder for each disk image (see Figure 15-24). These folders are named Disk1, Disk2, and so on. After the Wizard creates the folders, you simply copy all files from the Disk1 subfolder to the first disk, all files from the Disk2 subfolder to the second disk, and so on.

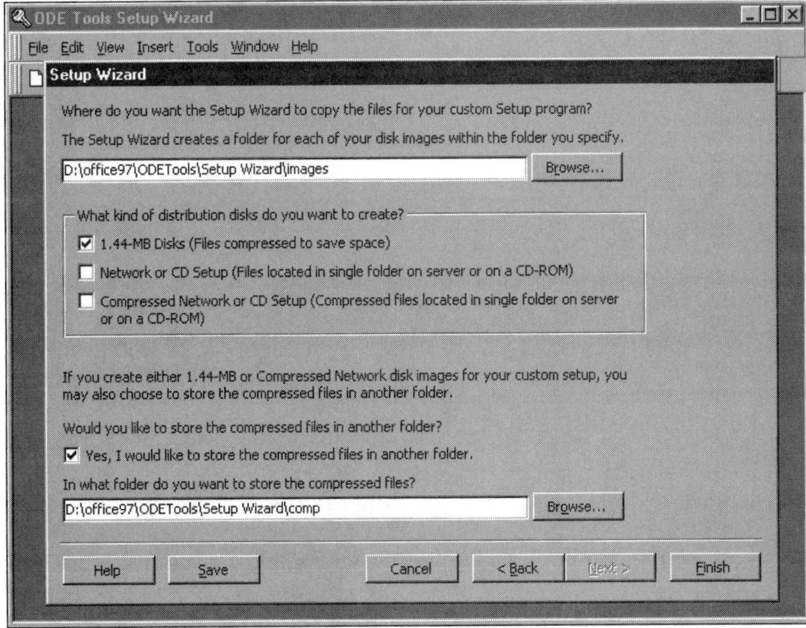

Figure 15-23: The final step of the Setup Wizard is defining what disk images to make and where to place them.

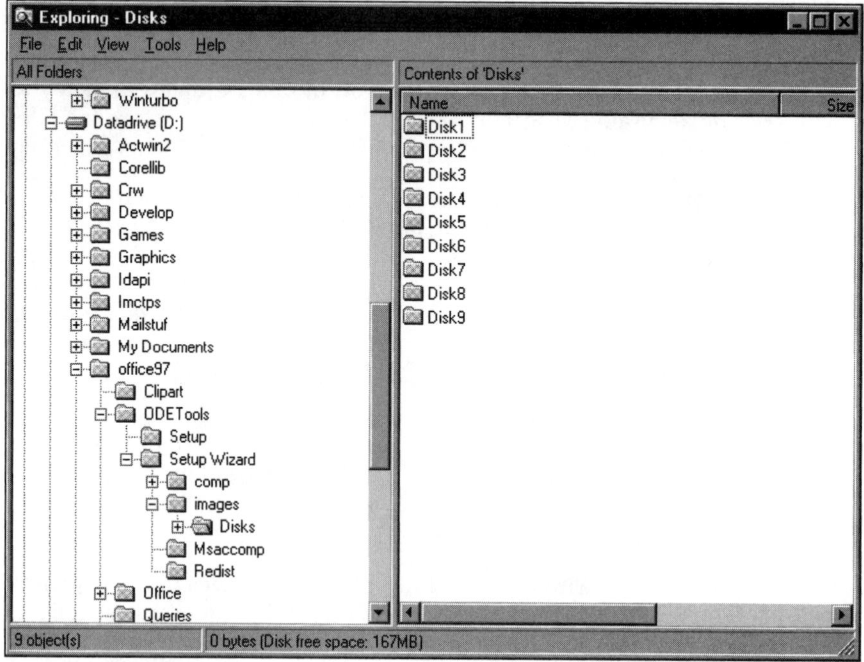

Figure 15-24: The Setup Wizard creates multiple subfolders under the folder you specify in which to create the images.

The Setup Wizard does not accept top level UNC Share paths (for example, \\server\share) for the folder where your custom Setup program disk images are to be created. You must specify a subfolder of the UNC share.

You can choose from the following three options for the type of installation to create:

- 1.44MB Disks
- Network or CD Setup
- Compressed Network or CD Setup

When you create a 1.44MB disk installation, the Setup Wizard compresses all files to save space. However, any files that you specifically marked to leave uncompressed are left uncompressed. In addition, any files that you specified to have installed on the first disk are placed in the Disk1 folder.

The Network or CD Setup compresses all files to be installed into one disk image and places them in their uncompressed state in a single folder. You can then move or copy this folder to your network or to a CD. When users want to install your application, they simply run your custom Setup program from the folder on the network. Moving or copying the folder is much faster and cheaper than distributing the Setup program on multiple disks to many users on a network.

The compressed Network or CD Setup is used the same way as the normal Network Setup, with the exception that all files are compressed in the disk image. It takes the Setup Wizard longer to create a Compressed Network or CD Setup than a normal Network or CD Setup, but the benefit is that the Compressed Network Setup is much smaller and therefore requires less space on the network drive or CD.

If you anticipate running the Setup Wizard again in the future (for new builds or product updates), you can have the Setup Wizard save a copy of all the compressed files on your hard drive. Then, the next time this setup definition is used to generate disk images, the Setup Wizard can use the existing compressed files rather than recompressing them again. Although using existing compressed files makes the consecutive builds much faster, it uses more disk space on your computer. If you elect to store the compressed files on your hard drive, you need to specify a folder in which to place them.

Warning

Verify that you have plenty of free space on the drive on which you are creating the images before clicking the Finish button. If the Setup Wizard runs out of disk space while compressing files, it will fail.

When you have supplied all the information on this page, you are ready to create your distribution disk images. Click on the Finish button to have the Setup Wizard create the images.

Note

If you included files with a one- or two-character extension in your distribution set, you need to rename them in the final image folders so that they contain three character extensions. For example, a file named READ.ME is named READ.M_ when compressed in the disk images. To correct your custom Setup program, rename this file READ.ME_. Note that this example assumes that READ.ME is a compressed file. If you included files with only one- or two-character extensions but elected not to compress them, you do not need to do anything with them at this point.

Running a custom Setup program

To install an application using a custom Setup program, users need to insert the first disk into their drives and run the Setup program. Users are then shown a screen similar to Figure 15-25. Users running your custom Setup program defined in the preceding example would see the following series of screen shots.

If the Setup program detects running applications that may interfere with the installation (such as a full version of Access), users would be alerted at this point. If no other applications conflict with the install, users can press the Continue button and are shown a form similar to Figure 15-26.

Figure 15-25: The custom Setup program starts with a welcome and a warning about shared files.

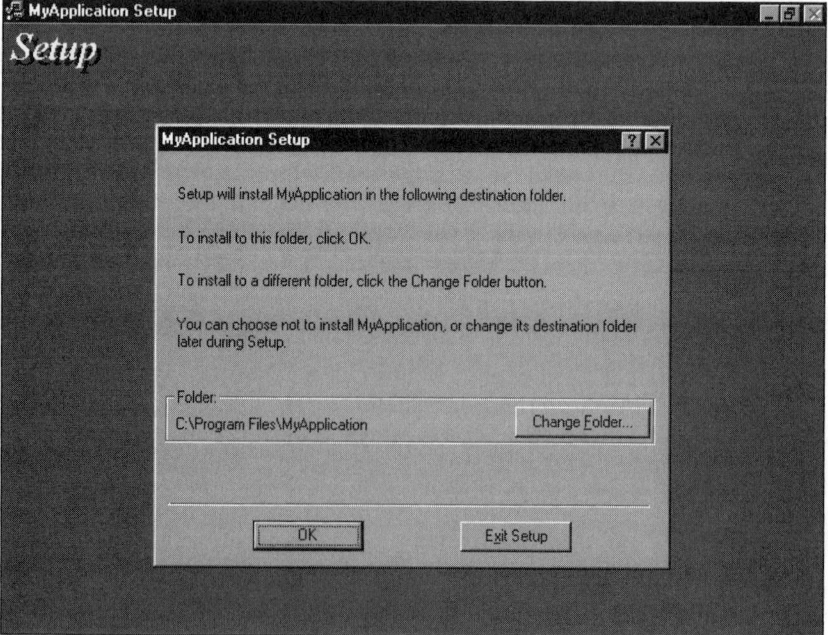

Figure 15-26: The Setup program suggests installing the application in the folder you specified in the Wizard.

On this form, users can accept the recommended installation folder that you designated in the Setup Wizard, or they can click on the Change Folder button and supply the name and path of a different folder. When users are satisfied with the folder selected, they click on the OK button to move to the installation type selection screen, shown in Figure 15-27.

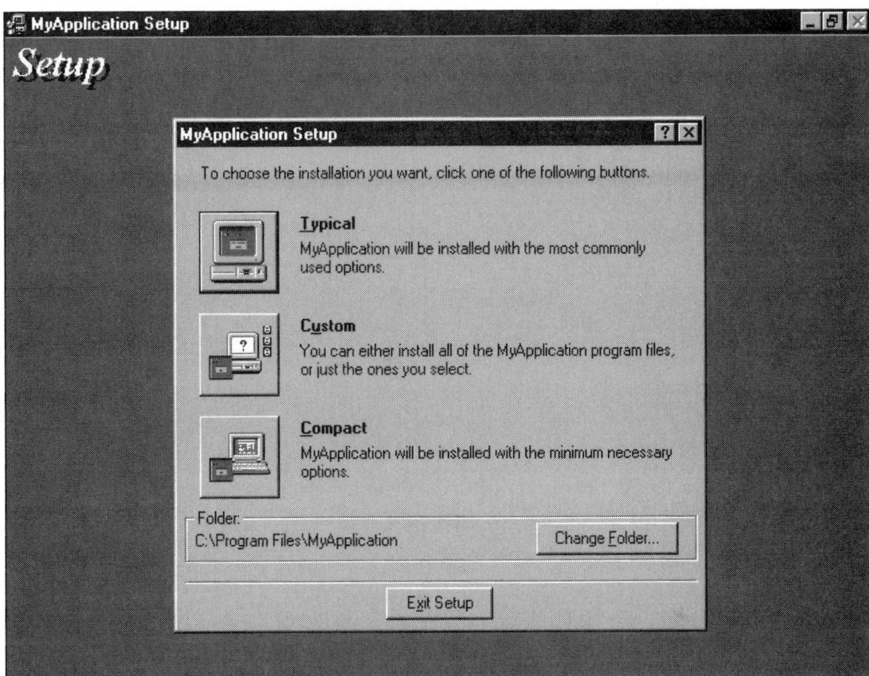

Figure 15-27: Your users can choose from three options how they want your installation performed — thanks to the new Setup Wizard.

From this form, users can elect to perform a typical installation, compact installation, or a custom installation. If they choose to perform a typical or compact installation, the Setup program installs all components that you designated as belonging to these types. If, however, users elect to perform a custom installation, they are shown a form similar to that in Figure 15-28.

Notice that these components are the ones designated as being displayed in the component list in the Setup Wizard. Highlighting a component displays its description text. The Setup program shows the amount of available space on the selected drive and the amount of space needed according to the components the user selects. When users are satisfied with their selections, they click on the Continue button to start the installation.

Figure 15-29 shows the result of running an executable at the end of the install. The Setup program actually tells the user that the installation has been successfully completed, as shown in Figure 15-30.

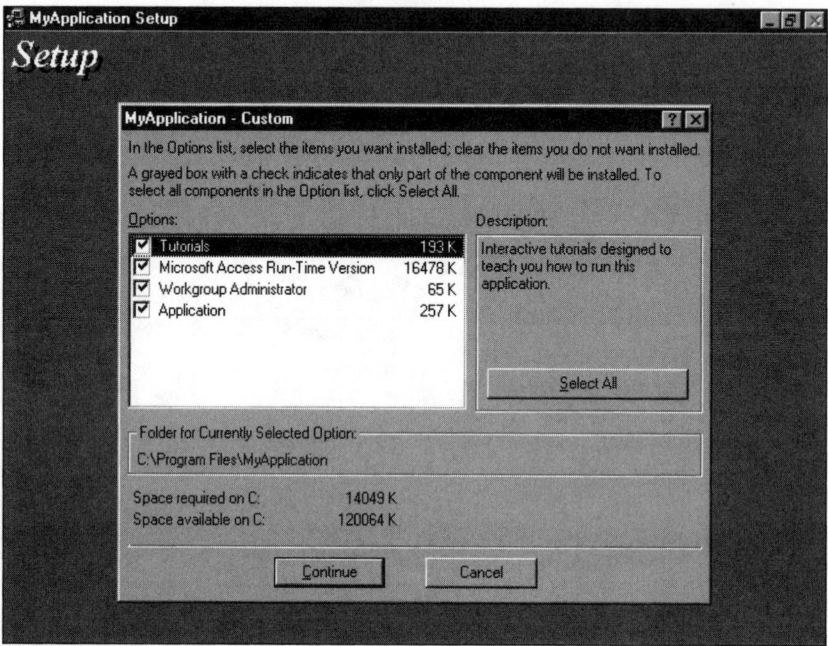

Figure 15-28: Choosing Custom Installation gives users the ability to decide which components get installed on their computers.

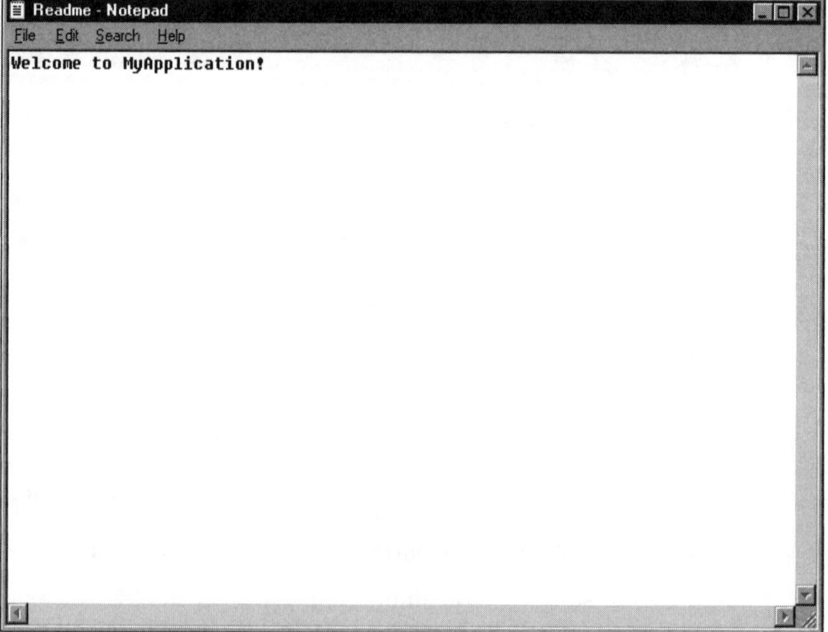

Figure 15-29: Having your custom Setup program display a README file on completion helps ensure (but does not guarantee) that your users will read the file.

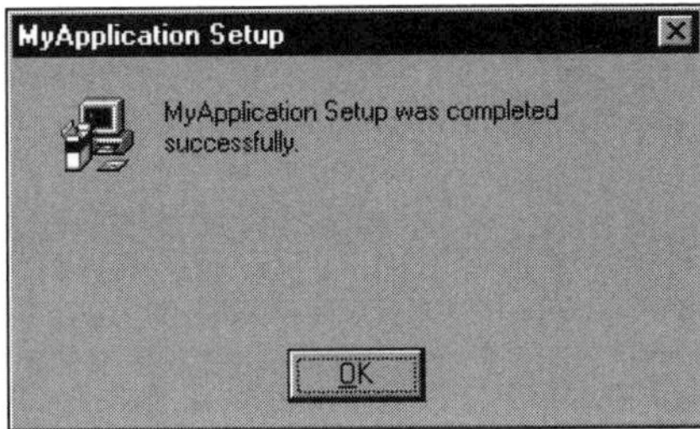

Figure 15-30: When your custom Setup program is complete, it informs the user that it is finished, then unloads itself from memory.

Figure 15-31 is provided to show you just what the Registry entry, shown earlier in the Setup Wizard, did. It created a path using the information provided in the Setup Wizard under the selected key HKEY_CURRENT_USER and stored a value of Light Gray for the color preference Registry entry.

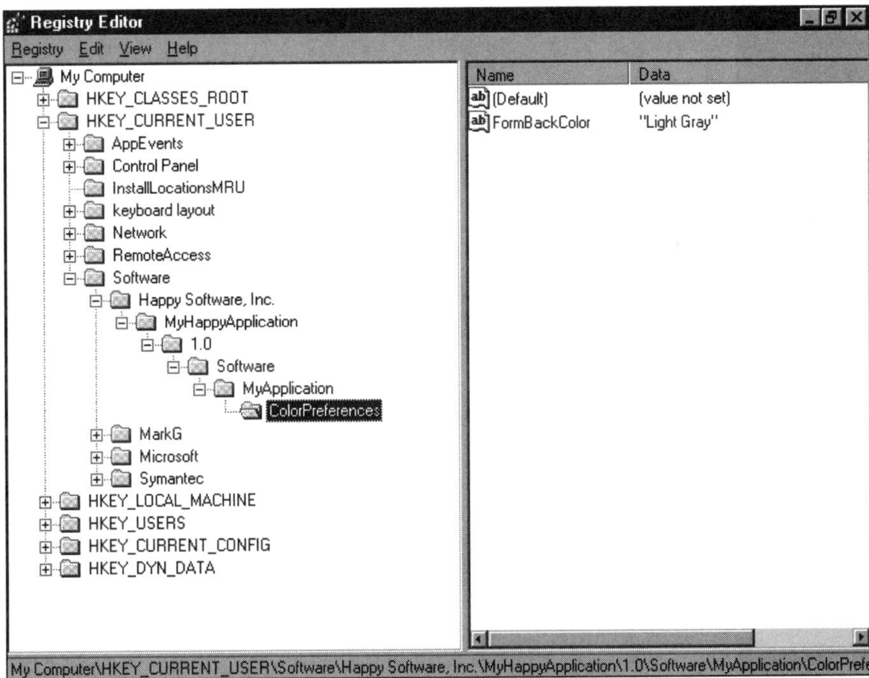

Figure 15-31: The Setup Wizard makes it easy to define custom Registry entries in which you can store almost an unlimited number of user parameters.

Although deciding what to distribute to your users and how to distribute it takes some time and considerable thought, taking the time to learn the Setup Wizard enables you to create perfect installations every time!

Many different steps are discussed here that are required to produce a top-notch distributed Access application. For each step, you can take dozens and dozens of shortcuts, but don't. It is not uncommon for a company to devote an entire week or longer just to prepare an application for distribution (not writing core code). It really shows when you take your time and do these things right, and your users will have a smooth-running, intuitive, dependable application that makes their tasks just a little bit easier.

Chapter 16

Exploring Add-Ins and Libraries

In This Chapter

- Understanding the types of add-ins
- Understanding libraries
- An overview of built-in add-ins in Access 97
- Understanding libraries and how to use them
- How to develop and install your own add-ins
- Exploring the Add-In Manager

Access 97 add-ins are databases containing procedures and associated objects that you can add to Access using the Add-In Manager. By doing so, you can enhance the functionality of Access or a custom application developed for the Access environment. There are three types of Access 97 add-ins: menu add-ins, builder add-ins, and wizard add-ins. This chapter provides an overview of the various add-ins prepackaged with Access and presents a hands-on look at building a custom add-in wizard that creates a table, form, and report.

Understanding Types of Add-Ins

Some add-ins are context-specific and are launched when the user attempts to perform some action in a particular context. Examples of context-specific add-ins include the Access form wizards, invoked when a user builds a new Autoform, and control wizards, invoked when a user inserts a new control on a form with the control wizards enabled. Context-specific add-ins are usually represented as wizard add-ins or builder add-ins.

Add-ins that are not context-specific are generally classified as menu add-ins. They appear on the pop-out menu when you choose Tools⇨Add-Ins, along with the menu add-ins that Access installs. In Access 97, you also can reference add-ins from any other menu or toolbar.

You can see the built-in menu add-ins and wizards installed by Access 97 by inspecting the system Registry. Using the Registry Editor (see Chapter 1, "Using Windows 95 Registry," for information on using the Registry Editor and the Registry architecture), expand the tree HKEY_LOCAL_MACHINE\Software\Microsoft\Office\8.0\Access. In this subtree, you see two subkeys, labeled Menu Add-Ins and Wizards. Expand these subkeys to see the various built-in add-ins in Access 97.

Later in this chapter, you'll explore a custom menu add-in and discover how to register this add-in in the Registry. For now, expand the Wizards subkey, the Control Wizards subkey, and the CommandButton subkey. Click once on the subkey labeled MSCommandButtonWizard to see the values registered for this add-in. Note the Library value. This is the database location of the database housing this add-in, the command button wizard. Also note the Function value, which specifies the function in the add-in that Access will call when a user invokes the add-in. You'll become more familiar with these entries when you explore the custom add-in.

A *wizard* is an add-in that helps you create objects such as tables, queries, reports, and forms. Some wizards create entire applications or sets of routines that you can integrate into your database. Access 97 has several built-in wizards, as you saw in the Registry, that you should find helpful. You'll find many more wizards available from third-party vendors. Wizards either are sold directly for an end-user's use, perhaps to produce a query or report, or are sold to enhance the productivity of Access application developers. As mentioned earlier, you also can build your own wizards.

Another type of add-in is a *builder*. Builders are tools that help simplify a task, such as building a formula for a control on a form or report or setting a control property. Builders are usually simpler than wizards in terms of the user interface and the resulting output of the add-in. Access 97 installs Property builders and an Expression builder, which you will find yourself using quite often as you build your applications.

The third type of add-in is the *menu* add-in. This type of add-in is not associated with any particular context in using Access. You install it to be a choice found on the Tools⇨Add-Ins menu (although you can place the add-in on other menus). An example of a menu add-in is the Switchboard Manager installed with Access.

Understanding Libraries

Add-ins live in a standard Access database and usually have either an .MDA or an .MDE extension. These databases are built with the sole purpose of housing one or more add-in procedures and associated database objects, such as forms, queries, and tables. These types of databases are known as *add-in databases* but sometimes are referred to as *libraries*.

Although add-ins can be considered library databases, the term library is generally reserved for databases that hold Visual Basic routines that provide utility across several Access applications. Using libraries will enable you to provide procedures that are customized for your business to all Access applications developed for the business, as well as to maintain the procedures in one common source, the library database.

Referencing library databases

To be used by Access 97 databases, library databases must be in Access 97 format and require that a reference be made to them from the calling database. Circular references are not allowed, meaning that you cannot establish a reference from YourAccountingLib.MDA to YourMathLib.MDA and have YourMathLib.MDA reference YourAccountingLib.MDA. These libraries can reference each other but not at the same time.

To establish a reference by using Access menus from YourApp.MDB to YourLib.MDA for example, follow these steps (refer to Chapter 6, "Working with OLE Objects and ActiveX Controls," for more information on references):

1. Open a module window in YourApp.MDB.
2. Choose References from the Tools menu and then click on the Browse button in the References dialog box.
3. In the Files of Type box, select Databases (*.mdb, *.mda, *.mde).
4. Locate your library database (YourLib.MDA in this example).
5. Click on OK.

You should see your library database name in the list of available references in the References dialog box. If your library contains a procedure with a name that is also found in another referenced library, a call to this procedure will invoke the first library in the references list to contain the procedure name. If your code is not being called, you can move your library higher on the list of referenced libraries or rename the procedure so that conflicts do not occur. You should take care in naming library procedures to reduce the risk of collisions with other libraries. Use a naming convention that has a good chance of being unique.

If you want to establish a reference at run time in Visual Basic code, use one of the `Create reference` methods of the `References` collection, as discussed in "Creating references in code" in Chapter 6, "Working with OLE Objects and ActiveX Controls."

Your application database can now call routines in the referenced database. The procedures called in your library must be Public procedures and must be resident in standard modules within the library database. Although your library procedures can use Private procedures in the library, the referencing database cannot use those Private procedures. Additionally, you cannot call functions contained in class modules within the library database. To use your library class methods, call public functions contained in standard modules that use the library class modules. Your library routines can be set up to return a calculated result and open Access objects stored in the library database. You can even use a library database to store custom toolbars.

The section "Exploring MDE files," later in this chapter, introduces the .MDE file type, which enables you to save your database as a compressed file with your source code removed. If you choose to save your library database as an .MDE file and your database references other databases, those referenced databases must also be in .MDE format before your save operation can be successful.

Calling functions in Dynamic Link Libraries

As you gain experience developing Access applications and libraries, sooner or later you'll find yourself needing a function that resides in a Windows 95 Dynamic Link Library (DLL) or some third-party DLL. It is quite common today to find Access applications containing calls to the Windows 95 Application Programming Interface (API) to take advantage of the power provided by the API. Chapter 6, "Working with OLE and ActiveX Controls," discusses Common Windows controls and the use of the comctl32.ocx and the comdlg32.ocx, which enable you to use the functions in the corresponding comctl32.dll and comdlg32.dll in your applications. One of the controls discussed in Chapter 6 is the `Common Dialog` control used for the File Open, File Save As, and Print dialog boxes. This section discusses the use of the File Open dialog box using an API call to the common dialog DLL (comdlg32.dll) instead of using the comdlg32.ocx.

To use functions contained in DLLs, you need to declare the functions to VBA. You use the `Declare` statement for this purpose. `Declare` informs VBA of the name of the DLL containing the function being declared as well as the arguments and argument types the function expects. This information enables VBA to check your function call at compile time for proper argument types. The following `Declare` statement is specified in CH16.MDA General Declarations section of the `General Functions` module to declare the common dialog `GetOpenFileName` function for opening a file (this code is included on the CD-ROM with this book):

```
Declare Function GetOpenFileName Lib "comdlg32.dll" Alias _
"GetOpenFileNameA" _
(pOpenfilename As OPENFILENAME) As Long
```

In the preceding `Declare` statement, `GetOpenFileName` is the name of the function being declared and is specified as residing in the DLL named by the `Lib` argument, comdlg32.dll.

The `Alias` argument specifies that `GetOpenFileNameA` is the actual name of the function in the comdlg32.dll. The program will use `GetOpenFileName`, but the actual function called will be `GetOpenFileNameA`.

The parentheses contain the arguments expected by the `GetOpenFileNameA` function. In this case, the function expects an `OPENFILENAME` structure to be passed into it. You need to declare this structure before the reference to it in the `Declare` statement.

The final As Long indicates to Visual Basic that GetOpenFileNameA returns a value of type Long. Alternatively, you can specify this return type as follows:

```
Declare Function GetOpenFileName& Lib "comdlg32.dll" Alias _
"GetOpenFileNameA" (pOpenfilename As OPENFILENAME)
```

Note the use of the & symbol at the end of the function name to designate the return type.

You can specify the arguments as Optional, ByVal, ByRef, or ParamArray to indicate the means of passing the arguments to the function, and each variable specified can also designate a type. Note that the variables specified in the Declare statement need not match those used in the actual call to the function, but the variables used in the call must match the type specified by position.

If you use Optional to specify an argument that may be passed to the function or omitted, you must designate the type of the argument as Variant and specify all remaining arguments as Optional also.

ByVal causes the variable's value to be passed to the function instead of to the variable's address. If an argument is designated as ByVal, the function cannot modify the argument variable (with the exception of String arguments, which are covered shortly).

ByRef causes the variable's address to be passed to the function. Argument variables passed in this manner can be modified by the called function. This is the manner in which you pass a variable to receive a return value other than that passed by the function's As Type specifier. In other words, some functions pass back a value indicating the success of the function execution in the function's As Type return value but also return other values into variables passed ByRef. If you don't specify an argument-passing method, the ByRef method is assumed.

The ParamArray specification can only be used as the last argument specifier and implies an Optional array of Variant elements. You may pass any number of arguments in place of this argument specification.

If a function does not require any arguments, you need only specify the parentheses with nothing inside of them.

Indicate the type of the argument after the argument name by using As Type, where Type can be any of the valid Visual Basic types, a user-defined structure as used in the GetOpenFileName function, an object type, or the generic type Object. If you use ByVal in front of a String type, Visual Basic passes a C-Type string, that is, a reference to a null-terminated string. This type of argument can be modified by the calling function.

Take a look at the `OpenFileDlg` function in the Ch16.MDA General Functions module. The function first sets up a string variable with the filters that will appear in the File of Type drop-down list in the `OpenFile` dialog box. These are the file types that will be listed in the directories chosen by the user of the File Open dialog box.

Next, various string variables are initialized, which will be assigned to members of the `OPENFILENAME` structure passed to the `GetOpenFileName` function. The `DlgTitle` string variable, for example, will be assigned to the `lpstrTitle` member of `OPENFILENAME` to display a custom title in the `FileOpen` dialog box when it appears.

After the initializations, the members of the variable `pOpenfilename` declared as an `OPENFILENAME` structure are given values before the actual call to the `GetOpenFileName` function. Note that some of the structure variables are assigned a value that is returned from another function, the `lstrcpy` function.

The `lstrcpy` function is another Windows API function found in kernel32.dll, as declared in the `Declare Function` statement in the General Declarations. This function copies the second argument string to the first argument string and returns the address (pointer) of the first argument string as a `Long`. This address is assigned to various member variables of the `OPENFILENAME` structure, which require an address value. Note that all of these member variables begin with the letters `lp`, which stand for *long pointer.* This naming scheme is generally followed throughout the Win32 API.

Not all structure members with names beginning with the letters `lp` are assigned the return value of `lstrcpy`. Some are assigned a value of zero. A zero value in variables storing long pointers is interpreted as a null pointer. If you are working with API calls that require input address values or pointers and they will accept null-valued pointers, you can assign zero and the function should be able to accept it.

When the `OPENFILENAME` structure has been set up for the call, the actual call to `GetOpenFileName` is made to open the `FileOpen` dialog box. The address of the file name chosen by the end user is returned in the `lpstrFile` member of `OPENFILENAME`. Again, `lstrcpy` assigns the file name to a string variable within the function. Because the `lpstrFile` points to a null-terminated string, one ending in `Chr$(0)`, the function strips the null character at the end of the file name using the `InStr` and `Left$` functions of VBA. The resulting string is passed back to the caller of `OpenFileDlg`. This file name contains the full path of the file.

Win32 API calls and calls to other DLLs can be very valuable in your Access applications. Of course, you have to know the API functions and their syntax before using them successfully in your application, and some are easier to use than others. If you do decide to use a Win32 API call, you can pick up its declaration statement, structure declarations, and constant declarations from the Win32 API Viewer application that ships with the Office Developers Edition. This application is located in the Office\ODE Tools\Win32 API

Viewer directory. It's a very handy tool for reducing function declaration errors as a result of typing the declaration statements manually.

An Overview of Access 97 Add-Ins

This section presents an overview of some of the Access 97 built-in add-ins. Three add-ins are explored here to give you a feel for the power of these tools: the Switchboard Manager add-in, the Form Wizard, and the Command Button control wizard.

Using the Switchboard Manager

Switchboards are forms in an application that present a road map of the application components or subsystems. Using a switchboard, the end user can easily choose the part of the application he or she wants to use, usually by clicking a button on the form. The switchboard is a main form presented to the user when the application starts up, or it can be a form buried in the application to help the end user through a series of tasks and can act as a checklist. More information on switchboards, including some interesting design options, is in Chapter 8, "User Interface Secrets and Techniques."

You can use the Switchboard Manager to build one or more switchboards for your application or to edit an existing switchboard built previously with the Manager. Use the following steps to create a new switchboard:

1. Choose Tools⇨Add-Ins and then select the Switchboard Manager.
2. If the Switchboard Manager doesn't find its Switchboard Items table resident in your database, it pops up a dialog box that asks if you would like to build a new switchboard. Click on Yes.
3. In the Switchboard Manager dialog box, the default switchboard, referred to as a *page,* is highlighted (see Figure 16-1). Click on the Edit button to add items to this switchboard.

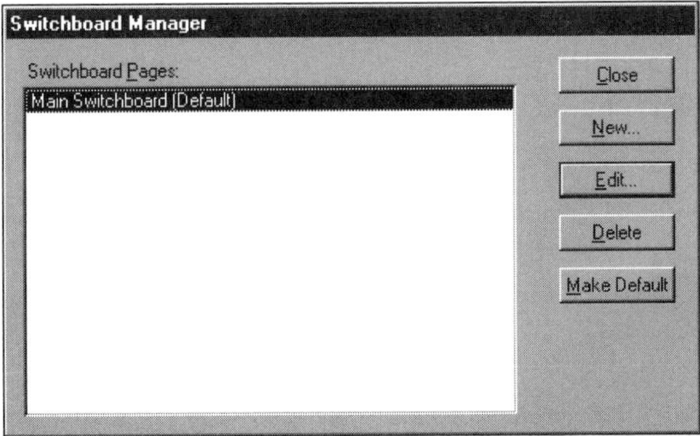

Figure 16-1: The Switchboard Manager dialog box.

4. In the Edit Switchboard Page dialog box, you can type a name for the switchboard in the Switchboard Name box to change the default name, or you can use the default name **Main Switchboard** (see Figure 16-2). Click on the New button to add a new item to this switchboard.

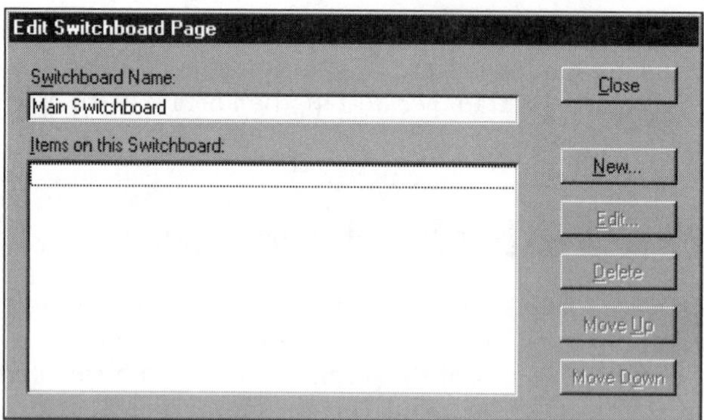

Figure 16-2: The Edit Switchboard Page dialog box.

5. The Edit Switchboard Item dialog box presents three choices for the switchboard item (see Figure 16-3). In the Text box, enter a name for the item. This name will appear on a switchboard button. In the Command combo box, select the command you want to activate when the user clicks on this button.

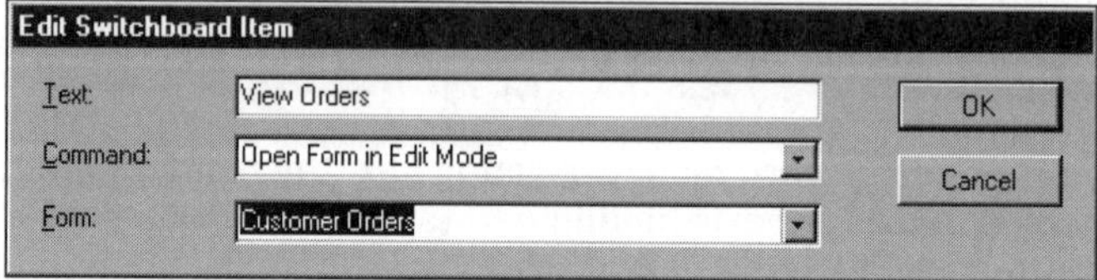

Figure 16-3: The Edit Switchboard Item dialog box.

The third entry on this dialog box changes with the selection in the Command combo box. If you select the command Go To Switchboard, for example, the third entry needs to specify the name of the switchboard to activate. If you specify a command of Run Code, the third entry needs to be the name of the function to run. Some command selections, such as Design Application, do not need a third entry.

6. After entering your choices for this switchboard item, click on OK. Repeat adding new items until you have completed your switchboard entries for this switchboard.

7. In the Edit Switchboard Page dialog box, you can edit an item by clicking on the Edit button, delete an item by clicking on the Delete button, or reposition an item by clicking on the Move Up or Move Down buttons.
8. When you have completed your switchboard, click on the Close button.

After you have completed these steps, you will notice that the Switchboard Manager has created a Switchboard Items table in your database and a form with the name you selected in the Edit Switchboard Page dialog box. Open the form to see the result of your work. Try out the choices to ensure that they do what you intended; if they don't, you can reopen the Switchboard Manager to edit your choices.

If you use the Switchboard Manager to create a switchboard form, you should also use the Manager to edit the form. This practice keeps the Manager's table of switchboard items in sync with the form and makes it easier to manage your switchboards.

Using the Form Wizard

The Form Wizard is one of seven wizards you can choose from when you elect to build a new form. This wizard is an example of an add-in that creates a form object and controls based on selected fields from the table or query you name in the New Form dialog box before launching the wizard.

The first page of the Form Wizard asks you to select the fields you want on the form (see Figure 16-4). You can choose to add all fields from the Available Fields list by clicking on the >> button, or you can choose specific fields and click on the > button for each field to move it to the Selected Fields list box.

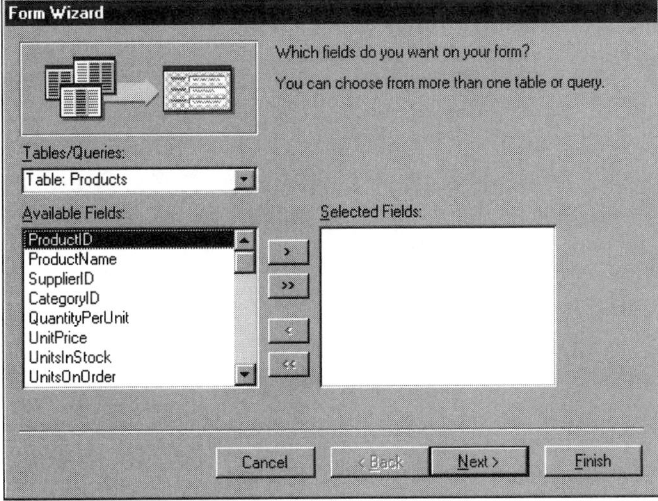

Figure 16-4: The first page of the Form Wizard that ships with Access 97.

If you have Relationships established in your database, you can choose fields from multiple tables by selecting those tables from the Tables/Queries drop-down combo box. If you select tables not in the relationships, the wizard asks if you want to edit the relationships. If you do elect to edit relationships at that point, you need to restart the Form Wizard to build your form.

The next page displayed by the wizard depends on the selections you made on the first page. If you selected fields from only one table or query, the second page displayed asks you what layout you want for the form (see Figure 16-5). You can choose from the options shown in Table 16-1.

Table 16-1 Form Wizard Layout Types

Layout Type	*Description*
Columnar	The selected fields are laid out in a column down the form; one record is displayed at a time.
Tabular	The selected fields are laid out across the form; multiple records are displayed.
Datasheet	The selected fields are laid out in datasheet format across the form width; multiple records are displayed.
Justified	The selected fields are laid out in tabular fashion across the form, but the fields are joined or justified and only one record is displayed at a time.

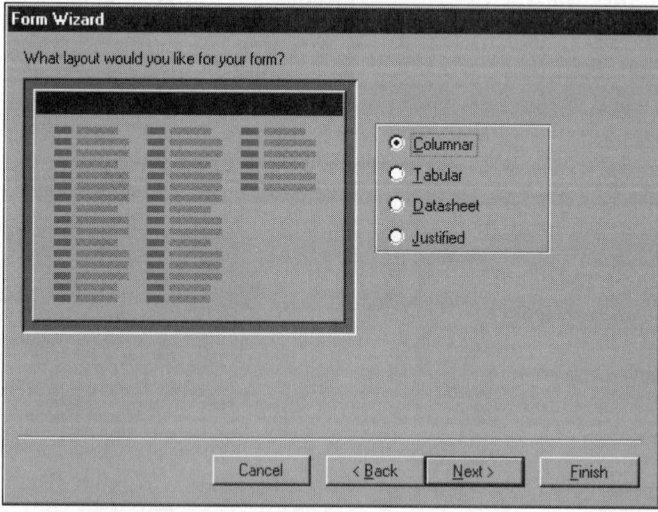

Figure 16-5: The Layout page of the Form Wizard.

If you selected fields from multiple tables/queries on page one of the wizard, the second page asks you for the type of view you want for each field source (see Figure 16-6). If a table selected in the list box is a one-side table in the defined relationships (a parent table), you can select Form with subform(s) or Linked forms for a view. Selecting a many-side table (a child table) in the list box enables you to choose Single form as a view.

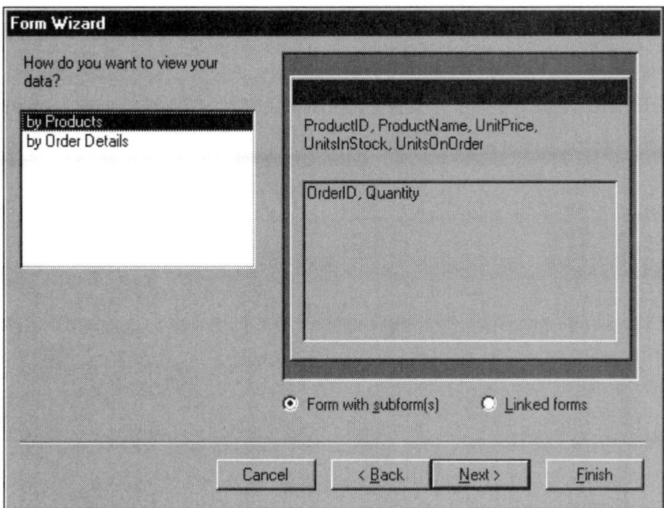

Figure 16-6: The View Selection page of the Form Wizard prompts you for a view type when you have selected fields from multiple related tables/queries.

For a parent table, choosing Form with subform(s) creates a parent form containing the fields you selected from the one side of the related tables and a subform for the fields you selected from the many side of the related tables. Selecting Linked forms as a view type creates a parent form for the one-side fields and a separate child form for the many-side fields linked by a command button on the parent form.

Choosing Form with subform(s) causes the next page of the wizard to prompt you for a layout of the subform. You can choose from Tabular or Datasheet.

After selecting the fields, the optional view, and the layout, the wizard asks you to select a style for the form and controls (see Figure 16-7). You have ten choices for styles. Selecting the styles from the list displays a preview in the left pane of the page.

The last page of the wizard asks you for a title for your form (see Figure 16-8). If you have linked forms, you can enter a title for each form. The last choice you have before creating the form is to open the form and view the data the form is based on or open the form in Design view to make changes. Click on the Finish button after making these choices to start the build process.

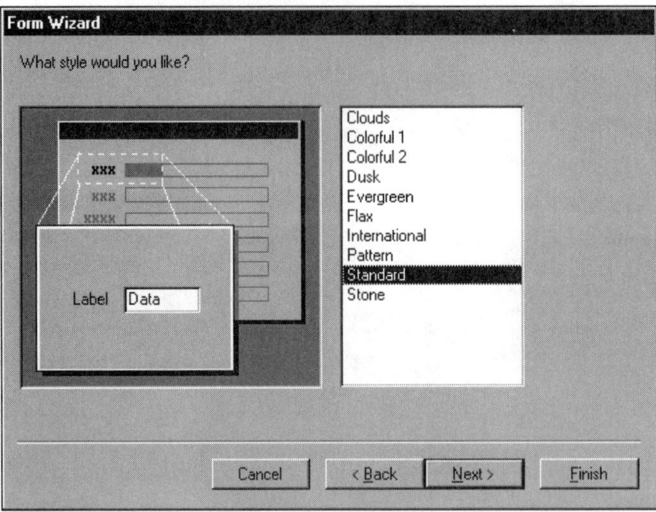

Figure 16-7: The Form Wizard page for selecting the form style applied to the form and controls.

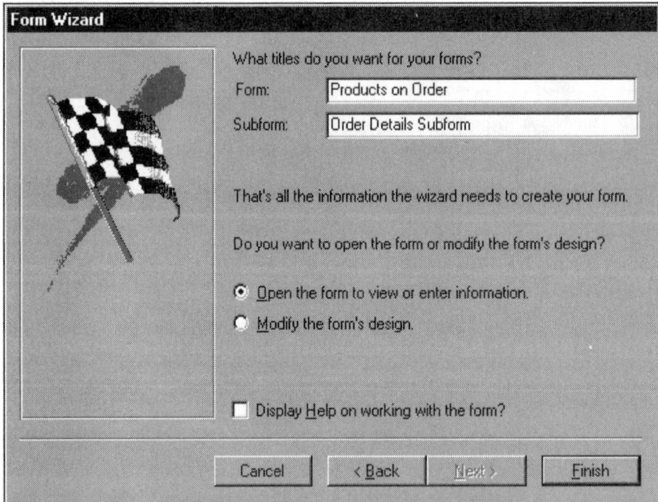

Figure 16-8: The last page of the Form Wizard prompts for a title and for the way you want the new form to open.

The Form Wizard does a good job with the information it collects, but like many of the wizards, you most likely will use the wizard as a starting point and make your own design changes to get the result you want.

Using the Command Button Wizard

If you enable control wizards by clicking the Control Wizards button on the Toolbox in form design mode, the Command Button Wizard will be launched when you insert a command button onto a form (see Figure 16-9).

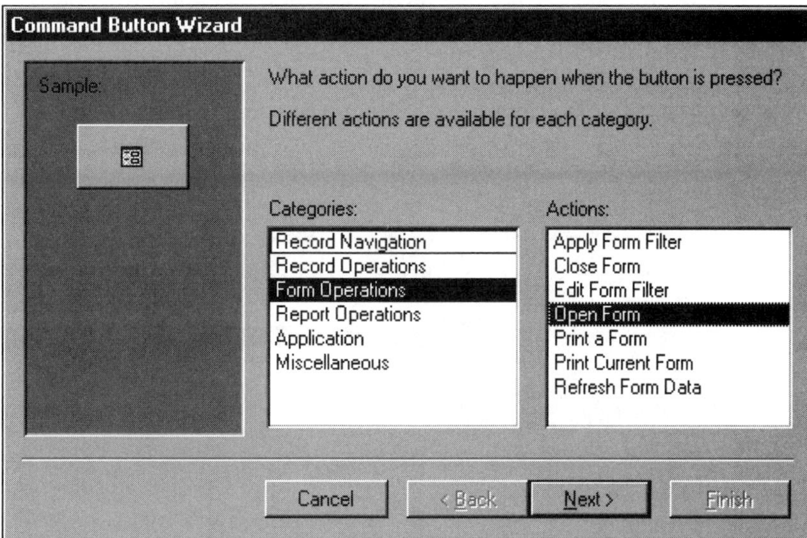

Figure 16-9: The first page of the Command Button Wizard asks you for an action to be associated with the click event of the command button.

The first page of the Command Button Wizard asks you to choose an action to run when a user clicks on the command button. There are six categories to choose from in the Categories list box. Selecting one of the categories causes the Actions list to be filled with actions in the selected category. Select an action and click on the Next button at the bottom of the wizard form. The available action categories are

- **Record Navigation:** Includes the actions Find Next, Find Record, Go to First Record, and others.
- **Record Operations:** Includes the actions Add New Record, Delete Record, and others.
- **Form Operations:** Includes the actions Edit Form Filter, Open Form, Print a Form, and others.
- **Report Operations:** Includes the actions Preview Report, Print Report, Send Report to File, and others.
- **Application:** Includes the actions Quit Application, Run Application, Run MS Excel, and others.
- **Miscellaneous:** Includes the actions Print Table, Run Macro, Run Query, and others.

Subsequent pages of the wizard depend on the selected action. For example, if you choose the Open Form action from the Form Operations category, the next page prompts you for a form name to be associated with the Open command. If you choose Run Query from the Miscellaneous category, the wizard prompts you for the query name to run.

Eventually, you get to choose between having text or a picture on the button (see Figure 16-10). If you choose Text, you can enter the text to be displayed on the button face. If you choose Picture, you can select a picture from the list or click the Browse button to find a picture file to be loaded and displayed on the button face.

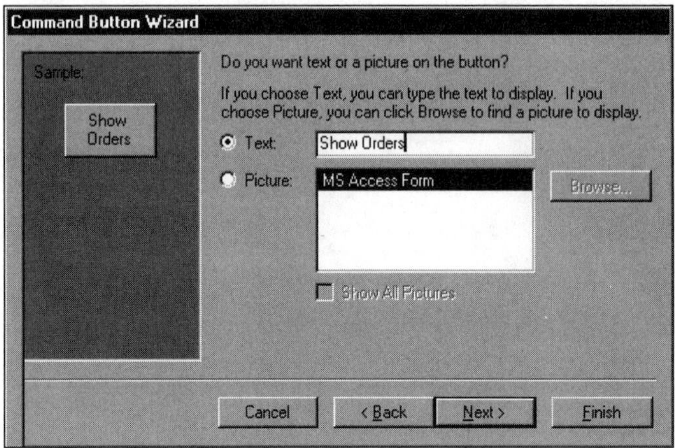

Figure 16-10: The Command Button Wizard dialog page for collecting your choice of having text or a picture displayed on the button face.

The final page of the wizard asks for the name you want to give to the command button. After entering the name, click on the Finish button to set the chosen properties. Canceling from this page only cancels the wizard; it does not cancel the insertion of the command button onto the form. To use the wizard again for this button, delete the button and reinsert a new one onto the form.

The Command Button Wizard is a good example of a property wizard that can help you set up your applications quickly. It also gives you an indication of what you can do with add-in technology.

Creating Your Own Add-Ins

This section presents an overview of the steps to create and install an add-in. The CD-ROM at the back of this book contains the file CH16.MDA as a sample add-in, which creates a table, form, and report object based on the selections you make in the wizard.

Following are the basic steps you take in developing an add-in:

1. Consider the purpose of the add-in and what type of add-in would best fit this purpose.
2. Design the add-in user-interface and the flow of control for the add-in.
3. Code the add-in by using code-behind-forms and modules.
4. Test your add-in.
5. Implement your add-in. This step includes the preparation of the add-in for use with the Add-In Manager.

The following sections discuss each step in order.

Considering the add-in purpose and type

The first task in developing your add-in is to decide what the add-in will do. What is the purpose of the add-in? Will it help the end user create some object, such as a report or form? Will it guide the end user through a series of steps toward the completion of some task? Will it aid in setting some property value or in selecting a value for a control?

Thinking about the purpose of the add-in and how it will be used helps you determine how to design the add-in and how it should be invoked.

If your add-in will create an Access object, such as a form or report, you may want to consider a form or report wizard invoked from the New button on the Form or Report tab of the database window. For this type of add-in, you need to query the end user for information about controls, such as their names and types, about data sources for the form, and about the look and feel of the form layout — just as the built-in Form Wizard does.

If you need to provide an aid to creating a property value or help decide on a value for a field based on the answers to a set of questions and values in the database, you might consider using a builder as an add-in launched in the context of a control on a form or in design mode for a form or report.

When your analysis determines that the add-in is not associated with any particular object or control context and should be generally available to the end user of Access or your application, you can choose to implement a Menu add-in that end users can choose whenever they need the tool.

Designing the add-in user interface and flow of control

In designing the add-in user interface and the flow of control within the add-in, you need to consider how the user will interact with the add-in to enter information in a logical manner as well as the dependencies among the information collected.

In this phase of the design process, you decide where to place prompts for information, which prompts to group together on a form, and in which order to present the prompts. As in the Form Wizard discussed earlier in this chapter, the second page to appear in the wizard is dependent on the user's selection(s) on the first page. When the user selects fields from only one data source, the wizard displays the page prompting for the layout to apply to the form. When the user selects fields from multiple data sources, the wizard displays a prompt for the type of view to use. This dependent action by a wizard may also be necessary in your add-in.

Diagramming flow of control

You may find it helpful to design your add-in flow of control on paper first. Start by drawing boxes to represent pages of dialog to present to the user. Connect those boxes by a line denoting direct passage of control from one page to the next, or by a diamond shape denoting one or more decisions. A diamond may be connected to any number of other boxes, one being chosen by the decision outcome.

The decisions you specify can range from very simple to very complex and may include decisions based on the outcome of edits on the entered data. If you need to perform edits on the entered data on a page-by-page basis, a decision point in the flow of control may direct the flow back to the same page if the edits fail (see Figure 16-11).

As you draw the boxes, label them with their names and purposes. When you are satisfied with the flow and the decisions controlling that flow, you can go back to the diagram and start designing the user interface for each page.

You may find that some add-ins need to present a means for the user to jump from one part of the add-in to another, possibly to skip a section that is not necessary for the task the end user wants to perform. In this case, you may provide a set of buttons on the add-in form to enable the end user to jump to the page of interest, or, if there are many choices, a drop-down list of pages from which the end user can choose. On your design diagram, you can designate the direct jump entry points by an arrow or other symbol at the page where the end user may jump to or enter.

Designing the interface

You may again want to do the preliminary design for each page by drawing a layout of controls on paper, labeled by the page name to correspond to the flow diagram, or you may want to design a prototype directly in Access form design mode to help you get the look you are after.

In designing your interface, try to keep it simple and consistent with the interface found in other Access add-ins. Don't try to cram too much into one dialog page. Keep the interface logical and collect information in a manner consistent with the way the typical end user would assume in entering the data. Be forgiving. If the end user makes a mistake, don't blow out of the add-in, making them reenter all the work they did up to that point. Instead, provide a message indicating the problem and give them a chance to fix it.

START

Page 1

Collect Name,
Template Load,
Date Placment,
Page #,
Orientation

Page 2

Collect,
Column,
Specification

Page 3

Collect,
Title,
Save Template,
Report Lines,
How To Open

Edits OK?

No

Go To 1st Page Containing Bad Data

Yes

Fill Column?

No

Generate Objects

FINISH

Yes

Page 4

Collect,
Fill,
Column,
Specification

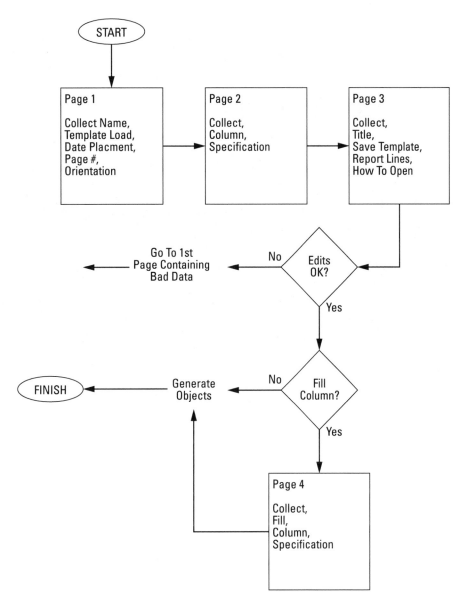

Figure 16-11: An example of a flow of control design for an add-in showing dialog pages and decision points.

Tip

We find it helpful in the design of our add-ins to put navigation buttons in a form footer and develop the pages of the interface as multiple pages of the same form. We usually provide a means for the end user to save and reload information entered into the wizard. This is especially useful when the add-in collects information that could be used in subsequent uses of the add-in. In a Form Wizard, for example, the end user may enter information to create a particular form and then want to go back later and create basically the same form but with some different choices. End users are very appreciative if they can simply load the add-in choices they made for the previous form and then make the changes they want for the new form.

Coding your add-in

When coding your add-in, you need to be aware of which objects you are referring to, those in the database that called the add-in or those in the database containing the add-in.

On CD-ROM

An example of the two reference requirements is found in the sample add-in from CH16.MDA on the CD-ROM. This add-in needs to refer to local tables in the add-in database for saving user entries that will be used in building the form and report. It doesn't make sense to create this table in the end user's database, because it is needed by the add-in only for creating the output objects. The output objects, table, form, and report, however, must be stored in the end-user database. You need a way to point your add-in to either the add-in database or the end-user database.

The `CodeDb` function returns a `Database` object that refers to the database in which the code is running. Because your add-in code is running to make the reference to the `CodeDb` function, the database returned is your add-in database. The `Name` property of this `Database` object is the full path and name of the add-in database. This is useful if you need to know where your add-in database resides on the user's hard disk.

The `Generate_Table` function in the CH16.MDA sample wizard needs a database object for the user database calling the wizard and a database object for the wizard database. The function starts out by setting two database objects using the familiar `DBEngine.Workspaces(0).Databases(0)` to refer to the user database and the `CodeDb` function to refer to the wizard database. The syntax is as follows:

```
Dim dbDatabase As Database, userdb As Database
...

Set dbDatabase = CodeDb()
Set userdb = DBEngine.Workspaces(0).Databases(0)
```

Access 97 provides several functions that you will find useful in coding your add-in. Table 16-2 shows these functions and their purpose.

Table 16-2 Add-In Functions for Creating Forms, Reports, and Controls

Function Name	*Purpose*
`CreateForm`	Creates a form in the user database and returns a `Form` object.
`CreateReport`	Creates a report in the user database and returns a `Report` object.
`CreateControl`	Creates a control on a form and returns a `Control` object. The form on which the control is placed must be open in Design mode.
`CreateReportControl`	Creates a control on a report and returns a `Control` object. The report on which the control is placed must be open in Design mode.
`CreateGroupLevel`	Creates a group on a report. The report must be open in Design mode.

You may specify a template in both the `CreateForm` and `CreateReport` functions. The template is typically used to provide a new form or report with a standard set of properties and controls. This reduces the amount of work the add-in must do to create the final result. If the `Create` functions do not specify a template, the one designated in the Forms/Reports tab of the Options dialog box is used as a template.

The sample wizard uses these functions to create the data entry form and the report, both of which are based on the table created in the user database. Refer to the functions `Generate_Form`, `Generate_Controls`, and `Generate_Report` to see these functions in action.

Cross-Reference

In addition to using DAO methods (discussed in Chapter 5, "Working with Data Access Objects") and the preceding functions for creating and manipulating database objects, you may find that you need to generate code to provide some special processing in the resulting objects. In the sample wizard, the `Generate_Code` function creates a series of statements that make up the `Print` event of the Detail section of the newly created report. This code draws lines around the report columns if the user specified this option in the wizard dialog box. Refer to the next section, "Coding on the run," to learn about the powerful module-editing capabilities you have available to your add-in.

You can run a preliminary test of your add-in by running the entry point function that's called by Access when your add-in is invoked by the user. Any objects generated by the add-in will end up in the add-in database because the user database and add-in (`CodeDb`) database are one and the same. Using this testing technique, you can at least test out the flow of control and generation of objects — but you must wait until after installation into a user environment to complete the tests.

Coding on the run

Your wizard or add-in may need to build or edit modules at run time. You may need to add code to a form module or, as the sample wizard does, add code to a report module. Or maybe you want to build some functions in a standalone module based on information entered by the user. Access 97 has added many new module-editing methods to help you build your modules at run time. This section explains these new methods associated with `Module` objects.

An Access 97 application contains a `Modules` collection of all open standard and class modules. Each `Module` object in the `Modules` collection can be accessed in any of the standard syntax for referencing collection members. Forms and Reports have `Module` properties that return a `Module` object that refers to their respective code modules. This property is used in the following discussion of the `InsertText` method. Within a `Modules` collection, an open form can also be referenced by using the following syntax:

```
Modules!Form_formname
```

Using InsertText

One method you can use to add code to a module at run time is to use the `InsertText` method. The syntax is as follows:

```
Module object.InsertText string
```

The object to which the `InsertText` method applies is either a Form, Report, standard module, or class module in your application database. This method inserts the text at the end of the designated module. You have no control over where to insert the code lines with this method.

The following example adds a command button and inserts a `Click Event Sub` procedure called `New_Customer_Click` into the Account form:

```
Dim sProcText As String
Dim cmdButton As Control

sProcText = "Private Sub New_Customer_Click()" & vbCrLf
sProcText = sProcText & "MsgBox ""A New Customer Added""" & vbCrLf
sProcText = sProcText & "End Sub" & vbCrLf

DoCmd.OpenForm "Account", acDesign

Set cmdButton = CreateControl("Account", acCommandButton, acDetail, _
"", "", (3.25 * 1440), (0.9583 * 1440), (1.0417 * 1440), (0.25 * 1440))
cmdButton.Name = "New_Customer"
cmdButton.OnClick = "[Event Procedure]"
cmdButton.Caption = "New Customer"
Forms![Account].Module.InsertText sProcText

DoCmd.Close acForm, "Account", acSaveYes
DoCmd.OpenForm "Account"
```

`sProcText` holds the text to be inserted into the module. `vbCrLf` is a constant defined by Visual Basic representing a carriage-return line-feed pair that forces line ends within the string.

This example only inserts a subprocedure that does nothing but present a message box when called, but you can code any valid statements to build a complete, meaningful procedure for your application. `InsertText` fails unless you insert at least one statement — even if it's no more than a comment — within the procedure being inserted.

The form that receives the text is opened in design mode by using the `DoCmd` object's `OpenForm` method. Use of the `InsertText` statement requires that the form be open in design mode.

After opening the form in design mode, the `CreateControl` function adds a command button that is used to add a new customer. `CreateControl` returns a `Control` object, which is assigned to an `Object` variable called `cmdButton`.

The `cmdButton` control sets the name of the command button and its caption and designates that the `OnClick` event references an event procedure.

The `InsertText` method is then executed to insert the Click event procedure into the form's module. The click event procedure receives the same name as the command button.

Now that the command button is on the form and tied to an event procedure, you can close the form by using the `Close` method of the `DoCmd` object. You specify an `acSaveYes` argument to save the form changes without prompting the user.

The Accounts form is then reopened to display the form with the new button. Clicking on the New Customer button displays the message inserted into the event procedure.

Using AddFromFile

Another method available to you for adding code to a module is the `AddFromFile` method, which adds lines from a text file into a module object. The syntax is as follows:

```
Module object.AddFromFile filename
```

Unlike the `InsertText` method — which inserts lines at the end of the module — the lines of the text file are inserted immediately after the declarations section and before the first procedure in the module designated by the module object. As in all module-editing methods, the module object must be open in design mode to enable editing.

The `AddFromString` method works exactly like the `AddFromFile` method but specifies a string as the source of the text lines instead of a file name.

Using CreateEventProc

The sample add-in discussed in this chapter needed to add an OnPrint event procedure to the report module being generated by the wizard. This procedure created borders around the printed text whenever the OnPrint event was fired by Access. As you see in the add-in, the entire procedure was built using the InsertText method. Another way to add event procedures to form or report modules starts off by using the CreateEventProc method. Its syntax follows:

```
Form/Report Module object.CreateEventProc(name of event, name of _
object)
```

CreateEventProc adds an event subprocedure shell for the event specified by the first argument to the object specified by the second argument. This method doesn't specify any code lines, so you need to use other methods of the Module object to insert the code you want to execute when the event is fired. To help in this endeavor, the CreateEventProc returns the line number of the first line of the procedure. This line number is relative to other procedures in the module.

Using InsertLines, ReplaceLine, and DeleteLines

To insert a line of code into the event procedure created with CreateEventProc, you can use the InsertLines method with the line number returned from the CreateEventProc. The syntax is as follows:

```
Module object.InsertLines starting line, string to insert
```

If you use a starting line number where code already resides, that code is pushed down below the inserted text. To replace a line, use the ReplaceLine method, which replaces the specified line number with the string argument. Its syntax is as follows:

```
Module object.ReplaceLine starting line, string to add
```

You may decide to house a module in your add-in database that contains a set of procedures you can use as templates in creating the code your add-in will insert into the target database. It's likely that these template procedures will contain more code than is necessary for a given target module and you'll need some way to delete certain lines from the templates as you build the target code. The module's DeleteLines method will come in handy for this purpose. Following is the syntax:

```
Module object.DeleteLines starting line, line count
```

DeleteLines deletes the number of lines specified by the line count argument, starting at the line specified by the starting line argument. Note that there is no designation of the procedure name in this method. The method works entirely by line numbers. If you know the name of the routine you want to delete, or maybe an offset from the first line of the routine, how do you get the line number so you can start deleting? The Find method is one method that can come to the rescue. Use the following syntax:

```
Module object.Find(text to find, starting line, starting column, _
ending line, ending column, _
optional wholeword, optional matchcase, optional pattern)
```

The `text to find` argument specifies the text to search for. When you have a module being used to hold template procedures in an add-in, as discussed previously, you can add comment lines or labels to the procedures or parts of procedures that designate sections you want to work with. To get the starting position of these procedures or sections, specify the label or keyword in the comment as the `text to find` in the `Find` method and nothing in the starting line argument. The `Find` method will return the line number of the text you are searching for, and you can add one to get the line after it.

If you know the `text to find` is beyond a given line in the module, you can set the `starting line` argument to that line number and `Find` will start its search at that line number. Whether the `starting line` argument is preset or not, the `Find` method returns the line number at which the search text was found in this argument. The `starting column` can be preset to the column of the starting line in which you want to start the search. `Find` will set the column number of the search text in this argument when it returns with a found condition.

`Ending line` and `ending column` work in a manner similar to `starting line` and `starting column`. You can specify the line you want the search to stop on in `ending line` and the column to stop search on in `ending column`. On return, `Find` will set the `ending line` argument to the line number the search text ends on and `ending column` to the column of that line at which the search text ends. The last three arguments are optional. `Wholeword` tells `Find` to search for whole words only. If you specify `port` as a `text to find` argument and set the `wholeword` argument to `True`, `Find` searches for `port` as a whole word. Setting `wholeword` to `False` or not specifying it at all causes `Find` to stop searching on any word containing `port`, such sup*port* or re*port*.

Setting the `matchcase` argument to `True` causes `Find` to match the case of the `text to find`, and a setting of `False` disregards case.

You can use wildcard characters such as * and ? in the `text to find` argument to do a pattern-matching search. To initiate pattern matching, set the `pattern` argument to `True`.

You can use `Find` to search through all occurrences of a text string by issuing the `Find` method with an empty `starting line` argument or an argument of `0`. If the `Find` method returns `True`, the text was found and the `starting line` argument is set to the line number where the text was found. Issuing the `Find` method again with this line number preserved in the `starting line` argument and `starting column` set to a value at least one greater than the value returned by `Find` causes the method to find the next occurrence of the text string. Continue with this technique until `Find` returns `False`.

Using ProcBodyLine and ProcStartLine

The ProcBodyLine property also returns the starting line number of a given procedure name. The syntax is as follows:

```
Module object.ProcBodyLine(name of proc, kind of proc)
```

Use one of the following predefined constants in the kind of proc argument:

Constant	*Procedure Type*
vbext_pk_Get	Property Get
vbext_pk_Let	Property Let
vbext_pk_Set	Property Set
vbext_pk_Proc	Sub or Function

ProcBodyLine returns the line number of the Proc statement. If you want the line number of the start of the procedure, which may include comments and compiler constants placed before the procedure statement, use the ProcStartLine property with the same arguments used in the ProcBodyLine.

If you need to retrieve one or more lines from a module, use the Lines property with the first argument set to the starting line number you want to retrieve and the second argument set to the number of lines to retrieve. Use this syntax:

```
Module object.Lines(starting line, number of lines)
```

Use any of the methods previously discussed to get the starting line number and then the Lines property to retrieve the number of lines you need into a string variable. You can then edit the string with standard VBA string editing functions and replace the lines back into the module or into another module.

Finding the number of lines in a module

Two properties are available to find the number of lines within a module. The ProcCountLines property returns the number of lines in a given procedure, including any comments and compiler constants immediately above the procedure statement. Following is the syntax:

```
Module object.ProcCountLines(name of proc, kind of proc)
```

The kind of proc argument is specified in the same way as for ProcBodyLine, discussed previously.

The `CountOfDeclarationLines` property is the second property that returns a line count. This property returns the number of lines in the declaration section of the referenced module. The syntax is as follows:

```
Module object.CountOfDeclarationLines
```

The number of lines returned is effectively the line number of the end of the module's `Declaration` section.

Compiling modules

After completing your module editing, you can force a compile of the modules by using the `RunCommand` method of the `DoCmd` or `Application` object. For example, to compile and save all modules, execute the following `RunCommand` before closing the edited modules:

```
DoCmd.RunCommand acCmdCompileAndSaveAllModules
```

When your add-in has finished its work, you should refresh the user's database window to display any new objects your add-in has added to their database. To do this, execute the `RefreshDatabaseWindow` method. This is a method of the application object, and there are no arguments to provide.

Preparing your add-in for installation

Now that you have your add-in designed, coded, and tested, you can turn your attention to distribution. This section deals with two topics: 1) preparing your add-in database so that the Add-In Manager can install it, and 2) saving your add-in as an .MDE file to protect your work and make a smaller file for distribution.

The first task to consider is setting up the necessary information in your database so that the Add-In Manager can determine what kind of add-in you want to install and provide the end user doing the installation with helpful information about your add-in.

Using the USysRegInfo table

The Add-In Manager uses a table called USysRegInfo and several database properties when installing your add-in. You can build the USysRegInfo from scratch or import it from any of the add-ins that ship with Access 97. The layout of the USysRegInfo table is shown in Table 16-3.

Table 16-3 Definition of the USysRegInfo Table

Field Name	*Field Type*	*Field Size*
SubKey	Text	255
Type	Number	Long Integer
ValName	Text	255
Value	Text	255

The records you insert into the USysRegInfo table depend on the type of add-in you have built. The first record in this table creates a key in the Registry to register your add-in.

The SubKey field of the first record is the key name and must be the same value on all records in the USysRegInfo table describing a given add-in. The SubKey starts with the root of the Registry tree under which you want to install your add-in. This value can be HKEY_LOCAL_MACHINE, or, if you are using a profile HKEY_CURRENT_ACCESS_PROFILE. (See "Using User Profiles" in Chapter 1, "Using the Windows 95 Registry," for information on setting up a profile in the registry.)

The next part of the SubKey entry depends on the type of add-in you are installing. If you are installing a builder, control wizard, or ActiveX control wizard, the next part of the SubKey must specify Wizards as the subkey under the root you previously chose, followed by the type of wizard, the subtype of wizard, and the name of the wizard, as shown here:

```
HKEY_LOCAL_MACHINE\Wizards\type wizard\subtype wizard\wizard name
```

For a control wizard, the type of wizard part of the string will be Control Wizards and the subtype of wizard will be the name of the control the wizard is associated with. Valid control names are the following:

- BoundObjectFrame
- CheckBox
- ComboBox
- CommandButton
- Image
- Label
- Line
- ListBox
- OptionButton

- `OptionGroup`
- `PageBreak`
- `Rectangle`
- `SubformSubreport`
- `TextBox`
- `ToggleButton`
- `UnboundObjectFrame`

If you are installing a builder, the type of wizard will be Property Wizards and the subtype of wizard will be the name of the property to associate the builder with. You can refer to the properties dialog box for an object in design mode to find the property name. Enter that name without spaces as the subtype of wizard.

For ActiveX control wizards, the type of wizard is ActiveX Control Wizards and the subtype of wizard is the value of the ActiveX control's `Class` property. To find the class name, select the ActiveX control in design mode and view its properties dialog box.

The SubKey format is a little different for wizards that create Access objects such as tables, forms, and reports. With these wizards, the SubKey specifies a type of wizard and wizard name but no subtype of wizard. The format of the SubKey is as follows:

```
HKEY_LOCAL_MACHINE\Wizards\type of wizard\name of wizard
```

The type of wizard may be one of the following values:

- Form Wizards
- Query Wizards
- Report Wizards
- Table Wizards

Menu add-ins have a SubKey format that registers your add-in under a Menu Add-Ins subkey rather than a Wizards subkey in the registry. The format of the SubKey is the following:

```
HKEY_LOCAL_MACHINE\Menu Add-Ins\name of add-in
```

The name of wizard for Access object wizards will appear in the New Object dialog box, and for a menu add-in, the name of add-in will appear in the Add-Ins submenu. For many of these menu add-ins, you will see an underlined letter in the add-in name. This is an access key for the add-in that enables the end user to access the menu add-in via the keyboard: Pressing Alt and then the underlined key launches the add-in. For example, to launch the Switchboard Manager add-in via the keyboard, you hold down the Alt key and press T for Tools, I for Add-Ins, and W for Switchboard Manager. To set an access key for your menu add-in, type **&** before the letter you want for an access key.

The Type field of the first record must be zero to denote that the subkey is to be added to the Registry, and the ValName and Value fields must be blank.

After the first record has been defined, subsequent records define values that are entered into the add-in entry in the Registry. All records must have the same SubKey value as the first record to identify them as belonging to that add-in.

The Type field on records following the first record denote the type of value to be entered into the registry. These types can be the following:

Type Field Value	*Type of Registry Value*
1	REG_SZ (String)
4	DWORD (REG_DWORD in the Windows NT Registry)

ValName specifies the name of the value to be entered, and Value contains the value itself. The number of values to add to the USysRegInfo table depends on the type of add-in being added. Table 16-4 lists the values you need to add for the various add-in types. (Remember that all SubKeys are the same as the first record in USysRegInfo for the add-in being defined.)

Table 16-4 Values to Add to the USysRegInfo Table for Add-Ins

Type Field	*ValName Field*	*Value Field*
Add-in Type: Control, ActiveX, or Builder Wizards		
4	Can Edit	1 = wizard can modify control or property; 0 = wizard cannot modify
1	Description	Text displayed in the Choose Builder dialog box when more than one add-in has been defined for the same control or property
1	Function	The name of the function that starts the add-in
1	Library	Specifies the path and name of the add-in database
Add-in Type: Access Object Wizards		
1	Bitmap	Specifies the path and name of the bitmap that is displayed for the wizard in the New Object dialog box

Type Field	ValName Field	Value Field
Add-in Type: Access Object Wizards		
4	Datasource Required	1 = user must specify a table or query name as the source of data for the object to be created by the wizard; 0 = datasource not required; this value is only necessary for Form and Report Wizards
1	Description	Text displayed in the New Object dialog box
1	Function	The name of the function that starts the add-in
4	Index	Specifies the order of the Description text displayed in the New Object dialog box; zero indicates the first entry in the dialog
1	Library	Specifies the path and name of the add-in database
Add-in Type: Menu Add-In		
1	Expression	The name of the function that starts the add-in preceded by an equal sign
1	Library	Specifies the path and name of the add-in database

On CD-ROM

The CH16.MDA sample add-in on the CD-ROM is an Object Wizard that creates a table, form, and report. The USysRegInfo records for this add-in are shown in Table 16-5.

Table 16-5 USysRegInfo Records Defining the CH16.MDA Sample Add-In

Subkey	Type	ValName	Value
HKEY_CURRENT_ACCESS_PROFILE\Menu Add-Ins\Secrets 97 Sample Wizard	0		
HKEY_CURRENT_ACCESS_PROFILE\Menu Add-Ins\Secrets 97 Sample Wizard	1	Expression	=StartWiz()
HKEY_CURRENT_ACCESS_PROFILE\Menu Add-Ins\Secrets 97 Sample Wizard	1	Library	ch16.mda

Setting database properties

Your second task in preparing your add-in for installation is to set some database properties. The information you provide in these properties will appear in the Add-In Manager dialog box to identify your add-in and your company. To set these properties, follow these steps:

1. Open the Database Properties dialog box by selecting Database Properties from the File menu or by right-clicking on the database container window and selecting Properties.
2. Click the Summary tab in Database Properties.
3. Enter a Title for your add-in, your Company name, and Comments. The Title will appear in the Available Add-Ins list in the Add-In Manager dialog box and in the Add-Ins menu after the end user adds your add-in. The Company Name will appear below the Available Add-Ins list box, and the Comments will appear directly below your company name.
4. Click on OK to close the Database Properties dialog box.

Cross-Reference

Now that you have prepared your add-in for installation by the Add-In Manager, you can create an installation disk set as described in Chapter 15, "Distributing Applications with the Office Developer Edition." Before you build your installation disk set, however, you may want to save your add-in in a smaller file size and at the same time protect your secrets by removing source code. The next section discusses how to save your database in a new format in Access 97: an .MDE file.

Exploring .MDE files

Saving your database as an .MDE file causes Access to compile your database, save it, remove source code, and compact the database. These actions result in a smaller, more efficient database due to source code removal and optimizations.

In the .MDE file format, your database code and objects cannot be viewed or modified by others, nor can they import the database forms, reports, and modules to another database. They can import tables, queries, and macros from your database, however. With these exceptions, your design is essentially locked up.

Secret

A drawback of the .MDE format is that because your source code is removed from the file, there is nothing to edit should your procedures use the module-editing features of VBA, as discussed in the "Coding on the run" section in this chapter. If your add-in needs to use module editing to add or change add-in code on the fly, you can't use the MDE format. If your add-in uses these VBA features to modify objects generated into the user database, however, an .MDE format is okay to use. This is generally what you will be doing in an add-in anyway.

If your database references other databases, such as a library database or another add-in database, those databases must also be in .MDE format. You cannot access .MDA formatted files from an .MDE file. Access will complain when you attempt to make an .MDE file that contains references to .MDB or .MDA files.

Building an .MDE file

To build the .MDE file, follow these steps:

1. Ensure that the database is closed by all possible users.
2. Choose Database Utilities from the Tools menu and click on Make MDE File.
3. Enter the name of the database you want to save in the Database To Save As MDE dialog box and click on Make MDE.
4. Enter a database name and choose the .MDE file location in the Save MDE As dialog box.

Tip

The action of creating an MDE file is a one-way street. After the file is created, it's only good for execution. If you need to modify the design or convert to a future version of Access, you will need the original database in non-MDE format. Be sure to save your original database in a safe place.

If you do not use the MDE format to distribute your database, be sure to compact the database before building your distribution disk set.

Using the Add-In Manager

With your USysRegInfo table and database properties set up, you are now ready to use the Add-In Manager to install your add-in. Note that the Add-In Manager can also be used to uninstall your add-in if necessary (but who would want to?).

Choose Add-Ins from the Tools menu and then click on Add-In Manager. The Available Add-Ins list in the Add-In Manager dialog box lists add-ins that are currently installed (those with an X next to them) and files in the Office directory with an .MDA or .MDE extension.

You can install one of the add-ins in the list by choosing it and clicking on Install, or you can add a new add-in by clicking on Add New. After installing the add-ins you want, click on the Close button to exit the Add-In Manager dialog box.

Cross-Reference

The Add-In Manager accesses your USysRegInfo table and enters the keys and values you specified there into the system Registry. You can use the Registry Editor as discussed in "Using the Registry Editor" in Chapter 1, "Using the Windows 95 Registry," to view your add-in entries. Figure 16-12 shows the Registry entries for the sample add-in in CH16.MDA.

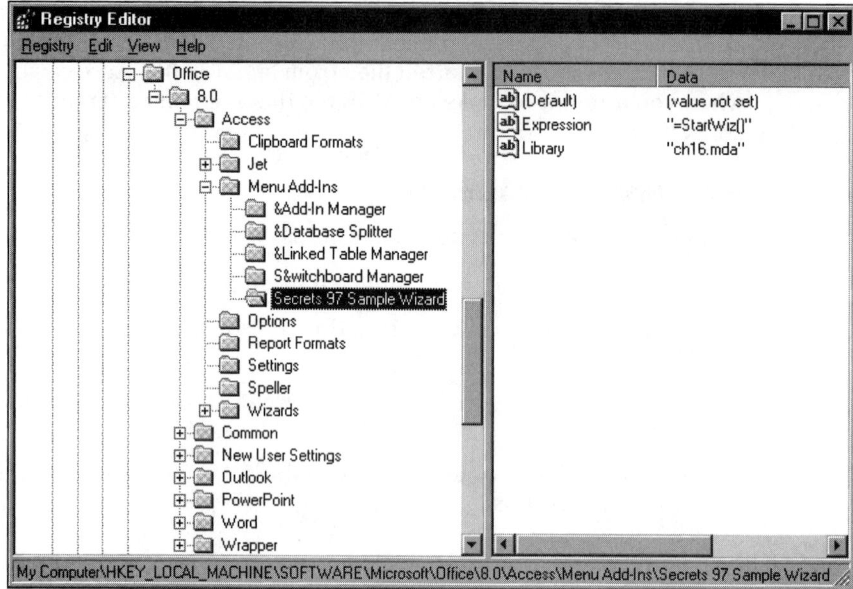

Figure 16-12: The Registry entries for the sample add-in from CH16.MDA on the CD-ROM.

With your add-in installed by the Add-In Manager, you can now run a complete test of the add-in to determine proper installation and functionality before distribution to your end users.

With the information provided in this chapter and the sample add-in in CH16.MDA, you'll be able to develop your own add-ins and libraries, which will substantially enhance the features of your Access 97 applications and ease the difficulty of your maintenance tasks.

Chapter 17

Securing an Access Application

In This Chapter

- Understanding Jet security
- Deciding on a security level to implement
- Creating a database password
- Using the /runtime option
- Using a database's Startup options
- Distributing an application as an .MDE file
- Manipulating users and groups
- Securing objects by using permissions
- Using the Access Security Wizard
- Encrypting a database
- Manipulating security by using DAO code

Although security options can be maintained in Access, Access is in fact manipulating the security of the Jet engine. The Jet security model has not changed much from Access 95. Jet's security is still a workgroup-based security model; all users in a workgroup are bound to the same security rules of the workgroup. The rules enforced for individual users, however, may vary from user to user, based on the permissions assigned each user.

Understanding Jet Security

Jet security is defined at the object level for individuals or groups of users. This security model of Jet/Access is rather complex, but it isn't too difficult to understand when broken down into its core components, which are as follows:

- Workgroups
- Groups
- Users
- Object owners
- Object permissions

Understanding workgroups

Jet stores security information for databases in workgroup files, usually named SYSTEM.MDW. The *workgroup file* is a special Access database that contains a collection of user names and passwords, user group definitions, object owner assignments, and object permissions. You can use the same workgroup file for multiple databases; after you enable security for a database, however, users must use the workgroup containing the security information. If users use a workgroup other than the workgroup used to define security, they are limited to logging in to the database as the Admin user — with whatever permissions the database administrator left for the Admin user.

Tip

When securing a database, one of the first things you need to do is to remove all permissions of the Admin user. Removing these permissions prevents other users from opening the database as the Admin user by using another Access workgroup file and obtaining the rights of the Admin user. Users can still open the database as the Admin user using a different workgroup, but they will not have any object permissions. This measure is discussed later in this chapter under Working with Workgroups.

Understanding permissions

The permissions in Jet security are defined at the object level; each object, such as a form or report, has a specific set of permissions. The system administrator defines what permissions each user, or group of users, has for each object. Users may belong to multiple groups, and they always inherit the highest permission setting of any of the groups to which they belong.

For example, every table object has a set of permissions associated with it: Read Design, Modify Design, Read Data, Update Data, Insert Data, Delete Data, and Administrator. (See Table 17-1 for a complete list of permissions and their meanings.) The database administrator has the ability to assign or remove any or all of these permissions for each user or group of users in the workgroup. Because the permissions are set at the object level, the administrator may give a user the ability to read data from Table A, read from and write data to Table B, and prevent the user from even looking at Table C. In addition, this complexity allows for unique security situations, such as having numerous users sharing data on a network, each with a different set of rights for the database objects. All security maintenance functions are performed from the Tools⇨Security menu item (see Figure 17-1).

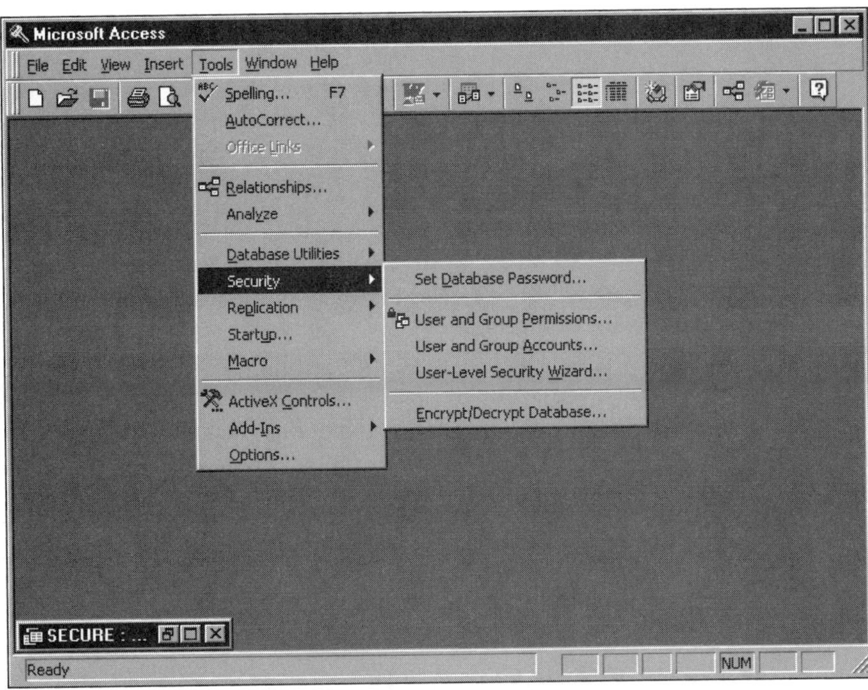

Figure 17-1: All Jet security functions are performed from the Tools➪Security menu.

Understanding security limitations

You must immediately be aware that you cannot depend on the Jet security model to be foolproof. Security holes in Access 2.0 have been discovered and exposed, in effect, *un*protecting every database distributed under the assumption that the code and objects were protected. Often, the amount of resources involved in developing an application is huge, and protecting that investment is essential. The most you can do for protection is to fully and properly implement the Jet 3.0 security model and use legally binding licensing agreements for all your distributed applications. Unfortunately, the future security of your databases is at the mercy of software hackers. As of the printing of this book, no *published* holes exist in the Jet 3.0 security model; however, as proven in the past, you are not guaranteed that this condition will not change.

Choosing a Security Level to Implement

As an Access developer, you must decide the level of security required for your application; not every database even needs security. If your application is used solely in-house, you may not need the powerful permission protection of Jet's security. When you do have an application database that you want to secure, you need to make the following decisions:

- What users are allowed to use the database?
- What groups do you need to create in the workgroup and what users will belong to each group?
- What object permissions need to be limited for each group or user?

After you have made these determinations, you are ready to begin implementing security in your application. Access includes a tool to help you implement security — the Security Wizard. This chapter teaches you how you can implement security by using Access's interface, discussing each security element in detail. Understanding the workings of the security model will greatly help you in your quest for total security. The wizard is discussed later in this chapter, after the nuts and bolts.

Creating a Database Password

You can use Jet security at its most basic level simply by controlling who can open the database. You control database access by creating a password for the databases you want to protect. When you set a database password for a database, users are prompted to enter the password each time they attempt to access the database. If they do not know the database password, they are not allowed access to the database. When using this form of security, you are not controlling specific permissions for specific users, you are merely controlling who can and cannot access the secured database.

To create a database password, follow these steps:

1. In Access, open the database that you want to secure. You must open the database exclusively in order to set the database password. To open a database exclusively, check the Exclusive checkbox on the Open dialog box.
2. Select Tools⇨Security⇨Set Database Password (refer to Figure 17-1).
3. In the Password field, type the password that you want to use to secure the database (see Figure 17-2).
4. In the Verify field, type the password again. This security measure ensures that you do not mistype the password (because you cannot see the characters you type) and mistakenly prevent everyone, including yourself, from accessing the database.

Figure 17-2: Creating a database password is the simplest way to secure your database.

5. Click on OK to save the password.

You cannot synchronize replicated databases that have database passwords. If you plan on using Jet's replication features and you need database security, you need to use user-level security.

After you save the database password, Access prompts every user of the database to enter the password prior to being allowed access to the database. Although this method controls *who* can access the database, it does not control *what* users are allowed to do with the objects and data after they have opened the database. To control objects, you need to fully implement Jet's user-level security, which is discussed in the following section.

To remove a database password, follow these steps:

1. In Access, open the database you want to unsecure. You must open the database exclusively to be able to unset the database password.
2. Select Tools⇨Security⇨Unset Database Password. This menu item was previously labeled Set Database Password but was changed when the database password was set.
3. In the password field, type the password of the database (see Figure 17-3).

Figure 17-3: You can remove a database password by retyping the password in the Unset Database Password dialog box.

4. Click on OK to unset the password.

If you remove a database password from an Access database, users are no longer required to enter a password to access the database unless you have enabled user-level security.

Any user who knows the database password has the ability to change or remove the database password. You can prevent this situation by removing the Administer permissions from the database for all users except the database administrator.

Using the /runtime Option

If you're not concerned with protecting your application but simply want to prevent users from mistakenly breaking your application by modifying or deleting objects, you can force your application to be run in Access's *runtime mode*. When a database is opened in Access in runtime mode, all the interface elements that allow changes to objects are hidden from the user. For example, it is impossible for a user to access the Database window in runtime mode. You must ensure that your application has a startup form that gives the users access to whatever objects you want them to be able to access.

You must have purchased and installed the Microsoft Office 97 Developer Edition tools (ODE) to use the /runtime switch.

To assign a form as a startup form, choose Tool⇨Startup and select the form you want to be the startup form from the Display Form drop-down list (see Figure 17-4).

To create a shortcut to start your application in Access's runtime mode, follow these steps:

1. Create a shortcut to start Access.
2. Right-click on the shortcut, select Properties, and then click on the Shortcut tab.
3. In the Target field, append to the path to MSACCESS.EXE a space, the path and filename of the database to open in runtime mode, another space, and then **/runtime**.

   The following command line starts Access and opens the Northwind database in runtime mode:

   C:\Program Files\Microsoft Office\Access\MSAccess.exe "c:\Program Files\Microsoft Office\Access\Samples\Northwind.mdb" /runtime

   The path and file name for the MSAccess.exe, as well as the /runtime switch, are not enclosed in quotes. However, you must enclose the path and file name for the database to open in quotes. If you enclose the /runtime switch in quotes, an error occurs when you attempt to execute the shortcut.

4. Distribute or re-create the shortcut for each user installation.

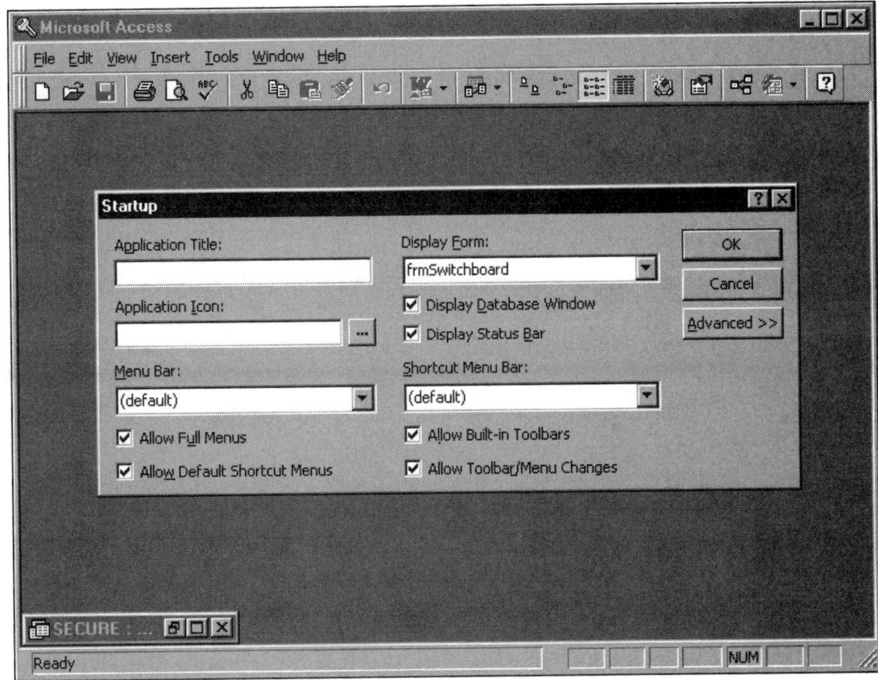

Figure 17-4: When running a database in Access's runtime mode, you must designate a startup form, usually a switchboard form from which your users can navigate your application.

You also can set database passwords by using VBA code. The following code changes the database password of the currently opened database:

```
Public Sub ChangeDatabasePassword()
On Error GoTo ChangeDatabasePasswordErr
Dim szOldPassword As String, szNewPassword As String
Dim db As Database

Set db = CurrentDb
szOldPassword = ""
szNewPassword = "shazam"

db.NewPassword szOldPassword, szNewPassword

Exit Sub

ChangeDatabasePasswordErr:
    MsgBox Err & ":  " & Err.Description
    Exit Sub

End Sub
```

If there is no database password set, you pass a zero-length string (" ") as the old password parameter. If there is a database password assigned and you want to remove the password, pass the database password as the old password parameter and pass a zero-length string (" ") as the new password.

Using a Database's Startup Options

A slightly more secure alternative to using the /runtime option is to set a database's Startup options. Although this provides greater security than the /runtime option, it is not a complete solution for situations where tight security is paramount. Figure 17-5 shows the Startup options dialog box with the Advanced options displayed. To access the Startup options dialog box, select Tools➪Startup.

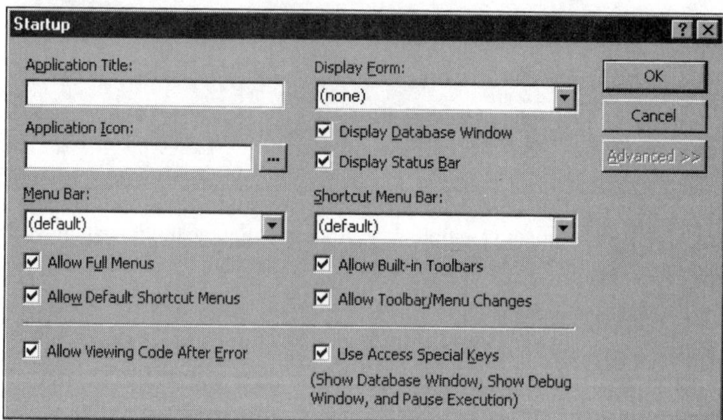

Figure 17-5: Using the Startup options dialog box gives you more security control than using the /runtime option.

On the Startup options dialog you can do the following:

- Prevent the Database window from being displayed
- Designate a menu bar to be used on startup of your application
- Designate a shortcut menu to be used on startup of your application
- Prevent Access's built-in menus from being displayed
- Prevent Access's built-in shortcut menus from being displayed
- Prevent Access's built-in toolbars from being displayed
- Prevent users from modifying toolbars

- Prevent users from being able to view code when an error is encountered (enter debug mode)
- Prevent users from using Access's special keys to display the Database window, display the debug window, or pause execution

Distributing a Database as an .MDE File

One way to ensure the security of your application's code, forms, and reports is to distribute your database as an .MDE file. When you save your database as an .MDE file, Access compiles all code modules (including form modules), removes all editable source code, and compacts the database. The new .MDE file contains no source code but continues to work because it does contain a compiled copy of all of your code. Not only is this a great way to secure your source code, it enables you to distribute databases that are smaller (because they contain no source code) and always keep their modules in a compiled state.

In addition to not being able to view your source code, end users cannot do the following to an .MDE file database:

- View, modify, or create forms, reports, or modules in Design view.
- Add, delete, or change references to object libraries or databases.
- Change your database's VBA project name using the Options dialog box.
- Import or export forms, reports, or modules. Note, however, that tables, queries, and macros can be imported from or exported to non-.MDE databases.

Because of these benefits/restrictions, it may not be possible to distribute your application as an .MDE file. For example, if your application creates forms at run time, you would not be able to distribute the database as an .MDE file.

There is no way to convert an .MDE file into a normal database file. Always save and keep a copy of the original database! When you need to make changes to the application, you must open the normal database and then create a new .MDE file before distribution. If you delete your original database, you will be unable to access any of your objects in design view!

Your database has to meet some requirements before it can be saved as an .MDE file. First, if security is in use, the user creating the .MDE file must have all applicable rights to the database. In addition, if the database is replicated, you must remove all replication system tables and properties before saving the .MDE file; you cannot create an .MDE file from a replicated database, but you can replicate an .MDE database. Last, you must save all databases or add-ins in the chain of references as .MDE files or your database will be unable to use them.

To create an MDE file, follow these steps:

1. Close the database if it is currently opened. If you do not close the current database, Access attempts to close it for you, prompting you to save changes where applicable. When working with a shared database, all users must close the database; Access needs exclusive rights to work with the database.
2. Select Tools⇨Database Utilities and then click on Make MDE File (see Figure 17-6).
3. In the Database to Save as MDE dialog box, specify the database you want to save as an .MDE file, and click on Make MDE (see Figure 17-7).

   If you have a database open when you select Make MDE File, this step is skipped and Access assumes you want to use the database that's open. If you want to use a different database, you need to cancel creating the MDE file, close the database, and select Make MDE File again. Then you will be asked for the database to save as an MDE file.

4. In the Database to Save as MDE dialog box, specify a name, drive, and folder for the database. Do not attempt to save the .MDE file with the same file name as the original database.

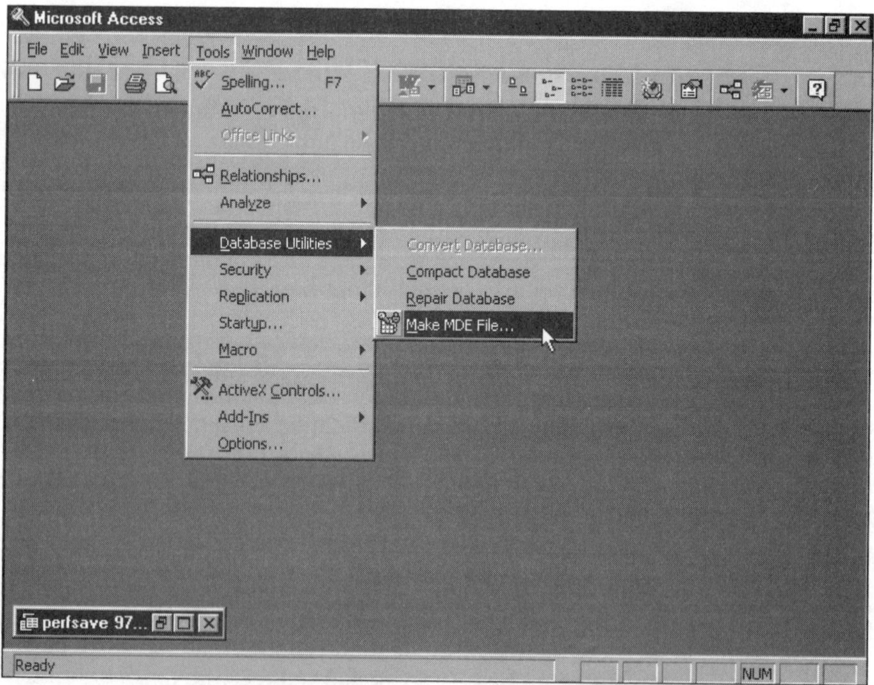

Figure 17-6: Access doesn't convert the existing database into an .MDE file, it creates a new .MDE file for the database.

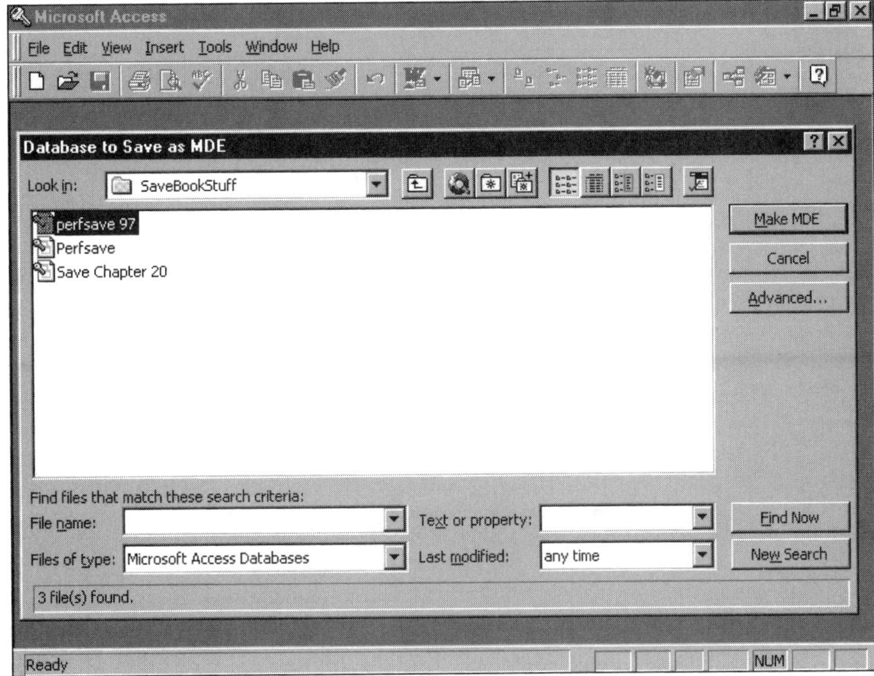

Figure 17-7: If you have a database open at the time you select Make MDE File, you do not see this form.

Warning

Do not delete or overwrite your original database! As stated previously, there is no way to convert an .MDE file to a normal database, and you cannot edit any objects in an .MDE file. If you delete or otherwise lose your original database, you will never again be able to access any of the objects in the design environment!

Using the Jet User-Level Security Model

Most often when security is required, setting a database password is simply not enough; you need to fully implement the user-level/object permissions security of Jet 3.0. To do this, you need to complete the following functions:

1. Select or create a workgroup database.
2. Define the workgroup database's security groups.
3. Create the users of the workgroup database.
4. Define permissions for each user and security group.
5. Enable security by setting an Admin user password.

Enabling security

Jet security is always on. When a new workgroup database is created, a user by the name of Admin is created within the workgroup. This Admin user has no password assigned to it. When the Admin password is blank, Access assumes that whenever a user attempts to open the database that user is the Admin user and automatically logs in to the database as the Admin user. To force Access/Jet to ask for a valid user name and password to log in to the database (see Figure 17-8), you simply need to create a password for the Admin user. To "turn security off," simply clear the Admin user's password. The security permissions you have designed are still in effect, but Access does not ask for a user name and password — it logs on all users as the Admin user with whatever permissions were assigned to the Admin user. Be careful about clearing the Admin user's password when you have modified the permissions of your users.

Figure 17-8: When you activate security, Jet forces all users to enter a valid user name and password to use the secured database.

If you have cleared the Admin password only to find out that some or all of the Admin user's permissions have been revoked and you need access to the restricted objects or if you need to log on as a different user, open the database and create a password for the Admin user, then exit and restart Access. When you restart Access, you are prompted to enter a user name and password.

Working with workgroups

A *workgroup* is a collection of users, user groups, and object permissions. You can use a single workgroup file for all your databases, or you may use different workgroups for different databases. The method you use depends on the level of security you need. If you give Administrative rights to users of some databases but not to users of other databases, you need to distribute separate workgroup files with each database. Access always uses a workgroup file when you open it. By default, this workgroup file is the SYSTEM.MDW workgroup file that comes with Access.

Creating a new workgroup

You can create new workgroups or join existing ones by using the Workgroup Administrator program that comes with Access (see Figure 17-9).

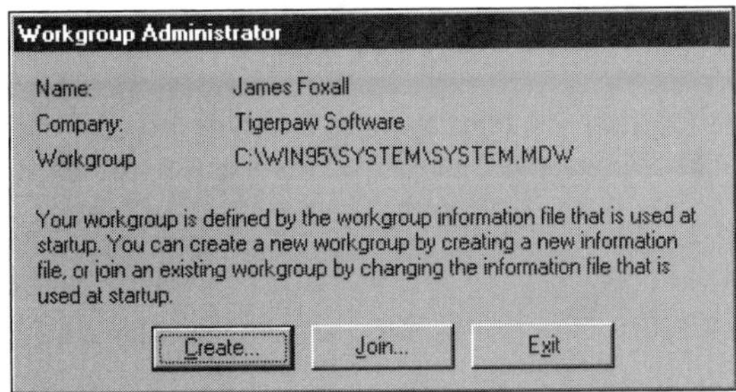

Figure 17-9: Use the Workgroup Administrator program to create new workgroups and to join existing workgroups.

You should completely close down Access when creating new or joining existing workgroups. When you use the Workgroup Administrator to join a workgroup, that workgroup is not actually used until the next time you start Access.

To create a new workgroup file, follow these steps:

1. Start MS Access Workgroup Administrator from the Taskbar or from Microsoft Explorer. If you use Explorer, the executable name to run is MS Access Workgroup Administrator, located in the directory in which you installed Access.
2. Click on the Create button in the Workgroup Administrator dialog box to display the Workgroup Owner Information dialog box.
3. The workgroup you create is identified by three components: Name, Organization, and Workgroup ID (see Figure 17-10). *In order to re-create the workgroup file in the event that it becomes corrupt or deleted, you need all three pieces of information.* For this reason, to ensure that no other user can create your workgroup and access your secured database, you should supply a unique, random string for the Workgroup ID. Someone may possibly guess the name and organization used in your workgroup file if he or she knows who you are, but to guess all three items, especially if you create a random, unique ID, is almost impossible.

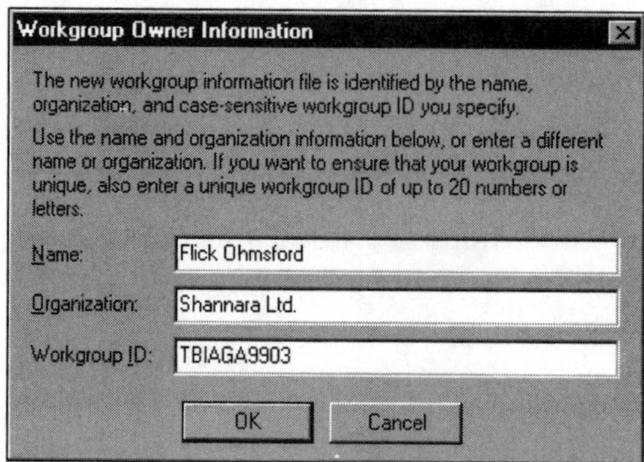

Figure 17-10: Workgroups are identified by these three key pieces of information. A workgroup cannot be re-created without all three of these items.

4. When you are satisfied with your entries, click on OK to display the Workgroup Information File dialog box.
5. Enter the name to save the new workgroup file as and click on OK to save the workgroup (see Figure 17-11).

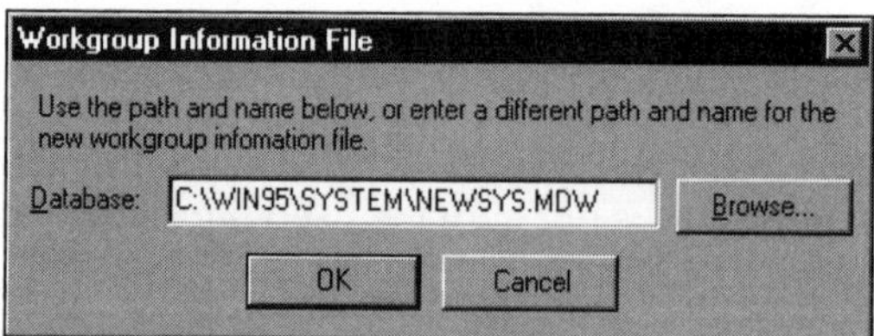

Figure 17-11: After defining your workgroup file, you need to give it a name in order to save it.

6. Before the Workgroup Administrator actually saves the workgroup, it shows you a confirmation dialog box (see Figure 17-12) that contains the information you entered for the new workgroup and explains the importance of writing down and storing the information. If you are satisfied with your entries, click on OK to save your workgroup.

In order to ensure that you can recover from the loss of your workgroup file, you should immediately make a copy of the workgroup file. In addition, you should write down the three pieces of information used to create the workgroup file exactly as they were entered in the event that you have to re-create the workgroup file from scratch. Store both the backup file copy and the written information in a secure place.

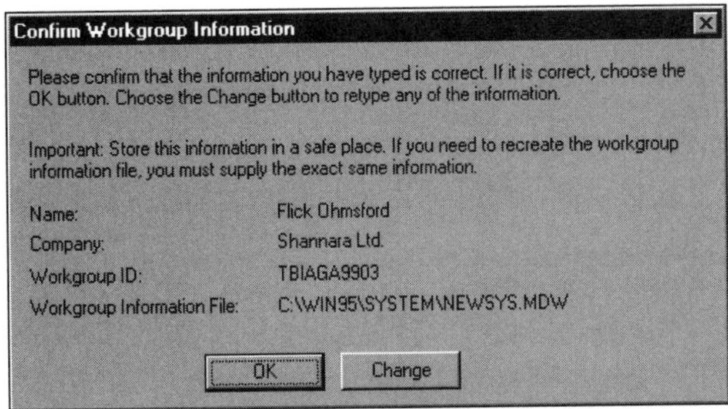

Figure 17-12: Do as this dialog box says and write down this information! You may need it if you ever have to re-create the workgroup file.

Joining an existing workgroup

When you create a new workgroup, Access automatically joins the new workgroup. If you do not want to use the new workgroup right away, or if at any time you need to use a workgroup other than the current workgroup, you need to join the desired workgroup by using the Workgroup Administrator.

To join an existing workgroup, follow these steps:

1. Run the Workgroup Administrator program.
2. The Workgroup Administrator dialog box shows you the currently joined workgroup (refer to Figure 17-9). Click on the Join button to select a workgroup file. If you are not sure of the file name, click on the Browse button to display a File dialog box in which to locate the workgroup file.
3. A prompt appears, enabling you to confirm or cancel joining the selected workgroup. Click on OK and then click on Exit to close the Workgroup Administrator program.

Working with users

Every time a user opens an Access (Jet) database, Jet must know the user opening the database. When security is "off" (in reality, security is never off — see the following section on enabling security), Jet always assumes that the Admin user is opening the database. When a new workgroup is created, Access automatically creates a default user with the name Admin; the Admin user is given full permissions to all objects in the database. Obviously, when you secure a database, you do not want everyone to be able to open the database with full permissions on all objects, so you must create additional users in the workgroup.

Adding and deleting user accounts

You add, delete, and edit user information on the User and Group Accounts dialog box (see Figure 17-13), accessed through the Tools➪Security➪User and Group Accounts menu item. The Users page of the User and Group Accounts dialog box consists of two sections. You use the first section to maintain user names and passwords; use the second section to assign users to security groups. Assigning users to groups is discussed in detail later in this chapter.

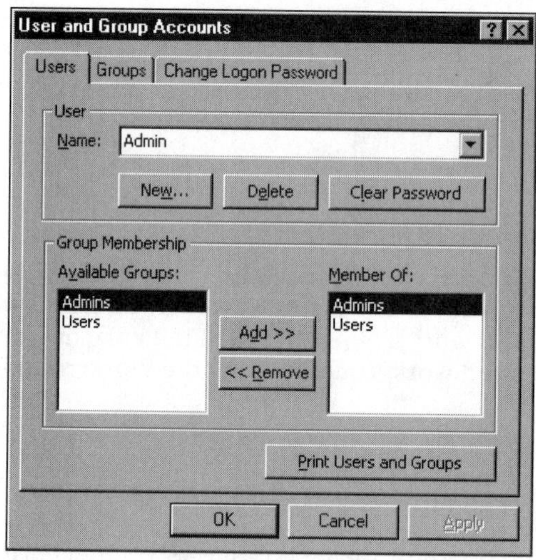

Figure 17-13: Users are maintained in the User and Group Accounts tabbed dialog box.

To fully secure your database with users and groups, follow these steps:

1. Create a new user.
2. Add the new user to the Admins group.
3. Remove the Admin user from the Admins group.
4. Assign all object ownerships to the new user.

When you create a user, you supply the user name and a personal identifier. Jet then combines these two items and processes them in a special algorithm, producing a unique SID — security ID. It is this SID that Jet uses to recognize users. In order to re-create a user in the workgroup, you need to know the user name and the PID (personal ID) used to create the user. Consequently, you should always write down and store all names and PIDs of users you create in a safe place.

To create a new user in a workgroup, follow these steps:

1. Open the database to secure in Access.
2. Select Tools⇨Security⇨User and Group Accounts to display the User and Group Accounts dialog box.
3. Click on the New button in the User section to display the New User/Group dialog box (see Figure 17-14).
4. Enter the name of the user and a unique personal ID. Write this information down and store it in a safe place; you will need it to re-create the user in the workgroup.
5. Click on OK to save the new user.

In order to fully secure your database, you must remove all permissions for the Admin user. All Admin users share the same SID in all workgroups, on all machines. If you do not remove the permissions for the Admin user, an unauthorized user using a different workgroup can open the database as the Admin user, with all permissions of the Admin user. The Admin user cannot be deleted, so the Admin user account needs to be adjusted accordingly.

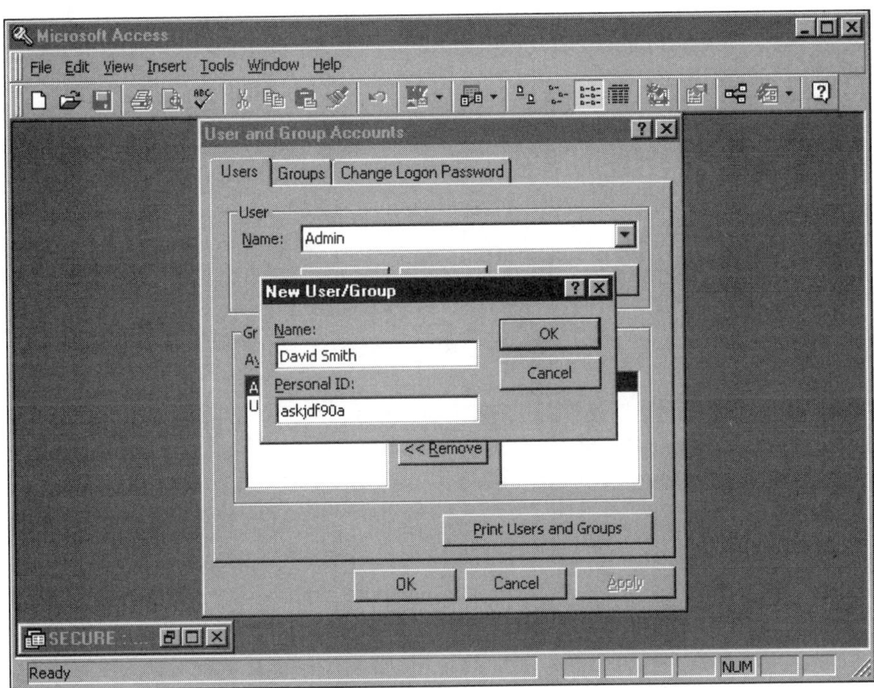

Figure 17-14: Jet employs the user name and personal identifier to create a unique SID for the user.

To remove all security rights from the Admin user, follow these steps:

1. Remove the Admin user from the Admins group (discussed in the section, "Working with groups").
2. Verify the permission settings for the Admin user for each object in your database (discussed in the section "Securing objects by using permissions").

Creating and changing user passwords

Any member of the Admins group can remove a password from any user account; however, no user can change or create a password for anyone other than himself; each user has the ability to change or create only his or her own password, regardless of security permissions. To create or change a user password, follow these steps:

1. Log on to the database as the user whose password you want to change.
2. Select Tools⇨Security⇨User and Group Accounts.
3. Click on the Change Logon Password tab (see Figure 17-15).
4. If a password exists for the user you are logged as, enter it in the Old Password field. If there is no password assigned to the user, leave the Old Password field blank.
5. Enter the new password in the New Password field.
6. You must enter the new password a second time in the Verify field in order to prevent typing errors, because you cannot see the characters you type for the password.

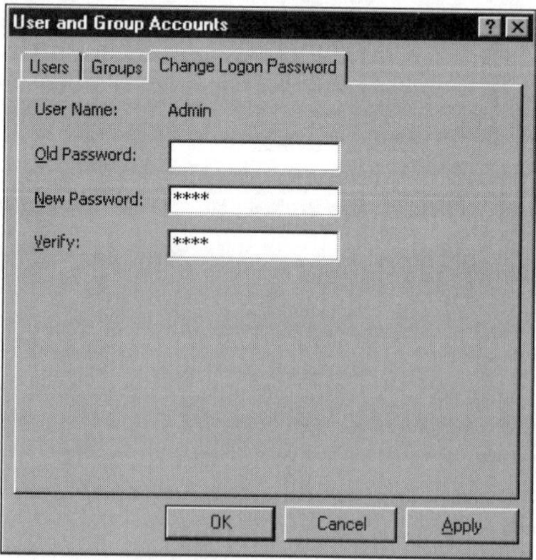

Figure 17-15: Users cannot create or change passwords for users other than themselves, regardless of their permission settings.

Working with groups

In addition to users, workgroups contain groups. *Groups* are collections of users; any user may belong to one or more groups. Groups enable you to easily set up object permissions for sets of users — enabling you to define the permissions once, versus having to assign them separately for each user. When you want a user to have the security permissions of a particular group, you simply add the user to the desired group.

For example, you may have a number of users in a credit department and in a sales department. If you want to allow all of these users to look at a customer's credit history but restrict the sales staff to viewing basic customer information, you have the following options:

- Allow all users in the credit department to log on as one user, and allow all users in the sales department to log on as a different user. You could then restrict the object permissions for each of these two users.
- Create an individual user account for all users in each department and assign object permissions for each user.
- Create an individual user account for all users in each department, and create a group account for each department. You could then make the permissions assignments for each of the two groups and place each user into his or her respective group to inherit the group's permissions.

The first method is straightforward and simple but presents many problems. If a user transfers from one department to another, he has user names and passwords for both departments and may be able to retrieve data he is no longer authorized to view. In addition, if an employee leaves, the user name and password need to be changed, and each user of the workgroup has to be made aware of the change. In a multiuser environment, creating a unique user account for each user and then grouping them accordingly is a much better solution.

Although the second method — creating a unique user account and assigning specific permissions to each user — would work, it is an administrator's nightmare. If policy dictates that one of the departments needs to have permissions added or revoked, the change has to be made to each user's account for that department. With the third option, the change can be made to the department group once, and all users inherit the new permission settings.

Adding and deleting groups

Just as Access creates a user called Admin in all new workgroups, it also creates two groups: Users and Admins. Every user account in the system belongs to the Users group; you cannot remove a user from the Users group. The Admins group is the all-powerful, "Big Daddy" group. Users of the Admins group have the ability to add and delete user and group accounts, as well as to assign and remove permissions for any object, for any user or group in the workgroup. In addition, a member of the Admins group has the ability to remove other user accounts from the Admin group. For this reason, you need to carefully consider which users you allow as members of the Admins group. The Admins group and the Users group are permanent groups; they can never be deleted.

Tip

Access does not enable you to remove all users from the Admins group; one user must belong to the Admins group at all times. If you were allowed to remove all users from the Admins group, you could set up security so tight that you would never be able to bypass it yourself! In general, when securing a database, you should only place one or two users in the Admins group.

Note

Unlike the Admin user's SID, which is identical in every Access Workgroup, the Admins group's SIDs are not identical from workgroup to workgroup, so unauthorized users using a workgroup other than the one you used to define security cannot access your database as a member of the Admins group. The Users group's SIDs are the same throughout all workgroups, however, so you need to remove all permissions for the Users group. If you do not remove permissions from the Users group, any user with any workgroup can open your database with the Users group's permissions.

To create a new group, follow these steps:

1. Select Tools➪Security➪User and Group Accounts to display the User and Group Accounts dialog box.
2. Click on the Groups tab.
3. Click on New to display the New User/Group dialog box (see Figure 17-16).
4. Just as you do to create users, enter a group name and personal ID. Also, just as before, write down this information and put it in a safe place; you will need it to re-create the group at a later time.
5. Click on OK to save the new group.

To delete a group, follow these steps:

1. Select Tools➪Security➪User and Group Accounts to display the User and Group Accounts dialog box.
2. Click on the Groups tab (refer to Figure 17-13).
3. From the drop-down list, select the group to delete.
4. Click on the Delete button to delete the selected group.

Assigning and removing group members

Assigning users to and removing users from groups is a simple process. All assignments and removals are performed on the Users tab of the User and Group Accounts dialog box. You may place any user in any group, and users may belong to more than one group. As stated earlier, you cannot remove a user from the Users group, nor can you remove all users from the Admins group; you must always have at least one user in the Admins group.

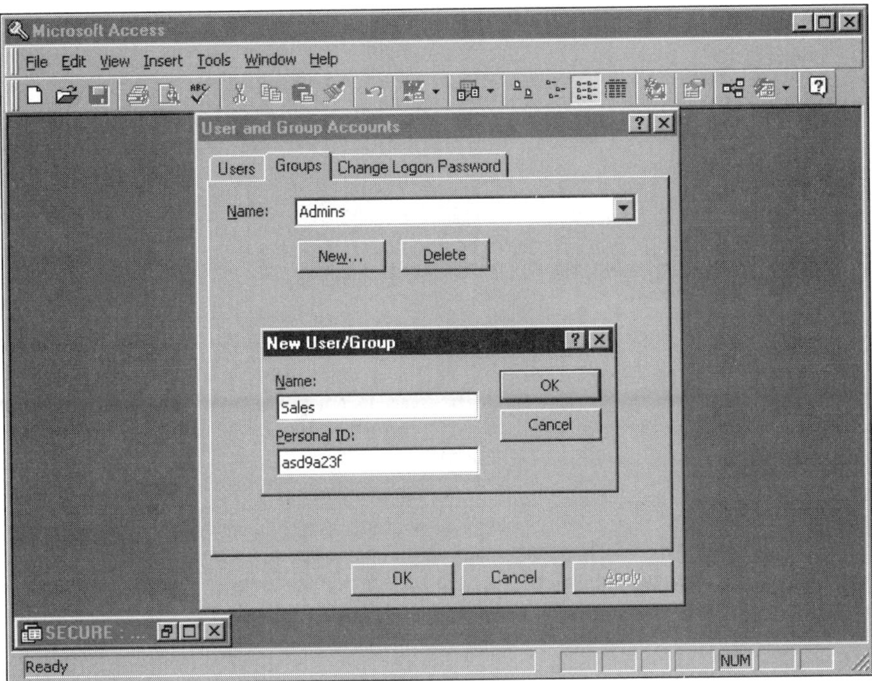

Figure 17-16: Jet uses the group name and personal identifier to create a unique SID for the security group, just as it does for user accounts.

To add or remove a user from a group, follow these steps:

1. Select Tools⇨Security⇨User and Group Accounts to display the User and Group Accounts dialog box.
2. From the drop-down list, select the user whose group assignments you want to modify.
3. If you want to assign users to a group or groups to which they do not currently belong, select the group(s) in the Available Groups list and click on the Add button (see Figure 17-17). The selected group (or groups) is then removed from the Available Groups list and moved to the Member Of list.
4. If you want to remove a user from a group or groups, select the group (or groups) in the Member Of list and click on the Remove button. The selected group is then removed from the Member Of list and moved to the Available Groups list.
5. Click on OK to save the new group assignments.

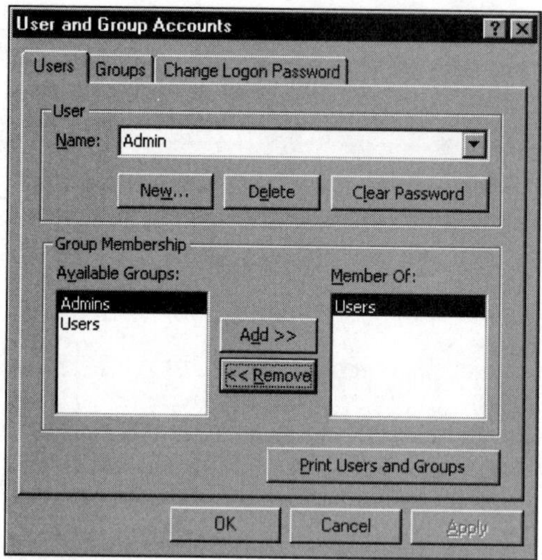

Figure 17-17: Assigning users to groups makes controlling object permissions much easier for the system administrator.

Because Jet uses the same SIDs for all Admin user accounts throughout all workgroups, you always need to remove the Admin user from the Admins group when securing a database. Figure 17-17 shows the Admin user removed from the Admins group. After removing the Admin user from the Admins group, all that is left to do is to verify that the Users group does not contain any permissions that you do not want unauthorized users to have and that no explicit permissions are assigned to the Admin user account (see the next section, "Securing objects by using permissions").

Securing objects by using permissions

After you have defined your users and groups, you must decide on the specific object permissions a user or group is to have. Permissions control who can view data, update data, add data, and work with objects in design view. Permissions are the heart of the Jet security system and can only be set by a member of the Admins group, by the owner of the object (see the next section), or by any user who has Administrator permission on the object in question.

Setting an objects owner

Every object in the database can have an owner. The *owner* is a user account in the workgroup that is designated to always have administrator rights to the object, regardless of the group to which they belong or the permissions explicitly applied to them for the object. You can designate one user to be the owner of all the objects in a database, or you may assign different owners to different objects.

OwnerAccess queries require special consideration when assigning owners to objects. When creating a query, you can set the `Run Permissions` property of the query to either `User's` or `Owner's` (see Figure 17-18). By default, this permission is set to `User's`, which limits the users of the query to seeing only the data that their security permissions permit. If you want to enable users to view or modify data for which they do not have permissions, you can set the `Run Permissions` property to `Owner's`. When the query is run with the Owner's permissions (`WITH OWNERACCESS OPTION` in an SQL statement), users inherit the permissions of the owner of the query when they run the query. These permissions are applicable only to the query and not throughout the database.

When a query's `Run Permissions` property is set to `Owner's`, only the owner can make changes to the query. If this restriction poses a problem, you may want to set the owner of the query to a group, rather than to a user account. Note that only the owner of an OwnerAccess query can change the query's owner.

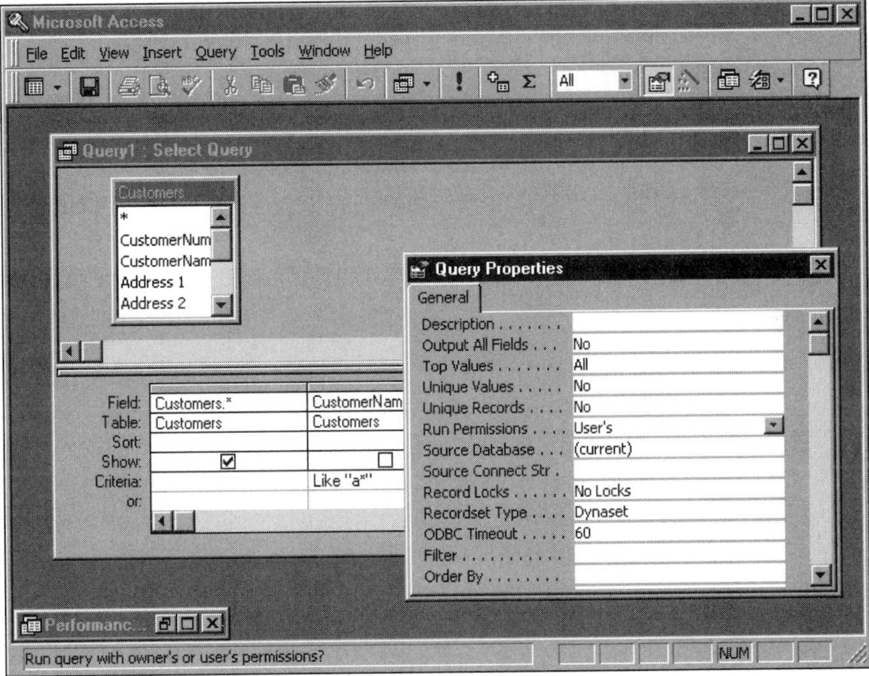

Figure 17-18: Judicious use of OwnerAccess queries enables you to temporarily grant object permissions to users who don't currently have those permissions.

To change the owner of an object, follow these steps:

1. Select Tools➪Security➪User and Group Permissions to display the User and Group Permissions dialog box.
2. Click on the Change Owner tab (see Figure 17-19).

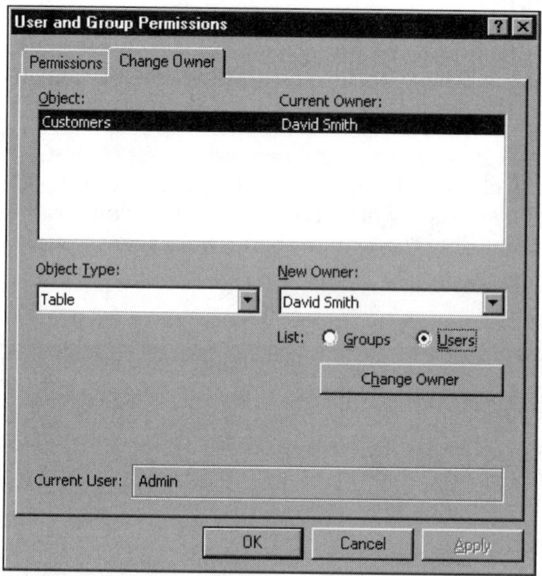

Figure 17-19: Controlling an object's owners is an important step in securing a database.

3. Select the object (or objects) whose ownership you want to transfer. You can select the type of objects to display by changing the Object Type field.
4. Select the user or group that you want to make the owner of the selected object.
5. Click on the Change Owner button to change the object's owner to the selected user or group.

In addition to the objects within a database each having an owner, the database itself has an owner. You can view the owner of the database by selecting Database from the Object Type drop-down list. You cannot change an object's owner by using Access's interface; the only way to change a database's owner is to log on as the user that you want to make the owner of the database, create a new database, and import the original database into the new database using the Import Database add-in. When you import a database, the current user is assigned as the new owner of the database and all of the database objects; this is essentially what the Security Wizard (discussed later in this chapter) does for you.

Setting object permissions

Object permissions, the heart of Jet security, can be set for users and groups and for one object or many objects at a time. When assigning permissions, you must keep in mind that some permissions automatically imply other permissions. For example, if you assign a user Read Data permission for a table, the Read Design permission is also granted, because a table's design must be available to access the data.

An object's permission assignments are persistent until one of the following conditions occurs:

- A member of the Admins group changes the object's permissions.
- The object is saved with a new name by using the Save As command from the File menu.
- The object is cut and pasted in the Database window.
- The object is imported or exported.

If any of the preceding conditions occurs, all permissions for the manipulated object are lost, and you have to reassign them. This loss of permissions occurs because you are actually creating a new object when you perform any of the actions, and new objects are assigned the default permissions defined for the object's type.

Understanding the two types of permissions is important:

- **Explicit permissions** are permissions granted directly to a user. When you explicitly assign a permission to a user, no other user's permissions are affected.
- **Implicit permissions** are permissions granted to a group. All users belonging to a group implicitly have the permissions of that group.

Because permissions can be assigned implicitly, and some permissions inherently grant other permissions (as mentioned in the previous discussion of the Read Data and Read Design permission relationship), users may be able to grant themselves permissions that they don't currently have. Because of this possibility, you must plan carefully when assigning permissions to groups of users and to individual users themselves.

To assign or revoke a user's permissions for an object, follow these steps:

1. Select Tools⇨Security⇨User and Group Permissions to display the User and Group Permissions dialog box.
2. Select the type of object whose permissions you want to change from the Object Type drop-down list.
3. Select the user or group account for which you want to modify the permissions.

4. Select the object (or objects) for which you want to modify the permissions.
5. Select or deselect the permissions of the object.
6. Click on Apply to commit the permission assignments.

Remember that Admin user SIDs are identical throughout all workgroups, so you need to remove all permissions for the Admin user in order to secure your database. Figure 17-20 shows the Admin user's permissions for all tables in the database. Note how all checkboxes have been cleared, preventing an Admin user from doing anything with the table object.

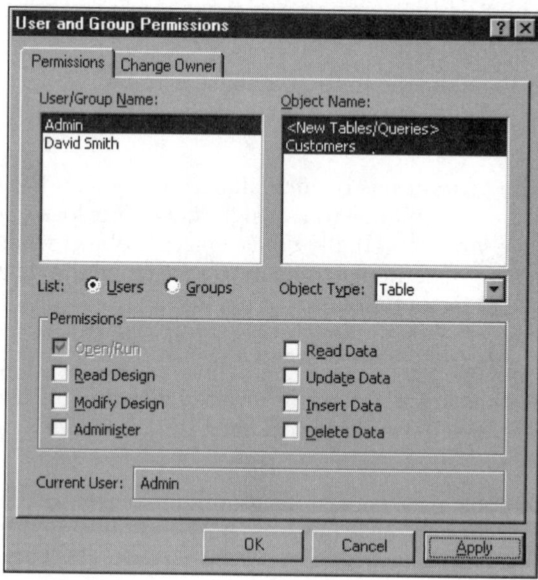

Figure 17-20: Removing all permissions for the Admin user is critical to securing your database.

Setting default object permissions

You can create default permission assignments for each type of object in a database. These default permissions are assigned when a new object is created, imported, or cut and pasted within the database container. You set the default permissions just as you would set any other object's permissions. You must select the user or group to which to assign default permissions, but you do not select a specific object. When you select the Object Type from the drop-down list, the first item in the Object Name list is <New OBJECT>, where OBJECT is replaced with the actual object type selected, such as <New Forms>. When you assign permissions for users and groups to these <New> items, the permissions are used as defaults for all new objects of that type.

When removing default permissions for table objects, if you have created make table queries, you must ensure that any users running the make table query have the ability to create new tables. If you remove a user's permission to create new tables, that user will not able to execute a make table query.

Setting database permissions

Each database has permissions, just as the objects in the database do. Selecting Database from the Object Type drop-down list displays the database permissions (see Figure 17-21). The database permissions enable you to control who has administrative rights to the entire database, who can open the database exclusively (locking out other users), and who can open or run the database.

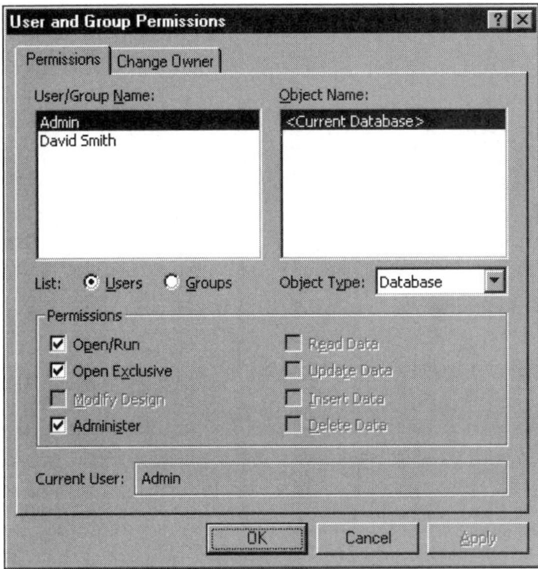

Figure 17-21: You can assign permissions for the entire database, not just for individual objects.

Securing your database for distribution: A basic approach

If you are securing a database for distribution, setting up detailed security for multiple users for all objects in your database may not be important to you. Often, the only concern with shipping a secured database is protecting your development investment by securing the design of your objects and code. If you need this protection, you can distribute your application as an .MDE file (see the section "Distributing a Database as an MDE File"), or you can follow these steps:

1. Create a workgroup to distribute with your database.

2. Remove the Admin user from the Admins group.
3. Remove all permissions for the Users group.
4. Remove any and all design permissions for the Admin user for all objects in the database.
5. Do not supply a password for the Admin user.

By not supplying a password for the Admin user, you tell Access to log on all users as the Admin user. Because the Admin user has no rights to the design of any objects, users cannot access your objects or code in design view.

If you use this method to secure the design of your objects, and you need to modify objects using DAO that the Admin user does not have rights for (such as QueryDefs, TableDefs, or reading data from a secured table), you need to create a temporary workspace as a user with administrative rights for the object.

For example, if you have a table called tblRegistration in which you keep registration and licensing information that you do not want the Admin user to be able to update, you can remove the Update Data permissions for the table. However, if you attempt to update the table using DAO, you receive an error because the logged-in user — the Admin user — does not have sufficient rights to manipulate the table. You can avoid this error by using a temporary workspace. Creating a temporary workspace is essentially logging in to the database as a user in Visual Basic; the login is valid for the scope of the workspace object that you dimension. The following is sample code that creates a temporary workspace and edits the data in tblRegistration. This example assumes that a valid user by the name of "David Hawkings" exists in the current workgroup and has the password "Pink Floyd":

```
Dim TempWorkspace As Workspace, MyDB As Database, tbl As Table
Set TempWorkspace = DBEngine.CreateWorkspace("TempWs", _
"David Hawkings", "Pink Floyd")
     DBEngine.Workspaces.Append TempWorkspace
     Set MyDB = TempWorkspace.OpenDatabase(CurrentDB().Name)
     Set tbl = MyDB.OpenTable("tblUsers")

    tbl.Edit
           tbl![Reg Name] = "John Davis"
    tbl.Update
```

The `CreateWorkspace` method of the `DBEngine` object accepts three parameters:

1. **A name to call the temporary workspace.** In the preceding code sample, the name assigned to the workspace is TempWs, but you can choose any name.
2. **The user name to log in as.** The preceding example creates a temporary workspace for the user David Hawkings.

3. **The user's password.** In the preceding example, David Hawkings' password is Pink Floyd.

Because you must supply the user's password when creating a temporary workspace, and the user has additional rights (or you wouldn't be following this procedure), it is absolutely critical that you secure the View Design permissions for all modules or forms that use the preceding code. If you do not secure objects that contain the code to create the temporary workspace, users can get the user name and password from your code and log into the database as that user.

Table 17-1 summarizes permissions that you can assign.

Table 17-1 Summary of Assignable Permissions

Permission	*Permits a User To*	*Applies To*
Open/Run	Open a database, form, or report, or run a macro.	Databases, forms, reports, and macros.
Open Exclusive	Open a database with exclusive access.	Databases.
Read Design	View objects in Design view.	Tables, queries, forms, reports, macros, and modules.
Modify Design	View and change the design of objects, or delete them.	Tables, queries, forms, reports, macros, and modules.
Administer	For databases, set database password, replicate a database, and change start-up properties. For database objects, have full access to objects and data, including the ability to assign permissions.	Databases, tables, queries, forms, reports, macros, and modules.
Read Data	View data.	Tables and queries.
Update Data	View and modify but not insert or delete data.	Tables and queries.
Insert Data	View and insert but not modify or delete data.	Tables and queries.
Delete Data	View and delete but not modify or insert data.	Tables and queries.

Using the Access Security Wizard

Access includes a tool to help you secure your databases: the Security Wizard. The Security Wizard enables you to select the objects to secure, and then it creates a new database containing secured versions of the selected objects. The Wizard assigns the currently logged in user as the owner of the objects in the new database and removes all permissions from the Users group for those objects. Finally, the Wizard encrypts the new database. The original database is not modified in any way. Only members of the Admins group and the user who ran the wizard have access to the secured objects in the new database.

When you use the Security Wizard, make sure that you are logged in as the user that you want to become the new database's owner.

To run the Security Wizard, select Tools⇨Security⇨User-Level Security Wizard (refer to Figure 17-1). The Wizard first requires you to designate all the objects you want to secure (see Figure 17-22).

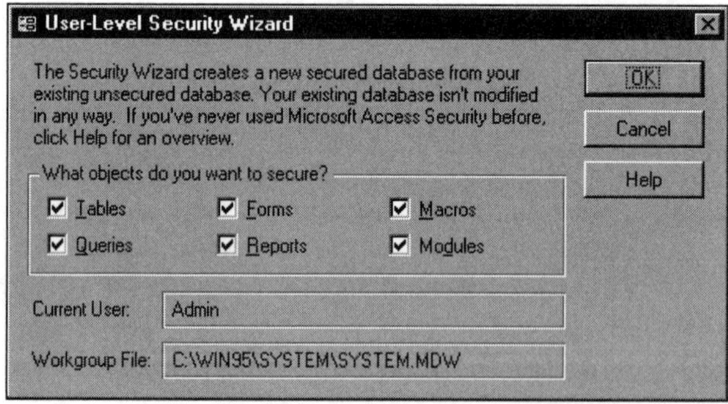

Figure 17-22: The Security Wizard helps jump start your security implementation.

If you deselect an object type (such as Tables or Forms), none of the objects of that type are exported to the secured database. If you do not want to restrict security permissions for a set of objects but still want those objects included in the new, secured database, you need to select the objects in the wizard and then modify the user and group permissions for those objects in the new secured database. When you are satisfied with your object selections, click on OK to continue.

After selecting the objects to secure, the Security Wizard requires you to provide a name for the new database (see Figure 17-23). Remember, the Security Wizard does not make any modifications to the current database; it creates an *entirely new* database with secured objects. When you distribute your secured application, make sure to distribute the database that the Security Wizard created for you.

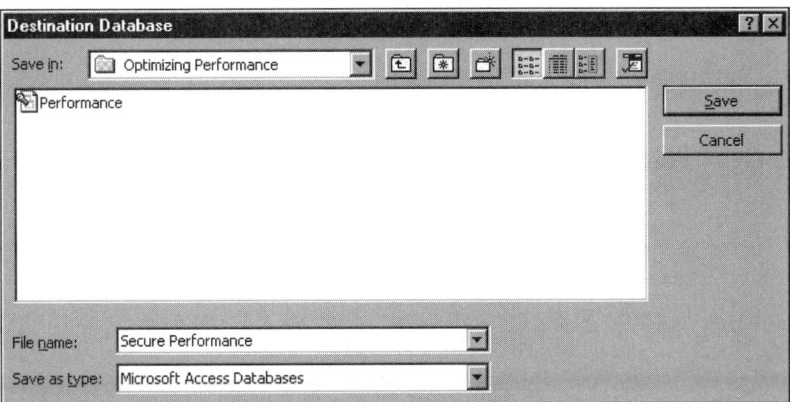

Figure 17-23: The Security Wizard does not affect your original database; it creates an entirely new database.

Generally, making a copy of the original database but working with the secured database is a good idea. If you make changes to the original database, you will need to run the Security Wizard again to create a secured version of the database. In addition, making a copy of the original database and then removing it from development helps prevent accidentally distributing the unsecured database. After entering the new database name, click on Save to save the secured database.

After supplying a name for the new database, the Security Wizard creates the database with the secured objects and gives you a summary of everything it did (see Figure 17-24).

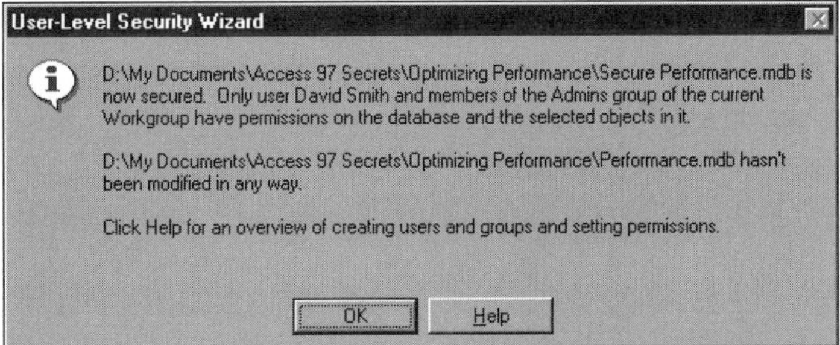

Figure 17-24: When finished, the Security Wizard shows you a summary of what it did.

The Security Wizard does not remove the Users group's Open/Run permission on the database itself. Although all of your objects are secure, any user can still open the database with Access. To completely secure the database from being opened by unauthorized users, remove the Users group's Open/Run permission on the database.

The Security Wizard gets you started securing your database. After running the wizard, you need to assign any appropriate privileges to the users or groups in the workgroup.

Encrypting a Database

When security is of utmost importance, one final step you need to take is to *encrypt* the database. Although it would take a great deal of skill (far more than the average computer user — or developer — possesses), using tools to view the actual database structure on the hard disk of the computer is possible. A skilled hacker could use this information to reconstruct SIDs and gain full access to your secured database.

Encrypting a database makes using such tools to gain any useful information about the database impossible. Only the database owner or a member of the Admins group can encrypt or decrypt a database.

To encrypt a database, follow these steps:

1. With no database open, select Tools⇨Security⇨Encrypt/Decrypt Database (see Figure 17-25).
2. Select the database to encrypt.
3. Provide a name for the new encrypted database.

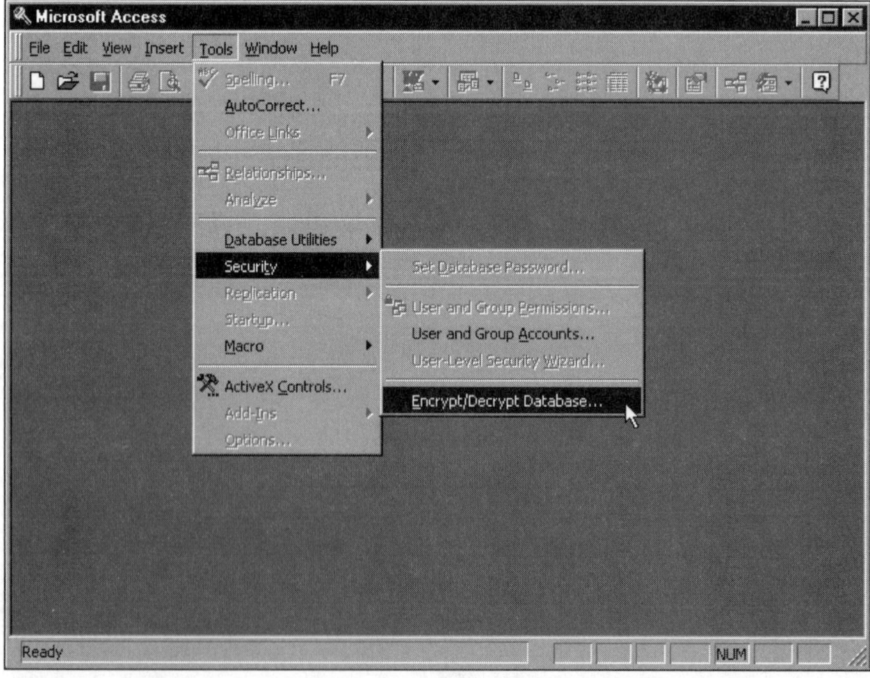

Figure 17-25: Encrypting a database helps ensure its security from highly skilled hackers.

Access does not modify the original database when it encrypts it; rather, it creates a clone of the database and encrypts the clone. As when using the Security Wizard, you should make a backup copy of the original database and store it somewhere safe to prevent accidentally distributing the unencrypted database.

In addition to encrypting a database using Access's interface, it is possible to encrypt a database using VBA code. The following code example can be used to encrypt a database:

```
Public Sub EncryptDatabase()
On Error GoTo EncryptDatabaseErr
Dim szDBName As String, szEncryptedDBname As String

szDBName = _
"c:\Program Files\Microsoft Office\Access\Samples\northwind.mdb"
szEncryptedDBname = _
"c:\Program Files\Microsoft Office\Access\Samples\encrypted.mdb"

DBEngine.CompactDatabase szDBName, szEncryptedDBname, dbLangGeneral, _
dbEncrypt

Exit Sub

EncryptDatabaseErr:
    MsgBox Err & ":  " & Err.Description
    Exit Sub

End Sub
```

As stated previously, few people have the ability or drive to hack a database in the way that encryption prevents, but encryption is a necessary step for securing highly sensitive databases. If you choose to encrypt a database, you have to accept the following drawbacks:

- Encrypted databases do not compress from their original size when used with compression programs such as PKZIP or the ODE Setup Wizard; encryption modifies the way the data is stored on the hard disk and renders the compression algorithms useless.
- Encrypted databases suffer some performance degradation (up to 15 percent). Depending on the size of your database and the speed of your computer, this loss may not be noticeable.

Encrypting a database should be performed as an *additional* step to securing a database using users, groups, and permissions. Simply encrypting a database does nothing to secure the database from users using Access. Encryption is an addition, not a complete solution, to securing a database.

Manipulating Security Objects Using DAO

An example presented earlier in this chapter demonstrates how to create temporary workspaces to gain the permissions of users other than the user you are logged in as. In addition, it is possible to create users and groups, remove or change passwords, change ownership of objects, and to assign permissions for objects — all using DAO in Visual Basic for Applications code.

Creating a user account using DAO

DAO includes a number of security objects that you can manipulate. First and foremost are the `User` and `Group` objects. Using these objects, you can create or delete users as well as change or remove user passwords. Users and Groups are created by defining the user or group and then appending it to the `User` or `Group` collection. The following code creates a new user account using DAO:

```
Public Sub CreateUser()
Dim usrNew As User, szUserName As String, szPID As String
Dim szPassword As String

szUserName = "Tabatha Thrush"
szPID = "MYPID105"
szPassword = "Shadow"

' Create a new user account.
Set usrNew = DBEngine.Workspaces(0).CreateUser(szUserName, _
szPID, szPassword)

' Save the new user account by appending it to Users collection.
DBEngine.Workspaces(0).Users.Append usrNew

End Sub
```

Changing a user's password using DAO

The password parameter of the `CreateUser` method is an optional parameter. Using the password property of the user object, the password can also be set as follows:

```
usrNew.PassWord = "Shadow"
```

This property must be set after the `CreateUser` method and prior to the `Append` method. To change the password of an existing user account, you need to use the `NewPassword` method of the `Users` object, as shown in the following procedure:

```
Public Sub ChangePassword()
On Error GoTo ChangePasswordErr
Dim szUserName As String, szOldPassword As String, szNewPassword As _
String

szUserName = "Tabatha Thrush"
szOldPassword = "Shadow"
szNewPassword = "Katie"
```

```
Workspaces(0).Users(szUserName).NewPassword szOldPassword, _
szNewPassword

Exit Sub

ChangePasswordErr:
    MsgBox Err & ":  " & Err.Description
    Exit Sub

End Sub
```

The NewPassword method accepts three arguments:

- The name of the user whose password is to be changed
- The existing password for the user
- The new password to assign to the user

If you create procedures that add or change passwords in code, you must protect or delete the code prior to distributing the application to prevent a user from obtaining other users' passwords.

Creating a group account using DAO

Creating a group account is much like creating a user account. The difference is that the Group object and collection are used in place of the User object and collection. The following code creates a new group account:

```
Public Sub CreateGroup()
On Error GoTo CreateGroupErr
Dim grpSales As Group, szGroupName As String, szPID As String

szGroupName = "Sales"
szPID = "GroupPID0456"

' Create the new Group object.
 Set grpSales = DBEngine.Workspaces(0).CreateGroup(szGroupName, _
 szPID)
' Create the new group by appending it to Groups collection.
 Workspaces(0).Groups.Append grpSales

Exit Sub

CreateGroupErr:
    MsgBox Err & ":  " & Err.Description
    Exit Sub

End Sub
```

Changing an object's owner using DAO

Ownership entitles users to certain irrevocable rights to objects in the database. You should take great care in protecting the ownership of the objects in your database. If you need to change an ownership through VBA code, you use the `Owner` property of a `Document` object, as follows:

```
Public Sub ChangeOwner()
On Error GoTo ChangeOwnerErr
Dim db As Database, ctrTemp As Container, docModule As Document
Dim szNewOwner As String

szNewOwner = "Tabatha Thrush"

' Return Database variable that points to current database.
 Set db = CurrentDb
' Return Container variable that points to Modules container.
 Set ctrTemp = db.Containers!Forms
' Return Document object that points to mdlUtilities module.
 Set docModule = ctrTemp.Documents!frmSwitchBoard
' Change the owner by setting the Owner property of the Document _
object
docModule.Owner = szNewOwner

Exit Sub

ChangeOwnerErr:
    MsgBox Err & ":  " & Err.Description
    Exit Sub

End Sub
```

Assigning object permissions using DAO

Permissions are manipulated by using the `UserName` and `Permissions` properties of a document or container object. For example, the function in the following code assigns full permissions on all modules for the user Laura Thrush:

```
Sub SetPermissions()
' This procedure is to demonstrate changing user permissions
' programmatically.
On Error GoTo SetPermissionsErr
Dim db As Database, ctr As Container, szUserName As String

szUserName = "Tabatha Thrush"

Set db = CurrentDb()
' Set the container to the table objects
 Set ctr = db.Containers!Modules

' Set UserName property to valid existing user account.
 ctr.UserName = szUserName

' Set permissions for all table objects
```

```
 ctr.Permissions = dbSecFullAccess

Exit Sub

SetPermissionsErr:
    MsgBox Err & ":  " & Err.Description
    Exit Sub

End Sub
```

Tables 17-2, 17-3, and 17-4 show all available permission constants. If you want to set multiple permissions, add the properties together as follows:

```
ctr.Permissions = dbSecDelete + dbSecReadSec
```

Table 17-2 General DAO Permissions Constants

Constant	*Description*
dbSecNoAccess	No access to the object
dbSecFullAccess	Full access to the object
dbSecDelete	Can delete the object
dbSecReadSec	Can read the object's security-related information
dbSecWriteSec	Can alter access permissions
dbSecWriteOwner	Can change the Owner property setting

The possible settings or return values for the Tables Container object or any Document object in a Documents collection are shown in Table 17-3.

Table 17-3 Constants Applicable Only to Tables Containers and Their Documents

Constant	*Description*
dbSecCreate	Can create new documents (valid only with a Container object)
dbSecReadDef	Can read the table definition, including column and index information
dbSecWriteDef	Can modify or delete the table definition, including column and index information
dbSecRetrieveData	Can retrieve data from the Document object
dbSecInsertData	Can add records
dbSecReplaceData	Can modify records
dbSecDeleteData	Can delete records

The possible settings or return values for the `Databases Container` object or any `Document` object in a `Documents` collection are shown in Table 17-4.

Table 17-4 Constants Applicable Only to Databases Containers and Their Documents

Constant	*Description*
`dbSecDBAdmin`	Gives the user permission to make a database replicable and to change the database password
`dbSecDBCreate`	Can create new databases (valid only on the `Databases Container` object in the system database [SYSTEM.MDW])
`dbSecDBExclusive`	Exclusive access
`DbSecDBOpen`	Can open the database

With a full understanding of the Jet security model and how to manage it, you can create databases that protect your development investment and your users' data.

Chapter 18

Creating Help Systems in Access 97

In This Chapter

- Understanding the Windows help structure
- Creating a Windows help program using Help Workshop
- Integrating graphics and sound in a Help system
- Compiling a Help system
- Integrating a Help system with your Access application
- Third-party help tools

One item of an application that is often overlooked entirely is the inclusion of a comprehensive Help system. Creating a complete and useful Help system is a skill unto itself, and often programmers don't take the time necessary to learn how to do it right. Understanding what makes a good Help system and how to create one can be a powerful tool in your development arsenal.

Understanding the Windows Help Structure

Great Help systems are more than just online documentation. A Help system needs to explain the how-to of your application in bits and pieces, and the user needs to be able to access a specific bit or piece of information related to the task at hand with minimum effort. In addition, these bits and pieces — called *topics* — need to be linked in a comprehensive web that enables a user to travel from one related topic to another with ease. Each topic can be linked to a form or control's `HelpContextId` property (see Figure 18-1) to provide instant access to the topic when the user presses F1 while the control or form has the focus.

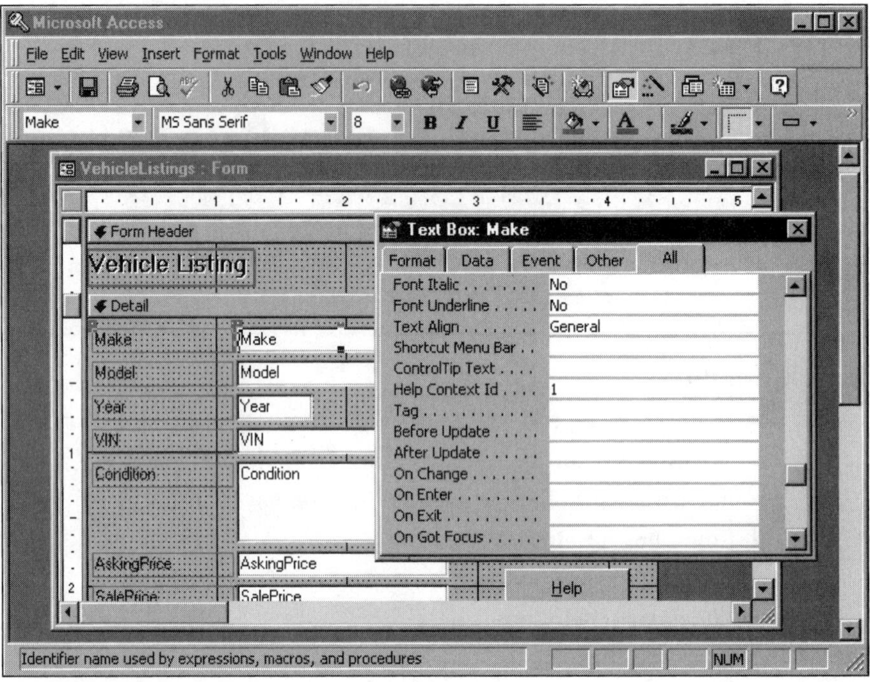

Figure 18-1: You can link Help topics to the form or control they relate to by using the HelpContextId property.

Help systems may consist of simple linked text topics, or they may contain graphics and multimedia to help educate the user. A good application of graphics in a Help system is the use of *hotspot graphics* to help explain an application's toolbars. Hotspot graphics, or *hypergraphics,* are graphic pictures that have links assigned to various regions of the graphic. Often, these regions are invisible; the user knows when the cursor is over a hotspot because the pointer turns into a pointing hand. When the user clicks on the hotspot, the topic linked to the hotspot is displayed. When creating a hypergraphic of a toolbar, you can link a related topic to each toolbutton in the toolbar graphic. Then users can simply click on the button they want help on to display the appropriate Help topic, just as they would click on the button on the toolbar.

The Windows Help system is a step forward from Windows 3.*x* Help in many ways. The differences become obvious from the moment you first run a new WinHelp 4.0 program. Besides the general look and feel being different, there are new features as well, including the following:

- **Help Topics Shortcut Menu.** When a user right-clicks on a Help window, a shortcut menu appears. This is the same menu that appears when the user clicks on the Options button in a Topic window.

- **New Access to Context-Sensitive Help.** In Windows 3.*x*, it was possible to display context-sensitive help by pressing the F1 key when the control or form in question had the focus. New to Windows 95 is the capability of displaying context-sensitive help by first clicking on the question-mark icon displayed in the title bar of a dialog box, and then clicking on the control or form in question. Many 3.*x* applications simulated this functionality with a toolbar button. Now, valuable toolbar real-estate no longer needs to be used.
- **Full-Text Search Engine.** Although you can still search for help based on keywords, just as you do for Windows 3.*x* applications, WinHelp 4.0 has the capability to let a user search all the text in each topic.

These new features greatly enhance the usability of the Help program for the end user of your application. The Help interface consists of numerous components; and understanding these components is key to mastering the designing of great Help files as well as to getting the most out of using a Help file.

The Help Topics dialog box

Help topics are the core element of a Help system. Each topic covered in your Help System should be contained in its own Help topic. Help topics are displayed in the Help Topics dialog boxes (see Figure 18-2). A Help Topics dialog contains information specific to the topic such as pertinent text, graphics, animation, or sound, and it may contain links to other Topics.

Topics Contents dialog box

Every Help system must have a *Contents file.* A Contents file defines the page displayed when a user clicks on Help Topics on your Help pull-down menu, clicks on the Contents tab of any Help topic, or double-clicks on your Help file in Windows Explorer. The Contents of a Help system is similar to the table of contents in a book (see Figure 18-3).

The Contents are shown in a collapsible outline format. Contents items that can be expanded are shown with a book icon, and actual topics that can be viewed have a document as their icon. Users use the Contents to locate items of interest. When users locate the items they want help on, they can double-click on the Help topic or select it and click on the Display button to view the Help topic.

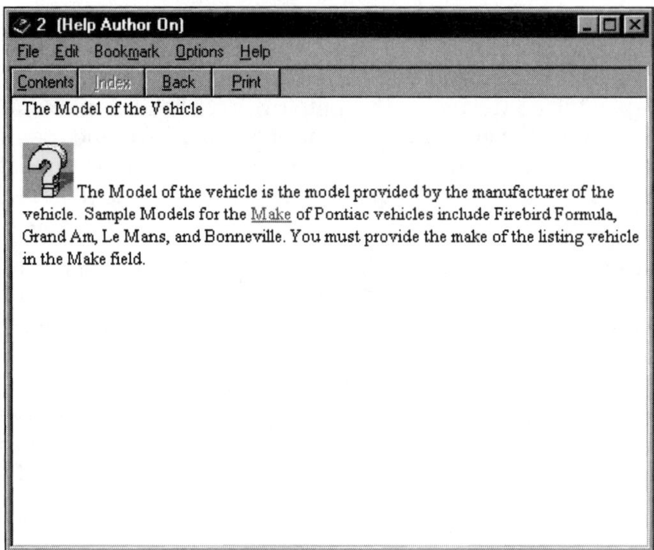

Figure 18-2: The Help Topics dialog box is where users of your Help system get the topical information they need.

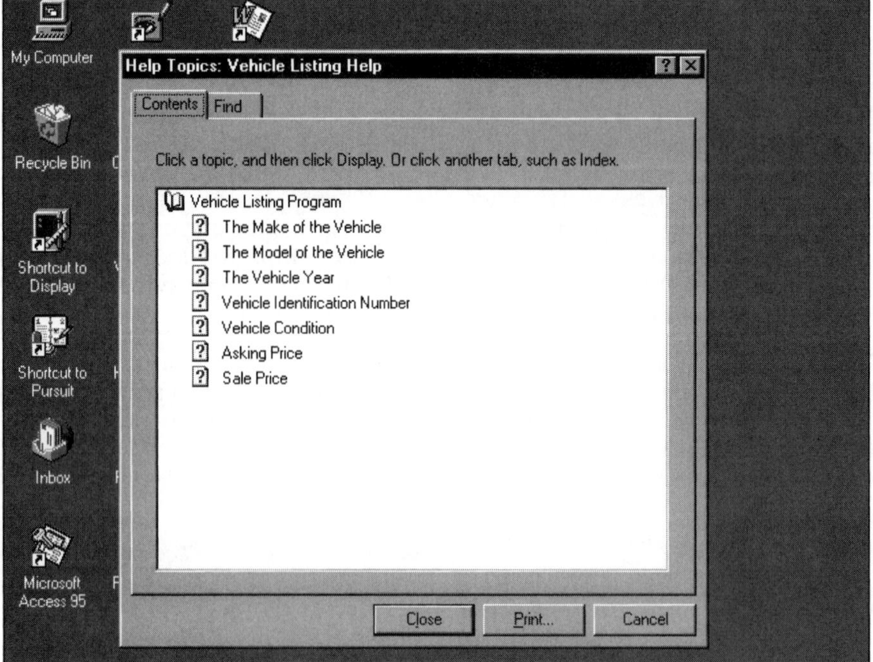

Figure 18-3: The Help Contents is where users of your Help file find the topics they're interested in.

Creating a Windows Help System

Creating Help systems for Windows involves the following:

- Using a word processor that supports Rich Text Format (.RTF) files to create your Topics
- Using the program that comes with the Access Developer's Toolkit, called Help Workshop, to define your Help project and contents files
- Using the Help Compiler (also included in the Access Developer's Toolkit) to compile your Help project into a distributable help program

Tip

You do not need to include all your Help topics in one Help file. The Help engine has the capability to use one index and one table of contents for multiple Help files — very useful when you have an application that consists of modular components. If WinHelp does not locate a referenced Help file on the end user's computer, that Help file's topics will not show up in the table of contents.

Creating Help topics

The most common element in a Help file is the Help topic. Topics must be created in a word processor that supports Rich Text Format files (.RTF files), such as Microsoft Word, which is used for the following examples. A single .RTF file can contain as many topics as you like; you are not limited to having to create a single .RTF for each topic.

To create an .RTF topic file, follow these steps:

1. Create a new document in Microsoft Word (or another word processor supporting .RTF files).
2. Enter the text to be displayed for each topic.
3. Separate each topic with a hard page break. You can create a hard page break in Microsoft Word by selecting Insert⇨Break and then selecting Page Break.
4. Save the file as a Rich Text Format (.RTF) file.

Tip

Before you begin typing the descriptive text for your topics, you should define a list of all the topics you want to include in your Help system. When you have created a list with all the topics for your Help system, organize them as best as possible (see Figure 18-4). This organization, in effect, creates a level 1 outline for your topics. After the topics are organized, simply type the topic's body text below each topic description in the list and add a hard page break at the end of the text. Creating your topics this way simplifies the effort in designing your topic structure.

In addition to text, your Help topics may also contain graphics or multimedia files. These additional items are discussed in their own sections later in this chapter.

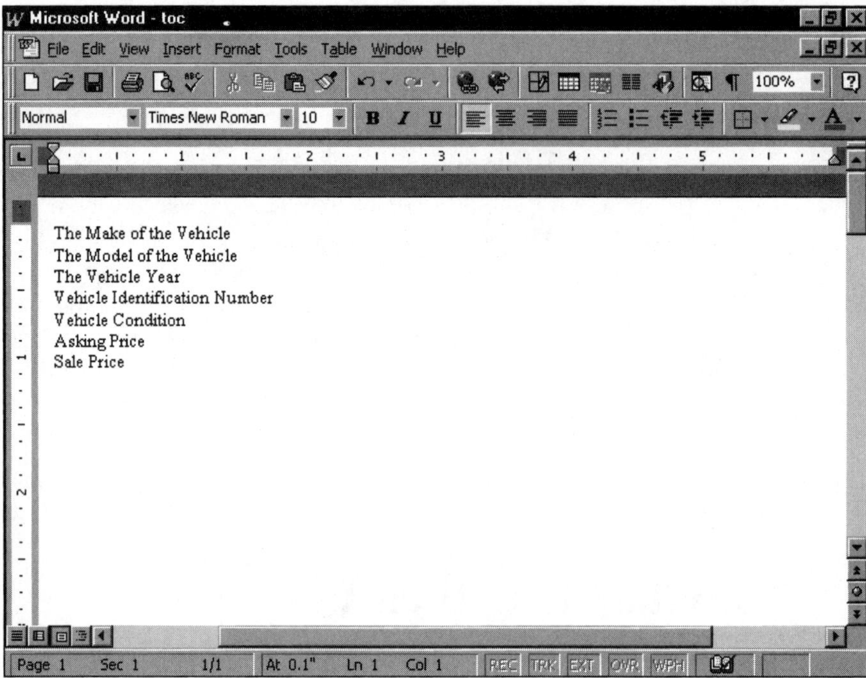

Figure 18-4: Organizing your topic list before you begin writing simplifies the design process.

Creating topic titles

All of your Help topics should have titles. Titles appear in the Topics Found dialog box, the Bookmark dialog box, and in the history window. Titles, like many other items in a topic, are created by using the footnote function of your word processor. The Help Compiler looks at the footnotes of each Topic and decides what to do with the footnote string based on its prefix. The prefix for a Topic Title is the dollar sign ($).

To create a Title footnote in Microsoft Word, follow these steps:

1. Place the cursor at the beginning of the text of the Topic to be titled.
2. Select Insert➪Footnote from the menu bar.
3. Select Custom Mark for the footnote.
4. Enter a dollar sign (**$**) as the custom mark and click on OK (see Figure 18-5). The $ sign footnote tells the Help Compiler that the footnote string is a Topic Title.
5. The cursor is placed at the bottom of the page (see Figure 18-6). Enter the topic title as the footnote text.

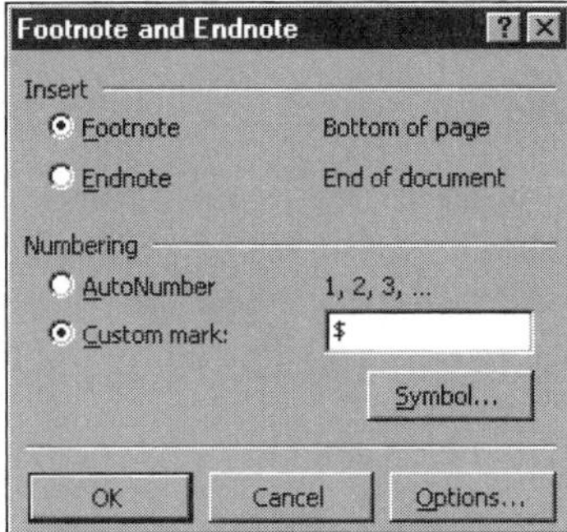

Figure 18-5: Footnote marks are used to create properties of the topic such as Title and Topic ID.

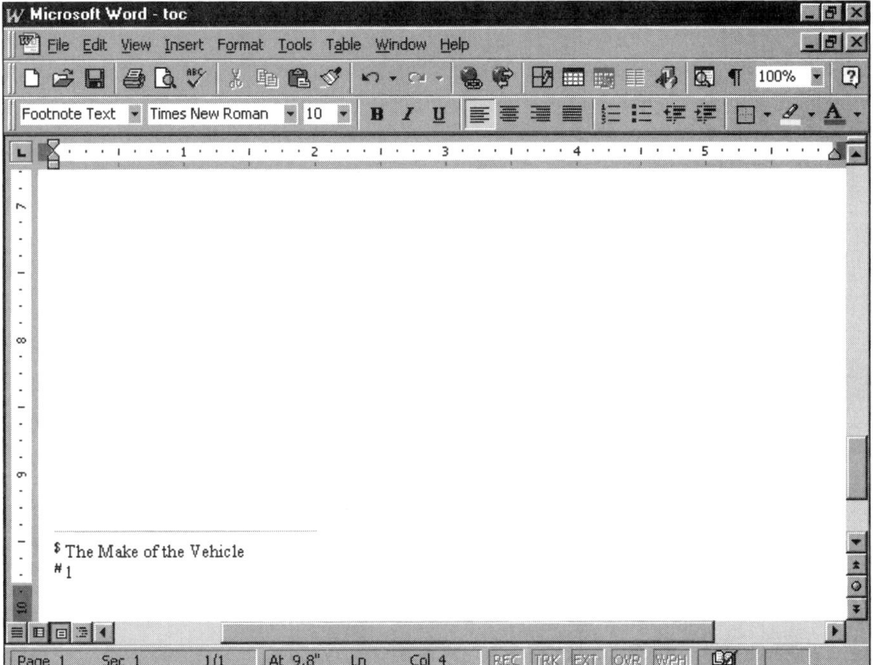

Figure 18-6: After creating the custom footnote mark, you enter the data required for the type of mark used.

You can use any string that you like for a topic title, but each title should be unique, and titles can be no more than 255 characters in length, including spaces.

Creating Topic IDs

Each topic may contain a Topic ID. Topic IDs are strings that uniquely identify a topic. When you link topics to forms and controls in your application to create context-sensitive help, you use the Topic IDs to create the link. Topic IDs are created by using the Footnote feature of your word processor.

To create a Topic ID in Microsoft Word, do the following:

1. Place the cursor at the beginning of the text of the topic for which you want to create an ID.
2. Select Insert⇨Footnote from the menu bar.
3. Select Custom Mark for the footnote.
4. Enter a pound sign (#) as the custom mark and click on OK. The # sign footnote tells the Help Compiler that the following string is a Topic ID.
5. The cursor is placed at the bottom of the page next to the # footnote mark. Enter the Topic ID as the footnote text (see Figure 18-6.)

Topic IDs can be almost any string that you want, but they must conform to the following rules:

- Topic IDs may contain spaces within the ID but should not contain leading or trailing spaces.
- Topic IDs should not contain any reserved characters (# =+&*%!).
- Topic IDs should consist of no more than 255 characters.

You can insert a Topic ID at a specific location in the Topic text, rather than just at the beginning, if you want users to be able to jump to a specific point in the text.

Creating non-scrolling regions in a topic

Often, help Topics become quite large and must be scrolled with a vertical scrollbar to be viewed entirely. This presents a problem in that important text that always needs to be seen, such as the topic's title, will eventually scroll out of view when the user uses the scroll bar. To prevent this from happening, you can create a *nonscrolling region* for any topic. A nonscrolling region is a region of text at the top of a Topic that always remains visible even if the user scrolls to the bottom of a long topic. The nonscrolling region is separated from the scrolling region by a thin black line. You may place bitmaps, hotspots, or text within the nonscrolling region. You create a nonscrolling region by applying the Keep with next paragraph style to each paragraph you want to keep in the nonscrolling region (see Figure 18-7).

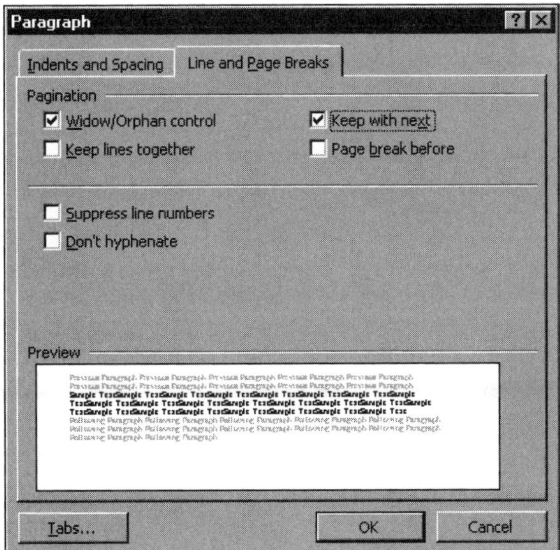

Figure 18-7: The Paragraph dialog box is used to set topic properties such as nonscrolling areas and nonwrapping text.

To create a nonscrolling region in Microsoft Word, do the following:

1. Place the cursor in a paragraph to include in the nonscrolling region.
2. Select Format⇨Paragraph.
3. Click on the Line and Page Breaks tab.
4. Check the Keep with next option box.
5. Click on OK.

Do not create nonscrolling regions for Topics that will be displayed in pop-up windows. They will not work and may cause errors on compiling the Help project field.

You can specify different background colors for nonscrolling and scrolling regions by opening your project (.HPJ) file in Help Workshop (discussed later in this chapter), clicking on the Windows button, and then clicking on the Color tab. If you use a transparent bitmap in both the scrolling region and the nonscrolling region of the same topic, however, the transparent area of both bitmaps is displayed using the background color of the scrolling region.

Preventing text from wrapping in a topic

One of the nice features of Windows Help is that users can stretch a Topic window to any size they want; WinHelp automatically wraps the text and adds scroll bars accordingly. At times, however, you do not want the text to wrap. For example, you may have a code example that becomes unreadable when the text in the example wraps. You can prevent a line from wrapping using the Keep lines together paragraph style.

To prevent a line of text from wrapping using Microsoft Word, follow these steps:

1. Place the cursor anywhere in a line of text that you do not want to wrap.
2. Select Format⇨Paragraph
3. Click on the Line and Page Breaks tab.
4. Check the Keep lines together option box.
5. Click on OK.

Defining topic keywords

Topic keywords are words that are listed in the index of a Help system. These keywords are used to quickly locate Topics; finding by keywords is faster than performing a full-text search. In addition, you can create keywords that do not even appear in the text of a topic, thereby allowing for many different ways to locate a topic of interest.

In general, you should specify any and all keywords a user might use to search for each topic. Put yourself in the user's seat for a little while and ask yourself this question: If I needed to find this information, what keywords would I expect to find it under? Consider using the following types of keywords:

- Nontechnical terms that are likely to occur to a beginning user
- Technical terms that are likely to occur to an advanced user
- Common synonyms for technical terms
- Words that describe the topic in a general manner
- Words that describe specific subjects within the topic
- Inverted forms of keyword phrases, such as "combining Help files" and "Help files, combining"

There are three kinds of keyword entries: *K-keywords, A-keywords,* and *multi-index keywords.* Each type of entry has its own corresponding topic footnote.

K-keywords

K-keywords are used for searches with the Index button. K-keywords are also used by the KLink macro to provide inter-topic jumps. K-keywords are denoted by the custom footnote mark K.

A-keywords

A-keywords are used for ALink macro jumps only. They do not appear in the index. A-keywords are denoted by the custom footnote mark A.

Both types of keywords must adhere to the following restrictions:

- Multiple keywords must be separated with a semicolon.
- Spaces before and after keywords are removed.
- You cannot use carriage returns when defining keywords.
- A keyword cannot contain more than 255 characters.

Consistency is very important to a user. If you want your index to look similar to those in Windows Help, consider the following:

- Always use the gerund form of verbs for keywords that begin with a verb, such as "Saving documents."
- Always use the plural form of nouns.
- Use synonyms consistently throughout a family of Help files.

To create index entries for a topic using Microsoft Word, do the following:

1. Place the cursor at the beginning of the text of the Topic for which you want to create the Index.
2. Select Insert⇨Footnote from the menu bar.
3. Select Custom Mark for the footnote.
4. Enter the letter **K** as the custom mark and click on OK. The K footnote tells the Help Compiler that the following string contains index entries.
5. The cursor is placed at the bottom of the page next to the K footnote mark. Enter the keywords for the topic as the footnote text.

When defining a keyword footnote, remember the following points:

- Separate keywords with a semicolon.
- Do not use spaces before or after keywords — they will be removed.
- Do not use carriage returns.
- Use no more than 255 characters per keyword.

To create second-level index entries for a topic, here's what you do:

1. Place the cursor at the beginning of the text of the topic for which you want to create the second-level index entry.
2. Select Insert⇨Footnote from the menu bar.
3. Select Custom Mark for the footnote.
4. Enter the letter **K** as the custom mark and click on OK. The K footnote tells the Help Compiler that the following string contains index entries.
5. The cursor is placed at the bottom of the page next to the K footnote mark. Type the first-level keyword entry followed by a semicolon (;).
6. Immediately after the semicolon, type the first-level entry again, followed by a comma or a colon (:), a space, the second-level entry, and a semicolon. For example, to create a second-level index entry called Getting Help under the index entry Help, you would create a footnote that contained the text `Help;Help, Getting Help`.

Keywords are case-sensitive, but Help Workshop assumes that two keywords that differ only in case are meant to be the same keyword. Help Workshop changes one of the keywords to agree with the other (it decides which one to use) and displays a warning message.

Entries appear alphabetically in the index, regardless of their order in footnote text.

Adding a topic to a Browse Sequence

When you have a series of topics that are designed to be viewed in a sequence, you can create a *browse sequence* for the topics. When a topic belongs to a browse sequence, browse buttons are displayed at the top of the topic's window. The user can then click on a browse button to view the previous or next topic in the browse sequence. You create browse sequences by using the footnote feature of your word processor.

To add a topic to a browse sequence using Microsoft Word, do the following:

1. Place the cursor at the beginning of the text of the Topic to add to a browse sequence.
2. Select Insert⇨Footnote from the menu bar.
3. Select Custom Mark for the footnote.
4. Enter a plus sign (+) as the custom mark and click on OK. The + sign at the beginning of the footnote tells the Help Compiler that the following string is a browse code.
5. The cursor is placed at the bottom of the page next to the + footnote mark. Type the text to be used for the *browse code.* A browse code is a number or character that specifies the topic's position in a browse sequence. The topics are sorted in ascending order by using the browse codes. When using numeric browse codes, include placeholding zeros (such as `001`, `002`, and `003`). See Figure 18-8 for an example.

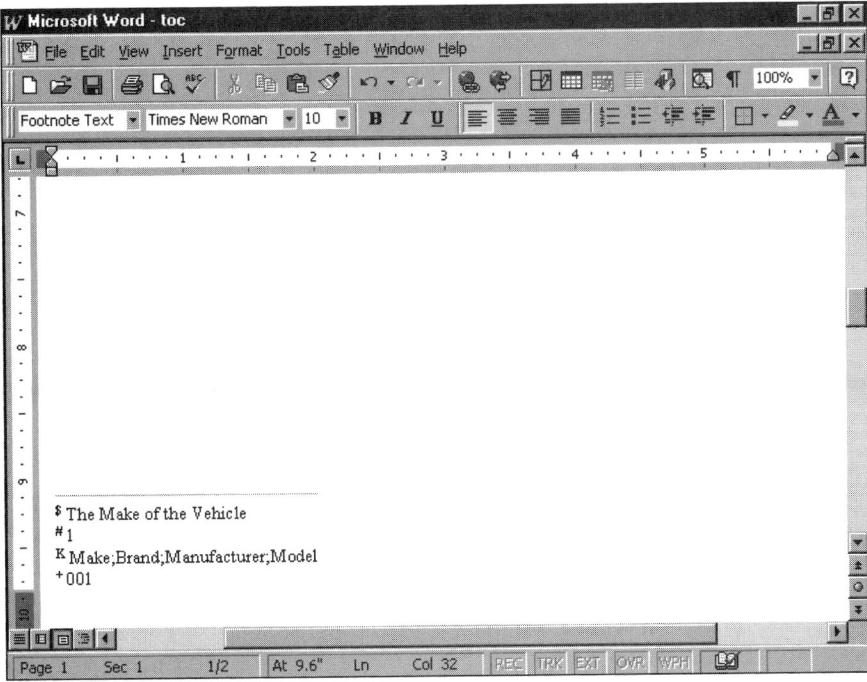

Figure 18-8: Footnotes are the foundation of creating Help topics, and you will create many different footnotes for each topic.

To use browse sequences, you must activate the browse buttons in the project file. In addition, WinHelp creates an auto-browse sequence for topics to which you have added a browse footnote (+) but for which you have not specified a browse code.

To make it easier to add topics at a later time, use the same browse name but do not provide a number for each browse footnote in a sequence. Help Workshop arranges your browse sequence in the order that the topics appear. To change the browse sequence, simply change the order in which topics appear in your .RTF file.

If your Help file has only one browse sequence, use `auto` as the browse code. Help Workshop automatically creates a browse sequence based on the order in which topics appear in your topic files.

Specifying a topics window type

Window types are discussed in detail later in this chapter. It is important to note here, however, that you specify the type of window a help topic appears in by using the footnote feature of your word processor.

To specify a topic's window type using Microsoft Word, follow these steps:

1. Place the cursor at the beginning of the text of the topic for which you want to designate a Window type.
2. Select Insert⇨Footnote from the menu bar.
3. Select Custom Mark for the footnote.
4. Enter a greater than sign (>) as the custom mark and click on OK. The > sign at the beginning of the footnote tells the Help Compiler that the following string is the name of a window type.
5. The cursor is placed at the bottom of the page next to the > footnote mark. Enter the name of the window type. Window types are created in the Help Project (.HPJ) file and are discussed later in this chapter.

Running a macro when a topic is opened

WinHelp has numerous macros that you can include within your Help systems. You can trigger a macro to execute when a Help topic is first opened to eliminate the need for the user to trigger the macro manually.

To specify a macro to run when a topic is first opened using Microsoft Word, do the following:

1. Place the cursor at the beginning of the text of the Topic to which you want to attach an opening macro.
2. Select Insert⇨Footnote from the menu bar.
3. Select Custom Mark for the footnote.
4. Start the footnote text with the bang sign (!). The ! at the beginning of the footnote tells the Help Compiler that the following string is the name of a macro to run when the Topic is opened.
5. After the ! sign, enter the name of the macro to run.
6. Click on OK to create the footnote.

Tip

You can trigger a string of macros to run when a Help topic is opened by listing all the macros to run in the browse footnote, separating them with a semicolon.

Creating jumps to other topics

Jumps are text that appear in a topic underlined and green. When the user clicks on jump text, the topic whose ID is associated with the selected jump is displayed. Alternately, a jump can display a topic as a pop-up window rather than remove the current topic and display the "jumped to" topic in its place.

To create a jump to a topic or *pop-up* topic using Microsoft Word, you do this:

1. Place the insertion point directly after the text or bitmap that you want to be the jump hotspot and then type the Topic ID of the topic you want to jump to. Do not put a space between the hotspot and the Topic ID.
2. Select the hotspot text. If the hotspot text ends in a punctuation mark, include the mark when you select the text. (Otherwise, a line break could cause the mark to appear at the beginning of a line.)
3. If you want another topic to be displayed, apply the double-underline character style to the jump text.
4. If you want a pop-up topic to be displayed, apply the single-underline character style to the jump text.
5. Select the topic ID and then apply the hidden character style. You hide text by first highlighting it, selecting Format➪Font, and then checking the hidden option box.

Note the underlined word `Make` in Figure 18-9. If a user clicks on this underlined text, the topic whose ID is associated with this jump is displayed in place of the current topic.

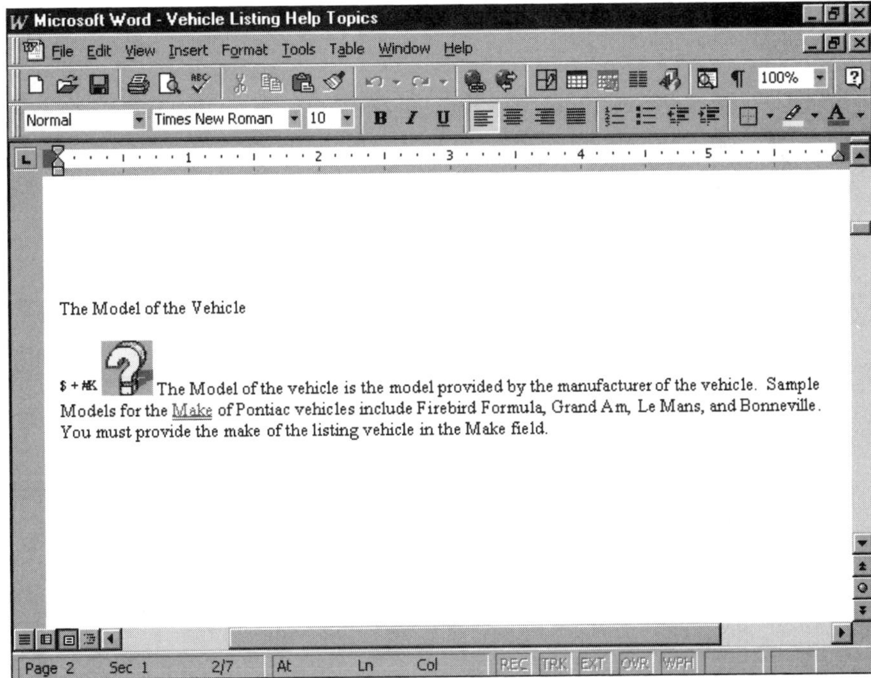

Figure 18-9: Jump text is shown in green and is underlined for easy recognition.

You have some additional control over the jumped text besides specifying whether the jump is a full jump or it displays a pop-up topic. You can change these other characteristics of the jump and displayed jump text:

- To display the jump in the default text color (non-green), insert an asterisk (*) at the beginning of the Topic ID. If you do this, be sure to hide the asterisk with the Topic ID.
- To display the jump in the default text color (non-green) without an underline, insert a percent sign (%) at the beginning of the Topic ID. Again, you must hide the % sign with the Topic ID.
- To create a jump to a topic in another Help file, insert an at sign (@) and the name of the other Help file at the end of the Topic ID and then hide them both with the Topic ID.
- To specify a window type for the topic you jump to, insert a greater than sign (>) and the window name at the end of the Topic ID and then hide them with the Topic ID.

Adding graphics to a topic

Although most of your Help topics will consist primarily of text, it is often beneficial to include graphics in your Help topics. For example, if you use lots of buttons with images on them (such as toolbar images), you can display the picture with its Topic text to help the user associate the image with its function.

You can include the following types of graphics in your Help Topics:

- Windows bitmaps (.BMP or .DIB)
- Windows metafiles (.WMF)
- Windows Help multiple-hotspot bitmaps created with Microsoft's SHED.EXE program (.SHG)
- Windows Help multi-resolution bitmaps (.MRB)

To include a graphic in a Topic using Microsoft Word, do this:

1. Place the cursor where you want the graphic to appear in the topic.
2. Open the graphic in the application it was created in and copy the graphic.
3. Select Edit⇨Paste in Word to paste the graphic at the desired location (refer to Figure 18-9).

If you do not have access to the application that created the graphic, or if you want to include multiple instances of the graphic, you can reference the graphic in the Topic text with the following syntax:

```
{bmx filename.bmp}
```

For x, specify one of the values listed in Table 18-1. For filename.bmp, specify the name of your bitmap file, including the path.

Table 18-1 Bitmap Alignment Specifiers

Value	Description
c	Aligns the bitmap as a text character
l	Aligns the bitmap with the left margin
r	Aligns the bitmap with the right margin

In addition, you can use the letter t with any of the preceding values. When you use the t indicator, the white pixels of the bitmap will be converted to the solid color closest to the background color of the window in which the Topic is displayed. You can use this feature only with 18-color bitmaps.

An example of a graphic reference is

```
{bmlt d:\graphics\MyPicture.bmp}
```

This line causes the bitmap d:\graphics\MyPicture.bmp to be displayed aligned with the left margin with all white pixels in the bitmap displayed as the closest matching color to the background of the topic window.

You can force WinHelp to display a bitmap that most closely matches the number of colors that can be displayed on the user's computer by first creating a single bitmap in each color mode you want available, and then referencing them as one string, with each bitmap separated by a semicolon. For example, if you wanted to include an 18-color version and a 256-color version of a bitmap and then have WinHelp decide at run time which file to display, you could create a bitmap reference like this one:

```
{bml c:\MyPicture16.bmp;c:\MyPicture256.bmp}.
```

Help Workshop automatically removes the aspect ratio from bitmap (.BMP) files so that WinHelp will not stretch or shrink them regardless of the aspect ratio of the user's monitor. Distorting bitmaps generally yields poor results; if you want text in a graphic to change depending on the aspect ratio of a user's monitor, use a metafile.

Adding video or animation to a topic

You can display video or animation in any topic by using the mci command. The mci command is similar to the bm command used to display bitmaps. All video and animation files inserted with the mci command must be video for Windows (.AVI) files.

To include video or animation in a Topic using Microsoft Word, follow these steps:

1. Place the cursor where you want to place the multimedia file.
2. Type in the reference to the multimedia file, using the following syntax:

```
{mci filename.ext}
```

You may also add any of the options listed in Table 18-2 when inserting a multimedia file using the `mci` command. If no options are specified, a play bar appears with a menu button, and the file is not played until the user requests it.

Table 18-2 Additional Parameters for Displaying Multimedia Files

Option	*Description*
EXTERNAL	Keeps the file outside of the Help file.
NOPLAYBAR	No play bar is shown (useful for auto-play and repeat).
NOMENU	No menu button is shown if there is a play bar.
REPEAT	The file automatically repeats when play is done.
PLAY	The file automatically plays when shown.

To use an option, enter the option after the `mci` identifier. If you want to use more than one option, separate the options by a space. Here is an example:

```
{mci PLAY NOMENU, MyVideo.avi}
```

Multimedia can really add pizzazz to your Help system. However, don't be taken in by the glitz of multimedia; if the video file has nothing to add to the topic to help the user, leave it out.

Using Help Workshop

After you have created your topics file using the word processor of your choice, you need to create a *Help project file.* A Help project file is an ASCII text file that contains all the information required by the Help Compiler to combine topic files, bitmaps, and other various files into a Help file. Help project files are saved with the extension .HPJ.

The *Office Developer Edition* tools CD-ROM includes a tool for you to create Help systems for your Access applications: Help Workshop (see Figure 18-10). Help Workshop is installed with the rest of the Office Developer Edition tools and you can run it by selecting Microsoft ODE Tools⇨ Microsoft Help Workshop from the task bar.

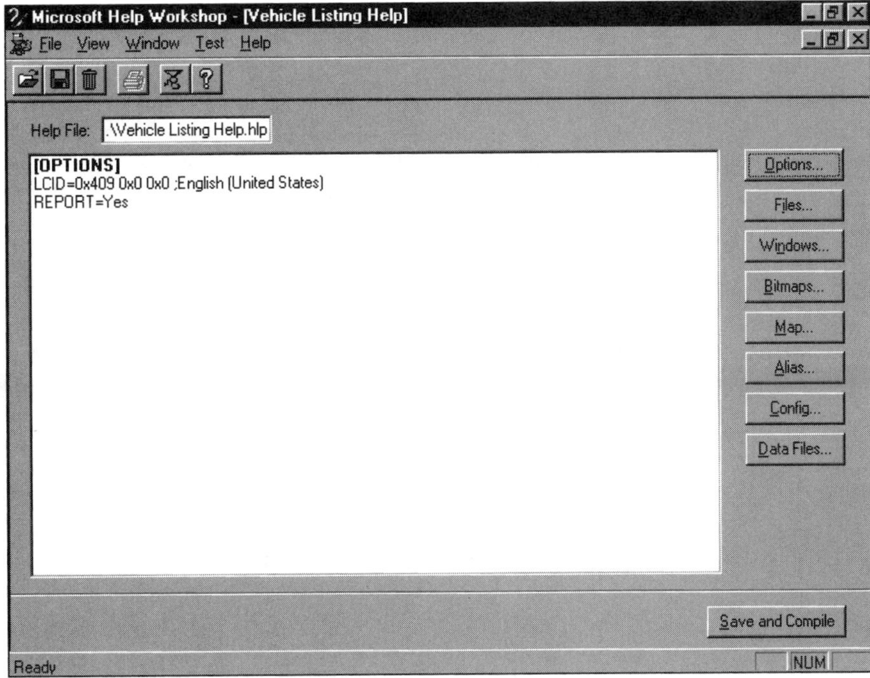

Figure 18-10: Help Workshop lets you create the Help project .HPJ files that the Help Compiler can use.

To create a new project file, first start Help Workshop from the Taskbar and then do the following:

1. Select File➪New.
2. Select Help Project and click on OK, or double-click on Help Project.
3. Enter the name of the new project file and click on OK.

When you first create a Help project file, it includes all the basic information necessary to compile (refer to Figure 18-10); however, you need to specify at least one topic file (.RTF) to include before the compile can be done.

Setting the Help project options

The first thing you should do when you create a new Help project is define the Options for the project. Click on the Options button on the Help Workshop main screen to access the project Options dialog box (see Figure 18-11).

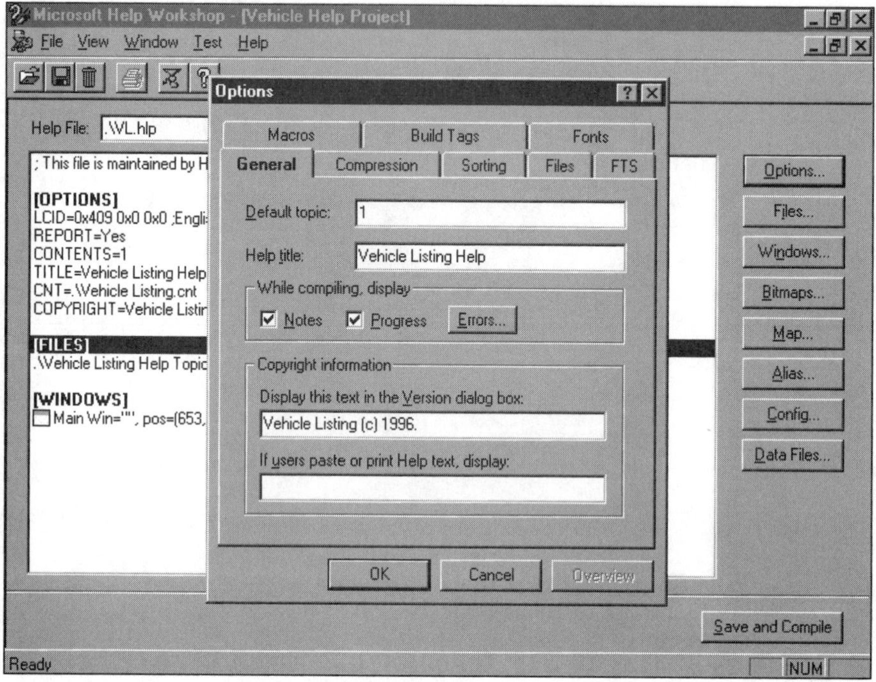

Figure 18-11: The Options dialog box is where you define parameters for your Help project, such as what table of contents to use.

Setting the General Options tab

The two main tabs to be concerned with at first are the General and the Files tabs. The General tab is the tab displayed when you first click on the Options button. On the General tab, you can modify these settings:

- **Default topic.** The *default topic* is the Topic ID (not the topic title) of the topic that WinHelp displays whenever an invalid jump is initiated. Help files that do not have an associated contents (.CNT) file display the default topic as the first topic when the Help file is opened and the Contents tab is clicked. If you do not specify a default topic, the first topic of the first file listed in the project (.HPJ) file is used as the default topic.
- **Help title.** This is the text string that appears in the title bar of your Help system. The words "Windows Help" are used if you leave this field blank and the contents (.CNT) file does not have a title specified. You should always provide a title specific to your Help program.
- **While compiling, display.** When you become more advanced at creating Help systems, you can "uncheck" these items to prevent the Compiler from displaying error messages and notes. Unless you have some specific reason not to, leave these boxes checked.

- **Copyright information.** You should always provide copyright text. This text is displayed when a user clicks on the Help menu in a main window and then clicks on Version. You may also specify text to have appended to any text copied from your Help file. You may want to include copyright information in this field as well.

You can include the date the Help file was compiled by adding a `%date` to the end of your copyright text.

Setting the Files Options tab

Clicking on the Files tab on the Help Workshop Options dialog box displays the page used to enter information about files associated with the current project (see Figure 18-12). The information you supply on this tab is discussed next, item by item. You need to be aware, however, that you must specify the Contents file to use on this tab or your Help system will not have a Contents! Although you have not created the Contents file yet, you may still specify the name of the Contents file you plan to create (with full path), or you may create the Contents file first and then reopen the project and supply the name.

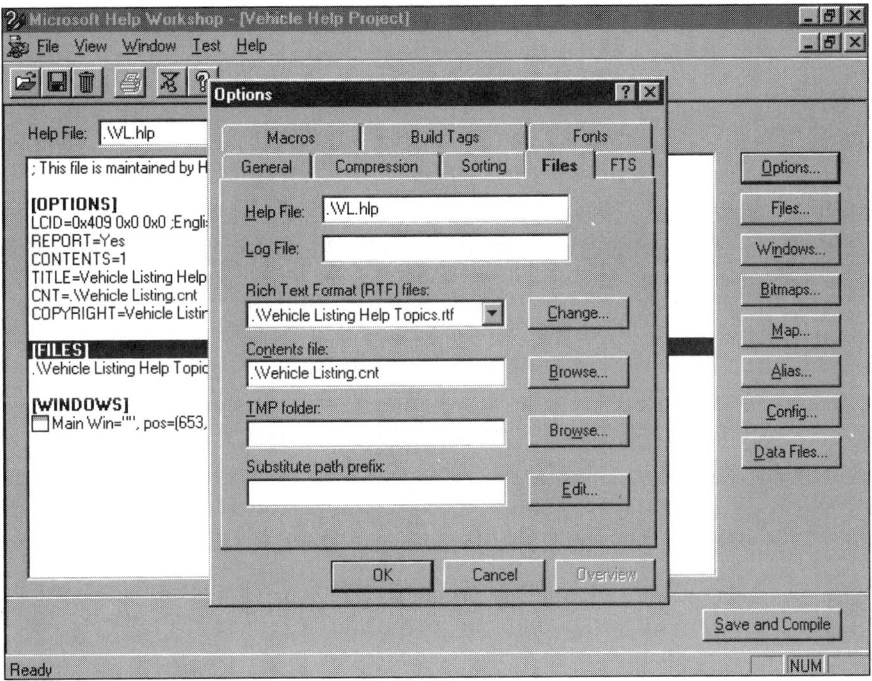

Figure 18-12: To include a Contents in your Help file, you must specify the Contents file name here.

The information you supply on the Files tab consists of the following:

- **Help File.** This is where you specify the name of the Help file to be created when the project is compiled. The Help file name may be anything you want, and it can even be a long file name; the only condition is that it must have the extension .HLP. Prefixing the file name with a .\ causes the Help file to be created in the same directory Help Workshop resides in. You may also provide this information on the main Help Workshop screen if you want, but you *must* supply a help file name to compile your project.
- **Log File.** You can have a text log file created when your Help project is compiled by specifying a valid file name here. This log file contains the information printed to the screen during compilation. For small projects, you may not need a log file, so you can leave this field blank. For larger projects, you may want to create a log file for you to review errors encountered when compiling the project.
- **Contents File.** You should always include a Contents for your Help project. Creating a Help Contents is discussed later in this chapter, but this is where you specify the full name and the path of the Contents file. You may fill this in at any time, but the specified Help Contents must exist when you compile the Help file.
- **TMP Folder.** By default, Help Workshop uses the folder that contains your topic (.RTF) files to store temporary files used to create your Help file. If you would like to use a different folder, you may specify it here. Note, however, that Help Workshop does not use this temporary location unless bitmaps are missing or your compiled Help file is larger than 8MB.
- **Substitute path prefix.** This field tells Help Workshop to use a path other than that specified in the project (.HPJ) file. If you move topic (.RTF) or bitmap (.BMP) files to a different drive or server, you can update this field instead of editing each individual path name. You can use the Edit button to locate the desired path.

Adding topic files to a Project file

When you have set up the Options to define your project, you need to add the topic (.RTF) files you want compiled into the Help file. You must supply at least one topic file in order to compile a Help project into a help file. To add topic files to, or remove topic files from, a Help project, you use the Topic Files dialog box, which you access by clicking on the Files button on the Help Workshop main screen (see Figure 18-13).

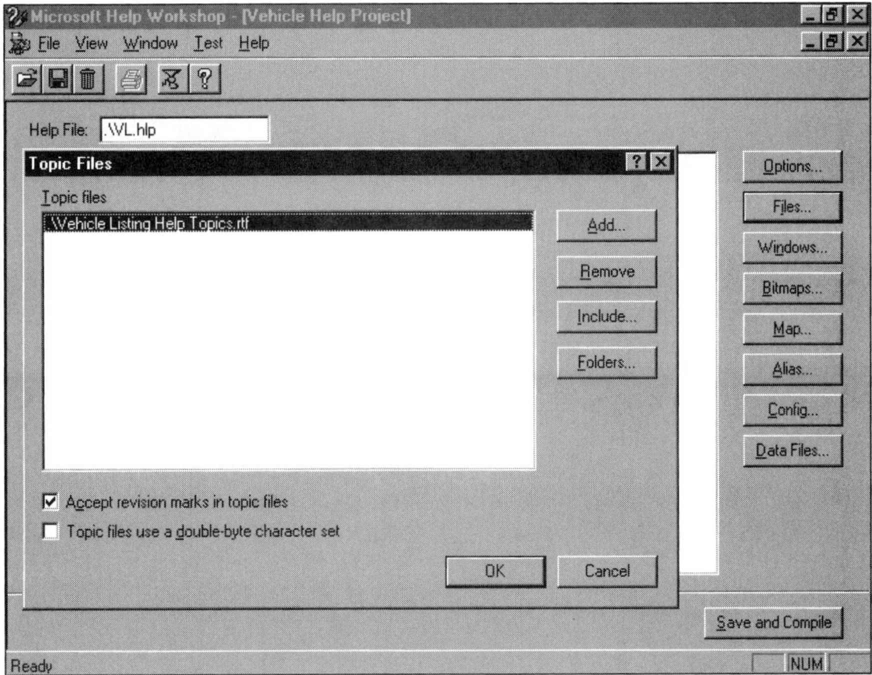

Figure 18-13: The Topic Files dialog box is used to add topics to or remove topic files from your Help project.

To add topic files to your Help project, first call up the Files dialog box by clicking on the Files button and then follows these instructions:

1. Click on the Add button.
2. Select the topic file you want to add to the Help project.
3. Click on the Open button to add the topic file to the project file. Files that you add to the project appear in the Help project definition script (see Figure 18-14).

To remove a topic file from your Help project, first call up the Files dialog box by clicking on the Files button and then do the following:

1. Select the file name you want to remove from the Help project.
2. Click on the Remove button.

Tip

If you have a large list of topic files to include in your Help project, you can create an ASCII text file with all the topic names (including paths) and use the Include button to select the ASCII file. This technique is very useful if you have large sets of topic files that are always used together in different Help projects.

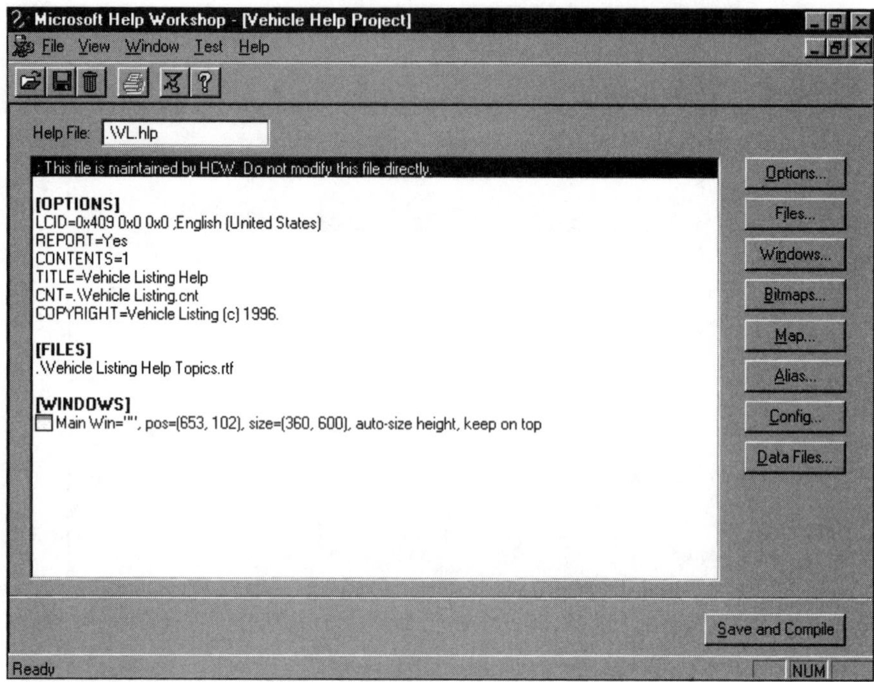

Figure 18-14: As you add files and change options, the text script that defines your Help project changes.

Creating a new Help Contents file

When you have finished adding all the topic files your help project will use, you need to create a Contents for your Help system. It is critical that you create a clear, concise, and comprehensive Contents for your Help system to make it easy for your users to locate the topics they need to get their job done. To create a Contents for your Help system, you create a Contents file with Help Workshop and then include this file in the Help project definition before compiling your Help project. Content files are ASCII files saved with the extension .CNT. Contents files consist of specifications of three items:

- Headings
- Topics
- Commands

To create a new contents file with Help Workshop, follow these steps:

1. Select File⇨New.
2. Select Help Contents and click on OK, or double-click on Help Contents to display the Contents editor of Help Workshop (see Figure 18-15).

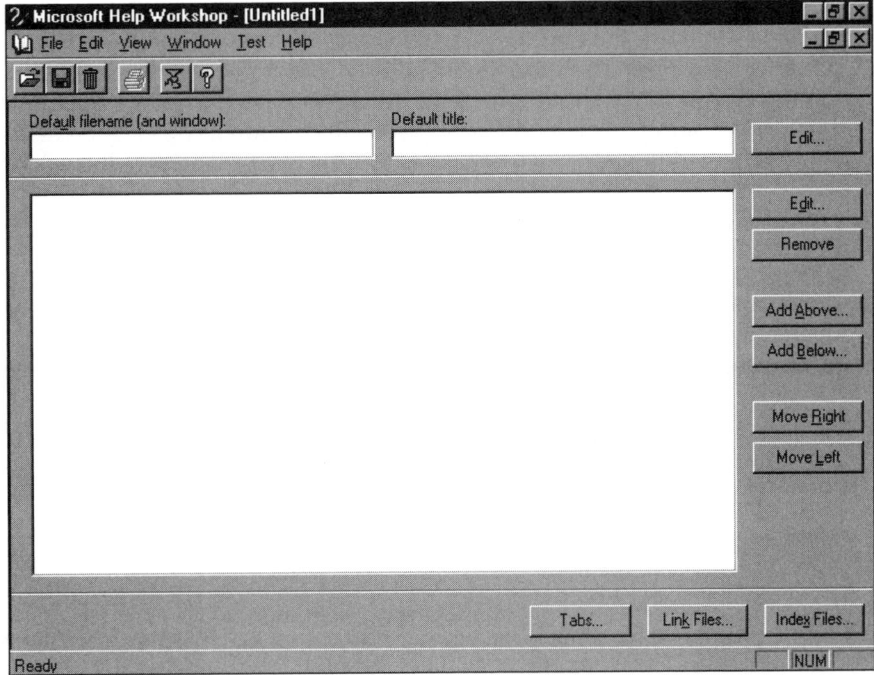

Figure 18-15: You create Contents files for your Help system using Help Workshop's Contents editor.

3. In the Default filename box, type the Help file name that most of your topics are in.
4. In the Default title box, type the text you want to appear in the title bar of the Help Topics dialog box. This text also appears in title bars that do not have a title specified in the `[WINDOWS]` section of the project file.
5. Click on the Save toolbutton.
6. Enter the name for the contents button and click on OK.

Help Contents are just like tables of contents in books: They are essentially outlines. The key to creating a usable Contents is to first create the first-level outline entries, called *headings*. Headings appear with book pictures in the Help Contents. If the user clicks on the book or the heading text, the Contents expands to show all items under the heading. You may create headings under headings as often as needed.

To create a heading entry in the Contents, follow these instructions:

1. Position the cursor in the Contents script where you want to create the heading. At first, the Contents script is empty, so you may skip this step.

2. Click on the Add Above button to add the heading above the selected line in the Contents script. When you first create the Contents file, the script is empty; just click on the Add Above button to create the first heading. If you want to insert the heading below the selected line in the script, click on the Add Below button. After you click on Add Above or Add Below, the Edit Contents Tab Entry dialog box is displayed (see Figure 18-16).
3. Click on the Heading radio button to denote this entry as a heading.
4. Enter the heading text in the title field.
5. Click on OK to create the heading.

After you have created the first-level headings in your Contents file, you need to create the topic entries used to jump to your Help topics. Topic entries appear with a picture of a help document and the title text you enter. When a user clicks on a topic entry, the Help system displays the topic associated with the entry.

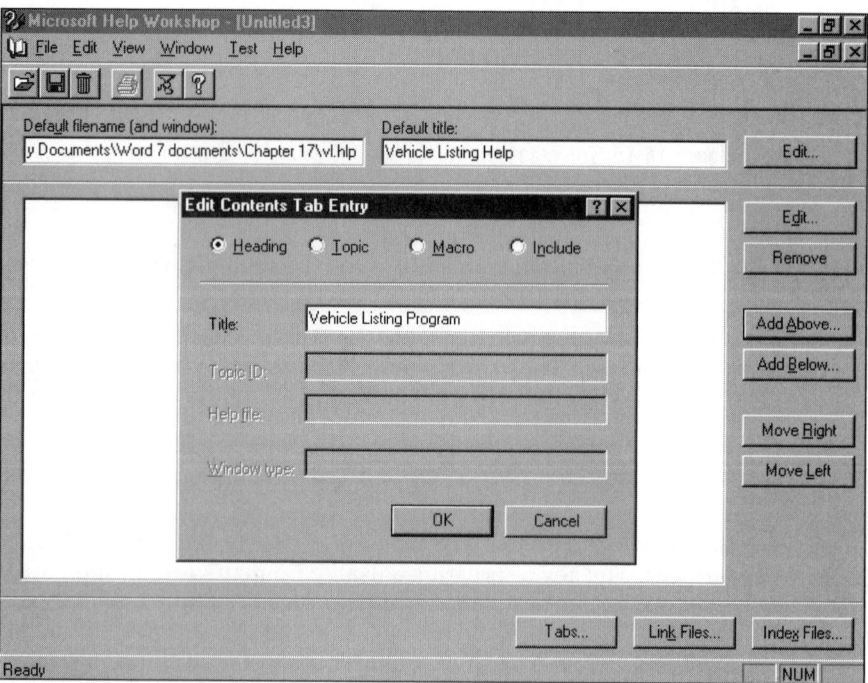

Figure 18-16: Headings are used to categorize topic entries in the Help system.

To create a topic entry in the Contents, do the following:

1. Position the cursor in the Contents script where you want to create the topic.
2. Click on the Add Above or Add Below button to add the topic entry in order to the display the Edit Contents Tab Entry dialog box.
3. Click on the Topic radio button to denote this entry as a topic entry (see Figure 18-17).
4. Enter the topic text in the title field.
5. Enter the ID of the topic to jump to when the user selects this topic entry.
6. If the specified Topic ID is not in the default Help file (the Help file this Contents is compiled in), this is where you need to specify the file name of the Help file in which it is located.
7. If you want to use a Window type other than the default window type, enter the type here.
8. Click on OK to create the topic.

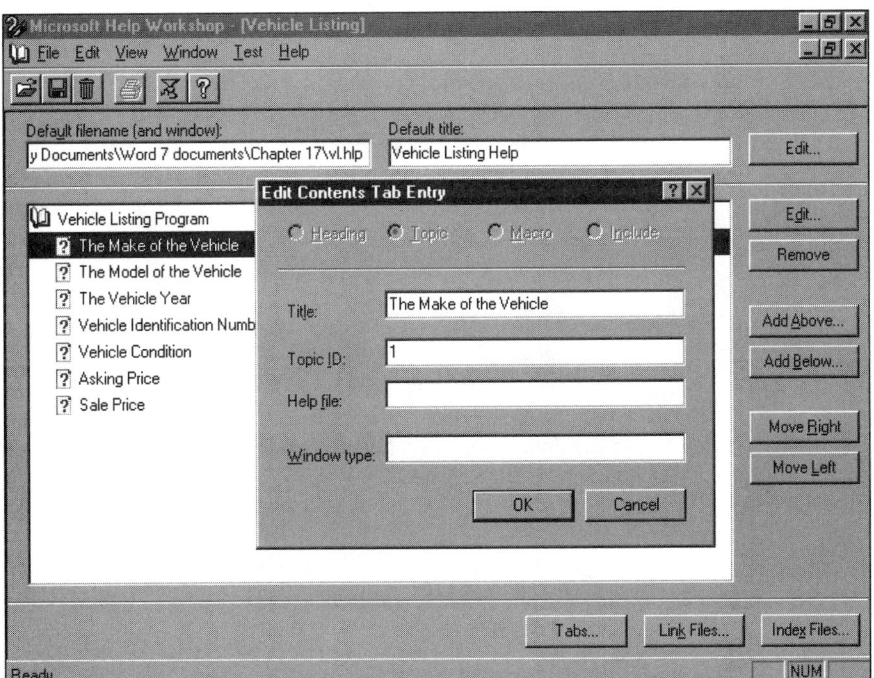

Figure 18-17: Topic entries are used to jump to Help topics within the current Help system or in other Help systems.

Tip

The Contents tab does not appear in the Help Topics dialog box unless the contents file contains at least one topic jump, so you probably want to create a valid entry right away to enable the Contents Tab on the Help Topics dialog box when testing your Help system.

You need to add topics and headings using the steps outlined previously until you have completely defined your Help Contents. As you create the Contents entries, your Contents will begin to take shape (see Figure 18-18). To change the level of a heading or topic, select the entry and click on the Move Right or Move Left button. All subordinate entries are moved in conjunction with the selected entry.

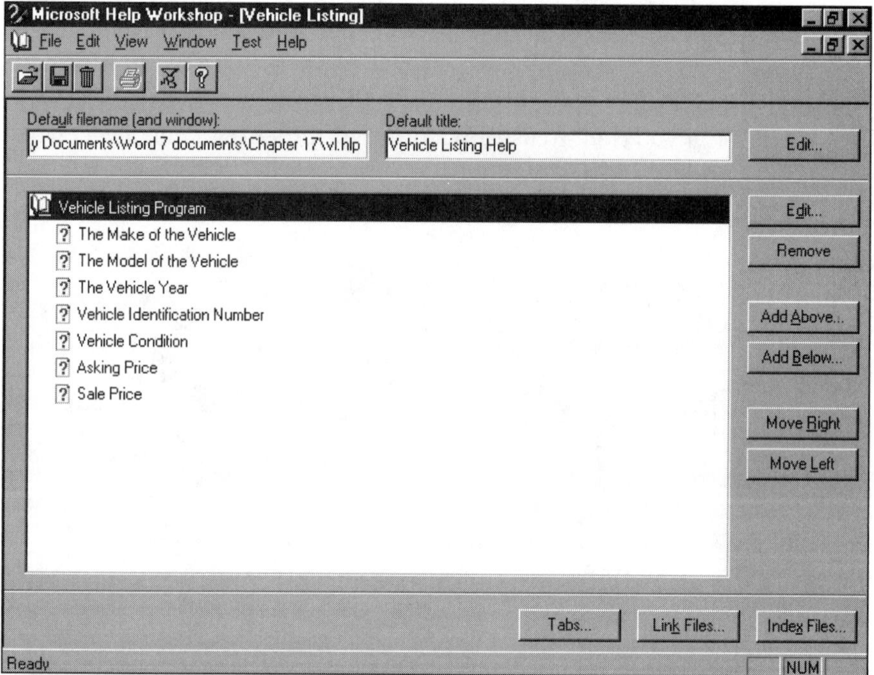

Figure 18-18: The Contents script shows you what the users of your Help system would see if they had all headings expanded.

Enabling full-text searching in your Help system

A powerful feature of WinHelp is the capability to perform full-text searches within a Help system. Ordinarily, when a user runs your Help system and clicks on the Find tab for the first time, the Find Setup Wizard appears. The wizard helps users set up a full-text search index on their computers. A full-text search index lists all the unique words in the Help file.

You can create the full-text index for your users and ship it with your Help files. The disadvantage to this is that it can greatly add to the disk space needed to distribute your Help file. You define your full-text search file by using the FTS tab of the Help project Options dialog box (see Figure 18-19).

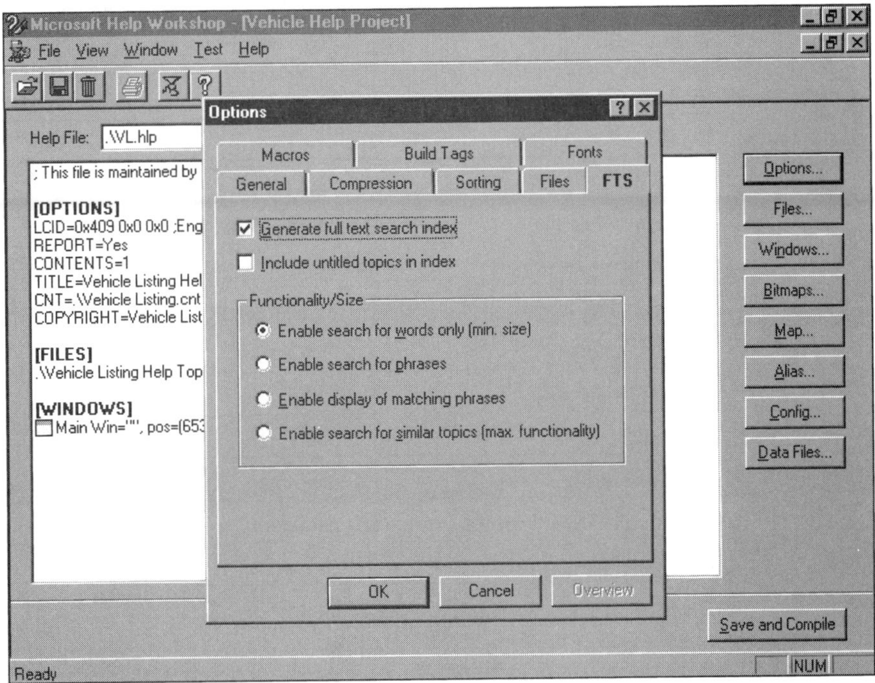

Figure 18-19: Use the FTS tab of the Help project Options dialog box to define full-text search files.

To create a full-text index for your help system, do the following:

1. Open your project (.HPJ) file in Help Workshop and click on the Options button.
2. Click on the FTS tab.
3. Check the Generate full text search index checkbox.
4. Set the Functionality/Size options to fit your situation. Each option increases the usability of your Help file but also increases the disk space required for it.
5. Click on OK to save your changes.

When you compile your project with maximum compression turned on, a full-text search (.FTS) file is created for your Help system. You need to distribute this file with your Help file.

WinHelp version 4.0 dramatically expands the capability of the Help system from Windows 3.*x*. However, there are still some limitations (see Table 18-3); although in most cases these limits are so large that they are not a factor in practice.

Table 18-3 WinHelp 4.0 System Limits

Item	*Limit*
Help file size	2GB
Topics per topic (.rtf) file	No practical limit
Topics per Help file	No practical limit
Topics per keyword	64,000
Topic footnote length	16,383 characters
Keyword length	255 characters
Hotspot hidden text	4,095 characters
Help title string	127 characters
Topic title string	127 characters
Custom window title string	50 characters
Custom window name	8 characters
Copyright string	255 characters
Browse string	50 characters
Referenced bitmaps	65,535 bitmaps per Help file
File name	259 characters
Font name	31 characters
Font ranges	20 ranges
Error log file	No limit
Citation string	2,000 characters
Window definitions	255 per Project file
Window caption	50 characters
Contents file entries	No practical limit
Contents headings	9 levels (indented)
Contents topic strings	255 characters (127 in a DBCS language)
Contents heading text	No practical limit

Compiling Your Help Project

After you have defined your topic (.RTF) files, Help project (.HPJ) file, and your Contents file (.CNT), you are ready to compile your project into a distributable Help file. When you compile a Help project, all the included topic files, bitmap files, and Contents file are placed into one Help file with the extension .HLP.

Setting the compression to use on compile

You may select one of several compression methods when compiling your Help project. The higher the compression used, the smaller the resulting Help file. The only drawback is that the higher the compression used, the greater the time required to compile the Help project. While testing your project, you may want to temporarily turn off compression to reduce the amount of time it takes to compile the project.

To specify the compression to use when compiling a project, follow these instructions:

1. Open the Help project in Help Workshop.
2. Click on the Options button to display the Help project's Options dialog box.
3. Click on the Compression tab to display the compression options (see Figure 18-20).
4. Select the compression type you want the compiler to use. When testing your project, you probably want to set the compression type to None to compile the project as quickly as possible. When you are ready to compile the project for distribution, use maximum compression.
5. Click on OK to save your changes.

Compiling your Help project

After you have set the compression settings to use on compiling, you are ready to compile your Help project. To compile a project, first open it in Help Workshop, and then click on the Save and Compile button located in the lower-right corner. Help Workshop then minimizes itself while compiling the project. When it is finished compiling, it redisplays itself, showing the results of the compilation (see Figure 18-21).

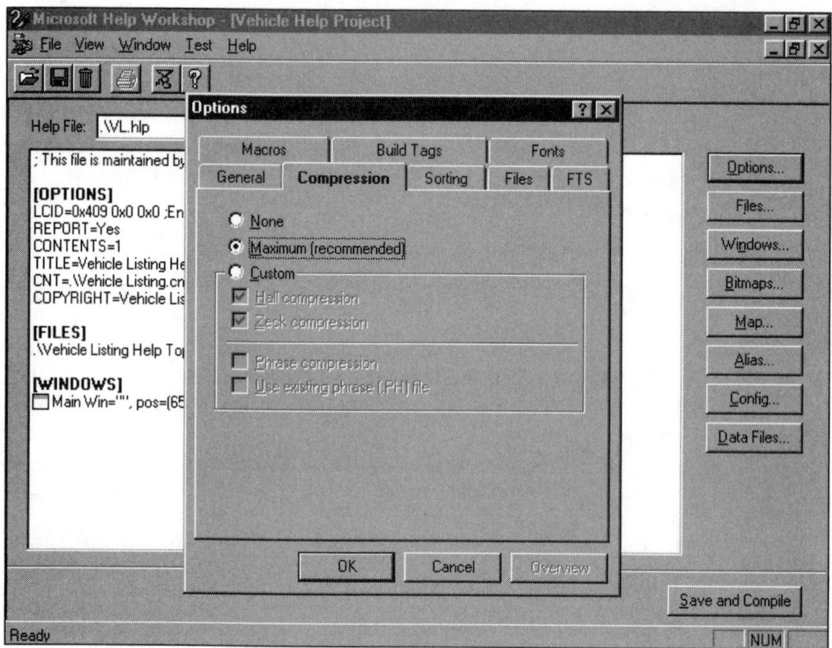

Figure 18-20: You can reduce the amount of disk space used by your Help file by setting the compression settings for the Help project.

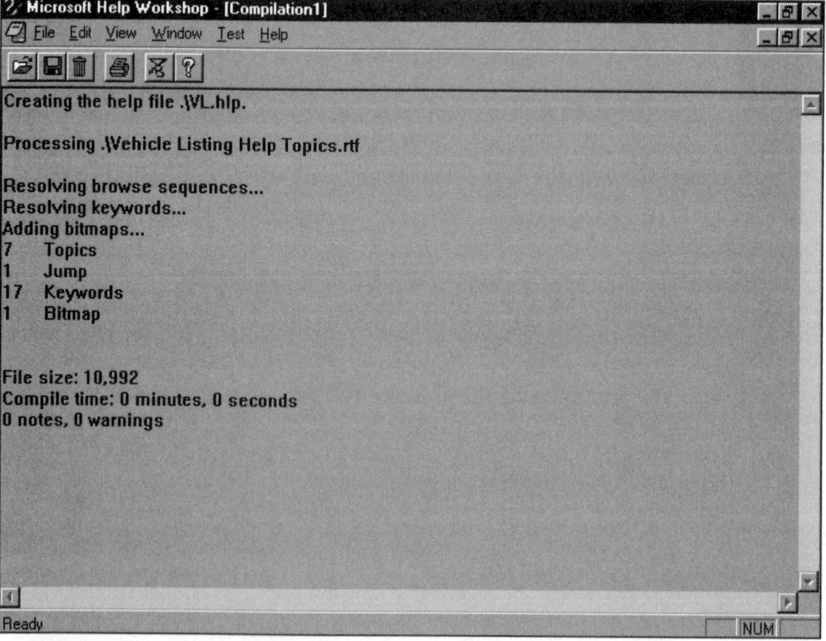

Figure 18-21: Help Workshop shows you results of your compile to help you troubleshoot if the project doesn't compile successfully.

If any errors are encountered, they are shown in this report. You must then close the report by clicking on the Trash Can and correcting the error in your Project file, Contents file, or Topic file(s).

Running your compiled Help file

To run your compiled Help file, click on the Run WinHelp button on the toolbar (the button with the yellow question mark on it). When you click on this button, Help Workshop displays the View Help File dialog box (see Figure 18-22). In this dialog box, you tell Help Workshop what Help file to run.

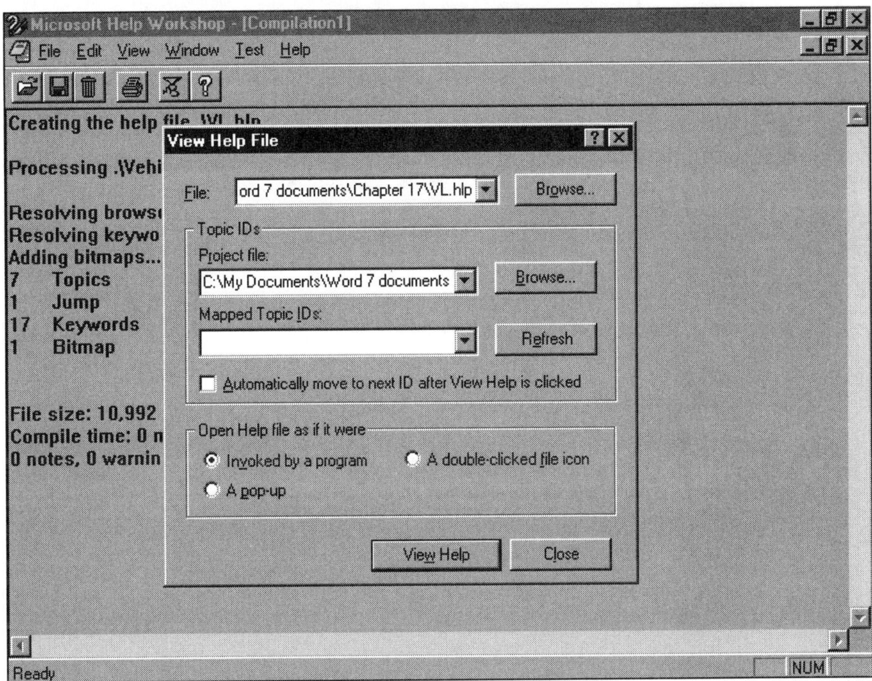

Figure 18-22: It is very important to thoroughly test your Help file before distributing it to your users.

In addition to the Help file you want to run, there are a number of additional options you may specify:

- **Topic IDs/Project file.** If you want to view mapped topics specified in your project file, you need to provide the name of the project (.HPJ) file for WinHelp to look in.
- **Topic IDs/Mapped Topic IDs.** If you specify a Project file in which to look for mapped topics, this field displays all the mapped topics. To view a mapped topic, click on its ID and then click on View Help. If you do not want to view a mapped topic, clear this box.

- **Open Help file as if it were.** You can have WinHelp open your file as though it were called from another program, as if it were a pop-up, or as if it were opened by double-clicking on its file icon. Use these settings to test how your Help file responds to the different ways it can be run.

When you are satisfied with the settings in this dialog box, click on the View Help button to run the Help file. If you selected a topic in the Topic IDs/ Mapped Topic IDs field, that topic is displayed. If your Help file is not displaying the Contents tab (because you displayed a map topic or changed the Open Help as if it were a parameter), click on the Contents tab to display it (see Figure 18-23).

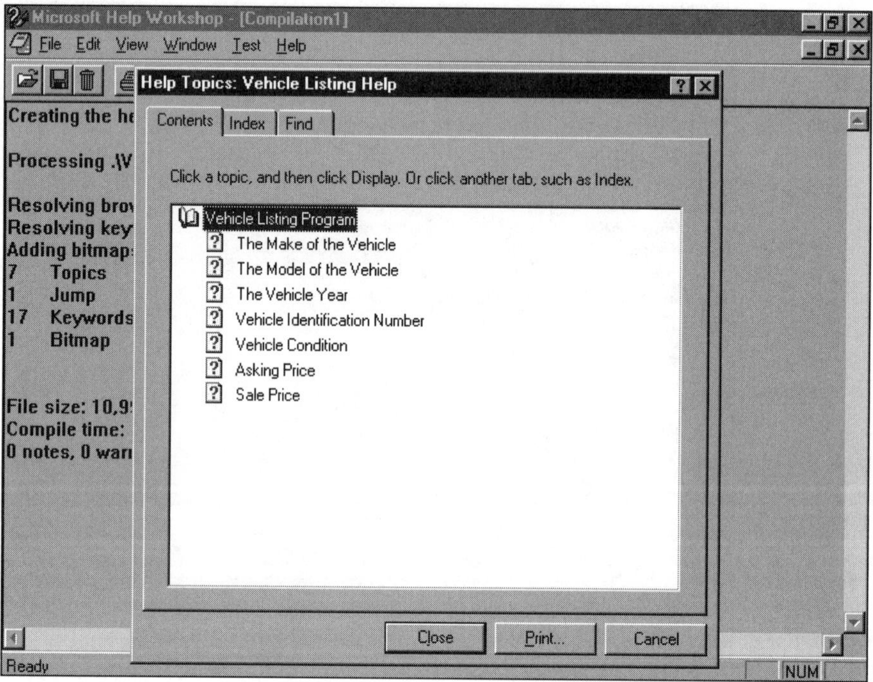

Figure 18-23: A finished Help file showing the Contents tab.

You can now test the contents and topic jumps in the Help file. If you click on the Index tab of the Help file's main window, you see a searchable list of all the K-keyword index entries you created for the topics (see Figure 18-24).

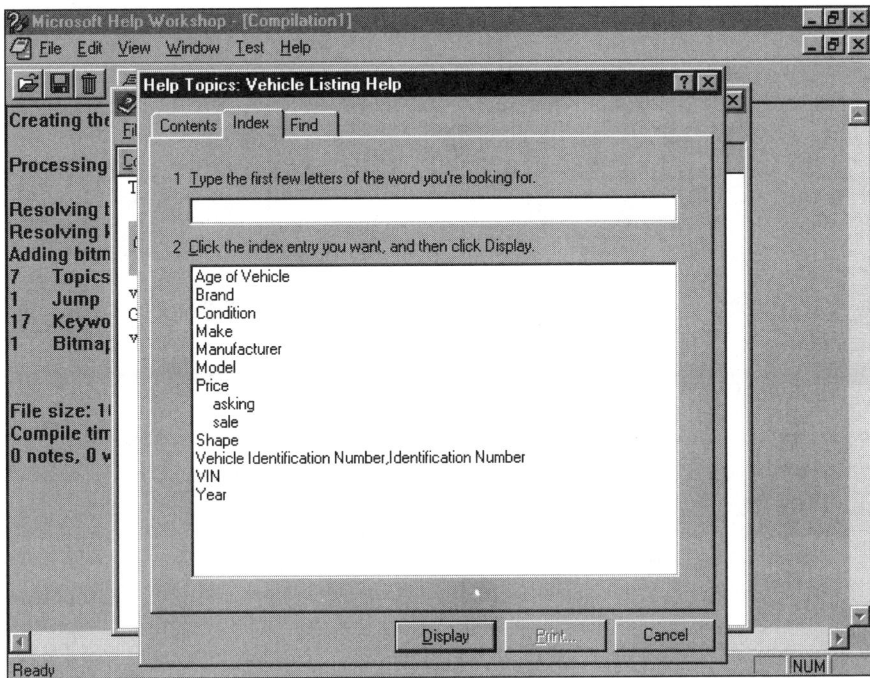

Figure 18-24: The K-keywords you create for topics appear in the index for the Help file.

Integrating a Help File with Your Application

After you have created and compiled a working Help file, it's time to integrate it with your Access application. You can tie controls, forms, command buttons, and menu items to specific Help topics by using the techniques described here.

The most common way to link an application to a Help file is to link forms or specific controls to topics in the Help file. You accomplish this task in two stages: first by specifying the Help file to use and then by setting the `Help Context ID` property on the forms and controls.

You must specify the Help file name on each form in your application to prevent Access Help from displaying. If you are distributing your application with the Office Developer Tools and you do not supply a Help file name, an error occurs when the user attempts to access help. If the Help file is located in a different folder than the running Access application, the Help File property on the form must include the full path to the Help file.

After you have set the Help File property on each form, you need to set the Help Context ID for the form. This should be the ID of a topic that talks about the form in general. After you have set the form's context (Topic) ID, you can set the Help Context IDs of all controls that you want to display a different topic than the topic to which the form is linked. If you do not want a control to display a unique topic, leave its Help Context ID = 0 and the form's topic will be displayed when the user presses F1 while the control has the focus; otherwise, the topic whose ID matches the Help Context ID of the control with the focus is displayed when the user presses F1.

Tip

If the user presses F1 in a control that has its Help Context ID set to 0 and the form's Help Context ID is also set to 0, Access help is displayed. If your application is distributed with the Office Developer Tools, Access's Help will not be displayed and an error will occur. For this reason, you should always link each form's Help Context ID to a valid topic.

Third-Party Help Tools

A number of tools on the market are designed specifically for creating Help files; most of them requiring Microsoft Word. Two of the most popular are Doc-2-Help and RoboHelp. These tools will save you days or weeks of work when creating large Help files. If you plan to create complex Help systems, the only reason not to invest in one of these tools is cost; they can be rather expensive. If you need to create large, in-depth Help files, however, you should invest in a Help authoring tool.

By supplying complete, accurate Help that is fully linked with your application, you will be providing a professional program that lowers the amount of support required for the application and greatly increases the application's usability.

Part VI

Enterprise Computing, Internet, and Client/Server Access

Chapter 19

Integrating with Microsoft Office

In This Chapter

- Using Automation to integrate with Office
- Creating Automation references
- Creating an instance of an Automation object
- Getting an existing object instance
- Working with Automation objects
- Closing an instance of an Automation object
- An Automation example using Microsoft Word 97
- Using Office's Macro Recorder
- Programming the Office Assistant

As companies standardize their computer practices and software selections, it is becoming more and more important to develop *total* solutions: solutions that integrate the many procedures of an organization. Usually, the different procedures are accomplished by using different software packages, such as Word for letter writing, Exchange for mailing and faxing, Excel for financial functions, and Pursuit for client and contact management. If the organization for which you are developing has standardized on the Microsoft Office suite, you can leverage your knowledge of Visual Basic for Applications to program for all these products.

Automation, formerly called OLE Automation, is a means by which an application can expose objects, each with it's own methods and properties, that other applications can create instances of and control through code. Not all commercial applications support Automation, but more and more applications are adopting Automation to replace the outdated DDE interface. Consult with a specific application's vendor to find out if it supports or plans to support OLE Automation in the program.

Using Automation to Integrate with Office

The applications mentioned previously all support Automation (sometimes referred to as OLE Automation). Using Automation, you can create objects in your code that represent other applications. By manipulating these objects (setting properties, calling methods), you can control the referenced applications as though you were programming directly in them; you can create seamless integrated applications using Automation.

Creating Automation references

Applications that support Automation provide information about their objects in an *Object Library*. The Object Library contains information about an application's classes (its internal objects), and their properties and methods. To reference an application's objects, Visual Basic must determine the type of object to which an object's variable in your code belongs. The process of determining the type of an object variable is called *binding*. You have two methods available to bind an object, *early binding* and *late binding*.

Early binding an object

Using the References dialog box in Access, you can explicitly reference an object library. When you explicitly reference an object library, you are performing early binding. Automation code executes much more quickly when you use early binding.

To create a reference, first open any module in your application database in Design view. When you have a module in Design view, a new command is available from the Tools pull-down menu: References (see Figure 19-1). Select Tools➪References to access the References dialog box (see Figure 19-2).

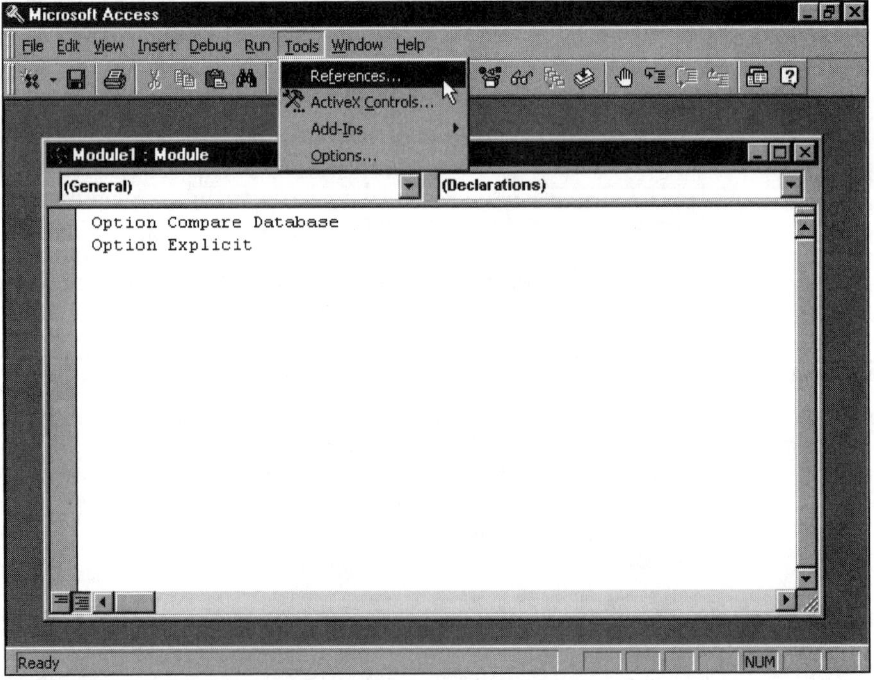

Figure 19-1: The Tools➪References menu item is only available when in module Design view.

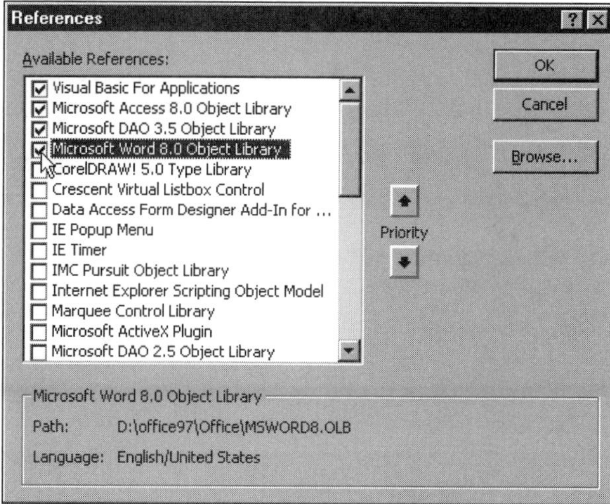

Figure 19-2: Early binding by setting references is the most efficient way to perform Automation.

In the References dialog box, you specify all the references your application needs for using Automation or for using other Access databases as library databases. To select or deselect a reference, click on its checkbox.

After you reference an application for Automation, you can explicitly dimension an object variable. The new coding help displays the available objects as you type, as shown in Figure 19-3. In addition, after you have selected the primary object and have entered a period (.), the new help feature of Access 97 enables you to select from the available class objects (see Figure 19-4).

Late binding an object

If you do not explicitly reference an object library using the References dialog box, you set an object's reference in code by first declaring a variable as an object and then using the `Set` command to create the object reference. This process is known as *late binding*.

To create an object to reference Microsoft Word 97, for example, you use code such as the following:

```
Dim WordObj As Object
Set WordObj = New Word.Application
```

The `Set` command is discussed in the next section.

If you create an object for an application that is not referenced, no drop-down help box such as the ones shown in Figures 19-3 and 19-4 is displayed.

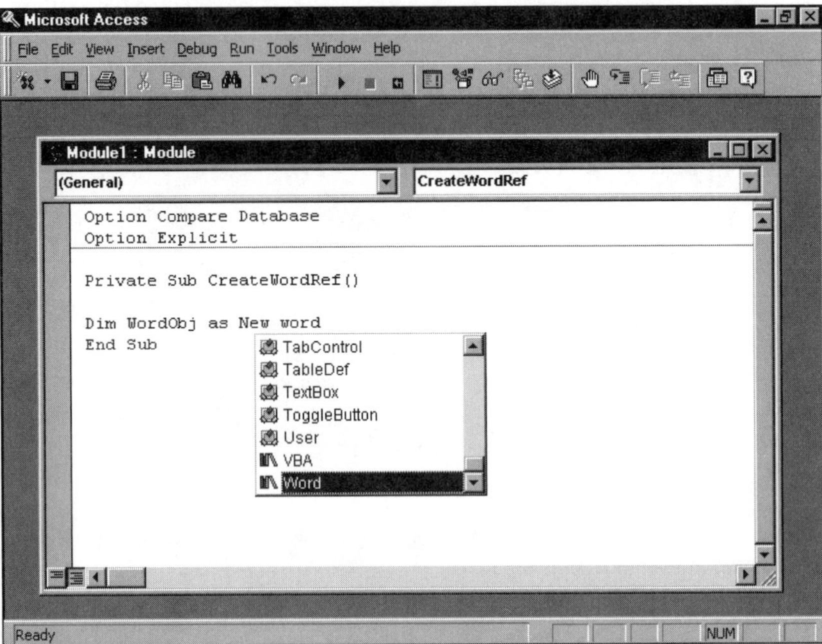

Figure 19-3: When an Automation Server is referenced, its objects are immediately known by Visual Basic.

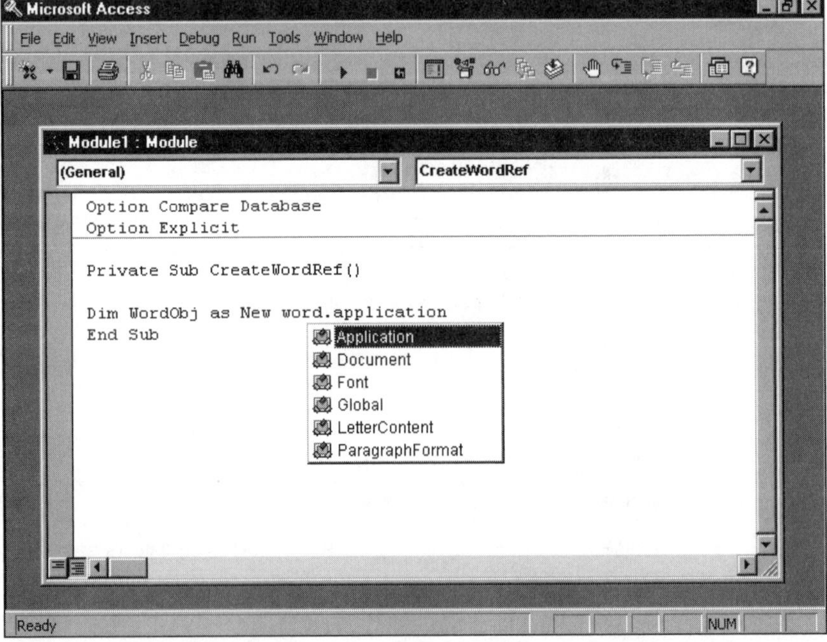

Figure 19-4: The new drop-down syntax help of Visual Basic makes using referenced Automation Servers easy.

Creating an instance of an Automation object

To perform an Automation operation, the operating system needs to start the application — if it isn't already started — and obtain a reference to it. Most applications that support Automation, called *Automation Servers,* expose an `Application` object. The `Application` object exists at the top of the object application's hierarchy and often contains many objects itself.

Using the New keyword to create a new instance

The simplest (and most efficient) method to create an Automation object is to bind the Automation Server: set a reference to it in Tools⇨References and then create a new instance of the object by using the `New` keyword in Visual Basic. In the preceding example, the variable `WordObj` is set to a new instance of Word's `Application` object.

Warning

If you do not create a reference to the Automation Server by using the References dialog box, Visual Basic does not recognize the object type and generates an error on compile.

Every time you create an instance of an Automation Server by using the `New` keyword, a new instance of the application is started. If you do not want to start a new instance of the application, use the `GetObject` function discussed in the section "Getting an existing object instance."

Not all Automation Servers support the `New` keyword. Consult the specific Automation Server's documentation to determine whether it supports the `New` keyword. If the `New` keyword is not supported, you need to use the `CreateObject` function discussed in the next section to create an instance of the Automation Server.

Using the CreateObject function to create a new instance

In addition to creating an instance of an object library by using the `New` keyword, you can create an instance of an object library using the `CreateObject` function. You use the `CreateObject` function to create instances of object libraries that do not support the `New` keyword. To use the `CreateObject` function, first declare a variable of the type equal to the type of object you want to create. Then use the `Set` statement in conjunction with the `CreateObject` function to set the variable to a new instance of the object library.

For example, Microsoft Binder does not support the `New` keyword, but it does provide an object library, so you can reference it by using the References dialog box. To early bind the object library of Binder, use the `CreateObject` function as shown in the following code:

```
Dim BinderObj As OfficeBinder.Binder
Set BinderObj = CreateObject("Office.Binder")
```

In the preceding example, the object library name for Binder is `OfficeBinder.Binder`, and the class instance is `"Office.Binder"`. You can view the names of object libraries and their available classes by using the Object Browser.

You can create an object instance with the `CreateObject` function that is late bound by not declaring the object variable as a specific type. For example, the following code creates an instance of the Binder object using late binding:

```
Dim BinderObj As Object
Set BinderObj = CreateObject("Office.Binder")
```

If you have different versions of the same Automation Server on your computer, you can specify the version to use by adding it to the end of the class information. For example, the following code uses Office 97 as the Automation Server:

```
Dim BinderObj As Object
Set BinderObj = CreateObject("Word.Application.8")
```

Although you could perform Automation in Word 95, Word 95 was not a true Automation Server. Because Word 97 is the first true Automation Server, you do not need to specify a version when creating instances of Word 97 object libraries; Word 97 is always used regardless of the other versions of Word on the computer. As a matter of fact, you get an error if you try to specify a version number.

Getting an existing object instance

As stated earlier, using the `New` keyword or the `CreateObject` function creates a new instance of the Automation Server. If you do not want a new instance of the server created each time you create an object, you use the `GetObject` function. The format of the `GetObject` function is as follows:

```
Set objectvariable = GetObject([pathname][, class])
```

The `pathname` parameter is an optional parameter. To use this parameter, you specify a full path and file name to an existing file for use with the Automation Server.

The specified document is then opened in the server application. Even if you omit the parameter, you must still include the comma (,).

The *class* parameter is the same as that used with the `CreateObject` function. See Table 19-1 for a list of some class arguments used in Microsoft Office.

Table 19-1 Class Arguments for Common Office Components

Component	Class Argument	Object Returned
Access	`Access.Application`	Microsoft Access Application object
Excel	`Excel.Application`	Microsoft Excel Application object
	`Excel.Sheet`	Microsoft Excel Workbook object
	`Excel.Chart`	Microsoft Excel Chart object
Word	`Word.Application`	Microsoft Word Application object
	`Word.Document`	Microsoft Word Document object

For example, to work with an existing instance of Microsoft Word but not a specific Word document, you use code such as the following:

```
Dim WordObj as Word.Application
Set WordObj = GetObject(, "Word.Application")
```

To get an instance of an existing Word document called `MyDoc.Doc`, you can use code such as the following:

```
Dim WordObj as Word.Application
Set WordObj = GetObject("c:\MyDoc.Doc", "Word.Application")
```

Working with Automation objects

After you have a valid instance of an Automation Server, you manipulate the object as though you were writing code within the application itself, using the exposed objects and their properties and methods.

For example, when developing directly in Word, you can use the following code to change the directory Word uses when opening an existing file:

```
ChangeFileOpenDirectory "D:\My Documents\"
```

Consult the development help for the Automation Server for specific information on the objects, properties, and methods available.

Just as in Access, Word is implicitly using its `Application` object; the command `ChangeFileOpenDirectory` is really a method of the `Application` object. Using the following code, you create an instance of Word's `Application` object and call the method of the object:

```
Dim WordObj As New Word.Application
WordObj.ChangeFileOpenDirectory "D:\My Documents\"
```

When using Automation, you should avoid setting properties or calling methods that cause the Automation Server to ask for input from the user via a dialog box. When a dialog box is displayed, the Automation code stops executing until the dialog is closed. If the server application is minimized or behind other windows, the user may not even be aware that he or she needs to provide input and might assume that the application is locked up.

Closing an instance of an Automation object

Automation objects are closed when the Automation object variable goes out of scope. Such a closing, however, does not necessarily free up all resources used by the object, so you should explicitly close the instance of the Automation object. You can close an Automation object by doing either of the following:

- Using the `Close` or `Quit` method of the object (consult the specific Automation Server's documentation for information on which method it supports).
- Setting the object variable to nothing, as follows:

```
Set WordObj = Nothing.
```

The very best way to close an instance of an Automation object is to combine the two techniques, like this:

```
WordObj.Quit
Set WordObj = Nothing
```

An Automation Example Using Word 97

Perhaps the most common Office application used for Automation is Word. Using Automation with Word, you can create letters that are tailored with information from databases. The following is an example of merging information from an Access database to a letter in Word by using Automation. This example is included in the thanks.dot template file on the CD-ROM that accompanies this book.

When you attempt to run this example, you must make sure that the path for the template in the Visual Basic code is the actual path in which the thanks.dot template file resides. This path may vary from computer to computer.

Items discussed in this Word Automation example include the following:

- Creating an instance of a Word object
- Making the instance of Word visible
- Creating a new document based on an existing template

- Using Bookmarks to insert data
- Activating the instance of Word
- Moving the cursor in Word
- Closing the instance of the Word object without closing Word

This example prints a thank you letter for an order. Figure 19-5 shows the data entry for Customers; Figure 19-6 shows the data entry form for Orders; Figure 19-7 shows the thanks.dot template; and Figure 19-8 shows a completed merge letter.

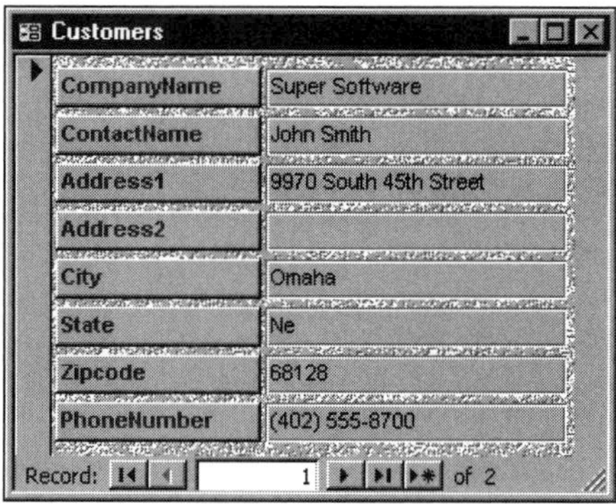

Figure 19-5: Customers used in the following Automation example are entered on the Customers form.

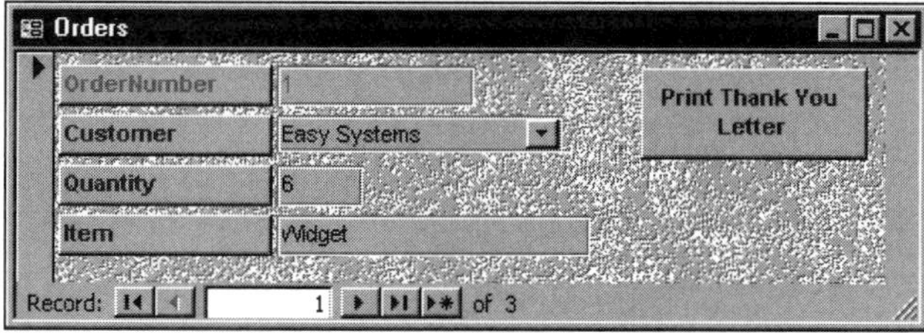

Figure 19-6: Each customer can have an unlimited number of orders. Thank you letters are printed from the Orders form.

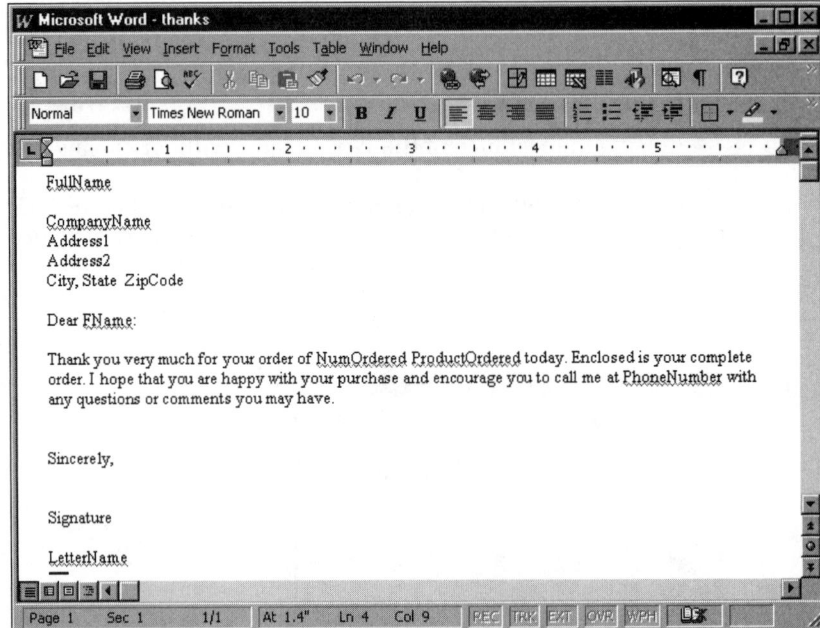

Figure 19-7: The thanks.dot template contains Bookmarks where the merged data is to be inserted.

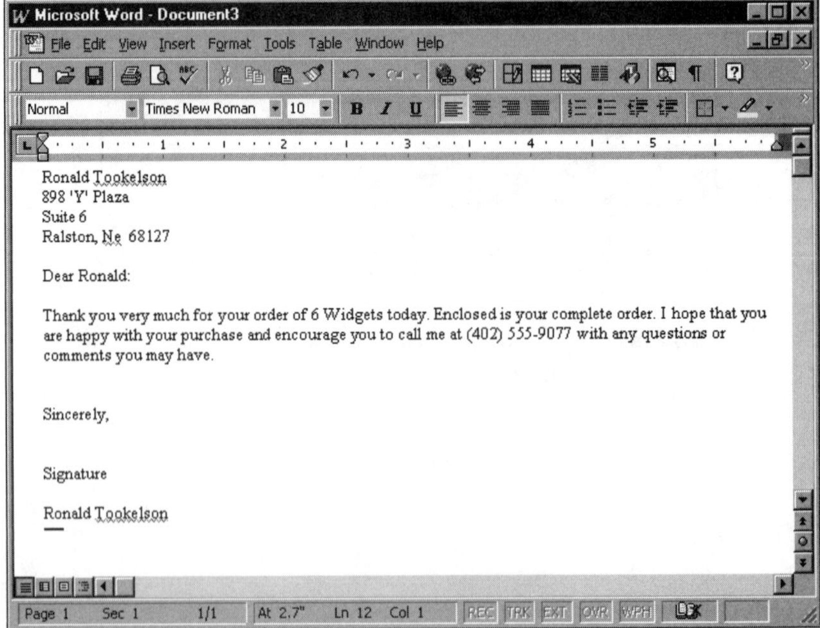

Figure 19-8: After a successful merge, all the Bookmarks have been replaced with their respective data.

When the user clicks the Print Thank You Letter button on the Orders form, Word 97 generates a thank you letter with all the pertinent information. Listing 19-1 shows the `MergetoWord` function in its entirety:

Listing 19-1 The MergetoWord Function

```
Public Function MergetoWord()
' This method creates a new document in MS Word 97 using Automation.
On Error Resume Next
Dim rsCust As Recordset, iTemp As Integer
Dim WordObj As Word.Application
Set rsCust = DBEngine(0).Databases(0).OpenRecordset("Customers", _
dbOpenTable)
rsCust.Index = "PrimaryKey"
rsCust.Seek "=", Forms!Orders![CustomerNumber]
    If rsCust.NoMatch Then
        MsgBox "Invalid customer", vbOKOnly
        Exit Function
    End If
DoCmd.Hourglass True
Set WordObj = GetObject(, "Word.Application")
If Err.Number <> 0 Then
    Set WordObj = CreateObject("Word.Application")
End If
WordObj.Visible = True
WordObj.Documents.Add Template:="D:\office97\Templates\thanks.dot",
NewTemplate:=False
WordObj.Selection.Goto what:=wdGoToBookmark, Name:="FullName"
    WordObj.Selection.TypeText rsCust![ContactName]
WordObj.Selection.Goto what:=wdGoToBookmark, Name:="CompanyName"
    WordObj.Selection.TypeText rsCust![CompanyName]
WordObj.Selection.Goto what:=wdGoToBookmark, Name:="Address1"
    WordObj.Selection.TypeText rsCust![Address1]
WordObj.Selection.Goto what:=wdGoToBookmark, Name:="Address2"
    If IsNull(rsCust![Address2]) Then
        WordObj.Selection.TypeText ""
    Else
        WordObj.Selection.TypeText rsCust![Address2]
    End If
WordObj.Selection.Goto what:=wdGoToBookmark, Name:="City"
    WordObj.Selection.TypeText rsCust![City]
WordObj.Selection.Goto what:=wdGoToBookmark, Name:="State"
    WordObj.Selection.TypeText rsCust![State]
WordObj.Selection.Goto what:=wdGoToBookmark, Name:="Zipcode"
    WordObj.Selection.TypeText rsCust![Zipcode]
WordObj.Selection.Goto what:=wdGoToBookmark, Name:="PhoneNumber"
    WordObj.Selection.TypeText rsCust![PhoneNumber]
WordObj.Selection.Goto what:=wdGoToBookmark, Name:="NumOrdered"
    WordObj.Selection.TypeText Forms!Orders![Quantity]
WordObj.Selection.Goto what:=wdGoToBookmark, Name:="ProductOrdered"
    If Forms!Orders![Quantity] > 1 Then
        WordObj.Selection.TypeText Forms!Orders![Item] & "s"
```

(continued)

(continued)

```
    Else
        WordObj.Selection.TypeText Forms!Orders![Item]
    End If
WordObj.Selection.Goto what:=wdGoToBookmark, Name:="FName"
    iTemp = InStr(rsCust![ContactName], " ")
    If iTemp > 0 Then
        WordObj.Selection.TypeText Left$(rsCust![ContactName], iTemp _
- 1)
    End If
WordObj.Selection.Goto what:=wdGoToBookmark, Name:="LetterName"
    WordObj.Selection.TypeText rsCust![ContactName]
DoEvents
WordObj.Activate
WordObj.Selection.MoveUp wdLine, 6
' Set the Word Object to nothing to free resources
Set WordObj = Nothing
DoCmd.Hourglass False
Exit Function
TemplateError:
   Set WordObj = Nothing
   Exit Function
End Function
```

Creating an instance of a Word object

The first step to using Automation is to create an instance of an object. The sample creates an object instance with the following code:

```
On Error Resume Next
...
Set WordObj = GetObject(, "Word.Application")
If Err.Number <> 0 Then
    Set WordObj = CreateObject("Word.Application")
End If
```

Obviously, you wouldn't want a new instance of Word created every time a thank you letter is generated, so some special coding is required. This code snippet first attempts to create an instance by using an active instance (running copy) of Word 97. If Word 97 is not a running application, an error is generated. Because this function has `On Error Resume Next` for error trapping, the code does not fail but rather proceeds to the next statement. If an error is detected (the `Err.Number` is not equal to `0`), an instance is created by using `CreateObject`.

Making the instance of Word visible

When you first create a new instance of Word 97, it runs invisibly. This approach enables your application to exploit features of Word 97 without the user even realizing Word 97 is running. In this case, however, it is desirable to let the user edit the merged letter, so Word 97 needs to be made visible by setting the object's `Visible` property to `True` by using this line of code:

```
WordObj.Visible = True
```

If you do not set the object instance's `Visible` property to `True`, you may create hidden copies of Word that use system resources and never shut down. A hidden copy of Word 97 does not show up in the Task tray or in the Task Switcher.

Creating a new document based on an existing template

Now that Word 97 is running, a blank document needs to be created. The following code creates a new document using the supplied template thanks.dot:

```
WordObj.Documents.Add Template:="D:\office97\Templates\thanks.dot", _
NewTemplate:=False
```

The thanks.dot template contains Bookmarks that tell this function where to insert data, as well as a generic thank you paragraph. You create Bookmarks in Word by highlighting the text you want to make a bookmark, selecting Edit⇨Bookmark, entering the bookmark name, and clicking on Add.

Using Bookmarks to insert data

Using Automation, you can locate Bookmarks in a Word document and replace them with the text of your choosing. To locate a Bookmark, you use the `Goto` method of the `Selection` object. When a Bookmark is located, the text making up the Bookmark is selected. By inserting text (using Automation or simply by typing directly into the document), you replace the Bookmark text. To insert text, use the `TypeText` method of the `Selection` object, as shown here:

```
WordObj.Selection.Goto what:=wdGoToBookmark, Name:="FullName"
WordObj.Selection.TypeText rsCust![ContactName]
```

You cannot pass a null to the `TypeText` method. If there is a possibility that a value may be `Null`, check ahead of time and make allowances. The preceding sample code checks the Address2 field for a `Null` value and acts accordingly. If you do not pass text to replace the Bookmark, even just a zero length string (" "), the Bookmark text remains in the document.

Activating the instance of Word

To allow the user to enter data in the new document, you must make Word the active application. If you do not make Word the active application, the user has to switch to Word from Access. You make Word the active application by using the `Activate` method of the Word object, as follows:

```
WordObj.Activate
```

Depending on the processing that is occurring at the time, Access may take the focus back from Word. You can help to eliminate this annoyance by preceding the `Activate` method with a `DoEvents` statement. Note, however, that this does not always work.

Moving the cursor in Word

You can control the cursor in Word. To move the cursor, use the `MoveUp` method of the `Selection` object. The following example moves the cursor up six lines in the document. The cursor is at the location of the last Bookmark when this code is executed:

```
WordObj.Selection.MoveUp wdLine, 6
```

Closing the instance of the Word object

To free up resources taken by an instance of an Automation object, you should always close the instance. In this example, the following code is used to close the object instance:

```
Set WordObj = Nothing
```

This code closes the object instance but not the instance of Word as a running application. In this example, the user needs access to the new document, so closing Word would defeat the purpose of this function. You could, however, automatically print the document and then close Word. If you were to do this, you might choose not even to make Word visible during this process. To close Word, use the `Quit` method of the Application object, as follows:

```
WordObj.Quit
```

Inserting pictures by using Bookmarks

It is possible to perform other unique operations by using Bookmarks. Basically, anything you can do within Word, you can do using Automation. The following code locates a Bookmark marking where a picture goes, and inserts a .PCX file from disk. You can use code such as the following to insert scanned signatures into letters:

```
WordObj.Selection.Goto what:=wdGoToBookmark, Name:="Picture"
WordObj.ChangeFileOpenDirectory "D:\GRAPHICS\"
WordObj. ActiveDocument.Shapes.AddPicture Anchor:=Selection.Range, _
FileName:= _
        "D:\GRAPHICS\PICTURE.BMP", LinkToFile:=False,
SaveWithDocument _
        :=True
```

Using Office's Macro Recorder

Using Automation is not a difficult process when you understand the fundamentals. Often, the toughest part of using Automation is knowing the proper objects, properties, and methods to use. Although the development help system of the Automation Server is a requirement for fully understanding the language, there is an even easier way to quickly create Automation for Office applications: the Macro Recorder.

Office 97 applications have a Macro Recorder located on the Tools menu (see Figure 19-9). When activated, the Macro Recorder records all events, such as menu selections and button clicks, and creates Visual Basic code from them.

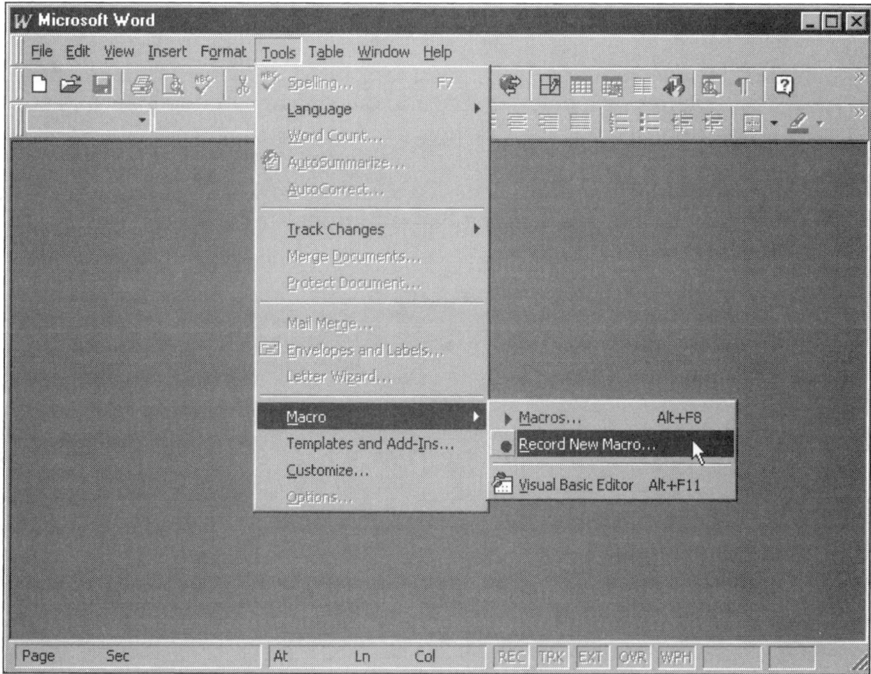

Figure 19-9: The Macro Recorder is a powerful tool to help you create Automation code.

After selecting Tools➪Macro➪Record New Macro, you must give your new macro a name (see Figure 19-10). In addition to a name, you can assign the macro to a toolbar or keyboard combination and select the template in which to store the macro. If you are creating the macro simply to create the Visual Basic code, the only thing you need to be concerned with is the macro name.

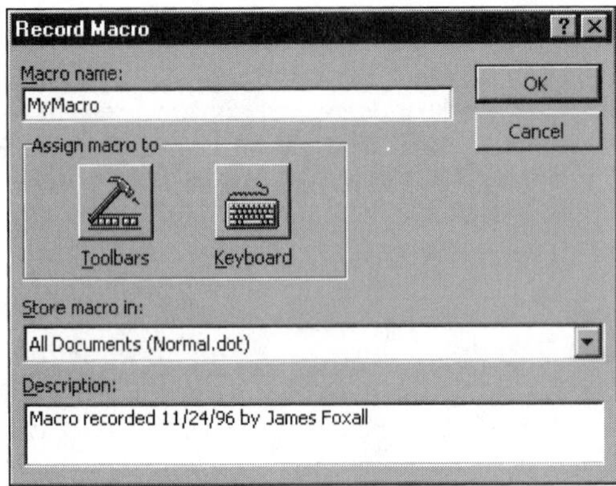

Figure 19-10: Enter a macro name and click on OK to begin recording the macro.

After entering a macro name and clicking on OK, the Macro Recorder begins recording events and displays a Stop Recording window, as shown in Figure 19-11. You can stop recording events by clicking on the Stop button (the button with a square on it). To pause recording events, click on the other button, which is the Pause button.

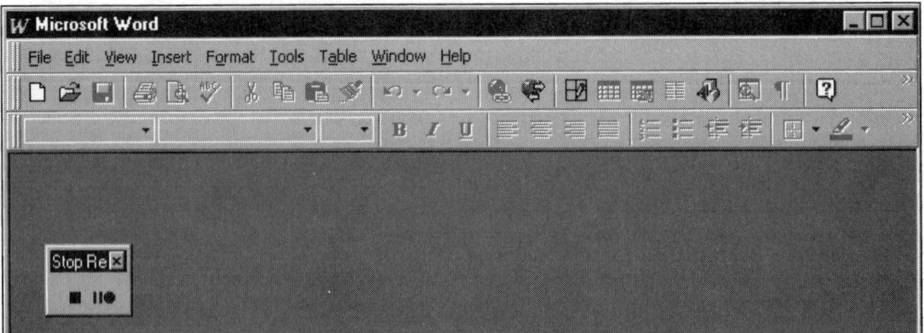

Figure 19-11: The Macro Recorder records all events until you click the Stop button.

After you have finished recording a macro, you can view the Visual Basic code created from your events. To view the code of a macro, select Tools➪Macro➪Macros to display a list of all saved macros. Then select the macro you recorded and click on the Edit button to display the Visual Basic editor with the macro's code. Figure 19-12 shows the Visual Basic editor with a macro that recorded creating a new document using the Normal template, and inserting a picture using the Insert➪Picture➪From File menu item.

In the application for which a macro is created, the Application object is used explicitly. When you use the code for Automation, you must create an Application object accordingly. For example, the preceding macro uses the following code to create a new document:

```
Documents.Add Template:="D:\office97\Templates\Normal.dot", _
NewTemplate:= False
```

This code implicitly uses the Application object. To use this code for Automation, you copy the code from the Visual Basic editor, paste it into your procedure, and create an object that you use explicitly, as follows:

```
Dim WordObj as New Word.Application
WordObj.Documents.Add Template:="D:\office97\Templates\Normal.dot", _
NewTemplate:= False
```

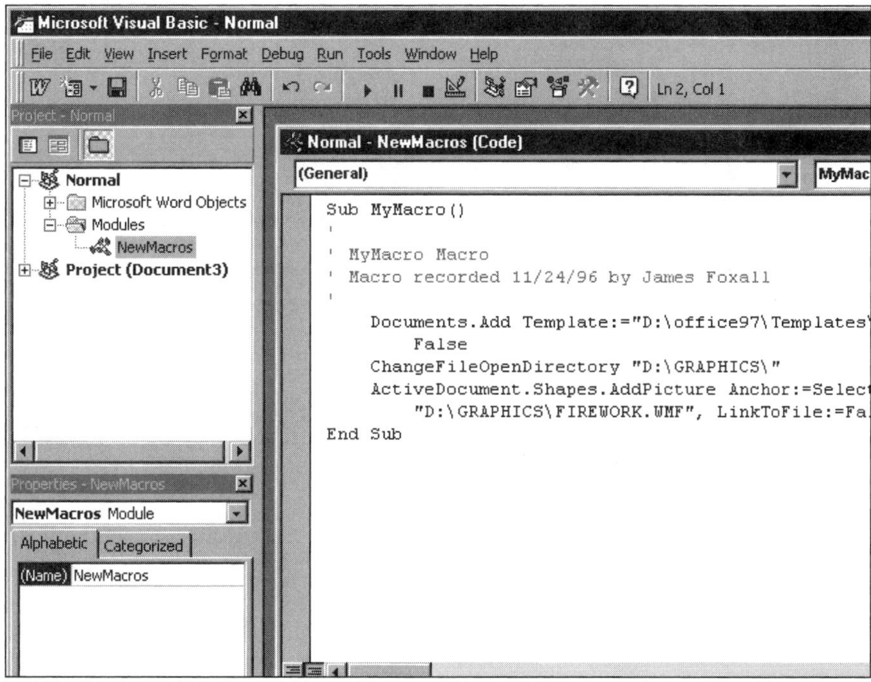

Figure 19-12: Macros are really Visual Basic event procedures.

The Macro Recorder enables you to effortlessly create long and complete Automation code without ever needing to read the Automation Server's documentation.

Programming the Office Assistant

Perhaps the most fun Automation Server yet is the Office Assistant. That's right, the Office Assistant is a fully programmable Automation Server! Using the techniques described in this chapter, you can completely control the Office Assistant. Included in the database for this chapter on the companion CD-ROM is an Office Assistant Automation Example form with all the code necessary to control the Office Assistant (see Figure 19-13).

To program the Office Assistant using Automation, you must first ensure that the Office Assistant is installed, and then you must create a reference to the Microsoft Office 8.0 Object Library (see Figure 19-14).

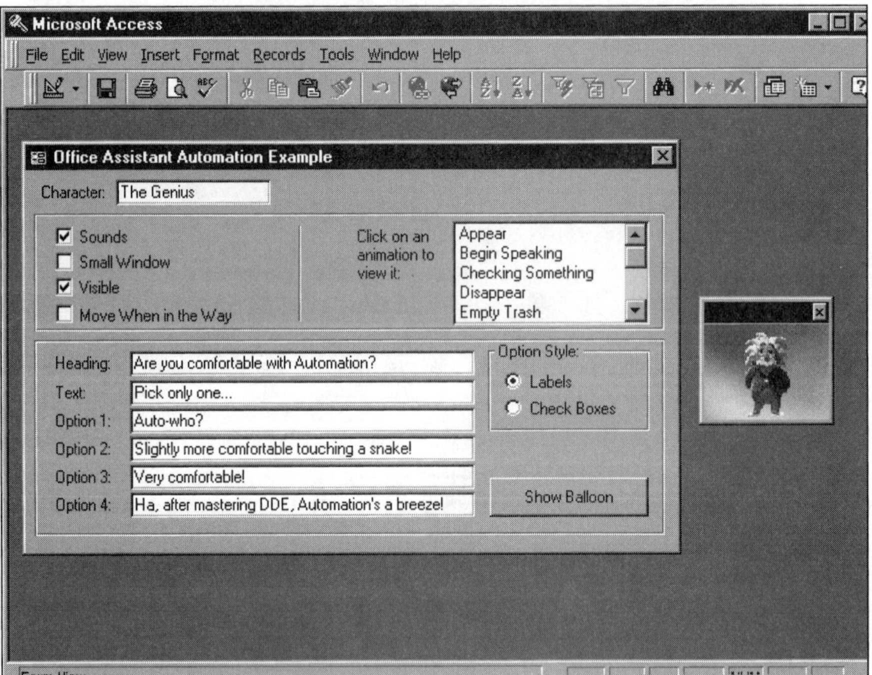

Figure 19-13: The Office Assistant Automation Example form contains all the code you need to control the Office Assistant.

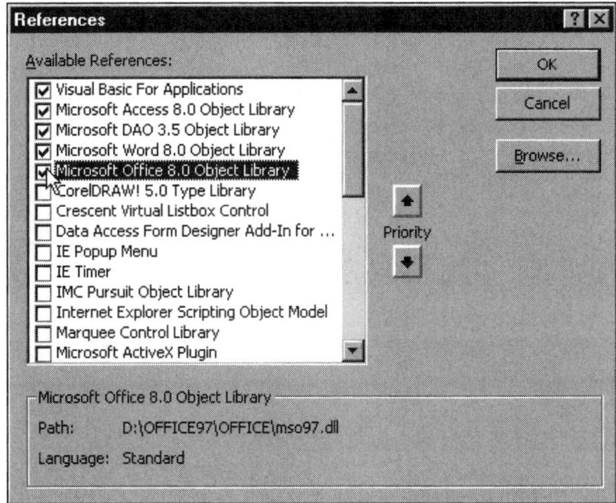

Figure 19-14: Programming the Office Assistant requires that the Office Assistant be installed and referenced in the database.

Displaying the Office Assistant in a small window

After the reference is added for the Microsoft Office 8.0 Object Library, you can directly access the Assistant object. As with other Automation object libraries, the Assistant Object contains objects, properties, and methods. You use these objects, properties, and methods to manipulate the Office Assistant. For example, the Office Assistant can be displayed in a large window, as shown in Figure 19-13, or in a small window, as in Figure 19-15. To display the assistant in a small window, you use the following code:

```
Assistant.Reduced = True
```

Hiding and showing the Office Assistant

You can completely hide the Office Assistant at any time by setting its `Visible` property to `False`, as follows:

```
Assistant.Visible = False
```

To show the Office Assistant, simply set the `Visible` property to `True`.

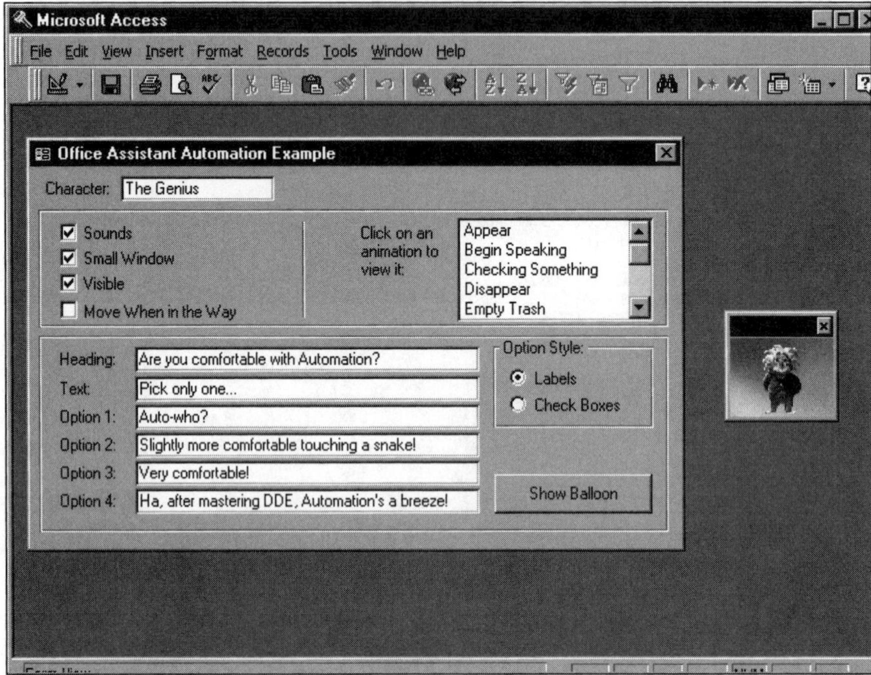

Figure 19-15: To save screen space, you can display the Office Assistant in a small window.

Keeping the Assistant out of the way

You can give the Office Assistant some smarts by instructing it to stay out of the way of other windows. To do this, use the following to set the Assistant's `MoveWhenInTheWay` property:

```
Assistant.MoveWhenInTheWay = True
```

When you set the `MoveWhenInTheWay` property to `True`, the Assistant recognizes when it is in the way of other windows — as they appear — and it attempts to move itself to a less obtrusive location. If you set the `MoveWhenInTheWay` property to `False`, the Office Assistant never moves itself.

Enabling and disabling the Assistant's sounds

You can programmatically enable and disable the Assistant's sounds by setting the Assistant's `Sounds` property. For example, to enable Assistant sounds, set the property to `True`, as follows:

```
Assistant.Sounds = True
```

To disable all Assistant sounds, set the property to `False`.

Displaying an Assistant animation

Of course, the coolest thing about the Office Assistant is its animation. To display an animation, you simply set the `Animation` property to the appropriate animation number. For example, to display the Empty Trash animation shown in Figure 19-16, you set the `Animation` property to `116`, as follows:

```
Assistant.Animation = 116
```

The sample database on the companion CD-ROM contains a table of all of the animations and their respective reference numbers.

Note

There are a number of different Assistants, ranging from a bouncing paper clip to a talking computer. Not every Office Assistant has an animation associated with each entry in the Animations table.

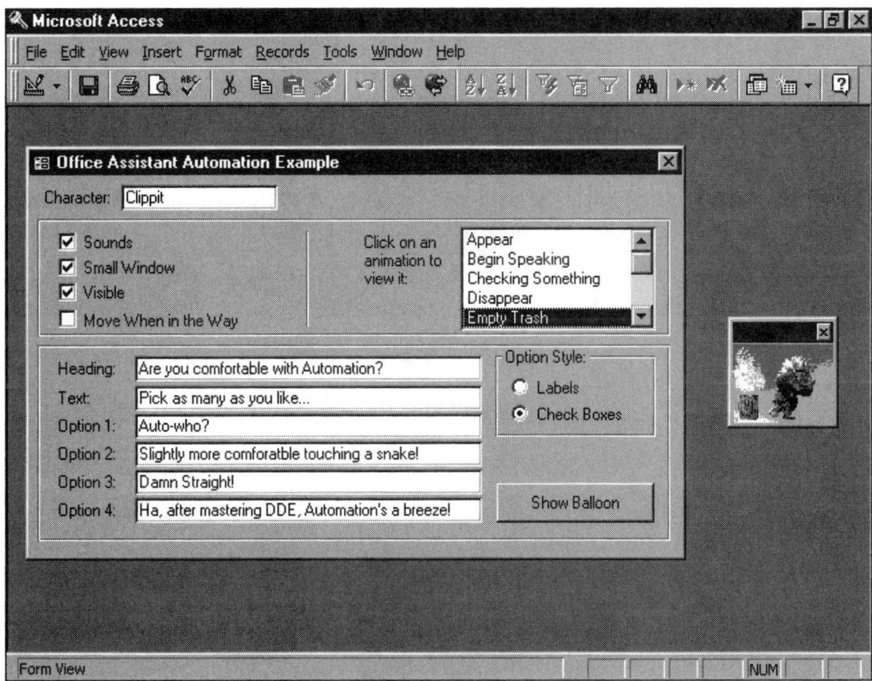

Figure 19-16: Displaying Office Assistant animation is as simple as setting a property.

Displaying information and getting user input using balloons

The Office Assistant isn't just a passive object taking up space on the desktop. You also can use the Assistant to display dialog boxes and to get user input (see Figure 19-17). These Assistant dialog boxes are called *balloons,* and you create them by using the `NewBalloon` method of the `Assistant` object.

Creating a new balloon

To create a balloon, first dimension a variable as a `Balloon` object. Then set the variable to a new balloon object by using the `NewBalloon` method of the `Assistant` object, as follows:

```
Dim objBalloon As Balloon
Set objBalloon = Assistant.NewBalloon
```

Specifying a balloon's heading and text

You then specify the heading and body text by using the `Heading` and `Text` properties of the new balloon object, as in the following example:

```
objBalloon.Heading = "This is heading text!"
objBalloon.Text = "This is body text."
```

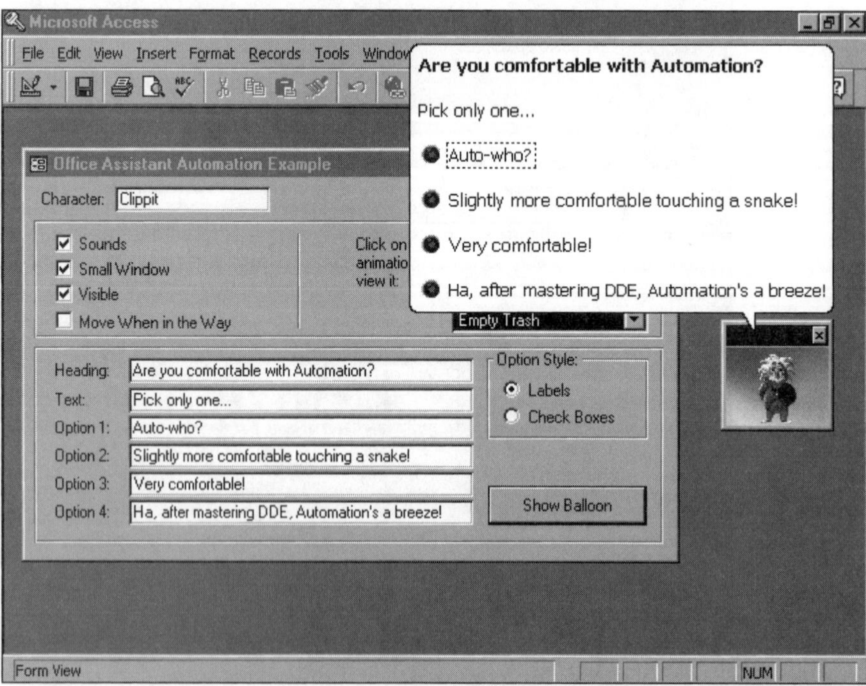

Figure 19-17: The Office Assistant becomes an active assistant when you use balloons.

Specifying a balloon's buttons

Specifying the buttons to be displayed is similar to specifying buttons for dialog boxes; you use a constant. Buttons are defined by setting the `Buttons` property, as follows:

```
objBalloon.Button = buttonconstant
```

The following are valid constants to use in place of `buttonconstant`:

- `msoButtonSetAbortRetryIgnore`
- `msoButtonSetBackClose`
- `msoButtonSetBackNextClose`
- `msoButtonSetBackNextSnooze`
- `msoButtonSetCancelmsoButtonSetNextClose`
- `msoButtonSetNonemsoButtonSetOK`
- `msoButtonSetOkCancel`
- `msoButtonSetRetryCancel`
- `msoButtonSetSearchClose`
- `msoButtonSetTipsOptionsClose`
- `msoButtonSetYesAllNoCancel`
- `msoButtonSetYesNoCancel`
- `msoButtonSetYesNo`

Creating balloon labels and checkboxes

You give the user selections from which to choose by defining a labels or checkboxes item. In Figure 19-17, labels are used. Labels are similar to radio buttons in that the user can select only one of a given set of labels. Instead of labels, you can allow a user to select a number of items by making them checkboxes (see Figure 19-18).

For each labels or checkboxes item on a balloon, you set a labels or checkboxes array item in code, as in the following:

```
objBalloon.Labels(1).Text = "Text for label 1"
objBalloon.Labels(2).Text = "Text for label 2"
...
or
objBalloon.checkboxes(1).Text = "Text for checkbox 1"
objBalloon.checkboxes(2).Text = "Text for checkbox 2"
...
```

There can be up to five labels and five checkboxes on a balloon.

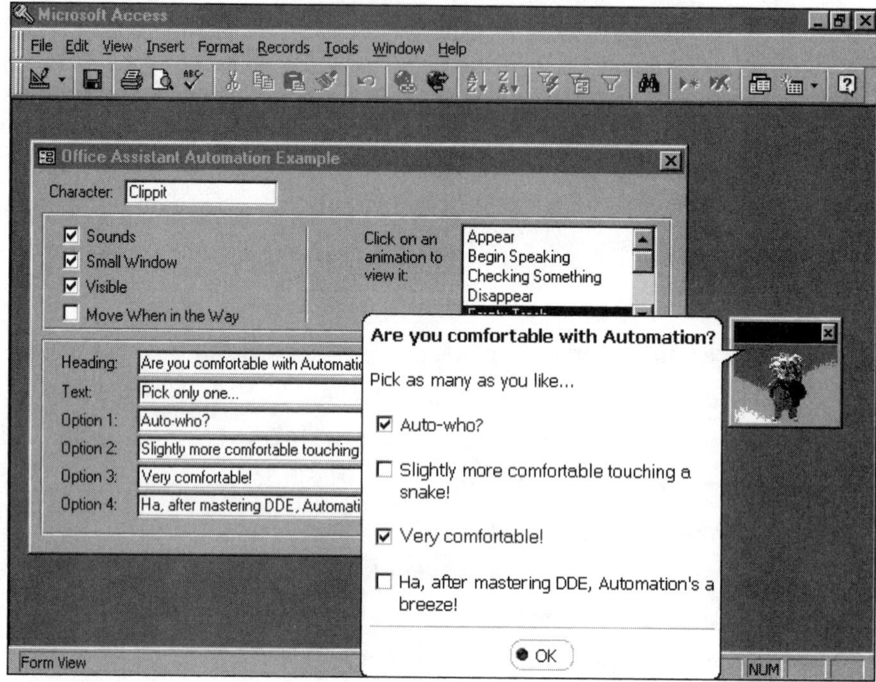

Figure 19-18: You can let a user select a number of items by using the checkboxes item.

Displaying a balloon

After the balloon is completely defined, you display the balloon by using the `Show` method of the `Balloon` object, as follows:

```
intRetval = objBalloon.Show
```

Note that the `Show` method returns a value. If the balloon contains labels, the return value is the index of the selected label. To find out which checkboxes are selected, you must look through the checkboxes items for the balloon, as follows:

```
Dim iCount as integer
For iCount = 1 To objBalloon.Checkboxes.Count
If objBalloon.Checkboxes(iCount).Checked = True Then
MsgBox "Checkbox #" & iCount & " is selected!", vbOKOnly
End If
Next iCount
```

Figure 19-19 shows the result of determining the selected item and creating a new balloon object to tell the user what it was.

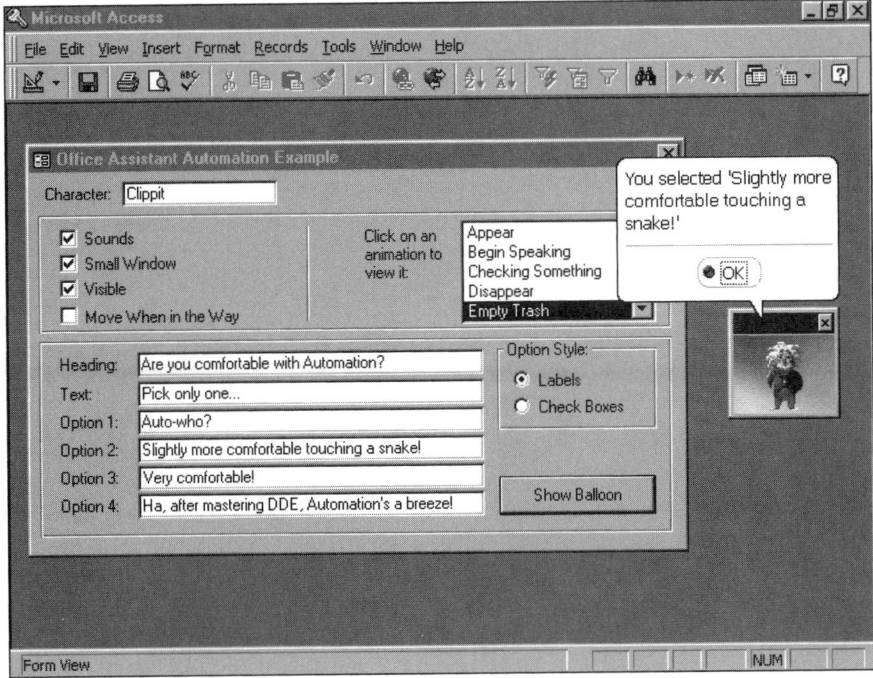

Figure 19-19: To display a new balloon, create a new balloon object.

Using the techniques discussed in this chapter, you can leverage your Visual Basic knowledge and create intelligent and powerful integrated applications.

Chapter 20

Working with External Data

In This Chapter

- Importing data and objects from other Access databases
- Importing data from other database sources
- Using the Text Import Wizard
- Importing data from delimited text files
- Importing data from fixed-width text files
- Importing data from line-feed delimited text files
- Saving and reusing import definitions
- Opening tables in other databases directly through VBA
- Using links to data from other database sources
- Working with HTML files

Importing Data

The most desirable method of using external data is to import the data into an Access database. After the database is imported, you have all of Access's powerful features at your disposal. If the data will never be updated outside of your Access application, you can import the data. If, however, the data will be updated from time to time from a different application that does not use the Jet engine, you will need to link to the external data.

Using Access, you can link to or import data in the following database formats:

- Any database created with the Microsoft Jet engine
- Open Database Connectivity (ODBC) databases, such as Microsoft SQL Server
- Paradox versions 3.x, 4.x, and 5.x
- dBASE II, dBASE IV, and dBASE 5.x
- Lotus 1-2-3® WKS, WK1, and WK3 spreadsheets

- Microsoft Excel 3.0, 4.0, 5.0, 7.0, and 8.0 worksheets
- Delimited and fixed-width text files in tabular format
- Tabular data in Hypertext Markup Language (HTML) files

Before you can import or link to data from sources other than Access (Jet), you must install the proper ODBC and ISAM drivers from the Access installation CD. In addition, when using ODBC, you will need to set up an ODBC datasource for each external data source by using the ODBC Manager. To start the ODBC manager, double-click 32-bit ODBC in Windows Control Panel.

Importing Databases Created with the Jet Engine

The simplest data to import is data stored in another Access database. When you import data from an Access database, you have the option of importing just the table definition or the table definition with data. In addition, you may import table relationships from the other Access database, enabling you to import multiple-table datasets completely intact.

Importing just a table's definition is a handy way of jump-starting table development in new databases. It is much faster to simply import the table definition than to import the table definition with all the table's data and then delete the data. It also saves you the step of compacting your database to free up the space used by the imported data after the data is deleted.

Importing tables

Often, data is stored in many different places throughout a company, and you are required to consolidate the data. If you're lucky and all the data is stored in various Access databases, consolidating the data is quite easy; you just import the tables into your database. If the data needs to be stored and maintained in separate databases, however, you are better off to link to the data.

To import data from another Access database into your Access database, select the menu item File⇨Get External Data⇨Import (see Figure 20-1). You always use this menu item to import data, regardless of the data source.

After selecting Import, you see the dialog box shown in Figure 20-2. Access enables you to import from many different database sources, but from only one source at a time. When you are first shown the Import dialog box, Microsoft Access is the default file type. Changing the file type (data source type) causes the dialog box to refresh its file list, showing you only the files that have the extension of your selected file type. To import an Access database, you select the database from this dialog box and click on Import.

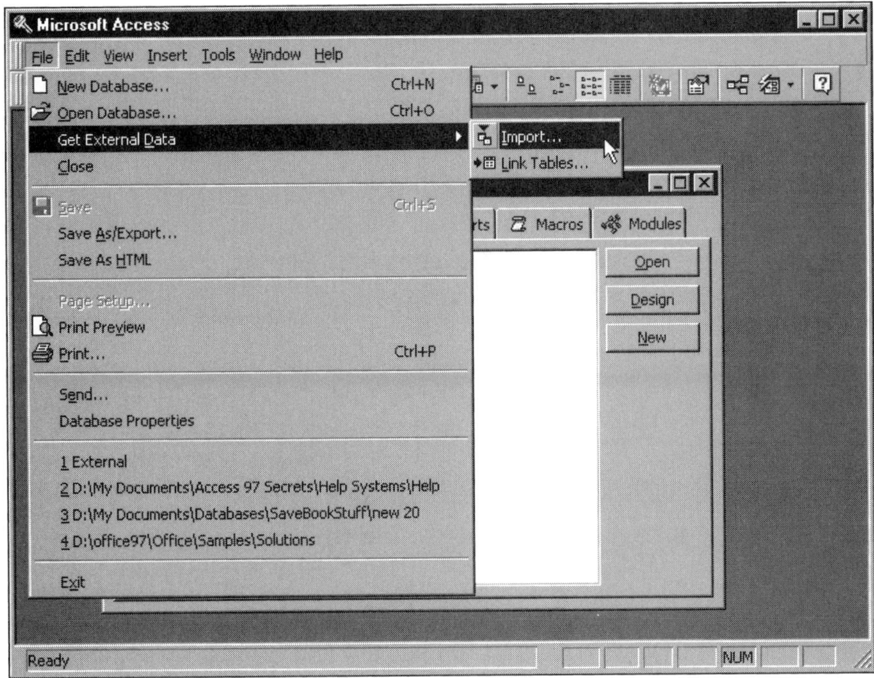

Figure 20-1: To import data into Access, regardless of its type, you always use the Get External Data menu item.

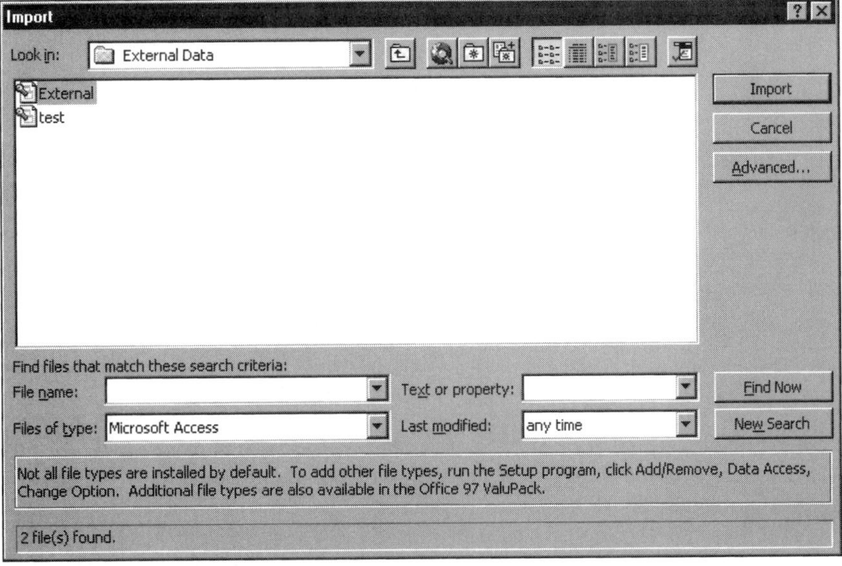

Figure 20-2: The Import dialog box enables you to choose to import from numerous data sources.

When you elect to import an Access database object, a secondary Database window is displayed (see Figure 20-3). This Database window shows all the objects in the source database. This window is modal; you cannot switch between it and the Database window for your application.

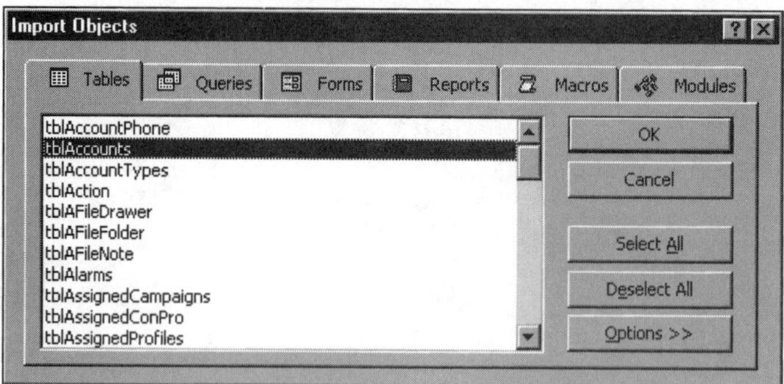

Figure 20-3: When importing objects from another Access database, you see a secondary Database window from which to choose the objects to import.

This secondary Database window, called the Import Objects dialog, has different buttons than the standard Database window. Instead of the buttons for Open, Design, and New, you may choose from the following buttons:

- **OK.** Clicking on this button ends the object selection process and imports the objects.
- **Cancel.** Clicking on this button cancels the import.
- **Select All.** This button selects all objects of the currently selected type. In Figure 20-3, clicking on this button selects all tables (in this case, there is only one).
- **Deselect All.** This button deselects all selected objects of the currently displayed type. It does not deselect objects of other types that you have selected.
- **Options.** Clicking on this button displays a form with additional options for importing Access objects.

Importing other Access objects

As stated earlier, when you import data from an Access database, you get additional options that are not available when importing from other data sources. Clicking on the Options button on the Import Objects dialog box displays these options (see Figure 20-4).

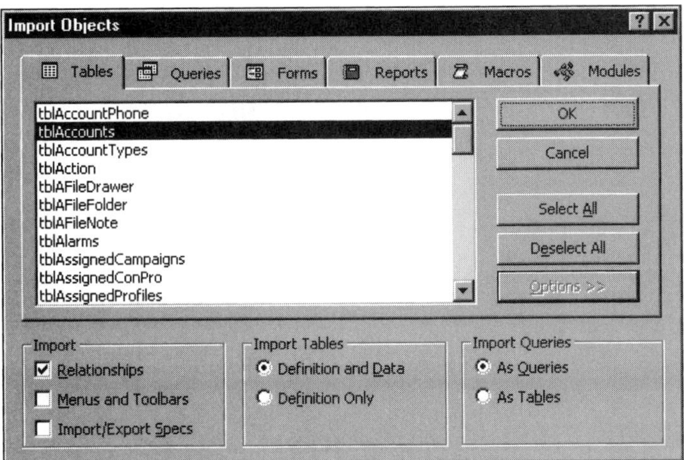

Figure 20-4: Additional options are available to you when you import objects or data from another Access database.

In addition to importing standard objects such as tables or queries, you can import table relationships, custom toolbars, and import/export specifications. Importing relationships can save you a great deal of time, which you would need to re-create the relationships when you import a number of tables from an Access database. If you have created custom toolbars that you want to use throughout your Access applications, here is the place to import them. Also, if you perform a large number of imports and exports and you want to continue to reuse your import definitions in different databases, you can import them here.

When importing table objects, you can choose to import the table definition without the data. This technique makes it easy to share common table structures throughout your applications.

Tip

If you find yourself only importing data structures and never modifying them, you should consider consolidating all your data in one database rather than having the same type of information stored in different databases.

The last additional option available to you when importing an Access database object is to import queries as queries or as tables. This feature can be very powerful if you need to import various datasets that consist of multiple tables. You could open the original database, create and run a make-table query, and then open your database and import the resultant table, or you could simply make the query a select query and import the query as a table.

After all selected objects are imported into your database, you are returned to your application's Database window (see Figure 20-5).

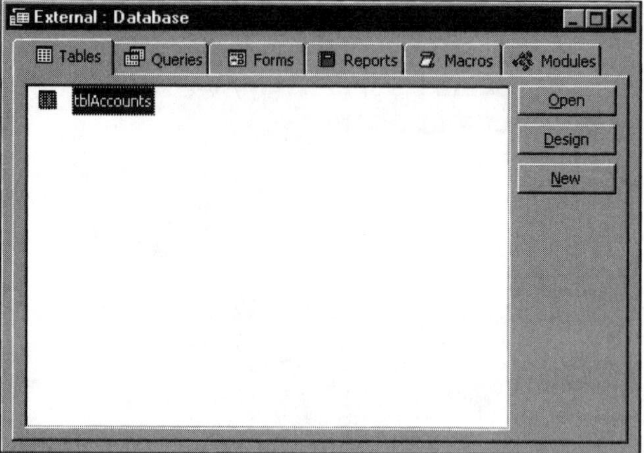

Figure 20-5: Access makes it easy to move data from one Access database to another.

Sometimes an Access database becomes so corrupted that a repair simply doesn't work. Often, it is possible to recover almost all of the data by creating a new, empty database and importing all the objects from the corrupted database. After you have imported all the objects, repair and compact the new database. This trick can save you an immense amount of time and serious unhappiness in the event of a major system crash if you don't have a current backup.

Importing Databases Not Created by the Jet Engine

Access makes it very easy not only to import from other Access databases, but from databases created by other database tools such as Paradox or dBASE. In addition, Access gives you great flexibility in importing delimited and fixed-width text files. Delimited and fixed-width text files have been around for a long time, and almost every application that maintains a database has the ability to export data into a delimited or fixed-width text file. Becoming proficient in importing text files is a wise thing to do if you anticipate regularly importing data from various, and sometimes unfamiliar, data sources; if you are unable to get at the data natively, often you can export the data to a delimited or fixed-width text file and then use the Text Import Wizard to get the data into Access.

Importing data from database sources other than Jet is very easy to do. First, select the menu item File➪Get External Data➪Import (refer to Figure 20-1) from the Database window's menu bar.

After selecting Import, you see the Import dialog box. Again, Microsoft Access is the default file type. The first thing you need to do is change the file type (data source type) from Microsoft Access to the data source type you want to import. For example, if you wanted to import a dBASE IV file, you select dBASE IV, as shown in Figure 20-6.

When you change the data source, the dialog refreshes its file list, showing you only the files that have the extension of your selected file type. You then select the drive, directory, and file name to import. When you have selected the file you want to import, click on the Import button.

Access imports the file you have selected into a new Access table. Whenever possible, Access preserves all indexes and primary keys.

Using the Text Import Wizard

When you import data from an Access database or from a supported third-party database (such as dBASE), Access understands the database format and requires little or no intervention on your part to bring the data into an Access table. When you import text files, however, Access needs you to hold its hand; you must define the data that is stored in the file as well as how the data is organized within the file.

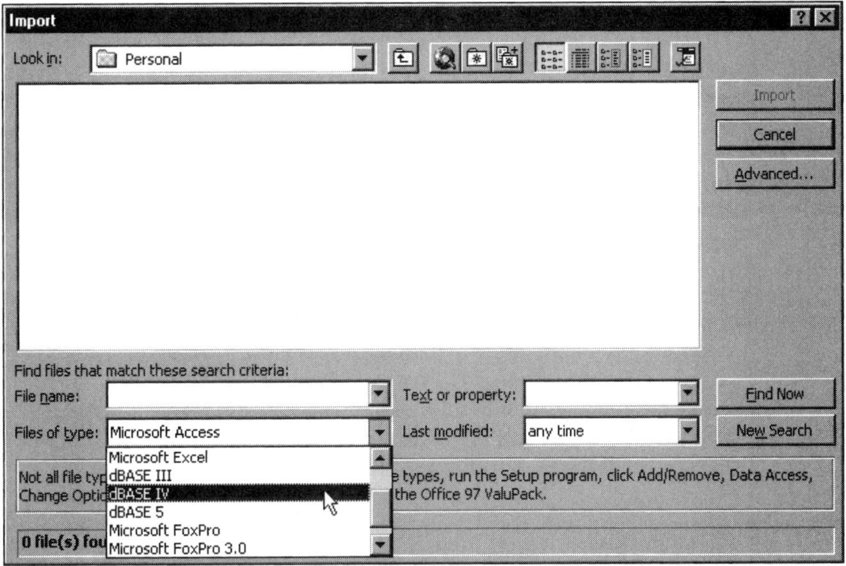

Figure 20-6: The Import dialog box enables you to select from many different data sources.

To import a text file with the Text Import Wizard, first select the menu item File➪Get External Data➪Import (refer to Figure 20-1) from the Database window's menu bar. Then select Files of type: Text File to list all the text files on your computer for the selected drive and directory (see Figure 20-7).

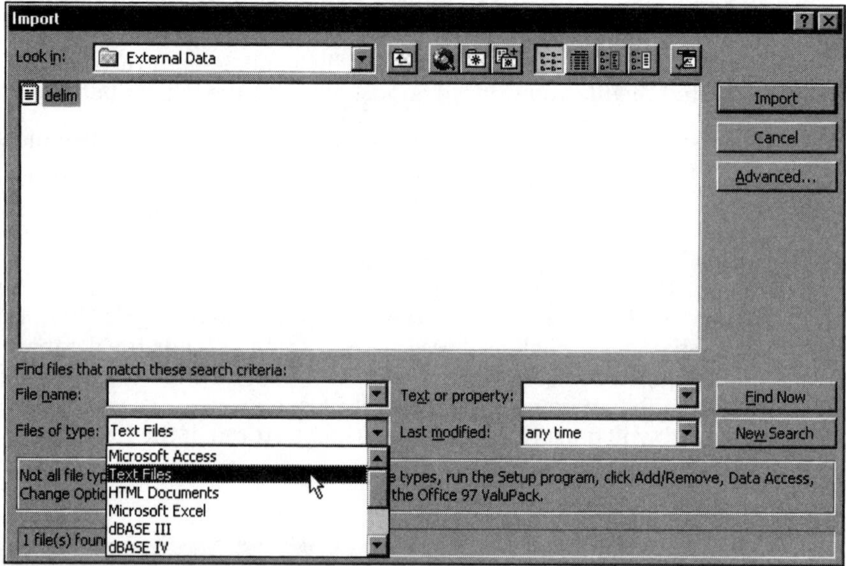

Figure 20-7: You specify the type of file for text files, just as you do for files created in other database formats.

After you change the file type, select the drive, directory, and file name of the text file you want to import, and then click on Import to display the Text Import Wizard.

Tip

Text files may contain any extension. By default, Access shows you files with the extensions .TXT, .CSV, .TAB, and .ASC. Even though they have different file extensions, these files are all the same type of file (a text file). In addition, text files may have arbitrary extensions, such as .BTF for Bob's Text File. If you know your file has an arbitrary extension, type *.XXX (where XXX is the extension) in the File Name field and press Enter. This action causes the Import dialog box to display all files with your specified type.

Specifying the text file format — delimited or fixed-width

The first page of the Text Import Wizard asks you for the format of the text file. Generally speaking, files with the extension .CSV are always comma-separated (delimited) files. The formats of the other text files may vary; they can be either comma-separated or fixed-width files. However, you should never assume the format of a text file. Figure 20-8 shows you a sample of the text file. If all the string-type data fields are surrounded by quotes and separated by commas, you are looking at a comma-separated (delimited) text file. If the data elements in the text file are separated by spaces and line up to form even columns, you are looking at a fixed-width file.

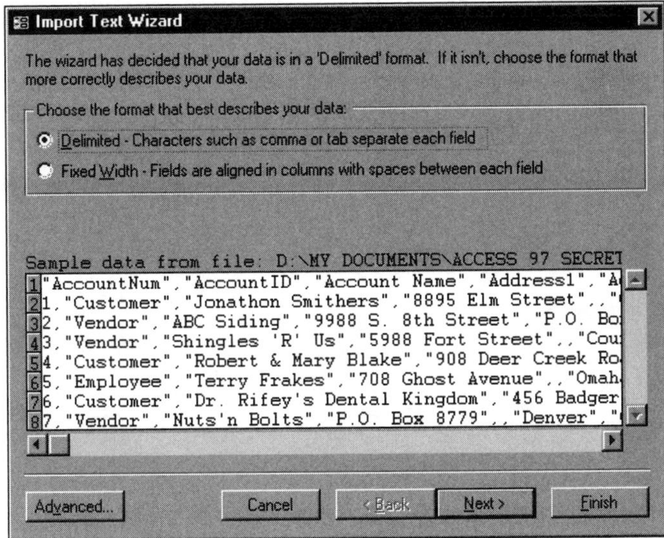

Figure 20-8: You can tell by the quotes and commas surrounding the data in this sample that this file is a delimited file.

Access attempts to detect the format of the selected file. You can choose to override the format that Access chooses, but you probably never will need to do so. After you have selected the format type of the file, click on Next.

Using the Text Import Wizard to import delimited text files

Delimited text files are used more often than fixed-width text files because delimited text files use much less disk space. The fields in delimited text files aren't "padded" with spaces to make them line up in columns. Delimited text files have their data elements separated by a special character. This *separator character* is most often a comma but can be just about anything. In addition, all text elements are surrounded by a *text qualifier.* The text qualifier is usually a set of double quotes. Numbers are not surrounded by quotes; but they are separated by the separator character.

Specifying the delimiter and text qualifier characters

You use the second page of the Text Import Wizard to define what constitutes the separator character and the text qualifier (see Figure 20-9). By default, the separator character is a comma (,) and the text qualifier is a set of double quotes (" "). You can easily tell what your text file is using as these two characters by looking at the sample at the bottom of the form. When in doubt, use the defaults.

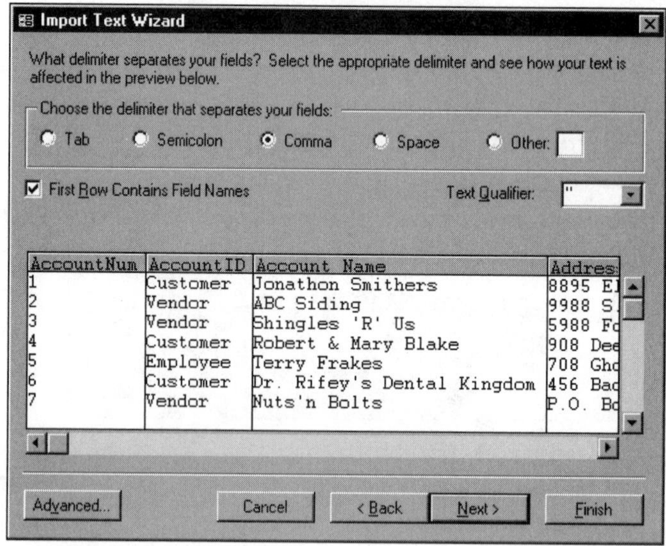

Figure 20-9: You can override the format definition defaults, but you probably never will need to do so.

Also on this page you can tell Access if the text file's first row contains field names. Often, programs that create delimited files put the field names in the first row of the text file so that anyone can later open the text file in a text editor such as Notepad and easily tell what fields are stored and in what order they appear. If the text file you are importing has field names in the first row, check the box. If you check the box that tells Access that the first row contains field names, Access removes the first row from the data displayed on the form and creates headers for each column, using the field names.

When you are ready to proceed, click on the Next button.

Electing to import data into a new or existing table

The third page of the Text Import Wizard is where you tell Access whether to import the data into an existing table or into a new table (see Figure 20-10). If you want to import the text file into an existing table, you must check the radio button labeled In an Existing Table and specify a table name.

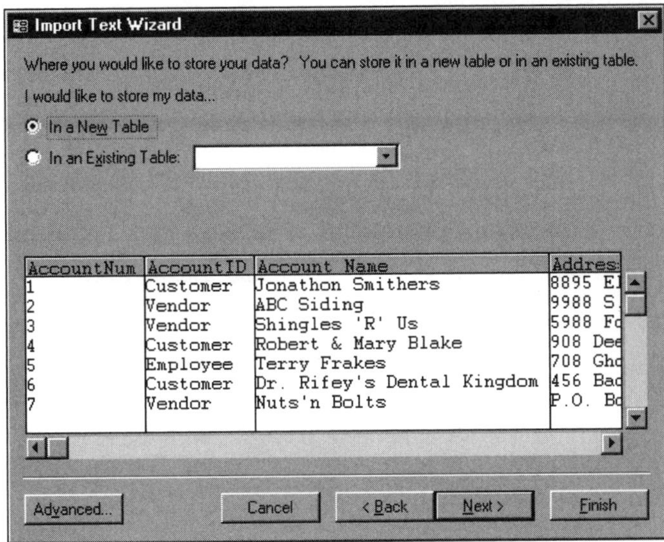

Figure 20-10: You have the option of importing the text file into an existing table or into a new table.

If the text file you are importing does not exactly match the format of the existing table into which you are importing, you will get errors upon importing (such as Type Mismatch errors), and the text file's data may or may not be imported correctly. If you are not sure that the text file matches an existing table's design, you should import the text file into a new table and use an append query to move the data into the existing table.

Again, after you have made your selection, click on Next to continue.

Specifying field options such as Name and Data Type

The fourth page of the Wizard allows you to define various field options (see Figure 20-11). The options that are available to you are:

- Field Name
- Data Type
- Indexed
- Do not import field (Skip)

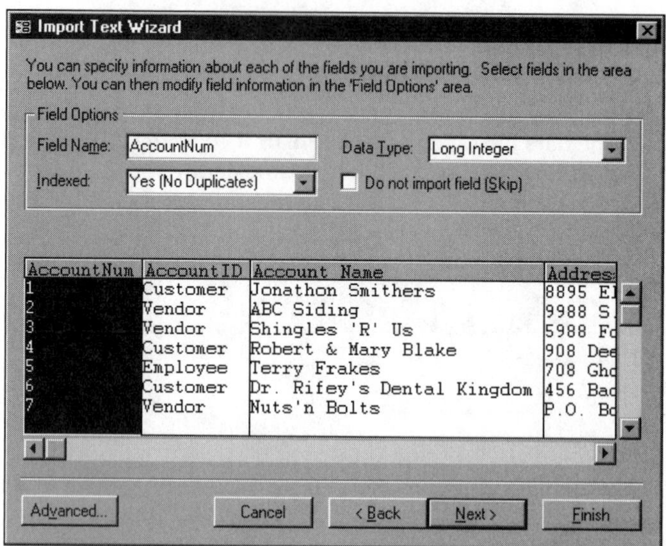

Figure 20-11: The Text Import Wizard gives you control over some of the field properties, saving you the trouble of having to change them in Table Design view.

If the text file's first row contains field names and you checked the appropriate option on the second page of the Text Import Wizard, you do not need to provide field names here. If the text file's first row does not contain field names, you probably will want to provide field names at this time. Access defaults the field names to Field1, Field2, and so forth. To change the name of a field, click on the column that contains the field and then enter a new field name.

Access makes its best guess at the type of data in each field. Although Access guesses correctly most of the time, you will occasionally need to change the type for a field. This situation occurs most often with date fields; Access sometimes interprets date fields as strings. To change the data type of a field, click on the column that contains the field and select the appropriate data type.

Although you can create indexes by opening the new table in Design view after the import is finished, Access's Text Import Wizard saves you time by enabling you to specify field indexes in the Wizard. To make a field an indexed field, click on the column that contains the field and specify the type of index for that field, just as you would in table design view.

You still need to edit the indexes in Table Design view if you want to create multiple field indexes.

Finally, you can tell Access to ignore a field altogether by clicking on the column that contains the field and checking the box that says Do not import field (Skip). Skipped fields are ignored completely and are not imported into your database.

After you have defined your fields, click on the Next button to continue.

Specifying a Primary Key

If you elected to import the text file into a new table, you have the option of designating a Primary Key (see Figure 20-12). You have the following options:

- Let Access add Primary Key
- Choose my own Primary Key
- No Primary Key

If the text file you are importing does not have a field that would make a good Primary Key, you can let Access create one for you by checking the first box (see Figure 20-12). If you let Access create a Primary Key for you, it creates a Primary Key field called ID of Type AutoNumber. The AutoNumber type replaces the Counter data type of Access 2.0.

If you want to use one of the fields in the text file as the Primary Key, simply select that field from the drop-down list provided. If you do not want a Primary Key, select the radio button next to No Primary Key. Unless you have a very specific reason not to have a primary key, you should always have one.

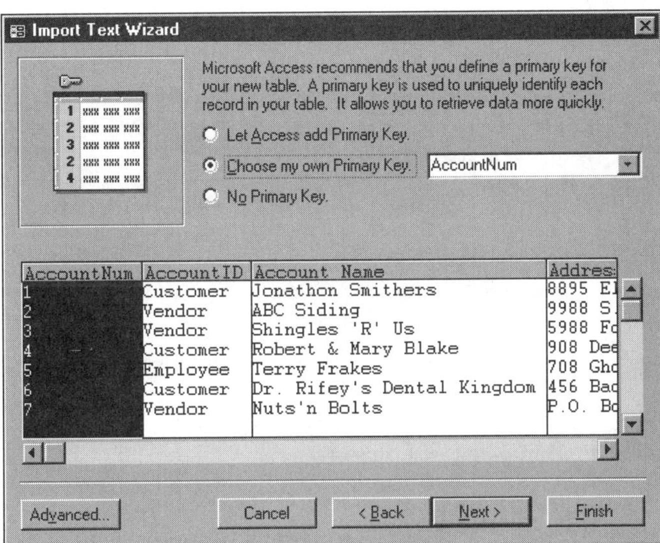

Figure 20-12: Importing into a new table gives you the additional option of designating a Primary Key for the new table.

If you designate a column as Primary Key and there are any records that would violate the key, the data for that field is imported but the key is not created. For example, suppose that you have a text file you are importing and you designate Field1, an integer field, as the Primary Key. If any records in the text file have text in Field1, Access makes that record's Field1 value a null because you cannot put text into a numeric field. Also, Access does not allow nulls in a Primary Key, so the result is that all records are imported, the record in question has a null in Field1, and no Primary Key is created.

After you have made your selection, click on the Next button to continue.

Designating the table into which to import

You use the sixth (and final) page of the Text Import Wizard to tell Access the name of the table into which you want to import the data. If you elected to import the data into an existing table, this field is locked and you cannot change the table name. If you elected to import the data into a new table, you specify the new table name here (see Figure 20-13).

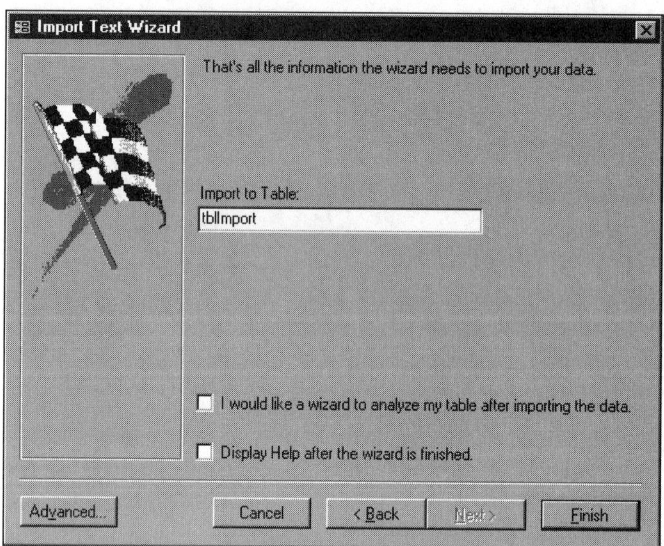

Figure 20-13: The last step of importing a text file is specifying the name of the table into which you want to import the data.

If you want Access to analyze your data by using the Table Analyzer Wizard after it is imported, check the box on the form. Chapter 2, "Relational Databases for Access 97 Developers," and Chapter 3, "Optimizing Performance," cover the Table Analyzer Wizard. Access also provides help that walks you through procedures that are often applied to imported data, such as:

- Customizing a table created by the Wizard
- Working with data in Datasheet view
- Troubleshooting importing problems
- Setting properties for a linked table

If you want Access to display these help topics, check the box next to Display Help after the wizard is finished.

After you have specified the table name and selected the desired options, click on the Finish button to import the data from the text file. After the importing is complete, you can open the table and view your imported data (see Figure 20-14).

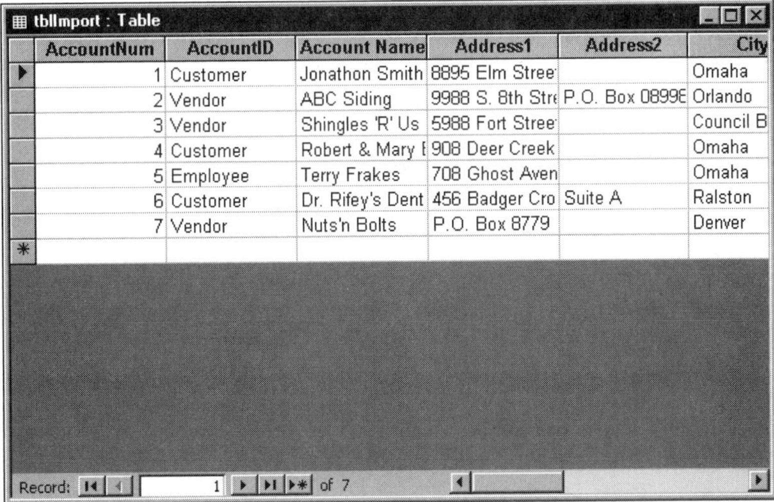

Figure 20-14: Data successfully imported from a delimited text file.

If any errors occur during the import, they are placed in a table named XXX_ImportErrors, where XXX is the name of the table into which you imported. If you get many errors on the first row but not on any other row, it is possible that the first row contained field names and you did not select this option in the Wizard. If you are importing into an existing table, you may receive field truncation errors. If this situation occurs, you have two choices: Leave the data as it is (truncated); or delete the imported data, increase the field sizes of the table you are importing into, and then re-import the data.

Using the Text Import Wizard's advanced options for delimited text fields

At any time while using the Text Import Wizard, you can click on the Advanced button to access the Wizard's advanced features (see Figure 20-15). On the Advanced import specification form, you can do the following:

- Specify the text file format (fixed-width or delimited)
- Specify the field delimiter and text qualifier
- Specify the file origin (Windows ANSI, DOS, or OS/2 PC-8)
- Specify the format of the dates and numbers in the text file
- Designate fields to be skipped

You can specify the format, field delimiter, text qualifier, and fields to be skipped on other pages of the Text Import Wizard; however, this page brings them all together; making defining your import a little easier and quicker.

The File Origin is very important when importing text files created with OS/2 or certain DOS programs. If you are importing a text file that is not in ANSI, you need to specify the file origin here. Also, different applications export dates in different formats. If the dates in your text file do not fit the standard date format of mm/dd/yy, you need to define the text file format in which they appear here.

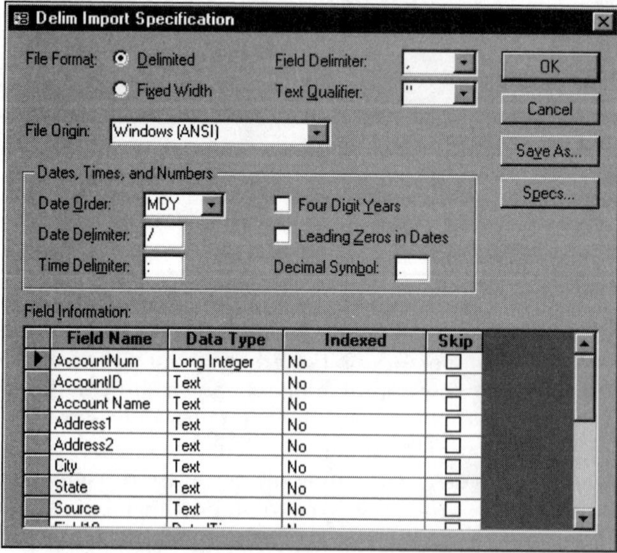

Figure 20-15: You can fine-tune certain aspects of your import through the Advanced options of the Text Import Wizard.

Saving and loading import specifications

You can save your import definition by clicking on the Save As button found in the Advanced Options of the Text Import Wizard. When you click on Save As, you are asked to provide a specification name. If you plan to perform many imports on text files of the same format, saving your import specification can save you a great deal of time and help you avoid mistakes. To load or delete an import specification, click on the Specs button.

The Text Import Wizard makes importing text files a quick and painless process. Mastering the Wizard makes importing data from different sources a snap. As long as an application can export its data into a text file, you can get the data into Access.

Using the Text Import Wizard to import fixed-width text files

Another common type of text data file is the fixed-width text file. A fixed-width text file has no separator or text qualifier characters. Instead, each field (column) contains a very specific number of characters. A typical fixed-width text file looks like the one in Figure 20-16.

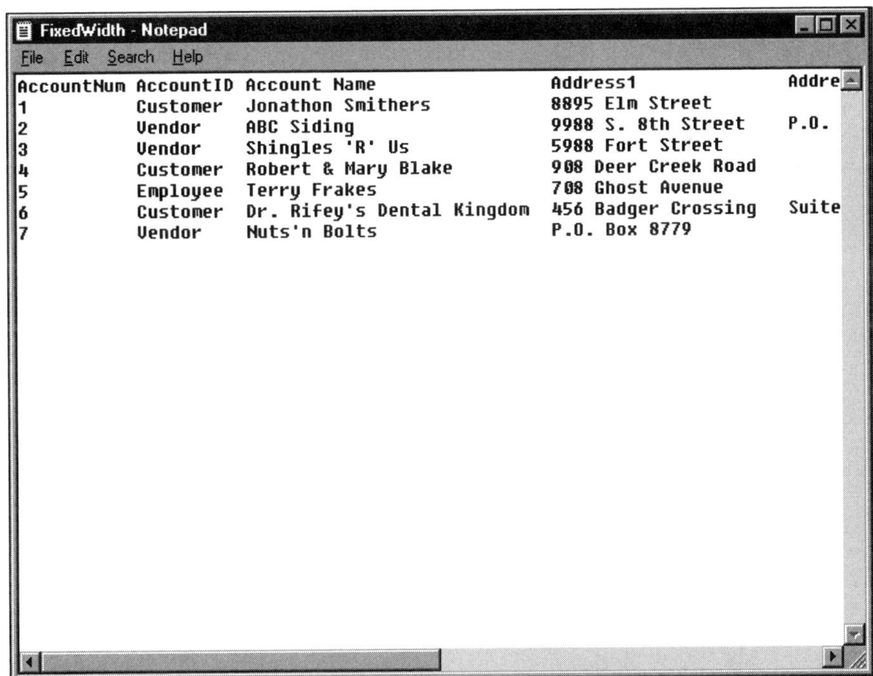

Figure 20-16: All fields in fixed-width files have specific lengths.

In this example, field1 (First Name) starts at the first character and contains 15 characters. Field2 (Last Name) starts at the sixteenth character and contains 15 characters. In a fixed-width text file, the fields need to have the spaces trimmed. For example, the first name Laura in the first record is actually "Laura ." Fixed-width fields often are used when the data contains quotes. For example, say that a field's data is the following:

> Jane said to Dick, "Dick, see me run."

If this text is exported to a comma-quote delimited file, it looks like this:

> "Jane said to Dick, "Dick, see me run."","Field 2 data","Field 2 data"

Programs that use comma-quote delimited files expect all string data to be enclosed in quotes and separated by commas. They do not know how to deal with the preceding example. One option is to use a character other than double-quotes as the text qualifier, but then you have to make sure that the text qualifier is not located in any of the data fields. A better solution is to export the data as a fixed-width file.

Access makes it very easy to import fixed-width files by using the Text Import Wizard. To import a fixed-width file, you start the Text Import Wizard the same way you do for delimited files. Follow these steps:

1. Select File⇨Get External Data⇨Import from the Database window's menu bar (refer to Figure 20-1).
2. Select Files of Type: Text File (*.txt, *.csv, *.tab, *.asc).
3. Select the drive, directory, and then the file name of the text file to import.
4. Click on the Import button.

Now you are on the first page of the Text Import Wizard (see Figure 20-17). The first page looks the same when importing fixed-width files as it does when importing delimited text files. However, the sample of the data in the text file looks different; instead of the fields being surrounded by quotes and separated by commas, the data is split into columns much like a spreadsheet.

Access usually detects correctly the format of the text file you are importing. If Access has mistaken a fixed-width file for a delimited file, you need to change the setting here. When you are satisfied that the proper format is selected, click on the Next button to continue.

Specifying field breaks

When importing fixed-width text files, you use the second page of the Text Import Wizard to define field breaks. As stated earlier, in a fixed-width text file, each field is composed of a specific number of characters. This fact causes the data to appear in columns (see Figure 20-18). Access does its best to guess where each column starts and stops in your selected text file, but it is almost never 100 percent correct. Making sure that the columns are correctly defined is crucial to importing the text file successfully.

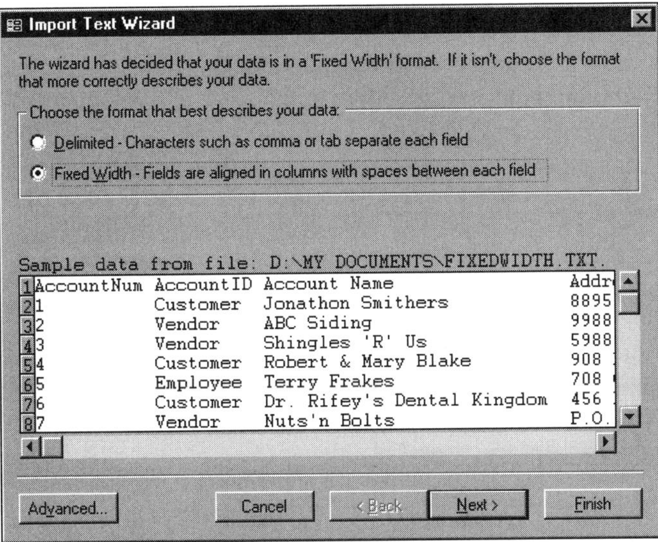

Figure 20-17: The Text Import Wizard begins in the same way for both fixed-width and delimited files. Only the data samples look different.

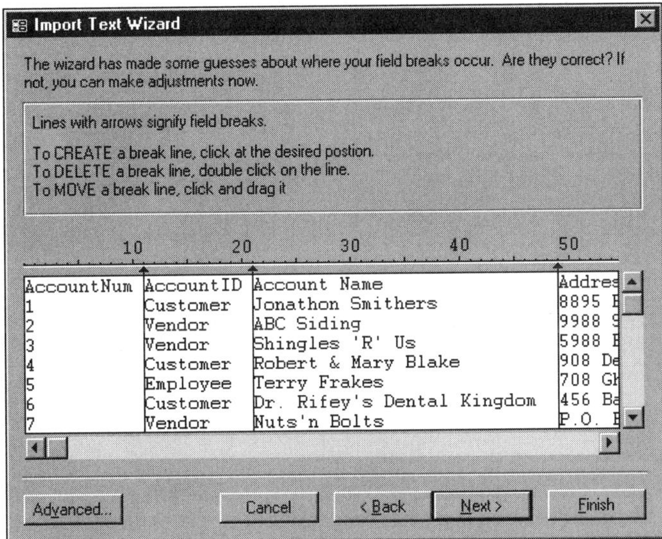

Figure 20-18: Correctly specifying the separation of columns is crucial to successfully importing fixed-width text files.

You have the ability to define columns by the following means:

- Moving an existing column marker by dragging it.
- Adding a column marker by clicking on the ruler/header where currently no marker exists.
- Deleting a column marker by double-clicking on the existing column marker you want to delete.

You do not need to place a column marker at the beginning of the first field or at the end of the last field, but you do need to have a column marker between each field in the text file. When you have finished placing the column markers, click on the Next button to continue.

Electing to import data into a new or existing table

Just as with importing delimited files, the third page of the Import Wizard is where you tell Access to import the data into an existing table or into a new table (see Figure 20-19). If you want to import the text file into an existing table, you must check the radio button labeled In an Existing Table and specify a table name. Please see the Secret in the previous section "Electing to import data into a new or existing table" for information on what happens if your existing table is not the same structure as the imported file. Again, when you are ready to continue, click on the Next button.

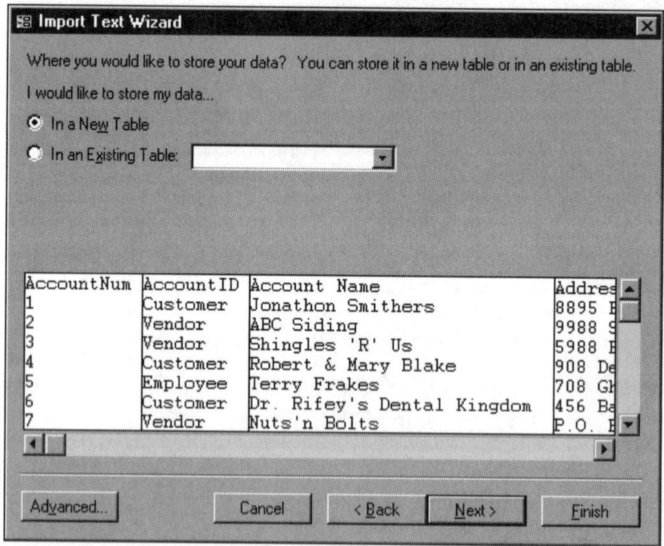

Figure 20-19: You can choose to import the text file into an existing table or into a new table. Notice that the Wizard continuously shows you a sample of the text file.

Specifying field options such as Name and Data Type

The next step of the Text Import Wizard is where you define field options, such as naming each field and specifying its data type. With delimited files, you always need to specify field names if you do not want to have them named Field1, Field2, and so on. With delimited text files, you are allowed to state that the first row contains names; you do not have this option when importing fixed-width text files. If the fixed-width text file you are importing contains the field names in the first row, you should delete the row from the text file before importing it. If you do not delete the row, chances are you will get errors when importing the text file. For example, if a field is named AccountNumber and you have assigned the data type of integer, the first row gets an error and the record has a null in the AccountNumber field because Access cannot place "AccountNumber" into a numeric data type. This situation is really not a problem because you can just delete the error table and delete the first row in your new Recordset. Refer to the previous section "Using the Text Import Wizard to import delimited text files" for more information on specifying field names and data types, creating indexes on imported fields, and choosing to skip fields during the import. When you have finished defining the field options, click on the Next button to continue.

Specifying a Primary Key

The final step in defining your import is to create (or choose not to create) a Primary Key. In general, you should never have a table that does not have a Primary key, but Access does allow you not to specify a Primary Key during the import. Refer to the previous section "Using the Text Import Wizard to import delimited text files" for information on specifying a Primary Key.

Designating the table into which to import

You use the final page of the Text Import Wizard to tell Access the name of the table into which you want to import the data. If you elected to import the data into an existing table, this field is locked and you cannot change the table name. If you elected to import the data into a new table, you specify the new table name here.

Using the Text Import Wizard's advanced options for fixed-width text files

The advanced options for fixed-width text files are very similar to that of delimited files (see Figure 20-20). The notable difference is that the Field Delimiter and Text Qualifier fields are disabled and you can see and change the Start Columns and Column Widths. Refer to the previous section "Using the Text Import Wizard to import delimited text files" for information on using the Advanced Options form.

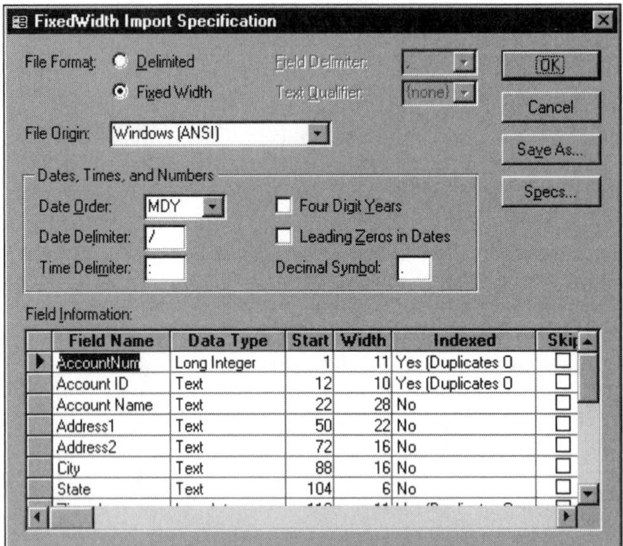

Figure 20-20: The Advanced Options form enables you to define many aspects of your import all at once.

Importing linefeed-delimited text files

You may encounter one other form of text file, the linefeed-delimited text file. A linefeed-delimited text file has one field per line — the fields are delimited by a linefeed (see Figure 20-21). Access has no built-in functionality to import linefeed-delimited files. If you need to import a linefeed-delimited file, you have to write code to do it.

To import a linefeed-delimited text file, you need to do the following:

1. Learn the order of the fields in the text file.
2. Define a table with the same structure as the data you are going to import.
3. Learn the number of fields (lines) per record.
4. Open the file with the `Open` statement.
5. Read one line at a time from the file, using the `Line Input#` statement.
6. Write the string you have just read from the text file out to the appropriate field in your database.
7. If the line you have just read is the last field of a record, test for end of file.
8. If you are not at the last field of a record or the end of file tests `False`, repeat steps 4, 5, 6, and 7.

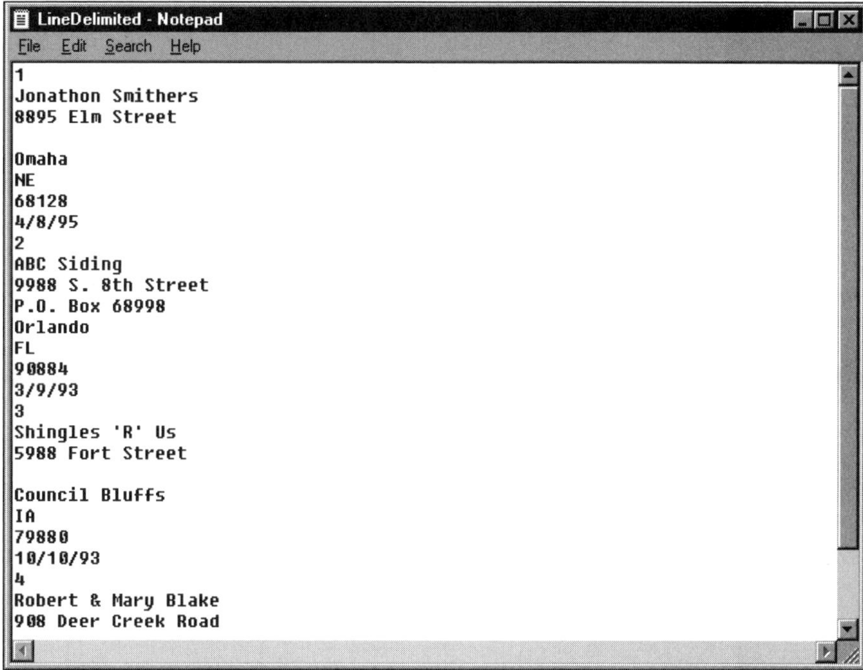

Figure 20-21: Linefeed-delimited files have one record per line.

One caveat about importing linefeed-delimited text files that may sound obvious but bears stating is that first and foremost you must start with a valid text file. Notice the blank line (three lines down) in the file shown in Figure 20-21. This record does not have an address 2, so it contains the blank line instead. Suppose that a blank line was not included where the address 2 field should be, like the following file:

```
1
Jonathon Smithers
8895 Elm Street
Omaha
NE
68128
4/8/95
```

The import will fail because the import must read each line sequentially and assume that each line corresponds to a specific field in the database (or is skipped all together). When the fourth line is read, it would assume that it was an Address 2 when in actuality it is the city for this record. This "misunderstanding" then throws all corresponding fields in every record off by one field. If this were to happen in another record, each field following would again be shifted by one field position. As you can see, even one field out of place in a linefeed-delimited file renders the file useless. To import a file like this one, you need to edit the file in a text editor prior to writing code to import it.

For example, assume that the preceding sample text file is a valid linefeed-delimited file that you want to import into your Access database. First, you need to decide where the data is to reside. You have two choices: Write code to import the data into an existing table, or create a table that matches exactly the format of the text file and import the file into that table (see Figure 20-22).

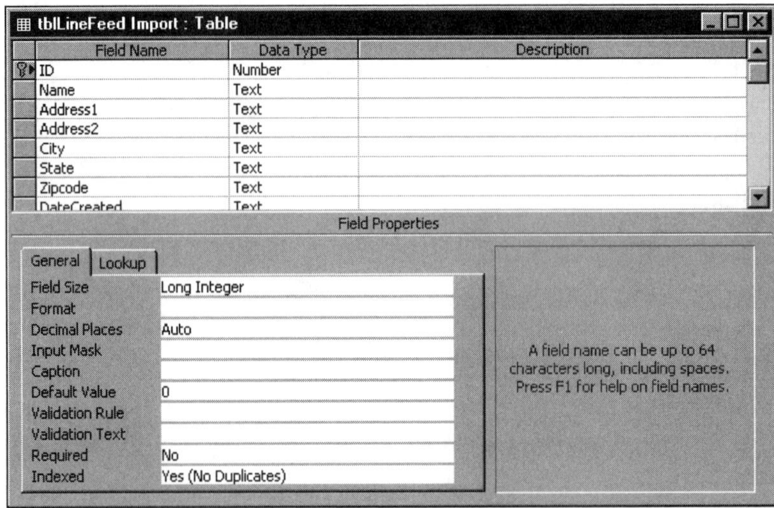

Figure 20-22: The first step to importing a text file through VBA code is to understand the data in the file and to create a table with a matching structure.

Tip

If you write an import routine that is to be distributed with an application you have created, you probably will want to write code that imports data directly into one of your existing tables. If, however, you are writing the import routine strictly for your own use and not for out-of-house use, you should create a new table to match the structure of the text file and import the data into that file. After the data is in the text file, you can look at the data to make sure it was imported correctly and message the data as needed. When you are satisfied with the imported data, use append queries to move the data to the appropriate tables in your database. Using this technique can save you many headaches if the imports don't go exactly as planned.

After you have created the table to match the structure of your text file, you will need to write the code to import the text file. Listing 20-1 is a module for importing the sample text file.

Listing 20-1 Code to Import Linefeed-Delimited Files

```
Sub ImportLFDelimitedFile()
   On Error Resume Next        ' You should always use error trapping!
   Dim szInput As String, db As DATABASE, rst As Recordset
```

```
   Set db = CurrentDb()
   Set rst = db.OpenRecordset("tblLineFeed Import")

   Open "C:\My Documents\LineDelimited.txt" For Input As 1

Do
   rst.AddNew
   Line Input #1, szInput
   rst![ID] = Val(szInput)
   Line Input #1, szInput
   rst![Name] = szInput
   Line Input #1, szInput
   rst![Address1] = szInput
   Line Input #1, szInput
   rst![Address2] = szInput
   Line Input #1, szInput
   rst![City] = szInput
   Line Input #1, szInput
   rst![State] = szInput
   Line Input #1, szInput
   rst![Zip] = szInput
   Line Input #1, szInput
   rst![DateCreated] = szInput
   rst.UPDATE
Loop Until EOF(1)

Close #1

End Sub
```

When you write code to perform imports, you need to make provisions for the data you are reading from the text file. When using the `Line Input` statement to read one line at a time, you always need to read the data into a string variable. Of course, not all the data types in your file will be strings.

In the preceding code example, you can see a provision made for the ID field. In the example table, the ID field is a numeric field, yet the line is read from the text file as a string. This situation is very easy to work around: Simply encapsulate the string in the `Val()` function. The `Val()` function returns the numeric equivalent of a string passed to it. You can use the `Val()` function whenever the data you are reading into a string variable needs to be converted to a number.

You may have to make other provisions as well. For example, when you create a new field in a table and assign the field the data type of string, Access by default sets the `Allow Zero Length` property to `False`. If you import a blank line such as the one discussed for Address2 of the first record in Figure 20-21, the string will be set as "" — a zero-length string. You need to either change the property in the table itself or write code that converts all zero-length strings to nulls when the data is written to the table field.

You may never have to import a linefeed-delimited file, but if you do, you are now prepared.

The key to importing text files is to do the following:

- Know the format of the text file.
- Know the fields and their order in the text file.
- Take your time! Use the Wizard whenever possible; simply read carefully and follow the directions.

By knowing how to import these three formats of text files, you should be able to import data from just about any data source.

Opening Tables in External Databases

Sometimes it is impractical to import external data into your Access database. This situation usually occurs when you have data that is accessed from applications other than your own Access application. When importing the data is not feasible, you have two options:

- Open the data directly
- Establish a Link to the external data

Understanding when to open tables directly

Opening tables from external databases is significantly slower than linking to the tables. When opening a table directly, you create a `Recordset` object for the external table, but when you link to the table, you create a `TableDef` object for the external table. In general, you should always link to external tables.

Sometimes, however, you may want to access a table directly rather than link to it, as in the following case:

1. You rarely need to access the table, and
2. The path to the table changes regularly (in this case, you may want to implement a File Open dialog box and let your user tell your application where the table is located), and
3. The table does not contain a large amount of information.

Opening the external database tables directly

To open tables from another database, you must use VBA code. In addition, you need to create the connection to the external tables each time your application runs. When you create a direct connection to external tables, they do not show up in the Database window. Therefore, you cannot view the tables in datasheet mode or access the tables by using the Query by Example editor. If you need to execute various queries on the tables, you should link to the tables.

To directly open a table in an external database, you need to perform two steps:

1. Open the external database, using the `OpenDatabase` method of the `Workspace` object.
2. Create a `Recordset` object for the external table, using the `OpenRecordset` method of the `Database` object.

For example, to open a FoxPro table called Orders in your existing Access database and create a new order record, you would use a procedure such as the one shown in Figure 20-23.

The `OpenDatabase` method has a total of four arguments:

- `Database Name`: Full path and file name of the database
- `Open Exclusive`: `True` or `False` flag
- `Read-Only`: `True` or `False` flag
- `Source`: The connect type (for example, `"FoxPro 2.5"`)

mdlUseExternal : Module

(General) OpenFoxPro

```
Sub OpenFoxPro()
Dim dbFox1 As Database, rstOrders As Recordset

' Open the external FoxPro table
Set dbFox1 = DBEngine.Workspaces(0).OpenDatabase("D:\Foxpro\", _
  False, False, "FoxPro 2.5")

' Open a Recordset for Orders table
Set rstOrders = dbFox1.OpenRecordset("Orders")

rstOrders.AddNew
    rstOrders![CustomerID] = 101
    rstOrders![ShipName] = "Simtuit Solutions"
    rstOrders![ProductID] = 302
    rstOrders![Quantity] = 10
    rstOrders![Unit] = "boxes"
rstOrders.UPDATE
End Sub
```

Figure 20-23: Opening a FoxPro table directly by using VBA code.

Tip

When using the `OpenDatabase` method to open a Jet database file, you specify the file name and extension in the `Database Name` argument. When accessing other external databases, such as FoxPro and dBASE files, you do not supply the file name, but rather you supply just the path where the table you want to open resides.

Opening text files as external tables directly

It is possible to open an ASCII text file as though it were an external table. The text file must be in a format that would be importable; the file must be fixed-width or delemited in a tabular format. In addition, you must create a *schema information file* for each text file you want to open directly.

Creating schema information files

Schema information files contain information that defines the format of the text file. Schema information files are always named Schema.ini and must be placed in the same folder as the text file you want to open. Access does not include any tool to create schema information files; you must create them with a text editor. The following is a list of the entries you create in a schema information file:

- The text file name
- The file format
- The field names, widths, and data types
- Special data type formats and conversions

There are some size limitations to take into consideration when opening text files:

Item	*Maximum size per text file*
Field	255 fields
Field Name	64 characters
Field Width	32,766 characters
Record Size	65,000 bytes

In addition, Access can only open text files exclusively; you cannot open a text file for shared access.

The following is a sample Schema.ini file. The various entries of the Schema.ini file are discussed in detail following the example.

```
[Text.txt]
ColNameHeader=False
Format=FixedLength
MaxScanRows=0
CharacterSet=ANSI
Col1="Customer Name" Text Width 100
Col2=Address Text Width 30
Col3=City Text Width 30
Col4=State Text Width 4
Col5=Zipcode Text Width 15
```

Because a Schema.ini file must reside in the same folder as the text file, and you may have multiple text files in the same folder, you can create multiple file specifications in a Schema.ini file. After the last entry of the first definition, create a blank line and start the next file specification beginning with the file name entry of the second file.

Specifying the text file name

In addition to having to place the Schema.ini file in the same folder as the text file, the first entry of the Schema.ini file must contain the text file name. The file name must be enclosed in square brackets like this:

```
[Test.txt]
```

Because the schema.ini files resides in the same folder as the text file, you do not include the path of the file, just the file name.

Specifying the text file format

Text files come in many different formats. For Access to be able to open your text file, it must know the format of the text file. The format entry must be one of the following values:

Format Value	*File Format*
`TabDelimited`	Fields in the text file are delimited by tabs.
`CSVDelimited`	Fields in the text file are delimited by commas.
`Delimited(*)`	Fields in the text file are delimited by the character in brackets (an asterisk in this example). You can substitute any character except the double-quote character (") in place of the asterisk as the delimiting character.
`FixedLength`	Fields in the text file have fixed-widths.

Specifying field names, widths, and data types

There are two ways to specify field names in delimited text files:

- Include the field names in the first record of the text file and set the `ColNameHeader` entry to `True`
- Specify each field by number and designate the field name and data type

If you set the `MaxScanRows` entry to `0`, Access will scan all of the rows in the text file to determine the data types of each field. If you want Access to scan only a certain number of rows, supply the number of rows for the `MaxScanRows` setting instead of `0`. If you set the `ColNameHeader` setting to `True`, Access starts scanning at the second row.

Defining field name, width, and data type information for fixed-width text files is a little more complicated. Each field in a fixed-width text file is called a column because the data lines up in columns when viewing the text file in a text editor that does not use proportional fonts. You must create a unique entry in the Schema.ini file for each column in the text file. The column entry has the following format:

```
Coln=ColumnName type [Width #]
```

The following table describes each part of the column entry:

Part	*Description*
`ColumnName`	The name of the field. If the field name contains spaces, you must enclose it in double-quotes.
`Type`	Specifies the data type of the field (see following table).
`Width`	This is a literal string and should not be changed. It denotes that the number following it is the number of characters in the field.
`#`	The number of characters of the column. Replace the # character with the proper number.

The following table lists the available values for the type setting:

Data Type
`Byte`
`Long`
`Currency`
`Single`
`Double`
`DateTime`
`Text`
`Memo`

For example, to specify five fields in a fixed-width text file, a 100-character customer name, a 50-character address, a 30-character state field, a 4-character state field, and a 15-character zip code field, add the following lines to the Schema.ini file:

```
Col1="Customer Name" Text Width 100
Col2=Address Text Width 30
Col3=City Text Width 30
Col4=State Text Width 4
Col5=Zipcode Text Width 15
```

Specifying a character set

Access allows you to specify the character set of the text file. You can specify an ANSI character set or an OEM character set. The entry required to denote the text file as an ANSI file is:

```
CharacterSet=ANSI
```

If you are unsure about the character set used, set the value to ANSI. If after opening the data source the character set is not correct, change the Schema.ini entry and open the database again.

Specifying data type formats and conversion

Text files can be created in a number of ways; they may have been created from scratch using a text editor or they may have been exported from one of many different types of databases. Because of this, various aspects such as date formats will vary from one text file to another. You can tailor the Schema.ini file to reflect these parameters. The following is a list of entries you can add to your Schema.ini file:

Entry	*Description*
`DateTimeFormat`	A format string that specifies the format dates and times appearing in the text file. Search Access's online Help for the `Format` command to see a list of all of the valid formats. If your dates and times do not share a consistent format in the text file, you cannot use this setting.
`DecimalSymbol`	Specifies the character used to separate the integer from the fractional portion of a number.
`NumberDigits`	Specifies the number of decimal digits in the fractional portion of numbers.
`NumberLeadingZeros`	Specifies whether a decimal value less than 1 and greater than –1should contain leading zeros; you can set this entry to `False` (no leading zeros) or `True` (use leading zeros).
`CurrencySymbol`	Specifies the currency symbol to be used for currency values in the text file. Examples include the dollar sign (`$`) and `Dm`.

(continued)

Entry	Description
CurrencyPosFormat	Specifies the position of the currency symbol. This value can be set to any of the following values:
0	Currency symbol prefix with no separation ($1)
1	Currency symbol suffix with no separation (1$)
2	Currency symbol prefix with one character separation ($ 1)
3	Currency symbol suffix with one character separation (1 $)
CurrencyDigits	Specifies the number of digits used for the fractional part of a currency amount.
CurrencyNegFormat	Specifies the format of negative currency values. This entry can be one of the following values:
0	($1)
1	-$1
2	$-1
3	$1
4	(1$)
5	-1$
6	1-$
7	1$-
8	-1 $
9	-$ 1
10	1 $-
11	$ 1-
12	$ -1
13	1- $
14	($ 1)
15	(1 $)
	The dollar sign is shown for purposes of this example, but it should be replaced with the appropriate CurrencySymbol value in the actual program.
CurrencyThousandSymbol	Specifies the single-character symbol to be used for separating currency values in the text file by thousands.

If you do not include one of the above entries in your Schema.ini file, Access uses the default value in Windows Control Panel.

Case-sensitive data sources

Some data sources such as Microsoft FoxPro, dBase, and Paradox are designed to be case-sensitive by default. You need to be conscious of this issue when designing queries that perform searches in case-sensitive databases. You can use the following methods to implement case-sensitivity:

- For Xbase databases such as Microsoft FoxPro or dBase, setting the value of the `Collating Sequence` setting in the \HKEY_LOCAL_MACHINE\SOFTWARE\Microsoft\Jet\3.5\Engines\Xbase key of the Windows Registry to `International` makes all operations case-insensitive; setting it to `Ascii` makes all operations case-sensitive.
- For Paradox databases, setting the value of the `Collating Sequence` setting in the \HKEY_LOCAL_MACHINE\SOFTWARE\Microsoft\Jet\3.5\Engines\Paradox key of the Windows Registry to `International`, `Norwegian-Danish`, or `Swedish-Finnish` makes all operations case-insensitive; setting it to `Ascii` makes all operations case-sensitive. The `Collating Sequence` setting's value must match the collating sequence of the database file (.db file) you want to open; if you open a .db file that was created with its collating sequence set to `Ascii`, even though the registry setting is set to `International`, all operations are still case-sensitive.
- Some ODBC servers can be configured for case-sensitivity. You must check with your server administrator to determine the setting of your ODBC server.

If you must work with case-sensitive data sources, you can use the `OR` operator when defining query criteria or search criteria to look for all of the possible case combinations such as `'Mr. OR mr. OR MR.'`.

Opening a secured Jet database

If you attempt to open a secured Jet database by using VBA code, you must create a new workspace for the database, using a valid user name and password, as in the following:

```
Dim wspSpecial As Workspace
Set wspSpecial = DBEngine.CreateWorkspace("SpecialWS","John Smith", _
"John's PW")
```

You then need to use this workspace in place of the default workspace (`Workspaces(0)`) when opening the database, as follows:

```
Set dbLink =wspSpecial.OpenDatabase("C:\MyDir\MyData.mdb")
```

Linking to External Data

The preferred way to use external data is to link to it. When you link to an external table, the table looks and performs much like an Access table in your current database, and you can create dynaset and snapshot Recordset objects with them. The connection information for the linked table is stored in a TableDef object. None of the external database data is stored in the current .MDB file, but rather the external database containing the linked tables is opened when you open your database .MDB file containing the links. Icons for the linked tables are displayed in the Database window, so you can open the tables in datasheet view and use them in the Query by Example editor.

Most commercial Access applications use table linking. When you develop an Access application that you plan to distribute to a user base, you should separate your program objects (forms, modules, queries, and macros) from your tables by placing all the tables into a second database and link to all the tables in your program database.

Why link to external tables

The greatest benefit of separating your program objects from your table objects is maintainability. When it is time to distribute an update of your program, you simply send the new program database file to your users. If you do not separate your program objects from your table objects, you must either manually convert the data from your old application by using Access or a combination of VBA code and queries to convert the data at the customer's location. The first option isn't even an option if your user base exceeds a half dozen or so locations. The second option is more portable but very tedious and time-consuming.

In addition to maintainability, it is essential that you separate the program objects from the table objects if you plan on having more than one user access the same shared data on a network. For maximum performance in a network setup, you don't want all users of your application to run the same instance of the application from the network. Instead, you want each workstation to have a copy of your application installed on it and have them all access the same data file from a network drive.

A third reason to separate your objects is due to Windows 95 itself. Most companies are migrating to Windows 95 one department at a time. Some companies are migrating one computer at a time. Because the new version of Jet (Version 3.0) that started shipping with Access 95 is strictly 32-bit, client machines on a network cannot access the Jet data if they are running Windows 3.1. For a department made up of computers running different operating systems, the 32-bit all-or-nothing approach may be unfeasible. If you plan to distribute your application for network use and you know that some of the machines that will need to use the data are still running a 16-bit operating system, you can migrate your program database to Access for Windows 95 but leave the data in a Jet 2.5 (Access 2.0) database format. This way, all computers can share the same data; computers running Windows 95 or Windows NT can take advantage of the new power and capabilities of Access for Windows 95, but not the improved speed of the new Jet engine.

You may decide to keep some user tables local in the program database (temporary tables used for short-term data manipulation are great candidates for keeping local), but, in general, when you plan to distribute your application to any user base, you should always separate the data to a different .MDB file and link to the data.

Although you can link to external database sources such as FoxPro and dBASE files, the following examples focus on linking to external Access database files. They teach you the tricks and techniques necessary to develop a distributable application that is easy to maintain. You will find information specific to linking to other database types, such as linking limitations, at the end of this chapter.

The time to start thinking about separating your program objects from your tables is when you first start to design your application. You should start right from the beginning by creating all your tables in one .MDB file and all your program objects in another .MDB file. In the following examples, the file name DATA.MDB refers to the database containing table objects, and PROGRAM.MDB refers to the database containing the program objects, such as forms and modules.

Preserving relationships in linked Jet tables

When you link to tables in another Access database, the relationships created in the database containing the actual TableDefs are maintained. Notice in Figure 20-24 that the Database window shows two linked tables, whereas the Relationships window shows their relationship to each other. This relationship was not added after the tables were imported but rather was created in the original .MDB file and imported along with the tables.

You can create a relationship between a linked table and a table created in your current Access database, but you cannot enforce any type of referential integrity between the tables. Referential integrity is enforced (if created) between two tables linked from the same database. This is why you should start your new Access projects by creating the tables and relationships in one database and your program objects in another.

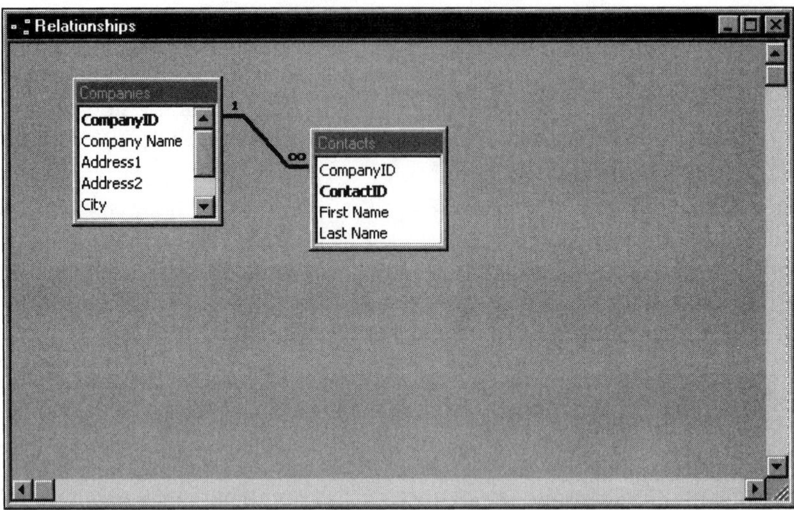

Figure 20-24: When you link to external tables, the table's relationships remain intact.

Splitting a database

If an application you created contains table objects and program objects that you want to split into two separate databases, you can manually separate the objects or you can use the Database Splitter Add-in. The Database Splitter is a small wizard that creates a new database that you name, moves all of the tables from the original database into the new database, and creates links to the tables in the new database. The Database Splitter can save you hours when splitting databases with large numbers of tables.

To split a database using the Database Splitter

1. Start the Database Splitter by selecting Tools➪Add-Ins➪Database Splitter.
2. On the Database Splitter form (see Figure 20-25), click on the Split Database button.
3. Enter the file name and path of the new database to house the tables.

After you click on the Split Database button, you cannot stop the splitting process. To undo the actions of the Database splitter, you will have to delete all of the links it created and import the tables and relationships from the newly created database. Always make a backup of your original database prior to using the Database Splitter.

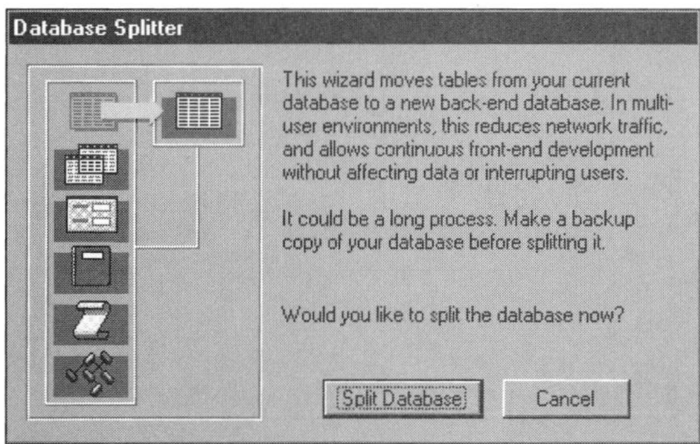

Figure 20-25: The Database Splitter add-in makes separating your code objects from your table objects a snap.

Creating links to external data

You can create links to external data by using the File➪Get External Data menu option of the Database window menu bar, or you can create the links by using VBA code. When you have the luxury of using the menu item to create links for you, you should take advantage of it. When you are designing an application for distribution and you need to link many tables to your program object database, use the menus.

To link to an external table by using the menus, first select File➪Get External Data from the Database window menu bar, shown in Figure 20-26, and then select Link Tables.

When you select Link Tables, you see the Link dialog box, which is similar to the File Open and Import dialog boxes (see Figure 20-27). In this dialog box, you specify the File of type (database type) to which you want to link. After you select the File type, the list refreshes to show all files of your selected type. Find and select the database file to which you want to link and click on the Link button.

If the database you have selected contains more than one table (such as Access databases do), you see the dialog box shown in Figure 20-28, which lists all the tables within the selected database.

This dialog box makes it very easy to link all tables from the selected database without having to link each table one at a time. Use the Select All button if you want to link all the tables. When you have selected all the tables to which you want to link, click on the OK button.

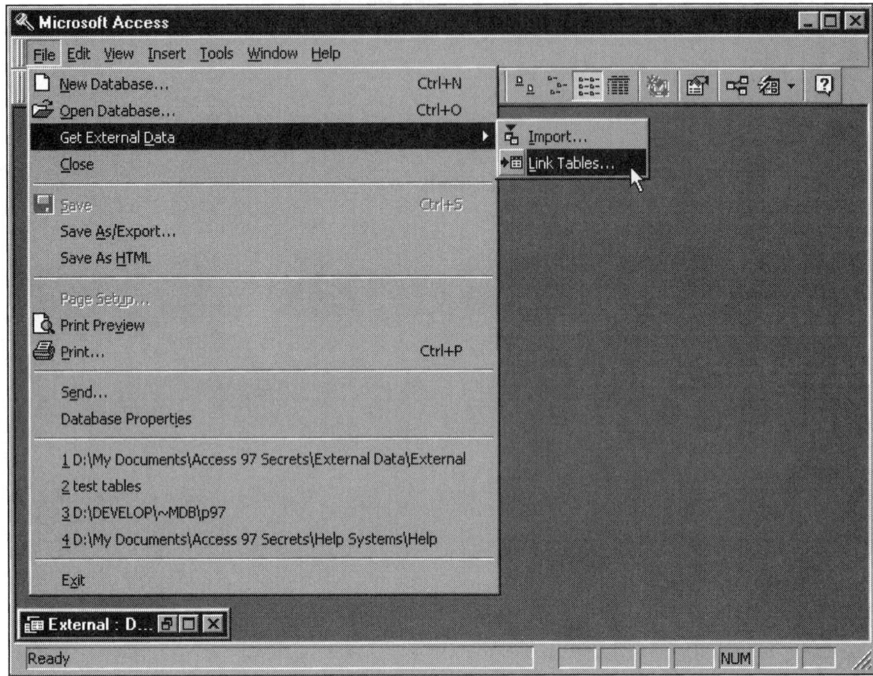

Figure 20-26: You access the linking function from the same submenu as you do the import functions.

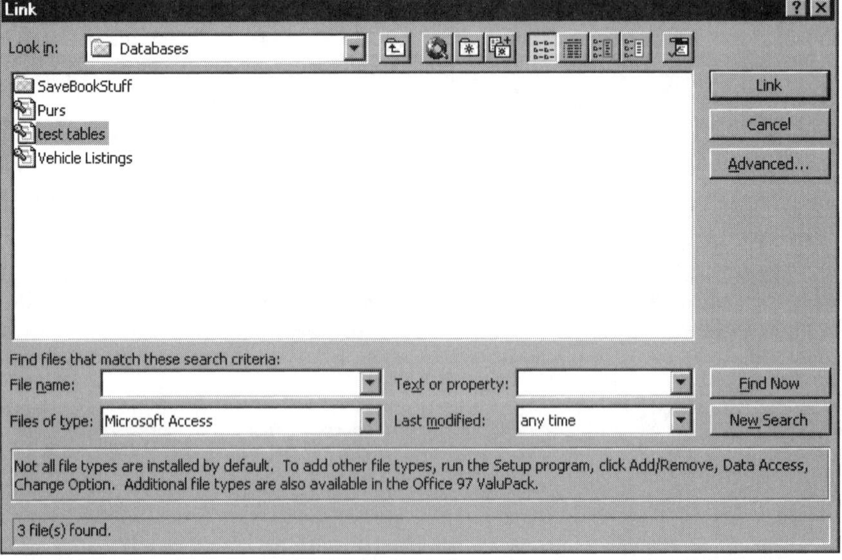

Figure 20-27: This dialog box should be familiar to you by now. Use it to select the database that contains the tables to which you want to link.

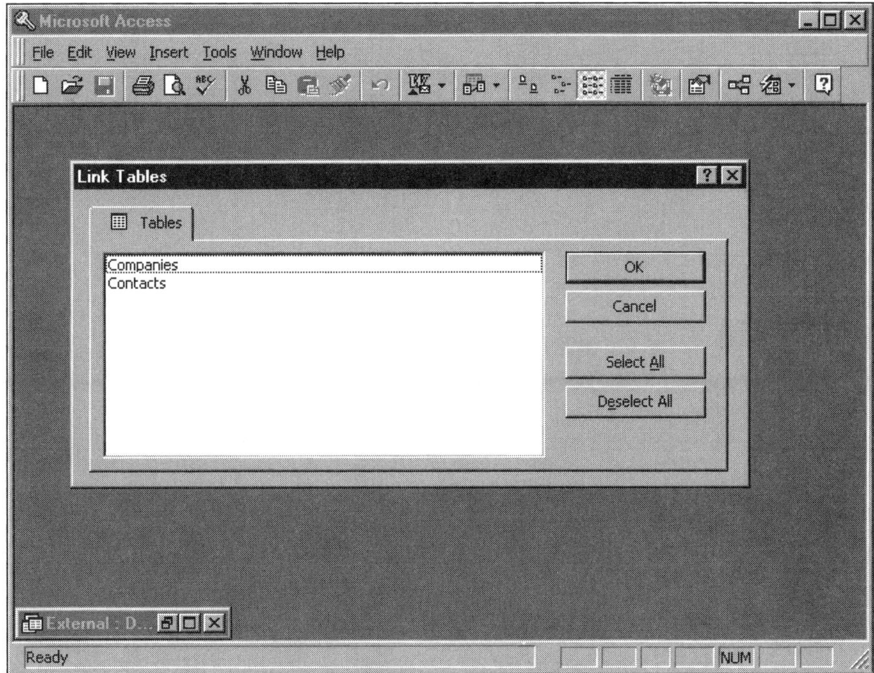

Figure 20-28: You can elect to import just one table from the selected database or as many as you like.

When you successfully link to an external table, the table shows up in the Database window with an icon representing its type (see Figure 20-29). All linked tables display an arrow to the left of the icon, showing that the table is linked. You can open the linked table and build queries by using the linked table, but you can make only certain design changes to the linked tables, as listed in Table 20-1.

Table 20-1 Editable Properties for Linked Tables

Property	*Effect*
`Format`	Controls how data is displayed in a field
`DecimalPlaces`	Controls the number of decimal places displayed
`InputMask`	Used to create a data input mask with separator characters and blanks to fill in
`Caption`	Changes the name used for a field's datasheet column heading, and specifies a default name to be used as a label when adding a field to a form

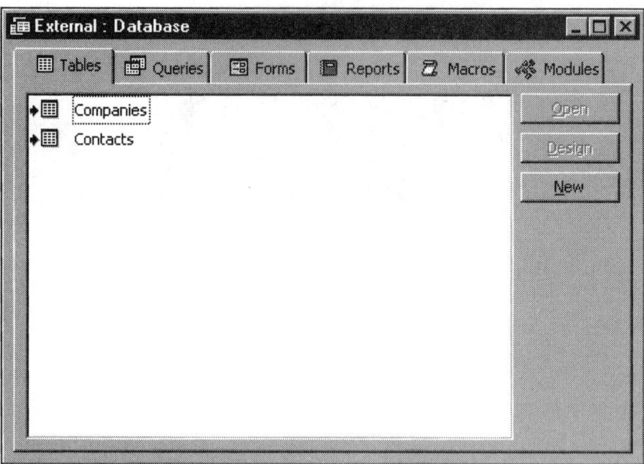

Figure 20-29: Linked tables appear in the database window with arrows to the left of their icons.

These changes affect only how your application handles and displays data from the linked tables; no changes are made to the original tables in the source database.

If you want more information on the linked table, right-click on the table and select Properties to display the table Properties sheet (see Figure 20-30). The Properties sheet tells you the type of table (in this case, Access), the date created, the date modified, and the owner of the table. You can also enter a description of this table and choose to hide the table in the database window.

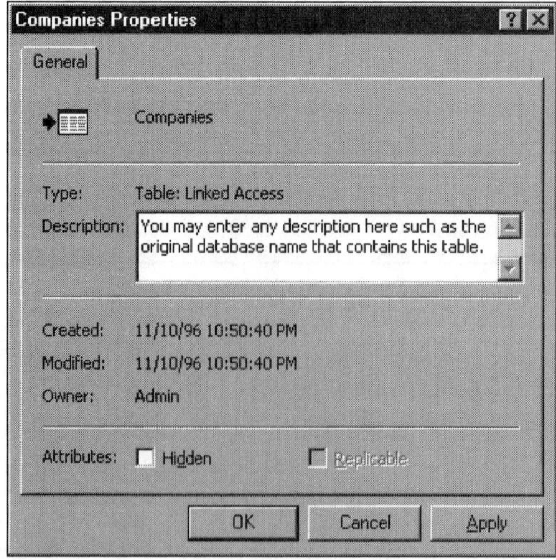

Figure 20-30: The table Properties sheet tells you that the table is linked and that it is an Access table.

You may want to enter the name of the original database that contains the linked table in the description field of the table Properties if your database contains links to many different external tables.

Linking to external data using VBA code

In addition to linking tables by using Access menus, you can link to external tables by using VBA code. This capability is useful if you do not know where the linked tables are at design time and you want to make your table-linking flexible at run time. Do not confuse this situation with not knowing where the tables will reside at run time; later in this chapter, you will learn how to write code that fixes broken links. In general, if the tables are tables that you will use every time you run your application, it is easier to link the tables manually and use the menus and custom code to fix any broken links that occur at run time.

Follow these steps to link an external database using VBA code:

1. Create a new `TableDef` for the linked table.
2. Set the `Connect` property of the newly created `TableDef`.
3. Set the `SourceTableName` property of the newly defined `TableDef`.
4. Append the newly defined `TableDef` to the `TableDefs` collection.

Creating the new TableDef

You need to create a new `TableDef` object for the linked table using the `CreateTableDef` method of the `Database` object, as follows:

```
Dim MyDB as DATABASE, tdfOrders as TableDef
Set MyDB = CurrentDB()

Set tdfOrders = MyDB.CreateTableDef("Linked Jet Table")
```

In the preceding line, when the `tdfOrders TableDef` is appended to the `TableDefs` collection, the new table is named `"Linked Jet Table"`. If you wanted the new table to be called `"Orders"`, you would use the following line of code:

```
Set tdfOrders = MyDB.CreateTableDef("Orders")
```

When you attempt to import a table with a name that is identical to an existing table in the database, Access imports the new table and gives it a numeric suffix (such as Orders1). When you attempt to link to a table by using VBA code and you assign a name to the `TableDef` using the `CreateTableDef` method and that name already exists for a table in the database, Access does not return an error. You receive an error, however, when you attempt to append the `TableDef` to the `TableDefs` collection.

Setting the new TableDefs source property

The next step is to supply the connection information by setting the `Connect` property.

```
tdfOrders.Connect = ";DATABASE=C:\MyDir\MyData.mdb"
```

The `Connect` property consists of two parts: the database type specifier and additional parameters (mainly the database path, but some ODBC data sources can have additional parameters). For databases created by Jet, the database type specifier is a zero-length string: "". If you are linking to tables from other data sources, you need to use the specifier listed in Table 20-2. In addition, if you are linking to a data source other than a Jet database, you need not supply the file name and extension; you supply only the path.

Table 20-2 Connect Property Database Specifiers

Database Type	*Specifier*	*Path*
Database using the Jet database engine	`"[database];"`	`"drive:\path\filename.mdb"`
dBASE III	`"dBASE III;"`	`"drive:\path"`
dBASE IV	`"dBASE IV;"`	`"drive:\path"`
dBASE 5	`"dBASE 5;"`	`"drive:\path"`
Paradox 3.x	`"Paradox 3.x;"`	`"drive:\path"`
Paradox 4.x	`"Paradox 4.x;"`	`"drive:\path"`
Paradox 5.x	`"Paradox 5.x;"`	`"drive:\path"`
FoxPro 2.0	`"FoxPro 2.0;"`	`"drive:\path"`
FoxPro 2.5	`"FoxPro 2.5;"`	`"drive:\path"`
FoxPro 2.6	`"FoxPro 2.6;"`	`"drive:\path"`
FoxPro 3.0	`"FoxPro 3.0;"`	`"drive:\path"`
Excel 3.0	`"Excel 3.0;"`	`"drive:\path\filename.xls"`
Excel 4.0	`"Excel 4.0;"`	`"drive:\path\filename.xls"`
Excel 5.0	`"Excel 5.0;"`	`"drive:\path\filename.xls"`
Excel 7.0	`"Excel 5.0;"`	`"drive:\path\filename.xls"`
Excel 8.0	`"Excel 8.0;"`	`"drive:\path\filename.xls"`
Excel 95	`"Excel 97;"`	`"drive:\path\filename.xls"`
HTML Import	`"HTML Import;"`	`"drive:\path\filename"`
HTML Export	`"HTML Export;"`	`"drive:\path\filename"`
Text	`"Text;"`	`"drive:\path"`

Note that both Excel 5.0 and Excel 7.0 spreadsheets use `'Excel 5.0'` as the specifier.

Specifying the source table name of the new TableDef

After setting the `Connect` property, you need to set the `SourceTableName` property. The `SourceTableName` is the actual name of the table as it is stored in the database in which it resides (the database you open with the `OpenDatabase` method). For example, if the table is called `Orders` in the source database, you set the `SourceTableName` property as follows:

```
tdfOrders.SourceTableName = "Orders"
```

Appending the new TableDef of the linked table

The final step to creating a link to an external table is to append the newly defined `TableDef` to the `TableDefs` collection. You accomplish this task by using the `Append` method of the `TableDefs` collection, as follows:

```
MyDB.TableDefs.Append tdfOrders
```

After you have appended the `TableDef` to the `TableDefs` collection of your database, the table shows up in the database window. Figure 20-31 shows a complete example of linking to an external FoxPro table by using VBA code.

If the current tab of the database window is the Tables tab showing the tables in your database, the newly linked table may not display immediately. To get the table to display, select another tab, such as the Forms tab, and then reselect the Tables tab to force Access to requery the `TableDef` collection and refresh the list of displayed tables.

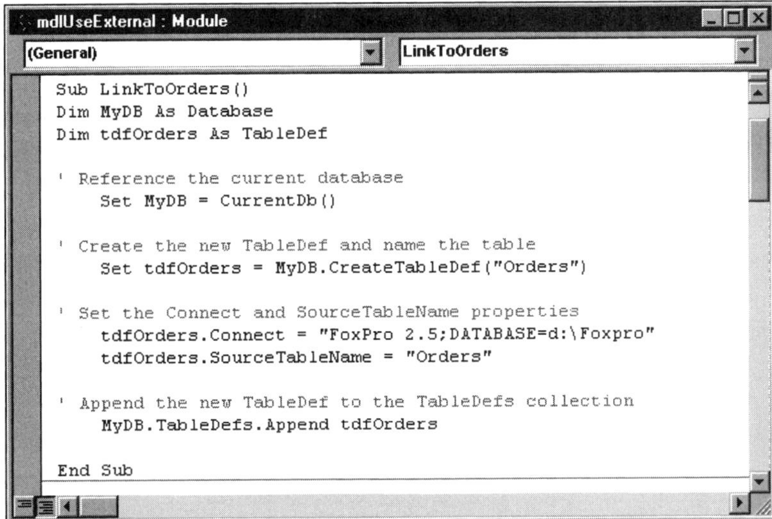

Figure 20-31: Linking to an external FoxPro table by using VBA code.

Using the optional parameters of the CreateTableDef method

When you are comfortable with setting the Connect and SourceTableName properties, you can save yourself a couple of lines of code by using the optional parameters of the CreateTableDef method. The full syntax for the CreateTableDef method is the following:

```
Set variable = database.CreateTableDef([name[, attributes[, source[, _
connect]]]])
```

The name attribute has been described previously; it is the name you want to assign to the linked table. You can omit the attributes argument, or it can be the sum of the Long integer constants listed in Table 20-3.

Table 20-3 CreateTableDef Attribute Constants

Constant	*Description*
dbAttachExclusive	For databases that use the Jet database engine; it indicates that the table is an attached table opened for exclusive use. You can set this constant on an appended TableDef object for a local table, but not for a remote table.
dbAttachSavePWD	For databases that use the Jet database engine; indicates that the user ID and password for the remotely attached table are saved with the connection information. You can set this constant on an appended TableDef object for a remote table, but not for a local table.
dbSystemObject	Indicates that the table is a system table provided by the Jet database engine. You can set this constant on an appended TableDef object.
dbHiddenObject	Indicates that the table is a hidden table provided by the Jet database engine. You can set this constant on an appended TableDef object.
dbAttachedTable	Indicates that the table is an attached table from a non-ODBC database, such as a Microsoft Jet or Paradox database (read-only).
dbAttachedODBC	Indicates that the table is an attached table from an ODBC database, such as Microsoft SQL Server (read-only).

For example, if you want to create a link to an external Jet table and you want the external table to be opened for exclusive use, you can use this line of code:

```
Set tdfOrders = MyDB.CreateTableDef("Orders", dbAttachExclusive)
```

Supplying a source parameter is the same as setting the `SourceTableName` property. For example, if you want to omit the line of code to set the `SourceTableName` property, you can specify the table name in the source argument of the `CreateTableDef` method, as follows:

```
Set tdfOrders = MyDB.CreateTableDef("Orders", 0, "Orders")
```

This example happens to use the same name for the linked table as the original name of the table in the source database, but you can specify a different name if you want.

Specifying a connect argument is the same as setting the `Connect` property of the `TableDef`. Therefore, you can create the new `TableDef` in the following manner:

```
Dim MyDB as DATABASE, tdfOrders as TableDef
Set MyDB = CurrentDB()

Set tdfOrders = MyDB.CreateTableDef("Linked Jet Table")
tdfOrders.Connect = ";DATABASE=C:\MyDir\MyData.mdb"
tdfOrders.SourceTableName = "Orders"

MyDB.TableDefs.Append tdfOrders
```

Alternatively, you can use the optional parameters of the `CreateTableDef` method and create the `TableDef` as follows:

```
Dim MyDB as DATABASE, tdfOrders as TableDef
Set MyDB = CurrentDB()

Set tdfOrders = MyDB.CreateTableDef("Linked Jet Table", 0,  _
   "Orders",";DATABASE=C:\MyDir\MyData.mdb")

MyDB.TableDefs.Append tdfOrders
```

Secret

If you do not want to supply attribute parameters but you want to provide connect information, you must enter a `0` for the attribute argument. Unlike most optional parameters in VBA methods, if you simply leave the argument blank, you will get an error. The error doesn't occur when you create the `TableDef` but rather when you attempt to append it to the `TableDefs` collection (see Figure 20-32). Take a good look at it and remember it if you plan on linking a large number of tables by using VBA code.

Refreshing links

Regardless of how you link your tables, whether you opt to link them using the menus or link them through VBA code, you need to enable your application to fix broken links. Links are broken when the source database containing the linked tables is moved to a different location.

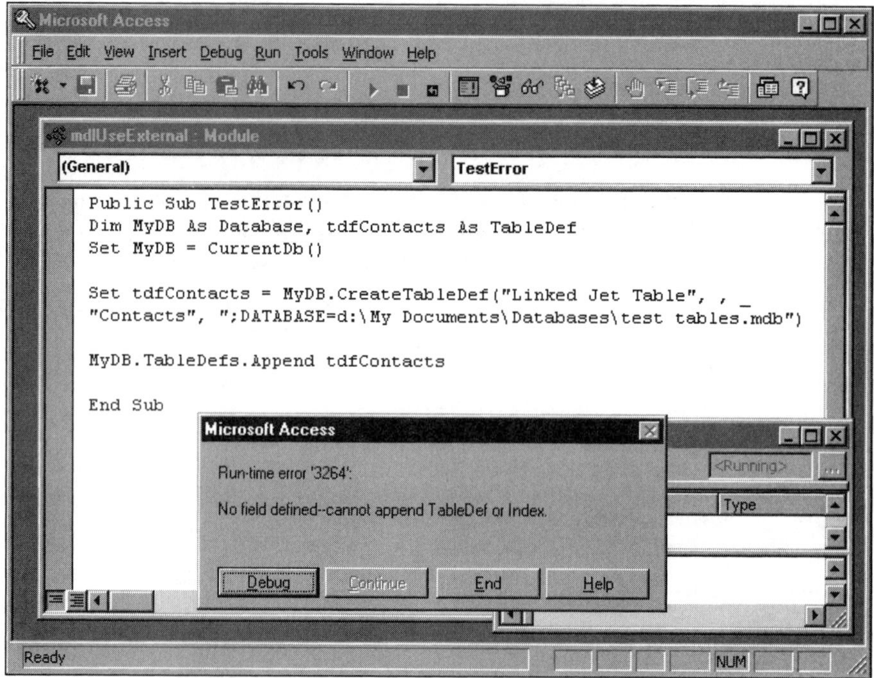

Figure 20-32: Without knowing that you must supply an attribute value of 0 rather than omit the parameter, you could spend hours trying to track this misleading error.

To refresh a link, follow these steps:

1. Set the `Connect` property to the new path.
2. Refresh the link by using the `Refresh` method of the `TableDef` object.

Refreshing a link is a fairly straightforward process. To make your application as friendly to the user as possible, however, your code should do the following:

- Detect when links are broken.
- Prompt the user for the new location of the source database.
- Refresh the links.

Detecting when a link is broken

One of the first things your application should do on start-up is to verify the links used in your application. Most often, you will link to a number of tables contained in one external database. When this situation is the case, it is usually sufficient to test the link of just one of the linked tables. If that link is broken, chances are that all the links to tables in that database are broken. Likewise, if the link is still sound, the other links should be sound as well.

To test the validity of a link, you simply attempt to reference a property of the `TableDef` of the linked table and trap any errors that occur. Suppose that the following error occurs:

```
Error 3265 - Item not found in this collection
```

This error indicates that you have lost your link. You can use the procedure in Figure 20-33 to test the validity of any link.

To use this procedure, simply pass the table name you want to test to the function, as in the following:

```
Dim bResult as Boolean
bResult = TestLink("Contacts")
```

The function returns `True` if the link is valid and `False` if the connection has been broken. If your application contains links to tables from multiple data sources, you should need to test only the link of one table per external database.

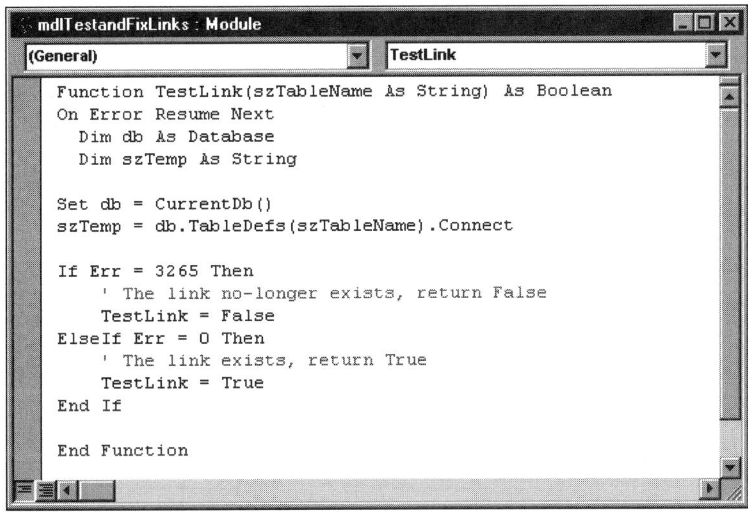

Figure 20-33: You can use the TestLink procedure to test the validity of any table's link.

Getting the new location of the linked tables

After you have determined that a link is broken, you need to find the new location of the external database. One way to find this information is to display a File dialog box and let your application's users point to the new location of the data. You may even decide to write code to search through the users' available drives in an attempt to locate the file. How you decide to retrieve the new location of the external database is up to you.

If you programmatically relocate the data, you may want to store the location of the external tables in a private .INI file or in the Windows registry. Then, if your application detects a broken link, it can retrieve the new location of the database and reestablish the links without any intervention from your users.

Refreshing the links

After you have found the new location of the external database of the broken link, you can reestablish the connection. To fix the broken link, you need to set the connect information, using the new location, and then trigger the `RefreshLink` method to relink the table. Figure 20-34 shows a procedure that you can use in your own code to reestablish any broken link.

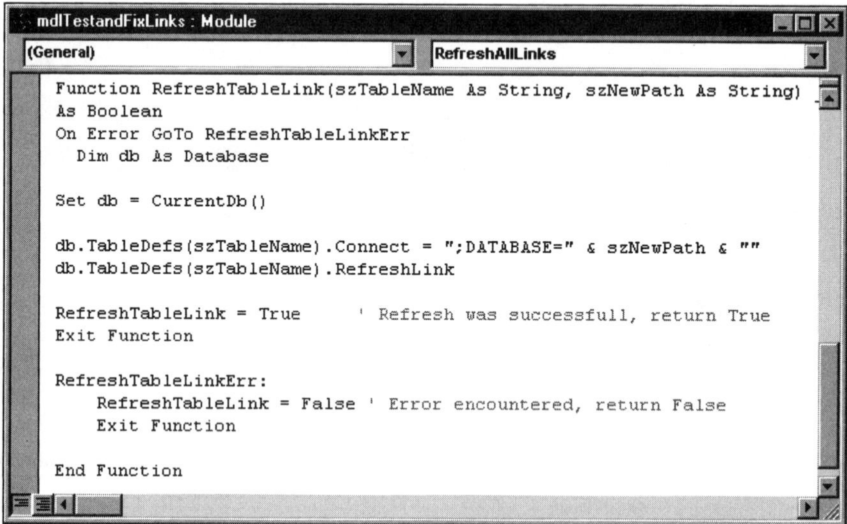

mdlTestandFixLinks : Module
(General)
RefreshAllLinks
Function RefreshTableLink(szTableName As String, szNewPath As String) _
As Boolean
On Error GoTo RefreshTableLinkErr
Dim db As Database
Set db = CurrentDb()
db.TableDefs(szTableName).Connect = ";DATABASE=" & szNewPath & ""
db.TableDefs(szTableName).RefreshLink
RefreshTableLink = True ' Refresh was successfull, return True
Exit Function
RefreshTableLinkErr:
RefreshTableLink = False ' Error encountered, return False
Exit Function
End Function

Figure 20-34: A small but flexible procedure to refresh a table's broken link.

To use this function to reestablish a broken link, you call the function passing it both the table name and the new path of the source database, as shown here:

```
Dim bResult as Boolean
bResult = RefreshTableLink "Mailing
List","c:\mydocu~1\access~1\testta~1.mdb"
```

The preceding line refreshes the link for the table `"Mailing List"` in the source database `"c:\mydocu~1\access~1\testta~1.mdb"`.

To refresh all broken links at one time, you need to move through the TableDefs collection one TableDef at a time and verify each connection. Code listing 20-2 shows a function that carries out this task. This function accepts a new path and file name and assumes that all TableDefs with broken links reside in the specified source database.

Listing 20-2 Refreshing Broken Links One at a Time

```
Sub RefreshAllLinks(szNewPath As String)
On Error Resume Next
Dim db As Database, iCount As Integer, tblDef As TableDef

Set db = CurrentDb()

For iCount = 0 To db.TableDefs.Count - 1
    Set tblDef = db.TableDefs(iCount)
    If tblDef.Connect <> "" Then
        tblDef.Connect = ";DATABASE=" & szNewPath
        Err = 0
        tblDef.RefreshLink
        If Err <> 0 Then
            If Err = 3011 Then                    ' Nonexistent table
                MsgBox "File does not contain required table '" &
tblDef.SourceTableName & "'", 16, "Refresh Error"
            ElseIf Err = 3024 Then                ' DATA.MDB not _
found
                MsgBox "Specified source database and path not _
found!", 16,
"Refresh Error"
            ElseIf Err = 3051 Then                ' Access denied
                MsgBox "Couldn't open source file (may be read- _
only).", 16,
"Refresh Error"
            ElseIf Err = 3027 Then               ' DATA.MDB is read- _
only
                MsgBox "Can't Refresh Links because source is read- _
only.",
16, "Refresh Error"
            End If
            Exit Sub
        End If
    End If
Next iCount

MsgBox "All Links were refreshed!", 64, "Refresh Successful"

End Sub
```

To call this function, you need to pass it the new source location and file name, as follows:

```
RefreshallLinks "c:\mydocu~1\testta~1.mdb"
```

If you have links to tables in different source databases, this code won't work. Most of your applications, however, probably link to tables in only one external database. If this is the case, this procedure works like a charm.

Referencing linked tables in VBA code

One thing that you need to take into consideration when linking to external tables is that although they show up in the database window, the tables do not actually reside in your application. Because they reside in the external database and not in your application, the following code doesn't work:

```
Dim db As DATABASE
Dim rst As Recordset

Set db = CurrentDb()
Set rst = db.OpenRecordset("tblContacts")
```

If you run this code and `tblContacts` is a linked table, you receive an `error 3024, Couldn't find file XXX`. If you anticipate manipulating your linked tables often by using VBA code, create a global variable called `dbAttachedData` of type `DATABASE`, as follows:

```
Global AttachedData As DATABASE
```

Then, in your initialization procedure, set this variable to point to the external data source, as in the following:

```
Set AttachedData = OpenDatabase("c:\mydocu~1\access~1\testta~1.mdb")
```

Now, whenever you need to manipulate the table by using VBA code, you substitute `AttachedData` for `CurrentDB`, as in the example in Figure 20-35.

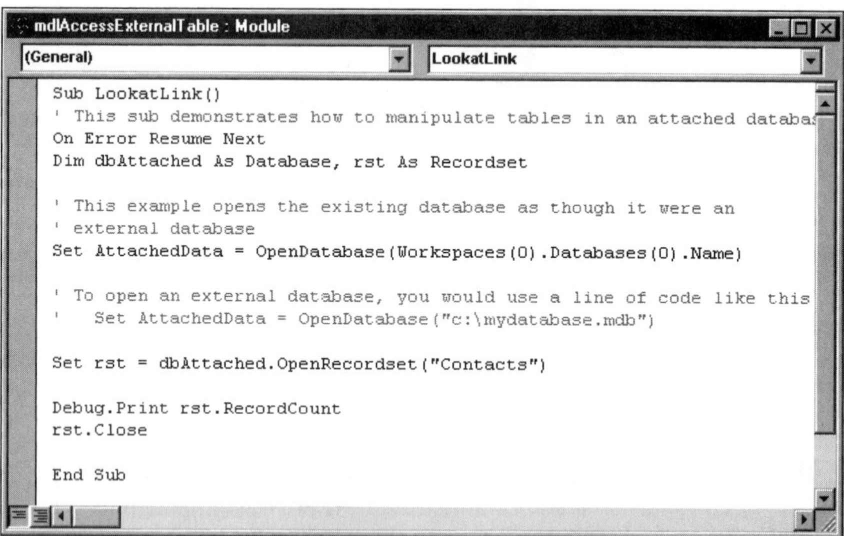

Figure 20-35: To work with an external database in code, you must reference the external database, not the current database (CurrentDB).

Removing links

You can remove a physical link in one of two ways:

- Select the table in the database window and press the Delete key
- Delete the TableDef in VBA code, using the `Delete` method of the `TableDefs` object

Links remain active until you delete the `TableDef` object from the `TableDefs` collection or move the source table. Even if you move the source table, however, the links still show up in the database window. The easiest way to remove a link is to delete the link just as you delete an ordinary table: by selecting it in the database window and pressing the Delete key. If you want to delete a link in VBA code, use the `Delete` method of the `TableDefs` collection, as follows:

```
MyDB.TableDefs.Delete "My Linked Table"
```

Creating a table in an external database

You can create tables in external databases through VBA code in the same manner you create them in your application: by using the `OpenDatabase` and `CreateTableDef` methods.

First, you need to open the external data source and perform the `CreateTableDef` method on the open database, as in the following:

```
Dim MyDB as DATABASE, tdfContacts as TableDef, TempField as Field
Set MyDB=DBEngine.Workspaces(0).OpenDatabase ("C:\data\MyData.mdb")
Set tdfContacts = MyDB.CreateTableDef("tblContacts")
```

A `TableDef` must contain at least one field before you can append it to the `TableDefs` collection. You can add fields to the `TableDef` by using the `CreateField` and `Append` methods, as shown here:

```
Set TempField = tdfContacts.CreateField("FirstName", dbText, 15)
tdfContacts.Fields.Append TempField
```

After you have defined a valid `TableDef`, you can append it to the `TableDefs` collection of the external database just as you do if you are appending it to your current database, as follows:

```
MyDB.TableDefs.Append tdfContacts
```

For clarity, here is the entire set of code to create the new table in the external database c:\data\MyData.mdb:

```
Set MyDB=DBEngine.Workspaces(0).OpenDatabase ("C:\data\MyData.mdb")
Set tdfContacts = MyDB.CreateTableDef("tblContacts")
Set TempField = tdfContacts.CreateField("FirstName", dbText, 15)
tdfContacts.Fields.Append TempField
MyDB.TableDefs.Append tdfContacts
```

Increasing linking performance

When you link external data in your application, you incur a slight performance penalty. This penalty is usually outweighed by the benefits gained by linking tables, and on small to medium tables the performance hit may be very small. However, you can do a few things to squeeze a little more performance out of your linked tables.

When using the `OpenRecordset` method to create snapshots of external data, use the `dbForwardOnly` switch if you plan to make only one forward pass through the data. This setting can help speed up your code, but here are a few caveats when writing procedures that use `dbForwardOnly` snapshots:

- You cannot use the `Bookmark` property.
- The following methods become unavailable for the Recordset: `Clone`, `FindFirst`, `FindLast`, `FindNext`, `MoveFirst`, `MoveLast`, `MovePrevious`, `OpenRecordset`, and `Move` (with any value other than `1`).

Also, if you're using a linked table on a network or in an SQL database, follow these guidelines whenever possible:

- View only the data you need.
- Use filters or queries to limit the number of records that you view in a form or datasheet. This way, Microsoft Access can transfer less data over the network.
- In queries that involve linked tables, avoid using functions in query criteria. Specifically, domain aggregate functions such as `DSum` cause Access to retrieve all the data in the linked table to execute the query.
- If you often add records to a linked table, create a form for adding records that has the `DataEntry` property set to `Yes`. When you open the form to enter new data, Access doesn't display any existing records and therefore doesn't need to retrieve all the records in the linked table.
- Avoid locking records longer than necessary when accessing shared tables on a network.

Working with HTML files

All of the Microsoft Office 97 applications have new features for dealing with the Internet, and Access 97 is no exception. Access now allows you to work with Hypertext Markup Language (HTML) files, the standard file format for creating web pages. HTML files are definitions containing everything necessary to display a web page, including text formatting and graphic placement. Web browsers such as Internet Explorer interpret HTML files to display web pages. You can link to HTML files or open them directly. Even though HTML files are handled in a similar manner as other text file formats, there are some unique issues involved with using HTML files.

Access cannot understand everything in an HTML file, but it can work with tabular information stored in the HTML file. Tabular data tables are embedded into HTML files with the <TD> and </TD> tags. For the most part, Access treats HTML files as it does text files; it uses the Text ISAM driver to access the HTML file.

How Access interprets data types, embedded images, hyperlinks

Actually Access doesn't really decide how to interpret the information in an HTML file, the Text installable ISAM driver used to access the HTML file does. Because of the way the ISAM driver decides a cell's data type, you may not always get the results you are hoping for. The ISAM driver scans all of the cells in a table, and assigns to each cell the data type that occurs most frequently for a cell. The driver then sets all cells that do not have data type that matches the majority data type (if there are any) to `Null`. Fortunately, the Text installable ISAM driver is smart enough to assign a `Long` or `Double` data type based on the data in numeric cells. If you want to control how the driver handles field data types, you can create a Schema.ini file (discussed earlier in this chapter) for the HTML file.

If the first row of the table in the HTML file contains field names, you may want to create a custom Schema.ini file because the ISAM driver always treats the table as though the first row does not contain field names. This may not pose a problem in some tables.

HTML documents can have graphics embedded into tables, referenced with the HTML `<IMG SRC ...>` tag. The Text installable ISAM driver is unable to read the graphics in this tag. If there is text within the cell with the graphic, the driver reads the text. If there is only the graphic and no text, the information in the cell is ignored.

Graphics may also be referenced in tables as hyperlinks with the `<A HREF-"...">TEXT</A>` tag. If there is no embedded text, the ISAM driver reads the hyperlink caption. If there is embedded text with the hyperlink, the ISAM driver ignores the hyperlink and reads the embedded text.

How Access interprets embedded lists and tables

Again, Access does not really decide how to handle embedded lists and tables, the Text installable ISAM driver used to access the HTML file does. HTML files can have lists or tables embedded into cells of other tables. If the ISAM driver encounters a list embedded within the cell of a table, it treats the list as one big text string with each item separated by a carriage return and line feed. If the ISAM driver encounters a table embedded within the cell of another table, it treats it as its own table and sets the cell in the parent table that contains the embedded table to `Null`.

Opening HTML files using VBA code

Opening HTML files is similar to opening text files in VBA code. You dimension a database object and use the `OpenDatabase` function, passing it the path and file name of the HTML file. The only difference between opening a text file and opening an HTML file is the data source specifier: `'HTML Import'` vs. `'Text'`.

There are a few constraints to opening HTML files directly:

- When opening an HTML file from a server, the Text installable ISAM driver creates a copy of the HTML file on the local workstation. The copy on the local workstation is the actual HTML file that Access uses, not the original on the server.
- Because you are working with a copy of the HTML file, the HTML data you view is a snapshot of the data created at the time you opened the HTML file. Any updates performed to the original HTML file will not show up in your snapshot; you must create a new snapshot by opening the HTML file again.
- You can only open HTML files as read-only; you cannot add or modify any of the data in the HTML table.

Tip

If you need to change the information in an HTML table, open the HTML information as a Recordset, save the Recordset contents to a native table within your database, make the necessary changes to the table, then export the table as a new HTML file. When Access exports information to an HTML file, it creates the minimum information necessary to make the file a valid HTML file. You will need to use an HTML authoring tool to merge the new HTML table into your existing HTML file.

When you reference a Recordset within an HTML file, you must give it a name. The name of the file is determined by one of the following:

- If the table within the HTML file has a caption, that caption is the table name.
- If the table does not have a caption and it is the only table within the HTML file, the title of the HTML document is the table name.
- If more than one table exists and none has a caption, the name of each table is prefixed with `'Table'`, with the suffix determined by the sequence of the table. For example, the second table in an HTML file would be called Table2.

The following code opens an HTML file and creates a Recordset from the HTML file:

```
Public Sub OpenHTMLFile()
Dim db As Database, rs As Recordset

Set db = OpenDatabase("http://www.imc.com/prodinfo/proda.html", _
False, False, "HTML Import;")

Set rs = db.OpenRecordset("Product Information")

End Sub
```

Linking to HTML files

Linking to HTML files is also similar to linking to ordinary text files (see "Creating links to external data," earlier in this chapter).

Chapter 21

Working with Client/Server Databases

In This Chapter

- Setting up ODBC data sources
- Creating links to ODBC data sources
- Linking with data access objects
- Linking queries to ODBC data sources
- Using SQL PassThrough queries
- Accessing remote stored procedures
- Capturing multiple result sets from stored procedures
- Using CacheSize, CacheStart, and FillCache
- ODBC and the Registry
- Managing connections
- Using transactions
- Exploring the MSysConf table
- Exploring ODBCDirect

The Access databases and many other ISAM-format databases accessed through the Jet database engine reside in *file server* type architectures. The engine that provides access to the database in response to an application's request for data services runs on the same machine as the application.

Even if the tables an application uses are located in a database on a remote machine over a network, the access to those tables is performed as though the tables were local to the requesting database application. All requests for table properties, selects, and updates travel over the network from Jet, sitting on the local machine. The remote machine provides file services so that the database file can be accessed remotely but provides no other facility for database processing. Recordsets then have no query compilation, no query execution, and no management performed on them at the server. As far as the remote machine is concerned, your .MDB file is just another file.

Another architecture in which databases reside is known as *client/server.* In this architecture, the database and the engine that provides the data services for the database are located on a machine in a network, and the application requesting data services resides on another machine in the network. This application is referred to as the *client* application; the data services engine is called the *server* application.

With client/server architecture, requests such as query compilation and execution are performed on the server machine by the data services engine, and the results are provided over the network to the requesting or client application.

Client/server provides a more efficient operation in that the amount of network traffic required to perform a particular database request is significantly less than the same request performed in a file server environment.

Examples of database systems that operate as client/server architectures are Microsoft SQL Server and Oracle. These products provide engines that run on network servers to access databases on those servers, and they provide libraries that client applications can use to request services from the remote engines.

Microsoft Jet provides access to these client/server database engines through a facility known as Microsoft Open Database Connectivity (ODBC).

ODBC provides an application program interface (API) that enables applications to work with databases for which an ODBC driver is available. The drivers translate ODBC API calls into the native language the database engine understands.

The ODBC API calls can be made by applications written in C or C++ or even by VBA applications. Jet uses ODBC and its associated drivers to access databases such as Microsoft SQL Server either directly or as attached tables. The architecture shown in Figure 21-1 enables Jet to mix databases of different types, including client/server databases, to provide a flexible data environment for your application.

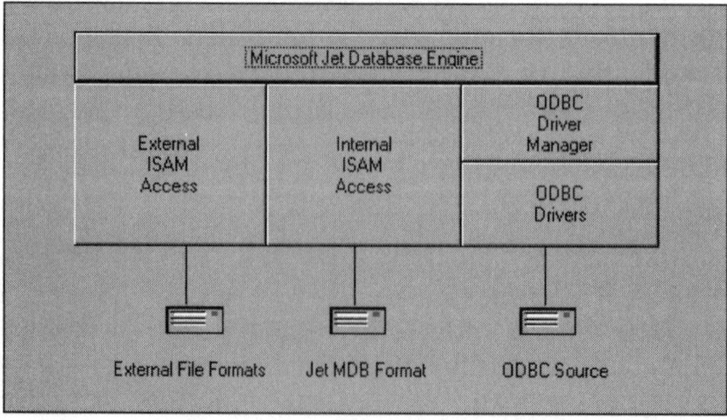

Figure 21-1: The Jet engine architecture provides access to an environment composed of different types of databases, including client/server databases accessed through ODBC.

This chapter looks at two technologies for accessing databases through ODBC. The first is Jet-connected ODBC, and the second is a new technique in Access 97 called ODBCDirect. The examples in this chapter use the pubs database that ships with Microsoft SQL Server 6.5.

Setting Up an ODBC Data Source

Before you can access SQL Server or any other ODBC data source from your Access database, you must provide information to enable a connection to the server. The information Jet needs to establish this connection can be provided by the use of DAO coding, the Control Panel ODBC Setup applet, or a combination of these methods.

To use the Control Panel applet to set up an SQL Server ODBC data source, open the Control Panel folder and double-click on the ODBC icon (see Figure 21-2).

Figure 21-2: The Windows 95 Control Panel contains the 32bit ODBC Administrator applet.

The User DSN Tab lists the data sources that are already defined, as shown in Figure 21-3. You can use this tab to edit an existing setup and to remove or add a data source.

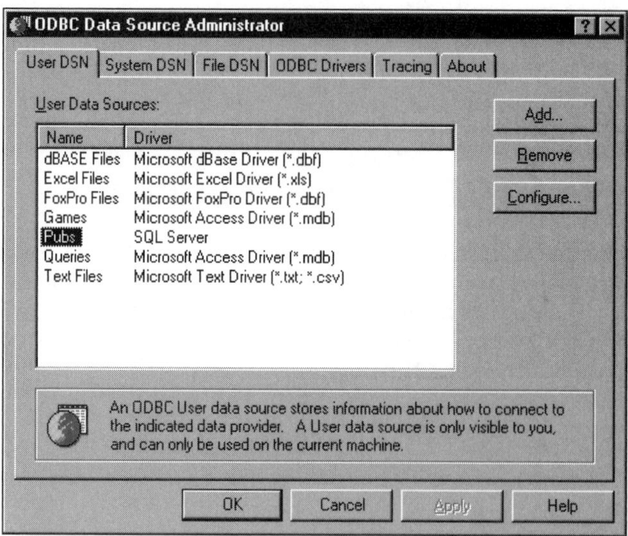

Figure 21-3: The User DSN tab of the ODBC Data Source Administrator dialog box enables you to manage data sources on your machine.

Click on the Add button to add a data source to the list. This action displays the Create New Data Source dialog box, as shown in Figure 21-4.

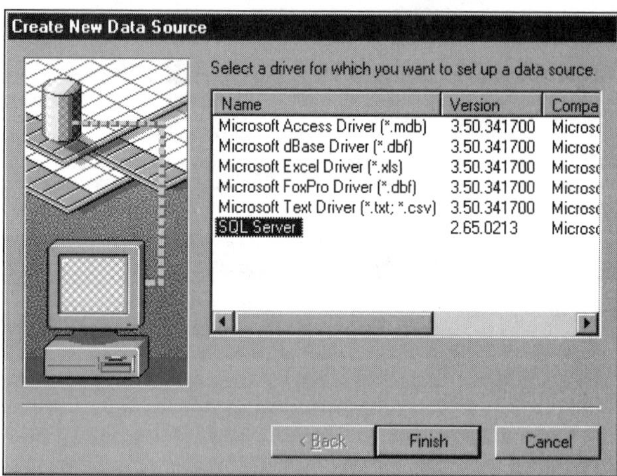

Figure 21-4: Add a new data source by selecting a driver previously installed.

The installed ODBC drivers list box lists the drivers you can use from your Access application database to access databases of the designated type. Note that the list in Figure 21-4 contains drivers for databases that Jet can access without the ODBC driver. Jet can access FoxPro databases, for example, directly through its ISAM drivers. It doesn't require an ODBC data source for this type of database; in fact, you cannot link to these types of databases through an ODBC data source. If you link these ISAM type databases in your Access database, choose their type directly in the Link dialog box. Do *not* choose ODBC as the type of database to link.

Choose SQL Server from the list of installed drivers and click on Finish. This action displays the ODBC SQL Server Setup dialog box, as shown in Figure 21-5.

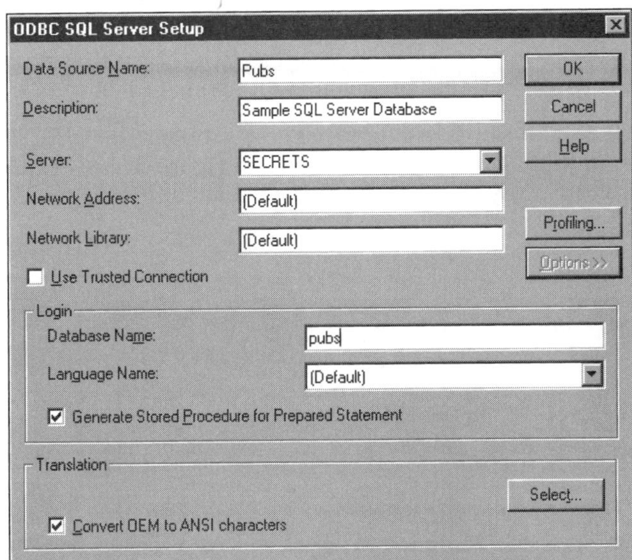

Figure 21-5: The ODBC SQL Server Setup dialog box.

Type a meaningful name for the data source in the Data Source Name text box, and enter a description of the data source in the Description text box.

In the Server drop-down list box, select or type the name of the server on which SQL Server is installed. The name (local) indicates that the server is the local machine on which Setup is running.

The Network Address box specifies the location of SQL Server. The form of the specification depends on the type of network and the net library you are using. If you are using the TCP/IP protocol, for example, this address is specified as an `IP-address,port`, as in `165.114.47.26,250`.

In the Network Library text box, specify the name of the SQL Server Net-Library the driver will use to communicate with the network. In the case of Microsoft SQL Server, you can leave these values as (Default).

You may also specify the database you want to associate with this data source name by clicking on the Options button and entering the database name in the Database Name text box. Because the examples in this chapter use the pubs database that ships as a sample database with SQL Server, `pubs` was entered as the database name.

Selecting the Generate Stored Procedure for Prepared Statement checkbox causes the SQL Server driver to create stored procedures for prepared statements. Using this option can be a benefit if you use the statements frequently in your application session. If this checkbox is cleared, the statement you send to SQL Server is prepared and executed on demand but is not stored as a stored procedure. Later in this chapter, you see how to cause queries to be prepared and saved as temporary stored procedures through the use of certain options in creating Recordsets and Querydefs.

Click on OK to add the data source. This step opens the ODBC Data Source Administrator dialog box again, as shown in Figure 21-3. Click the ODBC Drivers tab to display information about installed drivers, as shown in Figure 21-6.

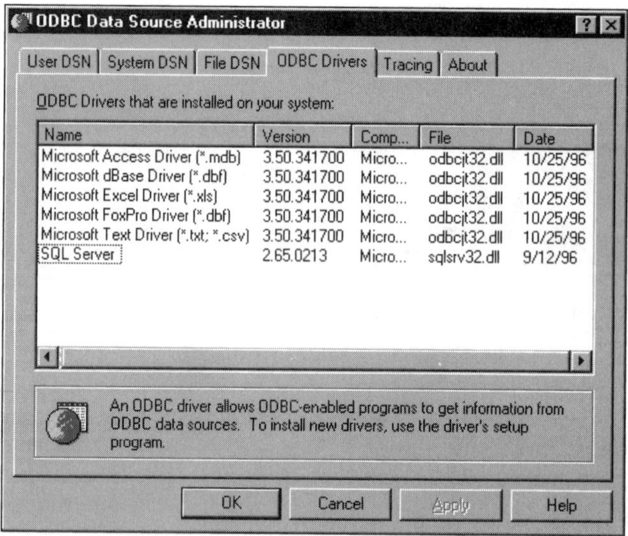

Figure 21-6: The ODBC Drivers tab displays information about installed ODBC drivers.

You can have the ODBC calls that Jet makes written to a log file by clicking on the Tracing tab and putting a check in the All the time checkbox or the One-time only checkbox (see Figure 21-7).

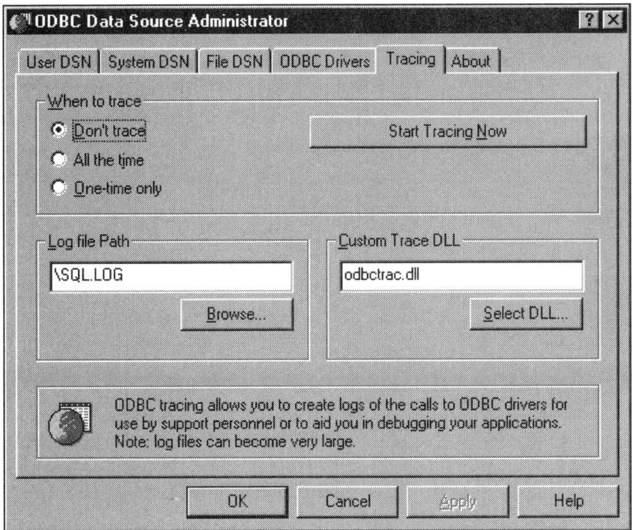

Figure 21-7: You can force the ODBC Driver Manager to trace the ODBC calls made by Jet to a file you can browse later.

When tracing is enabled, the ODBC Driver Manager writes to the file you specify in the Log file Path text box the ODBC calls made by any application. The default SQL.LOG file name is created in the root directory.

If you put a check in the One-time only checkbox, the trace is turned off after the ODBC Driver Manager detects the termination of the next connection. This option traces only the next connection.

The resulting data source is stored in the Registry under the HKEY_CURRENT_USER root directory as a user data source, as shown in Figure 21-8. The ODBC Data Sources subkey lists the data sources you see in the Data Sources list box on the User DSN tab. The data source details are listed in the subkey named after the data source name.

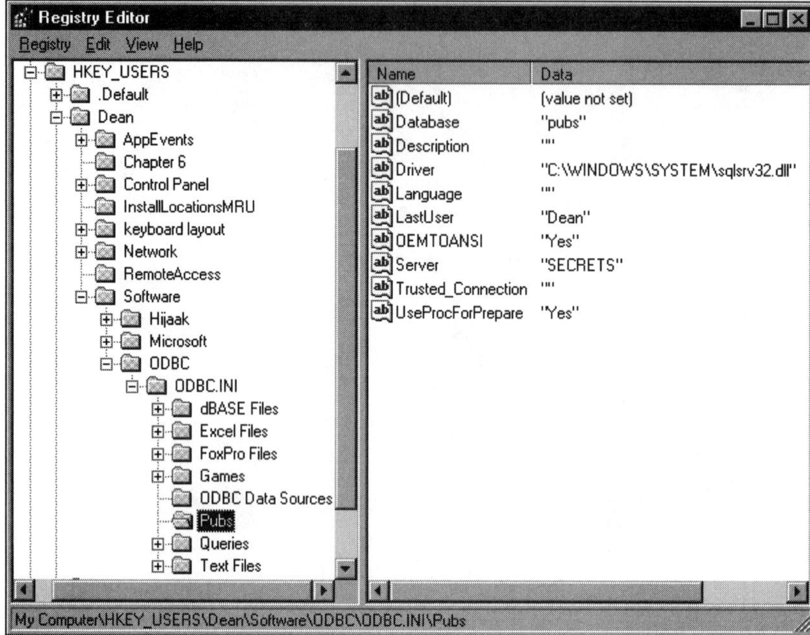

Figure 21-8: The Pubs data source as it appears in the Registry.

Linking to an ODBC Data Source

After defining your ODBC data source, you can refer to it when you link the tables and views located in the database the data source represents.

In Access, open your database that will contain the linked tables and choose Get External Data/Link Tables from the File menu.

In the Link dialog box, choose ODBC Databases from the Files of Type drop-down list. This step displays the Select Data Source dialog box, which contains a list of existing data sources. You should see in the list the data source you set up. The Pubs data source established in the preceding section appears in the list, as shown in Figure 21-9. Choose the data source you want to use and click on OK. If you click on the New button, you can set up a new ODBC data source, as you did with the Control Panel applet.

When you click on OK after choosing your data source, you are prompted for user and password information if the database requires a login, as shown in Figure 21-10. The login is necessary here because Access must obtain a list of tables and views from the external database so that you can choose which ones you want to link to your Access database.

After successfully logging in to the database, you see the Link Tables dialog box, as shown in Figure 21-11. Choose the tables you want to link and click on OK.

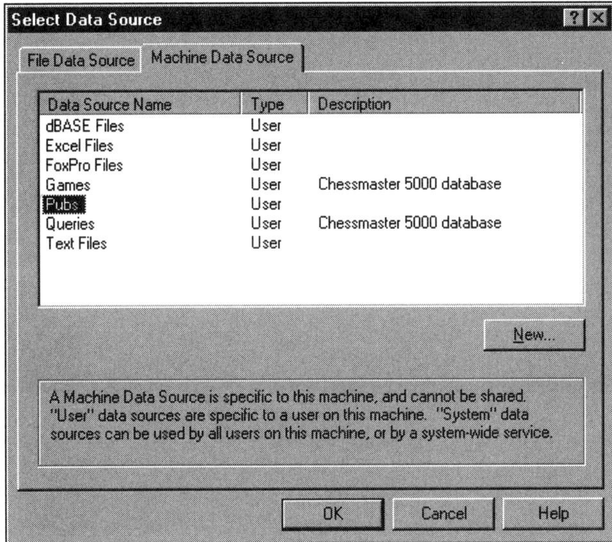

Figure 21-9: The Select Data Source dialog box lists the data sources you can use to link external tables.

Figure 21-10: Supplying your user ID and password information.

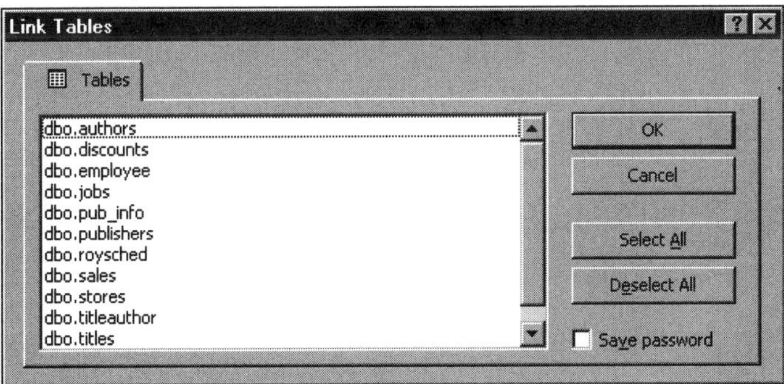

Figure 21-11: Choose the tables you want to link to your Access database and click on OK to establish the links.

Linking with DAO

Look at the Connect property of a table linked through the Access menus. You can look at this property by using DAO code or by opening one of the tables in Design mode and looking at Table Properties. The Description field in the Table Properties dialog box holds a copy of the Connect property, as follows:

```
Dim dbDatabase As DATABASE
   Dim tblTabledef As TableDef
   Set dbDatabase = DBEngine.Workspaces(0).Databases(0)
   Set tblTabledef = dbDatabase.TableDefs(txtTable.Value)
   txtConnect.Value = tblTabledef.Connect
   dbDatabase.Close
```

The Connect string for the dbo.authors table in the Pubs database looks like this:

```
ODBC;DSN=Pubs;APP=Microsoft Access;WSID=SECRETS;DATABASE=pubs
```

Connect strings for ODBC databases have this general form:

```
object.Connect = [ODBC;[ DSN=datasourcename _
;DATABASE=defaultdatabase; UID=user; PWD=password; _
LOGINTIMEOUT=seconds]]
```

The ODBC specification is the only parameter required for the Connect property to function as a link to an ODBC source. If you don't provide enough information in the connect string at the time the connection is attempted, you are prompted for the missing data. If the DATABASE parameter was specified in the Data Source setup named with the Data Source Name (DSN) parameter, you do not need to specify it in the connect string. Passing the user ID in the UID parameter and the associated password in the PWD parameter prevents the Login dialog box from being displayed as long as they are valid at the database.

The following code uses a partial Connect string to indicate that the new TableDef being defined is a linked table in an ODBC data source. The name of the table in the ODBC database is "dbo.sales"; in the Access database, it is called "dao_Remote_Sales".

```
Dim dbDatabase As DATABASE
   Dim tblTabledef As TableDef
   Dim strConnect As String
   strConnect = "ODBC;"
   Set dbDatabase = DBEngine.Workspaces(0).Databases(0)
   Set tblTabledef = dbDatabase.CreateTableDef("dao_Remote_Sales")
   tblTabledef.Connect = strConnect
   tblTabledef.SourceTableName = "dbo.sales"
   dbDatabase.TableDefs.Append tblTabledef
   dbDatabase.Close
```

When the new `TableDef` is appended to the `TableDefs` collection, you are prompted to select or create a data source in the SQL Data Sources dialog box and log in to the data source database. The linked table then appears in your Access Database window.

The user ID you use to log in to the ODBC database must have the proper permissions assigned to it in order to use the table or view you are attempting to link to. If a user doesn't have permission to access the table, the link attempt succeeds, but the user cannot open the table.

Refreshing links

You realize the benefit of creating linked tables in your Access database when you have Jet evaluate a query involving the remote data source. Having the information about the linked table cached locally in the database eliminates the need for Jet to request this information from the remote database. The local information speeds up Jet's query compilation and reduces network traffic.

Although it's not likely that an established remote database's objects will have their structure changed often, if they do, you have to refresh your links either manually, as discussed earlier, or in code, as follows:

```
On Error GoTo RefLnkErrHandler
Dim tblTabledef As TableDef
Dim Ndx As Integer
Set dbDatabase = DBEngine.Workspaces(0).Databases(0)
For Ndx = 0 To dbDatabase.TableDefs.Count - 1
    Set tblTabledef = dbDatabase.TableDefs(Ndx)
    If tblTabledef.Connect <> "" Then
        tblTabledef.RefreshLink
    End If
Next Ndx
dbDatabase.Close
Exit Sub
RefLnkErrHandler:
 MsgBox Err.Description
 Exit Sub
```

If the links to the changed objects are not refreshed after an object is changed (a column name change in a table, for example), you get an ODBC call failure when you attempt to access the linked object. Refreshing the link causes Jet to retrieve the new object attributes into the local database.

Linking Queries to an ODBC Data Source

In addition to linking a TableDef to a remote database, you can use the QueryDef's `Connect` property in a similar manner to link the query to a remote database. Using the QueryDef `Connect` property in this manner creates an SQLPassThrough query.

The QueryDef's `Connect` property provides Jet with the same information provided by the `Connect` property of a TableDef. It points to a remote data source to which Jet sends the query contained in the QueryDef.

The query contained in the `SQL` property of the QueryDef must be specified in the syntax of the remote database engine because Jet does not parse an SQLPassThrough query. It sends the query directly to the remote engine.

The use of an SQLPassThrough query has some benefits and limitations of which you should be aware. These are discussed in the following section.

Understanding SQLPassThrough Queries

A Recordset created from a static SQL string or a QueryDef against a linked table behaves in much the same way as a Recordset created from a local table. You can create dynasets and snapshots from linked tables, but you cannot open a Table-type Recordset against a linked table, whether or not it's an ODBC source. Use the following code:

```
Dim dbDatabase As DATABASE
   Dim rsRecordset As Recordset
   Dim qryQueryDef As QueryDef
   Set dbDatabase = DBEngine.Workspaces(0).Databases(0)
   ' ** The following results in an Invalid Operation error on the _
attached Customer table.
   'Set rsRecordset = dbDatabase.OpenRecordset("Customer", _
dbOpenTable)
   ' ** But using the following statement opens recordset as dynaset _
type by default.
   Set rsRecordset = dbDatabase.OpenRecordset("Customer")
```

Queries referencing the linked tables usually use an SQL syntax that Jet understands. Jet either executes the stored QueryDef SQL against the linked data source or parses and executes the static SQL string passed as an argument to the `OpenRecordset` method. In the case of an ODBC data source, Jet parses the SQL syntax and formats a request to the data source via the ODBC driver.

Jet offers another method of accessing data in the ODBC data source using the SQL syntax of the remote data source: SQLPassThrough.

When you're using an SQLPassThrough query, Jet doesn't bother to parse the SQL — it passes the statement to the remote database engine for it to figure out. If the remote engine likes the query, it executes it; otherwise, an ODBC error is returned. Not much different from Jet's parsing.

Like Jet's capability to execute stored QueryDefs, most database engines support the capability to store and execute a previously defined query. In SQL Server and other engines, these stored queries, called *stored procedures,* can often end up looking like entire BASIC programs, as in SQL Server's Transact-SQL language.

To create an SQLPassThrough query in Access, click on the New button on the Query tab in the Database window. Choose Design View and then click on Cancel to exit from the dialog box that asks you to choose a table.

Select the Query menu and then choose PassThrough from the SQL Specific pop-up menu. This step hides the Query Design window and displays the SQL edit window. Type your SQL statement in this window according to the syntax of the remote data source.

Click on the Properties button on the toolbar and note that the ODBC connect string contains only the ODBC specification. If you leave this connect string as is, you get a prompt for the data source when you run the query. To prevent this prompt from being displayed, add the data source to the connect string. In the Pubs example, you add `DSN=Pubs` after the semicolon that follows ODBC, as follows:

```
ODBC;DSN=Pubs
```

The pass-through query defaults to Returns Records. If your query doesn't return records, set the `Returns Records` property to `No`.

Close the SQL edit window and give the query a name in the Save As dialog box.

The code behind the ODBC Recordsets button on the Connect Lab form in CH21.MDB on the CD-ROM in the back of this book shows several examples of Recordsets created from an ODBC data source (the Pubs data source you created earlier in this chapter, in the section "Setting Up an ODBC Data Source").

One of these examples creates an SQLPassThrough QueryDef and uses it to create a snapshot Recordset. One of the limitations of SQLPassThrough queries is that you cannot create dynasets from them — they always result in a snapshot-type recordset. You can get around this limitation, as shown in this example:

```
   ' ** You can use the SQLPassThrough option to create a snapshot _
and then use Execute to
   ' ** run an Update against the remote table. This update will _
also be PassThrough.
   Dim dbDatabase As DATABASE
   Dim rsRecordset As Recordset
  Set dbDatabase = DBEngine.Workspaces(0).Databases(0)
  On Error GoTo updtErrHandler
  dbDatabase.Connect = "ODBC;DSN=Pubs"
  Set rsRecordset = dbDatabase.OpenRecordset _
("SELECT * FROM authors", _
      dbOpenSnapshot, dbSQLPassThrough)
  dbDatabase.Execute "UPDATE authors SET phone = '483-999-9999' _
WHERE au_id = '" & _
       rsRecordset![au_id] & "'", dbSQLPassThrough + dbFailOnError
```

This example passes a static SQL string to the remote engine by specifying the dbSQLPassThrough option in the OpenRecordset statement. The pass-through works because the Connect property of the database object on which the Recordset is being created contains a valid connect string. Without this specification, Jet doesn't know where to send the query, ignores the pass-through specification, and defaults to looking at the string itself. In this example, Jet requires a local table named authors; if it doesn't find one, it complains.

After the Recordset is opened, the next statement uses the database Execute method to update the current record through a reference to the current record's au_ID key field. The Update statement is also sent directly to the remote engine, because the database object's Connect property specifies the remote data source.

The code in Listing 21-1 creates an SQLPassThrough QueryDef. The QueryDef's Connect property announces to Jet that this is a pass-through QueryDef and that Jet should not attempt to parse it (Jet stores the query string as is):

Listing 21-1 Creating an SQLPassThrough QueryDef

```
   ' ** You can gain performance by using a querydef. Create the _
querydef and make it
   ' ** a SQLPassThrough query by setting the querydef's connect _
property to a valid
   ' ** odbc connect string. The same rule applies to a PassThrough _
querydef; it is not updatable.
   Dim dbDatabase As DATABASE
   Dim rsRecordset As Recordset
   Set dbDatabase = DBEngine.Workspaces(0).Databases(0)
   Set qryQueryDef = dbDatabase.CreateQueryDef("Remote Authors")
   ' ** If you use SQL syntax of the remote engine in the _
CreateQueryDef statement.
   ' ** Jet will complain. Assign the SQL after setting the Connect _
property.
   qryQueryDef.Connect = "ODBC;DSN=Pubs"
   qryQueryDef.SQL = "SELECT * FROM authors"
   ' ** Inform Jet that this query will return records. Error will _
result otherwise.
   qryQueryDef.ReturnsRecords = True
   dbDatabase.QueryDefs.Refresh
   ' ** Now use the PassThrough querydef.
   Set rsRecordset = dbDatabase.OpenRecordset("Remote Authors", _
dbOpenSnapshot)
```

Note in this example that it's not necessary to set the database object's Connect property, because that object is not referenced to acquire a valid connect string — the connection information is acquired from the QueryDef.

The new QueryDef is created with the CreateQueryDef method, and then its Connect property is set to designate it as a pass-through query. The SQL string is set after the Connect property is set to prevent Jet from parsing it.

The QueryDef's `ReturnsRecords` property is set to `True` to indicate to Jet that the query, which Jet hasn't looked at, will return records, as opposed to being an `Update` or `Delete` query.

When the QueryDef is used, a connection to the specified data source is made and the QueryDef's SQL string is sent to the remote engine. In this example, because no user ID or password was specified in the connect string, the process of creating the Recordset is temporarily interrupted by the display of a Login dialog box.

A stored procedure at the remote database can also be executed by using SQLPassThrough, as discussed in the following section.

Executing remote stored procedures

In the following example, an SQL Server stored procedure named `dbprocAuthors` is specified as the QueryDef's `SQL` property. Because the QueryDef is an SQLPassThrough query, any statement the remote engine understands can be specified in the SQL string. Because the name of a stored procedure is valid to SQL Server, this statement is excepted when Jet sends it to be executed.

Again, the example sets the QueryDef's `ReturnsRecords` property to indicate that records will come back from the server, as follows:

```
   Dim dbDatabase As DATABASE
   Dim rsRecordset As Recordset
   Dim qryQueryDef As QueryDef
   Set dbDatabase = DBEngine.Workspaces(0).Databases(0)
   ' ** A PassThrough querydef can also be used to run a remote _
stored procedure.
   Set qryQueryDef = dbDatabase.CreateQueryDef("SP_dbprocAuthors")
   qryQueryDef.Connect = "ODBC;DSN=Pubs"
   ' ** Set the SQL property to a valid stored procedure name in the _
remote database.
   qryQueryDef.SQL = "dbprocAuthors"
   qryQueryDef.ReturnsRecords = True
   dbDatabase.QueryDefs.Refresh
   ' ** Now use the PassThrough querydef.
   Set rsRecordset = dbDatabase.OpenRecordset("SP_dbprocAuthors", _
dbOpenSnapshot)
```

In addition to executing your own stored procedures, you can execute stored procedures that are shipped with the remote database manager. Microsoft SQL Server 6.5 contains several stored procedures, known as *system stored procedures,* that you may find useful.

Table 21-1 lists a few SQL Server 6.5 system stored procedures you can execute as SQLPassThrough queries. Consult SQL Server's Books OnLine for a complete list of available procedures. Note that execution of some of these procedures requires administrator or owner permissions.

Table 21-1 Stored Procedures Used in SQLPassThrough Queries

Name	*Syntax*	*Description*
sp_addlogin	sp_addlogin LoginID[, PassWord[, DefDB[,DefLang]]]	Adds a new user to the current database; the login ID must be added with sp_addlogin.
sp_adduser	sp_adduser LoginID[, UserName[, GroupName]]	Adds a new SQL Server user in master.dbo.syslogins.
sp_addtype	sp_addtype TypeName, SQLTypeName [,NullType]	Creates a user-defined datatype in the systypes table for use in CREATE TABLE and ALTERTABLE statements.
sp_changegroup	sp_changegroup GroupName, UserName	Adds the username to the group; GroupName must exist.
sp_configure	sp_configure [ConfigName	Displays or changes SQL Server configuration options.
sp_lock	sp_lock [SPID1 [,SPID2]]	Displays information about SQL Server locks; SPIDs are obtained with the sp_who stored procedure.
sp_monitor	sp_monitor	Displays SQL Server statistics.
sp_password	sp_password OldPswd, NewPswd [,LoginID]	Adds or changes a password for an SQL Server login ID; does not return records.
sp_spaceused	sp_spaceused [ObjName][[,] @UpdateUsage = {true | false}]	Displays the disk space used and reserved for the database or for the database table specified by ObjName.
sp_who	sp_who [LoginID | 'SPID']	Displays information about the current SQL Server users and processes.
sp_helptext	sp_helptext ObjName	Displays the text of the named stored procedure, rule, trigger, or view; the stored procedure must be unencrypted.

Capturing multiple results from stored procedures

Some stored procedures return multiple result sets to the client. If your code isn't set up to handle these multiple sets, you see only the first result set returned, which may not be the one you want.

Listing 21-2 deals with multiple result sets returned from a stored procedure. It uses a temporary make-table query to capture multiple results returned by an SQLPassThrough query that executes the remote stored procedure.

Listing 21-2 Multiple Result Sets Returned from a Stored Procedure

```
   Dim dbDatabase As DATABASE
   Dim rsRecordset As Recordset
   Dim qryQueryDef As QueryDef
   Dim qryQueryDef2 As QueryDef
   ' ** Create a passthrough query that returns multiple results.
   Set qryQueryDef = dbDatabase.CreateQueryDef("SP_dbprocTwoSets")
   qryQueryDef.Connect = "ODBC;DSN=Pubs"
   qryQueryDef.SQL = "dbprocTwoSets"
   qryQueryDef.ReturnsRecords = True
   dbDatabase.QueryDefs.Refresh
   ' ** Create and execute a temporary make-table query that stores _
multiple results
   ' ** from the SQLPassThrough query created above.
   Set qryQueryDef2 = dbDatabase.CreateQueryDef("")
   qryQueryDef2.SQL = "SELECT * INTO [MultSet] FROM _
[SP_dbprocTwoSets]"
   qryQueryDef2.Execute
   ' ** Create recordsets from the resulting tables.
   Set rsRecordset = dbDatabase.OpenRecordset("MultSet", _
dbOpenDynaset)
   ' ** Open other tables according to number returned.
   rsRecordset.Close
   Set rsRecordset = dbDatabase.OpenRecordset("MultSet1", _
dbOpenDynaset)
```

The stored procedure `SP_dbprocTwoSets` was added to the Pubs database and defined to return two result sets: one for all authors in the state of California and another for all authors in the state of Oregon.

`QueryDef SP_dbprocTwoSets` is defined as an SQLPassThrough query that executes the remote stored procedure named `dbprocTwoSets`.

A second QueryDef is defined as a temporary, no-name make-table query. The `SQL` property of this query is a simple `Select` from the pass-through query; the query inserts the results into one or more tables named `MultSetx` (where `x` is incremented sequentially from one to the number of result sets returned minus one). The first result set is stored without a number suffix in the table named MultSet.

The resulting tables are now local tables and may be used as any other local table from Access or code. No link exists to the source data of these tables. If you update the tables and expect those updates to be reflected in the original data source, you have to write code to handle the task.

Tip

This technique of creating local tables from a remote ODBC data source for your application to process improves, in some cases, the performance of your application. If you want your application only to read the data and you aren't concerned about whether the values are current to the second, loading the application into a local table at start-up eliminates the need to have it access the remote database every time you need the values. This capability can be especially helpful if your application accesses these values frequently.

Passing parameters in SQLPassThrough queries

You cannot pass parameters into an SQLPassThrough query the way you can with other queries. Because some stored procedures in the remote database require one or more parameters to be passed into them, you need some way to specify them when you execute the pass-through query.

On CD-ROM

The CH21.MDB Connect form on the CD-ROM at the back of this book contains a button labeled PassThrough Parameters that has the following code in its `On Click` event procedure:

```
  Set dbDatabase = DBEngine.Workspaces(0).Databases(0)
  Set qryQueryDef = dbDatabase.CreateQueryDef("")
  qryQueryDef.Connect = "ODBC;DSN=Pubs"
  qryQueryDef.SQL = "dbprocAuthorParm '" & txtAuthorState.Value & _
"'"
  Set rsRecordset = qryQueryDef.OpenRecordset()
  ' do something with results
  rsRecordset.Close
  dbDatabase.Close
```

This sample code creates a temporary QueryDef, as was done in the handling of multiple result sets. The `SQL` property of the query is set to the name of the stored procedure you want to execute, concatenated with values for the required parameters.

The stored procedure being executed in this example takes one parameter to specify the state and then returns the last names and phone numbers for authors in that state:

```
CREATE PROCEDURE dbprocAuthorParm @statein char(2) AS
 select au_lname,phone from authors where state = @statein
```

A Recordset is then opened and processed on the QueryDef.

Introducing CacheSize, CacheStart, and FillCache

When you're using a dynaset-type Recordset against a linked ODBC data source, you can improve the performance of record retrieval by using the Recordset properties `CacheSize` and `CacheStart`.

A *cache* is an allocation of local memory used to store records retrieved from the remote data source. If you have defined a cache for your dynaset, it is filled as you use `MoveNext` to move through the dynaset from the specified start of the cache to the limit of the cache size. After a record has been cached, Jet satisfies a request for that record from the cache rather than request it from the remote data source.

To create the cache, create a dynaset-type Recordset and then set the Recordset's `CacheSize` property to the number of records you want to hold locally. You may specify any number of records from 5 to 1,200 or up to the limits of memory.

You specify the first record to be cached by setting the `CacheStart` property of the Recordset equal to the `BookMark` property of the record you want. The record can be any record in the Recordset. To use `CacheStart`, you must specify as `Binary` the `Option Compare` method for the module in which you are using the property. If you don't use the `Binary` compare method, the current record will be set improperly.

You can cause the cache to be filled more quickly by using the Recordset's `FillCache` method. It retrieves records from the remote data source in blocks and fills the cache:

```
recordset.FillCache optional rows, optional start
```

The limiting factors on the size of the cache and the start of the cache are the `CacheSize` and `CacheStart` properties. You can specify a different size and start for the `FillCache` method, but the resulting range of records must be within the limits set for the cache. `FillCache` ignores records that fall outside the cache limits. If no optional parameters are specified, `FillCache` uses the `CacheSize` and `CacheStart` properties, as shown in Listing 21-3.

Listing 21-3 The CacheSize and CacheStart Properties

```
Dim dbDatabase As DATABASE
   Dim rsRecordset As Recordset
   Dim SQLStmt As String
   Set dbDatabase = DBEngine.Workspaces(0).Databases(0)
   SQLStmt = "SELECT au_lname,state,phone FROM dbo_authors"
   Set rsRecordset = dbDatabase.OpenRecordset(SQLStmt, _
dbOpenDynaset)
   ' Set the recordset cache
   rsRecordset.CacheSize = 75
```

(continued)

(continued)

```
rsRecordset.CacheStart = rsRecordset.Bookmark
' Fill the cache up to CacheSize records
rsRecordset.FillCache
Debug.Print "Time start with cache is ", Timer
Do While Not rsRecordset.EOF
   Debug.Print rsRecordset![au_lname], rsRecordset![phone]
   rsRecordset.MoveNext
Loop
Debug.Print "Time end with cache is ", Timer
' Set cache off
rsRecordset.CacheSize = 0
rsRecordset.MoveFirst
Debug.Print "Time start without cache is ", Timer
Do While Not rsRecordset.EOF
   Debug.Print rsRecordset![au_lname], rsRecordset![phone]
   rsRecordset.MoveNext
Loop
Debug.Print "Time end without cache is ", Timer
rsRecordset.Close
dbDatabase.Close
```

This code is behind the Cached Recordset button on the Connect Lab form in CH21.MDB on the CD-ROM at the back of this book. The code shows the difference in time between processing a Recordset with and without a cache. When you run the code, you can see that caching improves the performance of record retrieval.

Records that are cached do not reflect concurrent changes at the data source as do records in a nonattached Recordset. To refresh the cache from the remote data source, set the `CacheSize` property to zero, reset the `CacheSize` previously specified, and use the `FillCache` method. Set `CacheSize` to zero to turn off caching.

Using ODBC and the Registry

When Jet accesses an ODBC data source, it uses defaults built into Jet to control factors such as the amount of time to wait for an ODBC connection and the amount of time to wait for a query to finish.

If the Jet defaults are not satisfactory for your application, you can build entries in the system Registry to specify your own options. You must add the Registry tree to contain these values because the ODBC setup does not create them.

Add a tree to the Registry under the HKEY_LOCAL_MACHINE as follows:

```
\Software\Microsoft\Office\8.0\Access\Jet\3.5\Engines\ODBC
```

The values you can specify under the ODBC subkey are listed in Table 21-2.

Table 21-2 Allowable Settings for Jet's Use of an ODBC Data Source

Value Name	*Jet Default*	*Description*
`AsyncRetryInterval`	`500 milliseconds`	The number of milliseconds to wait between polls of the server to determine whether a query has completed when asynchronous processing is used; REG_DWORD.
`AttachableObjects`	`TABLE,VIEW, SYSTEM TABLE, ALIAS, SYNONYM`	The list of remote data source objects to which linking can occur; REG_SZ.
`AttachCaseSensitive`	`0`	An indicator of the type of match on an object name when objects are being linked. A `0` indicates a match regardless of case, and a `1` indicates a match in case; REG_DWORD.
`ConnectionTimeout`	`600 seconds`	The number of seconds a connection remains idle before being considered as timed out; REG_DWORD.
`DisableAsync`	`0`	An indicator of whether to use synchronous query execution (`1`) or asynchronous query execution (`0`); REG_DWORD.
`FastRequery`	`0`	An indicator of whether to use a prepared statement for parameterized queries. A `0` indicates `No`, and a `1` indicates `Yes`; REG_DWORD.

(continued)

Table 21-2 *(continued)*

Value Name	*Jet Default*	*Description*
JetTryAuth	1	An indicator of whether to use the Access login name and password to log in to the remote data source. A 0 indicates No, and a 1 indicates Yes; REG_DWORD.
LoginTimeout	20 seconds	The number of seconds a login attempt is allowed to continue before being considered as timed out; REG_DWORD.
PreparedInsert	0	An indicator of whether to use a prepared insert. A 0 indicates the use of an insert statement that inserts only non-null values, and a 1 indicates the use of a prepared insert that inserts into all columns; REG_DWORD.
PreparedUpdate	0	An indicator of whether to use a prepared update. A 0 indicates the use of an update that updates only changed columns, and a 1 indicates the use of a prepared update that updates all columns; REG_DWORD.
QueryTimeout	60 seconds	The number of seconds a query can run before being considered as timed out; REG_DWORD.

Value Name	Jet Default	Description
SnapshotOnly	0	An indicator of whether Recordsets are forced to be snapshots. A 0 indicates No (allow dynasets), and a 1 indicates Yes (snapshots only); REG_DWORD.
TraceODBCAPI	0	An indicator that turns on (1) the tracing of ODBC API calls Jet makes to an ODBC data source. The trace is written to ODBCAPI.TXT; REG_DWORD.
TraceSQLMode	0	An indicator that turns on (1) the tracing of SQL statements Jet sends to an ODBC data source. The trace is written to SQLOUT.TXT; REG_DWORD.

Note that these settings are under the 8.0/Access subkey and apply only to Jet by Access applications.

Managing Connections

The connection to an ODBC data source occurs when you first access the data source in your application. The user is then prompted for a login if you haven't provided the user ID and password in the connect string and if JetTryAuth is either not active or unsuccessful. After a successful connection, Jet caches the authorization until the application terminates.

The connection can take some time compared to the rest of your application. Rather than wait for the first access to occur to make the connection, you can *preconnect* at application start-up.

To preconnect to the data source, open the database your application uses and then close it. Although the database object is closed, Jet caches the connection and holds it. Then, when you first access the data source, Jet already has the connection open and uses it to run your query, as shown in this example:

```
Dim dbDatabase As Database
Dim strConnect As String
strConnect = "ODBC;DSN=Pubs"
Set dbDatabase = OpenDatabase("", False , False, strConnect)
dbDatabase.Close
```

If the connection remains idle for the time set by `ConnectionTimeout`, Jet drops the connection. If your application then accesses the data source, Jet uses the cached authentication to reconnect. No prompt occurs.

Handling Transactions

When you use statements (such as `Update` or `Insert`) that modify an ODBC data source, Jet automatically wraps the action in a transaction to ensure that the action as a whole will succeed or fail.

Jet's automatic transaction handling works well for simple actions against the data source. When you want to control multiple actions, however, you have to use explicit transactions with workspace transaction methods, as shown in Listing 21-4.

Listing 21-4 Explicit Transactions with Workspace Transaction Methods

```
On Error GoTo ErrHandler
Dim dbDatabase As Database
Dim wsWorkspace As Workspace
Dim qryQueryDef As QueryDef
Set wsWorkspace = DBEngine.Workspaces(0)
Set dbDatabase = wsWorkspace.Databases(0)
' Start a transaction
wsWorkspace.BeginTrans
Set qryQueryDef = dbDatabase.QueryDefs("SP_dbprocAuthor")
qryQueryDef.Execute
Set qryQueryDef = dbDatabase.QueryDefs("SP_dbprocTitle")
qryQueryDef.Execute
' Commit the activity and end the transaction
wsWorkspace.CommitTrans
dbDatabase.Close
Exit Sub
ErrHandler:
' Back out the actions that succeeded and end the transaction
wsWorkspace.Rollback
Exit Sub
```

The preceding code sets a workspace object and then uses the `BeginTrans` method to start a transaction in the workspace. Any action against the database between this statement and either a `Rollback` or `CommitTrans` statement is considered a unit of work.

Two queries, one against the `Authors` table and the other against the `Titles` table, are executed inside the unit of work. If an error is raised, the updates to the point of error are rolled back so that neither table is updated. If no errors occur, a `CommitTrans` statement commits the changes to both tables.

Tip

Although the use of transactions is critical to ensuring the integrity of the data, its use does cause locking to occur on the affected pages of data. The longer your transaction runs, the longer locks are held and other users of the data are prevented from doing their work. You should, therefore, keep your transactions as short as possible. Be sure not to include any unnecessary code within the transaction unit, and especially do not include any actions that require waiting on a user's entry.

Transactions against Access databases can be nested as many as five levels deep so that a commit on a transaction nested within another transaction may be rolled back by the outer transaction unit. With ODBC data sources, only one transaction unit may be active within a workspace. If you use nested transactions against ODBC data sources, only the outermost transaction is honored.

When you use transactions against ODBC data sources from different workspaces, the transactions are not managed separately, as they are against Access databases. The reason is the manner in which Jet manages the connection to the data source. To force Jet to manage the workspace transactions separately, set the `IsolateODBCTrans` property of the workspace to `True`.

Exploring the MSysConf Table

When you open a linked ODBC table in Access, the Recordset supporting the datasheet view is populated in the background by retrieving blocks of 100 records from the server. Access performs this background retrieval on a 10-second time interval during periods of inactivity by the user and when the user scrolls into the Recordset. The block retrieval continues until all records have been retrieved or until you close the datasheet.

You can change the default size of the block and the interval on which the block is retrieved by creating in the remote database a table called MSysConf. Each record in the MSysConf table specifies a configuration option that overrides the corresponding Access default.

Table 21-3 shows the column definitions you use when you create the MSysConf table.

Table 21-3 Column Definitions for the MSysConf Table in a Remote Database

Field	*Field Type*	*Should Allow Null Value?*
Config	2-byte integer	No
chValue	VARCHAR(255)	Yes
nValue	4-byte integer	Yes
Comments	VARCHAR(255)	Yes

When the table is completed, you can enter three records to override the Access defaults, which are described in Table 21-4.

Table 21-4 Record Values in MSysConf Table to Override Access Defaults

Config Value	*nValue Values Allowed*	*Description*
`101`	`0, 1`	A value of `0` indicates that no local storage of a login ID and password with attached tables is allowed. A value of `1` (the default) indicates that local storage of a login ID and password in attachments is allowed.
`102`	Delay interval in seconds	The interval between background retrieval operations to populate Recordsets by Access. The default is 10 seconds.
`103`	Record block size	The number of records to be retrieved in one block. The default is 100 records.

The MSysConf table should be added to each database you want to access in your application for which you want to provide overrides for the default background Recordset population parameters. You have to consider the trade-off between network traffic and performance at the client when you choose the override values. Choosing a small delay interval, for example, causes the blocks of records to be retrieved more quickly at the expense of increased network traffic between the client and server.

Exploring Database Access with ODBCDirect

The second technology of database access bypasses the Jet database engine and uses a new feature of DAO 3.5, called ODBCDirect. Much of what you have learned using a Jet-connected ODBC data source can be applied to an ODBCDirect workspace connection as well. ODBCDirect has its own hierarchy of objects, as shown in Figure 21-12, and, although similar to the Jet DAO hierarchy, has many features for fast and lean access to remote database servers through Level 2-compliant ODBC Drivers.

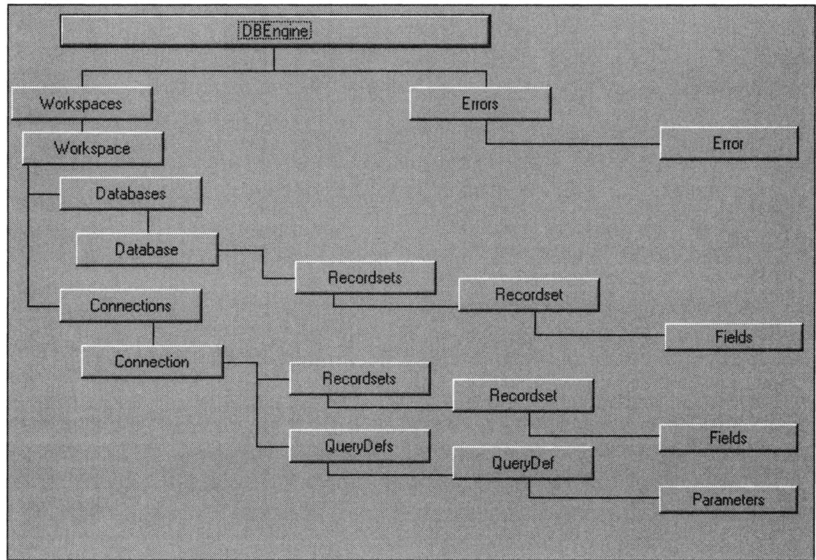

Figure 21-12: The DAO Object hierarchy of the ODBCDirect technology.

Specifying ODBC Workspaces and Connections

The ODBC `Workspace` object is created by using the `CreateWorkspace` method of the DBEngine, as follows:

```
Set workspaceobject = CreateWorkspace(name,user,password,type)
```

The type property can be one of the following:

ODBC Workspace Types	
`dbUseJet`	to create a Jet workspace
`dbUseODBC`	to create an ODBCDirect workspace

ODBC database cursors

Cursors in ODBC provide a means of keeping track of position within a result set. You can think of cursors as record pointers (introduced in Chapter 5), but ODBC cursors have a deeper meaning that affects how a result set may be processed.

ODBC defines four cursor types. The first cursor type is the *static* cursor. Static cursors maintain a Recordset that doesn't change from the time it is opened until it is closed. The record membership in a static cursor model is fixed. This is the type of cursor used for snapshot Recordsets.

A second type of cursor is the *keyset-driven* cursor. Keyset-driven cursors maintain a keyset of record identifiers for record members. The keyset itself is fixed until the Recordset (or cursor) is closed. Keys in the keyset will provide pointers to data so that the data can be fetched as needed by the cursor owner. If changes are made to the keyed record, no matter who makes the changes, those changes can be seen in the Recordset. If the record pointed to by a key is deleted, the key remains in the keyset. Visiting the key results in a "hole" in the dataset, that is, no record returned. Likewise, additions by other users that would normally qualify for membership in the result set are not shown, because their key is not in the fixed keyset. This type of cursor can support positioned updates. Dynasets are keyset-driven cursors.

The third type of cursor supported in ODBC is the *dynamic* cursor. With dynamic cursors, you never experience a "hole" in the dataset or miss additions by other users. The result set is constantly updated to show the true membership of the query. This type of cursor also maintains a keyset, but it is not fixed as it is in the keyset-driven cursor. Dynamic cursors are represented by Dynamic Recordsets in an ODBCDirect workspace.

The fourth type of cursor is the *mixed* cursor. Mixed cursors are a mix of keyset-driven cursors and dynamic cursors. They maintain a range of keys in a keyset (a subset of the entire result set keyset) and act like keyset-driven cursors within this keyset. After the limits of the keyset range are reached, the mixed cursor acts like a dynamic cursor, fetching a new keyset. The result set is thus maintained up-to-date as expected from a dynamic cursor, but done within a range of keys. This type of cursor has no corresponding Recordset in ODBCDirect.

If you have set the engine's `DefaultType` property to `dbUseODBC` prior to creating the workspace, you do not have to specify the type in the `CreateWorkspace` method.

The `DefaultCursorDriver` property of the ODBCDirect `Workspace` object specifies the type of cursor driver to be used when a `Connection` object is created in the workspace using `OpenConnection`. A cursor driver is used to create and define the behavior of Recordset cursors.

The `DefaultCursorDriver` can specify one of the values shown in Table 21-5 to take effect on `OpenConnections` subsequent to the setting of the property:

Table 21-5 DefaultCursorDriver Constants

Constant	*Description*
dbUseDefaultCursor	Use server-side cursors if supported by the remote DB engine, otherwise use ODBC Cursor Library.
dbUseODBCCursor	Use the ODBC Cursor Library.
dbUseServerCursor	Use server-side cursors.
dbUseClientBatchCursor	Use the client batch cursor library. Required for batch updates.
dbUseNoCursor	Recordsets opened as Forward-only, read-only.

A connection is similar to a database object. The Database property of a Connection object enables you to obtain a reference to the corresponding database object, whereas the Connection property of a Database object yields a reference to the corresponding Connection object. The OpenConnection method is used to connect to an ODBC data source. The resulting Connection object contains information about the connection, such as server name, data source name, and so on, as follows:

```
Dim WrkSpaceODBC As Workspace
Dim PubsConn As Connection
Set WrkSpaceODBC = _
CreateWorkspace("ODBCWorkSpace","admin","",dbUseODBC)
Set PubsConn =
WrkSpaceODBC.OpenConnection("PubsConn1",dbDriverNoPrompt,, _
    "ODBC;DATABASE=pubs;UID=sa;PWD=;DSN=Pubs")
```

The OpenConnection syntax is as follows:

```
Set connection =
workspace.OpenConnection(name,options,readonly,connect)
```

Options that may be specified in the OpenConnection are shown in Table 21-6.

Table 21-6 OpenConnection Constants

Constant	*Description*
dbDriverNoPrompt	ODBC Driver manager uses the connect string. Error occurs if not complete.
dbDriverPrompt	ODBC collects connection info from user.

(continued)

Table 21-6 *(continued)*

Constant	*Description*
`dbDriverComplete`	ODBC Driver manager uses connect string if complete; otherwise, prompts user for necessary info.
`dbDriverCompleteRequired`	ODBC Driver manager uses connect string and prompts user for incomplete info. Disables prompts for info collected from connect string.
`dbRunAsync`	Executes the `OpenConnection` asynchronously.

Note in the object hierarchy diagram shown in Figure 21-12 that a `Connection` object in an ODBCDirect workspace can contain a `QueryDefs` collection and a `Recordsets` collection, just as the `Database` object in a Jet workspace.

The `Cancel` method is used to cancel the `Asynchronous OpenConnection` method. Obviously, the connection cannot be referenced after the `Cancel` has been invoked.

A `Connection` can contain `QueryDef` objects and `Recordset` objects for access to the data source associated with the connection. Note that `Connection` objects in an ODBC workspace are not persistent, that is, they cannot be stored in the database across sessions. In that the connection is not persistent, its dependent objects also are not persistent. QueryDefs created on these ODBC connection objects last only for the duration of the connection. To create a QueryDef, you use the `CreateQueryDef` method of the `Connection` object.

Working with queries and Recordsets

The types of Recordsets available for use in ODBCDirect workspaces are the dynaset, snapshot, forward-only and dynamic Recordsets.

Cross-Reference

Dynasets, snapshots, and forward-only Recordsets have been explained in the context of Jet workspaces in Chapter 5, “Working with Data Access Objects.” These Recordset types correspond to keyset cursors, static cursors and forward-only cursors, respectively, when applied in an ODBCDirect workspace. The dynamic Recordset type is not available in a Jet workspace and corresponds to a dynamic cursor in the ODBCDirect workspace.

Dynamic Recordsets are similar to dynasets in that they hold a keyset buffer and a fetched data buffer. The difference lies in the membership of these buffers. Remember that a dynaset fills its keyset when you create the

Recordset. If other users delete records corresponding to keys in your dynaset and you move to that record, you effectively see a hole — that is, the key is in your keyset, but the record is not in the table to be fetched.

When other users add records to a table that would qualify for membership in your dynaset, but the add takes place after your dynaset has been created, you will never see these records until you requery the dynaset. After the dynaset has been created, the records in it are considered to be in a fixed membership.

With a dynamic Recordset, records that qualify for membership are always being evaluated. If another user adds or deletes a record that affects your Recordset, you see these additions and deletions as you navigate through the Recordset. This refetching of qualifying records takes place in conjunction with the dynamic cursor and affects the Recordset's keyset as well as the fetched data buffer.

Tip

Your choice between a dynaset and a dynamic Recordset depends on the requirements of your application. If your end user needs to see all changes by other users within the lifetime of your Recordset, then use a dynamic Recordset. Keep in mind, however, that this type of Recordset is the most expensive of all types available, due to its constant evaluation of Recordset members. If the dynaset will suffice, you should choose it instead.

You can create your Recordset on the `Connection` object with the `OpenRecordset` method, as follows:

```
    Set recordsetobject = connection.OpenRecordset(datasource, type, _
options, lockedits)
```

The `OpenRecordset` data source is an SQL statement, the name of a query or a table in the ODBC data source referenced by the `Connection`'s connect property.

The constants you can use to specify the type of Recordset are shown in Table 21-7.

Table 21-7 Constants Used to Specify Recordset Type

Constant	*Description*
`dbOpenDynaset`	a dynaset type Recordset
`dbOpenDynamic`	a dynamic type Recordset
`dbOpenSnapshot`	a snapshot type Recordset
`dbOpenForwardOnly`	a forward-only type Recordset

Table 21-8 lists the options you can specify in the `OpenRecordset` method for an ODBCDirect Recordset.

Table 21-8 OpenRecordset Options

Constant	*Description*
`dbRunAsync`	Causes the Recordset to be populated asynchronously
`dbExecDirect`	Forces the query to be executed without preparing a temporary stored procedure.

The use of `dbRunAsync` enables your code to do other processing while the Recordset is populated by the query. You need to check the `StillExecuting` property of the Recordset to determine whether the Recordset is available for accessing. If the `StillExecuting` property is `True`, the query has not yet finished. Referring to the Recordset while the query is still executing results in a run-time error. The query can be canceled by use of the `Cancel` method on the Recordset.

The `lockedits` argument is used to specify a locking strategy for the Recordset. The constants you can specify for this are shown in Table 21-9.

Table 21-9 Lockedits Constants in the OpenRecordset Method

Constant	*Description*
`dbReadOnly`	No changes to the Recordset are allowed.
`dbPessimistic`	Edit method applied to the Recordset causes the page containing the record being edited to be locked so that other users cannot change records in the page.
`dbOptimistic`	Update method applied to the Recordset causes a page lock until the updated record is committed to the table. Changes by other users cannot take place for the duration of the lock. Changes detected by row id or timestamp checking.
`dbOptimisticBatch`	Applies optimistic updating for batch updates.
`dbOptimisticValue`	Same concurrency as `dbOptimistic` but changes are detected by checking row values.

QueryDefs created from `Connection` objects in an ODBCDirect workspace are temporary. They are not saved to the database as Jet Database QueryDefs can be. The `sqlstmt` argument, shown in the following sample, can be an SQL string in a dialect known to the data source or the name of a stored procedure.

```
Set querydefobject = connectionobject.CreateQueryDef(name,sqlstmt)
```

By default, QueryDefs in an ODBCDirect workspace will be prepared as a temporary stored procedure when executed. This causes the initial execution to take on the overhead of the prepare before executing but speeds up executions of the query subsequent to the first. If you will be executing the query multiple times in an application, it is generally best to use the default setting for the `Prepare` property of the QueryDef. If you only need to execute the query once or you do not want to prepare a stored procedure, set the `Prepare` property to `dbQUnprepare` prior to setting the QueryDef's `SQL` property.

The `Prepare` property can be overridden in an `OpenRecordset` method or `Execute` method by setting the `dbExecDirect` option of these methods. This option causes the query to be executed without prepare regardless of what the `Prepare` property setting is.

You can limit the number of records to be returned from the query by setting the `MaxRecords` property to the number of records you want the Recordset to hold. Set the `MaxRecords` to zero to return all records in the result set — that is, no limit.

Tip

If you have data that is referenced often in your application — a lookup table, for example — you can enhance the performance of the lookup by caching the lookup table in local memory. With the records cached locally, DAO checks the cache before sending a data request to the server. If the requested records are found in the cache, they are returned; otherwise, the request is forwarded to the server. This is a good technique to use for lookup tables, which are generally read-only in an application.

Set the QueryDef's `CacheSize` property to a value between 5 and 1200 records to initiate the caching behavior. Turn off caching by setting `CacheSize` to zero. The `CacheStart` property and the `FillCache` method, covered in the section "Introducing CacheSize, CacheStart, and FillCache," are not supported in an ODBCDirect workspace.

In cases where your QueryDef accesses a remote stored procedure that takes or returns parameters, you may need to set the direction of those parameters before executing the query. Some ODBC drivers cannot determine or do not provide direction information on parameters. In this case, you need to specify the parameter direction before setting the parameter value and before executing the query.

Parameters by default are input parameters with their `Direction` property set to `dbParamInput`. If your stored procedure returns parameters or a return value, you can set the corresponding `Parameter Direction` property to one of the constants listed in Table 21-10.

Table 21-10 Direction Property Constants to Specify Parameter Direction for a Stored Procedure Parameter

Constant	*Description*
`dbParamInputOutput`	Passes parameter value into and receives value from the stored procedure.
`dbParamOutput`	Receives a value from the stored procedure.
`dbParamReturnValue`	Receives a return value from the stored procedure.

Listing 21-5 shows the code for the `ExecStoredProc` procedure found in CH21.MDB on the companion CD-ROM. This procedure creates a connection to the Pubs data source and creates a temporary QueryDef containing two parameters, as noted by the "?" placeholders in the `SQLStmtsql` statement.

Listing 21-5 Using the Direction Property for Stored Procedure Parameters

```
Sub ExecStoredProc()
    On Error GoTo ESPErr

    Dim wsODBC As Workspace
    Dim connODBC As Connection
    Dim qryTemp As QueryDef
    Dim SQLStmt As String
    Dim i As Integer
    ' Create an ODBC workspace

    Set wsODBC = CreateWorkspace("ODBCWorkspace", _
        "", "", dbUseODBC)

    ' Open a connection in the workspace

    Set connODBC = wsODBC.OpenConnection("Pubs", _
        dbDriverPrompt, False, _
        "ODBC;UID=Dean;DSN=Pubs")
    ' Set SQL string to call the st_auths stored procedure

   ' CREATE PROCEDURE st_auths @instate char(2), @outcount int
output
   ' AS
   ' select @outcount = count(*) from authors
   ' where state = @instate

    SQLStmt = "{ call st_auths(?,?) }"

    Set qryTemp = connODBC.CreateQueryDef("qry1", SQLStmt)

    ' Set the parameters
```

```
    qryTemp.Parameters(0).Direction = dbParamInput
    qryTemp.Parameters(0).Type = dbText
    qryTemp.Parameters(1).Direction = dbParamOutput
    qryTemp.Parameters(1).Type = dbInteger

   'Execute the query

    qryTemp.Parameters(0) = "CA"
    qryTemp.Execute
    ' Display the output parm
    MsgBox "Number of authors in " & qryTemp.Parameters(0) & _
      " is " & qryTemp.Parameters(1)

    connODBC.Close
    wsODBC.Close
    Exit Sub
ESPErr:
    MsgBox Err.Description
    Exit Sub
End Sub
```

The comments in this procedure describe the content of the stored procedure `st_auths`, which returns a count of rows in the pubs authors table having a state equal to the input state parameter. The count is returned in an output parameter. These two parameters are specified in the `SQLStmt` used in the `SQL` property of the QueryDef `qry1`.

The `Direction` property is set to describe each of the required parameters, one being an input parameter and the other being an output parameter. Both parameters are assigned a `Direction` property and a `Type` property in this procedure to document their use. The input parameter need not be dealt with, because the default `Direction` is `dbParamInput` — but it doesn't hurt to specify it.

After the parameters are described, the procedure assigns a value to the input parameter and executes the query. The output value from the stored procedure is found in the output parameter, `parameter(1)`, and is displayed in a message box at the end of the procedure.

Had the stored procedure defined a return value, the `SQLStmt` statement would need to be modified to inform DAO of the return value, as follows:

```
SQLStmt = "{ ? = call st_auths(?,?) }"
```

Given that there is one more placeholder in the `SQLStmt` syntax to deal with, you need to specify `parameter(0)` as having a direction of `dbParamReturnValue` and then offset the currently defined parameters by one to handle the input and output parameters.

Applying batch updates

Batch updating in an ODBCDirect workspace is a technique of updating a Recordset locally and then submitting those updates to the ODBC data source in a batch. This technique delays dealing with locking conflicts and change conflicts until the batch is submitted for update.

To use batch updating for a Recordset, you need to set the workspace `DefaultCursorDriver` property to `dbUseClientBatchCursor` and use the `dbOptimisticBatch` `Openrecordset` option.

When you submit the batch via the `dbUpdateBatch` option of the `Update` method, the records you updated may be in conflict with changes made by other users. You can detect the existence of conflicts by checking the Recordset's `BatchCollisionCount` property. If this property value is greater than zero, conflicts have occurred.

To find the records that had conflicts, you need to traverse the `BatchCollisions` array property. This array contains bookmarks to the records in the Recordset that experienced conflicts during the update attempt. Set the Recordset `Bookmark` property to an element in the `BatchCollisions` array to examine the record involved in the conflict.

You can deal with a conflict in one of three ways:

- Force the update of the change.
- Accept the current database record values made by another user.
- Change to the original record values that were present before your change was made.

When you want to force your change to overlay the current record value, you can reissue the update with the `RecordStatus` property set to `dbRecordModified`.

To accept the current record as modified by another user, set the `RecordStatus` property to `dbRecordUnmodified`.

To change the record to its original value prior to your change, set the `RecordStatus` to `dbRecordModified` and the changed fields to their `OriginalValue` property.

The updates can be applied on a record-by-record basis by issuing the update method with the `dbUpdateCurrentRecord` option, or you can resubmit the batch again after dealing with all conflicts.

Each time the batch update is submitted, DAO generates a batch of statements to send to the server. The number of statements that are sent to the server at a time is governed by the `BatchSize` property. By default, 15 statements are generated in a batch.

The statements DAO uses to perform the updates can be controlled somewhat by the `UpdateOptions` property. The default, `dbCriteriaKey`, causes the update statements to use key columns in the statement's `Where` clause, as in `Update authors set phone = '644-5891' Where name = 'Amo'`, given that `name` is a key column in the `authors` table.

Other constants you can specify in `UpdateOptions` are listed in Table 21-11.

Table 21-11 Constants That Specify UpdateOptions

Constant	*Description*
`dbCriteriaAllCols`	Use all columns in the `Where` clause.
`dbCriteriaModValues`	Use key columns and updated columns in the `Where` clause.
`dbCriteriaTimeStamp`	Use the `TimeStamp` column in the `Where` clause. `TimeStamp` column must be present in the Recordset or an error occurs.

In addition to the method of generating the `Where` clause of the update statements, you can also specify how the updates will be applied. Adding a `dbCriteriaDeleteInsert` constant to the `UpdateOptions` property causes updates to be applied as delete/insert combinations. Use of the `dbCriteriaUpdate` constant, the default, causes updates to be applied as pure updates.

Listing 21-6 shows a procedure implementing a batch update against the Pubs authors table. The `BatchUpdate` procedure first establishes an ODBCDirect connection to the Pubs data source in a workspace that has its `DefaultCursorDriver` property set to `dbUseClientBatchCursor` to specify batch updating.

Listing 21-6 A Procedure for Processing Batch Updates

```
Sub BatchUpdate()
    On Error GoTo BUErr
    Dim wsODBC As Workspace
    Dim connODBC As Connection
    Dim rsBatch As Recordset
    Dim i As Integer
    Dim Prompt As String
    Dim frmConflict As Form
    Set wsODBC = CreateWorkspace("ODBCWorkspace", _
        "", "", dbUseODBC)
    ' Set the DefaultCursorDriver for batch update

    wsODBC.DefaultCursorDriver = dbUseClientBatchCursor
    Set connODBC = wsODBC.OpenConnection("Publishers", _
```

(continued)

(continued)

```
        dbDriverPrompt, False, _
        "ODBC;UID=Dean;DSN=Publishers")
' Open a recordset with batch lockedits argument
    Set rsBatch = connODBC.OpenRecordset( _
        "SELECT * FROM authors", dbOpenDynaset, 0, _
        dbOptimisticBatch)
    With rsBatch
        ' perform updates in dynaset locally
        Do While Not .EOF

            If !state = "CA" Then
                .Edit
                !contract = 0   'bit field
                .Update
            End If
            .MoveNext

        Loop
        ' Submit batch update.
        .Update dbUpdateBatch
        ' Check for conflicts
        If .BatchCollisionCount > 0 Then
            Prompt = "Conflicts have occurred in update." & vbCrLf & _
                "Please correct errors. "
            DoCmd.OpenForm "Conflicts"
            Set frmConflict = Forms!Conflicts
            For i = 0 To UBound(.BatchCollisions)
                ' Go to first confict record
                .Bookmark = .BatchCollisions(i)
                frmConflict.userchange.Value = !contract
                frmConflict.currvalue.Value = !contract.VisibleValue
                frmConflict.origvalue.Value =
!contract.OriginalValue
                frmConflict.Refresh
                usersel = 0
                Do While usersel = 0
                   DoEvents
                Loop
                Select Case usersel
                   Case 1:
                        ' keep user change
                        .Update dbUpdateCurrentRecord, True
                   Case 2:
                        ' keep current value
                        !contract = !contract.VisibleValue
                        .Update dbUpdateCurrentRecord, True
                   Case 3:
                        ' keep original value
                        !contract = !contract.OriginalValue
                        .Update dbUpdateCurrentRecord, True
                End Select
            Next i
```

```
            DoCmd.Close acForm, "Conflicts"
        End If
        .Close
End With
    connODBC.Close
    wsODBC.Close
    Exit Sub
BUErr:
   MsgBox Err.Description
   Exit Sub
End Sub
```

After establishing a connection to the Pubs data source, the procedure opens a dynaset with the `lockedits` argument set to `dbOptimisticBatch`. This Recordset contains all fields of the authors table.

The update loop is performed to set the contract field to zero for each record containing a state equal to `"CA"`. This update is done locally. None of the updates are being sent to the server due to the batch update cursor.

After the updates have been applied to the Recordset, a batch update to the server is attempted, using the update option `dbUpdateBatch`. This causes DAO to generate update statements for ODBC and to send these updates to the server for processing. If the records to be updated at the server have changed since the local Recordset was created, conflicts occur and the Recordset's `BatchCollisions` array is loaded with bookmarks flagging the records that have changed.

The `BatchUpdate` procedure checks the `BatchCollisionCount` of the Recordset after issuing the batch update to determine whether there were conflicts. If there were, the user must determine how to deal with the errors. To do this, a conflict form is displayed with the field's current value from the local update, the field's current value from the server, and the original value of the field when the Recordset was created.

The user must elect to apply one of the displayed values to the database. When the user makes his or her decision, the `BatchUpdate` regains control and processes the choice.

To keep the user's change made to the local Recordset, the value currently in the record, the procedure executes another update method, this time using the `dbUpdateCurrentRecord` argument and setting the force flag to `True`.

To apply the value obtained from the server — the change made by another user since the local Recordset was opened — the field is updated to the `VisibleValue` property and applied to the database.

Finally, to update the database with the value of the field at the time the Recordset was created and before any change was made locally, the `OriginalValue` property is used to update the record.

This example is simplistic in that it only updates one field and displays optional values for that one field in the conflicts form. The same technique used here can be applied no matter how many fields you have to update, but you would want a more elaborate conflict form to display all of your changed fields as well as show some identifying fields so the user knows which record he or she is dealing with. You would then need to change the `BatchUpdate` to process each changed field according to the user's instructions.

Multiple Recordset processing

In Listing 21-2, multiple Recordsets are processed in a Jet-connected ODBC data source by creating tables to hold each of the Recordsets in the results of the query. The tables can then be processed individually at any time.

In an ODBCDirect workspace, you can use the same Recordset object to visit each of the Recordsets returned in the result of a multi-Recordset query. To use this feature, you specify a workspace `DefaultCursorDriver` property of `dbUseODBCCursor` and issue the `NextRecordset` method of the `Recordset` object to return the next Recordset in the result. Listing 21-7 shows an example of processing multiple Recordsets.

When the Recordset is opened, the first result set is available for processing. To get the subsequent result sets, issue the `NextRecordset` method. This action applied to a Recordset that has been specified with the `dbRunAsync` option will reset the `StillExecuting` property of the Recordset to `True` until the next result set is available.

If a subsequent result set is available, the `NextRecordset` method returns `True`; otherwise, a `False` is returned. Note that a `True` return value does not mean that the next Recordset has a record count greater than zero. It only means that another Recordset is present in the result.

Listing 21-7 Processing Multiple Recordsets with the NextRecordset Method

```
Public Sub GetMultiSet()
    On Error GoTo GMSErr

    Dim wsODBC As Workspace
    Dim connODBC As Connection
    Dim rsMult As Recordset
    Dim SQLStmt As String
    Dim moresets As Byte

    ' Create an ODBC workspace

    Set wsODBC = CreateWorkspace("ODBCWorkspace", _
        "", "", dbUseODBC)
    wsODBC.DefaultCursorDriver = dbUseODBCCursor
```

```
    ' Open a connection in the workspace

    Set connODBC = wsODBC.OpenConnection("Pubs", _
        dbDriverPrompt, False, _
        "ODBC;UID=Dean;DSN=Pubs")

    ' Open a recordset to return multiple results
    SQLStmt = "SELECT * FROM authors;" & _
              "SELECT * FROM titleview"
    Set rsMult = connODBC.OpenRecordset(SQLStmt, dbOpenForwardOnly)

    ' Process the recordsets
    moresets = True
    Do While moresets
       Do While Not rsMult.EOF
          ' process records in current recordset
          rsMult.MoveNext
       Loop
       ' Get the next recordset
       moresets = rsMult.NextRecordset
    Loop

    rsMult.Close
    connODBC.Close
    wsODBC.Close
    Exit Sub
GMSErr:
    MsgBox Err.Description
    Exit Sub
End Sub
```

The `GetMultiSet` procedure in Listing 21-7 opens a Forward-Only Recordset (the default) on a connection to the Pubs data source. The SQL specified for the Recordset selects all columns from the authors table to define the first Recordset and all columns from the titleview view to define the second Recordset.

Note that the procedure uses two loop constructs. The outer loop processes Recordsets returned by the initial `OpenRecordset` method and subsequently by the Recordset's `NextRecordset` method, until no more Recordsets are returned.

The inner loop processes the current Recordset until the `EOF` property indicates the end of file. Recordsets built in this manner are processed no differently than Recordsets built on a single query.

The advantage over the multiple table method shown in the Jet-connected ODBC example is that the same `Recordset` object is used to process all Recordsets. There are no tables to clean up after processing. At times, however, you may want to create tables for processing multiple Recordsets because the ODBCDirect Recordset only allows visiting Recordsets in a forward direction. Once populated, the Recordset needs to be requeried in order to visit a Recordset a second time; there is no `PreviousRecordset` method.

Chapter 22

Exploring Replication

In This Chapter

- Touring the replication components
- Creating replicas of your databases
- Synchronizing your replicas
- Resolving conflicts
- Creating a new Design Master

The *replication* feature of Microsoft Jet 3.5 provides a method for distributing your database, including all of its objects, to other users. The users of a replicated database may use it read-only or read-write, depending on the permissions you assign to the replica.

If a replicated database has been created as read-write, the changes made to it can be synchronized with the changes made to other replicas. This enables a database to be distributed to other machines and kept up-to-date with other distributed databases. Database changes can be synchronized directly among two replicas or, if direct connection is not possible, the changes can be stored for later update by the target Synchronizer. This feature goes well beyond a simple copy of the database, because changes to a copy are not easily synchronized back into the master database.

You can use replication to distribute your application code, tables, queries, forms, and reports. You can distribute your application's tables separate from the rest of your database objects, even if your master database contains all objects in a single database. Beginning with Access 97, you have the capability to create and synchronize partial replicas, which provide a means of distributing only the data required by a receiving site.

Replication may be used to provide a database or a part of a database to a portable computer, to other machines on the network, or to standalone machines. Even though other network-attached machines can be set up to access the same database, instances occur where you may want to have some of these machines access a replica of the database to improve performance.

You should precede the use of replication with solid planning. Replication does not come free. Several points within the scheme of replication require serious consideration before adopting this feature. This chapter addresses those considerations and looks at the components of replication and their management.

The Components of Replication

When you create a replica of your database, the database changes in several ways to support the synchronization of changes between the replica you create and the master database. Understanding these changes is your first task in deciding whether or not to use replication.

At the time you create a replica, Access needs to add several fields and objects to your database in order to track and synchronize updates. These additions increase the size of the database as described in the "Design Master" section of this chapter.

The original database that you are replicating becomes the *Design Master*. If you make any changes to the design of the database, meaning changes to the design of any object in the database, those changes should be made to the Design Master and then propagated to the replicas.

A replica of the Design Master can receive data changes, including additions, modifications, and deletions, but does not support changing the design of any of its replicated objects. Changes to the design of local objects, those created at the replica, are supported, however.

Multiple replicas can be created from either the Design Master or any replica created from the Design Master. All replicas related to the same Design Master are part of a group called the *Replica Set*.

Nonreplicable database

Your database requires the addition of several system tables, fields, and properties before it can be replicated. Without this additional information in your database, Access cannot keep track of changes and therefore cannot replicate those changes.

If your database has a password attached to it, you need to remove that password before making the database replicable. A password on the database prevents the synchronization of replicas among the replica set.

To convert your database to a replicable form, follow one of the procedures outlined in "Creating a Replica," later in this chapter.

Design Master

After your database has been made replicable, it is known in the newly created replica set as the Design Master database.

The Design Master and all replicas created from it contain internal IDs that are unique within the replica set. This set ID enables the replica set members to update each other but prevents updating members of other replica sets, even if those sets were created from the same nonreplicable database.

Any changes in design of replicated objects must be made at the Design Master. These changes are replicated to all the replicas in the set at the time of the next synchronization.

When the Design Master is created, new fields are added to your tables to support the replication of changes.

A field named s_Generation is added to track the number of changes occurring in a row. This field is incremented each time its containing row is updated, and it is used during synchronization to satisfy conflicts among other members of the replica set having updates to the same row.

An s_GUID field is added to give each row in a table a unique identifier. This field is an AutoNumber data type with a Replication ID field size, a 16-byte randomly generated field.

The s_GUID field is a Globally Unique ID generated by the operating system using time and machine information. A row existing at the time of replication is given an s_GUID that appears in all members of the replica set. New rows added to a table in a replica set member are given an ID that is randomly generated. Although unlikely, rows added to the same table in different replicas may possibly end up having the same s_GUID value. If this occurs, the synchronization process treats the rows as being one row instead of two different rows and selects one of the rows to keep in the replicas, while the other row is written to a *conflict table* for your review.

The s_Lineage field is added to hold information regarding the history of changes made to the row. This field plays a role in determining which changes to apply when multiple updates to the same record have been detected during synchronization.

Memo and OLE Objects are each given an additional field named Gen_fieldname. This field tracks changes to these objects separately from the rest of the row. If a row's changes do not include its memo or OLE object fields, those objects are not updated, which reduces the amount of traffic between the source and target of a synchronization process.

The conversion and synchronization processes add new system tables to your database, as described in Table 22-1.

Table 22-1 System Tables Added by the Creation and Synchronization of a Replica Set

Table Name	*Description*
MSysErrors	Holds the errors that occurred during the synchronization process.
MSysExchangeLog	Holds information about exchanges between replicas in the set.

(continued)

Table 22-1 *(continued)*

Table Name	*Description*
MSysGenHistory	Holds information about the generations of the containing replica.
MSysOthersHistory	Holds information about the generations of other replicas the containing database has synchronized with.
MSysRepInfo	Holds information about the replica set.
MSysReplicas	Holds information about each replica in the replica set.
MSysSchChange	Holds Design Master schema (design) changes to be replicated.
MSysSchedule	Holds synchronization schedule and details.
MSysTableGuids	Holds information about tables and their GUIDs used in synchronization.
MSysTombstone	Holds information about deletions to be replicated.
MSysTranspAddress	Holds information about replica set Transporters.
MSysSideTables	Holds the GUIDs of tables involved in conflicts and the names of their associated conflict tables holding the conflict records. Created at time of first conflict.
MSysSchemaProb	Holds information about schema (design) errors detected during synchronization.

When errors are detected during synchronization, they are recorded in the MSysErrors system table. When conflicts are detected, the conflicting records are added to the table indicated in the MSysSideTables. Conflict tables have names such as *tablename Conflict*, where *tablename* is the name of the table where the conflict was detected.

New properties are added to your database to give each replica set member a unique ID and to indicate whether the member is replicable or not. DesignMasterID is the GUID of the Design Master database, and ReplicaID is the ID of a replica database. A `True` value in the `Replicable` property indicates that the database is replicable.

If you have objects that you do not want to replicate, you can create a `KeepLocal` property and set it to `True` prior to creating the replica set. Any object with a `KeepLocal` property set to `True` does not appear in the replicas. If you later want to replicate these objects, add a `Replicable` property to the object and set it to `True`. When you next synchronize the database with other members, the object is replicated into the target replica. This also applies to objects created after a database becomes replicable, but only objects from the Design Master. Objects created within replicas cannot be replicated to other members.

Tip

If any of your tables have AutoNumber fields whose new values are assigned incrementally, these fields are changed to be assigned randomly during the conversion to the Design Master. If the AutoNumber field is a key field, keys are assigned randomly instead of sequentially to prevent the same key from being added in multiple replicas. Even though random values are assigned, the same value may possibly be generated in different replicas and may cause a data error when the replicas are synchronized. To eliminate this risk, use the s_GUID field as the key or a value that you can guarantee to be unique among all replicas in the set.

The addition of new fields and tables to your database increases the size of the database and raises some issues that you need to be aware of (see Table 22-2).

The addition of three fields, plus an additional field for each OLE Object and Memo field in the table, reduces the number of fields that your application can use due to the limit of 255 fields per table. Likewise, the additional data added to support replication could put the record size over the limit of 2048 bytes and, depending on update activity, could put the database over the total size limit of one gigabyte. Additionally, disk management needs to be addressed to ensure that sufficient space is available not only to add records but also to accommodate the replication support data.

Table 22-2 New Field Overhead

Field Name	*Description*
s_Generation	Long integer used to track changes to a record since the last synchronization
s_GUID	16-byte globally unique identifier
s_Lineage	OLE object used to track the versions and replicas updating a record
Gen_xxx	Long integer for each Memo or OLE field used to track changes to these fields in a record

Replicas

After you convert a nonreplicable database to a Design Master, you may then create as many replicas as needed.

Tip

You should not allow users to access the Design Master database. Keep this database protected so that no one can change it and cause those changes to be replicated to other replicas. Likewise, you should not allow the original nonreplicated database to be accessed so that new Design Masters and replica sets can be created. Too many replicas and multiple replica sets of the same database may cause confusion and possibly an environment that is out of synchronization.

Replicas can be created from the Design Master or from another replica in the set. Before creating a new replica, compress the database and synchronize all members of the set. Doing this ensures that the replica is created quickly and is up to date.

The replicas of a set can be synchronized only with the other members of the same set, including the Design Master. An error occurs if you attempt to synchronize a replica of one set with a replica of a different set.

If objects are created within a replica, they are marked as local and cannot be made replicable. If these objects are required to be replicated to other members, either create them in the Design Master or import them from their source database and set their `Replicable` property to `True`.

Creating a Replica

You have four options for creating a replica set for your database, as follows:

- *Access replication:* Access provides a Replication menu choice on the Tools menu. From this menu, you can create the Design Master and the first replica, create additional replicas, and synchronize and resolve conflicts.
- *Briefcase replication:* Dragging an Access .MDB file and dropping it on the Windows 95 Briefcase creates a Design Master and a replica, given that Access is installed on the machine. The Briefcase can also be used to synchronize the replica with the Design Master.

On CD-ROM

- *Replication using DAO:* DAO provides replication methods that enable you to create and maintain either full or partial replicas from code. The Replication Lab in CH22.MDB on the CD-ROM accompanying this book illustrates the use of these methods.
- *Replication Manager Utility:* The Microsoft Office Developer Edition contains a utility called Replication Manager. This utility provides access to all the replication functions, with the exception of creating a partial replica, which must be done in code, and offers a facility for scheduling the synchronization of replicas.

Access replication

To convert your database to a Design Master and create the first replica from within Access, select Tools➪Replication➪Create Replica.

The first message you see when converting your database is shown in Figure 22-1. This message merely informs you that the database must be closed before the replica can be created.

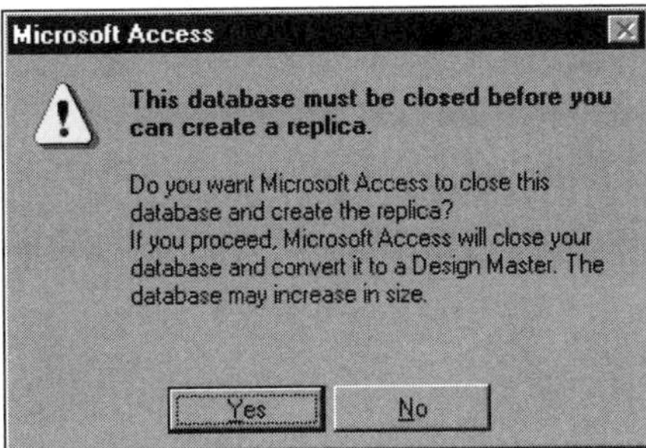

Figure 22-1: Access must close your database to create the Design Master.

Access then asks if you want to create a backup of the original nonreplicable database before it is converted (see Figure 22-2). Unless you have already made provisions for recovering your database back to a preconverted state, click Yes to answer this message.

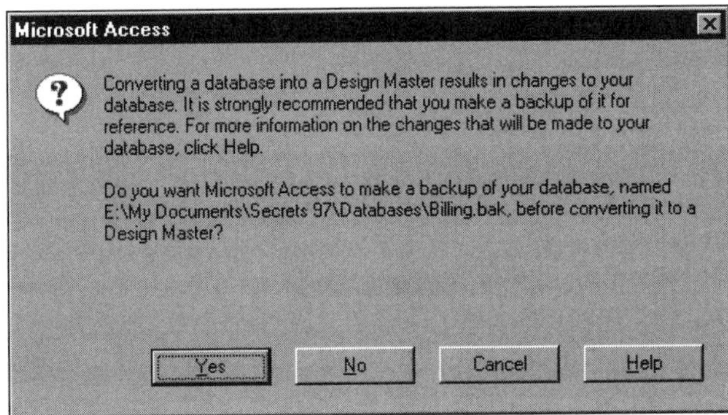

Figure 22-2: Access can make a backup of your nonreplicable database before converting it.

After your database is converted, the first replica is created. You are prompted for the name and location of this replica, as shown in Figure 22-3.

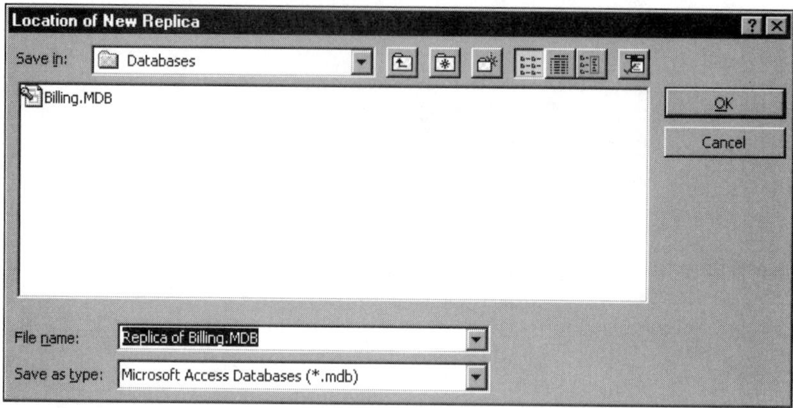

Figure 22-3: Enter the location and name of the first replica in the new set.

After the Design Master and the first replica have been created, you then see the success message shown in Figure 22-4.

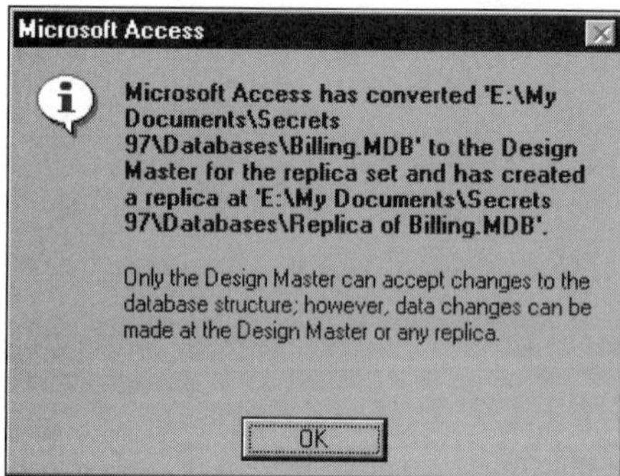

Figure 22-4: After the Design Master and first replica are created, the completion message is displayed.

Note that the Access title bar now identifies your open database as the Design Master. Click on the Tables tab in the database container and select Show System Objects from the Tools➪Options menu to see the new tables added to your database during conversion. Figure 22-5 shows the system tables after converting a database named Billing.

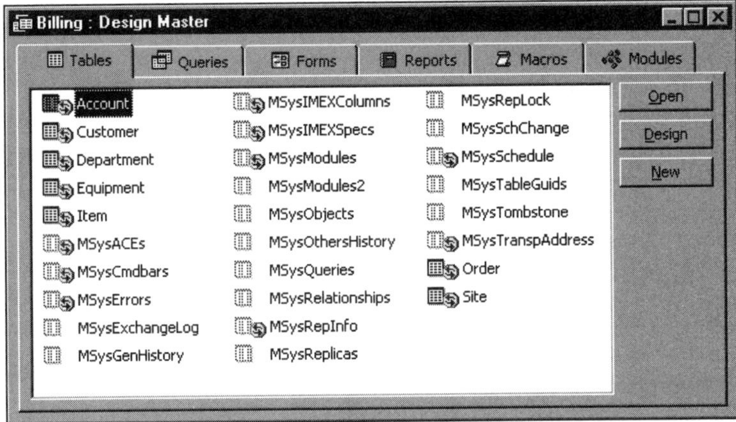

Figure 22-5: The Billing: Design Master tables tab in the database container showing system tables added during conversion.

Briefcase replication

If you installed the Briefcase Replication component when installing Access, you can use the Windows 95 Briefcase to convert your database to a replicable form and to synchronize that database with the briefcase replica.

When you install the Briefcase Replication component, it registers a reconciler ClassID with the briefcase, to be launched whenever an .MDB file is dropped onto the briefcase. The reconciler handles the database conversions and the synchronization of the briefcase replica with its associated replica whenever the user requests an update from the briefcase menu.

You can establish a briefcase icon on your Windows 95 desktop by right-clicking the mouse and selecting New Briefcase from the pop-up menu.

Convert your database by dragging it from an Explorer window to the briefcase icon and dropping it. The reconciler converts your database to the Design Master, leaving it in the source directory and creating a replica in the Briefcase. During this process, you are prompted to make two decisions (see Figure 22-6): Do you want to create a backup of the nonreplicable database before conversion; and which of the two databases should be the Design Master, the original in the source directory or the one in the Briefcase?

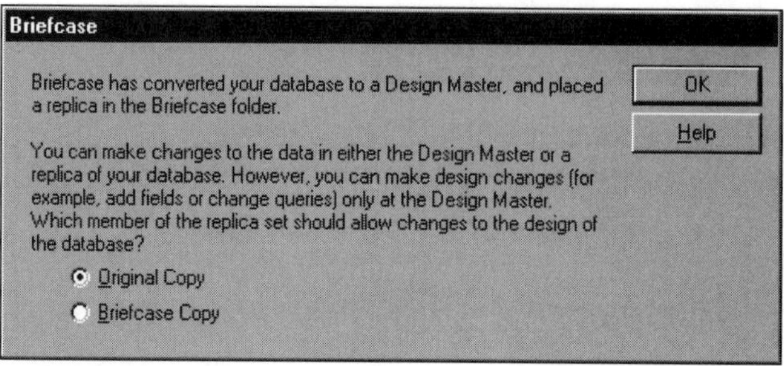

Figure 22-6: When the conversion is complete, you can choose which replica becomes the Design Master.

You can send the Briefcase to the diskette drive, for example, load it onto another computer, and update the replica. When you return the Briefcase to the desktop, you'll want to synchronize the replica updates in the Briefcase with the other replica in the source directory. See the section "Synchronizing from the Briefcase," later in this chapter, for details on Briefcase synchronization.

Replication using DAO

DAO provides methods that you can use to support either full or partial replication from code. Using these methods, you can convert a database to a Design Master, create additional replicas, synchronize replica members, and resolve conflicts.

On CD-ROM

CH22.MDB on the CD-ROM contains a replication lab form that illustrates the use of the replication methods, as shown in Figure 22-7.

To convert a database to a replicable form, type a database name into the Database text box or click on the Browse button to select one.

Click on the Make DB Replicable button to create and set the `Replicable` property on the selected database. This is done in the `MakeDesignMaster` procedure shown in Listing 22-1.

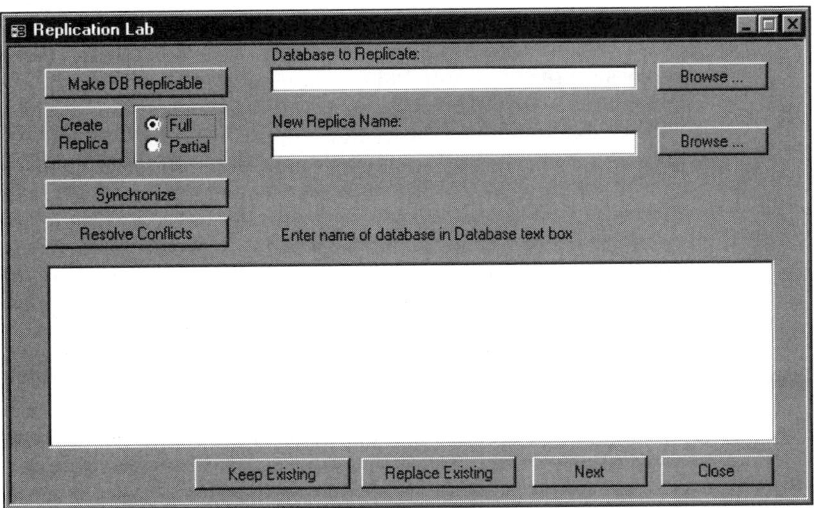

Figure 22-7: The Replication Lab form in CH22.MDB.

Listing 22-1 Function to Create and Set the Replicable Property

```
Public Function MakeDesignMaster(sDatabase As String)
On Error GoTo MDSErrHandler

Dim dbDatabase As Database
Dim dbProperty As Property

Set dbDatabase = DBEngine.Workspaces(0).OpenDatabase(sDatabase, _
True)
Set dbProperty = dbDatabase.CreateProperty("Replicable", dbText)
dbProperty.Value = "T"
dbDatabase.Properties.Append dbProperty
dbDatabase.Close
MakeDesignMaster = True
Exit Function
MDSErrHandler:
MsgBox Err.Description, vbCritical + vbOKOnly, "Conversion _
Error"
MakeDesignMaster = False
Exit Function
End Function
```

The `MakeDesignMaster` procedure creates the `Replicable` property and assigns the string value `"T"` to it. When the database is closed at the end of this procedure, the conversion to the Design Master occurs. Note that the database was opened exclusively.

Prior to converting a database, you should ensure that it has been reviewed to remove unwanted data. The existence of unnecessary data only lengthens the conversion process and makes replicas carry the burden of additional records that will never be used. Getting rid of these records prior to conversion is best, because then the system does not need to replicate the removal of these records across all replica set members some time after conversion.

To create a replica, enter the name of the database that will be the source of the replica in the Database to Replicate text box, and enter the path and name of the resulting replica in the New Replica Name text box. The database entered in the Database text box is expected to be either the name of the Design Master or of another existing replica.

Click either the Full or Partial option button and click on the Create Replica button to create the replica database. Selecting the Full option executes the `CreateReplica` procedure shown in Listing 22-2. The Partial option procedure is shown in Listing 22-3.

Listing 22-2 Function to Create a Full Replica of a Database

```
Public Function CreateReplica(sDatabase As String, sReplicaName As _
String)
On Error GoTo CRErrHandler
Dim dbDatabase As Database
Dim sDescription As String

Set dbDatabase = DBEngine.Workspaces(0).OpenDatabase(sDatabase)
sDescription = "Replica of " & sDatabase
dbDatabase.MakeReplica sReplicaName, sDescription
dbDatabase.Close
CreateReplica = True
Exit Function
CRErrHandler:
MsgBox Err.Description, vbCritical + vbOKOnly, "Create Error"
CreateReplica = False
Exit Function
End Function
```

The `CreateReplica` procedure assigns a description to the replica, then uses the `MakeReplica` method of the database object assigned by the `OpenDatabase` method on the database you entered in the Database text box.

If you want the replica to be ReadOnly, you can uncomment the `dbRepMakeReadOnly` constant, which can be passed as the third parameter to the `MakeReplica` method. You may want to add this as an option on the form.

When you designate a table as replicable and create a full replica of the database containing that table, all records in the table are replicated to the replica member. You may not need all records for a particular replica user. If this is the case, you can create a partial replica using the code in Listing 22-3.

Listing 22-3 Function to Create a Partial Replica of a Database

```
Public Function CreatePartial(sDatabase As String, sReplicaName As _
String)
   Dim db As Database, dbReplica As Database
   Dim td As TableDef
   Dim frmFilter As Form

   Set db = OpenDatabase(sDatabase)

   ' Create a replica to hold the partial data
   db.MakeReplica sReplicaName, _
       "Partial Replica of " & sReplicaName, dbRepMakePartial
   db.Close

   ' Set the ReplicaFilter property

   Set dbReplica = OpenDatabase(sReplicaName, True)

   ' Show modal dialog to collect table filter
  DoCmd.OpenForm ("CollectPartialFilter")
  Set frmFilter = Forms("CollectPartialFilter")
  Set td = dbReplica.TableDefs(frmFilter.sFilterTable)
  td.ReplicaFilter = frmFilter.sFilter
  dbReplica.Close

  ' Set the PartialReplica property on relationships here

  ' Create the partial replica
  Set dbReplica = OpenDatabase(sReplicaName, True)
  dbReplica.PopulatePartial sDatabase
  dbReplica.Close
  Exit Function
End Function
```

`CreatePartial` first creates a replica database to hold the partial replica. You do this by using the `MakeReplica` method of the source database.

The next step is to set the filter in the replica database. You accomplish this task by first collecting from the user the table to set a filter on and the filter specification. The lab example only allows one table and filter to be specified. The specifications collected from the `CollectPartialFilter` form are used to set the `ReplicaFilter` property of a table in the replica database.

After the `ReplicaFilter` is set, you can set relationships to pull records related to the filtered records. You do this by setting the `PartialReplica` property on all relations to participate in the partial population. The lab does not show the code to carry out this task.

The last step in creating a partial replica is to populate the replica with data according to the filter specification. The `PopulatePartial` method is used on the replica database to cause the `ReplicaFilter` on each table object to be applied to the database specified in the `PopulateReplica` method. This action pulls records from tables containing a ReplicaFilter property and related records in relations with a PartialReplica property. No other data is pulled into the partial replica. To remove a ReplicaFilter from a table, set the property to False.

Replication Manager Utility

The Replication Manager utility found in the Microsoft Office Developer Edition enables you to manage replica sets from the point of creating the set or additional replica members to synchronizing the set through a scheduled or manual synchronization. There is no facility for resolving conflicts, but you can determine which replicas experienced conflicts or errors and launch Access from within the Manager to resolve them.

Figure 22-8 shows the Replication Manager Synchronizer window displaying two Synchronizers. The Billing replica set is opened and there are two members of this set managed by the local Synchronizer named BAMO. One of those replicas is the Design Master, as indicated by the Design Master icon. Another Billing replica set member is managed by another Synchronizer named SECRETS, which, as indicated by its icon, is also an Internet Server Synchronizer.

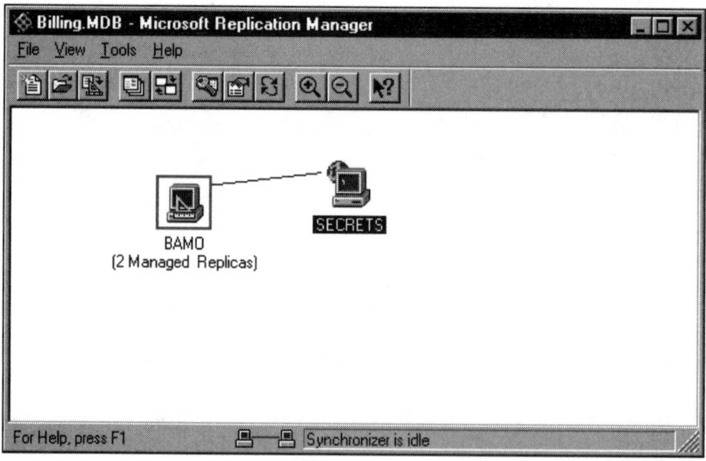

Figure 22-8: The Replication Manager utility window displaying one of its managed replica members.

In Figure 22-8, note at the bottom of the Manager window a status message indicating that the Synchronizer is idle. Later in this chapter, you'll see how the Synchronizer is scheduled.

A Synchronizer, MSTRAN35.EXE, is responsible for monitoring and synchronizing the replicas within one or more replica sets. You can assign as many replicas as necessary to a Synchronizer. As shown in Figure 22-8, when a replica set is opened, the number of replica members in that set managed by a Synchronizer is shown in parentheses below the Synchronizer icon.

When you first start the Replication Manager, it asks you to configure the Manager. This configuration designates various options the utility will use in managing replicas, such as the name of a shared network folder that will be used to cache transactions if a remote replica set member cannot be accessed during a synchronization and the path to the log file the Transporter will use to log its activity.

After the configuration is complete, the Synchronizer for the machine can be started and the Replication Manager can do its work. If the Synchronizer cannot be started, you cannot synchronize replicas with the utility; however, you can still synchronize by using one of the other methods discussed in this chapter.

Replicas may be located in any folder on the local machine and assigned to the local machine's Synchronizer, or they may be located in folders of other machines on the network and assigned to other Synchronizers, as is the case in Figure 22-8. The key to keeping these replicas in sync with each other is the knowledge of the Synchronizers regarding the member locations.

Tip

When using the Replication Manager to manage your replica sets, do not move replicas or create replicas outside of the Manager. Instead, use the Manager to create replicas and to move them to other folders on the network to ensure integrity of the set.

To start managing or to stop managing replicas, use the Managed Replicas dialog box of the Replication Manager (shown in Figure 22-9). The replicas selected in this dialog box will be managed by the machine's Synchronizer.

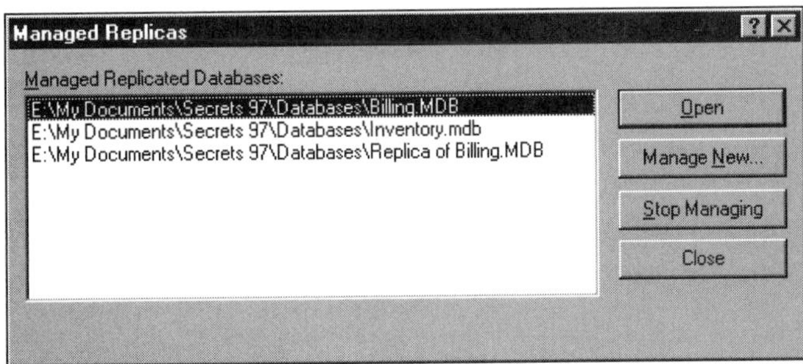

Figure 22-9: The Managed Replicas dialog box in the Replication Manager.

Figure 22-10 shows the dialog box in the Configuration Wizard for specifying the location of the *drop-box*, or shared network folder, where the Synchronizer leaves messages for a replica that cannot be accessed during a synchronization process.

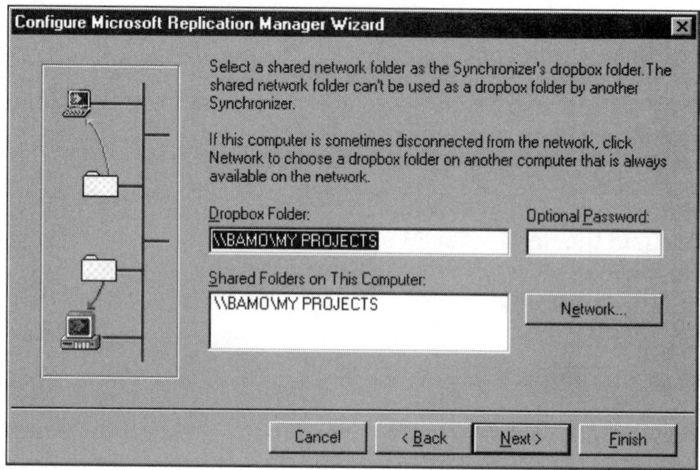

Figure 22-10: The drop-box folder selection dialog box of the Replication Manager Configuration Wizard.

The Synchronizer attempts to synchronize all managed members of a set by directly accessing the members itself and applying the necessary changes. If a replica in the set cannot be accessed for any reason, the Synchronizer cannot synchronize the replica with the other members of the set. In this case, the Synchronizer will leave messages for the remote Synchronizer of the disconnected member. The messages are placed in a drop-box to be picked up at a later time. Choose a drop-box folder to be available when the Synchronizer runs (see Figure 22-10). If the folder is not accessible when the Synchronizer launches, it does not start.

If the Synchronizer does run into problems during synchronization, it logs the problems, along with other messages regarding the status of the synchronization, in a Synchronizer Log file. This file and the path to it are specified in the wizard in the dialog box shown in Figure 22-11. You should choose a file location on the Synchronizer machine so that the log can be written, even if network connections are down.

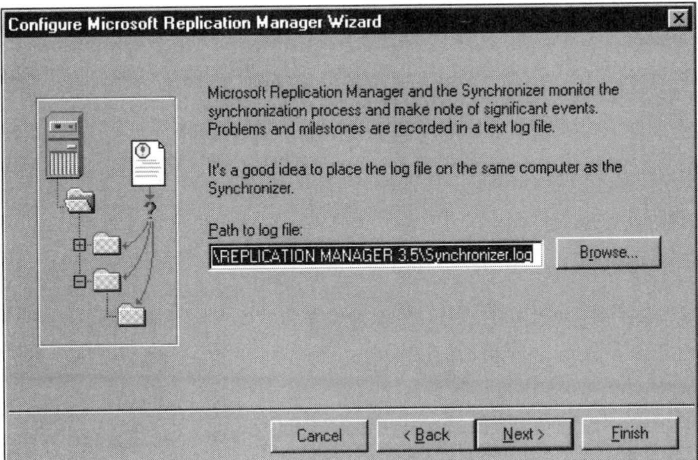

Figure 22-11: The Synchronizer log file path dialog box in the Replication Manager Configuration Wizard.

You can enter a name for the Synchronizer in the last dialog box of the Wizard (see Figure 22-12), which appears under the icon of the Synchronizer in the Replication Manager Synchronizer window. The machine name is a good choice for Synchronizer name.

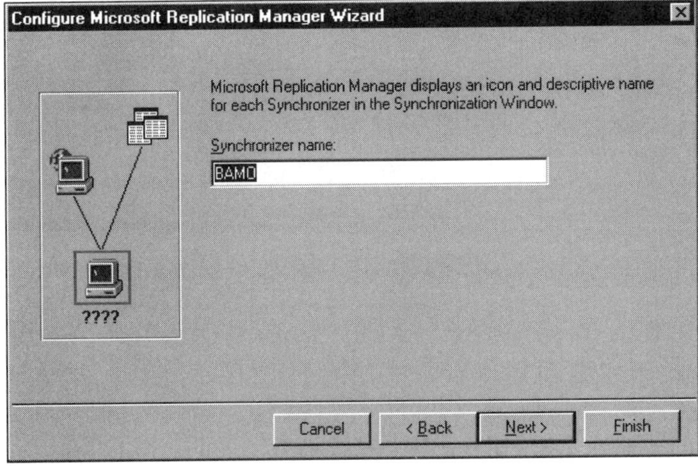

Figure 22-12: The last dialog box of the Configuration Wizard enables you to specify a name for the local Synchronizer.

After the configuration is completed, you are ready to start using the Manager to convert your databases and create and synchronize your replicas.

The Replication Manager does not require you to use its facilities for converting your database or creating new replicas. You may use any method presented in this chapter to create the replicas. After they are created, assign the replicas to a Synchronizer in the utility.

If you do choose to convert your database with the utility, select Convert Database To Design Master from the Replication Manager Tools menu. After selecting the database to convert, the Convert Database to Design Master Wizard appears.

In the first dialog box of the wizard, you are prompted to choose between making a backup of the selected database or not. If you haven't yet done so, have the wizard create a backup. The next dialog box asks you to enter a description for the entire replica set, as shown in Figure 22-13. This description appears in the title bar of the Replication Manager window whenever you select a member of the replica set.

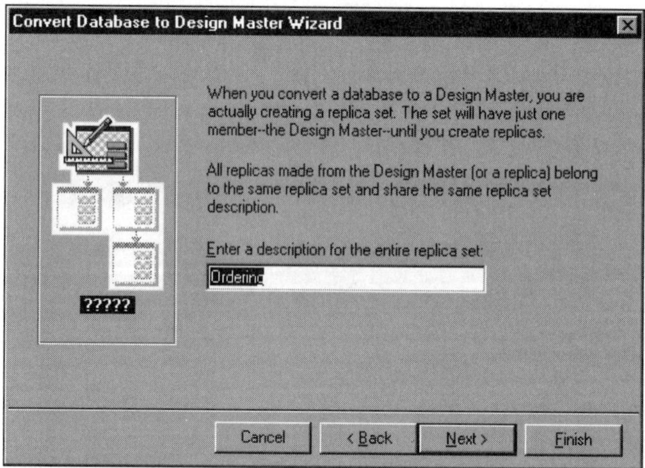

Figure 22-13: The second dialog box of the Convert Database Wizard is used to specify a description for the replica set.

The next dialog box of the wizard, shown in Figure 22-14, enables you to select the database objects you want replicated. You can choose to replicate all objects in the database or select specific objects. Consider the target users of the replicas and the objects they will need. Also consider the time required to synchronize replicas in making your choice of objects.

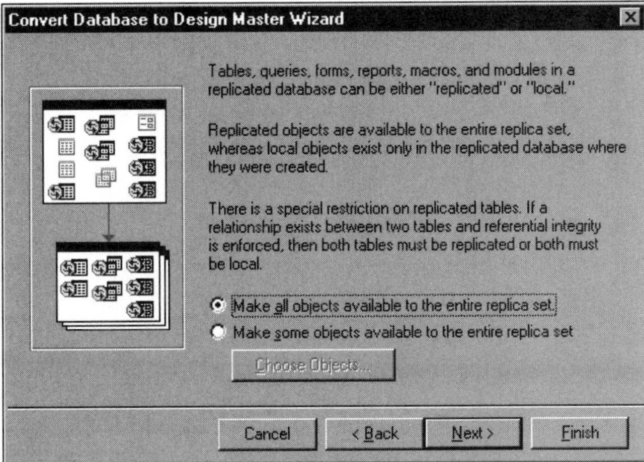

Figure 22-14: The third dialog box of the Convert Database Wizard enables you to select database objects to replicate.

If the data in your database supports partitioning, you could create separate partitions (tables) of the main database and then replicate those partitions to their target users. For example, if your database supports an organization that is broken down into regions, you may have data that is accessed only by users in a particular region and no one else. By creating a database that maintains only that subset of data, you could reduce the size of the replica and the time required to synchronize it. These partitions would need to be synchronized only with the main database tables to support global reporting and queries, because none of the replica data would overlap. Opportunities for other types of partitioning may exist as well, so give some thought to your target group and the data you need to support their requirements before you begin replicating databases. As an alternative to this approach, you can create partial replicas in DAO code.

In the next step of the conversion wizard, you are asked to choose between read-only and read-write replicas, as shown in Figure 22-15. Select the appropriate option for your intended usage of the replicas.

As shown in Figure 22-16, you have a choice of managing the Design Master with the local Synchronizer or deferring assignment to a Synchronizer until later.

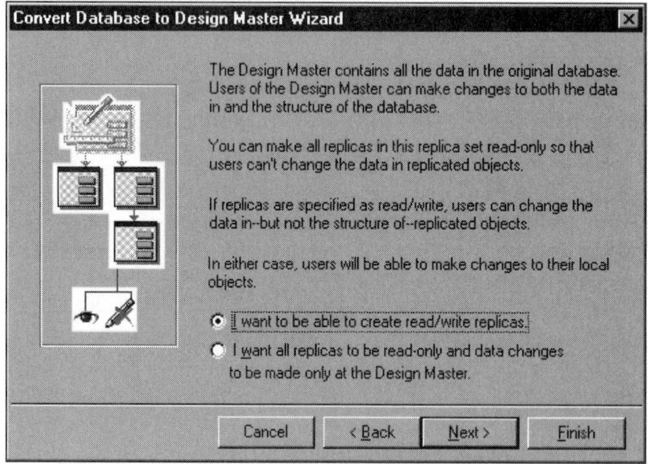

Figure 22-15: Replicas may be designated as read-only or read-write.

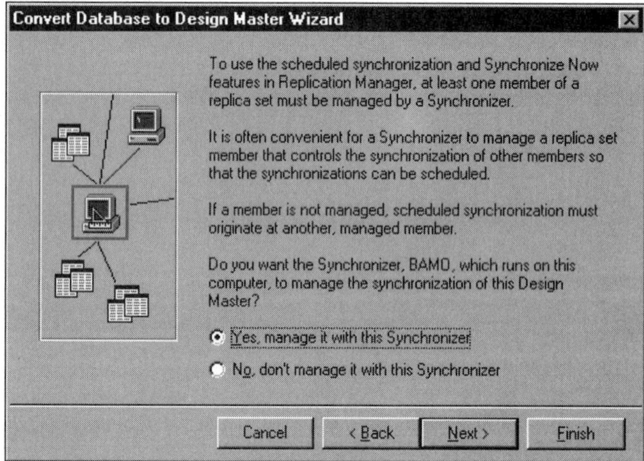

Figure 22-16: The Database Conversion Wizard gives you the opportunity to synchronize the Design Master with the local Synchronizer or to defer the assignment to later.

Clicking on the Finish button starts the conversion process and then opens the Design Master. Unlike the Access method and the Briefcase method, the Replication Manager does not automatically create a first replica member when it converts your database. The outcome of this process is the Design Master only.

To create replicas of your converted database, select New Replica from the File menu. The first dialog box of the New Replica Wizard enables you to select the Design Master as the source of the new replica or another member replica, as shown in Figure 22-17.

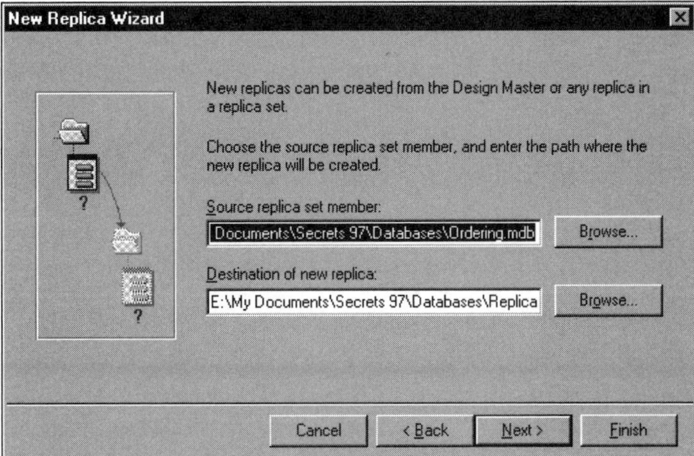

Figure 22-17: The first dialog box of the New Replica Wizard enables you to choose the source of the new replica.

The next dialog box of the wizard enables you to choose between read-only and read-write attributes for the new replica, as shown in Figure 22-18.

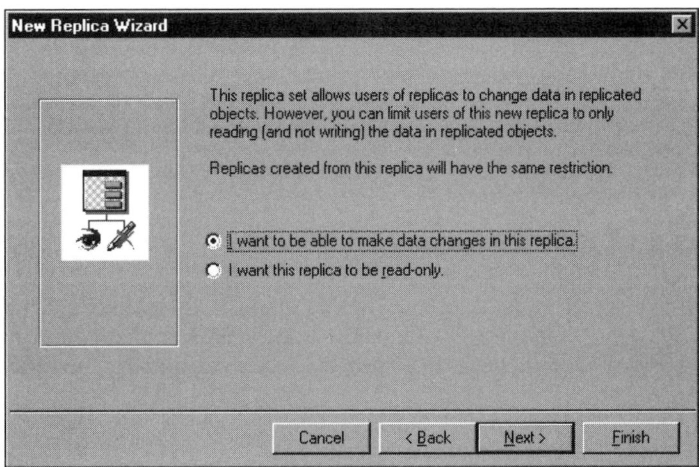

Figure 22-18: Designate the new replica as read-only or read-write.

The next New Replica Wizard dialog box asks you to choose the local Synchronizer or defer Synchronizer assignment for the new replica member, as shown in Figure 22-19. At least one member of the replica set needs to be assigned to a Synchronizer. If you have already assigned the Design Master to a Synchronizer, then you can defer assignment for this replica.

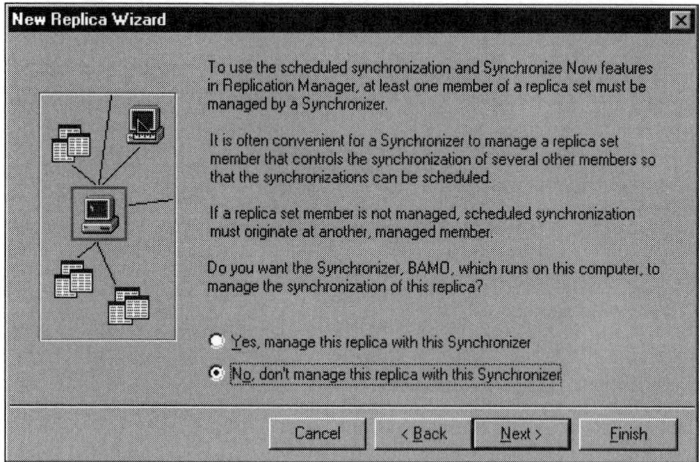

Figure 22-19: Assign the local Synchronizer to manage the new replica or defer assignment.

Click the Finish button to create the new replica, which appears in the Synchronization window as an additional count to managed replicas or as an unmanaged replica icon, according to your choice for Synchronizer assignment.

To view the objects contained in a replica, select the replica member in the Synchronization window and double-click or right-click the mouse to view properties. On the Open Database tab, click the View Object Status button. The Object Status dialog box displays the objects contained in the replica set and their status.

Synchronizing Replicas

All the replication facilities previously discussed — Access, Briefcase, DAO, and Replication Manager — offer the capability to synchronize members of the replica set. This next topic presents synchronization in each of these four facilities.

Synchronizing with Access

You can synchronize your open replica member with another selected member of the set by choosing Synchronize Now from the Tools⇨Replication menu in Access.

From the Synchronize Database dialog box, select another replica member to synchronize with from the drop-down list box, or click on the Browse button to specify a member not yet in the list, as shown in Figure 22-20.

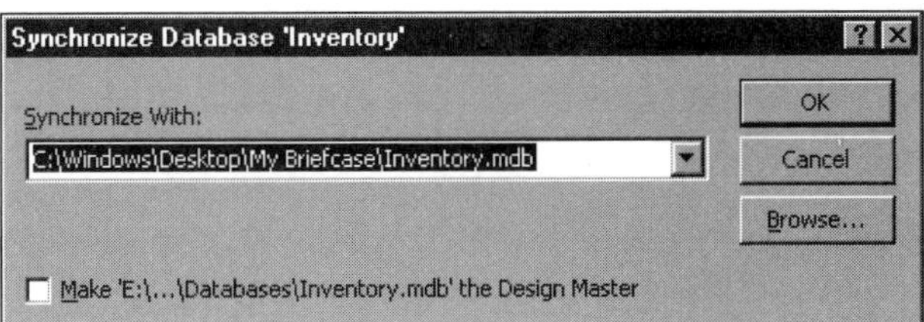

Figure 22-20: The Synchronize Database dialog box asks you to choose a target replica member to synchronize with the current database.

Replica set member names reside in the MSysReplicas table within each member database. A replica member becomes known to another member if one is created from the other or synchronized with the other. If a replica named Replica xxx1 creates a member replica named Replica xxx2, Replica xxx2 is immediately known to Replica xxx1 but is not known to Replica xxx or any other member until Replica xxx2 and Replica xxx are synchronized with each other. At that time, the existence of Replica xxx2 is entered into the MSysReplicas table of Replica xxx and vice versa.

You can remove a replica from a set by deleting the physical .MDB file. This action, however, does not remove the replica entry from the MSysReplicas table in remaining replica member databases, and the Synchronize Database dialog box continues to list the removed replica member in its drop-down list as a candidate for synchronization. To remove a replica from a set and from the candidate list in the synchronize dialog box, attempt to synchronize the current open replica with the deleted replica. Access will detect the missing database and remove the member from the replica set by removing the entry from the MSysReplicas table.

After deleting the file and removing it from the replica set, open Replication Manager and the managed replica set member or choose Refresh Synchronization Window from the Tools menu. You will no longer see the deleted replica member in the window. Attempting to remove a deleted replica from a managed set with the Replication Manager utility will only report a problem in its synchronization history details. It does not have the same effect as the synchronization from within Access.

Synchronizing from the Briefcase

Select the Details view from the Briefcase View menu to display the replica status information. To start the synchronization process, choose Update All or Update Selection from the Briefcase menu. For the .MDB replica in the Briefcase, a dialog box is presented that depicts the Briefcase replica and its target as well as the source from which the Briefcase replica was created, as shown in Figure 22-21. Click on the Update button to start synchronization.

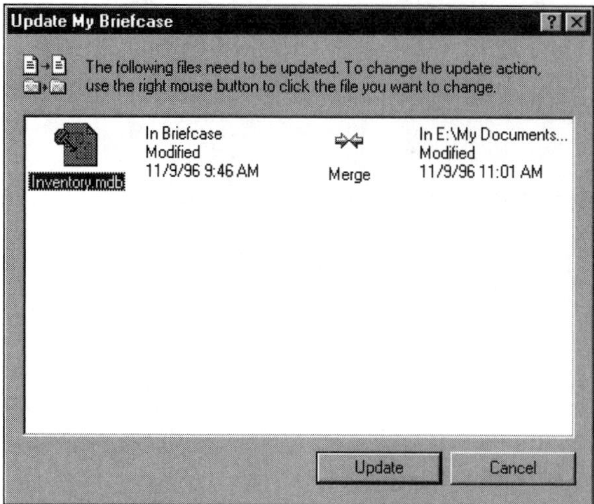

Figure 22-21: The Update My Briefcase dialog box prior to starting the synchronization process between the replicas displayed.

When the synchronization process ends, the status of the replica in the Briefcase changes to Up-to-date. Open the target database to verify that the briefcase database changes have been updated or to deal with the conflicts that may have been recorded. Be sure to check the Briefcase database as well if a bidirectional synchronization, changes passed between Briefcase and target and vice versa, has been performed.

If you subsequently make a design change to the Design Master, you again can select Update from the Briefcase menu to synchronize the design change with the replica, as shown in Figure 22-22.

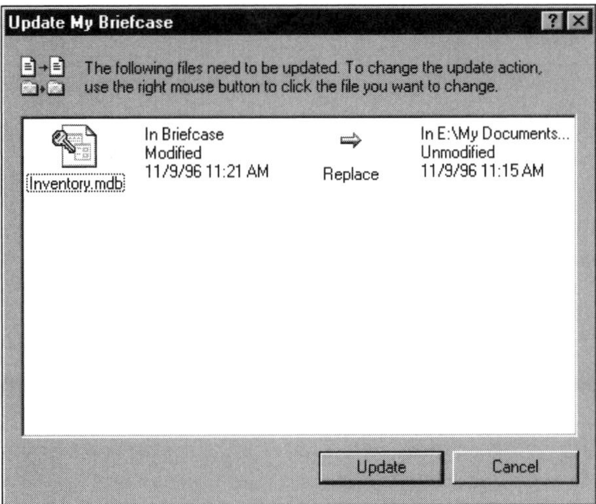

Figure 22-22: This Update dialog box indicates that the database in the Briefcase directory has been modified and needs to update the associated copy.

Synchronizing with DAO

On CD-ROM

On the Replication Lab form in CH22.MDB, included on the CD-ROM with this book, enter the names of the replicas in the Database and Replica Name text boxes and click on the Synchronize button.

The `SyncDBs` procedure shown in Listing 22-4 called from the Synchronize button's click event uses the `Synchronize` method of the database object. The `sSyncWithDB` string passed into the procedure is the name from the Replica Name text box, and it designates the other member with which the database object is to synchronize.

You may specify the direction of synchronization between the database object (dbDatabase) and the replica (sSyncWithDB) with the second parameter of the `Synchronize` method.

Use the `dbRepImpExpChanges` constant to replicate the changes in the `dbDatabase` database into the `sSyncWithDB` database.

Use `dbRepImportChanges` to replicate the changes in the sSyncWithDB database into the dbDatabase database.

The `dbRepImpExpChanges` constant used in the `SyncDBs` procedure yields a bidirectional exchange of changes between the two databases.

Listing 22-4 Function to Synchronize Two Replicas Using the Synchronize Method

```
Public Function SyncDBs(sDatabase As String, sSyncWithDB As String, _
RepType As Integer)
  On Error GoTo SDBErrHandler
  Dim dbDatabase As Database
  If RepType = 0 Then

     ' Full replica
     Set dbDatabase = _
DBEngine.Workspaces(0).OpenDatabase(sDatabase)
     dbDatabase.Synchronize sSyncWithDB, dbRepImpExpChanges
  Else

     ' Partial replica
     Set dbDatabase = _
DBEngine.Workspaces(0).OpenDatabase(sSyncWithDB)
     dbDatabase.PopulatePartial sDatabase
  End If
  dbDatabase.Close
  SyncDBs = True
  Exit Function
SDBErrHandler:
 MsgBox Err.Description, vbCritical + vbOKOnly, "Synchronization _
    Error"
 SyncDBs = False
 Exit Function
End Function
```

Note in Listing 22-4 the use of the `PopulatePartial` method to synchronize the changes contained in a partial replica indicated in the Replica Name text box with the database indicated in the Database Name text box. You use this method if you select the Partial option.

`PopulatePartial` synchronizes the changes in the partial replica member with the full database, clears the partial replica, and then repopulates it using the currently specified `ReplicaFilter` contained in the replica database. This portion of the `PopulatePartial` method is the same behavior used to create the partial replica, as discussed in the section "Replication using DAO," previously in this chapter.

Using `PopulatePartial` instead of `Synchronize` ensures that the partial is up to date with the full replica and that no orphaned records are left in the partial replica. Orphaned records can be created whenever a change in the partial replica data causes a record to no longer have the characteristics specified in the ReplicaFilter. Say, for example, your ReplicaFilter asks for all customers in Arizona at the time the partial replica was created. If the replica is updated to change a customer's state to New York, that customer no longer meets the Filter specifications. At synchronize time, `PopulatePartial` will pass the change to the full database and then receive new customers according to the current ReplicaFilter. If the ReplicaFilter still specifies Arizona customers, the customer changed to New York will not be pulled into the replica. Had the synchronization process merely exchanged changes, the New York customer would never be updated and therefore would be orphaned from the Arizona customers.

Synchronizing with Replication Manager

Using the Replication Manager, you have two options for synchronizing replicas. You can synchronize on demand or through a synchronization schedule, which you can customize to run on any 15-minute interval within a 24-hour clock.

To synchronize on demand, choose Synchronize Now from the Tools menu. This displays the Synchronize Now dialog box shown in Figure 22-23.

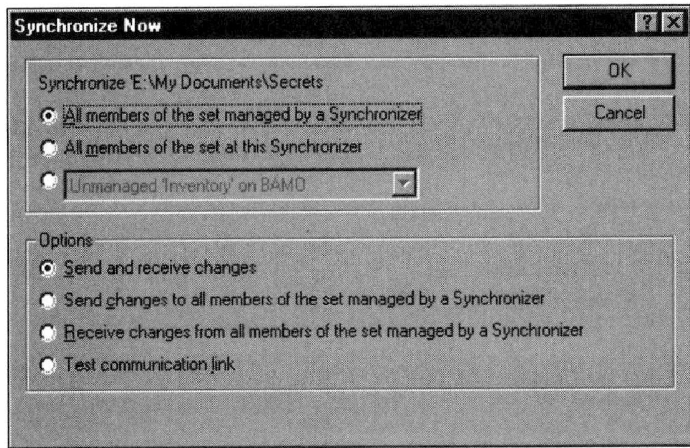

Figure 22-23: The Synchronize Now dialog box in Replication Manager enables you to specify the members to synchronize.

In the Synchronize Now dialog box, you specify the members to synchronize with the selected replica icon. You can synchronize with all other members managed by a Synchronizer, with all members of the set at the local Synchronizer, or with a specific member.

If you select All members of the set managed by a Synchronizer, you can select the exchange options in the Options frame. Only a bidirectional exchange is possible with the All members of the set at this Synchronizer option.

To set up a schedule for synchronizing members of replica sets managed by the local Synchronizer, right-click on a replica icon and select Edit Locally Managed Replica Schedule from the pop-up menu (see Figure 22-24).

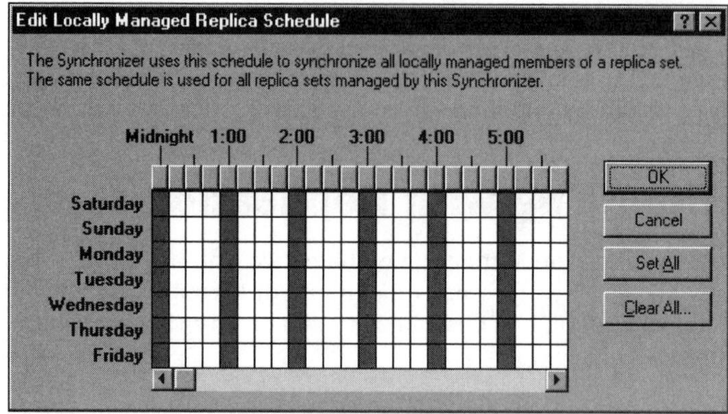

Figure 22-24: The Edit Locally Managed Replica Schedule can be set to automatically synchronize replica members at the local Synchronizer.

Click on the cells representing the time of day you want to schedule a synchronization. Click on the button at the top of the schedule grid to select all cells for the indicated time and have synchronization run at that time on every day of the week.

It is not necessary to have Replication Manager running for the synchronization schedule to take effect, but you do need to have the Synchronizer running.

Resolving Conflicts

When you synchronize replicas, you may detect conflicting changes that prevent one of the change records from being applied, or you may detect errors such as referential integrity errors or key errors.

Conflicts arise when the same record, identified by the GUID, is updated at two replica members in the set. The synchronization process selects one of the records to be applied to the two members being synchronized and writes the other record as a conflict record into a side-table created in the database that owns the conflict.

In the case of a conflict, Jet selects the record to apply to the table based on the version number in the record's s_Lineage field. This version number is updated each time the record is changed in each replica, and Jet selects the record having the highest version number, which is the record changed the most. If the version numbers are identical, then Jet must select one of the records to apply and write the other to the conflict side-table.

Errors can result whenever an update or design change from the Design Master violates a Jet- or Access-enforced rule, such as a unique key error or referential integrity error. The error is written into the MSysErrors table of the replica member where the error occurred. Before the members can be considered safely in sync, you must research and resolve all errors among the replicas and resynchronize the set to the point of no errors or conflicts.

Although you can use Replication Manager to determine the outcome of a synchronization, you cannot resolve the conflicts or errors within the utility. You can use Access or code your own DAO procedures to handle the resolution of problems.

To view the synchronization results of a replica, right-click on a replica icon and select View Local Synchronization History from the pop-up menu.

Resolving conflicts in Access

Opening a database after synchronization displays a message box informing you of any synchronization problems that occurred. You have the option to resolve the problems in this message box, or you can resolve the problems at a later time by choosing Resolve Conflicts from the Tools menu. Access displays a dialog box showing you the tables having problems and the types of problems experienced.

Resolving conflicts displays a dialog box showing the existing record and the conflict record, as shown in Figure 22-25. You are asked to choose between keeping the existing record or overwriting it with the conflict record. Either choice deletes the entry from the conflict side-table and either moves to the next conflict record or informs you that all conflicts have been processed.

Resolve Replication Conflicts - Customers

	Existing Record	Conflict Record
CustomerID:	1	1
CompanyName:	Let's Stop N Shop	Let's Stop N Shop
ContactFirstName:	Jaime	Jaime
ContactLastName:	Yorres	Yorres
BillingAddress:	87 Polk St.	87 Polk St.
City:	San Francisco	San Francisco
StateOrProvince:	CA	CA
PostalCode:	94117-	94117
Country:	USA	USA
ContactTitle:	Owner	Owner
PhoneNumber:	(415) 555-5997	4155555999
FaxNumber:	(415) 555-5939	(415) 555-5939
	Keep Existing Record	Overwrite with Conflict Record

Record: 1 of 1

Figure 22-25: The Resolve Replication Conflicts dialog box asks you either to choose to keep the existing record or to overwrite the existing record with the conflict record.

The Data Errors dialog box shows you the error details, such as duplicate values in a key field resulting from the same key being added to a table in the replicas. This error can arise if the key fields are not AutoNumber fields. The action you take depends on the type of error reported and may involve some extensive research with the replica users to determine how to resolve the error.

After resolving the reported problems, you should resynchronize the set to ensure that all problems have been resolved before releasing the databases into the production environment.

Resolving conflicts with DAO

If conflicts or errors result from the synchronization process, you can resolve them with your own procedures.

The Replication Lab form presents a method to resolve conflicts that is similar to the one used when you chose Resolve Conflicts from the Access Replication menu, but the method only illustrates the handling of conflicts. You can add procedures to handle errors by processing the MSysErrors table.

Processing the MSysErrors table enables you to find the tables that experienced conflicts and step through each conflict. The Replication Lab method asks you to choose either to keep the existing record (the one that was chosen by the synchronization process) or to overwrite it with the conflict record (the one that lost in the battle to become a row in the table).

On the Replication Lab form, enter the name of the database for which you want to resolve conflicts in the Database text box and click on the Resolve Conflicts button. The click event procedure for the Resolve Conflicts button calls the `ProcessConflicts` function to manage the display of conflicts.

The `ProcessConflicts` function shown in Listing 22-5 sets up the Recordsets needed to inspect the conflicts in all tables having conflicts. You can determine these tables by inspecting a table property called `ConflictTable`, which returns the name of the side-table holding the conflict records. Because this method would require visiting each TableDef in the database, the Replication Lab uses a more direct route to the conflicts by reading the MSysSideTables. This system table records the names of the side-tables holding the conflict records along with the GUID of the base table in which those conflicts occurred. To determine the name of the base table, another system table is used, MSysTableGuids, which holds the GUIDs and names of all tables in the database.

Listing 22-5 ProcessConflicts Manages the Collection and Display of Database Conflicts

```
Public Function ProcessConflicts(sDatabase As String)

On Error GoTo PCErrHandler

Set dbDatabase = DBEngine.Workspaces(0).OpenDatabase(sDatabase, _
True)
' Process Conflicts
On Error Resume Next
sSQLStmt = "SELECT [SideTable],[TableName] FROM _
MSysSideTables,MSysTableGuids WHERE MSysSideTables![TableGuid] = _
MSysTableGuids![s_GUID]"
Set rsSideTables = dbDatabase.OpenRecordset(sSQLStmt, _
dbOpenSnapshot)
   If Err = 0 Then
      If NextSideTable() = False Then
         rsSideTables.Close
           MsgBox "All conflicts have been processed"
      Else
         rc = NextConflict()
      End If
   End If
' Put Your Process Errors Code Here

ProcessConflicts = True
Exit Function

PCErrHandler:
ProcessConflicts = False
Exit Function
End Function
```

Replication Lab steps through each conflict record in the current side-table, presents each conflict record along with the existing record in the base table, and asks you to choose between those records. The base table record is selected using the conflict record's GUID field. This process is found in the `NextConflict` procedure shown in Listing 22-6.

Listing 22-6 Routine to Display the Existing Records and AssociatedConflict Records

```
Public Function NextConflict()
If Not rsConflicts.EOF Then
   Me!OLEControl10.ListItems.Clear
   rsBaseTable.Index = "s_GUID"
   rsBaseTable.Seek "=", rsConflicts![s_GUID]
   If rsBaseTable.NoMatch Then
'Record updated in Source not present in Target
   Else
'Record found is in conflict with the conflict table record
'Add existing record to view
```

(continued)

(continued)

```
     Set liItem = OLEControl10.ListItems.Add(, "K" & _
CStr(rsBaseTable.Name), CStr(rsBaseTable.Name))
     For i = 1 To rsBaseTable.Fields.Count
      liItem.SubItems(i) = rsBaseTable.Fields(i -1)   .Value
     Next i
   ' Add conflict record to view
     Set liItem = OLEControl10.ListItems.Add(, "K" & _
CStr(rsConflicts.Name), _
CStr(rsConflicts.Name))
     For i = 1 To rsConflicts.Fields.Count
       liItem.SubItems(i) = rsConflicts.Fields(i - 1).Value
     Next i
   End If
   rsConflicts.MoveNext
   NextConflict = True
Else
   NextConflict = False
End If
Exit Function
End Function
```

After all conflicts for a table are resolved, the next side-table is selected. The resolution process repeats until all side-tables have been inspected. The `NextSideTable` procedure in Listing 22-7 implements this process.

Listing 22-7 Function to Open a Conflict Table and Its Corresponding Base Table

```
Public Function NextSideTable()
If Not rsSideTables.EOF Then
' Open the Conflict Table
   Set rsConflicts = _
dbDatabase.OpenRecordset(rsSideTables![SideTable], dbOpenDynaset)
' Open the Base Table where conflict occurred
   Set rsBaseTable = _
dbDatabase.OpenRecordset(rsSideTables![TableName], dbOpenTable)
   Me!OLEControl10.ColumnHeaders.Clear
   Set colHeader = Me!OLEControl10.ColumnHeaders.Add(, "Table", _
"Table", 2000)
   For i = 0 To rsBaseTable.Fields.Count - 1
     Set colHeader = Me!OLEControl10.ColumnHeaders.Add(, _
(rsBaseTable.Fields(i).Name), _
(rsBaseTable.Fields(i).Name), 2000)
   Next i
' Get the next sidetable holding conflicts
   rsSideTables.MoveNext
   NextSideTable = True
Else
   NextSideTable = False
End If
Exit Function
End Function
```

If you click on the Replace Existing button, the existing record in the base table is replaced with the conflict record in the side-table. This process is found in the `ReplaceExistingRec` procedure listed in Listing 22-8.

Listing 22-8 Function Used to Replace a Base Table Record with a Conflict Record

```
Public Function ReplaceExistingRec()
'Replace existing base table record with conflict record
On Error Resume Next
rsConflicts.MovePrevious
rsBaseTable.Edit
For i = 0 To rsConflicts.Fields.Count - 1
   rsBaseTable.Fields(i).Value = rsConflicts.Fields(i).Value
Next i
rsBaseTable.Update
rsConflicts.MoveNext
Exit Function
End Function
```

After the conflict is resolved, the conflict record is removed from the side-table. When the side-table is empty, the table is deleted from the database. This process is implemented in the `RemoveConflict` procedure shown in Listing 22-9. This same function is also called when you elect to keep the existing record.

Listing 22-9 Function to Remove a Conflict Record from a SideTable

```
Public Function RemoveConflict()
' This procedure deletes the current conflict record. When the _
conflict
' table is empty, the table itself is deleted.
On Error Resume Next
rsConflicts.MovePrevious
rsConflicts.Delete
rsConflicts.MoveNext
If rsConflicts.EOF Then
   rsConflicts.Close
   rsSideTables.MovePrevious
   dbDatabase.TableDefs.Delete rsSideTables![SideTable]
   rsSideTables.MoveNext
End If
Exit Function
End Function
```

Building a New Design Master

If the Design Master becomes corrupted or lost, you can designate one of the other replicas as the new Design Master.

With one of the replica databases open in Access, choose Recover Design Master from the Tools➪Replication menu. A message box appears, informing you of the current Design Master name and asking you to verify that it has been lost or corrupted. Click on Yes to continue.

Access next tells you to synchronize the current database with all other replica members before designating it as the new Design Master. If you have already done this, click on Yes.

Access designates the current replica as the Design Master, which enables you to make design changes to the database and replicate those changes to other members in the set.

To designate the current database as the Design Master, Access changed the `DesignMasterID` property of the database to the ID of the replica. This can be accomplished in your own DAO procedures by assigning the current database `ReplicaID` value to the `DesignMasterID` property.

After changing a replica to the Design Master, you need to synchronize the replica with all other members of the set to update their DesignMasterIDs to point to the new Design Master.

Chapter 23

Using the Internet Features of Access 97

In This Chapter

- Tying the Internet features together in an application
- Exporting Access 97 objects to HTML
- Exploring access to an Access database on an Internet/intranet server using IDC/HTX
- Exporting objects using the Publish to Web Wizard
- Synchronizing Access 97 databases over the Internet
- Using hyperlinks in your application to jump between forms
- Using the Web Browser control to develop a mini-browser
- Displaying the Web Toolbar within Access 97

Hardly a day goes by without the average American seeing or hearing a reference to the Internet or World Wide Web. It seems as though every business, government, school, and hacker has a Web site. Of course, it's no secret that Microsoft is very dedicated to enhancing the power of the Internet/intranet, and the tools and functionality built into Microsoft Office 97 are testimony to that effort.

Access 97 uses a good portion of the new Microsoft Office 97 functionality to migrate Access objects such as forms, datasheets, and reports to Internet/intranet servers for viewing and even updating data from Access databases delivered by a browser, such as Microsoft Internet Explorer 3.0.

This chapter explores the various Internet features in Access 97 by means of a sample Product Inventory system for a sporting goods company. By examining this system, you learn about the use of hyperlinks to jump among Access 97 forms or between an Access 97 form and Internet Web-based forms. You also learn how to export your Access forms to a format that can be understood by Internet Information Server 2.0 or later and displayed in your browser. Finally, you explore the Web Browser control for displaying HTML documents in an Access form and synchronizing databases over an Internet connection.

A Product Inventory System

This chapter uses a simple product inventory system to illustrate the use of the Access 97 Internet features. The system discussed here is used by a sporting goods company and links to the Internet for entering orders directly to suppliers.

The client-side of the system, located in CH23.MDB on the CD-ROM accompanying this book, contains a switchboard, a form for editing customer orders, a form for editing products, and a form for viewing Internet documents.

The switchboard is used to navigate to the other forms in the system. Some of the navigation in this switchboard is implemented with standard `OpenForm` methods, whereas others are implemented using hyperlinks.

The products form lists all the products carried by the sporting goods company, the name of the supplier currently used for each product, and a hyperlink to each supplier's order form on the Internet. The supplier hyperlinks are stored as hyperlink data types in the suppliers table.

Clicking a hyperlink launches a form containing a Web Browser control. You use this form to retrieve a supplier's order form from the specified Internet address and to enter orders directly into the supplier's order system.

The interaction between the products form and the browser form is managed in code and uses `Hyperlink` object methods and events to navigate between forms and to control the browser's connection to the Internet.

The supplier's order forms and tables are found in CH23B.MDB on the CD-ROM. These forms and supporting tables will be exported to the Internet server using various export options, resulting in files suitable for hosting on Microsoft Internet Information Server 2.0, (an NT-based server that provides World Wide Web, FTP, Gopher, and other Internet services), which is used as the Web server in this chapter. The supporting tables will be migrated to the server via replication and synchronized using Internet synchronization. After these features have been covered, you can launch the order forms and view them in the client-side browser form or your favorite Internet browser.

Exporting the required Access objects to set up the supplier's order system on the Internet server is the first topic you explore.

Exporting Objects to HTML

The supplier's order forms are designed and built in Access and based on queries against local tables. CH23B.MDB contains the necessary forms to support order entry to a supplier of our sample sporting goods company.

Static and Dynamic HTML

The export of Access objects can result in either static or dynamic HTML documents. You should use the static HTML format when your data does not change frequently and your Web application does not require a form. *Static* data is data at a point in time. It displays the same information whenever the HTML page is displayed. Use dynamic format when your data changes frequently and your Web application needs to update and read live data from your Access database using a form. *Dynamic* data is data currently in the database. Each time the HTML page is displayed, you see current values from the database.

The order forms and their corresponding tables need to be placed on the Internet server and made available to Internet Information Server. After doing this, the client browser can request the form by requesting the form's URL (Uniform Resource Locator, which is essentially an address of a document).

Getting the required tables up to the server is accomplished through replication, which is covered in the "Synchronizing Databases over the Internet" section of this chapter. This section will deal only with exporting the forms.

Although the product inventory system doesn't require reports in HTML format, you can export reports to static HTML format, and you can export datasheets and forms to static or dynamic HTML format. Microsoft Access creates one Web page for each report page, datasheet, and form you export. Exporting objects to HTML format is useful for creating a simple Web application such as this one, verifying the format and appearance of an object's output, or adding files to existing Web applications.

Because you are exporting a form that accesses data in a table, the same functionality needs to be supported at the Internet server. The export of the order form then needs to do more than just ensure that labels and text boxes are placed on the Web page. As you'll see shortly, the Access 97 export features two technologies for accessing databases at the server.

The export of the order forms requires the selection of dynamic HTML output. Before you do this export, though, take a look at what static HTML output looks like.

Exporting a datasheet to static HTML format

To export a datasheet, such as the products datasheet from CH23.MDB, to a static HTML format, use the following steps:

1. In the Database window, click on the name of the table, query, or form you want to export, and then choose Save As⇨Export from the File menu.

2. In the Save As dialog box, click on To an External File or Database, and then click on OK.
3. In the Save as type combo box, select HTML Documents (*.html;*.htm) from the pull-down menu, as shown in Figure 23-1.

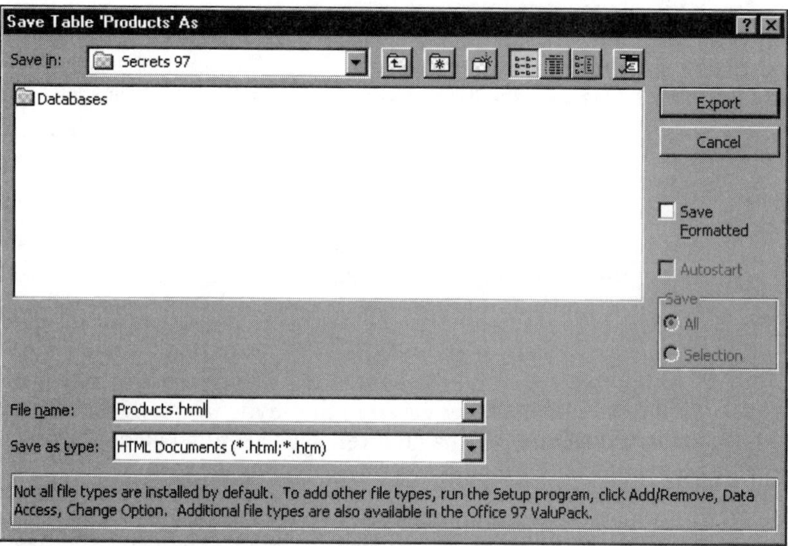

Figure 23-1: Selecting the HTML format in the Save As box.

4. Click the arrow to the right of the Save in box and select the drive or folder to which to export.
5. In the File name text box, enter the file name for the HTML file.
6. Select Save Formatted if you want to save the datasheet in a format similar to its appearance in Datasheet view. Select Autostart if you want to display the results in your default Internet browser.
7. Click on Export.

   If you selected Save Formatted in Step 6, the HTML Output Options dialog box is displayed. You can specify an HTML template to use. You also can define a default value for the HTML Template option. On the Tools menu, click on Options, and then click on the Hyperlinks/HTML tab, as shown in Figure 23-2.

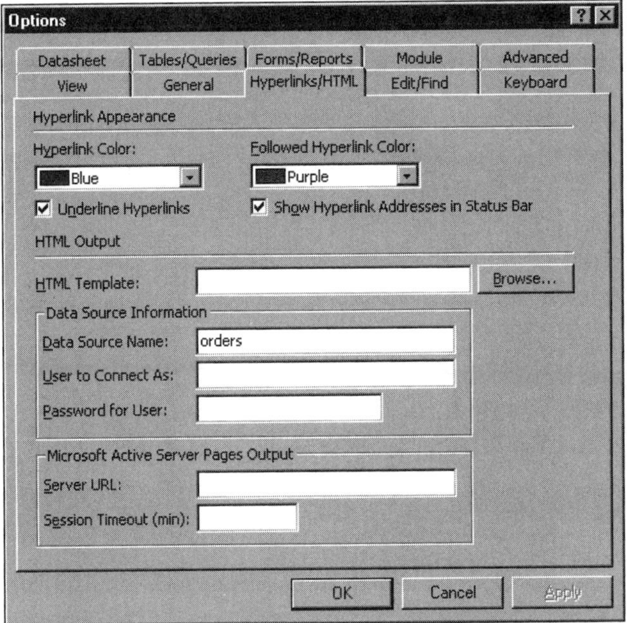

Figure 23-2: The Tools⇨Options⇨Hyperlinks/HTML tab.

The HTML file is based on the Recordset behind the datasheet, including any `OrderBy` or `Filter` property settings. If the datasheet contains a parameter query, Access first prompts you for the parameter values and then exports the results. If you selected Save Formatted in Step 6, the HTML table simulates as closely as possible the appearance of the datasheet by creating the appropriate HTML tags to retain attributes such as color, font, and alignment. Values from most fields (except OLE objects and Hyperlink fields) are output as strings and are formatted similar to how they appear in the datasheet, including defined `Format` or `InputMask` properties. Fields with a Hyperlink data type (see the section on Hyperlinks, later in this chapter) are output as HTML links using `<A HREF>` tags. All unformatted data types, except Text and Memo, are saved with right alignment as the default. Text and Memo fields are saved with left alignment by default.

Tip

The layout of the HTML page simulates the page orientation and margins set for the datasheet. To change these settings, display the datasheet, and then use the Page Setup command on the File menu before you export it. A large datasheet may take a long time to output and to display through a browser. Consider reducing the size of the datasheet, dividing the datasheet into smaller datasheets by using criteria such as a date field, or using a report or form to view the data.

Figure 23-3 shows the first portion of the HTML generated when exporting the data from the Products table.

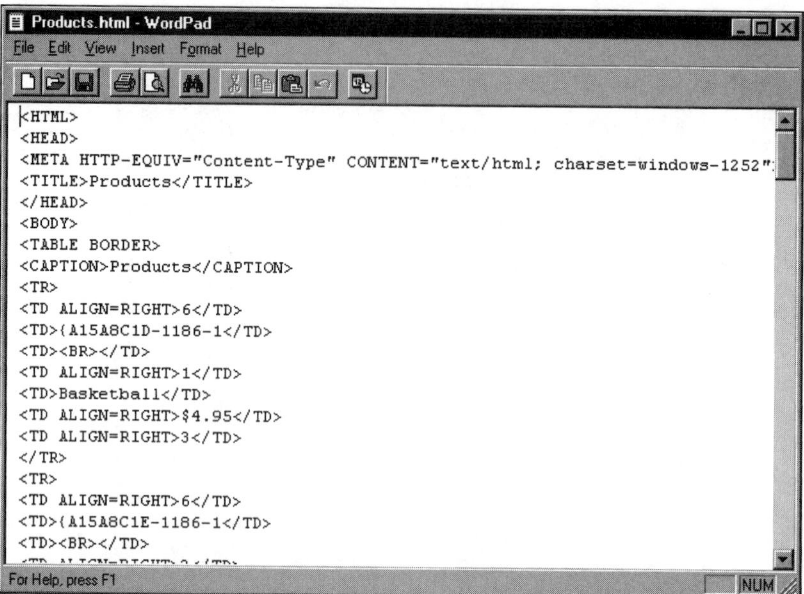


```
<HTML>
<HEAD>
<META HTTP-EQUIV="Content-Type" CONTENT="text/html; charset=windows-1252">
<TITLE>Products</TITLE>
</HEAD>
<BODY>
<TABLE BORDER>
<CAPTION>Products</CAPTION>
<TR>
<TD ALIGN=RIGHT>6</TD>
<TD>{A15A8C1D-1186-1</TD>
<TD><BR></TD>
<TD ALIGN=RIGHT>1</TD>
<TD>Basketball</TD>
<TD ALIGN=RIGHT>$4.95</TD>
<TD ALIGN=RIGHT>3</TD>
</TR>
<TR>
<TD ALIGN=RIGHT>6</TD>
<TD>{A15A8C1E-1186-1</TD>
<TD><BR></TD>
```

Figure 23-3: Viewing an HTML representation of the Products table.

Figure 23-4 shows the Products datasheet as displayed in the Internet Explorer 3.0 browser.

6	{A15A8C1D-1186-1	1	Basketball	$4.95	3
6	{A15A8C1E-1186-1	2	Football	$5.65	2
6	{A15A8C1F-1186-1	3	Soccer ball	$12.95	4
6	{A15A8C20-1186-1	4	Volleyball	$3.25	1
6	{A15A8C21-1186-1	5	6 Golf balls	$6.75	1
6	{A15A8C22-1186-1	6	Crystal ball	$45.55	2
6	{A15A8C23-1186-1	7	Baseball	$8.75	2
6	{A15A8C24-1186-1	8	Billiard balls	$127.45	3
6	{A15A8C25-1186-1	9	Tether ball	$9.65	3
6	{A15A8C26-1186-1	10	Foosball	$17.85	2
6	{3F9271D8-118C-1	18	Bowling ball	$54.95	3
6	{3F9271DB-118C-1	14	Bats	$29.87	4
6	{3F9271DC-118C-1	12	Gloves	$67.99	4

Figure 23-4: The Products datasheet as it appears in an Internet browser.

IDC/HTX and ActiveX Server Pages

Microsoft's Internet Information Server 2.0 currently (as of December 1996) supports Internet Database Connector (IDC) and HTML extension (HTX) technology for access to server-side databases through ODBC. Expected in early 1997 is Microsoft's release of the Microsoft ActiveX server framework, which will provide server-side scripting support and database access through server-side ActiveX components. The server-side script files to be processed by this framework contain VBScript, template directives, and HTML tags mixed together. These files have an .ASP extension, which stands for ActiveX Server Pages.

Exporting a datasheet to dynamic HTML format

The process of exporting a dynamic HTML format is essentially the same as exporting a static format except that you choose the Microsoft IIS 1-2 (*.htx;*.idc) or Microsoft ActiveX Server (*.asp) format instead of the HTML Documents choice in the Save Table As dialog box.

To export a datasheet to dynamic HTML format, follow the steps outlined in the preceding section, "Exporting a datasheet to static HTML format," but in the Save as type box, select Microsoft IIS 1-2 (*.htx;*.idc) or Microsoft ActiveX Server (*.asp), depending on which dynamic HTML format you want.

You must specify the system data source name that you will use on the Internet server, and, if required, a user name and password to open the database. If you are exporting to .ASP file format, you can enter the server URL of the location where the .ASP file will be stored on the server. For example, this example stores the .ASP files in the \Suppliers folder on the \\Secrets server, so type **http://Secrets/Suppliers/**.

If a form is in Datasheet view or its `Default View` property is set to `Datasheet` when you export to .ASP file format, then Microsoft Access outputs the form as a datasheet. If the form is in Form or Design view or its `Default View` property is set to `Single Form` or `Continuous Forms`, then Microsoft Access outputs the form as a form. The layout of the HTML page simulates the page orientation and margins set for the datasheet. To change these settings, display the datasheet, and then use the Page Setup command on the File menu before you export it.

Exporting a report to static HTML format

Reports are always output in a static HTML format. To export a report, follow these steps:

1. In the Database window, click on the name of the report you want to export, and then select Save As⇨Export from the File menu.

2. In the Save As dialog box, click To an External File or Database, and then click on OK.
3. In the Save as type text box, select HTML Documents (*.html;*.htm) from the pull-down menu.
4. Click on the arrow to the right of the Save In box and select the drive or folder to which you want to export.
5. In the File name text box, enter the name of the exported file.
6. Select Autostart to display the results in your default Internet browser.
7. Click on Export.

In the HTML Output Options dialog box, you can specify an HTML template to use. If you do not specify an HTML template file containing navigation tokens, Access 97 does not provide a default navigation scheme, and if you selected Autostart in Step 6, only the first page is displayed.

The HTML file is based on the Recordset behind the report, including any current `OrderBy` or `Filter` property settings. If the datasheet contains a parameter query, Access first prompts you for the parameter values and then exports the results. Most controls and features of a report, including subreports, are supported except the following: lines, rectangles, OLE objects, and subforms. You can, however, use an HTML template file to include report header and footer images in your output files.

The output files simulate as closely as possible the appearance of the report by creating the appropriate HTML tags to retain attributes such as color, font, and alignment. Microsoft Access 97 outputs a report, unlike a datasheet, as multiple HTML files, one file per printed page, using the object name and an appendix to create each file name; examples are Products.htm, ProductsPage1.htm, ProductPage2.htm, and so on. The layout of the HTML pages simulates the page orientation and margins set for the report. To change these settings, display the report in Print or Layout Preview, and then use the Page Setup command on the File menu before you export it.

Exporting a form to dynamic HTML format

The Customer Information form and Order form used to enter orders directly to the supplier will be exported in .ASP format. You can output several types of forms: View forms (to display records), switchboard forms (to act as the home page or to navigate to related pages), and data entry forms (to add, update, and delete records). To export a form in dynamic .ASP format, follow these steps:

1. In the Database window, click on the name of the form you want to export, and then select Save As⇨Export from the File menu.
2. In the Save Table As dialog box, click on To an External File or Database, and then click on OK.

3. In the Save as type text box, click on Microsoft ActiveX Server (*.asp).
4. Click on the arrow to the right of the Save In box and select the drive or folder to which you want to export.
5. In the File name text box, enter the name of the exported file.
6. Click on Export.

As you did in exporting a datasheet to dynamic HTML, you must specify the system data source name that you will use on the Internet server, and, if required, a user name and password to open the database. You can enter the server URL of the location where the .ASP file will be stored on the server. In this example, the server location for the .ASP files is the Suppliers folder on the Secrets server. Type **http://Secrets/Suppliers/** in the Server URL text box.

Access outputs a continuous form as a single form. Access outputs most controls as ActiveX controls but ignores any Visual Basic code behind them. Figure 23-5 shows the resulting .ASP file. This file contains template commands inside `<% %>` symbols and VBScript in addition to HTML tags.

If a form is in Datasheet view or its `Default View` property is set to `Datasheet` when you export to .ASP file format, then Access outputs the form as a datasheet. If the form is in Form or Design view or its `Default View` property is set to `Single Form` or `Continuous Form`, then Access outputs the form as a form.

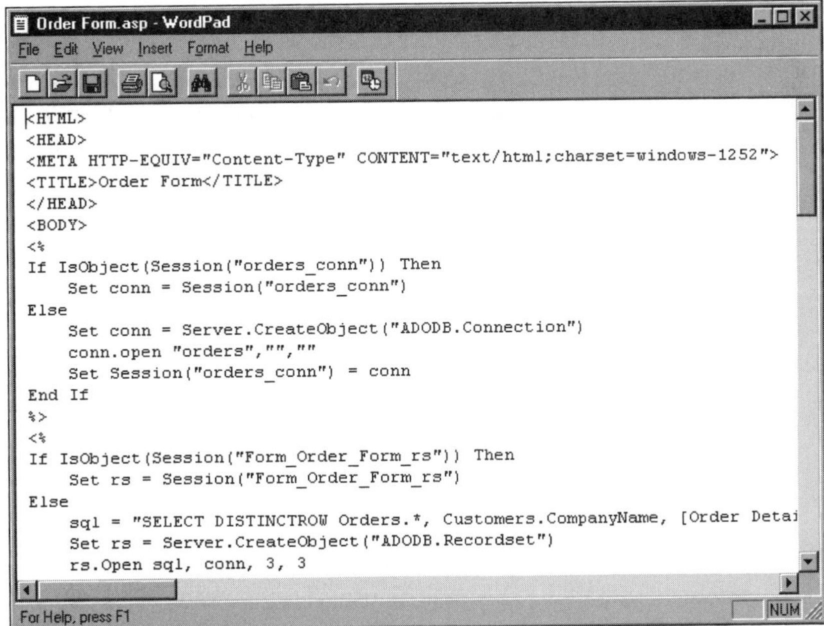

Figure 23-5: The .ASP file generated for the Orders form.

Figure 23-6 shows the Order form as it appears in the Internet Explorer 3.0 browser.

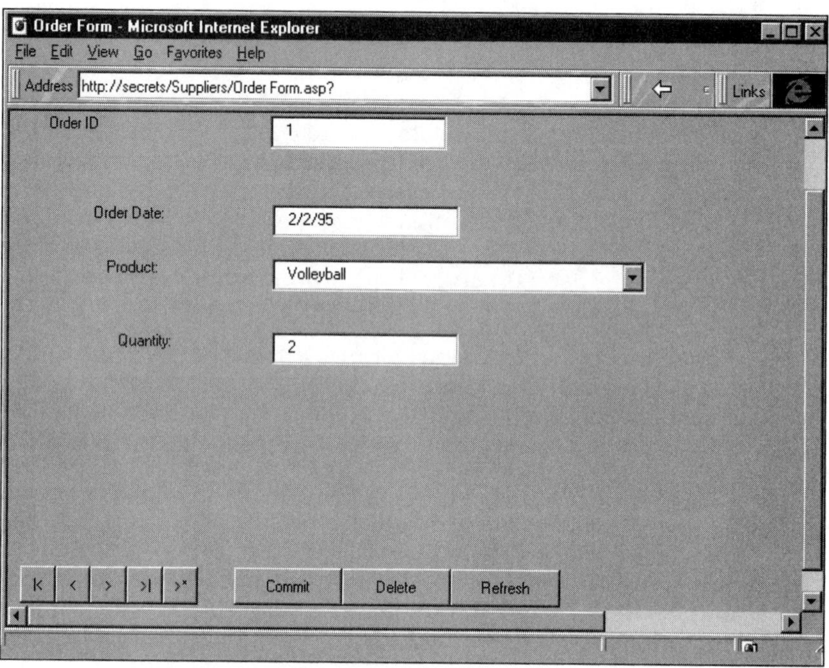

Figure 23-6: The Order form displayed in a browser.

After you have generated the forms, you need to place them in the proper folder on the server. You can do this yourself over a LAN or dial-up connection, provided you have permissions to do so, or you can send the files to your Webmaster (Internet server administrator) for placement into the server-side folder. The target folder needs to be defined with Read/Execute Access and can be set up with the Internet Service Manager on the server.

Using IDC/HTX

As an alternative to ActiveX Server Pages, you can use IDC/HTX as your data access method. This export choice creates an .IDC file to specify the required data from the data source named in the export steps and an .HTX file to specify the layout of the fields returned to the browser.

Follow the same steps as for exporting to an .ASP file format, but choose Microsoft IIS 1-2 (*.htx;*.idc) in the Save as type box. Figure 23-7 shows the resulting output .IDC file, and Figure 23-8 shows the .HTX file.

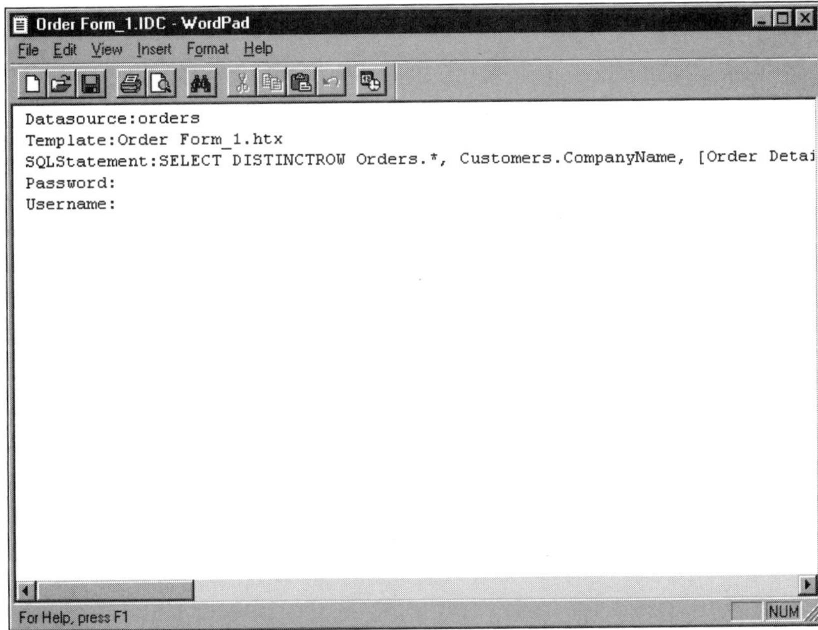

Figure 23-7: The .IDC file created by exporting to IDC/HTX format.

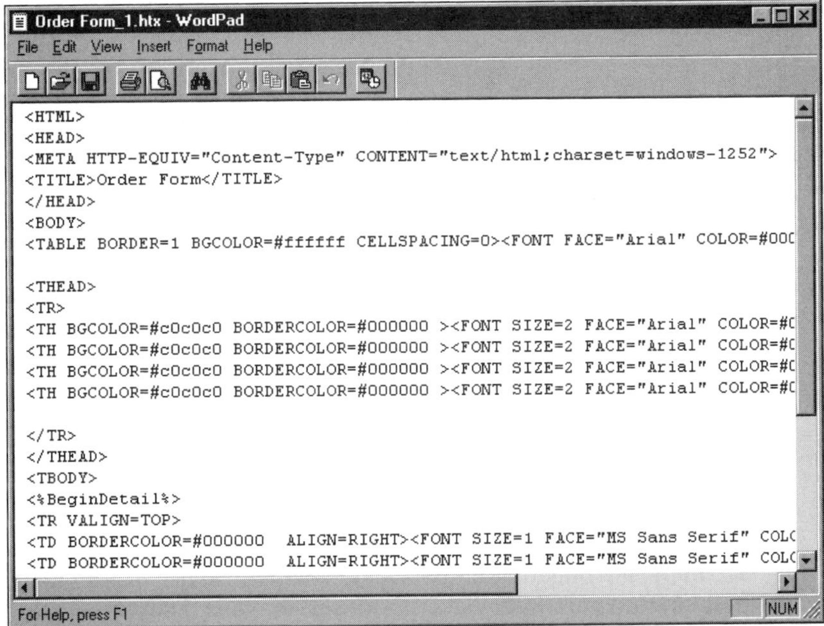

Figure 23-8: The .HTX file created by exporting to IDC/HTX format.

Exporting Objects Using the Publish to the Web Wizard

The Publish to the Web Wizard walks you through the steps of creating the HTML for selected database objects and of placing the generated HTML out on your Web site. You can export data from tables or query datasheets, forms, and reports.

Using this wizard, you can create either static or dynamic publications, publish them to the Web, create a home page, and even use templates to obtain a standard look and feel for all your HTML publications.

To start the Publish to the Web Wizard, go to the Database window and select Save As HTML from the File menu. The wizard starts, as shown in Figure 23-9.

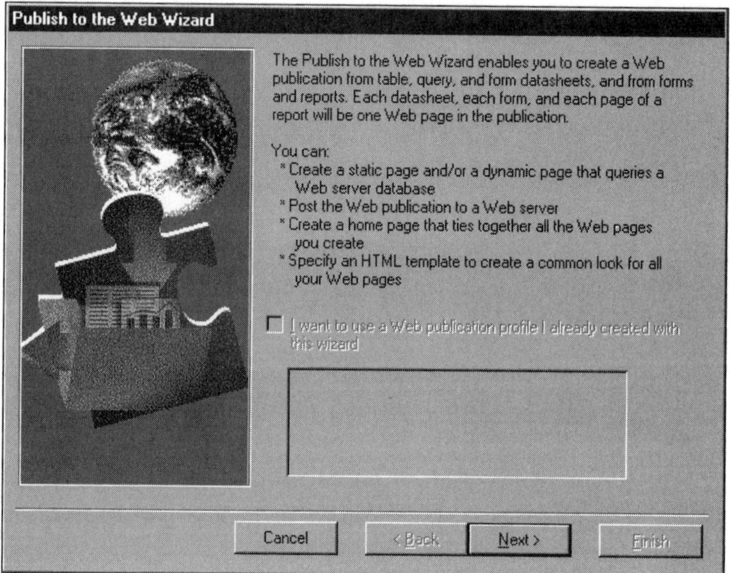

Figure 23-9: The Publish to the Web Wizard introductory screen.

The first screen simply gives you an introduction to the wizard and enables you to use a previously saved profile, which you have the opportunity to name and save each time you run the wizard. The Web publication profile is a set of all the selections you made when you used the wizard. As you can see in the introductory screen, you can create static pages of data (data at a point in time) or, if you have a Web server, you can create a page that queries the data for the latest data available each time the page is accessed. You also can create static or dynamic Web pages of report information as well as create a dynamic form, as was done for the supplier's Order form in this example.

Using the wizard, you also have the opportunity to create a home page that acts as a switchboard or menu to the other Web pages you create. You can create HTML templates that specify a common look for all of your Web pages that includes backgrounds and graphics on each page.

Click on the Next button to move to the next wizard screen.

The second Publish to the Web Wizard screen enables you to select the various objects you want to publish to the Web. As you can see in Figure 23-10, you have the option of selecting any or all of your tables, queries, forms, and reports.

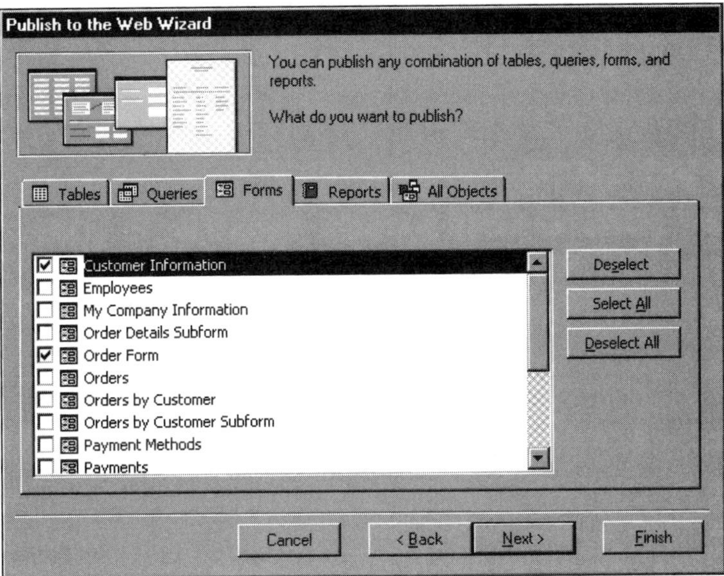

Figure 23-10: The Publish to the Web Wizard object selection screen.

In this screen, you can select as many objects as you want. Later, you can determine the purpose of each object when it is converted to an HTML equivalent. After you have selected the objects to be converted to HTML, you can display the next screen, in which you can select an HTML template file (see Figure 23-11).

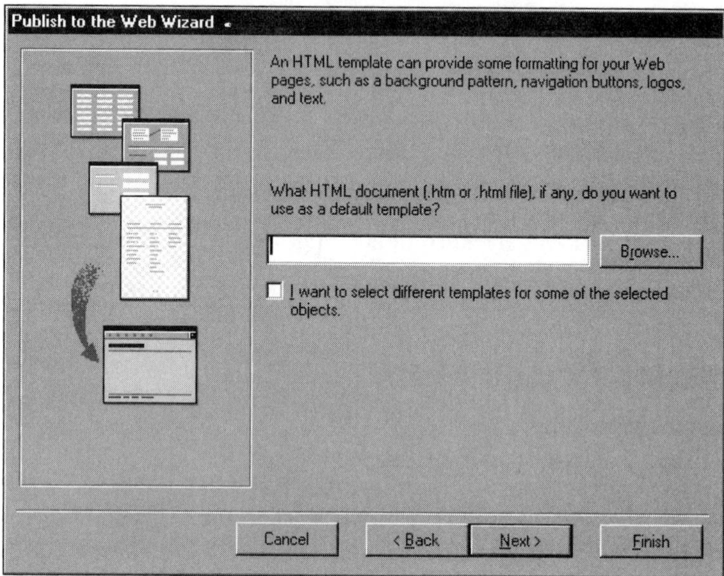

Figure 23-11: The Publish to the Web Wizard HTML template screen.

Using HTML templates

You may want to enhance the appearance and consistency of your Web application forms. You could decide to include a company logo in the header section, for example, or a company-approved background image in the body section of your Web pages. You can accomplish these effects through the use of HTML template files.

An HTML template can be any text file that includes HTML tags and tokens that indicate to Access the placement of data.

When you output a datasheet, form, or report by using the Publish to the Web Wizard or by exporting and you specify an HTML template file, Access merges the HTML template file with the files being created by replacing the tokens found in the template with the item indicated in Table 23-1.

Table 23-1 Template Tokens Recognized by Access

HTML Template Token	*Replaced With*
`<!-AccessTemplate_Title->`	The object name (placed in the title bar of the Web browser)
`<!-AccessTemplate_Body->`	The object output

HTML Template Token	***Replaced With***
<!–AccessTemplate_FirstPage–>	An anchor tag to the first page
<!–AccessTemplate_PreviousPage–>	An anchor tag to the preceding page
<!–AccessTemplate_NextPage–>	An anchor tag to the next page
<!–AccessTemplate_LastPage–>	An anchor tag to the last document page
<!–AccessTemplate_PageNumber–>	The current page number

HTML tags that specify files assume that the files reside in the same folder as the output files being created. The folder destination can be specified in the wizard. If you specify an HTML template file when you output an object to dynamic HTML format, it is merged with the .HTX or .ASP file during the output operation.

The next screen, shown in Figure 23-12, is very important to what you are actually creating. If you are creating HTML pages from data, you can create either static views of the data (at the point in time you complete the wizard) or dynamic views, which change each time the page is accessed at the server.

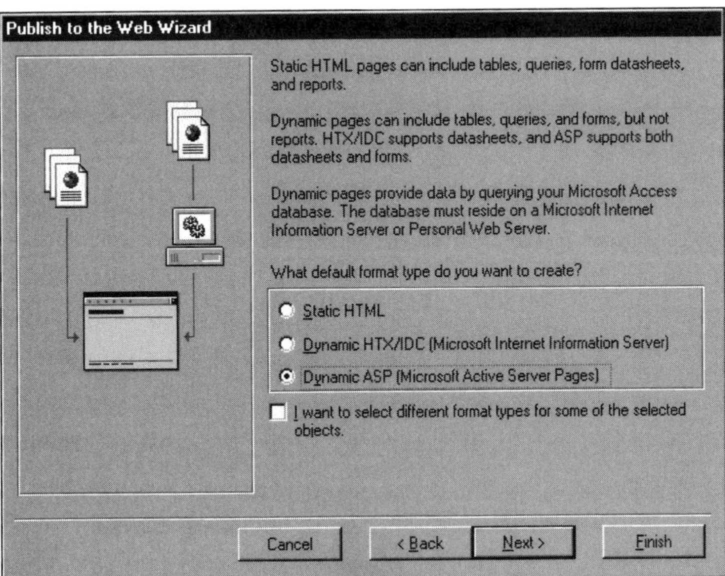

Figure 23-12: The Publish to the Web Wizard page determination screen.

Using static and dynamic views

You can create static HTML pages from table, query, and form datasheets, as well as from reports. The resulting HTML files are a snapshot of the data at the time you published your files. If your data changes, you must publish your files again to view the new data in your Web application.

When you output an object to IDC/HTX file format, instead of an .HTML file, Access creates an HTML extension file (.HTX) and an Internet Database Connector file (.IDC). The Internet Database Connector (httpodbc.dll) is a component of Microsoft Internet Information Server used to access an ODBC data source.

The .IDC file contains a query in the form of an SQL statement against a server-side ODBC data source — in the case of the supplier's order system in this example, an Access 97 database. The connection information includes the data source name and — if user-level security is required to open the database — the user name and password.

The .HTX file is an HTML file that contains formatting tags and instructions, and, instead of data, placeholders indicating where to insert the values returned from the query in the .IDC file.

After you publish your database and install your Web application, Microsoft Internet Information Server, upon request from a Web browser, opens the Access database (using the Microsoft Access Driver and the .IDC file connection information), runs the query in the .IDC file to access the data, and formats the results using the .HTX file specifications into HTML, which is sent back to the browser for display as a Web page.

Another type of dynamic output you can use is the ActiveX Server Page (.ASP) file, a component of Microsoft Internet Information Server 3.0 or later.

The .ASP file contains HTML tags interspersed with one or more queries in the form of SQL statements, template directives, and VBScript code containing references to ActiveX Server Controls. The .ASP file also contains ODBC connection information to connect to an ODBC data source. The connection information includes the data source name and — if required to open the database — the user name and password.

Using ActiveX Server Pages, the Microsoft Internet Information Server, upon request from a Web browser, runs the VBScript code, calls the ActiveX Server components, opens the Access database (using the Microsoft Access Driver and the .ASP file connection information), and runs the queries in the .ASP file to access the data. Then, the Server formats the results as HTML pages using the specifications in the alx.asp file (ordersalx.asp) referenced from the primary .ASP file (orders.asp), and returns the .HTML results to the Web browser for display as a Web page.

When you use dynamic HTML format files (either IDC/HTX or ASP), you need to do the following on the Internet Information Server to run your Web application:

- Define a system data source using the Access ODBC driver.
- Either copy the Microsoft Access database to the Web server or define its network location in the ODBC data source definition.
- Ensure that the users of your Web application can log on to the ODBC data source for your Access database.
- Ensure that the folder containing the .IDC or .ASP files has the necessary sharing properties, including `Read` and `Execute` for Microsoft Internet Information Server.

Tip

You can use the Publish to the Web Wizard to copy the Access database to its server destination, providing that your machine can connect to the target directory.

Cross-Reference

After you select either Static HTML (for tables and queries) or Dynamic IDC/HTX or ASP format, you can click the Next button to move to the screen, shown in Figure 23-13, which enables you to specify the Data Source and choose the ASP output options. You can create the Data Source you name in this dialog box by using the server-side ODBC setup, as discussed in Chapter 21, "Working with Client/Server Databases."

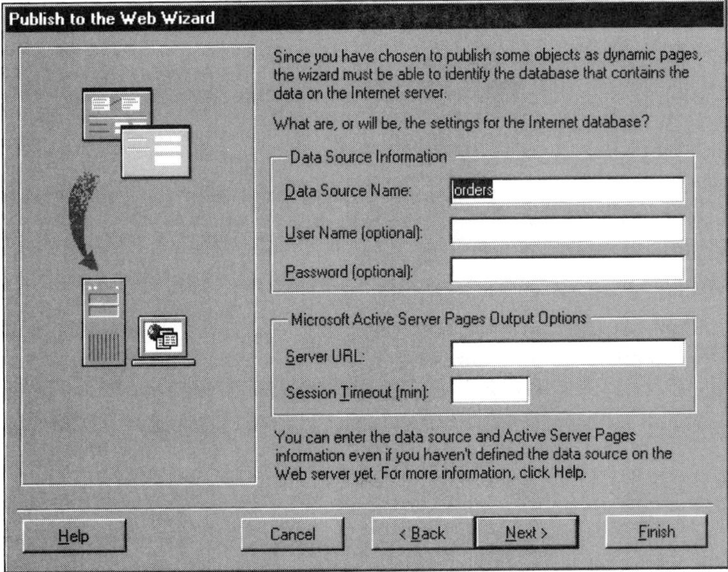

Figure 23-13: The Publish to the Web Wizard data source screen.

Click on the Next button to go to the screen shown in Figure 23-14, which enables you to select the path for the exported objects and to choose whether you want to publish Web objects locally or on an Internet server.

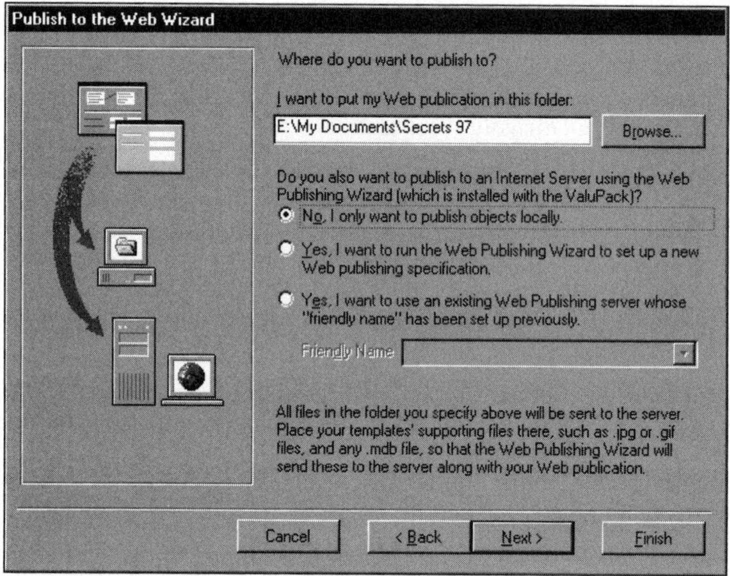

Figure 23-14: The Publish to the Web Wizard publish to screen.

If your template needs any support files, such as compressed icons or graphics (.GIF or .JPG), you must install them in the same directory specified at the top of the screen.

The next screen, shown in Figure 23-15, enables you to create a home page that can link all the published objects together. You simply give it a name and it is created for you. Of course, you can edit the HTML later and add to it whatever you want.

The last Publish to the Web screen enables you to save all the choices you made to a new profile, as you learned when reading about the first page of this wizard (see Figure 23-9). When you check the box, you can enter a new profile. If you use an existing name, the profile is updated, as shown in Figure 23-16.

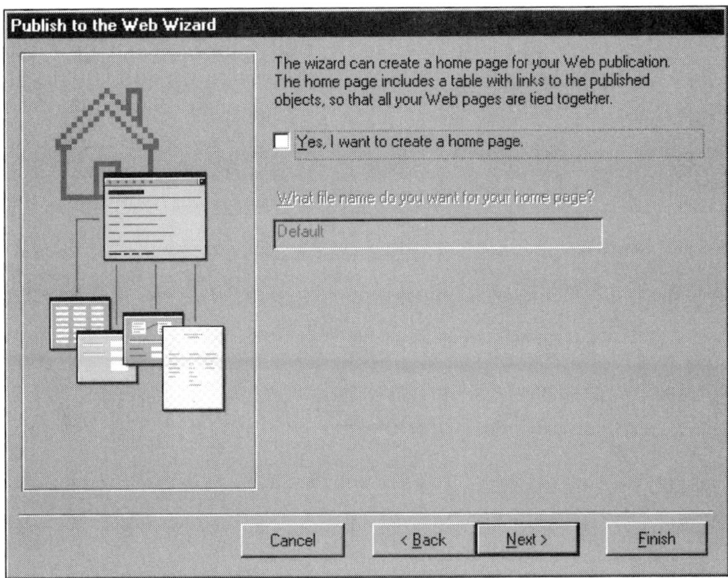

Figure 23-15: The Publish to the Web Wizard create a home page screen.

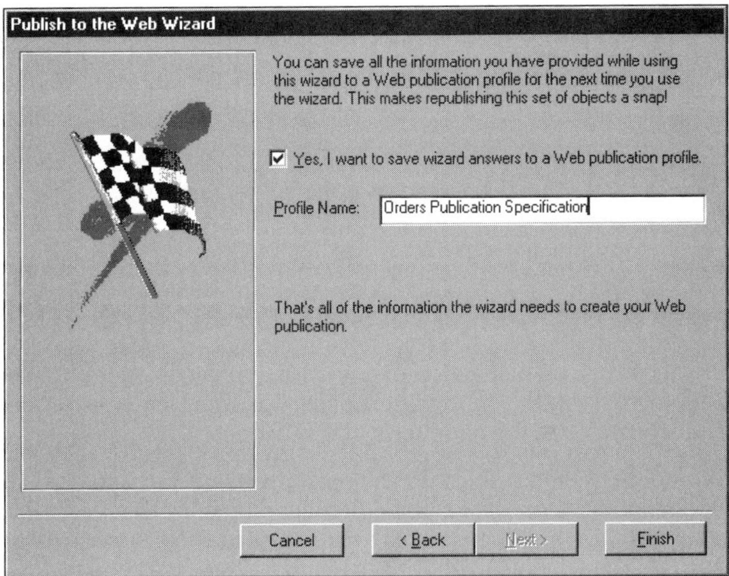

Figure 23-16: The Publish to the Web Wizard final screen.

You can display your home page or any of the other pages you published by specifying the page's URL in Microsoft Internet Explorer or other browser. Figure 23-17 shows the Order form displayed in the Internet Explorer.

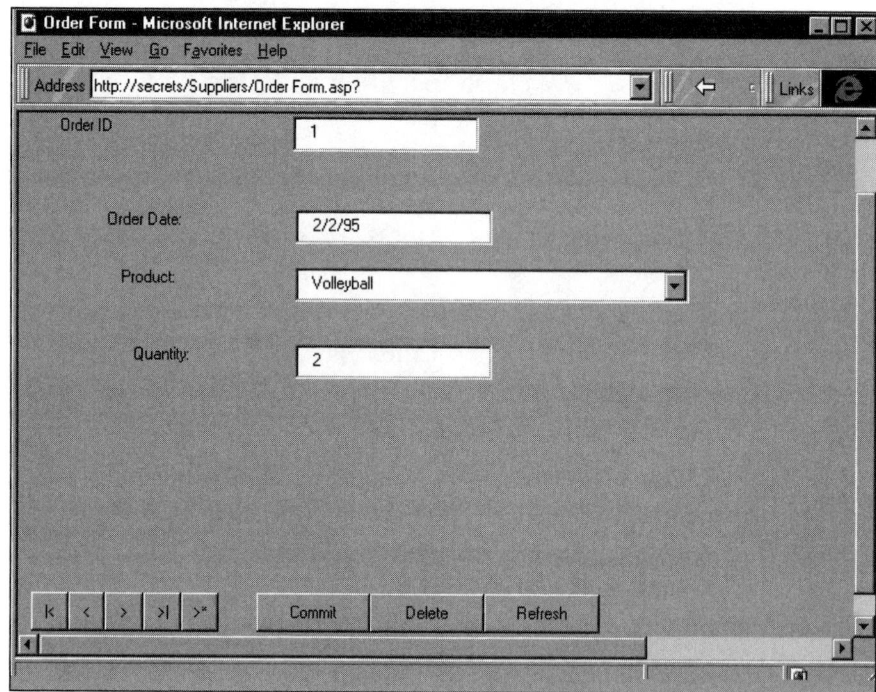

Figure 23-17: The Order form displayed in the Internet Explorer.

Synchronizing Databases over the Internet

As you can see by inspection of any of the exported .ASP files, the supplier's order forms residing on the Internet server require access to the orders and products tables in the supplier's order system.

On CD-ROM

The source of these tables for the example system is also the CH23B.MDB Access database on the CD-ROM that accompanies this book. Initially, the required tables are copied to the supplier's Internet server via creation or copy of a replica of CH23B.MDB through a direct LAN or dial-up connection to the server. The replica can also be copied over the Internet via FTP.

Cross-Reference

Any design changes to the tables are always made at the Design Master (see Chapter 22, "Exploring Replication," for details on working with replicas) and then replicated to the server-side replica. Likewise, if the supplier chooses to pull orders from the server-side replica into the main database for processing rather than access the replica directly, the replica can also be synchronized with the Design Master to retrieve these updates. If necessary, these synchronizations can be accomplished over the Internet via an indirect synchronization.

Indirect synchronization is done through the use of an FTP drop-box folder located on the server. Any changes from the client to be synchronized across the Internet are put into a message file, which is left in the FTP drop-box for the server-side Synchronizer to use in updating the server replica. The Synchronizer then puts the server replica changes — in this case, the order data — into a message file in the same drop-box and sends them to the client. The client then updates its replica to bring the two replica members in sync.

Before synchronization over the Internet can occur, you must perform a few setup steps. The first task is to set up the Internet server for replication. The steps for setting up Internet Information Server 2.0 are as follows:

1. Start the Internet Service Manager in the Microsoft Internet Server folder.
2. Ensure that both WWW and FTP services are running.
3. Select the WWW service icon and view Service Properties from the Properties menu.
4. Click on the Directories tab and select the Scripts directory. Click on Edit Properties and check the Execute checkbox. Close the Properties dialog box.
5. Select the FTP service icon and view Service Properties from the Properties menu.
6. Click on the Services tab and check the Allow Anonymous checkbox.
7. Click on the Directories tab and then click on the Add button to create a new directory for the message file drop-box.
8. Click on the Edit Properties button and check the Read and Write checkboxes.

In addition to the preceding steps, be sure that the Access 97 directory is on the system path.

The second task to prepare for Internet synchronization is to install Replication Manager 3.5 on the server. The steps for carrying out this task are the following:

1. After launching Replication Manager for the first time, you are asked to configure the Manager. If the Replication Manager is already installed, choose Configure Replication Manager from the Tools menu.
2. Specify the Scripts directory for Synchronizer installation.

3. Specify the FTP directory where the drop-box folder was created.
4. Create a replica of the database that will be synchronized over the Internet. The Design Master of CH23B.MDB was created at the client and its first replica stored in a shared folder at the server. The replica can be created either on the client or server, but it must be managed by the server-side Replication Manager.
5. You can now launch Replication Manager on a client machine and choose Synchronize Now across the Internet from the Tools menu. In the sample order system, the Design Master of CH23.MDB is managed by the Replication Manager on the client machine, and the Replica of CH23B.MDB is managed by the Replication Manager on the server machine.

Tip

If the Synchronize Now across the Internet option is not enabled after completing the preceding steps, try synchronizing the replicas via the LAN first and then attempt to Synchronize across the Internet.

Exploring Hyperlinks

In the sporting goods system, the Suppliers tables contains hyperlinks to each of the supplier's order forms resident on their Internet servers. These hyperlinks consist of two parts: display text and an Internet address. The *display text* is the text shown to the user of the form at the position of the hyperlink. As far as the user is concerned, this text represents the address. Hyperlink text is usually colored differently from the other text on the form and can be specified on the Hyperlinks/HTML tab of the Options dialog box.

The address component of a hyperlink specifies the absolute or relative path to a document in the network. This path can be an Internet URL, which specifies the network address or name corresponding to an address where the document can be found, or it can be a path on an intranet server. If a relative path is specified, it is relative to the path designated in the Hyperlink Base setting in the Database Properties dialog box.

Another component of a hyperlink that may be specified is known as a *subaddress*. The subaddress is a location within the document or page referenced by the address component. When you hyperlink from one form in your database to another form, the address component can be left blank and the subaddress component specifies the name of the form to display preceded by the object type, in this case, `Form`.

You may enter data into Hyperlink fields as `displaytext#address#optionalsubaddress`. In the suppliers table, the hyperlink for WA Sporting Goods is entered as `Order Form#http://secrets/Suppliers/Customer Information_1.asp#` with no subaddress specified.

When the supplier hyperlinks are displayed on the products form, placing the cursor over one of the Hyperlinks causes the cursor to change to a hand icon. Clicking the left mouse button opens the browser form and displays the selected customer form for entry of customer information prior to entering an order.

Working with Hyperlink Objects

Because some setup work is required prior to displaying the customer form in the browser control, clicking a hyperlink on the products form involves some code to process the `Hyperlink` object.

The hyperlinks are displayed as text boxes on the products form (combo box, label, command button, and image control are the other options for display of hyperlinks). When the text box is clicked, the click event is fired and the code in that event procedure opens the browser form.

After opening the browser form, the code needs to tell the `Web Browser` control — used to display the requested document — which document to retrieve. To do this, the text box's `Hyperlink` property is used to return a `Hyperlink` object.

The `Hyperlink` object has `Address` and `SubAddress` properties that can be inspected to extract the address information needed by the browser control. Listing 23-1 shows the hyperlink text box's click event procedure and the handling of the `Hyperlink` object address properties.

Although it is not required in this application, the `Hyperlink` object also has a method you can use to cause Access to evaluate the hyperlink address or follow it, as would have occurred had you not intercepted the click event. This method is called the `Follow` method.

Listing 23-1: The Order_URL OnClick Event Processing to Set Up the Web Browser Control

```
Private Sub Order_URL_Click()

   Dim hLink As Hyperlink

   Set hLink = Order_URL.Hyperlink
   DoCmd.OpenForm "Browser Form"
   Forms![Browser Form]!ActiveXCtl0.Navigate hLink.Address

End Sub
```

If you use a label, command button, or image control to display Hyperlinks, you can reference the control's `HyperlinkAddress` and `HyperlinkSubAddress` properties to obtain the same information returned by the `Hyperlink` object's `Address` and `SubAddress` properties, respectively.

At times, you may need to follow an address that is not associated with a hyperlink in a control. The same effect achieved with the `Hyperlink` object's `Follow` method can be achieved with the application object's `FollowHyperlink` method. Whereas the `Follow` method uses the Hyperlink's `Address` and `SubAddress`, the `FollowHyperlink` requires that you specify these address components as the first two arguments to the method. The `SubAddress` argument is optional.

If you want to save the address associated with a `Hyperlink` object to the Favorites folder, you can use the `AddToFavorites` method of the `Hyperlink` object. This is the same effect as selecting AddToFavorites on the Favorites menu found on the Web toolbar.

Using the Web Browser Control

On CD-ROM

The Browser form in CH23.MDB on the CD-ROM that accompanies this book uses a Web Browser control for displaying HTML documents, specifically, the Customer Information and Order forms from the supplier's Web site built earlier in this chapter.

The Web Browser ActiveX control is installed with Internet Explorer 3.0. To use the browser's properties and methods, set a reference to Microsoft Internet Controls in the References dialog box.

If you have installed Access 97 from the Microsoft Office Professional Edition 97 CD-ROM, you have access to a ValuPack directory on that CD-ROM. This directory contains database drivers for Lotus 1-2-3, Paradox, and Microsoft Exchange/Outlook. You also find an online version of "Building Applications with Microsoft Access 97" in HTML format, Microsoft Internet Explorer 3.0, the Web Publishing Wizard, Personal Web Server, and a help file for the WebBrowser control. The help file is found in the folder \ValuPack\Access\WebHelp.

The CH23.MDB Products form uses the Web Browser control's `Navigate` method as shown in Listing 23-1. The `Navigate` method causes the control to navigate to the URL specified as the first argument to the method. See Table 23-2 for a listing of the Navigate Flags constants. The full `Navigate` syntax is as follows:

```
WebBrowserControl.Navigate URL _
[Flags][,FrameName][,PostData][,Headers]
```

Table 23-2 Constants for Navigate Flags Argument

Constant	*Description*
`navNoHistory`	The resource is not added to the history list.
`navNoReadFromCache`	The disk cache is not used for navigation.
`navNoWriteToCache`	The disk cache is not updated with this navigation.

The optional `FrameName` is the name of a frame in which the resource is to be displayed. `PostData` is used for HTTP protocol resources and is the data the browser will send to the server in a `POST` transaction.

The `Headers` argument is also used for HTTP resources and specifies additional HTTP headers to be sent to the server in addition to the Internet Explorer header.

The Web Browser `OnUpdated` event is used to set the URL of the displayed document into the text box at the top of the browser form. To do this, the Web Browser's `LocationURL` property is accessed in the `OnUpdated` event procedure to retrieve the URL string of the current document. The text box in which this URL is displayed can also be edited by the user to enter a different URL. After the URL is entered by pressing the Enter or Return key, the form's `OnKeyDown` event detects the Return key and issues a `Navigate` method with the entered string as the new URL.

Using the Web Toolbar with Access 97

You can turn on the Web toolbar by right-clicking on the toolbar and selecting Web, or by selecting View⇨Toolbars⇨Web from any menu bar. When you have the Web toolbar displayed, you can use it to access Web sites on the Internet or your local intranet (see Figure 23-18). When you use the Web toolbar, you launch the default Web browser on your system.

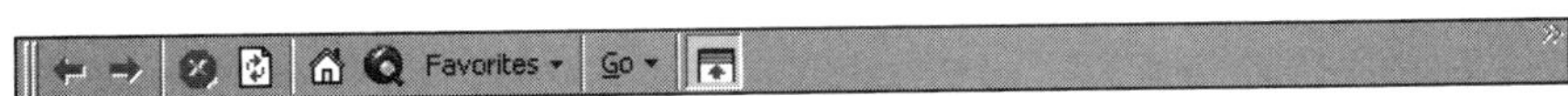

Figure 23-18: The Web Toolbar.

You can set the default home page by using the Set Start Page option from the Go menu on the Web toolbar. This is the document the browser will display on startup. Open the Start page by clicking on Start Page (a.k.a. Home Page) on the Web toolbar.

Search pages contain addresses of Internet or intranet documents and provide a means of finding a site and navigating to it. You can set the Search Page by displaying the document you want to use as the search page and then selecting Set Search Page from the Go menu. To open the search page, click on the Search the Web icon (the magnifying glass and globe) on the Web toolbar.

As you browse through the Internet/intranet, the browser keeps a list of documents you visit. This is the History list, which you can use to revisit a document without retyping the address. To revisit a document prior to your current position in the history list, click the Back arrow on the Web toolbar. To move forward from your current position, click the Forward arrow. When you have reached the bounds of the list, these arrows are disabled, to indicate that no more documents are in that direction.

Appendix A

What's New with Access 97

Access 97 has new features in every area of the product. One major change is the new Visual Basic for Applications language (Visual Basic or VBA for short). This language combines all the commands in Access Basic with some new functionality and consistency across other Microsoft Applications including Visual Basic, Excel, Word, and Project. This language, however, is only a small part of the added functionality in Access 97. Forms and tables have also been significantly enhanced from the Access 2.0 product.

The functionality added to Access 97 is not just a minimal upgrade from Access 2.0. Neither is it targeted solely at novice users or experienced developers. There are improvements for everyone: from wizards that are easier to use, more intuitive, and much more powerful for developers to the capability of programmatically opening multiple instances of a form where each one displays a different record. Furthermore, very important to many people is the capability to publish table data and even form objects on the Web.

Access 97 is a lot more than Access 2.0 with Windows 95 user interface changes. Some of the biggest changes were in the design and creation of tables, relationships, and the ease with which novices can normalize tables. Changes to forms have given developers the capability to create more efficient forms that can be controlled better than ever; new users can create fully functional forms with very little knowledge. Many of the most requested enhancements have made it into the product, including extended control types that use ActiveX controls (OCX) and the capability to change control types. A much needed tab control has now been integrated directly into the product. Finally, menus and toolbars have been replaced with Command Bars.

This appendix will cover the most important new features for both the serious developer and the new Access 97 user.

Forms for the Masses

Forms have undergone many changes. Some of the best changes include the capability to quickly build a prototype form, apply a variety of styles to it, instantly change control types, and then use it in an application that features far more control (pardon the pun) over the user interface elements and data display. Some of the features that have made this possible include

- Improved Wizards that sense relationships and automatically create subforms
- A Chart Wizard that everyone will understand
- Morphing control types (Text Box to Combo Box, Check Box to Option Buttons)
- Better links to the Table Designer, including default control types
- Multiselect list boxes
- Vastly improved performance on list/combo boxes
- New image controls for displaying unbound pictures with no OLE overhead
- Integrated tab control — no longer an OCX
- Background pictures and controlled elimination of section lines
- Easy publishing to the Web
- Hyperlinks that connect you to other places
- AutoFormat and Format Painter for globally changing control properties
- New special effects — Shadowed, Chiseled, and Etched
- The Startup Property dialog box replaces Autoexec macros and runtime options
- Integration with Office Spell Checker and AutoCorrect features
- New ways to handle a tab in the last control of a form (the `Cycle` property)
- Command Bars replace menu bars, toolbars, and pop-up menus
- New OLE custom controls that really work
- Ability to store an active filter and order by sort with the saved form
- Automatic Filter by Form and Filter by Selection
- New form properties for controlling adds, changes, and deletions to records
- On Error event to trap any error and create one global error routine
- Multiple-instance forms and using CBF anywhere

New and Improved Form Wizards Are Almost Magical

The wizards that create forms and reports have been expanded and improved. There are no longer separate wizards for different types of forms. The single form wizard asks you if you want to create a columnar, tabular, or datasheet type form. The main/subform wizard has also been eliminated.

Instead, all the form wizards let you access data from more than one table. This lets you create far more complex forms with wizards then ever before. Access 97 wizards recognize when fields from more than one table are used and when a one-to-many relationship exists and automatically creates a subform or linked form to handle the many side of the relationship. Figure A-1 shows the improved Field Selection Wizard dialog box.

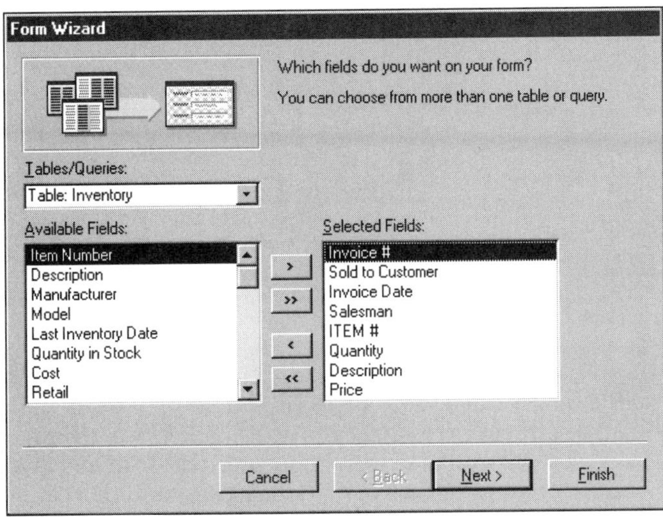

Figure A-1: Selecting fields from multiple tables.

Originally, the Invoice and the Invoice Lineitems table fields were displayed in the Available Fields list box. Some of these fields were selected and appear in the Selected Fields list box. The Tables/Queries combo box has been changed to Inventory, and these fields can now be selected for the form.

You can select fields from as many tables as you need. For this to work properly, the tables must either have predefined relationships or common fields that can be auto-joined when the forms are created.

After you have selected fields from all the tables you need, the Access form wizard detects that fields from multiple tables have been selected and asks you whether you want to create a form with a subform like Access 2.0 created or a linked form opened with a button. Figure A-2 shows this wizard screen.

Another major change in wizards is the change from a fixed number of styles (Standard, Chiseled, Shadowed, Boxed, and Embossed) to an unlimited number of totally customizable styles shown in Figure A-3. These resemble the templates in Word or PowerPoint combined with the power of formats in Excel. You can create your own styles which include custom backgrounds, colors, and properties for each different type of control.

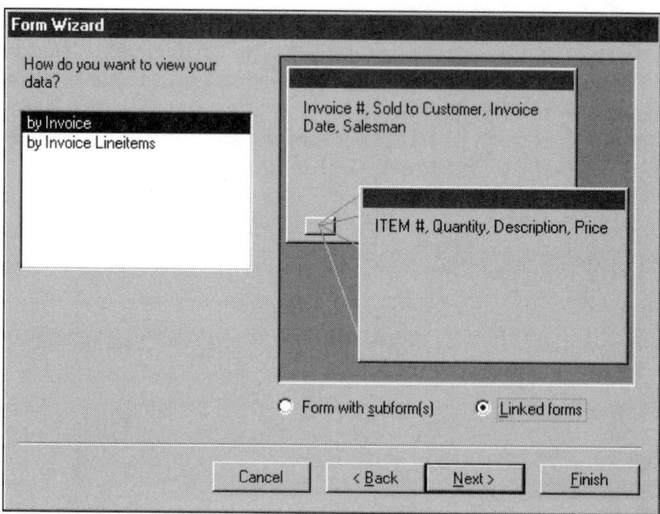

Figure A-2: Creating a multitable linked form.

Form wizards now include three types of AutoForm wizards (Columnar, Tabular, and Datasheet), the improved standard wizard, a new, easier to use Chart Wizard that really lets you create usable charts, and a Pivot Table form wizard for creating Excel-like cross-tabulations with hierarchical totals.

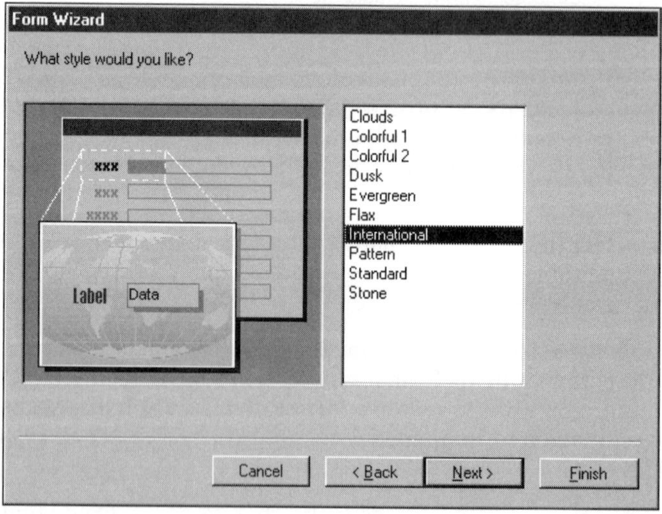

Figure A-3: Default Form Wizard styles.

The Chart Wizard in particular has undergone a complete makeover. Rather than go through the 10 cryptic wizard screens in Access 2.0 that required a doctorate in graphology, Access 97 uses just a few wizard screens that make creating a graph a drag and drop picnic. Figure A-4 shows the main graph wizard screen. You can create multiseries graphs in less than one minute. All the customization options are still available as the graph applet shared between all Office applications is largely unchanged in Office 97. One curious thing you should be aware of: The graph control button is not found in the forms toolbox. For some reason it was left out of the standard controls. Because the Toolbox in Access 97 is actually a toolbar, you can easily add it by using View⇨Toolbars⇨Customize⇨Toolbox and then dragging the chart wizard icon to the toolbox.

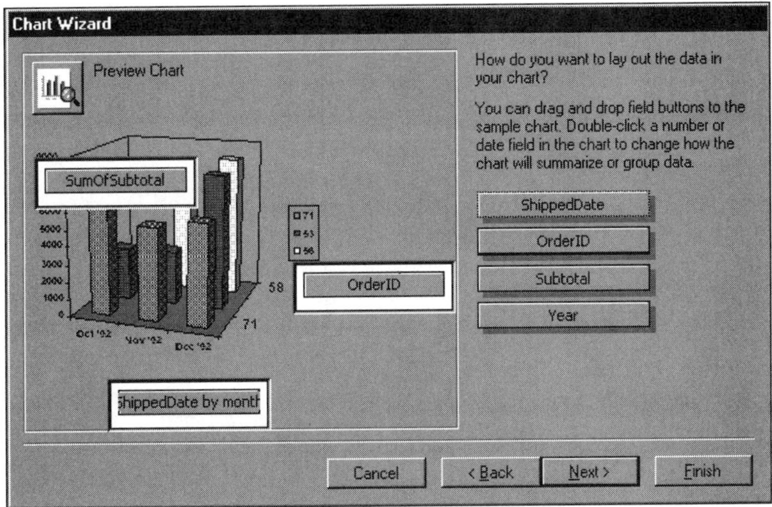

Figure A-4: The new Chart Wizard.

Control Wizards Also Have New Magic

Other wizards, such as the combo/list box, option group, and the command button wizards, are largely unchanged. In fact, some wizards have lost some functionality. You can no longer add pictures to the picture builder wizard by using a customize option (there is none), but you can add pictures directly to the wizard system table. The capability to customize any of the wizard *templates* that was found in Access 2.0 has been taken out. But, this has been replaced by more customizable options in the wizards themselves. Overall it is an increase in functionality and flexibility.

A new subform wizard has been added that walks you through the process of creating and setting the relationship of a subform. Additionally, you can still drag and drop a form onto another form or report and the subform wizard will take you through the process of building valid links between the forms either as an embedded subform or a linked form.

Control Improvements

There are many improvements to the controls that can be placed on forms. These include some functional and performance enhancements as well as an unlimited number of new controls through the use of OLE Custom Controls.

Control morphing allows instant control type changes

The first major improvement to controls is *control morphing*. Have you ever created a text box, set all the properties, colors, events, and then decided what you really wanted was a combo box? In Access 2.0, you would have to delete the control and then start again. In Access 97, you simply change the control type, complete a few different properties, and you have a new control with all the characteristics of the original control. Obviously, there are only certain control types you can use interchangeably. A text box can become a list box or combo box, and option buttons, toggle buttons, and check boxes are also interchangeable. You can do this by simply selecting the Format⇨Change To menu options.

Default control types and the Lookup Wizard make foreign keys readable

Also important is the new capability to define the default control type when you create the field in the table designer. For example, if you tell Access 97 that the default field type is a combo box, when you add the field to a form it will be a combo box with the default settings you have entered. A new Lookup Wizard is also used to automatically create combo boxes at table design time and to display a useful lookup value rather than a foreign key in the table itself.

For example, suppose you have a table named Invoice and one of the fields is named Sold to Customer, which is a foreign key lookup to a Customer table. When you view the Invoice data in a datasheet, you see some cryptic key value such as AN-4623 or 57243 in the Ship to Customer field. The Lookup Wizard can be used to display the customer's Company and Contact Name instead of the cryptic customer number. Even though the Ship To Customer number is stored in the field, any time the field is used it performs an immediate link to the field (or fields) specified in the lookup wizard (actual properties in the table as shown in Figure A-5).

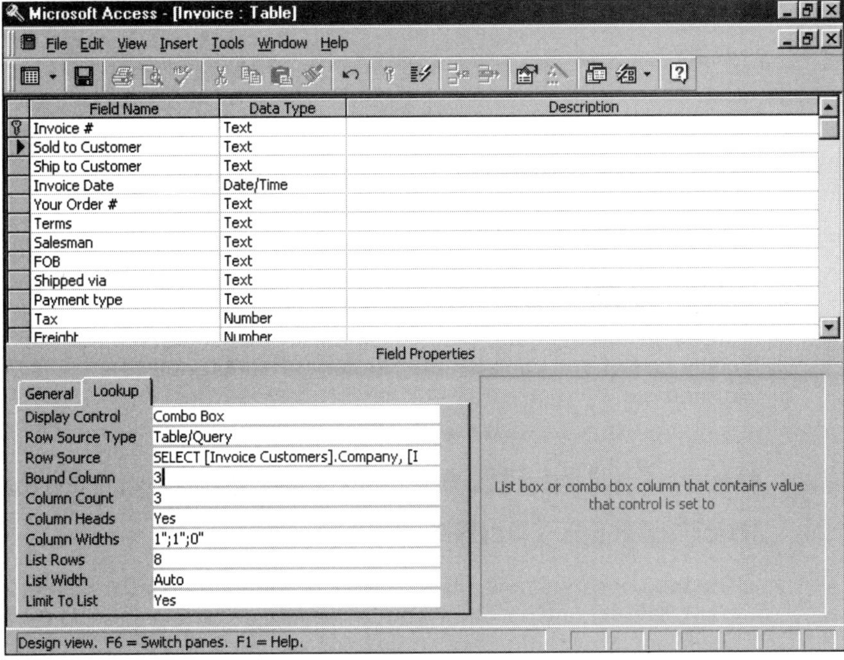

Figure A-5: Lookup Wizard properties used for foreign keys.

Multiselect list boxes add new flexibility

Another improvement to an existing control is the multiselect list box. In Access 2.0, only one selection could be made from a list box. Access 97's new `MultiSelect` property lets you select more than one value and process it in your application.

A list box becomes a multiselect list box by changing a single new property in the list box control. The new `MultiSelect` property has three choices:

- `None` — (Default) Multiple selection isn't allowed.
- `Extended` — Shift+Click or Shift+Arrow key extends the selection from the previously selected item to the current item. Ctrl+Click selects or deselects an item.
- `Simple` — Multiple items are selected or deselected by choosing them with the mouse or pressing the spacebar.

When the `MultiSelect` property is set to `Single`, the value of the list box control is equal to the selected item. You can use the `ListIndex` property to get the index for the selected item. When the `MultiSelect` property is set to `Extended` or `Simple`, you can use the list box's `Selected` or `ItemsSelected` properties to determine the items that are selected, as shown in the following code sample.

```
For Each intIndex In lstForms.ItemsSelected
    Set frm = colCustomerForms(intIndex + 1)
    frm.KeepMealive frm
Next intIndex
```

List and combo boxes are much faster and better

Thanks to new algorithms for querying data to fill list and combo boxes, you will see increased performance whenever you use list and combo boxes. Numeric bound columns and hidden bound columns will be especially faster. You can also exit combo boxes left null when LimitToList is turned on.

New, fully-integrated tab control makes multipage forms easy

The tab control is now a native Access control. It is no longer an OCX control. Tab controls allow you to present several pages of information as a single set. Now that the tab control is included as a standard Access control, you will find it easier to seamlessly take advantage of all that tab controls afford you within your applications. For example, you can display printing and customer information on one tab and the related orders in a subform on a second tab (see Figure A-6).

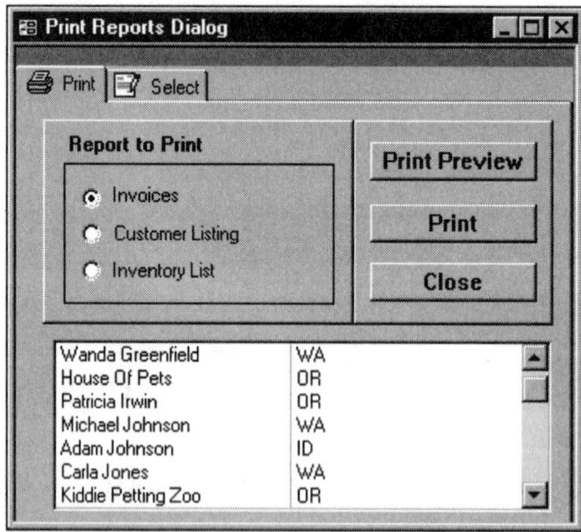

Figure A-6: The new integrated tab control.

Image controls save resources

A new image control has been added that is in addition to the unbound OLE object control. While the unbound OLE object is used to display pictures, sounds, video, or other OLE-enabled objects, in Access 2.0 the main use was to display pictures on forms or reports for logos or added pizzazz.

Many developers learned to use the Save As Picture menu item to break the OLE link and save some resources, but the truth is the OLE header that remained still used a lot of resources. The new image control uses virtually no resources and should always be used to display bitmap pictures.

Check boxes and option buttons — a triple play

In Access 2.0, there were two states to check boxes and option buttons: `On` and `Off`. However, null values were also shown as `No`. There was no way to tell whether a value was ever placed in one of these controls. In Access 97, a null state has been added. The values are now different for selected, unselected, and null.

Creating multiple controls is a lock

In Access 2.0, there was a lock button in the toolbox for creating multiple controls of the same type. You clicked the control you wanted, pressed the lock button and then created multiple controls. In Access 97, like Visual Basic, you merely have to double click the control icon in the toolbox to lock the control until you change it or click on the field selector icon.

The Internet Is Now Accessible to All of Us

Access is now full of features that allow you to easily make your applications Internet/intranet ready. With just a click of the mouse you can save tables, queries, reports, and form datasheets as HTML files. A Publish to the Web wizard allows even a neophyte to place the HTML code generated from an object out on a Web site, ready for the perusal of all who surf the Internet! Hyperlinks allow you and others to access your published data (and others' published data) as hypertext links, directly from your Access forms.

Easy publishing to the Web

Many people feel that the process of publishing data to the Web is something to be left to a Webmaster. Access 97 definitely turns this idea into a myth. The Publish to the Web wizard walks you through the steps of creating the HTML for selected database objects and of placing the generated

HTML out on your Web site. As seen in Figure A-7, by using the wizard you can create either static or dynamic publications, publish them to the Web, create a home page, and even use templates to obtain a standard look and feel for all your HTML publications!

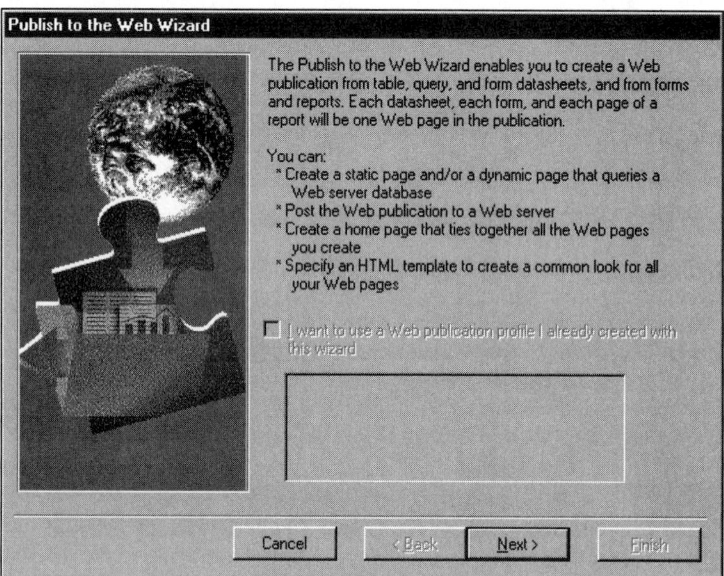

Figure A-7: The Publish to the Web Wizard.

Creating a hyperlink

Hyperlinks can be placed in forms, reports, and datasheets. They allow your users to quickly and easily jump to other objects within the current database, other databases, other applications, and even URLs out on the Web. Hyperlinks are added by setting two new properties of command buttons, labels, and pictures. These properties are `Hyperlink Address` and `Hyperlink Subaddress` (see Figure A-8). They allow you to specify the URL and location within the document to which you wish to jump (see Figure A-9).

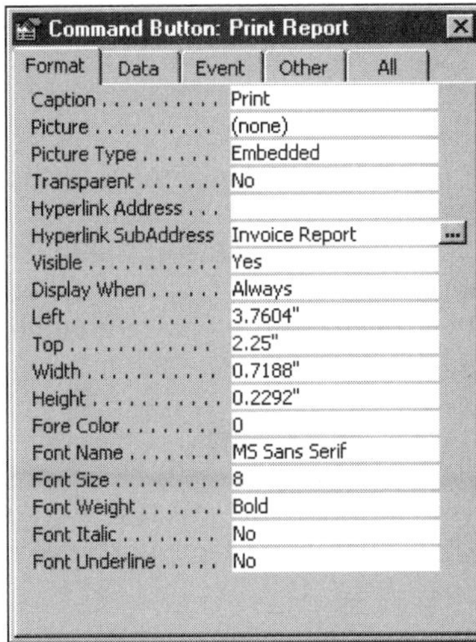

Figure A-8: New properties allow you to create hyperlinks.

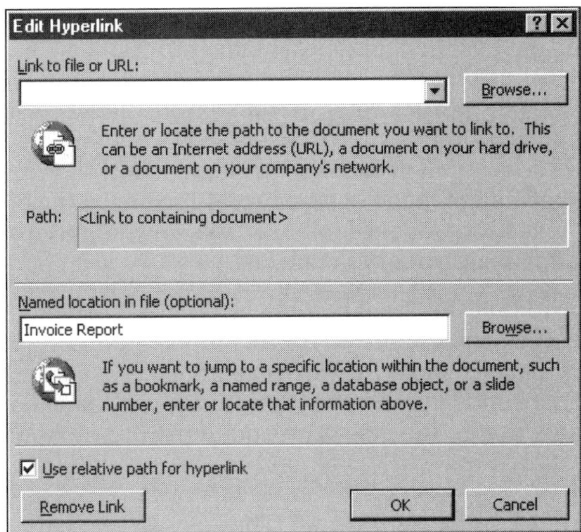

Figure A-9: Specifying the location of the hyperlink.

New and Enhanced Form Design Properties and Techniques

Many enhancements in Access 97 were made to the properties in forms and form controls. These include properties for both the visual look of forms and form controls as well as how forms operate. One of the first things you will notice is that the property window uses a tabbed dialog box to select the groups of properties instead of using a combo box to change groups.

Selecting properties is easier

A major change to form properties is the way you select them. As in Visual Basic, you can cycle through all the selections in a property by successively double-clicking on a property.

The palette is gone

The palette has been replaced by five independent movable palette windows and a new formatting toolbar consistent with Microsoft Office. The formatting toolbar has the font type and font size along with various font formatting property buttons. The windows let you control the foreground color, background color, border color, border width, and special effect. The less-used border style properties (`Transparent`, `Solid`, `Dashes`, `Short Dashes`, `Dots`, and so on) still must be set from the control property window. Another enhancement is the combo box at the beginning of the formatting toolbar used to select a control. This is especially important when you have controls hidden beneath other controls.

Notice in Figure A-10 that the Transparent button has replaced the Clear button for making the background of controls transparent. Previously, while label control backgrounds could be transparent, text box controls could not. In Access 97, all controls can have transparent backgrounds. This is especially important due to the new background picture capabilities described in the next section.

Background Pictures Give You the World (Or Anything Else You Want)

In Access 2.0, you could add an unbound OLE object picture to the background of a section; however, this took an enormous amount of resources and could only be used on a single section. You could not place a picture that transcended header, detail, and footer sections.

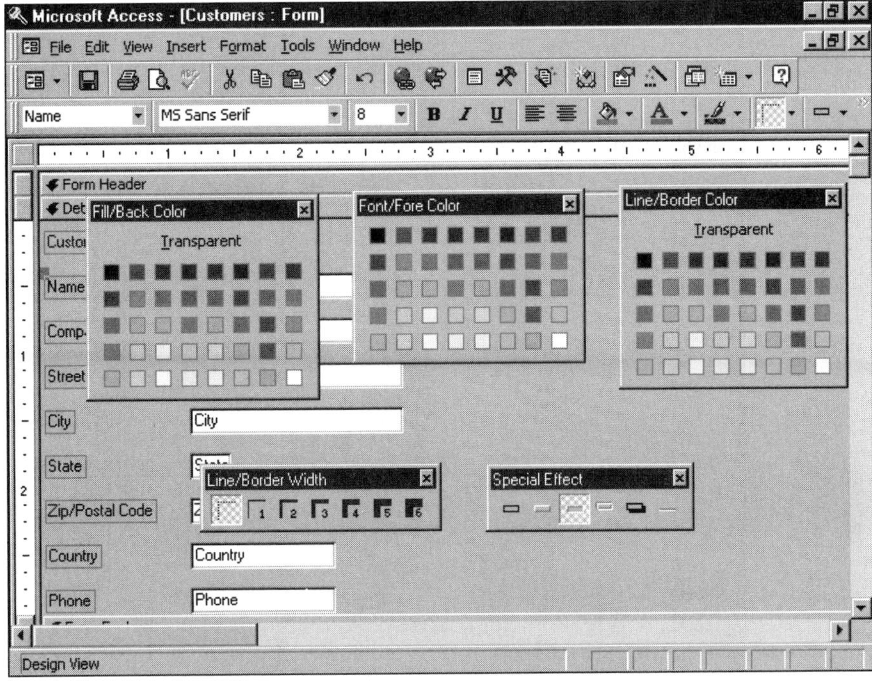

Figure A-10: The Formatting Toolbar and the Formatting Windows.

Controls placed on an unbound OLE object picture obscured the picture, giving it a rather choppy look. In Access 97, the new form `Picture` property solves all these problems. It uses very little resources, applies to the entire form, and, with the use of the new transparent control background, you don't obscure the picture beneath the control. In addition, you can control the alignment of the picture and the size mode. You can also add a small picture and have it automatically tile across the entire form. Figure A-11 shows a map of the world behind a simple form.

You can remove the dividing line between sections giving a seamless look to all sections of the form. The new `Dividing Lines` form property removes the section dividing lines. As you can see in Figure A-11, there is no line between the title in the Header section and the detail information. With these tools, you can also use scanned images as backgrounds for easy form fill-ins.

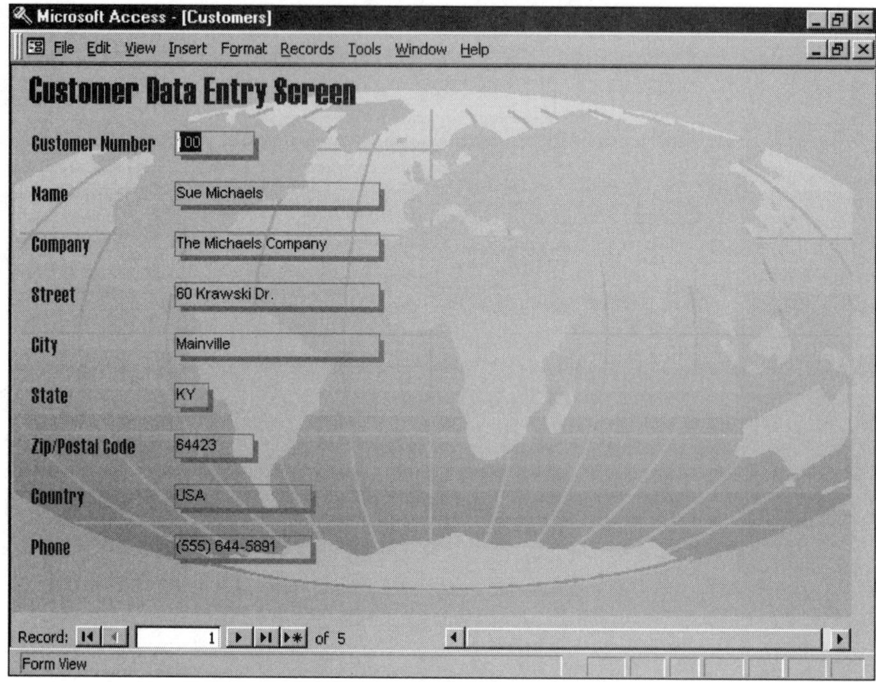

Figure A-11: Using a background form picture.

AutoFormat your forms

Access 97 contains technology formerly found in Word, Excel and PowerPoint to instantly change the formatting style of an entire form. When you select Format⇨AutoFormat, you can choose from a list of 10 predefined formats. These formats can change the colors, fonts, special effects, and even add a background picture if you like. Figure A-11 shows the International special effect. Figure A-3 showed a list of these AutoFormats. You can customize any of the formats and even create your own.

Format Painter copies single control formats

Besides being able to change the format of all the controls at once, you can copy all formatting from a single control and drop it on other controls to clone the formatting using the new Format Painter. On the main toolbar, this is the button with the paint brush next to the Cut, Copy, and Paste buttons.

Special effects are really special

In Access 2.0, you were limited to Normal (now called Flat), Sunken, and Raised special effects. You might have learned the secrets of creating chiseled, etched, or shadowed special effects, but they took a lot of work. In Access 97, these types of special effects are now built in.

Tool Tips are not just for toolbars anymore

Custom Toolbars in Access 97 can easily have Tool Tips added when the icon is added to the custom toolbar. There is now a form control property named `Control Tip Text` that allows you to enter a text string (called a control tip, like a Tool Tip) to appear when the cursor is passed over the control. Each control in a form can have a control tip.

Placing page numbers and dates just takes a second

Creating controls that contained page numbers, dates, or times was easy in Access 2.0 if you knew how to use the Function builder or the keywords for these calculated controls. Access 97 simplifies things by adding two new Insert menu options and dialog boxes to select and format the display of page numbers and date/time controls.

Startup properties jump-start your applications

The Autoexec macro is dead! The new Access 97 Startup Properties form, shown in Figure A-12, controls many of the properties that had to be set using Autoexec macro code and some properties that had to be set from an .INI file or Windows API call.

You can specify text for the title bar and an icon file to use when the application is minimized. These are options previously specified in an .INI file. Other properties include the starting menu bar name, starting form, starting toolbar, and whether or not to allow default shortcut menus, display the database window, display the status bar, allow toolbar changes, display a code window after a runtime error, or allow the special Access keys.

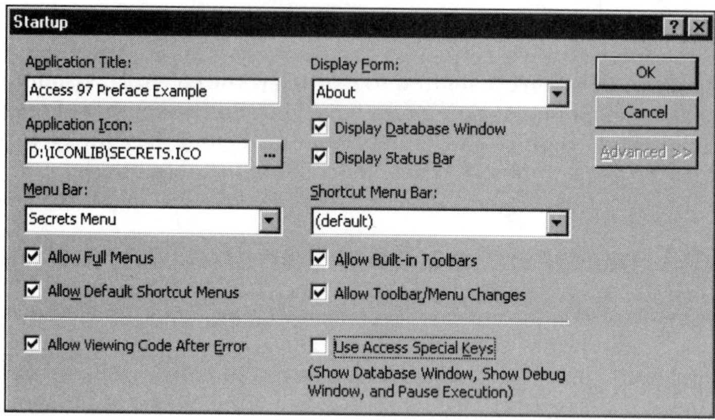

Figure A-12: The new Startup dialog box.

Is it Word or is it Access? Office comes to Access

Access 97 is not just integrated with Windows 95. It now shares many major components with Microsoft Office 97. If you are an Excel 97 or Word 97 user, you will be especially thrilled. The first shared component is the integrated Spell Checker, which is used to make sure that data stored in Access 97 tables is spelled correctly. The dictionary is shared across all Office 97 applications and includes custom words. Access 97 also shares the Office 97 AutoCorrect feature, which corrects errors while you type.

The Office 97 consistent look also includes toolbars, menus, tabbed option dialog boxes, and even the new File⇨Open and File⇨New dialog boxes. These dialog boxes allow for searching for databases using the Windows 95 file system. Even the cool, new animated delete is found in Access 97 datasheets, as the columns slowly close together after a deletion.

Tab stops can stop your navigation problems

Tab Stops have always been used to determine how the cursor moves from field to field when a keyboard user presses the Tab key. However, the last control in a form has always been a problem. Pressing the Tab key on the last control moves the cursor to the first control of the next record. This could always be stopped by writing a custom `KeyPress` trapping module. A new form property named `Cycle` has three selections, `All Records`, `Current Page`, and `Current Record`, to determine what happens when the Tab key is pressed on the last control of a form or form page. When set to `Current Page` or `Current Record`, it simply cycles back to the first control for that form page or form.

Menu and Toolbar Enhancements

Command Bars have now replaced the Menu Bars, Shortcut Menus, and Toolbars that we have all come to love (or hate). Command bars are a combination of menu bar and toolbar technologies. They enable you to access built-in and custom commands. They can be manipulated through the user interface or programmatically.

Menu bars and shortcut menus — no more macros!

Finally! Menu bars are no longer macros! Instead, a menu bar is a command bar that looks like a menu bar. For each menu item you can designate a caption, shortcut text, a Tool Tip, the action you want to take place when the menu item is selected, a style, a help file, and a help context Id (see Figure A-13). You can also specify a parameter and even a tag. Menu items can even contain pictures!

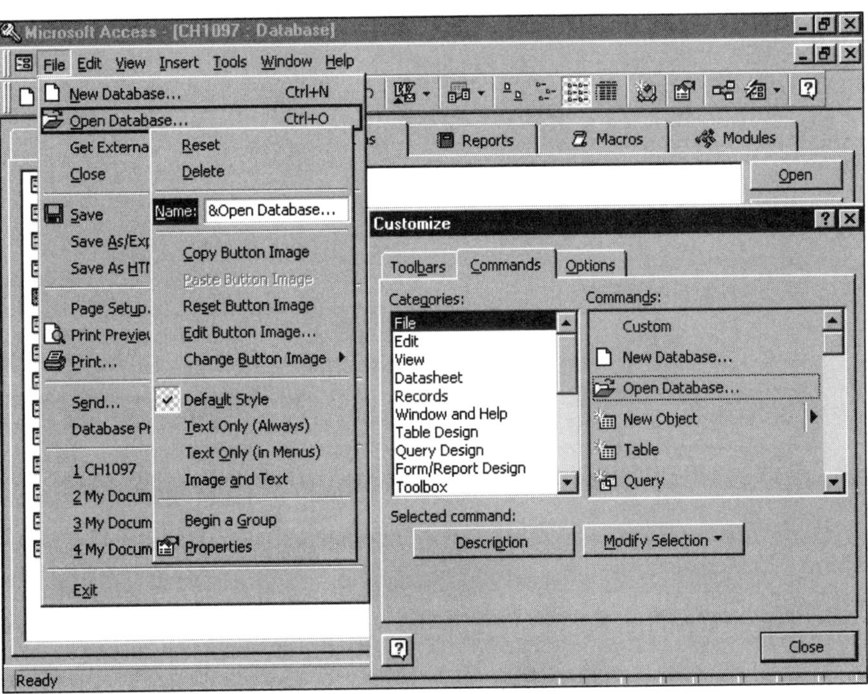

Figure A-13: Customizing a menu.

Toolbars — similar, but better

A toolbar is another type of command bar. Built-in toolbars can be modified, and new toolbars can be created (see Figure A-14). Access 97 toolbars are similar to their Access 2.0 counterparts but are now more flexible, powerful, and much easier to work with.

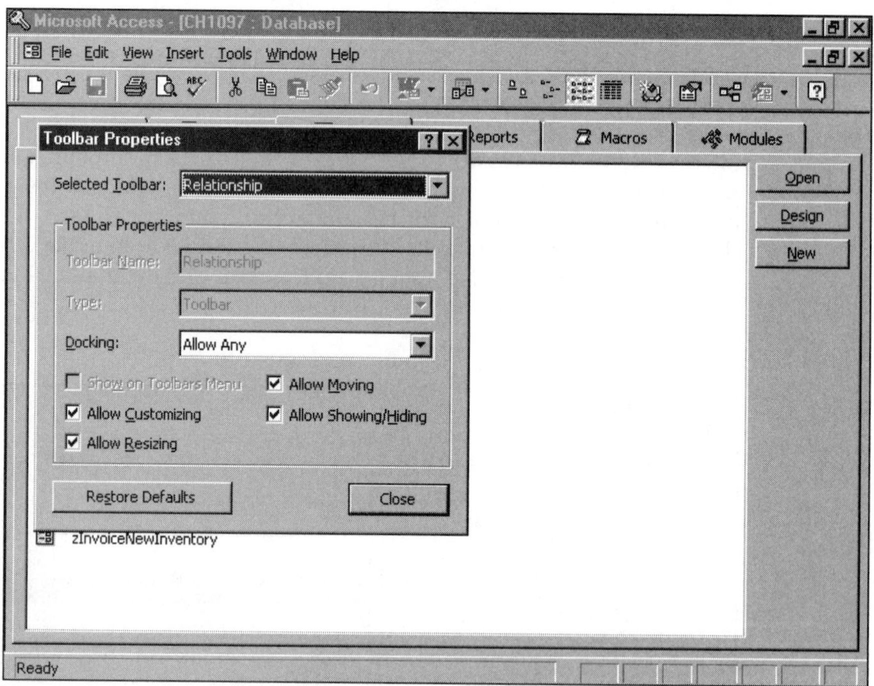

Figure A-14: The Toolbar Properties dialog box.

OLE Controls — A Mature Evolution

Virtually no one used OLE Custom Controls in Access 2.0. First, using them required the little-known Access 2.0 Service Pack. Secondly, only a few controls existed, and they were poorly documented, had limited functionality and were generally difficult to use. Most of the OLE Custom Controls, such as the Calendar Control and the Data Outline Control, came with the Access Developer's Toolkit. Other first-generation controls, such as the Tab Control, Spin Text Control, and MultiSelect List Box control found on CompuServe, were great for experimentation but not ready to be included in mission-critical applications. Using these controls required a special type of object and a separate set of properties. In Access 97, OLE Custom Control properties are integrated into the Other section of the tabbed property dialog box.

With the release of Visual C++ 2.1, true OLE Custom Controls started to appear. Access 97 comes with only one control, a new improved Calendar control. You simply drop this control onto a form, and you can easily select dates whose values can be stored in the underlying table. Many other OLE controls are soon to follow, and several, including Spin Box, Tab, Slider, Data Outline, and Common Dialog box OLE controls, will ship with the Access 97 Developer's Toolkit.

Figure A-15 shows the calendar and spin box controls. It also shows the OLE Custom Control property dialog box for the calendar control and the property window for the Other properties of this control. Each of these controls can be programmed in Access 97 using module code.

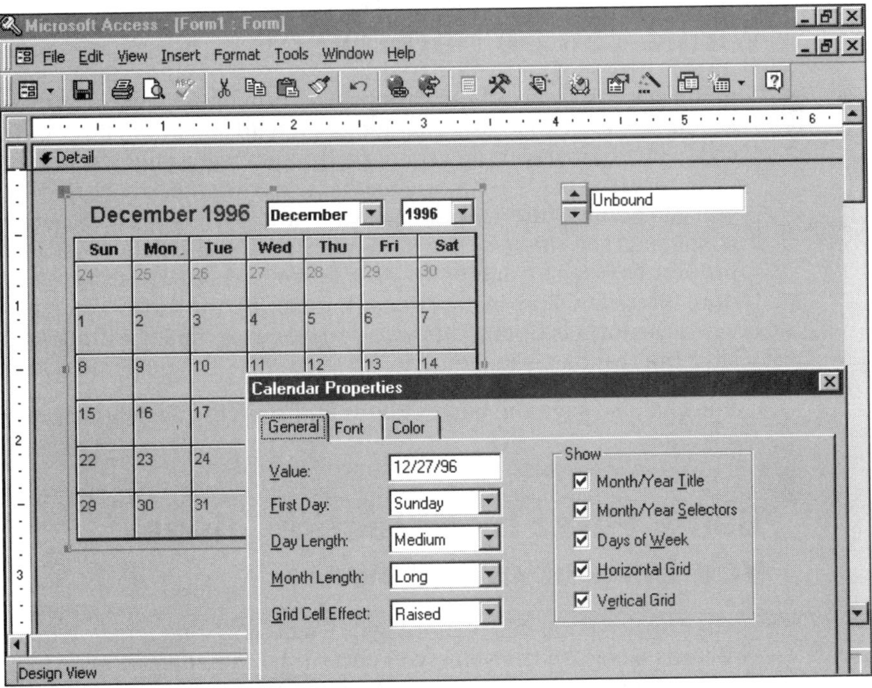

Figure A-15: Using Access 97 OLE Custom Controls.

Data and Query Enhancements to Forms

There have been a number of changes to forms that affect the data displayed on a form. These include new ways to search for data, enhancements to when data can be filtered and sorted, and new opportunities to save data in exactly the format you want after experimentation.

Queries no longer stop further analysis

Access has always offered the capability to click on one or more columns and instantly sort the data, but you could only do this on table data. If the results in a datasheet or form were from a query, you could not use the quick sort buttons to re-sort the data. This has been changed in Access 97. You can use the quick sort buttons at any time.

Using the Filter icons in the toolbar, you can display just the set of records with which you want to work. Now, this can also be done with results from a query or a table.

Saving temporary filters in forms can be permanent

In Access 2.0, you could always base a form on a query or further apply a secondary filter to a form that included field selection, filter criteria, and sort orders. However, any secondary filters were only temporary, as the form reverted back to its original data source when reopened. In Access 97, you can apply a filter and then save it and reapply it the next time the form is opened. The same is true for a quick sort of the data. Two new form properties, `Filter` and `Order By`, let you separately store with the form both filters and sort instructions that modify the `Record Source` property when the form is open. This way you can experiment with your data and still save the results permanently.

You can also save the current filter and sorting information as a query at any time.

Using Filter by Selection gives you instant drill down

Filter by Selection is a technology in Access 97 that lets you instantly select records based on the value you currently have selected. For example, suppose you move your cursor to a column named State that displays a list of valid states. When you click on the Sort Ascending button, the data is sorted by the state. Now you can highlight any of the records that contain the desired state (CA, for example). When you click on the Filter by Selection button on the toolbar, only the records for which the state equals CA will be selected.

Filter by Selection is also additive. If you then wanted to see only customers who live in Los Angeles, CA, you could click on the City column of one of the Los Angeles values and again click on the Filter by Selection button on the toolbar. This will show only customers who live in Los Angeles, CA . This feature allows you to drill down into increasingly specific layers of your data. The navigation button area lets you know that the database is currently filtered, and the Apply Filter/Remove Filter icon (the third filter icon, which looks like a large funnel) is depressed, indicating that a filter is in use. When you toggle this button, it removes all filters or sorts. The filter specification does not go away, however; it is simply turned off.

If you want to specify a selection and then see everything that *doesn't* match the selection, you can right click on the datasheet or form and select Filter Excluding Selection. This selects everything but the currently selected records. This is known as an inverse selection.

Using Filter by Form — no more combo code

Filter by Selection is just one of the ways to filter data in Access 97. Another way is known as Filter by Form. Selecting the second filter icon in the form or datasheet toolbar changes the form or datasheet to a single record in which every field is a combo box that allows you to select from a list of all values for that field. As you can see in Figure A-16, the bottom of the form lets you specify the Or conditions for each group of values you specify.

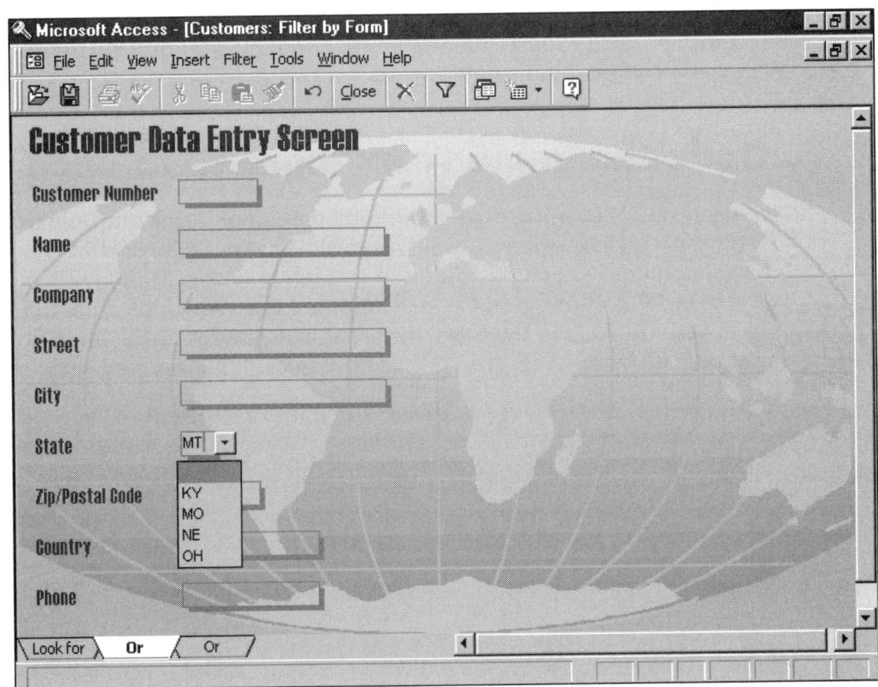

Figure A-16: Filter by Form.

In Figure A-16, you can see a form that mirrors the Customer form. After filling out the form, you can click on one of the Or tabs to enter a second set of conditions. Suppose you want to see all customers in the city of Harrison or the state of MT. You would select Harrison in the City field, click on the Or tab, and then select MT from the State combo box. When you click on the Apply Filter button (the large funnel), the data selection changes.

You can use as many conditions as you need. If you need even more advanced manipulation of your selections, you can still choose Records⇨Filter⇨Advanced Filter/Sort and get an actual QBE screen to enter more complex queries.

Control your editing and get a little dirty

Access 2.0 had a single control named Default Editing that controlled whether you could add new records or edit existing ones. Many developers found this confusing and limiting. Access 97 introduces three properties to more precisely control editing of data: `Allow Edits`, `Allow Deletes`, and `Allow Additions`.

A new `Dirty` property now lets you determine if a form has been changed. By using the `Dirty` property, you can better handle error and completion messages programatically.

Another new property named `NewRecord` lets you quickly determine whether you are on a new record.

Open the same form more than once

Access 97 allows the programmatic opening of forms multiple times. Each time the form is opened, a different underlying Recordset is created and maintained. Data can be updated in each Recordset independent of the others. This allows you to design applications in which a customer service representative can have two different customer records open at the same time.

Figure A-17 shows the same form open in three different records.

The following code accomplishes this task:

```
[General Declarations]
Option Compare Database

Option Explicit
'Collection to contain instances of the Customers form.
Dim colCustomerForms As New Collection

Sub cmdNewInstance
    Dim frmNewInst As Form_Customers
    Set frmNewInst = New Form_Customers
    colCustomerForms.Add Item:=frmNewInst, Key:=Me!CustomerID
End Sub
```

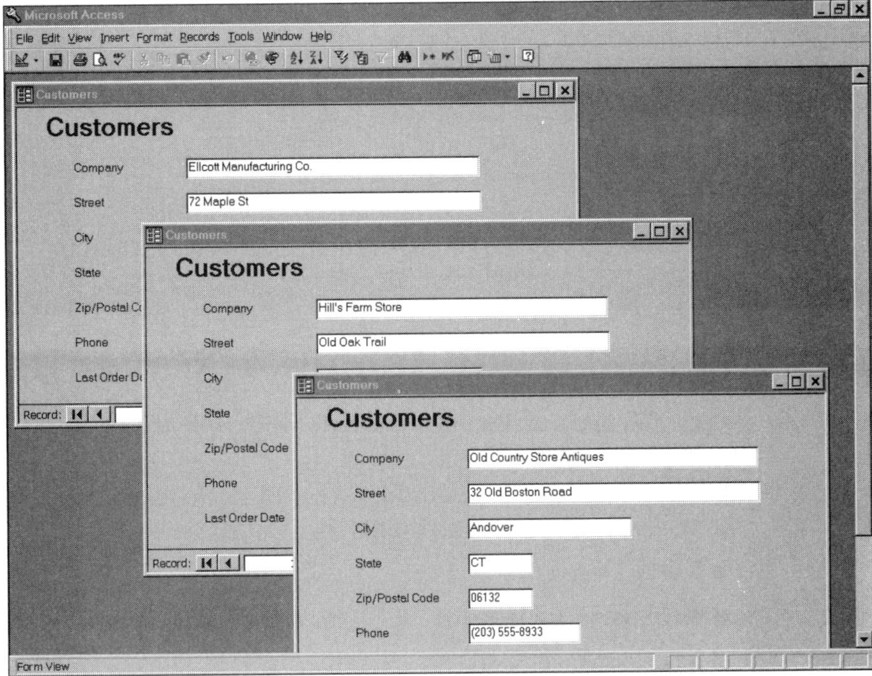

Figure A-17: Opening a form multiple times in different records.

Custom Form Properties and Methods Expose CBF

Access lets you create Visual Basic programs either in separate modules or as code behind forms (CBF). One limitation in previous versions of Access was that code behind forms could only be used by those forms. Though you could place common functions in common modules, those modules didn't get copied automatically in other databases when a form was copied.

In Access 97, you can declare public functions or properties so that form or report code is callable from other modules.

The following code is found in the Customers form:

```
Public Sub KeepMealive(frmWhoAmI As Form_Customers)
  'Indicates that this form should be kept open when CustomersDialog
closes.
  Set frmCustomers = frmWhoAmI
End Sub
```

It is called from the CustomersDialog form as follows:

```
Dim frm As Form_Customers
```

```
'Set the value of the user-defined KeepMeAlive property of _
the forms that should stay open.
intIndex = 1
'Determine which listbox items are selected.
For Each intIndex In lstForms.ItemsSelected
    Set frm = colCustomerForms(intIndex + 1)
    frm.KeepMealive frm
Next intIndex
```

Notice that the `KeepMealive` subroutine contained within the Customers form is called as a method of the form instance.

Creating and Using Tables — Never Better

Access 97 makes tables much easier to work with and create. Many new features have been added or enhanced to help make this happen. They include

- The capability to create a table from Datasheet view
- A Link Table Wizard
- An Import Data Wizard
- A Performance Analyzer
- A Table Analyzer
- A New Hyperlink Data Type

Help for the data-challenged

The average Microsoft Access user is not a data management expert. They are office workers, engineers, lawyers, doctors, self-employed entrepreneurs, students, or anyone who has found Microsoft Access to be incredibly useful to manage their data. However, their business is their expertise, not data management. Access 97 contains many new tools that help the data-challenged create usable, efficient tables.

Creating a new table has never been easier

There are many ways to create a table in Access 97. Of course, you can still go right to the Table Design view and enter your design, or you can use the Table Wizard, just like you did in Access 2.0. If you use the new, improved Table Wizard, you will notice that there are many more types of both Business and Personal tables. Nonetheless, there are three new ways to create a table in Access 97. First, you can start with an empty datasheet that looks exactly like an Excel worksheet. You can enter sample data in the rows and name the columns. When you save the datasheet, it asks you for a name for the new table. The new table design is automatically created using the sample data to determine the data type of each field.

The other two new ways to create a table design are actually wizards. The Link Table Wizard (formerly known as attach) helps you identify an external table to link (attach) to your current database. This creates the table link for you but does not actually create a table design. The Import Table Wizard lets you identify an external data source and imports the data, creating a new Access 97 table.

Changing a table can be as easy as using a datasheet

Datasheet columns work directly with the table designer. You can insert a column in a datasheet, and it will be added to the table design. You can name the column header, and, if you enter data, Access 97 will figure out the data type. This is very productive. You can delete a column from the table by selecting a datasheet column and deleting it. This is dangerous, but flexible.

Warning

Finally, you can rename a datasheet column header, which renames the underlying data field. If you delete or rename any fields that are used by forms, reports, macros, or modules, you will get errors the next time you use one of these objects. When you delete a column, you do get a warning message, and you can only delete one column at a time. *However, until Access 97 has a global search and replace for forms and reports, I do not suggest telling your end users about these features unless they are skilled developers.*

Importing Data Isn't Just for Wizards Anymore

Importing data in Access 2.0 required you to understand the type of data you were dealing with before you started. In Access 97, whenever you attempt to import non-Access data, a wizard analyzes the data and takes you through the process import process step by step. Even the difficult import/export specifications mandatory for fixed-width files have been wizardized.

Access 97 will automatically determine the type of data you are importing. For fixed-width data, it will let you select the columns as shown in Figure A-18. For delimited data, the wizard asks you to confirm how the file is delimited. You can place the data into a new or existing table and even define the table fields, data types, and sizes as you complete the wizard screens.

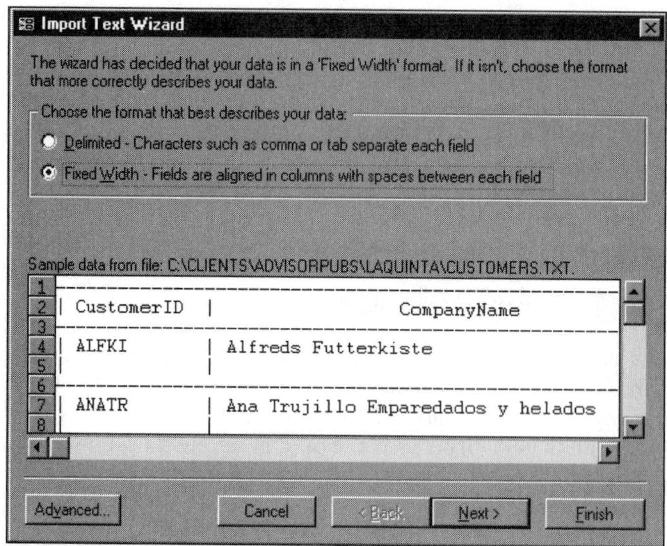

Figure A-18: Determining fixed-width import fields.

New Analysis Tools Help You Create Better Applications

There are several new tools in Access 97 that analyze your data and designs and help you work more efficiently. These include the new Performance Analyzer and the Table Analyzer.

The Performance Analyzer tells you off

After you have created a database, there are always ways to improve the performance of the tables, forms, and reports. Unless you have a lot of experience, it's often hard to know where to start. Some of the most common errors include not indexing fields in tables that are used for searching and creating a field with an inefficient data type. The Performance Analyzer is a tool that goes through selected objects in your database looking for areas where you could improve the speed of your application. Advice is split into four groups: Recommendations (you're only hurting yourself if you don't do this), Suggestions (this is a really good thing to do), Idea (this may or may not help), and Fixed (the Analyzer does it for you whether you want to or not). The most common advice is to convert all macros to Visual Basic, declare all variables in modules, index table fields, and change the Row Source of any combo boxes to a saved query.

The Table Analyzer almost makes a table normal

The Access 97 Table Analyzer (affectionately known as the Normalization Wizard) is used to analyze data in a flat file and split the data into as many tables as necessary to achieve proper database normalization. First, it searches for duplicate data that can be separated into lookup tables or one-to-many relations. This wizard also analyzes your data for spelling errors, incomplete values, and abbreviations and fixes the data. After the first step has been completed, the Table Analyzer shows you a relationship diagram of the new tables. Using drag and drop techniques, you can reintegrate tables into the original single table or perform further normalization, if you know how. This wizard will appeal to both the novice and the data professional as both a helper and a time-saver.

Figure A-19 shows a proposed layout from the table analyzer after analyzing a flat file of sales data containing invoice and invoice detail information, customer information, and product information.

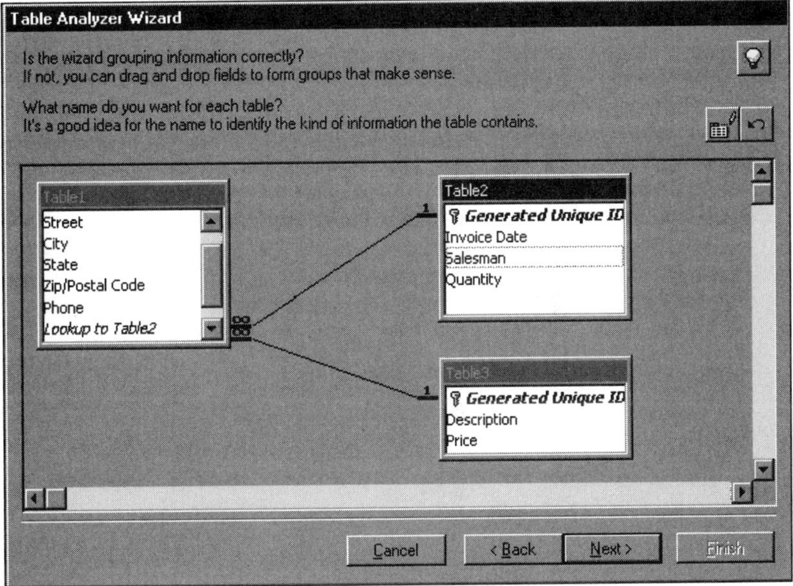

Figure A-19: The Table Analyzer's proposed layout.

The Table Analyzer has split the flat file into three tables. The first table, named Table1, contains information about the customer. The second table, named Table2, contains some information from the invoice and some from the detail of the invoice. The Table Analyzer Wizard has correctly moved the product data to a separate table, named Table3. Table1 also contains a foreign key (currently named Lookup to Table2) that is related to the primary key. You can rename the tables and even move a field from one table to another by simply dragging it from one table to another. Likewise, you can drag a field back from one table to another. You can also create a new table by dragging a field from one table to an empty area of the screen. This creates a new table, a primary key for the new table, and a new foreign key in the original table from which you dragged the field. You can eliminate a table by dragging all the fields from one table back to other tables. You can also change the order of the fields by selecting one and dragging it above or below other fields in the table.

Once you complete the wizard screen shown in Figure A-19 you can change the key fields that the table analyzer has created. The tables have been renamed, as shown in Figure A-20. Notice that the foreign key names have changed to reflect the renaming of the tables.

When you have completed setting all the primary key fields, you can begin a search for aberrant data. Misspellings and inconsistencies in like data are the most common types of problem data that the table analyzer can find. When performing the analysis, the Table Analyzer will also check your final field choices for fields that belong together.

If the Table Analyzer finds data that doesn't appear to fit the rest of the table data, you will get a warning message. You can go back and make further changes if you need to.

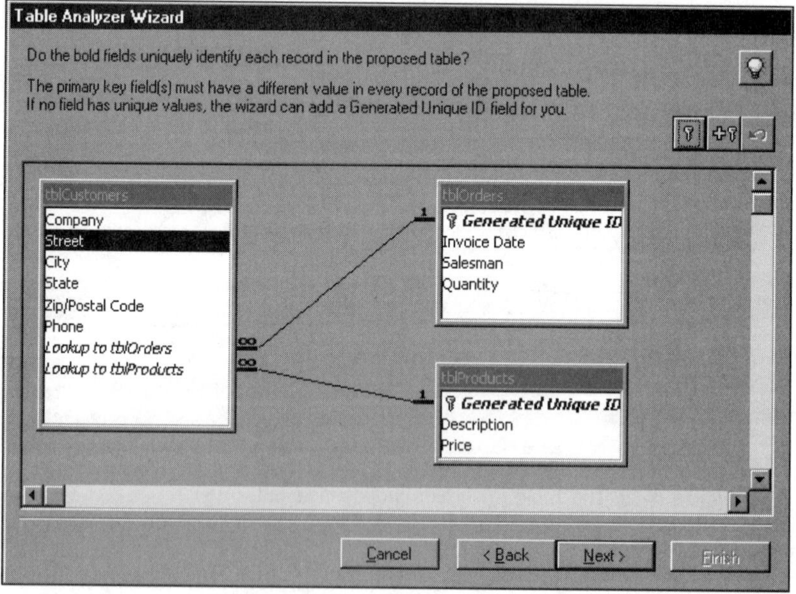

Figure A-20: The changed layout in the Table Analyzer.

The Table Analyzer will display a series of screens allowing you to correct what it believes are typographical errors.

After you enter all the corrections into the typo or primary key duplicate screens, you see the last Table Analyzer screen, which lets you complete the process. When you are through, Access 97 will display a tiled view of all the new tables. This way, you can see all the data in the new table designs.

The Table Analyzer can also create a query using the original name of your table but renaming the original table. This way you can continue to use your system but still take advantage of the relational table structure. This is especially important if you have existing forms or reports that used the original tables. When you create a form or report, you link those objects to specific table names. If you change these table names (or split one table into many tables), the forms or reports will no longer work. By creating a query that simulates your original environment, you can continue working without first redesigning forms and reports.

Though the Table Analyzer is not perfect, it is an outstanding way to normalize a data table with little effort and is probably the most advanced technology available for normalization today.

Table Enhancements Make Creating and Viewing Data Easier

There are a number of major changes in the table designer. You learned about the Lookup Wizard and default control types earlier in this appendix, but there are several more.

You can't count on the Counter field anymore

The Counter field has been replaced by the AutoNumber field. One enhancement is that you can now set the AutoNumber field to a value, and it will continue from there. Otherwise, this is just the Counter field with another name.

A new HTML field type makes any table Web-ready

A new HTML field type has been included in Access 97. This powerful field type allows you to store hyperlink addresses. The hyperlink address contains three parts. The Displaytext is the text that appears in the field or control. The Address is a path to a file (UNC) or page (URL). Finally, the SubAddress is a location within the file or page. When you click on a hyperlink in a field or text box, Access follows the hyperlink and opens the specified document, object, or page.

The Primary key — now it's there, now it's not

In Access 2.0, once you created a primary key, the only way to remove it was to open the Indexes window and delete the index line. In Access 97, you can simply toggle the primary key button on the toolbar.

The Database Splitter Wizard

Professional Access programmers never place tables and other objects together in the same database. Rather, tables are linked from the database containing queries, forms, reports, macros, and modules to the database containing the actual data tables. This process of linking Microsoft Access tables (formerly known as Attaching Tables) can be a very challenging assignment to the data-challenged. The Database Splitter wizard automates this process, creating two linked databases from a single database containing tables and other objects.

Figure A-21 shows the first screen that appears when you tell Access to split your tables. At the end of the process, you are asked to name the table that now contains just your table designs. This saves a lot of time and automates a critical step in the development process. You still have to watch out for operations that are not legal on linked tables such as using the SEEK command to retrieve data or importing data into a table programmatically. However, all these things can be worked around.

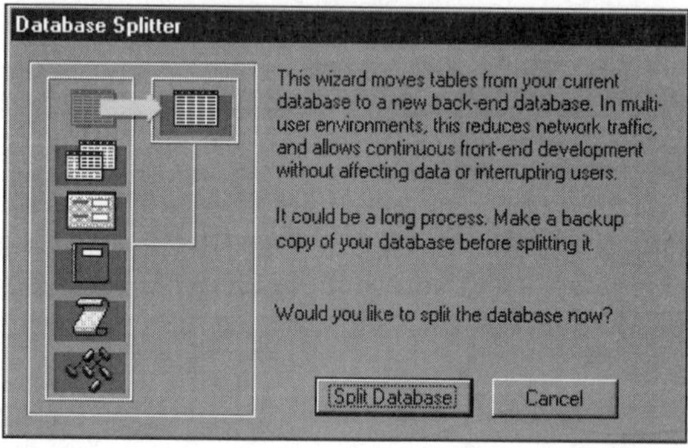

Figure A-21: Splitting the database tables.

This appendix provides a quick look at some of the new and enhanced form and table features in Access 97. By using the new features you will be able to create better systems with less work.

Appendix B

What's on the CD-ROM

The CD-ROM in the back of the book contains all the Access 97 databases used to create the examples in the book. It also contains several full-version products and other freebies from Cary Prague Books and Software, your Microsoft Access Superstore, as well as demo, trial, or limited-use versions of products from other vendors of Access 97 add-ons and ActiveX controls.

If you display the CD-ROM's directory tree using the Windows 95 or NT Explorer, you can access the software on the disc in one of two ways:

- Get into each directory and run the setup files you find there.
- Simply copy the files to your hard drive.

Instead of the standard name SETUP, most of the files use the abbreviated names of the actual products. To run the setup routines, simply select Run from the Windows 95 or NT 4.0 Start menu and then enter the name of the appropriate .EXE file you find on the CD-ROM. You can also double-click on the executable (.EXE) filename on the CD-ROM.

Some files were placed on the CD-ROM in their standard uncompressed .MDB format. For example, to run the Check Writer program, first display the \FREEBIES\CHECKWRT directory and then copy the file CHECKS97.MDB to your hard drive. You can then start Access 97 and open the CHECKS97 database.

Access 97 SECRETS Sample Database Files

The CD-ROM contains all the important example files used in the examples in the book. Each chapter's files are contained in a single chapter with the corresponding name. (For example, CH04.MDB contains the files for Chapter 4.) Some chapters have examples that we did not need to include on this CD-ROM, so you do not see them in the directory. You can find all the relevant chapter examples in the CD-ROM directory \CHAPTERS and they are not compressed in any way. To use these Access 97 database files, simply copy them to your hard drive and open them in Access 97.

All the .MDB files on the CD-ROM are Microsoft Access 97 files. They only work in Microsoft Access 97 and do not work in Microsoft Access 95, 2.0, 1.1, or 1.0.

Chapter 18 covers SQL Server and connecting to SQL Server files. The examples on the CD-ROM for CH18.MDB will only work if you have SQL Server installed on your computer.

Access Applications by Cary Prague Books and Software

Cary Prague Books and Software is the leader in business applications for Microsoft Access. We have placed a fully working version, with documentation, of our award-winning Check Writer program on the CD-ROM. We also have included demo versions of several of our other software products. If you would like our full-color catalog of books, videos, and add-on software products, call us at (860) 644-5891 or fax us at (860) 648-0710. You can download additional examples from our Web site at `www.caryp.com`.

The files in the \FREEBIES directory are given to you free of charge for your own use. These are all standard Access database files. To use them, simply copy them to your hard drive and open the database file.

Each is in its own directory and includes both the Access 97 program and full documentation in Word 6.0/95 format. You can use Word 97 to view or print the documentation as well.

Check Writer

Check Writer for Access 97 is a full-featured check-processing system that includes a visual check writer, check register, and a complete check reconciliation facility. This is not a demo but a complete product, including all documentation, ready to print in Word for Windows format. The Check Writer recently won an award from Microsoft Network for best Microsoft Access application.

To install Check Writer, go to the CD-ROM directory \FREEBIES\CHECKWRT and copy the files CHECKS97.MDB and CHECKWRT.DOC to your hard drive. You can get more information from the Cary Prague Books and Software Web site at `www.caryp.com` or by calling 860-644-5891. Check Writer normally costs about $79.

25 cool combo box tricks

This is a database of 25 of the coolest combo and list box techniques. To install the example database and complete documentation, go to the CD-ROM directory \FREEBIES\COOLCMBO and copy the files 25COMBOS7.MDB and 25COMBOS.DOC to your hard drive.

Access 97 Add-On Products

The CD-ROM contains a variety of demos of add-on products for use with Microsoft Access in the **\ADDONS** directory. These demos include

- An installation utility for creating standard Windows 95 or NT setup routines that install Access applications (or applications created with the Access Developer's Toolkit)
- A search-and-replace utility for changing Access 97 field names
- A set of Access functions, libraries, and frameworks for professional developers.

Business Forms Library

The Business Forms Library for Microsoft Access 97 is a sampler of three common business forms that demonstrate the flexibility and power of Microsoft Access 97 forms. This sampler includes Telephone Messages, Expense Form, and Card and Gift Tracker. Each form set includes tables, queries, forms, reports, and a simple macro library.

To use the Business Forms demo, go to the CD-ROM directory \ADDONS\BUSFRM and copy the file named BUSFRM.MDB. This is a standard Microsoft Access 97 database file. Simply open it and begin using it. The file BUSFRM.DOC contains sample documentation on how to use the forms. You can purchase the full version or get more information from the Cary Prague Books and Software Web site at `http://www.caryp.com` or by calling 860-644-5891. The Business Forms Library costs about $99.

Yes! I Can Run My Business, customizable business accounting product brochure

Yes! I Can Run My Business is the leading business accounting product for Microsoft Access 97. Built around an integrated double entry General Ledger, it takes basic business functions such as Quotations, Sales Order Entry, Invoices, Customer Tracking, Accounts Receivable, Inventory Control, Purchase Orders, Accounts Payable, Vendor Management, Chart Of Accounts, Bill Paying, and Bank Accounting (including Check Writing and Check Reconciliation) and automates them using simple Microsoft Access tables, forms, and reports. Best of all, because it's Microsoft Access, you can add your own reports and queries to customize everything.

If you like our products, we also have a complete set of stand-alone financial applications (including General Ledger and Inventory) starting at $189.95. Our fully integrated business accounting product is named *Yes! I Can Run My Business.* It includes invoice, quotations, purchase order, general ledger, payroll, inventory, accounts receivable and payable, and much more. A complete brochure is available in the ADDONS\YESICAN directory on the CD-ROM. You can download demos in any Microsoft Access format from our Web site (listed in the next paragraph).

You can purchase the full version, including over 500 pages of documentation, or get more information from the Cary Prague Books and Software Web site at `http://www.caryp.com` or by calling 860-644-5891. Yes! I Can Run My Business retails for $399 for the LAN license and $999.95 for the royalty-free developer's version. Mention our book and get Yes! I Can Run My Business Developer's Edition for only $795.00, a savings of over $200.

Command button images

There is also a set of Microsoft Office compatible button faces in the ADDONS\IMAGES directory on your CD-ROM for use in any Windows 95 or NT application. They can be used on Access 97 toolbars or command buttons. To use these button faces simply copy the files onto your hard disk or use the bitmaps as-is. The complete set of 2,500 bitmaps and the Image Editor is available from Cary Prague Books and Software. There are two image libraries which retail for $99.95 each as well as the Image Editor which also costs $99. Mention our book and receive all three for just $199. You can order these by calling (800) 277-3117 or (860) 644-5891. You can also order by sending e-mail to `caryp@caryp.com`.

The files named ACTxx.BMP are 32-by-32-pixel .BMPs that are perfect for Access command buttons. The files named ACTxx.B24 are 24-by-23-pixel .BMPs that are just as perfect for Access 97 toolbars and any Office-compatible application.

TabMaster Wizard

Creating a tabbed dialog box has always been a challenge in Microsoft Access. The TabMaster Wizard makes it easy to create great-looking tabbed dialog boxes and controls in any version of Access. On the ADDONS\TABMASTR directory is a file named TABDEM97.MDB. This contains both a live tutorial and a complete set of tabbed control examples — including tabbed dialog boxes within *other* tabbed dialog boxes.

You can purchase the full version, including 50 pages of documentation, or get more information from the Cary Prague Books and Software Web site at `http://www.caryp.com` or by calling 860-644-5891. The TabMaster Wizard retails for $149. Mention our book and get the new TabMaster Wizard for Access 97, with even more features than the demo — including programming for the new Access tab control for only $129.00.

Wise Installation System from Great Lakes Business Solutions

The Wise Installation System Version 5.0 is, in our opinion, the most flexible and easily usable product available for creating totally custom setup routines. Whether you're working from an easy-to-use wizard or editing a scripting-type language, you can create any type of installation for any type of application. You can add custom splash screens, billboards, or any graphics as the installation progresses. You can install ODBC and OLE and modify the Windows 95 Registry or Windows 3.1 .INI files. You can check for available disk space, perform version control, preserve overwritten files with backups, install an uninstall icon, and automatically add icons to the Windows 95 Start menu. Wise Installation creates setup routines for Windows 3.1, Windows 95, and Windows NT. The best part of this product is that it takes up only 60K and compresses your existing files by up to 90%.

To install the Wise Installation Demo, simply go to the CD-ROM directory \ADDONS\WISEINST and run the file named WISE.EXE. You can purchase the full version or get more information from the Great Lakes Business Solutions Web site at `http://www.glbs.com`. Wise Installation costs about $195. This is the product the authors of this book use to create custom setup routines.

Speed Ferret by Black Moshannon Systems

Speed Ferret is the only commercially available search-and-replace utility for Microsoft Access 97. When you change a table field name in Microsoft Access, your queries, forms, reports, and modules that reference that field name stop working. You can spend hours manually finding and changing these references, or you can do it in minutes with SpeedFerret for Access 97. Using a form-driven interface, you can choose to search all your forms, reports, and modules or just make replacements in selected objects. You can even check relationships and import/export specifications. A preview window lets you review and edit replacements, as well as undo replacements at a later time.

On the CD-ROM is a full product description of SpeedFerret 97 in a Windows 95 help file. To run the file, simply double-click on the file name SPEEDFER.HLP in the \ADDONS\SPEEDFER directory; your computer will do the rest. You can purchase the full version or get more information from Black Moshannon Systems by calling 814-345-5657. Speed Ferret costs about $99.

Start Developing by Moss Micro

Start Developing is an application framework that helps you reduce your development time. The product includes an Application Wizard, error handling, security, programmable table links and attaching routines, Win 32 API, registry manipulation, message handling, and much more. The product is written totally in Visual Basic for Applications, the language of Access 97.

To install the Start Developing demo, go to the CD-ROM directory \ADDONS\STARTDEV and run the file named SETUP.EXE. You can purchase the full version or get more information from Moss Micro's Web site at `http://www.mossmicro.com`. Start Developing costs about $199.

WinZip by Nico Mak Computing

WinZip has been the leader in compression utilities for many years. This is a shareware product. WinZip is a fully graphical implementation of the original PKZIP. Using 32-bit technology, WinZip 6.2 for Windows 95 makes creating and managing archive files easy. WinZip recognizes files created with PKZIP and .TAR, .LHA, .ARC, and .ARJ formats. WinZip95 includes long filename support, Internet support, and even virus-scanning support.

To install WinZip 6.2, go to the CD-ROM directory \ADDONS\WINZIP95 and run the file named SETUP.EXE. You can purchase the full version or get more information from Nico Mak Computing's Web site at `http://www.winzip.com` or by calling 713-242-4775. WinZip costs about $29 to register.

OCX Controls

Although VBX controls have long been the domain of Visual Basic, only now has this same functionality been available for Access 97 users. OLE controls, also known as OCX controls (and recently renamed ActiveX controls by Microsoft), enable you to extend the VBA language by providing Plug and Play components that work with your applications. Although a dozen OCX controls come with the Office 97 Developer's Edition, many others are also available from independent vendors. On the CD-ROM is a set of samplers from the biggest names in the business, such as MicroHelp, Crescent, and Visual Components.

Internet ToolPak by Crescent Software

The Crescent Internet ToolPak Version 2.0 consists of sixteen ActiveX controls and an Internet Mail Wizard to lead you through creating applications that exploit Internet capabilities. Included in the ToolPak are Mail

Controls (SMTP, POP, MIME, and UUEncode/Decode), an FTP control, newsgroup control, HTTP control, RAS (Remote Access Services) control, TCP/IP control, a Telnet form, and the Internet Mail Wizard.

To install the Internet ToolPak demo, go to the CD-ROM directory \CONTROLS\CRESCENT and run the CITPDEMO.EXE file. To order any of these products or request more information, visit Crescent's Web site at `http://www.crescent.progress.com` or call 617-280-3000. These tools cost from $89 to $395.

OLETools 5.0 from MicroHelp

OLETools contains more than a hundred 16- and 32-bit OCX controls in one package, including 23 data-aware controls and 3-D enhanced controls. You get enhanced label controls, text box controls, button controls, picture controls, gauges, list/file controls, timer controls, and special controls including calendars, common dialog boxes, and tab controls.

To install the OLETools 5.0 demo, go to the CD-ROM directory \CONTROLS\MICROHLP and run the file named MHSETUP.EXE. You can purchase the full version or get more information from the MicroHelp Web site at `http://microhelp.com` or by calling 770-516-0898. OLETools costs about $189.

Tools from Visual Components

The Visual Components Starter files on the accompanying CD-ROM include the following. You can run the demos by double-clicking on the SETUP files in each directory:

Formula One/NET

Formula One/NET is the first Internet spreadsheet component. After you have installed Formula One/NET on your system, you can view and manipulate live Formula One spreadsheets and charts embedded in Netscape Navigator 2.0 windows. Formula One/NET requires Netscape Navigator 2.0 and an *x*86 PC-compatible running Windows 3.1, Windows 95, or Windows NT with at least 800K of free RAM. Charting requires an additional 800K of free RAM. This evaluation copy of Formula One is available as a 32-bit OLE Custom Control (OCX). Formula One 3.1 gives you unmatched spreadsheet power, including the capability to create, import, and export Microsoft Excel 4.0 worksheets and 5.0 workbooks. Formula One can be integrated in applications that require advanced spreadsheet capabilities without the overhead associated with traditional spreadsheet applications.

VisualSpeller trial version

This evaluation copy of VisualSpeller is available as a 32-bit OLE Custom Control (OCX). VisualSpeller enables you to add spell-checking to your application with a minimum of programming. VisualSpeller is primarily a spell-checking engine tool used to add spell-checking functionality to a higher-level application. To use it, pass in the text for spell-checking and read the corrected text when the spell check is complete.

Index

(continued)

B

C

D

E

G

(continued)

H

I

(continued)

J

K

L

M

(continued)

N

P

Q

R

S

(continued)

(continued)

U

W

Z

IDG BOOKS WORLDWIDE, INC. END-USER LICENSE AGREEMENT

Read This. You should carefully read these terms and conditions before opening the software packet(s) included with this book ("Book"). This is a license agreement ("Agreement") between you and IDG Books Worldwide, Inc. ("IDGB"). By opening the accompanying software packet(s), you acknowledge that you have read and accept the following terms and conditions. If you do not agree and do not want to be bound by such terms and conditions, promptly return the Book and the unopened software packet(s) to the place you obtained them for a full refund.

1. **License Grant.** IDGB grants to you (either an individual or entity) a nonexclusive license to use one copy of the enclosed software program(s) (collectively, the "Software") solely for your own personal or business purposes on a single computer (whether a standard computer or a workstation component of a multiuser network). The Software is in use on a computer when it is loaded into temporary memory (i.e., RAM) or installed into permanent memory (e.g., hard disk, CD-ROM, or other storage device). IDGB reserves all rights not expressly granted herein.

2. **Ownership.** IDGB is the owner of all right, title, and interest, including copyright, in and to the compilation of the Software recorded on the CD-ROM. Copyright to the individual programs on the CD-ROM is owned by the author or other authorized copyright owner of each program. Ownership of the Software and all proprietary rights relating thereto remain with IDGB and its licensors.

3. **Restrictions on Use and Transfer.**

   (a) You may only (i) make one copy of the Software for backup or archival purposes, or (ii) transfer the Software to a single hard disk, provided that you keep the original for backup or archival purposes. You may not (i) rent or lease the Software, (ii) copy or reproduce the Software through a LAN or other network system or through any computer subscriber system or bulletin-board system, or (iii) modify, adapt, or create derivative works based on the Software.

   (b) You may not reverse engineer, decompile, or disassemble the Software. You may transfer the Software and user documentation on a permanent basis, provided that the transferee agrees to accept the terms and conditions of this Agreement and you retain no copies. If the Software is an update or has been updated, any transfer must include the most recent update and all prior versions.

4. **Restrictions on Use of Individual Programs.** You must follow the individual requirements and restrictions detailed for each individual program. These limitations are contained in the individual license agreements recorded on the CD-ROM. These restrictions may include a requirement that after using the program for the period of time specified in its text, the user must pay a registration fee or discontinue use. By opening the Software packet(s), you will be agreeing to abide by the licenses and restrictions for these individual programs. None of the material on this disk(s) or listed in this Book may ever be distributed, in original or modified form, for commercial purposes.

5. **Limited Warranty.**

   (a) IDGB warrants that the Software and CD-ROM are free from defects in materials and workmanship under normal use for a period of sixty (60) days from the date of purchase of this Book. If IDGB receives notification within the warranty period of defects in materials or workmanship, IDGB will replace the defective CD-ROM.

(b) **IDGB AND THE AUTHORS OF THE BOOK DISCLAIM ALL OTHER WARRANTIES, EXPRESS OR IMPLIED, INCLUDING WITHOUT LIMITATION IMPLIED WARRANTIES OF MERCHANTABILITY AND FITNESS FOR A PARTICULAR PURPOSE, WITH RESPECT TO THE SOFTWARE, THE PROGRAMS, THE SOURCE CODE CONTAINED THEREIN, AND/OR THE TECHNIQUES DESCRIBED IN THIS BOOK. IDGB DOES NOT WARRANT THAT THE FUNCTIONS CONTAINED IN THE SOFTWARE WILL MEET YOUR REQUIREMENTS OR THAT THE OPERATION OF THE SOFTWARE WILL BE ERROR FREE.**

(c) This limited warranty gives you specific legal rights, and you may have other rights which vary from jurisdiction to jurisdiction.

6. **Remedies**.

(a) IDGB's entire liability and your exclusive remedy for defects in materials and workmanship shall be limited to replacement of the Software, which may be returned to IDGB with a copy of your receipt at the following address: Disk Fulfillment Department, Attn: Access 97 SECRETS, IDG Books Worldwide, Inc., 7260 Shadeland Station, Ste. 100, Indianapolis, IN 46256, or call 1-800-762-2974. Please allow 3–4 weeks for delivery. This Limited Warranty is void if failure of the Software has resulted from accident, abuse, or misapplication. Any replacement Software will be warranted for the remainder of the original warranty period or thirty (30) days, whichever is longer.

(b) In no event shall IDGB or the author be liable for any damages whatsoever (including without limitation damages for loss of business profits, business interruption, loss of business information, or any other pecuniary loss) arising from the use of or inability to use the Book or the Software, even if IDGB has been advised of the possibility of such damages.

(c) Because some jurisdictions do not allow the exclusion or limitation of liability for consequential or incidental damages, the above limitation or exclusion may not apply to you.

7. **U.S. Government Restricted Rights**. Use, duplication, or disclosure of the Software by the U.S. Government is subject to restrictions stated in paragraph (c) (1) (ii) of the Rights in Technical Data and Computer Software clause of DFARS 252.227-7013, and in subparagraphs (a) through (d) of the Commercial Computer—Restricted Rights clause at FAR 52.227-19, and in similar clauses in the NASA FAR supplement, when applicable.

8. **General**. This Agreement constitutes the entire understanding of the parties and revokes and supersedes all prior agreements, oral or written, between them and may not be modified or amended except in a writing signed by both parties hereto which specifically refers to this Agreement. This Agreement shall take precedence over any other documents that may be in conflict herewith. If any one or more provisions contained in this Agreement are held by any court or tribunal to be invalid, illegal, or otherwise unenforceable, each and every other provision shall remain in full force and effect.

CD-ROM Installation

For information on installing and using the software on the *Access 97 SECRETS* CD-ROM, as well as a description of the programs, see Appendix B.